Exceptional Children

sixth edition

Exceptional Children

An Introduction to Special Education

William L. Heward
The Ohio State University

MERRILL
an imprint of Prentice Hall
Upper Saddle River, New Jersey *Columbus, Ohio*

Library of Congress Cataloging-in-Publication Data
Heward, William L.
Exceptional children : An introduction to special education / William L. Heward.—6th ed.
p. cm.
Includes bibliographical references and indexes.
ISBN 0-13-012938-0
1. Special education—United States. 2. Exceptional children—United States. I. Title.
LC3981.H49 2000
371.9′0973—dc21 99-34889
CIP

Cover Photo: Shelley Gazin Photography
Editor: Ann Castel Davis
Developmental Editor: Linda Ashe Montgomery
Production Editor: Mary M. Irvin
Design Coordinator: Diane C. Lorenzo
Associate Design Director: Karrie Converse-Jones
Text Design: STELLARViSIONS, Ceri Fitzgerald
Cover Design: Ceri Fitzgerald
Editorial Assistant: Pat Grogg
Photo Coordinator: Sandy Lenahan
Production Manager: Pamela D. Bennett
Electronic Text Management: Marilyn Wilson Phelps, Karen L. Bretz, Melanie N. King
Director of Marketing: Kevin Flanagan
Marketing Manager: Meghan Shepherd
Marketing Coordinator: Krista Groshong

This book was set in Garamond by Prentice Hall and was printed and bound by R. R. Donnelley & Sons Company. The cover was printed by Phoenix Color Corp.

Printed in the United States of America

10 9 8 7 6 5 4 3

ISBN: 0-13-012938-0

Prentice-Hall International (UK) Limited, *London*
Prentice-Hall of Australia Pty. Limited, *Sydney*
Prentice-Hall of Canada, Inc., *Toronto*
Prentice-Hall Hispanoamericana, S. A., *Mexico*
Prentice-Hall of India Private Limited, *New Delhi*
Prentice-Hall of Japan, Inc., *Tokyo*
Prentice-Hall (Singapore) Pte. Ltd., *Singapore*
Editora Prentice-Hall do Brasil, Ltda., *Rio de Janeiro*

This book is dedicated to John Cooper and Tim Heron.

Be it in the peleton, the bottling line, or a faculty meeting;

no better friends and colleagues could a guy have.

About the Author

William Lee Heward grew up in Three Oaks, Michigan, watching his hero Ernie Banks and the Chicago Cubs. He majored in psychology and sociology as an undergraduate at Western Michigan University, earned his doctorate in special education at the University of Massachusetts, and has been a member of the special education faculty at The Ohio State University since 1975. In 1985, Bill received Ohio State's highest honor for teaching excellence, the Alumni Association's Distinguished Teaching Award. He has had several opportunities to teach and lecture abroad, most recently in 1993 when he served as a Visiting Professor of Psychology at Keio University in Tokyo, Japan.

Bill's current research interests focus on "low tech" methods classroom teachers can use to increase the frequency with which each student actively responds and participates during group instruction and on methods for promoting the generalization and maintenance of newly learned skills. His research has appeared in many of the field's leading journals, including *Behavioral Disorders*, *Education and Training in Mental Retardation and Developmental Disabilities*, *Exceptional Children*, *Journal of Applied Behavior Analysis*, *Learning Disability Quarterly*, *Research in Developmental Disabilities*, *Teacher Education and Special Education*, and *Teaching Exceptional Children*.

Bill has co-authored five other textbooks, including *Applied Behavior Analysis* (Merrill/Prentice Hall, 1987). He has also written for the popular market. His book *Some Are Called Clowns* (Crowell, 1974) chronicled his five summers as a pitcher for the Indianapolis Clowns, the last of the barnstorming baseball teams.

Preface

Special education is the story of people. It is the story of a preschool child with multiple disabilities who benefits from early intervention services. It is the story of a child with mental retardation whose parents and teachers work together to ensure she participates in typical school activities with her peers. It is the story of a fourth-grader with learning disabilities who helps his parents and teachers plan his instructional program that teaches to his strengths and addresses his weaknesses. It is the story of the gifted and talented child who brings new insights to old problems, the high school student with cerebral palsy who is learning English as his second language, and the young woman who has recently moved into a group home after spending most of her life in a large institution. Special education is all of their stories, stories that portray the resiliency and triumphs of children and adults with exceptionalities.

The story of special education is yet unfinished. Professionals continue to strive to meet the challenges of special education and the people it serves. And, whether you are a beginner or a seasoned player, I hope that your study and involvement with children and adults with special needs will challenge you to seek better ideas to meet these needs.

Text Organization and Structure

With the sixth edition of *Exceptional Children*, I want to convey to you not only the diversity and excitement of special education but also to present you with an informative, readable, and responsible introduction to the professional practices, trends, and research that define contemporary special education. To this end, the book begins with A Personal View of Special Education—eight perspectives on the purpose and responsibilities of special education—followed by fifteen chapters organized into two parts.

Part One—Foundations for Understanding Special Education—presents an overview of terminology, laws, policies, and practices that are consistent with the 1997 amendments to the Individuals with Disabilities Education Act (IDEA) and the exceptional child's right to receive an appropriate education in the least restrictive environment. Chapter 2 examines the referral, assessment, and placement of students in special education. Chapters 3 and 4 describe how to acknowledge and appreciate the cultural and linguistic differences that some children with special needs bring to the classroom, and the important role parents and families play in the decision-making process for planning the individual education needs of their children. Part Two—Educational Needs of Exceptional Students—is organized around nine categorical chapters within a developmental, lifespan perspective. Thus, Part Two opens with a look at early childhood special education and the critical role early intervention plays in nurturing the development of young children with special needs. Part Two closes with a chapter on transition from secondary school and the responsibility educators and parents share in preparing students with exceptionalities for adulthood. Chapters 6 through 14, the chapters that fall between early childhood and transition, introduce you to the definitions, prevalence, causes, historical background, assessment techniques, instructional strategies, current issues, and future trends for eight disability categories and for giftedness and talent development. Autism, ADHD, and traumatic brain injury are covered within these chapters.

Key Text Features

Focus Questions

Each chapter begins with five questions that provide a framework for studying the chapter and its implications. These Focus Questions serve as discussion starters for introducing, overviewing, concluding, or reviewing. Open-ended questions can be found on the Message Board on the Companion Website **(http://www.prenhall.com/heward)**, which allows you to engage in interactive discussions with your classmates.

Teaching Strategies

Providing an instructional framework for this edition are "Teaching and Learning in School" boxes that describe a wide range of effective interventions—from classroom performance and classroom management to curriculum modifications and error correction and feedback. These strategies provide practical and clear guidelines for working with students in inclusive settings or in pull-out programs. Each of these strategies is supported by research that documents its effectiveness with students who have disabilities.

Teaching and Learning in School

Distributed throughout the text, "Teaching and Learning in School" boxes provide practical applications and intervention strategies for general classroom teachers and special educators.

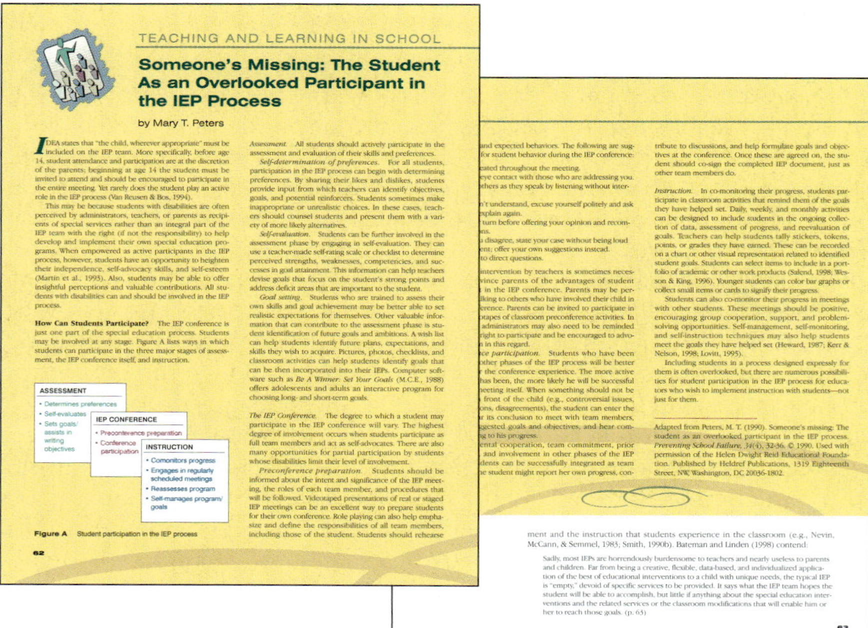

TEACHING AND LEARNING IN SCHOOL

Someone's Missing: The Student As an Overlooked Participant in the IEP Process

by Mary T. Peters

IDEA states that "the child, wherever appropriate" must be included on the IEP team. More specifically, before age 14, student attendance and participation are at the discretion of the parents; beginning at age 14 the student must be invited to attend and should be encouraged to participate in the entire meeting. Yet rarely does the student play an active role in the IEP process (Van Reusen & Bos, 1994).

This may be because students with disabilities are often perceived by administrators, teachers, or parents as recipients of special services rather than an integral part of the IEP team with the right (if not the responsibility) to help develop and implement their own special education programs. When empowered as active participants in the IEP process, however, students have an opportunity to heighten their independence, self-advocacy skills, and self-esteem (Martin et al., 1993). Also, students may be able to offer insightful perceptions and valuable contributions. All students with disabilities can and should be involved in the IEP process.

How Can Students Participate? The IEP conference is just one part of the special education process. Students may be involved at any stage. Figure A lists ways in which students can participate in the three major stages of assessment, the IEP conference itself, and instruction.

Figure A Student participation in the IEP process

Assessment. All students should actively participate in the assessment and evaluation of their skills and preferences.

Self-determination of preferences. For all students, participation in the IEP process can begin with determining preferences. By sharing their likes and dislikes, students provide input from which teachers can identify objectives, goals, and potential reinforcers. Students sometimes make inappropriate or unrealistic choices. In these cases, teachers should counsel students and present them with a variety of more likely alternatives.

Self-evaluation. Students can be further involved in the assessment phase by engaging in self-evaluation. They can use a teacher-made self-rating scale or checklist to determine perceived strengths, weaknesses, competencies, and successes in goal attainment. This information can help teachers devise goals that focus on the student's strong points and address deficit areas that are important to the student.

Goal setting. Students who are trained to assess their own skills and goal achievement may be better able to set realistic expectations for themselves. Other valuable information that can contribute to the assessment phase is student identification of future goals and ambitions. A wish list can help students identify future plans, expectations, and skills they wish to acquire. Pictures, photos, checklists, and classroom activities can help students identify goals that can be then incorporated into their IEPs. Computer software such as *Be A Winner: Set Your Goals* (M.C.E., 1988) offers adolescents and adults an interactive program for choosing long- and short-term goals.

The IEP Conference. The degree to which a student may participate in the IEP conference will vary. The highest degree of involvement occurs when students participate as full team members and act as self-advocates. There are also many opportunities for partial participation by students whose disabilities limit their level of involvement.

Preconference preparation. Students should be informed about the intent and significance of the IEP meeting, the roles of each team member, and procedures that will be followed. Videotaped presentations of real or staged IEP meetings can be an excellent way to prepare students for their own conference. Role playing can also help emphasize and define the responsibilities of all team members, including those of the student. Students should rehearse

62

...nd expected behaviors. The following are sug-
...for student behavior during the IEP conference:
...eated throughout the meeting.
...eye contact with those who are addressing you.
...thers as they speak by listening without inter-
...n't understand, excuse yourself politely and ask
...xplain again.
...turn before offering your opinion and recom-
...ns.
...u disagree, state your case without being loud
...ent; offer your own suggestions instead.
...to direct questions.
...intervention by teachers is sometimes neces-
...vince parents of the advantages of student
...in the IEP conference. Parents may be per-
...lking to others who have involved their child in
...erence. Parents can be invited to participate in
...otapes of classroom preconference activities. In
...administrators may also need to be reminded
...right to participate and be encouraged to advo-
...n in this regard.
...*ce participation.* Students who have been
...other phases of the IEP process will be better
...r the conference experience. The more active
...has been, the more likely he will be successful
...neeting itself. When something should not be
...front of the child (e.g., controversial issues,
...ons, disagreements), the student can enter the
...r its conclusion to meet with team members,
...ggested goals and objectives, and hear com-
...ng to his progress.
...ental cooperation, team commitment, prior
...and involvement in other phases of the IEP
...dents can be successfully integrated as team
...e student might report her own progress, con-

tribute to discussions, and help formulate goals and objectives at the conference. Once these are agreed on, the student should co-sign the completed IEP document, just as other team members do.

Instruction. In co-monitoring their progress, students participate in classroom activities that remind them of the goals they have helped set. Daily, weekly, and monthly activities can be designed to include students in the ongoing collection of data, assessment of progress, and reevaluation of goals. Teachers can help students tally stickers, tokens, points, or grades they have earned. These can be recorded on a chart or other visual representation related to identified student goals. Students can select items to include in a portfolio of academic or other work products (Salend, 1998; Wesson & King, 1996). Younger students can color bar graphs or collect small items or cards to signify their progress.

Students can also co-monitor their progress in meetings with other students. These meetings should be positive, encouraging group cooperation, support, and problem-solving opportunities. Self-management, self-monitoring, and self-instruction techniques may also help students meet the goals they have helped set (Heward, 1987; Kerr & Nelson, 1998; Lovitt, 1995).

Including students in a process designed expressly for them is often overlooked, but there are numerous possibilities for student participation in the IEP process for educators who wish to implement instruction with students—not just for them.

Adapted from Peters, M. T. (1990). Someone's missing: The student as an overlooked participant in the IEP process. *Preventing School Failure, 34*(4), 32-36. © 1990. Used with permission of the Helen Dwight Reid Educational Foundation. Published by Heldref Publications, 1319 Eighteenth Street, NW, Washington, DC 20036-1802.

ment and the instruction that students experience in the classroom (e.g., Nevin, McCann, & Semmel, 1983; Smith, 1990b). Bateman and Linden (1998) contend:

> Sadly, most IEPs are horrendously burdensome to teachers and nearly useless to parents and children. Far from being a creative, flexible, data-based, and individualized application of the best of educational interventions to a child with unique needs, the typical IEP is "empty," devoid of specific services to be provided. It says what the IEP team hopes the student will be able to accomplish, but little if anything about the special education interventions and the related services or the classroom modifications that will enable him or her to reach those goals. (p. 63)

63

Profiles of People/Perspectives of Issues

The "Profiles and Perspectives" boxes include two types of essays. One type highlights the personal struggles, triumphs, and stories of persons with disabilities, such as the interview of student leaders from Gallaudet University who share their position and passion on why the president of Gallaudet should be a member of the Deaf culture. In another box, Stephen Hawking, the famed physicist, contributes his thoughts on living with a degenerative disease that causes him to continually adapt his lifestyle but does not affect his intellectual ability. The other "Profiles and Perspectives" boxes are written by special educators, parents, and journalists who share their personal views about where special education is, or should be, going. Contributors to these boxes include Dr. Michael Giangreco, "Moving Toward Inclusive Education," and Dr. Richard D. Howell, who describes innovations in assistive technology with "Grasping the Future with Robotic Aids."

PROFILES AND PERSPECTIVES

Deaf President Now!

Gallaudet University in Washington, DC, is the world's only university dedicated exclusively to the education of deaf students. (Students with normal hearing are admitted into some of its programs.) A federally funded institution chartered by Congress in 1864, Gallaudet had never had a deaf president. When a presidential vacancy occurred in 1988, many Gallaudet students, faculty, and alumni expected that a deaf person would be appointed; however, an educator with normal hearing, who was unable to use sign language, was initially selected for the position. A week of turbulent protests and demonstrations ensued, with calls for a "Deaf President Now," focusing national and international attention on Gallaudet. We asked Bridgetta Bourne and Jerry Covell, two of the protest's four primary student leaders, to tell us the dramatic story.

Bridgetta Bourne When I identify myself as a deaf person, it's much like a black person identifying herself as black. All members of minority groups face certain challenges, and for the deaf the challenge is communication. As a deaf person, I feel disabled, even among groups including people with other disabilities. I still can't communicate with them without an interpreter.

There was recently a march from the White House to the Capitol in support of the Americans with Disabilities Act. There were many people with disabilities, but I didn't really feel like part of that community. Without an interpreter, I was basically lost. So the concept of oppression is one in which people in power are making decisions for me—about my life, about what I should do. Oppressed people have no voice.

Oppression is dangerous and pervasive. We even had it at Gallaudet, our own institution. Obviously, we should have a hand in running our own school, and that's why the Deaf President Now protest happened and was so successful. There had been so many years of struggle, so many years of deaf people being told they could not make decisions for themselves. You either have to release your anger at this oppression or just hold it in, as so many deaf people did in the past.

Jerry Covell Before the Deaf President Now movement, Gallaudet went through six presidents, all of them hearing men. These presidents served useful purposes, such as founding the college, expanding programs and services, creating new educational fields, and changing Gallaudet from college to university status. When the sixth president resigned and the board of trustees began a search for a new one, we all felt that the time was right for a deaf president.

Gallaudet is universally recognized and respected for its leadership in educating the deaf. Now we needed a deaf person to truly represent Gallaudet and the Deaf community. We needed a deaf person who could prove to hearing people that he or she was capable of carrying out the duties of a university president, thus opening the door to further opportunities for deaf people. There were qualified deaf people out there, with good backgrounds of education and experience. All but 4 of the 21 members of the board of trustees were hearing people. Many had good backgrounds in business, fund-raising, and public relations, and they contributed to Gallaudet in that way, but they had little or no understanding of deafness and Deaf culture. They needed to be convinced! So we held rallies. We got letters of support from many well-known people, including U.S. presidential candidates and senators. Public awareness grew. We felt confident, especially after the three finalists in the presidential search were announced: two deaf men and a hearing woman. Then the final selection was announced in a press release: "Gallaudet University Appoints First Woman President." We couldn't believe our eyes! We were shocked and upset. Please keep in mind, we didn't see this as a gender issue at all. It was strictly a hearing-deaf issue; a deaf woman president would have been great.

Bridgetta We marched downtown to the hotel where the chairman of the board of trustees was staying. We wanted a personal explanation of why they'd selected a hearing person over a deaf person. There was a reception going on at the hotel to introduce the new president. We hadn't planned a demonstration or a sit-in, but people were so angry! Sitting in the street was spontaneous. We didn't have a permit or anything; we just marched. The police came out with cars, barriers, and bullhorns to try to stop us. Signs and banners appeared. I remember a deaf couple who had a dog wearing a sign: "I understand sign language better than the new president of Gallaudet."

Jerry It was late by the time we got to the hotel, chanting and cheering. I remember seeing lights being turned on all over the hotel and people looking out the windows, wondering what was going on. Finally, the chairman came out. She couldn't understand sign language either. She said, "We felt this was the best decision for Gallaudet." We went round and round asking questions. We asked, "When will a deaf person get the chance to be president of Gallaudet?" "When will you allow this?" Eventually the chairman said, "Deaf people are not ready to function in a hearing world." Ooooh, that hurt! Everyone was stunned—even the interpreter. We were ready for real action after that. The infamous quote really pulled us together; it lit a flame under us. So in a way, we should thank the chairman.

We set out to shut Gallaudet down. On Monday morning, we put bike locks on the campus gates and parked cars in front of them. Students told everyone—administrators, faculty, staff, even board of trustees members—"Don't come in today. Go home. The campus is closed." When we took control of the campus, it showed how serious we were about the board's selection and the chairman's statement. The news media came in, and of course we took advantage of that.

Bridgetta As Jerry says, the protest brought people together. Before the protest, Gallaudet consisted of many different groups of deaf people. We came from various backgrounds. Some were interested in academics, others in sports, politics, or whatever. Some had gone to mainstream schools, others to deaf schools. Some were oral; others signed. But all rallied around the Deaf President Now movement, and our efforts were truly coordinated.

Jerry Our chants, in sign and speech, were important to the Deaf President Now movement. One of our chants was "Four! Four! Four!" We had four demands before we would release the university back. First, the hearing president had to be replaced by a deaf person. Second, the chairman of the board had to resign because of her statement. Third, a majority of the board had to consist of deaf people. Fourth, there must be no reprisals against faculty, staff, or students involved in the protest.

Toward the end of the week, the new president resigned or "stepped aside," as she put it. But she hadn't been replaced. So we changed our chant to "Three and a half! Three and a half!" That kept the motivation alive. We also chanted "Deaf and Proud!" and "Deaf Power!" We adapted that last one from the Black Power movement. We made the chant by putting one hand over an ear and raising the fist high in the air.

Bridgetta Bourne

Profiles and Perspectives

"Profiles and Perspectives" boxes silhouette cases—the personal journeys, joys, and obstacles of living with a disability or teaching students with disabilities. The hope is that by reading about the personal struggles or triumphs of people with disabilities or about the people in the field who are making a difference, you will be inspired to continue your study of special education.

New to This Edition

Integrated Videos

New to this edition are four inserts entitled "Teaching and Learning Video Connections." Each of these features begins by integrating the content of a video (available free to your professor) with teaching and learning strategies that will contribute to your development as an educator.

Teaching and Learning Video Connections

These features integrate the content of a video with the text and describe practical strategies for applying that content in a meaningful way.

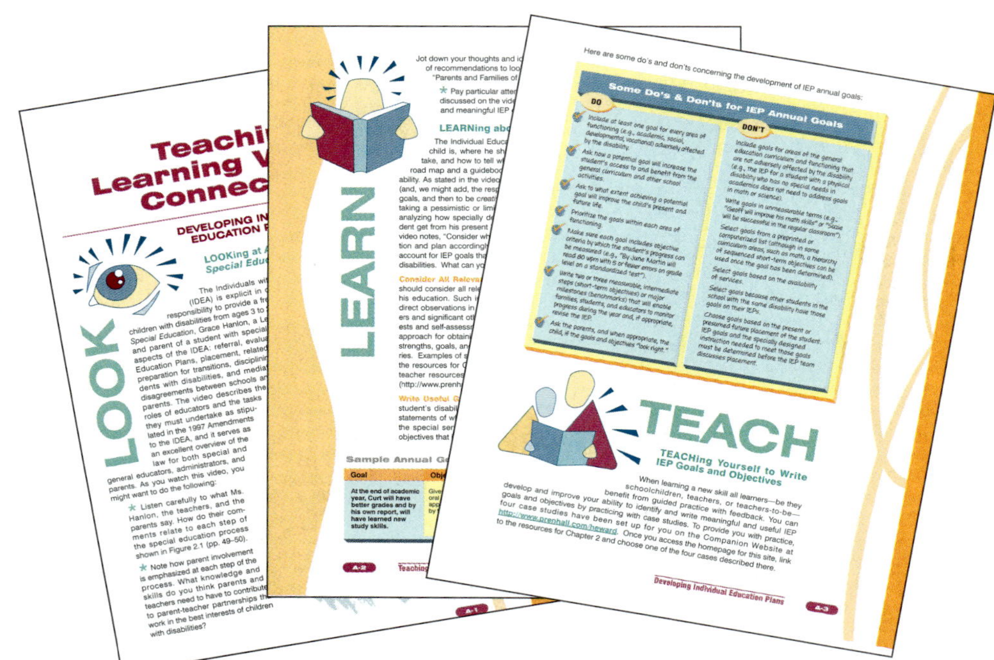

Video #1: A New IDEA for Special Education. The first of these inserts is entitled "Developing Individual Education Plans" and highlights the video *A New IDEA for Special Education,* through which you will learn about the critical aspects of the Individuals with Disabilities Education Act (IDEA). The insert further describes the essential components of writing the goals and objectives for individual education plans (IEPs). The teaching segment of this insert connects you to the Companion Website for this text **(http://www.prenhall.com/heward)**, where you can practice developing IEP goals and objectives for any one or more of four exceptional children who are profiled on the website.

Video #2: Together We Can! The second insert, "Classwide Peer Tutoring," introduces the video *Together We Can!* Following the viewing of the video, the Learn and Teach segments of the insert provide you with guidelines for designing and implementing a peer tutoring program in which every student in a general education classroom participates as both tutor and tutee.

Video #3: Small Differences. The third insert, "Small Differences," guides your viewing of the video of a small group of children with disabilities who want to raise your awareness of the *Small Differences* between people with and without disabilities. This feature asks you to examine closely your own preconceptions about the abilities of students with exceptionalities and apply strategies to develop positive images and attitudes.

Video #4: LifeLink. The fourth insert, "Learning to Live On My Own," highlights the video *LifeLink* and a program to provide opportunities for secondary students with disabilities to learn independent living skills and prepare for life in the adult community. In the Learn and Teach segments, you will find out how to teach for transition success.

Integrated Margin Notes

Also new to this edition are margin notes that direct you to the use of the Internet and a Companion Website **(http://www.prenhall.com/heward)** designed especially to accompany this text. Identified by the WWW logo, as shown here in the margin, these notes direct you to the Companion Website materials that will assist you in your study of each chapter. Long valued by users of previous editions of *Exceptional Children* is the wealth of information in the other margin notes. These notes provide additional commentary and perspectives on the accompanying content or links to related materials in other chapters or professional resources.

Companion Website

Accompanying this text is a user-friendly website that provides the professor and student a variety of meaningful resources and a study tool for you. Organized by chapter, this website includes:

Study Tools for Every Chapter

- **Chapter Objectives** – outlines key concepts from the text.
- **Interactive Self-quizzes** – complete with hints and automatic grading that provide immediate feedback to you. After you submit your answers for the interactive self-quizzes, the Companion Website **Results Reporter** computes a percentage grade, provides a graphic representation of how many questions you answered correctly and incorrectly, and gives a question-by-question analysis of the quiz. You are then given the option to send your quiz to up to four e-mail addresses (professor, teaching assistant, study partner, etc.).
- **Message Board** – serves as a virtual bulletin board to post or respond to questions or comments to/from a national audience. Some Focus Questions from the text have been added to get you started.
- **Web Destinations** – links to WWW sites that relate to chapter content

Access to the Course Syllabus

- **Syllabus Manage™** provides the instructor, with an easy, step-by-step process to create and revise syllabi, with direct links into Companion Website and other online content without having to learn HTML.
- You, as a student, may logon to the syllabus during any study session. All you need to know is the web address for the Companion Website and the password the professor has assigned to the syllabus. The address for this website is **http://www.prenhall.com/heward.**

- After your professor has created a syllabus using **Syllabus Manager**™, you may enter the syllabus for your course from any point in the Companion Website.
- Class dates are highlighted in white and assignment due dates appear in blue. By clicking on a date, you are shown the list of activities for the assignment. The activities for each assignment are linked directly to actual content.
- Adding assignments consists of clicking on the desired due date, then filling in the details of the assignment—name of the assignment, instructions, and whether or not it is a one-time or repeating assignment.
- In addition, links to other activities can be created easily. If the activity is online, a URL can be entered in the space provided, and it will link automatically to the final syllabus.
- The completed syllabus is hosted on the publisher's servers, allowing convenient updates from any computer on the Internet. Changes your professor makes to the syllabus are immediately available to you at your next logon.

Additional Supplements

Student Study Guide

A comprehensive review of the text content, the Student Study Guide provides you with a useful resource for learning about exceptional children, their families, and the field of special education. The chapter objectives, chapter overviews, chapter-at-a-glance tables, guided reviews, and self-check quizzes allow you to diligently study the course content.

Instructor's Manual

An expanded and improved Instructor's Manual is fully integrated with the text and includes numerous recommendations for presenting and extending the content of the chapters. The manual consists of chapter-by-chapter sections with chapter outlines, chapter-at-a-glance charts, chapter objectives, suggested answers to Focus Questions, introductory or enrichment activities, and recommendations for using the videos and video inserts, and other multimedia resources.

Transparencies

A package of nearly 150 two- and four-color acetate transparencies is available for use with the text. The transparencies highlight key concepts, summarize content, and illustrate figures and charts from the text. These transparencies are also available in Microsoft PowerPoint and can be accessed from the Companion Website, **http://www.prenhall.com/heward.**

Test Bank

A printed test bank of approximately 1,000 questions also accompanies the text. A variety of objective and essay questions are provided for each chapter. Computerized versions of the test bank are available in both Windows and Macintosh formats to enable professors to customize their exams.

Acknowledgments

The sixth edition of *Exceptional Children* has been enhanced by the combined efforts of a talented team of professionals at Prentice Hall Publishing Company. My Editor, Ann Castel Davis, has provided unwavering support and enthusiasm for the sixth edition—not to mention unrelenting pressure to "get the next chapter done." I really appreciate Ann for this; plus, she's a Cub fan. Developmental Editor Linda Montgomery was a tremendous help to me and a continuous source of good ideas throughout all stages of researching, conceptualizing, and revising the sixth edition. Among other things, Linda taught me how to organize content along a "critical path" for the reader. Dawn Potter copyedited the manuscript with a good balance of technical skill and respect for the author's writing style. The effective and meaningful portrayal of special education requires excellent photographs, and the contributions of Photo Editor Sandy Lenahan are evident throughout this edition. And if it were not for the hard work and professionalism of Production Editor Mary Irvin, the sixth edition would never have made it to the printing press. Mary (a.k.a. Ms. 24/7) can keep a lot of plates spinning at once, all the while displaying a rare and greatly appreciated graciousness.

No single author can capture the many perspectives and areas of expertise that make up a field as diverse and dynamic as special education. The currency and quality of this edition have been improved by Profiles and Perspectives and Teaching and Learning in School essays authored exclusively for this text by the following scholars and teachers: Sheila Alber, University of Southern Mississippi; Patty Barbetta, Florida International University; Sue Brewster and Lyn Dol, Toledo Public Schools; Judy Carta, Juniper Gardens Children's Center; John O. Cooper, Ohio State University; Vivian Correa, University of Florida; Jill Dardig, Ohio Dominican College; Glen Dunlap, Bobbie Vaughn, and Lise Fox, University of South Florida; Marsha Forest and Jack Pearpoint, Centre for Integrated Education and Community (Toronto); Douglas Fuchs and Lynn Fuchs, Vanderbilt University; Michael Giangreco, University of Vermont; Bonnie Grossen, University of Oregon; Stephen Hawking, Cambridge University; Dick Howell, Ohio State University; Carolyn Hughes, Vanderbilt University; Margo Mastropieri and Tom Scruggs, George Mason University; Catherine Maurice, author of *Let Me Hear Your Voice*; Jane Piirto, Ashland University; Diane Sainato, Ohio State University; Barbara Schirmer, Kent State University; Elaine Silliman and Jill Beasman, University of South Florida; Marti Snell, University of Virginia; Rachel Janney, Radford University; and John Umbreit, University of Arizona.

I am especially grateful to these colleagues and friends for their contributions to the four case studies introduced in the Teaching and Learning Video Connection, Developing Individual Educational Plans, and found in full on the companion website: Timothy Heron (Derek), Rebecca Morrison (Jeremy), Gayle Porterfield and Donald Tessman (Leanna), and Lynn Woolsey (Mwajabu). Because of their efforts, students will have opportunities to practice writing IEP goals and objectives for these real exceptional children.

Other individuals who provided me with material and information that greatly enriched the sixth edition are: Teresa Grossi, University of Indiana; Ronni Hochman Spratt, Upper Arlington Schools; Sandy Letham and Dennis Higgins, Zuni Elementary School, Albuquerque, NM; Diana Nielander, National Lekotek Center; and Sandie Trask, Westerville City Schools.

I would like to thank the reviewers of the sixth edition for their insights and comments: Michael Banks, Missouri Southern State College; Carrie Ann Blackaller, California State University—Dominguez Hills; Ann Boyer, Florida Atlantic University; Mary-Kay Crane, University of Georgia; Arthur R. Crowell, Jr., Bloomsburg University (PA); Lawrence Maheady, SUNY—College at Fredonia; Thomas F. McLaughlin, Gonzaga University (WA); Pam Robinson, Oklahoma Baptist University; Donald Stauffer, Slippery Rock University; and Marilyn Urquhart, University of South Dakota.

The following professors—all of whom have served as instructors of introductory special education courses at other colleges and universities—provided timely and helpful reviews of the previous edition: Bruce Baum, State University at Buffalo; Jim Burns, The College of St. Rose; Peter Carullias, II, University of Cincinnati; Carol Chase Thomas, Universtiy of North Carolina at Wilmington; Alice E. Christie, University of Akron; Sheila Drake, Kansas Wesleyan University; Pamela J. Gent, Clarion University of Pennsylvania; Joan M. Goodship, University of Richmond; Sheldon Maron, Portland State University; James M. Patton, College of William and Mary; Leonila P. Rivera, Southwest Missouri State University; James A. Siders, University of Southern Mississippi; and Scott Sparks, Ohio University. The perspectives, experience, and recommendations of these reviewers were instrumental in guiding the revision process.

I am indebted to Vivian Correa, University of Florida, for co-authoring Chapter 3—Special Education in a Culturally and Linguistically Diverse Society—and to my OSU colleague, Dick Howell, for co-authoring Chapter 14—Giftedness and Talent Development. Sheila Alber and April Miller, University of Southern Mississippi, co-authored the Student Study Guide. The Instructor's Manual and Test Bank were also written by Sheila and April, with contributions by their graduate students Kathleen Brennan, Sara Ernsbarger, and Pokey Stanford. This group of special educators produced a very strong set of ancillary materials, and I am confident instructors and students will appreciate and benefit from their hard work and creativity. I want to extend a special thank you to Joe Delquadri and Charlie Greenwood for producing the video on classwide peer tutoring that accompanies the sixth edition. The work on classwide peer tutoring by Charlie and Joe and their colleagues at the Juniper Gardens Children's Project over the past 20 years is a model of systematic research and development in education, and I am pleased that their video is part of the sixth edition.

Finally, I will always be grateful to Mike Orlansky, a former colleague, friend, and co-author of the first four editions of *Exceptional Children*.

Most of all, I appreciate and wish to acknowledge the support of my family—Jill, Lee, and Lynn—who (again) had to endure the unsightly aftermath of too many all-niters.

Bill Heward

Contents

Chapter 4

Part 2 *Educational Needs of Exceptional Students* 153

Chapter 5

Chapter 6

Mental Retardation 200

Chapter 7

Learning Disabilities 244

Chapter 8

Emotional and Behavioral Disorders 288

Chapter 9

Communication Disorders 326

Chapter 10

Hearing Loss 364

Chapter 11

Blindness and Low Vision 406

Chapter 12

Physical Impairments and Special Health Care Needs 442

Chapter 13

Severe Disabilities 484

Chapter 14

Giftedness and Talent Development 532

by Richard D. Howell and William L. Heward

Chapter 15

Transition to Adulthood 576

Postscript

Developing Your Own Personal View of Special Education 628

Special Features

TEACHING AND LEARNING IN SCHOOL

Strategy	*Application*	*Text Location*
Signaling for Help	Responding to individual student's requests for teaching assistance	36
Interactive Teaming	Guidelines for collaboration	54
Someone's Missing: The Student as an Overlooked Participant in the IEP Process	Including students in development of their own IEPs	62
An Ethnics Feelings Book	Developing cultural awareness	97
A Parent-Professional Partnership in Positive Behavioral Support	Using positive behavioral support in home and community	142
Selecting Toys for Young Children with Disabilities	Choosing toys for meaningful play	160
Idea Bunny Helps Preschoolers Be More Independent	Developing skills for independent learning	178
Including Preschool Children with Autism: Five Strategies That Work	Teaching young children with developmental disabilities skills for communication, social competence, and independence	192
How Many Can You Do in a Minute?	Building student's fluency in basic tool skills	228
What to Do When Students Make Mistakes	Providing effective and efficient error correction	232
Some Things We've Learned about Inclusion	Teacher modifications that make a difference	236
Six Principles for Early Reading Instruction	Teaching beginning readers	250
Tutoring Joe: Winning with the Precision Teaching Team	Using a daily record of progress to guide instruction	268
What Is Direct Instruction?	Using carefully designed, learner-tested curriculum that features active student response and immediate feedback	272
Mnemonic Strategies	Using memory-enhancing techniques	276
Using Response Cards to Increase Participation and Achievement	Providing frequent response opportunities to all children in the classroom	296
"Look, I'm All Finished!" Recruiting Teacher Attention	Teaching students why, when, and how to appropriately seek teacher attention	312
Leadership Roles Encourage Language in the Classroom	Developing language skills in young children	335
Helping the Child Who Stutters in the Classroom	Establishing a supportive speech environment for children with fluency disorders	347
Active Learning Dialogues for Students with Language Learning Disabilities	Linking problem solving with real-world experiences to develop verbal communication skills	350
Communication Partners: Strategies for Opening Doors to Communication	Employing nine specific strategies to increase communication effectiveness	360
Writer's Workshop: Teaching Process Writing to Students Who Are Deaf	Learning to manipulate the surface structure of English	382

PROFILES AND PERSPECTIVES

Prologue

EARN
Good Listeners
1. Look at the speaker
2. Do not start a conversation
with someone else while the
speaker is talking

A Personal View of Special Education

My primary goal in writing this book is to describe the history, practices, advances, problems, and challenges that make up the complex and dynamic field called special education in as complete, clear, up-to-date, and objective a manner as possible. This, of course, is much easier said than done: an author's personal views are surely implicit in those descriptions—between the lines, as they say. Because my personal beliefs and assumptions about special education—which are by no means unique, but neither are they universally held by everyone in the field—affect both the substance and the tone of the entire book, I believe I owe you an explicit summary of those views.

People with disabilities have a fundamental right to live and participate in the same settings and programs—in school, at home, in the workplace, and in the community—as do people without disabilities. That is, the settings and programs in which children and adults with disabilities learn, live, work, and play should, to the greatest extent possible, be the same settings and programs in which people without disabilities participate. People with and without disabilities have a great deal to contribute to and learn from one another. We cannot do that without regular, meaningful interaction.

Individuals with disabilities have the right to as much independence as we can help them achieve. Special educators have no more important teaching task than that of helping children with disabilities learn how to increase the level of decision making and control over their own lives. Thus, self-determination and self-advocacy skills should be significant curriculum components for all students with disabilities.

Special education must continue to expand its efforts to recognize and respond appropriately to all learners with exceptional educational needs. These include the gifted and talented child, the preschooler with disabilities and the infant who is at risk for a future learning problem, the exceptional child from a different cultural background, and the adult with disabilities. In support of this belief, this text includes a chapter on each of these critical areas of special education.

Both the meaningfulness and the effectiveness of special education are enhanced by a partnership between schools and families. Professionals have too long ignored the needs of parents and families of exceptional children, often treating them as patients, clients, or even adversaries instead of realizing that they are partners with the same goals. Some special educators have too often given the impression (and, worse, believed it to be true) that parents are there to serve professionals, when in fact the opposite is more correct. We have long neglected to recognize parents as a child's first—and in many ways best—teachers. Learning to work effectively with parents is one of the most important skills the special educator can acquire. Thus, a chapter is devoted to the parent-professional partnership.

The efforts of special educators are most effective when they incorporate the input and services of all of the disciplines in the helping professions. It is foolish to argue over territorial rights when we can accomplish more by working together within an interdisciplinary team that includes our colleagues in psychology, medicine, social services, and vocational rehabilitation.

All students have the right to an effective education. As educators, our primary responsibility is to design and implement effective instruction for personal, social, vocational, and academic skills. These skills are the same ones that determine the quality of our lives: working effectively and efficiently on our jobs; being productive members of our communities; maintaining a comfortable lifestyle in our homes; communicating with our friends and family; using our leisure time meaningfully and enjoyably. Instruction is ultimately effective when it helps the individuals we serve to acquire and maintain positive lifestyle changes. To put it another way, the proof of the process is in the product. Therefore . . .

Teachers must demand effectiveness from their instructional approaches. For many years conventional wisdom has fostered the belief that it takes unending patience to teach children with disabilities. I believe this view is a disservice to students with special needs and to the educators—both special and general education teachers—whose job it is to teach them. Teachers should not wait patiently for exceptional students to learn, attributing lack of progress to some inherent attribute or faulty process within the child, such as mental retardation, learning disability, attention-deficit disorder, or emotional disturbance. Instead, the teacher should use direct and frequent measures of the student's performance as the primary guide for modifying instruction in order to improve its effectiveness. This, I believe, is the real work of the special educator. Numerous examples of instructional strategies and tactics demonstrated to be effective through classroom-based research are described and illustrated throughout the text. Although you will not know how to teach exceptional children after reading this or any other introductory text, you will gain an appreciation for the importance of explicit, systematic instruction and an understanding of the kinds of teaching skills the special educator must have.

Finally, the future for individuals with disabilities holds great promise. We have only begun to discover the myriad ways to improve teaching, increase learning, prevent or minimize the conditions that cause disabilities, encourage acceptance, and use technology to compensate for disabilities. Although I make no specific predictions for the future, I am certain that we have not come as far as we can in learning how to help exceptional individuals build and enjoy fuller, more independent lives in the school, workplace, and community.

Part 1

Foundations for Understanding Special Education

Chapter 1

Defining Special Education

Focus Questions

- When is special education needed? How do we know?
- If categorical labels do not tell us what and how to teach, why are they used so frequently?
- Why have court cases and federal legislation been required to ensure that children with disabilities receive an appropriate education?
- Can a special educator provide all three kinds of intervention—*preventive*, *remedial*, and *compensatory*—on behalf of an individual child?
- What do you think are the three most important challenges facing special education today? Why? Read your answer again after finishing this book.

Educating children with special needs or abilities is a difficult challenge. Teachers and related professionals who have accepted that challenge—special educators—work in an exciting and rapidly changing field. To begin to appreciate some of the action and excitement that characterize this important and dynamic field, it is necessary to examine the concepts and perspectives that are basic to understanding exceptional children and special education.

Who Are Exceptional Children?

Go to the companion website at http://www.prenhall.com/heward and select Chapter 1 to review the chapter objectives.

All children exhibit differences from one another in terms of their physical attributes (e.g., some are shorter, some are stronger) and learning abilities (e.g., some learn quickly and are able to remember and use what they have learned in new situations; others need repeated practice and have difficulty maintaining and generalizing new skills). The differences among most children are relatively small, enabling these children to benefit from the general education program. The physical attributes and/or learning abilities of some children, however—those called **exceptional children**—differ from the norm (either below or above) to such an extent that an individualized program of adapted, specialized education is required to meet their needs. The term *exceptional children* includes children who experience difficulties in learning as well as those children whose performance is so superior that modifications in curriculum and instruction are necessary to help them fulfill their potential. Thus, *exceptional children* is an inclusive term that refers to children with learning and/or behavior problems, children with physical disabilities or sensory impairments, and children who are intellectually gifted or have a special talent. Definitions of several related terms will help you better understand the concept of exceptionality.

Disability refers to the reduced function or loss of a particular body part or organ; it is sometimes used interchangeably with the term *impairment.* A disability limits the ability to perform certain tasks (e.g., to see, to read, to walk) in the same way that most persons do. A person with a disability is not handicapped, however, unless the physical disability leads to educational, personal, social, vocational, or other problems. If a child who has lost a leg, for example, can learn to use an artificial limb and thus function in and out of school without problems, she is not handicapped. The term *students with disabilities* is more restrictive than *exceptional children* because it does not include gifted and talented children.

The word handicapped *is derived from "cap in hand" and conjures up the image of a person with disabilities begging in the street.* ***Handicapism*** *refers to the negative stereotyping and unequal and unjust treatment of people with disabilities.*

Handicap refers to a problem a person with a disability or impairment encounters in interacting with the environment. A disability may pose a handicap in one environment but not in another. The child with an artificial limb may be handicapped when competing against nondisabled peers on the basketball court but may experience no handicap in the classroom. Individuals with disabilities also experience handicaps that have nothing to do with their disabilities but are the result of negative attitudes and inappropriate behavior of others who needlessly restrict their access and ability to participate fully in school, work, or community activities. Although there are technical differences between *disability* and *handicap,* for many years the two terms have been used interchangeably (Vergason & Anderegg, 1997). The descriptor *with disabilities* is preferred today.

Physicians also use the term at risk *(or* high risk*) to identify pregnancies with a greater-than-normal probability of producing babies with disabilities. For example, a pregnancy may be considered high risk if the pregnant woman is above or below typical childbearing age, uses alcohol heavily, or is drug-dependent.*

At risk refers to children who, although not currently identified as having a disability, are considered to have a greater-than-usual chance of developing a disability. The term is often applied to infants and preschoolers who, because of conditions surrounding their births or home environments, may be expected to experience developmental problems at a later time. The term also refers to students who are experiencing learning problems in the regular classroom and are therefore at risk of school failure or of being identified for special education services.

Some exceptional children share certain physical characteristics and/or patterns of learning and behavior that may be related to special educational needs and services. These characteristics fall into the following so-called categories of exceptionality:

- Mental retardation
- Learning disabilities
- Emotional and behavioral disorders

- Communication (speech and language) disorders
- Hearing loss
- Blindness and low vision
- Physical and health impairments
- Severe disabilities
- Intellectual giftedness and special talents

As stated earlier, all children differ from one another in individual characteristics along a continuum; exceptional children are those whose differences from the norm are large enough to require an individually designed program of instruction—in other words, special education—if they are to benefit fully from education. It is a mistake, however, to think that there are two distinct kinds of children—that is, those who are special and those who are regular. Exceptional children are more like other children than they are different. Keep this critical point in mind as you read about the exceptional children described in this text.

Check your ongoing understanding of Chapter 1 concepts by using the guided review module at http://www.prenhall.com/heward.

How Many Exceptional Children Are There?

It is impossible to state precisely the number of exceptional children for many reasons: (1) the different criteria used by states and local school systems to identify exceptional children; (2) the relative resources and abilities of different school systems to provide preventive services so that an at-risk student does not become a special education student; (3) the imprecise nature of assessment and the large part that subjective judgment plays in interpretation of assessment data; and (4) the fact that a child may be identified as eligible for special education at one time in his school career and not eligible (or included in a different disability category) at another time.

The most complete and accurate information on how many exceptional children live in the United States is derived from the child count data in the U.S. Department of Education's annual report to Congress on the education of the country's children with disabilities. More than 5.7 million children and youth with disabilities, or 7.7% of the resident population ages 3 to 21, received special education services during the 1996–1997 school year (U.S. Department of Education, 1998). Table 1.1 shows the number of students ages 6 through 21 who received special education under each of the 12 disability categories used by the federal government.

Let's take a quick look at some other numerical facts about special education in the United States.

- The number of children and youth who receive special education has grown every year since a national count was begun in 1976, with an overall increase of 51% since the 1976–1977 school year.
- New early intervention programs have been major contributors to the increases since 1986. During the 1996–1997 school year, 559,902 preschoolers (ages 3 to 5) and 187,384 infants and toddlers (birth through age 2) were among those receiving special education.
- Children with disabilities in special education represent approximately 10.8% of the entire school-age population.
- The number of children who receive special education increases from age 3 through age 9. The number served decreases gradually with each successive age year after age 9 until age 17. Thereafter, the number of students receiving special education decreases sharply.
- Ninety-one percent of all children and youth ages 6 to 21 receiving special education are reported under four disability categories: (1) learning disabilities

Table 1.1 Number of students ages 6–21 who received special education services under the federal government's 12 disability categories (1996–1997 school year)

Disability Category	Number	Percent of Total
Specific learning disabilities	2,676,299	51.1
Speech or language impairments	1,050,975	20.1
Mental retardation	594,025	11.4
Emotional disturbance	447,426	8.6
Other health impairments	160,824	3.1
Multiple disabilities	99,638	1.9
Hearing impairments	68,766	1.3
Orthopedic impairments	66,400	1.3
Autism	34,101	0.7
Visual impairments	25,834	0.5
Traumatic brain injury	10,378	0.2
Deaf-blindness	1,286	<0.1
All disabilities	5,235,952	100.0

Source: From U.S. Department of Education. (1998). *Twentieth annual report to Congress on the implementation of the Individuals with Disabilities Act* (p. II-16). Washington, DC: Author.

What factors might be responsible for the huge increase in the number of children identified as learning disabled? Why has the number of children identified as mentally retarded decreased in recent years? Jot down your ideas and then compare them with what you learn later in Chapters 6 and 7.

(51.1%), (2) speech and language impairment (20.1%), (3) mental retardation (11.4%), and (4) emotional disturbance (8.6%).

- The percentage of students receiving special education under the learning disabilities category has grown dramatically (from 23.8% to 51.1%), whereas the percentage of students with mental retardation has decreased by more than half (from 24.9% to 11.4%) since the federal government began collecting and reporting child count data in 1976–77.
- About twice as many males as females receive special education.
- The vast majority—approximately 85%—of school-age children receiving special education have mild disabilities.
- The "typical" child receiving special education in the United States is a 9-year-old boy with learning disabilities who spends part of each school day in the regular classroom and part in a resource room (U.S. Department of Education, 1990).

Although special education for children who are gifted and talented is not mandated by federal law as it is for children with disabilities, by 1990 38 states reported serving more than 2 million students in K–12 gifted programs (U.S. Department of Education, 1993). This number ranks gifted and talented students as the second largest group of exceptional children receiving special education services. On the basis of an estimate that gifted and talented children may comprise as much as 5% of the school-age population, approximately 2.5 million additional gifted and talented children may need special education (Clark, 1997). This discrepancy between need and the level of service may make gifted and talented children the most underserved group of exceptional children.

Why Do We Label and Classify Exceptional Children?

Centuries ago, labeling and classifying people was of little importance; survival was the main concern. Those whose disabilities prevented their full participation in the activities necessary for survival were left on their own to perish or, in some instances, were

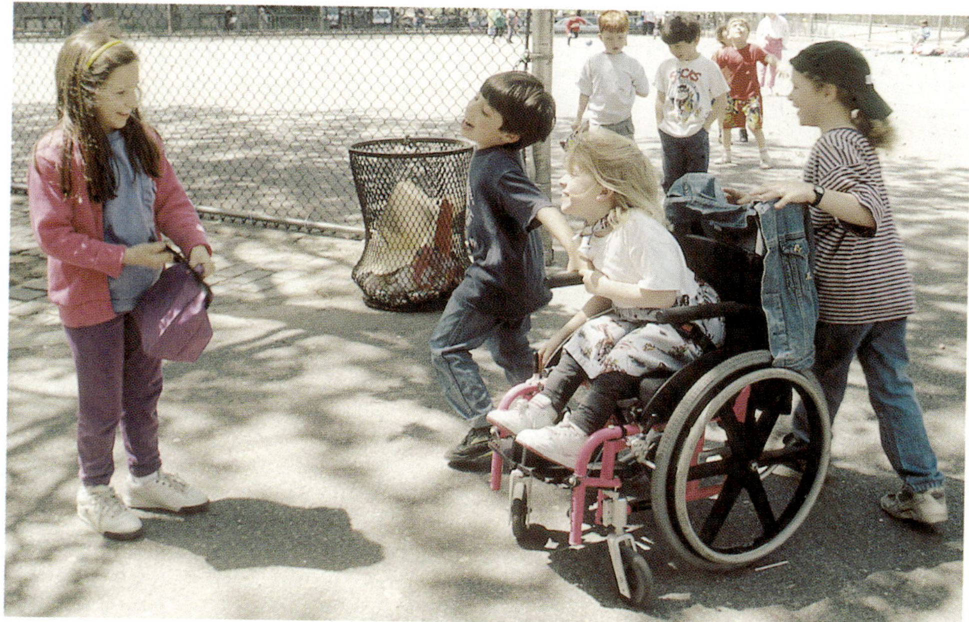

Although children with disabilities have special instructional needs, they are, above all, children.

even killed. In later years, derogatory labels such as "dunce," "imbecile," and "fool" were applied to people with mental retardation or behavior problems, and other demeaning words were used for persons with other disabilities or physical deformities. In each instance, however, the purpose of classification was the same: to exclude the person with disabilities from the activities, privileges, and facilities of everyday life.

Many educators believe that the labels used to identify and classify exceptional children stigmatize them and function to exclude them from the mainstream (e.g., Reschly, 1996; Reynolds, 1991; Stainback & Stainback, 1991). Others argue that a workable system of classifying exceptional children (or their exceptional learning needs) is a prerequisite to providing the special educational services those children require (e.g., Kauffman, 1998b; MacMillan, Gresham, Bocian, & Lambros, 1998). Classification is a complex issue involving emotional, political, and ethical considerations in addition to scientific, fiscal, and educational interests. As with most complex questions, there are valid perspectives on both sides. The reasons most often cited for and against the classification and labeling of exceptional children are the following:

Possible Benefits of Labeling

- Labeling recognizes meaningful differences in learning or behavior and is a first and necessary step in responding responsibly to those differences.
- Labeling may lead to a protective response in which children are more accepting of the atypical behavior of a peer with disabilities than they would be if that same behavior were emitted by a child without disabilities (MacMillan, 1982).
- Labeling helps professionals communicate with one another and classify and evaluate research findings.
- Funding and resources for research and other programs are often based on specific categories of exceptionality.
- Labels enable disability-specific advocacy groups (e.g., parents of children with autism) to promote specific programs and to spur legislative action.

A protective response—whether by peers, parents, or teachers—toward a child with a disability can be a disadvantage if it creates learned helplessness and diminishes the labeled child's chances to develop independence (Weisz, 1981; Weisz, Bromfield, Vines, & Weiss, 1985).

- Labeling helps make exceptional children's special needs more visible to policymakers and the public.

Possible Disadvantages of Labeling

- Because labels usually focus on disability, impairment, and performance deficits, some people may think only in terms of what the individual *cannot do* instead of what she *can or might be able to learn to do.*
- Labels may stigmatize the child and lead peers to reject or ridicule the labeled child.
- Labels may negatively affect the child's self-esteem.
- Labels may cause others to hold low expectations for and to differentially treat a child on the basis of the label, which may result in a self-fulfilling prophecy. For example, in one study, student teachers gave a child labeled "autistic" more praise and rewards and less verbal correction for *incorrect* responses than they gave a child labeled "normal" (Eikeseth & Lovaas, 1992). Such differential treatment could hamper a child's acquisition of new skills and contribute to the development and maintenance of a level of performance consistent with the label's prediction.
- Labels that describe a child's performance deficit often mistakenly acquire the role of explanatory constructs (e.g., "Sherry acts that way *because* she is emotionally disturbed").
- Even though membership in a given category is based on a particular characteristic (e.g., hearing loss), there is a tendency to assume that all children in a category share other traits as well, thereby diminishing the detection and appreciation of each child's uniqueness (Gelb, 1997).
- Labels suggest that learning problems are primarily the result of something wrong within the child, thereby reducing the systematic examination of and accountability for instructional variables as the cause of performance deficits. This is an especially damaging outcome when the label provides educators with a built-in excuse for ineffective instruction (e.g., "Jalen hasn't learned to read because he's ______ ").
- Special education labels have a certain permanence; once labeled, it is difficult for a child to ever again achieve the status of simply being just another kid.
- Labels may provide a basis for keeping children out of the regular classroom.
- Classifying exceptional children requires the expenditure of a great amount of money and professional and student time that might better be spent in planning and delivering instruction (Chaikind, Danielson, & Brauen, 1993).

Not all labels used to classify children with disabilities are considered equally negative or stigmatizing. One factor possibly contributing to the large number of children identified as learning disabled is that many parents view "learning disabilities" as a socially acceptable classification (Algozzine & Korinek, 1985; MacMillan, Gresham, Siperstein, & Bocian, 1996).

Clearly, there are strong arguments both for and against the classification and labeling of exceptional children. Although the pros and cons of using disability category labels have been widely debated for several decades, neither conceptual arguments nor research has produced a conclusive case for the total acceptance or absolute rejection of labeling practices. For example, while some educators contend that labeling stigmatizes children and hurts their self-esteem, research suggests that stigmatization and poor self-concept typically precede a child's identification for special education and that disability labels do not appreciably add to those effects (Hallahan & Kauffman, 1994). Still, research has shed little light on the problem. Most of the studies conducted to assess the effects of labeling have produced inconclusive, often contradictory, evidence and have generally been marked by methodological weakness (MacMillan, 1982). Let's look more closely at how the use of categorical labels affects a child's access to special education services and the quality of instruction that he receives.

Labeling and Eligibility for Special Education

On one level, the various labels given to children with special learning needs can be viewed as a means of organizing the funding and administration of special education services in the schools. Under current law, to receive special education services, a child must be identified as having a disability (i.e., labeled) and, with few exceptions, must be further classified into one of that state's categories, such as mental retardation or learning disabilities. In practice, therefore, a student becomes eligible for various kinds of special education and related services because of membership in a given category. If losing one's label also means loss of needed services, the trade-off is not likely to be beneficial for the child (Braaten, Kauffman, Braaten, Polsgrove, & Nelson, 1988). In the 1970s, for example, the definition of mental retardation was changed, and children who had previously been classified under the subcategory of "borderline mental retardation" no longer met the definition; as a result, they were no longer eligible for special education services designed for children with mental retardation. Although many of this large group of declassified youngsters receive services under other disability categories (notably learning disabilities), some do not receive needed services (MacMillan et al., 1998; Zetlin & Murtaugh, 1990).

Arguing that labels are a necessary first step in serving students with important differences in behavior and learning, Kauffman (1998b) writes:

> Although universal interventions that apply equally to all, regardless of their behavioral characteristics or risks of developing disorders, can be implemented without labels and risk of stigma, no other interventions are possible without labels. Either all students are treated the same or some are treated differently. Any student who is treated differently is inevitably labeled. . . . We need to use the least offensive labels that clearly describe the problem, but we need not believe the fantasy that the label *is* the problem or that a new label will fool people for long. . . . Some may argue that "person first" language (e.g., "child with behavioral disorder" or "person with mental retardation") is a partial solution, others that individuals do not actually *have* disabilities but are merely assigned them in some socially acceptable conspiratorial fashion or have merely developed a reputation for behaving in certain ways, or that we should label only programs or services, not the people who receive them. These are tortuous and self-serving philosophical games that delay and deny help to the suffering, whether they are individuals who exhibit the problem behavior, those who must live, learn, play, or work with them, or those who simply care about them. When we are unwilling for whatever reason to say that a person has a problem, we are helpless to prevent it. . . . Labeling a problem clearly is the first step in dealing productively with it. (p. 12)

Kauffman (1998b) contends that the issue of labeling is primarily a diversion and that our unwillingness to label children's behavior problems, especially young children who may be at risk for developing more serious problems, impedes prevention of more serious disabilities.

Impact on Instruction

What we can say about the possible benefits of classifying exceptional children? On the one hand, most are experienced not by individual children but by groups of children, parents, and professionals who are associated with a certain category. On the other hand, all of the potential negative aspects of labeling affect the individual child who has been labeled. Of the possible advantages of labeling listed earlier, only the first two could be said to benefit an individual child directly. However, the argument that labels associate diagnosis with proper treatment is tenuous at best, particularly when the kinds of labels used in special education are considered. Although written three decades ago, the following quotation states what many special educators continue to believe about the irrelevance of categorical labels to instructional planning:

> The children are given various labels including deaf, blind, orthopedically handicapped, trainable mentally retarded, educable mentally retarded, autistic, socially maladjusted, perceptually handicapped, brain-injured, emotionally disturbed, disadvantaged, and those with learn-

Children ages 3 to 9 can be identified as developmentally delayed and receive special education services without the use of specific disability labels.

ing disabilities. For the most part the labels are not important. They rarely tell the teacher who can be taught in what way. One could put five or six labels on the same child and still not know what to teach him or how. (Becker, Engelmann, & Thomas, 1971, pp. 435–436)

Although identification and classification of exceptional children are necessary, no one is happy with the current system of categorical labels (Speece & Harry, 1997). Reynolds, Wang, and Walberg (1987), who are strong opponents of the present system of identifying and labeling children for special education services, believe that "the boundaries of the categories have shifted so markedly in response to legal, economic, and political forces as to make diagnosis largely meaningless" (p. 396). Labels signify eligibility for services, but they have proven unreliable in many cases. For example, one study that examined the classification of 523 students with mild disabilities found that 24% had been given two or more labels during their school years and that 17% of those who were moved from their initial category to another category were later reassigned to their initial classification (Wolman, Thurlow, & Bruininks, 1989). Similar results were reported by Halgren and Clarizio (1993), who reported that 16.3% of 654 students with various disabilities in 10 school districts were reclassified during a three-year period.

For a critique and discussion of the possible merits and disadvantages of 20/20 Analysis, see Soodak and Podell (1994) and Reynolds, Zetlin, and Wang (1993).

A number of special educators have proposed alternative approaches to classifying exceptional children that focus on educationally relevant variables (e.g., Adelman, 1996; Hardman, McDonnell, & Welch, 1997; Iscoe & Payne, 1972; Sontag, Sailor, & Smith, 1977). For example, Reynolds and his colleagues have proposed a system they call "20/20 Analysis" as an alternative nonlabeling approach to the traditional, categorically driven model of special education (Reynolds, Zetlin, & Heistad, 1996). The lowest-achieving 20% and the highest-achieving 20% of students would be identified and eligible for broad (noncategorical) approaches to improvement of learning opportunities.

> In 20/20 Analysis, we begin with measuring progress of students in important areas of learning and identifying those at the margins—those who are not learning well and those showing top rates of learning. . . . At all times the focus is on outcome variables. . . . The idea is to look to the margins in learning progress and to identify those who most urgently require adapted instruction. (Reynolds & Heistad, 1997, p. 441)

Lovitt (1982) suggests classifying exceptional children according to the curriculum and skill areas they need to learn.

> "What should we call the special children who are sent to our classes?" This question might be asked by regular education teachers who are about to have special education children mainstreamed in their classes. Should they carefully study the dossiers of the children to figure out what others have called them? Should a regular teacher, for instance, try to remember that Roy, who will soon be sent to his regular class, was called emotionally disturbed by two school psychologists, a social worker, and a reading teacher (even though he was referred to as learning disabled by another school psychologist)? Should he hang on to the fact that Amy was called mentally retarded by most of the people who wrote reports for her folder? Likewise, should he make every effort to recall that Tim was most often referred to as learning disabled?
>
> No. Those labels do not help teachers design effective programs for the special children they will teach. They won't help teachers decide where to seat the children; they certainly won't help them to design educational and management strategies.
>
> But if we shouldn't refer to these special children by using those old labels, then how should we refer to them? For openers, call them Roy, Amy, and Tim. Beyond that, refer to them on the basis of what you're trying to teach them. For example, if a teacher wants to teach Roy to compute, read, and comprehend, he might call him a student of computation, reading, and comprehension. We do this all the time with older students. Sam, who attends Juilliard, is referred to as "the trumpet student"; Jane, who attends Harvard, is called "the law student." (Lovitt, 1979, p. 5)

In a system such as this, called **curriculum-based assessment,** students would be assessed and classified relative to the degree to which they are learning specific curriculum content (Deno, 1985, 1997; Howell, 1998; Salvia & Hughes, 1990). The fundamental question in curriculum-based assessment is "How is the student progressing in the curriculum of the local school?" (Tucker, 1985). Educators who employ curriculum-based assessment believe that it is more important to assess (and thereby classify) students in terms of acquisition of the knowledge and skills that make up the school's curriculum than to determine the degree to which they differ from the normative score of all children in some general physical attribute or learning characteristic.

Even though curriculum-based assessment is being used more frequently, use of the traditional labels and categories of exceptional children is likely to continue. The continued development and use of educationally relevant classification systems, however, make it more likely that identification and assessment will lead to meaningful instructional programs for children, promote more educationally meaningful communication and research by professionals, and perhaps decrease some of the negative aspects of the current practice of labeling children.

Why Are Laws Governing the Education of Exceptional Children Necessary?

An Exclusionary Past

It is said that a society can be judged by the way it treats those who are different. By this criterion, our educational system has a less than distinguished history. Children who are different because of race, culture, language, gender, or exceptionality have often been denied full and fair access to educational opportunities (Banks & Banks, 1997).

Past practices were not entirely negative. Long before there was any legal requirement to do so, many children with special needs were educated by devoted parents and teachers. See Safford and Safford (1996) for an interesting historical account of educators' attempts to help children with disabilities over the last several centuries.

Although exceptional children have always been with us, attention has not always been paid to their special needs. In the past, many children with disabilities were entirely excluded from any publicly supported program of education. Prior to the 1970s, many states had laws permitting public schools to deny enrollment to children with disabilities (Heward & Cavanaugh, 1997). Local school officials had no legal obligation to grant students with disabilities the same educational access that nondisabled students enjoyed. One state law, for example, allowed schools to refuse to serve "children physically or mentally incapacitated for school work"; another state had a law stipulating that children with "bodily or mental conditions rendering attendance inadvisable" could be turned away. When these laws were contested, the nation's courts generally supported exclusion. In a 1919 case, for example, a 13-year-old student with physical disabilities (but normal intellectual ability) was excluded from his local school because he "produces a depressing and nauseating effect upon the teachers and school children. . . . he takes up an undue portion of the teacher's time and attention, distracts attention of other pupils, and interferes generally with the discipline and progress of the school" (Johnson, 1986, p. 2). Many communities had no facilities or services whatsoever to help exceptional children and their families.

Gonder (1997) provides enlightening profiles of several pioneering special educators and their students from the 1940s to the present.

When local public schools began to accept a measure of responsibility for educating certain exceptional students, a philosophy of segregation prevailed—a philosophy that continued unchanged until recently. Inclusion of exceptional children into regular schools and classes is a relatively recent phenomenon. Children received labels—such as mentally retarded, crippled, or emotionally disturbed—and were confined to isolated and segregated classrooms, kept apart from the other children and teachers in the regular education program. One special education teacher describes the sense of isolation she felt and the crude facilities in which her special class operated in the 1960s:

What's in a Name? The Labels and Language of Special Education

Some years ago at the annual convention of the Council for Exceptional Children, hundreds of attendees were wearing big yellow and black buttons that were very popular that year. The buttons proclaimed "Label jars, not children!" Wearers of the buttons were presumably making a statement about one or more of the criticisms leveled at categorizing and labeling exceptional children, such as labeling is negative; it focuses only on the child's deficits in learning or behavior; labeling makes it more likely that others (teachers, parents, peers) will expect poor performance and bad behavior from the labeled child; and labels may hurt the child's self-esteem.

Labels, in and of themselves, are not the problem. The dictionary defines *label* as "a descriptive word or phrase applied to a person, group, theory, etc., as a convenient generalized classification" (*Webster's New World Dictionary,* 1986, p. 785). Most professionals in special education agree that a common language for referring to children who share common instructional and related service needs is necessary. The kinds of words that we use as labels, and even the order in which they are spoken or written, do, however, influence the degree to which a particular label serves as an appropriate generalized classification for communicating variables relevant to the design and delivery of educational and other human services. For example, although they may refer to a common set of educational needs, terms such as "the handicapped" or "the retarded" also imply negative connotations that are unwarranted and inappropriate. Such blanket labels imply that all persons in the group being labeled are alike; individuality has been lost (Gelb, 1997). At the personal level, when we describe a child as a "physically handicapped boy," we place too much emphasis on the disability, perhaps suggesting that the deficits caused by the disability are the most important thing to know about him.

How, then, should we refer to exceptional children? At the personal level, we should follow Tom Lovitt's advice and call them by their names: Linda, Shawon, and Jackie. Referring to a child as "Molly, a fifth-grade student with learning disabilities" helps us focus on the individual child and her primary role as a student. Such a description does not ignore or gloss over Molly's learning problems but acknowledges that there are other things we should know about her.

It is important for everyone, not just special educators, to speak, write, and think about exceptional children and adults in ways that respect each person's individuality and recognize strengths and abilities instead of focusing only on disabilities. Simply changing the way we talk about an individual with a disability, however, will not make the problems posed by her disability go away. Some disabled people have begun to speak out against the efforts of those without disabilities to assuage their feelings with language that may be politically correct but that ignores the reality of a disability. Judy Heumann, director of the U.S. Department of Education's Office of Special Education and Rehabilitation Services and a person who has used a wheelchair since she was 18 months old, explains her position:

> As our movement has evolved, we have been plagued by people, almost always not themselves disabled, attempting to change what we call ourselves. If we are "victims" of anything, it is of such terms as physically challenged, able-disabled, differently-abled, handi-capables, and people with differing abilities, to name just a few. Nondisabled people's discomfort with reality-based terms such as disabled led them to these euphemisms. I believe these euphemisms have the effect of depoliticizing our own terminology and devaluing our own view of ourselves as disabled people. . . .
>
> I have a physical disability that results in my inability to walk and perform a number of other significant tasks without the assistance of another person. This cannot be labeled away and I am not ashamed of it. I feel no need to change the word "disabled." For me, there is no stigma. I am not driven to call myself a "person with a disability." I know I am a person; I do not need to tell myself that I am. I also do not believe that being called a "person with a disability" results in my being treated any more like a human being. Maybe putting the word "disabled" first makes people stop and look at what, as a result of society's historical indifference to and/or hatred of people like me, is a critical part of my existence. . . .
>
> Let the disabled people who are politically involved and personally affected determine our own language. . . . A suggestion to those of you who do not know what to call me: ask!

Donald Cook, an educational researcher, contributed these comments to an Internet discussion of how to speak to and about people with disabilities:

> I am handicapped by post polio syndrome and must use a wheelchair and/or a walker. The other day I was

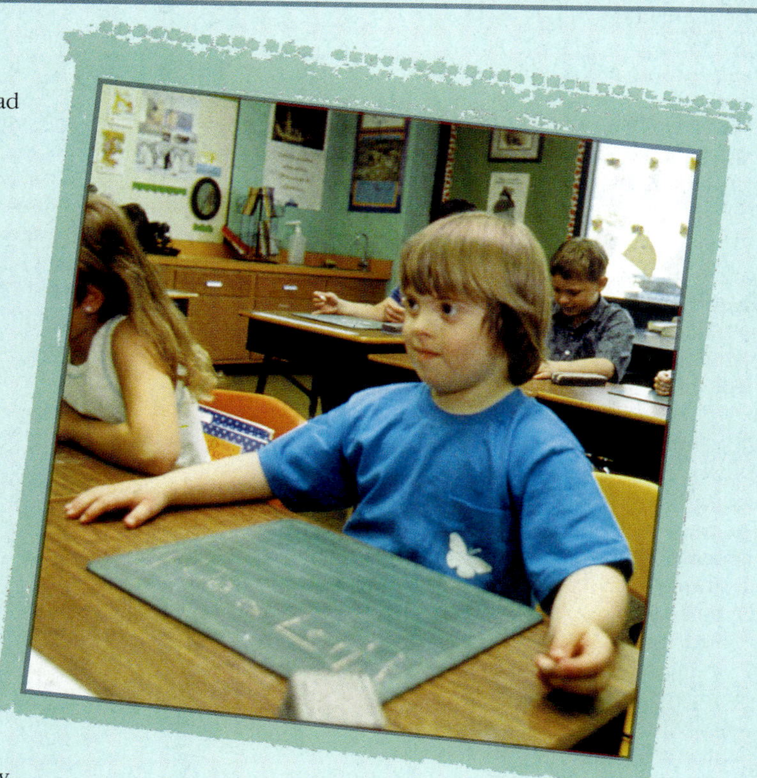

Changing the label used to identify or classify Jeffrey's disability won't lessen the impact of his disability. But referring to him as "Jeffrey, a third grader," instead of "a mentally retarded boy" helps us recognize his strengths and abilities—what he can do—instead of focusing on the disability as if it were his defining characteristic.

> referred to, for the first time, as "differently-abled." The context was benign: the speaker had noticed a beach with special wheelchairs that went across sand and into the water, and thought I would like to know about it. Still the term "differently-abled" stunned me. I asked whose feelings were being spared here, mine or hers? This question angered her—a possible sign of a question with a point. It seems clear to me that my condition is not merely different in some abstract dimension but one of a loss of function. So I prefer "handicapped" or some term which acknowledges that. It is NOT the case that there is some "compensation" such as the ability to extract square roots lightning fast with my left toe, or any other. (*CompuServe Education Forum,* July 11, 1994)

Bernard Rimland (1993a), director of the Autism Research Institute in San Diego and the father of a son with autism, is a severe critic of those who are trying to change the language of special education under the

> arrogant assumption of the moral high ground . . . certain that their way is the only way. . . . They insist that words such as "autistic," "retarded," and "handicapped" not be used. They insist that the silly euphemism "challenging" be used to describe severely self-injurious or assaultive behavior. . . . It deprives the handicapped of their most valuable asset—the recognition of their disability by the rest of us. Yes, there are people on the borderline between normal and handicapped. Does that mean that no one is handicapped? Yes, there are shades of gray. Does that mean there is no black and white? Does twilight disprove the difference between day and night? (p. 1)

Michael Goldfarb, executive director of the Association for the Help of Retarded Children, offers some provocative and insightful thoughts on the language of special education:

> Even after it had become fashionable to use the phrase "Down syndrome," Louis Striar insisted on calling his son a mongoloid. He enjoyed the shocked look on people's faces when he stubbornly clung to the old label. He consistently refused to trade in a phrase he was used to for one that was used by others. I always thought that Louie did this simply to shock people, because he enjoyed that.
>
> I now realize that his real goal, as a Board member of AHRC and as a parent of a disabled son, was to demonstrate that no new label, however popular, would solve his son's problem with society or society's problem with his son. No matter what label you used, Martin was retarded. Louie was attempting to teach us a very painful lesson, one which we still have not learned, namely, that linguistic reform alone can't really change the world. It has taken me a dozen years to figure out what he meant.

Consider the following lists of words:

crippled
handicapped
disabled
challenged

inmate
patient
resident
client
program participant

feeble minded
retarded
person with mental retardation
person

institution
state school
developmental center

Consider the words on the top of each list, the old and unfashionable ones. The names at the bottom are new and more acceptable. Many professionals in this field have made it a matter of deep personal commitment to get you to use the most up-to-date expressions.

Every one of these changes has been presented as an essential act of consciousness raising. Every one of these changes has been proposed by numbers of enlightened, progressive, and intelligent professionals with the genuine intent of changing the image and role of disabled people in this society. Every one of these linguistic reforms has been followed several years later by newer and "better" names. Every one of these changes has failed to make the world different.

Linguistic reform without systemic change conceals unhappy truths. Social problems may be reflected in the way we speak, but they are rarely, if ever, cured by changes in language. It is certainly true that liberals feel better when they use the most acceptable phrase, but this should not obscure the fact that the oppressed continue to be oppressed under any label. (Perhaps we should not call people "the oppressed"; perhaps it would be better to call them "people with oppression.")

Our real problem in this and many other societies is that we respect only intelligence, stylish good looks, and earning potential. This society denigrates people who are not intelligent, who are deemed unattractive, or who are poor. Referring to retarded people as "people with mental retardation" will not make them brighter, prettier, richer. These names leave the old prejudices intact. Society's attitudes and the values that underlie them must be changed. This will take far more than trivial linguistic changes. Can you imagine a Planning Board meeting at which a local resident says, "We don't want any retarded people living in our neighborhood! But people with mental retardation? That's different. They can move in anytime." I can't.

Changing attitudes and values is more difficult than changing language. Perhaps that is why we spend so much time changing language.

Source: Long excerpt reprinted from Heumann, J. (1993). Building our own boats: A personal perspective on disability policy. In L. O. Gostin & H. A. Beyer (Eds.), *Implementing the Americans with Disabilities Act: Rights and responsibilities of all Americans.* Baltimore: Brookes. Used by permission of the publisher and the author. Paul H. Brookes Publishing, P.O. Box 10624, Baltimore, MD 21285-0624.

Adapted from Goldfarb, M. (1990, spring). Executive director's report. *AHRC Chronicle.* Used by permission.

> I accepted my first teaching position, a special education class in a basement room next door to the furnace. Of the 15 "educable mentally retarded" children assigned to work with me, most were simply nonreaders from poor families. One child had been banished to my room because she posed a behavior problem to her fourth-grade teacher.
>
> My class and I were assigned a recess spot on the opposite side of the play yard, far away from the "normal" children. I was the only teacher who did not have a lunch break. I was required to eat with my "retarded" children while other teachers were permitted to leave their students. . . . Isolated from my colleagues, I closed my door and did my thing, oblivious to the larger educational circles in which I was immersed. Although it was the basement room, with all the negative perceptions that arrangement implies, I was secure in the knowledge that despite the ignominy of it all I did good things for children who were previously unloved and untaught. (Aiello, 1976, p. 14)

Children with mild learning and behavioral problems usually remained in the regular classroom but received no special help. If they did not make satisfactory academic progress, they were termed "slow learners" or simply "failures." If their deportment in class exceeded the teacher's tolerance for misbehavior, they were labeled "disciplinary problems" and suspended from school. Children with more severe disabilities—including many with visual, hearing, and physical or health impairments—were usually placed in segregated schools or institutions or kept at home. Gifted and talented children seldom received special attention in schools. It was assumed they could make it on their own without help.

Society's response to exceptional children has come a long way. As our concepts of equality, freedom, and justice have expanded, children with disabilities and their families have moved from exclusion and isolation to inclusion and participation. Although the speed of these changes has been described as a "painfully slow process of integration and participation" (Cremins, 1983, p. 3), the history of special education can be summarized as one of "progressive integration" (Reynolds, 1989, p. 7).

Society no longer regards children with disabilities as beyond the responsibility of the local public schools. No longer may a child who is different from the norm be turned away from school because someone believes that he is unable to benefit from typical instruction. Recent legislation and court decisions confirm that all children with disabilities have the right to a *free, appropriate program of public education in the least restrictive environment.*

The provision of equitable educational opportunities to exceptional children has not come about by chance. Many laws and court cases have had important effects on public education in general and on the education of children with special needs in particular. And the process of change is never finished; legal influences on special education are not fixed or static but fluid and dynamic (Yell, 1998).

Separate Is Not Equal

The recent history of special education, especially in regard to the education of children with disabilities in regular schools, is related to the civil rights movement. Special education was strongly influenced by social developments and court decisions in the 1950s and 1960s, especially the landmark case *Brown v. Board of Education of Topeka,* 347 U.S. 483 (1954). This case challenged the practice of segregating students according to race. In its ruling in the *Brown* case, the U.S. Supreme Court declared that education must be made available to all children on equal terms:

> Today, education is perhaps the most important function of state and local governments. Compulsory school attendance laws and the great expenditure for education both demonstrate our recognition of the importance of education to our democratic society. It is required in the performance of our most basic responsibilities. . . . In these days, it is doubtful that any child may reasonably be expected to succeed in life if he is denied the opportunity of an education. (*Brown v. Board of Education,* 1954)

The *Brown* decision and the ensuing extension of public school education to African American and white children on equal terms began a period of intense concern and questioning among parents of children with disabilities, who asked why the same principles of equal access to education did not apply to their children. Numerous court cases were initiated in the 1960s and early 1970s by parents and other advocates dissatisfied with an educational system that denied equal access to children with disabilities. Generally, the parents based their arguments on the Fourteenth Amendment to the Constitution, which provides that no state shall deny any person within its jurisdiction the equal protection of the law and that no state shall deprive any person of life, liberty, or property without due process of law. The concepts of equal protection and due process are so fundamentally important in special education that we discuss them in some detail.

Equal Protection

In the past, children with disabilities usually received differential treatment; that is, they were excluded from certain educational programs or were given special education only in segregated settings. Basically, when the courts have been asked to rule on the practice of denial and segregation, judges have examined whether such treatment is *rational* and whether it is *necessary* (Williams, 1977). One of the most historically significant cases to examine these questions was the class-action suit *Pennsylvania Association for Retarded Children v. Commonwealth of Pennsylvania* (1972). The association (PARC) challenged a state law that denied public school education to certain children considered "unable to profit from public school attendance."

A class-action lawsuit is one made on behalf of a group of people. In the PARC case, the class of people was school-age children with mental retardation living in Pennsylvania

The lawyers and parents supporting PARC argued that even though the children had intellectual disabilities, it was neither rational nor necessary to assume they were ineducable and untrainable. Because the state was unable to prove that the children were, in fact, ineducable or to demonstrate a rational need for excluding them from public school programs, the court decided that the children were entitled to receive a free, public education. In addition, the court maintained that parents had the right to be notified before any change was made in their children's educational program.

The wording of the *PARC* decision proved particularly important because of its influence on subsequent federal legislation. Not only did the court rule that all children with mental retardation were entitled to a free, appropriate public education, but the ruling also stipulated that placements in regular classrooms and regular public schools were preferable to segregated settings.

> It is the Commonwealth's obligation to place each mentally retarded child in a free, public program of education and training appropriate to the child's capacity. . . . placement in a regular public school class is preferable to placement in a special public school class and placement in a special public school is preferable to placement in any other type of program of education and training. An assignment to homebound instruction shall be re-evaluated not less than every 3 months, and notice of the evaluation and an opportunity for a hearing thereon shall be accorded to the parent or guardian. (*Pennsylvania Association for Retarded Children v. Commonwealth of Pennsylvania,* 1972)

In addition to the *Brown* and *PARC* cases, several other judicial decisions have had far-reaching effects on special education. The rulings of some of these cases have been incorporated into subsequent federal legislation, notably the Individuals with Disabilities Education Act.

The Individuals with Disabilities Education Act

Federal legislation is identified by a numerical system. P.L. 94–142, for example, was the 142nd bill passed by the 94th Congress. P.L. 94–142 was originally called the Education for All Handicapped Children Act. *Since it became law in 1975, Congress has amended P.L. 94–142 four times, most recently in 1997. The 1990 amendments renamed the law the Individuals with Disabilities Education Act—often referred to by its acronym, IDEA.*

In 1975 Congress passed Public Law 94–142, the Individuals with Disabilities Education Act (IDEA). Shortly after its passage, P.L. 94–142 was called "blockbuster legislation" (Goodman, 1976) and hailed as the law that "will probably become known as having the greatest impact on education in history" (Stowell & Terry, 1977, p. 475). These predictions have proven accurate; IDEA is a landmark piece of legislation that has changed the face of education in this country. This law has affected every school in the country and has changed the roles of regular and special educators, school administrators, parents, and many others involved in the educational process. Its passage marked the culmination of the efforts of a great many educators, parents, and legislators to bring together in one comprehensive bill this country's laws regarding the education of children with disabilities. The law reflects society's concern about treating people with disabilities as full citizens with the same rights and privileges that all other citizens enjoy.

The purpose of IDEA is to

> assure that all children with disabilities have available to them . . . a free appropriate public education which emphasizes special education and related services designed to meet

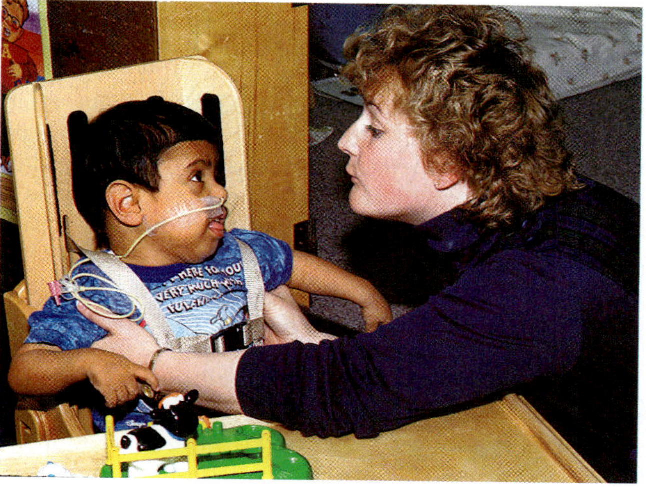

In the past, many children like Roberto were denied access to an education in public schools.

> their unique needs, to assure that the rights of children with disabilities and their parents or guardians are protected, to assist states and localities to provide for the education of all children with disabilities, and to assess and assure the effectiveness of efforts to educate children with disabilities. (IDEA, 20 U.S.C. § 1400[c])

More information about IDEA can be found by accessing the Resources Module for Chapter 1 at http://www.prenhall.com/heward and linking to "Laws" on the Special Ed Resource page.

IDEA is directed primarily at the states, which are responsible for providing education to their citizens. The majority of the many rules and regulations defining how IDEA operates are related to six major principles that have remained unchanged since 1975 (Turnbull & Cilley, 1999; Turnbull & Turnbull, 1998):

Six Major Principles of IDEA

Zero Reject Schools must educate all children with disabilities. This principle applies regardless of the nature or severity of the disability; no child with disabilities may be excluded from a public education. The requirement to provide special education to all students with disabilities is absolute between the ages of 6 and 17. If a state provides educational services to children without disabilities between the ages 3 to 5 and 18 to 21, it must also educate all children with disabilities in those age groups. Each state education agency is responsible for locating, identifying, and evaluating all children, from birth to age 21, residing in the state with disabilities or who are suspected of having disabilities. This requirement is called the *child find system*.

Nondiscriminatory Identification and Evaluation Schools must use nonbiased, multifactored methods of evaluation to determine whether a child has a disability and, if so, whether special education is needed. Testing and evaluation procedures must not discriminate on the basis of race, culture, or native language. All tests must be administered in the child's native language, and identification and placement decisions cannot be made on the basis of a single test score. These provisions of IDEA are known as *protection in evaluation procedures*.

Free, Appropriate Public Education (FAPE) All children with disabilities, regardless of the type or severity of their disability, shall receive a free, appropriate public education. This education must be provided at public expense—that is, without cost to the child's parents. An **individualized education program (IEP)** must be developed and implemented for each student with a disability. The IEP must be individually designed to meet the child's unique needs.

The individualized education program (IEP) *and the* least restrictive environment (LRE) *are examined in detail in Chapter 2.*

Least Restrictive Environment (LRE) IDEA mandates that students with disabilities be educated with children without disabilities to the maximum extent appropriate and that students with disabilities be removed to separate classes or schools only when the nature or severity of their disabilities is such that they cannot receive an appropriate education in a general education classroom with supplementary aides and services. IDEA creates a presumption in favor of inclusion in the regular classroom. The law requires that a student's IEP contain a justification and explanation of the extent, if any, to which a child will not participate with nondisabled peers in the general academic curriculum, extracurricular activities, and other nonacademic activities (e.g., lunch, recess, transportation, dances). To ensure that each student with disabilities is educated in the least restrictive environment appropriate for her needs, school districts must provide a continuum of placement alternatives.

Ann and Rud Turnbull (1998), who are special educators and parents of a young man with disabilities, describe due process as the legal technique that seeks to achieve fair treatment, accountability, and a new and more equal balance of power between professionals, who have traditionally wielded power, and families, who have thought they could not affect their children's education.

Due Process Safeguards Schools must provide due process safeguards to protect the rights of children with disabilities and their parents. Parental consent must be obtained for initial and all subsequent evaluations and placement decisions regarding special education. Schools must maintain the confidentiality of all records pertaining to a child with disabilities and make those records available to the parents. When parents of a child with disabilities disagree with the results of an evaluation performed by the school, they can obtain an independent evaluation at public expense. When the school and parents disagree on the identification, evaluation, placement, or special education and related services for the child, the parents may request a due process hearing. States are also required to offer parents an opportunity to resolve the matter through mediation by a third party prior to holding a due process hearing. Parents have the right to attorney's fees if they prevail in due process or judicial proceedings under IDEA.

Chapter 2 discusses strategies for working collaboratively with parents and families.

Parent and Student Participation and Shared Decision Making Schools must collaborate with parents and students with disabilities in the design and implementation of special education services. The parents' (and, whenever appropriate, the student's) input and wishes must be considered in placement decisions, IEP goals and objectives, and related services.

Other Provisions of the Law

Early intervention and IFSPs are described in Chapter 5.

Extending Special Education Services to Infants, Toddlers, and Preschoolers Noting that states were serving at most about 70% of preschool children with disabilities and that systematic early intervention services for infants and toddlers with disabilities from birth through age 2 were scarce or nonexistent in many states, Congress included provisions in the Education of the Handicapped Act Amendments in 1986 (P.L. 99–457) to expand services for these segments of the population. Beginning with the 1990–91 school year, each state was required to serve all preschool children with disabilities ages 3 to 5 fully—that is, with the same services and protections available to school-age children—or lose all future federal funds for preschoolers with disabilities.

P.L. 99–457 included an incentive grant program to encourage states to provide early intervention services to infants and toddlers with disabilities and their families—that is, children from birth through age 2 who need early intervention services because they are experiencing developmental delays or because they have a diagnosed physical or mental impairment likely to result in developmental delays. With the most recent reauthorization of IDEA in 1997 (P.L. 105–17), Congress reaffirmed the nation's commitment to a system of early intervention services. Rather than mandate special services for this age group, IDEA encourages each state to "develop and implement a statewide, comprehensive, coordinated, multidisciplinary, interagency program of early intervention services for infants and toddlers with disabilities and their families." The encouragement is in the form of a gradually increasing amount of federal money to be awarded to states that identify and serve all infants and toddlers with disabilities. Various education and human services agencies within each state work together to provide services such as medical and educational assessment, physical therapy, speech and language intervention, and parent counseling and training. These early intervention services are prescribed and implemented according to an **individualized family services plan (IFSP)** written by a multidisciplinary team that includes the child's parents.

Related Services and Assistive Technology Children with disabilities have sometimes been prevented from attending regular schools or benefiting from educational activities by circumstances that impede their access or participation. A child who uses a wheelchair, for example, may require a specially equipped school bus. A child with special health problems may require medication several times a day. A child with an orthopedic impairment may need physical therapy to maintain flexibility and use of her arms and legs. IDEA requires schools to provide any **related services** (e.g., special transportation, counseling, physical therapy) and **assistive technology**—devices and services such as visual aids, augmentative communication devices, specialized equipment for computer access—that a child with disabilities may need in order to access and benefit from special education. Table 1.2 provides definitions of the types of related services included in the IDEA regulations. The related services provision has been a highly controversial aspect of IDEA, creating much disagreement about what kinds of related services are necessary and reasonable for the schools to provide and what services should be the responsibility of the child's parents.

Federal Funding of Special Education Educating students with disabilities is expensive. Laws and regulations calling for special education would be of limited value if the schools lacked the necessary financial resources. Congress backed up its mandate for free, appropriate public education by providing federal funds to help

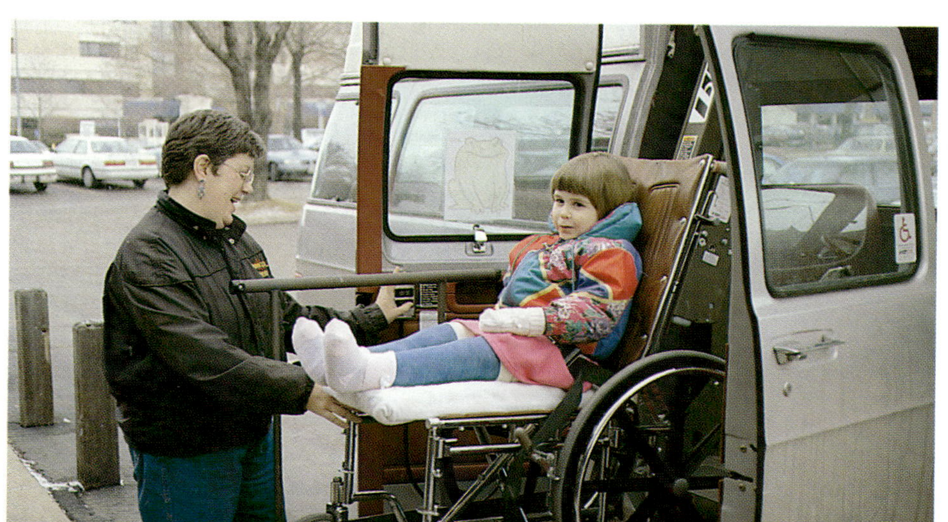

School districts must provide related services to students with disabilities—such as this adapted wheelchair lift that enables Tammy to travel to and from school—so they may have access to and benefit from a public education.

Related Service	Definition
Audiology	(1) Identifying children with hearing loss. (2) Determining the range, nature, and degree of hearing loss. (3) Providing habilitative activities, such as auditory training, speech reading, hearing evaluation, and speech conservation. (4) Creating and administering programs for prevention of hearing loss. (5) Counseling and guidance of pupils, parents, and teachers, regarding hearing loss. (6) Determining the child's need for group and individual amplification, selecting and fitting an appropriate hearing aid, and evaluating the effectiveness of amplification.
Counseling services	Services provided by qualified social workers, psychologists, guidance counselors, or other qualified personnel.
Early identification and assessment	Implementing a formal plan for identifying a disability as early as possible in a child's life.
Medical services	Services provided by a licensed physician to determine a child's medically related disability that results in the child's need for special education and related services.
Occupational therapy	(1) Improving, developing, or restoring functions impaired or lost through illness, injury, or deprivation. (2) Improving ability to perform tasks for independent functioning when functions are impaired or lost. (3) Preventing, through early intervention, initial or further impairment or loss of function.
Orientation and mobility services	Services provided to children who are blind or have visual impairments to assist them in traveling around their school or environment.
Parent counseling and training	Assisting parents in understanding the special needs of their child and providing parents with information about child development.
Physical therapy	Services provided by a qualified physical therapist.
Psychological services	(1) Administering psychological and educational tests, and other assessment procedures. (2) Interpreting assessment results. (3) Obtaining, integrating, and interpreting information about child behavior and conditions relating to learning. (4) Consulting with other staff members in planning school programs to meet the special needs of children as indicated by psychological tests, interviews, and behavioral evaluations. (5) Planning and managing a program of psychological services, including psychological counseling for children and parents.

Table 1.2 Types and definitions of related services that students with disabilities may need to benefit from education

school districts meet the additional costs of educating children with disabilities (many of whom had not previously been served by public schools). The funding provisions of IDEA (1997) provide each state up to $4.9 billion annually in federal dollars based on the number of children identified and served. If the $4.9 billion ceiling is reached, additional federal money is allocated based on a state's population and poverty level. States cannot use federal funds to serve more than 12% of their school-age students in special education. IDEA requires that 75% of the federal funds

Related Service	Definition
Recreation	(1) Assessment of leisure function. (2) Therapeutic recreation services. (3) Recreation programs in schools and community agencies. (4) Leisure education.
Rehabilitative counseling services	Services provided by qualified personnel in individual or group sessions that focus specifically on career development, employment preparation, achieving independence, and integration in the workplace and community.
School health services	Services provided by a qualified school nurse or other qualified person.
Social work services in the schools	(1) Preparing a social or developmental history on a child with a disability. (2) Group and individual counseling with the child and family. (3) Working with those problems in a child's living situation (home, school, and community) that affect the child's adjustment in school. (4) Mobilizing school and community resources to enable the child to learn as effectively as possible.
Speech pathology	(1) Identification of children with speech or language impairments. (2) Diagnosis and appraisal. (3) Referral for medical or other professional attention. (4) Provision of speech and language services for the habilitation and prevention of communicative problems. (5) Counseling and guidance of parents, children, and teachers regarding speech and language impairments.
Transportation	(1) Travel to and from school and between schools. (2) Travel in and around school buildings. (3) Specialized equipment if required to provide special transportation for a child with a disability (e.g., special or adapted buses, lifts, and ramps).
Assistive technology devices and services	Devices and related services that increase, maintain, or improve the functional capabilities of children with disabilities.

Table 1.2 *continued*

Source: IDEA regulations, 34 C.F.R. § 300.13.

received by the states be passed on to local school districts; 25% of the funds may be used by the state educational agency for administration, direct and supportive services for students with disabilities (e.g., support to state residential schools for students with sensory impairments), supervision, and compliance monitoring. In addition, each state is required to develop *a comprehensive system for personnel development,* including in-service training programs for regular education teachers, special education teachers, school administrators, and other support personnel.

State and local educational administrators contend that federal financial assistance for the education of students with disabilities has not been sufficient and that schools are hard pressed to meet the requirements in IDEA. When Congress passed IDEA in 1975, its intent was to provide federal funds for 40% of the total costs of educating children with disabilities. According to the most recent data reported by the U.S. Department of Education (1997), however, the federal government is providing only 7% of the average $5,435 needed to educate a student with disabilities over and above per-pupil expenditures to provide general education services.

Chaikind et al. (1993) reported a per-pupil annual cost of approximately $7,800 in 1989–90 dollars, or about 2.3 times the cost of educating each pupil in regular education. They found that costs of special education services varied considerably by disability category, ranging from under $1,000 per student with speech and language impairments to more than $30,000 per student with deaf-blindness.

Tuition Reimbursement Parents and school officials sometimes disagree about whether placement in a private school is the most appropriate way to meet the needs of a student with disabilities. IDEA stipulates that, in cases in which an appropriate education cannot be provided in the public schools, children with disabilities may be placed in private school programs at no cost to their parents. This has proven to be a particularly controversial aspect of the law (Yell, 1998).

Legal Challenges Based on IDEA

Although IDEA has resulted in dramatic increases in the number of students receiving special education services and in greater recognition of the legal rights of children with disabilities and their families, it has also brought about an ever-increasing number of disputes concerning the education of students with disabilities. Thousands of due process hearings and hundreds of court cases have been brought about by parents and other advocates. Due process hearings and court cases often place parents and schools in confrontation with each other and are expensive and time-consuming.

Turnbull and Turnbull (1998) and Yell (1998) provide in-depth but very readable explanations of special education law and related court cases.

It is difficult to generalize how judges and courts have resolved the various legal challenges based on IDEA. There have been many different interpretations of *free, appropriate education* and *least restrictive environment.* The law uses these terms repeatedly; but in the view of many parents, educators, judges, and attorneys, the law does not define them with sufficient clarity. Thus, the questions of what is appropriate and least restrictive for a particular child and whether a public school district should be compelled to provide a certain service must often be decided by judges and courts on consideration of the evidence presented to them. Some of the key issues ruled on by the courts are the extended school year, related services, disciplinary procedures, and the fundamental right to an education for students with the most severe disabilities.

Browder, Lentz, Knoster, and Wilansky (1988) discuss the extended school year.

Extended School Year Most public school programs operate for approximately 180 school days per year. Parents and educators have argued that, for some children with disabilities, particularly those with severe and multiple disabilities, a 180-day school year is not sufficient to meet their needs. In *Armstrong v. Kline* (1979), the parents of five students with severe disabilities claimed that their children tended to regress during the usual breaks in the school year and called on the schools to provide a period of instruction longer than 180 days. The court agreed and ordered the schools to extend the school year for these students. Several states and local districts now provide year-round educational programs for some students with disabilities, but there are no clear and universally accepted guidelines as to which students are entitled to free public education for a longer-than-usual school year.

The Rowley *case marked the first time a deaf attorney argued a case before the U.S. Supreme Court.*

Related Services The first case based on IDEA to reach the U.S. Supreme Court was *Board of Education of the Hendrick Hudson Central School District v. Rowley* (1982). Amy Rowley was a fourth grader who, because of her hearing loss, needed special education and related services. The school district had originally provided Amy with a hearing aid, speech therapy, a tutor, and a sign language interpreter to accompany her in the regular classroom. The school withdrew the sign language services after the interpreter reported that Amy did not make use of her services: Amy reportedly looked at the teacher to read her lips and asked the teacher to repeat instructions rather than get the information from the interpreter. Amy's parents contended that she was missing up to 50% of the ongoing instruction (her hearing loss was estimated to have left her with 50% residual hearing) and was therefore being denied an appropriate public school education. The school district's position was that Amy, with the help of the other special services she was still receiving, was passing from grade to grade without an interpreter. School personnel thought, in fact, that an interpreter might hinder Amy's interactions with her teacher and peers. It was also noted that this service would cost the school district as much as $25,000 per year. The Supreme Court ruled that Amy, who was making satisfactory progress in school without an interpreter, was receiving an adequate education and that the school district could not be compelled to hire a full-time interpreter.

The second P.L. 94–142 case to reach the Supreme Court was *Irving Independent School District v. Tatro* (1984). In this case, the Court decided that a school district was obligated to provide catheterization and other related medical services to enable a young child with physical impairments to attend school. (See Chapter 12 for further discussion of this case.)

Disciplining Students with Disabilities Some cases have resulted from parents' protesting the suspension or expulsion of children with disabilities. The case of *Stuart v. Nappi* (1978), for example, concerned a high school student who spent much of her time wandering in the halls even though she was assigned to special classes. The school sought to have the student expelled on disciplinary grounds because her conduct was considered detrimental to order in the school. The court agreed with the student's mother that expulsion would deny the student a free, appropriate public education as called for in IDEA. In other cases, expulsion or suspension of students with disabilities has been upheld if the school could show that the grounds for expulsion did not relate to the student's disability. In 1988, however, the Supreme Court ruled in *Honig v. Doe* that a student with disabilities could not be expelled from school for disciplinary reasons, which meant that, for all practical purposes, schools could not recommend expulsion or suspend a student with disabilities for more than 10 days.

The IDEA amendments of 1997 (P.L. 105–17) contain provisions that enable school districts to discipline students with disabilities in the same manner as students without disabilities, with a few notable exceptions. If the school seeks a change of placement, suspension, or expulsion in excess of 10 days, the IEP team and other qualified personnel must review the relationship between the student's misconduct and her disability. This review is called a **manifestation determination**. If it is determined that the student's behavior is not related to the disability, the same disciplinary procedures used with other students may be imposed. However, the school must continue to provide educational services in the alternative placement.

For a discussion of issues and considerations for disciplining students with disabilities in accordance with IDEA, see Katsiyannis and Maag (1998).

Right to Education The case of *Timothy W. v. Rochester School District* threatened the zero reject philosophy of IDEA. In July 1988, Judge Loughlin of the district court in New Hampshire ruled that a 13-year-old boy with severe disabilities and quadriplegia was ineligible for education services because he could not benefit from special education. The judge ruled in favor of the Rochester School Board, which claimed that IDEA was not intended to provide educational services to "*all* handicapped students." In his decision, the judge determined that the federal law was not explicit regarding a "rare child" with severe disabilities and declared that special evaluations and examinations should be used to determine "qualifications for education under PL 94–142."

The National School Boards Association (NSBA) defended the Rochester School Board when the district court's decision was appealed. The NSBA stated that local schools have no obligation to serve children on the "low end of the spectrum . . . because they have no capacity to benefit from special education."

In May 1989, a court of appeals overturned the lower court's decision, ruling that public schools must educate all children with disabilities regardless of how little they might benefit or the nature or severity of their disabilities. The three-judge panel concluded that "schools cannot avoid the provisions of EHA [Education of the Handicapped Amendments] by returning to the practices that were widespread prior to the Act's passage . . . unilaterally excluding certain handicapped children from a public education on the ground that they are uneducable." In summarizing the case, Buchanan and Kochar (1989) express the concerns of many parents and special educators:

> If the Loughlin decision stood, how would the language of PL 94–142 have changed? Would *all* have become *some*? Would the law only apply to "mildly and moderately impaired" children, and would "free appropriate public education" only be for students who were allowed to attend school? . . . If the Loughlin decision was upheld, years of research in education for new and innovative methods of teaching the handicapped may have been lost. . . . This case underscores the need for vigilance in our watch for shifts in interpretations of EHA that subtly modify the essential foundations of zero reject and protection from functional exclusion. (p. 3)

Table 1.3 summarizes key judicial decisions that have had significant impact on special education and the lives of individuals with disabilities.

Challenges to existing services and differing views on whether a particular program is appropriate or least restrictive are certain to continue. The high costs of providing special education and related services, although clearly not a valid basis for excluding students with disabilities, will likely be more often taken into consideration by judges and courts as they determine what schools may reasonably be expected to do. As Kauffman (1985) notes, one of the problems the field and society must resolve is "what the limits of special education are, where it stops" (p. 14). Some observers predict a lack of further expansion of related services for children with disabilities; others are more optimistic. Turnbull (1986), for example, notes that although the Supreme Court decided against the provision of related services in the *Rowley* case and in favor of them in the *Tatro* case, the decisions are consistent: the Court recognized the need for integration of children with disabilities with nondisabled children in both cases and kept the student's individualized education program as "the focal point of appropriateness" (p. 351). Although the courts will probably grant some requests in the future and deny others, it is now a well-established principle that each student with disabilities is entitled to a personalized program of instruction and supportive services that will enable him to benefit from an education in as integrated a setting as possible.

Related Legislation

Gifted and Talented Children Although IDEA does not apply to gifted and talented children, other federal legislation has addressed the specialized needs of these students. P.L. 95–561, the Gifted and Talented Children's Education Act of 1978, provides financial incentives for state and local education agencies to develop programs for students who are gifted and talented. The law provides for the identification of gifted and talented children and includes special procedures for identifying and educating those from disadvantaged backgrounds. The law makes funding available for in-service training programs, research, and other projects aimed at meeting the needs of gifted and talented students.

In 1982 the Education Consolidation Act phased out the federal Office of Gifted and Talented and merged gifted education with 29 other programs. Federal dollars to support these 30 wide-ranging education programs (K–12) are sent to the states in the form of block grants. Each state has the responsibility to determine what portion, if any, of the block grant funds will be used to support programs and services for students who are gifted and talented.

Congress passed the Jacob K. Javits Gifted and Talented Student Education Act in 1988 as part of the Elementary and Secondary Education Bill. This moderately funded act (approximately $10 million in 1996) provides federal money for special

Table 1.3 Major court cases that have influenced special education and the lives of individuals with disabilities

Date	Court Case	Educational Implications
1954	*Brown v. Board of Education of Topeka* (Kansas)	The case established the right of all children to an equal opportunity for an education.
1967	*Hobson v. Hansen* (Washington, DC)	The court declared the tracking system, in which children were placed into either regular or special classes according to their scores on intelligence tests, unconstitutional because it discriminated against African American and poor children.
1970	*Diana v. State Board of Education* (California)	A Spanish-speaking student in California had been placed in a special class for children with mental retardation based on the results of intelligence tests given in English. The court ruled that children cannot be placed in special education on the basis of culturally biased tests or tests given in other than the child's native language.
1972	*Mills v. Board of Education of the District of Columbia*	Seven children had been excluded from the public schools in Washington, DC, because of learning and behavior problems. The school district contended that it did not have enough money to provide special education programs for them. The court ruled that financial problems cannot be allowed to have a greater impact on children with disabilities than on students without disabilities and ordered the schools to readmit the children and serve them appropriately.
1972	*Pennsylvania Association for Retarded Citizens v. the Commonwealth of Pennsylvania*	This class-action suit established the right to free public education for all children with mental retardation.
1972	*Wyatt v. Stickney* (Alabama)	The decision declared that individuals in state institutions have the right to appropriate treatment within those institutions.
1979	*Larry P. v. Riles* (California)	The court ruled that IQ tests used to place African American children in special classes were inappropriate because they failed to recognize the children's cultural background and the learning that took place in their homes and communities. The court ordered that IQ tests could not be used as the sole basis for placing children into special classes.
1979	*Armstrong v. Kline* (Pennsylvania)	The case established the right of some children with severe disabilities to an extension of the 180-day public school year.
1982	*Board of Education of the Hendrik Hudson Central School District v. Rowley* (New York)	This was the first case based on P.L. 94–142 to reach the U.S. Supreme Court; while denying the plaintiff's specific request, the Court upheld for each child with disabilities the right to a personalized program of instruction and necessary supportive services.

Table 1.3 *continued*

Date	Court Case	Educational Implications
1983	*Abrahamson v. Hershman* (Massachusetts)	The court ruled that residential placement in a private school was necessary for a child with multiple disabilities who needed around-the-clock training and required the school district to pay for the private placement.
1984	*Department of Education v. Katherine D.* (Hawaii)	The court ruled that a homebound instructional program for a child with multiple health impairments did not meet the least-restrictive-environment standard and called for the child to be placed in a class with children without disabilities and provided with related medical services.
1984	*Irving Independent School District v. Tatro* (Texas)	The court ruled that catheterization was necessary for a child with physical disabilities to remain in school and that it could be performed by a nonphysician, thus obligating the school district to provide that service.
1984	*Smith v. Robinson* (Rhode Island)	The court ordered the state to pay for the placement of a child with severe disabilities in a residential program and ordered the school district to reimburse the parents' attorney fees. The U.S. Supreme Court later ruled that P.L. 94–142 did not entitle parents to recover such fees, but Congress subsequently passed an "Attorney's Fees" bill, leading to enactment of P.L. 99–372.
1985	*Cleburne v. Cleburne Living Center* (Texas)	The Supreme Court ruled unanimously that communities cannot use a discriminatory zoning ordinance to prevent establishment of group homes for persons with mental retardation.
1988	*Honig v. Doe* (California)	The court ruled that children with disabilities cannot be excluded from school for any misbehavior that is disability-related (in this case, "aggressive behavior against other students" on the part of two "emotionally handicapped" students) but that educational services could cease if the misbehavior is not related to the disability.
1989	*Timothy W. v. Rochester School District* (New Hampshire)	The U.S. Appeals Court upheld the literal interpretation that P.L. 94–142 requires that *all* children with disabilities be provided with a free, appropriate public education, unconditionally and without exception. The three-judge appeals court overturned the decision of a district court judge, who had ruled that the local school district was not obligated to educate a 13-year-old boy with multiple and severe disabilities because he could not benefit from special education.

projects, a national research center, and a position within the U.S. Department of Education with responsibility for gifted education.

Section 504 of the Rehabilitation Act of 1973 Another important law that extends civil rights to people with disabilities is Section 504 of the Rehabilitation Act of 1973. This regulation states, in part, that "no otherwise qualified handicapped individual shall, solely by reason of his handicap, be excluded from the participation in, be denied the benefits of, or be subjected to discrimination in any program or activity receiving federal financial assistance." This law, worded almost identically to the Civil Rights Act of 1964 (which prohibited discrimination based on race, color, or national origin), has expanded opportunities to children and adults with disabilities in education, employment, and various other settings. It requires provision of "auxiliary aids for students with impaired sensory, manual, or speaking skills"—for example, readers for students who are blind and people to assist students with physical disabilities in moving from place to place. This requirement does not mean that schools, colleges, and employers must have *all* such aids available at all times; it simply means that no person with disabilities may be excluded from a program because of the lack of an appropriate aid.

Section 504 is not a federal grant program; unlike IDEA, it does not provide any federal money to assist people with disabilities. Rather, it "imposes a duty on every recipient of federal funds not to discriminate against handicapped persons" (Johnson, 1986, p. 8). "Recipient," of course, includes public school districts, virtually all of which receive federal support. Most colleges and universities have also been affected; even many students in private institutions receive federal financial aid. The Office of Civil Rights conducts periodic compliance reviews and acts on complaints when parents, disabled individuals, or others contend that a school district is violating Section 504.

Architectural accessibility for students, teachers, and others with physical and sensory impairments is an important feature of Section 504; however, the law does not call for a completely barrier-free environment. Emphasis is on accessibility to programs, not on physical modification of all existing structures. If a chemistry class is required for a premedical program of study, for example, a college might make this program accessible to a student with physical disabilities by reassigning the class to an accessible location or by providing assistance to the student in traveling to an otherwise inaccessible location. All sections of all courses need not be made accessible, but a college should not segregate students with disabilities by assigning them all to a particular section regardless of disability. Like IDEA, Section 504 calls for nondiscriminatory placement in the "most integrated setting appropriate" and has served as the basis for many court cases over alleged discrimination against individuals with disabilities, particularly in their right to employment.

Table 1.4 summarizes federal legislation regarding the education and rights of individuals with disabilities.

Americans with Disabilities Act The Americans with Disabilities Act (P.L. 101–336) was signed into law on July 26, 1990. Patterned after Section 504 of the Rehabilitation Act of 1973, the Americans with Disabilities Act (ADA) extends civil rights protection of persons with disabilities to private sector employment, all public services, public accommodation, transportation, and telecommunications. A person with a disability is defined in ADA as a person (1) with a mental or physical impairment that substantially limits her in a major life activity (e.g., walking, talking, working, self-care); (2) with a record of such an impairment (e.g., a person who no longer has heart disease but who is discriminated against because of that history); or (3) who is regarded as having such an impairment (e.g., a person with significant facial disfiguration due to a burn who is not limited in any major life activity but is discriminated against). The major provisions of ADA are as follows:

Table 1.4 Federal legislation concerning the education and rights of exceptional children

Date	Legislation	Educational Implications
1958	National Defense Education Act (P.L. 85–926)	The law provided funds for training professionals to train teachers of children with mental retardation.
1961	Special Education Act (P.L. 87–276)	The law provided funds for training professionals to train teachers of deaf children.
1963	Mental Retardation Facility and Community Center Construction Act (P.L. 88–164)	The law extended support given in P.L. 85–926 to training teachers of children with other disabilities.
1965	Elementary and Secondary Education Act (P.L. 89–10)	The law provided money to states and local districts for developing programs for economically disadvantaged and disabled children.
1966	Amendment to Title I of the Elementary and Secondary Education Act (P.L. 89–313)	The law provided funding for state-supported programs in institutions and other settings for children with disabilities.
1966	Amendments to the Elementary and Secondary Education Act (P.L. 89–750)	The law created the federal Bureau of Education for the Handicapped (today's Office of Special Education).
1968	Handicapped Children's Early Assistance Act (P.L. 90–538)	The law established the "first chance network" of experimental programs for preschool children with disabilities.
1969	Elementary, Secondary, and Other Educational Amendments (P.L. 91–230)	The law defined learning disabilities and provided funds for state-level programs for children with learning disabilities.
1973	Section 504 of the Rehabilitation Act (P.L. 93–112)	The law declared that a person cannot be excluded on the basis of disability alone from any program or activity receiving federal funds.
1974	Education Amendments (P.L. 93–380)	Extending previous legislation, the law provided money to state and local districts for programs for gifted and talented students for the first time. It also protected the rights of children with disabilities and their parents in placement decisions.
1975	Developmental Disabilities Assistance and Bill of Rights Act (P.L. 94–103)	The law affirmed the rights of citizens with mental retardation and cited areas in which services must be provided for people with mental retardation and other developmental disabilities.
1975	Education for All Handicapped Children Act (EAHCA) (P.L. 94–142)	The law mandated free, appropriate public education for all children with disabilities ages 6 to 21, protected the rights of children with disabilities and their parents in educational decision making, required the development of an IEP for each child with a disability, and stated that students with disabilities must receive educational services in the least restrictive environment.

Date	Legislation	Educational Implications
1983	Amendments to the Education of the Handicapped Act (P.L. 98–199)	The law required states to collect data on the number of youth with disabilities exiting their systems and to address the needs of secondary students making the transition to adulthood. It also gave incentives to states to provide services to infants and preschool children with disabilities.
1984	Developmental Disabilities Assistance and Bill of Rights Acts (P.L. 98–527)	The law mandated the development of employment-related training activities for adults with disabilities.
1986	Handicapped Children's Protection Act (P.L. 99–372)	The law provided authority for the reimbursement of attorney's fees to parents who prevail in a hearing or court case to secure an appropriate education for their child.
1986	Education for the Handicapped Act Amendments of 1986 (P.L. 99–457)	The law required states to provide free, appropriate education to all 3- to 5-year-olds with disabilities who were eligible to apply for federal preschool funding. It included incentive grants to encourage states to develop comprehensive interdisciplinary services for infants and toddlers (birth through age 2) and their families.
1986	Rehabilitation Act Amendments (P.L. 99–506)	The law set forth regulations for the development of supported employment programs for adults with disabilities.
1988	Jacob K. Javits Gifted and Talented Students Education Act	The law provided federal funds in support of research, teacher training, and program development for the education of gifted and talented students.
1990	Americans with Disabilities Act (P.L. 101–336)	The law provides civil rights protection against discrimination to citizens with disabilities in private sector employment, access to all public services, public accommodations, transportation, and telecommunications.
1990	Individuals with Disabilities Education Act Amendments (IDEA) of 1990 (P.L. 101–476)	In addition to renaming the EAHCA, this amendment added autism and traumatic brain injury as new categories of disability, required all IEPs to include a statement of needed transition services no later than age 16, and expanded the definition of related services to include rehabilitation counseling and social work services.

Table 1.4 *continued*

Date	Legislation	Educational Implications
1997	Individuals with Disabilities Education Act (IDEA) of 1997 (P.L. 105-17)	The law restructured IDEA from nine subchapters into four parts and added several major provisions: it increased the emphasis on parent participation and shared decision making; the regular education teacher must be a member of the IEP team; students with disabilities must have access to the general education curriculum; beginning when the student reaches age 14 the IEP must identify transition services related to his course of study; the IEP must address positive behavior support plans where appropriate; students with disabilities must be included in state- or district-wide testing (assessment) programs; orientation and mobility services were added to the list of related services; if a school seeks to discipline a student with disabilities resulting in changes of placement, suspension, or expulsion for more than 10 days, a "manifestation determination" by the IEP team must find that the student's misconduct is not related to the disability.

- Employers with 15 or more employees may not refuse to hire or promote a person because of a disability if that person is qualified to perform the job. Also, the employer must make reasonable accommodations that will allow a person with a disability to perform essential functions of the job. Such modifications in job requirements or situation must be made if they will not impose undue hardship on the employer.
- All new vehicles purchased by public transit authorities must be accessible to people with disabilities. All rail stations must be made accessible, and at least one car per train in existing rail systems must be made accessible.
- It is illegal for public accommodations to exclude or refuse persons with disabilities. Public accommodations are everyday businesses and services, such as hotels, restaurants, grocery stores, and parks. All new buildings must be made accessible, and existing facilities must remove barriers if the removal can be accomplished without much difficulty or expense.
- Companies offering telephone service to the general public must offer relay services to individuals who use telecommunications devices for the deaf (e.g., TDDs) 24 hours per day, 7 days per week.

A timeline of the history of special education in the United States from 1817 through 1997 appears in the May 1997 issue of Teaching Exceptional Children.

What Is Special Education?

Special education can be defined from many perspectives. One may, for example, view special education as a legislatively governed enterprise. From this viewpoint, one would be concerned about issues such as the due process procedures for informing parents about their right to participate in decisions about their children's education programs and the extent to which all of the school district's IEPs include

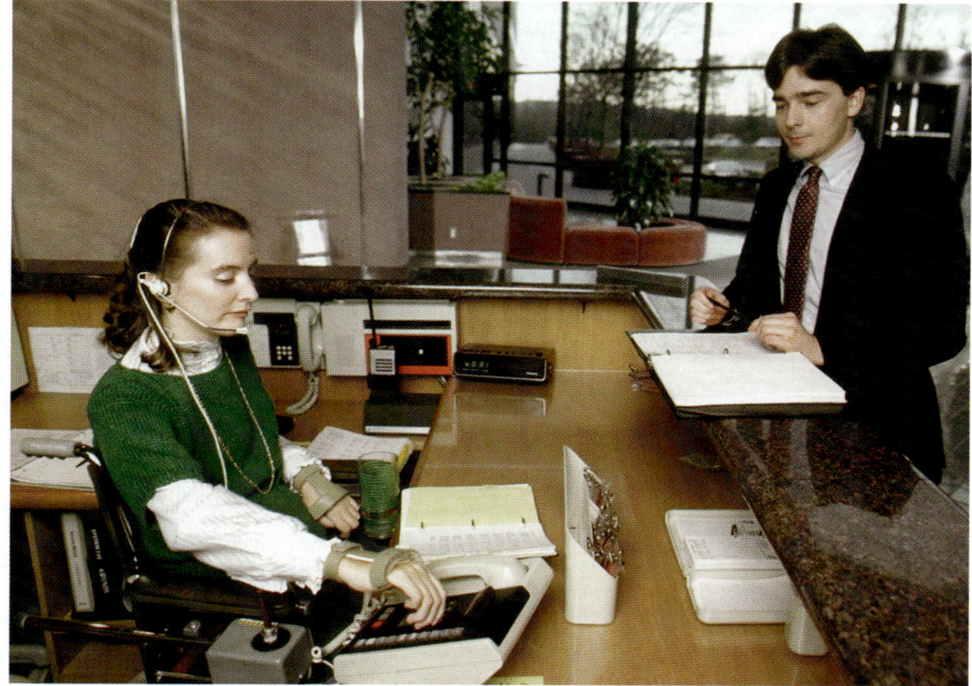

The Americans with Disabilities Act requires employers to make reasonable accommodations to allow a person with disabilities to perform essential job functions.

each component as required by IDEA. From a purely administrative point of view, special education can be seen as the part of a school system's operation that requires certain teacher-pupil ratios in the classroom and that uses special formulas to determine levels of funding for related services personnel. And from a sociopolitical perspective, special education can be seen as an outgrowth of the civil rights movement, a demonstration of society's changing attitudes about people with disabilities in general. Each of these perspectives has some validity, and each continues to play an important role in defining what special education is and how it is practiced. None of these views, however, reveals the fundamental purpose or essence of special education as instructionally focused intervention.

Special Education As Intervention

Special education is, first of all, purposeful intervention. Successful interventions prevent, eliminate, and/or overcome the obstacles that might keep an individual with disabilities from learning and from full and active participation in school and society. There are three basic types or levels of intervention:

- *Preventive*—intervening to keep potential or minor problems from becoming a disability
- *Remedial*—eliminating the effects of the disability through instruction
- *Compensatory*—teaching the use of skills or devices that enable successful functioning in spite of the disability

Prevention can occur at three levels. Primary prevention *consists of eliminating or counteracting risk factors so that a disability is never acquired.* Secondary prevention *is aimed at reducing or eliminating the effects of existing risk factors.* Tertiary prevention *involves intervention with a child with a disability to minimize the impact of the condition.*

Preventive Intervention Preventive efforts are most promising when they begin early—even before birth, in many cases. In later chapters, we explore some of the promising new methods for preventing disabilities. We also explore the efforts by social and educational programs to stimulate infants and very young children to acquire skills that most children learn without special help. Unfortunately, prevention programs have only just begun to affect the number and severity of disabilities in this country. And it is likely that we will be well into the 21st century before we achieve a significant reduction of disabilities. In the meantime, we must count on remedial and compensatory efforts to help people with disabilities achieve fuller and more independent lives.

Remedial Intervention Remedial programs are supported largely by educational institutions and social agencies. In fact, the word *remediation* is primarily an educational term; the word *rehabilitation* is used more often by social service agencies. Both have a common purpose: to teach the person with disabilities skills for independent and successful functioning. In school, those skills may be academic (reading, writing, computing), social (getting along with others; following instructions, schedules, and other daily routines), personal (eating, dressing, using the toilet without assistance), and/or vocational (career and job skills to prepare secondary students for the world of work). The underlying assumption of remedial intervention is that a person with disabilities needs special help (i.e., instruction) to succeed in typical settings.

Compensatory Intervention The third type of intervention involves teaching a substitute (i.e., compensatory) skill that enables a person to perform a task in spite of the disability. For example, although remedial instruction might help a child with cerebral palsy learn to use her hands for some tasks, a headstick and a template placed over a computer keyboard may compensate for her limited fine motor control and enable her to type instead of write lessons by hand. Compensatory interventions are designed to give the person with a disability an asset that nondisabled individuals do not need—whether it be a device such as a headstick or special training such as mobility instruction for a child without vision.

Special Education As Instruction

Ultimately, *teaching* is what special education is most about. But the same can be said of all of education. What, then, is *special* about special education? One way to answer that question is to examine special education in terms of the *who, what, how*, and *where* of its teaching.

Are there jobs in special education? Yes. There is a chronic annual shortage of about 29,000 certified special education teachers in the United States (Boe, Cook, Bobbitt, & Terhanian, 1998) and 25,000 special education personnel other than classroom teachers (U.S. Department of Education, 1996).

Who We have already identified the most important *who* in special education: the exceptional children whose educational needs necessitate an individually planned program of instruction. Teachers, both general education classroom teachers and special educators (those who have completed specialized training programs in preparation for their work with students with special needs), provide the instruction that is the heart of each child's individualized program of education. Working with special educators and regular classroom teachers are many other professionals (e.g., school psychologists, speech-language pathologists, physical therapists, counselors, and medical specialists) who help provide the educational and related services that exceptional children need. This interdisciplinary team of professionals, working together with parents and families, bears the primary responsibility for helping exceptional children learn despite their differences and special needs.

What Special education can sometimes be differentiated from general education by its curriculum—that is, by *what* is taught. Although every student with disabilities needs access to and support in learning as much of the general education curricu-

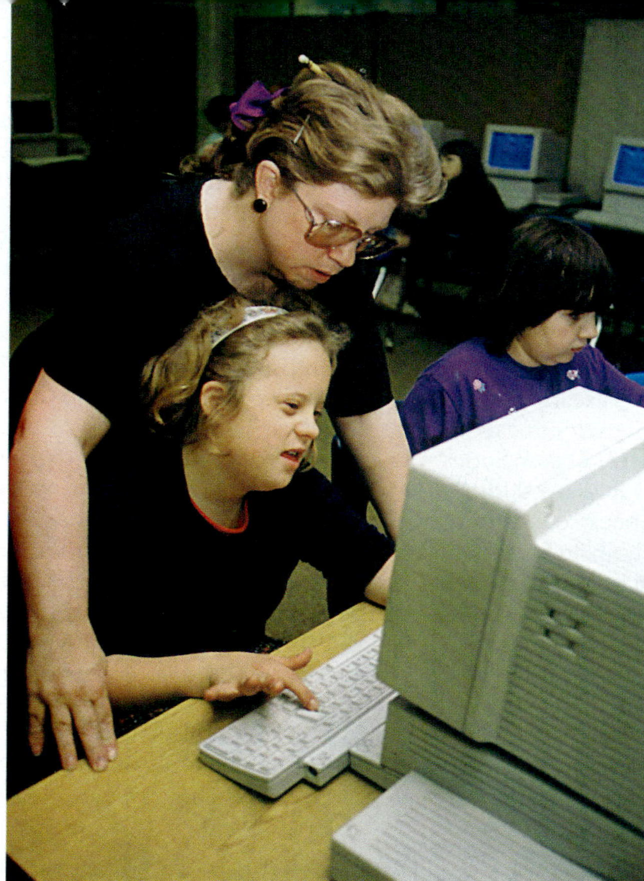

Most of all, special education is about teaching.

lum as possible, the IEP goals and objectives for some special education students will not be found in the school district's curriculum guide. Some children with disabilities need intensive, systematic instruction to learn skills that typically developing children acquire naturally. For example, self-help skills such as dressing, eating, and toileting are a critically important component of the school curriculum for many students with severe disabilities. Also, some children are taught certain skills to compensate for or reduce the handicapping effects of a disability. A child who is blind may be taught how to read and write in braille, whereas a sighted child does not need these skills.

The term functional curriculum *is often used to describe the knowledge and skills needed by students with disabilities to achieve as much success and independence as they can in daily living, personal-social, school, community, and work settings.*

How Special education can also be differentiated from general education by its use of specialized, or adapted, materials and methods. This difference is obvious when you observe a special educator use sign language with students who are deaf or witness another special educator teach a child how to communicate his wishes by pointing to pictures in a special booklet he carries with him. When watching a special educator gradually and systematically withdraw verbal and physical prompts while helping a student learn to perform the steps of a task, you may find the differentiated nature of special education instruction less obvious, but it is no less specialized.

Where Special education can sometimes be identified by *where* it takes place. Although most children with disabilities receive much of their education in regular classrooms, the others are someplace else—mostly in separate classrooms and separate residential and day schools. And many of those in regular classrooms spend a portion of each day in a resource room, where they receive individualized instruction. Special educators also teach in many environments not usually thought of as "school." An early childhood special educator may spend much of his time teaching parents how to work with their infant or toddler at home. Special education teachers, particularly those who work with students with severe disabilities, are increasingly conducting *community-based instruction,* helping their students learn and practice functional daily living and job skills in the actual settings where they must be used (Beck, Broers, Hogue, Shipstead, & Knowlton, 1994).

Table 1.5 lists the definitions of six educational placements used by the U.S. Department of Education.

Nearly three out of four school-age children with disabilities received at least part of their education in regular classrooms during the 1995–1996 school year (see Figure 1.1). This includes 45.4% who were served in the regular classroom and 28.7% who were served for part of each school day in a resource room, a special setting in which a special educator provides individualized instruction. About one-fifth of all children with disabilities are educated in separate classrooms within a regular school. About 3% of school-age students with disabilities—usually students with severe disabilities—are educated in special schools. Residential schools serve fewer than 1% of all children with disabilities, as do nonschool environments such as homebound or hospital programs.

Where students with disabilities are educated—in particular, the extent to which they are included as meaningful participants in the instructional and social life of the regular classroom—is the most hotly debated issue in special education today.

The vast majority of children in the two largest groups of students with disabilities spend at least part of the school day in regular classrooms: 82% of children with learning disabilities and 95% of children with speech or language impairments (see Table 1.6). In contrast, only 39% of children with mental retardation, 24% of children with multiple disabilities, and 21% of children with deaf-blindness were educated in

Table 1.5 Federal government's definitions of educational placements for students with disabilities

Placement	Definition
Regular class	Includes students who receive a majority of their education program in a regular classroom and receive special education and related services outside the regular classroom for less than 21% of the school day
Resource room	Includes students who receive special education and related services outside the regular classroom for at least 21% but no more than 60% of the school day
Separate class	Includes students who receive special education and related services outside the regular classroom for more than 60% of the school day
Separate school	Includes students who receive special education and related services in a public or private separate day school for students with disabilities, at public expense, for more than 50% of the school day
Residential facility	Includes students who receive special education in a public or private residential facility, at public expense, for more than 50% of the school day
Homebound/hospital environment	Includes students placed in and receiving special education in a hospital or homebound program

Source: Adapted from U.S. Department of Education. (1996). *Eighteenth annual report to Congress on the implementation of the Individuals with Disabilities Education Act* (p. 69). Washington, DC: Author.

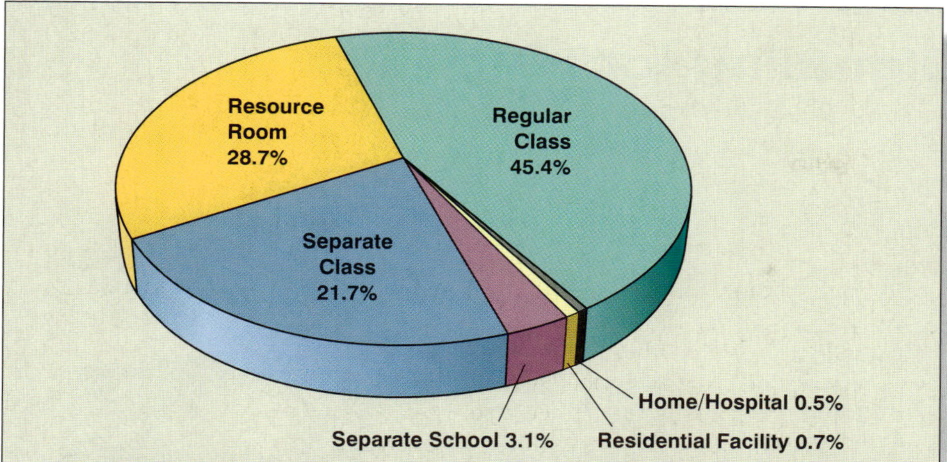

Notes: Separate school includes both public and private separate school facilities. Residential facility includes both public and private residential facilities

Figure 1.1 Percentage of all students with disabilities ages 6 through 21 served in six educational placements

Source: From U.S. Department of Education. (1998). *Twentieth annual report to Congress on the implementation of the Individuals with Disabilities Education Act*. Washington, DC: Author.

regular classrooms for part of each day during the 1995–1996 school year, although these figures represent increases over those of previous years.

Defining Features of Special Education

What, then, is special education? At one level, special education is an important part of society's response to the needs of exceptional children and the rights of individuals with disabilities—a response brought about by parental advocacy, litigation, legislation, and, increasingly, self-advocacy by disabled persons themselves. At another level, special education is a profession with its own history, cultural practices, tools, and research base

Table 1.6 Percentage of students with disabilities ages 6 through 21 served in six educational environments (1995–1996 school year)

Disability Category	Regular Classroom	Resource Room	Separate Classroom	Separate School	Residential Facility	Homebound or Hospital
Specific learning disabilities	42.4	39.3	17.4	0.6	0.1	0.2
Speech or language impairments	88.6	6.5	4.5	0.3	0.1	0.1
Mental retardation	10.3	28.6	54.0	6.0	0.6	0.5
Emotional disturbance	23.5	23.6	34.3	13.9	3.0	1.6
Other health impairments	43.2	30.2	18.4	1.7	0.2	6.2
Multiple disabilities	9.4	14.8	48.9	21.6	3.0	2.3
Hearing impairments	36.2	18.8	26.8	7.0	11.0	0.3
Orthopedic impairments	40.8	20.8	30.5	5.3	0.2	2.4
Autism	12.0	10.6	53.9	20.6	2.4	0.4
Visual impairments	47.7	20.6	17.1	5.4	8.6	0.6
Traumatic brain injury	28.5	24.8	30.6	11.5	2.1	2.4
Deaf-blindness	10.8	9.9	40.1	19.0	18.3	1.8
All disabilities	45.4	28.7	21.7	3.1	0.7	0.5

Source: From U.S. Department of Education. (1998). *Twentieth annual report to Congress on the implementation of the Individuals with Disabilities Education Act* (p. A-50–A-74). Washington, DC: Author.

Signaling for Help

Resource rooms are busy places. Students come and go throughout the school day, each according to an individualized schedule. Each student who comes to the resource room does so because of a need for intensive individualized instruction. The IEP objectives for any given group of students in a resource room at any one time typically cover a wide range of academic and social skills. Because of the varied skill levels and the ever-changing student groupings in the resource room, the special education teacher must often manage several types and levels of instruction at once. To accomplish this, students are often assigned individualized learning activities. Resource room teachers face a difficult challenge: the need to be in several places at once. While students work at their desks, learning centers, or computers, the teacher moves about the room, providing individual students with prompts, encouragement, praise, and corrective feedback as needed.

Students in a resource room are usually working on the skills for which they need the most help—that is, difficult material they have not yet mastered. Therefore, an effective and efficient system with which students can signal the resource room teacher for assistance is needed. Hand raising, the typical attention-getting signal, poses several problems. It is difficult to continue to work while holding one's hand in the air, a situation that results in a great deal of down time while students wait for the teacher to get to them. In addition, if several students are waving their hands in competition for the teacher's attention, it is distracting to other students and to the teacher. If unsuccessful in getting the teacher's help, students may give up trying whenever they run into difficulty. Even worse, students who are unsuccessful in obtaining the teacher's assistance may stop discriminating their need for help and simply continue to practice errors.

Students need an easy, quiet means of signaling for help that allows them to keep working with the assurance that their teacher will recognize their need for help. In Ronni Hochman Spratt's cross-categorical resource room for middle school students with disabilities, each student has a small flag made of colored felt, a dowel rod, and a 1 ¼-inch cube of wood. When one of Ronni's students needs assistance or wants her to check completed work, the student simply stands the flag up on his desk. While waiting for the teacher, the student can either go on to another item or work on materials in a special folder. With this simple and inexpensive system, down time is greatly reduced, and neither Ronni nor her students are distracted by hand waving or calling out. (An effective signaling device can also be made from an empty can wrapped with red and green construction paper [Kerr & Nelson, 1998]. Students turn the can on one end or the other to signal "I'm working" or "I need help.")

Signal flags are a simple and effective way for students to obtain teacher assistance and feedback.

Ronni asked her students to write what they thought of the signal flag system after using it for about three months.

> This is one of the best way to work in sted of raising your hand you raise your flag and keep on working but if you raise you hand you can't keep working. That is special because I get more work done. If she is working with some one els you raise it and she will get to you as fast as she can. (Brent)

> The flags in Miss Hochmans room are used for assistance from the teacher. When Miss Hochman is working you rais you flag and she will help you as soon as she has time. But you keep on working, like going on to the next problem. (Pam)

focused on the learning needs of exceptional children and adults. But at the level where exceptional children most meaningfully and frequently contact it, *special education is individually planned, specialized, intensive, goal-directed instruction*. When practiced most effectively and ethically, special education is also characterized by the use of research-based teaching methods, the application of which is guided by direct and frequent measures of student performance (Bushell & Baer, 1994; Greenwood & Maheady, 1997). Table 1.7 shows the dimensions and defining features of special education.

Current and Future Challenges

For thoughtful analyses of contemporary special education practice and the future of the field, see Kauffman (1998a) and Zigmond (1997).

Special education has accomplished a great deal during the past 30 years, and there is legitimate reason for those in the field to feel good about the progress. Much has been accomplished in terms of making a free, appropriate education available to many children with disabilities who were previously denied access to an education. Much has been learned about how to effectively teach children with severe disabilities—children who many previously had assumed were incapable of learning. Special educators and parents are learning to work as partners on behalf of exceptional children. Technological advances have helped many students overcome physical or communication disabilities. Throughout the remaining chapters, we describe many of these advances, but it is difficult to describe the state of the art of a large and ever-changing discipline such as special education. It is even more difficult to predict what special education will look like and be able to accomplish in the future.

Although the beginnings of special education can be traced back several centuries (Safford & Safford, 1996), in many respects the field is still in its formative years. There is a great deal that must be done to make special education most useful to those who need it most. Here are four areas that many in the field consider critical.

Bridge the Research-to-Practice Gap

To join the discussion on "What are the three most important challenges facing special education today?" go to the Message Board module at http://www.prenhall.com/heward

Special education can be nothing more, or less, than the quality of instruction provided by teachers. Contrary to the contentions of some, special education research has produced a significant and reliable knowledge base about effective teaching practices (Lloyd, Weintraub, & Safer, 1997). No knowledgeable person will argue that research has discovered everything that is important to know about teaching exceptional students. There are many questions to be answered, the pursuit of which will no doubt lead to other questions yet to be asked.

Table 1.7 Dimensions and defining features of special education instruction

Dimension	Defining Features
Individually planned	• Learning goals and objectives selected for each student based on assessment results and input from parents and student • Teaching methods and instruction materials selected and/or adapted for each student • Setting(s) where instruction will occur determined relative to opportunities for student to learn and use targeted skills
Specialized	• Sometimes involves unique or adapted teaching procedures seldom used in general education (e.g., constant time delay, token reinforcement, self-monitoring) • Incorporates a variety of instructional materials and supports—both natural and contrived—to help student acquire and use targeted learning objectives • Related services (e.g., audiology, physical therapy) • Assistive technology (e.g., adapted cup holder, head-operated switch to select communication symbols)
Intensive	• Instruction presented with attention to detail, precision, structure, clarity, and repeated practice • "Relentless, urgent" instruction (Zigmond, 1995) • Efforts made to provide incidental, naturalistic opportunities for student to use targeted knowledge and skills
Goal-directed	• Purposeful instruction intended to help individual students achieve the greatest possible personal self-sufficiency and success in present and future environments • Value/goodness of instruction determined by student attainment of outcomes
Research-based methods	• Recognizes that all teaching approaches are not equally effective • Instructional programs and teaching procedures selected on basis of research support
Guided by student performance	• Careful, ongoing monitoring of student progress • Frequent and direct measures/assessment of student learning that inform modifications in instruction

Instructional practices supported by scientific research are featured throughout this text.

While there is a significant gap between what is relatively well understood and what is poorly understood or not understood at all, the more distressing gap may be between what research has discovered about teaching and learning and what is practiced in many classrooms. For example, scientific research has helped us discover a great deal about areas such as how to design instruction to promote students' generalization and maintenance of what is taught, what features of early reading instruction will reduce the number of children who later develop reading problems, how to teach students the skills they need to more effectively self-determine and self-manage their lives, and what components of secondary special education programs increase students' success in making the transition from school to work. It is fundamentally and critically important for special education to bridge the research-to-practice gap regarding emphasis of effective instruction (Carnine, 1997).

Increase the Availability and Intensity of Early Intervention

It is better to intervene earlier than later. The recent growth in providing special education and family-focused services for infants, toddlers, and preschoolers who have disabilities or are at risk for developmental delay is a positive sign. Increased efforts must be made, however, to ensure that early intervention and special education preschool programs become more widely available and intensely delivered.

Improve Students' Transition from School to Adult Life

When special education is judged by its ultimate product—the youth who leave secondary school programs—it becomes clear how much further the field must progress. Too many young adults with disabilities are unsuccessful and unhappy in their postschool adjustment. Special education must improve the transition of youth with disabilities from school to life in their communities.

Improve the Special Education–General Education Partnership

It estimated that, in addition to the 10% to 12% of school-age children with disabilities who receive special education, another 10% to 20% of the student population have mild to moderate learning or behavior problems that interfere with their ability to progress and succeed in the general education program (Will, 1986). Both special and general educators must develop strategies for working together and sharing their skills and resources to prevent these millions of at-risk students from becoming failures of our educational system.

The ultimate effectiveness of special education must be measured by its ability to help secondary students with disabilities make a successful transition to adult life.

Using the Internet to Learn about Special Education and the Council for Exceptional Children

by Jill C. Dardig

The Council for Exceptional Children (CEC), the largest special education organization in the world, has more than 50,000 members, including teachers, specialists, administrators, and parents of children with disabilities and gifted and talented students. If you are preparing to become a special education teacher, consider joining CEC as student member. Membership includes subscriptions to two journals, *Exceptional Children* and *Teaching Exceptional Children*, and a quarterly newsletter, *CEC Today*.

Whether or not you are a member, you can find valuable information about a wide range of special education topics and issues on CEC's website (*http://www.cec.sped.org*), such as information on public policy and legislation, grant programs and special projects, job trends and openings, and current research. The site is linked to many other special education–related data bases as well. But like many complex websites, a quick surf through the site won't be very meaningful. With a little time, effort, and patience, however, you can fully navigate the site and find all that you are interested in. Playing the "20 Questions" game will help you explore the website and learn some useful things about special education. You will find many other interesting paths to follow beyond the questions listed below. Make use of both the home page links and the index (which is a shortcut method of finding the answers). The questions are fairly general because this site is updated regularly. Check back to the site periodically to see what new features have been added.

1. What is the mission of CEC?
2. What are three beliefs of CEC that you share?
3. When was the journal *Teaching Exceptional Children* started? Name the title and authors of an article in the current issue you might want to read.
4. Name five states that have a large demand for special education teachers.
5. What special education–related occupation(s) are predicted to experience a large increase in the next 5 to 10 years?
6. Who won the Clarissa Hug Teacher of the Year Award last year and why?
7. Name and describe one special project funded by CEC.
8. What is the purpose of the Minigrants for Educators program? What kind of project could you propose when you have your own classroom?
9. Which CEC division(s) might you like to join? Which additional journal(s) would you get if you did join?
10. Identify one teaching position in your home state that looks interesting.
11. Who is the state director of special education in your state? What is his or her address, phone number, and e-mail address?
12. State three Do's and three Don'ts when dealing with elected officials in your role as an advocate for students with disabilities.
13. Name one article or report summarized in the "Public Policy and Legislative Information" section that you might be interested in reading.
14. When and where will the upcoming annual CEC International Convention be held?
15. When and where will the CEC convention in your state be held?
16. List three topical areas that you are interested in that will be included in the upcoming annual convention program.
17. How does the *Teaching Exceptional Children* "Author On-Line" feature work?
18. Name one book or other material that you might like to order from the current CEC resource catalog. Give the title, author, and cost.
19. Describe and give the address for an interesting website that is linked to the CEC website. Visit it and browse around.
20. Use the search feature to locate a topic of personal or professional interest to you.

Jill C. Dardig is Professor of Education at Ohio Dominican College in Columbus, Ohio, where she trains special education teachers. Thank you to Dr. Tim Micek for sharing a similar idea.

These four areas are by no means the only important issues facing special education today. We could easily identify other challenges that many in the field would argue are equally important. For example:

- Increasing the availability and quality of special education programs for gifted and talented students
- Applying advances in assistive technology to greatly reduce or eliminate the disabling effects of physical and sensory impairments
- Combating the pervasive effects of childhood poverty on development and success in school (one in five American children under the age of 5 is living in poverty)
- Developing effective methods for providing education and related services to the growing numbers of children entering school whose development and learning are affected by prenatal exposure to drugs or alcohol
- Improving the behavior and attitudes of people without disabilities toward those with disabilities
- Opening up more opportunities for individuals with disabilities to participate in the full range of residential, employment, and recreational options available to nondisabled persons

Use the self-tests at http://www.prenhall.com/heward to assess your knowledge of the content of Chapter 1.

We do not know how successful special education will be in meeting these challenges. Only time will tell. And, of course, special educators do not face these challenges alone. General education; adult service agencies such as vocational rehabilitation, social work, and medicine; and society as a whole must all help find the solutions to these problems. But we do know that a large and growing group of people are working hard to respond to these challenges—people with and without disabilities, people within and outside special education. Whatever professional and personal goals you follow, I hope your introductory study of special education will encourage you to become part of that group.

Summary

Who Are Exceptional Children?

- *Exceptional children* are those whose physical attributes and/or learning abilities differ from the norm, either above or below, to such an extent that an individualized program of special education is indicated.
- *Disability* refers to the reduced function or loss of a particular body part or organ.
- *Handicap* refers to the problems a person with a disability or an impairment encounters when interacting with the environment.
- A child who is *at risk* is not currently identified as having a disability but is considered to have a greater-than-usual chance of developing a disability if intervention is not provided.

How Many Exceptional Children Are There?

- Children in special education represent approximately 10.8% of the school-age population.
- The four largest categories of children with disabilities receiving special education are learning disabilities, speech and language impairments, mental retardation, and emotional disturbance.
- The vast majority of children receiving special education have mild disabilities.
- Approximately 75% of students with disabilities receive at least part of their education in regular classrooms.

Why Do We Label and Classify Exceptional Children?

- Some believe that disability labels can have a negative effect on the child and on others' perceptions of her and can lead to exclusion; others believe that labeling is a necessary first step to providing needed intervention and that labels are important for comparing and communicating about research findings.
- In curriculum-based assessment, students are assessed and classified relative to the degree to which they are learning specific curriculum content.

Why Are Laws Governing the Education of Exceptional Children Necessary?

- Prior to the 1970s, many states had laws permitting public schools to deny enrollment to children with disabilities. When local public schools began to accept a measure of responsibility for educating certain exceptional students, a philosophy of segregation prevailed.
- Special education was strongly influenced by the case of *Brown v. Board of Education* in 1954 in which the U.S. Supreme Court declared that education must be made available to all children on equal terms.
- In the class-action lawsuit *PARC* (1972), the court ruled that all children with mental retardation were entitled to a free, appropriate public education and that placements in regular classrooms and regular public schools were preferable to segregated settings.
- All children are now recognized to have the right to equal protection under the law, which has been interpreted to mean the right to a free public education in the least restrictive environment.
- All children and their parents have the right to due process under the law, which includes the rights to be notified of any decision affecting the child's educational placement, to have a hearing and present a defense, to see a written decision, and to appeal any decision.
- Court decisions have also established the rights of children with disabilities to fair assessment in their native language and to education at public expense, regardless of the school district's financial constraints.

The Individuals with Disabilities Education Act

- The passage of IDEA by Congress in 1975 marked the culmination of the efforts of many educators, parents, and legislators to bring together in one comprehensive bill this country's laws regarding the education of children with disabilities. The law encompasses six major principles:
  - *Zero reject.* Schools must educate *all* children with disabilities. This principle applies regardless of the nature or severity of the disability.
  - *Nondiscriminatory identification and evaluation.* Schools must use nonbiased, multifactored methods of evaluation to determine whether a child has a disability and, if so, whether special education is needed.
  - *Free, appropriate public education.* All children with disabilities shall receive a free, appropriate public education at public expense. An individualized education program (IEP) must be developed and implemented for each student with a disability.
  - *Least restrictive environment.* Students with disabilities must be educated with children without disabilities to the maximum extent appropriate, and they should be removed to separate classes or schools only when the nature or severity of their disabilities is such that they cannot receive an appropriate education in a general education classroom.
  - *Due process safeguards.* Schools must provide due process safeguards to protect the rights of children with disabilities and their parents.
  - *Parent and student participation and shared decision making.* Schools must collaborate with parents and with students with disabilities in the design and implementation of special education services.
- IDEA requires states to provide special education services to all preschoolers with disabilities ages 3 to 5. This law also makes federal money available to encourage states to develop early intervention programs for disabled and at-risk infants and toddlers from birth to age 2. Early intervention services must be coordinated by an individualized family services plan (IFSP).
- Court cases have challenged the way in which particular school districts implement specific provisions of IDEA. No trend has emerged, but rulings from the various cases have established the principle that each student with disabilities is entitled to a personalized program of instruction and related services that will enable him to benefit from an education in as integrated a setting as possible.
- The Gifted and Talented Children's Education Act (P.L. 95–561) provides financial incentives to states for developing programs for gifted and talented students.
- Section 504 of the Rehabilitation Act forbids discrimination in all federally funded programs, including educational and vocational programs, on the basis of disability.
- The Americans with Disabilities Act (P.L. 101–336) extends the civil rights protections for persons with disabilities to private sector employment, all public services, public accommodations, transportation, and telecommunications.

What Is Special Education?

- Special education consists of purposeful intervention efforts at three different levels: preventive, remedial, and compensatory.
- Special education is individually planned, specialized, intensive, goal-directed instruction. When practiced most effectively and ethically, special education is also characterized by the use of research-based teaching methods and guided by direct and frequent measures of student performance.

Current and Future Challenges

- Four major challenges faced by special education are:
  - Bridging the research-to-practice gap
  - Making early intervention programs more widely available to infants, toddlers, and preschoolers who have disabilities or are at risk for developing disabilities
  - Improving the ability of young adults with disabilities to make a successful transition from school to community life
  - Working more effectively with general education to better serve the many students who have not been identified as disabled but who are not progressing in the general education program

For More Information

Journals

- *Education & Treatment of Children.* Published by PRO-ED, 8700 Shoal Creek Boulevard, Austin, TX 78758-6897. A quarterly journal devoted to the dissemination of information concerning the development and improvement of services for children and youths. Includes original research, reviews of the literature, and descriptions of innovative intervention and treatment programs.
- *Elementary School Journal.* Published five times per year by the University of Chicago Press, Journals Division, 5720 South Woodlawn Avenue, Chicago, IL 60637. A widely disseminated journal of research, reviews, and position papers concerning all aspects of elementary education.
- *Exceptional Children.* The official journal of the Council for Exceptional Children, published six times per year (see "Organization"). Publishes original research, position papers, debates, and reviews of the literature related to contemporary issues concerning the education of exceptional children. Designed to assist all professionals who work with exceptional children, including school psychologists, counselors, and administrators.
- *Intervention in School and Clinic.* Published five times per year by PRO-ED, 8700 Shoal Creek Boulevard, Austin, TX 78758-6897. An interdisciplinary journal directed toward an international audience of teachers, parents, educational therapists, and specialists in all fields who deal with the day-to-day aspects of special and remedial education.
- *Journal of Behavioral Education.* Published quarterly by Human Sciences Press, 233 Spring Street, New York, NY 10013-1578. Publishes original research as well as conceptual and review papers on the application of behavioral principles and technology to education and on the use of single subject replication designs to study educational issues, problems, and practices.
- *Phi Delta Kappan,* Eighth and Union, P.O. Box 789, Bloomington, IN 47402. A highly regarded journal that publishes articles of general interest on all aspects of education; a good source for information on current trends and issues.
- *Remedial and Special Education.* Published six times per year by PRO-ED, 8700 Shoal Creek Boulevard, Austin, TX 78758-6897. Devoted to discussion of issues involving the education of persons for whom typical instruction is not effective. Emphasizes interpretation of research literature and recommendations for the practice of remedial and special education.
- *Teacher Education and Special Education.* Published quarterly by the Teacher Education Division of the Council for Exceptional Children (see "Organizations"). Publishes research, program descriptions, and discussion articles on issues and methods pertaining to the education of teachers and other educational personnel for exceptional children.
- *Teaching Exceptional Children.* Published quarterly by the Council for Exceptional Children (see "Organization"). A practitioner's journal designed to assist both regular and special education classroom teachers of children with disabilities as well as those who are gifted and talented. Most articles feature practical methods and materials for classroom use. Also includes a teacher idea exchange, reviews of books and instructional materials, descriptions of selected materials from the ERIC Clearinghouse on Disabilities and Gifted Education, and information on national meetings and in-service training opportunities.
- *The Journal of Special Education.* Published quarterly by PRO-ED, 8700 Shoal Creek Boulevard, Austin, TX 78758-6897. Publishes articles from all disciplines; deals with research, theory, opinion, and reviews of the literature in special education.

Books

- Anderson, W., Chitwood, S., & Hayden, D. (1997). *Negotiating the special education maze: A guide for parents and teachers.* Reston, VA: Council for Exceptional Children.
- Cohen, M. K., Gale, M., & Meyer, J. M. (1994). *Survival guide for the first-year special education teacher* (rev. ed.). Reston, VA: Council for Exceptional Children.
- Council for Exceptional Children. (1998). *What every special educator must know: The international standards for the preparation and certification of special education teachers* (3rd ed.). Reston, VA: Author.
- Lovitt, T. C. (1995). *Tactics for teaching* (2nd ed.). Upper Saddle River, NJ: Prentice Hall.
- Pullen, P. L., & Kauffman, J. M. (1987). *What should I know about special education? Answers for classroom teachers.* Austin, TX: PRO-ED.
- Smarte, L., & McLane, K. (1994). *How to find answers to your special education questions* (rev. ed.). Reston, VA: Council for Exceptional Children.
- Turnbull, H. R., & Turnbull, A. P. (1998). *Free appropriate public education: The law and children with disabilities* (5th ed.). Denver: Love.
- Yell, M. L. (1998). *The law and special education.* Upper Saddle River, NJ: Merrill/Prentice Hall.
- Ysseldyke, J. E., Algozzine, B., & Thurlow, M. L. (1992). *Critical issues in special education* (2nd ed.). Boston: Houghton Mifflin.

Organization

- *Council for Exceptional Children (CEC),* 1920 Association Drive, Reston, VA, 22091-1589; (703) 620-3660; website: http://www.cec.sped.org. Membership includes more than 50,000 teachers, teacher educators, administrators, researchers, and other professionals involved in the education of exceptional children and adults.

Websites

- *Big Pages of Special Education Links,* http://www.mts.net/~jgreenco/special.html/. A signpost site that links to numerous other sites and organizations related to disabilities and special education.
- *National Information Center for Children and Youth with Disabilities,* http://www.nichcy.org/. A national information and referral center that provides information on disabilities and disability-related issues for families, educators, and other professionals.
- *Online Academy,* http://onlineacademy.org. Funded by a grant from the U.S. Office of Special Education to The University of Kansas; designed to enhance the education of all learners by providing teacher education programs with access to web-based modules on research-validated educational interventions in the areas of reading, technology, and positive behavioral support.
- *SpedTalk,* http://spedtalk@virginia.edu; subscribe to http://majordomo@virginia.edu. A listserve for discussion of current issues in special education.
- *U.S. Department of Education*, http://www.ed.gov. Nearly 2,000 ERIC research syntheses can be accessed at http://www.ed.gov/databases/ERIC_Digests/index/.
- *U.S. Office of Special Education and Rehabilitation Services*, http://www.ed.gov/offices/OSERS/.

Chapter 2

Planning and Providing Special Education Services

Focus Questions

- Why must the planning and provision of special education be so carefully sequenced and evaluated?
- Why are collaboration and teaming so critical to the effectiveness of special education?
- What is an individualized education program, and how should its quality be judged?
- Is the least restrictive environment always the regular classroom?
- Can high-quality, effective instruction be provided in any setting?

In Chapter 1, special education was defined as individually planned, specialized, intensive, goal-directed instruction. But how do teachers know what kinds of modifications to curriculum and instruction are needed by an individual child? And toward what goals should instruction be directed? In this chapter, we examine the basic process by which special education is planned, devoting particular attention to four critical aspects of educating students with disabilities: (1) the importance of teaming and collaboration among professionals, (2) the individualized education plan (IEP), (3) the least restrictive environment (LRE), and (4) inclusion.

The Process of Special Education

Federal law mandates a particular sequence of events that schools must follow when identifying and educating children with disabilities. Although the rules and regulations that state and local school districts must follow to implement IDEA are formal and sometimes redundant for legal purposes, the process is designed to answer a sequence of questions that makes both educational and common sense:

Go to the companion website at http://www.prenhall.com/heward and select Chapter 2 to review the chapter objectives.

- Which students might need special education?
- Does this particular child have a disability that adversely affects his educational performance? In other words, is this student eligible for special education? If the answer is yes, then. . . .
- What are the specific educational needs that result from the child's disability?
- What instructional modifications, related services, and supplementary supports are necessary to meet those needs so the student can be involved in and progress in the general curriculum and life of the school?
- Who is best suited to provide the special education and related services needed by the student?
- What educational placement is most appropriate for the student?
- Is special education helping the student make progress? Is it working?

Although not required to do so by IDEA, some states follow a process like the one shown in Figure 2.1 for planning individualized education programs for gifted and talented students.

Figure 2.1 identifies the major steps in the sequence of planning, implementing, and evaluating special education and highlights some of the key procedures, elements, or requirements of each step. With the exception of the first step, prereferral inter-

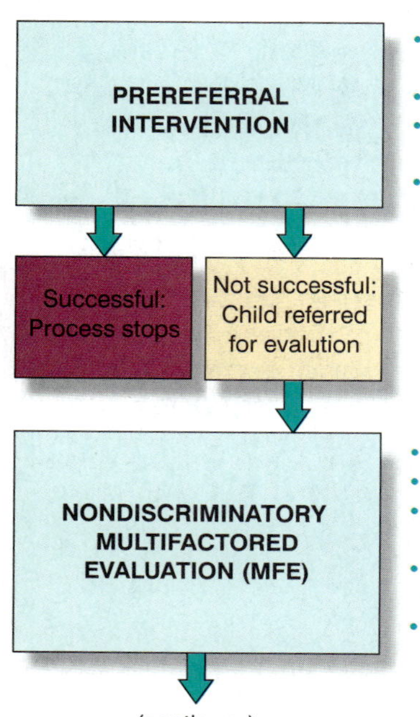

- Results of screening test indicate possible disability; or teacher (or parent) reports concern with child's learning, behavior, or development.
- Parents are notified.
- Intervention assistance team works with classroom teacher to plan modifications in curriculum and instruction in an attempt to solve the problem.
- Prereferral intervention is not required by IDEA; it may not be used to delay referral and evaluation of an eligible student.

- Parents' consent for testing and evaluation must be obtained.
- Evaluation must not discriminate on basis of race, culture, language, or gender.
- A multifactored evaluation considers all areas related to the suspected disability (e.g., academic performance, general intelligence, social behavior, vision, health).
- It uses a variety of assessment tools and strategies (e.g., formal tests, direct observations, parental input).
- It should provide information to help determine if the child has a disability, what kinds of services may be needed, and how the child can participate in the general education curriculum.

Figure 2.1 The basic steps in planning, providing, and evaluating special education

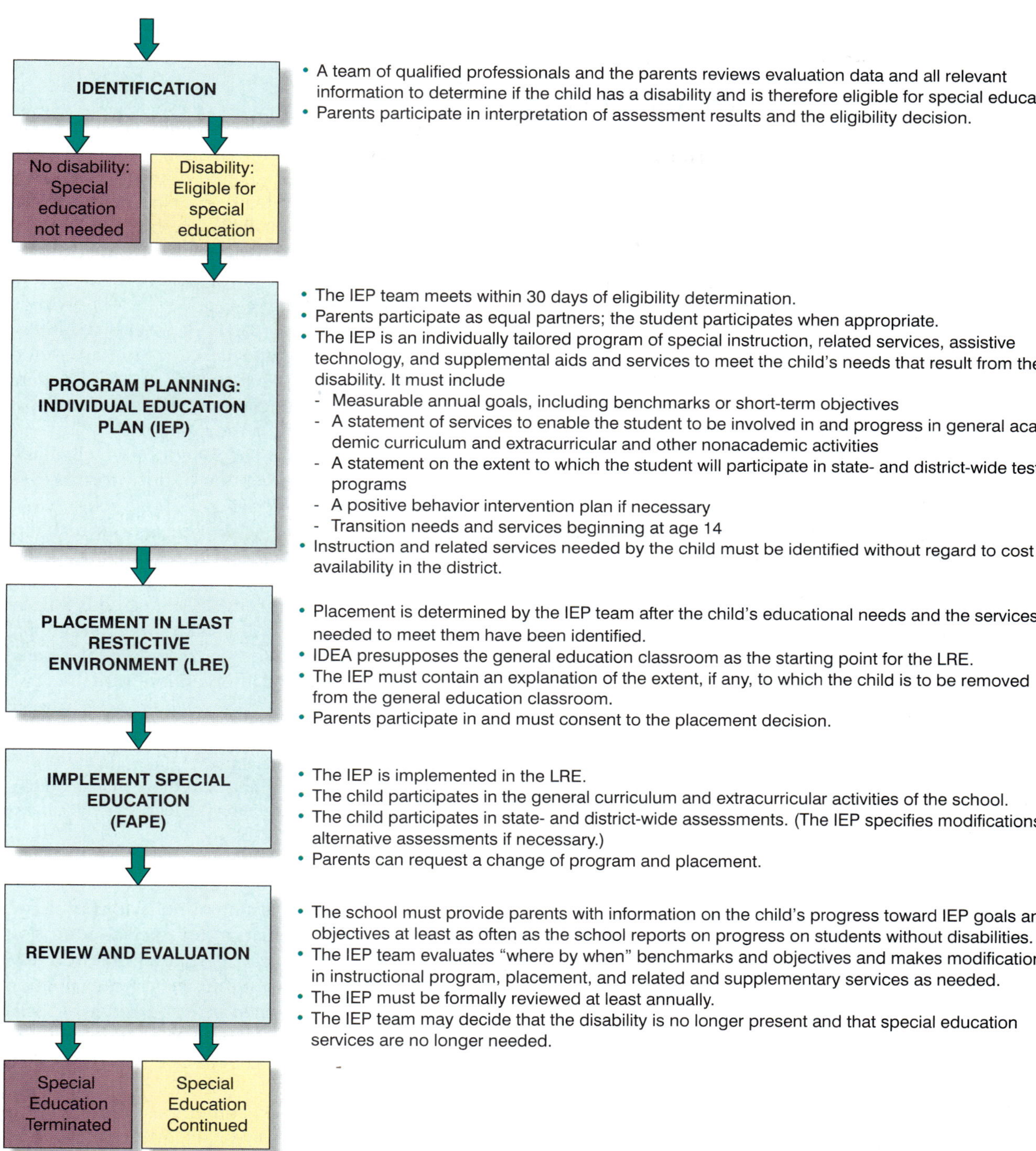

IDENTIFICATION
No disability: Special education not needed
Disability: Eligible for special education
PROGRAM PLANNING: INDIVIDUAL EDUCATION PLAN (IEP)
PLACEMENT IN LEAST RESTICTIVE ENVIRONMENT (LRE)
IMPLEMENT SPECIAL EDUCATION (FAPE)
REVIEW AND EVALUATION
Special Education Terminated
Special Education Continued
• A team of qualified professionals and the parents reviews evaluation data and all relevant information to determine if the child has a disability and is therefore eligible for special education.
• Parents participate in interpretation of assessment results and the eligibility decision.
• The IEP team meets within 30 days of eligibility determination.
• Parents participate as equal partners; the student participates when appropriate.
• The IEP is an individually tailored program of special instruction, related services, assistive technology, and supplemental aids and services to meet the child's needs that result from the disability. It must include
- Measurable annual goals, including benchmarks or short-term objectives
- A statement of services to enable the student to be involved in and progress in general academic curriculum and extracurricular and other nonacademic activities
- A statement on the extent to which the student will participate in state- and district-wide testing programs
- A positive behavior intervention plan if necessary
- Transition needs and services beginning at age 14
• Instruction and related services needed by the child must be identified without regard to cost or availability in the district.
• Placement is determined by the IEP team after the child's educational needs and the services needed to meet them have been identified.
• IDEA presupposes the general education classroom as the starting point for the LRE.
• The IEP must contain an explanation of the extent, if any, to which the child is to be removed from the general education classroom.
• Parents participate in and must consent to the placement decision.
• The IEP is implemented in the LRE.
• The child participates in the general curriculum and extracurricular activities of the school.
• The child participates in state- and district-wide assessments. (The IEP specifies modifications or alternative assessments if necessary.)
• Parents can request a change of program and placement.
• The school must provide parents with information on the child's progress toward IEP goals and objectives at least as often as the school reports on progress on students without disabilities.
• The IEP team evaluates "where by when" benchmarks and objectives and makes modifications in instructional program, placement, and related and supplementary services as needed.
• The IEP must be formally reviewed at least annually.
• The IEP team may decide that the disability is no longer present and that special education services are no longer needed.

Figure 2.1 *continued*

vention, each step in the process is required by IDEA and must be completed in the sequence shown.

Prereferral Intervention

Screening tests are relatively quick, inexpensive, and easy-to-administer assessments given to large groups of children to find out who might have a disability and need further testing. For example, most schools administer vision screening tests to all elementary children.

A child who may need special education usually comes to the attention of the schools because (1) a teacher or parent reports concern about differences in learning, behavior, or development or (2) the results of a screening test suggest a possible disability. Before referring the child for more formal testing and evaluation for special education, however, most schools initiate a process known as *prereferral intervention*.

Prereferral intervention is an informal, problem-solving process with two primary purposes: (1) to provide immediate instructional and/or behavior management assistance to the child and teacher and (2) to reduce the chances of identifying a child for special education who may not be disabled (Salvia & Ysseldyke, 1995). About 75% to 80% of children who are evaluated for special education are determined to have a disability (Algozzine, Ysseldyke, & Christenson, 1983; Galagan, 1985). When prereferral intervention is successful in ameliorating the problems that originally caused teachers or parents to be concerned for the child, it also prevents the costly and time-consuming process of assessment for special education eligibility. A school district may not, however, use prereferral intervention to delay formal evaluation and assessment of a student who is eligible for special education (Yell, 1998).

Descriptions of prereferral intervention models and related research can be found in Fuchs, Fuchs, and Bahr (1990); Graden (1989); and Pugach and Johnson (1989).

Many schools use *intervention assistance teams* to help classroom teachers devise and implement adaptations for a student who is experiencing either academic or behavioral difficulties so that she can remain in the regular classroom. Carter and Sugai (1989) found that, although not required by federal law, 23 states required prereferral interventions for students suspected of having a disability, and 11 additional states recommended that local school districts use prereferral systems. Fuchs, Fuchs, Bahr, Fernstrom, and Stecker (1990) note that prereferral intervention

> is often "brokered" by one or more support staff, such as a special educator or school psychologist, who works indirectly with a targeted difficult-to-teach student through consultation with the teacher. Implicit in this definition is a preventative intent; that is, (a) eliminating inappropriate referrals while increasing the legitimacy of those that are initiated and (b) reducing future student problems by strengthening the teacher's capacity to intervene effectively with a greater diversity of children. (p. 495)

Go to the Resource Module for Chapter 2 at http://www.prenhall.com/heward. Click on Special Ed Resource Page and access a search engine. Search for "Special Education and Assessment."

Evaluation and Identification

Teachers seldom refer children for minor or frivolous learning or behavior problems, and in practice about 90% of referrals lead to an evaluation for special education (Algozzine, Christenson, & Ysseldyke, 1982). IDEA requires that all children suspected of having a disability receive a nondiscriminatory multifactored evaluation (MFE). Either the school or parents can request that a child be evaluated for special education. Regardless of the source of the referral, the parents must be notified of the school's intent to test their child, and they must give their consent to the evaluation. IDEA is explicit in describing some do's and don'ts for the evaluation and identification of children for special education. These rules, sometimes referred to as *protection in evaluation procedures* (Yell, 1998), are shown in Figure 2.2.

The evaluation team may not determine that a child has a disability if the primary factor for the determination is "lack of instruction in reading or math or limited English proficiency" (IDEA, Sec. 1414[b][5]).

Assessment and evaluation are conducted by a school-based *evaluation team*, sometimes called a *multidisciplinary team* or *child study team*, which includes the child's parents. The team examines the test results and all other relevant information to determine if the child has a disability and needs special education. The multifactored evaluation must do more than just provide information on the existence of a

- The evaluation team must comprise a multidisciplinary team or group of persons, at least one of whom has knowledge in the child's suspected area of disability.
- Technically sound instruments must be used to assess the student across four domains: cognitive, behavioral, physical, and developmental.
- Tests must not discriminate on the basis of race or culture.
- Tests must be provided and administered in the child's native language or other mode of communication.
- Standardized tests must have been validated for the specific purpose for which they are used.
- Standardized tests must be administered by trained and knowledgeable personnel in accordance with any instructions provided by the publisher of the tests.
- The child is assessed in all areas related to the suspected disability.
- The evaluation process must not rely on any single procedure as the sole criterion for determining whether the student has a disability, the student's program, or placement.

Figure 2.2 IDEA rules for nondiscriminatory, multifactored evaluation and identification of children for special education
Source: IDEA, Sec. 1414(b).

disability for determining eligibility for special education. The IDEA amendments of 1997 require evaluation reports to also provide information about the child's educational needs and how to meet them.

Program Planning

Once the evaluation team has determined that a child has a disability that is adversely affecting his educational performance, an individualized education program (IEP) must be planned and provided. The IEP process determines the what (learning goals and objectives and related services), who (in terms of teachers and related service providers), and when (frequency of specialized instruction and related services) of a child's special education program. A critically important element of special education practice—some would say the centerpiece—the IEP will be described in some detail later in this chapter.

"Here's another idea we could try." Intervention assistance teams plan strategies to help children with learning or behavioral problems remain in the regular classroom.

Placement

After the child's educational needs and the special education and related services necessary to meet those needs are determined, the IEP team decides on the least restrictive environment (LRE) in which an appropriate education can be provided to the child. The placement of children with disabilities is one of the most debated and often misunderstood aspects of special education and IDEA and will be discussed in depth later in this chapter and throughout the text.

Should students with disabilities be graded the same way as other students? Even for modified assignments? For a discussion of grading practices for students with disabilities, see Bradley and Calvin (1998) and Christensen and Vogel (1998).

Evaluation

In addition to being specialized, intensive, and goal-directed education—when it is properly conducted—special education is also continuously evaluated education. All aspects of a child's IEP—achievement of goals and objectives, instructional methods, related services, placement—are reviewed and open for change. The IEP must be thoroughly and formally reviewed on an annual basis. However, schools must notify parents of their child's progress in the general curriculum and toward IEP goals and objectives at least as often as parents of nondisabled students receive information about their children's school performance.

No matter how appropriate the goals, benchmarks, and objectives specified on a student's IEP are, the document's usefulness is limited without direct and ongoing monitoring of student progress (Fuchs & Fuchs, 1986, 1996; Wesson, King, & Deno, 1984). Unfortunately, many teachers do not collect and use student performance data to evaluate the effectiveness of their instruction. Although three-fourths of the 510 special education teachers in one survey indicated that frequently collected student performance data are "important," many indicated they most often relied on anecdotal observations and subjective measures (e.g., checklists, letter grades) for determining whether or not IEP objectives were met, and 85% said they "never" or "seldom" collected and charted student performance data to make instructional decisions (Cooke, Heward, Test, Spooner, & Courson, 1991). Giek (1992) and Farlow and Snell (1994) describe a variety of practical procedures for obtaining and using student performance data to monitor student progress toward IEP objectives.

Check your ongoing understanding of Chapter 2 concepts by using the Guided Review Module at http://www.prenhall.com/heward.

The Importance of Collaboration and Teaming

Special education is a team game. The fourth-grade teacher who works with Sharelle in the regular classroom, the speech-language pathologist who meets with Sharelle's teacher each week to co-plan language activities, and the special education teacher who provides Sharelle with intensive reading instruction each day in the resource room and collaborates with her regular classroom teacher on instructional modifications for Sharelle in math and science are all members of a team that plans, delivers, and evaluates a program of special education and related services designed to meet the individual needs that arise from Sharelle's disability. Without open, honest, and frequent communication and collaboration between and among the members of Sharelle's team, the quality of her education is likely to suffer.

Collaboration

Once just a buzzword for futurists' conceptualizations of effective schools in the 21st century (Benjamin, 1989), collaboration has become common and necessary practice in special education. Teachers who work with students with disabilities and other students who are difficult to teach have discovered they are better able to diagnose and solve learning and behavior problems in the classroom when they work together.

Three ways in which team members can work collaboratively are through coordination, consultation, and teaming (Bigge, Stump, Spagna, & Silberman, 1999). *Coordination* is the simplest form of collaboration, requiring only ongoing communication and cooperation to ensure that services are provided in timely and systematic fashion. Although an important and necessary element of special education, coordination does not require service providers to share information or specifics of their efforts with one another. Fortunately for Sharelle, the three educators on her IEP team do much more than simply coordinate who is going to work with her when.

In *consultation,* team members provide information and expertise to one another. Consultation is traditionally considered unidirectional, with the expert providing assistance and advice to the novice. However, team members can, and often do, switch roles from consultant to consultee (or client) and back again. Sharelle's fourth-grade teacher, for example, receives expert advice from the speech-language pathologist on strategies for evoking extended language from Sharelle during cooperative learning groups but takes the consultant's role when explaining details of the science curriculum content to Sharelle's resource room teacher.

Heron and Harris (in press) describe a variety of consultation strategies special educators can use while working as team members with general education teachers and parents.

Teaming

Intervention assistance team, child study team, evaluation team, IEP team: each step of the special education process involves a group of people who must work together for the benefit of a child with special needs. For special education to be most effective, these groups must become functioning and effective teams. Teaming is the most difficult level of collaboration to achieve; it also pays the most dividends. *Teaming* "bridges the two previous modes of working together and builds on their strengths while adding the component of reciprocity and sharing of information among all team members through a more equal exchange" (Bigge et al., 1999, p. 13). There are several levels or ways in which this can happen. Table 2.1 shows examples of coordination, consultation, and teaming activities by professionals.

Although there are many variations of the team approach in terms of size and structure, each member of a team generally assumes certain clearly assigned responsibilities and recognizes the importance of learning from, contributing to, and interacting with the other members of the team. Many believe that the consensus and group decisions arising from a team's involvement provide a form of insurance against erroneous or arbitrary conclusions in the complex issues that face educators of students with disabilities. In practice, three team models have emerged (Giangreco, York, & Rainforth, 1989; Woodruff & McGonigel, 1988).

Paraprofessionals—*paid (and occasionally volunteer) workers who provide direct instructional and support services to students with disabilities under titles such as classroom aides and teacher assistants—are important members of many special education teams. Yet relatively little attention has been paid to their training and supervision (French & Pickett, 1997). For suggestions on how to effectively work with paraprofessionals in special education, see Blalock (1991); Courson and Heward (1988); French (in press); and Jones and Bender (1993).*

Multidisciplinary Teams *Multidisciplinary teams* are composed of professionals from different disciplines who work independently of one another. Each team member conducts assessments, plans interventions, and delivers services. Teams that operate according to a multidisciplinary structure risk the danger of not providing services that recognize the child as an integrated whole; they tend to "splinter" the child into segments along disciplinary lines. (An old saying described the child with disabilities as giving "his hands to the occupational therapist, his legs to the physical therapist, and his brain to the teacher" [Williamson, 1978].) Another concern is the lack of communication among team members.

To join in the discussion on "Why is collaboration and teaming so critical to the effectiveness of special education?" go to the Message Board Module at http://www.prenhall.com/heward.

Interdisciplinary Teams *Interdisciplinary teams* are characterized by formal channels of communication between members. Although each professional usually conducts discipline-specific assessments, the interdisciplinary team meets to share

Activity	Examples
Coordination	• special and general education teachers working out class schedules and support schedules for students • therapists and general and special education teachers working out schedules for therapy interventions • general and special education teachers coordinating grading procedures and policies • special education teachers working with job coaches and transition teachers to set community-based experience schedules for students
Consultation	• special education teachers assisting general education teachers • vocational education teachers working with community employers • related service personnel providing support to special education and general education teachers
Teaming	• special and general education teachers, administrators, counselors, support staff, and school psychologists working together on prereferral teams to design and implement interventions in general education classrooms • special and general education teachers co-teaching in the classroom • paraprofessionals working with general education teachers • special and general education teachers serving together on curriculum-planning teams • team of professionals working together to determine whether a child is eligible for special education services • IEP teams working together to assess the current performance of a student to determine continued eligibility for special education services

Table 2.1 Examples of coordination, consultation, and teaming activities in special education

Source: Reprinted from Bigge, J. L., Stump, C. S., Spagna, M. E., & Silberman, R. K. (1999). *Curriculum, assessment, and instruction for students with disabilities* (p. 14). Belmont, CA: Wadsworth. Used by permission.

information and to develop intervention plans. Each team member is generally responsible for implementing a portion of the service plan related to his discipline.

Regardless of the team model, team members must learn to put aside professional rivalries and work collaboratively for the benefit of the student. See "Interactive Teaming," which follows.

Transdisciplinary Teams The highest level of team involvement, but also the most difficult to accomplish, is the *transdisciplinary team*. Members of transdisciplinary teams seek to provide services in a uniform and integrated fashion by conducting joint assessments, sharing information and expertise across discipline boundaries, and selecting goals and interventions that are discipline-free (Gallivan-Fenlon, 1994; Giangreco, Edelman, & Dennis, 1991; Giangreco et al., 1989). Members of transdisciplinary teams also share roles (often referred to as *role release*); in contrast, members of multidisciplinary and interdisciplinary teams generally operate in isolation and may not coordinate their services to achieve the integrated delivery of related services.

Interactive Teaming

by Vivian I. Correa

Collaboration and teaming have become critical parts of how educators do their work in schools today. Solving the problems described in the three vignettes at the end of this box requires teaming and collaboration. Whether working with families, community agencies, or other educators, collaboration is a complex task that requires special knowledge and skills. We often assume that all education personnel and families know how to collaborate and team. It seems like common sense. Administrators, for example, often ask teachers to work together to solve a problem, assuming that they understand the intricacies of the collaboration process. Yet what often results from the interactions among the teachers are problems associated with poor interpersonal communication, role ambiguity, turf wars, lack of leadership support, and time constraints. Many educators have not learned the skills necessary for collaboration and lack the basic knowledge for understanding the dynamic process of interactive teaming.

Interactive teaming occurs when there is mutual or reciprocal effort among and between members of the team to meet the goal of providing the best possible education program for a student (Thomas, Correa, & Morsink, 1995). The purpose of interactive teaming is to share information and expertise to ensure that the best possible decisions are made and that effective programs are implemented.

Collaborating with professionals and families within an interactive team model has its benefits and barriers. The benefits of teaming, however, far outweigh the difficulties that may occur. For example, when individuals team, there is a sense of camaraderie, friendship, and mutuality. Effective teaming produces effective ideas and comprehensive solutions that one person alone may not have been able to achieve.

What are the important skills that education personnel need to become effective team members? Not surprisingly, one of the most important skills is the ability to communicate well. Effective *interpersonal communication* involves the ability to be empathic, genuine, positive, open, clear, and assertive. Both verbal and nonverbal communication skills can be developed in individuals through training and practice.

A second skill necessary for interactive teaming is *role clarification.* Each member of a team must understand her own role and responsibilities and those of other members. If confusion or overlapping interests occur among team members, effective teaming may be jeopardized. Members who are unsure of their roles and responsibilities may blame others by making statements such as "I thought that was what you were supposed to do" or "No one told me I was responsible for this." From the onset of interactive teaming, it is critical to avoid ambiguity of roles and responsibilities.

A third skill involved in interactive teaming relates to adult learning. Effective team members can *role release* to other members by teaching them about basic procedures and practices associated with their profession. For example, an occupational therapist can teach a classroom teacher and a parent how to implement oral motor exercises on a child before meals. Thus, educating and learning from other adults become core skills necessary for implementing the best integrated educational strategies for students.

Interactive team members must also become culturally competent. The first step for developing *cultural competence* is to become aware of one's own attitudes, values, biases, and stereotypes of ethnic minorities (e.g., African Americans, Native Americans, Asians, Hispanics) and non-ethnic minorities (e.g., individuals who are homeless, gays and lesbians, those living in poverty). Team members must understand the impact that ethnic or non-ethnic diversity has in the interactions among professional team members as well as among the students and families with whom they work. Teams must develop culturally responsive services for students and families from many diverse groups. (The characteristics of culturally responsive services are discussed in Chapter 3.)

Suggested Steps The following procedures are involved in interactive teaming. They may vary, however, depending on factors such as the age of the child, the severity of the problem, and the types of professionals available.

1. Designate a team leader and make sure all persons involved are notified of the meeting time and place.
2. Introduce all team members and state the purpose of the meeting.
3. Describe, in detail, the problem situation and allow team members to ask questions for clarification.
4. Reach consensus on a specific, measurable, and observational definition of the problem.
5. Prioritize the problems, if there are more than one, on the basis of the needs of the student and the family.
6. Determine the history and frequency of the problem.

7. Discuss any previous interventions that have been attempted.
8. Brainstorm possible interventions, encouraging full team participation.
9. Establish procedures for collecting data.
10. Determine how long the intervention will be applied.
11. Clarify the responsibilities of each team member.
12. Develop timelines for activities and schedule a follow-up meeting.
13. Evaluate the intervention regularly with team members and make modifications if necessary.
14. Provide consultative and collaborative assistance to each member as needed.
15. Evaluate the team's effectiveness and determine whether any changes need to be made in operating procedures, team composition, or other areas.

Interactive teaming can be extremely successful in solving problems for special education teachers working within today's inclusive school environments. The benefits of teaming are the development of effective strategies and solutions for students with disabilities and their families. The skills required for effective collaboration and teaming, however, are complex and must be demonstrated by all team members. It is imperative that college and university programs in teacher education teach the skills of teaming and collaboration and allow preservice students to practice them. As educators prepare for the increasing challenges of tomorrow's schools, a collaborative model like interactive teaming may well be the major pattern for future service delivery for students with disabilities and their families.

Application Activities

1. Think about the last time you worked on a project with a group of peers (e.g., planning a party or campus activity). Did everything go smoothly? Which individuals worked well together? Which ones did not? Why? What problems did you encounter? Why do you think those problems occurred? How were they resolved?
2. Form small teams and choose one of the following three vignettes to tackle. Have each person take a role (e.g., special educator, regular classroom teacher, parent) and role-play a problem-solving conference.

Gail Miller, the school liaison at a local elementary school, has asked that a team meeting be held to discuss the referral of Jacques, a 3-year-old Haitian child, to special education. Jacques was brought to the United States to live with his grandmother a year ago, and his diagnosis of cerebral palsy qualified him to receive early intervention services at a local day-care center. Gail is worried. Jacques is now eligible for preschool special education services at the elementary school, but no one at the school speaks French Creole and Jacques's custodial grandmother speaks little English. According to IDEA, children must be assessed in their native language. Gail is at a loss about what to do.

Claire, a 16-year-old with learning disabilities, is asking her parents to assist her in getting an after-school job at the mall where her friends work. Claire's parents ask Tom Greco, the high school transition specialist, to arrange a meeting with the principal and teachers regarding this request. Tom is concerned about this situation. What should he do?

Audrey is 8 years old and has been diagnosed with autism. Her teacher, Ms. Jones, is a beginning teacher at the local elementary school. Audrey's family members are concerned that Audrey's self-injurious behaviors have increased within the last few weeks. Ms. Jones has noticed this increase as well and has tried some strategies to redirect the behavior, with no positive results. She is worried about the situation and would like some assistance. What is she to do?

3. Use the steps described previously to come to some solutions. Share the results of your interactive teaming experience with the larger group. How did each team member feel about the conference? What problems or barriers emerged? How were they resolved? What were the solutions that resulted from the collaboration?

Vivian I. Correa is a professor of special education at the University of Florida and co-author of *Interactive Teaming: Consultation and Collaboration in Special Programs* (Thomas et al., 1995). She is well known for her work in helping teachers plan and deliver effective instruction for students from culturally and linguistically diverse backgrounds. Dr. Correa is also co-author of Chapter 3 of this text, "Special Education in a Culturally Diverse Society."

Individualized Education Program

The individualized education program (IEP) is the centerpiece of the special education process. IDEA requires that an IEP be developed and implemented for every student with disabilities between the ages of 3 and 21. The law is specific as to what an IEP must include and who is to take part in its formulation. Each IEP must be the product of the joint efforts of the members of an *IEP team*, which must include the following members:

(1) The parents (or surrogate parent) of the child;
(2) At least one regular education teacher of the child (if the child is, or may be, participating in the regular education environment);
(3) At least one special education teacher, or if appropriate, at least one special education provider of the child;
(4) A representative of the local education agency (LEA) who—
  i. Is qualified to provide, or supervise the provision of, specially designed instruction to meet the unique needs of children with disabilities;
  ii. Is knowledgeable about the general curriculum; and
  iii. Is knowledgeable about the availability of resources of the LEA;
(5) An individual who can interpret the instructional implications of evaluation results, who may be a member of the team described above;
(6) At the discretion of the parent or the school, other individuals who have knowledge or special expertise regarding the child, including related service personnel as appropriate; and
(7) The student, if age 14 or older, must be invited. Younger students may attend if appropriate. (34 CFR 300.344)

Individualized family service plans (IFSP) *are developed for infants and toddlers (from birth until age 3) with disabilities. IFSPs are described in Chapter 5.*

All IEPs must include the following seven components:

(1) A statement of the child's present levels of educational performance, including
  i. How the child's disability affects the child's involvement and progress in the general curriculum; or
  ii. For preschool children, as appropriate, how the disability affects the child' participation in appropriate activities;
(2) A statement of measurable annual goals, including benchmarks or short-term objectives, related to
  i. Meeting the child's needs that result from the child's disability to enable the child to be involved in and progress in the general curriculum; and
  ii. Meeting each of the child's other educational needs that result from the child's disability;
(3) A statement of the special education and related services and supplementary aids and services to be provided to the child, or on behalf of the child, and a statement of the program modifications or support for school personnel that will be provided for the child
  i. To advance appropriately toward attaining the annual goals;
  ii. To be involved in and progress in the general curriculum and to participate in extracurricular and other nonacademic activities; and
  iii. To be educated and participate with other children with disabilities and nondisabled children in [such] activities;
(4) An explanation of the extent, if any, to which the child will not participate with nondisabled children in the regular class and in the activities described in paragraph (3);
(5) A statement of
  i. Any individual modifications in the administration of State or district-wide assessments of student achievement that are needed in order for the child to participate in such assessment; and
  ii. If the IEP team determines that the child will not participate in a particular State or district-wide assessment of student achievement (or part of an assessment), a statement of

For ideas on increasing student participation in the IEP process, see "Someone's Missing" later in this chapter. Additional strategies for involving students in their IEPs can be found in Martin, Marshall, Maxson, and Jerman (1993) and Van Reusen and Bos (1990, 1994).

More information about developing IEPs can be found by accessing the Resources Module for Chapter 2 at http://www.prenhall.com/heward and the Special Ed Resource Page. Click on "Teacher Resources."

Jeremy takes an active role on his IEP team by indicating the learning goals most important to him.

(A) Why that assessment is not appropriate for the child; and
(B) How the child will be assessed;

(6) The projected date for the beginning of the services and modifications described in paragraph (3) and the anticipated frequency, location, and duration of those services and modifications; and

(7) A statement of
  i. How the child's progress toward the annual goals described in paragraph (2) will be measured; and
  ii. How the child's parents will be regularly informed (through such means as periodic report cards), at least as often as parents are informed of their nondisabled children's progress, of
    (A) Their child's progress toward the annual goals; and
    (B) The extent to which that progress is sufficient to enable the child to achieve the goals by the end of the year. (20 U.S.C., Sec. 1414[d][1][A])

IEPs for older students must also include information on how the child's transition from school to adult life will be supported:

> Beginning at age 14, and updated annually, a statement of the transition service needs of the child under the applicable components of the child's IEP that focuses on the child's courses of study (such a participation in advanced placement courses or a vocational education program);
>
> Beginning at age 16 (or younger if determined appropriate by the IEP team), statement of the needed transition services for the child, including, when appropriate, a statement of the interagency responsibilities or any needed linkages before the student leaves the school setting. (20 U.S.C., Sec. 1414[d][1][A])

Transition services are detailed in an individualized transition plan (ITP), *which becomes part of each student's IEP. Transition and ITPs are described in Chapter 15.*

The IEP is a system for spelling out where the child is, where she should be going, how she will get there, how long it will take, and how to tell when she has arrived. The IEP is a measure of accountability for teachers and schools. Whether a particular school or educational program is effective will be judged, to some extent, by how well it is able to help children meet the goals and objectives set forth in their

IEPs. Like other professionals, teachers are being called on to demonstrate effectiveness, and the IEP provides one way for them to do so. The IEP is not a legally binding contract. A child's teacher and school cannot be prosecuted in the courts if the child does not achieve the goals set forth in the IEP. Nevertheless, the school must be able to document that a conscientious and systematic effort was made to achieve those goals. The IEP is, however, much more than an accountability device. Its potential benefits are improved planning (including planning for the student's needs after he leaves school), consistency, regular evaluation, and clearer communication among parents, teachers, and others involved in providing services to the student.

IEP formats vary widely across school districts, and schools may go beyond the requirements of the law and include additional information. Bateman and Linden (1998) caution against overreliance on the use of a standardized form and using computers for creating IEPs. "Forms by their very nature tend to interfere with true individualization. . . . a proper form will contain all the required elements in the simplest way possible, allowing for the most flexibility and creativity" (p. 57). Figure 2.3 shows the "non-form" for IEPs recommended by Bateman and Linden. The first page identifies the student, IEP team members, and special factors to consider as required by the 1997 IDEA amendments. The "heart of the IEP" (p. 96) begins on the second page in the form of a three-column sequence from needs and present levels of performance, to services that will be provided, to goals and objectives. The IEP form concludes with additional IDEA requirements and, for older students, transition components.

Detailed procedures for systematic development and implementation of IEPs can be found in Bateman and Linden (1998) and Strickland and Turnbull (1993).

Figure 2.4 shows portions of the IEP for Curt, a ninth grader and low achiever seen by the school district as a poorly motivated student with a disciplinary problem and a bad attitude. Curt's parents see their son as a discouraged and frustrated student with learning disabilities, especially in written language.

One of the most difficult tasks for the child study team is determining how inclusive the IEP document should be. Strickland and Turnbull (1993) state that the definition of special education as "specially designed instruction" should be a key element in determining what should go into a student's IEP.

> The determination of whether instruction is "specially designed" must be made by comparing the nature of the instruction for the student with a disability to instructional practices used with typical students at the same age and grade level. If the instructional adaptations that a student with a disability requires are (1) significantly different from adaptations normally expected or made for typical students in that setting, and if (2) the adaptations are necessary to offset or reduce the adverse effect of the disability on learning and educational performance, then these adaptations should be considered "specially designed instruction" and should be included as part of the student's IEP, regardless of the instructional setting. (p. 13)

Of all the requirements of the IDEA, the IEP is "probably the single most unpopular aspect of the law, not only because it requires a great deal of work, but because the essence of the plan itself seems to have been lost in the mountains of paperwork" (Gallagher, 1984, p. 228). Several studies of actual IEPs seem to support Gallagher's contention (Fiedler & Knight, 1986; Schenck, 1980; Smith, 1990a). Smith and Simpson (1989), for example, evaluated the IEPs of 214 students with behavioral disorders and found that one-third of the IEPs lacked necessary mandated components.

*Over 55% of the 15,000 members surveyed by CEC's Division for Learning Disabilities reported that much of the paperwork required by the IDEA is unnecessary, duplicative, and costly (*DLD Times, *1994). These teachers believed that excessive paperwork interfered with time available for providing services to students and contributed to some special education teachers leaving the field.*

But properly including all of the mandated components in an IEP is no guarantee that the document will guide the student's learning and teachers' teaching in the classroom, as intended by IDEA. Although many educators agree that the idealized concept of the IEP is "grand and has great potential" (Morse, 1985, p. 182), inspection and evaluation of IEPs often do not reveal consistency between what is written on the docu-

INDIVIDUALIZED EDUCATION PROGRAM

Student's Name ______________________ **Date of IEP Meeting** ______________________
Date of Birth __________ **Grade** __________ **Primary Contact Person/Case Manager** ______________

Copies of this IEP will circulate among staff members who are working with this student.
Please observe the Federal and state laws that protect the student's right
to confidentiality of education records.
Do NOT share with unauthorized persons,
and do NOT include sensitive information such as disability category or IQ.

Participants

Signature	Position

Special Factors to Consider

For all students, consider:
- ❑ Strengths of the student
- ❑ Concerns of the parent(s)
- ❑ Need for assistive technology

If behavior impedes learning of the student or others, consider:
- ❑ Strategies, including positive behavioral interventions
- ❑ Supports to address behavior

If the student has limited English proficiency, consider:
- ❑ Language needs as they relate to the student's IEP

If the student is blind or visually impaired, consider:
- ❑ Instruction in the use of Braille (unless the IEP team decides instruction in Braille is inappropriate)

Consider communication needs (language & communication needs for students with hearing impairments), including:
- ❑ Opportunities for direct communication with peers and professionals in the student's language and communication mode
- ❑ Opportunities for direct instruction in the student's language and communication mode

Unique Educational Needs, Characteristics, and Present Levels of Performance (PLOPs)	**Special Education, Related Services, Supplemental Aids & Services, Assistive Technology, Program Modifications, Support for Personnel**	**Measurable Annual Goals & Short-Term Objectives or Benchmarks** • **To enable the student to participate in the general curriculum** • **To meet other needs resulting from the disability**
(include how the disability affects the student's ability to progress in the general curriculum)	***(include frequency, duration, & location)***	***(include how progress toward goals will be measured)***
[This is the most	*important part of the IEP. See Figure 2.4 for*	*sample entries.]*

Figure 2.3 Example of an IEP form

Progress Reports

The parents will receive regular reports about (the student's)
(a) progress toward achieving annual goals
(b) and the extent to which that progress is sufficient to enable achievement of goals by the end of the year
Progress reports will take the form of ______________

and the parents will receive them _____ times/year (which is at least as often as parents of children who are not on IEPs receive progress reports). Reports will include **specific** information about progress on each IEP goal.

Participants With Nondisabled Students

Explanation of the extent to which (the student) will **not** participate with nondisabled children in (a) regular classes ____

(b) special education services ______________

Participation in State- and District-Wide Assessments

(The student) needs the following modifications in the administration of state- or district-wide assessments ______

The IEP team has decided that (the student) will **not** participate in any state- or district-wide assessments
(a) because ______________

(b) (The student) will instead be assessed by ______________

Transition Planning

(The student) has reached age 14, and (his or her):
(a) goals for life after high school include ______________

(b) course of study is linked to student transition goals by ______________

(The student) has reached age 16, and:
(a) the following activities are needed to promote transition to post-high school life

- Instruction ______________
- Related services ______________
- Community experiences ______________
- Development of employment and other adult living objectives ______________
- Acquisition of daily living skills and functional vocational evaluation ______________

(b) (The student) does not need one or more of the activities listed above because ______________

(The student) will reach the age of majority under state law on (date). (He or she) has received notice (at least a year in advance) of all rights under the IDEA that will transfer to (him or her) at that time.

____
Student's Signature

Figure 2.3 *continued*

Source: Reprinted from Bateman, B. D., & Linden, M. L. (1998). *Better IEPs: How to develop legally correct and educationally useful programs* (pp. 97, 98, 99). Longmont, CO: Sopris West. Used by permission.

Someone's Missing: The Student As an Overlooked Participant in the IEP Process

by Mary T. Peters

IDEA states that "the child, wherever appropriate" must be included on the IEP team. More specifically, before age 14, student attendance and participation are at the discretion of the parents; beginning at age 14 the student must be invited to attend and should be encouraged to participate in the entire meeting. Yet rarely does the student play an active role in the IEP process (Van Reusen & Bos, 1994).

This may be because students with disabilities are often perceived by administrators, teachers, or parents as recipients of special services rather than an integral part of the IEP team with the right (if not the responsibility) to help develop and implement their own special education programs. When empowered as active participants in the IEP process, however, students have an opportunity to heighten their independence, self-advocacy skills, and self-esteem (Martin et al., 1993). Also, students may be able to offer insightful perceptions and valuable contributions. All students with disabilities can and should be involved in the IEP process.

How Can Students Participate? The IEP conference is just one part of the special education process. Students may be involved at any stage. Figure A lists ways in which students can participate in the three major stages of assessment, the IEP conference itself, and instruction.

ASSESSMENT

- Determines preferences
- Self-evaluates
- Sets goals/assists in writing objectives

IEP CONFERENCE

- Preconference preparation
- Conference participation

INSTRUCTION

- Comonitors progress
- Engages in regularly scheduled meetings
- Reassesses program
- Self-manages program/goals

Figure A Student participation in the IEP process

Assessment. All students should actively participate in the assessment and evaluation of their skills and preferences.

Self-determination of preferences. For all students, participation in the IEP process can begin with determining preferences. By sharing their likes and dislikes, students provide input from which teachers can identify objectives, goals, and potential reinforcers. Students sometimes make inappropriate or unrealistic choices. In these cases, teachers should counsel students and present them with a variety of more likely alternatives.

Self-evaluation. Students can be further involved in the assessment phase by engaging in self-evaluation. They can use a teacher-made self-rating scale or checklist to determine perceived strengths, weaknesses, competencies, and successes in goal attainment. This information can help teachers devise goals that focus on the student's strong points and address deficit areas that are important to the student.

Goal setting. Students who are trained to assess their own skills and goal achievement may be better able to set realistic expectations for themselves. Other valuable information that can contribute to the assessment phase is student identification of future goals and ambitions. A wish list can help students identify future plans, expectations, and skills they wish to acquire. Pictures, photos, checklists, and classroom activities can help students identify goals that can be then incorporated into their IEPs. Computer software such as *Be A Winner: Set Your Goals* (M.C.E., 1988) offers adolescents and adults an interactive program for choosing long- and short-term goals.

The IEP Conference. The degree to which a student may participate in the IEP conference will vary. The highest degree of involvement occurs when students participate as full team members and act as self-advocates. There are also many opportunities for partial participation by students whose disabilities limit their level of involvement.

Preconference preparation. Students should be informed about the intent and significance of the IEP meeting, the roles of each team member, and procedures that will be followed. Videotaped presentations of real or staged IEP meetings can be an excellent way to prepare students for their own conference. Role playing can also help emphasize and define the responsibilities of all team members, including those of the student. Students should rehearse

appropriate and expected behaviors. The following are suggested rules for student behavior during the IEP conference:

- Remain seated throughout the meeting.
- Maintain eye contact with those who are addressing you.
- Respect others as they speak by listening without interruption.
- If you don't understand, excuse yourself politely and ask them to explain again.
- Wait your turn before offering your opinion and recommendations.
- When you disagree, state your case without being loud or impatient; offer your own suggestions instead.
- Respond to direct questions.

Creative intervention by teachers is sometimes necessary to convince parents of the advantages of student involvement in the IEP conference. Parents may be persuaded by talking to others who have involved their child in the IEP conference. Parents can be invited to participate in or view videotapes of classroom preconference activities. In some cases, administrators may also need to be reminded of students' right to participate and be encouraged to advocate for them in this regard.

Conference participation. Students who have been involved in other phases of the IEP process will be better prepared for the conference experience. The more active the student has been, the more likely he will be successful in the IEP meeting itself. When something should not be discussed in front of the child (e.g., controversial issues, policy decisions, disagreements), the student can enter the meeting near its conclusion to meet with team members, listen to suggested goals and objectives, and hear comments relating to his progress.

With parental cooperation, team commitment, prior preparation, and involvement in other phases of the IEP process, students can be successfully integrated as team members. The student might report her own progress, contribute to discussions, and help formulate goals and objectives at the conference. Once these are agreed on, the student should co-sign the completed IEP document, just as other team members do.

Instruction. In co-monitoring their progress, students participate in classroom activities that remind them of the goals they have helped set. Daily, weekly, and monthly activities can be designed to include students in the ongoing collection of data, assessment of progress, and reevaluation of goals. Teachers can help students tally stickers, tokens, points, or grades they have earned. These can be recorded on a chart or other visual representation related to identified student goals. Students can select items to include in a portfolio of academic or other work products (Salend, 1998; Wesson & King, 1996). Younger students can color bar graphs or collect small items or cards to signify their progress.

Students can also co-monitor their progress in meetings with other students. These meetings should be positive, encouraging group cooperation, support, and problem-solving opportunities. Self-management, self-monitoring, and self-instruction techniques may also help students meet the goals they have helped set (Heward, 1987; Kerr & Nelson, 1998; Lovitt, 1995).

Including students in a process designed expressly for them is often overlooked, but there are numerous possibilities for student participation in the IEP process for educators who wish to implement instruction with students—not just for them.

Adapted from Peters, M. T. (1990). Someone's missing: The student as an overlooked participant in the IEP process. *Preventing School Failure, 34*(4), 32-36. © 1990. Used with permission of the Helen Dwight Reid Educational Foundation. Published by Heldref Publications, 1319 Eighteenth Street, NW, Washington, DC 20036-1802.

ment and the instruction that students experience in the classroom (e.g., Nevin, McCann, & Semmel, 1983; Smith, 1990b). Bateman and Linden (1998) contend:

> Sadly, most IEPs are horrendously burdensome to teachers and nearly useless to parents and children. Far from being a creative, flexible, data-based, and individualized application of the best of educational interventions to a child with unique needs, the typical IEP is "empty," devoid of specific services to be provided. It says what the IEP team hopes the student will be able to accomplish, but little if anything about the special education interventions and the related services or the classroom modifications that will enable him or her to reach those goals. (p. 63)

Unique Educational Needs, Characteristics, and Present Levels of Performance (PLOPs)	Special Education, Related Services, Supplemental Aids & Services, Assistive Technology, Program Modifications, Support for Personnel	Measurable Annual Goals & Short-Term Objectives or Benchmarks • To enable student to participate in the general curriculum • To meet other needs resulting from the disability
(include how the disability affects the student's ability to progress in the general curriculum)	***(include frequency, duration, & location)***	***(include how progress toward goals will be measured)***
Study Skills/Organizational Needs: How to read text Note taking How to study notes Memory work Be prepared for class, with materials Lengthen and improve attention span and on-task behavior Present Level: Curt currently lacks skill in all these areas.	1. Speech/lang: therapist, resource room teacher, and content area teachers will provide Curt with direct and specific teaching of study skills, i.e. Note taking from lectures; Note taking while reading text; How to study notes for a test; Memorization hints; Strategies for reading text to retain information. 2. Assign a "study buddy" for Curt in each content area class. 3. Prepare a motivation system for Curt to be prepared for class with all necessary materials. 4. Develop a motivational plan to encourage Curt to lengthen his attention span and time on task. 5. Provide aide to monitor on-task behaviors in first month or so of plan and teach Curt self-monitoring techniques. 6. Provide motivational system and self-recording form for completion of academic tasks in each class.	Goal: At the end of academic year, Curt will have better grades and, by his own report, will have learned new study skills. Obj. 1: Given a 20-30 min. lecture/oral lesson, Curt will take appropriate notes as judged by that teacher. Obj. 2: Given 10-15 pgs. of text to read, Curt will employ an appropriate strategy for retaining info.—i.e., mapping, webbing, outlining, notes, etc.—as judged by the teacher. Obj. 3: Given notes to study for a test, Curt will do so successfully as evidenced by his test score. Goal: Curt will improve his on-task behavior from 37% to 80% as measured by a qualified observer at year's end. Obj.1: By 1 month, Curt's on-task behavior will increase to 45%. Obj. 2: By 3 months, Curt's on-task behavior will increase to 60%. Obj. 3: By 6 months, Curt's on-task behavior will increase to 80% and maintain or improve until end of the year.
Academic Needs/Written Language: Curt needs strong remedial help in spelling, punctuation, capitalization, and usage. Present Level: Curt is approximately 2 grade levels behind his peers in these skills. Adaptations to Regular Program: • In all classes, Curt should sit near the front of the class. • All teachers should help Curt with study skills as trained by spelling/language specialist and resource room teacher. • Curt should be called on often to keep him involved and on task. • Teachers should monitor Curt's work closely in the beginning weeks/months of his program.	1. Provide direct instruction in written language skills (punctuation, capitalization, usage, spelling) by using a highly structured, well-sequenced program. Services provided in small group of no more than four students in the resource room, 50 minutes/day. 2. Build in continuous and cumulative review to help with short-term rote memory difficulty. 3. Develop a list of commonly used words in student writing (or use one of many published lists) for Curt's spelling program.	Goal: Within one academic year, Curt will improve his written language skills by 1.5 or 2 full grade levels. Obj. 1: Given 10 sentences of dictation at his current level of instruction, Curt will punctuate and capitalize with 90% accuracy (checked at the end of each unit taught). Obj. 2: Given 30 sentences with choices of usage, at his current instructional level, Curt will perform with 90% accuracy. Obj. 3: Given a list of 150 commonly used words in writing, Curt will spell with 90% accuracy.

Figure 2.4 Portions of the IEP for Curt, a ninth grader with learning disabilities and a history of disciplinary problems

Source: Reprinted from Bateman, B. D., & Linden, M. L. (1998). *Better IEPs: How to develop legally correct and educationally useful programs* (pp. 128–129). Longmont, CO: Sopris West. Used by permission.

Special and regular educators are working together to create procedures for developing IEPs that go beyond compliance with the law and actually serve as a meaningful guide for the specially designed instruction a student with disabilities needs. Several tools have been developed to assist IEP teams in the critical process of designing a truly appropriate education. For example, Giangreco, Cloninger, and Iverson (1998) have developed and field-tested an IEP process called *Choosing Outcomes and Accommodations for Children (COACH)*, which guides child study teams through the assessment and planning stages of IEP development in a way that results in goals and objectives directly related to functional skills in integrated settings.

One step of the COACH process is described and illustrated in Chapter 13.

Least Restrictive Environment

IDEA requires that every student with disabilities be educated in the **least restrictive environment (LRE).** Specifically, the law stipulates that

> to the maximum extent appropriate, children with disabilities, including children in public or private institutions or other care facilities, [will be] educated with children who are not disabled, and that special classes, separate schooling or other removal of children with disabilities from the regular educational environment [may occur] only when the nature or severity of the disability is such that education in regular classes with the use of supplementary aids and services cannot be achieved satisfactorily. (20 U.S.C. § 1412[a][5])

Thus, the LRE is the setting that is closest to a regular school program and that also meets the child's special educational needs. Least restrictive environment is a relative concept; the LRE for one child might be inappropriate for another. Since the passage of IDEA, there have been many differences of opinion over which type of setting is least restrictive and most appropriate for students with disabilities. Some educators and parents consider any decision to place a student with disabilities outside the regular classroom to be overly restrictive; most, however, recognize that full-time placement in a regular classroom can be restrictive and inappropriate if the child's educational needs are not adequately met.

The least restrictive environment is a relative concept; the LRE for one child may be inappropriate for another.

The definitions of six educational placements used by the U.S. Department of Education are shown in Chapter 1.

A Continuum of Services

Children with disabilities and their families need a wide range of special education and related services. Today, most schools provide a *continuum of services*—that is, a range of placement and service options to meet the individual needs of students with disabilities. The continuum is often symbolically depicted as a pyramid, with placements ranging from regular classroom placement at the bottom to special schools and residential programs at the top (see Figure 2.5). The fact that the pyramid is widest at the bottom indicates that the greatest number of children are served in regular classrooms and that the number of children who require more intensive and specialized placements gets smaller as we move up. As already noted, the majority of children receiving special education services have mild disabilities. The number of children with mild mental retardation, for example, is far greater than those who experience severe retardation. Likewise, children with mild or moderate behavior problems greatly outnumber those with severe emotional and behavioral disorders. As the severity of the disability increases, the need for more specialized services also increases, but the number of students involved decreases.

Five of the seven placement options depicted in Figure 2.5 are available in regular public school buildings. Children at the first four placements attend general education classes with peers without disabilities; supportive help is given by special teachers who provide consultation to the children's regular teachers or in special resource rooms. In a *resource room*, a special educator provides instruction to students with disabilities for part of the school day, either individually or in small groups. Children who require full-time placement in a *separate classroom* are with other children with disabilities for most of the school day and only interact with children without disabilities at certain times, such as during lunch, recess, or perhaps art and music. Although the separate classroom provides significantly fewer opportuni-

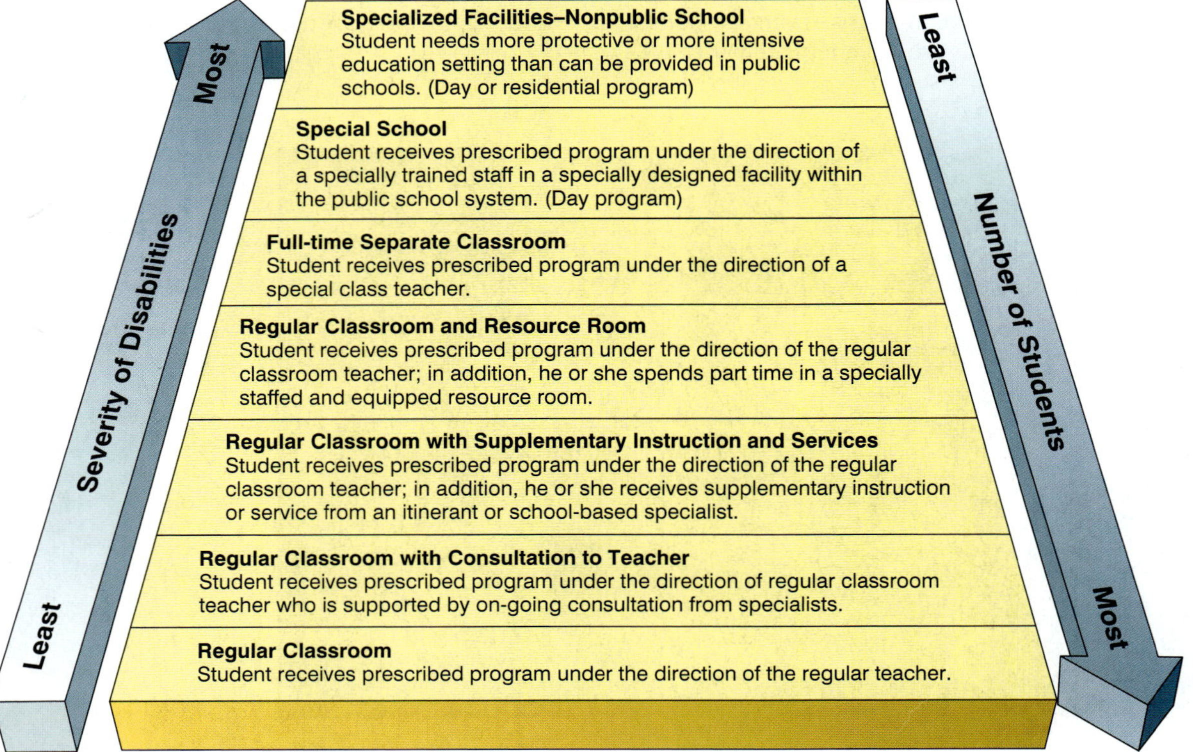

Severity of Disabilities
Most
Least
Number of Students
Least
Most
Specialized Facilities–Nonpublic School
Student needs more protective or more intensive education setting than can be provided in public schools. (Day or residential program)
Special School
Student receives prescribed program under the direction of a specially trained staff in a specially designed facility within the public school system. (Day program)
Full-time Separate Classroom
Student receives prescribed program under the direction of a special class teacher.
Regular Classroom and Resource Room
Student receives prescribed program under the direction of the regular classroom teacher; in addition, he or she spends part time in a specially staffed and equipped resource room.
Regular Classroom with Supplementary Instruction and Services
Student receives prescribed program under the direction of the regular classroom teacher; in addition, he or she receives supplementary instruction or service from an itinerant or school-based specialist.
Regular Classroom with Consultation to Teacher
Student receives prescribed program under the direction of regular classroom teacher who is supported by on-going consultation from specialists.
Regular Classroom
Student receives prescribed program under the direction of the regular teacher.

Figure 2.5 Continuum of educational services for students with disabilities.
Source: From Montgomery County Public Schools, Rockville, MD. Used by permission.

ties for interaction with nondisabled children than the regular classroom does, it provides more integration than does placement in a *special school* or *residential facility* attended only by children with disabilities.

Maynard Reynolds, who was among the first to propose the continuum of services concept, believes that it is time to make some changes in the model—specifically, to do away with the two most restrictive placements.

> In this writer's view, we are prepared now to lop off the top two levels of the continuum. . . . [I]t is now well demonstrated that we can deliver special education and related services within general school buildings and at a continuum level no higher than the special class. Thus, we can foresee the undoing or demise of special schools (day and residential) as delivery mechanisms for special education—at least in the United States. (Reynolds, 1989, p. 8)

Not all special educators agree with Reynolds. As we will see throughout this text, the relative value of providing services to students with disabilities outside the regular classroom, especially in separate classrooms and schools, is a hotly contested issue in special education.

Determining the LRE

The IEP team determines the proper placement for a child *after* the child's needs as a result of the disability and the special education and related services necessary to meet those needs have been determined. For many years special education operated like this: (1) a student found eligible for special education was labeled with a disability category; (2) the student was placed into a program for students with that particular disability; and (3) a not-so-individualized version of the already-in-place program was written down and presented as the student's IEP, even though the program continued as usual whether the "new" student was in it or not. This is the wrong way, and has been the wrong way since IDEA first went into effect in 1977.

The legally mandated and educationally sound process goes like this: (1) the school must determine whether the child has a disability and is therefore eligible for special education; (2) the child's needs must be determined and an IEP developed that specifies the special education and related services that will be provided to meet those needs; and (3) the child is then placed in the least restrictive environment in which an appropriate program can be provided and the child can make satisfactory educational progress.

Bateman and Linden (1998) describe the difference between the wrong way and the IDEA way:

> For many, the old way is deeply ingrained and it seems practical. . . . for example, "Joe is learning disabled, so we'll put him in the resource room for learning disabled students and then have the resource teacher write up one more copy of the ongoing program in that room and call it the IEP." Instead, one should have said, "Joe is eligible, Joe's individual needs are X, Y, Z, and can be met by services A, B, C (his IEP) which we can implement in placement P." Districts have tried to fit children into programs, . . . rather than flexibly and creatively designing new programs one child at a time. (p. 67)

Placement of a student with disabilities should not be viewed as "all or nothing" at any one level on the continuum. The IEP team should consider the extent to which the student can effectively be integrated into each of three dimensions of school life: the general academic curriculum, extracurricular activities (e.g., clubs), and other school activities (e.g., recess, meal times). The LRE "provision allows for a 'mix and match' where total integration is appropriate under one dimension and partial integration is appropriate under another dimension" (Turnbull & Cilley, 1999, p. 41).

In addition, placement must not be regarded as permanent. The continuum concept is intended to be flexible, with students moving from one placement to another as dictated by their individual educational needs. The IEP team should peri-

Champagne (1993) has developed a sequence of steps that schools can use to make placement decisions consistent with the LRE requirements of IDEA.

odically review the specific goals and objectives for each child—they are required to do so at least annually—and make new placement decisions if warranted. The child's parents must be informed whenever any change in placement is being considered so that they can either consent or object to the change and can present additional information if they wish.

Because neither IDEA nor the regulations that accompany it specify exactly how a school district is to determine LRE, numerous conflicts have arisen; some have led to court cases. After reviewing the rulings of four LRE disputes that reached U.S. courts of appeals, Yell (1995) concluded that IDEA does not require the placement of students with disabilities into the regular classroom but does fully support the continuum of services.

> At times, the mainstream will be the appropriate placement; however, IDEA and case law interpreting the LRE mandate are clear that for some students with disabilities, the appropriate and least restrictive setting will not be the regular education classroom. As the *Daniel* court stated, "Mainstreaming a child who will suffer from the experience would violate [IDEA's] mandate for a free appropriate public education." . . . The IEP team, as the courts have indicated, needs to employ a balancing test, weighing the desirability of integration against the obligation to furnish an appropriate education. (p. 402)

Inclusive Education

Although often confused, the terms inclusion *and* least restrictive environment *are not synonymous. Inclusion means educating students with disabilities in regular classrooms; the LRE principle requires students with disabilities be educated in settings as close to the regular class as possible in which an appropriate program can be provided and the child can make satisfactory educational progress.*

The terms **mainstreaming** and, more recently, **inclusion** describe the process of integrating children with disabilities into regular classrooms. Much discussion and controversy and many misconceptions have arisen regarding the inclusion of students with disabilities in regular classes—the so-called mainstream of our public school system.

Many parents of children with disabilities strongly support the placement of their children in regular classes; others have resisted it just as strongly, thinking that the regular classroom does not offer the intense, individualized education their children need. For example, a recent study found that most parents of elementary students with learning disabilities who received reading instruction in resource rooms had strong positive attitudes toward the resource room program and were reluctant to have their children reintegrated into general education classes for reading instruction (Green & Shinn, 1995).

As we have seen, what the law does call for is the education of each child with disabilities in the least restrictive environment, removed no farther than necessary from the regular public school program. IDEA does not require placement of all children with disabilities in regular classes, call for children with disabilities to remain in regular classes without necessary supportive services, or suggest that regular teachers should educate students with disabilities without help from special educators and other specialists. Although not all children with disabilities attend regular classes, it is true that regular classroom teachers are expected to deal with a much wider variety of learning, behavioral, sensory, and physical differences among their students than was the case just a few years ago. Thus, provision of in-service training for regular educators is an important (and sometimes overlooked) requirement of IDEA. Regular classroom teachers are understandably wary of having children with disabilities placed in their classes if little or no training or support is provided. The role of regular classroom teachers is already a demanding one; they do not want their classes to become any larger, especially if they perceive exceptional children as unmanageable. Regular classroom teachers are entitled to be involved in decisions about children who are placed in their classes and to be offered continuous consultation and other supportive services from administrators and their special education colleagues (Heron & Harris, in press; West & Idol, 1990). IDEA does, however, specifically call for regular and special educators to cooperate in providing an equal educational opportunity to every student with disabilities.

We know that simply placing a child with disabilities in a regular classroom does not mean that the child will learn and behave appropriately or be socially accepted by children without disabilities (Gresham, 1982; Hallenbeck & Kauffman, 1995). It is important for special educators to teach appropriate social skills and behavior to the child with disabilities and to educate nondisabled children about their classmates. Examples of effective mainstreaming and inclusion programs can be found at age levels ranging from preschool (Esposito & Reed, 1986; Jenkins, Speltz, & Odom, 1985) to high school (Warger, Aldinger, & Okun, 1983), and they include children whose disabilities range from mild (Algozzine & Korinek, 1985; Thomas & Jackson, 1986) to severe (Brinker, 1985; Condon, York, Heal, & Fortschneider, 1986). Numerous strategies for including students with disabilities in the general education program can be found in Beninghof (1998), Friend and Bursuck (1999), Lewis and Doorlag (1995), Salend (1998), and Wood (1998).

Arguments For and Against Full Inclusion

Some special educators believe that the continuum of services should completely give way to regular classroom placement for all students with disabilities. For example, Taylor (1988) makes the following suggestions about the LRE and continuum of services model:

1. *Legitimates restrictive environments.* To conceptualize services in terms of restrictiveness is to legitimize more restrictive settings. As long as services are conceptualized in this manner, some people will end up in restrictive environments. Some people will continue to support institutions and other segregated settings merely by defining them as the LRE for certain people.
2. *Confuses segregation and integration with intensity of services.* As represented by the continuum, LRE equates segregation with the most intensive services and integration with the least intensive services. The principle assumes that the least restrictive, most integrated settings are incapable of providing the intensive services needed by people with severe disabilities. However, segregation and integration on the one hand and intensity of services on the other are separate dimensions.
3. *[Is] based on a "readiness model."* Implicit in LRE is the assumption that people with developmental disabilities must earn the right to move to the least restrictive environment. In other words, the person must "get ready" or "be prepared" to live, work, or go to school in integrated settings.
4. *Supports the primacy of professional decision making.* As Biklen (1988) notes, integration is ultimately a moral and philosophical issue, not a professional one. Yet LRE invariably is framed in terms of professional judgments regarding "individual needs." The phrase "least restrictive environment" is almost always qualified with words such as "appropriate," "necessary," "feasible," and "possible" (and never with "desired" or "wanted").
5. *Sanctions infringements on people's rights.* When applied to people with disabilities, the LRE principle sanctions infringements on basic rights to freedom and community participation beyond those imposed on nondisabled people. The question imposed by LRE is not whether people with disabilities should be restricted, but to what extent.
6. *Implies that people must move as they develop and change.* As LRE is commonly conceptualized, people with disabilities are expected to move toward increasingly less restrictive environments. Even if people moved smoothly through a continuum, their lives would be a series of stops between transitional placements.
7. *Directs attention to physical settings rather than to the services and supports people need.* By its name, the principle of the LRE emphasizes facilities and environments designed specifically for people with disabilities. The field has defined the

mission in terms of creating "facilities," first large ones and now smaller ones, and "programs," rather than providing the services and supports to enable people with disabilities to participate in the same settings used by other people. (pp. 45–48)

See "Moving toward Inclusive Education" later in this chapter.

There is no clear consensus in the field about the meaning of inclusion (Kauffman & Hallahan, 1995). To some, inclusion means full-time placement of all students with disabilities into regular classrooms; to others, the term refers to any degree of integration into the mainstream. Stainback and Stainback (1992), strong advocates and leaders of the inclusion movement, define an *inclusive school* as "a place where everyone belongs, is accepted, supports, and is supported by his or her peers and other members of the school community in the course of having his or her educational needs met" (p. 3). Giangreco, Cloninger, Dennis, and Edelman (1994) contend that inclusive education is in place only when all five components shown in Figure 2.6 "occur on an ongoing, daily basis" (p. 321).

Figure 2.6 Components of inclusive education

Source: Reprinted from Giangreco, M. F., Cloninger, C. J., Dennis, R. E., & Edelman, S. W. (1994). Problem-solving methods to facilitate inclusive education. In J. S. Thousand, R. A. Villa, & A. I. Nevin (Eds.), *Creativity and collaborative learning: A practical guide to empowering students and teachers* (p. 322). Baltimore: Brookes. Used by permission.

Inclusive education is in place when each of these five features occurs on an ongoing, daily basis.

1. *Heterogeneous Grouping* All students are educated *together* in groups where the number of those with and without disabilities approximates the *natural proportion.* The premise is that "students develop most when in the physical, social, emotional, and intellectual presence of nonhandicapped persons in reasonable approximations to the natural proportions" (Brown, Ford, Nisbet, Sweet, Donnellan, & Gruenewald, 1983, p. 17). Thus, in a class of 25 students, perhaps there is one student with significant disabilities, a couple of others with less significant disabilities, and many students without identified disabilities working at various levels.
2. *A Sense of Belonging to a Group* All students are considered members of the class rather than visitors, guests, or outsiders. Within these groups, students who have disabilities are welcomed, as are students without disabilities.
3. *Shared Activities with Individualized Outcomes* Students share educational experiences (e.g., lessons, labs, field studies, group learning) at the same time (Schnorr, 1990). Even though students are involved in the same activities, their learning objectives are individualized and, therefore, may be different. Students may have different objectives in the same curriculum area (e.g., language arts) during a shared activity. This is referred to as *multi-level instruction* (Campbell, Campbell, Collicott, Perner, & Stone, 1988; Collicott, 1991; Giangreco & Meyer, 1988; Giangreco & Putnam, 1991). Within a shared activity, a student also may have individualized objectives from a curriculum area (e.g., social skills) other than that on which other students are focused (e.g., science). This practice is referred to as *curriculum overlapping* (Giangreco & Meyer, 1988; Giangreco & Putnam, 1991).
4. *Use of Environments Frequented by Persons without Disabilities* Shared educational experiences take place in environments predominantly frequented by people without disabilities (e.g., general education classrooms, community worksites).
5. *A Balanced Educational Experience* Inclusive education seeks an individualized balance between the academic/functional and social/personal aspects of schooling (Giangreco, 1992). For example, teachers in inclusion-oriented schools would be as concerned about students' self-image and social network as they would be about developing literacy competencies or learning vocational skills.

Teaching & Learning Video Connections

LOOK

DEVELOPING INDIVIDUAL EDUCATION PLANS

LOOKing at *A New IDEA for Special Education*

The Individuals with Disabilities Education Act (IDEA) is explicit in detailing the public schools' responsibility to provide a free appropriate education to all children with disabilities from ages 3 to 21. In the video *A New IDEA for Special Education*, Grace Hanlon, a Learning and Behavior Specialist and parent of a student with special needs, explains some critical aspects of the IDEA: referral, evaluation, Individual Education Plans, placement, related services, preparation for transitions, disciplining students with disabilities, and mediating disagreements between schools and parents. The video describes the roles of educators and the tasks they must undertake as stipulated in the 1997 Amendments to the IDEA, and it serves as an excellent overview of the law for both special and general educators, administrators, and parents. As you watch this video, you might want to do the following:

* Listen carefully to what Ms. Hanlon, the teachers, and the parents say. How do their comments relate to each step of the special education process shown in Figure 2.1 (pp. 49–50)?

* Note how parent involvement is emphasized at each step of the process. What knowledge and skills do you think parents and teachers need to have to contribute to parent-teacher partnerships that work in the best interests of children with disabilities? Jot down your

Shelley Gazin

thoughts and ideas and be as specific as you can. Save your list of recommendations to look at again after you've read Chapter 4, "Parents and Families of Children with Special Needs."

* Pay particular attention to and think about ways each topic discussed on the video contributes to the identification of appropriate and meaningful IEP goals.

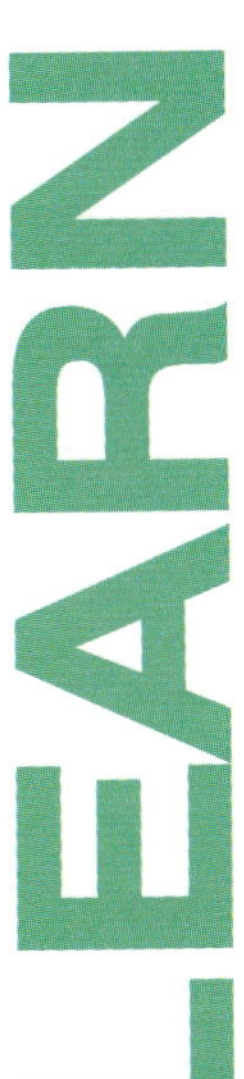

LEARNing about IEP Goals and Objectives

The Individual Education Plan (IEP) is a system for spelling out where the child is, where he should be going, how he will get there, how long it will take, and how to tell when he has arrived. Thus, a good IEP serves as both a road map and a guidebook for meeting the challenges posed by a student's disability. As stated in the video, the IEP provides teachers and parents the opportunity (and, we might add, the responsibility) to first be *realistic* about the child's needs and goals, and then to be *creative* about how to meet them. Being realistic doesn't mean taking a pessimistic or limited view of the child's capabilities or potential. It means analyzing how specially designed instruction and related services can help the student get from his present levels of performance to future goals. As one parent in the video notes, "Consider where you would like to see your child at the end of his education and plan accordingly." Parents and educators must work together to plan and account for IEP goals that serve as road maps to improve the futures of students with disabilities. What can you, as an educator, do to help plan for more meaningful IEPs?

Consider All Relevant Information. In determining annual goals, the IEP team should consider all relevant information about the child's disability and its effects on his education. Such information includes results of standardized tests, data from direct observations in the classroom and at home, anecdotal observations by teachers and significant others, parents' input, and, when appropriate, the student's interests and self-assessment (see "Someone's Missing" on pp. 62–63). One systematic approach for obtaining information from parents and students about their interests, strengths, goals, and concerns related to IEP planning is the use of profiling inventories. Examples of student and parent profile instruments can be found by accessing the resources for Chapter 2 at http://www.prenhall.com/heward and linking to the teacher resources on the Merrill Education Special Education Resource Page (http://www.prenhall.com/specialed).

Write Useful Goals. Each area of functioning that is adversely affected by the student's disability must be represented by an annual goal on the IEP. Goals are statements of what the IEP team believes the student can accomplish in one year if the special services provided are effective. Goals are supported by measurable objectives that identify the concepts or processes necessary for reaching goals.

Sample Annual Goal and Objectives

Goal	Objective 1	Objective 2	Objective 3
At the end of academic year, Curt will have better grades and by his own report, will have learned new study skills.	Given a 20-30 min. lecture/oral lesson, Curt will take appropriate notes as judged by that teacher.	Given 10-15 pages of text to read, Curt will employ an appropriate strategy for retaining information—i.e., mapping, webbing, outlining, notes, etc.—as judged by the teacher.	Given notes to study for a test, Curt will do so successfully as evidenced by his test score.

Here are some do's and don'ts concerning the development of IEP annual goals:

Some Do's & Don'ts for IEP Annual Goals

DO

- Include at least one goal for every area of functioning (e.g., academic, social, developmental, vocational) adversely affected by the disability.
- Ask how a potential goal will increase the student's access to and benefit from the general curriculum and other school activities.
- Ask to what extent achieving a potential goal will improve the child's present and future life.
- Prioritize the goals within each area of functioning.
- Make sure each goal includes objective criteria by which the student's progress can be measured (e.g., "By June Martin will read 80 wpm with 5 or fewer errors on grade level on a standardized test").
- Write two or three measurable, intermediate steps (short-term objectives) or major milestones (benchmarks) that will enable families, students, and educators to monitor progress during the year and, if appropriate, revise the IEP.
- Ask the parents, and when appropriate, the child, if the goals and objectives "look right."

DON'T

Include goals for areas of the general education curriculum and functioning that are not adversely affected by the disability (e.g., the IEP for a student with a physical disability who has no special needs in academics does not need to address goals in math or science).

Write goals in unmeasurable terms (e.g., "Geoff will improve his math skills" or "Suzie will be successful in the regular classroom").

Select goals from a preprinted or computerized list (although in some curriculum areas, such as math, a hierarchy of sequenced short-term objectives can be used once the goal has been determined).

Select goals based on the availability of services.

Select goals because other students in the school with the same disability have those goals on their IEPs.

Choose goals based on the present or presumed future placement of the student. IEP goals and the specially designed instruction needed to meet those goals must be determined before the IEP team discusses placement.

TEACH

TEACHing Yourself to Write IEP Goals and Objectives

When learning a new skill all learners—be they schoolchildren, teachers, or teachers-to-be—benefit from guided practice with feedback. You can develop and improve your ability to identify and write meaningful and useful IEP goals and objectives by practicing with case studies. To provide you with practice, four case studies have been set up for you on the Companion Website at http://www.prenhall.com/heward. Once you access the homepage for this site, link to the resources for Chapter 2 and choose one of the four cases described there.

CHAPTER 2
Resources

Introduction | Evaluation Results | Additional Information | IEP Planning

Jeremy. Jeremy is four years old. His parents report that he developed "normally" for the first two and a half years of his life, but then he stopped talking and interacting with others. He frequently engages in repetitive rocking motions and sometimes strikes his face and head with his fists. When his parents and teachers speak to him, he sometimes repeats the same words back to them. Jeremy attends an early childhood program for five days per week which is attended by children with and without disabilities.

Derek. Derek is 10 and in the fourth grade. He was held back one year, repeating the third grade. He is frequently inattentive in class, has difficulty following instructions and staying engaged with a task for more than a few minutes, and seldom turns in completed homework. Derek's teacher has referred him for an evaluation to determine if he is eligible for special education. He does passing work in math, but is failing social studies and science. Results of standardized tests show he has average to above average general intelligence and is reading on the second grade level.

Mwajabu. Mwajabu and her family have just moved from East Africa, and it is her first year in the school district. She is 14 years old and in the eighth grade. Although instruction was often provided in English in the schools she attended in Africa, her reading and written language are very poor. She is noncompliant with her teachers' requests, and several incidences of her hitting other students have been reported. An auditory screening test given to all new students revealed a potential hearing loss. Results of a subsequent audiometry test found that Mwajabu has a severe hearing loss.

Leanna. Tenth-grader Leanna is 16, gets along well with everyone, and is eager to please her teachers and parents. Academically, she functions at the second to third grade level. Leanna attends a resource room for about half of each school day, is included in several general education classes, and spends two afternoons per week at a community-based job site. She has had an IEP since she entered kindergarten.

Go to the Web!

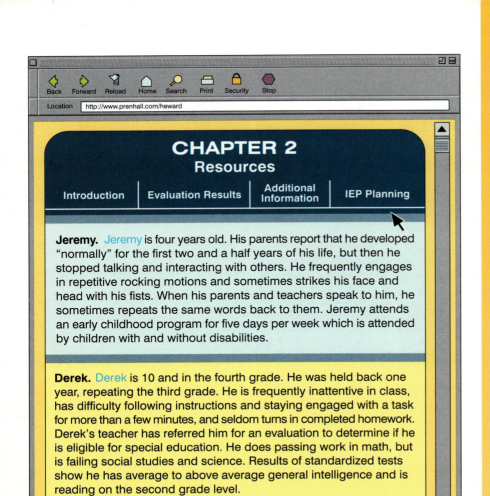

- Review the introduction to each child and the results of their multifactored evaluation; present levels of performance (PLOPs) across each academic, social, communication, functional living, or other area adversely affected by the child's disability; information from their teachers; and profiles of the parents' and student's interests, concerns, and goals.
- Click on the "IEP Planning" section and follow the directives to enter your ideas for IEP goals and objectives and related services for your chosen case. Write at least one annual goal with its relevant short-term objectives or benchmarks for each area of functioning impacted by the child's disability.
- Describe any related services or assistive technology needed to respond to the problems caused by the student's disability and to increase access to an appropriate education.
- Send your ideas via email to your instructor or some of your peers and ask for feedback to ensure that you have written IEP goals appropriately and completely.

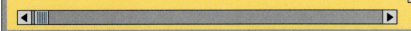

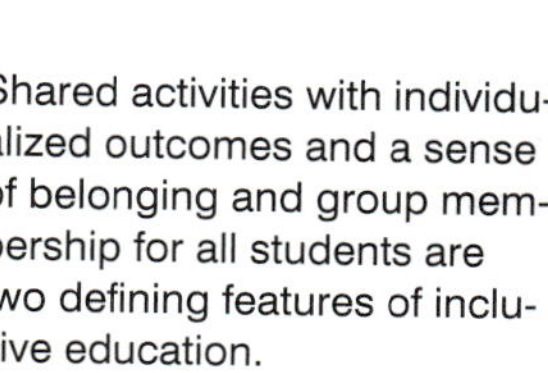

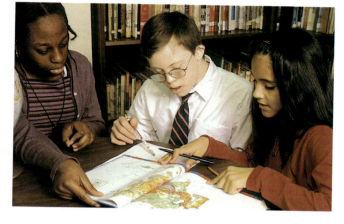

Shared activities with individualized outcomes and a sense of belonging and group membership for all students are two defining features of inclusive education.

Virtually all special educators support the responsible inclusion of students with disabilities in regular classrooms and the development and evaluation of new models for working more cooperatively with general educators to serve all students (e.g., Smith & Hilton, 1997; Vaughn, Schumm, & Brick, 1998). Descriptions of many research-backed model programs and strategies for successfully and meaningfully including students with disabilities as full members in the academic and social life of regular classrooms are provided throughout this text.

Most special educators, however, are not in favor of eliminating the LRE concept and dismantling the continuum of alternative placements. The Council for Exceptional Children, the major professional organization in special education, supports inclusion as a "meaningful goal" to be pursued by schools but believes that the continuum of services and program options must be maintained and that IEP planning teams must make placement and decisions based on the student's individual educational needs (see Figure 2.7).

Position statements on inclusion by the Council for Learning Disabilities, the Learning Disabilities Association of America, and The Association for Persons with Severe Handicaps (TASH) can be found in Chapters 7 and 13. The discussion of inclusion and where students with disabilities are best served continues throughout the text.

Figure 2.7 CEC policy on inclusive schools

Source: Reprinted from the supplement to *Teaching Exceptional Children, 25*(4), May 1993. Used by permission.

The Council for Exceptional Children (CEC) believes all children, youth, and young adults with disabilities are entitled to a free and appropriate education and/or services that lead to an adult life characterized by satisfying relations with others, independent living, productive engagement in the community, and participation in society at large. To achieve such outcomes, there must exist for all children, youth, and young adults with disabilities a rich variety of early intervention, educational, and vocational program options and experiences. Access to these programs and experiences should be based on individual educational need and desired outcomes. Furthermore, students and their families or guardians, as members of the planning team, may recommend the placement, curriculum option, and the exit document to be pursued.

CEC believes that a continuum of services must be available for all children, youth, and young adults. CEC also believes that the concept of inclusion is a meaningful goal to be pursued in our schools and communities. In addition, CEC believes children, youth, and young adults with disabilities should be served whenever possible in general education classrooms in inclusive neighborhood schools and community settings. Such settings should be strengthened and supported by an infusion of specially trained personnel and other appropriate supportive practices according to the individual needs of the child.

Inclusion versus Full Inclusion

by Douglas Fuchs and Lynn S. Fuchs

Full inclusion is the most important and contentious issue in special education today. In this discussion, we first define the term by comparing it to a similar-sounding but different idea: inclusion. Second, we explain why full inclusion is undesirable and why it will not succeed as a movement.

What Is Inclusion? Inclusionists believe it is the job of regular classroom teachers and special educators to help children with disabilities acquire important skills, knowledge, and behaviors that, for many, will facilitate high school—or even college—graduation and a good job. Such achievement, say inclusionists, depends on the existence of a continuum of special education placements, which includes the regular classroom.

In principle, each special education placement in the continuum (from residential facilities, to special day schools, to self-contained classes, to resource rooms) offers specialized, individualized, and intensive instruction that is continuously evaluated for its effectiveness. Teachers in these special settings are instructional experts. For example, they know multiple ways to teach reading, not just one way. To the fullest extent appropriate, these special educators and their students work on the general education curriculum and have a clear understanding of the level of academic accomplishment and social behavior necessary for success in regular classrooms.

Implicit in the inclusionist position is this: the regular classroom's capacity to change is finite. Whereas classrooms *can* and *should* be made more flexible and responsive to a broad range of children's instructional needs, including those of many students with disabilities, there is a limit on how much a given classroom can be expected to change, on how many students to whom any teacher can responsibly provide direct individualized instruction. Inclusionists express several reasons for this belief, the first of which is the large number of children in regular classrooms, typically ranging from 25 to 40. Project Star (Finn & Achilles, 1990), widely acknowledged as the best research exploring relations between class size and student achievement, showed that students' academic performance increased only when class size was reduced to between 13 and 17 students. Inclusionists wonder, however, whether such small classes are possible in the foreseeable future?

Second, the 25 to 40 students are not all performing on grade level. According to Rodden-Nord and Shinn (1991), a typical fifth-grade classroom includes a few students reading below second grade, a handful of students reading above sixth grade, and most students reading somewhere in between. Researchers have found few teachers who differentiate their instruction to address this broad range of academic achievement (Baker & Zigmond, 1990; Fuchs, Fuchs, & Bishop, 1992; McIntosh, Vaughn, Schumm, Haager, & Lee, 1993). Instead, according to the researchers, many teachers present the same lesson and instructional materials to all students.

One reason for this is that teachers infrequently use research-backed instructional methods, such as cooperative learning or classwide peer tutoring. When teachers implement these or other best practices, their responsiveness to diversity increases as does student achievement, including the achievement of many special-needs children. Even so, about 30% of participating children with disabilities typically fail to respond to these best practices, suggesting that even very knowledgeable and dedicated teachers using best practices cannot address the special instructional needs of all children.

Given (1) the large numbers of students per class, (2) the dramatic variability of academic accomplishment among *nondisabled* children, and (3) the fact that a significant number of students with disabilities are not helped by best practices, inclusionists believe the academic needs of some children with disabilities will not be served by full-time placement in regular classes. Some children with disabilities require special education placements to obtain an appropriate education.

What Is Full Inclusion? Full inclusionists believe the primary job of educators is to help children with disabilities establish friendships with nondisabled persons. Moreover, say full inclusionists, within the context of friendship making, educators should (1) help change stereotypic thinking about disabilities among normally developing children and (2) help children with disabilities develop social skills, which in turn will enable them to interact more effectively within an increasingly broad network of acquaintances, coworkers, family members, and friends as the children grow older. Friendship making, attitude change, and social skills development can only occur, say full inclusionists, in regular classes for the simple reason that these objectives require the presence of age-appropriate, nondisabled children, and such children are absent in separate classes, special schools, and other special education placements.

In addition, full inclusionists claim that the placement of special-needs children in regular classrooms must be full-time (e.g., Lipsky & Gartner, 1991; Stainback & Stainback, 1992). They offer two reasons for this. First, only full-time placement confers legitimacy on special-needs children's membership and place in regular classrooms. Second, full inclusionists fear that as long as special education placements exist, educators will use them as dumping grounds for the difficult-to-teach student. Full inclusionists predict that by eliminating special education placements, classroom teachers will have no choice but to transform their classes into settings responsive to all children—including Title I, gifted and talented, and bilingual students. Full inclusionists concede, however, that this will require fundamental changes in the roles of special and regular educators and in the entire teaching and learning process.

The fundamental changes many full inclusionists describe include a radical constructivist vision of teaching and learning and a concomitant deemphasis, if not outright rejection, of standard curricula, directed instruction, and accountability standards. Stainback and Stainback (1992), two well-known full inclusionists, write: "From a holistic, constructivist perspective, all children simply engage in a process of learning as much as they can in a particular subject area; how much and exactly what they learn will depend upon their backgrounds, interests, and abilities" (p. 72).

For some students with disabilities, separate placements such as resource rooms and self-contained classrooms may provide more of the intensive, systematic instruction they need than does the regular classroom.

Many Children, Many Needs How does one explain the dramatic differences between the inclusionists and the full inclusionists? We believe the answer is surprisingly simple: inclusionists and full inclusionists advocate for different children with different needs. Most inclusionists speak for children with sensory impairments and high-incidence disabilities such as learning disabilities, behavior disorders, and mild mental retardation. Most full inclusionists represent children with severe disabilities. So when full inclusionists argue for regular class placements for children with disabilities, they are motivated by the concern that "their" children make friends, influence attitudes about disability, and improve social skills. If the children's learning of academic, functional, or vocational skills suffer, this is a sacrifice many full inclusionists seem willing to make. Inclusionists, by contrast, are primarily concerned that "their" children get appropriate academic instruction; if this is most likely to happen in a separate class or special day school, most inclusionists say, "So be it."

Why the Full Inclusion Movement Will Not Succeed There are several reasons why the full inclusion movement will not succeed.

Uncompromising and presumptive. To ensure a place in regular classrooms for children with severe disabilities, full inclusionists have pressed for an elimination of special education placements for *all* children with disabilities. Their antipathy toward special education placements is based on a conviction that, as long as such programs exist, children with severe disabilities—their children—will most likely be assigned to and confined in them. This uncompromising position—regular classes for all, special education classes for none—reflects a willingness and presumption to speak on behalf of parents and professional advocates of deaf children, blind children, and children with learning disabilities, behavior disorders, and mild mental retardation. It puts full inclusionists in direct conflict with many in the disability community. For example, Bernard Rimland (1993b), a well-known advocate and father of a child with autism, writes: "I have no quarrel with [full] inclusionists if they are content to insist upon inclusion for their children. But when they try to force me and other unwilling parents to dance to their tune, I find it highly objectionable and quite intolerable. Parents need options" (p. 3).

Full inclusionists' willingness to speak for Rimland and everyone else unwittingly makes committed opponents of people who were once their comrades. It appears unlikely that full inclusionists will achieve the elimination of special education placements when so many equally motivated and politically connected advocates oppose their efforts.

Accommodating all in one place. A second major weakness in the full-inclusion position is an unquestioned belief in the capacity of regular education to accommodate all children. The dubiousness of this proposition can be argued with respect to many children with many kinds of special needs. The limits of the regular classroom and need for a variety of special education placements is recognized even in Vermont, a state with nearly double the national average of students with disabilities in regular classrooms and long known as a leader in inclusive education (Sack, 1997). Two years ago, Rutland, Vermont, school officials began The Success School, a separate program for disruptive students in grades 6 through 12. According to Rutland's director of special services, Ellie McGarry, the goal for most students is to return to the regular classroom full time. For others it is gaining the skills necessary to find a job. A handful of students, Ms. McGarry said, "wouldn't be in school at all if it weren't for [The] Success [School]" (Sack, 1997, p. 6). The district's superintendent, David Wolk, says The Success School is "a common-sense way to help the inclusion pendulum settle in the middle. It's clear this is the best environment for those children" (p. 3).

Special education accountability. In arguing against full inclusion, we are not arguing for the status quo. We acknowledge that there are major problems with how special education is practiced in many school districts. For example, few special educators document their effectiveness in teaching basic and higher-order skills to students with disabilities. A second problem is that separate special education placements become terminal assignments in the educational careers of too many children. In other words, there is insufficient evidence that special education teachers facilitate movement along the continuum of special education services so that children in special day schools, for example, transition into resource rooms or that children in resource rooms reintegrate into mainstream classrooms, where eventually they may be decertified.

For too long, accountability in special education has been defined in terms of process—for example, by whether school districts can produce legally correct IEPs. Our field, however, is currently in the midst of redefining accountability in terms of student progress in academic, social, and school-behavior domains. Although this redefinition will be difficult to accomplish—for both conceptual and practical reasons—it is a most important endeavor. We are confident that time will tell that student progress requires options in instruction, curricula, materials, and placements.

Douglas Fuchs and Lynn Fuchs are professors of special education at Vanderbilt University. Their research interests focus on developing classroom-based techniques such as curriculum-based measurement and peer-assisted learning strategies that strengthen the academic performance and social integration of students with and without disabilities. They are the coeditors of *The Journal of Special Education*.

Fuchs and Fuchs (1994), who are concerned that reform in special education is being "radicalized" by a minority who want to do away with all special education placements in favor of full inclusion, write:

> Special education has big problems. Not the least of which is that it must redefine its relationship with general education. Now is the time to hear from inventive pragmatists, not extremists on the right or the left. Now is the time for leadership that recognizes the need for change; appreciates the importance of consensus building; looks at general education with a sense of what is possible; respects special education's traditions and values and the law that undergirds them; and seeks to strengthen the mainstream, as well as other educational placements that can provide more intensive services, to enhance the learning and lives of all children. (p. 305)

Where Does Special Education Go from Here?

The promise of a free, appropriate public education for all children with disabilities is indeed an ambitious one. The process of bringing this goal about has been described in such lofty terms as a "new Bill of Rights" and a "Magna Carta" for children with disabilities (Goodman, 1976). Weintraub and Abeson (1974) wrote more than 25 years ago in support of IDEA: "At the minimum, it will make educational opportunities a reality for all handicapped children. At the maximum, it will make our schools healthier learning environments for all our children" (p. 529). Today, most observers acknowledge that substantial progress has been made toward fulfillment of that promise.

IDEA has had far-reaching effects. As Turnbull and Turnbull (1997) observe, the student is no longer required to meet the requirements of the school, but the school is required to fit the needs of the student. Schools today provide far more than academic instruction. In effect, they have become diversified agencies offering services such as medical support, physical therapy, vocational training, parent counseling, recreation, special transportation, and in-service education for staff members. In place of the once-prevalent practice of excluding children with disabilities from programs, schools now seek the most appropriate ways of including them. Schools are committed to providing wide-ranging services to children from differing backgrounds and with differing characteristics.

Many citizens—both within and outside the field of education—have welcomed the recognition of the rights of children with disabilities in their schools and communities. Additionally, the greater involvement of parents and families in the educational process and the emphasis on team planning to meet individual needs throughout the life span are widely regarded as positive developments. Reports from teachers and students, as well as a growing number of data-based studies, indicate that many children with disabilities are being successfully educated in regular schools and that, for the most part, they are well accepted by their nondisabled schoolmates.

Despite this ample evidence of progress toward providing equal educational opportunity, it is equally true that many people—again, inside and outside the field of education—have detected significant problems in the implementation of IDEA. Many school administrators maintain that the federal government has never granted sufficient financial resources to the states and local school districts to assist them in providing special services, which are often very costly. Special education teachers express dissatisfaction over excessive paperwork, unclear guidelines, and inappropriate grouping of students with disabilities. General education teachers contend that they receive little or no training or support when students with disabilities are placed in their classes. Some parents of children with disabilities have voiced opposition to full inclusion. Some observers find that the schedules and procedures used in some inclusion programs actually allow for relatively little integration (Sansone & Zigmond, 1986). There are many other problems, real and perceived, and no quick fix or easy solution can be offered.

Special education is at a crossroads. Once, access to educational opportunity was the primary issue for children with disabilities. Would they receive an education at all? Could they be served in their local community? Some access problems persist (e.g., particularly for children who live in poverty or in extremely isolated areas), but now the primary issue of concern is the appropriateness and effectiveness of special education received by students.

Can we fulfill the promise of a free, appropriate public education for all students with disabilities? The answer depends on the readiness of professionals to work together, assume new roles, communicate with each other, and involve parents, families, and individuals with disabilities themselves.

Ultimately, educators must realize that regardless of where services are delivered, the most crucial variable is the quality of instruction that children receive.

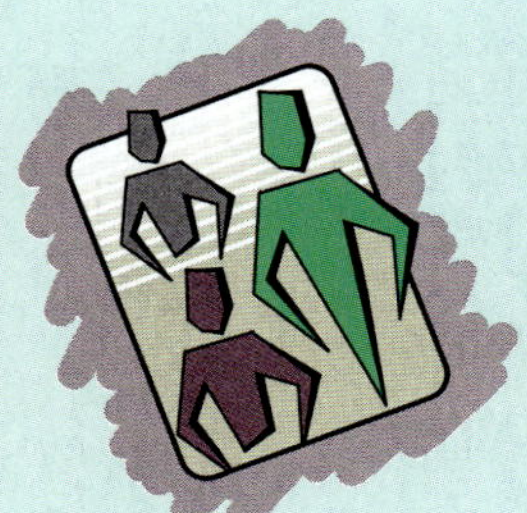

PROFILES AND PERSPECTIVES

Moving Toward Inclusive Education

by Michael F. Giangreco

In the early 1980s, when I first heard about early efforts to include students with moderate and severe disabilities within general education classrooms, I must admit I was somewhat skeptical. I wondered how the educational needs of the students in my own special education class, who had labels such as autism, deaf-blindness, severe mental retardation, and multiple disabilities, could be appropriately addressed within a general education classroom. I knew it wouldn't be enough merely to have students physically present in a classroom, separated within the class, or programmatically isolated from their peers.

Over the next few years I had opportunities to help develop inclusive educational opportunities for students with disabilities by working collaboratively with other team members (e.g., parents, general educators, related services staff, paraprofessionals). Despite the initial apprehensions of some school staff, once people got to know their new student with disabilities and designed appropriately individualized curriculum and instruction, they usually felt positive about the situation. Equally as important, many teachers came to realize that the steps they had taken to ensure educational integrity and appropriate inclusion of the student with disabilities (e.g., collaborative teamwork, activity-based learning, cooperative experiences, data-based instruction, creative problem solving, peer-to-peer supports) were also applicable for meeting the widely differing educational needs of students without disability labels. Qualified general education teachers with inclusive attitudes and appropriate supports found that they could successfully teach students with disabilities, in part because the basic principles of teaching and learning are the same whether a student has a disability label or not.

WHAT ARE YOU IN FOR?
CEREBRAL PALSY, BUT THEY SAID WITH GOOD BEHAVIOR I COULD BE OUT IN 3 TO 5.
8
INSPIRED BY ROBERT HOLLAND
© 1998 MICHAEL F. GIANGRECO, ILLUSTRATION BY KEVIN RUELLE
PEYTRAL PUBLICATIONS, INC. 612-949-8707
"PAROLE APPROACH" TO SCHOOL INCLUSION

In recent years the term *inclusive education* has been a source of some controversy. Sometimes people's concerns about inclusive education are based on speculation rather than actual experiences with inclusion. Other times their concerns are less about inclusion than they are about the process of change. Often they had been exposed to something labeled "inclusive education" when it wasn't. Some of these well-intentioned but mislabeled situations were only partial implementation efforts. Too often they were simply examples of bad educational practice. As my colleague, Michael Hock, likes to say about inclusive education, "Doing it wrong doesn't make it wrong." So when someone tells me a horror story about a student with a disability who was dumped into a classroom, or how the teacher wasn't supported, or how a student's needs weren't met, I remind them that such situations are inaccurately labeled as inclusive education.

Inclusive education means:

1. All students are welcomed in general education classes in their local schools. Therefore, the general education classroom in the school that a student would attend if he did not have a disability is the first placement consideration, given individually appropriate supports and services.
2. Students are educated in classes where the number of those with and without disabilities is proportional to the local population (e.g., 10% to 12% have identified disabilities).
3. Students are educated with peers in the same age groupings available to those without disability labels.

4. Students with varying characteristics and abilities participate in shared educational experiences while pursuing individually appropriate learning outcomes with necessary supports and accommodations. In cases where students have substantially different learning outcomes, this can occur through differentiated instruction, multilevel instruction, or curriculum overlapping.
5. Shared educational experiences take place in settings predominantly frequented by people without disabilities (e.g., general education classroom, community worksites).
6. Educational experiences are designed to enhance individually determined, valued life outcomes for students and therefore seek an individualized balance between the academic/functional and social/personal aspects of schooling.
7. Inclusive education exists when each of the previously listed characteristics occurs on an ongoing daily basis.

FRANK LEARNS THAT INCLUSION DOESN'T HAVE TO BE ROCKET SCIENCE.

At its core, inclusive education is a set of values, principles, and practices that seeks more effective and meaningful education for all students, regardless of whether they have exceptionality labels or not.

People occasionally ask me, "Are there any students who cannot successfully be included in general education?" If you are looking for the rare exception, it can usually be found. At the same time, it is important to acknowledge that where such exceptions exist it is usually because we, as a field, have not yet figured out how to include certain students or have chosen not to. The exclusion of many students with disabilities often has less to do with their characteristics than ours. For example, 20 years ago it was quite rare for students with Down syndrome to be educated in general education classrooms. Today in many school districts it is commonplace. The range of characteristics presented by students with Down syndrome are the same now as they were then. What has changed are our attitudes and practices. But clearly more needs to be done.

Our attention and energy may be more constructively focused on asking questions such as "How can we successfully include more students with disabilities who are still being educated in unnecessarily restrictive environments such as special education schools and classes?" We know that far too many students are unnecessarily excluded because children with similar characteristics and needs who live in one community are educated in general education classes with supports while in other communities they continue to be sent to special education classes and schools, often without any real consideration being given to general class placement. Being included should not depend on where you live, but currently it does. We need to continually remind ourselves that special education—namely, specially and individually designed instruction—is a portable service, not a place.

We have moved beyond knowing whether inclusive education is viable; it has been demonstrated to be so for an ever widening array of students in increasing numbers of schools over many years. As this change progresses it will require a continued shift in how we think about educating diverse groups of students and how schools operate. Students' lives should be better as result of having been in school. Inclusive education provides a foundation for that to occur for students with disabilities in ways that are not possible in special education schools and classes. Ultimately, this job will be easier, approached with greater enthusiasm, and maybe even with a greater sense of urgency, when we demonstrate that we truly value people with disabilities by including them, welcoming them, and helping them learn skills and develop supports that result in meaningful outcomes in their lives.

Michael F. Giangreco is a research associate professor at the Center on Disability and Community Inclusion at the University of Vermont. His research and writing focus on the education of students with disabilities in inclusive classrooms and community settings.

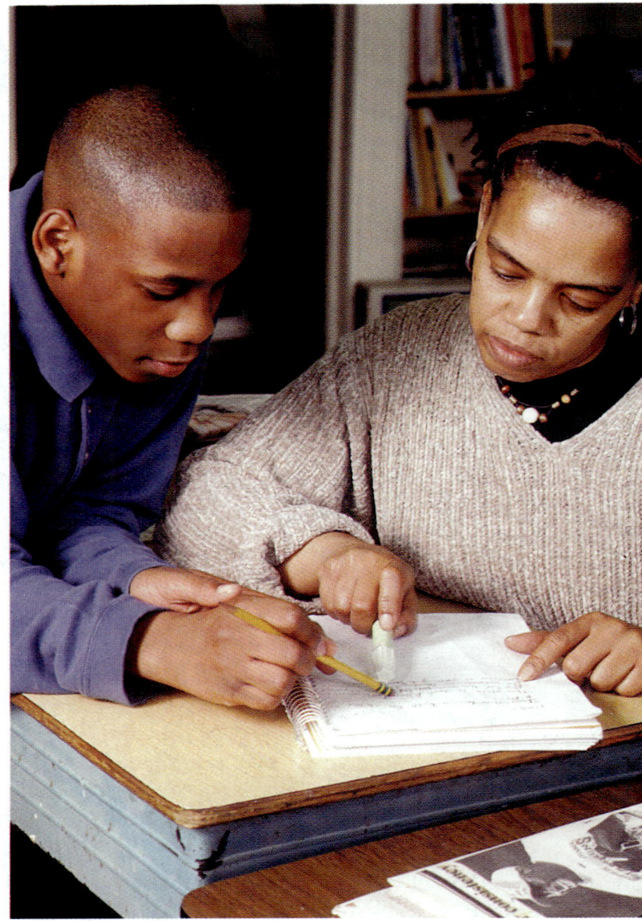

Regardless of where services are delivered, the most crucial variable is the quality of instruction that each child receives.

Use the self-tests at http://www.prenhall.com/heward to assess your knowledge of the content of Chapter 2.

Keogh's (1990) conclusion regarding the greatest challenge for special education reform is right on target:

> It is clear that major changes are needed in the delivery of services to problem learners, and that these services need to be the responsibility of regular as well as special educators. It is also clear that teachers are the central players in bringing about change in practice. It follows, then, that our greatest and most pressing challenge in the reform effort is to determine how to improve the quality of instruction at the classroom level. (p. 190)

Special education is serious business. The learning and adjustment problems faced by students with disabilities are real, and their prevention and remediation require effective intervention. Regardless of who does it or where it takes place, good teaching must occur. Exceptional children deserve no less.

Summary

The Process of Special Education

- IDEA mandates a particular sequence of events that schools must follow in identifying and educating children with disabilities.
- Prereferral intervention is an informal, problem-solving process used by many schools to (1) provide immediate instructional and/or behavior management assistance to the child and teacher and (2) reduce the chances of identifying a child for special education who may not be disabled.
- All children suspected of having a disability must receive a nondiscriminatory multifactored evaluation (MFE) for determining eligibility for special education and to provide information about the child's educational needs and how to meet them.
- An individualized education program (IEP) must be planned and provided for each child with a disability that is adversely affecting her educational performance.

The Importance of Collaboration and Teaming

- Coordination, consultation, and teaming are three modes of collaboration that team members can use.
- Three models for teaming are multidisciplinary, interdisciplinary, and transdisciplinary. Transdisciplinary teams conduct joint assessments, share information and expertise across discipline boundaries, and select discipline-free goals and interventions.

Individualized Education Program

- An IEP planning team must include at least (1) the parents of the child; (2) one regular education teacher of the child; (3) one special education teacher; (4) a representative of the local education agency; (5) an individual who can interpret the instructional implications of evaluation results; (6) other individuals who have knowledge or special expertise regarding the child, including related service personnel as appropriate; and (7) the student, if age 14 or older. (Younger students may attend if appropriate.)
- Although the formats vary widely from district to district, each IEP must include these seven components: (1) the child's present levels of educational performance; (2) measurable annual goals, including benchmarks or short-term objectives; (3) the special education and related services and supplementary aids and services to be provided to the child; (4) an explanation of the extent, if any, to which the child will not participate with nondisabled children in the regular class; (5) any individual modifications in the administration of state- or district-wide assessments of student achievement that are needed for the child to participate in such assessment (or alternative assessments); (6) the projected date for the beginning of the services and modifications described in number 3 and the anticipated frequency, location, and duration of those services and modifications; and (7) how the child's progress toward the annual goals will be measured and how the child's parents will be regularly informed of their child's progress.
- Beginning when the student reaches age 14, IEPs must also include information on how the child's transition from school to adult life will be supported.
- Without direct and ongoing monitoring of student progress toward IEP goals and objectives, the document's usefulness is limited.
- The IEP is a measure of accountability for teachers and schools; however, a teacher and school cannot be prosecuted if the child does not achieve all of the goals set forth in the IEP.

The Least Restrictive Environment

- The LRE is the setting closest to the regular classroom that also meets the child's special educational needs.
- The LRE is a relative concept; the LRE for one child might be inappropriate for another.
- The continuum of services is a range of placement and service options to meet the individual needs of students with disabilities.
- The IEP team must determine the LRE after it has designed a program of special education and related services to meet the child's unique needs.

Inclusive Education

- Inclusion (formerly called mainstreaming) describes the process of integrating children with disabilities into regular schools and classes.
- Studies have shown that well-planned, carefully conducted inclusion can be generally effective with students of all ages, types, and degrees of disability.
- A few special educators believe that the LRE principle should give way to full inclusion, in which all students with disabilities are placed full time in regular classrooms.
- Most special educators and professional organizations, such as CEC, support inclusion as a goal but believe that the continuum of services and program options must be maintained and that placement decisions must be based on the student's individual educational needs.

Where Does Special Education Go From Here?

- The promise of a free, appropriate public education for all children with disabilities is an ambitious one, but substantial progress has been made toward fulfillment of that promise.
- Implementation of IDEA has brought problems of funding, inadequate teacher training, and opposition by some to the inclusion of children with disabilities into regular classes.
- Regardless of where services are delivered, the most crucial variable is the quality of instruction that each child receives.

For More Information

Journals

- All of the journals listed at the end of Chapter 1 are relevant to the content of Chapter 2.
- *Journal of Disability Policy Studies.* Published quarterly by the Department of Rehabilitation Education and Research, University of Arkansas, 346 North West Avenue, Fayetteville, AK 72701. Publishes research, discussion, and review articles addressing a broad range of topics on disability policy from the perspective of a variety of academic disciplines.
- *Journal of Educational and Psychological Consultation.* Published quarterly by the Association for Educational and Psychological Consultation, Lawrence Erlbaum Associates, 365 Broadway, Hillsdale, NJ 07642. Publishes both research and practitioner-oriented articles on the process and outcomes of consultation.

Books

- Bigge, J. L., Stump, C. S., Spagna, M. E., & Silberman, R. K. (1999). *Curriculum, assessment, and instruction for students with disabilities*. Belmont, CA: Wadsworth.
- Friend, M., & Bursuck, W. D. (1999). *Including students with special needs: A practical guide for classroom teachers* (2nd ed.). Needham Heights, MA: Allyn & Bacon.
- Giangreco, M. F., Cloninger, C. J., & Iverson, V. S. (1998). *Choosing options and accommodations for children* (2nd ed.) Baltimore: Brookes.
- Goodlad, J. I., & Lovitt, T. C. (Eds.). (1993). *Integrating general and special education*. Upper Saddle River, NJ: Merrill/Prentice Hall.
- Heron, T. E., & Harris, K. C. (in press). *The educational consultant: Helping professionals, parents, and mainstreamed students* (4th ed.). Austin, TX: PRO-ED.
- Howell, K. W. (1998). *Curriculum-based evaluation: Teaching and decision making* (3rd ed.). Monterey, CA: Brooks/Cole.
- Kauffman, J. M., & Hallahan, D. P. (Eds.). (1995). *The illusion of full inclusion: A comprehensive critique of a current special education bandwagon.* Austin, TX: PRO-ED.
- Lewis, R. B., & Doorlag, D. H. (1995). *Teaching special students in the mainstream* (4th ed.). Upper Saddle River, NJ: Merrill/Prentice Hall.
- Salend, S. J. (1998). *Effective mainstreaming: Creating inclusive classrooms* (3rd ed.). Upper Saddle River, NJ: Merrill/Prentice Hall.
- Stainback, S., & Stainback, W. (Eds.). (1992). *Curricular considerations in inclusive classrooms: Facilitating learning for all students*. Baltimore: Brookes.
- Strickland, B. B., & Turnbull, A. P. (1993). *Developing and implementing individualized education programs* (3rd ed.). Merrill/Prentice Hall.
- Thomas, C. C., Correa, V. I., & Morsink, C. V. (1995). *Interactive teaming: Consultation and collaboration in special programs* (2nd ed.). Upper Saddle River, NJ: Merrill/Prentice Hall.
- Thousand, J. S., Villa, R. A., & Nevin, A. I. (Eds.). (1994). *Creativity and collaborative learning: A practical guide to empowering students and teachers*. Baltimore: Brookes.
- Wood, J. W. (1998). *Adapting instruction for mainstreamed students and at-risk students* (3rd ed.). Upper Saddle River, NJ: Merrill/Prentice Hall.

Chapter 3

Special Education in a Culturally Diverse Society

by Vivian I. Correa and William L. Heward

Focus Questions

- Why are culturally and linguistically diverse students disproportionately represented in special education?
- What initial steps can a teacher take to become culturally responsive?
- What must educators realize and be sensitive to when attempting to involve culturally and linguistically diverse families in school activities?
- How should assessment, curriculum, and instructional methods differ for students from culturally or linguistically different backgrounds?
- If a student cannot speak, read, or write English well enough to progress in the school curriculum, does it make any difference whether the limited English proficiency is caused by cultural differences or by a disability?

The United States is a society composed of people from many cultural groups, and the students in our schools reflect this great diversity. Because the achievement of ethnic groups such as African Americans, Hispanics, and Native Americans is similar to white students' in the early grades but falls further behind the longer the students stay in school (Banks, 1994b), there is reason for concern over the role our educational system may be playing in limiting the achievement of students from different cultural groups.

Another reason for concern over the role of our educational system is the fact that culturally and linguistically diverse students are dropping out of school at a much higher rate than white students are. Overall, 5 out of every 100 young adults enrolled in high school drops out of high school. In 1996, the dropout numbers were higher for racial and ethnic groups, with 9% of Hispanics leaving school before completing a high school program compared to 6.7% of blacks and 4.1% of whites (National Center for Education Statistics, 1997). It is also estimated that 55% of Native American students eventually will drop out of school (Gollnick & Chinn, 1998). Furthermore, African American and Latino students who do manage to graduate from high school are much less likely than whites to go to college (Education Trust, 1996). Compounding this problem is the fact that "about 1 in 4 special education students drop out of high school; 43% of those who graduate remain unemployed three to five years after high school, and nearly one third—primarily those with learning and emotional disabilities—are arrested at least once after leaving high school" (Shapiro, Loeb, Bowermaster, & Toch, 1993, p. 56).

The postsecondary school adjustment of young adults with disabilities is examined in Chapter 15.

The distinguishing characteristics of ethnic background and disability place culturally and linguistically diverse students with disabilities in double jeopardy for dropping out of school and not attaining success in postschool settings. In fact, Utley (1995) observed that some culturally and linguistically diverse students "face quadruple jeopardy due to a combination of factors, such as poverty, language, culture, and/or disabling condition and this has devastating effects on their educational opportunities and makes them vulnerable to placement in special education" (p. 303).

Go to the companion website at http://www.prenhall.com/heward and select Chapter 3 to review the chapter objectives.

Further, some students with disabilities still experience discrimination or receive a less-than-adequate education *because* of their racial, ethnic, social class, or other differences. We are not implying that belonging to a cultural or linguistic group that differs from the majority culture is a disability. Rather, we recognize that even though cultural diversity is a strength of our society, being a member of a minority group too often means discrimination and misunderstanding, closed doors, and lowered expectations.

In addition, culturally and linguistically diverse students continue to be both underrepresented and overrepresented in special education (Artiles & Trent, 1994; Artiles & Zamora-Durán, 1997; Baca & Cervantes, 1998; Correa, Blanes-Reyes, & Rapport, 1995; Ford, 1998; MacMillan & Reschly, 1998; Patton, 1998). Consider the following:

- In the 1992 school year, 32.5% of the total school population was minority, while 39.2% of the those identified as having mild mental retardation, and 41.4% of those identified as having moderate mental retardation were minority.
- African American students constitute about 16.3% of the general school population but more than 31% of students with mild mental retardation and 23.7% of students with severe emotional disturbance.
- Latinos are overrepresented in programs for students with learning disabilities and speech-language impairments.
- Native Americans are in classes for students with learning disabilities in disproportionately high numbers, whereas their representation in classes for students who are gifted is consistently low (Chinn & Hughes, 1987; Ford, 1998).
- Ethnically diverse students constitute about 32.5% of the general school population but only about 22.6% of all students who are identified as gifted and talented (U.S. Department of Education, Office of Civil Rights, 1994).
- Asian Pacific students are generally underrepresented in disability categories and overrepresented in gifted and talented programs.

- Approximately 500,000 migrant students live in the United States, but only 10.7% of them with mild disabilities appear to be identified (Smith & Luckasson, 1995).
- Culturally different males are significantly overrepresented in classes for students with mental retardation, severe emotional disturbance, and specific learning disabilities.

The Division for Culturally and Linguistically Diverse Exceptional Learners (DDEL), a division of CEC, serves the interests of professionals working with culturally and linguistically diverse students with disabilities and their families.

Special educators, in facing these challenges, seek to provide a relevant, individualized education to students with disabilities from culturally diverse backgrounds. Our public school system is based, after all, on a philosophy of equal educational opportunity. IDEA is only one of many significant steps toward implementing equal educational opportunity. Court decisions and legislation, besides prohibiting discrimination by schools because of intellectual or physical disability, have forbidden discrimination in education and employment on the basis of race, nationality, gender, or inability to speak English. Special programs now provide financial support and assistance to schools that serve refugee and migrant students and that provide self-determination in education for Native Americans.

Despite these important efforts, equal educational opportunity for all is not yet a reality (Banks & Banks, 1997; Grossman, 1995). Interestingly, the following statement from the U.S. Department of Education further emphasizes the problem of the high disproportion of minority children in special education—a problem that continues to be an issue of national concern and debate:

> Congress . . . suggested that the use of standardized assessment instruments which are racially biased are, at least in part, responsible. Some observers contend that school professionals are more likely to refer and place minority and poor children in special education because of lower expectations regarding the educability of these children. Other observers have noted, however, that it is logical to expect a disproportionate number of poor, minority children being placed in special education given that these children are more likely to have experienced poor prenatal and early childhood nutrition and health care, resulting in actual disabilities. (U.S. Department of Education, 1992, p. 15)

Each student in this classroom benefits from the diverse cultural and ethnic perspectives, values, and problem-solving approaches they experience by working with one another.

The problem of disproportionate numbers of culturally diverse students in special education is not simple, and the solutions require significant changes for schools and communities (Artiles & Trent, 1994; Artiles & Zamora-Durán, 1997; Delpit, 1995; Gollnick & Chinn, 1998; Harry, 1994). However, understanding the multivariate nature of the problem is a first step in identifying effective solutions to improving educational services for all culturally and linguistically diverse students and their families.

Why Are There Disproportionate Placements of Culturally Diverse Students in Special Education?

For extensive literature reviews and discussions of the disproportionate representation of minority students in special education, see Kauffman, Hallahan, and Ford (1998).

Go to the Resources Module for Chapter 3 at http://www.prenhall.com/heward. Click on Special Ed Resource Page and access a search engine. Search for "cultural bias and special education."

The fact that culturally diverse children constitute a high percentage of special education students and are identified as having mental retardation, emotional disturbance, or learning disabilities is not, in itself, a problem. Students with special needs should be served in special programs, whatever their ethnic background. The presence of large numbers of culturally diverse students, however, raises several important concerns about our education practices. Three areas that have been identified as integral to this problem include (1) incongruence in interactions between teachers and culturally diverse students and families, (2) inaccuracy of the assessment and referral process for culturally diverse students in special education, and (3) ineffective curriculum and instructional practices for culturally diverse students. The second part of this chapter addresses possible solutions to these three concerns.

Incongruence Between Teachers and Culturally Diverse Students

Teachers, administrators, school psychologists, and counselors generally require or expect certain behaviors of students. For example, they assume that most children will learn to respond to the teacher's instructions and will be positively motivated by verbal praise and attention. Children, however, are strongly influenced by their early contacts with family members, neighbors, and friends. If the expectations and values of home and school environments are vastly different, children may have serious problems. Behaviors considered problems by school personnel might be related to differences between the standards of behavior in the home and standards of the school. For example, a teacher might characterize a silent and shy child as overly withdrawn and refer him to a school counselor. In fact, however, the child may be behaving according to the standards of his home.

The idea of cultural incongruence between home and school can also be seen in instruction. A common mode of instruction in mainstream U.S. classrooms is analytical and verbal, whereas the language-learning style of some culturally diverse learners is more imaginative and nonverbal (Harry, 1992a). For example, culturally diverse students might find it difficult to recite mathematics facts in front of the whole class and compete to "win" on the weekly spelling bee. However, the same students might become more engaged in instruction if the math facts were imbedded in an ethnic cooking activity with small groups of peers and the spelling bee were turned into a dramatic play activity where they were asked to perform the history of their ancestors using the week's spelling words. Such conflicts can interfere with a child's learning and behavior and are thus a legitimate concern of all special educators. Without a solid understanding of how culture influences both students and school personnel, the cultural conflict between the home and school will continue to exist. School staff can better understand cultural incongruence with students and families from diverse cultures if they recognize the definition of culture, the heterogeneity within cultures, and the existence of microcultures.

Definition of Culture Culture "refers to the many different factors that shape one's sense of group identity: race, ethnicity, religion, geographical locations, income status, gender, and occupations" (Turnbull, Turnbull, Shank, & Leal, 1995, p. 8). Because a social group adapts to and modifies the environments in which it lives, **culture** can be defined as "the way of life of a social group; the human-made environment. Although culture is often defined in a way that includes all the material and nonmaterial aspects of group life, most social scientists today emphasize the intangible, symbolic, and ideational aspect of culture. . . . Cultures are dynamic, complex, and changing" (Banks, 1994a, pp. 50–51).

A culture, then, is determined by the "world view, values, styles, and above all language" shared by members of a social group (Hilliard, 1980, p. 585). Although an outsider can learn to speak the language of another social group or to use some of its tools, such accomplishments do not confer complete access to or understanding of the group's culture. While the language, artifacts, and other things associated with a particular group are sometimes presented as its culture, this view is only partly accurate. Chopsticks, for example, are an important part of the Chinese culture but are not culture in and of themselves.

> Unless we know the meaning of an action such as using chopsticks, these implements remain just bits of wood, bone, or ivory. We have to acquire the knowledge and ideas about what they mean and what they are used for. . . . If we are members of the social group that uses such implements, we will know the code by virtue of knowing the culture. A stranger in the group would have to watch chopstick-using behavior or ask for instructions. . . . Even then, the stranger might not learn all the subtleties of chopstick use immediately but would have to be acquainted with the social group for a long time before finding out that there are rules of politeness and etiquette surrounding the apparently simple process of eating with chopsticks. (Bullivant, 1993, p. 35)

People who share a particular culture's ideas and values usually interpret events in similar ways. Although membership in a specific cultural group does not determine behavior, members are exposed to (socialized by) the same set of expectations and consequences for acting in certain ways. As a result, certain types of behavior become more probable (Banks, 1994b; Skinner, 1974). Gollnick and Chinn (1998) outline four basic characteristics of culture that give us a background for considering the special needs of culturally diverse students with disabilities and their families.

> 1. *Our cultural heritage is learned.* It is not innately based on the culture in which we are born. Vietnamese infants adopted by Italian American, Catholic, middle-class parents will share a cultural heritage with middle-class Italian American Catholics, rather than Vietnamese in Vietnam.
> 2. *Culture is shared.* Shared cultural patterns and customs bind people together as an identifiable group and make it possible for them to live together and function with ease. Groups may not realize the common cultural aspects as existent in the cultural group—the way they communicate with each other and the foods they eat.
> 3. *Culture is an adaptation.* Cultures have developed to accommodate certain environmental conditions and available natural and technological resources. Thus, Eskimo who live with extreme cold, snow, ice, seals, and the sea have developed a culture different from the Pacific Islander. The culture of urban residents differs from rural residents, in part because of the resources available in the different settings.
> 4. *Culture is dynamic system that changes continuously.* For example, the replacement of industrial workers by robots is changing the culture of many working-class communities. (pp. 5–6)

Heterogeneity within a Culture The importance of understanding and respecting inter- and intraindividual differences cannot be stressed too strongly. Cultural groups can be extremely heterogeneous; for example, Native Americans today comprise 510 federally recognized tribes and 278 reservations (including pueblos, rancherias, and communities) and speak 187 languages (Coburn et al., 1995). Although many Native Americans share a certain cultural heritage and world view, "tribal differences are very real and tribal affiliations are quite important to Indian people. . . . There is no such thing as a single 'Indian' culture. Navajos are as different culturally from the Sioux as Canadians are from Mexicans" (Little Soldier, 1990, pp. 66, 68). Asian Americans are an even more diversified group, coming from more than 24 countries and speaking more than 1,000 languages and dialects (Leung, 1988).

Microcultures The degree to which a student inherits a distinct cultural background varies immensely. Remember, a student's cultural group is just one of the social groups that influence her values and behavior. Each student is simultaneously a member of a number of microcultures such as race, ethnicity, social class, religion, gender, and disability. Each of these groups exerts various degrees of influence on a student's ways of interpreting and responding to the world.

> For example, a child in the classroom is not just Asian-American, but also male and middle-class. Therefore, his view of reality and his actions based on that view will differ from those of a middle-class Asian-American girl or a lower-class Asian-American boy. A teacher's failure to consider the integration of race, social class, and gender could lead at times to an oversimplified or inaccurate understanding of what occurs in schools. (Grant & Sleeter, 1989, p. 49)

Pazcual Villaronga, a bilingual teacher in New York City's "El Barrio," reflects on his own culture in the poem "The So Called." He states, "The poem's energy is not so much out of anger, but rather more out of a burning desire to celebrate the many cultures within. And especially the ones that make me who I am!" (Villaronga, 1995, p. 260).

Although this chapter emphasizes issues related to culturally and linguistically diverse students from African American, Hispanic, Asian, and Native American backgrounds, it is important to define diversity in a much broader way.

> [Diversity] encompasses not only those individuals whose ethnic heritage originates in another country, but also those among us who may have special educational and other needs . . . , those who may share significantly different lifestyles (rural and urban children, children who live in extreme poverty, drug dependents), those whose identity is critically influenced by gender, and those who are significantly influenced by variations in class and religion. (Cusher, McClelland, & Safford, 1992, p. 7)

In other words, as we think about diversity, we must remember that Appalachian, gay and lesbian, homeless, or Muslim students deserve the same respect, understanding, and acceptance from educators as other ethnically diverse groups do.

Inaccurate Assessment and Referral

A second major reason for the disproportionate numbers of culturally diverse students in special education is bias in assessing and referring these students. Tests are widely used in special education. However, the testing methods used to identify students for special education services are an inexact science at best and at times little more than guesswork (Correa et al., 1995). The likelihood of obtaining valid, accurate, and unbiased assessment results is less when the student in question is from a culturally different background. Figueroa (1989) calls the current practice of psychological testing of children from culturally and linguistically diverse groups "random chaos" because it is so fraught with problems.

Brown (1982) discusses several ways in which standardized tests—traditionally normed on white, English-speaking, middle-class children—may discriminate against those from different cultural backgrounds.

- *The tests use formats and items that are more germane to one group than another.* For example, the test may include restrictive time limits, vocabulary

The So Called

by Pazcual Villaronga

I am mixture
similar to h2O
I am american pie
the black-eyed peas
with plenty of salsa

I am the rhythm and blues
the classical lines
the pru-cu-ta-ca-ca-mambo

I am a potpourri of values and attitudes
the fact that men don't cry
but in reality they do
and don't die

I am a mixture
of beautiful paints
that picture
psychedelic tones
african blood
spanish blood
and Indian blood

transported
by economical
social
or political fact

from an island of joy
under a damn
cynical
implemented
ploy

to a jungle of cement
metal
and glass

to become a confused entity
a confused being
of meatloaf
and oxtails
and arroz con pollo

of Beethoven
Isaac Hayes
and eddi palmieri

to struggle with my culture
their culture
and the loss of mine

goodbye three kinds
hello christmas
and its mad capitalistic
season

the dropping of my accent
the implementation of
another language

I am Puerto Rico
the u.s. of a.
and new york

spinning
trying to lose myself
in the sun
on the penthouse
in my place
in my slums
trying to become
what will constantly be denied

I am black
white
brown
uptown
downtown
all around
the damn town

I am here
I am there
I am everywhere
spread thin
so that my existence
my consistency
my reality

can be denied
mesmerized
until I boil down to nothing
at the bottom of the pot
"El Pegao"

which they don't know is the best
part of the meal
especially because I survive
to eat it

I am the music you can't exploit
because you don't
understand
comes from our corazones
speaks of our culture
our history
our minds

in a language you find
easier to destroy
because yours is better

I am caught in a flight
over a sea
of controversy

I am a piece of a puzzle
that doesn't fit
here or there

because both my vehicles of expression
are dulled and
downed
by my own
and my own

I am what has always been there
only with a different name
to fit the purpose
to play the game
for someone's fame
other than mine

I am the P.R.
the rican
the spic
the new click
the so called New-Yor-Rican

Pazcual Villaronga is a bilingual teacher in the Lola Rodriguez School in Manhattan's District 4, in New York City's "El Barrio."

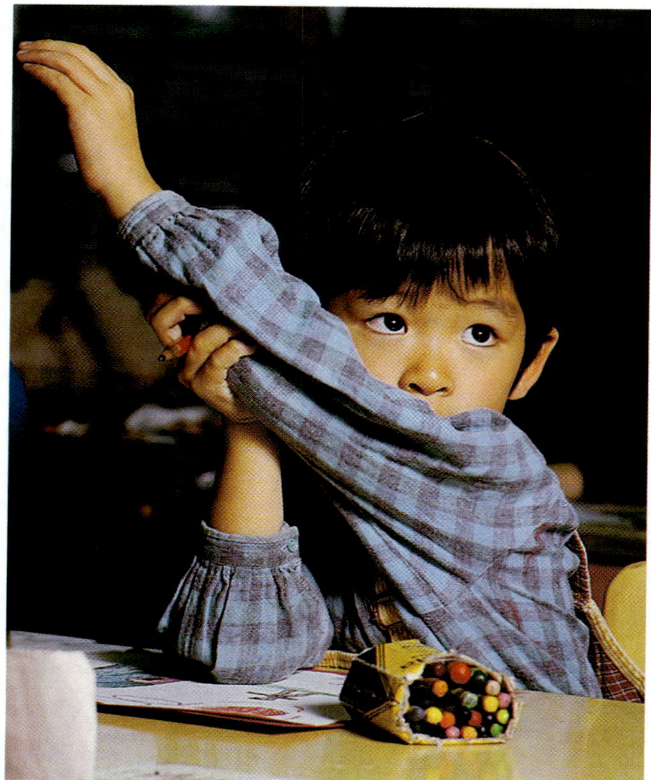

This student's behavior and values are influenced not only by his membership in a specific cultural group but by his social class, gender, and exceptionality.

tasks that require the child to read the word, and items that require a child to read in a task designed to measure listening comprehension ability.

- *Children have differing amounts of "test wiseness," which is more likely to be a problem with the preschool-age child than with the school-age child.* For example, white, middle-class, preschool-age children tend to be familiar with question-and-answer formats, puzzles, and pointing and naming tasks often included on tests. The same degree of familiarity cannot be assumed when evaluating a child from a low socioeconomic background.
- *The skills reflected by the test items may not be relevant to the skills demanded from children in low socioeconomic and/or culturally different environments.* "The tests, rather than assessing the disadvantaged child's ability, measure the extent to which such children have assimilated aspects of the dominant culture" (p. 164).

Issues in IQ testing are discussed more fully in Chapters 6 and 14.

The practice of placing children in special education programs for students with disabilities or giftedness solely because of their performance on standardized intelligence tests is rapidly disappearing. Past overreliance on IQ tests probably resulted in the inappropriate labeling and placement of many students from diverse cultural backgrounds; IQ tests do not present a fair or complete measure of the intelligence of culturally diverse students.

Hilliard (1975) called attention to sources of cultural bias in several widely used tests of cognitive ability. These tests appear to be based on the faulty premise that every child comes to the test with a similar background of life experiences. Hilliard cited the following examples of potentially unfair test items:

> On one test, a child must be familiar with such words as wasp, captain, hive, casserole, shears, cobbler, or hydrant. On another test, a child must know the distance from Boston to London [and] why icebergs melt. . . . The child, in order to get the answers correct, must assume that women are weak and need protection, that policemen are always nice, that labor laws are just. How is the examiner to distinguish ignorance from disagreement? (p. 22)

A child's performance in testing situations may be heavily influenced by the environment and the examiner. Labov (1975) presents a case study of the verbal behavior of an 8-year-old African American child named Leon. When Leon was tested in school by a white interviewer who placed objects on a table and said, "Tell me everything you can about this," his response was minimal, consisting mostly of silence and one-word utterances. It appeared that Leon was functioning well below his age level and perhaps had a serious communication disorder or mental retardation. On another occasion, however, Leon was interviewed by an African American examiner who took him to an apartment in a familiar neighborhood, brought along Leon's best friend and a supply of potato chips, and sat down on the floor with the child. In this situation, Leon spoke much more fluently; he had a great deal to say to the adult and to his friend. Labov has also performed a detailed linguistic analysis of the nonstandard English used by many African American children and has concluded that traditional classroom tests and tasks have little relevance or accuracy. "There is no reason to believe that any nonstandard vernacular is in itself an obstacle to learning" (Labov, 1975, p. 127).

Although Labov's case study illustrates that one child responded differently to different examiners, we should not assume that the race, gender, or age of a teacher or examiner will inevitably affect a child's performance. Brown (1982) reviewed several studies of the effects of examiner race on the performance of culturally diverse children and found no general tendency of African American and Hispanic students to score higher or lower when tested by white, African American, or Hispanic examiners. Characteristics such as the examiner's "ability to evidence a warm, responsive, receptive, but firm style" were found to be more important than race or ethnic group in motivating children to do their best. "This does not preclude the possibility that ethnic or racial variables can influence performance, but it does suggest that to study race alone—without considering other interactional variables—is likely to be futile" (Brown, 1982, p. 165).

Ineffective Curriculum and Instruction

A third reason that disproportionate numbers of culturally diverse students are placed in special education may be because educators do not provide effective academic instruction to students from diverse backgrounds. "Traditional schools require conformity, passivity, quietness, teacher-focused activities, and individualized, competitive, noninteractive participation of students" (Shade & New, 1993, p. 318). The idea that curriculum and instructional strategies that are effective for white middle-class students will benefit all students has dominated American education (Winzer & Mazurek, 1998). However, since the context of a culturally diverse student's life is often different from a middle-class student's, the "sameness of treatment does not always equate with equality of treatment" (p. 126).

If the student's cognitive functions, learning styles, and communication modes do not conform to the traditional educational patterns, the student is likely to lag behind expected learning benchmarks. Educators who do not adapt the curriculum for the diversity in schools today will most likely perpetuate the referral of students into special education. If one believes that diverse cultures foster diverse learning styles, then providing a "one size fits all" instructional approach to education will most likely create a mismatch between the learners' style and the instructional style. For example, field-independent (analytical) students learn well through books, lectures, and worksheets. Field-dependent students (often members of underrepresented groups), on the other hand, learn best in context through hands-on, authentic tasks rather than out of context (Gollnick & Chinn, 1998; Ramirez & Castañeda, 1974). The teacher's own instructional style (especially if he comes from the dominant white, middle-class culture) may be incompatible with the natural learning styles of students from diverse cultural backgrounds. For example, Latino students may not respond well to timed tests and may fail to complete an examination within the allotted time. This does not mean that students from cultural backgrounds cannot, or should not, be taught to perform academic tasks at faster rates.

Further accentuating the problems between the traditional curriculum and culturally diverse students are the textbooks selected by teachers for instruction. Many educators do not evaluate the validity of a textbook's content. Yet the vast majority of all classroom activity is regulated by textbooks (Starr, 1989). "At least six forms of bias are found in classroom materials: invisibility of certain groups, stereotyping, selectivity and imbalance, unreality, fragmentation and isolation of non-dominant cultures, and linguistic bias" (Gollnick & Chinn, 1998, p. 322). Curriculum materials that do not reflect the images and voices of culturally diverse students may fail to engage such students in active classroom participation. Furthermore, teaching styles that clash with the unique characteristics of culturally diverse students will most likely result in referral to special education or discrimination and bias against students.

> The ultimate goal of multicultural education is to meet the individual learning needs of each student so that all students can progress to their fullest capacity. This goal has not been reached in the past, partly because educators have been unable to effectively use the cultural backgrounds of students in providing [appropriate curriculum materials] and classroom instruction. (Gollnick & Chinn, 1998, p. 331)

Check your ongoing understanding of Chapter 3 concepts by using the guided review module at http://www.prenhall.com/heward.

Understanding the complex issues related to the disproportionate numbers of culturally diverse students in special education requires that educators understand the problems with incongruence between a teacher's interactions with students and families from diverse cultures, the assessment and referral process in special education, and ineffective instructional practices. To better meet the needs of students with disabilities from culturally diverse backgrounds three areas should be addressed. First, school staff must become culturally responsive to students and families. Second, school staff must implement appropriate assessment strategies for determining the educational needs of culturally diverse students. Third, educators should implement culturally responsive practices that support a multicultural approach to curriculum and instruction.

Becoming a Culturally Responsive Educator

Before teachers and other school staff members can implement culturally responsive assessment, curriculum, and instructional procedures, they must develop self-awareness and an appreciation of diversity. The following story helps illustrate this idea.

> **A Non-Indian Story.**
> You are a "non-Indian." When you arrive in class, the "Indians" are all at the front of the room chatting with the teacher. She looks up. "Ah, the new student. Welcome! Have a seat. You're a non-Indian, aren't you? We were just talking about your people." The children turn to look at you. They giggle and whisper to each other. None of the people in the room look or sound like your family. You look around the room. No dolls in the beds

or pictures on the book covers have eyes or hair or noses like those of your family members. Only one of the pictures of faces on the bulletin board looks similar to yours. The bulletin board says "Thanksgiving: A Non-Indian Holiday" and has a grotesque picture of a non-Indian woman in Reeboks and a Pilgrim hat, holding a dead turkey in one hand and a machine gun in the other. Your classmates giggle when they look at the bulletin board. "Look at those funny shoes," they whisper. (You look down at your favorite pair of Reeboks and stuff your feet under your chair.)

"Now class, it's very important to remember that our non-Indian friends are not responsible for what their forefathers did. They stole our land and ruined our forests, but that was a long time ago. We're not going to talk about that today. Who knows what kind of houses non-Indians live in? Yes, that's right. They live in square houses with red tile roofs. Who lives in these houses? Mother and father and sister and brother. Yes, that is right. Grandmother? No; they don't live with their grandmothers like we do. They send their grandmothers to special places called retirement homes. Why? I don't know.

"Next week, during Thanksgiving, we'll have a unit on non-Indians. We'll all make a non-Indian town out of clay. It's called a suburb. Can you say suburb? Non-Indians sleep in separate rooms, and they have little houses to keep their cars in. Now this is a non-Indian hat." The teacher pulls out a Pilgrim's hat. "Non-Indians wore these when they first came to our land." (Clark, DeWolf, & Clark, 1992, pp. 4–9)

Teacher Awareness and Development

See "A Cultural Journey" later in this chapter.

To understand and appreciate fully the diversity that exists among the students and families that special educators serve, we must first understand and appreciate our own cultures. All cultures have built-in biases, and there are no right or wrong cultural beliefs. Cultural self-awareness is the bridge to learning about other cultures. "It is not possible to be truly sensitive to someone else's culture until one is sensitive to one's own and the impact that cultural customs, values, beliefs, and behaviors have on practice" (Lynch & Hanson, 1998, p. 39).

Self-awareness is the first step on the journey toward cross-cultural competence. Educators must also become aware of their own biases and prejudices: "Teachers are human beings who bring their cultural perspective, values, hopes, and dreams to the classroom. They also bring their prejudices, stereotypes, and misconceptions to the classroom. The teacher's values and perspective mediate and interact with the teacher and influence the way that messages are communicated and perceived by their students" (Banks, 1994b, p. 159).

Fortunately, multicultural education is becoming a required component in many teacher education programs, and educators are learning how to become more accepting and supportive of cultural differences. As a measure of their beliefs about culture and its importance to teaching, for example, both practicing and prospective teachers can complete an instrument such as the Multicultural Self-Report Inventory (Slade & Conoley, 1989) (see Figure 3.1). Items with a zero in the far lefthand

Having students teach one another about their ethnic, linguistic, and historical backgrounds is a good way to increase multicultural understanding and appreciation by teachers and students.

MULTICULTURAL SELF-REPORT INVENTORY

SA = Strongly Agree
MA = Moderately Agree
U = Undecided
MD = Moderately Disagree
SD = Strongly Disagree

			SA	MA	U	MD	SD
	1.	I am interested in exploring cultures different from my own.	1	2	3	4	5
(–)	2.	I have enough experience with cultures different from my own.	1	2	3	4	5
(0)	3.	I seem to like some cultures and ethnic groups better than others.	1	2	3	4	5
(–)	4.	Part of the role of a good teacher is to encourage children to adopt middle class values.	1	2	3	4	5
(–)	5.	I feel that cultural differences in students do not affect students' behavior in school.	1	2	3	4	5
(–)	6.	As students progress through school, they should adopt the mainstream culture.	1	2	3	4	5
	7.	I am comfortable around people whose cultural background is different from mine.	1	2	3	4	5
	8.	I can identify attitudes of my own that are peculiar to my culture.	1	2	3	4	5
	9.	I believe I can recognize attitudes or behaviors in children that are a reflection of cultural or ethnic differences.	1	2	3	4	5

Figure 3.1 Multicultural Self-Report Inventory

"Never judge another man until you have walked a mile in his moccasins." This North American Indian proverb suggests the importance of understanding the cultural background and experiences of other persons rather than judging them by our own standards (Gollnick & Chinn, 1994, p. 8).

column have no positive or negative relevance and are included to lessen the probability of giving answers just because they are socially acceptable. Items with a minus are scored negatively. The lower the score, the more accepting and supportive the person's attitude about cultural differences. A low score indicates less multicultural bias; a high score suggests greater discomfort with the concept. Slade and Conoley describe several activities that are part of a two-week module used in a preservice teacher-training course designed to develop positive attitudes toward cultural diversity in the classroom.

Once teachers are aware of their own ethnic attitudes, behaviors, and perceptions, they can begin an action program designed to change their behavior if necessary (Banks, 1994b) and gain knowledge about other cultures. Methods for gathering information about cultures include but are not limited to reading books, searching the Internet, studying ethnograms, and interviewing cultural informants (persons from a particular culture who are familiar with families' beliefs and patterns). Teachers can increase their understanding and appreciation of different ethnic and cultural groups by studying the following concepts (Banks, 1994a, pp. 53–58):

- Origins and immigration
- Shared culture, values, and symbols

		SA	MA	U	MD	SD
	10. I feel I can take the point of view of a child from a different culture.	1	2	3	4	5
(–)	11. It makes me uncomfortable when I hear people talking in a language that I cannot understand.	1	2	3	4	5
(–)	12. Values and attitudes learned in minority cultures keep children from making progress in school.	1	2	3	4	5
(–)	13. Only people who are part of a culture can really understand and empathize with children from that culture.	1	2	3	4	5
(–)	14. I have had few cross-cultural experiences.	1	2	3	4	5
	15. Multicultural education is an important part of a school curriculum.	1	2	3	4	5
(0)	16. I am prejudiced in favor of some ethnic or cultural group or groups.	1	2	3	4	5
(–)	17. Some ethnic groups make less desirable citizens than others.	1	2	3	4	5
	18. Some ethnic groups are more reluctant to talk about family matters than other cultural groups.	1	2	3	4	5
	19. Children from differing ethnic groups are likely to differ in their attitudes toward teacher authority.	1	2	3	4	5
(–)	20. Personally, I have never identified any prejudice in myself.	1	2	3	4	5
(–)	21. I am prejudiced *against* some ethnic or cultural groups.	1	2	3	4	5
(–)	22. In the United States, given equal intelligence and physical ability, every individual has equal access to success.	1	2	3	4	5

Figure 3.1 *continued*

Source: From "Multicultural Experiences for Special Educators" by J. C. Slade & C. W. Conoley. *Teaching Exceptional Children, 22*(1), 1989, p. 62. © 1989 by the Council for Exceptional Children. Reprinted with permission.

- Ethnic identity and sense of peoplehood
- Perspectives, worldview, and frames of reference
- Ethnic institutions and self-determination
- Demographic, social, political, and economic status
- Prejudice, discrimination, and racism
- Intraethnic diversity
- Assimilation and acculturation
- Revolution
- Knowledge construction

Understanding Verbal and Nonverbal Communication Styles Another important aspect of teacher awareness and cultural competence involves understanding the patterns of verbal and nonverbal communication of ethnic groups. Although mainstream American teachers will probably not find it feasible to adopt the nonverbal behaviors of another culture, teacher-student and teacher-parent communication may be enhanced by some knowledge of the different significance attached to touch, interpersonal distance, silence, dress, and gestures.

It is important to note, however, that "simply recognizing ethnic and cultural diversity is not enough. Understanding and respect for diverse values, traditions, and

PROFILES AND PERSPECTIVES

A Cultural Journey

Culture is not just something that someone else has. All of us have cultural, ethnic, and linguistic heritages that influence our current beliefs, values, and behaviors. To learn more about your own heritage, take this simple cultural journey.

Origins

- When you think about your roots, what country(ies) other than the U.S. do you identify as a place of origin for you or your family?
- Have you ever heard any stories about how your family or your ancestors came to the U.S.? Briefly, what was the story?
- Do you or someone else prepare any foods that are traditional for your country(ies) of origin? What are they?
- Does your family continue to celebrate any celebrations, ceremonies, rituals, or holidays that reflect your country(ies) of origin? What are they? How are they celebrated?
- Do you or anyone else in your family speak a language other than English because of your origin? If so, what language?
- Can you think of one piece of advice that has been handed down through your family that reflects the values held by your ancestors in the country(ies) of origin? What is it?

Beliefs, Biases, and Behaviors

- Have you ever heard anyone make a negative comment about people from your country(ies) of origin?
- As you were growing up, do you remember discovering that your family did anything differently from other families because of your culture, religion, or ethnicity that seemed unusual to you?
- Have you ever been with someone in a work situation who did something because of his or her culture, religion, or ethnicity that seemed unusual to you? What was it? Why did it seem unusual?
- Have you ever felt shocked, upset, or appalled by something that you saw when you were traveling in another part of the world? If so, what was it? How did it make you feel? Pick some descriptive words to explain your feelings. How did you react? In retrospect, how do you wish you would have reacted?
- Have you ever done anything that you think was culturally inappropriate when you have been in another country or with someone from a different culture? In other words, have you ever done something that you think might have been upsetting or embarrassing to another person? What was it? What did you do to try to improve the situation?

Imagine

- If you could be from another culture or ethnic group, what culture would it be? Why?
- What is one value from that culture or ethnic group that attracts you to it?
- Is there anything about that culture or ethnic group that concerns or frightens you? What is it?
- Name one concrete way in which you think your life would be different if you were from that culture or ethnic group.

Source: Reprinted from Lynch, E., & Hanson, M. (1998). *Developing cross-cultural competence* (2nd ed., pp. 87–89). Published by Paul H. Brookes Publishing, P.O. Box 10624, Baltimore, MD 21285-0624. Used by permission of the publisher and the authors.

behaviors are essential if we are to fully actualize our nation's democratic ideals" (Banks, 1994b, p. 287).

Understanding Multicultural Terminology In preparing to work with culturally and linguistically diverse students and their families, school personnel must also have a common understanding of correct terminology for working with a diverse population. Many terms have been applied to members of culturally diverse populations. As we have learned elsewhere in this book, it is difficult to use labels effectively. Although labels can sometimes serve a useful purpose in identifying relevant factors, they are just as likely to convey misleading or inaccurate generalizations. This unfortunate effect is especially evident in several terms that have been used to refer to children from different cultural backgrounds.

An Ethnic Feelings Book

by B. A. Ford and C. Jones

The self-contained classroom for students with developmental disabilities consisted of four boys and eight girls from 9 to 12 years old. All of the children were African Americans. Their teacher, Charles Jones, was concerned about his students' self-perceptions and levels of self-esteem. Their informal verbal discussions about themselves, their aspirations, and their interpersonal interactions with each other were often negative. When frustrated academically or socially, the students frequently engaged in ethnic name calling, which was often associated with skin color and their African heritage (e.g., "You're black"; "I'm not black"; "You're like those dirty Africans"; "My ancestors don't come from Africa!"). Self-deprecating statements, such as "I'm crazy," were also heard. When asked, "What do you want to do for a living when you're an adult?" the children's responses typically involved sports, working in a fast-food restaurant, and motherhood, suggesting a limited view of future possibilities. Collectively, the students did not feel good about themselves, nor did they appear comfortable with their ethnicity. Difficulty in performing academic tasks seemed to reinforce their feelings of inadequacy in general and their negative perceptions of their ethnicity in particular.

Working with Bridgie Alexis Ford, a faculty member in special education at the University of Akron, Mr. Jones developed and implemented a cultural awareness project for his students. The project was designed to help the students learn factual information about the historic experiences and contributions of African Americans. Jones and Ford believed that as a result of learning about their ancestors' experiences and examining their own feelings about those experiences, the students would develop positive feelings about their ethnic heritage.

The cultural awareness unit took 30 to 45 minutes each day for 10 weeks and revolved around the creation of an ethnic feelings book. The feelings book included both factual information about African Americans and the students' interpretations of the feelings of their ancestors during various periods. The unit began with the positive aspects of African life before the slave-trade era, discussed slavery and segregation, identified actions by African Americans to create freedom and equal opportunity, and focused on the students' positive characteristics and capabilities. After covering each part of the unit, the students created another section of their feelings book. The emphasis throughout the unit was on highlighting positive aspects and contributions and dispelling negative stereotypes.

Historical information and personal accounts were presented via low-vocabulary, high-interest, well-illustrated books and filmstrips, recordings, and West African artifacts. African American leaders from the local community also visited the classroom and discussed their accomplishments and feelings with the students. These were some of the instructional activities that were part of the unit:

- *Brainstorming.* This helped the teachers acquire background information about what the students already knew about their African ancestors.
- *Adoption of a tribe.* Each student adopted one of the tribes portrayed in the books or filmstrips and prepared a report about it. The class selected one of the reports, edited it, and included it in the feelings book.
- *Discussions about negative terminology and stereotypes assigned to slaves.* Ethnic name calling was also discussed.
- *Segregation simulation.* At the beginning of one school day, half the class tied blue strings around their waists to designate themselves as segregated students (SS). Throughout the rest of that day, these students were treated in a discriminatory manner: they did not get to use recreational equipment during recess, they could not use the rest rooms at the times the non-SS students were using them, and they received no verbal attention or tangible reinforcement during normal class routines. The next day, the students switched roles so that everyone experienced the feelings of segregation.
- *Identification of positive attributes.* Positive characteristics of relatives and community leaders whom the students admired were discussed. The students submitted typed paragraphs describing their talents and interests and indicating the types of jobs they believed they could pursue.

The students exhibited a great deal of enthusiasm and cooperative behavior throughout the project. Name calling decreased; and when it did occur, the students began to reprimand one another.

Multicultural activities are often restricted to a special day or week during the school year. For students with developmental disabilities, Ford and Jones believe that an ongoing, systematic approach to cultural awareness is imperative.

Source: Adapted from Ford, B. A., & Jones, C. (1990). An ethnic feelings book: Created by students with developmental handicaps. *Teaching Exceptional Children, 22*(4), 36–39.

> *American Indian or Alaskan Native*—a person having origins in any of the original peoples of North America and who maintains cultural identification through tribal affiliation or community recognition.
>
> *Asian or Pacific Islander*—a person having origins in any of the original peoples of the Far East, Southeast Asia, the Pacific Islands, or the Indian subcontinent (e.g., China, India, Japan, Korea, the Philippine Islands, Samoa).
>
> *Hispanic*—a person of Mexican, Puerto Rican, Cuban, Central or South American, or other Spanish culture or origin, regardless of race.
>
> *Black* (not of Hispanic origin)—a person having origins in any of the black racial groups of Africa.
>
> *White* (not of Hispanic origin)—a person having origins in any of the original peoples of Europe, North Africa, or the Middle East.

Figure 3.2 Classification of racial groups according to the Office of Civil Rights

Source: From U.S. Office of Civil Rights. (1987). *1986 elementary and secondary school civil rights survey: National summaries.* Washington, DC: DBS.

In the United States, the term *minority* essentially represents an attempt to categorize by race, not by culture (Harry, 1992a). Figure 3.2 identifies the U.S. Office of Civil Rights' (1987) classification of racial groups. These classifications, however, do not address the common occurrence of mixed race origins. Furthermore, the term *minority* implies that the racial group being referred to constitutes a recognizable minority in society. Yet in many communities and regions of the country, "minorities" constitute the predominant population. An African American child in Detroit, a Hispanic child in Miami, or a Navajo child on a reservation in Arizona could be considered part of a minority only in respect to the national population, a comparison that would have little relevance to the child's immediate environment. The *majority* of students now enrolled in the 25 largest public school systems in the United States are from ethnically diverse "minority" groups (Zawaiza, 1995). In addition to suggesting that the population of the group is small, the term *minority group* carries some "negative connotations of being less than other groups with respect to power, status, and treatment" (Chinn & Kamp, 1982, p. 383).

The term *culturally diverse* is preferred when referring to children whose backgrounds are different enough to require, at times, special methods of assessment, instruction, intervention, or counseling. This term implies no judgment of a culture's value and does not equate cultural diversity with disability. Furthermore, the names used to describe ethnic groups have also changed. *Asian American* has replaced *Oriental; African American* has replaced *black; Latino* in some parts of the country has replaced *Hispanic;* and specific tribal names, rather than *Native American,* are preferred. It is important for special educators to respect and keep up with changes that represent increasing group identity and empowerment (Lynch & Hanson, 1998).

More information about families can be found by accessing the Resources Module for Chapter 3 at http://www.prenhall.com/heward and the Special Ed Resource Page.

Working with Culturally and Linguistically Diverse Families

Family involvement in the educational process is important for students' success in school. The positive influence of parental involvement on children's academic achievement and school adjustment should be of great concern to school staff. A strong correlation between parental involvement in school and the at-risk child's development of self-confidence, motivation, and sense of cohesiveness is evident in the literature (Henderson, Marburger, & Odom, 1986; Hidalgo, Siu, Bright, Swap, & Epstein, 1995; Reynolds, 1992). Furthermore, Rumberger, Ghatak, Polous, Ritter, and

Dornbush (1990) reported that families of students who did not drop out and who succeeded in school participated in their children's school decisions, demonstrated a motivating and nonpunitive action concerning grades, and were involved to different degrees within the school environment.

Involving families who come from diverse backgrounds in school activities is often challenging. Often the demands and challenges faced by families who are less educated, poor, or isolated from the mainstream American culture prevent them from becoming actively involved in school partnerships. The literature on culturally diverse families supports the following six notions about these families (Correa, 1992; Harry, 1992b; Lynch & Hanson, 1998; Thomas, Correa, & Morsink, 1995):

The parent-professional partnership is examined in detail in Chapter 4.

1. *Many families may be potentially English proficient, less well educated, have low socioeconomic status, or be undocumented immigrants.* Thus, practitioners should provide materials in both the native and English language and preferably communicate with the family directly through home visits or by telephone. Some parents are not able to read their native language and may depend on older children who are English-dominant to translate materials for them.

2. *Practitioners must understand that although the parents may not have finished school or are unable to read, they are "life educated" and know their child better than anyone else does.* In Spanish, the term *educado* (educated) does not mean "formal schooling" but means that a child is skilled in human relations, well mannered, respectful of adults, and well behaved.

3. *If families are suspected to be undocumented immigrants, they are naturally fearful of interaction with anyone representing authority.* Our role as special educators is not to engage in the activities of the Office of Immigration and Naturalization Services. Our focus is on educating children who, by law, are *not a suspect class* (Correa, Gollery, & Fradd, 1988). Building families' trust and cooperation, even if they are undocumented immigrants, is important.

4. *Families from culturally diverse backgrounds tend to be family-oriented.* Extended family members—*compadres* or *padrinos* (godparents) in the Hispanic culture—may play important roles in child rearing and family decisions. A child's disability or even a mild language problem may be an extremely personal subject for discussion with outsiders, and solutions for problems may lie within the family structure. It is important for educators to respect this informal kinship system of support and to understand that we may represent a much more formal and impersonal support service for these families. Dunst, Trivette, and Deal (1988) contend that this close, insular aspect in a family is a strength that assists the family in functioning and coping with the stresses sometimes associated with raising a child with a disability.

5. *It is important to know that culturally diverse families may have different experiences and views about disability, and some may hold idiosyncratic ideologies and practices about the cause and treatment of disability.* For example, in some Hispanic cultures, parents may believe that God sent the child with disabilities to them as a gift or blessing, while others may believe the child was sent as a test or a punishment for previous sins. In a recent study by Bailey, Skinner, Rodrigues, and Correa (in press), Latino families acknowledged transforming their lives since the birth of their child by becoming better parents. Most families were positive in describing the child with disabilities, and very few reported the presence of the child with disabilities as a negative sign or punishment from God for sins. The role of faith in God was extremely important for families coping with the child, more so than formal religious activities such as church attendance or Bible studies (Bailey et al., in press). Interestingly, among many Native American groups, it is not considered negative or tragic to have a child born with a disability: "It is assumed the child has the

The role religion plays in supporting families of children with disabilities has been documented by other researchers (Fewell, 1986; Haworth, Hill, & Gillen, 1996; Heller, Markwardt, Rowitz, & Farber, 1994; Rogers-Dulan, 1998; Weisner, Beizer, Stolze, 1991).

Culture is only one influence on a family's reaction to having a child with a disability. Other influences, such as financial status, intactness of the family, external and internal support systems, and coping mechanisms, must also be considered (Correa, 1992; Harry, 1992a, b; Lynch & Hanson, 1998).

prenatal choice of how he wishes to be born and, if [disabled], is so by choice" (Stewart, 1977, p. 439).

Although previous literature has reported the existence of folk beliefs and alternative treatments for disabilities in some cultural groups, Bailey et al. (in press) did not find this prevalent in the Latino families they studied. Families did report knowing about *el mal ojo* (the evil eye) or *el susto* (a scare or fright experienced by the pregnant mother) as explanations given for disabilities but did not believe them to be true of their own children with disabilities. They reported that some family members (usually the elders) might believe that, to cure the child, the family must make *mandas* (offerings to God or a Catholic saint) or seek the help of a *curandero* (a local healer). However, almost all families interviewed used traditional western medicine to treat the child with disabilities.

6. *The educational system—in particular, the special education system—may be extremely intimidating to the family.* Although this may be true for many white families as well, for the family from a non-English language background or one that is less well educated and poor, professionals' use of educational language and jargon, their nonverbal communication, and possible insensitivity may be especially intimidating. Furthermore, parents with disabilities may also find themselves just as disenfranchised from their child's special education program, often not wanting to engage in any school-home interaction. Some families may even put the professional on a pedestal and, believing the professional is the expert, not question or comment on their own wishes for their child's education.

Florian (1987) states that ethnically diverse parents of children with disabilities have seldom used the modern idea of consumer involvement in service delivery. Parents or caregivers may not participate in a partnership with us because (for example) parent education groups do not address their needs or the ways in which we educate and propose solutions to child rearing issues may be inappropriate or impractical for the culturally diverse family.

Christensen (1992) advised that teachers should understand a broad range of families' cultural aspects. She reported that the top 12 areas that teachers thought were necessary for understanding families from culturally diverse backgrounds included the following:

- General understanding of culture
- Child rearing practices
- Family patterns
- Views of exceptionality
- Availability and use of community resources
- Linguistic differences
- Acknowledging own culture and biases
- Beliefs about professionals
- Nonverbal communication styles
- Views of medical practices

A culturally responsive educator strives to develop awareness of and sensitivity for the beliefs and values held by parents and family members from different cultural groups.

- Sex roles
- Religion

Additionally, Dennis and Giangreco (1996) advised that teachers should understand a broad range of families' cultural aspects. A good way to gain knowledge and an understanding of family values and priorities for a child with disabilities is to conduct family interviews. Dennis and Giangreco suggest that professionals seek help from cultural interpreters before the interview and carefully ascertain the literacy and language status of family members. In conducting the interview, professionals should be prepared to adapt the time frame to meet the needs of the family and to be flexible and responsive to the family's interaction style.

Appropriate Assessment of Culturally Diverse Students

Alternative, nonstandardized methods of assessment with multiple criteria seem to be more appropriate and effective for some ethnic and linguistically diverse students. Alternative assessment models integrate a variety of measures and data collection methods (e.g., observations, self-reports, checklists, portfolios, inventories, curriculum-based assessment). This approach provides teachers with relevant and useful information regarding student performance and is valuable in making appropriate instructional decisions (Baca & Cervantes, 1998; Fradd & McGee, 1994; Gollnick & Chinn, 1998; Hamayan & Damico, 1991). For example, Rueda (1997) identifies several types of portfolios that can be used as the basis for collecting and examining achievement as well as meeting the accountability demands usually achieved by more formal testing procedures (p. 13):

1. *Student portfolios* inform the student and document self-reflection.
2. *Working portfolios* are designed for the teacher's daily use and as a primary tool for developing and modifying instruction on a short-term basis.
3. *Showcase portfolios* inform the parents and surrounding educational community.
4. *Cumulative portfolios* are designed for accountability and evaluative purposes.

Furthermore, alternative assessment allows for exploration of the numerous factors and confounding variables (e.g., environmental deprivation, poverty, health problems, language and cultural differences) that affect the performance of culturally diverse students and that could result in a misdiagnosis.

Ishil-Jordan (1997) states that behavior is culture-related; and when there is "a great disparity between a cultural interpretation of a child's behavior and the school's interpretation of that behavior, there is also likely to be a disagreement on how that behavior is viewed and handled" (p. 30). Along with objective observation and recording of behavior, a child's social and cultural background should be taken into account when assessing performance. What is normal and acceptable in a child's culture may be regarded as abnormal or unacceptable in school and may result in conflict, mislabeling, or punishment.

See "Refugee Children from Vietnam" later in this chapter.

Gallimore, Boggs, and Jordan (1974) offer the example of several native Hawaiian children who sought help from other children on tests and tasks and seemed to pay little attention to the teacher. This behavior was interpreted as cheating and inattentiveness. Closer observation of the children's home and community environments, however, revealed that the Hawaiian children were typically peer-oriented. It was normal for them to share in the responsibility of caring for each other, and they often worked cooperatively on tasks rather than following the directions of an adult. Some Asian American students internalize their reactions to environmental and intrapersonal stimuli by not expressing how they are feeling or demonstrating nega-

PROFILES AND PERSPECTIVES

Refugee Children from Vietnam: Adjusting to American Schools

Tam Thi Dang Wei is a school psychologist who is Vietnamese. Wei points out that many Vietnamese refugee children encounter emotional, social, and educational problems in the United States because of different cultural traditions and expectations. The following incidents illustrate some cross-cultural difficulties that have arisen as Vietnamese students and American schools adjust to each other. Wei interprets each incident.

Incident: A Vietnamese girl in the 10th grade in Missouri reportedly refused to go to her gym class. When the gym teacher asked for a valid reason, the girl simply said she did not like gym. Only much later did the real reason appear. She revealed to a Vietnamese friend that she objected to being seen bare-legged wearing gym shorts.

Interpretation: Coming from a region of Vietnam where old customs and traditions were still strong and where women, both young and old, were never seen bare-legged, this girl confessed to an intense feeling of discomfort during gym class. To add a sense of measure to this interesting case, however, we must also consider the case of two Vietnamese high school girls, one in Georgia and the other in Maryland, who were drum majorettes for their respective high school bands.

Incident: An 8-year-old Vietnamese boy in an elementary school in Maryland complained of a stomach ache every day after lunch. His teacher was mystified because the same food and milk did not make any other child in the class sick. The cause was later identified to be the fresh milk, which was perfectly good but to which the boy's digestive system was not accustomed.

Interpretation: Food habits are different from one culture to the next. Rice is a staple in the Vietnamese diet, whereas bread is a staple in the American diet. Pork is preferred to beef by most Vietnamese; the reverse is true in the United States. Fresh milk is likely to give some Vietnamese an upset stomach. They are used to boiled rather than homogenized milk, and their bodies are said not to produce the necessary enzyme to digest fresh milk.

Incident: A teacher thought his Vietnamese student had an auditory discrimination problem. He found out later that some sounds in the English language do not exist in the Vietnamese language. The student simply could not hear them and thus could not pronounce them correctly. Another teacher was surprised to see a Vietnamese child color pictures of eggs brown and cows yellow. The surprise turned into laughter when a Vietnamese friend told the teacher that Vietnamese eggs are brown in color and that there are more yellow cows in Vietnam than black or brown cows.

Interpretation: The language problem is still a major handicap for students. It is complicated further by the cultural trait of face saving, which affects the pride and self-esteem of the Vietnamese and causes them frustration and a loss of motivation. It is important that American teachers understand the consequence of failure for these students.

Refugee children are a unique challenge for educators not only because they can be misdiagnosed, misclassified, or misunderstood but also because they may not receive appropriate services when they indeed have disabling conditions.

Source: Adapted from Wei, T. T. D. (1983). The Vietnamese refugee child: Understanding cultural differences. In D. R. Omark & J. G. Erickson (Eds.), *The bilingual exceptional child* (pp. 197–212). San Diego: College-Hill. Used by permission.

tive emotions. Educators might interpret this behavior negatively as docile and unhealthy.

Nondiscriminatory assessment requires that decisions be based on varied and accurate information. Building rapport with children before testing them; observing their behavior in school, home, and play settings; and consulting with their parents can help teachers and examiners become more aware of cultural differences and reduce the number of students inappropriately placed in special education programs. Paraprofessional personnel or volunteers who are familiar with a child's language and/or cultural background have proven to be valuable assistants in many testing situations (Mattes & Omark, 1984).

Attention to Language As Brown (1982) notes, limited use of language is not synonymous with limited intellectual ability: "Some culturally different children are virtually silent in the testing situation, and the examiner may need to listen to the child in play with other children to hear a representative sample of the child's language" (p. 170). Standardized tests in English are not likely to give an accurate picture of a child's abilities if he comes from a non-English-speaking home. "If the student's primary language is Spanish, Navajo, or Thai, the only justification for testing in English is to determine the student's facility in this second language" (Lewis & Doorlag, 1991, p. 361).

IDEA specifies that assessment for the purpose of identifying and placing children with disabilities must be conducted in the child's native language. Figueroa, Fradd, and Correa (1989), however, point out a serious flaw in the way the law can be implemented:

IDEA also requires that notice of IEP and placement meetings and other important conferences be given to parents in their native language.

> A curious and perhaps vicious anomaly exists between the law and its regulations. Whereas the actual legislation defines "native language" as the language of the home, . . . the regulations degenerate the intent of the law by defining "native language" as the language normally used by the child in school. Most bilingual children quickly acquire a conversational English that may not support academic development in English. For them, the regulations in P.L. 94–142 preclude any primary language support. As it has turned out, the act's brand of special education for Hispanic children from native language homes has perpetuated preexisting problems. (p. 175)

Unfortunately, when an examiner does wish to use the child's native language, few reliable tests are available in languages other than English, and translation or adaptation of tests into other languages poses certain problems (Cummins, 1989). Alzate (1978), for example, reviewed several studies of the performance of Spanish-speaking children on translated versions of English tests and concluded that translated tests are generally unreliable. DeAvila (1976) points out the great variety in language within Hispanic populations and notes that when Mexican American children were given a test in Spanish that was developed with a population of Puerto Rican children, they performed even more poorly than on an admittedly unfair English test. To illustrate the confusion that may result from inappropriate translations, DeAvila observes that a Spanish-speaking child may use any one of several words to describe a kite, depending on the family's country of origin: *cometa, huila, volantin, papalote,* or *chiringa.* Thus, although translation of tests and other materials into a child's native language may be helpful in many instances, care must be taken to avoid an improper translation that may actually do a disservice to the linguistically different child.

It is not always easy to distinguish between children whose learning and communication problems result from disabilities and those who are solely in need of instruction in English. The high number of language-minority students in special education classes, however, implies a need for tests and referral procedures that will "help teachers to distinguish differences from exceptionalities for language minority students" and to accommodate the differences in the least restrictive educational setting (Teacher Education Division, 1986, p. 25).

Language-proficiency tests coupled with an analysis of real or authentic conversational factors provide the opportunity to assess communicative competence. Figure 3.3 provides a checklist for assessment of communicative competence skills in four areas: grammatical competence, sociolinguistic competence, discourse competence, and strategic competence.

Avoiding Discrimination and Bias Bias and discrimination can also occur in the referral process, when children's records are reviewed and decisions are made about what type of services to provide. In the opinion of some educators, a child's race, family background, and economic circumstances—rather than actual performance and needs—unfairly influence the label she is likely to receive and the degree to which she will be removed from the regular classroom.

The prereferral process shown in Figure 3.4 was initially developed by Ortiz and Garcia (1988) as a means of making sure that curriculum and instruction are responsive to the linguistic and cultural needs of Hispanic students who are experiencing difficulty in the regular classroom *before* they are referred for formal assessment to determine special education placement. Although the model was presented in reference to Spanish-speaking students, it is a sound approach to improving the quality of regular education for any student who is experiencing academic difficulty. By systematically addressing the questions as illustrated in the model, both special and regular

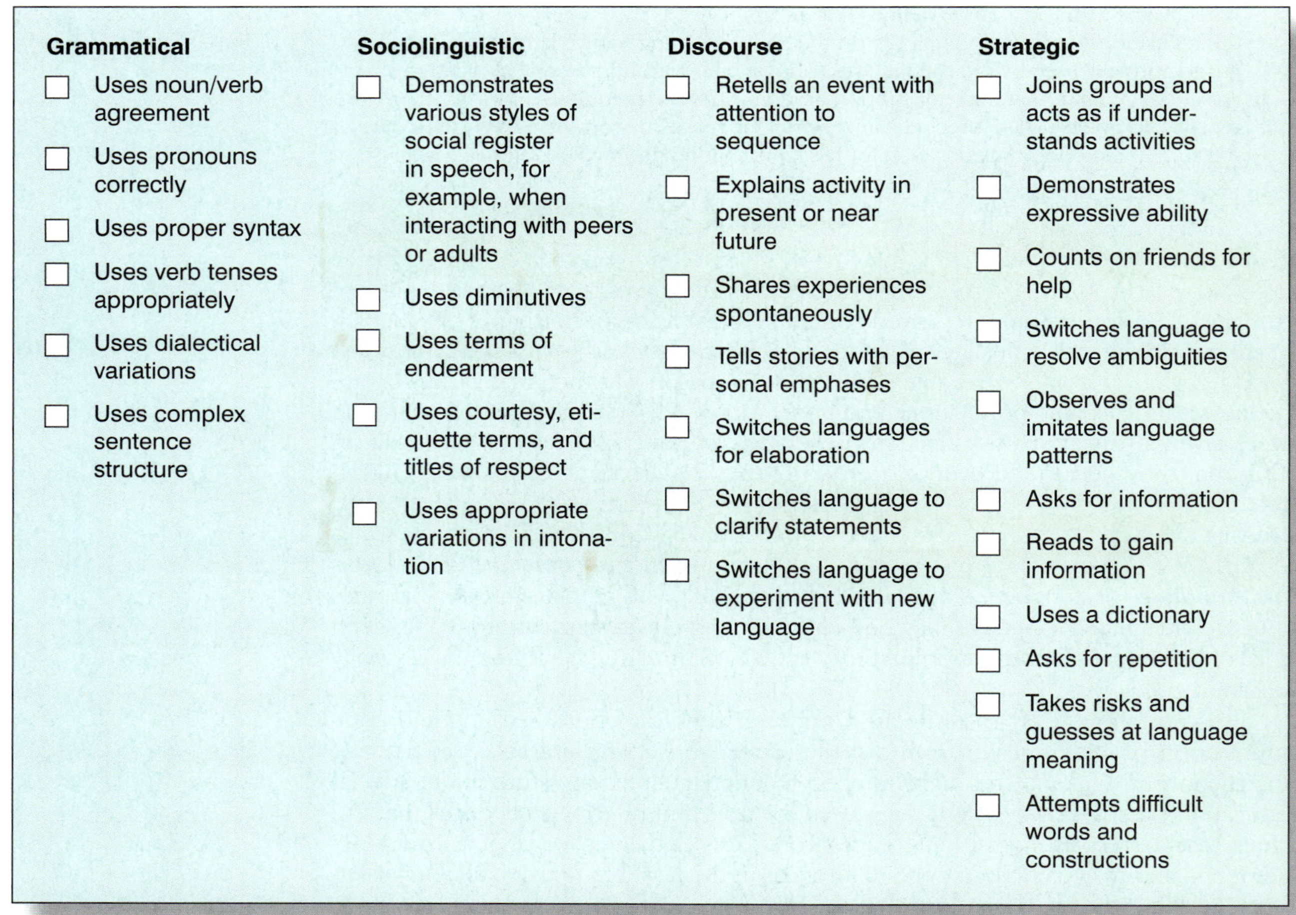

Grammatical

- ☐ Uses noun/verb agreement
- ☐ Uses pronouns correctly
- ☐ Uses proper syntax
- ☐ Uses verb tenses appropriately
- ☐ Uses dialectical variations
- ☐ Uses complex sentence structure

Sociolinguistic

- ☐ Demonstrates various styles of social register in speech, for example, when interacting with peers or adults
- ☐ Uses diminutives
- ☐ Uses terms of endearment
- ☐ Uses courtesy, etiquette terms, and titles of respect
- ☐ Uses appropriate variations in intonation

Discourse

- ☐ Retells an event with attention to sequence
- ☐ Explains activity in present or near future
- ☐ Shares experiences spontaneously
- ☐ Tells stories with personal emphases
- ☐ Switches languages for elaboration
- ☐ Switches language to clarify statements
- ☐ Switches language to experiment with new language

Strategic

- ☐ Joins groups and acts as if understands activities
- ☐ Demonstrates expressive ability
- ☐ Counts on friends for help
- ☐ Switches language to resolve ambiguities
- ☐ Observes and imitates language patterns
- ☐ Asks for information
- ☐ Reads to gain information
- ☐ Uses a dictionary
- ☐ Asks for repetition
- ☐ Takes risks and guesses at language meaning
- ☐ Attempts difficult words and constructions

Figure 3.3 Checklist for skills that illustrate communicative competencies

Source: From "From Tests to Talking in the Classroom: Assessing Communicative Competence" by G. Zamora-Durán & E. Reyes. In A. Artiles & G. Zamora-Durán (Eds.), *Reducing Disproportionate Representation of Culturally Diverse Students in Special and Gifted Education* (1997, pp. 51). Reston, VA: Council for Exceptional Children. © 1997 by the Council for Exceptional Children. Reprinted with permission.

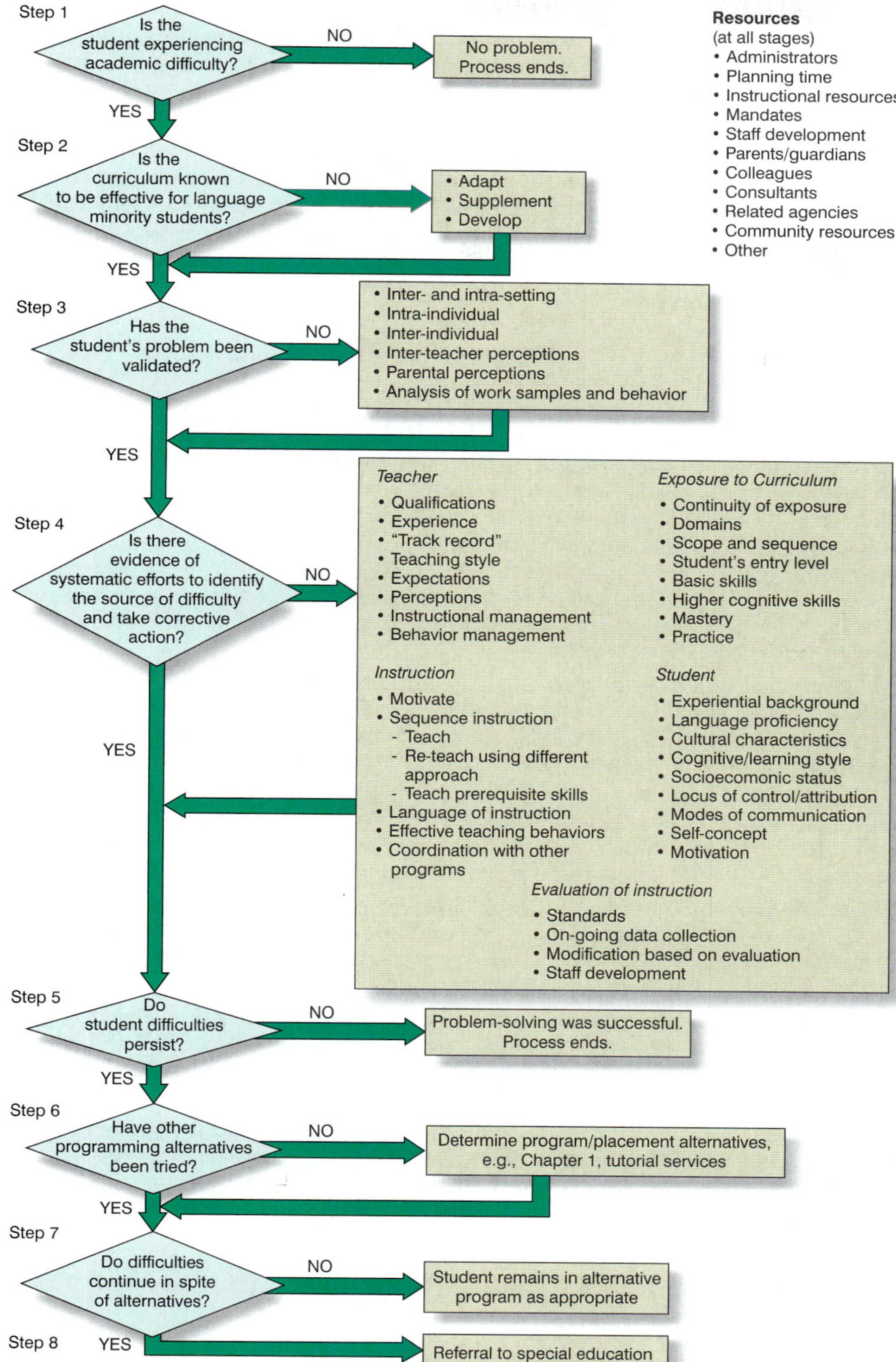

Figure 3.4 A prereferral process for preventing inappropriate placements of culturally diverse students in special education

Source: From "A Prereferral Process for Preventing Inappropriate Placements of Culturally Diverse Students in Special Education" by A. A. Ortiz & S. B. Garcia. In A. A. Ortiz & B. A. Ramirez (Eds.), *Schools and the Culturally Diverse Exceptional Student: Promising Practices and Future Directions* (1988, p. 9). Reston, VA: Council for Exceptional Children. © 1988 by the Council for Exceptional Children. Reprinted with permission.

educators can work together to improve the student's performance in the mainstream classroom before moving him to a more restrictive environment.

Ortiz (1991a, 1991b) further developed and evaluated the efficacy of the model by addressing the issues of prereferral, assessment, and intervention of students from non-English language background. The Assessment and Intervention Model for the Bilingual Exceptional Student (AIM for the BESt) model is a comprehensive service delivery model that was pilot-tested in four elementary schools in central Texas. Two of the schools served as intervention sites; two served as comparison or control sites. The steps and features of the AIM for the BESt model are listed in Figure 3.5.

The Assessment and Intervention Model for the Bilingual Exceptional Student (AIM for the BESt) describes a service delivery system designed to (1) improve the academic performance of limited English proficient (LEP) students in regular and special education programs, (2) reduce the inappropriate referral of LEP students to special education, and (3) ensure that assessment produces are nonbiased. AIM for the BESt consists of six major steps:

Step 1: The regular classroom teacher uses instructional strategies known to be effective for language-minority students. The project staff trained general, bilingual, and special education teachers on using a reciprocal interaction approach to oral and written communication that emphasized higher-order thinking and problem solving. In particular, the teachers were introduced to the shared literature (Roser & Firth, 1983) and writing workshop approaches (Graves, 1983).

Step 2: When a student experiences difficulty, the teacher attempts to resolve the difficulty and validates the problem. The project staff trained the teachers in diagnostic/prescriptive approaches that included sequencing instruction by (a) observing and analyzing student performance to design instructional programs, (b) implementing the program, (c) monitoring the progress, and (d) redesigning instruction as necessary.

Step 3: If the problem is not resolved, the teacher requests assistance from a school-based, problem-solving team. The project staff, teachers, and support personnel formed cooperative teams to assist teachers with student-related problems by developing interventions and follow-up plans to resolve the difficulties.

Step 4: If the problem is not resolved by the school-based, problem-solving team, a special education referral is initiated. The team's records describing the intervention plans from Step 3 accompanied the referral for special education services. The records were beneficial in assisting the referral team in designing appropriate evaluations and making recommendations.

Step 5: Assessment personnel incorporate informal assessment procedures into the comprehensive individual assessment. Project staff trained personnel in using alternative assessment instruments and strategies to support standardized testing. In particular, curriculum-based assessment in both the native language and English were used with the students.

Step 6: If the child had a disability, special educators used instructional strategies known to be effective for language-minority students. Special education teachers used the reciprocal interactive strategies for instruction. The holistic strategies described in Step 1 also included (a) encouraging expression of students' experiences, language background, and interests to foster success and pride and (b) peer collaboration and peer approval.

Figure 3.5 The AIM for the BESt model for culturally diverse students

Source: Adapted from Ortiz, A. A., & Wilkinson, C. Y. (1991). Assessment and Intervention Model for the Bilingual Exceptional Student (AIM for the BESt). *Teacher Education and Special Education, 14,* 35–42. Used by permission.

Culturally Responsive Curriculum and Instruction

Culturally and linguistically diverse students come to school with rich and complex cultural backgrounds that may be influenced by the family, home, and local community. Culturally responsive educators struggle with the balance between accepting and respecting the unique characteristics of students from diverse backgrounds and preparing them for postschool environments in the mainstream American culture. In fact, Brower (1983) suggests that culturally and linguistically diverse students may need to be taught about American expectations and values so that they can become more forthright and assertive in educational and employment situations.

A Culturally Responsive Pedagogy

To join in the discussion on "What initial steps can a teacher take to become culturally responsive?" go to the Message Board Module at http://www.prenhall.com/heward.

Culturally responsive instructional practices enhance students' opportunities to reach their fullest potential. The need for a culturally responsive pedagogy is even more critical when referring to culturally diverse students with disabilities (Moll, 1992). The place to begin to prepare students for the real world is the classroom. Teachers can begin to balance respect for one's culture and preparedness for postschool settings by accommodating and adapting their instructional programs and curricula and by adopting a culturally responsive pedagogy. Correa et al. (1995) describe the characteristics of a culturally responsive pedagogy:

- *Context-embedded instruction.* Context-embedded instruction facilitates the development of responsive classroom environments for all children by providing meaningful content that is culturally responsive and that uses students' experiences as tools for building further knowledge (Baca & Cervantes, 1998; Bennett, 1990; Cummins, 1989; Scarcella, 1990). Delpit (1995) reported that African American teachers who successfully taught mathematics to African American students who speak a dialect confirmed that the use of cultural context and students' prior experience is essential in helping students learn. In one case, Delpit found that students connected with mathematics problems that related to a familiar locale and the amount of money needed to buy a leather jacket more than to a problem that involved unfamiliar locales and the number of milk cans needed by a farmer.
- *Content-rich curriculum.* Researchers have shown that students who receive instruction within a content-rich curriculum develop a positive attitude about learning, a heightened self-concept, and pride in their culture (Duran, 1988; Scarcella, 1990). In addition, a content-rich curriculum should be integrated across broad fields of subject matter. For example, Gonzalez, Brusca-Vega, and Yawkey (1997) describe the P.I.A.G.E.T. programs, where preK–12 teachers incorporate all subject matter around the thematic units of self, family, living things, and transportation. The orientation provides meaningful experiences from multiple perspectives focused on a unitary set of common learning (e.g., transportation). The classroom becomes a "mosaic of students' personalities along with their social, emotional and cultural overlays" (p. 87).
- *Equitable pedagogy.* An equitable pedagogy, which varies according to students' needs and teachers' styles, focuses on providing an appropriate educational experience for all children regardless of their disability or ethnolinguistic background. Instructional practices that facilitate and promote academic success among students within a pluralistic and democratic setting allow students to

Teachers are most effective when curriculum content and instructional methods are responsive to the cultural, ethnic, and linguistic diversity among their students.

develop positive ethnic and national identifications (Villegas, 1988). In fact, Banks (1994a) advocates for a "*transformative curriculum* that challenges the basic assumptions and implicit values of the Eurocentric, male-dominated curriculum institutionalized in U.S. schools, colleges, and universities. It helps students to view concepts, events, and situations from diverse racial, ethnic, gender, and social-class perspectives. The transformative curriculum also helps students to construct their own interpretations of the past, present, and future" (p. 103).

Siccone (1995) describes more than 75 multicultural activities to enhance self-worth, self-respect, and self-confidence in K–8 students.

- *Interactive and experiential teaching.* Interactive and experiential teaching approaches have been reported by researchers to promote feelings of responsibility, self-pride, and belongingness in diverse learners (Obiakor, Algozzine, & Ford, 1993; Voltz & Damiano-Lantz, 1993). This hands-on approach empowers learners as they share the responsibility for the learning process while teachers provide guidance in the construction of knowledge.
- *Classroom materials and school environment.* Classroom materials and school environment should reflect students' diverse backgrounds (Freeman & Freeman, 1993). Materials selected on the basis of their content and their relevance and significance to the student's cultural background generate a more meaningful and student-centered learning experience.

The BUENO Center for Multicultural Education at the University of Colorado is an excellent source of materials and information for building cultural awareness in students with disabilities. See "For More Information" at the end of this chapter.

Bilingual Special Education

It is especially challenging for students who are both linguistically different and disabled to succeed in school. Not only must they work to overcome the difficulties posed by their disability, but they also must do so in an environment in which instruction occurs in a foreign language and opportunities to use their native language are infrequent. For these children, a program of bilingual special education may be needed. Baca and Cervantes (1998) define bilingual special education as

> the use of the home language and the home culture along with English in an individually designed program of special instruction for the student in an inclusive environment. Bilingual special education considers the child's language and culture as foundations upon which an appropriate education may be built. The primary purpose of bilingual special education is to help each individual student achieve a maximum potential for learning. (p. 21)

Some people object to bilingual special education on the basis that it is too much to ask special educators, who already face the difficult task of teaching basic skills to a child with a disability, to also teach in a second language. Baca and Cervantes (1998) reply that the opposite is true:

> The imparting of basic skills may be facilitated considerably if one understands that the child's culture and language are the foundations upon which an appropriate education may be built. . . . Building on children's existing knowledge base is fundamental to sound educational practice. In actuality, Anglo cultural skills and English are the new subject matters for the linguistically or culturally different child. (p. 21)

Most general bilingual education programs emphasize either a *transitional* or a *maintenance* approach. In a transitional program, the student's first language and culture are used only to the extent necessary to function in the school until English is mastered sufficiently for all instruction. Transitional programs are an assimilationist approach in which the limited English proficient (LEP) student is expected to learn to function in English as soon as possible (Gollnick & Chinn, 1998). The home language is used only to help the student make the transition to English. The native language is gradually phased out as the student learns to speak English.

The maintenance approach to bilingual education, however, helps the LEP student function in both the native language and English, encouraging the student to become bilingual and bicultural in the process. Cummins (1989) stresses the importance of encouraging children to develop their first language (L1) skills. He cites several studies suggesting that a major predictor of academic success for linguistically different students is the extent to which their native language and culture are incor-

Figure 3.6 lists several specific strategies by which school staff can create a climate for promoting children's use of their first language (L1).

- Reflect the various cultural groups in the school district by providing signs in the main office and elsewhere that welcome people in the different languages of the community.
- Encourage students to use their L1 around the school.
- Provide opportunities for students from the same ethnic group to communicate with one another in their L1.
- Recruit people who can tutor students in their L1.
- Provide books written in the various languages in the classroom and in the school library.
- Incorporate greetings and information in the various languages in newsletters and other school communications.
- Provide bilingual and multilingual signs.
- Display pictures and objects of the various cultures in the school.
- Create study units that incorporate the students' L1.
- Encourage students to write contributions in their L1 for school newspapers and magazines.
- Provide opportunities for students to study their L1 in elective subjects and in extracurricular clubs.
- Encourage parents to help in the classroom, library, playground, and in clubs.
- Invite second-language learners to use their L1 during assemblies and other official school functions.
- Invite people from ethnic minority communities to act as resource people and to speak to students in both formal and informal settings.

Figure 3.6 Strategies for encouraging children to develop proficiency in their first language (L1)

Source: From New Zealand Department of Education. (1988). *New Voices: Second Language Learning and Teaching: A Handbook for Primary Teachers*. Wellington: Author; cited in "A Theoretical Framework for Bilingual Special Education" by J. Cummins. *Exceptional Children, 56,* 1989, pp. 113–114. © 1989 by the Council for Exceptional Children. Reprinted with permission.

porated into the school program. Cummins states that even where programs of bilingual education are not offered, school staff can encourage and promote children's skills and pride in their first language.

Although most bilingual educators support the maintenance approach to bilingual education, the majority of programs in existence are transitional (Gollnick & Chinn, 1998). In fact, all state and federal laws providing support for bilingual education favor only transitional models. However, as Baca and Cervantes (1998) point out, the laws do not prevent school districts from offering maintenance programs if their staff members desire to do so.

A *restoration* model of bilingual education seeks to restore the students' ancestral language and cultural heritage that have been lost or diminished through cultural assimilation. *Enrichment* programs of bilingual education are designed to teach a new language and cultural ways to a group of monolingual students; for example, some school districts now offer language immersion schools in which all or most instruction is provided in a second language. (Spanish and French are the most common.)

Educators disagree about the most effective methods for teaching bilingual students. Former U.S. Secretary of Education William J. Bennett (1986) wrote that some children "come from families who encourage their acquisition of English; some run in peer groups where the native language is a matter of pride. Some arrive speaking languages from which the transition to English is relatively easy; others speak languages whose entire structure is perplexingly different from ours" (p. 62). Bennett maintains that the choice of specific methods to teach bilingual children should be a local decision, but he argues strongly that "all American children need to learn to speak, read, and write English as soon as possible" (p. 62). Some professionals and

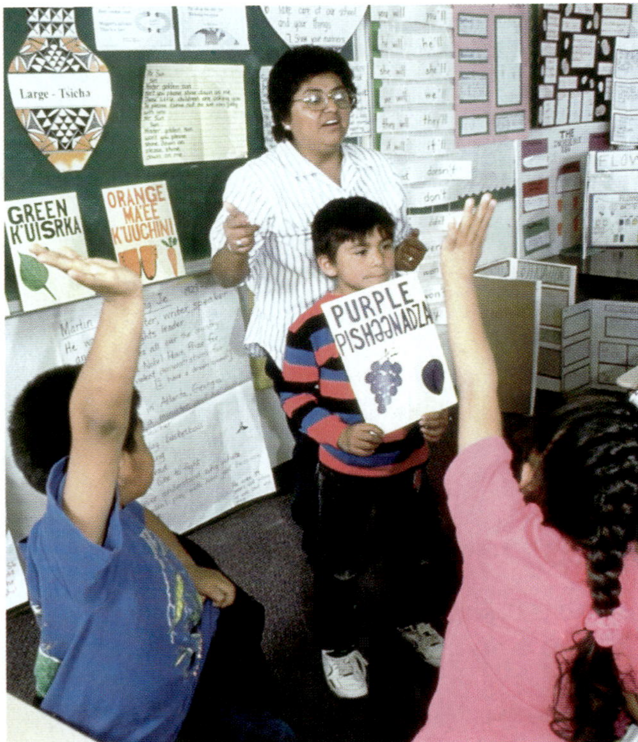

Some bilingual education programs help students function in both their native language and English, encouraging the child to become bilingual and bicultural.

legislators have called for the designation of English as the exclusive official language of the United States. Adopting such a policy, however, would probably discourage schools from offering instruction in students' native languages.

Conversely, the English Plus group advocates for linguistic pluralism and encourages educational programs to offer opportunities to learn a second language and develop cultural sensitivity (National Council for Languages and International Studies, 1992). Banks (1994b) observes that the nation's language policies and practices are at a crossroads and exemplify the second-language ambivalence held by people in the United States.

Research in bilingual education has not provided clear guidelines for methodology. There is general agreement, however, that children acquire English most effectively through interactions with teachers, parents, and peers. A child who engages in and talks about interesting experiences will be more likely to develop good English skills than a child who is limited to classroom instruction and teacher correction of errors. Efforts should be made to give bilingual exceptional children a variety of opportunities to explore the world through language. Briggs (1991) recommends that teachers use the following strategies for getting their point across when working with LEP students:

- Use gestures.
- Use visuals.
- Write down important information.
- Check frequently for understanding.
- Actively involve students.
- Use cooperative learning and other types of pair and group work.
- Focus on communication.
- Discuss learning strategies.
- Use students' experiences and interests.
- Have varied ways of assessing your students.
- Make sure you and your students are organized.
- Allow more time for reaction.
- Use the students' primary language.
- Use notes and tapes.
- Give the students as much support as you can in class.

Thinking about Your Own Practice

How can educators prevent the inappropriate referral and placement of culturally diverse students in special education while providing special education to all students who need services? The answer is not simple. But it must begin with culturally responsive curriculum and instructional practices in the general education classrooms that enable all students to achieve at their highest potential. And achievement (i.e., learning meaningful academic and social skills) should be the focus of every classroom activity. Focusing on achievement—learning—helps us recognize another fundamental form of diversity in the classroom:

> While gender, social class, race, ethnicity, and language difference increasingly characterize U.S. classrooms and influence equitable access to the benefits of educational programs, every classroom can also be characterized by students' *skill diversity*. Some children learn quickly and easily apply what they learn to new situations. Other children must be given repeated practice to master a simple task and then may have difficulty successfully completing the same task the next day. Some children are popular and have

many friends. Others are ostracized because they have not learned how to make friends. (Heward & Cavanaugh, 1997, p. 301)

For the most part, good systematic teaching is good systematic teaching. But when a student with disabilities has the additional challenge of learning in a new or different culture or language, it is even more important for her teacher to plan individualized, culturally responsive activities; convey expectations clearly; observe and record behavior precisely; and provide specific, immediate reinforcement and feedback in response to performance. These procedures, coupled with a helpful and culturally sensitive attitude, will increase the culturally different child's motivation and achievement in school.

The most effective teachers are, by definition, responsive to change (or lack of change) in an individual student's performance. Therefore, it can also be argued that the effective teacher needs as many different ways of teaching as there are students in the classroom—regardless of cultural backgrounds. This argument is basically true. But it pushes us to question how cultural and language differences affect a child's responsiveness to instruction and, hence, whether those effects warrant different approaches to teaching. So although the basic methods of systematic instruction remain the same, teachers who will be most effective in helping children with disabilities from culturally diverse backgrounds to achieve will be those who are sensitive to and respectful of their students' heritage and values. A teacher does not have to share his students' culture and native language to serve them effectively, but he will likely be quite ineffective in helping his students achieve in the classroom if he ignores those differences.

Use the self-tests at http://www.prenhall.com/heward to assess your knowledge of the content of Chapter 3.

The teacher of culturally diverse children with disabilities should adopt a flexible teaching style, establish a positive climate for learning, and use a variety of approaches to meet individual student needs. With a caring attitude, careful assessment and observation of behavior, and the use of appropriate materials and community resources, the teacher can do a great deal to help culturally and linguistically diverse children with disabilities and their families experience success in school.

Summary

Why Are There Disproportionate Placements of Culturally Diverse Students in Special Education?

- Although cultural diversity is a strength of our society, many students with disabilities still experience discrimination because of cultural, social class, or other differences from the majority. Educators must avoid stereotypes based on race or culture and become culturally responsive to differences in students from diverse backgrounds.
- Students who are members of culturally diverse groups are typically underrepresented in gifted programs and overrepresented in special education.
- Three factors may account for the disproportionate placement of students in special education: (1) incongruence in interactions between teachers and culturally diverse students and families, (2) inaccuracy of the assessment and referral process for culturally diverse students in special education, and (3) ineffective curriculum and instructional practices implemented for culturally diverse students.

Becoming a Culturally Responsive Educator

- It is necessary for educators to become culturally self-aware before becoming responsive to students and families from diverse backgrounds.
- Teacher education programs should include curriculum and field-based experiences related to teaching culturally diverse students.
- Understanding family values and beliefs about education, disabilities, and the school involvement of culturally diverse students informs teachers about their diverse students.

Appropriate Assessment of Culturally Diverse Students

- Assessment of students for placement in special education should be fair; referral should be based on each child's needs rather than on background.
- Language plays a major role in the assessment of a student's educational and emotional needs.

Culturally Responsive Curriculum and Instruction

- Multicultural approaches to curriculum include an equitable pedagogy that matches the student's learning style and the teacher's teaching styles and focus on providing an appropriate educational experience for all children regardless of their disability or ethnolinguistic background.
- Cooperative learning can be an effective strategy for students from diverse backgrounds.
- Bilingual special education uses the child's home language (L1) and home culture along with English in an individually designed education program.
- Most bilingual special education programs take either a transitional or a maintenance approach.

Thinking about Your Own Practice

- Skill diversity is a fundamental form of diversity in the classroom.
- Regardless of their cultural background, all children benefit from good, systematic instruction.
- The teacher must be sensitive to the effect of cultural and language differences on a child's responsiveness to instruction.

For More Information

Journals

- *Multicultural Education.* Published by the National Association for Multicultural Education by Caddo Gap Press, 3145 Geary Boulevard, Suite 275, San Francisco, CA 94118.
- *Teaching Tolerance.* Published by the Southern Poverty Law Center, 400 Washington Avenue, Montgomery, AL 36104.

Books

- Artiles, A., & Zamora-Durán, G. (1997). *Reducing disproportionate representation of culturally diverse students in special and gifted education*. Reston, VA: Council for Exceptional Children.
- Baca, L. M., & Cervantes, H. T. (1998). *The bilingual special education interface* (3rd ed.). Upper Saddle River, NJ: Merrill/Prentice Hall.
- Banks, J. A. (1994a). *An introduction to multicultural education.* Needham Heights, MA: Allyn & Bacon.
- Banks, J. A. (1994b). *Multiethnic education: Theory and practice* (3rd ed.). Needham Heights, MA: Allyn & Bacon.
- Banks, J. A., & Banks, C. A. M. (Eds.). (1997). *Multicultural education: Issues and perspectives* (3rd ed.). Boston: Allyn & Bacon.
- Cheng, L. L. (1987). *Assessing Asian language performance.* Rockville, MD: Aspen.
- Council on Interracial Books for Children. (1984). *Guidelines for selecting bias-free textbooks and story books.* New York: Author.
- Cusher, K., McClelland, A., & Safford, P. (1992). *Human diversity in education.* New York: McGraw-Hill.
- Delpit, L. (1995). *Other people's children: Cultural conflict in the classroom*. New York: New Press.
- Derman-Sparks, L., & the A.B.C. Task Force. (1989). *Anti-bias curriculum: Tools for empowering young children.* Washington, DC: National Association for the Education of Young Children.
- Fradd, S. H., & Tikunoff, W. J. (Eds.). (1987). *Bilingual education and bilingual special education: A guide for administrators.* Boston: Little, Brown.
- Gollnick, D. M., & Chinn, P. C. (1998). *Multicultural education in a pluralistic society* (5th ed.). Upper Saddle River, NJ: Merrill/Prentice Hall.
- Grant, C. A. (1995). *Educating for diversity: An anthology of multicultural voices.* Needham Heights, MA: Allyn & Bacon.
- Kitano, M. K., & Chinn, P. C. (Eds.). (1986). *Exceptional Asian children and youth.* Reston, VA: Council for Exceptional Children.
- Mattes, L. J., & Omark, D. R. (1984). *Speech and language assessment for the bilingual handicapped.* San Diego: College-Hill.
- Ortiz, A. A., & Ramirez, B. A. (Eds.). (1988). *Schools and the culturally diverse exceptional student: Promising practices and future directions.* Reston, VA: Council for Exceptional Children.
- Putnam, J. W. (1993). *Cooperative learning and strategies for inclusion: Celebrating diversity in the classroom.* Baltimore: Brookes.
- Siccone, F. (1995). *Celebrating diversity: Building self-esteem in today's multicultural classrooms.* Needham Heights, MA: Allyn & Bacon.
- Tiedt, P. L., & Tiedt, I. M. (1986). *Multicultural teaching: A handbook of activities, information, and resources* (2nd ed.). Needham Heights, MA: Allyn & Bacon.
- Willig, A. C., & Greenberg, H. F. (1986). *Bilingualism and learning disabilities: Policy and practice for teachers and administrators.* New York: American Library.
- Winzer, M. A., & Mazurek, K. (1998). *Special education in multicultural contexts*. Upper Saddle River, NJ: Merrill/Prentice Hall.

Organizations

- *BUENO Center for Multicultural Education,* College of Education, University of Colorado, Boulder, CO 80309-0249 (Leonard Baca, director). Conducts research, implements pre- and in-service teacher training programs, and disseminates information about multicultural education through various publications.
- *Division for Culturally and Linguistically Diverse Exceptional Learners (DDEL),* Council for Exceptional Children, 1920 Association Drive, Reston, VA 22091. One of the newest divisions of CEC; publishes the biannual *DDEL Newsletter* and an annual monograph on the needs of culturally diverse exceptional children.
- *ERIC Clearinghouse on Rural Education and Small Schools,* New Mexico State University, Las Cruces, NM 88004. Publishes a directory of organizations and programs involved in the education of migrant students.
- *Interstate Migrant Education Council,* Education Commission of the States, 1860 Lincoln Street, Denver, CO 80203. A forum for developing policy issues and disseminating information about migrant education.
- *National Association of Multicultural Education,* Caddo Gap Press, 3145 Geary Boulevard, Suite 275, San Francisco, CA 94118; (415) 750-9978.
- *National Association of State Directors of Migrant Education,* 200 West Baltimore Street, Baltimore, MD 21201. Provides information for teachers and parents about delivery of services to migrant students.
- *National Clearinghouse for Bilingual Education,* http://www.ncbe.gwu.edu. Publishes a web journal, *NCBE Newsline,* on issues related to the education of linguistically and culturally diverse students.
- *Teachers of English to Speakers of Other Languages (TESOL),* 1600 Camron Street, Suite 300, Alexandria, VA 22315-2751; (703) 836-0774.

Chapter 4

Parents and Families of Children with Special Needs

Focus Questions

- What can a teacher learn from the parents and families of students with disabilities?
- How does a child with disabilities affect parenting?
- How can an educator who is not the parent of a child with a disability communicate effectively and meaningfully with parents of exceptional children?
- How might the nature or severity of a child's disability change the objectives of parental and family involvement?
- How much parent and family involvement is enough?

The family is the most powerful and pervasive influence in a young child's life. Long before a professional with the job title "teacher" arrives, parents and family members help the child learn hundreds of skills. A parent is a child's first teacher, the person who gives encouragement, prompts, praise, and feedback. No one ever knows or cares about a child as much as a parent does. Yet only recently have special educators begun to understand these fundamental truths.

For years, many educators viewed parents as either troublesome (if they asked too many questions or, worse, offered suggestions about their child's education) or uncaring (if they did not jump to attention whenever the professional determined the parent needed something—usually advice from the professional). Parents, too, have often seen professionals as adversaries. But today, parent involvement and family support are viewed as essential elements of special education. Special educators have given up the old notions that parents should not be too involved in their children's educational programs or that they should not try to teach their children for fear of doing something wrong. Teachers now realize that parents and families are powerful and necessary allies.

Support for Parent and Family Involvement

Go to the companion website at http://www.prenhall.com/heward and select Chapter 4 to review the chapter objectives.

Recently, a number of forces have combined to focus attention on the importance of a strong parent-teacher partnership based on mutual respect and participation. Although many factors have contributed to the increased emphasis on collaboration between parents and teachers in the education of exceptional children, three issues are clear: (1) parents want to be involved, (2) research and practice have shown that educational effectiveness is enhanced when parents and families are involved, and (3) the law requires collaboration.

Parents Advocate for Change

*An **advocate** is someone who speaks for or pleads the case of another.*

For many years, parents of exceptional children have advocated for equal access to educational opportunities for their children, and they have done so with impressive effectiveness. As we learned in Chapters 1 and 2, parents played the primary role in bringing about litigation and legislation establishing the right to a free and appropriate public education for *all* children with disabilities. Not surprisingly, parents themselves have been most responsible for their greater involvement in planning and evaluating the special education services their children receive. The first parent group organized for children with disabilities was the National Society for Crippled Children, formed in 1921. The United Cerebral Palsy Association, organized in 1948, and the National Association for Retarded Citizens (now called The Arc), organized in 1950, are two national parent organizations largely responsible for making the public aware of the special needs of children with disabilities. The Learning Disabilities Association of America (LDA), formed in 1963, also organized by and consisting mostly of parents, has been instrumental in bringing about educational reform. Parent members of The Association for Persons with Severe Handicaps (TASH), founded in 1975, have been forceful and effective advocates for family-focused educational services and the inclusion of students with severe and multiple disabilities in neighborhood schools and general education classrooms.

Families believe they have the greatest vested interest in their children and the most knowledge about their needs. The developers of a highly regarded program for planning and implementing inclusive educational programs for students with disabilities agree. They present four powerful arguments for viewing active family involvement as the cornerstone of relevant and longitudinal educational planning:

- *Families know certain aspects of their children better than anyone else does.* As educators, we must remind ourselves that we spend only about half the days of the year with our students, seeing them less than a third of each of those days. Nonschool time may provide key information that has educational implications, such as the nature of a student's interests, motivations, habits, fears, routines, pressures, needs, and health. By listening to parents, educators can gain a more complete understanding of a student's life outside school.
- *Families have the greatest vested interest in seeing their children learn.* In our eagerness to help

A parent is a child's first teacher.

children learn, we sometimes convey the message to parents that teachers care more about children than parents do. Of course, this is rarely the case.

- *The family is likely to be the only group of adults involved with a child's educational program throughout her entire school career.* Over the course of a school career, a student with special educational needs will encounter so many professionals that it will be difficult for the family to remember all the names. Professionals must build upon a family-centered vision for the child rather than reinvent a student's educational program each year.
- *Families must live with the outcomes of decisions made by education teams all day, every day.* People rarely appreciate having someone else make decisions that will affect their lives without being included in the decision making. As professionals making decisions, we must constantly remind ourselves that these decisions are likely to affect other people besides the child and have an effect outside of school. (Giangreco, Cloninger, & Iverson, 1993, pp. 6–7)

More information about families can be found by accessing the Resources Module for Chapter 4 at http://www.prenhall.com/heward and the Special Ed Resource Page.

Educators Strive for Greater Effectiveness and Significance

Educators have recognized the necessity of expanding the traditional role of the classroom teacher to meet the special needs of children with disabilities. This expanded role demands that we view teaching as more than "standing and delivering" the three Rs. Teachers now realize that self-care, social, vocational, and leisure skills are critical to the successful functioning of a student with disabilities. Today's special educator attaches high priority to designing and implementing instructional programs that enable students with disabilities to use and maintain those functional skills in school, at home, at work, and in community settings. Implementing this priority requires teachers to look beyond the classroom for assistance and support, and parents and families are natural and necessary allies.

Extensive evidence shows that the effectiveness of educational programs for children with disabilities is increased when parents and families are actively involved (e.g., Cronin, Slade, Bechtel, & Anderson, 1992; Guralnick, 1997; Hardin & Littlejohn, 1995). At the very least, teachers and students benefit when parents provide information about their children's use of specific skills outside the classroom. But parents can do much more than just report on behavioral change. They can work with teachers to provide extra skill practice at home and to teach their children new skills. When parents are involved in identifying what skills their children need to learn (and, just as important, what they do not need to learn), the hard work expended by teachers is more likely to produce outcomes with real significance in the lives of children and their families. For example, in an IEP conference,

> the mother of a moderately retarded child questioned why her son was being taught to label prehistoric animals verbally. The parent asked the teachers what type of job they expected the child to have as an adult. The teachers replied that they had never really considered job opportunities for the child, since he was only 10. To the teachers, 10 seemed young; to the parents, 10 meant that almost half his formal education was completed. As the meeting progressed, it was clear that the parents were specifying objectives related to independence as an adult (telling time, reading survival words, sex education) that were different from the more traditional curriculum proposed by the teachers. Through sharing evaluation data, goals for the child, and special problems, all parties involved created a curriculum that met everyone's approval. (Turnbull, 1983, p. 22)

Legislators Mandate Parent and Family Participation

As we learned in Chapter 1, in 1975 Congress heard the parent advocates and mandated parent involvement as a key element in the Education of All Handicapped Children Act (P.L. 94–142), the original federal special education law. Parent and family participation in the education of children with disabilities was strengthened further in P.L.

105–17, the most recent reauthorization of IDEA. Congress reaffirmed its belief in the importance of parent and family involvement in this introduction to IDEA 1997: "Over 20 years of research and experience has demonstrated that the education of children with disabilities can be made more effective by . . . strengthening the role of parents and ensuring that families of such children have meaningful opportunities to participate in the education of their children at school and at home" (601[c][5][B]).

Parent participation in the form of shared decision making is one of six basic rules, or principles, of IDEA that form the general framework for carrying out national policies for the education of children with disabilities. IDEA provides statutory guidelines that schools must follow with parents of children with disabilities with regard to referral, testing, placement, and program planning and evaluation. In addition, the law provides due process procedures if parents believe that their child's needs are not being met.

Check your ongoing understanding of Chapter 4 concepts by using the Guided Review Module at http://www.prenhall.com/heward.

We've identified three factors responsible for increased parent and family involvement in the education of exceptional children: parents want it, educators know it's a good idea, and the law requires it. But the most important reasons why parents and educators strive to develop working partnerships are the benefits to the child with disabilities:

- Greater consistency and support in the child's two most important environments
- Increased opportunities for learning and development
- Access to expanded resources and services

Understanding Parents and Families of Children with Disabilities

To join the discussion "How can an educator who is not a parent of a child with a disability communicate effectively and meaningfully with parents of exceptional children?" go to the Message Board Module at http://www.prenhall.com/heward.

When parents and teachers work together for the mutual benefit of a child with disabilities, they make a powerful team. To work together, they must communicate with one another. Effective communication is more likely when each party understands and respects the responsibilities and challenges faced by the other. For educators, the first step in developing a partnership with parents and families is to strive for an understanding of how a child with disabilities influences the family system and alters the many interrelated roles of parenthood.

The Impact of a Child with Disabilities on the Family

Consider this parent's feelings: "All I wanted was a baby and now I've got doctors' appointments, therapy appointments, surgeries, medical bills, a strained marriage, no more free time. . . . When you have a handicapped child, you don't just have to deal with the child and the fact that he's handicapped. You have to adjust to a whole new way of life. It's a double whammy" (Simon, 1987, p. 15).

Based on their observations of 130 participants in two parent support groups over a period of several years, Anderegg, Vergason, and Smith (1992) have developed a revised model of Blacher's work they call the grief cycle, *which consists of three stages: confronting, adjusting, and adapting.*

The birth of a baby with disabilities or the discovery that a child has a disability is an intense and traumatic event. Evidence suggests that many parents of children with disabilities experience similar reactions and emotional responses and that most go through an adjustment process, trying to work through their feelings (Eden-Piercy, Blacher, & Eyman, 1986; Frey, Fewell, & Vadasy, 1989; Johnson, 1993). Blacher (1984) found three consistent stages of adjustment. First, parents experience a period of emotional crisis characterized by shock, denial, and disbelief. This initial reaction is followed by a period of emotional disorganization that includes alternating feelings of anger, guilt, depression, shame, lowered self-esteem, rejection of the child, and overprotectiveness. Finally, parents reach a third stage in which they accept their child.

Poyadue (1993) suggests a stage beyond acceptance that involves appreciation of the positive aspects of family life with a child with a disability—as when, for example, a child learns a new skill. There is some research evidence supporting this concept. For example, Patterson and Leonard (1994) interviewed couples whose children required intensive home care routines because of chronic and complex health care needs and found roughly equal numbers of positive and negative responses. Among the positive responses was that caregiving brought the couple closer together and created a stronger bond among family members. In another study, the majority of 1,262 parents of children with disabilities agreed with the following statements about being the parent of a child with a disability: "The presence of my child is very uplifting. Because of my child, I have many unexpected pleasures. My child is the reason I am a more responsible person" (Behr, Murphy, & Summers, 1992, p. 26).

Sandler and Mistretta (1998) believe that the focus on positive family adaptation "represents an effort to both more accurately portray 'how it is' for families, and learn from the experience of successful families to better serve those families experiencing difficulty" (p. 123).

Turnbull and Turnbull (1985) offer a collection of moving personal stories from parents of children with disabilities.

But emphasizing stages of adjustment as the basis for planning or delivering family services poses two potential problems. First, it is easy to assume that all parents must pass through a similar sequence of stages and that time is the most important variable in adjustment. In fact, parents react to the arrival of a child with disabilities in many ways (Allen & Affleck, 1985). For some parents, years may pass, but they still are not comfortable with their child. Others report that having a child with disabilities has strengthened their life or marriage (Bradley, Knoll, & Agosta, 1992). The sequence and time needed for adjustment are different for every parent. The one common thread is that almost all parents and families can be helped during their adjustment by sensitive and supportive friends and professionals.

A second concern is that the various stages of adjustment have a distinct psychiatric flavor, and professionals may mistakenly assume that parents must be maladjusted in some way. As Roos (1985) notes, some educators seem to assume that all parents of children with disabilities need counseling.

> It may be that many parents do respond in ways that are well-described by the stage model. But it is dangerous to impose this model on all parents. Those who exhibit different response patterns might be inappropriately judged as "deviant." Parents who do not progress as rapidly through the "stages" might be considered slow to adjust. And those who exhibit emotions in a different sequence might be thought of as regressing. (Allen & Affleck, 1985, p. 201)

The Many Roles of the Exceptional Parent

Parenthood is an awesome responsibility, and parenting any child requires tremendous physical and emotional energy. All parents share a great deal in common. Hart and Risley (1995), who conducted a longitudinal study of 42 families with young children, noted: "Raising children made all the families look alike. All the babies had to be fed, changed, and amused. As we went from one home to another we saw the same activities and lives centered on caregiving. . . . Most impressive of all that the parents had in common was the continual and incredible challenge a growing child presents" (pp. 53, 55).

Parents of children with disabilities, however, sometimes experience added stress caused by a child's physical, emotional, and financial demands. Educators who are not parents of a child with disabilities or chronic illness cannot know the 24-hour reality of being the parent of such a child. Nonetheless, they should strive to understand how a child with special needs affects (and is affected by) the family system.

Parents of children with disabilities must fulfill nine varied and demanding roles:

Singer and Powers (1993) describe a variety of interventions to help families cope with everyday challenges of having a family member with disabilities.

Caregiver Taking care of any young child can be a nonstop task. But the level of caregiving required by some children with disabilities can be tremendous and cause added stress:

> Mike sleeps when he wants to, mostly during the day. He sleeps with a heart monitor on which alarms several time per night, because he stops breathing frequently. Usually I'm up by 8:00 and often cannot go to bed until 12:00 or 1:00 because of Mike's feedings, medication. It's hard to fit all of this into a day and still have time for sleep.
>
> Douglas's tube caught on the door handle and his trach came out. I panicked, but Douglas's father was home and he "simply" reinserted the trach and reattached the tube to the ventilator machine. Douglas meanwhile had turned gray, then blue for just a minute or less. I was crying as he began breathing again and his color came back. (Bradley et al., 1992)

Provider Food, clothing, shelter, music lessons: parents pay a lot of money to raise a typically developing child from birth to adulthood. Providing for a child with disabilities, however, often means additional expenses, sometimes in the thousands of dollars. While some families receive federal, state, and/or private assistance for such extra expenses, most families have to pay their own way. For example, consider these parents of a child with physical disabilities and chronic health problems:

> We had to find another place to live with first floor bedroom, widened doorways, enlarged front porch, central air, ramp, van. House renovation: $10,000. Van: $18,500. Air: $1,450. Porch: $1,400. Ramp: $1,000. Furnishings to accommodate supplies: $800. We've got the following equipment: Suction machine, portable suction machine, generator for emergency power, hospital bed, air pressure mattress, wheelchair, room monitor, humidifier, bath chair, oxygen, air cleaner, gastronomy tube pump, breathing treatment machine. And all the following expenses have gone up: formula, diapers, appliances, utility bills, medications. (Bradley et al., 1992)

Teacher Most children learn many skills that no one tries to teach them. Children with disabilities, however, often do not acquire new skills as naturally or independently as their typically developing peers do. In addition to learning systematic teaching techniques, some parents must learn to use and/or teach their children to use special equipment and assistive devices such as hearing aids, braces, wheelchairs, and adapted eating utensils (Parette & Brotherson, 1996).

Counselor All parents are counselors in the sense that they deal with their developing children's changing emotions, feelings, and attitudes. But in addition to all of the normal joys and pains of raising a child, parents of a child with disabilities must deal with the feelings their child has as a result of his particular disability: "Will I still be deaf when I grow up?" "I'm not playing outside anymore; they always tease me." "Why can't I go swimming like the other kids?" Parents play an important role in how the child with disabilities comes to feel about himself. Their interactions can help develop an active, outgoing child who confidently tries many new things or a withdrawn child with negative attitudes toward himself and others.

To learn how educators and one family worked together to provide positive behavioral support for a young boy with challenging behavior, see "A Parent-Professional Partnership in Positive Behavioral Support" later in this chapter. Further discussion and examples of positive behavioral support appear in Chapter 13.

Behavior Management Specialist All children act out from time to time, and all parents are challenged and frustrated by their children's noncompliance and misbehavior. But the frequency and severity of challenging behaviors exhibited by certain children with disabilities can make it nearly impossible for some families to experience and enjoy normal routines of daily life (Dunlap, Robbins, & Darrow, 1994). Turnbull and Ruef (1996) interviewed 14 families with children with mental retardation who frequently exhibited problem behavior. The parents reported that their children frequently engaged in at least one of four categories of problem behavior: aggression toward others, property destruction, self-injurious behavior, or pica (eating inedible objects). The children's problem behavior fell into one of two domains, according to the behavior's impact on the child and the family: dangerous behavior (e.g., "He punches his face a lot on the jaw line—his cheek bone, his mouth, occasionally his forehead. . . . He will eventually bleed from his mouth") and difficult behavior (e.g., "When I am around him it is constant noise. He talks or squawks. By afternoon I am frazzled") (p. 283). Such behavior demands specialized and consistent treatment, and some parents of exceptional children must become highly skilled in behavior management techniques to achieve a semblance of normal family life (e.g., Derby et al., 1997; Dunlap & Fox, 1996; Richman, Harrison, & Summer, 1995; Vaughn, Clarke, & Dunlap, 1997; Werle, Murphy, & Budd, 1993).

For suggestions on how to plan and conduct workshops and support groups for siblings of children with disabilities, see Cramer, Erzkus, Mayweather, Pope, Roeder, & Tone, (1997); Summers, Bridge, and Summers (1991); and Meyer, Vadasy, and Fewell (1994).

Parent of Siblings without Disabilities Children are deeply affected by having a brother or a sister with special needs (Caro & Derevensky, 1997; Wilson, Blacher, & Baker, 1989). Brothers and sisters of a child with disabilities often have concerns about their sibling's disability: uncertainty regarding the cause of the disability and its effect on them, uneasiness about the reactions of friends, a feeling of being left out or being required to do too much for the child with disabilities (Dyson, Edgar, & Crnic, 1989).

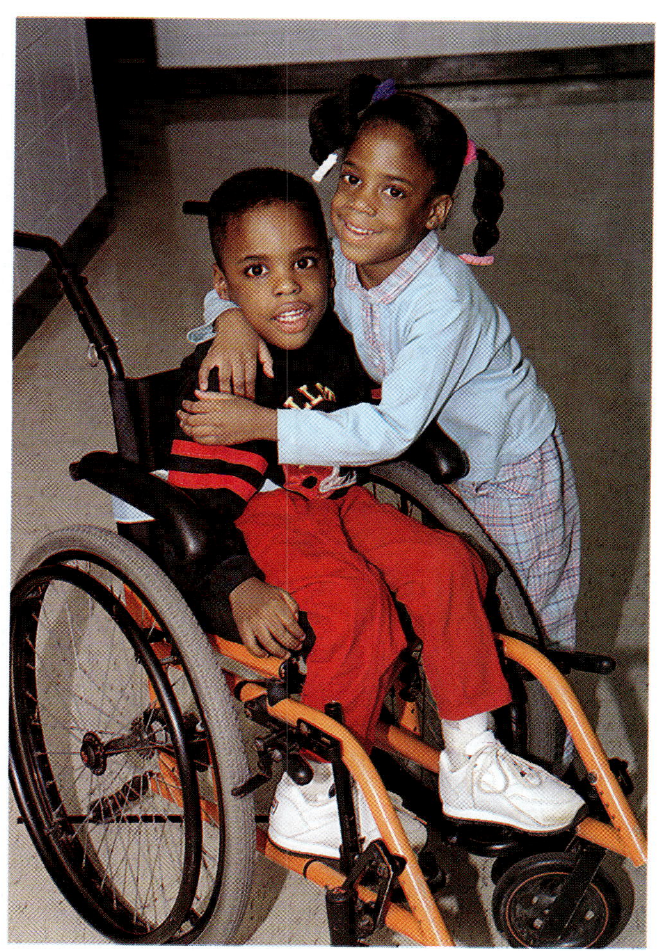

Nondisabled brothers and sisters often have special needs and concerns because of their sibling's disability.

Abuse and Neglect of Children with Disabilities

Consider the following cases:

> Travis hit all the kids on the school bus, on the playground and everyone he could reach as he bound into my kindergarten class. Every day. Travis had witnessed his mother deliberately scalding his 3-year-old sister with a kettle of boiling water. She was injured terribly.
>
> Brevard's drug-addicted mother had burned his genitalia with her cigarette. She has blond hair. He was frightened of every blond-haired woman, among his many emotional problems.
>
> Kim said Christmas wasn't as much fun as usual, with the cops coming and taking Daddy to jail for stabbing Mommy's tummy.
>
> Ernestine never smiled or laughed the whole year, not even when going down the slide or catching a ball. Her arms twitched nervously most of the time. Her mom had left her with a neighbor "while she went to the store." She never returned. Ernestine has lived in the green house, the white one, the apartment and had been in three schools before she entered my kindergarten from the brown house. (Craig Wall, kindergarten teacher, Columbus, OH; quoted in the *Columbus Dispatch,* August 28, 1998, p. 7A)

Child maltreatment covers a spectrum of behaviors committed by parents or significant others. It includes verbally intimidating or shaming a child, neglecting a child's physical and health care needs, causing physical harm by striking or burning a child, and sexually abusing a child. Maltreatment takes a tremendous toll on a child's development. "Other than malnutrition or disease, there is probably no risk factor for children that has greater consequences for their development than maltreatment by their parents" (Groves, 1997, p. 86).

Child abuse and neglect occur with alarming frequency in the United States. Here are some statistics for 1996 (U.S. Department of Health and Human Services, 1998):

- State child protection service agencies investigated an estimated 2 million reports that involved the alleged maltreatment of approximately 3 million children.
- Almost 1 million children were victims of substantiated or indicated child abuse and neglect, an approximate 18 percent increase since 1990.
- The national rate of victimization was 15 victims per 1,000 children.
- An estimated 1,077 child maltreatment fatalities occurred in the 50 states and the District of Columbia

Because the majority of child abuse and neglect cases are never reported, it is impossible to know the true extent of the problem. Some professionals think the number of actual cases is at least twice the number of those reported (Straus, Gelles, & Steinmetz, 1980).

Data from a study using nationally representative samples showed that children with disabilities are 1.7 times more likely to be abused and neglected by family members and other caregivers (Crosse, Kaye, & Ratnofsky, 1993). Not only are children with disabilities overrepresented in child abuse samples (Sullivan & Knutson, 1994), but they are more likely to be abused for a longer period. "Whereas the infant with colic may increase family stress for a limited period, the child with cerebral palsy, or any other long-term or permanent handicap, presents a potential long-term family crisis. . . . It is no wonder, then, that children with handicaps are disproportionately represented in child abuse samples" (Zirpoli, 1987, p. 44).

Is a child abused and neglected because of a disability, or do abuse and neglect produce a disability in an otherwise normally developing child? "In many cases, to ask the question . . . is something akin to the old question of which came first—the chicken or the egg" (Morgan, 1987, p. 45). In most instances, however, it would be a mistake to say simply that a child's disability caused the abuse and neglect. Researchers have concluded that child abuse and neglect have no single cause but are the product of complex interactions among numerous variables, only one of which concerns the child's characteristics (Kairys, 1996; Sobsey, 1994; Zirpoli, 1987, 1990). Factors also include a parent's own abuse as a child, alcohol or drug dependency, unemployment, poverty, and marital discord; seldom is any one factor the lone cause of child abuse. For example, although poverty increases the probability of abuse and neglect, most children from poor families receive loving and nurturing care from their parents. Likewise, the great majority of parents of children with disabilities provide a loving and nurturing environment.

Educators' Responsibility to Report Suspected Abuse There must be greater awareness of the problem of child abuse and neglect, especially among professionals who work with children and families. Because teachers see children daily for most of the year, they are in the best position to identify and report suspected cases of abuse. All 50 states require that teachers and other professionals who frequently deal with children report suspected cases of abuse and neglect (Meddin & Rosen, 1987). Indeed, many state laws require any citizen who suspects abuse and neglect to report it, and most states impose criminal penalties for failure to do so. People who, in good faith, report suspected cases are immune from civil or criminal liability. All educators should become familiar with child abuse laws in their state and learn how to recognize and report indicators of abuse and neglect. Pearson (1996) provides specific information on detecting and reporting signs of physical abuse, sexual abuse, and neglect and describes classroom policies and practices to protect teachers from unwarranted allegations of abuse.

Support for Families with Histories of Abuse and Neglect One successful program for preventing and treating child abuse and neglect is Project 12-Ways, developed by Lutzker and colleagues at the University of Southern Illinois (Lutzker & Campbell, 1994; Lutzker & Newman, 1986). The project's guiding philosophy is that family problems can be eased by eliminating stress-producing factors (e.g., unemployment) and teaching both children and parents the skills necessary for getting along without abuse and neglect. Recognizing the multidimensional factors involved and understanding the entire family as a dynamic system, the project employs an ecobehavioral approach to treatment. That is, rather than prescribing a standard treatment regimen consisting of one or two components, a counselor conducts a thorough assessment of the family's needs and resources. After assessment, family and counselor jointly determine goals and then implement an individualized program of family support services.

Repucci, Britner, and Wollard (1997) have studied 25 programs for helping abusive and neglectful parents and offer numerous suggestions for planning, conducting, and evaluating such programs.

Information on detecting signs of child abuse and neglect can be obtained from Child Help USA. Anyone can and should report a suspected case of child abuse; reports can be filed anonymously. If you do not know the appropriate local agency to contact, call the toll-free Child Help USA hotline: (800) 422-4453.

Marriage Partner Having a child with disabilities can put stress on a marriage (Frey, Greenberg, & Fewell, 1989). Specific stressors can be as diverse as arguing over whose fault the child's disability is; disagreeing about expectations for the child's behavior; and spending so much time, money, and energy on the child with disabilities that little is left for each other (Cohen, Agosta, Cohen, & Warren, 1989). It is a mistake, however, to assume that the presence of a child with disabilities has a negative effect on marital relations. Some studies have found that a child with disabilities strengthens a marriage (Abbot & Meredith, 1986; Kazak & Marvin, 1984).

Respite care can reduce the mental and physical stress on parents and families created by the day-to-day responsibilities of caring for a child with disabilities (see Figure 4.1).

Information Specialist/Trainer for Significant Others Grandparents, aunts and uncles, neighbors, the school bus driver: all of these people can have an important influence on a child's development. While parents of a child without disabilities can reasonably expect her to receive certain kinds of treatment from significant others, parents of children with disabilities know they cannot necessarily depend on others' appropriate actions and reactions. These parents must try to ensure that, as much as possible, other people interact with their child in a way that facilitates the acquisition and maintenance of adaptive behaviors. Schulz (1985) describes her response to anyone who stares at her son with Down syndrome: she looks the person squarely in the eye and says, "You seem interested in my son. Would you like to meet him?" (p. 6). This usually ends the staring and often creates an opportunity to provide information or begin a friendship.

George (1988) describes a group support program designed to help grandparents and extended family members of children with disabilities develop positive and supportive roles that help the child and the parents.

Advocate for School and Community Services IDEA not only defines the rights of parents of children with disabilities but requires specific efforts and respon-

Figure 4.1 Respite care: Support for families

Parents of nondisabled children frequently hire others to care temporarily for their children. The range of day care and baby-sitting options available to families of children with disabilities, however, is severely limited. Many parents of children with severe disabilities identify the availability of reliable, high-quality child care as their single most pressing need (Grant & McGrath, 1990). In response to this need, many communities have developed respite care programs. **Respite care** is the short-term care of a family member with disabilities to provide relief for parents from caretaking duties.

Quality respite care can reduce the mental and physical stress on parents and families created by the day-to-day—in some cases, moment-to-moment—responsibilities of caring for a child with disabilities. Respite care has also been correlated with reduced requests for long-term residential placement of children with disabilities and improved family functioning (Neef, Parrish, Egel, & Sloan, 1986). The mother of a son born with a neurological condition that produces frequent seizures and extreme hyperactivity describes her family's experience with respite care:

> During the first four years of Ben's life, we averaged four hours of sleep a night. We were wearing ourselves out; I have no doubt we would have completely fallen apart. My husband, Roger, used his vacations for sleeping in. The respite program came along just in time for us. It was hard at first. There's an overwhelming guilt that you shouldn't leave your child. We didn't feel like anyone else could understand Ben's problems. But we had to get away. Our church gave us some money, with orders to take a vacation. It was the first time Roger and I and our 12-year-old daughter, Stacy, had really been together since Ben was born.

Another parent expressed what respite care has meant to her family:

> Our son Tom's autism has meant a lot of restrictions in our family life for the past 25 years, bringing with it many problems and much resentment. At last we have been given a no-strings-attached, low-cost way to loosen some of those restrictions. Funny thing is, our Tom is such a nice guy—it's sure good to be able to get far enough away every so often to be able to see that.

To locate respite service providers in their communities, families and their advocates can call the National Respite Locator Service at this toll-free number: (800) 773-5433.

Anderson, Chitwood, and Hayden (1997) and Cutler (1993) use everyday language to explain the intricacies of special education and offer step-by-step advice for parents on how to make the system work for children with disabilities. A Parent Handbook for Individualized Education Programs *(1996) is available from the Beach Center on Families and Disability. See "For More Information" at the end of this chapter.*

sibilities. Although some involvement in the educational process is desirable for all parents, involvement is a must for parents of exceptional children. They must acquire special knowledge (e.g., the differences between a norm-referenced and a criterion-referenced test) and learn special skills (e.g., how to participate effectively in IFSP/IEP meetings). In addition, many parents of children with disabilities have concerns over and above those of most parents; they must often advocate for services and opportunities for their children in a society that devalues persons with disabilities. For example, while all parents may be concerned about having adequate community playgrounds, the parents of a child who uses a wheelchair may find themselves having to fight long and hard for an accessible playground.

Changing Needs As Children Grow

Another way to understand how a child with disabilities affects his or her family and vice versa, is to examine the likely impact of the child's changing needs at various ages. Turnbull and Turnbull (1997) describe the possible issues and concerns that parents and siblings face during four life-cycle stages. Table 4.1 outlines their analysis

Table 4.1 The four life-cycle stages of a person with disabilities: Issues and strategies for family members

	LIFE-CYCLE STAGES	
	Early Childhood, ages 0–5	**Childhood, ages 6–12**
Issues for Parents	• Obtaining an accurate diagnosis • Informing siblings and relatives • Locating early intervention services • Participating in IFSP meetings • Seeking to find meaning in the exceptionality • Clarifying a personal ideology to guide decisions • Addressing issues of stigma • Identifying positive contributions of exceptionality • Setting great expectations	• Establishing routines to carry out family functions • Adjusting emotionally to educational implications • Clarifying issues of mainstreaming versus special class placement • Advocating for inclusive experiences • Participating in IEP conferences • Locating community resources • Arranging for extracurricular activities • Developing a vision for the future
Issues for Siblings	• Less parental time and energy for sibling needs • Feelings of jealousy because of less attention • Fears associated with misunderstandings about exceptionality	• Division of responsibility for any physical care needs • Oldest female sibling may be at risk • Limited family resources for recreation and leisure • Informing friends and teachers • Possible concern about younger sibling surpassing older • Issues of mainstreaming into same school • Need for basic information on exceptionality
Enhancing Successful Transitions	• Begin preparing for the separation of preschool children by periodically leaving the child with others. • Gather information and visit preschools in the community. • Encourage participation in Parent to Parent programs. (Veteran parents are matched in one-to-one relationships with parents who are just beginning the transition process.) • Familiarize parents with possible school (elementary and secondary) programs, career options, or adult programs so they have an idea of future opportunities.	• Provide parents with an overview of curricular options. • Ensure that IEP meetings provide an empowering context for family collaboration. • Encourage participation in Parent to Parent matches, workshops, or family support groups to discuss transitions with others.

Table 4.1 *(continued)*

	LIFE-CYCLE STAGES	
	Adolescence, ages 12–21	**Adulthood, ages 21–**
Issues for Parents	• Adjusting emotionally to possible chronicity of exceptionality • Identifying issues of emerging sexuality • Dealing with physical and emotional changes of puberty • Addressing possible peer isolation and rejection • Planning for career/vocational development • Arranging for leisure activities • Expanding child's self-determination skills • Planning for postsecondary education	• Address supported employment and living options • Adjusting emotionally to any adult implications of dependency • Addressing the need for socialization opportunities outside the family • Initiating career choice or vocational program • Planning for possible need for guardianship
Issues for Siblings	• Overidentification with sibling • Greater understanding of differences in people • Influence of exceptionality on career choice • Dealing with possible stigma and embarrassment • Participation in sibling training programs • Opportunity for sibling support groups	• Possible issues of responsibility for financial support • Addressing concerns regarding genetic implications • Introducing new in-laws to exceptionality • Need for information on career/living options • Clarify role of sibling advocacy • Possible issues of guardianship
Enhancing Successful Transitions	• Assist families and adolescents to identify community leisure activities. • Incorporate into the IEP skills that will be needed in future career and vocational programs. • Visit or become familiar with a variety of career and living options. • Develop a mentor relationship with an adult with a similar exceptionality and an individual who has a career that matches the student's strengths and preferences.	• Provide preferred information to families about guardianship, estate planning, wills, and trusts. • Assist family members in transferring responsibilities to the individual with an exceptionality, other family members, or service providers as appropriate. • Assist the young adult or family members with career or vocational choices. • Address the issues and responsibilities of marriage and family for the young adult.

Source: From FAMILIES, PROFESSIONALS, AND EXCEPTIONALITY: 3/E, A SPECIAL PARTNERSHIP by Turnbull/Turnbull 111, ©1997. Reprinted by permission of Prentice-Hall, Inc., Upper Saddle River, NJ.

along with suggested strategies that support family transitions across the stages. A study by Wikler (1986) lends support to the concept that parents and siblings face different challenges at different life-cycle stages of the child with disabilities. Wikler's study of 60 families found higher levels of family stress at the onset of adolescence and adulthood.

Parents of children with disabilities face various challenges, but in the end they adjust—striving simply to have a family life. A research team asked families of young children with developmental delays to tell their stories, asking, "How is it going for you?" The team concluded:

> Many issues concern these parents. What concerns them most is something beyond specific problems, something more comprehensive. This more general adaptive problem appears again and again in parents' accounts of living with a child who exhibits developmental delays early in life: The creation of a sustainable and meaningful daily routine of family life. (Gallimore, Weisner, Bernheimer, Guthrie, & Nihira, 1993, p. 186)

Parent-Teacher Communication

Regular two-way communication with parents is the foundation of an effective parent-teacher partnership. Without open, honest communication between teacher and parent, many of the positive outcomes we have examined cannot be achieved. "A good conversation is neither a fight nor a contest. Circular in form, cooperative in manner, and constructivist in intent, it is an interchange of ideas by those who see themselves not as adversaries but as human beings come together to talk and to listen and to learn from one another" (Martin, 1985, p. 10).

Principles of Effective Communication

Wilson (1995) recommends five principles for effective communication between educators and parents:

Accept Parents' Statements Accepting parents' statements means conveying through verbal and nonverbal means that what parents say is valued. Parents are more likely to speak freely and openly when they believe that what they say is respected. Acceptance means conveying "I understand and appreciate your point of view." It does not mean the teacher must agree with everything that a parent says.

Listen Well Good listeners attend to a conversation partner in a sincere and genuine manner. A good listener not only pays attention to the content of what is being said but notes who said it and how he said it. For example, in an IFSP/IEP conference attended by extended family members, an educator should notice if a grandparent seems to be speaking for the child's parents or if the mother and father express different opinions about an issue through tones of voice or body language.

Question Effectively To the extent possible, educators should use open-ended questions when communicating with parents, especially during conferences. For example, an open-ended question such as "What did Sharena do with her homework project last week?" is more likely to evoke a descriptive and informative reply from parents than is the closed-ended question "Is Sharena having trouble with her homework?" which might result in a yes or no response.

Encourage It is important for parents to hear good news about their son or daughter. Describing or showing parents specific instances of their child's good behavior or improved performance encourages parental involvement. When parents

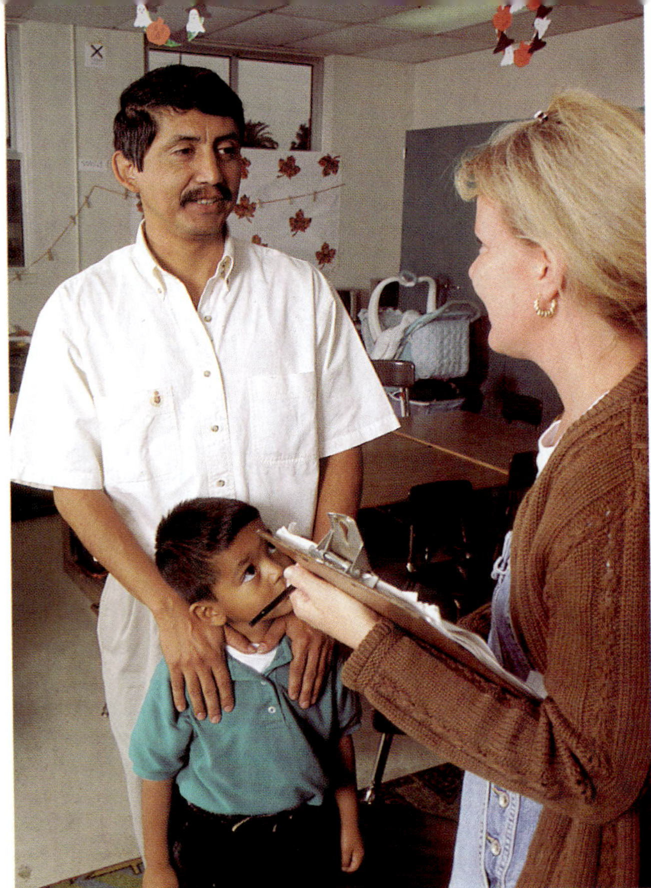

Parent-teacher communication is enhanced when teachers value what parents say and listen well.

need to be informed of an academic or behavioral problem, educators might use the "sandwich" technique: presenting the concern between two positive comments or examples of progress.

Stay Focused Although greetings and some small talk are desirable before getting down to business, conversations between parents and teachers should focus on the child's educational program and progress. Educators must be sensitive to cultural differences and the idiosyncratic conversational styles of individual families (Dennis & Giangreco, 1996; Wilson & Hughes, 1994). But they must also learn to distinguish when extended small talk is drifting too far from the purpose at hand so that they can refocus the conversation.

For suggestions on interacting with angry parents and resolving conflicts and disagreements, see Fish (1990), Margolis and Brannigan (1990), and Simpson (1996).

Barriers to Effective Parent-Teacher Communication

Let's face it: parents and teachers do not always cooperate. They may sometimes even seem to be on opposite sides, battling over what each thinks is best for the child. The child, unfortunately, never wins that battle. She needs to have the people responsible for the two places where she spends most of her life—home and school—work together to make those environments consistent and supportive of her job of learning. Some parents and teachers make assumptions about and hold attitudes toward one another that are counterproductive. Parents may complain that educators are negative, unavailable, or patronizing. Teachers may complain that parents are uninterested, uncooperative, or hostile.

Some professionals hold stereotypes and false assumptions about what parents of children with disabilities must be like and what they need (Adelman, 1994; Dyson, 1996; Voltz, 1994). These attitudes often lead to poor relationships between parents and professionals (see Figure 4.2). Of course, most teachers do not act so negatively toward parents. But when they do, parents may feel intimidated, confused, angry, or hostile.

But the factors working against positive parent-teacher relationships cannot all be attributed to professional mishandling. Some parents are genuinely difficult to work with or unreasonable.

There are situations in which parents fight long and hard for services for their child. But after services are found and the child is receiving an appropriate education, the parents continue their intense advocacy until minor issues with professionals become major confrontations. One mother stated, "For years I have scrapped and fought for services. Now I come on like gangbusters over issues that are really not that important. I don't like what has happened to me. I've ended up to be an aggressive, angry person" (Bronicki & Turnbull, 1987, p. 10). This posture leads to unproductive interactions between parents and professionals.

Although some teachers voice concern that parents of children with disabilities are unrealistic and make too many demands of schools (e.g., Chesley & Calaluce, 1997), most recognize that these parents, like all parents, are simply advocating for the best possible educational services and outcomes for their children. Simons (1998), the mother of a freshman daughter enrolled in honors classes and a senior

Parent as vulnerable client. Professionals who see parents only as helpless souls in need of assistance make a grave mistake. Teachers need parents and what they have to offer as much as parents need teachers.

Professional distance. Most professionals in human services develop some degree of distance to avoid getting too involved with a client—supposedly to maintain objectivity and credibility. But aloofness or coldness in the name of professionalism has hindered or terminated many parent-teacher relationships. Parents must believe that the professional really cares about them.

Parent as patient. Some professionals make the faulty assumption that having a child with disabilities causes a parent to need therapy. A father writes, "I had suddenly been demoted from the role of a professional to that of parent as patient and had experienced the common assumption of many professionals that parents of a problem child are emotionally maladjusted and are prime candidates for counseling, psychotherapy, or tranquilizers" (Roos, 1985, p. 246).

Parent's responsibility for the child's condition. Some parents do feel responsible for their child's disability and, with a little encouragement from a professional, can be made to feel completely guilty. A productive parent-professional relationship focuses on collaborative problem solving, not on laying blame.

Parent as less intelligent. Parents' information and suggestions are given little recognition. Parents are considered too biased, too involved, or too unskilled to make useful observations. Some professionals concede that parents have access to needed information but contend that parents are not able to, or should not, make any decisions based on what they know.

Parent as adversary. Some teachers expect the worst whenever they interact with parents. Even when that attitude can be partially explained by previous unpleasant encounters with unreasonable parents, it often becomes a self-fulfilling prophecy and is at best a negative influence on new relationships.

Parent in need of a label. Some educators seem eager to label parents (and students). If parents disagree with a diagnosis or seek another opinion, they are *denying*; if parents refuse a suggested treatment, they are *resistant*; and if parents insist that something is wrong with their child despite test evidence to the contrary, they are *anxious*.

Figure 4.2 Roadblocks to partnership: Professionals' attitudes and assumptions about parents

Source: Adapted from Sonnenschein, P. (1981). "Parents and professionals: An uneasy relationship." *Teaching Exceptional Children, 14,* pp. 62–65. Used by permission of the Council for Exceptional Children, Reston, VA.

son with mental retardation who spends much of his school day in general education classrooms, reminds us:

> There are meddlesome parents of children at all achievement levels. Parents of children with special needs do not have a corner on the market. Just visit any competitive public high school in the United States. There you will find . . . some of the most unrealistic parents in America. They are playing with homogeneous groups, they are asking for untimed SATs, they are overruling teachers' placement decisions in honor classes, they are hiring tutors, and they are stopping at nothing to demand anything that will ensure their child's school success. So why are parents of children with special needs held to a higher and unattainable standard? (p. 322)

We should examine factors that cause friction between parents and teachers not to determine fault but to identify what we can change and improve. Professionals who recognize that some of their own behaviors may diminish the potential for productive relationships with parents are in a better position to change their actions and obtain the benefits that such relationships can provide. Perhaps the first and most important step for the teacher is to avoid sweeping generalizations about parents of exceptional children and to treat them with respect as individuals. After all, isn't that how teachers want to be treated?

Methods of Home-School Communication

Parent-teacher conferences, written messages, and telephone conversations are the three most common methods of home-school communication.

The strategies recommended in this section are relevant to all types of parent-teacher meetings. However, IEP and IFSP planning and evaluation meetings, which are discussed in Chapters 2 and 5 respectively, entail additional procedural requirements.

Parent-Teacher Conferences Although parent-teacher conferences are as common to school as recess and homework, they are not always an effective vehicle for communication. Too often, parent-teacher conferences are stiff, formal affairs with anxious teachers and worried parents who wonder what bad news they will hear this time. Fortunately, parents and teachers are learning to talk with one another in more productive ways. In a face-to-face meeting, parents and teachers can exchange information and coordinate their efforts to assist the child with disabilities at home and in school. Parent-teacher conferences should not be limited to the beginning and end of the school year but scheduled regularly.

Preparing for the Conference. Preparation is the key to effective parent-teacher conferences. It entails establishing specific objectives for the conference, obtaining and reviewing a computer printout or list of the student's grades, selecting examples of the student's work and perhaps a graph or chart showing the student's cumulative progress, and preparing an agenda for the meeting (Courson & Hay, 1996; Dodd, 1996; Stephens & Wolf, 1989). Figure 4.3 shows a parent-teacher conference outline that can be used for preparing an agenda and recording notes of the meeting.

For detailed descriptions of how to plan and conduct parent-teacher conferences, see Kroth and Edge (1997), Simpson (1996), and Turnbull and Turnbull (1997). Edens (1997) offers guidelines for holding conferences in parents' homes.

Conducting the Conference. Most parent-teacher conferences for school-age children are held in the child's classroom because (1) the teacher feels comfortable in familiar surroundings; (2) the teacher has ready access to student files and instructional materials; (3) the classroom itself serves as a reminder to the teacher of things the child has done; and (4) the classroom, with its desks, chairs, and teaching materials, reminds both teacher and parents that the purpose of the conference is their mutual concern for improving the child's education (Bennett & Hensen, 1977). Wherever parent conferences are held, the area should be arranged so that it is conducive to partnership interactions (Courson & Hay, 1996). Teachers should not make

Conference Outline

Date 2-14-01 Time 4:30 - 5:00

Student's Name Jeremy Wright
Parents' Name(s) Barbara and Tom Wright
Teacher's Name Tim G.
Other Staff present None

Objectives for Conference: (1) Show graph of J's reading progress, (2) find out about spelling program, (3) get parents' ideas: intervention for difficulties on playground/in gym, (4) share list of books of leisure reading

Student's Strengths
- good worker academically, wants to learn
- excited about progress in reading fluency

Area(s) Where Improvement is Needed:
- continue w/spelling @ home
- arguments & fighting w/other kids

Questions to Ask Parents:
- Interactions w/friends while playing in neighborhood?
- How would they feel about f'dback from classmate re: playground/gym behavior?
- Consequences?

Parent's Responses/Comments:
- very pleased w/reading - want to build on it.
- wondering how long w/in-home spelling?
- willing to give rewards @ home: playground/gym

Examples of Student's Work/Interactions:
- graph of corrects/errors per min.: reading
- weekly pre- & post test scores: spelling.

Current Programs and Strategies Used by Teacher:
- reading: silent read, two 1-min. time trials, self-charting comprehension practice
- spelling: practice w/tape recorder, self-checking

Suggestions for Parents:
- continue spelling games (invite friends)
- Show interest in/play fantasy games (Dung. & Dragons) W/J

Suggestions from Parents:
- Try using some high-interest spelling words (e.g., joust, castle)
- Matt & Amin could help with playground/gym program

Follow-up Activities: (Agreed to in conf)

Parents:
- Continue to play spelling game 2 nights per week
- Take J to library for adventure books

Teacher:
- Ask J for high-interest words & use 3-4 in his weekly list.
- Develop peer intervention strategy w/Matt, Amin & J (group contingency?)

Date to Call for Follow-up:

Feb. 28 (Wednesday) ________ (check when called)

Figure 4.3 Outline for a parent-teacher conference
Source: Adapted from Heward, W. L., Dardig, J. C., & Rossett, A. (1979). *Working with parents of handicapped children* (p. 233). Upper Saddle River, NJ: Merrill/Prentice Hall. Used by permission.

the mistake of hiding behind their desks, creating a barrier between themselves and the parents, or of seating parents in undersized chairs meant for students.

Stephens and Wolf (1989) recommend a four-step sequence for parent-teacher conferences:

1. *Build rapport.* Establishing mutual trust and the belief that the teacher really cares about the student is important to a good parent-teacher conference. A minute or two should be devoted to relevant small talk. The teacher might begin with something positive about the child or family instead of a superficial statement about the weather or traffic.

2. *Obtain information.* Parents can provide teachers with important information for improving instruction. As suggested earlier, teachers should use open-ended questions that cannot be answered with a simple yes or no. For example, "Which activities in school has Felix mentioned lately?" is better than "Has Felix told you what we are doing now in school?" The first question encourages the parent to provide more information; the teacher is trying to build conversation, not preside over a question-and-answer session. Throughout the conference, the teacher should show genuine interest in listening to parents' concerns, avoid dominating the conversation, and stay focused on the purpose of the meeting. Above all, teachers should refrain from making comments that lecture ("Do you realize. . . . "), criticize or judge ("That was a mistake. . . . "), or threaten ("Unless you take my advice. . . . "), all of which block communication (Simpson, 1996; Turnbull & Turnbull, 1997; Wilson, 1995).

3. *Provide information.* The teacher should give parents concrete information about their child in jargon-free language. The teacher should share examples of schoolwork and data on student performance—what has already been learned and what needs to be learned next. If the student has not made much progress, parents and teacher should look together for ways to improve it.

4. *Summarize and follow up.* The conference should end with a summary of what was said. The teacher should review strategies agreed on during the conference and indicate the follow-up activities that either party will do to help carry out those strategies. Some teachers record notes on a laptop computer during the conference,

By showing parents specific examples of their children's progress, teachers set the occasion for parental praise and approval of student effort.

printing out a copy at the conclusion of the meeting so that parents will also have a record of what was said or agreed to.

Written Messages Although much can be accomplished in face-to-face meetings, they require time to plan and conduct, so they cannot take place frequently. But parent-teacher conferences should not be the sole means of home-school communication. Written messages, especially when part of a systematic form of ongoing information exchange, can be an excellent way of maintaining home-school communication.

Happy Grams. The easiest and quickest type of home-school written message are short notes informing parents of something positive their child has accomplished at school. Many teachers regularly send happy grams home with their students, giving parents an opportunity to praise the child at home and stay abreast of activities in the classroom. A book by Kelly (1990) includes tear-out masters of school-home notes that can be duplicated and used for a variety of communication purposes.

Two-Way Home-School Note Systems. A two-way parent-teacher communication system can be built around a reporting form or notebook the child carries between home and school. Teachers can develop and use a standard form or checklist, such as the one shown in Figure 4.4, to inform parents about their child's homework assignments and behavior in the classroom (Cronin et al., 1992; Olympia, Andrews, Valum, & Jensen, 1993; Sicley, 1993). Parents sign the form to indicate they have received it and can use the form themselves to provide information or request assistance from the teacher(s). To be most effective, home-school communication forms should be simple to use, with spaces for teachers and parents to circle or check responses and to write short notes to one another.

Home-school dialogue notebooks offer another form of written communication between parents and teachers. Williams and Cartledge (1997) describe a notebook system that Williams used to communicate regularly with the parents of children with emotional and behavioral disorders. The children attended an urban school, and all came from low socioeconomic backgrounds. Williams and Cartledge emphasize the importance of being organized, persistent, and flexible in expectations for parent participation.

To learn about the importance of regular parent-teacher communication (including a home-school notebook) to one student's family and his teacher, see "In Support of Jay" later in this chapter.

> Parent responses are needed to make the notebook system work. How did we get parents to respond regularly and meaningfully? The secret is the teacher's consistency, persistence, and caring. . . . I found that to make the system work, I had to be well-organized and disciplined. I had to read 10 notebook entries every day and make my own entries. In my classroom, I placed a basket near the door. . . . As soon as the students entered the classroom, they were to put their notebook in the basket before going to breakfast. I would read the parent notes while the students were eating breakfast, and I also used lunch or periods when students attended art, music, and physical education classes as times to review parent messages. I usually wrote to the parents during the afternoon recess period.
>
> Needless to say, not all parents immediately embraced this communication system. This is where persistence became important; I refused to give up. I always tried to respond positively to every parent, and I worked to help them gradually increase their levels of participation. Some parents were comfortable with just signing their names on the notebook to let me know that they had read my message; some were comfortable writing about their child's activities during the previous night; and some would go further to share special or personal events that they felt would be of significance to their child's schooling. (p. 32)

Figure 4.5 shows some sample parent-teacher notebook exchanges.

Assignment Monitoring Sheet

Name ______________________________ Date: ______________________

PERIOD	ASSIGNMENT	FEEDBACK			COMMENT	SIGNATURE
1		HWC HWNC	CWC CWNC	AB UB		
2		HWC HWNC	CWC CWNC	AB UB		
3		HWC HWNC	CWC CWNC	AB UB		
4		HWC HWNC	CWC CWNC	AB UB		
5		HWC HWNC	CWC CWNC	AB UB		
6		HWC HWNC	CWC CWNC	AB UB		
7		HWC HWNC	CWC CWNC	AB UB		

KEY:
HWC = HomeWork Completed
CWC = ClassWork Completed
AB = Acceptable Behavior
HWNC = HomeWork Not Completed
CWNC = ClassWork Not Completed
UB = Unacceptable Behavior

****

Parent Feedback/Assistance Request

Feedback or Issue of Concern:

____

____

____

Action Requested:
phone conference ______
conference at school ______
none ______

Best day/time to contact:
day: __________
time: __________

Parent Signature: ______________________________ Phone: ______________________

Figure 4.4 Home-school communication form for monitoring homework and in-school behavior
Source: From Cronin, M. E., Slade, D. L., Bechtel, C., & Anderson, P. (1992). Home-school partnerships: A cooperative approach to intervention. *Intervention in School and Clinic, 27*(5), 286–292. © 1992 by PRO-ED, Inc. Reprinted by permission.

Home-School Contracts. A home-school contract specifies parent-delivered rewards for the child contingent on her behavior or academic performance in the classroom (Smith, 1994). For example, Kerr and Nelson (1998) describe a home-school contract developed by the teacher and parents of a child who interrupted the teacher and disrupted other students during math and social studies classes. The student received a checkmark for each class period that he participated in class discussions instead of disrupting others; when he earned 50 checkmarks, his parents agreed to buy him a

The teacher said:
William had a great first day at school. He did as much as he could with his hand. Please go through the papers that he brought home and explain them to him. He had a great start, and I am sure that he is just going to do fine.

Then the parent said:
William had a great evening. He was very anxious about school. His goal for this semester is to have straight *A*s. Thanks so much for being so kind with him.

The teacher said:
Mrs. R, thank you very much for attending our class feast yesterday. That was very nice of you, and I want you to know that it was greatly appreciated. I am pleased that Jason is making progress both academically and socially—which could not have happened without your support and cooperation.

Then the parent said:
Mrs. W., thank you very much for the lunch. It was very good. I am glad that Jason is making progress especially with his behavior. I hope this will continue. Jason misplaced his homework and could not find it. Would you please send another homework home today so that he will be able to get the credit?

The parent said:
I checked some of Jermain's papers. Please don't accept sloppy work. He is making some mistakes, and I think he is not paying attention to his work. He loves to come to school, and he is making some new friends. He said you have been very helpful. He had a great weekend.

Then the teacher said:
Jermain had a pleasant day at school today. He did his assignments and followed directions. I talked with him about his writing and taking time with his work. He promised to do better. Let me know when you want to come in for the conference so that I can make time to be available for you before Thursday.

The parent said:
Matt practiced his spelling words. He finally gave me his spelling book this morning. When is the science project due? Matt could not remember when. He read a cookbook for a half-hour and made out a grocery list for supper from the recipes.

Then the teacher said:
Matt's day at school was fine. He did his assignments and followed directions on the playground. The science project is due in tomorrow morning. He is concerned that he might not be able to put it together before tomorrow. I told him that he should do his best and bring whatever he has in. We will be doing our cooking on Friday, and you are welcome to attend if it is convenient for you.

Figure 4.5 Sample parent-teacher notebook exchanges

Source: Reprinted from Williams, V. L., & Cartledge, G. (1997). Passing notes to parents. *Teaching Exceptional Children, 30*(1), 32. Used by permission of the Council for Exceptional Children, Reston, VA.

gerbil. Home-school contracts use parent-controlled rewards, build in parent recognition and praise of the child's accomplishments, and involve the teacher and parents together in a positive program to support the child's learning.

Teachers should never rely on written messages, regardless of their form, as the sole method of communicating with parents. Teachers must also be sensitive to the cultural and linguistic backgrounds and educational levels of parents. For example, Harry (1992a) reports that because one group of Hispanic parents had to spend a great deal of time translating and trying to understand a school's written messages, they viewed those messages as a nuisance that further alienated them from their children's school.

Class Newsletters and Websites. Class newsletters or websites are additional methods of fostering home-school communication. Even though putting together a class newsletter or designing a website requires a lot of work, in many cases it is worth the effort. Most teachers today have access to a computer and word processing software. A one- to three-page monthly newsletter can give parents—especially those who do not attend meetings or open houses—information that is too long or detailed to give over the telephone. A newsletter is also an excellent way to recognize parents who participate in various activities. By making the newsletter or website a class project, the teacher can include student-written stories and news items and can create an enjoyable learning activity for the entire class.

Telephone Calls Regular telephone calls can be an effective and efficient way to maintain home-school communication and parent involvement (Gartland, 1993). A brief conversation that focuses on a child's positive accomplishments lets parents and teachers share the child's success and recognize each other's contributions. Short, positive calls from the teacher also reduce parents' fear that calls from school always indicate a problem. Teachers should set aside time on a regular basis so that each child's parent receives a call at least once every two or three weeks. Teachers should ask parents what times they prefer to receive calls. Keeping a log helps to maintain the schedule and reminds teachers of any necessary follow-up.

Telephone trees can be an efficient way to get information to all parents associated with a class. The teacher calls two or three parents, each of whom calls two or three more, and so on. A telephone tree gets parents actively involved and gives them an opportunity to get to know one another.

Telephone answering machines are a convenient, low-cost technology for home-school communication. By recording daily messages on an answering machine, teachers can give parents a great deal of information for relatively little cost. Parents can call and listen at their convenience, literally 24 hours a day. Recorded telephone messages can provide schoolwide and classroom-by-classroom information, good news (e.g., citizen of the month), and suggestions for working with children at home (Heward, Heron, Gardner, & Prayzer, 1991; Minner, Beane, & Prater, 1986; Test, Cooke, Weiss, Heward, & Heron, 1986). Parent callers can also leave messages on the machine, pose a question, offer an idea or suggestion for the teacher, and so on.

Heward and Chapman (1981) used daily recorded telephone messages to increase parent-teacher communication. The teacher of a primary learning disabilities class recorded brief messages on an automatic telephone answering machine. Parents could call five nights per week from 5:00 P.M. until 7:00 A.M. and hear a recorded message like this one:

> Good evening. The children worked very hard today. We are discussing transportation. They enjoyed talking about the airport and all the different kinds of airplanes. The spelling words for tomorrow are train, t-r-a-i-n; plane, p-l-a-n-e; truck, t-r-u-c-k; automobile, a-u-t-o-m-o-b-i-l-e; and ship, s-h-i-p. Thank you for calling. (p. 13)

The number of telephone calls the teacher received from the parents of the six children in the class each week was recorded for the entire school year. The teacher received a total of only 5 calls for the 32 weeks when the recorded messages were not available (0.16 calls per week) compared with 112 calls during the 6 weeks the message system was in operation (18.7 per week). During the nonmessage portions of the study, the next day's spelling list was sent home with the children each day, and parents were asked to help their children with the words. Nonetheless, scores on the daily five-word spelling tests improved for all six students only when the recorded messages were available.

Teachers can also use recorded telephone messages to help parents carry out home-based tutoring. One teacher of junior high students with learning disabilities used an answering machine to mediate a summer writing program (Hassett, Engler, Cooke, Test, Weiss, Heward, & Heron, 1984). Parents of several of her students wanted to help their children maintain or extend their writing skills over the summer. Each day during the nine-week program, the teacher recorded instructions for the session and a story-starter idea (e.g., "You are going up the river in a boat. You feel safe because the unfriendly natives are on the far shore. Suddenly you notice a leak. . . . "). Parent and student called and listened to the taped message together, the student wrote for 10 minutes on that day's story starter, and the parent scored the student's writing according to criteria provided by the teacher. The parents rewarded their children for progress and recorded the results for the teacher after listening to the next day's message.

To get an idea of how this program worked, compare the two stories shown in Figure 7.1 in Chapter 7. Story 8 was written by James before his parents started the program to help him write more action words and adjectives. Story 33 was the sixth story written after his parents began to reward adjectives.

While no single mode of communication will be effective or even appropriate with every parent and family, teachers can increase the number of families they reach by making several methods of home-school communication available to parents. Some parents and families prefer face-to-face meetings; others appreciate receiving written message or phone calls; still others communicate more frequently and efficiently via e-mail or fax machine. Teachers should ask parents which methods of communication they prefer.

Ammer and Littleton (1983) asked 217 parents of exceptional children to check which methods they preferred for receiving regular information from school. Letters were most popular, checked by 69% of parents. The next most popular were parent-teacher conferences (51%) and telephone calls from teachers (45%). Home visits (19%) were the least preferred method of establishing or improving home-school communication.

Regardless of the mode or form of parent-teacher communication, the suggestions in Figure 4.6 can serve as valuable guidelines for educators in their interactions with parents and families.

Other Types of Parent Involvement

Parents As Teachers

Typically developing children learn many skills that children with disabilities do not learn without systematic instruction. For children with disabilities, the casual routines of everyday life at home and in the community may not provide enough practice and feedback to teach them important skills. Many parents of exceptional children have responded to this challenge by systematically teaching their children self-help and daily living skills or by providing home-based academic tutoring to supplement classroom instruction.

Contrast the communication styles suggested in Figures 4.2 and 4.6. With whom would you rather work?

Parents can serve as effective teachers for their children, a conclusion supported by numerous research studies and parent involvement projects in which parents have successfully taught their children at home (e.g., Barbetta & Heron, 1991; Leach & Siddall, 1992; Thurston & Dasta, 1990). Research shows that parents can enhance the development of children with disabilities by teaching them at home (e.g., Baker, 1989; Snell & Beckman-Brindley, 1984; Wedel & Fowler, 1984). And the majority of parents who participate in systematic home tutoring programs describe it as a positive experience for them and their children. A mother and father who participated in a home tutoring program organized by their child's school wrote: "We really enjoyed teaching M. to tell time, and he enjoyed working with us. He learned so quickly and we were so happy and proud to see the progress he was making. We have two other children. Doing this program allowed us to spend time alone with M." (Donley & Williams, 1997, p. 50).

Usually, if parents wish to tutor their children at home, they can and should be helped to do so. Properly conducted, home-based parent tutoring strengthens a child's educational program and gives enjoyment to both child and parent. It is important, however, for professionals to consider carefully to what extent parent tutoring is appropriate. Not all parents want to teach their children at home or have the time to learn and use the necessary teaching skills—and professionals must not

Don't assume that you know more about the child, his needs, and how those needs should be met than the parents do. If you make this assumption, you will usually be wrong and, worse, will miss opportunities to obtain and provide meaningful information.

Junk the jargon. Educators who use technical terminology will have difficulty communicating effectively with parents (or with anyone else, for that matter). Speak in clear, everyday language and avoid the alphabet soup of special education (e.g., FAPE, IFSP, MFE).

Don't let generalizations about parents of children with disabilities guide your efforts. If you are genuinely interested in what a father or mother feels or what she wants, ask. Do not assume a parent is in the *x, y,* or *z* stage and therefore needs *a, b,* or *c*.

Be sensitive and responsive to the cultural and linguistic backgrounds of parents and families. The information and support services desired by families from different cultural and ethnic groups may vary, and majority educators must work to be sensitive to those differences (Sontag & Schacht, 1994). Suggestions for interviewing families from diverse cultural backgrounds can be found in Dennis and Giangreco (1996); Harry (1992a); and Wayman, Lynch, and Hanson (1990).

Don't be defensive toward or intimidated by parents. No, unless you are one, you cannot ever really know what being the parent of a child with disabilities is like. But as a trained teacher, you do know something about helping children with disabilities learn. That's your job; it's what you do every day with lots of children. Offer the knowledge and skills you have without apology, and welcome parents' input.

Maintain primary concern for the child. If you are a child's teacher, you interact with parents and families in an effort to improve the child's educational program. In that role, you are not a marriage counselor or a therapist. If a parent or a family member indicates the need for non-special-education services, offer to refer him to professionals and agencies qualified to provide those services.

Help parents strive for realistic optimism. Children with disabilities and their families benefit little from professionals who are doom-and-gloom types or who minimize the significance of a disability. Help parents analyze, plan, and prepare for their child's future (Giangreco et al., 1998; Turnbull & Turnbull, 1997).

Start with something parents can be successful with. For many parents, involvement in their child's educational program is a new experience. When parents show an interest in helping their child at home, don't set them up to fail by giving them complicated materials, complex instructions, and a heavy schedule of nightly tutoring. Begin with something simple that is likely to be rewarding to the parent and the child.

Don't be afraid to say, "I don't know." Sometimes parents will ask questions that you cannot answer or request services you cannot provide. The mark of a real professional is knowing the limits of your expertise and when you need help. It is okay to say, "I don't know." Parents will think more highly of you.

Figure 4.6 Guidelines for communicating and working with families of children with disabilities

interpret that situation as an indication that parents do not care enough about their children. Hawkins and Hawkins (1981) write:

> Training and motivating parents to carry out a small number of teaching tasks each day does seem appropriate. These should be tasks that have most of the following characteristics: (1) they are brief, usually requiring no more than three or four minutes each; (2) the ultimate value of them to the parent is obvious (thus self-dressing, but perhaps not

block-stacking); (3) they fit the daily routine almost automatically, not requiring a special, noticeable training "session" (thus self-bathing, but not basic communication-board training); (4) they are tasks that cannot be accomplished readily at school alone, either because the opportunities are infrequent or absent (getting up in the morning, toileting), or because training must occur at every opportunity if it is to achieve its objective (mealtime behaviors, walking appropriately with family). (pp. 17–18)

Bowen, Olympia, and Jensen (1996) and Lovitt (1982) suggest these guidelines for home-based parent tutoring:

- *Keep sessions short.* Aim for 15- to 20-minute sessions three or four days per week.
- *Make the experience positive.* Parents should praise the child's attempts.
- *Keep responses to the child consistent.* By praising the child's successful responses (materials and activities at the child's appropriate instructional level are a must) and providing a consistent, unemotional response to errors (e.g., "Let's read that word again, together"), parents can avoid the frustration and negative results that can occur when home tutoring is mishandled.
- *Use tutoring to practice and extend skills already learned in school.* For example, use spelling or vocabulary words from school as the questions or items for an adapted board game (Wesson, Wilson, & Higbee Mandelbaum, 1988).
- *Keep a record.* Parents, like classroom teachers, can never know the exact effects of their teaching unless they keep records. A daily record enables both parents and child to see gradual progress that might be missed if subjective opinion is the only basis for evaluation. Most children do make progress under guided instruction, and a record documents that progress, perhaps providing the parent with an opportunity to see the child in a new and positive light.

For specific programs and techniques teachers can use to help parents who wish to tutor their children at home, see Bowen et al. (1996) and Miller, Barbetta, and Heron (1994). For suggestions on working with parents to help their children with homework and study skills, see Jayanthi, Bursuck, Epstein, and Polloway (1997); Jensen, Sheridan, Olympia, and Andrews (1994); and Luckner (1994).

Parent Education and Support Groups

Education for parenting is not new; programs date back to the early 1800s. But as a result of greater parent involvement in the education of children with disabilities, many more programs are offered for and by parents. Parent groups can serve a variety of purposes: from one-time-only dissemination of information on a new school policy, to make-it-and-take-it workshops in which parents make instructional materials to use at home (e.g., a math facts practice game), to multiple-session programs on participation in IEP/IFSP planning or child behavior management.

Properly conducted, home-based parent tutoring sessions strengthen the child's educational program and are enjoyable for both child and parent.

A Parent-Professional Partnership in Positive Behavioral Support

by Glen Dunlap, Bobbie J. Vaughn, and Lise Fox,
University of South Florida

Our research group at the University of South Florida has focused on children and families affected by disabilities and problem behavior. We have tried to find effective and efficient ways for resolving serious behavior problems that result in durable, meaningful changes for the child and concerned family members, friends, and professionals. Millie Bucy was a part-time member of our group. She helped families enrolled in our early intervention program understand their children's challenges and obtain needed services from schools and agencies. Millie was well suited to this role because she is the mother of a 9-year-old boy with a severe disability.

Her son Jeffrey was born with Cornelia de Lange Syndrome, a condition associated with significant, chronic medical challenges and severe intellectual disabilities. Jeffrey had a history of disruptive and destructive behaviors. He did not talk; he communicated through gestures, vocalizations, and behaviors that included whining, scratching, yelling, biting, hitting, throwing, and head banging. For example, when his mother tried to move him from his favorite spot near the doors of the grocery store, he cried, screamed, and dropped to the floor. If she tried to pick him up, he scratched her face and arms and banged his head on the floor. Yet despite his challenging behaviors, he was a fun-loving child with a great smile.

Jeffrey often exhibited intense aggression and tantrums, especially in public, which increased the difficulties for Millie, her husband Bob, and Jeffrey's 11-year-old brother Chris. Scratched and bruised by Jeffrey's attacks, Millie was reluctant to let him accompany her on errands. Bob, a truck driver, was often out of town, and Millie had no reliable help with Jeffrey.

When she eventually revealed the severity of her son's behavior, we formed a support team that included Millie, ourselves, and our colleague Shelley Clarke, an experienced researcher and support provider. As a team, we agreed to pursue two goals: (1) develop and implement a plan to reduce Jeffrey's problem behaviors and help him establish more congenial patterns of public interaction and (2) document the process carefully so that our experience might benefit other families in similar circumstances. Existing research literature gives little insight into the actual experiences of families affected by a child's severe behavior problems, and little is known about the impact of behavioral support programs on families' day-to-day functioning as well as feelings, expectations, and hopes.

Our work with Millie and Jeffrey was a true partnership. Millie participated as a full member of the behavioral support and research team. Each member had different roles and expertise, but all views were respected and incorporated into decisions. Millie was involved in assessment and intervention. She made final decisions about settings and procedures, and her views and preferences were instrumental in determining specifics of the research.

To address Jeffrey's behavior, we used **positive behavioral support,** which uses findings from applied research literature (especially applied behavior analysis) to construct a comprehensive, individualized program of intervention designed to reduce (or eliminate) problem behaviors while developing alternative patterns more agreeable to the child and the people around him. Positive behavioral support is based on person-centered values. Procedures are intended to preserve the child's dignity and promote his ability to engage with the environment while striving for outcomes that enhance his lifestyle. Positive behavioral support plans are individualized to the child and his circumstances. Specific intervention procedures are derived from a **functional assessment** process that produces an individualized understanding of the child and how his behavior relates to the environment.

For Jeffrey, functional assessment included conversations with Millie and observations in the three community settings that she identified as most problematic: a large grocery store, a fast-food restaurant, and a drive-through bank. The process involved two weeks of information gathering and team discussion. Observations confirmed that Jeffrey exhibited high rates of severe problem behaviors in the three settings. Particularly serious tantrums occurred when he was expected to go through store and restaurant doorways. The team surmised that tantrums occurred because he liked the doorways very much (especially the electronic doors), and disruptions prolonged his proximity to them. We hypothesized that his aggression and tantrums in the store, restaurant, and bank related to boredom and an absence of interesting, reinforcing things to occupy his attention.

We linked our assessment-based hypothesis statements to intervention strategies that were (1) appropriate for the designated settings and (2) Millie considered feasible to use while she was running errands. A number of components were tailored to each of the settings. The plan included techniques for increasing the positive features of Millie's interactions with Jeffrey (e.g., reducing her number of corrections) and promoting appropriate engagement with the routines. When he needed to wait (e.g., in the car at the bank, in the booth at the restaurant, in line at the grocery store), he was given toys to secure his attention and interest or a special picture book depicting favored items and activities. To encourage his participation in shopping, he had a pictorial shopping list so that he could anticipate and identify items to be placed in the grocery cart. To reduce tantrums during transitions through doorways, we provided a powerful, competing reward. Immediately before a transition, he was handed a picture of a highly desired, noisy toy that would be waiting for him in the car. This motivated him to move quickly through the doors.

Although Millie always implemented the support plan as if she were alone with Jeffrey, the support team was on site for coaching during the first few sessions in each setting. During subsequent sessions, members were present to inconspicuously collect data but remained in the background. After an average of seven sessions per setting over a period of about three months, Millie was handling the community outings without any on-site assistance. Formal follow-up observations were conducted five to six months after intervention began.

Support efforts produced important outcomes for Jeffrey and his family. His severe behaviors were virtually eliminated in each targeted setting. The store took longer than the other settings, perhaps because he was learning to use the picture schedule while participating actively in shopping. Tantrums during transitions were reduced substantially. Millie's instructions and interactions with Jeffrey changed positively, with reprimands declining and activity-specific praise increasing over the course of the study. She described the changes as extremely significant and reported restored confidence in being able to manage Jeffrey's behavior, even in awkward circumstances. She felt a new sense of hope for his future as a member of her family and the community:

> I'm feeling a lot more optimistic now and I think that things are really working. I'm seeing differences every day in Jeffrey, little things that he's learning to do. This has just had a really powerful impact on him and on us too.
>
> We decided that we would stop in the grocery store on the way home. . . . it was amazing how well he did. . . . And another thing that was kind of rewarding was that people in the store recognized him and said "hi" to him. . . . I think that helps me and hopefully helps him to feel like he's a part of the community and that was one of our major goals.

We learned a great deal from Millie and Jeffrey and from our efforts to work as partners in seeking meaningful solutions to difficult problems. We gained an appreciation for the value of respectful collaboration and learned that trusting relationships with family members can yield valuable insights. We also learned more about the deep impact that severe problem behaviors can have on all aspects of a family's life. As we learn more about supporting children and their families, we must remain sensitive to the many challenges they encounter every day. That sensitivity will help us be even more effective partners in working with families to make life with their children more rewarding, productive, and satisfying.

For a more detailed account of this case, see Vaughn, Dunlap, Fox, Clarke, and Bucy (1997).

Most parent groups are designed to accomplish one or more of the following purposes (Miller & Hudson, 1994):

1. To disseminate information and suggestions to assist parents in the challenge of raising a child with disabilities
2. To provide a forum for parents to share information with and support one another
3. To exchange information from parents that will enhance their child's education program

There is consistent agreement in parent education literature on the importance of involving parents in planning and, whenever possible, actually conducting parent groups (Baker, 1989; Kroth & Edge, 1997; Turnbull & Turnbull, 1997). To determine what parents want from a parent program, educators should use both open and closed needs assessment procedures. An *open needs assessment* consists of questions like these:

The best family time for my child is when we __________.
I will never forget the time that my child and I __________.
When I take my child to the store, I am concerned that she will __________.
The hardest thing about having a special child is __________.
I wish I knew more about __________.

Baker (1989) describes a 10-session "parents as teachers" training program in which parents of children with mental retardation and other disabilities learn principles for teaching self-help and play skills and decreasing behavior problems. Books such as Steps to Independence: Teaching Everyday Skills to Children with Special Needs *(Baker & Brightman, 1997) and classic parenting manuals such as* Parents Are Teachers *(Becker, 1971/1998) and* Living with Children: New Methods for Parents and Teachers *(Patterson, 1979/1998) are excellent resources for "parents as teachers" training programs. For a review of the literature on parent education programs and research, see Dangle and Polster (1984).*

Parents' responses to open-ended questions can provide a tremendous amount of information about what kinds of parent training programs might be needed and appreciated.

A *closed needs assessment* asks parents to choose, from a list of possibilities, topics they would like to learn more about. For example, educators can give parents a list of topics (e.g., bedtime behavior, interactions with siblings, homework, making friends, planning for the future) and ask them to check any item that is something of a problem and circle any topics that are of major concern or interest.

Bailey and Simeonsson (1988a) have developed the family needs survey, consisting of 35 items organized into six categories (e.g., information, support, finances, family functioning). Because they have obtained different profiles of responses for mothers and fathers, they recommend that both mothers and fathers complete the survey. They also recommend combining open-ended questions with an overall assessment of family needs. They simply ask parents to list on a piece of paper their five greatest needs as a family. By examining the results of needs assessment questionnaires, parents and professionals together can plan parent education groups that respond to parents' real needs.

Parent to Parent Groups

Parent to Parent programs help parents of children with special needs become reliable allies for one another (Santelli, Turnbull, Marquis, & Lerner, 1997). Parent to Parent gives parents of children with disabilities the opportunity to receive support from a veteran parent who is experiencing similar circumstances and challenges. The program carefully matches trained and experienced parents in a one-to-one relationship with parents who have been newly referred to the program. "Because the two parents share so many common disability and family experiences, an immediacy of understanding is typically present in the match. This makes the informational and emotional support from the veteran parents all the more meaningful" (Santelli et al., 1997, p. 74) The first Parent to Parent program, called Pilot Parents, was formed in 1971 by the parent of a young child with Down syndrome in Omaha, Nebraska. Today, more than 35,000 parents have participated in 500 active local Parent to Parent groups and 25 statewide programs.

Turnbull and Turnbull (1997) provide a conversation guide of more than 70 questions that educators might ask parents and family members in an effort to learn more about the family's needs and wishes regarding their child with disabilities.

Parents As Research Partners

Researchers in special education are concerned about the social validity of their studies. Are they investigating socially significant variables? Are the methods used to change student performance acceptable? Did the changes observed make any real difference in the child's life? (Schwartz & Baer, 1991; Wolf, 1978). Who better than parents to identify meaningful outcomes, observe and measure performance in the home and community, and let researchers know if their ideas and findings have any real validity.

A model research-partnership program conducted at the Fred S. Keller School in New York embraces parents as full partners in conducting action research with their children. "The parents are the scientists, and they conduct empirical studies under

For postal and Internet addresses and telephone numbers of state and local Parent to Parent programs, see "For More Information" at the end of this chapter.

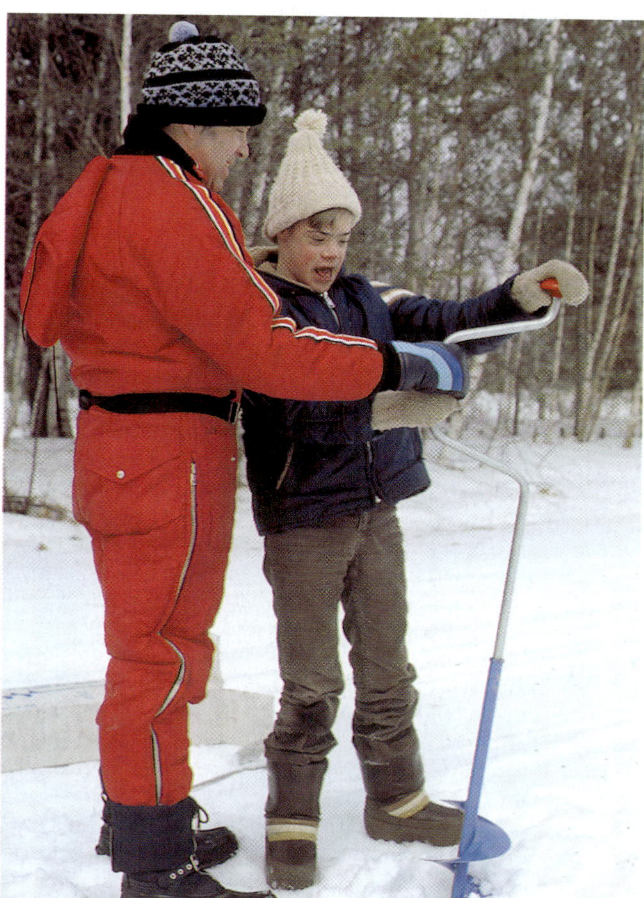

When helping families assess their strengths and needs, professionals must not overlook the importance of leisure time.

the supervision of the schools' parent educators" (Donley & Williams, 1997, p. 46). Parents are assisted in the development of their research projects by their child's teachers, other parents, and a paid parent educator. The experience culminates with a poster session presentation at the end of the school year during which the parent-scientists display the academic, social, and affective gains achieved by their children. Donley and Williams recognize that some school programs do not have the resources to hire a parent educator. They provide several suggestions for schools with more limited resources to approximate their model.

Kay and Fitzgerald (1997) believe that collaborative action research projects foster closer bonds between teachers and parents and provide parents with the satisfaction of knowing what works with their child and why. They recommend that parents participate in action research by helping brainstorm research questions, collect performance data on their children, and share the outcomes with other parents and teachers. Kay and Fitzgerald recognize that involving parents in home-based research experiences can, at times, be overwhelming, but they view the benefits as far outweighing the disadvantages. Whether the parents participate as paid or volunteer members of a research team, they are involved in collecting performance data on their children, talking about these data on a regular basis with other parents, and displaying them in an informal and supportive environment at the end of the year (Donley & Williams, 1997).

In Support of Jay

by Ann P. Turnbull and Mary E. Morningstar

Ann's Perspective Jay was in Mary's class for the last year of his high school program, and it was a very positive experience for him and our entire family. The first evening that our family met Mary, we were impressed with her energy, state-of-the-art knowledge, and obvious commitment to her students. Mary quickly earned our confidence in terms of the programming that she was doing, and we were totally together in our values for integration, productivity, and independence.

Mary organized an in-service program that allowed teachers and parents to work together and to share information about disabilities with the typical students in the school to help prepare them for positive interactions. It gave us a chance to go to classes, meet students and teachers, and feel like part of the school. Right away, Mary got Jay established as a manager of the football team, helped facilitate relationships between Jay and typical students (an opportunity he had never really had before), and helped him dress cool, walk cool, and generally fit into the school.

In terms of family contact, Mary treated us, Jay's parents and sisters, with respect and dignity. There have been times in the past when I have felt judged by teachers, and often it made me feel defensive. To the contrary, I always felt that Mary was able to see my strengths and to value how conscientiously our family was trying to support Jay.

We exchanged a notebook back and forth, and I always looked forward to reading Mary's positive messages. It was a great source of connection and camaraderie for all of us. It was as if we had a visit each day.

I also remember how wonderful it was for Mary to bring Jay and his classmates to our house a couple of days a week for their domestic training. It was a bonus for Jay to be able to learn domestic skills in his own setting, and it was certainly a bonus for our family to have assistance in housekeeping.

One of the confidences that I had throughout the entire year was that Jay was in a quality program and that Mary knew exactly what she was doing. It was an incredible relief for our family to not feel that we had to advocate during every spare minute to ensure opportunities for Jay. We knew that Mary was doing a good job, and we could relax and spend time in family recreation rather than in evening advocacy meetings. What a relief from previous years!

Mary's Perspective The most crucial part of my school program always started during that first meeting with the family. I have always preferred that my first visit take place in the family's home. This puts the family more at ease, lets me get a feel for how the family lives, and lets me meet the brothers and sisters.

As with all of my families, my first visit with Ann, Rud, Jay, Kate, and Amy included completing a parent inventory and a skills preference checklist. The inventory included such items as Jay's daily schedule. What did he do each day? What did he need help with? What was important to him and to his family? I also identified his level of performance and past experiences with certain functional activities, such as grocery shopping, domestic chores, riding a public bus, and having a job. Finally, it looked at future goals. Where did Jay want to work? Where was he going to live? Who would be his friends?

From this inventory, we moved to the preference checklist. On the basis of Jay's activities and skill levels, we figured out what Jay should spend his time learning while in school. Once all of this was done, we picked specific goals and objectives to work on for that year and plugged them into a weekly schedule. What seemed to me to be "just doing my job as a special education teacher" often had a profound effect on families. I remember Ann and Rud's being awed by this process. As parents of a young man with disabilities, they greatly valued the opportunity to work with the schools to tailor a program for their son. Their enthusiasm and excitement about Jay's program helped sustain me through some of the more trying school days.

Continued communication with the family is critical to the success of any school program. Like all of my students, Jay carried his home-school communication notebook back and forth with him each day. This was my lifeline with the family. Any issues, problems, great ideas, changes in schedule, or good things that happened were written down in that notebook. In fact, it was such an important chronicle of our school year that when Jay graduated, we fought over who would keep the notebook! Our compromise was to make a copy for me as a keepsake.

Parent-professional partnerships require give-and-take on both sides. What was most important to me in my relationship with the Turnbulls was their willingness to support me and follow through with Jay's program at home. Ann mentioned that Jay was the manager of the football team, but what she left out was that Rud and Kate enthusiastically attended just about every game, both home and away. They were there not only to cheer the Whitman Vikings but also to support Jay and, through Jay, me and my program.

Knowing that Ann and Rud were there to support my efforts was the most critical component of Jay's successful year. Their involvement provided me with the sustenance to continue my efforts and to improve my program. A school- and community-based program requires more than an eight-hour day. It touches the lives of not only the student and teacher but also the family, school friends, neighbors, employers, store workers, bus drivers, and all who come into contact with that student and family. Establishing a positive and mutually beneficial family-professional partnership requires much effort and skill, but the outcomes of such a relationship far outweigh the efforts.

Source: Adapted from Turnbull, A. P., & Morningstar, M. E. (in press). Family and professional interaction. In M. E. Snell & F. Brown (Eds.), *Instruction of students with severe disabilities* (5th ed.). Upper Saddle River, NJ: Merrill/Prentice Hall.

How Much Parent Involvement?

It is easy for educators to get carried away by a good concept, especially one like parent and family involvement, which has so much promise for positive outcomes. But teachers and everyone else involved in providing special education services to children with disabilities must not take a one-sided, unidirectional view of parent involvement. Sometimes the time and energy required for parents to participate in home-based tutoring programs or parent education groups cause stress among family members or guilt if the parents cannot fulfill teachers' expectations (Callahan, Rademacher, & Hildreth, 1998; Winton & Turnbull, 1981). The time required to provide additional help to a child with disabilities may take too much time and attention away from other family members (Turnbull & Turnbull, 1982).

Kroth and Edge (1997) describe the mirror model for parent involvement (see Figure 4.7), which recognizes that parents have a great deal to offer as well as a need to receive services from special educators. The model attempts to give parents an equal part in deciding what services they need and what services they might provide to professionals or other parents. The top half of the model assumes that professionals have certain information, knowledge, and skills that should be shared with parents to help them with their children. The bottom half of the model assumes that parents have information, knowledge, and skills that can help professionals be more effective in assisting children. The model assumes that not all parents need everything that professionals have to offer and that no parent should be expected to provide everything. All parents should be expected to provide and obtain information, most parents will be active participants in IEP planning, and fewer parents will participate or contribute to workshops and extended parent education groups.

Cone, Delawyer, and Wolfe (1985) developed the parent/family involvement index to objectively measure 12 types of parent involvement in a special education program.

Current Issues and Future Trends

Special educators and families of children with disabilities will continue to develop more effective ways of working together. These efforts will be increasingly driven by values such as those suggested by the Syracuse University Center on Human Policy (1987):

1. Families should receive the supports necessary to maintain their children at home.
2. Family services should support the entire family.
3. Family supports should maximize the family's control over the services and supports they receive.

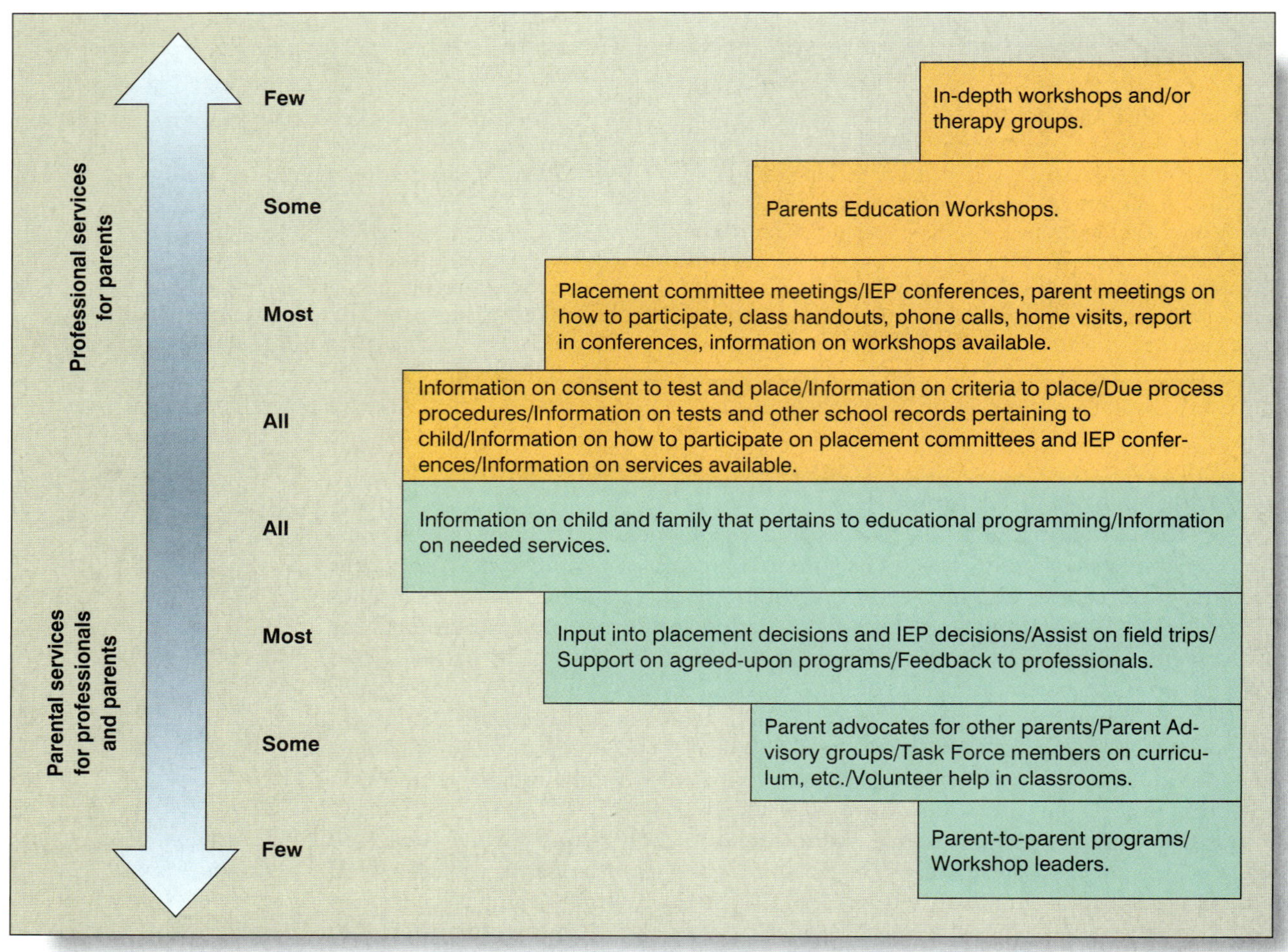

Figure 4.7 Mirror model for parent involvement

Source: From Kroth, R. L., & Edge, D. (1997). *Strategies for communicating with parents of exceptional children* (3rd ed.). Denver: Love. Reprinted by permission.

Dunlap and Fox (1997) define ***family supports*** *as "any and all actions that serve to strengthen and sustain the family system, especially as these actions pertain to the family's assimilation and understanding of the child's disability" (p. 4).*

Thus, family preservation and empowerment have become the goals of working with families of children with disabilities. Family-centered services are predicated on the belief that the child is part of a family system and that effective change for the child (who is one part of the system) cannot be achieved without helping the entire family (the whole system) (Turnbull & Turnbull, 1997).

The rationale for family empowerment is based on the belief that families are the primary and most effective social institution, that families cannot be replaced, that parents are and should remain in charge of their families, and that the role of professionals is to help parents in their capacity as family leaders (Callister, Mitchell, & Talley, 1986). Empowerment can be viewed as a process of enabling families to take control of their lives by providing information and resources and helping families learn to use them. The specific actions and supports that result in meaningful and effective empowerment will vary across families and even change across time and instances within a specific family (Jones, Garlow, Turnbull, & Barber, 1996).

Another emerging perspective, particularly with families involved in early intervention programs for infants and toddlers, is the movement toward a **strength-based approach** to conceptualizing and providing family supports:

> A strength-based philosophy is a critical belief, an all-pervasive attitude that informs all of the professional's interactions with families. It assumes that all families have strengths they can build on and use to meet their own needs, to accomplish their own goals, and to promote the well-being of family members. The family-professional relationship starts not from an assessment of problems related to the child with a disability but from an attempt to fully understand the way in which the family successfully accomplishes its goals and manages its problems. (Powell, Batsche, Ferro, Fox, & Dunlap, 1997, p. 4)

Professionals and parents are working to develop and provide a wide range of supportive services for families of children with disabilities. Programs are being implemented to help parents plan effectively for the future; develop problem-solving skills; and acquire competence in financial planning, coping with stress, locating and using community services, and finding time to relax and enjoy life—to name just a few areas of emphasis.

Parents and family are the most important people in a child's life. Effective and caring teachers should be next in importance. Working together, teachers, parents, and families can and do make a difference in the lives of exceptional children.

Use the self-tests at http://www.prenhall.com/heward to assess your knowledge of the content of Chapter 4.

Summary

Support for Parent and Family Involvement

- Three factors are responsible for the increased emphasis on parent and family involvement in the education of children with disabilities: parent advocacy, educators' desire to increase their effectiveness, and legislators.
- A successful parent-teacher partnership provides benefits for the professional, the parents, and—most important—the child.

Understanding Parents and Families of Children with Disabilities

- All parents and family members must adjust to the birth of a child with disabilities or the discovery that a child has a disability. This adjustment process is different for each parent, and educators should not make assumptions about an individual parent's stage of adjustment.
- There are nine roles and responsibilities that parents of children with disabilities must fulfill: caregiver, provider, teacher, counselor, behavior management specialist, parent of siblings without disabilities, marriage partner, information specialist for significant others, and advocate for school and community services.
- A family member's disability affects parents and siblings without disabilities in different ways during the different life-cycle stages.
- Respite care—the temporary care of an individual with disabilities by nonfamily members—is a critical support for many families of children with severe disabilities.
- Children with disabilities are overrepresented among reported cases of child abuse and neglect. The presence of a disability, however, is just one of a complex set of variables related to child abuse. Most parents of children with disabilities provide a loving and supportive home.

Parent-Teacher Communication

- Five principles for effective communication between educators and parents are accepting what is being said, listening, questioning appropriately, encouraging, and staying focused.
- The three most common modes of home-school communication are parent-teacher conferences, written messages, and telephone calls.
- Here are some guidelines for working with parents and families of children with disabilities:
  - Don't assume you know more about a child than the parents do.
  - Junk the jargon and speak in plain, everyday language.
  - Don't use generalizations or assumptions.
  - Be sensitive and responsive to cultural and linguistic differences.
  - Don't be defensive toward or intimidated by parents.
  - Keep concern for the child at the forefront.
  - Help parents strive for realistic optimism.
  - Start with something that parents can be successful with.
  - Don't be afraid to say, "I don't know."

Other Types of Parent Involvement

- Many parents can and should learn to help teach their child with disabilities.
- Parents and professionals should work together in planning and conducting parent education groups.
- Parent to Parent groups give parents of children with disabilities support from a veteran parents who are experiencing similar circumstances and challenges.
- Parents who serve as action research partners help brainstorm research questions, collect performance data on their children, and share those data with other parents and teachers.

- The mirror model of parent involvement assumes that not all parents need everything that professionals have to offer and that no parent should be expected to participate in everything.

Current Issues and Future Trends

- Professionals who work with parents should value family needs and support families in maintaining control over the services and supports they receive.
- The rationale for family empowerment is based on the belief that families are the primary and most effective social institution, that families cannot be replaced, that parents are and should remain in charge of their families, and that the role of professionals is to help parents in their capacity as family leaders.
- Family-centered services are predicated on the belief that the child is part of a family system and that effective change for the child cannot be achieved without helping the entire family.
- A strength-based approach to family supports assumes that all families have strengths they can build on and use to meet their own needs, accomplish their own goals, and promote the well-being of family members.

For More Information

Journals/Magazines/Newsletters

- *Exceptional Parent*, 555 Kinderkamack Road, Oradell, NJ 07649; (800) 247-8080; website: http://www.familyeducation.com/. Mission of this monthly magazine is to empower mothers and fathers of children with disabilities by providing practical information and emotional support. Contains articles for parents and professionals on subjects such as improving parent-professional relationships, maintaining family relationships, and managing financial resources.
- *Families and Disability Newsletter*. Free newsletter published three times a year by the Beach Center on Families and Disability (see "Organizations").
- *Sibling Information Network Newsletter*. Published by the Sibling Information Network (see "Organizations").

Books

- Alper, S. K., Schloss, P. J., & Schloss, C. N. (Eds.). (1994). *Families of students with disabilities: Consultation and advocacy.* Needham Heights, MA: Allyn & Bacon.
- Anderson, W., Chitwood, S., & Hayden, D. (1997). *Negotiating the special education maze: A guide for parents and teachers*. Reston, VA: Council for Exceptional Children.
- Cutler, B. C. (1993). *You, your child, and "special" education: A guide to making the system work.* Baltimore: Brookes.
- Gartner, A., Lipsky, D. K., & Turnbull, A. P. (1990). *Supporting families with a child with a disability*. Baltimore: Brookes.
- Harry, B. (1992). *Cultural diversity, families, and the special education system*. New York: Teachers College Press.
- Kroth, R. L., & Edge, D. (1997). *Strategies for communicating with parents of exceptional children* (3rd ed.). Denver: Love.
- Lutzker, J. R., & Campbell, R. (1994). *Ecobehavioral family interventions in developmental disabilities*. Pacific Grove, CA: Brooks/Cole.
- Meyer, D. J., Vadasy, P. F., & Fewell, R. R. (1996). *Living with a brother or sister with special needs: A book for sibs* (2nd ed.). Seattle: University of Washington Press.
- Mullins, J. (1987). Authentic voices from parents of exceptional children. *Family Relations, 36,* 30–33. Journal article lists 60 books written by parents of children with various disabilities.
- Neef, N. A., et al. (1998). *Caring for persons with developmental disabilities: A training program for respite care providers*. Champaign, IL: Research Press.
- Powell, T. H., & Gallagher, P. A. (1992). *Brothers and sisters: A special part of exceptional families.* Baltimore: Brookes.
- Pueschel, S., Scola, P. S., Weidenman, L., & Bernier, J. (1995). *The special child: A sourcebook for parents and children with developmental disabilities* (2nd ed.). Baltimore: Brookes.
- Repucci, N. D., Britner, P. A., & Wollard, J. L. (1997). *Preventing child abuse and neglect through parent education.* Baltimore: Brookes.
- Salisbury, C. L., & Intaglia, J. (1986). *Respite care support for persons with developmental disabilities and their families*. Baltimore: Brookes.
- Shea, T. M., & Bauer, A. M. (1993). *Parents and teachers of children with exceptionalities* (2nd ed.). Needham Heights, MA: Allyn & Bacon.
- Simpson, R. L. (1996). *Working with families and parents of exceptional children and youth: Techniques for successful conferencing and collaboration* (3rd ed.). Austin, TX: PRO-ED.
- Singer, G. H. S., & Powers, L. E. (Eds.). (1993). *Families, disability, and empowerment: Active coping skills and strategies for family interventions*. Baltimore: Brookes.
- Singer, G. H. S., Powers, L. E., & Olson, A. L. (Eds.). (1996). *Redefining family support: Innovations in public-private partnerships*. Baltimore: Brookes.
- Stray-Gundersen, K. (1995). *Babies with Down syndrome: A new parents' guide*. Bethesda, MD: Woodbine House.

- Turnbull, A. P., & Turnbull, H. R. (1997). *Families, professionals, and exceptionality: A special partnership* (3rd ed.). Upper Saddle River, NJ: Merrill/Prentice Hall.
- Turnbull, H. R., & Turnbull, A. P. (1985). *Parents speak out: Then and now* (2nd ed.). Upper Saddle River, NJ: Merrill/Prentice Hall.

Organizations

- *ARCH National Resource Center for Crisis Nurseries and Respite Care Services,* Chapel Hill Training Outreach Project, 800 Eastowne Drive, Suite 105, Chapel Hill, NC 27514; National Respite Locator Service: (800) 773-5433.
- *Beach Center on Families and Disability,* University of Kansas, 3111 Haworth Hall, Lawrence, KS 66045; phone, V/TTY: (913) 864-7600; e-mail: beach@dole.lsi.ukans.edu; website: http://www.lsi.ukans.edu/beach/beachhp.htm. Conducts research and training to enhance families' empowerment and disseminates information to families, individuals with disabilities, educators, and the general public. Provides technical assistance to national network of Parent to Parent support programs.
- *National Center on Child Abuse and Neglect*, U.S. Department of Health and Human Services, P.O. Box 1182, Washington, DC 20013; Child Help USA hotline: (800) 422-4453.
- *National Information Center for Handicapped Children and Youth (NICHCY),* P.O. Box 1492, Washington, DC 20013; phone, TTY: (800) 695-0285; e-mail: nichcy@aed.org; website: http://www.nichcy.org. Disseminates free information about children and youth with disabilities; provides referrals to state and national disability groups, advocacy organizations, and parent groups.
- *National Parent Network on Disabilities*, 1727 King Street, Suite 305, Alexandria, VA 22314; phone, V/TTY: (703) 684-6763. A consortium and clearinghouse of information about parent training and information centers, parent groups, and professional organizations with interest in parent and family issues.
- *National Parent CHAIN*, 515 West Giles Lane, Peoria, IL 61614. A volunteer organization to establish a national information and education network for citizens with disabilities and their families.
- *National Parent to Parent Support and Information System,* (706) 632-8822; toll-free for parents: (800) 651-1151; website: http://www.nppsis.org. Maintains data base of thousands of parents and matches people with parents whose children have similar rare disabilities.
- *Parents Educational Advocacy Center*, 116 West Jones Street, Raleigh, NC 27611.
- *PEP (Parents Educating Parents) Project*, Georgia Association for Retarded Citizens, 1851 Ram Runway, Suite 104, College Park, GA 30337.
- *Sibling Information Network,* A. J. Pappanikou Center, University of Connecticut, 249 Glenbrook Road, U64, Storrs, CT 06269-2064; (860) 486-5035.
- *Technical Assistance to Parents Programs (TAPP) Network,* 95 Berkeley Street, Suite 104, Boston, MA 02116; phone, V/TTY: (617) 482-2915. Information on national network of more than 70 parent training and information centers funded by the U.S. Department of Education.
- *Federation of Families for Children's Mental Health,* 1021 Prince Street, Alexandria, VA 22314-2071. National parent-run organization focused on the needs of children and youths with emotional, behavioral, or mental disorders and their families.

Websites

- Anderson, K. M., & Anderson, C. L. (1997). Helpful web sites for parents of children with disabilities. *Intervention in School and Clinic, 33*(1), 40–42.
- *Compact for Learning: An Action Handbook for Family-School-Community Partnerships,* http://www.ed.gov/pubs/compact/. Helps teams of school staff, teachers, parents, and others develop and use compacts outlining the shared responsibilities of school partners for children's learning.
- *General links,* http://nucleus.com/parent.html/. Information sites for new and expecting parents, support groups, etc.
- *Parents' Guide to the Internet,* http://www.ed.gov/pubs/parents/internet/. Intended to help parents and families, regardless of their technological know-how, use the Internet as a tool for learning.
- *Sibling Support Project,* http://www.chmc.org/departmt/sibsupp/. Assistance and resources for brothers and sisters of those with special needs, advice for their parents, and a directory of support programs.

Part 2

Educational Needs of Exceptional Students

Chapter 5

Early Childhood Special Education

Focus Questions

- Why is it so difficult to measure the impact of early intervention?
- How can we provide early intervention services for a child whose disability is not yet present?
- What are the goals of early childhood special education? Which do you think are most important?
- In what ways might a program based entirely on developmentally appropriate practices not always be sufficient for a young child with disabilities?
- How can a play activity or an everyday routine be turned into a specially designed learning opportunity for a child with disabilities?

Most children learn a phenomenal amount from the time they are born until they enter school. They grow and develop in orderly, predictable ways, learning to move about their world, communicate, and play. As their ability to manipulate their environment increases, so does their level of independence. Normal rates and patterns of child development contrast sharply with the progress experienced by most children with disabilities. If they are to master the basic skills that most children acquire naturally, many preschoolers with disabilities need carefully planned and implemented early childhood special education services.

Early childhood experts agree that the earlier intervention begins, the better. Child development expert Burton White, who has conducted years of research with typically developing infants and preschoolers at Harvard University's Preschool Project, believes that the period between 8 months and 3 years is critical to cognitive and social development: "to begin to look at a child's educational development when he is 2 years of age is already much too late" (White, 1975, p. 4). If the first years of life are the most important for children without disabilities, they are even more critical for the child with disabilities, who, with each passing month, risks falling even further behind nondisabled age mates. Yet parents concerned about deficits in their child's development used to be told, "Don't worry. Wait and see. She'll probably grow out of it."

Over the past 25 years, the "extraordinary vulnerability of young children at risk for developmental problems . . . as well as those with established disabilities has been recognized" (Guralnick, 1998, p. 319). Today, early childhood special education has become one of the most prominent components in education, and the creation of an effective system of early intervention services has become a national priority.

Go to the companion website at http://www.prenhall.com/heward and select Chapter 5 to review the chapter objectives.

The Importance of Early Intervention

Early intervention consists of a wide variety of educational, nutritional, child care, and family supports, all designed to reduce the effects of disabilities or prevent the occurrence of learning and developmental problems later in life for children presumed to be at risk for such problems. McConnell (1994) provides an excellent definition of early intervention:

> Early intervention can be defined as a loosely structured confederation of publicly and privately funded home- and classroom-based efforts that provide (1) compensatory or preventative services for children who are assumed to be at risk for learning and behavior problems later in life, particularly during the elementary school years, and (2) remedial services for problems or deficits already encountered. . . . Simply put, early intervention must provide early identification and provision of services to reduce or eliminate the effects of disabilities or to prevent the development of other problems, so that the need for subsequent special services is reduced. (pp. 75, 78)

*Early intervention sometimes refers to services provided to infants and toddlers, from birth through age 2, and their families. In this book, the terms **early childhood special education** and **early intervention** are used interchangeably to describe special education services provided to children from birth to age 5.*

More simply, early intervention includes all of our "efforts to improve the development of vulnerable children and their families through deliberate intervention in their life space" (Gallagher, 1997, p. 88).

Does early intervention work? If so, what kinds of interventions work best? Hundreds of studies have been conducted in an effort to answer these questions. We'll look at a few of those studies here.

First-Generation Research

Let's consider two widely cited examples of what Guralnick (1997) calls first-generation research: studies that try to answer the question, "Does early intervention make a difference for children and their families?"

Intelligence testing and IQ scores are discussed in Chapter 6.

Skeels and Dye The earliest and one of the most dramatic demonstrations of the critical importance and potential impact of early intervention was conducted by Skeels and Dye (1939). They found that intensive stimulation, one-to-one attention, and a half-morning kindergarten program with 1- to 2-year-old children who were classified as mentally retarded resulted in IQ gains and eventual independence and success as adults when compared to similar children in the institution who received adequate medical and health services but no individual attention. The Skeels and

Dye study can be justly criticized for its lack of tight experimental methodology. Nevertheless, it challenged the widespread belief that intelligence was fixed and that little could be expected from intervention efforts, and it served as the catalyst for many subsequent investigations into the effects of early intervention. Figure 5.1 tells more about the work of Skeels and Dye.

For 15 years the Milwaukee Project provided education and family support services to children born of low-IQ mothers. A book by Garber (1988), the coordinator of the project's research team, describes significant improvements in intelligence, language performance, and academic achievement for the children who received services, compared with a control group of disadvantaged children from mothers of average intelligence.

The Milwaukee Project The goal of the Milwaukee Project was to reduce the incidence of mental retardation through a program of parent education and infant stimulation for children considered at risk for retarded development because of their mothers' levels of intelligence (IQs below 70) and conditions of poverty (Garber & Heber, 1973; Heber & Garber, 1971; Strickland, 1971). The mothers received training in child care and were taught how to interact with and stimulate their children. Beginning before the age of 6 months, the children also participated in an infant stimulation program conducted by trained teachers. By the age of 3½, the experimental children tested an average of 33 IQ points higher than did a control group of children who did not participate in the program.

Hailed by the popular media as the "miracle in Milwaukee," this study is sometimes offered as proof that a program of maternal education and early infant stimulation can reduce the incidence of mental retardation caused by psychosocial disadvantage. Although the Milwaukee Project has been criticized for its research methods (e.g., Page, 1972), Garber and Heber (1973) claim:

> Infant testing difficulties notwithstanding, the present standardized test data, when considered along with performance on learning tasks and language tests, indicate an unquestionably superior present level of cognitive development on the part of the experimental group. Also, the first wave of our children are now in public schools. None have been assigned to classes for the retarded. (p. 114)

Psychosocial disadvantage, *a combination of social and environmental deprivation early in a child's life, is generally believed to be the cause of most cases of mild mental retardation.*

Second-Generation Research

Second-generation research seeks to find what factors make early intervention more or less effective for particular target groups of children (Guralnick, 1997).

A stimulating, language-rich environment enhances the social and cognitive development of all young children.

Because an orphanage in the mid-1930s had no room, two "hopeless" baby girls, ages 13 months and 16 months, were transferred from an orphanage to a ward of adult women in an institution for persons with mental retardation. "The youngsters were pitiful little creatures. They were tearful, had runny noses, and coarse, stringy, and colorless hair; they were emaciated, undersized, and lacked muscle tone or responsiveness. Sad and inactive, the two spent their days rocking and whining" (Skeels, 1966, p. 5). At the time of their transfer, the two children had IQs estimated between 35 and 46, which classified them in the moderate to severe range of mental retardation. After living with the older women for six months, the girls' IQs were measured at 77 and 87, and a few months later, both had IQs in the mid-90s.

Such regular intelligence testing was not a common procedure in those days, but because of their unusual placement, the two girls were observed closely. Hearing of the girls' remarkable improvement, Skeels and Dye looked for possible causes. They learned that the children had received an unusual amount of attention and stimulation. Ward attendants had purchased toys and books for the girls, and residents had played and talked with them continuously. Excited by the possibilities, Skeels and Dye convinced state authorities to permit an unusual experiment.

Thirteen 1- to 2-year-old children were selected. All but two were classified as mentally retarded (average IQ of 64) and, because of a prevailing state law, were judged unsuitable for adoption. The children in this experimental group were removed from the unstimulating orphanage and placed in the one-to-one care of teenage girls with mental retardation who lived at the institution. Each adolescent "mother" was taught how to provide basic care and attention for her baby—how to hold, feed, talk to, and stimulate the child. The children also attended a half-morning kindergarten program at the institution. A group of 12 children, also under 3 years of age, remained in the orphanage. Children in this contrast group received adequate medical and health services but no individual attention. The children in the contrast group had an average IQ of 86 at the beginning of the study; only two were classified as mentally retarded.

Figure 5.1 The potential impact of early intervention: A powerful demonstration

Weisberg (1994) describes a successful early intervention prevention program in which preschoolers from low-income backgrounds received two years of intensive reading instruction based on the Direct Instruction model and materials (see Chapter 7) before they entered kindergarten.

The Abecedarian Project The Abecedarian Project was designed as an experiment to test whether mental retardation caused by psychosocial disadvantage could be prevented by intensive, early education preschool programs (in conjunction with medical and nutritional supports) beginning shortly after birth and continuing until children enter kindergarten (Martin, Ramey, & Ramey, 1990). Children in the Abecedarian Project received early intervention that was both intensive and long: a full-day preschool program, 5 days per week, 50 weeks per year. Compared with children in a control group who received supplemental medical, nutritional, and social services but no daily early educational intervention services, children in the early intervention group made positive gains in IQ scores by age 3, were 50% less likely to fail a grade, and scored higher on IQ and reading and mathematics achievement tests at age 12.

A related finding was that children of low-IQ mothers benefited most from early intervention. For the mothers with IQs below 70 who were in the control condition, all but one of their children had IQs in the mentally retarded or borderline intelligence range at age 3. In contrast, all of the children in the early intervention group tested in the normal range of intelligence (above 85) by age 3.

> This finding supports the concept of *targeted intervention,* which indicates that primary prevention of childhood disorders is more likely for certain subgroups than for others (Landesman & Ramey, 1989). Because the majority of children with mild and moderate mental retardation come from families with extremely low resources and with parents

Two years later, the children in both groups were retested. The experimental group showed an average *gain* of 27.5 IQ points, enough for 11 of the 13 children to become eligible for adoption and be placed in good homes. The children in the contrast group who stayed in the orphanage had *lost* an average of 26 IQ points.

Twenty-five years later, Skeels (1966) located all of the subjects in the original study. What he discovered was even more impressive than the IQ gains originally reported. Of the 13 children in the experimental group, 11 had married; the marriages had produced nine children, all of normal intelligence. The experimental group's median level of education was the 12th grade, and four had attended college. All were either homemakers or employed outside the home, in jobs ranging from professional and business work to domestic service (for the two who had not been adopted). The story of the 12 children who had remained in the orphanage was less positive. Four were still institutionalized in 1965, and all but one of the noninstitutionalized subjects who were employed worked as unskilled laborers. The median level of education for the contrast group was the third grade. Skeels (1966) concluded his follow-up study with these words:

> It seems obvious that under present-day conditions there are still countless infants with sound biological constitutions and potentialities for development well within the normal range who will become retarded and noncontributing members of society unless appropriate intervention occurs. It is suggested by the findings of this study and others published in the past 20 years that sufficient knowledge is available to design programs of intervention to counteract the devastating effects of poverty, sociocultural, and maternal deprivation. . . . The unanswered questions of this study could form the basis for many life-long research projects. If the tragic fate of the twelve contrast group children provokes even a single crucial study that will help prevent such a fate for others, their lives will not have been in vain. (p. 109)

Figure 5.1 *continued*

> who have limited intellectual resources themselves, these families are the ones that are most in need of early intervention and are those that benefit the most in terms of outcomes valued by society. (Ramey & Ramey, 1992, p. 338)

Project CARE Project CARE compared the effectiveness of home-based early intervention in which mothers learned how to provide developmental stimulation for their infants and toddlers with center-based early intervention like that provided in the Abecedarian Project (Wasik, Ramey, Bryant, & Sparling, 1990). Children who received the full-day, center-based preschool program five days per week, supplemented by home visits, showed gains in intellectual functioning almost identical to those found in the Abecedarian Project. A disappointment was that the intellectual functioning of children in the home-based–only treatment group did not improve. Ramey and Ramey (1992) suggest, "One plausible interpretation of these results is that the home-based treatment was not sufficiently intensive, on a day-to-day basis, to produce the same benefits that occur when a more formally organized and monitored center-based program is provided year round" (p. 339).

The Infant Health and Development Program The Infant Health and Development Program provided early intervention services to infants who were born prematurely and at low birth weight (less than 2,500 grams, or about 5½ pounds), two condi-

TEACHING AND LEARNING IN SCHOOL

Selecting Toys for Young Children with Disabilities

In 1916, John Dewey said, "Children learn by doing." He might just have well have said, "Children learn by playing." Play provides children with natural, repeated opportunities for critical learning. It is the way they explore the world and discover their own capabilities. An infant bats a mobile with her hand, repeats the action, and begins learning about her world. As a toddler, her interactions with play materials teach her to discriminate and compare shapes and sizes and to learn concepts such as cause and effect and fast and slow (Hughes, Elicker, & Veen, 1995). A preschooler's increasingly complex play develops gross and fine motor skills, requires her to communicate and negotiate plans with others, and exposes her to pre-academic math and literacy skills (Morrison, 1999; Weber, Behl, & Summers, 1994).

If play is the work of childhood, then toys are the child's tools. Ideally, play materials, whether store-bought toys or everyday household items such as pots and pans, should provide meaningful, motivating activities that serve as a precursor to more complex learning (Brewer & Kieff, 1996; Mann, 1996; Perlmutter & Burrell, 1995). Not all toys, however, are accessible to children with disabilities.

The National Lekotek Center is a nationwide, nonprofit network of play centers, toy lending libraries, and computer loan programs dedicated to making play accessible for children with disabilities and to those living in poverty. Diana Nielander, planning and information officer at Lekotek, recommends keeping the following 10 tips in mind when selecting toys for young children with disabilities:

1. *Multisensory appeal.* Does the toy respond with lights, sounds, or movements. Are there contrasting colors? Does it have scent? Texture?
2. *Method of activation.* Will the toy provide a challenge without frustration? What force is required to activate it? What are the number and complexity of steps required?
3. *Adjustability.* Does the toy have adjustable height, sound, volume, speed, level of difficulty?
4. *Opportunities for success.* Can play be open-ended with no definite right or wrong way?
5. *Child's individual characteristics.* Does the toy provide activities that reflect both developmental and chronological ages? Does it reflect the child's interests?
6. *Self-expression.* Does the toy allow for creativity and choice making? Will it give the child experience with a variety of media?
7. *Potential for interaction.* Will the child be an active participant during use? Will the toy encourage social and language engagement with others?
8. *Safety and durability.* Are the toy and its parts sized appropriately given the child's size and strength? Can it be washed and cleaned? Is it moisture resistant?

tions that place children at risk for developmental delays (Ramey, Bryant, Wasik, Sparling, Fendt, & LaVange, 1992). This large-scale study involved nearly 1,000 children and their families in eight locations throughout the United States. Home visits were conducted from shortly after birth through age 3. Because of health problems associated with prematurity and low birth weight, the children did not begin attending the center-based early education program until 12 months of age and continued until age 3. Improvements in intellectual functioning were noted, with babies of comparatively higher birth weight showing increases similar in magnitude to those found in the Abecedarian Project and Project CARE.

This study found a positive correlation between how much children and their families participated in the early intervention and the intellectual development of the chil-

9. *Where the toy will be used.* Will the toy be easy to store? Is there space in the home? Can the toy be used in a variety of positions (e.g., by a child lying on his side) or on a wheelchair tray?
10. *Current popularity.* Is it a toy almost any child would like? Does it tie in with popular books, TV programs, or movies?

Information on specific toys can be found in the Lekotek's *Toy Guide for Differently-Abled Kids!*, a free resource published in conjunction with Toys "R" Us and endorsed by the National Parent Network on Disabilities. The catalog includes pictures and descriptions of more than 100 toys that have been tested with preschoolers with disabilities. Each toy is identified according to its likelihood of promoting growth in 10 developmental or skill areas: auditory, language, visual, tactile, gross motor, fine motor, social skills, self-esteem, creativity, and thinking.

Information about Lekotek and its services to families can be obtained at its website (http://www.lekotek.org). Lekotek also operates a toy resource helpline at (800) 366-PLAY, a toll-free service that anyone can use to talk directly to trained play experts who will recommend appropriate toys and play activities for a particular child as well as make referrals to other disability-related resources for families.

Play provides children with natural, repeated opportunities for critical learning.

dren. The percentages of children whose IQ scores fell in the mental retardation range based on tests administered at age 3 for each of the groups were 17% for the control group, 13% for those with low participation, 4% for medium participation, and less than 2% for high participation. The most active participants had an almost ninefold reduction in the incidence of mental retardation compared to the control group.

Together, these three second-generation studies provide strong evidence that children at risk for developmental delays and poor school outcomes respond favorably to systematic early intervention. They also point to two factors that appear highly related to the outcome effectiveness of early intervention: the *intensity* of the intervention and the *level of participation* by the children and their families (Ramey & Ramey, 1992).

Summarizing the Research Base

Numerous methodological problems make it difficult to conduct early intervention research in a scientifically sound manner. Among the problems are the difficulties in selecting meaningful and reliable outcome measures; the wide disparity among children in the developmental effects of their disabilities; the tremendous variation across early intervention programs in curriculum focus, teaching strategies, length, and intensity; and the ethical concerns of withholding early intervention from some children so that they may form a control group for comparison purposes (Bricker, 1986; Fewell & Glick, 1996; Guralnick, 1998; Strain & Smith, 1986).

White, Bush, and Casto (1986) conducted a "review of reviews" and found that 94% of a sample of 52 previous reviews of the literature concluded that early intervention resulted in substantial immediate benefits for children with disabilities, those at risk, and those living in impoverished environments.

Despite these problems, most educators agree with Guralnick (1998), who concluded that, when taken as whole, contemporary comprehensive early intervention programs reveal a "consistent pattern of effectiveness as these programs are able to reduce the decline in intellectual development that occurs in the absence of intervention" (p. 323). Our national policymakers also believe that early intervention produces positive results for young children with disabilities, those who are at risk for developmental delays, and their families. Citing research and testimony from families, Congress identified the following outcomes for early intervention in the 1997 amendments to IDEA (P.L. 105–17, Sec. 1431):

a. to enhance the development of infants and toddlers with disabilities and to minimize their potential for developmental delay;
b. to reduce the educational costs to our society, including our Nation's schools, by minimizing the need for special education and related services after infants and toddlers with disabilities reach school age;
c. to minimize the likelihood of institutionalization of individuals with disabilities and maximize the potential for their independently living in society;
d. to enhance the capacity of families to meet the special education needs of their infants and toddlers with disabilities; and
e. to enhance the capacity of State and local agencies and service providers to identify, evaluate, and meet the needs of historically underrepresented populations, particularly minority, low-income, inner-city, and rural populations.

Go to the Resources Module for Chapter 5 at http://www.prenhall.com/heward. Click on Special Ed Resource Page and go to the "For Kids" link. Go to the section on "toys" and review those appropriate for kids with specific disabilities.

In addition to helping young children with disabilities make developmental gains, early intervention can help prevent secondary disabilities, provide needed support for parents and families, and reduce the need for special education services when children reach school age.

IDEA and Early Childhood Special Education

When Congress passed P.L. 94–142 in 1975 (the original IDEA), it mandated a free, appropriate public education for all school-age children with disabilities, ages 6 through 21. The law also required a state to provide special education services to all preschool children ages 3 to 5 with disabilities if that state already provided general public education for children in that age group. To encourage states to begin programs for preschoolers with disabilities, P.L. 94–142 included an incentive grant program that provided funds for establishing or improving preschool programs for children with disabilities.

Check your ongoing understanding of Chapter 5 concepts by using the Guided Review Module at http://www.prenhall.com/heward.

Since 1975, Congress has enacted four bills reauthorizing and amending the original IDEA. The second of those bills, P.L. 99–457, has been called "the most important legislation ever enacted for developmentally variable children" (Shonkoff & Meisels, 1990, p. 19). Before passage of this law, Congress estimated that states were serving at most about 70% of preschool children with disabilities, and systematic early intervention services for infants and toddlers with disabilities from birth through age 2 were scarce or nonexistent in many states. P.L. 99–457 included a mandatory preschool component for children ages 3 to 5 and a voluntary incentive grant program for early intervention services to infants and toddlers and their families. With the most recent reauthorization of IDEA in 1997 (P.L. 105–17), Congress reaffirmed the nation's commitment to a system of early intervention services.

Table 5.1 identifies other legislation and some key historical events in early childhood special education. For a chronology of federal legislation and support of early childhood special education, see Hebbeler, Smith, and Black (1991).

Early Intervention for Infants and Toddlers

If a state chooses to provide early intervention services to infants and toddlers and their families, it can receive federal funds under IDEA's early intervention provisions. The law covers any child under age 3 who meets the following guidelines:

a. Needs early intervention services because of developmental delays (as measured by appropriate diagnostic instruments or procedures) in one or more of areas of cognitive development, physical development, social or emotional development, or adaptive development
b. Has a diagnosed physical or medical condition that has a high probability of resulting in developmental delay
c. Each State may also, at its discretion, serve infants and toddlers who are at risk of experiencing a substantial developmental delay if early intervention services are not provided.

Thus, IDEA has three categories of eligibility under which states can provide early intervention services to infants and toddlers: developmental delay, established conditions, and documented risk (Shonkoff & Meisels, 1991). Developmental delay includes children with significant delays or atypical patterns of development. Each state's definition of developmental delay must be broad enough to include all disability categories covered by IDEA, but children do not need to be classified or labeled according to those categories to receive early intervention services. Established conditions include children with a diagnosed physical or medical condition that almost always results in developmental delay or disability. Examples of established conditions are **Down syndrome, fragile-X syndrome,** and other conditions associated with mental retardation, brain or spinal cord damage, sensory impairments, fetal alcohol syndrome (FAS), and maternal acquired immune deficiency syndrome (AIDS).

FAS is described in Figure 5.2.

Although not required to do so, states may also use funds from IDEA to provide early intervention for infants and toddlers who fall under two types of documented risk. Children considered biologically at risk have a greater than usual probability of

Table 5.1 A history of early childhood special education: Key events and implications

Date	Historical Event	Educational Implications
1939	Skeels and Dye reported that intensive stimulation, one-to-one attention, and a half-morning kindergarten program with 1- to 2-year-old children who were classified as mentally retarded resulted in IQ gains and eventual independence and success as adults.	This landmark study challenged the widespread belief that intelligence was fixed and that little could be expected from intervention efforts, and it served as the catalyst for many subsequent investigations into the effects of early intervention.
1958	Kirk found that children with mental retardation who received two years of preschool training in social and cognitive development gained between 10 and 30 IQ points.	This often-cited study found that IQ scores of children in the control group declined and differences between the groups were maintained over a period of years.
1965	Head Start was established to provide day care, developmental enhancement, meals, medical and dental screening, and family support to children ages 3 to 5 from poverty environments.	Head Start was the nation's first public commitment to young children with special needs. Currently there are more than 1,300 Head Start programs serving over 450,000 children.
1968	The first federal law written exclusively for preschoolers with disabilities, the Handicapped Children's Early Childhood Assistance Act (P.L. 90–538), was passed by Congress.	The law created the Early Education Program for Children with Disabilities (EEPCD) to develop model early intervention programs for children with disabilities from birth through age 8. Since it began, EEPCD has funded more than 600 projects in all 50 states and several U.S. territories.
Early 1970s	The first reports of the Milwaukee Project were published (Garber & Heber, 1973; Heber & Garber, 1971). Mothers with IQs of below 70 received training in child care and learned to interact with and stimulate their babies. By age 3½, children who received early intervention tested an average of 33 IQ points higher than a control group of children did.	Results from this 15-year project suggests that a program of maternal education and early infant stimulation can reduce the incidence of mental retardation caused by psychosocial disadvantage (Garber, 1988).
1972	The Economic Opportunity Act required Head Start to reserve at least 10% of its enrollment capacity for children with disabilities.	Today, 13.4% of the children enrolled in Head Start programs across the country are children with disabilities.
1973	The Division for Early Childhood (DEC) was established within the Council for Exceptional Children.	With more than 7,000 members, DEC is the fourth-largest division of CEC.
1975	Individuals with Disabilities Education Act (IDEA) (P.L. 94–142) mandated a free, appropriate public education for all school-age children with disabilities and required that all children ages 3 to 5 with disabilities receive special education services if state law or practice already provides general public education for children in that age group.	To stimulate other states to begin programs for preschoolers with disabilities, IDEA included an incentive grant program that provided funds for establishing or improving preschool programs for children with disabilities.

Date	Historical Event	Educational Implications
1986	P.L. 99–457 required states to provide preschool services to all children with disabilities ages 3 to 5.	The law prescribed family-focused early intervention services delivered according to an Individualized Family Services Plan (IFSP).
1987	NAEYC published developmentally appropriate practice (DAP) guidelines for early childhood programs.	DAP guidelines provide national standards and a context for assessment.
Early 1990s	Well-controlled studies evaluating the effects of intensive early intervention were conducted—e.g., the Abecedarian Project, Project CARE, and the Infant Health and Development Program.	Results of these second-generation studies provided strong evidence that children at risk for developmental delays and poor school outcomes respond favorably to systematic, intensive early intervention.
1997	Amendments to IDEA (P.L. 105-17) confirmed and strengthened the nation's commitment to early intervention for infants and toddlers and their families.	The law required that early intervention services be family-centered and provided in natural environments.

Figure 5.2 Two prenatal risk factors that should be prevented

Fetal Alcohol Syndrome

Alcohol use by a pregnant woman can have devastating effects on the fetus that result in developmental delays and other disabilities. **Fetal alcohol syndrome (FAS),** caused by excessive alcohol use during pregnancy, often produces serious physical defects and developmental delays. FAS is diagnosed when the child has two or more craniofacial malformations and growth is below the 10th percentile for height and weight (Griesbach & Polloway, 1990). Children who have some but not all of the diagnostic criteria for FAS and a history of prenatal alcohol exposure are sometimes diagnosed with **fetal alcohol effects (FAE).** The incidence of FAS is estimated at one to three infants per 1,000 live births; however, FAS birth rates among alcoholic women are about 25 per 1,000 (Burd & Martsolf, 1989).

FAS is one of the leading known causes of mental retardation and has an incidence higher than Down syndrome, cerebral palsy, and spina bifida (Streissguth, Aase, Clarren, Randels, La Due, & Smith, 1991). In addition to problems in physical development, many children with FAS have neurological damage that contributes to cognitive and language delays. Other problems include sleep disturbances, motor dysfunctions, hyperirritability, challenging behaviors such as aggression and conduct problems, and poor academic achievement (Burgess & Streissguth, 1992; Howard, Williams, & McLaughlin, 1994). For an excellent overview of FAS and guidelines for early intervention, see Carmichael Olson (1994).

Despite rising awareness of the hazards of alcohol during pregnancy, each year several thousand children are born in the United States with birth defects caused by prenatal alcohol exposure. Although research has shown that the fetus is most vulnerable to the effects of alcohol or other toxins during the first trimester and that children with FAS are usually born to mothers who are heavy drinkers, research has determined no safe level of drinking during pregnancy.

Prenatal Exposure to Cocaine

Use of illegal drugs during pregnancy, especially cocaine, has reached epidemic proportions and is reported at all economic and educational levels. The president's National Drug Control Strategy Report estimates that 100,000 babies are born to cocaine-using women each year (Kusserow, 1990). Miller (1989) reports that hospital surveys show that 17% of women used cocaine during pregnancy. Shocking as this figure is, self-reported use of an illegal substance is almost certain to produce an underestimate. Indeed, Frank et al. (1988) found that 24% of the pregnant women they interviewed failed to report cocaine use that was later verified by urine tests. Hospitals that conduct urine tests on newborns are finding 10% to 15% positive for cocaine (Miller, 1989), yet presence of the drug in the urine of newborns only indicates cocaine use within 48 hours before delivery. Cocaine-exposed infants project distress signals such as increased respiration and movement and high-pitched crying, and they often show little ability to interact with caretakers or respond to comforting (Williams & Howard, 1993).

It has been estimated that about one-third of children prenatally exposed to cocaine experience delays in language and/or problems with attention and self-regulation (Griffith, 1992). These problems are likely to be compounded, if not overshadowed, by the debilitating effects of the combination of poor prenatal care, poverty, and impoverished learning environments that the majority of these children also experience (see "Educating Young Children Prenatally Exposed to Illegal Drugs" later in this chapter). For a description of behavioral interventions with children prenatally exposed to alcohol and cocaine, see Howard et al. (1994).

Women who are pregnant or anticipating pregnancy should abstain from drinking alcohol or taking nonprescribed drugs in any amount.

Figure 5.2 *continued*

Smoking during pregnancy and inadequate prenatal care increase the risk of ***sudden infant death syndrome (SIDS),*** *the leading cause of death in the United States for infants from 1 month to 1 year old. Sleep position is also a risk factor. The incidence of SIDS has dropped sharply in countries that advocate back or side sleeping. The U.S. Department of Health has begun a campaign to encourage parents to put babies to sleep on their back or side. The Back to Sleep Program to increase SIDS prevention and awareness has a toll-free hotline: (800) 505-CRIB.*

developmental delay or disability because of their pediatric histories or current biological conditions (e.g., significantly premature birth, low birth weight). Children may be considered environmentally at risk for developmental delay because of factors such as extreme poverty, parental substance abuse, homelessness, abuse or neglect, or parental intellectual impairment.

Individualized Family Services Plan

IDEA prescribes family-focused early intervention services, delivered according to an **Individualized Family Services Plan (IFSP).** The IFSP is developed by a multidisciplinary team that includes the child's parents and family and must include each of the eight elements shown in Figure 5.3.

The IFSP must be evaluated once a year and reviewed with the family at six-month intervals. Recognizing the critical importance of time for the infant with disabilities, the law allows for initiation of early intervention services before the IFSP is completed if the parents give their consent. The IFSP effectively defines the family as being the recipient of early intervention services rather than the child alone. Figure 5.4 shows portions of an IFSP written with the family of an 18-month-old child with developmental disabilities.

Special Education for Preschoolers

IDEA requires states to provide special education services to all children with disabilities ages 3 to 5. The regulations governing these programs are similar to those for school-age children, with the exceptions in the list beginning on p. 167:

Educating Young Children Prenatally Exposed to Illegal Drugs

by Judith J. Carta

About 10 years ago, several of my colleagues in the Juniper Gardens Children's Project became aware that children who had been identified as being prenatally exposed to drugs, especially cocaine, were entering our local preschool and child care settings. The media were publishing reports describing a new population of children like no other previously seen in classrooms. They were described as out of control, with no ability to focus attention; lacking in affect; and unable to tell the difference between right and wrong. Teachers were afraid and unequipped to handle these children, and potential foster and adoptive parents were hesitant to open their homes and families to them.

These fears were based on several myths about children who may have been prenatally exposed to drugs. Such misconceptions are conveyed in questions that people frequently asked about children prenatally exposed to drugs.

Do they all have behavior problems or learning difficulties? Children whose prenatal histories include their mothers' use of drugs are not a homogeneous group but represent a wide range of abilities. Some have physical and mental disabilities; others appear to be unaffected. Some are passive and socially withdrawn; others are aggressive. Some are unattached; others constantly seek attention and affection. No profile or set of characteristics defines this group; the children do not have an easily identifiable syndrome. Some group studies of these children have reported that approximately 30% perform at a lower level than typically developing children. But this average figure fails to account for variation in how individuals may be affected and all the other factors from their pre- or postnatal environments that may account for developmental outcomes.

What accounts for the growing number of inner-city children's sudden episodes of violence, difficulties in attention, or lack of social skills, which appear more often in our classrooms? Aren't these problems caused by mothers' drug use? It is interesting that only behavior problems in inner-city schools are being linked to prenatal drug use. Such a conclusion suggests that only mothers in the inner city use drugs. In reality, the problem is not unique to the inner city or to any particular racial or ethnic group. No one group "owns" the problem of prenatal substance exposure. It is as likely to occur in rural areas as in urban areas or the suburbs.

Although prenatal substance exposure may be a factor in explaining the wide-ranging types of problems occurring with greater frequency in our schools, many risk factors associated with living in poverty and less-than-adequate caregiving may also be responsible. For example, two other factors are associated with a drug-using lifestyle in poverty: violence and drug trafficking. Violence is a fact of life in communities where trafficking occurs. A large percentage of children witness violence in neighborhoods as well as homes. Mothers are often victims of abuse, as are children themselves. A growing body of research on the effects of exposure to violence or maltreatment of children points to many of the same behavioral symptoms attributed to prenatal drug exposure.

Another factor associated with behavioral and learning difficulties is the quality of caregiving that children receive in a substance-using lifestyle. Unfortunately, substance abuse often results in behaviors that conflict with high-quality, nurturing caregiving. Substance abusers are often inconsistent caregivers, behaving one way toward their children when they are straight, another when they are high or coming down. Attempting to get straight often requires a period of separation from children because many residential treatment centers do not allow them. Parents are often socially isolated and lack a network of friends or family. They have difficulty getting the things they need for themselves and their children, including services, child care, jobs, and education. The lack of support, resources, and sometimes bare necessities challenges any parent's caregiving.

These risk factors and many others can act in combination with prenatal exposure to drugs, as well as with each other, to produce behavior and learning problems. Such factors can threaten a child's developmental and educational outcomes and challenge teachers, caregivers, and parents, who affect a child's development and educational success.

Will children prenatally exposed to drugs require specialized interventions that have not yet been developed? No evidence currently exists to suggest that these children exhibit a unique set of problems requiring a special curriculum or set of educational or caregiving procedures. All of these children do not have problems, and when they do, their difficulties are ones that are exhibited by other children. Some children who are prenatally exposed may have language or social problems; others may have cognitive, motor, or adaptive deficits. Interventions are available that have been documented as effective in improving skills in each of these areas. We expect that these interventions will be as effective for children with a history of prenatal exposure to illegal drugs as they have been for other children. We do not need a curriculum or intervention aimed at the population of children who have been drug exposed; what we do need is a set of instructional procedures to address the problem behaviors and skill deficiencies exhibited by these children. Therefore, our suggested approach to determining interventions for children who are prenatally exposed to illegal drugs is identical to the approach we use for all children:

- Identify specific behaviors that require remediation.
- Determine specific interventions that address those behaviors.
- Systematically implement those interventions.
- Monitor the effects of the interventions on the specified behaviors.

What require special attention, however, are the risks these children face growing up in drug-using lifestyles. Until we begin to comprehensively address the risks associated with living in concentrated poverty, our efforts to provide interventions for children will have little chance of producing lasting effects.

Judith J. Carta, Ph.D., is a principal investigator at the Early Childhood Research Institute on Substance Abuse, a research consortium of the University of Kansas, the University of Minnesota, and the University of South Dakota. The institute's goal is to develop interventions for children at risk for developmental delays because of prenatal exposure to alcohol or other drugs.

Figure 5.3 Required components for an IFSP
Source: P.L. 105–17, Sec. 1436.

The plan shall be in writing and contain

1. a statement of the child's present levels of physical development, cognitive development, communication development, social or emotional development, or adaptive development, based on objective criteria;
2. a statement of the family's resources, priorities, and concerns relating to enhancing the development of the family's infant or toddler with a disability;
3. a statement of the major outcomes expected to be achieved for the infant or toddler and family, and the criteria, procedures, and timelines used to determine the degree to which progress toward achieving the outcomes is being made and whether modifications or revision of the outcomes or services are necessary;
4. a statement of the specific early intervention services necessary to meet the unique needs of the infant or toddler and family, including frequency, intensity, and method of delivering the services;
5. a statement of the natural environments in which early intervention services shall appropriately be provided, including a justification of the extent, if any, to which the services will not be provided in a natural environment;
6. the projected dates for initiation of services and anticipated duration of services;
7. the identification of the service coordinator from the profession most immediately relevant to the infant's or toddler's or family's needs who will be responsible for implementation of the plan and coordination with other agencies and persons; and
8. the steps to be taken to support a successful transition of the toddler with a disability to preschool or other appropriate services.

Outcome: #1

Jesse will improve his gross motor skills by 3 months.

Strategies/Activities:

1. Bella will meet with the physical therapist and the team to get new ideas about encouraging Jesse to stand with support. These activities will be shared with the Websters on the next home visit.
2. The Websters would like to continue the current crawling, rolling, sitting, and standing activities for the next month.
3. Jesse will be supported in standing while he manipulates toys at the coffee table. Jenny will show Walton how to do this properly and ask him to create an activity that he and Jesse can do while she is preparing dinner. This will begin next week.
4. Weekly home visits will continue to focus on Jesse's full development while promoting standing, with support, whenever possible.

Criteria/Timelines:

Timelines are indicated next to each strategy/activity.

Outcome: #2

The Websters want more information about future services for Jesse, particularly when he is a young adult.

Strategies/Activities:

1. The Websters will meet with representatives of the area Association for Retarded Citizens (ARC) to discuss and visit supported employment sites and adult homes in the community. Michael Webster will set this up.
2. The Websters will get information about waiting lists for these services.
3. The Websters will meet some workers with Down syndrome at the local sheltered workshop to try to get more understanding of the quality of their lives.
4. The Websters will visit the public schools to observe their programs.

Criteria/Timelines:

The Websters will make these visits by September. If more information is needed, the Websters will call their service coordinator.

Figure 5.4 Portion of an IFSP written with the family of an 18-month-old child with developmental disabilities

Source: Adapted from from Raver, S. A. (1999). *Intervention strategies for infants and toddlers: A team approach* (2nd ed., pp. 384–368). Upper Saddle River, NJ: Merrill/Prentice Hall. Used by permission.

- Preschool children do not have to be identified and reported under existing disability categories (e.g., mental retardation, orthopedic impairments) to receive services.
- Each state, at its discretion, may also serve children (from ages 3 through 9) who are

  a. experiencing developmental delays as defined by the State and as measures by appropriate diagnostic instrument and procedures in one or more of the following areas: physical development, cognitive development, communication development, social or emotional development, or adaptive development; and
  b. who, by reason thereof, need special education and related services. (Sec. 1401)

This provision of IDEA allows, but does not require, states to serve at-risk students from ages 3 through 9 (Turnbull & Cilley, 1999).

Outcome: #3

Jenny Webster wants more written information about Down syndrome and wants to participate in personal counseling to discuss her adjustment to Jesse's condition.

Strategies/Activities:

1. Marie (the service coordinator) will give Jenny a list of counselors and counseling centers by June 15th.
2. Marie will give Jenny information about financial assistance for counseling services by June 15th.
3. By September, Jenny will ask the Down syndrome support group to have a counselor as a speaker at one of their meetings to discuss family adjustments.
4. Jenny will discuss her feelings and concerns with her family, and her neighbor, Mrs. Brooke, in the next two weeks.
5. Marie will loan Jenny a book and some pamphlets on Down syndrome by June 15.

Criteria/Timelines:

The timelines are listed next to each activity. Jenny will reevaluate the need for counseling in 6 months.

Figure 5.4 *continued*

- IEPs must include a section with instructions and information for parents.
- Local education agencies may elect to use a variety of service delivery options (home-based, center-based, or combination programs), and the length of the school day and year may vary.
- Preschool special education programs must be administered by the state education agency; however, services from other agencies may be contracted to meet the requirement of a full range of services.

IDEA requires states to provide special education to all children with disabilities ages 3 to 5.

Screening, Identification, and Assessment

Assessment and evaluation in early childhood education is conducted for at least four different purposes, with specific evaluation tools for each purpose (Bricker, Pretti-Frontczak, & McComas, 1998; McLean, Bailey, & Wolery, 1996):

Screening: quick, easy-to-administer tests to identify children who may have a disability and who should receive further testing

Diagnosis: in-depth, comprehensive assessment of all major areas of development to determine a child's eligibility for early intervention or special education services

Program planning: curriculum-based, criterion-referenced assessments to determine a child's current skill level, identify IFSP/IEP objectives, and plan intervention activities

Evaluation: curriculum-based, criterion-referenced measures to determine progress on IFSP/IEP objectives and evaluate the program's effects

Screening Tools

Before young children and their families can be served, they must be identified. Some children's disabilities are so significant that no test is needed. As a general rule, the more severe a disability, the earlier it can be detected. In the delivery room, medical staff can identify certain disabilities, such as microcephaly, cleft palate, and other physical deformities, as well as most instances of Down syndrome. Within the first few weeks, other physical characteristics such as paralysis, seizures, or rapidly increasing head size can signal possible disabilities. But most children who experience delays in development are not immediately identifiable by obvious physical characteristics or behavioral patterns, especially at very young ages. That is where screening tools come into play.

The Apgar Scale The Apgar scale, a screening test for newborn infants, measures the degree of prenatal asphyxia (oxygen deprivation) an infant experiences during birth. The Apgar is administered to virtually all babies born in U.S. hospitals. The test administrator—nurse, nurse anesthesiologist, or pediatrician—evaluates the newborn twice on five physiological measures: heart rate, respiratory effort, response to stimulation, muscle tone, and skin color. The child is given a score of 0, 1, or 2 on each measure according to the criteria described on the scoring form (see Figure 5.5).

The first administration of the test, which is conducted 60 seconds after birth, measures how the baby fared during the birth process. If the newborn receives a low score on the first test, the delivery room staff takes immediate resuscitation action. The scale is given again five minutes after birth. At that point a total score of 0 to 3 (out of a possible 10) indicates severe asphyxia, 4 to 6 moderate asphyxia, and 7 to 10 mild asphyxia. Some stress is assumed on all births, and the five-minute score measures how successful any resuscitation efforts were. A five-minute score of 6 or less indicates follow-up assessment to determine what is causing the problem and what interventions may be needed.

The Apgar has been shown to identify high-risk infants—those who have a greater than normal chance of developing later problems. Research has shown that oxygen deprivation at birth contributes to neurological impairment, and the five-minute Apgar score correlates well with eventual neurological outcomes.

Although most newborns are evaluated in terms of gestational weight and age and are screened for certain specific disorders, the Apgar scale is at present the only screening test universally used with infants. Another widely practiced screening procedure is the analysis of newborn blood and urine samples to detect metabolic disorders, such as PKU, that produce mental retardation. Many hospitals also routinely analyze newborn blood and urine samples to detect the presence of illegal drugs and other toxins.

Developmental Screening Tests One of the most widely used screening tools for developmental delays is the Denver II (Frankenburg, Dodds, & Fandal, 1975). It can be used with children from 2 weeks to 6 years of age, using both testing-observa-

			60 sec.	5 min.
Heart rate	Absent	(0)		
	Less than 100	(1)		
	100 to 140	(2)	1	2
Respiratory effort	Apneic	(0)		
	Shallow, irregular	(1)		
	Lusty cry and breathing	(2)	1	1
Response to catheter stimulation	No response	(0)		
	Grimace	(1)		
	Cough or sneeze	(2)	1	2
Muscle tone	Flaccid	(0)		
	Some flexion of extremities	(1)		
	Flexion resisting extension	(2)	1	2
Color	Pale, blue	(0)		
	Body pink, extremities blue	(1)		
	Pink all over	(2)	0	1
		Total	4	8

Figure 5.5 The Apgar evaluation scale

Screening tests have also been developed for the early detection of behavioral disorders and autism. See Chapter 8 for a description of Systematic Screening for Behavior Disorders (SSBD), which has been adapted for use with preschoolers (Walker, Severson, & Feil, 1994). Two widely used screening instruments for autism are the Autism Behavior Checklist (ABC) (Krug, Arick, & Almond, 1980) and the Childhood Autism Rating Scale (CARS) (Schopler, Reichler, & Renner, 1988).

Parental involvement in screening has been found to reduce the number of misclassifications (Henderson & Meisels, 1994). For a review of research on the use of parental input during screening and assessment of young children, see Diamond and Squires (1993).

tion and a parent report format. The Denver II assesses 125 skills arranged in four developmental areas: gross motor, fine motor–adaptive, language, and personal-social. Each test item is represented on the scoring form by a bar showing at what ages 25%, 50%, 75%, and 90% of normally developing children can perform that skill. The child is allowed up to three trials per item. A child's performance on each item is scored as "pass" or "fail" and then interpreted as representing "advanced," "OK," "caution," or "delayed" performance by comparing the child's performance with those of the same age in the standardized population. The Denver II is most often administered by physicians, and the test form was designed to fit the schedule of well-baby visits recommended by the American Academy of Pediatrics.

No one observes a child more often, more closely, and with more interest than his parents. Mothers' estimates of their preschool children's levels of development often correlate highly with those that professionals produce by using standardized scales (Gradel, Thompson, & Sheehan, 1981). Recognizing this fact, early childhood specialists have developed a number of screening tools for use by parents. One such tool is the Ages and Stages Questionnaire (ASQ) (Bricker & Squires, 1999). The ASQ includes 11 questionnaires to be completed by the parents when the child is 4, 6, 8, 12, 16, 18, 20, 24, 30, 36, and 48 months old. Each consists of 30 questions covering 5 areas of development: gross motor, fine motor, communication, personal-social, and adaptive. Many of the questions include illustrations to help the parents evaluate their child's behavior. Figure 5.6 shows part of the 8-month questionnaire. Parents are instructed to try each item with their child before scoring it.

Diagnostic Tools

When the results of a screening test raise suspicion that a disability may be present, the child is referred for diagnostic testing. The specific diagnostic tests to be used depend upon the suspected delay or disability. In general, tests that seek to determine if a child is experiencing a developmental delay measure performance in six major developmental areas or domains (see Figure 5.7). Generally, these six areas are broken down into specific, observable tasks and sequenced developmentally—that is, in the order in which most children learn them. Sometimes each task is tied to a specific age at which a child should normally be able to perform it. This arrangement allows the examiner to note significant delays or gaps, as well as other unusual patterns, in a high-risk child's development. These developmental domains are not mutually exclusive. There is considerable overlap between domains as well as across subskills within a specific domain. Most activities by children in everyday settings

III. Fine Motor *(Be sure to try each activity with your child.)*

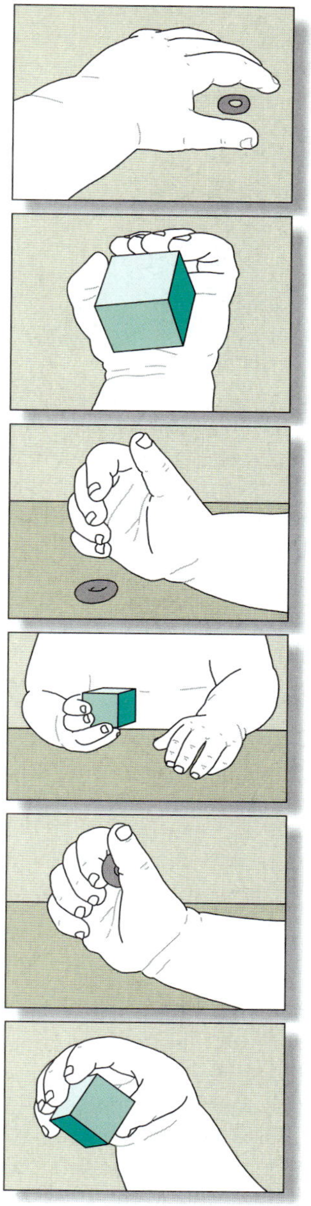

	Yes	Sometimes	Not Yet	
1. Does your baby reach for a crumb or Cheerio and touch it with her finger or hand? (If she already picks up a small object, check "yes" for this item.)	☐	☐	☐	____
2. Does your baby pick up a small toy, holding it in the center of her hand with her fingers around it?	☐	☐	☐	____
3. Does your baby ***try*** to pick up a crumb or Cheerio by using her thumb and all her fingers in a raking motion, even if she isn't able to pick it up? (If she already picks up a crumb or Cheerio, check "yes" for this item.)	☐	☐	☐	____
4. Does your baby usually pick up a small toy with only one hand?	☐	☐	☐	____
5. Does your baby ***successfully*** pick up a crumb or Cheerio by using her thumb and all her fingers in a raking motion? (If she already picks up a crumb or Cheerio, check "yes" for this item.)	☐	☐	☐	____
6. Does your baby pick up a small toy, with the ***tips*** of her thumb and fingers? You should see a space between the toy and her palm.	☐	☐	☐	____

Figure 5.6 Sample items from the 8-month Ages and Stages Questionnaire

Source: Reprinted from Bricker, D., & Squires, J. (1999). *Ages and Stages Questionnaire: A parent-completed, child-monitoring system* (2nd ed.). Baltimore: Brookes. Used by permission.

1. *Cognitive skills.* Children use cognitive skills when they attend to stimuli, perform preacademic skills such as sorting or counting, remember things they have done in the past, plan and make decisions about what they will do in the future, integrate newly learned information with previously learned knowledge and skills, solve problems, and generate novel ideas.
2. *Motor skills.* The ability to move one's body and manipulate objects within the environment provides a critical foundation for all types of learning. Motor development involves improvements in general strength, flexibility, endurance, and eye-hand coordination and includes large-muscle movement and mobility (such as walking, running, throwing) and small-muscle, fine motor control (like that needed to pick up a toy, write, tie a shoe).
3. *Communication and language skills.* Communication involves the transmission of messages, information about needs, feelings, knowledge, desires, and so forth. Children use communication and language skills when they receive information from others, share information with other individuals, and use language to mediate their actions and to effectively control the environment. This domain encompasses all forms of communication development, including a child's ability to respond nonverbally with gestures, smiles, or actions and the acquisition of spoken language—sounds, words, phrases, sentences, and so on.
4. *Social competence and play skills.* Children who have developed competence in social skills with one another share toys and take turns, cooperate with others, and resolve conflicts.
5. *Affective and emotional development.* Children should feel good about themselves and know how to express their emotions and feelings.
6. *Self-care and adaptive skills.* As young children develop self-care and adaptive skills such as dressing/undressing, eating, toileting, toothbrushing, and handwashing, their ability to function independently across multiple environments increases, which provides and enhances opportunities for additional kinds of learning.

Figure 5.7 Six key domains of child development

For detailed descriptions and comparisons of numerous screening, diagnostic, and assessment tests for infants and preschoolers with disabilities, see McLean et al. (1996).

involve skills from multiple domains. For example, playing marbles typically requires a child to use skills from the cognitive, motor, communication, and social domains.

Two widely used tests for diagnosing developmental delays are the Battelle Developmental Inventory (Newborg, Stock, Wnek, Guidubaldi, & Suinicki, 1988) and the Bayley Scales of Infant Development—II (Bayley, 1993). The Battelle can be administered to children with and without disabilities, from birth through age 8, and it has adapted testing procedures for use with children with different disabilities. The Bayley II evaluates development in motor, adaptive, language, and personal-social in infants from 2 to 30 months.

Program Planning and Evaluation Tools

See Bagnato, Neisworth, and Capone (1986) for a description and rationale of CBA as well as a review of 21 assessment measures useful for CBA in early childhood special education programs.

A growing number of early intervention programs are moving away from assessments based entirely on developmental milestones to curriculum-based assessment (CBA). CBA tools enable early childhood teams to (1) identify a child's current levels of functioning, (2) select IFSP/IEP goals and objectives, (3) determine the most appropriate interventions, and (4) evaluate the child's progress (McLean et al., 1996). Each item in a CBA relates directly to a skill in the program's curriculum, thereby providing a direct link among testing, teaching, and progress evaluation (Bagnato, Neisworth, & Munson, 1997).

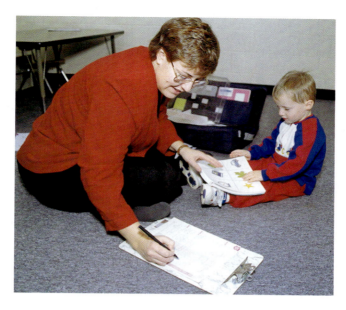

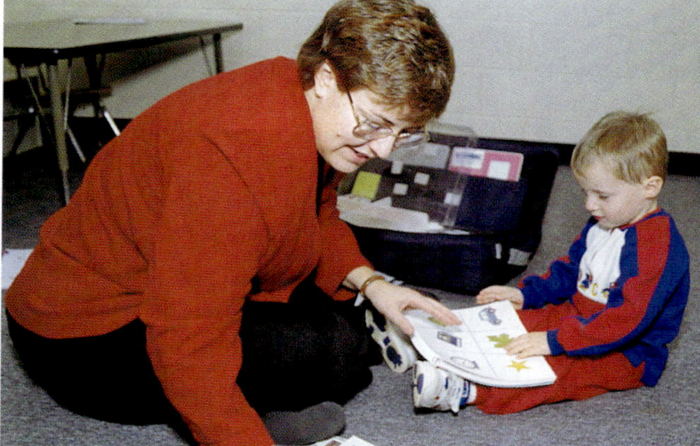
The Bayley Scales can be used to diagnose developmental delays in children from 2 to 30 months.

One thoroughly developed and empirically tested CBA tool is the Assessment, Evaluation, and Programming System: For Infants and Young Children (AEPS). The AEPS is divided into two levels: one for infants and toddlers from birth to 3 years (Bricker, 1993), one for children from 3 to 6 years (Bricker & Pretti-Frontczak, 1996). The AEPS is divided into six domains: fine motor, gross motor, adaptive, cognitive, social-communication, and social. Each domain is divided into strands that group related behaviors and skills considered essential for infants and young children to function independently. The AEPS tests can be used in conjunction with the associated AEPS curricula (Bricker & Waddell, 1996; Cripe, Slentz, & Bricker, 1993) or with other similar early childhood curricula such as the Carolina Curriculum for Preschoolers with Special Needs (Johnson-Martin, Attermeier, & Hacker, 1990).

Curriculum Goals in Early Childhood Special Education

Bricker et al. (1998) propose the following general goal or purpose for early intervention/early childhood special education: "to orchestrate environmental input, both physical and social, to maximize children's motivation to acquire and generalize targeted information and skills that will enhance their independence, problem-solving skills, and adjustment across a range of changing conditions and settings" (p. 187).

More specifically, early childhood special education programs should be designed and evaluated with respect to the following outcomes or goals (Bailey & Wolery, 1992; Bricker et al., 1998; DEC, 1993; Wolery & Sainato, 1993, 1996):

1. *Support families in achieving their own goals.* Although the child with special needs is undoubtedly the focal point, a major function of early intervention is helping families achieve the goals most important to them. Professionals realize that families function as a system and that separating the child from the system results in limited and fragmented outcomes (Turnbull & Turnbull, 1997).

2. *Promote child engagement, independence, and mastery.* Early childhood special education seeks to minimize the extent to which children are dependent on others and different from their age mates. Intervention strategies should "promote

To read how preschoolers with disabilities can learn to be more independent, see the "Idea Bunny" later in this chapter.

active engagement (participation), initiative (choice making, self-directed behavior), autonomy (individuality and self-sufficiency) and age-appropriate abilities in many normalized contexts and situations" (Wolery & Sainato, 1993, p. 53). In situations in which independence is not safe, possible, or practical, support and assistance should be provided to enable the child to participate as much as she can. "For example, in getting ready for a bath, a 3-year-old child should not be expected to adjust the water to the appropriate temperature, but could be expected to help get ready for the bath (e.g., getting bath toys, assisting in taking off clothing)" (Wolery & Sainato, 1993, p. 53).

3. *Promote development in all important domains.* Successful early intervention programs help children make progress in each of the key areas of development already described (e.g., cognitive, motor, communication, social). Because young children with disabilities are already behind their typically developing age-mates, Wolery and Sainato (1993, 1996) suggest that early childhood special educators should only use instructional strategies that lead to rapid learning. Strategies that produce rapid learning help the child with disabilities by saving time for other goals and moving closer to normal developmental levels.

4. *Build and support social competence.* Social skills, such as learning to get along with others and making friends, are among the most important skills anyone can learn. Most children learn such skills naturally, but many children with disabilities do not learn to interact effectively and properly simply by playing with others (McEvoy & Yoder, 1993). In fact, one leader in the field of early childhood special education suggests that "understanding and promoting the social competence of young handicapped children may well be the most important challenge to the field of early intervention in the decade of the 1990s" (Guralnick, 1990, p. 3).

Several strategies for promoting the generalization and maintenance of learning are described in Chapter 6.

5. *Facilitate the generalized use of skills.* As effortlessly as most typically developing children seem to generalize what they learn at one time in one situation to another place and time, many children with disabilities have extreme difficulty remembering and using previously learned skills in other situations. "Early interventionists should not be satisfied if children learn new skills; they should only be satisfied if children use those skills when and wherever they are appropriate" (Wolery & Sainato, 1993, p. 54).

6. *Prepare and assist children for normalized life experiences with their families, in school, and in their communities.* Early intervention should be characterized by the principle of normalization; that is, services should be provided in settings that are as much like the typical settings in which young children without disabilities play and learn as is possible. A large and growing body of published research literature demonstrates the benefits of integrated early intervention to children with disabilities and their families and suggests strategies for effective mainstreaming programs (Miller, Strain, Boyd, McKinley, Hunsicker, & Wu, 1992; Peck, Odom, & Bricker, 1993; Sainato & Strain, 1993; Wolery & Wilbers, 1994).

7. *Help children and their families make smooth transitions.* A transition occurs when a child and his family move from one early intervention program or service delivery mode to another. For example, program transitions typically occur at age 3 when a child with disabilities moves from a home-based early intervention program to an early childhood special education classroom and again at age 5 when the child moves from a preschool classroom to a regular kindergarten classroom. Preparing and assisting children and their families for smooth transitions ensures continuity of services, minimizes disruptions to the family system, and is another important way for promoting the success of young children with disabilities as they move into more normalized environments (Carta, Atwater, Schwartz, & Miller, 1990; Fowler, Schwartz, & Atwater, 1991). Cooperative planning and supports for transitions must

come from professionals in both the sending and the receiving programs (Chandler, 1993; Hadden & Fowler, 1997).

8. *Prevent or minimize the development of future problems or disabilities.* Prevention of future problems is a major goal of early intervention. Indeed, early intervention programs that serve at-risk infants and toddlers are designed entirely with prevention as their primary goal.

As we have noted, preventative efforts are most effective when intervention services are begun early, conducted systematically and intensively, and provided over a significant period of time (McEachin, Smith, & Lovaas, 1993; Ramey & Ramey, 1992).

Developmentally Appropriate Practice

Virtually all early childhood educators—whether they work with typically developing children or those with disabilities—share a common philosophy that learning environments, teaching practices, and other components of programs that serve young children should be based on what is typically expected of and experienced by children of different ages and developmental stages. This philosophy and the guidelines for practice based on it are called *developmentally appropriate practice* (DAP) and are described in widely disseminated materials published by the National Association for the Education of Young Children (NAEYC) (Bredekamp, 1987; Bredekamp & Copple, 1997). The DAP guidelines were created partially in response to concerns that too many early childhood programs were focusing on academic preparedness and not providing young children with enough opportunities to engage in the less structured play and other activities that typify early childhood. "For example, some people considered it developmentally appropriate for 4- and 5-year-olds to do an hour of seatwork, toddlers to sit in high chairs with dittos, or babies in infant seats to 'do' the calendar" (Bredekamp, 1993, p. 261).

DAP recommends the following guidelines for early childhood education programs:

- Activities should be integrated across developmental domains.
- Children's interests and progress should be identified through teacher observation.
- Teachers should arrange the environment to facilitate children's active exploration and interaction.
- Learning activities and materials should be real, concrete, and relevant to the young child's life.
- A wide range of interesting activities should be provided.
- The complexity and challenges of activities should increase as the children understand the skills involved.

Most early childhood special educators view the DAP guidelines as providing a foundation or context within which to provide early intervention for children with special needs, but the guidelines by themselves are inadequate to ensure the individualized intervention that such children need. Wolery, Ault, and Doyle (1992) suggest four reasons why a curriculum based entirely on DAP may not be sufficient for young children with disabilities:

For a discussion and debate concerning the role of the NAEYC's developmentally appropriate practice (DAP) for early childhood special education, see Bredekamp (1993); Carta, Atwater, Schwartz, and McConnell (1993); and Johnson and Johnson (1993). For a description of explicit practices recommended by leaders in early childhood special education, see DEC Recommended Practices *(DEC, 1993).*

1. Many children with special needs have delays or disabilities that make them dependent upon others.
2. Many children with special needs have delays or disabilities that keep them from learning well on their own.
3. Many children with special needs develop more slowly than their typically developing peers.
4. Many children with special needs have disabilities that interfere with how they interact; and as a result, they often acquire additional handicaps.

Although Bricker et al. (1998) find "a basic congruence and compatibility" (p. 213) between DAP and the focused activity-based intervention used by many early childhood special educators, they note two significant differences between the

Idea Bunny Helps Preschoolers Be More Independent

by Diane M. Sainato, Marie C. Ward, Jamie Brandt, Jill McQuaid, and Tamara C. Timko

Picture the scene that follows:

> When the flurry of the children's arrival at preschool subsided, their teacher gathered them together for morning circle time. They sang the "good morning" song, charted the weather, and handed out jobs for the day. Just before circle time ended, the teacher said, "Today during free-choice time we have many fun things to do. Please remember: only a few children at a time should be at each center. When you take an activity off the shelf, be sure to return it to the same place. Now everyone find something to do. I will be here to help you."
>
> Most of the children immediately chose activities. The teacher had to remind some children about "waiting your turn" and "using inside voices." Most children were appropriately and actively engaged during the 15-minute center time; however, Sally, who chose a matching and sorting task, dumped a variety of colored bears onto the table and promptly forgot what to do next. Quickly frustrated by waiting for the teacher to notice her, she wandered off without finishing the task. When the teacher noticed Sally, she took her by the hand and brought her back to the table with the bears. The teacher reminded Sally about what to do, showed her how, and moved to help another child. Sally matched several bears by color. Then, growing bored with the task, she carried the bucket of bears to the water table and dumped them into the water.
>
> The teacher sternly said, "Sally, what are you supposed to be doing?"
>
> Sally replied, "I don't know."

Learning to perform tasks without teacher direction is necessary for successful transition and inclusion into many typical classrooms. These skills are important not only in kindergarten but throughout a child's education (Sainato & Lyon, 1989). To help preschool children develop independent performance skills, we built on the work of other researchers who had successfully used auditory prompting systems with older students with disabilities (Alberto, Sharpton, Briggs, & Stright, 1986; Trask-Tyler, Grossi, & Heward, 1994). In previous studies, students used a foot pedal or hand-operated switch to work a small tape recorder, which played instructions about performing components of tasks such as meal preparation (see "I Made It Myself and It's Good!" in Chapter 11). We adapted the auditory prompting system to make it more appropriate for preschool children and called it the Idea Bunny—a soft, stuffed toy with a small tape recorder sewn inside. A foot pedal was attached to the recorder through a small opening in the bunny's underside. The bunny was placed on a table close to a bookshelf that held a variety of activity materials.

Task Analyses and Scripts We developed a task analysis to determine the component steps for each table-top activity. For example, these are the steps for a picture completion task:

1. Choose the basket containing picture pieces from the shelf.
2. Take the basket to the table.
3. Place the pieces on the table to show the picture.
4. Choose one piece and find another to make a picture.
5. Put the picture at the top of the table.
6. Put the pieces back into the basket.
7. Return the basket to the shelf.

We then created a script of instructions that included the steps for each learning task. The Idea Bunny "said" one step when the child pressed the foot pedal. Children were taught to use the bunny to help them complete steps in the activity. A beep sounded to signal the end of each specific step. At the end of the task, the Idea Bunny asked the child to stick its ears together to show the teacher that the child was finished.

The Bunny Talks! This was the bunny's script for the picture completion task:

> Hello! I'm happy you came to see Idea Bunny today. I have a great idea for you to try. Today we are going to complete pictures together. Go to the shelf and find the yellow basket of pictures that are cut in half. Bring the basket back to the table. [beep]
>
> Take all of the pieces out of the basket and turn them around so that you can see the picture on each piece. [beep] Choose one piece and pick another piece so that it makes a picture. Match the two pieces together and put them at the top of the table. [beep]
>
> Keep on matching the pieces together until they have all been matched to make pictures. [beep]

Great job! Now that you are finished matching the pieces, pick them up and place them in the basket. [beep]

Take the basket of picture pieces back to the shelf where you found them. [beep]

Now, put my ears together so the teacher knows you have finished your work. We had a great time today! Let's play again tomorrow. [beep]

"Hello, Rondell! I'm happy you came to see Idea Bunny. Today we are going to complete pictures together."

Research Results We have conducted three studies using the Idea Bunny as an auditory prompting device in preschool classrooms for young children with developmental disabilities (Brandt, 1992; Stemley, 1993; Ward, 1994). Results show that even though children are initially able to do the tasks, they require a great deal of teacher direction. Children have to be taught to use the Idea Bunny. At first, the children in our studies often played the whole tape just to listen to the bunny talk. Then they forgot what the bunny had first told them to do. We found that in the baseline condition (without the Idea Bunny), the children were engaged in the task but required many teacher prompts to keep on task. We then trained each child to use the Idea Bunny in a one-to-one situation with the teacher. During the intervention phase, we noted that children were much more engaged with the task and the rate of teacher prompts was low and stable.

These studies showed that preschoolers with developmental disabilities were able to learn to use the auditory prompting device. Independent engagement increased and, more important, was maintained when the prompting device was removed. Children appeared to enjoy the Idea Bunny and often patted him on the head and kissed him before they left the center. Sometimes they would talk back to the bunny. One day when the bunny said, "Good morning, I'm glad you came to see me today," a child replied, "Hi, Bunny, I'm happy to see you, too."

Suggestions for Using Idea Bunny in the Classroom

- Begin with skills in the child's repertoire. This activity should be for practice, not introducing new skills.
- Design a space for the center away from general play areas.
- Create a task analysis for each activity and develop scripts to match.
- Try out the scripts first to see whether the steps are too long.
- Teach children to use the prompting device.
- Monitor children to see that they understand the task.
- Place all of the materials needed to complete the task near the children.

Diane Sainato is a member of the special education faculty at The Ohio State University, where she directs a master's degree program in early childhood education and conducts research on the Idea Bunny and other ways to increase young children's independence. Marie Ward directs the Disability Services Center at the University of Nebraska. Jamie Brandt and Jill McQuaid are early childhood special education teachers. Tamara Timko is a faculty member in the Special Education Department at the University of Missouri, St. Louis.

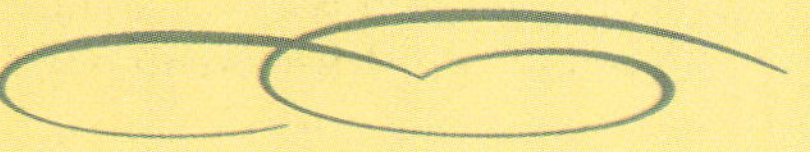

approaches. First, special educators must target specific goals and objectives to meet the unique developmental needs of individual children, while DAP is concerned with more general developmental goals (e.g., improve language skills or self-esteem) that are applicable to a broad range of children. Second, early childhood special educators use comprehensive and repeated assessments to determine learning objectives and to monitor progress according to stated performance criteria. DAP, by contrast, does not require the use of assessment or evaluation tools.

More information about IEPs for young children can be found by accessing the Resources Module for Chapter 5 at http://www.prenhall.com/heward and linking to "Teacher Resources" on the Special Ed Resource Page.

Selecting IFSP/IEP Objectives

The breadth of developmental domains and the activities that young children typically engage in provide an almost unlimited number of possibilities for instructional objectives. Notari-Syverson and Shuster (1995) recommend that potential IFSP/IEP objectives for infants and young children be evaluated according to five criteria:

1. *Functionality.* A functional skill (a) increases the child's ability to interact with people and objects in her daily environment and (b) may have to be performed by someone else if the child cannot do it.
2. *Generality.* In this context, a skill has generality if it (a) represents a general concept as opposed to a particular task, (b) can be adapted and modified to meet the child's disability, and (c) can be used across different settings, with various materials, and with different people.
3. *Instructional context.* The skill should be easily integrated into the child's daily routines and taught in a meaningful way that represents naturalistic use of the skill.
4. *Measurability.* A skill is measurable if its performance or a product produced by its performance can be seen and/or heard. Measurable skills can be counted or timed and enable objective determination of learning progress.
5. *Relation between long-range goals and short-term objectives.* Short-term objectives should be hierarchically related; the achievement of short-term objectives should contribute directly to the attainment of long-term goals.

For a description of general curriculum and intervention strategies used in early childhood special education, see Bailey and Wolery (1992) and Odom and McLean (1996).

Figure 5.8 shows 11 questions that can be used to assess potential IFSP/IEP objectives according to those five criteria.

To join in the discussion "Why is it so difficult to measure the impact of early intervention?" go to the Message Board Module at http://www.prenhall.com/heward.

Intervention Strategies in Early Childhood Special Education

Like their colleagues who work with elementary and secondary students with disabilities, early childhood special educators are, first and foremost, teachers who must be skilled in using a wide range of instructional strategies and tactics. In this section, we briefly look at three instructional challenges that all early childhood special educators must deal with: promoting the communication and language skills of young children, increasing children's social competence, and planning an activity schedule.

For a rationale and instructional guidelines for using signing to increase the communication and language development of children in inclusive preschools, see Heller, Manning, Pavur, and Wagner (1998) and Zeece and Wolda (1995).

Developing Language in Preschoolers with Disabilities

Learning the native language of their community is a major developmental task of children. Most children learn to speak and communicate effectively with little or no formal teaching. But children with disabilities often do not acquire language in the spontaneous, seemingly effortless manner of their peers without disabilities. And as children with disabilities slip further and further behind their peers, their language deficits make social and academic development even more difficult. Preschoolers with disabilities need opportunities and activities directed at language use and development throughout the day (Goldstein, Kaczmarek, & Hepting, 1994).

■ FUNCTIONALITY

1. Will the skill increase the child's ability to interact with people and objects within the daily environment?

The child needs to perform the skill in all or most of the environments in which he or she interacts.

Skill: Places object into container.

Opportunities: Home—Places sweater in drawer, cookie in paper bag.
School—Places lunch box in cubbyhole, trash in trash bin.
Community—Places milk carton in grocery cart, rocks and soil in flower pot.

2. Will the skill have to be performed by someone else if the child cannot do it?

The skill is a behavior or event that is critical for completion of daily routines.

Skill: Looks for object in usual location.

Opportunities: Finds coat on coat rack, gets food from cupboard.

■ GENERALITY

3. Does the skill represent a general concept or class of responses?

The skill emphasizes a generic process, rather than a particular instance.

Skill: Fits objects into defined spaces.

Opportunities: Puts mail in mailbox, places crayon in box, puts cutlery into sorter.

4. Can the skill be adapted or modified for a variety of disabling conditions?

The child's sensory impairment should interfere as little as possible with the performance.

Skill: Correctly activates simple toy.

Opportunities: Motor impairments—Activates light, easy-to-move toys (e.g., balls, rocking horse, toys on wheels, roly-poly toys).
Visual impairments—Activates large, bright, noise-making toys (e.g., bells, drums, large rattles).

5. Can the skill be generalized across a variety of settings, materials, and/or people?

The child can perform the skill with interesting materials and in meaningful situations.

Skill: Manipulates two small objects simultaneously.

Opportunities: Home—Builds with small interlocking blocks, threads laces on shoes.
School—Sharpens pencil with pencil sharpener.
Community—Takes coin out of small wallet.

■ INSTRUCTIONAL CONTEXT

6. Can the skill be taught in a way that reflects the manner in which the skill will be used in daily environments?

The skill can occur in a naturalistic manner.

Skill: Uses object to obtain another object.

Opportunities: Uses fork to obtain food, broom to rake toy; steps on stool to reach toy on shelf.

7. Can the skill be elicited easily by the teacher/parent within classroom/home activities?

The skill can be initiated easily by the child as part of daily routines.

Skill: Stacks objects.

Opportunities: Stacks books, cups/plates, wooden logs.

■ MEASURABILITY

8. Can the skill be seen and/or heard?

Different observers must be able to identify the same behavior.

Measurable skill: Gains attention and refers to object, person, and/or event.

Nonmeasurable skill: Experiences a sense of self-importance

Figure 5.8 Five criteria for evaluating IEP/IFSP objectives for infants, toddlers, and preschoolers with disabilities

Source: Adapted from Notari-Syverson, A. R., & Shuster, S. L. (1995). Putting real-life skills into IEP/IFSPs for infants and young children. *Teaching Exceptional Children, 27*(2), 31. Used by permission of the Council for Exceptional Children, Reston, VA.

(Figure 5.8 continues on p. 182.)

9. **Can the skill be directly counted (e.g., by frequency, duration, distance measures)?**
The skill represents a well-defined behavior or activity.
Measurable skill: Grasps pea-sized object.
Nonmeasurable skill: Has mobility in all fingers.

10. **Does the skill contain or lend itself to determination of performance criteria?**
The extent and/or degree of accuracy of the skill can be evaluated.
Measurable skill: Follows one-step directions with contextual cues.
Nonmeasurable skill: Will increase receptive language skills.

■ HIERARCHICAL RELATION BETWEEN LONG-RANGE GOAL AND SHORT-TERM OBJECTIVE

11. **Is the short-term objective a developmental subskill or step thought to be critical to the achievement of the long-range goal?**
Appropriate: Short-Term Objective—Releases object with each hand. Long-Range Goal—Places and releases object balanced on top of another object.
Inappropriate: 1. The Short-Term Objective is a restatement of the same skill as the Long-Range-Goal, with the addition of an instructional prompt (e.g., Short-Term Objective—Activates mechanical toy with physical prompt. Long-Range Goal—Independently activates mechanical toy) or a quantitative limitation to the extent of the skill (e.g., Short-Term Objective—Stacks 5 1-inch blocks; Long-Range-Goal—Stacks 10 1-inch blocks).
2. The Short-Term Objective is not conceptually or functionally related to the Long-Range Goal (e.g., Short-Term Objective—Releases object voluntarily; Long-Range Goal—Pokes with index finger).

Figure 5.8 *continued*

Creating sociodramatic play scripts that require children to interact with one another (e.g., customer and clerk at a shoe store or a hamburger stand) can be effective in promoting communication skills (Goldstein, 1993).

Research has shown that the more a child talks, the better he talks (Hart & Risley, 1995). Teachers of preschool children should plan activities that encourage children to develop and use language skills all day long. The basic measure of a language intervention's success should be how much the child talks. Allen (1980a) says that good teachers do three things to ensure effective intervention for language-delayed children:

1. They arrange the environment in ways that are conducive to promoting language: by providing interesting learning centers (blocks, housekeeping and dramatic play, creative and manipulative materials); by balancing child-initiated and teacher-structured activities; and by presenting materials and activities that children enjoy.
2. They manage their interactions with children so as to maximize effective communication on the part of each language-impaired child and use every opportunity to teach "on the fly."
3. They monitor the appropriateness of environmental arrangements, their own behavior, and that of the children to validate child progress and thus program effectiveness.

Two approaches that teachers can use for systematically encouraging and developing language use throughout the school day are the *incidental teaching model* (Hart, 1985; Hart & Risley, 1980) and the *mand model* (Rogers-Warren & Warren, 1980; Warren, McQuarter, & Rogers-Warren, 1984.) The essential feature of the incidental teaching model is that when the child wants something from the teacher (help, approval, information, food, or drink), the teacher takes the opportunity to promote language use. In other words, whenever the child initiates an interaction with the teacher, the teacher uses that opportunity to get the best possible language from the child. Allen (1980b) offers the following example of an incidental teaching episode described by Hart:

> A four-year-old girl with delayed language stands in front of the teacher with a paint apron in her hand. The teacher says, "What do you need?" (Teacher does not anticipate the child's need by putting the apron on the child at the moment.)
>
> If the child does not answer, the teacher tells her and gives her a prompt: "It's an apron. Can you say 'apron'?" If the child says "apron," the teacher ties it while giving descriptive praise, "You said it right. It is an apron. I am tying your apron on you." The teacher's last sentence models the next verbal behavior, "Tie my apron," that the teacher will expect once the child has learned to say "apron."
>
> If the child does not say "apron," the teacher ties the apron. No further comments are made at this time. The teacher must not coax, nag or pressure the child. If each episode is kept brief and pleasant, the child will contact the teacher frequently. Thus, the teacher will have many opportunities for incidental teaching. If the teacher pressures the child, such incidental learning opportunities will be lost. Some children may learn to avoid the teacher—they will simply do without; other children may learn inappropriate ways, such as whining and crying, to get what they want. (unpaged)

Through repeated interactions of this type, children learn that language is important; it can get them what they want, and teachers listen when they speak and want to hear more about things of interest to them. An important guideline in incidental teaching is to keep interactions brief and pleasant so that there will be many more opportunities. The child should never be interrogated or put on the spot (Allen, 1980a).

Warren and Gazdag (1990) combined incidental teaching and mand-model techniques into a *milieu instructional approach* to teach two 3-year-olds with developmental delays various language forms during naturalistic play. The authors describe the differences between the two complementary techniques:

> The distinction between the two procedures centers on who (trainer or child) initiates the instructional interaction. With the mand-model the teacher is in the role of facilitator, initiating the interaction by "manding" a target response, typically by asking a target probe question about the event or activity to which the child is attending. In the incidental teaching procedure, the child initiates the interaction either verbally or nonverbally. The trainer then elicits the target response by prompting a more elaborate response. (p. 70)

Table 5.2 shows examples of instructional episodes using incidental teaching and mand-model techniques. The methods have much in common. Both view the teacher as (1) an astute and systematic observer and recorder of children's language, (2) a sensitive and willing listener, and (3) a systematic responder who helps the child "say it better" through differential feedback (Allen, 1980a).

Promoting the Social Competence of Preschoolers with Disabilities

Many young children with disabilities exhibit problems interacting with others. One survey of preschool special education teachers found that 75% of the children with disabilities in their classes had social skill deficits (Odom, McConnell, & McEvoy, 1992). When placed in inclusive settings, many preschoolers with disabilities interact infrequently and incompetently with other children. In recent years, special education practice, especially in early childhood special education, has placed increasing

Table 5.2 Examples of language-promoting episodes using mand-model and incidental-teaching procedures

Example 1	Example 2
Mand Model	
Context: Child is scooping beans with a ladle and pouring them into a pot. Trainer: "What are you doing?" (target probe question) Child: No response. Trainer: "Tell me." (mand) Child: "Beans." Trainer: "Say, *pour beans*."(model) Child: "Pour beans." Trainer: "That's right, you're pouring beans into the pot." (verbal acknowledgement + expansion)	Context: Trainer gives each child a turn to blow bubbles. Trainer: (holds the wand up to the child's mouth) "What do you want to do?" (target probe question) Child: "Bubbles." Trainer: "*Blow* bubbles." (model) Child: "Blow bubbles." Trainer: "OK, you want to blow bubbles. Here you go." (verbal acknowledgement + expansion + activity participation)
Incidental Teaching	
Context: Making pudding activity. Trainer gives peer a turn at stirring the pudding as the subject looks on. Child: "Me!" (child initiates) and reaches for ladle. Trainer: "Stir pudding." (model) Child: "Stir pudding." Trainer: "All right. You stir the pudding, too." (verbal acknowledgement + expansion + activity participation)	Context: Trainer and subject are washing dishes together in a parallel fashion. Child: "Wash." (Child initiates with an action-verb, partial target response) Trainer: "Wash what?" (elaborative question) Child: "Wash" (incorrect response). Trainer: "Wash *what*?" (elaborative question) Child: "Wash cups." Trainer: "That's right. We're washing cups." (verbal acknowledgement + expansion)

Source: From Warren, S. F. (1992). Facilitating basic vocabulary acquisition with milieu teaching procedures. *Journal of Early Intervention, 16,* 242. Reprinted by permission.

To learn several strategies for teaching preschoolers with disabilities how to make friends, see Cooper and McEvoy (1996); English, Goldstein, Kaczmarek, and Shafer (1996); and Kohler and Strain (1993).

McConnell, McEvoy, and Odom (1992) describe 49 interventions for increasing social interaction skills of young children with disabilities.

emphasis on the development of peer relationships and friendships by children with special needs (Richardson & Schwartz, 1998).

Strain and his colleagues (Sainato, Goldstein, & Strain, 1992; Strain & Odom, 1986) have investigated the use of peer social initiations as a means of increasing the social competence of preschoolers with disabilities. The procedure involves teaching nondisabled peers to direct social overtures to their classmates with disabilities. Strain and Odom (1986) recommend that peer intervention agents be taught to make initiations to children with disabilities in the form of (1) play opportunities, (2) offers to share, (3) physical assistance, and (4) affection. These initiations are recommended on the basis of naturalistic studies of the social interactions of both preschoolers with and without disabilities; the studies showed that such initiations were followed by a positive response more than 50% of the time and that responding to the social bids of others increased a child's social acceptability.

The strategy requires careful arrangement of the classroom environment to encourage greater social interaction. For example, the probability of social interaction can be increased by limiting the number of toys so that to participate children must share and by requiring children to play within a confined area. The key feature of the procedure, however, is the careful training of the peers who are chosen to serve as confederates. Training sessions usually take between 20 and 25 minutes and incorporate teacher modeling and both teacher and confederate role playing of the desired social initiation. Figure 5.9 shows a sample script for an initial training session in

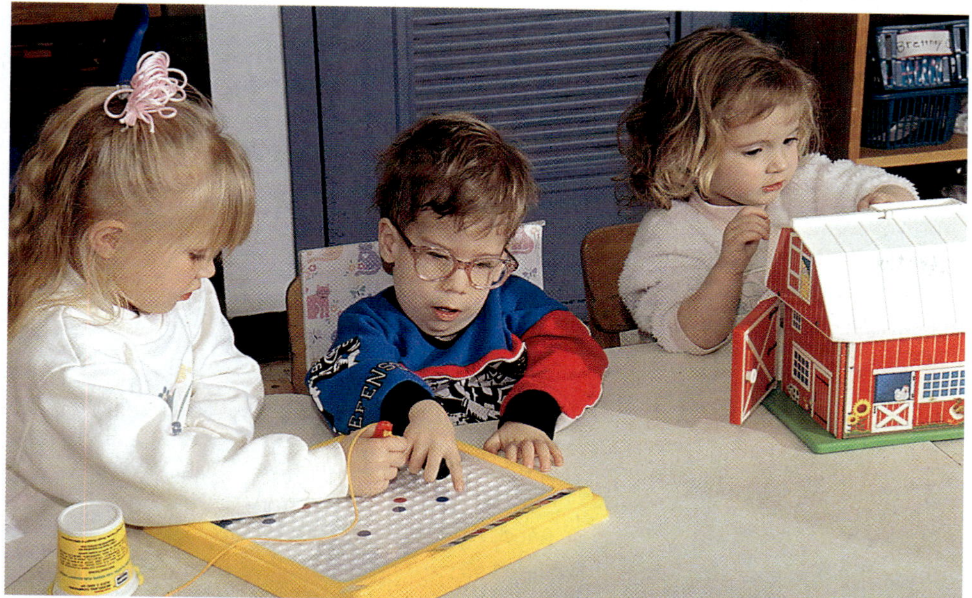

The systematic use of play activities and the use of peer "confederates" can increase the language skills and social competence of preschoolers with disabilities.

which children learn how to initiate sharing. Training is followed by daily intervention sessions, in which the teacher arranges an activity for the children that is conducive to social interaction and then prompts and verbally reinforces the confederate for being a good teacher and the target child with disabilities for being a good player.

Developing a Preschool Activity Schedule

Teachers in preschool programs for children with disabilities face the challenge of organizing the program day into a schedule that meets each child's individual learning needs and provides children with many opportunities to explore the environment and communicate with others throughout the day. The schedule should include a balance of child-initiated and planned activities, large- and small-group activities, active and quiet times, and indoor and outdoor activities; it should allow easy transition from activity to activity. In short, the schedule should provide a framework for maximizing children's opportunities to develop new skills and practice what they have learned previously while remaining manageable and flexible. In addition, how activities are scheduled and organized has considerable effect on the frequency and type of interaction that occurs between children with and without disabilities (Harris & Handleman, 1994) and on the extent to which children with disabilities benefit from instructional activities (O'Connell, 1986).

Even the time between activities can be used for learning and practicing important skills. Transition-based teaching, *presenting a single instructional trial as a child begins to leave one activity to go to another, has been found effective (Werts, Wolery, Venn, Demblowski, & Doren, 1996; Wolery, Anthony, & Heckathorn, 1998).*

Lund and Bos (1981) suggest that teachers begin planning a preschool schedule by determining the basic activities and time blocks. The next steps in constructing the schedule are filling in the approximate amount of time to spend on each activity each day, sequencing the components, scheduling children for individual and group activities, and assigning staff (teachers, aides, and volunteers). Bricker et al. (1998) describe an activity-planning and scheduling process that combines children's individual IFSP/IEP objectives with group activity plans. Figure 5.10 shows how children's goals and objectives in the social-communication domain were integrated into group activities in one preschool classroom.

O'Connell (1986) offers suggestions for structuring the physical arrangement of small-group learning activities in inclusive preschool classrooms.

The physical arrangement of the classroom itself must support the planned activities. Figure 5.11 shows an example of a preschool classroom layout with a variety of

TEACHER: "Today you are going to learn how to be a good teacher. Sometimes your friends in your class do not know how to play with other children. You are going to learn how to teach them to play. What are you going to do?"

CHILD RESPONSE: "Teach them to play."

TEACHER: "One way you get your friend to play with you is to share. How do you get your friend to play with you?"

CHILD RESPONSE: "Share."

TEACHER: "Right! You share. When you share, you look at your friend and say. 'Here,' and put a toy in his hand. What do you do?" (Repeat this exercise until the child can repeat these three steps.)

CHILD RESPONSE: "Look at friend and say, 'Here,' and put the toy in his hand."

ADULT MODEL WITH ROLE-PLAYER: "Now, watch me, I am going to share with ________. Tell me if I do it right." (Demonstrate sharing.) "Did I share with ________? What did I do?"

CHILD RESPONSE: "Yea! ________ looked at ________, said 'Here ________' and put a toy in his hand."

ADULT: "Right. I looked at ________ and said, 'Here ________' and put a toy in his hand. Now watch me. See if I share with ________." (Move to the next activity in the classroom. This time provide a negative example of sharing by leaving out the "put in hand" component. Put the toy beside the role-player.) "Did I share?" (Correct if necessary and repeat this example if child got it wrong.) "Why not?"

CHILD RESPONSE: "No. You did not put the toy in ________'s hand."

ADULT: "That's right. I did not put the toy in ________'s hand. When I share, I have to look at ________ and say, 'Here ________' and put the toy in his hand." (Give the child two more positive and two more negative examples of sharing. When the child answers incorrectly about sharing, repeat the example. Vary the negative examples by leaving out different components: looking, saying 'Here,' and putting in hand.)

CHILD PRACTICE WITH ADULTS: "Now ________, I want you to get ________ to share with you. What do you do when you share?"

CHILD RESPONSE: "Look at ________ and say. 'Here ________,' and put a toy in his hand."

ADULT: "Now, go get ________ to play with you." (For those practice examples, the role-playing adult should be responsive to the child's sharing.) (To the other confederates:) "Did ________ share with ________? What did she/he do?"

CHILD RESPONSE: "Yes/No. Looked at ________ and said, 'Here ________' and put a toy in his hand."

ADULT: (Move to the next activity.) "Now, ________, I want you to share with ________."

Introduce Persistence

TEACHER: "Sometimes when I play with ________, he/she does not want to play back. I have to keep on trying. What do I have to do?"

CHILD RESPONSE: "Keep on trying."

TEACHER: "Right, I have to keep on trying. Watch me. I am going to share with ________. Now I want you to see if I keep on trying." (Role-player will be initially unresponsive.) (Teacher should be persistent until child finally responds.) "Did I get ________ to play with me?" **CHILD:** "Yes." **TEACHER:** "Did he want to play?" **CHILD:** "No." **TEACHER:** "What did I do?" **CHILD:** "Keep on trying. No?" **TEACHER:** "Right, I kept on trying. Watch. See if I can get ________ to play with me this time." (Again, the role-player should be unresponsive at first. Repeat above questions and correct if necessary. Repeat the example until the child responds correctly.)

Figure 5.9 Sample script for an initial training session in which children learn how to initiate sharing
Source: Reprinted from Strain, P. S., & Odom, S. L. (1986). Peer social interactions: Effective intervention for social skills development of exceptional children. *Teaching Exceptional Children, 52,* 547. Used by permission of the Council for Exceptional Children, Reston, VA.

Child	Goals and objectives	Daily Program Activities: Social Communication				
		Arrival	Lunch	Outdoor play	Circle time	Discovery time
Darin **Sam** **Mikail** **Aaron**	Shares or exchanges objects	Shares umbrella with peer while walking from bus to classroom	Exchanges plates/bowls of food with peers	Shares or trades objects when enough are not available		• Shares watercolor palette • Trades objects in any area selected • Shares large paper to paint/write/draw • Shares big blocks • Trades puppets
Sam	Knows gender of self and others	• Walks in line with boys to classroom from bus • Places attendance card on bulletin board next to a boy's or a girl's card			Responds to song directions specifically for boys	• Plays doctor's office in dramatic area that requires practice in giving identifying information such as name, address, gender
Jamal **Marisa** **Cody**	Accurately identifies own affect/emotions	Responds to questions, "How do you feel today?" "How do you think (blank) feels today?"	Identifies likes and dislikes	Identifies affect/emotion of children experiencing conflict or injury	Identifies affect/emotion of people in books	
Alex	Asks what and where questions	Smells food cooking for lunch and asks, "What is for lunch?"	Notices absent peer or adult and asks, "Where is (blank)?"	Plays Hide and Seek and asks peer/adult "Where is (blank)?"	• Asks what and where questions about objects brought for sharing day • Participates in animal charades asking, "Where do you live and what do you eat?"	Asks where are objects when too few objects are present in areas
Jorge **Dahlia**	Uses adjectives to make comparisons	Describes texture and color of clothing on self and others	Describes textures and colors of food items served		Describes items felt in feely bag	Describes and compares completed project of peer/self

Figure 5.10 Example of an activity schedule in the social-communication domain

Source: Reprinted from Bricker, D., Pretti-Frontczak, K., & McComas, N. (1998). *An activity-based approach to early intervention* (2nd ed., pp. 103–104). Baltimore: Brookes. Used by permission.

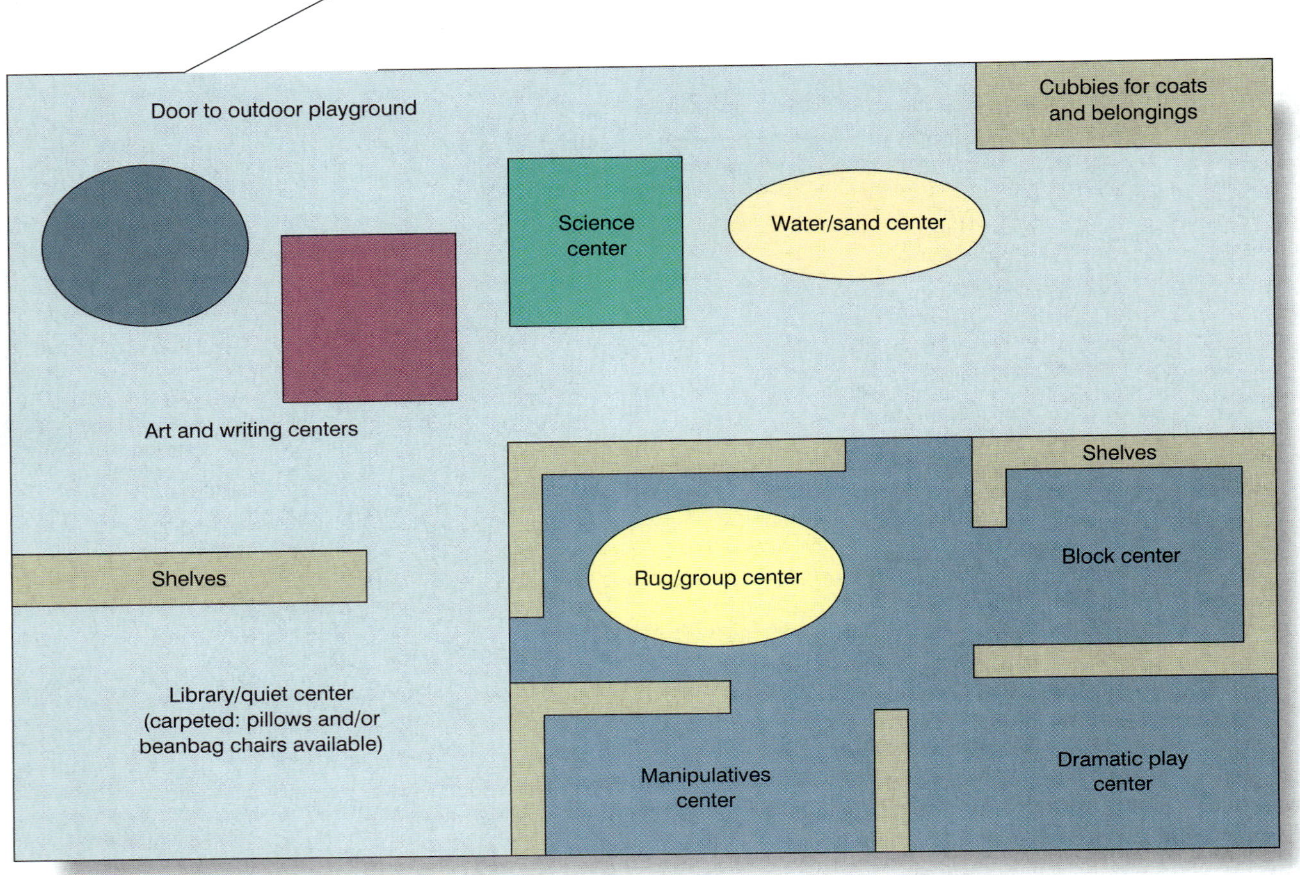

Figure 5.11 Example of a preschool classroom layout with a variety of activity centers
Source: From Bricker, D., & Waddell, M. (1996). *AEPS curriculum for three to six years* (p. 27). Baltimore: Brookes. Reprinted by permission.

activity centers. Suggestions for setting up a preschool classroom include the following (Bricker et al., 1998; Johnson-Martin et al., 1990; Lund & Bos 1981; Morrison, 1998):

- Organize the classroom into a number of different well-defined areas to accommodate different kinds of activities (e.g., quiet play, messy play, dramatic play, constructive play, active play).
- Locate quiet activities together, away from avenues of traffic, and loud activities together.
- Equip each area with abundant, appropriate materials that are desirable to children.
- Locate materials where children can easily retrieve them and are not dependent on adults.
- Have an open area, perhaps on a large rug, where large-group activities such as circle time and story reading can be conducted.
- Label or color-code all storage areas so that aides and volunteers can easily find needed materials.
- Arrange equipment and group areas so that students can move easily from one activity to another. Pictures or color codes can be applied to various work areas.
- Provide lockers or cubbies for students so they know where to find their belongings. Again, add picture cues to help students identify their lockers.

Service Delivery Alternatives for Early Intervention

Where early intervention takes place varies, depending on the age of the child and the special supports she and her family need. Early intervention services for infants and newborns with significant disabilities are often provided in hospital settings. Most early childhood special education services, however, are provided in the child's home, in a center- or school-based facility, or in a combination of both settings.

IDEA requires that early intervention services be provided in natural environments to the greatest extent possible. Natural environments are the same home, school, and community settings that typically developing children inhabit (Noonan & McCormick (1993).

Hospital-Based Programs

Increasingly, early intervention services are being provided to hospitalized newborns and their families. Low-birth-weight and other high-risk newborns who require specialized health care are placed in neonatal intensive care units (NICUs). Many NICUs now include a variety of professionals, such as neonatologists who provide medical care for infants with special needs, nurses who provide ongoing medical assistance, social workers or psychologists who help parents and families with emotional and financial concerns, and infant education specialists who promote interactions between parents and infants (Brown, Thurman, & Pearl, 1993; Flynn & McCollum, 1989).

For suggestions for developing IFSP/IEPs for children who are technology dependent, see Prendergast (1995).

Home-Based Programs

As the name suggests, a home-based program depends heavily on parental training and cooperation. The parents assume the primary responsibility of caregivers and teachers for their child with disabilities. Parent training is usually provided by a teacher or trainer who visits the home regularly to guide the parents, act as a consultant, evaluate the success of intervention, and regularly assess the child's progress. Home visitors (or home teachers or home advisors, as they are often called) in some programs are specially trained paraprofessionals. They may visit as frequently as several times a week but probably no less than a few times a month. They sometimes carry the results of their in-home evaluations back to other professionals, who may recommend changes in the program.

The Portage Project, one of the best-known and most widely replicated home-based programs, was begun nearly 30 years ago by a consortium of 23 school districts in south-central Wisconsin (Shearer & Shearer, 1972). A project teacher typically visits the home one day each week to review the child's progress during the previous week, describe activities for the upcoming week, demonstrate to the parents how to carry out the activities with the child, observe the parent and child interacting, offer suggestions and advice as needed, summarize where the program stands, and indicate what records parents should keep during the next week. The Portage Project has produced its own assessment materials and teaching activities, *The Portage Guide to Early Education*, based on 450 behaviors, sequenced developmentally and classified into self-help, cognition, socialization, language, and motor skills.

Home-based early intervention programs have several advantages:

- The home is the child's natural environment, and it is often true that a parent can give more time and attention to the child than even the most adequately staffed center or school.
- Other family members, such siblings and perhaps even grandparents, have more opportunity to interact with the child, for both instruction and social contact. These significant others can play an important role in the child's growth and development.
- Home learning activities and materials are more likely to be natural and appropriate.

- Parents who are actively involved in helping their child learn and develop clearly have an advantage over parents who feel guilt, frustration, or defeat at their seeming inability to help their child.
- Home-based programs can be less costly to operate without the expenses of maintaining a facility and equipment and transporting children to and from the center.

Home-based programs, however, can have disadvantages:

- Because programs place so much responsibility on parents, they are not effective with all families. Not all parents are able or willing to spend the time required to teach their children, and some who try are not effective teachers.
- Early childhood special education programs must learn to serve more effectively the large and growing number of young children who do not reside in the traditional two-parent family—especially the many thousands of children with teenage mothers who are single, uneducated, and poor. Many of these infants and preschoolers are at risk for developmental delays because of the impoverished conditions in which they live, and it is unlikely that a parent struggling with the realities of day-to-day survival will be able to meet the added demands of involvement in an early intervention program (Turnbull & Turnbull, 1997).
- Because the parent—usually the mother—is the primary service provider, children in home-based programs may not receive as wide a range of services as they would in a center-based program, where they can be seen by a variety of professionals. (Note, however, that the services of professionals such as physical therapists, occupational therapists, and speech therapists are sometimes provided in the home.)
- The child may not receive sufficient opportunity for social interaction with peers.

Center-Based Programs

Center-based programs provide early intervention services in a special educational setting outside the home. The setting may be part of a hospital complex, a special day care center, or a preschool. Some children may attend a specially designed developmental center or training center that offers a wide range of services for children with varying types and degrees of disabilities. Wherever they are, these centers offer the combined services of many professionals and paraprofessionals, often from several different fields.

The curricula, teaching methods, daily activity schedule, approaches to integration, methods of parent involvement, and transition planning used by 10 different preschool programs for children with autism are described by Harris and Handleman (1994).

Most center-based programs encourage social interaction, and some try to integrate children with disabilities and typically developing children in day care or preschool classes. Some children attend a center each weekday for all or most of the day; others may come less frequently, although most centers expect to see each child at least once a week. Parents are sometimes given roles as classroom aides or encouraged to act as their child's primary teacher. A few programs allow parents to spend time with other professionals or take training while their child is somewhere else in the center. Virtually all effective programs for young children with disabilities recognize the critical need to involve parents, and they welcome parents in every aspect of the program.

A good example of a center-based program is the Precise Early Education of Children with Handicaps (PEECH) project originally developed at the University of Illinois. Designed for children ages 3 to 5 with mild to moderate disabilities, PEECH combines classroom instruction for up to 10 children with disabilities and 5 nondisabled children. A team approach to intervention and parental involvement includes a classroom teacher and a paraprofessional aide, a psychologist, a speech-language pathologist, and a social worker. Children spend two or three hours in class each day, with some time in large and small groups and individualized activities. Parents are included in all stages of the intervention, including policymaking. The project offers a lending library and a toy library for parents to use as well as a parent newsletter. The project's ultimate goal is to successfully integrate youngsters with disabilities into regular kindergarten classes whenever possible. Early childhood special educators at 200 replication sites in 36 states have received training in various components of the PEECH program (Karnes, Beauchamp, & Pfaus, 1993).

Another model center-based program is the Alice H. Hayden Preschool at the University of Washington (see "Including Preschool Children with Autism" later in this chapter). For extensive and helpful information on inclusion of preschoolers with disabilities, contact the Early Childhood Research Institute on Inclusion, listed in "For More Information" at the end of this chapter.

Center-based programs generally offer three advantages that are difficult to build into home-based efforts:

- Increased opportunity for a team of specialists from different fields—education, physical and occupational therapy, speech and language pathology, medicine, and others—to observe each child and cooperate in intervention and continued assessment. Some special educators feel that the intensive instruction and related services that can be provided in a center-based program are especially important for children with severe disabilities (Rose & Calhoun, 1990).
- The opportunity for contact with typically developing peers makes center programs especially appealing for some children.
- Most parents involved in center programs feel some relief at the support they get from the professionals who work with their child and from other parents with children at the same center.

Disadvantages of a center-based program include the expense of transportation, the cost and maintenance of the center itself, and the probability of less parent involvement than in home-based programs.

Combined Home-Center Programs

Many early intervention programs combine center-based activities and home visitation. Few center programs take children for more than a few hours a day, for up to five days per week. But because young children with disabilities require more intervention than a few hours a day, many programs combine the intensive help of a variety of professionals in a center with the continuous attention and sensitive care of parents at home. Intervention that carries over from center to home clearly offers many of the advantages of the two types of programs and negates some of their disadvantages.

St. Mark's Circle School in Charlotte, North Carolina, offers a combination home- and center-based early intervention program for infants and toddlers with severe/profound disabilities. The program is based on the social reciprocity model, which views

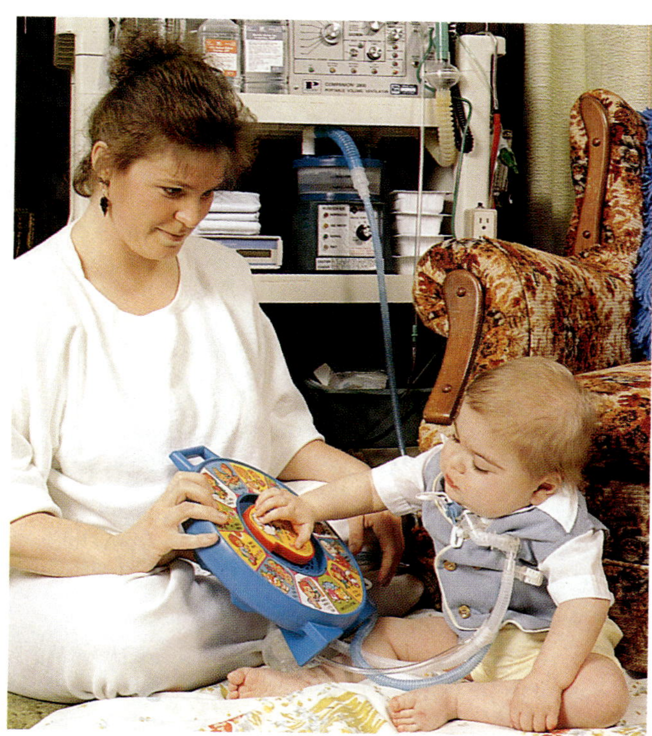

Programs like the St. Mark's Circle Project in North Carolina teach parents to identify and increase the frequency of positive behaviors by their infants such as smiling or imitating.

Including Preschool Children with Autism: Five Strategies That Work

by Ilene S. Schwartz, Felix F. Billingsley, and Bonnie M. McBride

Children with autism and other developmental disabilities are included in the Alice H. Hayden Preschool at the University of Washington, a comprehensive program for approximately 150 children from birth through age 6 and their families. Each classroom has 15 children: 9 qualifying for special education services, 6 typically developing. The classrooms serve children with a wide range of abilities, from severe disabilities to mild language delay to giftedness. About 30% of the children with disabilities have autism. Each class has a head teacher, an assistant teacher, and at least one aide.

We consider five strategies central to providing educational services for young children with disabilities in inclusive settings. They are tricks of the trade for helping children with autism and other developmental disabilities acquire skills, develop relationships, and participate as full class members.

Teach Communication and Social Competence Without communication and social interactions among children, an inclusive program may provide little more than parallel instruction.

- *Use the Picture Exchange Communication System (PECS) to help children without functional verbal skills communicate effectively.* PECS teaches children to communicate with pictures and symbols (Bondy & Frost, 1994; Schwartz, Garfinkle, & Bauer, 1998). It also teaches persistence, an important skill for many communicative and social interactions. Most children with autism quickly learn to use PECS to communicate in understandable and acceptable ways about the things that are important to them while acquiring speech skills.
- *Provide systematic instruction in imitation skills.* Imitation is critical to learning from and relating to others. Embed imitation training throughout the day, in small groups, opening circle, gym, outdoor play, and free choice.
- *Plan opportunities for students with disabilities to interact directly with typically developing peers.* At opening circle, begin with a desirable toy such as bubbles and then help all children share the toy directly with other children instead of passing the toy from child to teacher to child.

Here's an example:

> Mark, who has autism, sits at the art center with several classmates. He sees that his favorite painting utensil, Dot Art paints, is next to Mary, who is typically developing and new to the class. Mark uses his symbols to build the sentence "I want Dot Art paint" and extends it toward Mary. Ben, who has been in Mark's class for a year, sees that he is trying to communicate with Mary, who is painting and doesn't notice. Ben turns to Mary and says, "Mary, Mark is talking to you. Take the sentence from him and see what he wants." Mary takes Mark's sentence strip, looks at the picture, and gives him the Dot Art paint. Ben says, "If you want it back, you can just ask Mark for it. We have to share in our class."

Use Instructional Strategies That Maintain the Class's Natural Flow Rather than isolating children with disabilities to provide individualized instruction, teach within the context of developmentally appropriate activities and routines.

- *Draw peers into the instructional situation.*
- *Use naturalistic teaching procedures.* Instruction should involve activities that are interesting to students, take advantage of child-initiated interactions, and use naturally occurring consequences.
- *Use different cues and prompts to ensure each child receives adequate support.* But take care to provide only what help is required so the children do not become dependent on teacher assistance.

Here's an example:

> One of Jacob's IEP objectives is to learn to match similar objects. During small-group time his class made collages using various art supplies. Before the activity, his teacher placed five shapes of different colors on his collage. As the activity began, the teacher gave him five corresponding color shapes to match. The teacher provided sufficient prompts for him to complete the matching task as independently as possible. He continued to work on his collage alongside his classmates.

Teach and Provide Opportunities for Independence While interdependence is appropriate and normal in human relationships, we also expect children to become increasingly independent as they grow.

- *Give children choices whenever possible and teach choice making when necessary.*

- *Picture schedules can help some children learn to follow the sequence and duration of daily activities.* Visual cues can ease transitions between activities, increase engagement, and provide structure for trying new activities and play materials. Over time, the schedules can be faded.
- *Because it is easy to overlook nonverbal children, give them frequent chances to respond to teacher initiations.*
- *Maintain high expectations for all children.* Celebrate small victories and immediately "up the ante," all the while believing that the child has the ability to reach the next objective. Don't say, "He can't"; instead, say, "How can we help him to . . . ?

Here's an example:

It is free-choice time in Jon's classroom, and he has been having a difficult day. Transitions are always challenging for him, but today there has been more crying and mild self-injury than we have seen in six weeks. When the teacher announces that everyone can make his first choice, Jon walks to the wall and looks at his schedule. It has his name and six picture/symbols on it representing activity centers that are open during free choice. The first two pictures show centers in which Jon is developing play skills; the third is his favorite—the computer center. The next two are less preferred areas, and the last picture shows "Jon's choice," which means he can pick any activity he wants. Although he is still whimpering, he looks at the schedule, touches the first picture, sets a kitchen timer next to the schedule, and walks to a center. As he engages in this routine, he calms down. He plays in the center with other children until the timer goes off. Then he walks back to the schedule, takes off the first picture and puts it in the "finished pocket" at the bottom, and repeats the routine.

Build a Classroom Community That Includes All Children Classrooms are learning communities where everyone can make a valuable contribution and has something to learn. Both large-group activities (e.g., opening circle, songs, stories, plays) and small-group activities (e.g., cooperative games, art projects, pre-academic activities) help create a classroom community.

- *Use activities that will engage children with a large range of abilities.* Plan open-ended activities that use preferred materials, support many responses, and address strengths of children with disabilities.
- *Allow every child to have a turn and play a role.* For example, every child, including children with autism, take turns being in charge of handing out materials. This puts the children with disabilities on an equal footing with others in the group and requires them to be communicative partners with peers as they request materials.

Here's an example:

It is "show and share" day, and Sophie, a 5-year-old with autism, is ready. In her lap she has a special toy from her grandmother and a cue card with words and symbols her teacher has prepared. When it's her turn, she walks to the front of the circle, holds up her toy, looks at the notecard, and follows the routine of telling her classmates two things about her toy. Then she asks, "Any questions?" After calling on classmates and answering two questions, she returns to her seat, puts her toy and cue card behind her, and picks up the notecard at her place. The teacher prepared this card with cues to support Sophie's participation as an audience member. Anthony then tells the class about the toy he brought to school and asks, "Any questions?" Sophie looks at the card in front of her, raises her hand, and looks at Anthony. When Anthony calls on Sophie, she asks, "Where did you get it?" Anthony answers the question, calls on another classmate, and "show and share" time continues.

Promote Generalization and Maintenance of Skills Unless skills are demonstrated across a variety of situations and maintained over time, children will have limited ability to participate meaningfully in inclusive environments.

- *Target skills that will be useful in each child's life.* Skills a child needs in many situations and those typically enjoyed by same-age children will be practiced with many persons in different situations over time. Useful skills are also likely to be generalized and maintained because they often produce naturally reinforcing outcomes and reduce the need for artificial reinforcers.
- *Use instructional prompts judiciously and fade them rapidly.* To keep children from depending on adult assistance and direction, use the least directive and intrusive prompt that ensures successful skill performance. Fade the prompt as quickly as possible without disrupting performance.
- *Distribute learning trials naturally.* Capitalize on teaching opportunities that occur within natural school routines and activities. This increases the likelihood of generalization and maintenance because it "duplicates the occasions in which the skill should occur after instruction ceases" (Billingsley, Liberty, & White, 1994, p. 90).
- *Use common materials for instruction.* Teach with materials frequently found in preschools, child care settings, and the homes of young children. Arrange for chil-

dren to practice with these materials across many settings in the classroom.

Here's an example:

Joey has difficulty in the dramatic play area. To promote skill development, his teacher provides systematic instruction of a pretend play sequence during small-group time, using a simple play script with pictures and words and the same materials available in the dramatic play center this week. The teacher models the sequence, following the pictures in the script book and reciting corresponding words. Then Joey takes a turn while the teacher helps. Later, during free play, he enters the dramatic play area and sees the familiar pretend play props and his picture script book. He begins following the sequence without adult assistance. Next week, the teacher will use a similar script with different materials.

Successfully embedding effective instructional strategies into developmentally appropriate preschool routines and supporting children with disabilities in inclusive classrooms have taught us two important lessons:

1. *We have learned to view children holistically.* Our students with autism constantly show us their strengths and skills. Our staff has learned to work with them and their families to develop individualized programs that address children's needs and build on their strengths.
2. *We have learned to view the outcomes of inclusion and effective instruction broadly.* Although developing, implementing, and evaluating discrete IEP objectives are important, we encourage our staff to look beyond children's learning and generalizing of discrete skills to understand how the skills affect the child's and family's lifestyle (Billingsley, Gallucci, Peck, Schwartz, & Staub, 1996).

Source: Adapted from Schwartz, I. S., Billingsley, F. F., & McBride, B. M. (1998). Including children with autism in inclusive preschools: Strategies that work. *Young Exceptional Children, 1*(2), 19–26. Used by permission.

For a summary of research on the social reciprocity model in early intervention and step-by-step guidelines for interventions, including parent handouts in both English and Spanish, see Calhoun, Rose, and Prendergast (1991).

the child's behavior as affecting the parent, whose behavior in turn affects the behavior of the child—hence the "circle" in the program's name. Nonresponsiveness, nonvocal behavior, irritability, lack of imitation responses, and the need for special health-care routines (e.g., tube feeding, suctioning) all present special challenges to normal infant-parent interactions; behaviors associated with these problems are often viewed negatively. The program attempts to identify and increase the frequency of alternative positive behaviors that will cause parents to want to continue their interactions with their child (Calhoun & Kuczera, 1996; Calhoun, Rose, Hanft, & Sturkey, 1991; Rose & Calhoun, 1990). The center-based component of classroom instruction occurs from 9:00 A.M. to 1:00 P.M. throughout the year. The home-based/family services component entails monthly home visits; the visits include family-focused assessment and planning, demonstrations of instructional techniques, and provision of information and other support. Between regularly scheduled home visits, ongoing individualized consultation and collaboration with parents and families are available as needed.

Who Can Help?

For discussions of different team models used in early childhood programs, see Raver (1999) and Thomas, Correa, and Morsink (1995).

The success of efforts to prevent disabilities in children and to identify, assess, and intervene with children who have special needs as early as possible requires the training, experience, and cooperation of a wide range of professionals. Current best practice guidelines for early childhood services call for a transdisciplinary approach to the delivery of related services in which parents and professionals work together in assessing needs, developing the IFSP or IEP, providing services, and evaluating outcomes (DEC, 1993).

Physicians and Other Health Professionals

No other professional has as great an opportunity to prevent certain disabilities as the obstetrician. Knowing many of the conditions that predict possible disabilities, the obstetrician can examine the family history and recommend genetic counseling if there appears to be a significant risk. Because this physician sees an expectant mother several times during pregnancy, he can monitor any possible problems that arise, perform or refer her for amniocentesis if necessary, and generally ensure the kind of prenatal care that reduces the risk of problems at birth. In the delivery room, the doctor's concern for possible birth trauma can contribute to preventing problems or identifying them early.

In the same way, the pediatrician (or perhaps the family doctor) has the chance to see the infant soon after birth and then regularly during the first months of life. Because most moderate to severe disabilities and sensory impairments are recognizable at birth or soon afterward, the pediatrician's role is critical. Other conditions, such as parental neglect or abuse, may also be evident to the attentive physician. For the same reasons, nurses and nurse practitioners can be of enormous help in noting and questioning possible conditions in the home that might lead to a disability.

Later, other health professionals also contribute to identification, assessment, or treatment of specific problems that can cause disabilities. An ophthalmologist can detect early vision problems and fit a child with corrective lenses (as can an optometrist). An audiologist can assess a child's hearing and prescribe a hearing aid or other treatment if there is a loss.

Other Early Intervention Specialists

Increasingly, early intervention services are being provided to hospitalized newborns and their families. NICUs now include a variety of professionals, such as neonatologists who provide medical care for infants with special needs, nurses who provide ongoing medical assistance, social workers or psychologists who help parents and families with emotional and financial concerns, and infant education specialists who promote interaction between parents and infant (Flynn & McCollum, 1989).

A psychologist can evaluate a child's socioemotional skills and cognitive development. Psychologists often participate in a child's initial assessments and frequently administer standardized tests. Staff psychologists often participate in team planning for a child. Although school psychologists have traditionally been trained to provide standardized assessments for school-age students and consultation to classroom teachers, their participation in preschool programs for children with disabilities is likely to increase as the public schools provide more early childhood special education services (Widerstrom, Mowder, & Willis, 1989).

Because so many mild disabilities stem from social and cultural factors, a social worker can be instrumental in helping children receive much needed services. It is often the social worker who is admitted to many homes in low socioeconomic areas, which correlate with higher incidences of mild retardation and learning problems. The case worker can observe young children whose behavior suggests future problems and refer them for assessment and possible treatment. Later, the social worker may help explain, monitor, or evaluate the progress of a home-based intervention.

A speech-language pathologist is an important part of almost every intervention team. Speech and language specialists usually assess every child referred for services, and they participate in the intervention plans for many children.

For children who have physical or multiple disabilities, a physical therapist is important. Physical therapy can help prevent further deterioration of muscles; it can also be applied to teaching a child gross and fine motor coordination. Likewise, an occupational therapist contributes to the intervention program for children with physical, multiple, or other severe impairments. She provides instruction in movement, self-help skills, and the use of adaptive equipment.

Early Childhood Educators

Teachers and other staff in regular preschools and day care centers may be the first to identify certain delays in development or problems such as mild sensory impairments, socioemotional problems, learning difficulties, or language problems. Prompt referral for special education services can often get children with mild disabilities the help they need before they fall significantly behind their peers. As more children with disabilities are integrated into regular preschools, the role of general education teachers and paraprofessionals in these settings has become even more critical. Regular preschool and kindergarten teachers also play important roles in supporting a child's transition into a mainstream setting.

The Division for Early Childhood recommends specific training and certification requirements for early childhood special educators (DEC, 1993).

The actual delivery of services, whether in a home or center program, is most often the province of the special teacher, regardless of what title that person has. The special teacher must be the most knowledgeable about a child's instructional goals and objectives, the specific strategies and activities that will accomplish them, and the child's day-to-day progress. He must be well trained in observing, analyzing, selecting, and sequencing learning tasks so that the child overcomes delays rather than falls further behind. He must be imaginative and willing to try new things but patient enough to give a program a chance once it has begun. The teacher must be able not only to find what motivates and reinforces a child but also to relate to all of the other individuals involved in the child's program. In a home-based program, the home teacher or visitor must be able to train parents to take primary responsibility for teaching their child. In center-based programs, a large share of the center's parent-training efforts may fall to the special teacher.

Families: Most Important of All

Of all the people needed to make early intervention work, parents and families are the most important. Given enough information and support, parents can help prevent many risks and causes of disabilities—before pregnancy, before birth, and certainly before a child has gone months or years without help. Given the chance, parents can take an active role in determining their children's educational needs and goals. And given some guidance, training, and support, many parents can teach their children at home and even at school.

It is no wonder, then, that all successful intervention programs for young children with disabilities take great care to involve parents (Harris & Handleman, 1994; Raver, 1999). Parents in early intervention programs frequently assume roles as members of

Of all the people needed to make early intervention effective, parents are the most important.

advisory councils for the programs, consumers who inform others, staff members, primary teachers, recruiters, curriculum developers, counselors, assessment personnel, evaluators, and record keepers.

Parents are the most frequent and constant observers of their children's behavior. They usually know better than anyone else what their children need, and they can help educators set realistic goals. They can report on events in the home that outsiders might never see—for instance, how a child responds to other family members. They can monitor and report on their children's progress at home, beyond the more controlled environment of the center or preschool. In short, they can contribute to their children's programs at every stage—assessment, planning, classroom activities, and evaluation. Many parents even work in classrooms as teachers, teacher aides, volunteers, or other staff members.

Most early intervention programs focus on the home as the best and most natural learning environment and on the parent as the best and most natural teacher for the child. Even center-based programs rely heavily on parents as teachers who carry the center program into the home. But in our efforts to involve parents, we should heed this warning:

> Early childhood professionals, in their zeal to attain those all-important early developmental gains, should not push parents to the point of burn-out. Early childhood professionals will pass the child on to new programs; their task will be finished when the child reaches school age. But the family will only be beginning a lifetime of responsibility. For early childhood programs, a task equally as important as the achievement of developmental gains is the preparation of families for the long haul. Families must learn to pace themselves, to relax and take time to meet everyone's needs. They must learn that the responsibility of meeting an exceptional child's needs is not a 100-yard dash to be completed in one intensive burst of effort. It is more like a marathon, where slow and steady pacing wins the race. (Weyhing, 1983)

Finally, as Hutinger, Marshall, and McCarten (1983) remind us, we must not forget that early childhood is supposed to be a fun, happy time for children and for the adults who are fortunate enough to work with them.

> We as professionals who work with young handicapped children sometimes are so serious about the magnitude of our mission that any element of fun, humor or pleasure is absent in our work with both children and their families.
>
> Part of our mission as professionals in the field of early childhood special education is to possess an art of enjoyment ourselves and to help instill it in the young children and families with whom we work.
>
> Early childhood comes but once in a lifetime. . . . Let's make it count!

Use the self-tests at http://www.prenhall.com/heward to assess your knowledge of the content of Chapter 5.

Summary

The Importance of Early Intervention

- Research has documented that early intervention can provide both intermediate and long-term benefits for young children with disabilities and those at risk for developmental delay. Benefits of early intervention include
  - Gains in physical development, cognitive development, language and speech development, social competence, and self-help skills
  - Prevention of secondary disabilities
  - Reduction of family stress
  - Reduced need for special education services or placement during the school year
  - Savings to society of the costs of additional educational and social services that would be needed later without early intervention
  - Reduced likelihood of social dependence in adulthood
- The effectiveness of early intervention is increased when it begins early in life, is intensive, and lasts for a long time.

IDEA and Early Childhood Special Education

- IDEA requires states to provide special education services (via IEPs) to all preschool children with disabilities, ages 3 through 5.

- States may also use IDEA funds to serve infants and toddlers (via IFSPs) from birth to age 3 who are experiencing developmental delays or are at risk for acquiring a disability.

Screening, Identification, and Assessment

- Four major types of assessment purposes/tools are used in early childhood special education:
  - Screening involves quick, easy-to-administer tests to identify children who may have a disability and who should receive further testing.
  - Diagnosis requires in-depth, comprehensive assessment of all major areas of development to determine a child's eligibility for early intervention or special education services.
  - Program planning uses curriculum-based, criterion-referenced assessments to determine a child's current skill level, identify IFSP/IEP objectives, and plan intervention activities.
  - Evaluation uses curriculum-based, criterion-referenced measures to determine progress on IFSP/IEP objectives and evaluate a program's effects.
- Many early intervention programs are moving away from assessments based entirely on developmental milestones and are incorporating curriculum-based assessment, in which each item relates directly to a skill included in the program's curriculum. This provides a direct link among testing, teaching, and program evaluation.

Curriculum Goals in Early Childhood Special Education

- Early intervention and education programs for children with special needs should be designed and evaluated according to these outcomes or goals:
  - Support families in achieving their own goals
  - Promote child engagement, independence, and mastery
  - Promote development in all important domains
  - Build and support social competence
  - Facilitate the generalized use of skills
  - Prepare for and assist children with normalized life experiences in their families, schools, and their communities
  - Help children and their families make smooth transitions
  - Prevent or minimize the development of future problems or disabilities
- Developmentally appropriate practices provide a foundation or context within which to provide early intervention for children with special needs, but by themselves the guidelines are inadequate to ensure the individualized intervention such children need.
- IEP/IFSP objectives for infants and young children can be evaluated according to their functionality, generality, instructional context, measurability, and relation between short- and long-range goals.

Intervention Strategies in Early Childhood Special Education

- Promoting language development (helping children learn to talk) is a primary curriculum goal for preschoolers with disabilities. The incidental-teaching model and the mand-model procedure are two methods for encouraging and developing language use throughout the school day.
- Many young children with special needs require instruction to develop social competence.

Service Delivery Alternatives for Early Intervention

- In home-based programs, a child's parents act as the primary teachers, with regular training and guidance from a teacher or specially trained paraprofessional who visits the home.
- In center-based programs, a child comes to the center for direct instruction, although the parents are usually involved. Center programs allow a team of specialists to work with the child and enable the child to meet and interact with other children.
- Many programs offer the advantages of both models by combining home visits with center-based programming.

Who Can Help?

- A wide range of professionals should be involved in a team that works with young children with disabilities, including obstetricians, pediatricians, nurses, psychologists, social workers, and teachers.
- Parents are the most important people in an early intervention program. They can act as advocates, participate in educational planning, observe their children's behavior, help set realistic goals, work in the classroom, and teach their children at home.

For More Information

Journals

- *Day Care and Early Education.* Published bimonthly by Behavioral Publications, 72 Fifth Avenue, New York, NY 10016. Directed at day-care personnel; focuses on innovative ideas for educating preschool children.
- *Infants and Young Children.* Published quarterly by Aspen Publishers, 7201 McKinney Circle, Frederick, MD 21701.
- *Journal of Early Intervention.* Published by the Division for Early Childhood, Council for Exceptional Children (see "Organizations").

- *Topics in Early Childhood Special Education.* Published quarterly by PRO-ED, 5341 Industrial Oaks Boulevard, Austin, TX 78735.
- *Young Children.* Published bimonthly by the National Association for the Education of Young Children (see "Organizations"). Spotlights current projects, theory, and research in early childhood education as well as practical teaching ideas.

Books

- Allen, K. E., & Schwartz, I. S. (1996). *The exceptional child: Inclusion in early childhood education*. Albany, NY: Delmar.
- Bailey, D. B., & Wolery, M. (1992). *Teaching infants and preschoolers with disabilities* (2nd ed.). Upper Saddle River, NJ: Merrill/Prentice Hall.
- Bricker, D. (1998). *An activity-based approach to early intervention*. Baltimore: Brookes.
- Cook, R. E., Tessier, A., & Klein, M. D. (1992). *Adapting early childhood curricula for children with special needs* (3rd ed.). Upper Saddle River, NJ: Merrill/Prentice Hall.
- Guralnick, M. J. (1997). *The effectiveness of early intervention*. Baltimore: Brookes.
- Harris, S. L., & Handleman, J. S. (Eds.). (1994). *Preschool programs for children with autism.* Austin, TX: PRO-ED.
- Johnson, L. J., Gallagher, R. J., LaMontagne, M. J., Jordan, J. B., Gallagher, J. J., Hutinger, P. L., & Karnes, M. B. (Eds.). (1994). *Meeting early intervention challenges: Issues from birth to three.* Reston, VA: Council for Exceptional Children.
- Johnson, L. J., LaMontagne, M. J., Elgas, P. M., & Bauer, A. M. (1998). *Early childhood education: Blending theory, blending practice*. Baltimore: Brookes.
- McLean, M. E., Bailey, D. B., & Wolery, M. (1996). *Assessing infants and preschoolers with special needs* (2nd ed.). Upper Saddle River, NJ: Merrill/Prentice Hall.
- Meisels, S. J., & Shonkoff, J. P. (1990). *Handbook of early childhood intervention.* New York: Cambridge University Press.
- Noonan, M. J., & McCormick, L. (1993). *Early intervention in natural environments.* Pacific Grove, CA: Brooks/Cole.
- Odom, S. L., McConnell, S. R., & McEvoy, M. A. (Eds.). (1992). *Social competence of young children with disabilities: Nature, development, and intervention.* Baltimore: Brookes.
- Odom, S. L., & McLean, M. E. (1996). *Early intervention/Early childhood special education: Recommended practices*. Austin, TX: PRO-ED.
- Raver, S. A. (1999). *Intervention strategies for infants and toddlers with special needs: A team approach* (2nd ed.). Upper Saddle River, NJ: Merrill/Prentice Hall.
- Rosenkoetter, S. E., Hains, A. H., & Fowler, S. (1994). *Bridging early services for children with special needs and their families.* Baltimore: Brookes.
- Umansky, W., & Hooper, S. R. (1998). *Young children with special needs* (3rd ed.). Upper Saddle River, NJ: Merrill/Prentice Hall.
- Wolery, M., & Wilbers, J. S. (Eds.). (1994). *Including young children with special needs in early childhood programs.* Washington, DC: National Association for the Education of Young Children.
- Zirpoli, T. J. (1995). *Understanding and affecting the behavior of young children.* Upper Saddle River, NJ: Merrill/Prentice Hall.

Organizations

- *Early Childhood Research Institute on Inclusion (ECRII),* website: http://www.inform.umd.edu/educ/.www/depts/ecrii. A five-year, federally funded project conducted by researchers at five universities to study the inclusion of preschool children with disabilities. Numerous resources and research reports are available.
- *Division for Early Childhood (DEC),* Council for Exceptional Children, 1920 Association Drive, Reston, VA 22091.
- *National Association for the Education of Young Children (NAEYC)*, 1509 16th Street, NW, Washington, DC 20036; e-mail: naeyc@naeyc.org; website: http://www.naeyc.org.
- *National Center for Clinical Infant Programs (NCCIP),* 2000 14th Street North, Suite 380, Arlington, VA 22201-2500; (703) 528-4300.
- *National Early Childhood Technical Assistance System (NEC-TAS),* Suite 500, NCBC Plaza, Chapel Hill, NC 27514; (919) 962-2001.
- *National Head Start Resource Access Program Administration for Children, Youth, and Families, Office of Human Development Services,* P.O. Box 1182, Washington, DC 20013.

Websites

- *Toys and Play for Children,* http://www.lekotek.org.
- *ERIC Research Digest: Developmentally Appropriate Practice: What Does Research Tell Us,* http://www.ed.gov/databases/ERIC_Digests/index/.
- *How Can Families Choose Early Childhood Programs That Encourage Family Involvement?* http://www.ed.gov/offices/OERI/ECI/digests/98may.html.

Chapter 6

Mental Retardation

Focus Questions

- What is most important in determining a person's level of adaptive functioning: intellectual capability or a supportive environment?
- What should a curriculum for students with mental retardation emphasize?
- What are the characteristics of effective instruction?
- Is inclusion a good thing for every student with mental retardation?
- How can environmental supports, the principle of normalization, and self-determination interact to influence successful functioning in the community?

During the past 25 years, we have witnessed significant improvements in the education and treatment of children and adults with mental retardation. After more than a century of almost complete exclusion and segregation from everyday society, people with mental retardation are beginning to experience some of the benefits and responsibilities of participation in the mainstream.

Most people have some notion of what mental retardation is and what people with mental retardation must be like. Unfortunately, although there is considerable and growing public awareness of mental retardation, much of that awareness still consists of misconceptions, oversimplifications, and fear. For example, undergraduate special education majors gathered and recorded these statements by people outside the university, who were making everyday references to mental retardation:

> After telling a fellow waitress about her career plans to teach children labeled as having mental retardation, . . . her co-worker's response was, "Why would you want to teach children who cannot learn?" . . .
>
> A hair dresser burned herself on a hot curling iron. "I must be retarded," she remarked. "I always burn myself on this thing." . . .
>
> Two co-workers discussed the location of a bar in another part of the city. . . . The listener . . . had some idea of where the bar was located. He asked a question to confirm his idea, "Is it across the street from the funny farm?" The co-worker confirmed that the bar was, in fact, across from the "funny farm," a residential facility for persons with mental retardation. . . .
>
> She expressed many things to me as I explained special education including being scared of those people. . . . She told me over and over how she felt sorry for them. (Danforth & Navarro, 1998, pp. 36–40)

Orr and associates (1997) provide an annotated bibliography of books about people with mental retardation and developmental disabilities for children pre-K through grade 8.

Defining Mental Retardation

Go to the companion website at http://www.prenhall.com/heward and select Chapter 6 to review the chapter objectives.

Some children and adults are so clearly deficient in academic, social, and self-care skills that it is obvious to anyone who interacts with them that they require special services and educational programming. For these individuals, how mental retardation is defined is not much of an issue; they experience pervasive and substantial deficits in all or most areas of development and functioning. But this group forms only a small portion of the total population of persons with mental retardation. The largest segment consists of school-age children with mild retardation. Thus, how mental retardation is defined determines what special educational services many thousands of children are eligible (or ineligible) to receive. As MacMillan (1982) notes, disagreements among professionals over what constitutes mental retardation are "not merely academic exercises in semantics" (p. 35). A subtle difference between two definitions can determine whether the label *mental retardation* is associated with a particular child and whether or not appropriate educational supports are provided (MacMillan, Gresham, Siperstein, & Bocian, 1996).

*The term **mental retardation** is, above all, a label used to identify an observed performance deficit—failure to demonstrate age-appropriate intellectual and social behavior. Mental retardation describes performance; it is not a "thing" that a person is born with or possesses.*

First, we will look at a definition of mental retardation based primarily on the concept of the degree of measured intelligence. After discussing how intelligence is measured and how the results can be used to classify individuals with mental retardation, we will examine the most recent definition of mental retardation—one intended to change the way people think about mental retardation, moving away from deficits within the individual toward the environment and the kinds and levels of supports needed for the individual to function effectively.

AAMR's IQ-Based Definition

AAMR is an interdisciplinary organization of professionals (in education, medicine, psychology, social work, speech pathology, and so forth) as well as students, parents, and others concerned with the study, treatment, and prevention of mental retardation. Its more than 9,500 members are from 55 countries.

In 1973, the American Association on Mental Retardation (AAMR) published a definition of mental retardation that was incorporated into IDEA and continues to serve today as the basis by which most states identify children for special education services under the disability category of mental retardation. That definition, with minor rewording, was retained in the organization's 1983 manual on terminology and classification of mental retardation: "Mental retardation refers to significantly subaverage general intellectual functioning resulting in or associated with deficits in adaptive behavior and manifested during the developmental period" (Grossman, 1983, p. 11).

The definition includes three criteria: First, "significant subaverage intellectual functioning" must be demonstrated before mental retardation is diagnosed. The word *significant* in the definition refers to a score of two or more standard deviations below the mean on a standardized intelligence test. Second, an individual must be well below average in both intellectual functioning *and* adaptive behavior; that is, intellectual functioning is not intended to be the sole defining criterion. Third, the definition specifies that the deficits in intellectual functioning and adaptive behavior must occur during the developmental period to help distinguish mental retardation from other disabilities (e.g., impaired performance by an adult due to head injury).

Go to the Resource module for Chapter 6 at http://www@prenhall.com/heward. Click on Special Ed Resource Page and go to "general & disability information" to link to the AAMR homepage.

Measuring Intellectual Functioning

Intellectual functioning is most often measured by a standardized intelligence (IQ) test. An IQ test consists of a series of questions and problem-solving tasks assumed to require certain amounts of intelligence to answer or solve correctly. Although an IQ test samples only a small portion of an individual's skills and abilities, the test taker's performance on those items is used to derive a score representing her overall intelligence.

An earlier definition published by AAMR (Heber, 1961) required an IQ score of only one standard deviation below the mean for the diagnosis of mental retardation.

Normal Curve and Standard Deviation IQ scores seem to be distributed throughout the population according to a phenomenon called the **normal curve,** shown in Figure 6.1. To describe how a particular score varies from the mean, or average score, of all the scores in the norm sample, a mathematical concept called the **standard deviation** is used. By applying an algebraic formula to the scores achieved by the norm sample on a test, it can be determined what value equals one standard deviation for that test. A person's IQ test score can then be described in terms of how many standard deviations above or below the mean it is. Theoretically, each standard deviation above and below the mean score includes a fixed portion of the population. About 2.3% of the population falls two or more standard deviations below the mean, which the AAMR calls "significantly subaverage."

On the two most widely used intelligence tests, the Stanford-Binet Intelligence Scale (Thorndike, Hagen, & Sattler, 1986) and the Wechsler Intelligence Scale for Children—Revised (WISC-R) (Wechsler, 1974), the norm, or average score, is 100. One standard deviation on the Stanford-Binet is 16 points, on the WISC-R 15 points. (The difference stems from the difference in the distribution of scores obtained

A standardized test consists of the same questions and tasks always presented in a certain, specified way, with the same scoring procedures used each time the test is administered.

An IQ test has also been normed—that is, administered to a large sample of people selected at random from the population for whom the test is intended. Test scores of the people in the random sample are then used as norms, or averages of how people generally perform on the test.

Which student has mental retardation? The term *mental retardation* identifies substantial limitations in functioning: it is not something inherent within the individual.

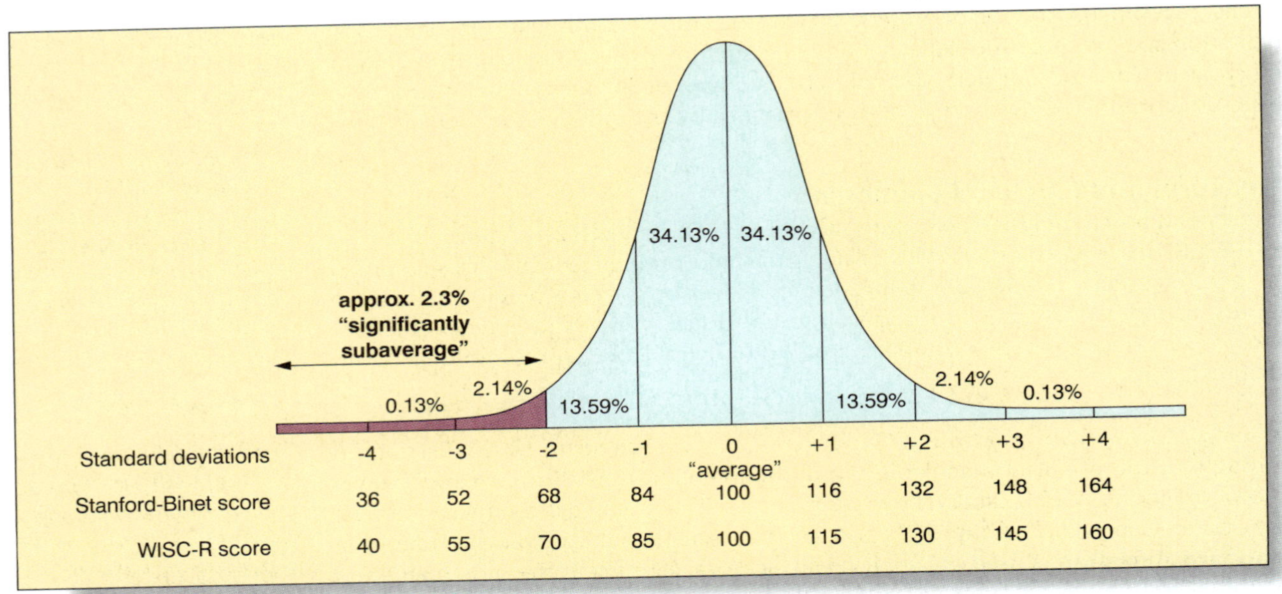

Figure 6.1 The normal curve, along which IQ scores seem to be distributed throughout the population

from the samples of children used to derive the norms for the two tests.) Thus, according to the AAMR's definition, a diagnosis of mental retardation requires an IQ score at least two standard deviations below the mean, which is approximately 70 or less on the two tests.

The AAMR manual emphasizes that the IQ cutoff score of 70 is intended only as a guideline and should not be interpreted as a hard-and-fast requirement. A higher IQ score of 75 or more may be associated with mental retardation if, according to a clinician's judgment, the child exhibits deficits in adaptive behavior thought to be caused by impaired intellectual functioning.

Support for the Shift to IQ 70 Many professionals supported the AAMR's shift to a more conservative definition of mental retardation requiring a score of at least two standard deviations (approximately 70 or less) below the mean on an IQ test. Here are some of their reasons:

1. *The mental retardation label can be stigmatizing.* Some educators believe that when a child receives the official label *mental retardation,* the damage done by the label itself outweighs any positive effects of special education and treatment that result from the label. Although recent studies have shown that children and adults continue to hold negative misconceptions about mental retardation (e.g., Antonak, Fiedler, & Mulick, 1989; Danforth & Navarro, 1998), research on whether the label itself is responsible for negative stereotyping has yielded mixed results (MacMillan, Jones, & Aloia, 1974; Rowitz, 1981).

2. *Intelligence tests can be culturally biased.* Both the Binet and Wechsler IQ tests have been heavily criticized for being culturally biased. The tests tend to favor children from the population on which they were normed—primarily white, middle-class children. Some of the questions on an IQ test may tap learning that only a middle-class child is likely to have experienced. Both tests, which are highly verbal, are especially inappropriate for children for whom English is a second language. Mercer (1973a) points out that when an IQ test is used to identify children for special class placement, many more African American, Hispanic, and poor children are identified than are white, middle-class children.

3. *IQ scores can change significantly.* Several studies have shown that IQ scores can change, particularly in the 70–85 range that formerly constituted borderline retardation (MacMillan, 1982). Hence, observers are hesitant to use the label *mental retardation* on the basis of a test score that might increase by 15–20 points after a period of intensive, systematic intervention.

4. *Intelligence testing is not an exact science.* Even though the major intelligence tests are among the most carefully developed and standardized of all psychological tests, they are still far from perfect. Among the many variables that can affect an individual's IQ score are motivation, the time and location of the test, and inconsistency or bias on the test giver's part in scoring responses that are not precisely covered by the test manual. Even the choice of which test to use can be critical. For example, Wechsler (1974) reports that the WISC-R and the revised Stanford-Binet correlate with each other at about the 0.70 level. This means that it is possible for a child's performance on one test to fall in the range defined by mental retardation but not if the other test is used.

When the upper IQ limit was reduced from 85 to 70, the largest group of children previously served, those with borderline mental retardation, were no longer identified. Although this may have appeared to be an "overnight cure" of a large portion of mental retardation, some special educators were (and remain today) concerned that many children with borderline mental retardation "reside in an educational 'DMZ,' or 'no man's land' where students are ineligible for any special educational services" (MacMillan, 1989, p. 14) because they no longer qualify for the special education they needed.

Advantages and Disadvantages of IQ Tests Clearly, intelligence tests have both advantages and disadvantages. Here are several more important considerations:

- *The concept of intelligence is a hypothetical construct.* No one has ever seen a thing called intelligence; it is not a precise entity but something we infer from observed performance. We assume it takes more intelligence to perform some tasks than it does to perform others.
- *There is nothing mysterious or all-powerful about an IQ test.* An IQ test consists of a series of questions and/or problem-solving tasks.
- *An IQ test measures only how a child performs at one point in time on the items included in one test.* We infer from that performance how a child might perform in other situations.
- *IQ tests have proven to be a good predictor of school achievement.* Because IQ tests are composed largely of verbal and academic tasks—the same things a child must master to succeed in school—they correlate highly with school achievement.
- *In the hands of a competent school psychologist, IQ tests can provide useful information.* They are particularly useful for objectively identifying an overall performance deficit.
- *Results of an IQ test should never be used as the sole basis for labeling and classifying a child.* They should not be the only criterion for making a decision on the provision or denial of special education services.
- *Results from an IQ test are generally not useful for determining educational objectives or designing instructional strategies for a student.* Results of teacher-administered, criterion-referenced assessments of a student's performance of curriculum-specific skills are generally more useful for planning what

A possible negative outcome of being labeled as mentally retarded is that peers may be more likely to avoid or ridicule the child. To find out what two young researchers did to improve children's attitudes about people with mental retardation, read A. Turnbull and Bronicki (1986) and K. Turnbull and Bronicki (1989).

Traditional methods of standardized assessment do not allow the examiner to give prompts or cues or to interact in any way that might "teach" the child how to respond correctly during the test itself. Some psychologists and educators believe that such strict testing methods do not reveal the child's true learning potential. They recommend an alternative approach to assessment called dynamic assessment *in which the examiner uses various forms of guided learning activities to determine the child's potential for change. To learn more about dynamic assessment, see Jitendra and Kameenui (1993).*

MacMillan and colleagues provide some thoughtful discussions on the plight of borderline students with subaverage general intelligence as a result of current identification and classification practices by public schools (MacMillan, Gresham, Siperstein, & Bocian, 1996; MacMillan, Gresham, Bocian, & Lambros, 1998; MacMillan, Siperstein, & Gresham, 1996).

to teach. Results of direct and frequent measurement of a student's performance during instruction provide needed information for evaluating and modifying teaching practices. In their analysis of intelligence testing in general, and use of the WISC-R in particular, Macmann and Barnett (1992) conclude:

> It is difficult to imagine a plausible set of circumstances in which inferences about a student's intellectual processing (based on the analysis of WISC-R scores) could markedly improve the quality of instruction that may be afforded through sound instructional principles and the alteration of methods and materials based on careful monitoring of intervention outcomes. (p. 156)

A criterion-referenced test *for basic math skills, for example, might include 10 single-digit addition problems. Rather than judging the child's ability to compute single-digit math problems by comparing his performance with other children's (as in norm-referenced testing) or inferring it from his work on other types of math problems, the child's performance on the skill in question is compared with a standard criterion. For example, if the criterion is 9 and the child gets 9 or 10 correct, instruction will not be necessary on that skill; if he gets fewer than 9 correct, a teaching program for single-digit addition problems would be implemented.*

Measuring Adaptive Behavior

To be classified as mentally retarded, an individual must exhibit clear deficits in adaptive behavior. Recognizing that some people score below 70 on an IQ test yet function well in school, home, and the community, MacMillan (1982) notes, "It would be pointless to identify and classify as mentally retarded a person who faces no unusual problems or whose needs are met without professional attention. Such people are not mentally retarded, and should not be labeled as such" (p. 42).

Adaptive behavior is "the effectiveness or degree with which the individual meets the standards of personal independence and social responsibility expected of his age and social group" (Grossman, 1983, p. 157). Measurement of adaptive behavior is important for reasons other than the diagnosis of mental retardation. The severity of maladaptive behavior exhibited by persons with mental retardation is one of the most critical factors in determining the supports they require for success in most school, work, and residential settings (Campbell, Smith, & Wool, 1982).

Adaptive Behavior Scale A frequently used instrument for assessing adaptive behavior by school-age children is the AAMR Adaptive Behavior Scale—School (ABS-S) (Lambert, Nihira, & Leland, 1993). The ABS-S consists of two parts. Part 1 contains nine domains related to independent functioning and daily living skills; Part 2 assesses the individual's level of maladaptive (inappropriate) behavior (see Figure 6.2).

The ABS-S is long: 104 items with multiple questions per item. A shorter (75-item) adaptation of the scale, called the Classroom Adaptive Behavior Checklist, has been developed by Hunsucker, Nelson, and Clark (1986). Another form, the ABS-RC, assesses adaptive behavior in residential and community settings (Nihira et al., 1993).

Vineland Social Maturity Scale The Vineland Social Maturity Scale (Doll, 1965) is another widely used method for assessing adaptive behavior. The Vineland has recently undergone substantial revision and is now available in three versions under the name Vineland Adaptive Behavior Scales (Sparrow, Balla, & Cicchetti, 1984). Two versions, the Interview Editions in Survey Form or Expanded Form, are administered by an individual, such as a teacher or a direct caregiver, who knows well the person being assessed. The Classroom Edition is designed to be completed by a teacher.

Assessment of Social Competence One of the most recent adaptive behavior assessment instruments to be developed is the Assessment of Social Competence (ASC) (Meyer, Cole, McQuarter, & Reichle, 1990). The ASC, which is intended to measure social competence at all levels of social and intellectual functioning, consists of 252 items organized within 11 social functions (e.g., initiates interactions, follows rules, indicates preferences). Each function is further broken down into eight levels, with the highest level representing performance at an adult level of mastery.

Measurement of adaptive behavior has proven difficult, in large part because of the relative nature of social adjustment and competence: what is considered appropriate in one situation or by one group may not be in or by another. Nowhere is there a list that everyone would agree describes exactly those adaptive behaviors all

Part One

I. Independent functioning
  A. Eating
  B. Toilet use
  C. Cleanliness
  D. Appearance
  E. Care of clothing
  F. Dressing and undressing
  G. Travel
  H. Other independent functioning
II. Physical development
  A. Development
  B. Motor development
III. Economic activity
  A. Money handling and budgeting
  B. Shopping skills
IV. Language development
  A. Expression
  B. Verbal comprehension
  C. Social language development
V. Numbers and time
VI. Prevocational/vocational activity
VII. Self-direction
  A. Initiative
  B. Perseverance
  C. Leisure time
VIII. Responsibility
IX. Socialization

Part Two

X. Social behavior
XI. Conformity
XII. Trustworthiness
XIII. Stereotyped and hyperactive behavior
XIV. Self-abusive behavior
XV. Social engagement
XVI. Disturbing interpersonal behavior

Figure 6.2 Domains of adaptive functioning covered by the Adaptive Behavior Scale—School (ABS-S)

Source: Reprinted from Lambert, N., Nihira, K, & Leland, H. (1993). *Adaptive Behavior Scale—School* (2nd ed.). Austin, TX: PRO-ED. Reprinted by permission.

of us should exhibit. As with IQ tests, cultural bias can be a problem in adaptive behavior scales; for instance, one item on some scales requires a child to tie a laced shoe, but some children have never had a shoe with laces. Ongoing research on the measurement of adaptive behavior may help resolve these problems.

Some professionals have argued against inclusion of adaptive behavior in the definition of mental retardation. Zigler, Balla, and Hodapp (1984) contend that mental retardation should be determined solely by a score of less than 70 on a standardized IQ test. In a rebuttal that probably reflects the position of most professionals in the field, Barnett (1986) attacks Zigler et al.'s proposal by explaining the necessity of retaining adaptive behavior in the definition of mental retardation if the concept is to remain socially valid.

Despite the fact that most professionals view adaptive behavior as an important component of mental retardation, a child's IQ score remains the primary variable in identifying her as mentally retarded (Beirne-Smith, Ittenbach, & Patton, 1998). A survey of state departments of education found that although assessment of adaptive behavior is mentioned in the procedures used by 44 states to identify children with mental retardation, 36 of those states used no specific criteria or cutoff scores (Frankenberger & Fronzaglio, 1991). By contrast, only one state allows a child to be identified with mental retardation without falling under a specific cutoff score on an IQ test.

Classifying Mental Retardation Based on Intellectual Ability

Many systems have been proposed for classifying mental retardation by type or degree of severity. Some systems classify mental retardation according to **etiology** (cause) or clinical type (e.g., Down syndrome). Although these classification systems are useful to physicians, they have limited utility for educators. For example, two children might be classified as having Down syndrome, but one child functions with little assistance in a regular second-grade classroom while the other is unable to perform the most basic self-help tasks.

An examination of the guidelines issued by state departments of education found that only 56% of states used the term mental retardation; *the remaining states classified students with terms such as* developmental disabilities, developmental handicaps, *or* mental disabilities *(Utley, Lowitzer, & Baumeister, 1987).*

Mental retardation has traditionally been classified by the degree or level of intellectual impairment, as measured by an IQ test. The most widely used classification method cited in the professional literature consists of four levels of mental retardation according to the range of IQ scores shown in Table 6.1. The range of scores representing the high and low ends of each level indicates an awareness of the inexactness of intelligence testing and the importance of clinical judgment in determining level of severity.

Educators use different terms for the various levels of mental retardation. For many years, students with mental retardation were classified as either *educable mentally retarded* (EMR) or *trainable mentally retarded* (TMR), which refer to mild and moderate levels of retardation, respectively. (Because children with severe and profound mental retardation were often denied a public education, they were not considered in this two-level classification system.) Although one may still encounter the terms *EMR* or *TMR* today, most educators consider their use inappropriate because of the connotations of predetermined achievement limits.

Mild Mental Retardation Children with mild retardation have traditionally been educated in self-contained classrooms in the public schools. Today many children with mild mental retardation are being educated in regular classrooms, with a special educator helping the classroom teacher with individualized instruction for the child and providing extra tutoring in a resource room as needed. Many children with mild retardation are not identified until they enter school and sometimes not until the second or third grade, when more difficult academic work is required.

For a review of research on teaching reading to students with mental retardation, see Conners (1992).

Career education is discussed in Chapter 15.

Carroll, Burnworth, Chambers, Cousino, Mahaney, and Trent (1991) describe how students with disabilities can learn needed functional academic and vocational skills by operating a "classroom company."

Traditionally, school programs for students with mild mental retardation stressed the basic academic subjects—reading, writing, and arithmetic—during the elementary years, with a shift in emphasis to vocational training and work-study programs in junior high and high school. Today, the important outcomes of special education for students with mild mental retardation focus on successful employment, development of independence and life skills, and involvement in the community (Patton et al., 1996). As a result, schools have begun to provide career education (Brolin, 1995) and instruction on community living skills (Dever, 1989) in the elementary grades. Most students with mild mental retardation master academic skills up to about the

Table 6.1 Classification of mental retardation by measured IQ score

Level	Intelligence Test Score
Mild retardation	50–55 to approximately 70
Moderate retardation	35–40 to 50–55
Severe retardation	20–25 to 35–40
Profound retardation	Below 20–25

Source: Based on the AAMR's *Classification of Mental Retardation* (Grossman, 1983) and the *Diagnostic and Statistical Manual of Mental Disorders (DSM-IV)* (American Psychiatric Association, 1994).

sixth-grade level and are able to learn job skills well enough to support themselves independently or semi-independently. Some adults who have been identified with mild mental retardation develop excellent social and communication skills and once they leave school are no longer recognized as having a disability.

Moderate Mental Retardation Children with moderate retardation show significant delays in development during their preschool years. As they grow older, discrepancies in overall intellectual development and adaptive functioning generally grow wider between these children and age mates without disabilities. Approximately 30% of individuals with moderate mental retardation have Down syndrome, and about 50% have some form of brain damage (Neisworth & Smith, 1978). People with moderate mental retardation are more likely to have physical disabilities and behavior problems than are individuals with mild retardation.

For information on the prevalence, evaluation, and treatment of individuals with a dual diagnosis of mental retardation and mental illness, see the Journal of Consulting and Clinical Psychology, 62*(1) (1994).*

Instruction for children with moderate mental retardation typically focuses on daily living skills, social skills, and academics such as development of a basic sight-word vocabulary (e.g., survival words such as "exit," "don't walk," "stop"), some functional reading skills (e.g., simple recipes), and basic number concepts. In the past, most persons with moderate mental retardation were removed from society and placed in large institutions, where they had little opportunity to develop and learn how to get along in the world. Today most people with moderate retardation are receiving the individualized levels of support and supervision they require to live and work in the community.

Mental retardation is seldom a time-limited condition. Although many individuals with mental retardation make tremendous advancements in adaptive skills (some to the point of functioning independently and no longer being considered under any disability category), most are affected throughout their life span (Mulick & Antonak, 1994). In Chapter 15, we examine in detail the transition to adult life by individuals with disabilities.

Severe and Profound Retardation Individuals with severe and profound mental retardation are almost always identified at birth or shortly afterward. Most of these infants have significant central nervous system damage, and many have additional disabilities and/or health conditions. Although IQ scores can serve as the basis for differentiating severe and profound retardation from one another, the difference is primarily one of functional impairment. Until recently, education for individuals with severe retardation focused entirely on self-care skills—toileting, dressing, eating, and drinking—and communication development. Recent developments in instructional technology and the creation of environmental support systems, however, are enabling many persons with severe mental retardation to learn skills previously thought to be beyond their capability—even to the point of becoming semi-independent adults able to live and work in the community. A person with profound mental retardation may not be able to care for personal needs, have limited or no independent mobility, and require 24-hour nursing care.

Students with severe disabilities are the focus of Chapter 13.

Until recently, children with severe and profound mental retardation were virtually shut out by the U.S. educational system. Fortunately, this situation is changing. Litigation and legislation ensuring the rights of individuals with disabilities, regardless of type or degree, and advances in educational methods (Cipani & Spooner, 1994; Snell & Brown, in press) have contributed to this change. The outlook for these children is improving. An effective advocacy group of researchers, teachers, parents, and other interested individuals—The Association for Persons with Severe Handicaps (TASH)—is working to help that future.

Alternative Definitions That Emphasize Individualized Need for Supports

Numerous alternative definitions of mental retardation have been proposed, spurred in part by questions about the nature and meaning of what is measured by intelligence tests and the steady gains in adaptive functioning by individuals with

Children with mild or moderate mental retardation are now often placed in inclusive classrooms where teachers can support their learning of academic skills in elementary years.

mental retardation as a result of new understandings about how to design and provide effective instruction and increased opportunities to participate in inclusive schools and community settings (Hilton & Ringlaben, 1998). Four prominent alternative definitions conceptualize mental retardation from behavioral, sociological, or instructional perspectives.

Bijou's Behavioral Definition Sidney Bijou (1966) proposed a strictly behavioral definition: "A retarded individual is one who has a limited repertoire of behavior shaped by events that constitute his history" (p. 2). Bijou's view of mental retardation attributes a limited (retarded) behavioral repertoire to the hampering effects of biomedical impairment, handicapping sociocultural conditions, or both. This perspective maintains that if the person's environment provides the proper supports, the deficits in functioning associated with mental retardation can be replaced with more adaptive, age-appropriate behavior.

Mercer's Sociological Definition Jane Mercer, a sociologist, believes that the concept of mental retardation is a sociological phenomenon and that the label *mental retardation* is "an achieved social status in a social system" (Mercer, 1973a, p. 3). Mercer's research (1973a, 1973b) shows that many children identified as mildly retarded by the school system, especially children from cultural minorities, are labeled because their behavior does not meet the norms of the white, middle-class social system.

Discussions and case-study examples of mental retardation as a socially constructed concept can be found in Bogdan and Taylor (1994) and Trent (1995).

Mercer has developed a system for diagnosing mental retardation in children from minority groups. Called the System of Multicultural Pluralistic Assessment (SOMPA), it is designed to eliminate cultural bias in intelligence testing. Using SOMPA, the examiner converts the child's WISC-R IQ score into what is called an *estimated learning potential* (ELP) score. The ELP score is affected by variables such as ethnic group membership and family size and structure. Although some school districts use SOMPA, research has not determined how valid and ultimately useful it may be.

Gold's Social Responsibility Definition Marc Gold (1980) proposed a definition of mental retardation encompassing both a behavioral and a sociological perspective. According to Gold, mental retardation should be viewed as society's failure to provide sufficient training and education rather than a deficit within the individual.

> Mental retardation refers to a level of functioning which requires from society significantly above average training procedures and superior assets in adaptive behavior, manifested throughout life. The mentally retarded person is characterized by the level of power needed in the training process for [the person] to learn, and not by limitations on what [the person] can learn. The height of a retarded person's level of functioning is determined by the availability of training technology and the amount of resources society is willing to allocate and not by significant limitations in biological potential. (Gold, 1980, p. 148)

Gold's "social responsibility" perspective is a highly optimistic one in its claim that the ultimate level of functioning of a person with mental retardation is determined by the technology available for training and the amount of resources devoted to the task.

Dever's Instructional Definition Recognizing that definitions both reflect the perceptions of their developers and help shape the perceptions of people entering the field, Dever (1990) believes that mental retardation should be conceptualized from an instructional perspective. He offers the following definition to guide the efforts of personnel who work directly with individuals with mental retardation after they have been identified according to an "administrative" definition such as the AAMR's: "Mental retardation refers to the need for specific training of skills that most people acquire incidentally and that enable individuals to live in the community without supervision" (p. 149).

The alternative definitions of mental retardation proposed by Bijou, Mercer, Gold, and Dever are important ones. Each defines mental retardation as a relative phenomenon that should not be viewed as a permanent condition. Each emphasizes the fundamental notion that mental retardation represents a current level of performance; it is not something a person has in the same way one has measles or red hair. Furthermore, performance can often be altered significantly by manipulating certain aspects of the environment (teaching adaptive, age-appropriate behavior or, in Mercer's view, altering one's own culturally biased perspective of what constitutes adaptive behavior).

The story of Daniel, an 11-year-old with Down syndrome, offers powerful support of Bijou's and Gold's belief in the potential of systematic, intensive teaching. See "Positive Expectations and 10,000 Hours," which follows.

AAMR's Definition Based on Needed Supports: The 1992 System

Although none of the alternative definitions was widely adopted, each of the perspectives they represented helped lay the foundation for the AAMR's newest definition of mental retardation. Called the "1992 System" by its developers, the new definition represents a shift away from conceptualizations of mental retardation as an inherent trait or permanent state of being to a description of the individual's present functioning and the environmental supports needed to improve it.

> *Mental retardation* refers to substantial limitations in present functioning. It is characterized by significantly subaverage intellectual functioning, existing concurrently with related limitations in two or more of the following applicable adaptive skill areas: communication, self-care, home living, social skills, community use, self-direction, health and safety, functional academics, leisure, and work. Mental retardation manifests before age 18.
>
> The following four assumptions are essential to the application of the definition:
>
> 1. Valid assessment considers cultural and linguistic diversity as well as differences in communication and behavioral factors;

PROFILES AND PERSPECTIVES

Positive Expectations and 10,000 Hours

"Hey, hey, hey, Fact Track!" The 11-year-old chose one of his favorite programs from the table next to the computer in his parents' dining room. He inserted the floppy disk, booted the system, and waited for the program to load.

"What is your name?" appeared on the monitor.

"Daniel Skandera," he typed. A menu scrolled up, listing the program's possibilities. Daniel chose multiplication facts, level 1.

"How many problems do you want to do?" the computer asked.

"20."

"Do you want to set a goal for yourself, Daniel?"

"Yes, 80 sec."

"Get ready!"

Daniel Skandera, Jr., was born with Down syndrome, a chromosomal abnormality that usually results in moderate to severe mental retardation. Daniel's father explained, "A psychologist tested Daniel at 12 months and told us he was three standard deviations below normal. That assessment was the basis for Daniel's being denied enrollment in an infant stimulation program. We accepted the challenge of teaching Daniel ourselves. Between Marie [Daniel's mother] and me, we had spent about 10,000 hours working with Daniel by the time he was 5. It's paid off a million times over. He's an inspiration and a joy."

"We believed that we had learned enough about how Daniel learns to work with him confidently," said Marie. "If something doesn't work, if he becomes frustrated, we are challenged to try another approach. Daniel is an only child, and we were older when he was born. When we're gone, we want him to be able to take care of himself, to be a taxpayer instead of a tax burden."

Randomly generated multiplication facts flashed on the screen: "4 × 6," "2 × 9," "3 × 3," "7 × 6." Daniel responded, deftly punching in his answers on the computer's numeric keypad. Twice he recognized errors and corrected them before inputting his answers.

Daniel attends a regular fourth-grade classroom. Academically, he performs at grade level except for two subjects. For math and spelling, his best subjects ("Hooray, I love spellin'!"), he leaves the fourth-grade classroom each day and moves to the fifth grade. Daniel is not a special education student; he has no IEP. His extracurricular activities are those of his classmates and neighborhood friends: riding his bicycle, working out on his regulation-size trampoline, playing along with tape-recorded rock and roll on his six-piece drum set, rough-housing, spending the night at a buddy's.

"Positive expectations are the key words," agreed Daniel's parents. "With Daniel, it might take a little longer, but we get there."

The computer tallied the results. "You completed 20 problems in 66 seconds. You beat your goal. Problems correct = 20. Congratulations, Daniel!" And with that the 11-year-old retreated hastily to the TV room. It was almost tipoff time for an NBA championship game, and Daniel wanted to see the first half before bedtime.

2. The existence of limitations in adaptive skills occurs within the context of community environments typical of the individual's age peers and is indexed to the person's individualized needs for supports;
3. Specific adaptive limitations often coexist with strengths in other adaptive skills or other personal capabilities; and
4. With appropriate supports over a sustained period, the life functioning of the person with mental retardation will generally improve. (Luckasson, Coulter, Polloway, Reiss, Schalock, Snell, Spitalnick, & Stark, 1992, p. 1)

Figure 6.3 shows how the three key elements of the new definition are interrelated. *Capabilities,* on the left side of the triangle, show that functioning is related specifically to limitations in intelligence and adaptive skills. The right side of the triangle represents the *environments* in which limited functioning is meaningful. The bottom of the triangle shows that the presence and absence of supports influence *functioning.* The equilateral triangle emphasizes that all three aspects are necessary

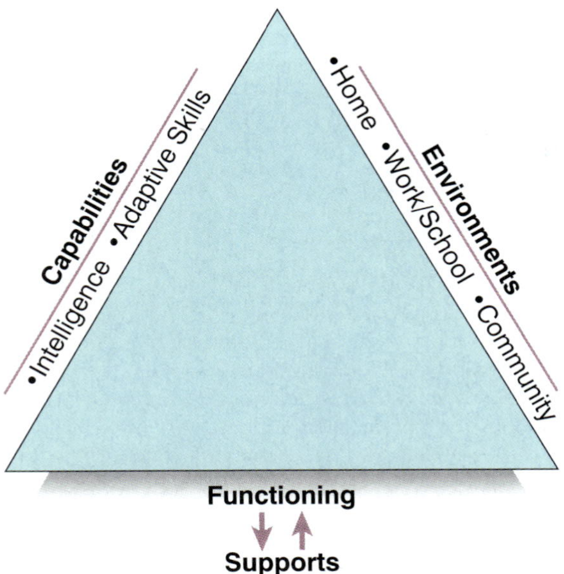

Figure 6.3 General structure of the 1992 AAMR definition of mental retardation

Source: Reprinted from the American Association on Mental Retardation (AAMR). (1992). *Mental retardation: Definition, classification, and systems of supports* (9th ed., p. 10). Washington, DC: Author. Used by permission.

for a full understanding of mental retardation. Mental retardation is defined within the context of the environments in which the individual lives; it exists as a disability (limitations in functioning) as a result of the interaction between limitations in capabilities and demands of the environment.

Classification Based on Intensity of Needed Supports

The AAMR's 1992 system is more than a definition of mental retardation. It also provides conceptual and procedural recommendations for functionally classifying mental retardation according to a profile of needed supports. This approach represents a change from classifying mental retardation on the basis of estimates of an individual's deficiencies to estimating the intensities of supports needed to improve functioning in the environments in which the individual lives, goes to school or works, and plays. Needed supports are identified and classified by an interdisciplinary team according to the four levels of intensities shown in Table 6.2.

Although Kelly needs extensive supports in some areas of life functioning, only limited supports are needed in communication and social skills.

Table 6.2 Definitions of intensities of supports for individuals with mental retardation

Intermittent	Supports on an "as needed basis." Characterized by episodic nature, person not always needing the support(s), or short-term supports needed during life-span transitions (e.g., job loss or an acute medical crisis). Intermittent supports may be high or low intensity when provided.
Limited	An intensity of supports characterized by consistency over time, time-limited but not of an intermittent nature, may require fewer staff members and less cost than more intense levels of support (e.g., time-limited employment training or transitional supports provided during the school to adult period).
Extensive	Supports characterized by regular involvement (e.g., daily) in at least some environments (such as work or home) and not time-limited (e.g., long-term support and long-term home living support).
Pervasive	Supports characterized by their constancy and high intensity; provided across environments; potential life-sustaining nature. Pervasive supports typically involve more staff members and intrusiveness than do extensive or time-limited supports.

Source: Reprinted from the American Association on Mental Retardation (AAMR). (1992). *Mental retardation: Definition, classification, and systems of supports* (9th ed., p. 26). Washington, DC: Author. Used by permission.

An interdisciplinary team develops a profile of the types and intensity of needed supports within each of four dimensions: intellectual functioning and adaptive skills, psychological/emotional considerations (e.g., behavioral problems), physical/health/etiology considerations, and environmental considerations (e.g., mobility/access). Figure 6.4 is an example of what the profile and intensities of needed supports might look like for Jared, an upper-elementary student who has intellectual limitations and behavioral problems. In developing this profile, the interdisciplinary team incorporated the results of various assessments of Jared's current functioning and knowledge of his experiences and his parents' desires for placement, including the following:

- He frequently displays stereotypic movements of the hands and body.
- He seldom smiles, laughs, or shows affection toward others.
- He has a congenital heart problem.
- He does not initiate routine self-care tasks without prompting and reminding.
- He has been attending a self-contained classroom in a separate school for students with mental retardation since he was 5 years old, despite the fact that he has to ride the bus for one hour each way.
- His friends are limited to his immediate family, relatives, and two neighborhood children who sometimes visit.
- His parents are eager for him to attend school with his siblings, neighbors, and peers, and they have noted favorable changes in behavior when he is with peers.
- His teachers have recently reduced his tantrum behavior by equipping him with a radio headset.
- He has acquired some practical skills when taught in community settings (e.g., crossing the street, purchasing a snack).

Name *Jared* Date *9/20/00*

List the support function, the specific activity, and the level of intensities needed in each of the areas and/or dimensions. (See Activities listed on the back of this page.)

Levels of intensity are: I–Intermittent; L–Limited; E–Extensive; P–Pervasive

Dimension I: Intellectual Functioning and Adaptive Skills

Dimension/Area	Support Function	Activity	Level of Intensity I L E P
Communication	Befriending	Establish an augmentative communication system.	E
Self-care	Health assistance	Assist in developing independent grooming and hygiene.	L
Social skills	Behavior support	Modeling and social skills programming to teach functional communication and other replacement skills, and to decrease escape behaviors.	E
Home living	Behavior support	Teach him to make bed, prepare his sack lunch.	L
Community use	Community access and use	Provide opportunities for recreation and community use activities.	L
Self-direction	Behavior support	Teach problem-solving skills and decision-making.	E
Health and safety	Health assistance	Procure on-going medical/physical exams.	I
Functional academics	Student assistance	Evaluate the efficacy of computer assisted instruction. Provide activity-based instruction in functional academics.	P
Leisure	Community access and use Befriending	Attend and participate in as many games and recreation programs as possible.	I
Work N/A			

Figure 6.4 Profiles and intensities of support for Jared, an upper-elementary student with mental retardation

Source: Reprinted from the American Association on Mental Retardation (AAMR). (1992). *Mental retardation: Definition, classification, and systems of supports* (9th ed., pp. 24–25). Washington, DC: Author. Used by permission.

(Figure 6.4 continues on p. 216.)

Dimension II: Psychological/Emotional Considerations

Dimension/Area	Support Function	Activity	Level of Intensity I L E P
	Behavioral support	Teach replacement skills matched to functional assessment. Employ non-aversive strategies.	E

Dimension III: Physical/Health Considerations

Dimension/Area	Support Function	Activity	Level of Intensity I L E P
	Health assistance	Procure annual physical. Monitor heart defect.	I

Dimension IV: Environment Considerations

Dimension/Area	Support Function	Activity	Level of Intensity I L E P
	Community access and use	Move into a regular integrated school.	E

Figure 6.4 *continued*

Criticisms of the AAMR's New Definition of Mental Retardation

The conception of mental retardation has undergone numerous changes in terminology, IQ score cutoff, and the relative role of adaptive functioning during the past four decades. In each case, those changes have reflected an ongoing attempt to better understand mental retardation in order to achieve more effective and reliable systems of identification, classification, research, and habilitation. In a paper describing the implications of the new definition for the field of mental retardation, the members of the AAMR Ad Hoc Committee on Terminology and Classification recognize the need for and inevitability of ongoing change (Schalock, Stark, Snell, Coulter, Polloway, Luckasson, Reiss, & Spitalnick, 1994):

> The reactions to the 1992 System are not unlike the reactions to a scientific revolution discussed by Kuhn (1970), in which there are doubts or difficulties with a particular approach, conflict between the "old" and "new" approaches, and the eventual acceptance of a new paradigm whose major characteristics include attracting converts, being sufficiently open-ended so that it is testable, and being attractive and hopeful. . . . the field of mental retardation is in the middle of a paradigm shift and it will continue to undergo significant future changes. . . . There is already evidence that the 1992 System is taking root. . . . Change never comes easy. However, the challenges and opportunities provided by the changing conception of mental retardation and the 1992 System set an important agenda for the next decade. (pp. 189–190)

Not all professionals in the field of mental retardation share the same level of enthusiasm and optimism for the new definition (e.g., Borthwick-Duffy, 1994; Greenspan, 1994; Jacobsen & Mulick, 1992, in press; MacMillan, Gresham, & Siperstein, 1993; Vig & Jedrysek, 1996). Some of the concerns are as follows:

- IQ testing will remain a primary (and in practice perhaps the only) means of diagnosis.
- The new definition may fail to differentiate subgroups of mental retardation, particularly whether the condition is caused by organic impairment or environmental influence.
- The 10 adaptive skill areas do not consider developmental factors and cannot be reliably measured with current assessment methods.
- The levels of needed supports are too subjective.
- Classification will remain essentially unchanged in practice because the four intensities of supports—intermittent, limited, extensive, and pervasive—will simply replace the four levels of retardation based on IQ scores—mild, moderate, severe, and profound.

In response to these and other criticisms of the new definition, Reiss (1994), a member of the AAMR committee that developed the new definition, writes: "There is no intent to change who is and who is not considered to have mental retardation. Instead, the intent was to change how people *think* about mental retardation: the old deficiency model is replaced with a new support model" (p. 1).

CEC's Division on Mental Retardation and Developmental Disabilities cautiously supports the AAMR 1992 definition. In an official position statement adopted by its board of directors (Smith, 1994), CEC-MRDD praises the new definition for focusing greater attention on the needs of individuals instead of on degrees of deficiency residing within the person with mental retardation and for providing the field with a positive stimulus for debate on issues critical to persons with mental retardation. The statement notes, however, that the changes required by and the implications of the new definition are so profound that they "require the most careful consideration before they are implemented in special education practices" (p. 179).

Smith (1994) concludes his presentation and discussion of CEC-MRDD's position on the new definition with this observation:

> The new definition should not be viewed as either tug-of-war or as dogma. . . . while the revised definition may be a paradigm shift it must be remembered that unlike physics, for example, where a paradigm shift from the worldview of Newton to that of Einstein does nothing to change the reality of the physical universe, a paradigm shift in the field of mental retardation may have profound implications for the education, care and treatment of perhaps millions of human beings. (p. 179)

Check your ongoing understanding of Chapter 6 concepts by using the guided review module at http://www.prenhall.com/heward.

The debate over the definition of mental retardation will surely continue. We end this discussion of definition with the words of the late Burton Blatt, one of the field's most prolific, influential, and controversial figures, who argues that when all is said and done, mental retardation is best viewed as an administrative category. In his final book, *The Conquest of Mental Retardation* (1987), Blatt writes, "Simply stated, someone is mentally retarded when he or she is 'officially' identified as such" (p. 72).

Prevalence

Changing definitions of mental retardation, the schools' reluctance to identify some children with mild mental retardation, and the changing status of schoolchildren with mild mental retardation (most are no longer counted after leaving school) contribute to the difficulty of estimating the number of people with mental retardation. Historically, the federal government estimated the prevalence at 3% of the general population, although recent analyses find little objective support for this figure. If prevalence figures are based on IQ scores alone, theoretically 2.3% of the population scores in the retarded range—two standard deviations below the mean (see Figure 6.1).

Prevalence rates vary greatly from state to state. For example, the prevalence of mental retardation as a percentage of total school enrollment ranged from a low of 0.28% (New Jersey) to a high of 2.52% (Alabama). Such large differences in prevalence are no doubt a function of the widely differing criteria for identifying students with mental retardation (Frankenberger & Fronzaglio, 1991). Prevalence figures also vary considerably among districts within a given state (McDermott, 1994).

Basing prevalence estimates on IQ scores only, however, ignores the other necessary criteria for mental retardation—deficits in adaptive functioning and the need for supports. Some professionals believe that if adaptive behavior is included with intellectual ability when estimating prevalence, the figure would drop to about 1%. In fact, a recent national study estimated the prevalence rate of mental retardation at 1.1% of the U.S. population (Fujiura & Yamaki, 1997).

The 1% estimate is consistent with data reported by the U.S. Department of Education (1998) on the number of children receiving special education. During the 1996–1997 school year, 594,025 students ages 6 through 21 received special education under the disability category of mental retardation. These students represented 11.4% of all school-age children in special education, or about 0.96% of the total school-age population.

Causes of Mental Retardation

More than 250 causes of mental retardation have been identified. Figure 6.5 lists just some of the many hundreds of disorders associated with mental retardation that are categorized by the AAMR (Luckasson et al., 1992) as **prenatal** (occurring before birth), **perinatal** (occurring during or shortly after birth), or **postnatal** causes. All of these etiologic factors associated with mental retardation can be classified as either organic (biological or medical) or environmental.

Table 6.3 lists some key historical events and their implications for the education of children with mental retardation.

Authors of a review of 13 epidemiological studies concluded that for approximately 50% of cases of mild mental retardation and 30% of cases of severe mental retardation, the cause is unknown (McLaren & Bryson, 1987). Nevertheless, knowledge of etiology is critical to efforts designed to prevent the incidence of mental retardation (Coulter, 1996) and may have implications for some educational interventions (MacMillan, Gresham, & Siperstein, 1993).

The term syndrome *refers to a number of symptoms that occur together and that provide the defining characteristics of a given disease or condition. Down syndrome and fragile-X syndrome are the two most common causes of inherited mental retardation. For a discussion of the educator's role in identification, intervention, and prevention of fragile-X syndrome, see Santos (1992).*

Organic Causes

All of the known causes of retardation are biological or medical, and these conditions are referred to as *clinical mental retardation* (brain damage). It is important to understand that none of the etiologic factors shown in Figure 6.5 *is* mental retardation. These disorders, syndromes, and conditions are commonly associated with mental retardation, but they may or may not result in the deficits of intellectual and social functioning that define mental retardation. Indeed, one or more of these etiologic factors are found in many individuals who do not experience mental retardation.

Environmental Causes

Individuals with mild mental retardation make up 80% to 85% of all persons with mental retardation. In the vast majority of those cases, etiology is unknown; that is, there is no demonstrable evidence of organic pathology—no brain damage or other

Table 6.3 A history of the education of children with mental retardation: Key events and implications

Date	Historical Event	Educational Implication
1794	Jean Marc Gaspard Itard published an account of his work with Victor, the Wild Boy of Aveyron.	Itard showed that intensive treatment could produce significant learning. Many consider Itard to be the father of special education.
1848	Edouard Seguin helped establish the Pennsylvania Training School.	This was the first educational facility for persons with mental retardation in the United States.
1850	Samuel Gridley Howe began the School for Idiotic and Feeble Minded Youth.	This was the first publicly funded residential school in the United States.
1896	The first public school class for children with mental retardation began in Providence, RI.	This began the special class movement, which grew to 1.3 million children in 1974, the year before IDEA.
1905	Alfred Binet and Theodore Simon developed a test in France to screen those students not benefiting from the regular curriculum.	The test enabled empirical identification of students with mental retardation and contributed to the growth of the special class movement.
1916	Lewis Terman of Stanford University published the Stanford-Binet Intelligence Scale in the United States.	Many schools adopted IQ testing as a means of identifying children with below-average general intelligence.
1935	Edgar Doll published the Vineland Social Maturity Scale.	It provided a standardized method for assessing a person's adaptive behavior, which later became part of the definition of mental retardation.
1950	Parents formed the National Association for Retarded Children (known today as The Arc).	The Arc remains a powerful and important advocacy organization for persons of all ages with mental retardation.
1959	AAMR published its first manual on the definition and classification of mental retardation, with diagnosis based on an IQ score of one standard deviation below the mean (approximately 85) (Heber, 1959).	Many students were identified in the borderline category of mental retardation and served in special classes for "slow learners" or EMR students.
1961	John F. Kennedy established the first President's Panel on Mental Retardation.	The panel's first report (Mayo, 1962) made recommendations that helped guide national policy with respect to mental retardation (e.g., citizenship, education, prevention).
1969	Bengt Nirje published a key paper defining normalization. Wolf Wolfensberger championed normalization in the United States.	Normalization became a leading philosophy guiding the development and delivery of educational, community, vocational, and residential services for persons with mental retardation.
1973	AAMR published a revised definition that required a score on IQ tests of two standard deviations below the mean (approximately 70 or less) and concurrent deficits in adaptive behavior.	This effectively eliminated mild mental retardation.
1992	AAMR published "System '92," a radically different definition of mental retardation based on intensities of supports.	The impact of AAMR's newest definition and classification system on special education is not yet clear.

I. PRENATAL CAUSES
   A. Chromosomal disorders (e.g., Trisomy 21 [**Down syndrome**], **fragile-X syndrome, Turner's syndrome, Klinefelter syndrome**)
   B. Syndrome disorders (e.g., **Duchenne muscular dystrophy**, **Prader-Willi syndrome**)
   C. Inborn errors of metabolism (e.g., **phenylketonuria** [PKU], **Tay-Sachs disease**)
   D. Developmental disorders of brain formation (e.g., **anencephaly**, **spina bifida, hydrocephalus**)
   E. Environmental influences (e.g., maternal malnutrition, fetal alcohol syndrome, **juvenile diabetes mellitus,** irradiation during pregnancy)
II. PERINATAL CAUSES
   A. Intrauterine disorders (e.g., maternal anemia, premature delivery, abnormal presentation, umbilical cord accidents, multiple gestation)
   B. Neonatal disorders (e.g., intracranial hemorrhage, neonatal seizures, respiratory disorders, **meningitis, encephalitis,** head trauma at birth)
III. POSTNATAL CAUSES
   A. Head injuries (e.g., cerebral concussion, contusion, or laceration)
   B. Infections (e.g., encephalitis, meningitis, malaria, measles, **rubella**)
   C. Demyelinating disorders (e.g., postinfectious disorders, postimmunization disorders)
   D. Degenerative disorders (e.g., Rett syndrome, Huntington disease, Parkinson's disease)
   E. Seizure disorders (e.g., **epilepsy**)
   F. Toxic-metabolic disorders (e.g., **Reye's syndrome**, lead or mercury poisoning)
   G. Malnutrition (e.g., protein-calorie malnutrition)
   H. Environmental deprivation (e.g., psychosocial disadvantage, child abuse and neglect, chronic social/sensory deprivation)
   I. Hypoconnection syndrome

Figure 6.5 Disorders in which mental retardation may occur

Source: Adapted from the American Association on Mental Retardation (AAMR). (1992). *Mental retardation: Definition, classification, and systems of supports* (9th ed., pp. 81–91). Washington, DC: Author. Used by permission.

The term developmental retardation *is also used as a synonym for* psychosocial disadvantage *to refer to mental retardation thought to be caused primarily by environmental influences such as minimal opportunities to develop early language, child abuse and neglect, and/or chronic social or sensory deprivation.*

physical problem. When no organic damage is evident in an individual with mental retardation, the cause is presumed to be psychosocial disadvantage**,** the combination of a poor social and cultural environment early in the child's life. Although there is no direct proof that social and environmental deprivation causes mental retardation, it is generally believed that these influences cause most cases of mild retardation.

Research conducted at the Juniper Gardens Children's Project has led to a hypothesis of developmental retardation as an intergenerational progression in which the cumulative experiential deficits in social and academic stimulation are transmitted to children from low socioeconomic status (SES) environments during their preadult life span (Greenwood, Carta, Hart, Kamps, Terry, Delquadri, Walker, & Risley, 1992; Greenwood, Hart, Walker, & Risley, 1994). Figure 6.6 illustrates the progression of developmental retardation in terms of low academic achievement and early school failure. There are several key contributors to this cycle of environmentally caused retardation (Greenwood et al., 1994):

1. limited parenting practices that produce low rates of vocabulary growth in early childhood,
2. instructional practices in middle childhood and adolescence that produce low rates of academic engagement during the school years,
3. lower rates of academic achievement and early school failure, early school dropout, and finally
4. parenthood and continuance of the progression into the next generation.

> Although this progression represents one of undoubtedly many specific developmental pathways leading to developmental retardation, it does represent an increasingly sophisticated guide for knowing where, when, and why environmental variables affect behavior and outcomes. (p. 216)

*A **longitudinal study** follows the same subjects over a period of years.*

This model is much more than intellectual theorizing and conjecture. The Juniper Gardens research team has obtained more than 25 years of research data that show clearly the relationships among parenting, early vocabulary growth, and school failure. For example, a longitudinal study of 42 infants and their families from their home environment through their early schooling examined the relations between SES status and parent-child language interactions (Hart & Risley, 1995). The results showed strong correlations between SES status and the amount of exposure to language at home. Young children from poor environments verbally interacted with their parents less often and were exposed to less vocabulary than were children from middle- and upper-SES homes. Hart and Risley also found that observations of natural language use in the home during the first 7 to 36 months of age could be used to predict children's measured IQ and academic achievement at the end of first grade.

Additional support for the hypothesis of developmental retardation is provided by McDermott (1994), who has found that much of the variability in prevalence rates of mental retardation reported by different school districts is explained by SES sta-

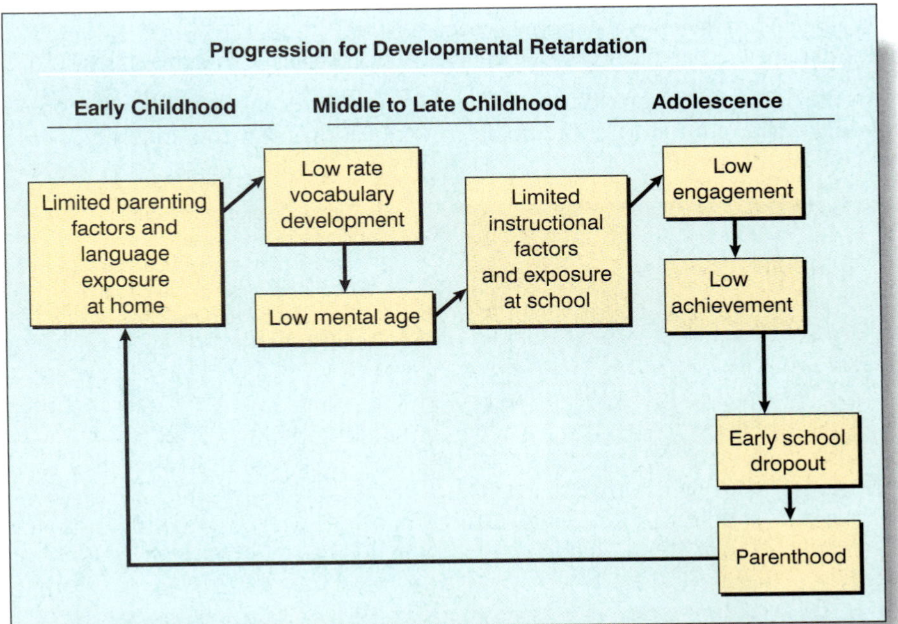

Figure 6.6 Schematic illustration of the intergenerational progression of developmental retardation

Source: Reprinted from Greenwood, C. R., Hart, B., Walker, D., & Risley, T. (1994). The opportunity to respond and academic performance revisited: A behavioral theory of developmental retardation and its prevention. In R. Gardner, III, D. M. Sainato, J. O. Cooper, T. E. Heron, W. L. Heward, J. W. Eshleman, & T. A. Grossi (Eds.), *Behavior analysis in education: Focus on measurably superior instruction* (p. 216). Reprinted with permission of Wadsworth Publishing, a division of International Thomson Publishing. Fax 800-730-2215.

tus. Her findings are "consistent with the notion that a large percentage of mental retardation is based on environmental causes, most notably, deprivation in the early years of life" (p. 182).

Educational Approaches

Curriculum Goals

What do individuals with mental retardation need to learn? Not too many years ago, children with mild mental retardation were presented with a slowed- and/or watered-down version of the general education curriculum that focused largely on traditional academic subjects. For example, a group of children with mild mental retardation might spend several weeks on a geography unit learning the 50 states and their capitals. Students with moderate and severe retardation spent many hours putting pegs into pegboards and sorting plastic sticks by color because observers believed that these isolated skills were developmental prerequisites for more meaningful activities. Unfortunately, knowing that Boise is the capital of Idaho or being able to sort by color did not help these students become more independent.

Functional Academics In recent years, identifying functional curriculum goals for students with mental retardation has become a major priority for special educators. Learning activities in a functional curriculum are chosen because they help students acquire skills that can be used in everyday home, community, and work environments. As Clark (1994) points out, however, what is functional for one student may not necessarily be so for another student. He suggests that teachers determine functional knowledge or skills by seeking answers to these questions:

- Does the content focus on necessary knowledge and skills to function as independently as possible in the home, school, or community?
- Does the content provide a scope and sequence for meeting future needs?
- Do the student's parents think the content is important for both current and future needs?
- Does the student think the content is important for both current and future needs?
- Is the content appropriate for the student's chronological age and current intellectual, academic, or behavioral performance level(s)?
- What are the consequences to the student of not learning the concepts and skills? (p. 37)

An even simpler approach to determining whether any given skill represents functional curriculum is to contemplate this question from the student's perspec-

"That'll be eighty-five cents, please." Ben's teacher is helping him learn functional vocational skills in the bagel shop that he and his classmates operate.

tive: "Will I need it when I'm 21?" (Beck, Broers, Hogue, Shipstead, & Knowlton, 1994). The answer to this question are critical; because when educators fail to relate curriculum for a student with mental retardation to outcomes with direct relevance to that student's eventual independence and lifestyle quality, "years of valuable opportunities for meaningful learning can be wasted" (Knowlton, 1998, p. 96).

Community Living Skills One organized statement of functional outcomes that can be used as the framework from which to build a functional curriculum is *Community Living Skills: A Taxonomy* (Dever, 1988). The taxonomy includes more than 300 instructional goals structured around five domains that represent the person as she lives, works, plays, and moves through the community: personal maintenance and development, homemaking and community life, vocational, leisure, and travel. Figure 6.7 shows how the five domains relate to one another; Figure 6.8 lists the major goals for two of the domains.

Instructional Methodology

Using the scientific method to discover effective and reliable teaching methods for students with mental retardation began with Itard in the late 18th century. Although this work is far from finished—we must continually search for better teaching methods—research has developed an instructional approach that reliably produces improvements in the lives of individuals with mental retardation. This approach is known as applied behavior analysis.

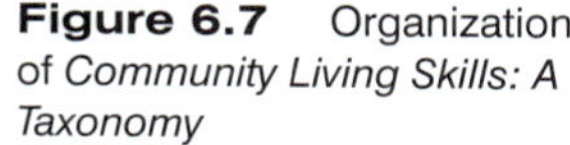

For a list of textbooks describing behavioral teaching methods and journals that regularly publish applications of behavior analysis with learners with mental retardation, see "For More Information" at the end of this chapter.

Applied behavior analysis can be defined as systematically arranging environmental events to produce desired learning. Applied behavior analysis is not a single technique but a systematic approach to teaching based on scientifically demonstrated principles that describe how the environment affects learning (Alberto & Troutman, 1999; Cooper, Heron, & Heward, 1987; Wolery, Bailey, & Sugai, 1988). Teaching methods derived from applied behavior analysis are used effectively not

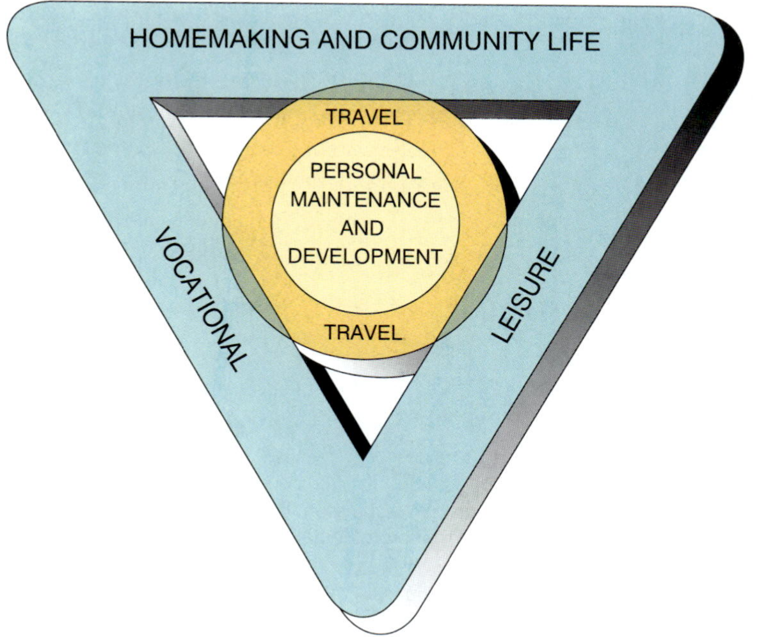

Figure 6.7 Organization of *Community Living Skills: A Taxonomy*

Source: Reprinted from Dever, R. B. (1988). *Community living skills: A taxonomy.* Washington, DC: American Association on Mental Retardation. © 1988 by the American Association on Mental Retardation. Used by permission.

DOMAIN P
PERSONAL MAINTENANCE AND DEVELOPMENT

I. The learner will follow routine body maintenance procedures
   A. Maintain personal cleanliness
   B. Groom self
   C. Dress appropriately
   D. Follow appropriate sleep patterns
   E. Maintain nutrition
   F. Exercise regularly
   G. Maintain substance control

II. The learner will treat illnesses
   A. Use first aid and illness treatment procedures
   B. Obtain medical advice when necessary
   C. Follow required medication schedules

III. The learner will establish and maintain personal relationships
   A. Interact appropriately with family
   B. Make friends
   C. Interact appropriately with friends
   D. Cope with inappropriate conduct of family and friends
   E. Respond to sexual needs
   F. Obtain assistance in maintaining personal relationships

IV. The learner will handle personal "glitches"
   A. Cope with changes in daily schedule
   B. Cope with equipment breakdowns and material depletions

DOMAIN H
HOMEMAKING AND COMMUNITY LIFE

I. The learner will obtain living quarters
   A. Find appropriate living quarters
   B. Rent/buy living quarters
   C. Set up living quarters

II. The learner will follow community routines
   A. Keep living quarters neat and clean
   B. Keep fabrics neat and clean
   C. Maintain interior of living quarters
   D. Maintain exterior of living quarters
   E. Respond to seasonal changes
   F. Follow home safety procedures
   G. Follow accident/emergency procedures
   H. Maintain foodstock
   I. Prepare and serve meals
   J. Budget money appropriately
   K. Pay bills

III. The learner will co-exist in a neighborhood and community
   A. Interact appropriately with community members
   B. Cope with inappropriate conduct of others
   C. Observe requirements of the law
   D. Carry out civic duties

IV. The learner will handle "glitches" in the home
   A. Cope with equipment breakdowns
   B. Cope with depletions of household supplies
   C. Cope with unexpected depletions of funds
   D. Cope with disruptions in routine
   E. Cope with sudden changes in the weather

Figure 6.8 List of major curriculum goals from *Community Living Skills: A Taxonomy*

Source: Reprinted from Dever, R. B. (1988). *Community living skills: A taxonomy.* Washington, DC: American Association on Mental Retardation. © 1988 by the American Association on Mental Retardation. Used by permission.

only with learners who experience mental retardation and other disabilities but also with students in general education.

Although literally hundreds of specific teaching tactics are based on behavior analysis (e.g., Lovitt, 1995), most share the following six features:

1. Precise definition and *task analysis* of the new skill or behavior to be learned
2. *Direct and frequent measurement* of the student's performance of the skill
3. Frequent opportunities for *active student response* during instruction
4. Immediate and *systematic feedback* for student performance
5. Procedures for achieving the *transfer of stimulus control* from instructional cues or prompts to naturally occurring stimuli
6. Strategies for promoting the *generalization and maintenance* of newly learned skills to different, nontraining situations and environments

Task Analysis An initial step in the behavioral approach to instruction is to specify exactly what skills, or behaviors, the learner is to acquire. **Task analysis** means breaking down complex or multiple-step behaviors or skills into small, easier-to-teach subtasks. The subskills or subtasks are then sequenced, either in the natural order in which they are typically performed or from the easiest to most difficult. Assessing a student's performance on a sequence of task-analyzed subskills helps pinpoint exactly where instruction should begin.

During the task analysis stage of instructional planning, it is important to consider the extent to which the natural environment requires performance of the target skill for a given duration or at a minimum rate. For example, Test, Spooner, Keul, and Grossi (1990) included specific time limits for each of the 17 steps in a task analysis used to teach two secondary students with severe mental retardation to use the public telephone to call home. The specific sequence of steps and the time limit for each one were determined by having two adults without disabilities use the telephone (see Table 6.4).

Excellent descriptions and examples of how to perform and validate task analyses can be found in Bailey and Wolery (1984); Bellamy, Horner, and Inman (1979); Moyer and Dardig (1978); Snell (2000); and Test and Spooner (1996). A task-analytic procedure based on 17 fundamental motions known as therbligs *can also be used by special educators (Browder, Lim, Lin, & Belfiore, 1993).*

Table 6.4 Task analysis and time limits for performing each task of using a public telephone

	Step	Time Limit
1.	Locate the telephone in the environment	2 minutes
2.	Find the telephone number	1 minute
3.	Choose the correct change	30 seconds
4.	Pick up the receiver using left hand	10 seconds
5.	Put receiver to left ear and listen for dial tone	10 seconds
6.	Insert first coin	20 seconds
7.	Insert second coin	20 seconds
8.-14.	Dial seven-digit number	10 seconds per
15.	Wait for telephone to ring a minimum of five times	25 seconds
16.	If someone answers, initiate conversation	5 seconds
17.	If telephone is busy, hang up phone and collect money	15 seconds

Source: Reprinted from Test, D. W., Spooner, F., Keul, P. K., & Grossi, T. A. (1990). Teaching adolescents with severe disabilities to use the public telephone. *Behavior Modification, 14,* 161. Used by permission.

__Precision teaching__, a method of direct and frequent assessment of student performance with specific decision rules indicating when instruction should be modified, is described in Chapter 7.

Direct and Frequent Measurement Behaviorally oriented teachers verify the effects of their instruction by directly and frequently measuring student performance. Measurement is *direct* when it objectively records the learner's performance of the behavior of interest in the natural environment for that skill. Measurement is *frequent* when it occurs on a regular basis; ideally, measurement should take place as often as instruction occurs. Academic achievement tests have traditionally been the major source of data for evaluating educational programs. Although achievement data are important, they are not useful for day-to-day planning and evaluation of instruction. Achievement tests are usually given only once or twice a year, and the information they provide is indirect, requiring that inferences be made about the student's actual classroom performance.

> Two errors of judgment are common for [teachers] who do not collect direct and frequent measurements of their student's performance. First, many ineffective intervention programs are continued. . . . Second, many effective programs are discontinued prematurely because subjective judgment finds no improvement. For example, teachers who do not use direct and frequent measures might discern little difference between a student's reading 40 words per minute with 60% accuracy and 48 words per minute with 73% accuracy. However, direct and frequent data collected on the rate and accuracy of oral reading would show an improved performance. Decision making in education must be based upon performance data; the individual's behavior must dictate the course of action. (Cooper et al., 1987, p. 60)

For guidelines on how to make instructional decisions based on student performance data, see Farlow and Snell (1994).

Only through diligent direct and frequent measurement of student performance are teachers able to provide the individualized instruction so vital to the growth and progress of students with mental retardation.

Active Student Response Contemporary educational research is unequivocal in its support of the positive relationship between the amount of time children spend actively responding to academic tasks and their subsequent achievement. Students who make many responses during a lesson learn more than students who make few responses or, worse, passively observe the teacher or other students respond. Providing instruction with high levels of active student participation is important for all learners, but it is particularly important for students with disabilities: "For children who are behind to catch up, they simply must be taught more in less time. If the teacher doesn't attempt to teach more in less time . . . the gap in general knowledge between a normal and handicapped student becomes even greater" (Kameenui & Simmons, 1990, p. 11).

Various terms such as *active student response, opportunity to respond,* and *academic learning time* are used to refer to this important variable.

For reviews of research showing the relationship between student participation and achievement in both general and special education, see Brophy and Good (1986); Fisher and Berliner (1985); Greenwood, Delquadri, and Hall (1984); Greenwood et al. (1994); Greer (1994); Heward (1994); and Rosenshine and Stevens (1986).

> **Active student response (ASR)** can be defined as an observable response made to an instructional antecedent. To say it less technically, ASR occurs when a student emits a detectable response to ongoing instruction. The kinds of responses that qualify as ASR are as varied as the kinds of lessons that are taught. Depending upon the instructional objective, examples of ASR include words read, problems answered, boards cut, test tubes measured, praise and supportive comments spoken, notes or scales played, stitches sewn, sentences written, workbook questions answered, and fastballs pitched. The basic measure of how much ASR a student receives is a frequency count of the number of academic responses emitted within a given period of instruction. (Heward, 1994, p. 286)

When all variables are held constant (e.g., quality of curriculum materials, students' prerequisite skills, motivational variables), an ASR-rich lesson will generally result in more learning than does a lesson in which students make few or no

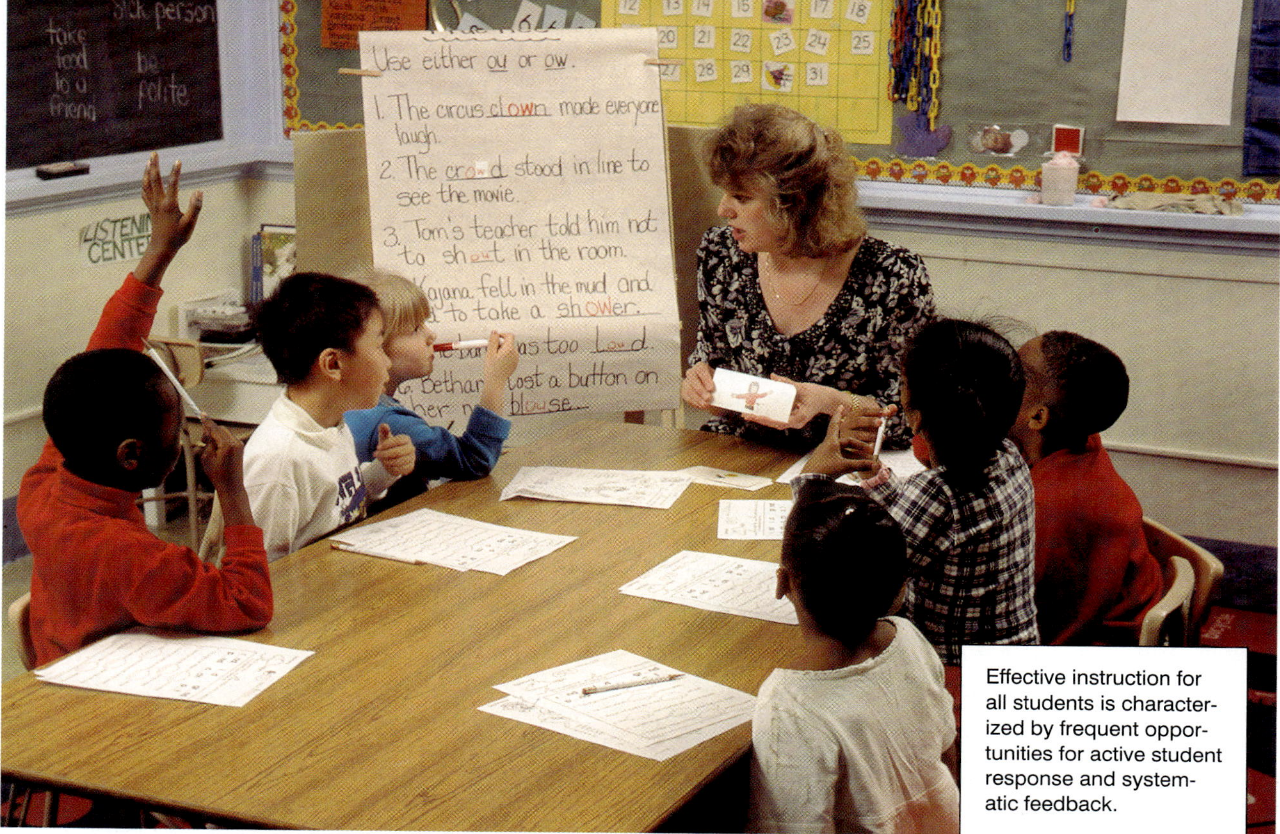

Effective instruction for all students is characterized by frequent opportunities for active student response and systematic feedback.

responses. Frequent ASR is a fundamental characteristic of numerous instructional methods with empirical support for their effectiveness with students with disabilities, including the following:

- Choral responding (Heward, Courson, & Narayan, 1989; Kamps, Dugan, Leonard, & Daoust, 1994; Sainato, Strain, & Lyon, 1987)
- Response cards (see "Everyone Participates in This Science Class," Chapter 8)
- Guided notes (see Chapter 7)
- Repeated reading (O'Shea, Sindelar, & O'Shea, 1985; Weinstein & Cooke, 1992)
- Fluency-building activities such as time trials (see "How Many Can You Do in One Minute?" which follows)
- Peer tutoring (Refer to the Teaching and Learning Video Connections insert entitled "Classwide Peer Tutoring.")
- Computer-assisted instruction (Lewis, 1995)
- Direct instruction (see Chapter 7) (Becker, 1992; Gersten, Carnine, & White, 1984; Weisberg, 1994)

Systematic Feedback Reith and Evertson (1988) note that all major reviews of the literature on effective teaching describe feedback as among the most critical instructional variables. Instructional feedback—information provided to students on some aspect of their performance—falls into two broad categories: praise and/or other forms of **positive reinforcement** for correct responses, and error correction for incorrect responses. Feedback is generally most effective when it is specific, immediate, positive, frequent, and differential (comparing the student's present performance with past performance; e.g., "You read 110 words today, Jermon. That's five more than yesterday.") (Van Houten, 1980, 1984). But what does *immediate*

Several studies have found that instructive feedback *can increase the efficiency of instruction for students with mental retardation and other disabilities (Werts, Wolery, Gast, & Holcombe, 1996). When giving feedback to students on their responses to targeted items, the teacher intentionally and methodically presents extra information. For example, when praising students' correct responses when reading the word "corn," the teacher might say, "You're right! That word is corn; it is a vegetable." The instructive feedback is the statement "it is a vegetable."*

How Many Can You Do in One Minute?

The conventional wisdom goes something like this: students with mental retardation can learn, but because they learn at a slower rate than students without disabilities, they should be given more time to complete their work. Although it is true that children with mental retardation acquire new skills more slowly, teachers may be doing students with disabilities a disservice by always providing plenty of time for them to do their work. Accuracy measures alone do not provide a complete picture of learning. For instance, whereas two students might each complete a page of math problems with 100% accuracy, the one who finishes in two minutes is more accomplished than the one who needs five minutes to answer the same problems. To be functional, many of the skills we use every day in the home, community, or workplace must be performed at a certain rate of speed.

Providing students with practice to build fluency is an important part of teaching. After the initial **acquisition stage of learning,** when a student learns how to perform the skill correctly, the student progresses to the **practice stage of learning,** in which the focus should shift to building **fluency**—the accuracy and rate with which a skill is performed. "The teacher does not push fluency when the student cannot yet work the problems correctly. Similarly, when teaching a student to be fluent, techniques used to promote accuracy are not used. During fluency instruction, elaborate explanations and corrections are not needed; in fact, they might even slow the student down. Instead, the teacher talks about and rewards fluency" (Howell & Lorson-Howell, 1990, p. 21).

Time trials—giving students the opportunity to perform a skill as many times as they can in a brief period—can be an excellent way to build fluency. Several studies have shown that both general and special education students not only benefit from time trials but also like to be timed (see Van Houten, 1980). For example, Miller, Hall, and Heward (1995) evaluated the effects of two procedures for conducting one-minute time trials on the rate and accuracy with which 11 elementary students with mild mental retardation wrote answers to single-digit math facts. During the first two weeks of the study, when the students were told to complete as many problems as they could during an untimed 10-minute work period, the students answered correctly an average of 8.4 problems per minute. During the next phase, in which a series of seven one-minute time trials was conducted with a 20-second rest period between each time trial (equaling a total of 10 minutes, as in the first phase), the students' correct rate increased to 13.2 per minute. Fluency improved to 17.3 problems per minute during a final phase, when immediate feedback and self-correction were conducted immediately after each of two consecutive time trials. Figure A illustrates the results.

Did working faster harm students' accuracy? Not at all: the students answered correctly 85% of all the problems they attempted during the 10-minute work period, but their accuracy improved to 89% when time trials were used. When asked which method they preferred, 10 of the 11 students indicated they liked time trials better than the untimed work period.

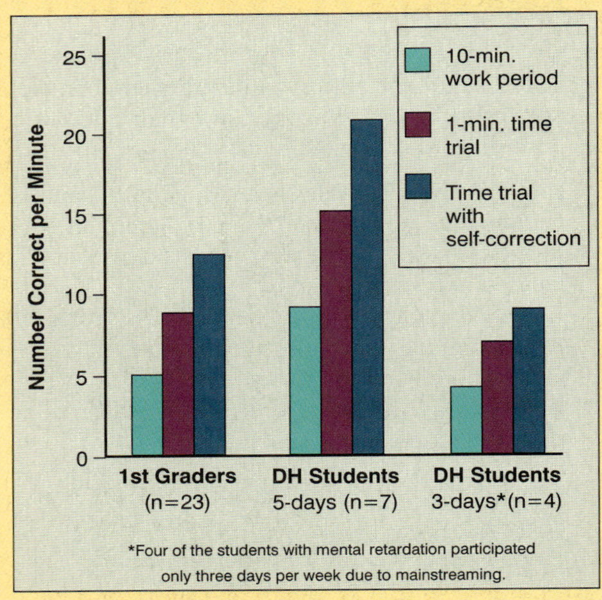

Figure A Mean number of math facts answered correctly per minute by first graders and elementary students with mental retardation (shown here as "DH students")

Source: Reprinted from Miller, A. D., Hall, S. W., & Heward, W. L. (1995). Effects of sequential 1-minute time trials with and without inter-trial feedback and self-correction on general and special education students' fluency with math facts. *Journal of Behavioral Education,* p. 340. Used by permission.

Fluency training in the form of one-minute time trials or counting periods has been used successfully to help individuals with disabilities improve a wide range of academic, vocational, and other skills (e.g., Beck, Conrad, & Anderson, 1995; Binder, 1996; Johnson & Layng, 1994; McCuin & Cooper, 1994; Stump, Lovitt, Fister, Kemp, Moore, & Schroeder, 1992; Tam & Heward, 1999; Weinstein & Cooke, 1992).

Guidelines for Conducting Time Trials

- Keep the time for each trial short. One minute is sufficient for most academic skills.
- Do time trials every day. For example, a series of two or three one-minute oral reading time trials could be conducted at the end of each day's lesson.
- Make time trials fun. Time trials should not be presented as a test; they are a learning activity that can be approached like a game.
- Use time trials only during the practice stage of learning, after students have learned how to do the skill correctly.
- Follow time trials with a more relaxed activity.
- Feedback to students should emphasize proficiency (total number correct), not simply accuracy (percentage correct).
- Have each student try to beat his own best score.
- Have students keep track of their progress by self-graphing.
- Consider using a performance feedback chart to provide both individual and group feedback during a time trial program (Van Houten, 1980, 1984).

Source: Adapted from Miller, A. D., & Heward, W. L. (1992). Do your students really know their math facts? Using daily time trials to build fluency. *Intervention in School and Clinic, 28,* 98–104. Used by permission.

mean, what aspects of the student's performance should be attended to, and how frequently must feedback be delivered to be effective?

The Learning Trial or Learn Unit. The point of contact between the learner and systematic instruction is a three-term relationship called a learning trial or learn unit (Greer, 1994). A **learning trial** consists of three major elements: (1) an instructional antecedent (e.g., a question or item from the curriculum or lesson), (2) the student's response to that item, and (3) instructional feedback following the response. The learning trial serves as a basic unit for analyzing and examining teaching and learning from both the teacher's perspective (as an opportunity to teach) and the student's perspective (as an opportunity to learn) (Heward, 1994). The concept of the three-term learning trial is not limited to structured, teacher-directed instruction. Learning trials occur during incidental teaching, community-based instruction, on the playground, and with social as well as academic skills.

See "What to Do When Students Make Mistakes" later in this chapter.

Two Stages of Learning. Effective teachers change the focus and timing of the feedback they provide as a student progresses from initial attempts at learning a new skill through practicing a newly acquired skill. Figure 6.9 illustrates two ways in which a series of learning units can take place within the ongoing dimension of time. When a student is first learning a new skill or content knowledge, feedback ideally follows each response. Feedback during this initial acquisition stage of learning should focus on the accuracy and topography of the student's response. By providing feedback after each response, the teacher reduces the likelihood of the student practicing errors (Van Houten, 1984).

During the practice stage of learning, when the student can perform the new skill with accuracy, a series of responses can and should be emitted before feedback is obtained (as shown in the bottom half of Figure 6.9). Feedback during the practice

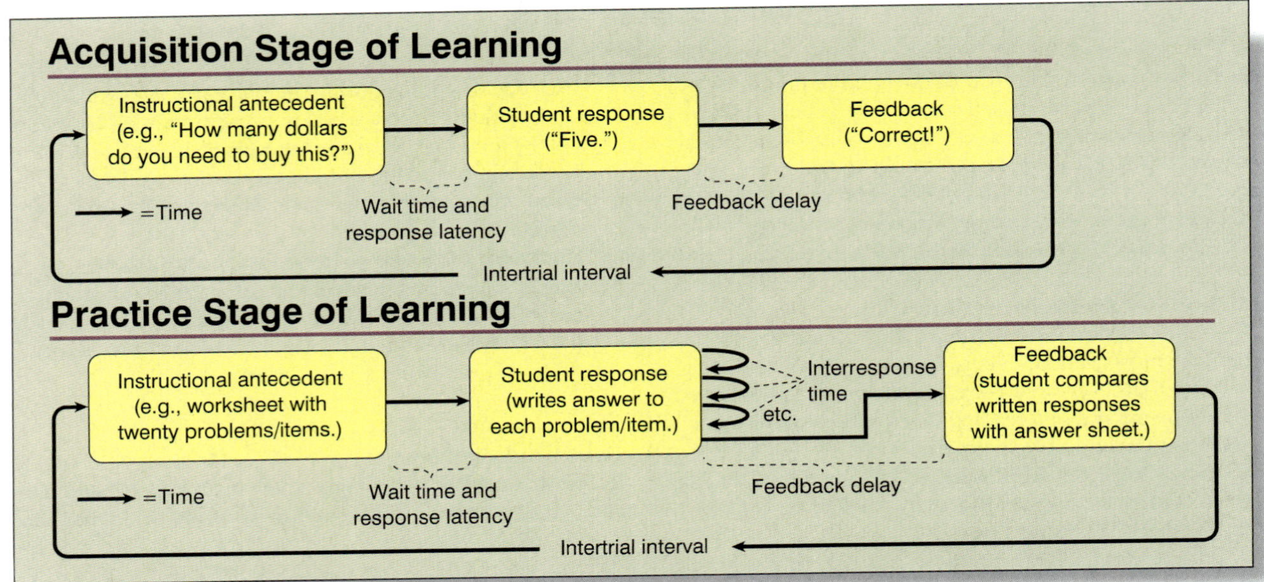

Figure 6.9 Feedback within a series of learn units during the acquisition and practice stages of learning

Source: Reprinted from Heward, W. L. (1994). Three "low-tech" strategies for increasing the frequency of active student response during group instruction. In R. Gardner, III, D. M. Sainato, J. O. Cooper, T. E. Heron, W. L. Heward, J. W. Eshleman, & T. A. Grossi (Eds.), *Behavior analysis in education: Focus on measurably superior instruction* (p. 284). Reprinted with permission of Wadsworth Publishing, a division of International Thomson Publishing. Fax 800-730-2215.

stage should emphasize the rate or speed at which the student performs the target skill. Providing feedback after each response during the practice stage of learning may actually have a detrimental effect by blocking the student's chance to develop fluency by "going fast."

Recent studies have found that individuals with mental retardation can use self-operated prompting systems to help them learn and perform a variety of academic, domestic, and vocational tasks (e.g., Barfels, Heward, & Al-Attrash, 1999; Briggs et al., 1990; Grossi, 1998; Mechling & Gast, 1997). See "I Made It Myself and It's Good!" in Chapter 11.

Transfer of Stimulus Control Trial-and-error learning is difficult and frustrating at best for students without disabilities. For students with mental retardation and other learning problems, it is likely to be a complete waste of time. Instead of waiting to see whether the student will make a correct response, the effective teacher provides a prompt (e.g., physical guidance, verbal directions, picture cues, prerecorded auditory prompts) that makes a correct response very probable. For example, Wood, Frank, and Hamre-Nietupski (1996) provided picture prompts for students to help them correctly perform each step in a task analysis for opening a combination lock found on student lockers. The correct response is reinforced, the prompt is repeated, and another correct student response is reinforced. The response prompts are then gradually and systematically withdrawn, and the student's behavior comes under the **stimulus control** of the curriculum content, or things in the natural environment that typically serve as cues for that skill.

One method for transferring stimulus control is **constant time delay,** a procedure in which the teacher begins by simultaneously presenting the stimulus being taught and a controlling response prompt. For example, as the teacher holds up a flashcard with the word "ball" printed on it, he says, "Ball," which successfully prompts a correct response by the student. After a number of zero-second delay trials, the teacher waits for a fixed amount of time (e.g., four seconds) between presentation of the instructional stimulus and the response prompt. Learning trials are

Teaching & Learning Video Connections

LOOK

CLASSWIDE PEER TUTORING

LOOKing at *Together We Can!*

Meaningful inclusion of students with disabilities into the academic and social life of the regular classroom presents a difficult challenge. The regular classroom teacher is not only accountable to deliver individualized instruction to these and other students whose learning is at risk, but is also expected to ensure all other learners' academic success and integrate the whole class socially. In-class tutoring is one method that has been used to individualize instruction without requiring students to leave the classroom. An often untapped but always available source of tutoring help in every classroom is the students themselves.

Although the idea of peer tutoring (same-age classmates teaching one another) is not new (Lancaster, 1806), it has recently become the focus of renewed interest and research. Traditional peer tutoring involves singling out students who have not mastered a particular skill for special help from a few high-achieving students who are assigned as tutors. In contrast, **classwide peer-tutoring (CWPT)** includes low achievers and students with disabilities as full participants in an ongoing whole-class activity. In the video *Together We Can! Classwide Peer Tutoring for Basic Academic Skills,* you will observe students participating in a CWPT program. Depicted in this video is a diverse group of students engaged in the learning/teaching process, where all students have the opportunity to tutor and be tutored.

Scott Cunningham/Merrill

LEARN

LEARNing the Characteristics of Effective Classwide Peer Tutoring

The classwide peer tutoring system you saw in *Together We Can!* is one of several CWPT models that reliably produce significant academic gains by students with disabilities in regular classrooms. These systems all have several characteristics in common.

* ***Clearly defined learning tasks/responses.*** CWPT programs are based on clearly defined learning tasks and explicitly defined peer tutoring roles and teaching responsibilities. Tutoring procedures are often scripted, and each tutor is expected to use highly similar procedures with little variation.

* ***Individualized instruction.*** In CWPT, teachers give frequent pre- and posttests to determine learning tasks that match the current needs of each student. In addition, because CWPT uses a one-on-one tutor/pupil ratio, each learner's performance can be observed, checked, and redirected in ways not otherwise possible in traditional teacher-led instruction.

* ***High rates of active student responding (ASR).*** Well-designed CWPT programs provide each student with many opportunities to respond. Depending on the learning task, students may make 100 or more responses during a 10-minute peer tutoring session. Total ASR is increased further in reciprocal CWPT programs because each student responds to the academic task in the role of tutee (initial responses to tutor's prompts, and repeating missed items) and tutor (prompting responding, discriminating between correct and incorrect responses, and providing instructional feedback).

* ***Immediate feedback and praise for correct responses.*** Peer tutors provide immediate feedback and praise to their tutees; and the teacher provides feedback to the tutors as a means of promoting high-quality peer teaching and learning during CWPT sessions. Formal point/reward systems are used in many CWPT programs to motivate participation and make learning fun.

* ***Systematic error correction.*** Tutors immediately and systematically correct mistakes by their tutees. Accurate error correction by tutors who themselves are learning the material can be achieved by using materials that show the correct response to the tutor or by a "tutor huddle" procedure described on the following page.

* ***Ongoing tracking of student progress.*** All CWPT programs incorporate direct and frequent measurement of each student's progress. These data are obtained in a variety of ways, such as daily end-of-session assessments given by tutors, regularly scheduled teacher-administered "check outs" of students' performance, and weekly pre- and posttests. In some programs, items missed on follow-up assessments are put back into the student's folder for additional practice.

Setting Up a Classwide Peer Tutoring Program

To better understand how a classwide peer tutoring could be applied, review the following practical procedures a first grade teacher used in a CWPT program to increase her students' sight-reading vocabulary. In this class of 28 children, each child served as both tutor and student each day. When in the role of student, each child practiced words from an individualized list of unknown words determined by a teacher-given pretest.

Tutoring Folders. Every student in the class had a tutoring folder containing 10 sight vocabulary word cards. Each card identified one word to be taught by a child's tutoring partner. These word cards were placed in a GO pocket on one side of the folder. Also in the folder was "a track" to record the tutee's progress during testing, markers to use for recording, and a STOP pocket to collect words that were learned after three tutoring sessions.

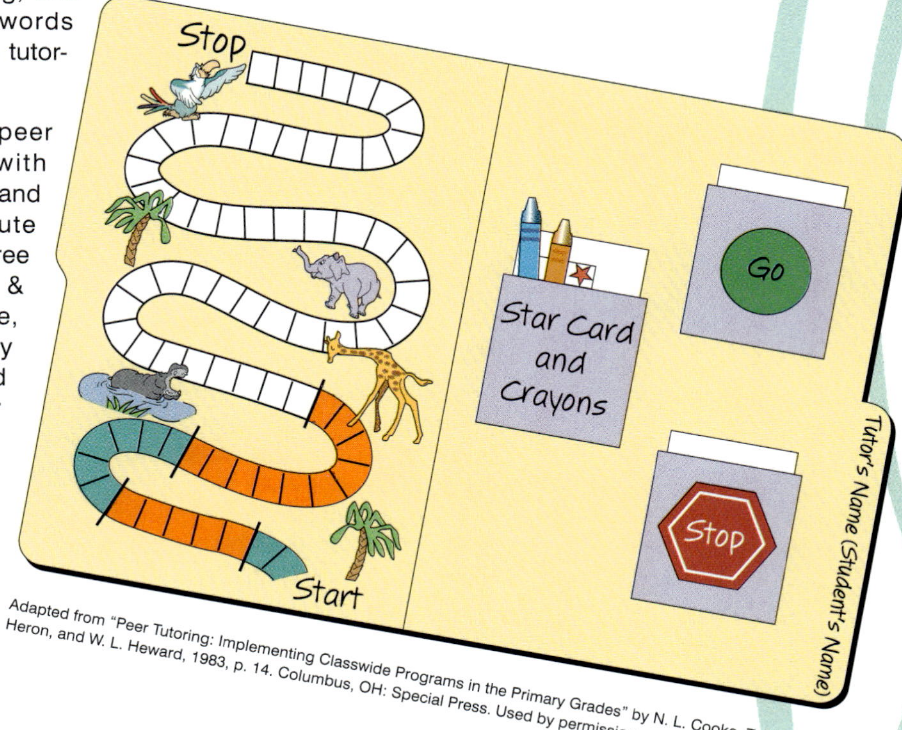

Adapted from "Peer Tutoring: Implementing Classwide Programs in the Primary Grades" by N. L. Cooke, T. E. Heron, and W. L. Heward, 1983, p. 14. Columbus, OH: Special Press. Used by permission.

Tutor Huddle. The daily peer tutoring session began with children getting their folders and participating in a five-minute "tutor huddle" with two or three other tutors (Heward, Heron, & Cooke, 1982). In the huddle, the tutors took turns orally reading the words they would shortly be responsible for teaching to their partners. (Meanwhile, their partners were in other tutor huddles working on the words they, too, would soon be teaching.) The teacher circulated around the room, helping tutor huddles that could not identify or agree on a given word.

Practice. After tutor huddle, partners joined each other on the floor to practice their words. One child began in the role of tutor, presenting the set of word cards as many times as possible during a five-minute practice period. Tutors were trained to praise their students from time to time for correct responses. When a student made an error, the tutor said, "Try again." If the student still did not respond correctly, the tutor said, "The word is *tree*; say *tree*." A timer signaled the end of the first practice period, and the partners switched roles. While students were tutoring their partners, the teacher walked around the room, answering questions and generally supervising the activity.

Testing. After the second practice period, the students reversed roles again and the first tutor tested her partner by presenting each sight word once, providing no prompts or cues. The teacher provided tutors about five minutes each to test and record their tutee's progress. Cards for the words the tutee read correctly were placed in one pile, and missed word cards were put in another pile. A small star was made on the back of each word card that was identified correctly. Then, the tutors tracked the tutees' daily progress. For example, in the illustration note how on the first day, one tutee was able to identify two words correctly. On a subsequent day, a different color marked the tutee's score of five. Once a child correctly read a word on the test for three consecutive sessions, that word was considered learned and its card was moved to the folder's STOP pocket. When all 10 words had been learned, a new set of word cards was placed in the GO pocket. At the end of each session, tutors praised each other for their good work.

Examining Results. Over a five-month period the children learned sight words at a rapid, consistent pace. The class average on 10-word review tests given one week after each set of words was learned was 8.9 words correct. Of particular interest was the performance of two children with disabilities. A boy in the class with learning disabilities successfully functioned as both student and tutor. A girl with mental retardation, who did not serve as a tutor, learned at the rate of almost one new word per day. Her sight vocabulary increased from a score of 4 to 51 learned words.

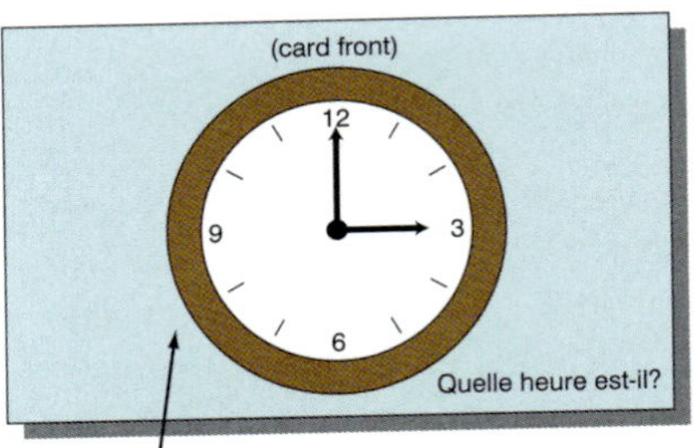

Quelle heure est-il?

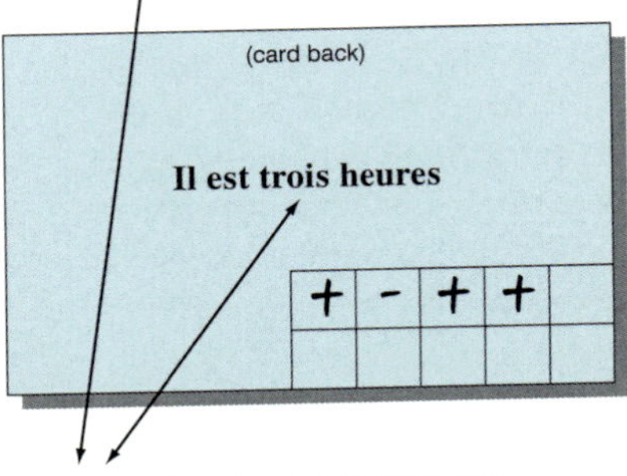

(card front)

Vary cards to show other clock faces and times

TEACHing Students How to Tutor Their Peers

TEACH

Effective classwide peer tutoring programs can be conducted in just about any classroom, no matter how diverse the students' skills and abilities. Work with a teacher in an elementary, middle school, or secondary classroom and set up a CWPT program. Discuss with the teacher which academic skills students could use help with. Do students need extra practice in basic math facts or reading fluency? Could peer tutoring help students practice problem-solving tasks or facts related to science or social studies data? Once you determine the class needs, work with the teacher to develop pretests to determine individual learning needs. Then create your own peer tutoring materials: peer tutoring folders and task cards. Shown on this page are examples of peer tutoring task cards for a variety of curriculum areas and levels of difficulty. Adapt your ideas to match these kinds of materials. Write a script identifying what tutors and tutees should say and do during each part of a peer tutoring session. Train the students by modeling and role playing the tutoring procedures. You might begin by pilot testing your system with just one or two pairs of students. Track the students' progress and use those data, as well as suggestions from the children, to make changes and improvements in your peer tutoring program. Include a sample tutoring folder, data on student learning, and comments from the children about their peer tutoring experiences in your teaching portfolio.

The video *Together We Can! Classwide Peer Tutoring for Basic Academic Skills* was developed by Charles R. Greenwood, Joseph Delquadri, & Judith J. Carta for Juniper Gardens Children's Project, University of Kansas. CWPT studies cited include Heron, Heward, Cooke, & Hill, 1983; Cooke, Heron, Heward, & Test, 1982; Cooke, Heron, & Heward, 1983; Maheady, Harper, & Mallette, 1991; Mathes, Fuchs, Fuchs, Henley, & Sanders, 1994; Miller, Barbetta, & Heron, 1994.

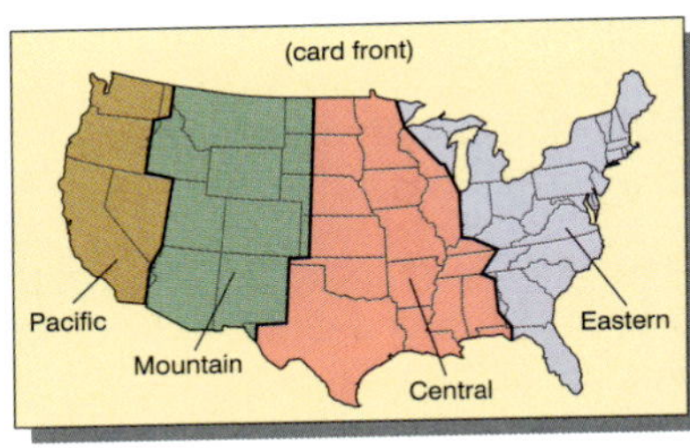

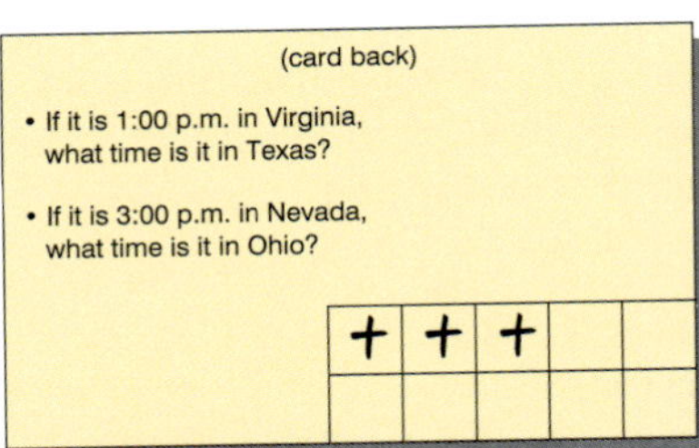

(card front)

(card back)
Il est trois heures
• If it is 1:00 p.m. in Virginia, what time is it in Texas?
• If it is 3:00 p.m. in Nevada, what time is it in Ohio?
+ + +

Vary to include generalization questions: If you left California at 10:00 a.m. traveling 600 miles per hour, and you flew for 5 hours to New York, what time would it be when you arrived. (Give reverse problem).

Adapted from "START Tutoring: Designing, training, implementing, adapting, and evaluating tutoring programs for school and home settings" by A. D. Miller, P. M. Barbetta, & T. E. Heron, 1994. In R. Gardner III, D. M. Sainato, J. O. Cooper, T. E. Heron, W. L. Heward, J. Eshelman, & T. A. Grossi (Eds.), *Behavior analysis in education: Focus on measurably superior instruction* (pp. 274-275). Pacific Grove, CA: Brooks/Cole. Used by permission.

repeated with the constant delay until the student begins to respond correctly before the teacher's prompt; that is, the student's behavior has come under the control of the instructional stimulus (the printed word), and the response prompt is no longer needed.

Time delay is one of the most well researched strategies for teaching students with mental retardation and severe disabilities (Ault, Gast, Wolery, & Doyle, 1992; Kratzer, Spooner, Test, & Koorland, 1993). See Wolery, Ault, and Doyle (1992) for detailed information on how to use response-prompting strategies with students who have moderate and severe disabilities.

Constant time delay may sound like a difficult procedure, but it's not. One study found that second- and fourth-grade students could successfully use constant time delay to teach sight words to three peers with mental retardation and other disabilities (Wolery, Werts, Snyder, & Caldwell, 1994).

Generalization and Maintenance *Generalization* and *maintenance* refer to the extent to which students extend what they have learned across settings and over time. Students with disabilities often have trouble remembering what they have learned and using their new knowledge and skills in settings or situations different from the ones in which they were taught. During the past 20 years, behavior analysts have designed and evaluated a number of effective alternatives to the "train and hope" method of teaching (Stokes & Baer, 1977; Stokes & Osnes, 1989). Although there is still much to be learned about helping students with disabilities get the most out of what they learn, the promising beginnings of a reliable "technology of generalization" have been developed. Here are four strategies used by special educators to promote the generalization and maintenance of new skills and knowledge:

Generalization and maintenance of skills in the regular classroom can be enhanced by training students with disabilities to recruit teacher praise and attention for their good behavior (Alber & Heward, 1997). See "Look, I'm All Finished!" in Chapter 8.

- *Aim for naturally occurring contingencies of reinforcement.* The most basic of all strategies for promoting generalization and maintenance is to increase the probability that a student's new skill will be reinforced in the natural environment (e.g., the regular classroom, the playground, the community, recreational and work settings) (Kohler & Greenwood, 1986; Rosales & Baer, 1998). This can be accomplished by (1) teaching only functional skills that are needed and likely to be valued by people in the natural environment and (2) teaching students to perform new skills with enough accuracy and fluency necessary to produce reinforcement in the natural environment.
- *Use a general case strategy to select teaching examples.* Instructional examples that systematically represent the full range of response requirements and stimulus variations found in the natural environment should be selected and incorporated into lessons (Horner, Williams, & Steveley, 1987; Sprague & Horner, 1984). Incorporating negative teaching examples—situations in which the student should not perform the behavior—can also improve the student's success in the natural environment (Horner, Eberhard, & Sheehan, 1986).
- *Program common stimuli.* If the generalization setting (e.g., the regular classroom or community setting) differs greatly from the setting in which teaching takes place (e.g., a special class), the student may not perform the new behavior. Programming common stimuli is accomplished by (1) incorporating into the teaching situation as many typical features of the generalization setting as possible and/or (2) creating a new common stimulus that the student learns to use in the teaching setting and that is transportable to the generalization setting, where it prompts or assists performance of the target skill (Anderson-Inman, Walker, & Purcell, 1984; Trask-Tyler, Grossi, & Heward, 1994; van den Pol, Iwata, Ivancic, Page, Neef, & Whitley, 1981).
- *Teach self-management skills.* The only person who is with the learner at all times and in all places is the learner's own self. Students can use self-management to promote the generalization and maintenance of their new knowledge and skills (Agran, 1997; Hughes, 1994; Rhode, Morgan, & Young, 1983).

Two excellent sources of how-to information for planning and implementing instruction for generalized outcomes are Rosales and Baer (1998) and Horner, Dunlap, and Koegel (1988).

What to Do When Students Make Mistakes

Students make mistakes, even during carefully planned lessons using well-designed instructional materials. They answer incorrectly, give incomplete answers, or do not respond at all. The importance of providing feedback when students make errors is well documented (e.g., Brophy, 1986; Christenson, Ysseldyke, & Thurlow, 1989; Fisher et al., 1980). Nevertheless, relatively little experimental research on error correction exists, and what does exist is inconclusive. Teachers are left knowing the importance of correcting student errors but receiving little empirically supported guidance for how to do so.

Don't Let Students Practice Errors During the Acquisition Stage of Learning Students learn by doing, but if errors are repeated, they may be learning how to perform skills incorrectly. Students learn better by "doing with feedback." The biggest problem with delayed feedback is that it allows students to practice errors (Van Houten, 1980, 1984). Practicing errors also wastes valuable instructional time because of the reteaching and relearning that eventually must take place.

Most errors are made during the acquisition stage of learning, when the student is learning how to perform a new skill or to remember and use new knowledge correctly. It is important that feedback be provided *before the student is required to use the skill/knowledge again.* Feedback should be qualitative, focusing on the accuracy of the student's response. For example: "Excellent, Robin. You removed all of the leaves with dark spots. But there's still too much sand on them to serve to our customers. Let me show you again how to wash it off. Then you can show me."

For behaviors that produce a permanent product (e.g., a completed workbook page, a sanded piece of wood), it is usually not critical that feedback occur within a few seconds or minutes of a student's response. Feedback received even a day or two later may still be helpful as long as it occurs before the student must respond again.

Teachers can ensure that students receive feedback after each response by using instructional strategies such as these:

- *Collaborative learning.* Use a peer tutoring system or small-group activities in which peers provide feedback and error correction to one another after each response (Miller, Barbetta, & Heron, 1994) (see the Teaching and Learning Video Connections insert entitled "Classwide Peer Tutoring").
- *Learning centers.* Use instructional materials and computer software that provide feedback after each response.
- *Self-correction.* Teach students to self-score their work and self-correct any errors before proceeding to the next problem or item (Goddard & Heron, 1998; Morten, Heward, & Alber, 1998).
- *Homework.* Avoid assigning homework or independent seatwork activities that do not contain self-scoring and self-correcting components until the student can perform the target skill with some accuracy.

When Errors Occur, Provide Effective and Efficient Error Correction When handled properly, errors can provide good opportunities for teaching and learning. But too often error correction is carried out ineffectively (the student is still wrong the next time) and inefficiently (it is time-consuming and reduces the total number of learn units that can be conducted during the lesson). Although much remains to be learned about how teachers should respond when students make mistakes during instruction, the combined results of several experimental studies provide some guidance. Research suggests that error correction will be more effective and efficient under the following conditions:

Done Right Now. Errors should be corrected before going to the next item or problem. Teachers may hesitate to delay instruction when a student errs during group instruction, preferring instead to work individually with her after the lesson. But this may allow the student to make the same mistake for the rest of the lesson. Two recent studies compared "right now" and "end-of-the-lesson" error correction during sight-word lessons with primary students with mental retardation and science vocabulary lessons with upper elementary-age students with learning disabilities. Error correction immediately after each error was more effective, even when the postlesson error correction consisted of repeated trials (Barbetta, Heward, Bradley, & Miller, 1994; Kleinman, Heckaman, Kimball, Possi, Grossi, & Heward, 1994).

Direct. Error correction is direct when the feedback relates to the target skill. Several studies have shown that the effectiveness of error correction is improved when students are provided with complete information or a direct model of the missed item (Barbetta, Heward, & Bradley,

1993; Espin & Deno, 1989). That is, instead of offering incomplete or indirect feedback, tell, show, and/or guide the student through the correct response.

Quick. Error correction is quick when the teacher rapidly tells, shows, and/or demonstrates the correct response (e.g., "No. This word is 'circus.'"). Correcting an error in three or four seconds is better than discussing the student's mistake for a minute or longer. In trying to help students understand their error, teachers often spend a great deal of time talking. Although detailed explanations are sometimes necessary and helpful, often students just get confused or lose interest. Time would be better used conducting several more complete learning trials (Heron, Heward, Cooke, & Hill, 1983).

Ends with the Student Making the Correct Response. When a student errs, teachers often hint, probe, tell, show, and eventually provide the correct response or ask another student to answer. The student who made the original error passively observes. Results from several studies show that feedback is more effective when the student who erred is given an opportunity to emit the corrected response (Barbetta & Heward, 1993; Dalrymple & Feldman, 1992; Drevno, Kimball, Possi, Heward, Gardner, & Barbetta, 1994). For example, Barbetta, Heron, and Heward (1993) examined the effects of active student response during the correction of errors made by primary students with mental retardation during sight-word lessons. Half of each week's set of 20 unknown words were taught with "no response" (NR) error correction (after each error, the teacher modeled the correct response while the student looked at the word); the remaining 10 words were taught with "active student response" (ASR) error correction (the student repeated the word after the teacher's model). ASR error correction was more effective for all six children on all five measures of performance: number and percentage of correct responses during instruction, same-day tests, next-day tests (see Figure A), maintenance tests given 2 weeks after instruction, and words read in sentences.

The error correction episode should end with the student making the correct response. Instead of providing or showing the correct response and then asking the student, "Now do you understand?" have the student repeat the correct response (e.g., teacher: "No. This word is 'circus.' What is this word?" Student: "Circus." Teacher: "Good.").

Evaluate the Effects of Error Correction As with any instructional technique, teachers should evaluate their error correction procedures. First, what is the procedure's *effectiveness* in helping students respond correctly in the future? This can be directly and simply determined by observing how the student responds to the same item or task the next time it is presented. Second, how *efficient* are the error correction procedures? A complex, time-consuming procedure may be effective (the student responds correctly in the future) but too inefficient because it limits the total number of learn units during the lesson. Like most questions concerning effective instructional practices, the question of how error correction should be conducted is an empirical one. Its answer lies in student performance.

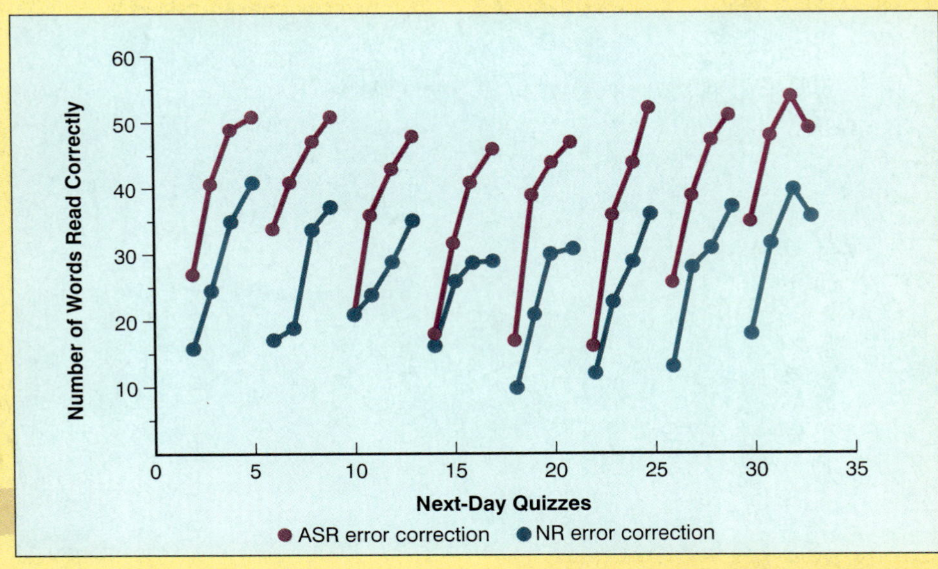

Figure A Total number of sight words read correctly by six primary students with mental retardation on tests given one day after instruction (breaks in data paths separate word sets)

Source: Reprinted from Barbetta, P. M. (1991). Active error correction during sight words drills by students with developmental handicaps. Unpublished doctoral dissertation, The Ohio State University. Used by permission.

Educational Placement Alternatives

Traditionally, students with mild mental retardation (EMR) were educated in a separate classroom with 12 to 18 other EMR students. Children with moderate and severe mental retardation were usually excluded from the local public school and placed in a special school for children with disabilities or an institution. Although the regular public schools are changing their ways of providing services to students with mental retardation, they are doing so slowly.

Polloway (1984) provides a comprehensive review of history and research concerning the most effective classroom placement for students with mild retardation.

For many students today, the label of mental retardation still results in a placement decision, and more often than not that placement is a separate class. Even though IDEA mandates that children with disabilities be educated with their nondisabled peers to the greatest extent possible, only slightly more than one in three students with mental retardation spends all or part of the school day in the regular classroom. During the 1995–1996 school year, only 10% of students with mental retardation were educated in the regular classroom, with 29% being served in resource room programs and 54% in separate classes (U.S. Department of Education, 1998).

In Chapter 13 we examine the case for educating children with severe disabilities in their neighborhood schools.

About 7% of students with mental retardation continue to attend special schools or residential facilities. Sometimes a number of small neighboring school districts pool their resources to offer a special school program for students with moderate/severe/profound mental retardation. Some special educators today believe, however, that separate schools prohibit students from obtaining an education in the least restrictive environment and that all children should attend their local neighborhood schools regardless of the type or severity of their disability (e.g., Baumgart & Giangreco, 1996; Brown, Long, Udvari-Solner, Davis, VanDeventer, Ahlgren, Johnson, Gruenewald, & Jorgensen, 1989a; Snell, 1991).

Inclusive Classrooms

As we saw in Chapter 2, simply putting a child with disabilities into a regular classroom does not necessarily mean that he will be accepted socially or receive the most

Community-based instruction provides these secondary students with mental retardation an opportunity to acquire employment skills in a real work setting.

appropriate and needed instructional programming. This may be especially true for students with mental retardation, whose presence in the regular classroom represents a novel challenge for many teachers. For example, although 97% of general education teachers who responded to a national survey about grading practices reported that they had taught students with learning disabilities and 73% had taught students with behavior disorders, only 23% indicated they had taught students with mental retardation (Bursuck, Polloway, Plante, Epstein, Jayanthi, & McConeghy, 1996).

More information about inclusive schools can be found by accessing the Resources module for Chapter 6 at http://www.prenhall.com/heward and linking to the Special Ed Resource Page.

Many special and regular educators, however, are developing programs and methods for integrating the instruction of students with mental retardation with that of their nondisabled classmates. Systematically planning for the focus student's inclusion in the classroom through team games and group investigation projects and directly training all students in specific skills for interacting with one another are just some of the methods for increasing the chances of a successful regular class placement (Giangreco, 1997; Janney & Snell, 1996, 1997; Putnam, 1998; Stainback & Stainback, 1996).

Peer tutoring and peer buddy programs have also proven effective in promoting the instructional and social inclusion of students with mental retardation into regular classrooms (Delquadri, Greenwood, Whorton, Carta, & Hall, 1986; Hughes, Killian, & Fischer, 1996; Staub, Spaulding, Peck, Gallucci, & Schwartz, 1996). For example, Cooke et al. (1982) implemented a classwide peer tutoring system in a first-grade classroom in which a student with Down syndrome participated. During the course of this five-month study, she not only interacted directly and positively with her peer tutor but also learned more than 40 sight words from her classmate.

To learn how nondisabled high school students supported the inclusion of classmates with mental retardation and other disabilities, see the "The Metropolitan Nashville Peer Buddy Program" in Chapter 13.

Students with mental retardation often benefit from similar programs for students who are not disabled. During the early elementary grades, students with mental retardation, as well as their chronological age peers, need instruction in basic academic skills. Reading, mathematical calculations, and writing are core curricular areas that should be included in programs for all students. During this period, many students with mental retardation benefit from full or partial inclusion in regular classroom settings.

> As students get older, their needs begin to differ and thus curricular differentiation becomes an important consideration. . . . Rather than being integrated into a world history class, many students with mental retardation may be better served by learning the necessary functional skills for independent living. Skills such as job readiness, how to use leisure time, how to budget and shop, how to cook and how to maintain a household are important. While all individuals must learn these skills in order to be independent, most students learn them on their own, without specific instructional activities that focus on these areas. Students with mental retardation, on the other hand, often need structured learning experiences in order to learn these skills. (Smith & Hilton, 1994, pp. 6–7)

The relative appropriateness of inclusion in the regular classroom may change for some students as they move from the elementary grades to the secondary level when opportunities for community-based instruction in vocational and life skills are critical. The extent to which a student with mental retardation, like all students with disabilities, is educated in a general education classroom should be determined by the student's individual needs. "School inclusion can then be seen as a means (as opposed to just a goal unto itself) toward the ultimate objective of community inclusion and empowerment" (Polloway, Smith, Patton, & Smith, 1996, p. 11).

See "Some Things We've Learned about Inclusion" later in this chapter.

Some Things We've Learned about Inclusion

by Martha E. Snell, University of Virginia, and Rachel E. Janney, Radford University

Not everyone thinks of inclusion in the same way, so let's start by defining it. *Inclusion involves creating a mainstream where everyone fits and learns. Inclusion affects the location of students, the supports provided, the roles school staff fill, and the ways teachers interact with each other.* In inclusive schools:

- All students attend their neighborhood school.
- Students with disabilities are members of general education classrooms with their age peers; their numbers reflect the natural proportion of students with disability.
- Special education supports follow students into the mainstream.
- Inclusion is planned individually to enable active and meaningful participation in learning and social activities (classes and schedule, amount and kinds of support, accommodations and modifications, pullout services versus peer supports).

Benefits of Inclusion Most educators agree that inclusion involves complex change, but knowing what inclusion is still may not convince people to make the change. Why include students with disabilities, especially those with extensive support needs? There are benefits to students with disabilities, typical students, and teachers.

For students with disabilities, benefits are psychological, social, and cognitive: not being separated from typical peers but sharing class membership; having increased social interactions; gaining positive social relationships; expanding a peer network and making friends; and having peers who can be models for communication, social skills, dress, and style. Cognitive benefits include increased alertness to improved academic learning and motivation for learning.

For typical students, benefits cluster in the personal growth domain (Staub & Peck, 1995). Students demonstrate improvements in attitudes toward people different from them, increased social responsibility, and self-confidence. They have an opportunity to expand peer networks and form meaningful relationships with students in the mainstream (Staub, Schwartz, Gallucci, & Peck, 1994). Lou Brown, an inclusion advocate at the University of Wisconsin, notes the long-term benefits of improving student attitudes toward those with disabilities: they will be the future voters, taxpayers, parents of children with and without disabilities, and politicians leading our cities, states, and countries.

General education teachers describe unanticipated rewards from their own interactions with focus students; these teachers are positively motivated by discovering that students with disabilities had personalities, can learn, and can contribute in class.

Most benefits of inclusion depend on how schools plan for, implement, and support change and then sustain outcomes. Searching the literature for supportive evidence produces a mixed bag of findings. It seems that the challenges of including students with extensive cognitive and/or physical disabilities may be fewer than those of including students prone to emotional outburst or aggression. But categorizing students as "easier to include" or "harder to include" is an error-prone strategy. Only by planning needed supports on an individual basis can educators help inclusion yield benefits.

Unwritten Agreements between Teachers Observations and interviews with teachers and students from 10 classrooms in elementary schools practicing inclusion have taught us a great deal (Janney & Snell, 1996, 1997). For example, classroom teachers and special education teachers have unwritten contracts about the roles they play to support the students with moderate and severe disabilities included in their classrooms:

1. Classroom teachers continued to have primary authority for the class and the included child when he was treated like classmates—for example, during class activities, recess, P.E., circle time, reading and math, and field trips.
2. Special education teachers or classroom aides assumed primary responsibility when the focus child was treated differently from classmates: for example, during individualized tutoring or related services for health or physical needs.
3. When including students with more extensive support needs, the teachers would, as much as possible, (a) keep focus students near their peers, (b) treat them like their classmates, and (c) provide them with the same or similar activities and materials.

After all, as these teachers told us, inclusion is about students having membership in classrooms with nondisabled peers. So why separate them or treat them differently? That made good sense to us!

Inclusion should be planned to enable active and meaningful participation in the learning and social activities of the classroom.

Teachers' Modifications To implement these assumptions, teachers made three kinds of changes. First, they modified their typical roles because the focus student was shared between two teachers; the regular classroom teacher now had at least one (and usually more) new staff member in and out of the classroom. Second, they modified class routines and the classroom itself. For example, peers were allowed to walk with focus students and help them stay with the class on the way to lunch, P.E., and other activities; schedules allowed time for students with physical disabilities to make transitions; reading circles were moved so positioning equipment would fit. Third, teachers modified instructional activities to enable focus students to participate academically and socially. Sometimes changes were simplifications (fewer spelling words); sometimes they involved different materials (specialized scissors) or response modalities (listening to a taped story rather than looking at a book because of visual impairments). Sometimes instructional activities were modified to enable the focus child to participate socially, not academically: just sitting with a group doing math activities or holding a book that others were reading. Finally, special education teachers used parallel activities that differed from classmates' activities, were carried out separately but in the classroom, and in which only the focus child participated (e.g., working on money skills while classmates did addition and subtraction). Inclusion was successful when students fit in both socially and instructionally.

Lessons about Helping and Socialization Observations also taught us about how teachers use peer interactions to include students with disabilities in their elementary general education classrooms. We learned that classroom teachers developed rules for peers to help the focus child:

- *Who to help with class work.* They can't help each other, but they can help the focus student.
- *When to help the focus student.* They can help if they are helper of the day or asked by the teacher, not when the teacher is teaching or if the focus student rejects assistance.
- *How to help.* They can help in ways that let the focus student participate as much as she can. "Don't do it for her" was a guideline teachers taught peers (but did not always follow themselves).

We have repeatedly observed general and special education teachers teach three important lessons that facilitate socialization between students and their classmate with disabilities. The main teaching approach was to model lessons through their own behavior toward the focus student—to "practice what they preached."

Lessons	**Examples**
Just another student Treat focus students like other students as much as possible.	Use greetings, joking styles as with other students; include them in all class activities; and apply the same rules for everyone's behavior.
Age appropriate Encourage focus students to look and act in ways that reflect their actual age, not like babies. Use the same rule to guide peer interactions.	Use age-appropriate greetings, tone of voice, teaching and leisure materials, and clothes.
Back off Adults should draw peers into academic or social activities with focus children and then back off to avoid hampering their interactions.	Pull peers into the activity and make it fun; then leave. Or help a focus student into the sandbox among peers; then move away and monitor from a distance.

To join the discussion, "Is inclusion a good thing for every student with mental retardation?" go to the Message Board module at http://www.prenhall.com/heward.

Current Issues and Future Trends

In its 1976 report, the President's Committee on Mental Retardation outlined the country's major objectives in the field of mental retardation for the remainder of the century. Here were four key objectives:

- Attainment of citizenship status in law and in fact for all mentally retarded individuals in the United States, exercised to the fullest degree possible under the conditions of disability
- Reduction of the incidence of mental retardation from biomedical causes by at least 50% by the year 2000
- Reduction of the incidence and prevalence of mental retardation associated with social disadvantage to the lowest level possible by the end of the century
- Achievement of a firm and deep public acceptance of persons with mental retardation as members in common of the social community and as citizens in their own right

As we begin a new century, let us review the progress made over the past 25 years. Although a great deal remains to be done to realize these goals, significant accomplishments have been made in each key area.

Rights of Persons with Mental Retardation

We have come a long way since the time when people with mental retardation were exterminated, ridiculed, or employed as court jesters, but we still have a long way to go. Of all the goals of the first President's Committee on Mental Retardation, the goal of legal rights for persons with mental retardation has come closest to being reached.

To learn how you might go about getting to know an adult with disabilities, see "A Friendship Program for Future Special Education Teachers" in Chapter 15.

Numerous court decisions have advanced the position that a person with mental retardation has and should be able to exercise, with assistance from society if necessary, the same rights and freedoms as a nondisabled citizen. Many states have organized citizen advocacy programs to aid individuals with mental retardation. An **advocate** is a volunteer committed to becoming personally involved with the welfare of a person with a disability and knowledgeable about the services available for that person. In a sense, an advocate is an informed friend who can legally take a stand to see that his friend's rights are not abused and that the necessary educational and other services are in fact delivered. Being an advocate can be an excellent way to serve a citizen with mental retardation and in the process learn much about the field. Persons with disabilities are increasingly using self-advocacy as a means of improving their quality of life.

Prevention of Mental Retardation

The December 1992 issue of the journal Mental Retardation *is devoted to articles on prevention.*

Each week in this country, more than 2,000 babies are born who are or at some point will be diagnosed with mental retardation. As scientific research, both medical and behavioral, has generated new knowledge about the causes of mental retardation, procedures and programs designed to prevent its occurrence have increased.

Probably the biggest single preventive strike against mental retardation (and many other disabling conditions, including blindness and deafness) was the development of an effective rubella vaccine in 1962. When rubella (German measles) is contracted by mothers during the first three months of pregnancy, it causes severe damage in 10% to 40% of the unborn children (Krim, 1969). Fortunately, this cause of mental retardation can be eliminated if women are vaccinated for rubella before becoming pregnant.

Phenylketonuria (PKU) is a genetically inherited condition in which a child is born without an important enzyme needed to break down the amino acid phenylalanine, which is found in many common foods. Failure to break down this amino acid causes brain damage that results in severe mental retardation. By analyzing the concentration of phenylalanine in a newborn's blood plasma, doctors can diagnose PKU and treat it with a special diet. Most children with PKU who receive a phenylalanine-restricted diet early enough have normal intellectual development (Berman & Ford, 1970).

Toxic exposure through maternal substance abuse and environmental pollutants (e.g., lead poisoning) are two major causes of preventable mental retardation that can be combated with education and training (Schroeder, 1987).

Advances in medical science have enabled doctors to identify certain genetic influences strongly associated with mental retardation. One approach to prevention offered by many health service organizations is **genetic counseling,** a discussion between a specially trained medical counselor and prospective parents about the possibility that they may give birth to a child with disabilities on the basis of the parents' genetic backgrounds.

For a discussion of the ethical and legal issues involved in genetic counseling, see Pueschel (1991).

Amniocentesis is a procedure in which a sample of fluid is withdrawn from the amniotic sac surrounding the fetus during the second trimester of pregnancy (usually the 14th to 17th week). Fetal cells are removed from the amniotic fluid and grown in a cell culture for about two weeks. At that time, a chromosome and enzyme analysis is performed to identify the presence of about 80 specific genetic disorders before birth. Many of these disorders, such as Down syndrome (O'Brien, 1971), are associated with mental retardation.

A new technique for prenatal diagnosis that may eventually replace amniocentesis is **chorion villus sampling (CVS).** A small amount of chorionic tissue (a fetal component of the developing placenta) is removed and tested. The most significant advantage of CVS is that it can be performed earlier than amniocentesis (during the 8th to 10th week of pregnancy). Because fetal cells exist in relatively large numbers in the chorion, they can be analyzed immediately without waiting for them to grow for two to three weeks. Although CVS is being used more often, it has been associated with a miscarriage rate of about 10 in 1,000 (compared with 2.5 in 1,000 for amniocentesis) and is still considered experimental. The relative safety and risks of CVS are discussed by Rhoads et al. (1989).

For a discussion of the ethical and legal issues involved in the abortion of fetuses with Down syndrome, see Glover and Glover (1996).

Medical advances such as these have noticeably reduced the incidence of mental retardation caused by some of the known biological factors, but huge advancements in research are needed to reach the goal of lowering the incidence of biomedical mental retardation by 50%. The authors of a recent analysis of prevention strategies concluded that full use of currently available prevention measures could reduce the prevalence of severe mental retardation by 20% (Stevenson, Massey, Schroer, McDermott, & Richter, 1996). While noting that progress toward the 50% prevention goal has been significant, Stevenson et al. concluded: "At the present time, the technological capacity to prevent 50% of cases of mental retardation does not exist. The greatest shortfall is the capacity to determine causation" (p. 187).

As we noted earlier, most children with mental retardation are in the mild range, and their developmental delays have no clearcut etiology. These are the children whose mental retardation is thought to be primarily the result of a poor environment during their early years. The poor environment may be a result of parental neglect, poverty, disease, bad diet, and other factors—many of which are completely out of the hands of the child's parents. In Chapter 5 we discussed two of the most well-known and long-running research and intervention programs aimed at reducing the incidence of developmental retardation: the Milwaukee Project and the Juniper

Gardens Children's Project. Although measuring the effects of programs that aim to prevent psychosocial retardation is much more difficult than measuring the decreased number of children suffering from a disease like PKU, the preliminary results of these projects are encouraging, and some models of effective early intervention have been identified (Ramey & Ramey, 1992).

Wolf Wolfensberger (1983), the best-known champion of the normalization principle, has proposed the term social role valorization *to replace* normalization. *He writes, "The most explicit and highest goal of normalization must be the creation, support, and defense of valued social roles for people who are at risk of social devaluation" (p. 234).*

Use the self-tests at http://www.prenhall.com/heward to assess your knowledge of the content of Chapter 6.

Normalization and Self-Determination

The principle of **normalization** refers to the use of progressively more normal settings and procedures "to establish and/or maintain personal behaviors which are as culturally normal as possible" (Wolfensberger, 1972, p. 28). Normalization is not a single technique or set of procedures but an overriding philosophy. It says that persons with mental retardation should, to the greatest extent possible, be both physically and socially integrated into the mainstream of society regardless of the degree or type of disability.

Perhaps the greatest current expression and extension of the normalization concept can be found in the growing movement toward teaching self-determination skills to individuals with mental retardation. Self-determination involves acting as the primary agent in one's life and "making choices and decisions regarding one's quality of life free from undue influence or interference" (Wehmeyer, Kelchner, & Richards, 1996, p. 632). Because special educators are realizing that self-determination is a key ingredient for successful transition from school to adult life, more teachers are gearing specific teaching strategies and curriculum objectives toward this goal (Wehmeyer, Agran, & Hughes, 1998). As support for normalization grows among both educators and the public, the time draws nearer when all persons with mental retardation will experience the benefits of humane and effective treatment and education in integrated school, community, and, employment settings.

Summary

Defining Mental Retardation

- The definition incorporated into IDEA states that mental retardation involves both significantly subaverage general intellectual functioning and deficits in adaptive behavior manifested between birth and age 18. Intellectual functioning is usually measured with a standardized intelligence test and adaptive behavior with an observation checklist or scale.
- The most recent AAMR definition of mental retardation, the "1992 System," represents a shift away from conceptualizations of mental retardation as an inherent trait or permanent state of being to a description of the individual's present functioning and the environmental supports needed to improve it.
- There are four degrees of mental retardation as classified by IQ score: mild, moderate, severe, and profound.
- Children with mild mental retardation may experience substantial performance deficits only in school. Their social and communication skills may be normal or nearly so. They are likely to become independent or semi-independent adults.
- Most children with moderate mental retardation show significant developmental delays during their preschool years. Most school children with moderate mental retardation are educated in self-contained classrooms, and most live and work in the community as adults if individualized programs of support are available.
- Most persons with severe and profound mental retardation are identified in infancy. Some adults with severe and profound mental retardation can be semi-independent; others need 24-hour support throughout their lives.
- Classification in the AAMR's "1992 System" is based on four levels and intensities of supports needed to improve functioning in the environments in which the individual lives: intermittent, limited, extensive, and pervasive.

Prevalence

- Theoretically, 2.3% of the population would score two standard deviations below the norm on IQ tests, but this does not account for adaptive behavior, the other criterion for diagnosis of mental retardation. Many experts now cite an incidence figure of approximately 1% of the total population.
- During the 1996–1997 school year, approximately 1% of the total school enrollment received special education services under the disability category of mental retardation.

Causes of Mental Retardation

- All of the more than 250 known causes of mental retardation are biological.
- Etiology is unknown for most individuals with mild mental retardation. Increasing evidence, however, suggests that psychosocial disadvantage in early childhood is a major cause of mild mental retardation.

Educational Approaches

- Curriculum should focus on functional skills that will help the student be successful in self-care, vocational, domestic, community, and leisure domains.
- Applied behavior analysis is widely used in teaching students with mental retardation. Major components include task analysis, direct and frequent measurement, repeated opportunities to respond, systematic feedback, transfer of stimulus control from teacher-provided cues and prompts to natural stimuli, and programming for generalization and maintenance.

Educational Placement Alternatives

- Although some children with mental retardation attend special schools, most are educated in their neighborhood schools—either in special classes or in regular classes where they receive special help or attend a resource room for part of the day.
- Many children with mild retardation are educated in regular classrooms, with extra help provided as needed. They can generally master standard academic skills up to about a sixth-grade level.
- Students with moderate mental retardation are usually taught communication, self-help and daily living skills, and vocational skills, along with limited academics. Most children with moderate mental retardation are educated in self-contained classrooms.
- Despite their severe disabilities, people with severe and profound mental retardation can learn. Curricula stress functional communication and self-help skills.

Current Issues and Future Trends

- Recent court cases have extended and affirmed the rights of persons with mental retardation. Advocates can help protect the rights of individuals with mental retardation.
- Recent scientific advances—including genetic counseling, amniocentesis, CVS, virus vaccines, and early screening tests—are helping reduce the incidence of clinical or biologically caused retardation.
- Although early identification and intensive educational services to high-risk infants show promise, there is still no widely used technique to decrease the incidence of mental retardation caused by psychosocial disadvantage.
- The current goal is to make the lives of people with mental retardation—at home, in school, and at work—as normal as possible. Thus, we must develop normalized and effective training and transition programs and community services for individuals with mental retardation and work to change public attitudes.

For More Information

Journals

- *American Journal on Mental Retardation.* Published bimonthly by the American Association on Mental Retardation, 1719 Kalorama Road, NW, Washington, DC 20009. Publishes empirical studies, reviews of research, and theoretical articles dealing with the behavioral, social, and biological aspects of mental retardation.
- *Education and Training in Mental Retardation and Developmental Disabilities.* Published four times per school year by the Division on Mental Retardation, Council for Exceptional Children, 1920 Association Drive, Reston, VA 22091-1589. Publishes experimental studies and discussion articles dealing with the education of individuals with mental retardation.
- *Mental Retardation.* Published bimonthly by the American Association on Mental Retardation, 1719 Kalorama Road, NW, Washington, DC 20009. Concerned with new approaches to methodology, critical summaries, essays, program descriptions, and research studies dealing with all aspects of mental retardation.
- *Research in Developmental Disabilities.* Published quarterly by Pergamon Press, Maxwell House, Fairview Park, Elmsford, NY 10535. Publishes original behavioral research and theory on severe and pervasive developmental disabilities. Also covers the legal and ethical aspects of applying treatment procedures to children and adults with mental retardation.
- The following journals regularly publish applications of behavior analysis with learners who have mental retardation: *Behavior Modification, Journal of Applied Behavior Analysis, Journal of The Association for Persons with Severe Handicaps,* and *Journal of Behavioral Education.*

Books on Mental Retardation

- Beirne-Smith, M., Ittenbach, R., & Patton, J. R. (1998). *Mental retardation* (5th ed.). Upper Saddle River, NJ: Merrill/Prentice Hall.
- Hickson, L., Blackman. L. S., & Reis, E. M. (1995). *Mental retardation: Foundations of educational programming.* Boston: Allyn & Bacon.

- Hilton, A., & Ringlaben, R. (1998). *Best and promising practices in developmental disabilities*. Austin, TX: PRO-ED.
- McLaughlin, P. J., & Wehman, P. (1996). *Mental retardation and developmental disabilities* (2nd ed.). Austin, TX: PRO-ED.
- Mulick, J. A., & Antonak, R. (Eds.). (1985–1994). *Transitions in mental retardation* (Vols. 1–5). Norwood, NJ: Ablex.
- Robinson, G. A., Patton, J. R., Polloway, E. A., & Sargent, L. R. (Eds.). (1989). *Best practices in mild mental disabilities.* Reston, VA: Council for Exceptional Children.
- Smith, J. D. (1995). *Pieces of purgatory: Mental retardation in and out of institutions.* Pacific Grove, CA: Brooks/Cole.

Books on Applied Behavior Analysis and Behavioral Teaching Methods

- Alberto, P. A., & Troutman, A. C. (1999). *Applied behavior analysis for teachers* (5th ed.). Upper Saddle River, NJ: Merrill/Prentice Hall.
- Cooper, J. O., Heron, T. E., & Heward, W. L. (1987). *Applied behavior analysis.* Upper Saddle River, NJ: Merrill/Prentice Hall.
- Lovitt, T. C. (1995). *Tactics for teaching* (2nd ed.). Upper Saddle River, NJ: Merrill/Prentice Hall.
- Schloss, P. J., & Smith, M. A. (1994). *Applied behavior analysis in the classroom.* Needham Heights, MA: Allyn & Bacon.
- Sulzer-Azaroff, B., & Mayer, G. R. (1991). *Behavior analysis for lasting change.* New York: Holt, Rinehart, & Winston.
- Wolery, M., Ault, M. J., & Doyle, P. M. (1992). *Teaching students with moderate to severe disabilities.* New York: Longman.
- Wolery, M., Bailey, D. B., & Sugai, G. M. (1988). *Effective teaching: Principles and procedures of applied behavior analysis.* Needham Heights, MA: Allyn & Bacon.

Organizations

- *American Association on Mental Retardation* (AAMR), 444 North Capital Street, NW, Suite 486, Washington, DC 20001-1512; (202) 387-1968 or (800) 424-3688; fax: (202) 387-2193; e-mail: info@aamr.org; website: http://www.aamr.org. The oldest and largest interdisciplinary organization of professionals (researchers, teacher educators, and psychologists) concerned about mental retardation and related disabilities. Mission is to advance the knowledge and skills of professionals in the field of mental retardation by exchanging information and ideas.
- *The Arc* (formerly the Association for Retarded Citizens), 500 East Border Street, Suite 300, Arlington, TX 76010; (817) 261-6003; fax: (817) 277-3491; website: http://TheArc.org. An advocacy organization consisting primarily of parents and family members, with active local chapters in most states. Promotes the general welfare of individuals with mental retardation of all ages and in all settings.
- *Division on Mental Retardation and Developmental Disabilities* (MRDD), Council for Exceptional Children, 1920 Association Drive, Reston, VA 22091. With more than 7,500 members, MRDD works to promote professional growth and research to advance programs for persons with mental retardation and developmental disabilities.
- *National Association for Down Syndrome,* P.O. Box 4542, Oak Brook, IL 60522-4542; (708) 325-9112; website: http://www.nads.org. Founded by parents in 1961 to create a better environment and bring about understanding and acceptance of people with Down syndrome.

Chapter 7

Learning Disabilities

Focus Questions

- Why has the concept of learning disabilities proven so difficult to define?
- Do most students who are identified as learning disabled have a true disability? Or are they just low achievers or victims of poor instruction?
- What are the most important skills for an elementary-age student with learning disabilities to master? A secondary student?
- How do basic academic skills and learning strategies relate to each other?
- Should all students with learning disabilities be educated in the regular classroom?

No area of special education has experienced as much rapid growth, extreme interest, and continuing controversy as learning disabilities. The number of children identified as learning disabled has nearly tripled since the passage of IDEA, making this category the largest in special education and fueling an ongoing debate over the nature of the learning disability concept. Some believe the increase in the number of children identified as learning disabled indicates the true extent of the disability. Others contend that too many low achievers—children without a disability who are simply doing poorly in school—have been improperly identified as learning disabled, placing a severe strain on the limited resources available to serve those students challenged by true learning disabilities.

The term learning disabilities *was coined by Samuel Kirk in an address in 1963 to a group of parents whose children were experiencing serious difficulties in learning to read, were hyperactive, or could not solve math problems.*

Go to the companion website at http://www.prenhall.com/heward and select Chapter 7 to review the chapter objectives.

More information about learning disabilities can be found by accessing the Resources Module for Chapter 7 at http://www.prenhall.com/heward and linking to the Special Ed Resource Page and the "general and disability information."

To see how learning disabilities are defined from the perspectives of adults with learning disabilities, see Reiff, Gerber, and Ginsburg (1993). The August/September 1992 issue of Journal of Learning Disabilities *and the summer 1993 issue of* Learning Disability Quarterly *are devoted to issues and programs concerning adults with learning disabilities.*

There is considerable confusion and disagreement among professionals and parents on even the most basic question: what is a learning disability? In some ways, learning disabilities brings out both the worst and the best that special education has to offer. Learning disabilities has served as a breeding ground for fads and miracle treatments ("New Vitamin and Diet Regimen Cures Learning Disabilities!"). At the same time, some of the most innovative teachers and scholars in special education have devoted their careers to learning disabilities. And numerous methods of instruction first developed for students with learning disabilities have influenced and benefited the entire field of education.

Defining Learning Disabilities

More than 40 definitions for learning disabilities have been proposed, but none has been universally accepted. The two definitions that have had the most influence are the federal definition in IDEA and a definition proposed by the National Joint Committee on Learning Disabilities.

The Definition in IDEA

IDEA defines *specific learning disability* as

> a disorder in one or more of the basic psychological processes involved in understanding or in using language, spoken or written, which may manifest itself in an imperfect ability to listen, think, speak, read, write, spell, or to do mathematical calculations. The term includes such conditions as perceptual handicaps, brain injury, minimal brain dysfunction, dyslexia, and developmental aphasia. The term does not include children who have learning problems which are primarily the result of visual, hearing or motor handicaps, of mental retardation, or of environmental, cultural, or economic disadvantages. (U.S. Office of Education, 1977b, p. 65083)

The NJCLD Definition

The National Joint Committee on Learning Disabilities (NJCLD), a group composed of official representatives from 10 professional organizations involved with students with learning disabilities, believes that the federal definition of learning disabilities contains several inherent weaknesses (Myers & Hammill, 1990):

1. *Exclusion of adults.* Learning disabilities can occur at all ages, and the IDEA definition refers only to school-age children.
2. *Reference to basic psychological processes.* Use of the phrase "basic psychological processes" has generated extensive and perhaps unnecessary debate over how to teach students with learning disabilities, and how to teach is a curricular issue, not a definitional one. The NJCLD believes the intent of the original phrase was only to show that a learning disability is intrinsic to the person affected.
3. *Inclusion of spelling as a learning disability.* Because spelling can be subsumed under "written expression," it is redundant and should be eliminated from the definition.
4. *Inclusion of obsolete terms.* The NJCLD believes that inclusion of terms such as *dyslexia, minimal brain dysfunction, perceptual impairments,* and *developmental aphasia,* which historically have proven difficult to define, only adds confusion to the definition.
5. *Wording of the exclusion clause.* The final clause in the IDEA definition suggests that learning disabilities cannot occur along with other disabilities. A more accurate statement, according to the NJCLD, is that a person may have a learning disability along with another disability but not *because of* another disability.

In response to these problems with the federal definition, the NJCLD proposed the following definition:

> Learning disabilities is a general term that refers to a heterogeneous group of disorders manifested by significant difficulties in the acquisition and use of listening, speaking, reading, writing, reasoning, or mathematical abilities. These disorders are intrinsic to the individual and presumed to be due to central nervous system dysfunction, and may appear across the life span. Problems in self-regulatory behaviors, social perception, and social interaction may exist with learning disabilities but do not themselves constitute a learning disability. Although learning disabilities may occur concomitantly with other handicapping conditions (for example, sensory impairment, mental retardation, serious emotional disturbance) or with extrinsic influences (such as cultural differences, insufficient or inappropriate instruction), they are not the result of those conditions or influences. (National Joint Committee on Learning Disabilities, 1989, p. 1)

The NJCLD's requirement that the disorder is "intrinsic to the individual and presumed to be due to central nervous system dysfunction" can be seen as an effort to limit the use of the term learning disabilities *to the "hard core" or severely learning disabled. For additional rationale and discussion of the NJCLD definition, see Hammill (1990), Myers and Hammill (1990), and the summer 1998 issue of* Learning Disability Quarterly.

Putting the Definition to Work

When operationalizing the definition for the purpose of identifying students with learning disabilities, most states and school districts require that three criteria be met:

1. A severe discrepancy between the student's intellectual ability and academic achievement
2. An exclusion criterion
3. A need for special education services

Mercer, Jordan, Allsopp, and Mercer (1995) surveyed all 50 states and found that the majority use the IDEA definition of learning disabilities or some variation of it.

IQ-Achievement Discrepancy Learning disabilities are characterized by an unexpected difference between general ability and achievement—a discrepancy that would not be predicted by the student's general intellectual ability. Children who are having minor or temporary difficulties in learning should not be identified as learning disabled. The term is meant to identify children with a true disability, which, according to federal guidelines, is evidenced by a "severe discrepancy between achievement and intellectual ability" (U.S. Office of Education, 1977b, p. 65083). The most common practice for determining if a severe discrepancy exists involves comparing a student's score on an IQ test with his score from a standardized achievement test. While such a comparison seems simple on the surface, in practice it is fraught with problems.

The federal government proposed several mathematical formulas for determining a severe discrepancy. All of the proposed formulas were eventually rejected, and the final rules and regulations for IDEA did not contain a specific definition of and formula for determining a severe discrepancy. This left states to find their own criteria for implementing the definition of learning disabilities. For example, the Ohio Department of Education devised the following formula for determining if the severe discrepancy criterion is met:

(ii) The following shall be used in computing the discrepancy score:
  (a) From:
    (i) The score obtained for the measure of intellectual ability,
    (ii) Minus the mean of the measure of intellectual ability,
    (iii) Divided by the standard deviation of the measure of intellectual ability.
  (b) Subtract:
    (i) The score obtained for the measure of achievement,
    (ii) Minus the mean of the measure of achievement,
    (iii) Divided by the standard deviation of the measure of achievement.
  (c) The result of this computation equals the discrepancy score. If the discrepancy score is two or greater than two, a severe discrepancy exists. (Rules for the Education of Handicapped Children, effective July 1, 1982, p. 69)

"The various additions, subtractions, divisions, and ratios generated by these formulas are essentially meaningless and, in all cases, misleading" (Reynolds, 1992, p. 4). Confusion and disagreement over exactly how a severe discrepancy should be determined have led to widely differing procedures for identifying and classifying students as learning disabled (Finlan, 1992; Stanovich, 1991). As a result, the percentage of children identified as learning disabled ranges across states from a low of 2.9% of the total school-age population in Georgia to 9.2% in Massachusetts (U.S. Department of Education, 1997).

For detailed discussion of the problems associated with the discrepancy concept and recommended approaches and alternatives, see Fletcher et al. (1998) and Mercer (1997).

The Council for Learning Disabilities (CLD, 1986) published a position statement citing eight reasons for opposing the use of discrepancy formulas, making these recommendations: (1) that discrepancy formulas be phased out as required procedure for identifying individuals with learning disabilities; (2) that when discrepancy formulas must be used, they be used with extreme caution; and (3) that the results of discrepancy formulas should never be used to dictate whether an individual has a learning disability. In lieu of discrepancy formulas, CLD recommends improved comprehensive multidisciplinary assessment of all areas of learning disabilities identified by federal rules and regulations (oral expression, listening comprehension, and writing expression, in addition to reading and mathematics).

The May 1997 issue of Journal of Learning Disabilities *contains a special series of articles discussing the co-occurrence of learning disabilities with other disability conditions.*

Exclusion The IDEA definition of learning disabilities is meant to identify students with significant learning problems that are not "primarily the result" of mental retardation, sensory impairment, emotional disturbance, or lack of opportunity to learn due to environmental, cultural, or economic conditions. The word "primarily" in the definition recognizes that learning disabilities can coexist with other disabilities; but when that is considered the case, the student typically receives services under the other disability category. For example, some children whose primary diagnosis is mental retardation do not achieve up to their expected potential (Polloway, Patton, Smith, & Buck, 1997).

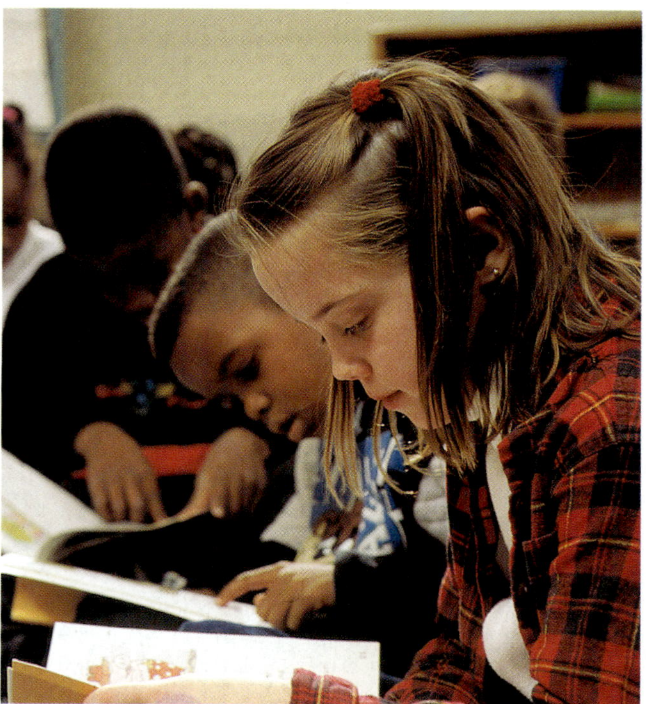

Students with learning disabilities experience significant learning difficulties that cannot be explained by mental retardation, sensory impairment, emotional disturbance, or lack of educational opportunity.

Need for Special Education Students with learning disabilities are those who show specific and severe learning problems despite normal educational efforts and therefore need specially designed instruction that is tailored (i.e., specially designed) to meet their unique needs (Simmons, Kameenui, & Chard, 1998). This criterion is meant to avoid the overidentification of children who have not had the opportunity to learn (NJCLD, 1998). Such children should progress normally as soon as they receive typically effective instruction at a curricular level appropriate to their current skills.

Fuchs and Fuchs (1998) describe how curriculum-based measurement can be used to distinguish students with learning disabilities from students whose low achievement is due primarily to ineffective instruction.

Characteristics of Students with Learning Disabilities

To describe the various categories of exceptionality, observers typically list the physical and psychological characteristics often exhibited by the individuals who make up that group. The inherent danger in such lists is the tendency to assume, or at least to look for, *each* of those characteristics in *all* of the children considered to be in the category. This danger is especially troublesome with learning disabilities because the category includes children who exhibit a wide range of learning, social, and emotional problems. In fact, Mercer (1997) suggests that it is theoretically possible for an individual with learning disabilities to exhibit one of more than 500,000 combinations of cognitive or socioemotional problems.

Check your ongoing understanding of Chapter 7 concepts by using the Guided Review Module at http://www.prenhall.com/heward.

Most students with learning disabilities show one or more of the following characteristics: reading problems, deficits in written language, underachievement in math, social skills deficits, problems with attention and hyperactivity, and behavioral problems.

*For example, early in the field's history a task force commissioned to identify the characteristics of children with learning disabilities (the term **minimal brain dysfunction** was used to describe these children at that time) found that 99 separate characteristics were reported in the literature (Clements, 1966).*

Reading Problems

Difficulty with reading is by far the most common characteristic of students with learning disabilities. It is estimated that at least 80% of all children identified as learning disabled are referred for special education services because of reading problems (Lerner, 1993). Some professionals now believe the term *learning disabilities*, because it encompasses so many different types of learning problems, hinders our understanding of the causes, developmental courses, and outcomes of the reading problems experienced by many children (Lyon, 1995; Stanovich, 1993). They recommend developing specific definitions and research bases in each type of learning disability (e.g. reading disabilities, math disabilities).

*The term **dyslexia** is also used to refer to reading disabilities. For a discussion and definition of dyslexia as a distinct type of learning disabilities, see Lyon (1995).*

Evidence suggests that reading disabilities are a persistent deficit, not simply a developmental lag in linguistic or basic reading skills (Grossen, 1998). Children who fail to learn to read by the first grade tend to fall farther and farther behind their peers, not only in reading but in general academic achievement as well. For example, longitudinal studies have found that 74% of children who are diagnosed as learning disabled because of reading problems remain disabled in the ninth grade (Fletcher et al., 1994; Stanovich & Siegel, 1994).

Recent research has begun to reveal a great deal about the fundamental nature of children's reading disabilities and the type of instruction most likely to prevent and remediate reading problems (Stanovich & Stanovich, 1995; Torgesen, in press). In summarizing this research, Torgesen and Wagner (1998) state that (1) the "most severe reading problems of children with learning disabilities lie at the word, rather than the text, level of processing" (i.e., inability to accurately and fluently decode single words), and (2) the most common cognitive limitation of these children involves a dysfunction in the awareness of the phonological structure of words in oral language (p. 226).

To learn what research tells us about how to prevent reading disabilities in young children, see "Six Principles for Early Reading Instruction."

Six Principles for Early Reading Instruction

by Bonnie Grossen

Extensive research by the National Institute of Child Health and Human Development (NICHD) over the last 30 years has produced more than 2,000 peer-reviewed journal articles about early reading acquisition and reading difficulties (see Lyon [1995] for a review). Six key principles of effective beginning reading instruction can be derived from this growing body of highly replicable scientific findings (Grossen, 1997):

1. *Begin teaching phonemic awareness directly in kindergarten.* Phonemes are the individual sounds in words that make a difference in meaning if changed. Children and adults who cannot read are not aware of phonemes. Children and adults who can read are aware of phonemes. A child is phonemically aware if she can do some of these things (Stanovich, 1994):

   - *Phoneme deletion.* What word would be left if the /k/ sound were taken away from "cat"?
   - *Word to word matching.* Do "pen" and "pipe" begin with the same sound?
   - *Blending.* What word would we have if you put these sounds together: /s/, /a/, /t/?
   - *Sound isolation.* What is the first sound in "rose"?
   - *Phoneme segmentation.* What sounds do you hear in the word "hot"?
   - *Phoneme counting.* How many sounds do you hear in the word "cake"?
   - *Odd word out.* What word starts with a different sound: "bag," "nine," "beach," "bike"?
   - *Sound to word matching.* Is there a /k/ sound in "bike"?

   If phonemic awareness does not develop by age 5 or 6, it is unlikely to develop later without instruction. In other words, don't wait for this crucial reading readiness skill to develop. Phonemic awareness activities such as rhyming games have a positive effect on reading acquisition and spelling for nonreaders (Torgesen, 1998). It has been estimated that reading disabilities could be reduced from the current level of 20% to less than 2% of the population with explicit instruction in phonemic awareness in kindergarten. Teachers should start teaching phonemic awareness before beginning instruction in letter-phoneme relationships and continue phonemic awareness activities while teaching the letter-phoneme relationships.

2. *Teach each letter-phoneme relationship explicitly.* Phonemic awareness alone is not sufficient. Explicit, systematic instruction in common letter-sound correspondences is also necessary for many children. Telling the children explicitly what single sound a given letter or letter combination makes prevents reading problems better than encouraging the child to figure out the sounds for the letters by giving clues. Many children have difficulty figuring out the individual letter-phoneme correspondences if they hear them only in the context of words and word parts. Therefore, phonemes must be separated from words for instruction. For example, the teacher should show the children the letter "m" and say, "This letter says /mmm/."

   A new phoneme and other phonemes the children have learned should be briefly practiced for about five minutes each day in isolation. The rest of the lesson should use these phonemes in words and stories composed of only the letter-phoneme relationships the children have learned in isolation up to that point.

3. *Teach frequent, highly regular letter-sound relationships systematically.* Only about 40 to 50 letter-sound relationships are necessary to read. (Writing requires about 70 letter-sound relationships.) Figure A shows the 48 most regular letter-phoneme relationships. (The given sounds for each of the letters and letter groups are either the most frequent sound or occur at least 75% of the time.)

   To teach systematically means coordinating the introduction of the letter-phoneme relationships with the material the children are asked to read. The words and stories should be composed of only the letter-phoneme relationships they have learned, so all the children must be taught using the same sequence. The order of the introduction of letter-phoneme relationships should be planned to allow reading material composed of meaningful words and stories as soon as possible. For example, if the first three letter-phoneme relationships the children learn are /a/, /b/, /c/, the only real word the children can read is "cab." But if the first three letter-phoneme relationships are /m/, /a/, /s/, the children can read "am," "Sam," "mass," "ma'am."

The integration of phonics and reading can only occur with decodable text.

4. *Show children exactly how to sound out words.* After children have learned two or three letter-phoneme relationships, teach them how to blend the sounds into words. Show them how to move sequentially from left to right through spellings as they sound out each spelling. Every day practice blending words composed of only the letter-phoneme relationships the children have learned.
5. *Give children connected, decodable text to practice the letter-phoneme relationships.* Children need extensive practice applying their knowledge of letter-phoneme relationships to the task of reading. This integration of phonics and reading can only occur with the use of *decodable text*—text composed of words that use the letter-phoneme relationships the children have learned to that point and a limited number of sight words that have been systematically taught. As the children learn more letter-phoneme relationships, the texts become more sophisticated in meaning.

Texts that are less decodable do not integrate phonological knowledge with actual reading. For example, the first sentence children read in one meaning-based pro-

a as in "fat"	**i** as in "sit"	**r**	**er** as in "fern"
g as in "goat"	**c** as in "cat"	**o-e** as in "pole"	**qu** as in "quick"
v	**w** as in "well"	**z**	**ai** as in "maid"
m	**f**	**ch** as in "chip"	**ay** as in "hay"
l	**b**	**ou** as in "cloud"	**sh** as in "shop"
e	**j**	**kn** as in "know"	**ar** as in "car"
t	**a-e** as in "cake"	**ea** as in "beat"	**igh** as in "high"
h	**n**	**oy** as in "toy"	**th** as in "thank"
u-e as in "use"	**i-e** as in "pipe"	**oa** as in "boat"	**au** as in "haul"
s	**d**	**ee** as in "need"	**ew** as in "shrewd"
u	**k**	**ph** as in "phone"	**ir** as in "first"
p	**y** as in "yuck"	**oi** as in "boil"	**aw** as in "lawn"

Figure A The 48 most regular letter-sound relationships

gram that added an unintegrated phonics component was "The dog is up." The sound-letter relationships the children had learned up to this point were /d/, /m/, /s/, /r/, /t/. By applying their phonics knowledge, the children could only read "_____ d_____ _____ _____." But if children have learned /a/, /s/, /m/, /b/, /t/, /h/, /f/, /g/, /i/, they can read "Sam has a big fist." The sentence is 100% decodable because the phonics component has been integrated properly into the child's real reading.

Text that is less decodable requires children to use prediction or context to figure out words. Though prediction is valuable in comprehension for predicting the next event or predicting an outcome, research indicates that it is not useful in word recognition. Consider the following sample of authentic text by Jack London. One child was able to decode approximately 80% of the text; the parts he was unable to decode accurately are omitted.

> He had never seen dogs fight as these w_____ish c_____ f_____t, and his first ex_____ t_____t him an unf_____able l_____n. It is true, it was a vi_____ ex_____, else he would not have lived to pr_____it by it. Curly was the v_____. They were camped near the log store, where she, in her friend_____ way, made ad_____ to a husky dog the size of a full-_____ wolf, th_____ not half so large as _____he. _____ere was no w_____ing, only a leap in like a flash, a met_____ clip of teeth, a leap out equal_____ swift, and Curly's face was ripped open from eye to jaw.

The use of predictable text rather than decodable text might allow children to use prediction to figure out a passage. However, the strategy would not transfer to real reading, as the London passage demonstrates. Predictable text gives children false success. While such success may motivate many children, ultimately they will not be successful readers if they rely on text predictability to read.

6. *Use interesting stories to develop language comprehension.* Research does not rule out the use of interesting, authentic stories to develop language comprehension. But it does recommend not using these stories as reading material for nonreaders. Any text controlled for decodability or vocabulary will not provide entire coherent stories in the early stages of reading acquisition. During this stage, children can benefit from stories the teacher reads to them. Teacher-read stories play an important role in building children's oral language comprehension, which ultimately affects their reading comprehension. Story-based activities should be structured to build comprehension skills, not decoding skills.

Using real stories to develop comprehension should be balanced with the decoding instruction described in the first five principles. While children are learning to decode, instruction for comprehension and instruction for decoding should be conducted separately; but both types of instruction should occur. In other words, balance but don't mix. A common misconception is that the teacher should teach letter-phoneme relationships in the context of real stories. This mixture of decoding and comprehension instruction in the same instructional activity is clearly less effective, even when the decoding instruction is fairly structured. The inferiority of instructional activities with mixed goals (embedded phonics) has been demonstrated in several studies (Foorman, Francis, Fletcher, Schatschneider, & Mehta, 1998; Torgesen, Wagner, & Rashotte, 1997).

During the early stages of reading acquisition, children's oral language comprehension level is much higher than their reading comprehension level. The stories read to children to build their comprehension should be geared to their oral language comprehension level. The material used to build children's decoding should be geared to their decoding skills, with attention to meaning. Though decodable text can be meaningful and engaging, it will not build children's comprehension skills nor teach them new vocabulary to the extent that might be needed. Comprehension strategies and new vocabulary should be taught using orally presented stories and texts that are more sophisticated than the early decodable text the children read. The teacher should read these stories to the children and discuss the meaning with them. After the children become fluent decoders, they can apply these comprehension strategies to their own reading.

Bonnie Grossen is a research associate at the University of Oregon. Her interests include identifying the best interventions for solving educational problems, especially in the areas of reading and science instruction, critical thinking, and problem solving for diverse learners.

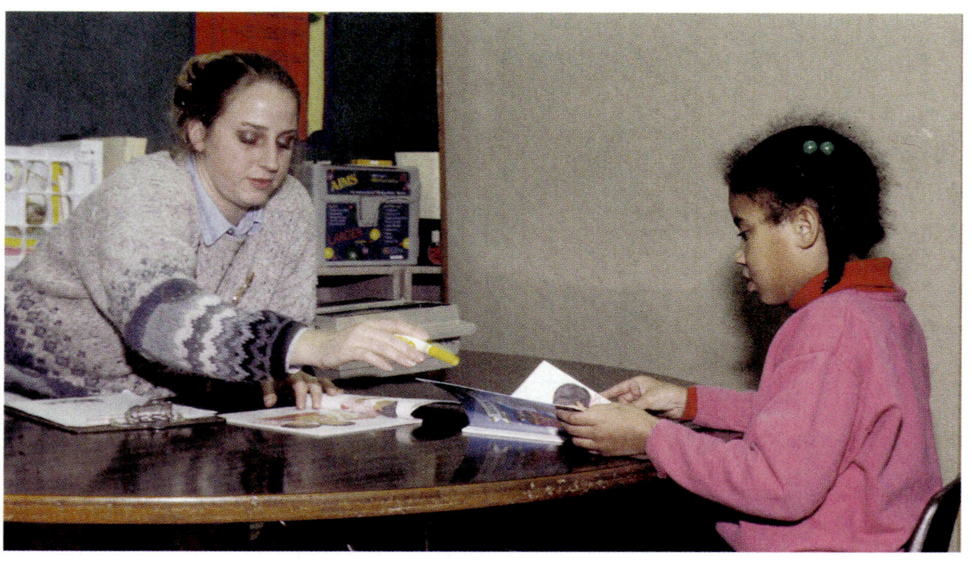

Learning to read is the most common academic problem experienced by students with learning disabilities.

Written Language Deficits

Many students with learning disabilities have problems with writing and spelling. When compared to their peers without disabilities, students with learning disabilities perform significantly lower across most written expression tasks, especially vocabulary, grammar, punctuation, and spelling (Newcomer & Barenbaum, 1991) (see Table 7.1).

Compounding the weak language base that many students with learning disabilities bring to the writing task is an approach to the writing process that involves minimal planning, effort, and metacognitive control (Englert, Raphael, Anderson, Anthony, Stevens, & Fear, 1991; Graham & Harris, 1993). Many of these students use a "retrieve-and-write" approach in which they retrieve from immediate memory "whatever seems appropriate and write it down" (De La Paz & Graham, 1997, p. 295). They seldom use the self-regulation and self-assessment strategies of competent writers: setting a goal or plan to guide their writing, organizing their ideas, drafting, self-assessing, and rewriting. As a result, they produce poorly organized compositions containing a few poorly developed ideas (Sexton, Harris, & Graham, 1998).

Fortunately, the writing and spelling skills of most students with learning disabilities can be improved through explicit instruction that includes frequent opportunities to practice writing with feedback (Goddard & Heron, 1998; Graham & Harris, 1988; Heward, Heron, Gardner, & Prayzer, 1991). For example, the two stories in Figure 7.1 show noticeable improvements in the writing of a 13-year-old student with learning disabilities. He wrote Story 8 before instruction and Story 33 after 21 days of explicit instruction focusing on the use of adjectives.

For ideas on how to help students use the Internet to improve their writing skills, see Smith, Bone, and Higgins (1998).

Table 7.1 Written language sample from a 10-year-old student in response to the prehistoric illustration story starter from the Test of Written Language—2 (Hammill & Larsen, 1988).

Sean's Written Story	Sean's Oral Reading of His Story
A loge tine ago they atene a cosnen they head to geatthere on fesee o One day tere were sane evesedbeats all gaseraned tesene in cladesn they hard a fest for 2 meanes.	A long time ago there were ancient cave men. They had to get their own food. One day there were some wildebeests. They all gathered them and killed them. They had a feast for two months.

Source: Courtesy of Timothy E. Heron, The Ohio State University.

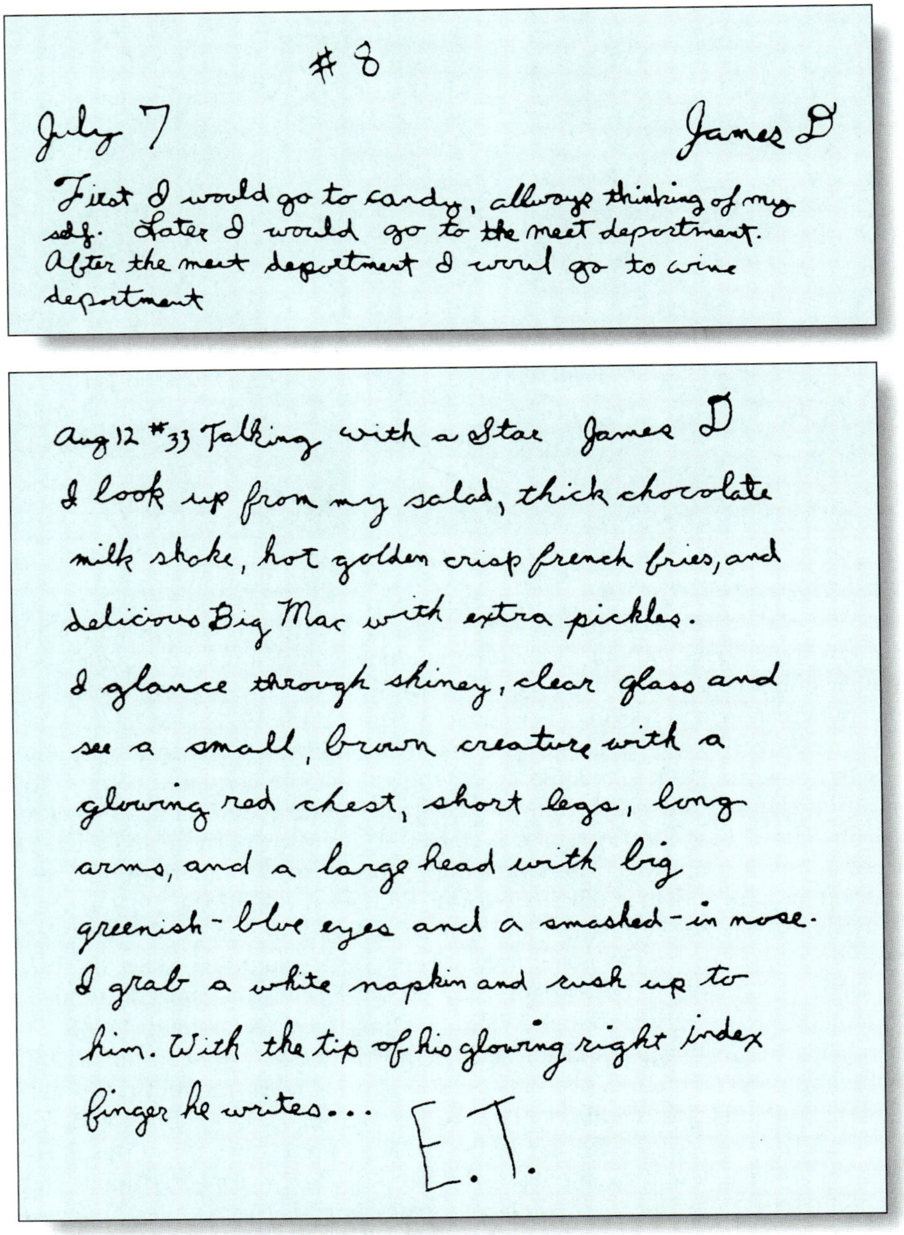

#8

July 7 James D

First I would go to candy, allways thinking of my self. Later I would go to the meet deportment. After the meet depottment I woul go to wine department

Aug 12 #33 Talking with a Star James D

I look up from my salad, thick chocolate milk shake, hot golden crisp french fries, and delicious Big Mac with extra pickles. I glance through shiney, clear glass and see a small, brown creature with a glowing red chest, short legs, long arms, and a large head with big greenish-blue eyes and a smashed-in nose. I grab a white napkin and rush up to him. With the tip of his glowing right index finger he writes... E.T.

Figure 7.1 Two stories written by a 13-year-old student with learning disabilities
Source: Adapted from Hassett, M. E., Engler, C., Cooke, N. L., Test, D. W., Weiss, A. B., Heward, W. L., & Heron, T. E. (1984). A telephone-managed, home-based summer writing program for LD adolescents. In W. L. Heward, T. E. Heron, D. S. Hill, & J. Trap-Porter (Eds.), *Focus on behavior analysis in education* (pp. 84–103). Upper Saddle River, NJ: Merrill/Prentice Hall. Used by permission.

The winter and spring 1996 issues of LD Forum *are devoted to teaching math to students with learning disabilities.*

Math Underachievement

Numerical reasoning and calculation pose major problems for many students with learning disabilities. One large-scale study of the characteristics of students with learning disabilities reported an average math score at approximately the 30th percentile (Kavale & Reese, 1992). As with reading and writing, direct instruction that provides repeated, meaningful practice with feedback usually improves the math performance of students with learning disabilities (e.g., Marsh & Cooke, 1996).

Tim's daily session in the "writing room" is spent practicing, self-evaluating, and self-editing the specific writing skills he needs to master.

Social Skills Deficits

After reviewing 152 different studies, Kavale and Forness (1996) concluded that about 75% of students with learning disabilities exhibit deficits in social skills. Poor social skills often lead to rejection, low social status, difficulty making friends, and loneliness—all of which are experienced by many students with learning disabilities regardless of classroom placement (Gresham & Reschly, 1986; Haager & Vaughn, 1995; Ochoa & Palmer, 1995).

Some students with learning disabilities, however, experience no problems getting along with their peers and teachers. After reviewing the published studies on the social status of learning disabled students, Dudley-Marling and Edmiaston (1985) concluded that, as a group, learning disabled individuals are at greater risk for attaining low social status but that some students with learning disabilities are, in fact, popular. Sabornie and Kauffman (1986) reported no significant difference in the sociometric standing of 46 learning disabled high school students and 46 peers without disabilities. Moreover, they discovered that some of the students with learning disabilities enjoyed socially rewarding experiences in inclusive classrooms.

One interpretation of these contradictory findings is that social competence and peer acceptance is not a characteristic of learning disabilities but an outcome of the different social climates created by teachers, peers, parents, and others with whom students with learning disabilities interact. This interpretation is supported by the authors of a study of 210 students with and without learning disabilities in grades 3 to 10. The authors found that students with learning disabilities in classes where they are accepted by their teachers were not less well liked or less well known by their classmates than students from other achievement groups (Vaughn, McIntosh, Schumm, Haager, & Callwood, 1993). In fact, Vaughn et al. found that approximately 90% of the students in their study had a mutual best friend, which was slightly better than either low-achieving or high-achieving students without disabilities.

Another interpretation is that the concept of learning disabilities is poorly defined and functions as a catch-all category for any student who is experiencing learning problems and who does not meet eligibility requirements for other disability categories.

Coleman and Minnett (1992) recommend "studying children who are socially successful despite limited academic success [as] a profitable avenue for identifying social skills that may be useful to other children with LD" (p. 244). Toward that end, researchers have begun to identify the types of problems experienced by children with learning disabilities who are ranked low in social acceptance and to discover instructional arrangements that promote the social status of students with learning disabilities in the regular classroom (Bryan, 1997; Vaughn, Elbaum, & Schumm, 1996).

More information about ADHD can be found by accessing the Resources Module for Chapter 7 at http://www.prenhall.com/heward and linking to the Special Ed Resource page and the "general and disability information."

Attention Problems and Hyperactivity

Attention deficit (the inability to attend to a task) and hyperactivity (high rates of purposeless movement) are frequently cited as characteristics of children with learning disabilities. The term currently used to describe this combination of behavioral traits is

See "Signaling for Help" in Chapter 1 to find out how one learning disabilities resource room teacher helps her students stay on task while working at their desks.

attention-deficit hyperactivity disorder (ADHD). Children are diagnosed as having ADHD according to criteria found in the *Diagnostic and Statistical Manual of Mental Disorders (DSM-IV)* (American Psychiatric Association, 1994). "The essential feature of attention-deficit/hyperactivity disorder is a persistent pattern of inattention and/or hyperactivity-impulsivity that is more frequent and severe than is typically observed in individuals at a comparable level of development" (p. 78). To diagnose ADHD, a physician must determine that a child consistently displays six or more symptoms of either inattention or hyperactivity-impulsivity for a period of at least six months (see Figure 7.2).

The diagnostic criteria for ADHD are so diverse and subjective (e.g., how does one decide if a person is "on the go"?) that a child who is not diagnosed by one physician may very well be diagnosed by the next doctor who evaluates her. Parents have been known to engage in "physician shopping," taking their child from one doctor to another until a diagnosis of ADHD is made (Reid, Maag, & Vasa, 1994). Goodman and Poillion's (1992) review of 48 articles and books on ADHD written by leading authorities revealed that 69 characteristics and 38 different causes of ADHD were proposed. Goodman and Poillion concluded that ADD was an acronym for "*A*ny *D*ysfunction or *D*ifficulty" (p. 37).

Estimates of the prevalence of ADHD range from 3% to 5% of all school-age children (American Psychiatric Association, 1994). These figures suggest that the typical classroom will have from one to three children either diagnosed as ADHD or presenting the problems typically associated with ADHD (DuPaul, Stoner, Tilly, & Putnam, 1991). A random national sample of family practitioners found that approximately 5% of all elementary students screened received a diagnosis of ADHD (Wolraich, Lindgren, Stromquist, Milich, Davis, & Watson, 1990).

The October/November 1993 issue of Exceptional Children *and the spring 1997 issue of* Teacher Education and Special Education *are devoted to the education of students with ADHD. Bender (1997) provides teachers and parents with practical strategies for teaching and living with children with ADHD.*

Although a considerable percentage of children with ADHD are also identified as having a learning disability—25% to 50% depending upon the school district (Shelton & Barkely, 1994)—it is important to stress that ADHD is not the same as a learning disability. Although some children with learning disabilities are hyperactive and inattentive (Silver [1990] estimates that 15% to 20% of children with learning disabilities have ADHD), many are calm and work hard at learning tasks. Many children without learning disabilities also have trouble attending and sitting still. Likewise, numerous children who display impulsivity, inattention, and/or hyperactivity do well in school. Although ADHD is not a disability category recognized by IDEA, children with ADHD can be served under the "other health impairments" category if the disorder results in limited alertness and adversely affects academic performance (U.S. Department of Education, 1997). Children with ADHD may also be eligible for services under Section 504 of the Rehabilitation Act.

Drug Therapy The most commonly prescribed treatment for ADHD is drug therapy. Methylphenidate, a member of the amphetamine family sold under the trade name Ritalin, is the most prescribed medication. Although amphetamines are stimulants that normally increase a person's activity level, they produce a paradoxical effect in many children; that is, a reduced level of activity typically follows ingestion of the drug.

An extended discussion of the use of psychotropic medication (behavior- and/or mood-altering drugs) is beyond the scope of this text. Gadow's (1986) book is an excellent source of information on this important topic for educators.

The number of children on stimulant medication has increased tremendously. A survey by the Baltimore County Health Department found that 5.9% of all elementary-age schoolchildren were receiving drug treatment for hyperactivity/inattentiveness (Safer & Krager, 1988). Given the results of nine previous biannual surveys, this figure represents a doubling of the rate of medication treatment for hyperactive/inattentive students every four to seven years. Singh and Ellis (1993) estimate that more than 1 million U.S. schoolchildren are given daily doses of stimulant medication in an effort to control hyperactivity and attention deficits.

Diagnostic Criteria for Attention-Deficit/Hyperactivity Disorder

A. Either (1) or (2):

(1) six (or more) of the following symptoms of *inattention* have persisted for at least 6 months to a degree that is maladaptive and inconsistent with developmental level:

Inattention

(a) often fails to give close attention to details or makes careless mistakes in schoolwork, work, or other activities
(b) often has difficulty sustaining attention in tasks or play activities
(c) often does not seem to listen when spoken to directly
(d) often does not follow through on instructions and fails to finish schoolwork, chores, or duties in the workplace (not due to oppositional behavior or failure to understand instructions)
(e) often has difficulty organizing tasks and activities
(f) often avoids, dislikes, or is reluctant to engage in tasks that require sustained mental effort (such as schoolwork or homework)
(g) often loses things necessary for tasks or activities (e.g., toys, school assignments, pencils, books, or tools)
(h) is often easily distracted by extraneous stimuli
(i) is often forgetful in daily activities

(2) six (or more) of the following symptoms of *hyperactivity-impulsivity* have persisted for at least 6 months to a degree that is maladaptive and inconsistent with developmental level:

Hyperactivity

(a) often fidgets with hands or feet or squirms in seat
(b) often leaves seat in classroom or in other situations in which remaining seated is expected
(c) often runs about or climbs excessively in situations in which it is inappropriate (in adolescents or adults, may be limited to subjective feelings of restlessness)
(d) often has difficulty playing or engaging in leisure activities quietly
(e) is often "on the go" or often acts as if "driven by a motor"
(f) often talks excessively

Impulsivity

(g) often blurts out answers before questions have been completed
(h) often has difficulty awaiting turn
(i) often interrupts or intrudes on others (e.g., butts into conversations or games)

B. Some hyperactive-impulsive or inattentive symptoms that caused impairment were present before age 7 years.

C. Some impairment from the symptoms is present in two or more settings (e.g., at school [or work] and at home).

D. There must be clear evidence of clinically significant impairment in social, academic, or occupational functioning.

E. The symptoms do not occur exclusively during the course of a Pervasive Developmental Disorder, Schizophrenia, or other Psychotic Disorder and are not better accounted for by another mental disorder (e.g., Mood Disorder, Anxiety Disorder, Dissociative Disorder, or a Personality Disorder).

Figure 7.2 Diagnostic criteria for attention-deficit hyperactivity disorder (ADHD)
Source: Reprinted with permission from the Diagnostic and Statistical Manual of Mental Disorders, Fourth Edition. Copyright 1994, American Psychiatric Association.

Although many physicians, parents, and teachers report positive results with stimulant therapy for children with learning disabilities or ADHD, results of controlled studies are mixed (Gadow, 1986; Swanson et al., 1993). After examining 341 published reviews of research on the effects of stimulant medication on children with ADHD, Swanson et al. (1993) reported these generalizations about what should be expected:

- Temporary management of overactivity, inattention, and impulsivity
- Temporary improvement of deportment, aggression, and increased academic output
- No improvement in long-term adjustment (academic achievement, arrest rate)
- Side effects such as increases in tics, disruptions in eating and sleeping patterns; possible negative effects on cognition

Howell, Evans, and Gardiner (1997) provide educators with guidelines for the safe use of stimulant medications in the classroom with optimal benefits.

A promising technique for evaluating the effects of drugs and determining appropriate dosage levels is direct and daily measurement of a student's performance on academic tasks during alternating drug and placebo conditions (e.g., Northup, Fusilier, Swanson, Roane, & Borrero, 1997; Stoner, Carey, Ikeda, & Shinn, 1994). It is difficult to predict the effects of stimulant medication on an individual child. The child's age, size, or weight cannot be used to determine the optimum dosage in terms of the desired effects on hyperactivity and safety.

Additional problems have been reported with children not taking their medication as prescribed, trying to catch up on missed pills by taking too many pills at once, and trading or even selling their medications (Hancock, 1996). Given the questionable benefits of drug therapy with children and the fact that undesirable side effects are sometimes noted (e.g., insomnia, decreased appetite, headaches, disruption of normal growth patterns, irritability, reduced emotional affect, increased blood pressure), some professionals now view drug treatment as an inappropriate, easy way out that might produce short-term improvements in behavior but result in long-term harm. "When stimulants work in the short-term, pharmacological intervention may be used as a crutch and may postpone or prevent the use of non-pharmacological interventions, which may be more effective in the long run" (Swanson et al., 1993, p. 158).

Behavioral Problems

Regardless of the interrelationships of these characteristics, teachers and other caregivers responsible for planning educational programs for students with learning disabilities need skills in dealing with social and behavioral difficulties as well as academic deficits. Some of these important teaching skills are described in Chapter 8.

Some students with learning disabilities display behavioral problems in the classroom. Research by Epstein and Cullinan and their colleagues has consistently found a higher-than-normal rate of behavioral problems among students with learning disabilities (Epstein, Bursuck, & Cullinan, 1985; Epstein, Cullinan, & Lloyd, 1986; Epstein, Cullinan, & Rosemier, 1983). In a study of 790 students enrolled in K–12 learning disabilities programs in Indiana, the percentage of students with behavioral problems (15%) remained consistent across grade levels (McLeskey, 1992). Although these data definitely show increased behavioral problems among children with learning disabilities, the relationships between the students' problem behavior and academic difficulty are not known. In other words, we do not know whether the academic deficits or the behavioral problems cause the other difficulty. As with ADHD, many children with learning disabilities exhibit no behavioral problems at all.

The Defining Characteristic

Although students who receive special education under the learning disabilities category are an extremely heterogeneous group, it is important to remember that the fundamental, defining characteristic of students with learning disabilities is *specific and significant achievement deficiency in the presence of adequate overall intelli-*

gence. By the time they reach high school, students with learning disabilities are the lowest of the low achievers, performing below the 10th percentile in reading, written language, and math (Hock, Schumaker, & Deshler, in press). The difficulties experienced by children with learning disabilities—especially for those who cannot read at grade level—are substantial and pervasive and usually last across the life span (see Table 7.2). As Hallahan (1998) points out, the tendency of many educators to think of learning disabilities as a mild disability detracts from the real needs of these students.

> Our reference to a learning disability as one of the "mild" disabilities reinforces the notion that a learning disability is little more than a minor inconvenience rather than the serious, life-long condition it often is. Such a nonchalant attitude toward learning disabilities, coupled with the slogan, "All children can learn," used by so many reformers has lulled many into thinking that students with learning disabilities will respond to a quick fix. Yes, all children can learn, but some do not learn as well as others, and some require intensive instruction to learn even the most basic skills. (p. 4)

Prevalence

Learning disabilities is by far the largest of all special education categories. During the 1996–1997 school year, 2.67 million children ages 6 to 21 received special education under the specific learning disabilities category (U.S. Department of Education, 1998). This figure represents 51% of all school-age children with disabilities and means that about 5 of every 100 students in the United States has a learning disability (U.S. Department of Education, 1998).

Males outnumber females by a 3-to-1 ratio across primary, elementary, and secondary age levels (Cone, Wilson, Bradley, & Reese, 1985; McLeskey, 1992).

The number of students identified with learning disabilities has grown tremendously since the passage of IDEA. The current number is nearly triple the number of students with learning disabilities who received special education in 1976–1977, the first year the federal government reported such data. Among the reasons cited by the government for the growth in the number of children with learning disabilities are "eligibility criteria that permit children with a wide range of learning problems to be classified as learning disabled; social acceptance and/or preference for the learning disabled classification; the reclassification of some mentally retarded children as learning disabled; and the lack of general education alternatives for children who are experiencing learning problems in regular classes" (U.S. Department of Education, 1986, p. 5).

During this same period, the percentage of school-age students receiving special education services under the category of mental retardation dropped from approximately one in every four students in 1976–1977 to one in nine students in 1996–1997. What factors might account for these changes? Do you think the two trends are related?

Many educators are alarmed by the rising prevalence figures for learning disabilities. They believe the ever-increasing numbers of students classified as learning disabled are the result of overidentification and misdiagnosis of low-achieving students, which reduces the resources available to serve the students who are truly learning disabled. Some authorities, however, believe the current number of students being served as learning disabled may not be a gross overestimate and may be closer to the truth than most people have previously thought. Hallahan (1992) points to the newness of the field of learning disabilities and social/cultural changes in society as two possible reasons for the increase in prevalence figures:

Table 7.3 lists some key historical events and their implications for students with learning disabilities.

> We have been engaged in the formal study of learning disabilities for only 20 to 30 years. Although 20 to 30 years may seem like a long time to a culture obsessed with youth, it is not much more than an eye blink to scientists engaged in serious study of a phenomenon as complex as learning disabilities, or to educators grappling to come up with the best ways to identify and educate these children. . . . The dramatic increase in students served as learning disabled may not be due to identification procedures run amok, as critics would have us believe. Instead, the increase may be, in part, a reflection of professionals' and parents' growing recognition of the condition of learning disabilities and how to deal with it. . . . I hypothesize that social/cultural changes over the past 20 to 40 years may have led to an increase in the prevalence of learning disabilities in two ways. First,

Table 7.2 A life-span view of learning disabilities

	Preschool	Grades K–1	Grades 2–6	Grades 7–12	Adult
Problem Areas	Achievement of developmental milestones (e.g., uses sentences) Receptive language Expressive language Visual perception Auditory perception Attention span Hyperactivity Self-regulation Social skills Concept formation	Academic readiness skills (e.g., alphabet knowledge) Receptive language Expressive language Visual perception Auditory perception Reasoning Motor development Attention span Hyperactivity Social skills	Reading skills Arithmetic skills Written expression Verbal expression Receptive language Attention span Hyperactivity Socio-emotional Reasoning Problem solving Self-regulation	Reading skills Arithmetic skills Written expression Verbal expression Listening skills Study skills Metacognition Socio-emotional/delinquency Problem solving Self-regulation	Reading skills Arithmetic skills Written expression Verbal expression Listening skills Study skills Socio-emotional Metacognition Vocational skills Life skills
Assessment Focus	Prediction of high risk for later learning problems within ecocultural perspective	Prediction of high risk for later learning problems within ecocultural perspective	Identification of learning disabilities within ecocultural perspective	Identification of learning disabilities within ecocultural perspective	Identification of learning disabilities within ecocultural perspective
Primary Treatment Types*	Preventative Collaborative	Preventative Corrective Collaborative	Remedial Corrective Collaborative Strategic	Remedial Corrective Collaborative Compensatory Strategic Proactive	Remedial Corrective Collaborative Compensatory Strategic Proactive
Treatments with Most Research or Expert Support	Direct instruction in language skills Behavioral management Parent education and involvement	Direct instruction in academic and language areas Behavioral management Parent education and involvement Cooperative learning	Direct instruction in academic areas Behavioral management Parent education and involvement Learning strategies Cooperative learning	Direct instruction in academics, social skills, and learning strategies Tutoring in academics Compensatory instruction Self-instruction training Teaming instruction Curriculum modifications	Direct instruction in academics, social skills, and learning strategies Tutoring in academics or vocational areas Compensatory instruction Self-instruction training Teaming instruction

**Collaborative*, from the teacher's perspective, primarily refers to instruction generated via teachers teaming; from the student's perspective it involves students teaming with each other during the learning process.

Strategic primarily refers to instruction that helps learners identify task demands, set goals, develop plans, coordinate resources, implement the plan, evaluate the plan, and modify the plan. It includes learning strategy instruction in metacognition and problem solving.

Proactive primarily refers to instruction that empowers the learners via self-instruction. The learners use resources and strategies to teach themselves.

Source: From Mercer, C. D. (1997). *Students with learning disabilities* (5th ed., pp. 20–21). Upper Saddle River, NJ: Merrill/Prentice Hall. Reprinted with permission.

Table 7.3 A history of the education of children with learning disabilities: Key events and implications

Date	Historical Event	Educational Implications
late 1930s–early 1940s	Research by Alfred Strauss and colleagues with children with mental retardation and brain injury at the Wayne County Training School in Michigan found relationships between brain injury and disorders that interfered with learning: perceptual disorders, perseveration, disorders of conceptual thinking, and behavioral problems such as hyperactivity and impulsivity.	In the book, *Psychopathology and Education of the Brain-Injured Child,* Strauss and Lara Lehtinen (1947) recommended strategies for relieving perceptual and conceptual disturbances of children with brain injury and thus reducing their symptomatic learning problems.
1950s–1960s	By the early 1950s, most public schools had established special education programs for children with mental retardation, sensory impairments, physical disabilities, and behavioral disorders. But there remained a group of children who were having serious learning problems at school, yet did not fit into any of the existing categories of exceptionality. They did not "look" disabled; the children seemed physically intact, yet they were unable to learn certain basic skills and subjects at school.	In searching for help with their children's problems, parents turned to other professionals—notably doctors, psychologists, and speech and language specialists. Understandably, these professionals viewed the children from the perspectives of their respective disciplines. As a result, terms such as *brain damage, minimal brain dysfunction, neurological impairment, perceptual handicap, dyslexia,* and *aphasia* were often used to describe and to account for the children's learning and behavior problems.
1963	The term *learning disabilities* was coined by Samuel Kirk in an address to a group of parents whose children were experiencing serious difficulties in learning to read, were hyperactive, or could not solve math problems.	The parents liked the term and, that very evening, voted to form the Association for Children with Learning Disabilities (ACLD).
1966	A national task force identified 99 different characteristics of children with *minimal brain dysfunction* (the term used at the time) reported in the literature (Clements, 1966).	The inherent danger in such lists is a tendency to assume that *each* of those characteristics is exhibited by *all* of the children considered to be in the category. This danger is especially troublesome with learning disabilities, because the children who make up the category are an extremely heterogeneous group.
mid 1960s–1970s	The concept of process, or ability, testing grew out of the belief that learning disabilities are caused by a basic underlying difficulty of the child to process, or use, environmental stimuli in the same way that children without disabilities do. Two of the most widely used process tests used for diagnosing and assessing learning disabilities were developed during this time: the Illinois Test of Psycholinguistic Abilities (ITPA) (Kirk, McCarthy, & Kirk, 1968) and the Marianne Frostig Developmental Test of Visual Perception (Frostig, Lefever, & Whittlesey, 1964).	The ability training approach dominated special education for children with learning disabilities, from the field's inception through the 1970s. The three most widely known ability-training approaches were psycholinguistic training, based on the ITPA; the visual-perceptual approach (Frostig & Horne, 1973); and the perceptual-motor approach (Kephart, 1971).

Table 7.3 *continued*

Date	Historical Event	Educational Implications
1968	The National Advisory Committee on Handicapped Children drafted and presented to Congress a definition of learning disabilities.	This definition was later incorporated into IDEA and used to govern the dispersal of federal funds for support of services to children with learning disabilities.
1968	The Division for Children with Learning Disabilities (DCLD) was established within the Council for Exceptional Children (CEC).	DCLD has become the largest division of CEC.
1969	The Children with Learning Disabilities Act (part of P.L. 91–230) was passed by Congress.	This legislation authorized a five-year program of federal funds for teacher training and the establishment of model demonstration programs for students with learning disabilities.
late 1970s–early 1980s	Reviews of research showing the ineffectiveness of psycholinguistic training (Hammill & Larsen, 1978), the visual-perceptual approach (Myers & Hammill, 1976), and perceptual-motor approaches (Kavale & Mattison, 1983) are published.	Process testing and ability training gradually gave way to increased use of a skill training, or task-analysis, approach. If a student has not learned a complex skill (e.g., reading a sentence) and has had sufficient opportunity and wants to succeed, a skill trainer would conclude that the student has not learned the necessary prerequisite skills (e.g., sounding out letters, reading single words) and provides direct instruction and practice on those prerequisite skills.
1975	Congress passed the Individuals with Disabilities Education Act (P.L. 94-142)	Learning disabilities was included as one of the disability categories in IDEA.
1980s and 1990s	Research on instructional design (e.g., Kameenui & Carnine, 1998), content enhancements (e.g., Scruggs & Mastropieri, 1992), and learning strategies (e.g., Schumaker & Deshler, 1992) provides additional knowledge on effective teaching methods for students with learning disabilities.	Skill training approach supplemented with increased emphasis on helping students with learning disabilities have meaningful contact with the general curriculum through explicit instruction, content enhancements, fluency-building, and the use of learning strategies and self-management skills.

social/cultural changes [e.g., poverty, substance abuse by pregnant women] have put the development of children's central nervous systems at increasing risks of disruption. Second, they have placed an increasing degree of psychological stress on children and their families. . . . Exactly what proportion of the increase represents bogus cases of learning disabilities is open for speculation and future research. In the meantime, we should be open to the idea that at least some of the increase represents students who are in very real need of learning disabilities services. (Hallahan, 1992, pp. 523–528)

Causes of Learning Disabilities

In almost every case, the cause (etiology) of a child's learning disability is unknown. Many causes have been proposed, a situation that probably reflects the highly diverse nature of students with learning disabilities. Just as there are different types of learning disabilities (e.g., dyslexia, math disabilities), there are likely to be different causes. Four suspected causal factors are brain damage, heredity, biochemical imbalance, and environmental causes.

Brain Damage

Spivak (1986) has estimated that as many as 20% of children with learning disabilities have sustained a prior brain injury, either before (prenatal), during (perinatal), or after (postnatal) birth. Some students with learning disabilities show definite signs of brain damage, which may well be the cause of their learning problems (Hynd, Marshall, & Gonzalez, 1991). Recent advances in neuroimaging technology have enabled researchers to discover that specific regions of the brains of some individuals with reading disabilities show activation patterns during phonological processing tasks that are different from the patterns found in the brains of nondisabled individuals (Shaywitz et al., in press).

Some professionals believe that all children with learning disabilities suffer from some type of brain injury or dysfunction of the central nervous system. Indeed, this belief is inherent in the NJCLD definition of learning disabilities, which states that learning disorders are "presumed to be due to central nervous system dysfunction." In cases in which actual evidence of brain damage cannot be shown (and this is the situation with the majority of children with learning disabilities), the term *minimal brain dysfunction* is sometimes used, especially by physicians. This wording implies brain damage by asserting that the child's brain does not function well.

Most special educators place little value on theories linking learning disabilities to brain damage, for two major reasons. First is lack of evidence: not all children with learning disabilities display clinical (medical) evidence of brain damage, and not all children with brain damage have learning disabilities. The second problem is that the brain-damage assumption can serve as a built-in excuse for ineffective instruction. When a student with suspected brain damage fails to learn, her teachers may be quick to presume that the brain injury prevents her from learning and slow to analyze and change instructional variables.

The concern that teachers do not let diagnoses of real or suspected neurological problems sway their educational judgments is shared by virtually all professionals in learning disabilities, even those who believe that a true learning disability is caused by central nervous system damage or dysfunction. Myers and Hammill (1990) conclude their discussion of etiology with these cautionary words:

> For the teacher or clinician who is not engaged in systematic research, the primary concerns are to handle the correlative symptoms . . . to teach the children to read, speak, write, and so on. Whether learning disabilities in an individual case are symptoms that result from brain injury or developmental delay will not essentially alter the methods of teaching the student. . . . Isolation of definite or presumed etiologies for the observed disabilities is of only tangential interest and value to the teacher-clinician and plays a minor role in the preparation of instructional programs. (p. 22)

Heredity

Siblings and children of persons with reading disabilities have a slightly greater than normal likelihood of having reading problems. There is growing evidence that heredity may account for at least some family linkage with dyslexia (Pennington, 1995). Research has located possible chromosomal loci for the genetic transmission of phonological deficits that may predispose a child for reading problems later (Cardon et al., 1994).

Biochemical Imbalance

Biochemical disturbances within a child's body have been suspected as a cause of learning disabilities.

Food Additives Feingold (1975a, 1975b, 1976) received much publicity for his claims that artificial colorings and flavorings in many of the foods children eat can cause learning disabilities and hyperactivity. He recommended a treatment for learning disabilities that consisted of a diet with no foods containing synthetic colors or flavors. A number of research studies were conducted to test the Feingold diet, some claiming positive results (Connors, Goyette, Southwick, Lees, & Andrulonis, 1976; Cook & Woodhill, 1976). However, in a comprehensive review of diet-related studies, Spring and Sandoval (1976) concluded that very little scientific evidence supported Feingold's theory. Many of the studies were poorly conducted, and the few experiments that were scientifically sound concluded that only a small portion of hyperactive children might be helped by the special diet.

In response to the controversy over diet treatments, the American Council on Science and Health (1979) issued the following statement:

> Hyperactivity will continue to be a frustrating problem until research resolves the questions of its cause, or causes, and develops an effective treatment. The reality is that we still have a great deal to learn about this condition. We do know now, however, that diet is not the answer. It is clear that the symptoms of the vast majority of the children labeled "hyperactive" are not related to salicylates, artificial food colors, or artificial flavors. The Feingold diet creates extra work for homemakers and changes the family lifestyle . . . but it doesn't cure hyperactivity. (p. 5)

Although it is possible, or even probable, that biochemistry may affect a student's behavior and learning in the classroom, no reliable scientific evidence exists today revealing the nature or extent of that influence. It is understandable that claims of cure create a great deal of excitement and interest among both professionals and parents. Rooney (1991), who reviewed and critiqued a number of controversial therapies claiming to cure or remediate the learning and/or behavioral problems experienced by children with disabilities, suggests that we "read the fine print" before accepting a discovery.

Vitamins Cott (1972) hypothesized that learning disabilities can be caused by the inability of a child's bloodstream to synthesize a normal amount of vitamins. Some physicians began megavitamin therapy with children with learning disabilities. Megavitamin treatment consists of massive daily doses of vitamins in an effort to overcome the suspected vitamin deficiencies. Two studies designed to test the effects of megavitamin treatment with learning disabled and hyperkinetic children found that huge doses of vitamins did not improve the children's performance (Arnold, Christopher, Huestis, & Smeltzer, 1978; Kershner, Hawks, & Grekin, 1977). And several researchers have noted the potential risks of large doses of vitamins. Toxic effects such as scurvy, cardiac arrhythmia, headaches, and abnormalities of the liver may result, especially from megadoses of certain B vitamins (Eastman, 1978; Golden, 1980).

Environmental Factors

Although very difficult to document as primary causes of learning disabilities, environmental factors—particularly impoverished living conditions early in a child's life and poor instruction—probably contribute to the achievement deficits experienced by many children in this special education category. The tendency for learning disabilities to run in families suggests a correlation between environmental influences on children's early development and subsequent achievement in school. Evidence appears in longitudinal research such as that conducted by Hart and Risley (1995), who found that infants and toddlers who received infrequent communication exchanges with their parents were more likely to show deficits in vocabulary, language use, and intellectual development prior to entering school.

Another environmental variable that is likely to contribute to children's learning problems is the quality of instruction they receive. "Perhaps 90 percent or more of the children who are labeled 'learning disabled' exhibit a disability not because of anything wrong with their perception, synapses, or memory, but because they have been seriously mistaught. Learning disabilities are made, not born" (Engelmann, 1977, pp. 46–47).

Although the relationship between poor instruction and learning disabilities is not clear, there is a great deal of evidence showing that many students' learning problems can be remediated by direct, systematic instruction. It would be naïve to think, however, that the achievement problems of all children with learning disabilities are caused entirely by inadequate instruction. Perhaps Engelmann's other 10% are those children whose learning disability is the result of a malfunctioning central nervous system. Nevertheless, from an educational perspective, intensive, systematic instruction should be the treatment of first choice for all students with learning disabilities.

Assessment

Four types of assessment are frequently used with students with learning disabilities: norm-referenced achievement tests, criterion-referenced tests, informal reading inventories, and curriculum-based measurement.

In the 1960s and 1970s, tests designed to assess psycholinguistic, perceptual-motor, or visual-perceptual abilities were often used with children with learning disabilities. Such process tests are seldom used today; research has shown that instruction designed to improve the abilities assessed by the tests is ineffective (e.g., Hammill & Larsen, 1978; Kavale & Mattson, 1983).

Norm-Referenced Achievement Tests

Norm-referenced tests are designed so that one student's score can be compared with the scores of other students of the same age who have taken the same test. Because a deficit in academic achievement is the major characteristic of students with learning disabilities, standardized achievement tests are widely used. Some standardized achievement tests are designed to measure a student's overall academic achievement—e.g., the Iowa Tests of Basic Skills (Hoover, Hieronymus, Frisbie, & Dunbar, 1993), the Peabody Individual Achievement Test (Markwardt, 1989), the Woodcock-Johnson Psychoeducational Battery (Woodcock & Johnson, 1989), and the Wide Range Achievement Test—3 (WRAT) (Wilkinson, 1989). Scores on these tests are reported by grade level; a score of 3.5, for example, means that the student's score equaled the average score by those students in the norm group who were halfway through the third grade.

Some norm-referenced tests are designed to measure achievement in certain academic areas. Frequently administered reading achievement tests include the Durrell Analysis of Reading Difficulty (Durrell & Catterson, 1980), the Gates-McKillop Reading Diagnostic Test (Gates, McKillop, & Horowitz, 1981), the Gray Oral Reading Tests (Wiederholt & Bryant, 1992), the Spache Diagnostic Reading Scales (Spache, 1981), and the Woodcock Reading Mastery Tests (Woodcock, 1987). Norm-referenced tests used to assess mathematics achievement include KeyMath—Revised: A Diagnostic Test of Essential Skills (Connolly, 1988), the Stanford Diagnostic Mathematics Test (Beatty, Madden, Gardner, & Karlsen, 1995), and the Test of Mathematical Abilities (Brown, Cronin, & McEntire, 1994).

Texts by McLoughlin and Lewis (1994) and Salvia and Ysseldyke (1995) describe special education assessment practices in detail and examine many widely used tests. For an excellent discussion of assessment for instructional planning (that is, for using assessment to determine what to teach and how to teach), see Howell, Fox, and Morehead (1993).

Criterion-Referenced Tests

Criterion-referenced tests differ from norm-referenced tests in that a child's score on a criterion-referenced test is compared with a predetermined criterion, or mastery level, rather than with normed scores of other students. The value of criterion-referenced tests is that they identify the specific skills the child has already learned and the skills that require instruction. One criterion-referenced test widely used by special educators is the Brigance Comprehensive Diagnostic Inventory of Basic Skills (Brigance, 1983), which includes 140 skill sequences in four subscales: readiness, reading, language arts, and math. Some commercially distributed curricula now include criterion-referenced test items for use both as a pretest and posttest. The pretest assesses the student's entry level to determine which aspects of the program he is ready to learn; the posttest evaluates the effectiveness of the program. Criterion-referenced tests can be, and often are, informally developed by classroom teachers.

Informal Reading Inventories

Teachers' growing awareness of the inability of formal achievement tests to provide useful information for planning instruction has led to greater use of teacher-developed and -administered tests, particularly in the area of reading. An informal reading inventory usually consists of a series of progressively more difficult sentences and paragraphs that a student is asked to read aloud. By directly observing and recording aspects of the student's reading skills—such as mispronounced vowels or consonants, omissions, reversals, substitutions, and comprehension—the teacher can determine the level of reading material that is most suitable for the child and the specific reading skills that require remediation.

For a list of children's literature recommended for students with learning disabilities, see Higbee Mandlebaum (1992).

Curriculum-Based Measurement

Curriculum-based measurement involves frequent assessment of a student's progress in learning the objectives that make up the actual curriculum in which the student is participating (Deno, 1985; Fuchs & Fuchs, 1996). Curriculum-based measurement is a *formative evaluation* method in that it provides information on student learning as instruction takes place over time. Curriculum-based measurement can occur as often as every day for some skills.

By contrast, the result of a summative evaluation *cannot be used to inform instruction because it is conducted after instruction has been completed (e.g., at the end of a grading period or school year).*

Direct Daily Measurement Direct daily measurement means observing and recording a child's performance on the specific skill being taught, each day that it is taught. In a program teaching multiplication facts, for example, the student's performance of multiplication facts would be assessed each day that multiplication was taught. Measures such as correct rate (number of facts stated or written correctly per minute), error rate, and percent correct are often recorded.

Two advantages of direct daily measurement are clear. First, it gives information about the child's performance on the skill under instruction. Second, this information is available on a continuous basis so that the teacher can modify instruction in accordance with changing (or unchanging) performance, not because of intuition, guesswork, or the results of a test that measures something else. Direct and frequent measurement is the cornerstone of the behavioral approach to education introduced in Chapter 6 and is becoming an increasingly popular assessment and evaluation technique in all areas of special education.

See Bushell and Baer (1994) for a powerful argument in support of making direct and frequent measurement of student performance an integral part of educational practice.

Precision Teaching. **Precision teaching** is a system for direct daily measurement of student academic performance originally developed by Ogden Lindsley (1971) and used often with students with learning disabilities. Precision teachers make curricular decisions based on the changing frequency of a student's performance (i.e., count per unit of time) as plotted on a standard graphic display called the **standard celeration chart** (Pennypacker, Koenig, & Lindsley, 1972). The chart shows a student's progress from day to day. Precision teaching is neither a specific method of teaching nor a curriculum; it is a way of evaluating the effects of instruction and making instructional decisions. As such, it can augment any instructional system, from whole language instruction to direct instruction.

More information about precision teaching can be found in Beck, Conrad, and Anderson (1995); Kubina and Cooper (in press); Lindsley (1996); Potts, Eshleman, and Cooper (1993); West, Young, and Spooner (1990); and the Journal of Precision Teaching.

Precision teachers use the following procedures to identify learning objectives, monitor student progress, and make decisions about teaching and learning:

1. *Pinpoint the performance.* For example, the performance might be writing digits or saying words.
2. *Count correct and incorrect performances.* Recording both correct and incorrect responses gives a more complete picture of learning.

To see how precision teaching was used to help a student with learning disabilities improve his reading skills, see "Tutoring Joe" later in this chapter.

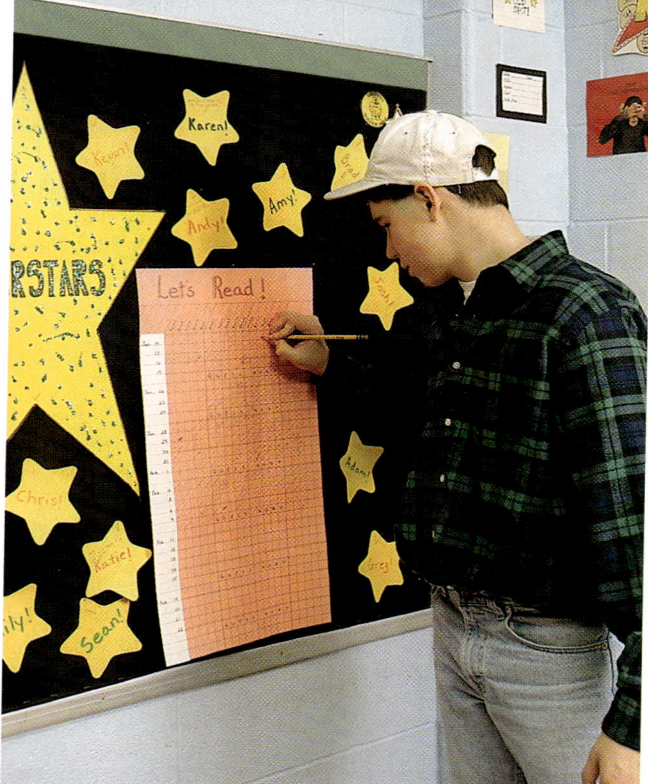

Self-recording and self-graphing daily measures of academic performance are excellent ways to motivate and involve students in their own learning.

3. *Identify the learning channel.* Learners receive and send information in many ways. They can receive information by seeing, hearing, tasting, touching, thinking, and feeling; they can send information by saying, writing, matching, pointing, and thinking. Reading sight words, for example, uses the "see/say" learning channel. Identifying learning channels when designing instruction does the following (Kubina & Cooper, in press):
   - Extends skill applications by teaching and practicing many exemplars of the skill area
   - Facilitates planning for instruction and practice
   - Tells others in plain English about our instruction
   - Reminds us that students learn in many ways
   - Helps us select instructional and practice activities for learners with special needs
   - Adds variety to our teaching and practice
4. *Plan for a counting time.* A one-minute assessment is sufficient for most academic skills (see "How Many Can You Do in One Minute?" in Chapter 6).
5. *Specify a performance standard or instructional aim.* Without an instructional aim, instruction is aimless. Precision teachers aim for performance standards that correlate with students' retention, endurance, application, and stability of new knowledge and skills (Binder, 1996).
6. *Arrange before and after events.* What happens before the learner's performance (e.g., curriculum materials, teacher directions, learning channels for receiving information) and what happens after the performance (e.g., instructional feedback, self-charting, and celebrating improvements) influence learning.
7. *Make curricular decisions.* Teachers must accept the responsibility for arranging instruction so students will learn. Make an instructional change if students do not progress.

Tutoring Joe: Winning with the Precision Teaching Team

by John O. Cooper

Precision teachers are guided by four basic tenets:

- Frequency (a count per unit of time) provides a universal measure of performance.
- Count each time you teach.
- Display student performance on the standard celeration chart to evaluate teaching and learning.
- The learner knows best.

Of these four principles, "the learner knows best" is most important. This principle needs some explanation, however, because of its common, and much different, use in child-directed teaching methods (see Grossen, 1998). With child-directed teaching methods this principle means that a learner knows best what to learn, how to study, when to practice, whether to practice, and so on. To precision teachers, "the learner knows best" simply means that when a learner makes academic progress, the practice and instruction are right for that learner. If the learner does not make progress, then something about the instruction is inappropriate for that learner. The precision teaching team (learner, teacher, and chart) must find another way to practice and learn. Thus, the learner's *behavior* knows best. Precision teachers only trust the learner's actual progress to guide the development and refinement of appropriate instruction.

Joe (a fifth-grader with learning disabilities who attends an inclusive classroom in an inner-city elementary school) and I used precision teaching to improve his reading skills. We worked together in an after-school tutoring program on Tuesdays and Fridays. Each session lasted about 45 minutes.

Charting one-minute timed readings. During his first tutorial, Joe orally read 62 correct and 8 incorrect words per minute from a grade-level chapter book, *The Wish Giver*. We set his "see/say" reading aim at 180 to 200 correct words with 5 or fewer incorrect words per minute. In just eight tutoring sessions over the next four weeks, Joe reached his aim and selected a new book at the same grade level, *Stone Fox*. He began the new book at 89 correct and 8 incorrect words per minute, almost 30 more correct words per minute than he read four weeks earlier. On the second book, he achieved his aim in six sessions. We moved to a new book at the same grade level, *The War with Grandpa*. During the first counting time, Joe read 124 correct words, with 1 incorrect word, per minute. It took just three practice sessions for Joe to achieve his instructional aim on this book.

Sprinting. Each session began with Joe reading one or two chapters to me. Before the 1-minute counting time, he practiced by reading shorter passages with 10-second timings. Precision teachers call these shorter timings *sprints*. Academic sprinting can help to develop fluent performances and build academic endurance (Binder, Haughton, & Van Eyk, 1990). Joe and I looked for fluency blockers during the sprint practices. (Precision teachers call anything that keeps a student from performing smoothly and accurately a *fluency blocker*.) Teacher-paced flash cards, reading books with many pictures, underdeveloped phonemic awareness, and teacher instructions to slow down are common fluency blockers for reading. Joe found that big words such as "nothingness" and "dimension" blocked his fluency development. He deliberately practiced reading these words until he read them automatically.

Segmenting long words. Joe practiced ways to look for smaller parts in longer words by breaking the word into syllables. He practiced breaking words into syllables using the precision teaching practice sheets called "Segmentation and Blending of Syllables and Words" (Freeman & Haughton, 1996). He practiced dividing three or four syllable words and answered questions about the order of the syllables in each word. Joe reached the aim of 30 segmentation responses per minute for the three or four syllable words in only four sessions. He said he liked doing the segmentation practice!

Celebrating accomplishments. Joe worked hard to reach his oral reading aim of 180 to 200 words per minute. He made reading more enjoyable and interesting by choosing the books he wanted to read, striving for a personal best performance each session, and charting his performance on the standard celeration chart (see Figure A). After charting, Joe and I would celebrate his personal best performances.

Joe's improved reading fluency raised his academic performance in the classroom. The more fluently he read, the more time he could give to thinking about the meaning of the words and sentences. Fluent reading correlates highly with reading comprehension (Downs & Morin, 1990).

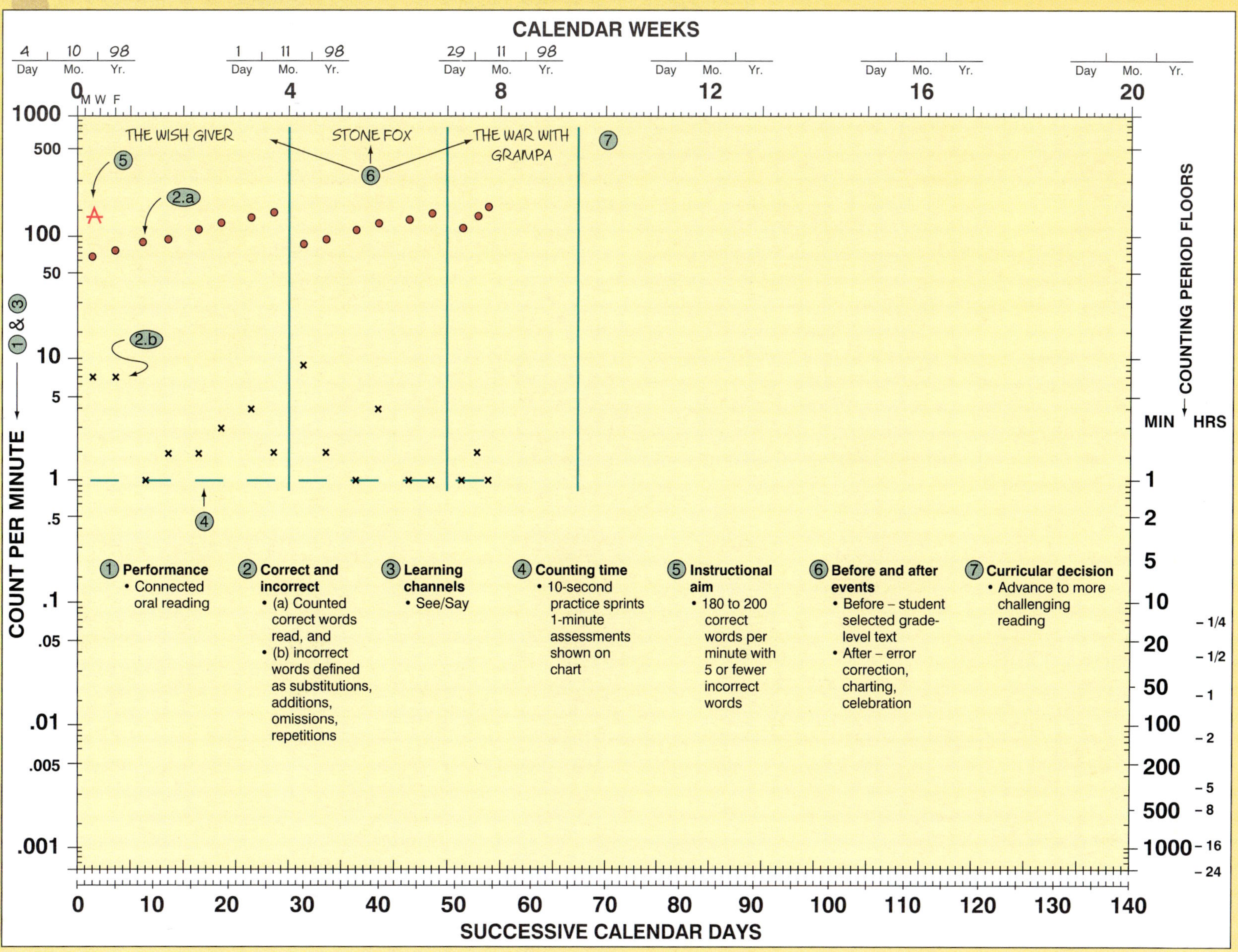

Figure A Joe's standard celeration chart

Joe's progress in reading made me very happy and proud of his accomplishments. On his last day of tutoring, he had his best reading day ever. He read big words like "intelligence" without hesitation. When he came to a word he didn't know by sight, he would say, "Don't tell me; I will get it!" and then use his new skills to sound out the word.

Joe's precision teaching team (teacher, student, and chart) made the instructional decision to advance to more challenging, higher-grade-level books.

John O. Cooper is Professor of Special Education at The Ohio State University, where he conducts research in applied behavior analysis and trains teachers in the use of precision teaching.

Educational Approaches

Not long ago, instruction of students with learning disabilities emphasized the remediation of basic skills deficits, often at the expense of providing opportunities for students to express themselves, to learn problem-solving skills, or to contact the general education curriculum in a meaningful way. "The overemphasis on the 'basics' with the exclusion of any creative or cognitively complex activities provides many students with LD an unappealing intellectual diet" (Gersten, 1997, p. 163).

In recent years, however, the field has begun to shift its instructional focus, from a remediation-only mode to an approach designed to give students with learning disabilities meaningful access to the core curriculum. Researchers have recognized that these students (1) have difficulty organizing information on their own, (2) bring limited stores of background knowledge to many academic activities, and (3) require a large amount of practice and feedback to learn and retain abstract information. Thus, contemporary best practice in educating students with learning disabilities is characterized by explicit instruction, content enhancements, and learning strategies (Gersten, 1997; Hock et al., in press).

Explicit Instruction

Direct Instruction (discussed later in this chapter) is a thoroughly developed model of explicit instruction.

Explicit instruction involves carefully designed materials and activities that provide structures and supports that enable students to make sense of new information and concepts. According to Cazden (1992), teachers should be "explicit about what needs to be done, or said, or written—rather than leaving it to learners to make inferences from experiences that are unmediated by help" (p. 111). In other words, explicit instruction is anything but learning by trial and error. Teachers use explicit instruction when they do the following (Carnine, Jones, & Dixon, 1994; Gersten, 1998):

1. Provide students with a sufficient range of examples to illustrate a concept or problem-solving strategy.
2. Provide models of proficient performance, including step-by-step strategies (at times) or broad, generic questions and guidelines that focus attention and prompt deep processing.
3. Have students explain how and why they make decisions.
4. Provide frequent, positive feedback for student performance so students persist in activities.
5. Provide adequate practice opportunities that entail interesting and engaging activities.

Content Enhancements

Educating students with learning disabilities at the secondary level is difficult. Lectures and assigned readings in textbooks are widely used in middle and high school classrooms to present academic content to students. The teacher talks (or assigns a portion of the text), and students are held responsible for obtaining, remembering, and using the information later (usually on a quiz or test). Poor listening, note-taking, reading, and study skills, compounded by a poor store of background knowledge, limit the ability of students with learning disabilities to obtain needed information from lectures, reading, and homework assignments. *Content enhancement* is the general name given to a wide range of techniques to help students organize, comprehend, and retain critical curriculum content (Crank & Bulgren, 1993; Hock et al., in press; Hudson, Lignugaris/Kraft, & Miller, 1993; Lenz & Bulgren, 1995). This section describes four content enhancements helpful to students with learning disabilities.

Content enhancements make instruction more effective for all *students; their use should not be restricted to students with learning disabilities.*

Graphic Organizers and Visual Displays *Graphic organizers*—visual-spatial arrangements of information containing words or statements connected graphically—can help students see meaningful hierarchical and comparative relationships (Horton, Lovitt, & Bergerud, 1990). *Visual displays* can be effective for teaching abstract concepts to students with disabilities. For example, the visual map in Figure 7.3 helps students see how the concept of convection operates in similar fashion across a number of applications.

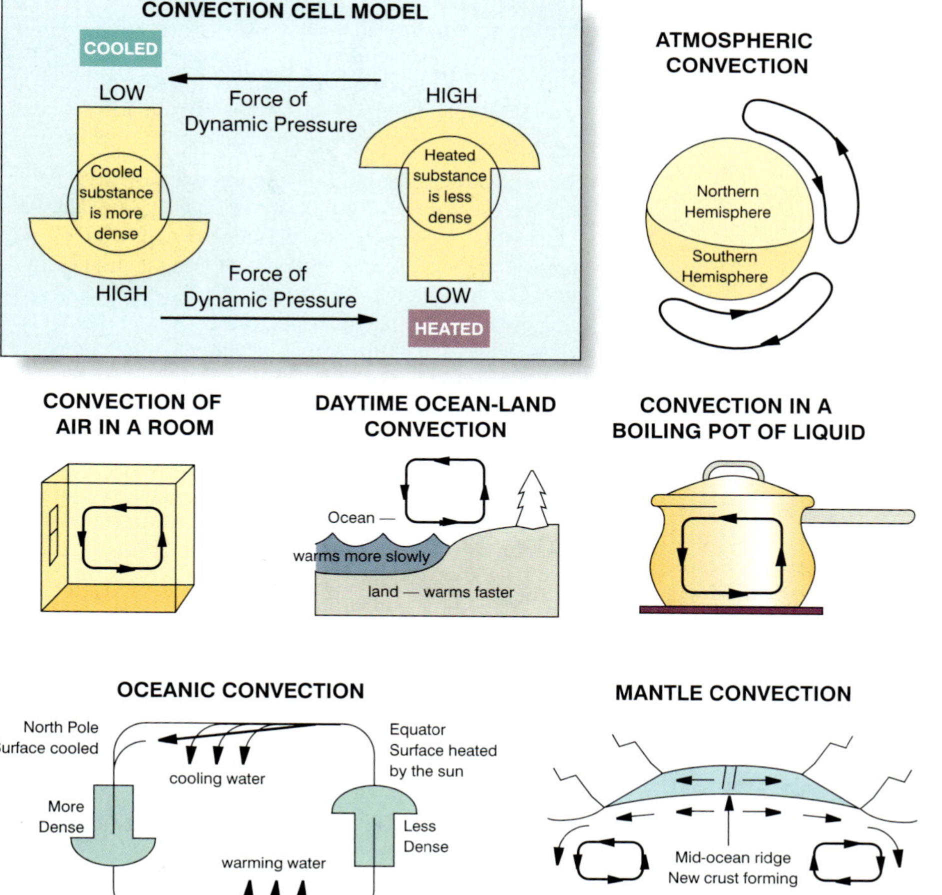

Figure 7.3 Visual display showing how the concept of convection applies across applications

Source: From Grossen, B. J., Carnine, D. W., Romance, N. R., & Vitale, M. R. (1998). Effective strategies for teaching science. In E. J. Kameenui & D. W. Carnine (Eds.), *Effective teaching strategies that accommodate diverse learners* (p. 121). Upper Saddle River, NJ: Merrill/Prentice Hall. Reprinted by permission.

What Is Direct Instruction?

The Direct Instruction (DI) model is the most carefully developed and thoroughly tested program for teaching reading, math, writing, spelling, and thinking skills to children. Siegfried Engelmann and Wesley Becker developed DI at the University of Illinois in the 1960s. It was further developed by Engelmann, Doug Carnine, Bonnie Grossen, Ed Kameenui, Jerry Silbert, and others at the University of Oregon. Research and development on the model continues today throughout the country. Two major rules underlie DI: (1) teach more in less time, and (2) control the details of the curriculum.

Teaching more in less time recognizes that even if students with disabilities are taught by an effective program that enables them to progress at the same rate as their nondisabled peers, they will always remain behind. Only by teaching at a *faster rate* can the achievement gap be reduced (Kameenui & Simmons, 1990).

High rates of student engagement. Although some DI programs are designed for whole-class instruction, DI is typically conducted with 5 to 10 children, which is more efficient than one-to-one instruction and allows more teacher attention, feedback, and individualization than does large-group instruction. High rates of active student response are generated by having students chorally respond (in unison) to a rapid series of teacher-presented items (Carnine, 1976; Heward, Courson, & Narayan, 1989). Individual turns are interspersed within group responses. To help both the pacing and the simultaneous participation of all students, teachers use signals (e.g., hand movements, claps) to cue students when to respond.

Immediate feedback. Correct responses are praised, and materials have been designed so that 70% of first-time responses are correct (Engelmann, 1997). All errors are corrected immediately via a model-lead-test procedure that ends with the student making the correct responses. This firming continues until the student(s) who erred responds correctly and independently. A good DI teacher does not move to the next task in a lesson (or from one lesson to the next) until the students have demonstrated their mastery of the current task.

Scripted lessons. Scripts indicate what the teacher should do and say for each item or task in the lesson. They ensure consistent, quality instruction across teachers and help reduce the amount of unnecessary teacher talk. DI developers found that children learn best by working through a sequence of tasks with carefully timed comments from the teacher. They learn little from listening to teacher talk, which often causes confusion by changing the focus of the tasks, thereby hampering students' acquisition of the larger generalization. It also draws out the length of the lesson unnecessarily and reduces the number of practice trials. When the teacher is talking, students are not responding, and students learn most when they are actively responding.

Scripted presentations are part of the whole lesson, and DI lessons are part of the whole school day. Lessons also include opportunities for group and independent work. A good DI teacher creates additional activities that allow students to make use of their learning in various situations.

Learner-tested curriculum design. A first-time observer of a well-taught DI lesson is immediately struck by its high energy level: rapid pacing, the teacher's use of verbal and visual signals, and the children's choral responding stand out from typical teaching methods. But the observer is seldom aware of the curriculum design—the selection and sequencing of instructional examples—that is at the heart of DI.

> Direct Instruction is an intensive intervention designed to increase not only the amount of learning but also its quality by systematically developing important background knowledge and explicitly applying it and linking it to new knowledge. Direct Instruction designs activities that carefully control the background knowledge that is required so that all students can "build hierarchies of understanding," not just those students who come to school with the appropriate background knowledge. In the process, mechanistic skills evolve into flexible strategies, concepts combine into schemata, and success in highly structured situations develops into successful performance in naturalistic, unpredictable, complex environments. (Carnine, Grossen, & Silbert, 1995)

Curriculum examples are selected and sequenced based on the finding that if children respond perfectly to a smaller set of carefully engineered tasks, they generalize their learning to untaught examples and situations (Engelmann & Carnine, 1982). For example, children who learn to spell 600 word parts called morphographs and know three rules for connecting them can spell 12,000 words. Children who rehearse the 600 word parts and three rules to a level of automaticity can spell any of the 12,000 words with ease.

DI designers test the programs carefully before publishing them. Each DI program is extensively field-tested and revised based on student performance data. The goal is to include every piece necessary to make the lessons successful.

DI curriculum materials are available for teaching reading (Engelmann & Bruner, 1988), mathematics (Engelmann & Carnine, 1992), and language arts (Engelmann & Silbert, 1993) in grades K to 6. There is even a DI program that parents can use to teach preschoolers to read: *Teach Your Child to Read in 100 Easy Lessons* (Engelmann, Haddox, & Bruner, 1983). Recent textbooks provide teachers with thorough explanations and examples of how to apply DI curriculum design and instructional principles to teaching reading (Carnine, Silbert, & Kameenui, 1998) and math (Stein, Silbert, & Carnine, 1997).

Powerful results. The effectiveness of DI is supported by an impressive body of research. An evaluation of the model was conducted by the nationwide Follow Through program and involved more than 8,000 children in 20 communities who were taught by one of nine different models. (Follow Through is a nationwide, comprehensive educational program for economically disadvantaged children, grades K to 3. Many Head Start children enter Follow Through programs.) Children who participated in the DI model made significant gains in academic achievement, catching up to or even surpassing the national norms on several arithmetic, reading, and language skills (Bock, Stebbins, & Proper, 1996; Gersten, Carnine, & White, 1984). None of the other eight educational approaches evaluated by the Follow Through program was nearly as effective as DI. Perhaps even more impressive are the results from two follow-up studies showing long-term benefits of DI. When they were in high school, the children who had participated in DI through the third grade had higher graduation rates (60% to 40%), lower dropout rates, more promotions to the next grade, and more acceptances to college than a comparison group of children with similar disadvantaged backgrounds (Darch, Gersten, & Taylor, 1987; Meyer, Gersten, & Gutkin, 1983). All of these differences were statistically significant. For more information on the effectiveness of DI, see Adams and Engelmann (1996) and Weisberg (1994).

Myths and misconceptions. There are many myths and misconceptions about DI (Engelmann, 1997; Tarver, 1998). Here are four:

- *DI is good for teaching decoding and word recognition but does not improve reading comprehension or instill a love of books.* Wrong. Because they have learned to rapidly and effortlessly decode printed text, DI students are able to concentrate on the meaning of authentic literature, thereby enjoying and truly benefiting from whole language activities (Carnine, Silbert, & Kameenui, 1998).
- *DI relegates the teacher to a person who simply reads a script.* Wrong. First, just reading the script will not teach students anything. Even though DI programs are carefully tested and scripted, there is nothing simple about using them successfully. Good DI teachers must learn special presentation techniques and make many on-the-fly decisions in response to the children's performance. Second, while scripts are used by other highly skilled professionals (e.g., surgeons and musicians) for some reason the education profession expects teachers to create their own method of instruction. Imagine how comfortable you would feel if the pilot of your next flight decided to experiment with his "new idea" for landing the plane. Yet every day teachers experiment with the futures of children by trying first one approach, then another.
- *DI is effective for teaching rote memory skills but does not teach higher-order thinking skills or problem solving.* Wrong. DI curriculum design principles have been used successfully to teach higher-order skills such as deductive and inductive reasoning in history, literary analysis, chemistry, earth science, legal reasoning, problem solving, critical thinking, and ratio and proportions (Kameenui & Carnine, 1998).
- *DI has a detrimental effect on students' self-esteem and their attitudes toward learning.* Wrong. In fact, data from the Follow-Through study show just the opposite. Children in DI programs had the highest scores on measures of self-concept, higher even than programs designed to enhance self-concept (Watkins, 1996). This is not surprising. Children who are competent readers, writers, and math calculators are more likely to feel good about themselves than are children whose academic difficulties make each day in school a hardship.

If you think that content enhancements such as guided notes are "spoon-feeding" students and making learning too easy, consider this: when students use guided notes, they are actively responding and interacting with the curriculum content. Teachers make it too easy when they allow students to passively attend to ongoing instruction.

Guided Notes Students who take good notes and study them later consistently receive higher test scores than students who only listen to the lecture and read the text (Baker & Lombardi, 1985; Norton & Hartley, 1986). The listening, language, and, in some cases, motor-skill deficits of many students with learning disabilities, however, make it difficult for them to identify what is important and write it down correctly and quickly enough during a lecture. While trying to choose and write one concept in a notebook, the student with learning disabilities might miss the next two points. Although various strategies and formats for effective note taking have been identified, they are seldom taught to students (Saski, Swicegood, & Carter, 1983).

Guided notes is a method for organizing and enhancing curriculum content and providing students with disabilities and their regular classroom peers with a means of actively participating during a lecture (Heward, 1994; Lazarus, 1996). Guided notes are teacher-prepared handouts that guide students through a lecture with standard cues and specific spaces in which to write key facts, concepts, and/or relationships (see Figure 7.4). More than 10 studies in elementary, middle school, and secondary classrooms have consistently found that students at all achievement levels

Figure 7.4 Portion of guided notes used by a fifth-grade teacher for a U.S. history lesson

Source: From Pados, G. E. (1989). A comparison of the effects of students' own notes and guided notes on the daily quiz performance of fifth-grade students. Unpublished master's thesis, The Ohio State University, Columbus. Reprinted by permission.

American History Guided Notes Name ___________________

Road to Revolution II

A. *New Problems and New Troubles*
   1. The French and Indian War ______________________________
      a. The British thought the colonists ______________________
      b. Britain also thought the colonists ______________________
   2. In 1764, Parliament decided to ____________ the colonists to help pay the bills for the war.
      a. Colonists had to pay a tax on ______________ and ______________
      b. ____________ collected the taxes.
   3. ____________ —the British lawmaking group
   4. ____________ —the people who collected the taxes. They were allowed to keep part of the taxes themselves.

B. *The Stamp Act (1765)*
   1. Under this law, colonists had to buy ______________ for all kinds of paper products.
      a.
      b.
      c.

C. *"Taxation without Representation"*
   1. "Taxation without Representation" means ____________ by a lawmaking group in which you have no representation.
      a. Colonists could not ______________________________
      b. Colonists also could not ___________________________
   2. James Otis, a young lawyer from Massachusetts, referred to the Stamp Act as ______________________________

earn higher test scores when using guided notes than they earn when taking their own notes (e.g., Beckley, Al-Attrash, Heward, & Morrison, 1999; Courson, 1989; Pados, 1989; see Heward [1994] for a review). Figure 7.5 lists some advantages of guided notes and suggestions for using them.

See "Mnemonic Strategies" later in this chapter.

Mnemonic Strategies Recent research has demonstrated that *mnemonic strategies* (memory-enhancing strategies) are a promising method for improving students' recall of specific academic content (Mastropieri & Scruggs, 1998). For example, Nagel, Schumaker, and Deshler (1986) used a first-letter mnemonic strategy, TEENS, to help students remember the five sense organs: *t*ongue, *e*ars, *e*yes, *n*ose, and *s*kin. Scruggs and Mastropieri (1992) reported that 19 middle school students with learning disabilities performed better on delayed-recall tests when life science facts were taught with mnemonic pictures that symbolically represented those facts. The students also learned to successfully generate and apply their own mnemonic strategies to novel content. Similarly, students with learning disabilities have used mnemonic strategies to learn information about U.S. presidents (Mastropieri, Scruggs, & Whedon, 1997).

Learning Strategies

Proficient learners approach tasks and problems systematically. They identify what needs to be done, make a plan, and evaluate their progress. An accomplished writer knows how to identify and organize the content of a paper to enhance its persuasive-

Figure 7.5 Guided notes: Advantages and suggestions

Advantages of Guided Notes

- Students retain more course content and have higher scores on quizzes and tests.
- Students must actively respond to and interact with the lesson's content.
- Students are better able to determine whether they are "getting it" and are more likely to ask the teacher to clarify.
- Students produce a standard and accurate set of notes for study and review.
- Students may acquire improved note-taking skills (White, 1991).
- Teachers must plan the lesson or lecture carefully.
- Teachers are more likely to stay on task with content and sequence of lecture.

Suggestions for Using Guided Notes

- Include all facts, concepts, and relationships students are expected to learn.
- Include background information so that students' note taking focuses on the important facts, concepts, and relationships they need to learn.
- Provide consistent cues (e.g., asterisks, lines, bullets) so that students will know where, when, and how many concepts they should record.
- Don't require students to write too much, or the lesson will bog down.
- Produce notes on a word processor so that changes and updates can be easily made.
- Consider gradually fading the use of guided notes to help students learn to take notes in classes in which they are not used.
- Provide follow-up activities to ensure that students study and review their notes (e.g., daily quiz, collaborative review activity) (Lazarus, 1991).

Mnemonic Strategies

by Margo A. Mastropieri and Thomas E. Scruggs

Success in school is strongly associated with the ability to learn and remember verbal information. For example, students are frequently expected to remember states and capitals, multiplication facts, U.S. presidents, science vocabulary, and mathematical formulas. Unfortunately, many students with mild cognitive disabilities have difficulty remembering verbal information. Some researchers have linked these problems to difficulties in effectively using appropriate learning strategies to improve recall by more effectively encoding, storing, and retrieving information.

We have been studying mnemonic (memory-enhancing) strategies and evaluating their effectiveness with students who have difficulty remembering academic information. We primarily have studied the use of these strategies by students with learning disabilities; however, we have also found that they can be useful for students with mild mental retardation and behavioral disorders as well as normally achieving and gifted students.

The Keyword Method The keyword method is one of the most versatile mnemonic strategies. It is useful when linking a new, unfamiliar word with familiar information. For example, to remember that the Italian word *mela* (may-LA) means "apple," first construct a keyword for *mela*. A keyword sounds like the new word but is familiar and easy to picture. In this case, "mailbox" would be a good keyword for mela because it sounds like it and is easy to picture. Next, draw (or ask students to imagine) a picture of the keyword and its referent doing something together—e.g., a mailbox with an apple in it. Finally, students study the picture and are told, when asked for the meaning of mela, to think of the keyword "mailbox," remember the picture with the mailbox in it, remember *what else* was in the picture, and retrieve the correct answer, "apple." Although there are several steps to successful retrieval, research has shown that students with learning difficulties can easily use the keyword method and remember far more information when they do so.

To help remember that George M. Cohan wrote the patriotic song "Over There" during World War I, students could use the picture shown in Figure A. In this picture, "cone" is the keyword for Cohan. When a child asks, "Where did you get the cone?" the other child points and sings, "Over there." Students who have studied the picture and its mnemonic strategy can then remember the answer to the question "Who was George M. Cohan?"

Sometimes two keywords can be used. For example, to teach that Annapolis is the capital of Maryland, construct keywords of both Annapolis ("an apple") and Maryland ("marry") and show a picture of apples getting married.

Sometimes keywords are not necessary because the words are already familiar. Sometimes pictures can be *mimetic*, or direct representations. For example, to show that sponges attach themselves to the ocean floor, draw a mimetic picture in which sponges are attached to the ocean floor. Sometimes *symbolic* pictures are needed when the information is familiar but abstract. For example, to show that birds are warm-blooded, show a picture of a bird sitting in warm sunshine. In this case, the sun is a symbol for warm-blooded. In contrast, cold-blooded fish and reptiles can be pictured in cold scenes. This method of using mimetic, symbolic, or acoustic (keyword) reconstructions has been called *reconstructive elaborations.* It can be used to adapt a wide variety of content information.

The Pegword Method The pegword method employs rhyming words for numbers (1 is "bun," 2 is "shoe," 3 is

Figure A Mnemonic picture for remembering that George M. Cohan wrote the song "Over There"

Source: From Mastropieri, M. A., & Scruggs, T. E. (1991). *Teaching students ways to remember: Strategies for learning mnemonically* (p. 49). Cambridge, MA: Brookline. Reprinted with permission.

"tree," etc.) when information to be remembered is numbered or ordered. For example, to remember that an example of a third-class lever is a rake, create a picture of a rake leaning against a tree (3). To remember that insects have six legs, create a picture of insects on sticks (6). To remember that Newton's first (or, number 1) law of motion is that objects at rest tend to stay at rest, show a picture of a bun (1) resting.

Pegwords can be combined with keywords. For example, to remember that the mineral rhodochrosite is number 4 on the Mohs's hardness scale, show a picture of a road (keyword for rhodochrosite) going through a door (pegword for 4).

Letter Strategies Most people can remember using letter strategies to remember information—for example, using the acronym HOMES to remember the names of the Great Lakes: Huron, Ontario, Michigan, Erie, and Superior. However, this strategy is effective only if students are familiar with the names of the Great Lakes because they just have the first letters as a prompt. Another helpful letter strategy is the acronym FARM-B to remember the classes of vertebrates: fish, amphibians, reptiles, mammals, birds.

Acrostics and related strategies can also be helpful. For example, the sentence "My very educated mother just served us nine pizzas" can be used to remember the planets in order: Mercury, Venus, Earth, Mars, Jupiter, Saturn, Uranus, Neptune, Pluto.

Letter strategies can also be combined with keywords. For example, the countries of the Central Powers in World War I included Turkey, Austria-Hungary, and Germany. These countries can be represented by the acronym TAG, which Figure B shows being played in Central Park, keyword for Central Powers.

Recommendations Here are some guidelines for incorporating mnemonic strategies into classroom teaching for students with learning difficulties:

1. *Teach a small number of strategies at first.* Explain every step of the strategy very carefully and monitor for understanding. When students begin to show facility in using the method, more strategies can be included.
2. *Monitor for comprehension.* Students need to be made aware that they are learning two things: important content information and the strategies for remembering that information. This can be prompted by asking for each separately: "What is the capital of New Hampshire, Mary?" "Good. How did you remember that?" Additionally, students should not be taught to remember information they do not understand. Ensure comprehension of the information before applying memory strategies.
3. *Mnemonic pictures do not need to be great works of art.* They simply need to portray the relevant information clearly. However, if you are certain that you cannot draw at all, use stick figures or cutouts from magazines, employ a student artist, ask students to draw their own pictures, or encourage student use of imagery.
4. *Teach students to generalize mnemonic strategies to their own independent use.* However, they should first be well acquainted with a variety of teacher-developed mnemonic strategies. Promote group brainstorming of keywords and interactive pictures and carefully explain the steps to constructing mnemonic strategies. Then prompt strategy construction and provide feedback.

For further information, see Mastropieri, M. A., & Scruggs, T. E. (1991). *Teaching students ways to remember: Strategies for learning mnemonically.* Cambridge, MA: Brookline.

Margo A. Mastropieri and Thomas E. Scruggs are professors in the Graduate School of Education, George Mason University. They are co-editors of the research annual *Advances in Learning and Behavioral Disabilities*.

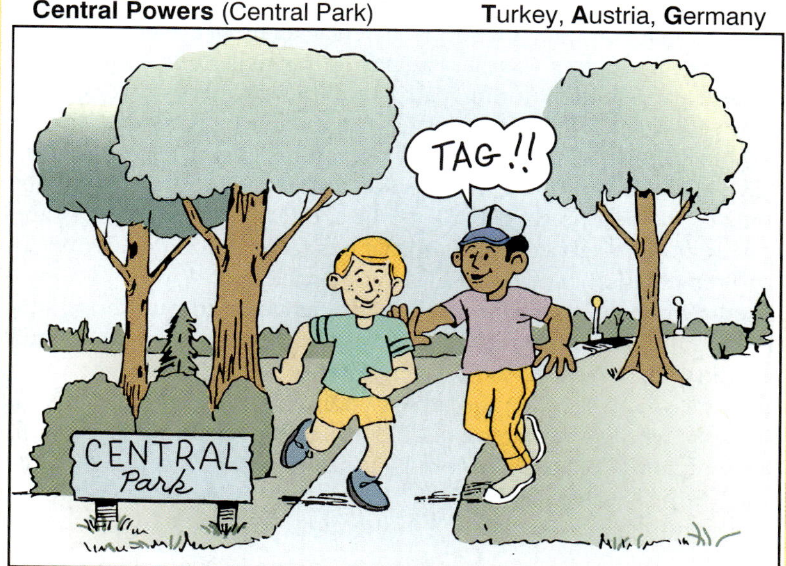

Central Powers (Central Park)
Turkey, **A**ustria, **G**ermany
TAG!!
CENTRAL
Park

Figure B Mnemonic picture for remembering the names of the countries in the Central Powers during World War I: Turkey, Austria-Hungary, and Germany

Source: From Mastropieri, M. A., & Scruggs, T. E. (1991). *Teaching students ways to remember: Strategies for learning mnemonically* (p. 119). Cambridge, MA: Brookline. Reprinted with permission.

ness. When adding a series of unlike fractions, a skilled math student immediately looks to see if all of the denominators are even numbers. Unless they are explicitly taught, however, many students with learning disabilities are unaware of the learning strategies, or "tricks of the trade," that proficient learners use (Deshler & Schumaker, 1993).

The learning strategies approach does not mean teachers can abandon explicit instruction in basic skills. "If the skills tool box is empty, learning strategies will be ineffective" (Deshler, 1998, n.p.).

A *learning strategy* can be defined as "an individual's approach to a learning task. A strategy includes how a person thinks and acts when planning, executing, and evaluating performance on a task and its outcomes" (Deshler & Lenz, 1989, p. 205). Donald Deshler and Jean Schumaker and their colleagues at the University of Kansas (Schumaker & Deshler, 1992) have conducted extensive research on how to help students with learning disabilities acquire and use effective learning strategies. They have developed, field-tested, and validated a learning strategies curriculum for adolescents with learning disabilities (Ellis, Deshler, Lenz, Schumaker, & Clark, 1991).

The June/July 1993 issue of the Journal of Learning Disabilities *is devoted to articles on learning strategies instruction.*

Task-specific strategies help students guide themselves successfully through a learning task. The Sentence Writing Strategy (Schumaker & Sheldon, 1985), for example, provides students with a set of steps for using a variety of formulas when writing sentences. Case, Harris, and Graham (1992) taught fifth- and sixth-grade students with learning disabilities to use a five-step self-instructional strategy to solve addition and subtraction word problems. The students learned to (1) read the problem aloud, (2) look for important words and circle them (e.g., "how many left," "how much more"), (3) draw pictures to help tell what is happening, (4) write down the math sentence, and (5) write down the answer. In a related study, nine elementary students with learning disabilities used tape-recorded cues with their own voices to remind them of a 10-step problem solving strategy for math problems (Wood, Rosenberg, & Carran, 1993). The students continued to use the self-instructional strategy to solve problems when the tape-recorded cues were withdrawn in the study's final phase.

Educational Placement Alternatives

Regular Classroom

During the 1995–1996 school year, 42% of students with learning disabilities were served in the regular classroom (U.S. Department of Education, 1998).

IDEA requires that students with disabilities be educated with their nondisabled peers and have access to the core curriculum to the maximum extent possible and that they be removed from the regular classroom only to the extent that their disability necessitates. A number of methods can be used singly or in combination to help make the regular classroom an effective learning environment for many students with learning disabilities. For example, adapting curricular materials (Hudson et al., 1993), modifying testing procedures (Garjía, Salend, & Henrick, 1994), increasing the frequency of student participation during instruction (Heward, 1994), using mastery learning (Guskey, Passaro, & Wheeler, 1995), and employing classwide peer-tutoring programs (Miller, Barbetta, & Heron, 1994; Simmons, Fuchs, Fuchs, Hodge, & Mathes, 1994) have all been shown to increase the academic success of students with learning disabilities in the regular classroom. In addition, school districts are providing teachers with more in-service training programs focusing on the identification, assessment, and remediation of children's learning problems.

Another strategy for increasing the likelihood of successful inclusion is to interview successful students to find out their secrets for success in a particular teacher's classroom (Monda-Amaya, Dieker, & Reed, 1998).

Ellet (1993) asked 89 regular education high school teachers to rate those student skills and behaviors they believed were most important for success in the regular education classroom. Table 7.4 lists the 10 things those teachers thought were most important for success. This list identifies at least some of the skills special educators must help students who have learning disabilities learn in order to succeed in the regular classroom: organizational skills and how to use their time wisely (Shields & Heron, 1989), note taking (Suritsky & Hughes, 1991), study skills (Hoover, 1989), completing homework on time (Cavanaugh, 1990; Trammel, Schloss, & Alper, 1994),

Student Skill/Behavior	Mean Rating*
Follows directions in class	3.72
Comes to class prepared with materials	3.48
Uses class time wisely	3.48
Makes up assignments and tests	3.43
Treats teachers and peers with courtesy	3.40
Completes and turns in homework on time	3.37
Works cooperatively in student groups	3.19
Completes tests with a passing grade	3.19
Appears interested in subject	2.90
Takes notes in class	2.88

*Skills are ordered from most to least important as ranked by teachers; 4 is the highest possible score.

Source: Reprinted from "Instructional Practices in Mainstreamed Secondary Classrooms" by L. Ellet, 1993, *Journal of Learning Disabilities, 26,* 59. © by 1993 PRO-ED, Inc. Used by permission.

Table 7.4 The 10 most important things a student with learning disabilities should do to achieve success in a regular education classroom

politely requesting teacher assistance (Alber, Heward, & Hippler, 1999), and getting along with others (Cartledge & Milburn, 1995).

Many school districts employ a collaborative teaching model to support the full inclusion of students with learning disabilities. Collaborative teaching involves in-class support by a special education teacher who provides instructional assistance to students with disabilities and perhaps some co-teaching with the general education teacher. Data from two recent studies, however, question the effectiveness of this model. Boudah, Schumaker, and Deshler (1997) found that both the general education teachers and the special education teachers devoted more than half of their time to noninstructional tasks and spent less than 10% of their time presenting curriculum content. Not surprisingly, Boudah et al. also reported disappointing outcome measures for the students with learning disabilities who were included in those classrooms. The authors of another study that examined the experiences of 25 elementary students with learning disabilities who participated in a full inclusion program concluded that "full-time placement in the general education classroom with in-class support from special education teachers is not sufficient to meet the needs of these students. They require combined services that include in-class support and daily intensive, one-on-one instruction from highly trained personnel" (Klingner, Vaughn, Hughes, Schumm, & Elbaum, 1998, p. 159).

WWW

To join in the discussion "Should all students with learning disabilities be educated in the regular classroom?" go to the Message Board Module at http://www.prenhall.com/heward.

Consultant Teacher

A consultant teacher provides support to regular classroom teachers and other school staff who work directly with students with learning disabilities. The consultant teacher helps the regular teacher select assessment devices, curriculum materials, and instructional activities. The consultant may even demonstrate teaching methods or behavior management strategies. A major advantage of this model is that the consultant teacher can work with several teachers and thus indirectly provide special education services to many children. A major drawback is that the consultant has little or no direct contact with the children. Heron and Harris (in press) describe procedures consultant teachers can use to increase their effectiveness in supporting mainstreamed children.

During the 1995–1996 school year, a resource room was the primary educational placement for 39% of all students with learning disabilities (U.S. Department of Education, 1998).

Resource Room

A resource room is a specially staffed and equipped classroom where students with learning disabilities come for one or several periods during the school day to receive individualized instruction. A resource room teacher serves an average of 20 students with disabilities (U.S. Department of Education, 1989).

The resource teacher is a certified special educator whose primary role is to teach needed academic skills, social skills, and learning strategies to the students who are referred to the resource room. Most of the students are in general education classrooms for part of the school day and come to the resource room only for specialized instruction in the academic skills and/or social skills they need to smooth their integration into the regular classroom and benefit from the general curriculum of the school. Other students may receive all of their academic instruction in the resource room and attend the regular classroom only for periods such as art and music. In addition to teaching students with learning disabilities, the resource teacher also works closely with each student's regular teacher to suggest and help plan each student's program in the regular classroom.

Ronni Hochman Spratt (1999), a middle school learning disabilities resource room teacher, offers these suggestions for placing a student with learning disabilities into the regular classroom:

> I think a key to a resource room is identifying where the student's successes are and initially putting him back into the regular classroom only in the areas in which he can experience a great amount of success. I use the student's time in the resource room to build those skills he needs to learn to be completely integrated into the regular classroom—whether it's learning to read better or learning to complete an independent seatwork task. (personal communication)

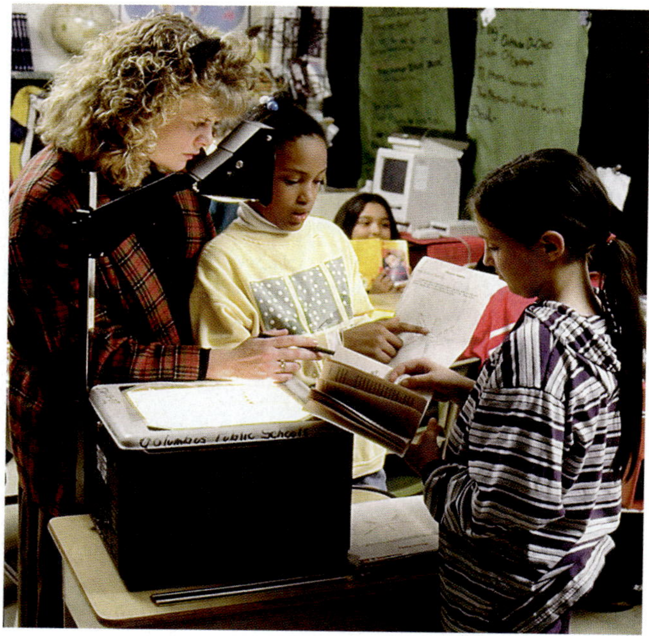

A resource room can provide students with learning disabilities with intense, individualized instruction on the academic and social skills they need for success in the mainstream.

Some advantages of the resource room model are that (1) students do not lose their identity with their peer group, which reduces the chance they will be stigmatized as "special"; (2) students can receive the intense, individualized instruction they need every day, which might be impossible for the regular teacher to provide; and (3) flexible scheduling allows the resource room to serve a fairly large number of students (Wiederholt, Hammill, & Brown, 1983).

Several disadvantages of resource rooms are that they (1) require students to spend time traveling between classrooms, (2) may result in inconsistent instructional approaches between settings, and (3) make it difficult to determine whether students should be held accountable for what they missed while out of the regular classroom (Lieberman, 1982).

Separate Classroom

In a separate classroom the learning disabilities teacher is responsible for all educational programming for a group of 8 to 12 students with learning disabilities. The academic achievement deficiencies of some children with learning disabilities are so severe that they need full-time placement in a learning setting with a specially trained teacher. In addition, poor work habits and inappropriate social behaviors make some students with learning disabilities candidates for the separate classroom, where distractions can be minimized and individual attention stressed. It is important, however, that placement in a separate classroom not be considered permanent. A student should be placed in a separate classroom only after legitimate and supported attempts to serve her effectively in other less restrictive environments have proven unsuccessful.

During the 1995–1996 school year, 17% of students with learning disabilities were served in separate classrooms (U.S. Department of Education, 1998).

Although the effectiveness and appropriateness of separate classrooms have been the focus of much debate, some students benefit from full-time instruction in a separate classroom. For example, a follow-up study of 10 high school students five to six years after they had been enrolled for a year in a self-contained learning disabilities program showed them to be performing as well as nondisabled students in a comparison group (Leone, Lovitt, & Hansen, 1981). Even though the students' performances varied considerably, their oral reading ability, free-time and occupational interests, and general success in high school were within the normal range. The results of this study suggest that placement in a separate classroom because of significant academic deficits in the elementary grades does not preclude success in high school.

Fewer than 1% of students with learning disabilities are served in separate schools (U.S. Department of Education, 1998).

Current Issues and Future Trends

The study of learning disabilities is so dynamic and controversial that an entire book could be devoted to a discussion of current issues. These include what terminology to use (is a reading disability the same as a learning disability?), the concern for the special needs of adults with learning disabilities, what kind of training learning disabilities teachers should receive, how federal and state funds should be appropriated, and what to do about the proliferation of controversial cures for learning disabilities. We will briefly discuss two issues: the continuing debate over defining and identifying the "true nature" of learning disabilities, and where students with learning disabilities should be taught (full inclusion). The chapter closes with an observation on the importance of maintaining a positive approach in our work with children with learning disabilities.

Will the Real Student with Learning Disabilities Please Stand Up?

The field of learning disabilities continues to struggle with defining the nature of the unexpected learning problems it was created to study and treat. Although virtually everyone in education recognizes that present definitions of learning disabilities are inadequate, finding a definition that provides clearcut criteria for identification and serves as a standard by which to interpret and assess research findings has "proven easier said than done" (Conte & Andrews, 1993, p. 149).

The widely different prevalence rates for learning disabilities from state to state and district to district illustrate the lack of a standard operational definition. Some prominent special educators believe that the trend toward expanding the learning disabilities classification to include more and more children indicates a misunderstanding of the concept and detracts from and weakens services to children who have severe learning problems. Myers and Hammill (1990), for example, believe that far too many students are identified as learning disabled:

> A number of teachers will note readily that many, possibly most, of the "learning disabled" students enrolled in their programs do not satisfy either the 1977 USOE or the NJCLD definition. This is because, in many school districts, all students who are thought to be able to profit from tutoring or remedial education are arbitrarily called learning disabled. As a consequence of such definitional liberality, the learning disability programs have become glutted with underachieving students, culturally different students, and poorly taught students. (p. 13)

To Tell the Truth was a popular TV game show in the 1960s. A panel of celebrities asked questions of three contestants, only one of whom was actually the person all were pretending to be. In some respects, the search to find the truly learning disabled among the many students who do poorly in school is like that TV game show. Many questions (in the form of achievement tests, intelligence tests, and more tests) are given to the contestants (students), whose answers are judged by a panel of experts (teachers, school psychologists, and administrators) charged with picking out the "real" students with learning disabilities from the "pretenders." The differences, of course, are also significant. On the game show, the consequences for a wrong answer were no more serious than a loud buzzer and a consolation prize; but in the game of identifying students with learning disabilities, mistakes are costly. A "no, he's not learning disabled" answer can be devastating for the student who truly needs specially designed instruction to meet his individual learning needs. If the team of selection experts concludes "yes, there is one" when the student's achievement deficits are simply a result of insufficient contact with appropriate general education curriculum and instruction, then the limited resources available to help students with learning disabilities are stretched further.

The discussion of what constitutes a true learning disability will no doubt go on for some time. We close this discussion of the difficulties in defining learning disabilities by recognizing a central truth: labeling does not cause disabilities, nor will the removal of a label cure them (Lerner, 1993). From an educator's standpoint, the most important issue should not revolve around whether to consider the academic deficiencies exhibited by a student as evidence of learning disabilities (Macht, 1998). Instead, we should focus our resources and energies on determining how to go about assessing and effectively remediating the specific academic and social skill deficits in each student's repertoire. What a child's learning problem is called is not so important; what is important is that schools provide an educational program responsive to the individual needs of all children who have difficulty learning.

Should All Students with Learning Disabilities Be Educated in the Regular Classroom?

IDEA mandates that all students with disabilities receive a program of special education services tailored to meet their individual needs in the least restrictive environment. For the majority of students with learning disabilities, the least restrictive environment for all or most of the school day is the regular education classroom attended by their same-age peers. The popular movement toward full inclusion of all students with disabilities in regular classrooms, however, has many professionals and advocates for students with learning disabilities worried. They think that although the full inclusion movement is based on strong beliefs and has the best intentions of children with disabilities at heart, little research supports it (Division for Learning Disabilities, 1993; Kauffman & Hallahan, 1994; Martin, 1993; Silver, 1993). They fear that the special education services for students with learning disabilities guaranteed by IDEA—particularly the meaningful development and implementation of IEPs and the identification of the least restrictive environment for each student along a continuum of placement options—will be lost if full inclusion becomes reality. They wonder how, for example, a middle school student with learning disabilities who spends the entire school day in regular education subject matter classes will receive the individualized reading instruction at the second-grade level that she needs. With full inclusion comes the general education curriculum (Pugach & Warger, 1993). The regular education classroom for some students with learning disabilities may actually be more restrictive than a resource room or special class placement when the instructional needs of the student are considered—and remember that academic deficit is the primary characteristic and remedial need of students with learning disabilities (Baker & Zigmond, 1995).

Dan Hallahan, a long-time leader and contributor to the field of learning disabilities, shared his concerns about full inclusion in this message posted on the Internet:

> It is important that students with learning disabilities have access to the general education curriculum. A very legitimate criticism of the resource room model of the 1980s is that far too often the special education teacher and his or her students had no idea what was transpiring in the general education classroom. I fear, however, that folks are going to translate the 1997 IDEA emphasis on the general education classroom to mean exclusive placement in general education classrooms. Why can't students with learning disabilities learn the general education curriculum with the help of special educators in special education settings? Furthermore, let's not forget that failure in the general education curriculum is what got many of these students into special education in the first place. Just maybe there's something wrong with the general education curriculum. Access to the general education curriculum is great, but how about access to instruction? (LD-Online, 1998)

See "Full Inclusion versus Inclusion" in Chapter 2.

All of the major professional and advocacy associations concerned with the education of children with learning disabilities have published position papers against full inclusion (CLD, 1993; DLD, 1993; LDA, 1993 [see Figure 7.6]; NJCLD; 1994). Each group recognizes and supports the placement of students with learning disabilities in regular classrooms to the maximum extent possible, given that the instructional and related services required to meet each student's individualized educational needs are provided, but they strongly oppose policies that mandate the same placement and instruction for all students with learning disabilities. Each group believes that special education for students with learning disabilities requires a continuum of placement options that includes the possibility of some or even all instruction taking place outside the regular classroom.

Maintaining a Positive Focus

With its unending stream of claims, counterclaims, and controversy, the area of learning disabilities at times seems to lose sight of its fundamental goals and some commonsense truths. Tom Lovitt, who contributed classroom-based research on virtually every aspect of the education of children with learning disabilities for more than 30 years, once wrote that, all things being equal, a teacher who imparts many skills to many children is good, and one who does not is not (Lovitt, 1977). After all, teaching is helping children learn new things. Although Lovitt believed that the development of children's academic and social skills is the primary purpose for teachers and students coming together, he also warned us to not become so concerned with fixing everything we believe is wrong with the student that we forget about building upon all that is positive.

> Although we don't know how to really define LD youngsters (and heaven knows we've tried), we do know that they don't do as well as their non-LD mates in oral and silent

"Full inclusion," "full integration," "unified system," and "inclusive education" are terms used to describe a popular policy/practice in which all students with disabilities, regardless of the nature or severity of their disability and need for related services, receive their total education with the regular education classroom in their home school. The Learning Disabilities Association of America does not support "full inclusion" or any policies that mandate the same placement, instruction, or treatment of all students with learning disabilities. Many students with learning disabilities benefit from being served in the regular education classroom. However, the regular education classroom is not the appropriate placement for a number of students with learning disabilities who may need alternative instructional environments, teaching strategies, and/or materials that cannot or will not be provided with the context of a regular classroom placement.

LDA believes that decisions regarding educational placement of students with learning disabilities must be based on the needs of each individual student rather than administrative convenience or budgetary considerations and must be the result of a cooperative effort involving educators, parents, and the student when appropriate.

LDA strongly supports the Individuals with Disabilities Act (IDEA) which mandates:

- a free and appropriate public education in the least restrictive environment appropriate for the student's specific learning needs
- a team-approved Individualized Education Program (IEP)
- a placement decision must be made on an individual basis and considered only after the development of the IEP
- a continuum of alternative placements to meet the needs of students with disabilities for special education and related services
- a system for the continuing education of regular and special education and related services personnel to enable these personnel to meet the needs of children with disabilities

LDA believes that the placement of all children with disabilities in the regular classroom is as great a violation of IDEA as is the placement of all children in separate classrooms on the basis of their type of disability.

Figure 7.6 Learning Disabilities Association of America position statement on full inclusion

Source: Reprinted from Learning Disabilities of America Association. (1993, March/April). Position paper on full inclusion of all students with learning disabilities in the regular classroom. *LDA Newsbrief, 28*(2). © 1993 by the Learning Disabilities of America Association, Pittsburgh, PA. Used by permission.

reading, reading comprehension, spelling, mathematics, history, science, geography, industrial arts, music, or family living. Because of these many deficits and deviations, we teachers, in all good faith, set out to remediate as many of the "shortfalls" as possible so that learning disabled youth will be as normal and wonderful as we are. We should reconsider this total remedial approach to learning disabilities. One reason for considering an alternative might be obvious if we thought of a day in the life of an LD youth. First, the teacher sets out to remediate his reading, then his math, and then his language, social skills, and soccer playing. Toward the end of the day, she attempts to remediate his metacognitive deficits. That lad is in a remediation mode throughout the day. Is it any wonder that the self-concepts, self-images, self-esteems, and attributions of these youngsters are out of whack?

Use the self-tests at http://www.prenhall.com/heward to assess your knowledge of the content of Chapter 7.

We should spend some time concentrating on these youngsters' positive qualities. If, for example, a girl is inclined toward mechanics, or a boy to being a chef, we teachers should nurture those skills. And if an LD child doesn't have a negotiable behavior, we should locate one and promote it. I can't help but think that if every youngster, LD or otherwise, had at least one art, trade, skill, or technique about which he or she was fairly competent, that would do more for that youngster's adjustment than would the many hours of remediation to which the child is subjected. Perhaps that accent on the positive would go a long way toward actually helping the remediation process. If children knew they could excel in something, that might help them become competent in other areas as well. (Lovitt, 1989, p. 477)

Summary

Defining Learning Disabilities

- There is no universally agreed-on definition of learning disabilities. Most states require that three criteria be met: (1) a severe discrepancy between potential or ability and actual achievement, (2) learning problems that cannot be attributed to other disabilities, and (3) special educational services needed to succeed in school.
- No matter which definition is used, educators should focus on each student's specific skill deficiencies for assessment and instruction.

Characteristics of Students with Learning Disabilities

- Most students with learning disabilities show one or more of the following characteristics: reading problems, deficits in written language, underachievement in math, social skills deficits, problems with attention and hyperactivity, and behavioral problems.
- The fundamental, defining characteristic of students with learning disabilities is specific and significant achievement deficiency in the presence of adequate overall intelligence.

Prevalence

- Learning disabilities form the largest category in special education. Students with learning disabilities represent about 5% of the total school enrollment in the United States and half of all students receiving special education.

Causes of Learning Disabilities

- Although the actual cause of a specific learning disability is seldom known, four types of suspected causal factors are brain damage, heredity, biochemical imbalance, and environmental factors such as poverty, child-rearing practices, and poor instruction.

Assessment

- Norm-referenced tests compare a child's score with the scores of other age mates who have taken the same test.
- Criterion-referenced tests, which compare a child's score with a predetermined mastery level, are useful in identifying specific skills the child has learned as well as skills that require instruction.
- Teachers use informal reading inventories to observe directly and record a child's reading skills.
- Curriculum-based measurement is a formative evaluation method that measures a student's progress in the actual curriculum in which she is participating.
- Direct and daily measurement involves assessing a student's performance on a specific skill each time it is taught.
- Precision teaching is a special case of direct and daily measurement in which the standard celeration chart is used to guide instructional decisions based on count per unit of time.

Educational Approaches

- Contemporary best practice in educating students with learning disabilities includes approaches such as explicit instruction, content enhancements, and learning strategies.
- Direct Instruction programs consist of carefully scripted, field-tested lessons in which students respond, both chorally and individually, to a fast-paced series of learning tasks presented by the teacher. The careful selection and sequencing of tasks in DI lessons helps students systematically acquire important background knowledge so they can explicitly apply it and link it to new knowledge.
- Content enhancements, such as graphic organizers, visual displays, guided notes, and mnemonic strategies, help make curriculum content more accessible to students with learning disabilities.
- Learning strategies help students guide themselves successfully through specific tasks or general problems.

Educational Placement Alternatives

- Most students with learning disabilities spend at least part of each school day in the regular classroom.
- In some schools, a consultant teacher helps regular classroom teachers work with children with learning disabilities.
- In the resource room, a specially trained teacher works with children on particular skill deficits for one or more periods per day.
- A few children with learning disabilities attend separate classrooms. This placement option, however, should be used only after legitimate attempts to serve the child in a less restrictive setting have failed, and it should not be considered permanent.

Current Issues and Future Trends

- The discussion and debate over what constitutes a true learning disability are likely to continue. It is important for schools to respond to the individual needs of all children who have difficulty learning.

- Most professionals and advocates for students with learning disabilities do not support full inclusion, which would eliminate the continuum of service delivery options.
- In addition to their academic and social skills deficits, students with learning disabilities possess positive attributes and interests that teachers should identify and try to strengthen.

For More Information

Journals

- *Intervention in School and Clinic.* Published five times a year by PRO-ED, 8700 Shoal Creek Boulevard, Austin, TX 78758-6897. An interdisciplinary journal directed at teachers, parents, educational therapists, and specialists in all fields who deal with the day-to-day aspects of special and remedial education.
- *Journal of Learning Disabilities.* Published 10 times a year by PRO-ED, 8700 Shoal Creek Boulevard, Austin, TX 78758-6897. Publishes research and theoretical articles relating to learning disabilities.
- *Journal of Precision Teaching.* Published by the Center for Individualized Instruction, Jacksonville State University, Jacksonville, AL 36265. A multidisciplinary journal dedicated to a science of human behavior that includes direct, continuous, and standard measurement. Publishes both formal and informal articles describing precision teaching projects.
- *Learning Disabilities Research and Practice.* Published four times a year by the Division for Learning Disabilities, Council for Exceptional Children (see "Organizations").
- *Learning Disability Quarterly.* Published four times a year by the Council for Learning Disabilities (see "Organizations"). Emphasizes practical implications of research and applied research dealing with learning disability populations and settings.

Books

- Bender, W. (Ed.). (1998). *Professional issues in learning disabilities: Practical strategies and relevant research findings.* Austin, TX: PRO-ED.
- Bley, N. S., & Thornton, C. A. (1995). *Teaching mathematics to students with learning disabilities* (3rd ed.). Austin, TX: PRO-ED.
- Deshler, D., Ellis, E., & Lenz, K. (1996). *Teaching adolescents with learning disabilities: Strategies and methods* (2nd ed.). Denver: Love.
- Dowdy, C. A., Patton, J. R., Smith, T. E. C., & Polloway, E. A. (1998). *Attention-deficit/hyperactivity disorder: A practical guide for teachers.* Austin, TX: PRO-ED.
- DuPaul, G. J., & Stoner, G. (1994). *ADHD in the schools: Assessment and intervention strategies.* New York: Guilford.
- Hallahan, D. P., Kauffman, J. M., & Lloyd, J. W. (1999). *Introduction to learning disabilities* (2nd ed.). Boston: Allyn & Bacon.
- Lerner, J. W. (1993). *Learning disabilities: Theories, diagnosis, and teaching strategies* (6th ed.). Boston: Houghton Mifflin.
- Lerner, J. W., Lowenthal, B., & Lerner, S. R. (1995). *Attention deficit disorders: Assessment and teaching.* Pacific Grove, CA: Brooks/Cole.
- Mercer, C. D. (1997). *Students with learning disabilities* (5th ed.). Upper Saddle River, NJ: Merrill/Prentice Hall.
- Myers, P. I., & Hammill, D. D. (1990). *Learning disabilities: Basic concepts, assessment practices, and instructional strategies* (4th ed.). Austin, TX: PRO-ED.
- Smith, T. E. C., Dowdy, C. A., Polloway, E. A., & Blalock, G. E. (1997). *Children and adults with learning disabilities.* Needham Heights, MA: Allyn & Bacon.

Organizations

- *Learning Disabilities Association of America (LDA),* 4156 Library Road, Pittsburgh, PA 15234. Founded in 1963 as the Association for Children with Learning Disabilities (ACLD). A large, active organization of parents and educators that advocates for services to children with learning disabilities.
- *Council for Learning Disabilities (CLD),* P.O. Box 40303, Overland Park, KS 66204. An independent organization of professionals who work with individuals with learning disabilities. Publishes *Learning Disabilities Quarterly,* holds semiannual conferences to disseminate research and information, and promotes standards for learning disabilities professionals.
- *Division for Learning Disabilities (DLD),* Council for Exceptional Children, 1920 Association Drive, Reston, VA 22091. Includes teachers, teacher educators, researchers, and other members of CEC who work with or on behalf of individuals with learning disabilities.

Website

- *LD Online,* http://www.ldonline.org. A service of the Learning Project at WETA, Washington, DC, in association with the Coordinated Campaign for Learning Disabilities. Includes *What's New,* highlighting new information, research findings, and political news in the field of learning; *Audio Clips,* featuring learning disabilities experts; *Bulletin Boards* for parents, teachers, and students to share their experiences with learning disabilities; *LD In-Depth,* providing information on every aspect of learning disabilities; and *Ask the Expert,* offering opportunities to communicate directly with experts in the field of learning disabilities through a special bulletin board.

Chapter 8

Emotional and Behavioral Disorders

Focus Questions

- Why should a child who behaves badly be considered disabled?
- Who is more severely disabled: the acting-out, antisocial child or the withdrawn child?
- How are behavior problems and academic performance interrelated?
- How can a teacher's efforts to diffuse a classroom disturbance contribute to an escalation of misbehavior?
- What are the most important skills for teachers of students with emotional and behavioral disorders?

Childhood should be a happy time: a time for playing, making friends, and learning—and for most children it is. But some children's lives are in constant turmoil. Some children strike out at others, sometimes with disastrous consequences. Others are so shy and withdrawn that they seem to be in their own worlds. In either case, playing with others, making friends, and learning all the things a child must learn are extremely difficult for these children. These are children with emotional and behavioral disorders. They are referred to with a variety of terms: emotionally disturbed, socially maladjusted, psychologically disordered, emotionally handicapped, or even psychotic if their behavior is extremely abnormal or bizarre.

Children without disabilities sometimes act in the same ways as children with emotional and behavioral disorders, but not as often or with such intensity. And, of course, many children with emotional and behavioral disorders are likable.

Many children with emotional and behavioral disorders are seldom really liked by anyone—their peers, teachers, siblings, even parents. Sadder still, they often do not even like themselves. The child with behavioral disorders is difficult to be around, and attempts to befriend him (most are boys) may lead to rejection, verbal abuse, or even physical attack. Although most children with emotional and behavioral disorders are of sound mind and body, their noxious or withdrawn behavior is as serious an impediment to their functioning and learning as the physical and developmental disabilities that challenge other children with disabilities. Children with emotional and behavioral disorders make up a significant portion of students who need special education.

Defining Emotional and Behavioral Disorders

McIntyre (1992, 1993a, 1995) has written extensively on the influence of cultural differences on behavioral norms and expectations.

Like their colleagues in mental retardation and learning disabilities, special educators who work with students with emotional and behavioral disorders have been struggling to reach consensus on a definition. A clear definition of behavioral disorders is lacking for numerous reasons. First, disordered behavior is a social construct; there is no clear agreement about what constitutes good mental health. All children behave inappropriately at times. So how often and with how much intensity must a student engage in a particular behavior before she is considered disabled because of the behavior? Second, different theories of emotional disturbance use concepts and terminology that do little to promote meaning from one definition to another. Third, expectations and norms for appropriate behavior are often quite different across ethnic and cultural groups. Finally, disordered behavior sometimes occurs in conjunction with other disabilities (most notably mental retardation and learning disabilities), making it difficult to tell whether one condition is the result or the cause of the other.

Although many definitions of behavioral disorders have been proposed (see Forness & Kavale [1997] for a comparative review), the two that have had the most influence are the definition in IDEA used by the federal government to determine eligibility for special education services and a definition proposed by a coalition of professional associations concerned with children with behavior problems.

Go to the companion website at http://www.prenhall.com/heward and select Chapter 8 to review the chapter objectives.

IDEA Definition of Emotional Disturbance

Serious emotional disturbance is one of the disability categories in IDEA under which children may receive special education services.

(I) The term means a condition exhibiting one or more of the following characteristics over a long period of time and to a marked degree that adversely affects educational performance:
  (a) An inability to learn which cannot be explained by intellectual, sensory, and health factors;
  (b) An inability to build or maintain satisfactory interpersonal relationships with peers and teachers;
  (c) Inappropriate types of behavior or feelings under normal circumstances;
  (d) A general pervasive mood of unhappiness or depression; or
  (e) A tendency to develop physical symptoms or fears associated with personal or school problems.

(II) The term includes schizophrenia. The term does not apply to children who are socially maladjusted, unless it is determined that they have an emotional disturbance. (IDEA, 1997)

At first glance, this definition may seem straightforward enough. It identifies three conditions that must be met: *chronicity* ("over a long period of time"), *severity* ("to a marked degree"), and *difficulty in school* ("adversely affects educational performance"); and it lists five types of problems that qualify. But in fact, the definition is extremely vague and leaves much to the subjective opinion of the authorities who surround the child. How does one operationalize terms such as "satisfactory interpersonal relationships," "normal," "inappropriate," and "pervasive"? And how does one determine that some behavior problems represent "social maladjustment" whereas others indicate true "emotional disturbance"? This determination is critical because children who are socially maladjusted are not considered disabled under IDEA and are therefore ineligible for special education services. Eli Bower (1960), who wrote an earlier definition that was later used as the basis for the IDEA definition, never intended a distinction between emotional disturbance and social maladjustment. Indeed, Bower (1982) has stated that the five components of the definition were, in fact, meant to be indicators of social maladjustment.

It is difficult to conceive of a child who is sufficiently socially maladjusted to have received that label but who does not display one or more of the five characteristics (especially *b*) included in the federal definition. As written, the definition seemingly excludes children on the very basis for which they are included. The inclusion in the federal definition of this illogical criterion for ineligibility has been heavily criticized (Center, 1990; Cline, 1990; Kauffman, 1997; Peterson, Benson, Edwards, Rosell, & White, 1986). A harsh critic of federal policy toward the education of children with emotional and behavioral disorders, Kauffman (1982) has written, "The federal definition is, if not claptrap, at least dangerously close to nonsense" (p. 4).

CCBD Definition of Emotional or Behavioral Disorders

The Council for Children with Behavioral Disorders (CCBD) (1989) drafted substitute terminology (see Figure 8.1) and a definition that was adopted by the National Mental Health and Special Education Coalition (NMHSEC) and subsequently submitted to the U.S. Congress as a proposed replacement for the IDEA definition of serious emotional disturbance. This definition describes *emotional or behavioral disorder* as a disability characterized by the following:

The NMHSEC is a coalition of more than 30 professional mental health and education associations concerned with the education and welfare of children with emotional and behavioral disorders.

1. Behavioral or emotional responses in school programs so different from appropriate age, cultural, or ethnic norms that they adversely affect educational performance, including academic, social, vocational or personal skills. Such a disability is

   (a) more than a temporary, expected response to stressful events in the environment;
   (b) consistently exhibited in two different settings, at least one of which is school-related; and
   (c) unresponsive to direct intervention in general education, or the condition of the child is such that general education interventions would be insufficient.

2. Emotional and behavioral disorders can co-exist with other disabilities.
3. This category may include children or youth with schizophrenic disorders, affective disorders, anxiety disorders, or other sustained disorders of conduct or adjustment, when they adversely affect educational performance as described in paragraph (1). (Forness & Knitzer, 1992, p. 13)

The proposed definition clarifies the educational dimensions of the disability (McIntyre & Forness, 1996). Perhaps most important, it does not require "meaningless distinctions between social and emotional maladjustment, distinctions that often waste diagnostic resources when it is already clear that serious problems exist" (Forness & Kavale, 1997, p. 49).

Check you onging understanding of Chapter 8 concepts by using the Guided Review Module at http://www.prenhall.com/heward.

Even though no definition of behavioral disorders proposed so far has provided a consistent, universally agreed-on standard for identification, diagnosis, communication, and research, they all agree that a child's behavior, to be considered disor-

The Council for Children with Behavioral Disorders (CCBD) has officially adopted the position that the term *behaviorally disordered* is more appropriate than the term *emotionally disturbed*. The CCBD endorses use of *behaviorally disordered* because (1) it does not suggest any particular theory of causation or set of intervention techniques, (2) it is more representative of the students who are disabled by their behavior and are being served under IDEA, and (3) it is less stigmatizing (Huntze, 1985). The concern about stigmatization may have some merit, at least in terms of how teachers perceive children. Two studies found that the label *behaviorally disordered* implies less negative dimensions to teachers than does *emotionally disturbed* (Feldman, Kinnison, Jay, & Harth, 1983; Lloyd, Kauffman, & Gansneder, 1987). Both pre- and in-service teachers indicated they thought children labeled as behaviorally disordered were more teachable and likely to be successful in a regular classroom than were children identified as emotionally disturbed.

Figure 8.1 *Emotionally disturbed* or *behaviorally disordered*? Does it make a difference?

dered, must differ markedly (extremely) and chronically (over time) from current social or cultural norms.

Characteristics of Children with Emotional and Behavioral Disorders

Children with emotional or behavioral disorders are characterized by behavior that falls "significantly outside the norm of their peer group on two broadband dimensions commonly referred to as externalizing and internalizing" (Kauffman, 1983, p. 24). Both patterns of aberrant behavior have adverse effects on children's academic achievement and social relationships.

Externalizing Behaviors

The most common pattern of behavior by children with emotional and behavioral disorders consists of antisocial, or *externalizing behaviors*. In the classroom, children with externalizing behavior problems frequently do the following (adapted from Walker, 1997, p. 13):

White and Koorland (1996) describe procedures for dealing with cursing in the classroom.

- Get out of their seats
- Yell, talk out, and curse
- Disturb peers
- Hit or fight
- Ignore the teacher
- Complain
- Argue excessively
- Steal
- Lie

- Destroy property
- Not comply with directions
- Have temper tantrums
- Are excluded from peer-controlled activities
- Not respond to teacher corrections
- Not complete assignments

Rhode, Jensen, and Reavis (1998) describe noncompliance as the "king-pin behavior" around which other behavioral excesses revolve. "Noncompliance is simply defined as not following a direction within a reasonable amount of time. Most of the arguing, tantrums, fighting, or rule breaking is secondary to avoiding requests or required tasks" (p. 4). Clearly, an ongoing pattern of such behavior presents a major challenge for teachers of antisocial children. "They can make our teaching lives miserable and single-handedly disrupt a classroom" (Rhode et al., 1998, p. 3).

Go to the Resources Module for Chapter 8 at http://www.prenhall.com/heward. Click on Special Ed Resource Page and link to the search engine section. Search for additional information about "emotional disturbances."

All children sometimes cry, hit others, and refuse to comply with requests of parents and teachers, but children with emotional and behavioral disorders do so frequently. Also, the antisocial behavior of children with emotional and behavioral disorders often occurs with little or no provocation. Aggression takes many forms—verbal abuse toward adults and other children, destructiveness and vandalism, and physical attacks on others. These children seem to be in continuous conflict with those around them. Their own aggressive outbursts often cause others to strike back. It is no wonder that children with emotional and behavioral disorders are seldom liked by others and find it difficult to establish friendships.

Many believe that most children who exhibit deviant behavioral patterns will grow out of them with time and become normally functioning adults. Although this popular wisdom holds true for many children who exhibit problems such as withdrawal, fears, and speech impairments (Rutter, 1976), research indicates that it is not so for children who display consistent patterns of aggressive, coercive, antisocial, and/or delinquent behavior (Patterson, Cipaldi, & Bank, 1991; Robins, 1979; Wahler & Dumas, 1986; Walker, Colvin, & Ramsey, 1995). Robins (1966) conducted a classic follow-up study of more than 500 adults who as children had been seen by clinic staff members because of behavior problems. Structured interviews were used to gather information such as work history, alcohol and drug use, performance in the armed services, arrest, social relationships, and marital history. A control group of 100 adults who grew up in the same communities as the subjects was used for comparison. The results were significant. Of those adults who had been referred to a clinic for behavior problems as children, 45% had five or more antisocial traits. Only 4% of those in the control group showed that many antisocial characteristics. In analyzing the results further, Robins found that those who as children had been referred to the clinic for antisocial behavior (e.g., theft, fighting, discipline problems in school, truancy) had the most difficulty adjusting as adults. Furthermore, as adults, they tended to raise children who had a higher incidence of problem behaviors than normal, thus continuing the cycle. As Walker et al. (1995) note, a pattern of antisocial behavior early in a child's school career is the best single predictor of delinquency in adolescence:

Students with emotional and behavioral disorders are 13.3 times more likely to be arrested during their school careers than nondisabled students are (Doren, Bullis, & Benz, 1996a), and 58% are arrested within five years of leaving high school (Chesapeake Institute, 1994).

> Preschool children, particularly boys, engage in oppositional, overly active, pestering, random, and unfocused forms of behavior that do not seem serious at this developmental level. However, the manifestations of this behavior pattern in adolescence are *very* different and have great salience and impact. . . . It is very important to note that preschoolers who show the early signs of antisocial behavior patterns do not grow out of them. Rather, as they move throughout their school careers, they grow *into* these unfortunate patterns with disastrous results to themselves and others. This myth that preschoolers will outgrow antisocial behavior is pervasive among many teachers and early educators and is

very dangerous because it leads professionals to do nothing early on when the problem can be effectively addressed. (p. 47)

Internalizing Behaviors

Students with emotional and behavioral disorders who have poor social skills are much more likely to be victims of personal violence, sexual abuse, and other criminal acts during and after their high school careers (Doren, Bullis, & Benz, 1996b).

Some children with emotional and behavioral disorders are anything but aggressive. Their problem is the opposite—too little social interaction with others. They are said to have *internalizing* behavioral disorders. Although children who consistently act immature and withdrawn do not present the threat to others that antisocial children do, their behavior creates a serious impediment to their development. These children seldom play with others their own age. They usually do not have the necessary social skills to make friends and have fun, and they often retreat into daydreams and fantasies. Some are fearful of things without reason, frequently complain of being sick or hurt, and go into deep bouts of depression. Obviously, such behavioral patterns limit a child's chances to take part in and learn from the school and leisure activities in which normal children participate.

Because children who manifest internalizing behaviors may be less disturbing to classroom teachers than antisocial children are, withdrawn children are in danger of not being identified (Walker & Fabre, 1987). Happily, the outlook is fairly good for the child with mild or moderate degrees of withdrawn and immature behavior who is fortunate enough to have competent teachers and other school professionals responsible for his development. Carefully outlining the social skills the child should learn and gradually and systematically arranging opportunities for and rewarding those behaviors often prove successful.

Social skills training is discussed later in this chapter.

School Achievement and Intelligence

The disruptive and defiant behavior of students with emotional and behavioral disorders "almost always leads to academic failure. This failure, in turn, predisposes them to further antisocial conduct" (Hallenbeck & Kauffman, 1995, p. 64). It is estimated that only 30% of students with behavioral disorders are performing at or above grade level (Knitzer, Sternberg, & Fleisch, 1990). Two nationwide studies reported the following academic outcomes for students with emotional and behavioral disorders (Chesapeake Institute, 1994; Valdes, Williamson, & Wagner, 1990):

- Two-thirds could not pass competency exams for their grade level.
- They had the lowest grade-point average of any group of students with disabilities.
- They had highest absenteeism rate of any group of students.
- Only 42% earned a high school diploma, compared to 50% of all students with disabilities and 76% of all youth in the general population.
- As many as 48% dropped out of high school, compared with 30% of all students with disabilities and 24% of all high school students.

Even when IQ scores are taken into account, children with emotional and behavioral disorders achieve below the levels suggested by their scores. See Chapter 6 for a discussion of IQ tests.

Many more children with emotional and behavioral disorders score in the slow learner or mildly retarded range on IQ tests than do normal children. Two surveys that used national samples reported average IQ scores for students with emotional and behavioral disorders. Valdes et al. (1990) reported a mean IQ of 86, with about half of their sample scoring between 71 and 90. The students in a study by Cullinan, Epstein, and Sabornie (1992) had an average mean IQ score of 92.6. On the basis of his review of research related to the intelligence of children with emotional and

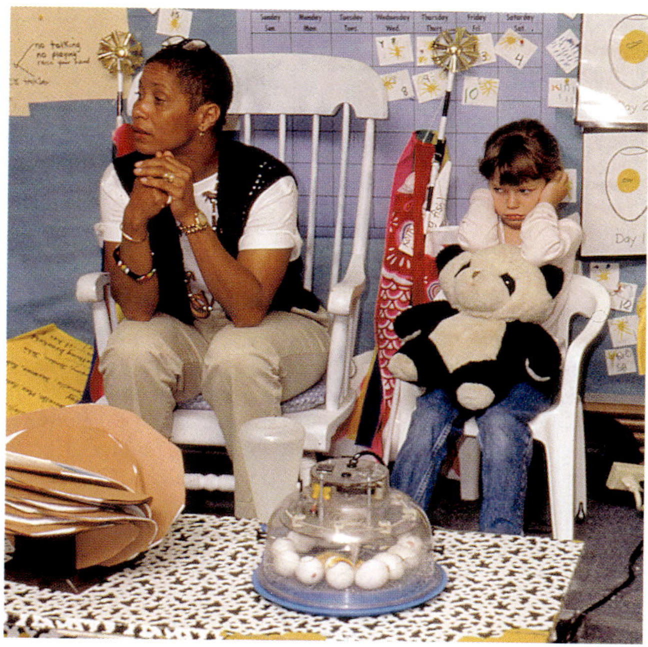

The immature and withdrawn behavior of children with internalizing behavior disorders poses a serious impediment to their learning and development.

behavioral disorders, Kauffman (1997) concluded: "We have accumulated enough research on these students' intelligence to draw this conclusion: although the majority fall only slightly below average in IQ, a disproportionate number, compared to the normal distribution, score in the dull normal and mildly retarded range, and relatively few fall in the upper ranges" (p. 243).

Whether children with emotional and behavioral disorders actually have any less real intelligence than normal children is difficult to say. An IQ test measures only how well a child performs certain tasks. It is almost certain that the disturbed child's inappropriate behavior has interfered with past opportunities to learn many of the tasks included on the test. Rhode et al. (1998) estimate that the average student actively attends to the teacher and her assigned work approximately 85% of the time but that students with behavior disorders are on task only about 60% or less of the time. This difference in on-task behavior can have a dramatic impact on academic learning.

Providing students with frequent response opportunities during instruction increases both on-task behavior and achievement. See "Using Response Cards" later in this chapter.

Social Skills and Interpersonal Relationships

The ability to develop and maintain interpersonal relationships during childhood and adolescence is an important predictor of present and future adjustment. As might be expected, many students with emotional and behavioral disorders experience great difficulty in making and keeping friends (Cartledge & Milburn, 1995). A study comparing the social relationships of secondary students who have behavioral disorders with those of same-age peers who do not have behavioral disorders reported lower levels of empathy toward others, participation in fewer curricular activities, less frequent contacts with friends, and lower-quality relationships for the adolescents with behavioral disorders (Schonert-Reichl, 1993).

To learn how puppetry can help students with emotional and behavioral disorders develop social and affective awareness and social skills, see Caputo (1993). Storytelling can also be an effective means for helping students learn to understand and express their emotions (Bauer & Balius, 1995).

Using Response Cards to Increase Participation and Achievement

Rashawn raised his hand for the last time. He wanted to answer several of his teacher's questions, especially when she asked whether anyone could name the clouds that look like wispy cotton. But it wasn't his day to get called on. He tried to follow along but after a while lost interest and laid his head on his desk.

Dean did get called on once, but he didn't raise his hand too often. It was easier just to sit there. If he were quiet and still like Rashawn, then he wouldn't have to think about learning all this weather stuff. But it got too hard for Dean to just sit, so he started acting out. This got his teacher's attention.

"Dean, please pay attention!"

"Stop that, Dean!"

"Dean, how do you expect to learn this material for tomorrow's test if you're not part of the group?"

The next day, Rashawn and Dean both did poorly on the test of meteorology concepts. Each boy had a long history of poor school achievement, and teachers sometimes used *slow learner*, *attention deficit disorder*, *learning disabilities*, *emotional disturbance*, and *behavioral disorders* as explanations for their lack of success. But perhaps their poor scores, as well as their chronic underachievement, were directly influenced by the quality of instruction they received.

Neither boy had actively participated during the previous day's lesson. Instead of being active learners who responded frequently to the lesson's content, both boys were at best passive observers. Educational research has shown that students who respond actively and often usually learn more than students who passively attend to instruction (Fisher & Berliner, 1985; Greenwood, Delquadri, & Hall, 1984). Although most teachers recognize the importance of active student participation, it is difficult during group instruction. A common strategy is for the teacher to pose a question to the entire class and then call on one student to answer. This technique often results in frequent responses by high-achieving students and few or no responses by low-achieving students such as Rashawn and Dean (Maheady, Mallete, Harper, & Saca, 1991). Response cards (RCs) are one alternative to the traditional hand-raising (HR) and one-student-participating-at-a-time method of group instruction (Heward et al., 1996).

Response Cards **Response cards** are cards, signs, or items that are simultaneously held up by all students to display their responses to a question or problem presented by the teacher. There are two basic types: preprinted and write-on. When using preprinted RCs, each student selects from a personal set of cards the one with the answer he wishes to display. Examples include *yes/true* and *no/false* cards, numbers, colors, traffic signs, molecular structures, and parts of speech. Instead of a set of different cards, a single preprinted RC with multiple answers can be given to each student (e.g., a card with clearly marked sections identified as proteins, fat, carbohydrate, vitamins, and minerals for use in a lesson on healthful eating habits). In its humblest version, the preprinted RC with multiple responses is a "pinch card": the student responds by holding up the card and pinching the part displaying her answer. Brightly colored clothespins also make excellent pinching tools. Preprinted RCs may also have built-in devices for displaying answers, such as a cardboard clock with movable hour and minute hands.

When using write-on RCs, students mark their answers on blank cards that are erased between learning trials. A set of 40 durable write-on RCs can be made from a four-by-eight-foot sheet of white laminated bathroom board (available from most builders' supply stores). The cost is generally less than $20, including the charge for cutting the sheet into 9-by-12 inch RCs. Dry-erase markers (e.g., EXPO brand) are available at most office supply stores, and paper towels or tissues will easily wipe the RCs clean.

Students can also use small chalkboards as write-on RCs, but responses may be difficult for the teacher to see in a full-size classroom. Write-on RCs can be custom-made to provide background or organizing structure for responses. For example, music students might mark notes on an RC that has permanent treble and bass clef scales; students in a driver's education class could draw where their car should go on RCs with permanent street intersections.

Research RCs have been evaluated through a series of studies in both regular and special education classrooms at the elementary, middle, and secondary levels (e.g., Cavanaugh, Heward, & Donelson, 1996; Narayan, Heward, Gardner, Courson, & Omness, 1990; Rindfuss, Al-Attrash, Morrison, & Heward, 1998). For example, Gardner, Heward, and Grossi (1994) compared the use of write-on RCs with HR during whole-class science lessons in an inner-city fifth-grade classroom. The study produced three major findings.

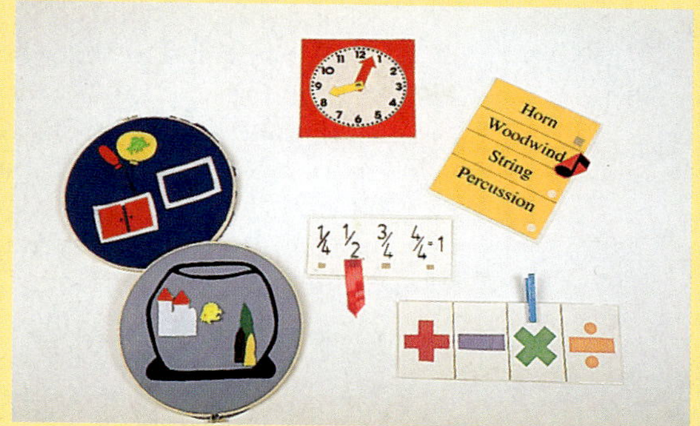

With write-on response cards, each student in the class can answer every question the teacher asks about the story just read.

First, when RCs were used students responded to teacher-posed questions an average of 21.8 times per 30-minute lesson, compared to a mean of 1.5 academic responses when the teacher called on individuals. The higher participation rate takes on additional significance when its cumulative effect is calculated over the course of a 180-day school year. If RCs were used instead of HR for just 30 minutes per day, each student in the class would make an additional 3,700 academic responses during the school year.

Second, all 22 students scored higher on next-day quizzes and two-week review tests that followed lessons with RCs than they did on quizzes and tests that followed lessons with HR.

Third, all but one student preferred RCs over raising their hands to be called on.

General Suggestions for Using RCs

- Model several question-and-answer trials and give students practice on how to use RCs.
- Maintain a lively pace throughout the lesson; keep intervals between trials short.
- Give clear cues when students are to hold up and put down their cards.
- Remember that students can learn from watching others; do not let them think it is cheating to look at classmates' RCs.

Specific Suggestions for Using Preprinted RCs

- Design and construct the cards to be as easy to see as possible (e.g., consider size, print type, color codes).
- Make the cards easy for students to manipulate and display (e.g., put answers on both sides of the cards so that students can see what they are showing the teacher, attach a group of related cards to a ring).
- Begin instruction on new content with a small set of fact/concept cards (perhaps only two), gradually adding additional cards as skills improve.

Specific Suggestions for Using Write-On RCs

- Limit language-based responses to one or two words.
- Keep a few extra markers on hand.
- Be sure students do not hesitate to respond because they are concerned about making spelling mistakes: (1) provide several practice trials with new terms before the lesson begins; (2) write new terms on the chalkboard and tell students to refer to them during the lesson; or (3) use the "don't worry" technique, telling students to try their best but that misspellings will not count against them.
- Students enjoy doodling on their response cards. After a good lesson, let students draw on the cards for a few minutes.

Prevalence

Estimates vary tremendously as to how many children have emotional and behavioral disorders. On the basis of his widely cited survey of California schools, Bower (1981) concluded that two or three children in the average classroom (about 10%) can be expected to show signs of emotional disturbance. In a longitudinal study by Rubin and Balow (1978), 7.4% of the 1,586 children in the sample were considered to have a behavior problem by every teacher who rated them over a three-year period. After reviewing studies on prevalence, Koyanagi and Gaines (1993) concluded that between 3% and 5% of children have emotional and behavioral problems sufficient to warrant intervention.

Such widely varying estimates suggest that different criteria are being used to decide whether a child is behaviorally disordered. Differences in prevalence figures, however, stem as much from how the data are collected as from the use of different definitions (Kauffman, 1997). Most surveys ask teachers to identify students in their classes who display behavior problems at that point in time. Many children exhibit inappropriate behavior for short periods, and such one-shot screening procedures will identify them, as in the Rubin and Balow (1978) study in which more than half of all students were identified as having behavior problems by at least one teacher at some time during their elementary school careers. As Hewett and Taylor (1980) observe:

> In our experience, when you walk into any elementary classroom, you can usually pick out two or three children who are "not with it" and who are visible enough to stand out from other members of the class in terms of their problem behavior. And if you stay long enough, you can usually determine if they "fit" within the teacher's range of tolerance for behavioral differences. Whether they would be the same children a week or semester later is debatable. Thus, we get almost no meaning from incidence figures. (p. 42)

A major study of education for children with emotional and behavioral disorders that investigated 26 programs in 13 states during the 1987–89 school years supports the "two or three children per classroom" figure: "Estimates suggest 10% of the child population has behavior problems serious or sustained enough to warrant intervention, [and] 3% to 5% are judged to be seriously emotionally disturbed" (Knitzer et al., 1990, n.p.).

Annual reports from the federal government, however, show far fewer children being served. The 447,426 children ages 6 to 21 who received special education under the IDEA category of serious emotional disturbance during the 1996–1997 school year represented only about 0.7% of the school-age population (U.S. Department of Education, 1998). Although this figure marked the greatest number of children with emotional and behavioral disorders ever served and ranked emotional disturbance as the fourth-largest disability category in special education (8.6% of all students ages 6 through 21 served under IDEA), it means that only 20% to 30% of children with emotional and behavioral disorders are being served.

The number of children being served represents less than half of the 2% estimate the federal government used previously in its estimates of funding and personnel needs for students with emotional and behavioral disorders. Kauffman (1997) believes that social policy and economic factors caused the government to first reduce (from 2% to 1.2%) its estimate of the prevalence of behavioral disorders and then to stop publishing an estimate altogether. "The government obviously prefers not to allow wide discrepancies between prevalence estimates and the actual number of children served. It is easier to cut prevalence estimates than to serve more students" (p. 50).

Regardless of what prevalence study one turns to, it is evident there are many thousands of schoolchildren whose disordered behavior is handicapping their educational progress but who are not presently receiving the special education they need. Although IDEA clearly mandates that all children with disabilities receive individualized special education services, the uncertain meaning of many aspects of the definition allows determination of whether a child is behaviorally disordered to be more a function of a school district's available resources (its ability to provide the needed services) than a function of the child's actual needs for such services.

> Faced with a shortage of adequately trained personnel and insurmountable budget problems, what can we expect of school officials? They cannot risk litigation and loss of federal funds by identifying students they cannot serve. . . . The social policy mandate changes the question, at least for those who manage budgets, from "How many students with emotional and behavioral disorders are there in our schools?" to "How many can we afford to serve?" And to save face and try to abide by the law, it is tempting to conclude that there are, indeed, just as many students with emotional and behavioral disorders as one is able to serve. (Kauffman, 1997, p. 51)

Gender

Boys are much more likely than girls to be identified as emotionally or behaviorally disordered. Surveys of school-age children with behavioral disorders have found a male-to-female ratio of approximately 4:1 (Cullinan, Epstein, & Kauffman, 1984; Cullinan et al., 1992). Boys identified as emotionally or behaviorally disordered are likely to have externalizing disorders and to exhibit antisocial, aggressive behavior. Girls with emotional and behavioral disorders are more likely to show internalizing disorders such as anxiety and social withdrawal.

Juvenile Delinquency

The word *delinquent* is a legal term; however, the offenses that an adolescent commits to be labeled delinquent constitute a behavioral disorder. Although the overall rate of crime in the United States has been declining, the rate and seriousness of crimes committed by juveniles have been increasing. Even though juveniles comprise only about 20% of the total population, they commit 40% of all violent crimes (Snarr & Wolford, 1985). Arrest rates for juveniles increase sharply during the junior high years. This pattern probably reflects both the greater harm adolescents can cause to society as a result of their inappropriate behavior and the fact that younger children are often not arrested (and therefore do not show up on the records) for committing the same acts that lead to the arrest of an older child.

Younger children, however, are being arrested, and they are committing more serious and violent crimes than in the past (National Center for Juvenile Justice, 1998). Children under the age of 15 account for 5.2% of all arrests, but they are responsible for 11.1% of all arrests for serious crimes (U.S. Department of Commerce, 1990a). Although boys have generally committed crimes involving aggression (e.g., assault, burglary) and girls have been associated with sex-related offenses (e.g., prostitution), more and more violent offenses are being committed by girls (Siegel & Senna, 1994).

About half of all juvenile delinquents are *recidivists* (repeat offenders). Recidivists are more likely to begin their criminal careers at an early age (usually by age 12), commit more serious crimes, and continue a pattern of repeated antisocial behavior as adults (Farrington, 1995; Tolan & Thomas, 1995). Because only a fraction of the total number of criminal acts committed by juveniles are reported (i.e., around 12% to 15% [Henggler, 1989]), it is impossible to know the extent of the problem. The information in Table 8.1 (originally intended to show the ability of positive peer-culture counseling groups to provide confidentiality and to generate a feeling of trust among the youths and their adult leader) gives some idea of the multiple crimes committed by individual juvenile offenders that go unreported to the authorities.

Offenses Known to Court	Offenses Not Known to Court Discussed in Group
Student A Petty larceny; brutality (holding 9-year-old boy over burning trash barrel).	Auto theft; breaking and entering.
Student B Beyond control of parent; sexual intercourse with 12-year-old sister.	Auto theft; attempted rape; stealing; shoplifting; breaking and entering; vandalism; sexual acts with animals; incest with mother.
Student C Shoplifting; disorderly conduct; grand larceny; breaking and entering; destroying private property; truancy.	Habituation to drugs; grand larceny; petty larceny; arson; auto theft; carrying concealed weapons.
Student D Curfew violation; auto theft; breaking and entering; public intoxication; operating motor vehicle without license.	Carrying deadly weapon; robbery; arson; auto theft; multiple breaking and entering; three instances of assault and battery.
Student E Truancy; runaway; obtaining merchandise under false pretenses.	Habituation to drugs; shoplifting; auto theft; vandalism; "rolling queers" for money (assault, battery, robbery).
Student F Petty larceny; contempt of court; curfew violation; breaking and entering.	Malicious cutting and wounding; housebreaking; stealing; forgery; shoplifting.
Student G Breaking and entering; attempted safe burglary; safe burglary.	Carrying a deadly weapon; malicious cutting and wounding; burglary; concealing stolen property; fraud; stealing from automobiles.
Student H Shoplifting; runaway; violation of probation.	Breaking and entering; stealing.
Student I Public intoxication; petty larceny; carrying concealed deadly weapon; burglary; attempted safecracking.	Shoplifting; driving without license; breaking and entering.

Table 8.1 Reported and unreported crimes by juvenile offenders

Source: Reprinted from Vorath, H. H., & Brendtro, L. K. (1985). *Positive peer culture* (2nd ed., p. 84). New York: Aldine de Gruyter. © 1985 by Harry H. Vorath & Larry K. Brendtro. Used with permission.

Causes of Emotional and Behavioral Disorders

Several theories and conceptual models have been proposed to explain abnormal behavior. Regardless of the conceptual model from which behavioral disorders are viewed, the suggested causes of disordered behavior can be grouped into two major categories: biological and environmental.

Biological Factors

For the vast majority of children with emotional and behavioral disorders, there is no evidence of organic injury or disease; that is, they appear to be physically healthy and sound. Some experts believe that all children are born with a biologically determined temperament. Although a child's inborn temperament may not in itself cause a behavior problem, it may predispose the child to problems. Thus, certain events that might not produce abnormal behavior in a child with an easygoing temperament might result in disordered behavior by the child with a difficult temperament.

Restlessness in infants and young children has been associated with increased likelihood of later behavior problems (Morgan & Jensen, 1988). Even when a clear biological impairment exists, however, no one has been able to say with certainty whether the physiological abnormality actually causes the behavior problem or is just associated with it in some unknown way.

Environmental Factors

Environmental factors involve events in the child's life that affect the way he acts. Dodge (1993) has identified three primary causal factors that contribute to the development of conduct disorder and antisocial behavior: (1) an adverse early rearing environment, (2) an aggressive pattern of behavior displayed when entering school, and (3) social rejection by peers. Considerable research evidence supports Dodge's contention that these causal factors occur in sequence (Patterson, Reid, & Dishion, 1992; Wahler & Dumas, 1986). The settings in which these events occur are the home, community, and school.

Child abuse, which is discussed in Chapter 4, is also correlated with a higher-than-usual incidence of antisocial behavior.

The Influence of Home The relationship that children have with their parents, particularly during the early years, is critical to the way they learn to act. Observation and analysis of parent-child interaction patterns show that parents who treat their children with love, are sensitive to their children's needs, and provide praise and attention for desired behaviors tend to have normal children with positive behavioral characteristics. More than two decades of research have shown that antisocial children are more likely to come from homes in which parents are inconsistent disciplinarians, use harsh and excessive punishment to manage behavior problems, spend little time engaged in prosocial activities with their children, do not monitor the whereabouts and activities of their children, and show little love and affection for good behavior (Biglan, 1995; Dumas, 1989; Patterson et al., 1992; Walker et al., 1995). In a longitudinal study examining the behavior and school performance of seventh-grade boys as a correlate of various factors present during the fourth grade, ineffective discipline and infrequent parental involvement with the child proved the best predictor of delinquency in the seventh grade (Walker, Stieber, Ramsey, & O'Neill, 1991).

Because of the research on the relationship between parental child rearing practices and behavior problems, some mental health professionals have been quick to pin the blame for children's behavior problems on parents. But the relationship between parent and child is dynamic and reciprocal; in other words, the behavior of the child affects the behavior of the parents just as much as the parents' actions affect the child's actions (Patterson, 1980, 1982, 1986; Sameroff & Chandler, 1975). Therefore, at best it is not practical, and at worst it is wrong, to blame parents for abnormal behavior in young children. Instead, professionals must work with parents to help them systematically change certain aspects of the parent-child relationship in an effort to prevent and modify these problems.

The Influence of Peers When students associate with peers who exhibit antisocial behavior, they are more likely to experience additional trouble in the community and at school. Gang membership, drug and alcohol abuse, and deviant sexual behavior are factors in the community context that contribute to the development and maintenance of an antisocial lifestyle (Biglan, 1995; Walker et al., 1995).

The Influence of School School is where children spend the largest portion of their time outside the home. Therefore, it makes sense to carefully observe what takes place in schools in an effort to identify other events that may cause problem behavior.

Classroom practices that may contribute to the development of emotional and behavioral problems include unclear rules and expectations and inconsistent and punitive discipline practices.

Also, because most children with emotional and behavioral disorders are not identified until they are in school, it seems reasonable to question whether the school actually contributes to the incidence of behavioral disorders. Schooling practices that are likely to contribute to the development of emotional and behavioral problems in children include ineffective instruction that results in academic failure, unclear rules and expectations for appropriate behavior, inconsistent and punitive discipline practices, and failure to individualize instruction to accommodate diverse learners (Colvin, Kameenui, & Sugai, 1993; Mayer, 1995).

There is no question that what takes place in the classroom can maintain and actually strengthen deviant behavioral patterns even though the teacher is trying to help the child. Consider the all-too-common interaction between teacher and student illustrated in Figure 8.2 (Rhode et al., 1998). It begins with a teacher request that the student ignores and follows a predictable and escalating sequence of teacher pleas and threats that the student counters with excuses, arguments, and eventually a full-blown tantrum. The aggression and tantruming is so aversive to the teacher that she withdraws the request (thereby reinforcing and strengthening the student's disruptive behavior) so the student will stop tantruming (thereby reinforcing the teacher for withdrawing the request). This process has been called *coercive pain control* because the child learns to use painful behavior (e.g., arguing, making excuses, tantruming, property destruction, even physical aggression) to get what he wants (Patterson, 1982).

For specific suggestions on how to prevent student-teacher interactions that escalate out of control, see Rhode et al. (1998) and Walker and Sylvester (1998).

Children's emotional and behavioral problems are no doubt the product of a combination of etiologic factors. As Walker (1997) points out, however, effective intervention and treatment do not require precise knowledge of causal factors:

> It is apparent that a child's behavior pattern at school is the result of a complex interaction of (1) the behavior pattern the child has been taught at home, including attitudes toward school; (2) the experiences the child has had with different teachers in the school setting; and (3) the relationship between the child and his/her current teacher(s). Trying to determine in what proportion the child's behavior pattern is attributable to each of these learning sources is an impossible *and* quite unnecessary task. Disruptive child behavior can be changed very effectively without knowing the specific, original causes for its acquisition and development. (p. 20)

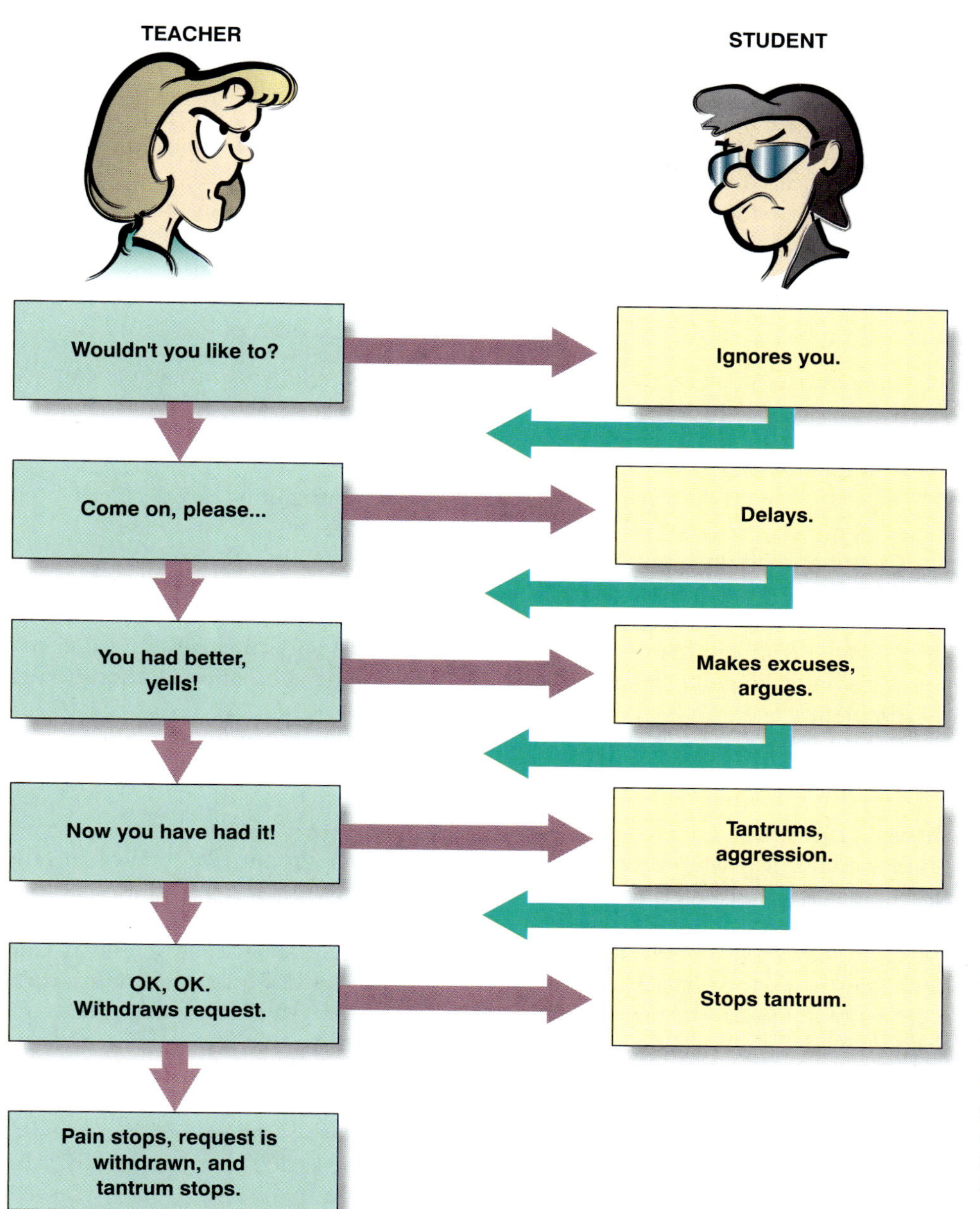
TEACHER
STUDENT
Wouldn't you like to?
Ignores you.
Come on, please...
Delays.
You had better, yells!
Makes excuses, argues.
Now you have had it!
Tantrums, aggression.
OK, OK. Withdraws request.
Stops tantrum.
Pain stops, request is withdrawn, and tantrum stops.

Figure 8.2 Coercive pain control

Source: Reprinted from Rhode, G., Jensen, W. R., & Reavis, H. K. (1992). *The tough kid book: Practical classroom management strategies* (p. 5). Longmont, CO: Sopris West. Used with permission.

Identification and Assessment

Assessment of emotional and behavioral disorders, as with all disabilities, should answer four basic questions concerning special education services:

1. Who might need help?
2. Who really does need help (who is eligible)?
3. What kind of help is needed?
4. Is the help benefiting the student?

In practice, however, many school districts do not use any systematic method for identifying children with emotional and behavioral disorders. This is because most children with emotional and behavioral disorders identify themselves. Antisocial children seldom go unnoticed: "To have one in your classroom is to recognize one" (Rhode et al., 1998, p. 3). This does not mean, however, that identification is a sure thing. Identification of emotional disturbance is always more difficult with younger children because the behavior of all young children changes quickly and often. Also, there is danger that some children with internalizing behaviors go undetected because their problems do not draw the attention of parents and teachers.

Walker (1997) recommends that school-related assessment of children with behavior problems should include the following (adapted from pp. 72–73):

- Whenever possible, address the specific reason(s) underlying problematic or deficient student behavior
- Provide a road map to guide the design and implementation of effective interventions
- Always give high priority to the vast reservoir of information teachers have about student performance and behavioral characteristics
- Use more than one method (e.g., rankings, checklists, direct observations), occur in more than one setting (e.g., classroom, playground, home), and involve more than one social agent (e.g., parents, teachers, peers)
- Consider teacher judgment as one of the most valid and valuable sources of decision-making information available for developing alternative solutions to the problem
- Collect only the essential information necessary to understand the school-related problems

The primary purpose of initial assessment is not to determine whether the child has *something called an emotional and behavioral disorder but to see whether the child's behavior is* different enough to warrant special services *and, if so, to indicate what those services should be.*

Many districts now require an intermediate step between screening and full-scale assessment. This step consists of interventions designed to maintain the child in the regular classroom and to prevent a suspected or developing problem from getting worse.

Screening Tests

Children who display patterns of antisocial behavior upon entering school run the risk of developing more serious and longstanding behavior problems as they progress through school and life (Patterson et al., 1991; Wehby, Dodge, & Valente, 1993). Walker et al. (1995) stress the importance of systematically screening and identifying as early as possible those children who are at risk for developing serious patterns of antisocial behavior. **Screening** is the process of differentiating between children who are not likely to be disabled and those who either show signs of behavioral disturbance or seem to be at risk for developing behavior problems. Children identified through a screening process then undergo more thorough assessment to determine their eligibility for special education and their specific educational needs.

Most screening devices consist of behavior rating scales or checklists that are completed by teachers, parents, peers, and/or children themselves. A good screening instrument has been normed across a large number of children of different ages and cultural backgrounds, uses standardized and easy-to-follow procedures for administration and scoring, and is economical and easy to use. Descriptions of three widely used screening tests for emotional and behavioral disorders follow:

1. *Behavior Rating Profile (BRP-2).* This test includes six subtests that can be used independently or in any combination (Brown & Hammill, 1990). The Teacher Rating Scale includes 30 items that teachers rate on a four-point scale from "very much like the student" to "not at all like the student" (e.g., "Doesn't follow class rules."). Parents complete the 30-item Parent Rating Scale in a similar manner (e.g., "Is shy, clings to parents."). Students answer true/false questions on the three Student Rating Scales (Home, School, and Peer) (e.g., "Other kids don't seem to like me very

much."). The Sociogram is a peer-nomination activity in which each student in the class identifies three classmates in response to questions such as "Which of the girls and boys in your class would you most (or least) like to work with on a class project?"

2. *Child Behavior Checklist (CBCL).* This test comes in teacher report, parent report, and child report forms and can be used with children ages 5 through 18 (Achenbach & Edelbrock, 1991). The teacher's form includes 112 behaviors (e.g., "cries a lot," "not liked by other pupils") that are rated on a three-point scale: "not true," "somewhat or sometimes true," or "very true or often true." The CBCL also includes items representing social competencies and adaptive functioning such as getting along with others and acting happy.

3. *Systematic Screening for Behavioral Disorders (SSBD).* This test is the most systematic, fully developed instrument presently available for screening children for possible emotional and behavioral disorders. The SSBD employs a three-step **multiple-gating screening** process for progressively narrowing down the number of children suspected of having serious behavior problems (Walker & Severson, 1990). In Gate I, classroom teachers rank-order every student in their classrooms according to behavioral profiles on two dimensions: externalizing problems (antisocial behavior, acting out, aggression) and internalizing problems (withdrawal, anxiety, little interaction with peers). The top three students on each teacher's list progress to Gate II, the Critical Events Index.

> Critical events are behavioral pinpoints of high salience and intensity that do not depend on frequency to define their severity. Any occurrence of these target behaviors is viewed as an indicator of major disruption of social-behavioral adjustment processes in school. Critical events have been characterized as analogous to "behavioral earthquakes" in terms of their ecological disruptiveness and severity. Because of their salience and low base rates of occurrence, critical events are viewed as indicative of serious behavioral pathology and may strongly reinforce negative peer and teacher social perception biases toward students who exhibit them. (Todis, Severson, & Walker, 1990, pp. 75–76)

The 33 items that make up the Critical Events Index were developed from previous research on teachers' standards and behavioral expectations (Walker & Rankin, 1983). They include externalizing behaviors such as "is physically aggressive with other students" and "makes lewd or obscene gestures" and internalizing behaviors such as "vomits after eating" and "has auditory or visual hallucinations." Students who exceed normative criteria on the Critical Events Index advance to Gate III of the SSBD, which consists of direct and repeated observations during independent seatwork periods in the classroom and on the playground during recess. Children who meet or exceed cutoff criteria for either or both observational measures are referred to child study teams for further evaluation.

The Early Screening Project *is an adaptation of the SSBD for use with preschool children ages 3 to 5 (Walker, Severson, & Feil, 1994).*

Projective Tests

A **projective test** consists of ambiguous stimuli (e.g., "What does this inkblot look like to you?") or open-ended tasks (e.g., "Complete this sentence for me: 'Most girls like to. . . . '"). It is assumed that responses to items that have no right or wrong answer will reveal a person's true personality characteristics.

The most famous projective test is the Rorschach Test (Rorschach, 1942), which consists of a set of 10 cards, each containing an inkblot, the left and right halves being mirror images of each other. The subject is shown one card at a time and told, "Tell me what you see, what it might be for you. There are no right or wrong answers."

Another well-known projective test is the Thematic Apperception Test (TAT) (Morgan & Murray, 1935). A person taking the TAT is shown a series of pictures and asked to make up a story about each picture, telling who the people are; what they are doing, thinking, and feeling; and how the situation will turn out.

A projective test specifically developed for screening children with emotional disorders is the Draw a Person: Screening Procedure for Emotional Disturbance, in which the child is asked to draw three pictures: a man, a woman, and herself (Naglieri, McNeish, & Bardos, 1991). Studies have shown that children in programs for students with emotional and behavior problems include in their drawings a statistically higher frequency of signs associated with emotional disturbance (e.g., distorted body parts, frowning mouth) than do nondisabled children (McNeish & Naglieri, 1993; Naglieri & Pfeiffer, 1992).

Although sometimes interesting, the results of projective tests have proven to be of minimal value in prescribing appropriate intervention. Children often do not respond in a testing or interview situation in the same way they do in the classroom or at home. Also, projective tests assess an indirect and extremely limited sample of a child's behavioral repertoire and, just as important, do not assess how the child typically acts over a period of time. One-time measures—whether they are direct or indirect—are not sufficient as a basis for either identifying the presence of an emotional or behavioral disorder or planning education and treatment.

Detailed explanation of procedures for measuring behavior can be found in Alberto and Troutman (1999) and Cooper, Heron, and Heward (1987).

Direct Observation and Measurement of Behavior

In assessment by direct observation and measurement, the actual behaviors that cause concern about a child are clearly specified and observed in the settings in which they normally occur (e.g., in the classroom, on the playground). Behavior can be measured objectively along several dimensions: rate (or frequency), duration, latency, topography, and magnitude (see Figure 8.3).

The advantage of assessing and describing emotional and behavioral disorders in terms of these dimensions is that identification, design of instructional strategies, and evaluation of the effects of treatment can all revolve around objective measurement. This approach leads to a direct focus on the child's problem—the inappropriate behavior—and ways of dealing with it as opposed to concentrating on some presumed (and unreachable) problem within the child.

Kauffman (1997) makes a strong case for direct and frequent measurement with children with emotional and behavioral disorders:

> The teacher who cannot or will not pinpoint and measure the relevant behaviors of the students he or she is teaching is probably not going to be very effective. . . . Not to define precisely and to measure these behavioral excesses and deficiencies, then, is a fundamental error; it is akin to the malpractice of a nurse who decides not to measure vital signs (heart rate, respiration rate, temperature, and blood pressure), perhaps arguing that he or she is too busy, that subjective estimates of vital signs are quite adequate, that vital signs are only superficial estimates of the patient's health, or that vital signs do not signify the nature of the underlying pathology. The teaching profession is dedicated to the task of changing behavior—changing behavior demonstrably for the better. What can one say, then, of educational practice that does not include precise definition and reliable measurement of the behavioral change induced by the teacher's methodology? *It is indefensible.* (p. 514)

IDEA recommends that functional assessments be conducted as part of designing positive behavioral support plans for students with disabilities. Functional assessment is described further in Chapter 13.

Functional Assessment

The purpose of functional assessment is to obtain information about when, where, and why problem behaviors occur as well as when, where, and why they do not occur (O'Neill, Horner, Albin, Sprague, Storey, & Newton, 1997; Sugai, Horner, &

Rate (or frequency): how often a particular behavior is performed. All children cry, get into fights with other children, and sulk from time to time; yet we are not apt to think of them as emotionally disturbed. The primary difference between children with behavioral disorders and other children is the frequency with which these behaviors occur. Although disturbed children may not do anything their nondisabled peers do not do, they do certain undesirable things too often (e.g., crying, hitting others) and/or engage in adaptive behaviors too infrequently (e.g., playing with others).

Duration: how long a child engages in a given activity. The amount of time children with behavioral disorders engage in certain activities is often markedly different—either longer or shorter—from that of other children. For example, most young children have temper tantrums, but the tantrums generally last no more than a few minutes. A child with emotional and behavioral disorders may tantrum for over an hour at a time. The problem may also be one of too short a duration. For example, some children with emotional and behavioral disorders cannot stick to a task for more than a few seconds at a time.

Topography: the physical shape or form of behavior. For instance, printing your name in block letters and signing your name in cursive have different topographies. Some children with emotional and behavioral disorders emit behaviors that are seldom, if ever, seen in typical children (setting fires, self-abuse). These behaviors may be maladaptive, bizarre, or dangerous to the child or others.

Latency: the time that elapses between the opportunity to respond and the beginning of the behavior. The latency of a child's behavior may be too long (e.g., several minutes elapse before beginning to comply with the teacher's request) or too short (e.g., the child immediately begins screaming and tantruming at the slightest provocation or frustration, thus having no time to consider more appropriate alternative behaviors).

Magnitude: the strength or intensity of behavior. The magnitude of a child's responses may be too little (e.g., talking in a volume so low that he cannot be heard) or too much (e.g., slamming the door).

Figure 8.3 Five measurable dimensions of behavior

Sprague, in press). Functional assessment involves interviews with significant others and direct observation to determine the environmental events that typically occur before and after the behavior(s) of concern. It may also involve experimental manipulation of one or more antecedent or consequent events surrounding the target behavior in an attempt to verify the function of the behavior for the child (e.g., systematically varying the difficulty of academic tasks to test if the child's oppositional behavior is triggered by difficult tasks). This information can then be used to improve the effectiveness and efficiency of behavioral intervention (Lalli, Browder, Mace, & Brown, 1993; Umbreit, 1995). For example, knowing that a student's tantrums are maintained by teacher attention will suggest a different intervention than would be indicated for misbehavior that is maintained by escape from challenging academic tasks.

Educational Approaches

Theoretical and Conceptual Models

On the basis of the work of Rhodes and his colleagues (Rhodes & Head, 1974; Rhodes & Tracy, 1972a, 1972b), Kauffman (1997) has identified six conceptual models for understanding and treating emotional and behavioral disorders (see Figure 8.4).

For examples of research on behavioral interventions, see the journals Behavioral Disorders, Education and Treatment of Children, Journal of Applied Behavior Analysis, *the* Journal of Behavioral Education, *and the* Journal of Applied Behavior Interventions.

Few teachers use only the techniques suggested by one model; most employ an *eclectic* approach, which means they combine a number of theories, philosophies, and methods in their work with students with emotional and behavioral disorders (Beare, 1991). The models themselves are not entirely discrete; they overlap in certain areas. Sometimes the difference is mostly a matter of wording; the actual classroom practices of teachers using the different models may be quite similar.

Our main purpose here is to make you aware of these different approaches. It is beyond the scope of this text to do justice to a description of each model and to compare and contrast them. We will say, however, that little empirical evidence attests to

Figure 8.4 Conceptual models for emotional and behavioral disorders

Biogenic: views deviant behavior as a physical symptom of genetic or medical causes. Implies that these causes must be cured to treat the emotional disturbance. Treatments include drug therapy, dietary control, exercise, surgery, and biofeedback.

Psychodynamic: disordered behavior conceptualized as a symptom of a pathological imbalance of hypothetical mental processes (ego, id, and superego); unconscious motivation for behavior must be understood for the problem to be resolved. Treatment entails psychotherapy for the child (and sometimes the parents) and stresses a permissive and accepting classroom environment.

Psychoeducational: concerned with "unconscious motivations and underlying conflicts (hallmarks of psychodynamic models) yet also stresses the realistic demands of everyday functioning in school, home, and community" (Kauffman, 1997, p. 115). Intervention focuses on therapeutic discussions, such as life-space interviews, to allow children to understand their behavior rationally and to plan to change it (Gardner, 1990a, 1990b; Long, 1990; Wood & Long, 1991).

Humanistic: suggests that the child with emotional and behavioral disorders is not in touch with her own feelings and cannot find self-fulfillment in traditional educational settings. Treatment takes place in an open, personalized setting where the teacher serves as a nondirective, nonauthoritarian "resource and catalyst" and the child has free choice of educational goals and activities (Rogers, 1983).

Ecological: stresses the interaction of the child with the people around him and with social institutions. Treatment involves teaching the child to function within the family, school, neighborhood, and larger community (Hobbs, 1966).

Behavioral: views disordered behavior as the primary problem in its own right; assumes that maladaptive behavior has been learned and is being maintained by current events in the environment. Treatment involves the use of applied behavior analysis techniques to help the child learn new adaptive behaviors and eliminate inappropriate ones (Alberto & Troutman, 1999; Cooper et al., 1987; Kerr & Nelson, 1998; Rhodes et al., 1998; Walker, 1997).

the effectiveness of treatment approaches based on the psychodynamic model of underlying subconscious causes of children's behavior problems. Cullinan, Epstein, and Lloyd (1991) compared the effectiveness of the psychoeducational, behavioral, and ecological models with respect to desired improvements in behavior at the time and place of intervention. They concluded that there was weak scientific support for the psychoeducational model and too little research available on which to evaluate the ecological model. "In contrast, there is a substantial body of good research demonstrating that many behavioral interventions can bring about swift, fairly reliable, and often dramatic improvements in problem behaviors" (pp. 153–154).

Curriculum Goals

What should students with emotional and behavioral disorders be taught? An obvious but only partially correct answer is they should learn to control their antisocial behavior. For many years, programs serving students with behavioral disorders focused on treating maladaptive behavior at the expense of academic instruction. As a result, students who already possessed deficient academic skills fell even farther behind their peers (Knitzer et al., 1990). Special education for these students must also include instruction in the social and academic skills required for success in integrated classroom, community, and vocational settings.

Learning how to recruit teacher attention for good behavior is a social skill that can lead to success in the classroom. See "Look, I'm All Finished!" later in this chapter.

Social Skills Social skills instruction is an important curriculum component for students with emotional and behavioral disorders. Many of these students have difficulty holding a conversation, expressing their feelings, participating in group activities, and responding to failure or criticism in positive and constructive ways. They often get into fights and altercations because they lack the social skills needed to handle or defuse provocative incidents. The slightest snub, bump, or misunderstood request—which would be laughed off or ignored by most children—can precipitate an aggressive attack from some students.

For detailed information on how to teach social skills, see Alberg, Petry, and Eller (1994); Cartledge and Milburn (1995); Rutherford, Chipman, DiGangi, and Anderson (1992); and Serna (1993). For a review of 27 studies that examine specific social skills interventions and their effects on students with behavior problems, see Zaragoza, Vaughn, and McIntosh (1991).

Knapczyk (1992) taught four secondary students with behavioral disorders positive alternative responses to situations that previously had precipitated aggressive outbursts (see Table 8.2). Instruction consisted of individualized videotape modeling and behavioral rehearsal. Two male students who were leaders in the school served as actors for the videotapes—one playing the role of the subject, simulating his usual reactions to provoking situations and demonstrating appropriate alternative responses; the other acting out the usual reactions of classmates. After watching the videotapes, the students discussed the circumstances of the incidents with their special class teacher and practiced specific alternative responses. Not only did treatment result in a decreased frequency of aggressive acts by all four students across several settings, but observers noted a concurrent decrease in the number of provoking antecedent events.

Numerous social skills curricula and training programs have been published; several recommended ones are described in Figure 8.5.

In the process of learning how to participate in collaborative learning activities and serving as academic tutors for one another, students with emotional and behavioral disorders may also learn better social and affective skills (Cartledge & Cochran, 1993; Cochran, Feng, Cartledge, & Hamilton, 1993).

Academic Skills A continuing concern in the field of emotional and behavioral disorders is poor academic achievement. Although students with emotional and behavioral disorders require the help of a specially trained teacher to work on their specific behavior problems and social skills deficits, academic instruction cannot be neglected. Most children with emotional and behavioral disorders are already achieving at a rate below that of their nondisabled peers; ignoring the three Rs only puts them further behind. Reading, writing, and arithmetic are as important to children with emotional and behavioral disorders as they are to any child who hopes to function successfully in society.

Table 8.2
Examples of alternative behaviors a student can learn to emit in response to provoking antecedent events

Antecedent Events	Alternative Responses
Participant initiates a greeting and is ignored or called a name	1. Repeat the greeting 2. Greet another person 3. Walk away without saying anything else
Participant requests an object and request is denied	1. Make request of another person 2. Work on another activity that does not require object
Participant reaches for an object and person tries to retain it	1. Ask politely for object 2. Ask someone else for object 3. Work on another activity until person finishes using object
Participant asks person to engage in an activity and the request is turned down	1. Suggest another activity 2. Ask someone else 3. Start an activity that does not involve another person
Participant touches another person and is pushed or hit by the person	1. Ignore the incident 2. Say "Excuse me" to person 3. Engage person in a conversation or appropriate activity

Source: Reprinted from Knapczyk, D. R. (1992). Effects of developing alternative responses on the aggressive behavior of adolescents. *Behavioral Disorders, 17,* 249. Used by permission of the Council for Exceptional Children, Reston, VA.

Fortunately, most students with emotional and behavioral disorders learn when presented with direct, systematic instruction (see Chapters 6 and 7). And effective instruction is the first and fundamental element for effective classroom management. Students who are actively engaged during instruction exhibit less off-task and disruptive behavior than do students who are expected to passively observe (Gunter, Hummel, & Conroy, 1998; Miller, Hall, & Heward, 1995).

Alterable Variables The twofold task of the teacher of children with emotional and behavioral disorders is helping students replace antisocial and maladaptive behaviors with more socially appropriate behaviors and acquire academic knowledge and skills. The frequent displays of antisocial behavior, the absence of appropriate social skills, and the academic deficits exhibited by many students with emotional and behavioral disorders make this a staggering challenge. The challenge is made all the more difficult because the teacher seldom, if ever, can control (or even know) all of the factors affecting a student's behavior. There is typically a host of contributing factors over which the teacher can exert little or no influence (e.g., the delinquent friends with whom the student associates before and after school). But it does little good to bemoan the student's past (which no one can alter) or to use all of the things in the student's current life that cannot be changed as an excuse for failing to help the student in the classroom. Special educators should focus their attention and efforts on those aspects of a student's life that they can effectively control.

Getting Along with Others (Jackson, Jackson, & Monroe, 1983): includes 32 lessons across 17 social skills areas such as following directions, handling name calling and teasing, and offering to help. Available from Research Press, Department 95, P.O. Box 9177, Champaign, IL 61826.

Skillstreaming the Adolescent: A Structured Learning Approach to Teaching Prosocial Skills (Goldstein et al., 1980): activities designed to increase self-esteem and develop competence in dealing with peers, family, and authority figures. Skillstreaming programs for elementary and preschool children are also available. Available from Research Press (see above).

Taking Part: Introducing Social Skills to Children (Cartledge & Kleefeld, 1991): helps students in preschool classrooms through third grade learn social skills in six units: making conversation, communicating feelings, expressing oneself, cooperating with peers, playing with peers, and responding to aggression and conflict. Published by American Guidance Service, 4201 Woodland Road, Circle Pines, MN 55014.

The Prepare Curriculum: Teaching Prosocial Competencies (Goldstein, 1988): designed for students who are aggressive, withdrawn, or otherwise deficient in social competencies. Activities and materials for middle and high school students in 10 areas, such as problem solving, anger control, stress management, and cooperation. Published by Research Press (see above).

The Walker Social Skills Curriculum: includes *ACCEPTS: A Curriculum for Children's Effective Peer and Teacher Skills* (Walker et al., 1983), for children grades K–6, and *ACCESS: Adolescent Curriculum for Communication and Effective Social Skills* (Walker, Todis, Holmes, & Horton, 1988) for students at the middle and high school levels. Available from PRO-ED, 8700 Shoal Creek Boulevard, Austin, TX 78757.

Working Together (Cartledge & Kleefeld, 1994): incorporates stories and activities based on folk literature to teach social skills to students in grades 3–6 and older students with special needs. Published by American Guidance Service (see above).

Figure 8.5 Recommended social skills curricula

Bloom (1980) calls these "alterable variables": ones that both make a difference and can be affected by teaching practices.

> The primary focus of the special educator's concern must be on the contributing factors that the teacher can alter. Factors over which the teacher has no control may determine how the child or youth is approached initially, but the teacher is called upon to begin working with specific pupils after disorders have appeared. The special educator has two primary responsibilities: first, to make sure that he or she does no further disservice to the student; and second, to manipulate the student's present environment to foster development of more appropriate behavior in spite of unalterable past and present circumstances. Emphasis must be on the present and future, not the past. And although other environments may be important, the teacher's focus must be on the classroom environment. Certainly teachers may profitably extend their influence beyond the classroom, perhaps working with parents to improve the home environment or using community resources for the child's benefit. But talk of influence beyond the classroom, including such high-sounding phrases as *ecological management* and *wraparound services*, is patent nonsense until the teacher has demonstrated that he or she can make the classroom environment conducive to improved behavior. (Kauffman, 1997, p. 513)

"Look, I'm All Finished!" Recruiting Teacher Attention

by Sheila R. Alber and William L. Heward

Preparation of students with disabilities for inclusion in general education classrooms should include instruction in classroom survival skills. Attending to instruction, following directions, and completing assigned seatwork are likely to enhance a student's acceptance and success in the regular classroom (Anderson-Inman, Walker, & Purcell, 1984). Because teachers value such "good student" behaviors, students are also likely to receive teacher praise and attention for exhibiting them.

But classrooms are busy places, so important academic and social behaviors by students can easily be overlooked by teachers. Research shows that teachers are more likely to pay attention to a disruptive student than to one who is working quietly and productively (Walker, 1997). It is hard for teachers to be aware of students who need help, especially low-achieving ones who are less likely to ask (Newman & Golding, 1990).

Although teachers in general education classrooms are expected to adapt instruction to serve students with disabilities, this is not always the case. Most secondary teachers interviewed by Schumm et al. (1995) believed that students with disabilities should take responsibility for obtaining the help they need. Thus, politely recruiting teacher attention and assistance can help students with disabilities function more independently and actively influence their quality of instruction they receive.

Recruiting Can Work Students of various ages and abilities have learned to recruit teacher attention for performing a wide range of tasks in classroom and community settings: preschoolers with developmental delays for completing preacademic tasks and staying on task during transitions (Connell, Carta, & Baer, 1993; Stokes, Fowler, & Baer, 1978) as well as students with learning disabilities (Alber, Heward, & Hippler, 1999; Todd, Horner, & Sugai, in press), behavioral disorders (Morgan, Young, & Goldstein, 1983), and mental retardation (Craft, Alber, & Heward, 1998) while performing academic tasks in regular classrooms and secondary students with mental retardation (Mank & Horner, 1987) for improved work performance in vocational training settings. (For a review, see Alber and Heward [in press].)

For example, Craft et al. (1998) taught four fourth graders with mental retardation to recruit teacher attention while they worked on spelling assignments in a general education classroom. They were taught to show their work to the teacher two to three times per session and to make statements such as "How am I doing?" or "Look, I'm all finished!" Recruitment training, which was conducted in the special education classroom, increased the frequency of each student's recruiting, the frequency of teacher praise, the percentage of worksheet items completed, and the accuracy with which the students completed the assignments. After the study the general education teacher stated, "They fit in better, they were more a part of the group, and they weren't being disruptive because they were working."

Who Should be Taught to Recruit?

Withdrawn Willamena. Willamena seldom asks a teacher anything. Because she is so quiet and well behaved, her teachers sometimes forget she's in the room. Withdrawn Willamenas are prime candidates for recruitment training.

In-a-Hurry Harry. Harry's usually half-done with a task before his teacher finishes explaining it. Racing through his work allows him to be the first to turn it in. But his work is often incomplete and error-filled, so he doesn't hear much praise from his teacher. Harry would benefit from recruitment training that includes self-checking and self-correction.

Shouting Shelly. Shelly has just finished her work, and she wants her teacher to look at it—*right now!* But Shelly doesn't raise her hand. She gets her teacher's attention—and disrupts most of her classmates—by shouting across the room. Students like Shelly should be taught appropriate ways to solicit teacher attention.

Pestering Pete. Pete always raises his hand, waits quietly for his teacher to come to his desk, and then politely asks, "Have I done this right?" But he can repeat this routine a dozen times in a 20-minute period, so his teachers find it annoying. Positive teacher attention often turns into reprimands. Recruitment training for Pete, and for all students, will teach him to limit the number of times he cues his teachers for attention.

Teaching Students to Recruit

1. *Identify target skills.* Students should recruit teacher attention for target skills that are valued and therefore likely to be reinforced—e.g., writing neatly and legibly, working accurately, completing assigned work, cleaning up at transitions, and making contributions when working in a cooperative group.

2. *Teach self-assessment.* Students should self-assess their work before recruiting teacher attention (e.g., Sue asks herself, "Is my work complete?"). After the student can reliably distinguish between complete and incomplete work samples, she can learn how to check the accuracy of her work with answer keys, checklists of the steps or components of the academic skill, or spot checking two or three items before asking the teacher to look at it.
3. *Teach appropriate recruiting.* Teach students when, how, and how often to recruit and how to respond to the teacher after receiving attention.
   - *When?* Students should signal for teacher attention after they have completed and self-checked a substantial part of their work. Students should also be taught when *not* to try to get their teacher's attention (e.g., when the teacher is working with another student, talking to another adult, taking the lunch count).
   - *How?* The traditional hand raise should be part of every student's recruiting repertoire. Other methods of gaining attention should be taught depending upon teacher preferences and routines in the general education classroom (e.g., have students signal they need help by standing up a small flag on their desks; expect students to bring their work to the teacher's desk for help and feedback).
   - *How often?* While helping Withdrawn Willamena learn to seek teacher attention, don't turn her into a Pestering Pete. How often a student should recruit varies across teachers and activities (e.g., independent seatwork, cooperative learning groups, whole-class instruction). Direct observation in the classroom is the best way to establish an optimal rate of recruiting; it is also a good idea to ask the regular classroom teacher when, how, and with what frequency she prefers students to ask for help.
   - *What to say?* Students should be taught several statements that are likely to evoke positive feedback from the teacher (e.g., "Please look at my work." "Did I do a good job?" "How am I doing?"). Keep it simple, but teach the student to vary her verbal cues so she will not sound like a parrot.
   - *How to respond?* Students should respond to their teacher's feedback by establishing eye contact, smiling, and saying, "Thank you." Polite appreciation is very reinforcing to teachers and will increase the likelihood of more positive attention the next time.
4. *Model and role-play the complete sequence.* Begin by providing students with a rationale for recruiting (e.g., the teacher will be happy you did a good job, you will get more work done, your grades might improve). Thinking aloud while modeling is good way to show the recruiting sequence. While performing each step, say, "Okay, I've finished my work. Now I'm going to check it. Did I put my name on my paper? Yes. Did I do all the problems? Yes. Did I follow all the steps? Yes. Okay, my teacher doesn't look busy right now. I'll raise my hand and wait quietly until she comes to my desk." Have another student pretend to be the regular classroom teacher and come over to you when you have your hand up. Say, "Mr. Patterson, please look at my work." The helper says, "Oh, you did a very nice job." Then smile and say, "Thank you, teacher." Role-play with praise and offer corrective feedback until the student accurately performs the entire sequence on several consecutive trials.

Politely recruiting teacher attention and assistance is one way students can actively influence the quality of instruction they receive.

Prepare Students for Alternate Responses Of course, not every student cue will result in teacher praise; some efforts to recruit may even be followed by criticism (e.g., "This is all wrong. Pay better attention the next time."). Use role playing to prepare students for these possibilities and have them practice polite responses (e.g., "Thank you for helping me with this."). For more information on teaching students to recruit teacher attention, see Alber and Heward (1997).

Sheila R. Alber is a faculty member in the Department of Special Education at the University of Southern Mississippi.

Source: Adapted from Alber, S. R., & Heward, W. L. (1997). Recruit it or lose it! Training students to recruit contingent teacher attention. *Intervention in School and Clinic, 5,* 275–282. Used with permission.

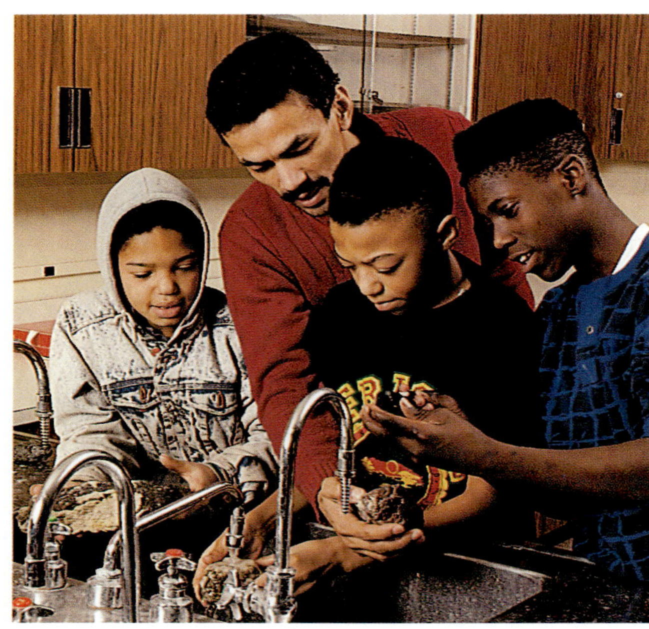

The academic development of students with behavior disorders must not be ignored.

An explanation of these techniques is beyond the scope of this book. A number of excellent books are available for the teacher who wishes to learn more about classroom and behavior management (e.g., Alberto and Troutman, 1999; Kameenui & Darch, 1995; Kerr & Nelson, 1998; Rhode et al., 1998; Sprick & Howard, 1997; Zirpoli & Melloy, 1997).

Behavior Management

Managing the classroom environment for students with emotional and behavioral disorders requires a great deal of knowledge and skill. Teachers must know when and how to use behavioral teaching strategies such as **positive reinforcement**, **shaping, contingency contracting, extinction** (ignoring disruptive behavior), **differential reinforcement of other behavior** (reinforcing any behavior except the undesirable response), **response cost, time out** (restricting students' access to reinforcement for a brief time following an inappropriate behavior), and **overcorrection** (requiring restitution beyond the damaging effects of the antisocial behavior, as when a child who takes another child's cookie must return it plus one of her own). These techniques should not be implemented as isolated events but incorporated into an overall instructional and classroom management plan that might include a **token economy** and/or a *level system* to help each student learn greater independence and earn more privileges (Anderson & Katsiyannis, 1997; Barbetta, 1990a, 1990b; Smith & Farrell, 1993).

When designing and implementing classroom management strategies, teachers of students with emotional and behavioral disorders must be careful not to create an environment in which coercion is the primary means by which students are motivated to participate and follow rules. Coercive environments, in addition to promoting escape and avoidance behavior by those being coerced, do not teach what to do as much as they focus on what not to do (Sidman, 1989). Teachers of students with emotional and behavioral disorders must strive to design classroom environments that not only are effective in decreasing antisocial behavior but also increase the frequency of positive teacher-student interactions (Gunter, Denny, Jack, Shores, & Nelson, 1993; Shores, Gunter, & Jack, 1993).

The vast majority of classroom behavior problems can be prevented by the use of proactive behavior management. *Proactive strategies* are preplanned interventions that anticipate behavior problems and stop them before they occur. "It is much more difficult to remediate the problems caused by a Tough Kid than to prevent them. Once

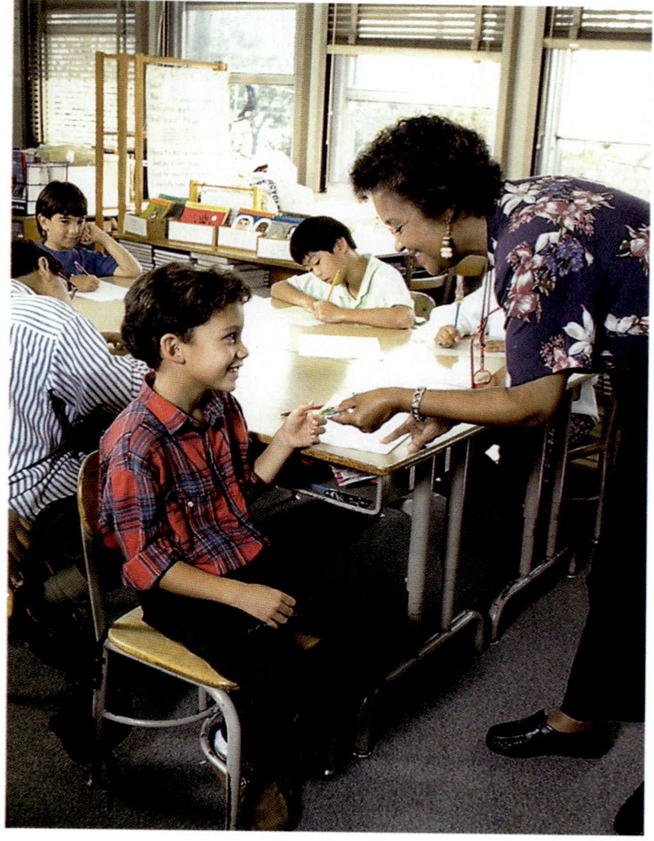

Proactive behavior management strategies include the use of positive reinforcement to increase the frequency of desired behavior.

a teacher has lost the management tempo in a classroom and things are out of control, it is far more difficult to reestablish control" (Rhode et al., 1998, p. 19).

Proactive strategies include structuring the physical environment of the classroom (e.g., have the most difficult students sit nearest the teacher), establishing clear rules and expectations for appropriate behavior, scheduling and sequencing lesson activities to minimize down time, presenting instructions and requests to students in a manner that increases the likelihood of compliance, and effectively using positive reinforcement to "catch students being good" and motivate desired behavior (Rhode et al., 1998). Two other examples of proactive classroom management approaches are teaching self-management skills to students and using peer mediation and support.

Self-management research with students with emotional and behavioral disorders is reviewed by Nelson, Smith, Young, and Dodd (1991).

Self-Management Teaching self-management skills is an excellent way to help students learn responsibility and self-determination (Agran, 1997; Wehmeyer, Agran, & Hughes, 1998). Many children with emotional and behavioral disorders think they have little control over their lives. Things just seem to happen to them, and being disruptive is their means of reacting to a world that is inconsistent and frustrating.

For a review of research on self-monitoring as a behavior management technique, see Webber, Scheuerman, McCall, and Coleman (1993).

Numerous studies have demonstrated that students with behavior problems can effectively use self-monitoring and self-evaluation to help regulate their behavior (e.g., Carr & Punzo, 1993; DiGangi & Maag, 1992; Dunlap et al., 1995; Wood, Murdock, Cronin, Dawson, & Kirby, 1998). **Self-monitoring** is a relatively simple procedure in which the student observes and records the occurrence (and sometimes the nonoccurrence) of his own behavior; *self-evaluation* involves comparing one's behavior against a standard or goal.

Self-management is also appealing from the standpoint of generalizing treatment gains from one setting to another. An external control agent (e.g., a special education teacher in the resource room) cannot go with the student to all of the settings in which she needs to exhibit newly learned behavior (e.g., staying in her seat and completing a whole workbook page). But the one person who is always with the student is the student's own self (Baer & Fowler, 1984).

An impressive study demonstrating the potential of self-management techniques for the generalization of improved behavior across classroom settings was conducted by Rhode, Morgan, & Young (1983). Six students with emotional and behavioral disorders learned to bring their highly disruptive and off-task behaviors under control in a resource room with a combination of techniques that featured self-monitoring and self-evaluation. Initially, the teacher rated each student and awarded points at 15-minute intervals on a scale from 5 (great) to 0 (poor) for classroom behavior and academic work. Then the students began to evaluate their own behavior with the same rating system (see Figure 8.6). The teacher continued to rate each student.

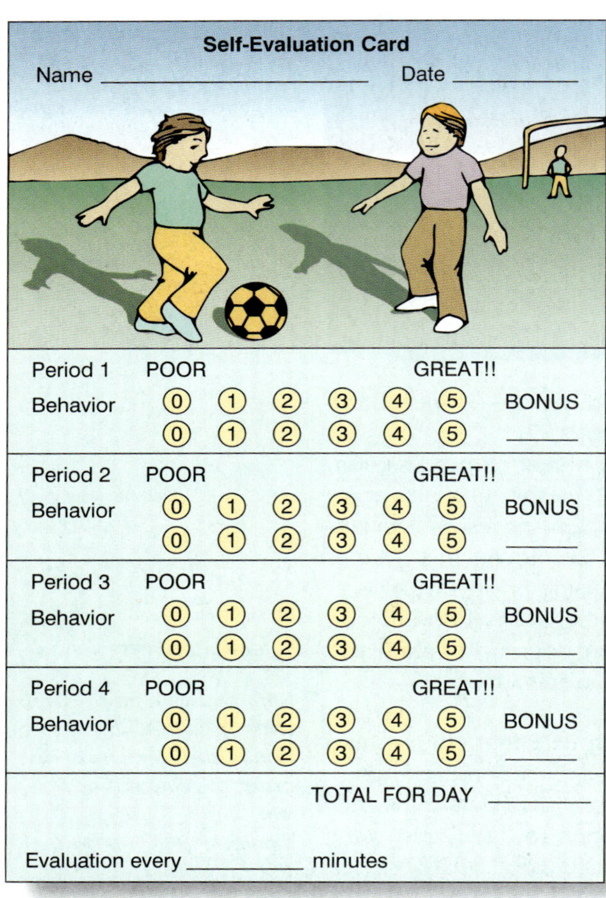

Front of Card

Back of Card

Figure 8.6 Card used for student self-evaluation

Source: Reprinted from Rhode, G. (1981). Generalization and maintenance of treatment gains on behaviorally/emotionally handicapped students from resource rooms to regular classrooms using self-evaluation procedures (p. 157). Unpublished doctoral dissertation, Utah State University. Used by permission.

Teacher and students compared their ratings. If the student's rating was within one point of the teacher's, he received the number of points he had given himself. If teacher and student matched exactly, the student earned an additional bonus point. The teacher then began to fade the number of times she also rated the students. After the students were behaving at acceptable levels and accurately self-evaluating their behavior, they began to self-evaluate once every 30 minutes in the regular classroom. Eventually, the self-evaluation cards and point system were withdrawn, and students were encouraged to continue to self-evaluate themselves privately. During the study's final phase, the students' level of appropriate behavior in the regular classroom was as high as their nondisabled peers.

Peer Mediation and Support The power of the peer group can be an effective means of producing positive changes in students with behavioral disorders (Barbetta, 1990a; Coleman & Webber, 1988). Specific strategies for teaching peers to help one another decrease inappropriate behavior include *peer monitoring* (a student is taught to observe and record a peer's behavior and to provide the peer with feedback) (Fowler, Dougherty, Kirby, & Kohler, 1986; Smith & Fowler, 1984) and *peer confrontation* (peers are trained to confront one another when inappropriate behavior occurs or is about to occur, explaining why the behavior is a problem and suggesting or modeling an appropriate alternative response) (Salend, Jantzen, & Giek, 1992; Sandler, Arnold, Gable, & Strain, 1987).

Implementing a peer support, or *group process,* model is much more complicated than bringing together a group of children and hoping they will benefit from positive peer influence. Most children with serious emotional and behavioral disorders have not been members of successfully functioning peer groups in which appropriate behavior is modeled and valued (Hallenbeck & Kauffman, 1995), nor have many such children learned to accept responsibility for their actions (Rockwell & Guetzloe, 1996). The teacher's first and most formidable challenge is helping promote group cohesiveness. Barbetta (1991) recommends some basic rules for fostering the development of group cohesiveness:

- Every child is an equal member of the group and, as such, is accountable and responsible to the group.
- As often as possible, the group "moves" as one.
- The group works out all major decisions and problems together.
- All major rewards are earned and shared by the group.
- Only in rare instances is a student "removed" from the group (i.e., no longer accountable to the group for her behavior).
- The teacher functions as a member of the group but has veto power when necessary.

Although group process treatment programs take many forms, most incorporate group meetings and group-oriented contingencies. Two types of group meetings are usually held daily. A planning meeting is held each morning in which the group reviews the daily schedule, each group member states a behavioral goal for the day, peers provide support and suggestions to one another for meeting their goals, and a group goal for the day is agreed on. An evaluation meeting is held at the end of each day to discuss how well the individual and group goals were met, and each group member must give and receive positive peer comments. Problem-solving meetings are held whenever any group member, including the teacher, feels the need to discuss a problem. The group identifies the problem, generates several solutions, discusses the likely consequences of each solution, develops a plan for the best solution, and makes

For one teacher's personal reflections on teaching students with emotional and behavioral disorders with a group process approach, see "My Return Voyage" on pp. 318-319.

My Return Voyage

by Patricia M. Barbetta

The power of the peer group can be an effective means of producing positive changes in children with emotional and behavioral disorders. Patty Barbetta, now chairperson of the Department of Special Education at Florida International University, spent 11 years as a teacher, teacher supervisor, and education director at the Pressley Ridge School, a special school for children and adolescents with severe emotional and behavioral disorders in Pittsburgh. Here Patty describes some of her experiences implementing a behavior analytic group process model.

What was I doing? Returning to a frontline position in a classroom for children with emotional and behavioral disorders after five years as a program supervisor? My co-workers, friends, and family asked these questions—and for very good reasons. They recalled my early teaching experiences with these children: the hours I spent restraining Jeremy, who never thought twice before hitting me hard; the day the fire chief threatened to fine me when Sam falsely set off the alarm once too often; the time I developed a behavioral contract for Connie to follow her mother's directions, only to have her run away from home. And my biannual trips to the emergency room for a tetanus shot necessitated by student bites.

Reasons for Returning My reasons for returning to the classroom were many, but I will mention just two. First was the progress we had made during my first year of teaching. Don't get me wrong. We still had behavior problems right through the last day of school. But by the end of the year, the problems were less frequent and typically were resolved quickly. In our second year (we virtually had the same group), we managed to function well enough to earn money for a field trip to Washington, DC—a three-day trip that (even though the entire group had to take a time out at Arlington Cemetery) went off without major incident. We were by far the best-behaved group at the Smithsonian (much better than some of the general education groups). Witnessing our hard-earned gains was very rewarding.

Second, I had an interest in directly implementing group process techniques as a new component of the treatment program at Pressley Ridge. I admit I didn't readily buy into the group model at first. The idea of handing over control to a group of students with behavioral disorders scared me. These students working together as a group? I simply couldn't imagine it. Most of them had never been part of a successfully functioning peer group. When they did participate as a group, they usually shoplifted, hung out on the street corner harassing passersby, or picked on timid students in the school cafeteria.

"That's His Problem, Not Mine!" As I had feared, things did not go well when I first tried a group approach. The students, accustomed to individualized, teacher-designed and -directed classroom management systems, resented being asked to be involved in their own treatment. And they especially resented being held accountable to each other. The students were not very good at working together, problem solving, or encouraging each other to behave appropriately. In fact, they were *terrible* at these skills. Most did everything they could to undermine the group effort by intentionally losing points needed to earn group activities. They often refused to get involved in each other's problems: "That's his problem, Miss, not mine." Furthermore, many of them intentionally encouraged inappropriate behaviors by laughing at and suggesting even more creative ways for misbehaving. As for us teachers, we thought it was much simpler to just do things ourselves. There were many very unhappy students and teachers in that early transition period, but we have since learned how we could have made that transition much smoother.

Three Important Lessons I learned three very important lessons during the transition to a group programming model. First, implementing a successful group process program is much more complicated than simply bringing together a group of students. Teachers and students have to work very hard to develop well-functioning groups. Second, the peer group is an extremely powerful resource—one that we cannot afford to waste. When the groups at our school started to gel, we observed some positive and powerful group pressure at work. I remember watching Danaire, a young man with a history of acting out, calmly and effectively de-escalating Louie (a new group member) on many occasions when he was about to assault a staff person. And I recall the first time Rico, a tough inner-city kid, shook Chad's hand when he finally learned his multiplication facts. Why was this so amazing? You see, Chad was pretty much the class nerd, and it took several weeks for Rico to even recognize his existence. The two never became best friends, but they were able to help each other out on occasion. And finally, and maybe most important, I learned that involving the students in their treatment was not giving up control. As teachers, we sometimes kid ourselves into thinking we are in control. Every student in the room contributes to each other's behaviors; their influence already exists. The effective use of group process program strategies helped us guide this peer influence.

So what was my return to the classroom like? Frustrating, exciting, challenging, exhausting, and rewarding are a few descriptors that come to mind. You might think that after eight years in the field it would have been simple. Working with students with behavioral disorders is often rewarding, but it is never simple. The Voyagers (my group that return year) reminded me of this.

The Voyagers Who were the Voyagers? Well, they were 12 very different 13- to 15-year-old boys who were referred to our program for a variety of behavior problems. Why did they decide to call themselves the Voyagers? They said it was because they would be "voyaging smoothly through their year to return quickly to their public schools." Well, not quite. Things did start out great (commonly referred to as the "honeymoon period"), but we quickly hit a few meteor storms.

Just a few examples. Eric, who referred to himself as "the King of Going Off" (the "Go-Off Master" for short) was very big for his age. He enjoyed staring down, shoving, and hitting students and staff, and he did so often. Then there was Mark, the class thief, who stole anything that wasn't tied down. Then he would hide the stolen item in a fellow Voyager's desk to try to get him in trouble. Gary lived in a rough neighborhood with his alcoholic mother. He often came to school tired and angry. On a bad day, even the simplest request would set him off. What did he do when he was "off"? Usually, he threw his desk across the room. Russell, the class clown, occasionally felt the need to run into the woods, gather sticks and leaves, attach them to his clothes, and come back into the classroom acting like Rambo. This was sometimes funny but hardly appropriate. And don't let me forget James, whose favorite activity was hanging and swinging from the doorway while making funny noises combined with the most creative combinations of swear words you could imagine. Remember, I've described only 5 of the 12 Voyagers.

Were we ever able to function as a group? Yes, we were on many occasions but only after many disappointing moments, terribly difficult days, and frequent opportunities to practice pulling it together as a group. We spent numerous days with restricted privileges because of poor group performances, but no group was more pleased to earn top-level privileges. We may not have made it to the Halloween party, but we did win the Christmas door-decorating contest. And it might have taken us 55 minutes to walk back into school after we lost an intramural football game in the fall, but no group could touch us at the tug-of-war during Spring Field Day.

Was I crazy to go back into the classroom? Probably. Was I sorry I did? No way. I learned more that year about effective strategies for working with students with emotional and behavioral disorders than ever before. And along the way I managed to help a few troubled kids. It was a rough return voyage but a very rewarding one.

verbal commitments to carry out the plan. **Group-oriented contingencies** specify certain rewards and privileges that are enjoyed by the group if their behavior meets certain criteria (Barbetta, 1990a). The criteria for earning the rewards, as well as the rewards themselves, are determined by the group.

Affective Traits of a Good Teacher

To join in the discussion "What are the most important skills for teachers of students with emotional and behavioral disorders?" go to the Message Board Module at http://www.prenhall.com/heward.

In addition to academic and behavior management skills, the teacher of children with emotional and behavioral disorders must be able to establish healthy child-teacher relationships. Morse (1976) believes that teachers need two important affective characteristics to relate effectively and positively to students with behavior problems. He calls these traits differential acceptance and an empathetic relationship.

Differential acceptance means the teacher can receive and witness frequent and often extreme acts of anger, hate, and aggression from children without responding similarly. Of course, this is much easier said than done. But the teacher of students with emotional and behavioral disorders must view disruptive behavior for what it is—behavior that reflects the student's past frustrations and conflicts with himself and those around him—and try to help the child learn better ways of behaving. Acceptance should not be confused with approving or condoning antisocial behav-

Most effective teachers of students with emotional and behavioral disorders are expert at recognizing and using nonverbal cues that are part of every teacher-student interaction. See Banbury and Hebert (1992) for a discussion of body language and gestures in classroom interactions.

ior; the child must learn that he is responding inappropriately. Instead, this concept calls for understanding without condemning.

Having an *empathetic relationship* with a child refers to a teacher's ability to recognize and understand the many nonverbal cues that often are the keys to understanding the individual needs of emotionally disturbed children. Kauffman (1997) stresses the importance of teachers' communicating directly and honestly with behaviorally troubled children. Many of these children have already had experience with supposedly helpful adults who have not been completely honest with them. Children with emotional and behavioral disorders can quickly detect someone who is not genuinely interested in their welfare.

The teacher of children with emotional and behavioral disorders must also realize that his actions serve as a powerful model. Therefore, it is critical that the teacher's actions and attitudes be mature and demonstrate self-control. Hobbs (1966) describes the kind of person he believes would make a good teacher and model for students with emotional and behavioral disorders:

> A decent adult; educated, well trained; able to give and receive affection, to live relaxed, and to be firm; a person with private resources for the nourishment and refreshment of his own life; not an itinerant worker but a professional through and through; a person with a sense of the significance of time; of the usefulness of today and the promise of tomorrow; a person of hope, quiet confidence, and joy; one who has committed himself to children and to the proposition that children who are emotionally disturbed can be helped by the process of reeducation. (pp. 1106–1107)

Educational Placement Alternatives

Like other students with disabilities, students with emotional and behavioral disorders are served across the continuum of educational placements. During the 1995–1996 school year, approximately 34% of school-age children with emotional and behavioral disorders were served in a separate classroom, 24% in a resource room, 23% in a regular classroom with consultation, 14% in a special school, and 5% in a residential or homebound placement (U.S. Department of Education, 1998). In a national survey, Cullinan et al. (1992) found that nearly 50% of students with emotional and behavioral disorders were included in regular classrooms for an average of 2.6 hours per day. Only 19% of the students in their study spent no time in the regular classroom. By contrast, an earlier study reported that just 17% of students with emotional and behavioral disorders spent up to half of the school day in regular classrooms, and 44% had no mainstream time (Kauffman, Cullinan, & Epstein, 1987). The results of the more recent survey may reveal an increasing willingness on the part of regular classroom teachers to accept students with emotional and behavioral disorders into their classrooms.

The challenge of educating students with emotional and behavioral disorder is to arrange an environment in which both academic and social skills can be learned at acceptable rates (Brigham & Kauffman, 1998). A study comparing middle school students who spent the entire school day in separate classrooms with students who participated in various classes in regular classrooms for at least one hour per day found that the mainstreamed students had better academic records and better work habits than the students who spent the entire day in a special class (Meadows, Neel, Scott, & Parker, 1994). Although these results seem to support the contention that all students with emotional and behavioral disorders should be included in regular classrooms, the authors point out that the mainstreamed students did not exhibit the extreme aggression, lack of self-control, or degree of withdrawal that the students who stayed in the special class did. They also noted that placement in general education classrooms typically represents "a major reduction, . . . if not a complete cessation, of differential pro-

The challenge of educating students with emotional and behavioral disorders is arranging an environment in which both academic and social skills can be learned at acceptable rates.

gramming" (p. 178). That is, the general education teachers did not make instructional or management accommodations to meet the needs of the mainstreamed students. Thus, it is hard to imagine how students with severe emotional and behavioral disorders would receive an appropriate education in the regular classroom.

A similar conclusion has been drawn by Schneider and Leroux (1994), who reviewed 25 studies comparing the progress of students with emotional and behavioral disorders in different educational placements. Acknowledging the difficulties in comparing and collapsing the results of studies done with different students and different methodologies, they report that special programs (which included resource rooms, self-contained classrooms, special schools, and treatment centers) appear to be more effective in promoting academic achievement, but comparisons between types of special programs are inconclusive. Better gains in children's self-concept are noted for less restrictive settings. Discussing the least restrictive alternative for students with emotional and behavioral disorders, Schneider and Leroux (1994) write:

> The first conclusion we can draw is that youngsters with behavioral disorders require more support than is available to the regular classroom teacher unassisted by at least resource room personnel. Second, it would appear that most youngsters with behavioral disorders will require ongoing support for a number of years. . . . For these youngsters, the least restrictive setting *possible* would appear to be a well-equipped resource room in a regular school. However, not enough research has been conducted on the capabilities of resource rooms to manage various problematic behaviors. Pending more conclusive data, one might speculate that some pupils may display behaviors too disruptive to be managed in this type of setting. On the other hand, there are clear drawbacks to more self-contained special settings, especially with regard to children's self-concept. (pp. 201, 203)

Epstein, Foley, and Cullinan (1992) conducted a national survey of programs for adolescents with emotional and behavioral disorders. On the basis of teachers' descriptions of their programs, Epstein et al. report five types of programs for students with emotional and behavioral disorders in grades 7 through 12:

- *Mainstreaming/inclusion* (34%). Primary importance is placed on increasing students' time in the regular classroom; academic curriculum and activities parallel the regular classroom; the student-teacher ratio is low; students with other high-incidence disabilities often are part of the program.

- *Classroom structure* (30%). Students are taught to be respectful to one another in a positive, supportive, and nonthreatening atmosphere; classroom rules and consequences are explicitly communicated and enforced; daily activities follow a predictable routine; one-to-one academic instruction is designed to meet individual needs.
- *Social and school survival skills* (16%). Emphasis is on how to get along with others, manage one's own thoughts and feelings, use problem-solving skills, and demonstrate responsibility for self; students are taught study skills, learning strategies, and time management; life-space interviewing, reality therapy, and crisis interventions are used; academics are addressed through tutoring.
- *Instruction in nontraditional content* (12%). Interpersonal and school-coping skills are approached through an affective curriculum of vocational, career, outdoor, and/or leisure educational experiences; academics emphasize functional skills for independent living; team teaching and multidisciplinary student evaluations are used.
- *Individualized communication and instruction* (8%). Comprehensive diagnostic assessment is used to develop an individualized treatment program for each student; considerable communication is done with parents and mainstream teachers; counseling is provided for areas such as psychological, vocational, and substance abuse problems; consequences for inappropriate behavior may include in-school and out-of-school suspensions.

Current Issues and Future Trends

Special education for students with emotional and behavioral disorders faces a number of critical and ongoing issues. Foremost among the concerns of many experts is revising the federal definition of this disability so that all children with emotional and behavioral disorders will be eligible for special education. The major problem with the current federal definition of "seriously emotionally disturbed" is that it attempts to distinguish between students who exhibit "true" emotional disturbance (considered a disability covered under IDEA) and those whose disordered and antisocial behaviors are thought to be the result of social maladjustment, who are not eligible for special education. A related concern is ensuring that traditionally underserved groups of children and youths not be denied services for emotional and behavioral disorders, particularly those who are poor, from historically oppressed minorities, and homosexual (McIntyre, 1993a).

See Nelson, Rutherford, and Wolford's (1987) book Special Education in the Criminal Justice System.

Development of an effective system of special education services for school-age youths with disabilities in correctional institutions, an increasing number of whom have emotional and behavioral disorders, is another important challenge; 20% of students with emotional and behavioral disorders are arrested at least once before they leave school, compared with 9% for all students with disabilities and 6% of all students (Chesapeake Institute, 1994). About 450,000 delinquent youths are placed in detention centers or training schools each year in the United States, with another 300,000 sent to adult jails (Leone, Rutherford, & Nelson, 1991). The educational outlook is bleak for juveniles with disabilities who find themselves in jails and detention centers. Although it can be argued that adjudicated delinquents are, by virtue of the behaviors that precipitated their arrest, behaviorally disordered, most juvenile offenders receive few or no special education services (McIntyre, 1993b). Those incarcerated youths who do receive special education services typically receive substandard services (Leone, 1994).

Although the challenges faced by those who work with students with emotional and behavioral disorders appear daunting and unrelenting, the field has also experienced significant advancements and successes. A group of nationally known leaders in the field of emotional and behavioral disorders met to review the field's knowledge base and to make recommendations for the improvement of policy and practice (Peacock Hill Working Group, 1991). In addition to identifying and describing the key characteristics of a number of successful intervention programs from around the country, the group cited the following strategies that, when used in combination, are likely to result in successful programming for students with emotional and behavioral disorders:

- *Systematic, data-based interventions.* It is critical that interventions be selected and evaluated on the basis of data regarding their effectiveness.
- *Continuous assessment and monitoring of progress.* Curriculum-based assessment and direct, daily measurement are two strategies for attaining the level of measurement required for success.
- *Provision for practice of new skills.* Skills taught in isolation, without provision for practicing them in everyday situations, are unlikely to be retained.
- *Treatment matched with the problem.* A student whose primary problem is getting along with others needs intensive instruction in social skills, not an exclusive focus on academics or the suppression of a particular noxious behavior. Treatment must also address the relevant settings in the student's life and not be confined to the school setting alone.
- *Multicomponent treatment.* The additive effects of different classroom interventions and related treatment modalities are often critical to successful outcomes. For some disorders, long-term outcome has been measurably better when combinations of instructional, behavior, psychopharmacological, and/or family treatments are systematically coordinated.
- *Programming for generalization and maintenance.* Interventions must include strategies for the maintenance and transfer of treatment gains to new settings.
- *Commitment to sustained intervention.* Some disorders of emotion and behavior may require interventions over the individual's life span. One-shot cures simply are not now available, nor are they likely to be developed in the future. Programs should provide follow-up and continued intervention as needed.

Use the self-tests at http://www.prenhall.com/heward to assess your knowledge of the content of Chapter 8.

Summary

Defining Emotional and Behavioral Disorders

- There is no single, widely used definition of emotional and behavioral disorders. Most definitions require a child's behavior to differ markedly (extremely) and chronically (over time) from current social or cultural norms.
- Many leaders in the field do not like the federal definition of "seriously emotionally disturbed" in IDEA because students who are socially maladjusted are not eligible for special education services.
- The CCBD and the NMHSEC have proposed a definition of *emotional and behavioral disorders* as a disability characterized by "behavioral or emotional responses in school programs so different from appropriate age, cultural, or ethnic norms that they adversely affect educational performance."

Characteristics of Children with Emotional and Behavioral Disorders

- On the average, students with emotional and behavioral disorders score somewhat below normal on IQ tests and achieve academically below what their scores would predict.
- Many students with emotional and behavioral disorders have difficulty developing and maintaining interpersonal relationships.
- Children with externalizing problems frequently exhibit antisocial behavior; many become delinquents as adolescents.
- Children with internalizing problems are overly withdrawn and lack social skills needed to interact effectively with others.

Prevalence

- Although the U.S. Department of Education has traditionally estimated that children with emotional and behavioral disorders comprise 2% of the school-age population, the number of children served is less than half of the 2% estimate.
- The ratio of boys to girls in programs for students with emotional and behavioral disorders is approximately 4:1. Although there are many exceptions, boys are more likely to have externalizing problems, and girls are more likely to have internalizing problems.

Causes of Emotional and Behavioral Disorders

- The two groups of causes suggested for behavioral disorders are biological and environmental.
- Because of its central role in a child's life, the school can also be an important contributing factor to a behavior problem.

Identification and Assessment

- Although several screening tests have been developed, many school districts do not use any systematic method for identifying children with emotional and behavioral disorders.
- Whereas antisocial children stand out, withdrawn children may go unnoticed.
- Screening should be conducted as early as possible and include information from multiple agents and settings.
- Projective tests often yield interesting results, but they are rarely useful in planning and implementing interventions.
- Direct and continuous observation and measurement of specific problem behaviors within the classroom is an assessment technique that indicates directly whether and for which behaviors intervention is needed. Five measurable dimensions of behavior are rate, duration, latency, topography, and magnitude.

Educational Approaches

- Six conceptual models of children's emotional and behavioral disorders have been proposed: biogenic, psychodynamic, psychoeducational, humanistic, ecological, and behavioral. Although each approach has a distinct theoretical basis and suggests types of treatment, many teachers use techniques from more than one of the models.
- Research supports the behavioral and ecological models, which analyze and modify the ways in which a child interacts with the environment.
- Teachers should concentrate their resources and energies on alterable variables—those things in a student's environment that the teacher can influence.
- Many students with emotional and behavioral disorders benefit from systematic social skills training.
- Self-management skills can help students develop control over their environment, responsibility for their actions, and self-direction.
- A good classroom management system uses proactive strategies to create a positive, supportive, and noncoercive environment that promotes prosocial behavior and academic achievement.
- Group process approaches use the power of the peer group to help students with emotional and behavioral disorders learn to behave appropriately.
- Two important affective traits for teachers of students with emotional and behavioral disorders are differential acceptance and empathetic relationship.

Educational Placement Alternatives

- Most students with emotional and behavioral disorders are served in self-contained or resource classrooms.
- Nearly half of students with emotional and behavioral disorders spend up to half of the school day in regular classrooms.
- Comparing the behavioral and academic progress of students with emotional and behavioral disorders in different educational placements in an effort to determine which setting is the best is difficult because students with milder disabilities are included first and more often, whereas those students who exhibit more severe behavioral disturbances tend to remain in special classes.

Current Issues and Future Trends

- Special education services are needed for the many incarcerated adolescents with emotional and behavioral disorders.
- Successful programs for students with emotional and behavioral disorders are characterized by systematic, data-based interventions; continuous assessment and monitoring of student progress; provision for practice of new skills; matching treatment with the problem; multicomponent treatments; programming for generalization and maintenance of newly learned skills; and commitment to follow-up and continued intervention as needed.

For More Information

Journals

- *Behavior Therapy.* Published five times a year by Academic Press for the American Association for the Advancement of Behavior Therapy (see "Organizations").
- *Behavioral Disorders.* Published quarterly by the Council for Children with Behavioral Disorders, Council for Exceptional Children (see "Organizations"). Publishes research and discussion articles dealing with behavioral disorders in children.
- *Beyond Behavior: A Magazine for Exploring Behavior in Our Schools.* Published three times a year by the Council for Children with Behavioral Disorders, Council for Exceptional Children (see "Organizations"). Presents commentary, essays, and first-person accounts related to understanding and working with students with emotional and behavioral disorders.
- *Education and Treatment of Children.* Published quarterly by Pressley Ridge School, 530 Marshall Avenue, Pittsburgh, PA 15214. Includes experimental studies, discussion articles, literature reviews, and book reviews covering a wide range of education and treatment issues with children.
- *Journal of Applied Behavior Analysis.* Published quarterly by the Society for the Experimental Analysis of Behavior, Department of Human Development, University of Kansas, Lawrence, KS 66045-2133. Publishes original experimental studies demonstrating improvement of socially significant behaviors. Many studies involve children with emotional and behavioral disorders as subjects.
- *Journal of Emotional and Behavioral Disorders.* Published quarterly by PRO-ED, 8700 Shoal Creek Boulevard, Austin, TX 78757-6897. A multidisciplinary journal featuring articles on research, practice, and theory.
- *Journal of Positive Behavior Interventions.* Published by PRO-ED, 8700 Shoal Creek Boulevard, Austin, TX 78757-6897. Features research on developing and evaluating positive behavior support plans.
- *Reclaiming Children and Youth: Journal of Emotional and Behavioral Problems.* Published by PRO-ED, 8700 Shoal Creek Boulevard, Austin, TX 78757-6897. Features a strength-based approach in which problems are viewed as opportunities for teaching prosocial behavior and values.

Books

- Algozzine, B., Serna, L., & Patton, J. R. (1998). *Childhood behavior disorders: Applied research and educational practice*. Austin, TX: PRO-ED.
- Bauer, A. M., & Shea, T. M. (1999). *Learners with emotional and behavioral disorders: An Introduction*. Upper Saddle River, NJ: Merrill/Prentice Hall.
- Kameenui, E. J., & Darch, C. B. (1995). *Instructional classroom management: A proactive approach to behavior management.* White Plains, NY: Longman.
- Kauffman, J. M. (1997). *Characteristics of emotional and behavioral disorders of children and youth* (6th ed.). Upper Saddle River, NJ: Merrill/Prentice Hall.
- Kerr, M. M., & Nelson, C. M. (1998). *Strategies for managing behavior problems in the classroom* (3rd ed.). Upper Saddle River, NJ: Merrill/Prentice Hall.
- Long, N. J., Morse, W., & Newman, R. G. (1996). *Conflict in the classroom: The education of at-risk and troubled students* (5th ed.). Austin, TX: PRO-ED.
- Rhode, G., Jensen, W. R., & Reavis, H. K. (1998). *The tough kid book: Practical classroom management strategies.* Longmont, CO: Sopris West.
- Walker, H. M. (1997). *The acting out child: Coping with classroom disruption*. Longmont, CO: Sopris West.
- Walker, H. M., Colvin, G., & Ramsey, E. (1995). *Antisocial behavior in schools: Strategies and best practices.* Pacific Grove, CA: Brooks/Cole.
- Walker, J. E., & Shea, T. M. (1995). *Behavior management: A practical approach for educators.* Pacific Grove, CA: Brooks/Cole.
- Whelen, R. J. (1997). *Emotional and behavioral disorders: A 25-year focus*. Denver: Love.
- Young, K. R., West, R. P., Smith, D. J., & Morgan, D. P. (1997). *Teaching self-management strategies to adolescents.* Longmont, CO: Sopris West.
- Zirpoli, T. J., & Melloy, K. J. (1997). *Behavior management: Applications for teachers and parents* (2nd ed.). Upper Saddle River, NJ: Merrill/Prentice Hall.

Organizations

- *American Association for the Advancement of Behavior Therapy,* 15 West 36th Street, New York, NY 10018. Includes psychologists, educational researchers, and educators (primarily at the university level).
- *Council for Children with Behavioral Disorders* (CCBD), Council for Exceptional Children, 1920 Association Drive, Reston, VA 22091. With more than 8,500 members, the second largest of CEC's 17 divisions. Includes teachers, teacher educators, and researchers interested in promoting the general welfare and education of children with emotional and behavioral disorders.
- *Federation of Families for Children's Mental Health,* 1021 Prince Street, Alexandria, VA 22314-2071. A national parent-run organization focused on the needs of children and youths with emotional, behavioral, or mental disorders and their families.

Chapter 9

Communication Disorders

Focus Questions

- How can a true communication disorder be differentiated from a communication difference?
- How can a teacher use what is known about typical language development to support children with language impairments?
- What are the most important functions of an alternative and augmentative communication system?
- What are common elements of effective interventions for speech disorders?
- Why are naturalistic interventions more likely to result in maintenance and generalization of a child's new speech and language skills?

Imagine trying to go through an entire day without speaking. How would you make contact with other people? You would be frustrated when others did not understand your needs and feelings. By the end of the day, besides feeling exhausted from trying to make yourself understood, you might even start to question your ability to function adequately in the world.

Although relatively few people with communication disorders are completely unable to express themselves, an exercise such as the one just described would increase your awareness of some of the problems and frustrations faced every day by children and adults who cannot communicate effectively. Children who cannot absorb information through listening and reading and/or cannot express their thoughts in spoken words are virtually certain to encounter difficulties in their schools and communities. When communication disorders persist, it may be hard for children to learn and develop and to form satisfying relationships with other people.

Communication, Language, and Speech

Before we discuss specific types of communication disorders and their effects on learning, some definitions of basic terms are necessary.

Go to the companion website at http://www.prenhall.com/heward and select Chapter 9 to review the chapter objectives.

Communication

Communication is the exchange of information and ideas. It involves encoding, transmitting, and decoding messages. It is an interactive process requiring at least two parties, each playing the dual roles of sender and receiver. Each interaction includes three elements needed to qualify as communication: (1) a message, (2) a sender who expresses the message, and (3) a receiver who responds to the message.

Although speech and language form the message system most often used in human communication, spoken or written words are not necessary for communication to occur. Both paralinguistic behaviors and nonlinguistic cues are used in human communication. *Paralinguistic behaviors* are nonlanguage sounds (e.g., "oohh," laughter) and speech modifications (e.g., variations in pitch, intonation, rate of delivery, pauses) that change the form and meaning of the message. *Nonlinguistic* cues include body posture, facial expressions, gestures, eye contact, head and body movement, and physical proximity.

*The study of nonlinguistic behaviors that augment language is called **kinesics.***

Lindfors (1987) has enumerated several important functions of communication, particularly between teachers and children:

1. *Narrating.* Children need to be able to tell (or follow the telling of) a story—that is, a sequence of related events connected in an orderly, clear, and interesting manner. Five-year-old Cindy tells her teacher, "I had a birthday party. I wore a funny hat. Mommy made a cake, and Daddy took pictures." Fourteen-year-old David tells the class about the events leading up to Christopher Columbus's first voyage to America.
2. *Explaining/informing.* Teachers expect children to interpret the explanations of others in speech and in writing and to put what they understand into words so that their listeners or readers will be able to understand it too. In a typical classroom, children must respond frequently to teachers' questions: "Which number is larger?" "How do you suppose the story will end?" "Why do you think George Washington was a great president?"
3. *Expressing.* It is important for children to express their personal feelings and opinions and to respond to the feelings of others. Speech and language can convey joy, fear, frustration, humor, sympathy, anger. A child writes, "I have just moved. And it is hard to find a friend because I am shy." Another tells her classmates, "Guess what? I have a new baby brother!" Through such communicative interactions, children gradually develop a sense of self and an awareness of other people.

Language

Language is a common system used by a group of people for giving meaning to sounds, words, gestures, and other symbols to enable communication with one another. Lahey (1988) defines language as "a code whereby ideas about the world are expressed through a conventional system of arbitrary signals for communication" (p. 2). A child may learn to identify a familiar object, for example, by hearing the spoken word "tree," seeing the printed word "tree," viewing the sign language gesture for "tree," or encountering a combination of these signals. When we hear, speak, read, or write with language, we transmit information.

The symbols and the rules governing language are essentially arbitrary no matter what language is spoken, and English is no exception. The arbitrariness of language means there is usually no logical, natural, or required relationship between a set of sounds and the object, concept, or action it represents. The word "whale," for example, brings to mind a large mammal that lives in the sea, but the sound of the word has no apparent connection with the creature. "Whale" is merely a symbol we use for this particular mammal. A small number of onomatopoeic words—such as "tinkle," "buzz," and "hiss"—are considered to sound like what they represent, but most words have no such relationship. Likewise, some hand positions or movements in sign language, called *iconic signs,* look like the object or event they represent (e.g., tipping an imaginary cup to one's lips is the manual sign for "drink"). Remember, language is used to express descriptions of and relations between objects and events; it does not reproduce those objects and events.

Phonemes are represented by letters or other symbols between slashes. For example, the phoneme /n/ represents the "ng" sound in "sing"; /i/ represents the long "e" as in "see."

Five Dimensions of Language Language is often described along five dimensions: phonology, morphology, syntax, semantics, and pragmatics. *Phonology* is the study of the linguistic rules governing a language's sound system. Phonological rules describe how sounds can be sequenced and combined. The English language uses approximately 45 different sound elements, called **phonemes.** Only the initial phoneme prevents the words "pear" and "bear" from being identical, for example; yet in one case we think of a fruit, in the other a large animal.

The *morphology* of a language governs how the basic units of meaning are combined into words. Phonemes, the individual sounds, do not carry meaning. A **morpheme** is the smallest element of language that carries meaning. The word *baseball,* for example, consists of two morphemes: "base" and "ball." The "-s" added to make "baseballs" would be a third morpheme.

Syntax is the system of rules governing the meaningful arrangement of words into sentences. If morphemes could be strung together in any order, language would be an unintelligible tangle of words. Syntactical rules are language-specific (e.g., Japanese and English have different rules), and they specify relations among the subject, verb, and object. For example, "Help my chicken eat" conveys a meaning much different from "Help eat my chicken."

Semantics is a system of rules that relates phonology and syntax to meaning; that is, semantics describes how people use language to convey meaning.

Finally, **pragmatics** is a set of rules governing how language is used. Lahey (1988) describes three kinds of pragmatic skills: (1) using language to achieve various communicative functions and goals, (2) using information from the conversational context (e.g., modifying one's message according to listener reactions), and (3) knowing how to use conversational skills effectively (e.g., beginning and ending a conversation, taking turns).

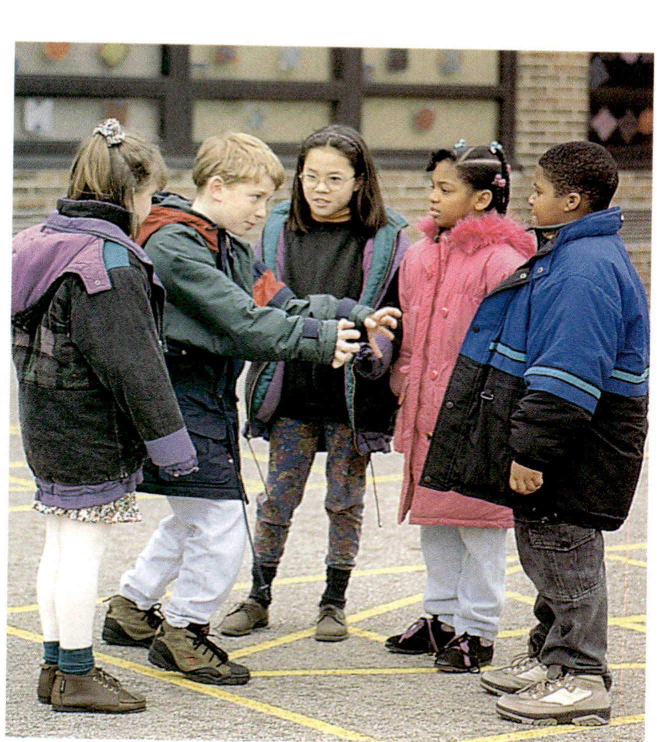

Good communicators use nonlinguistic cues such as body postures and gestures and pragmatic conversational skills such as turn taking.

One model of language, developed by Bloom and Lahey (1978), describes three components of language—form, content, and use—that make up an integrated system. The *form* of the language is its surface structure that connects sound and meaning (phonology, morphology, syntax). The *content* is based on knowledge of the world and our feelings about it. Thus, the form of language allows us to express and understand content (semantics). The *use* of language refers to the ways in which language functions in communication (pragmatics). It includes both our purposes in communicating and how we choose a specific form to express a particular message.

This model can be helpful in understanding and treating a child's communication disorder.

Speech

Speech is the behavior of producing a language code by making appropriate vocal sound patterns. Although it is not the only possible vehicle for expressing language (gestures, manual signing, pictures, and written symbols can also be used), speech is an effective and efficient method. Speech is also one of the most complex and difficult human endeavors. Speech sounds are the product of four separate but related processes (Hulit & Howard, 1993): *respiration* (breathing provides the power supply for speech), *phonation* (the production of sound when the vocal folds of the larynx are drawn together by the contraction of specific muscles, causing the air to vibrate), *resonation* (the sound quality of the vibrating air, shaped as it passes through the throat, mouth, and sometimes nasal cavities), and **articulation** (the formation of specific, recognizable speech sounds by the tongue, lips, teeth, and mouth). Figure 9.1 shows the normal speech organs.

American Sign Language—a visual-spatial language—is described in Chapter 10.

Most languages start out in oral form, developed by people speaking with each other. Reading and writing are secondary language forms that use graphic symbols to represent the oral form. There is no one-to-one correspondence, however, between **graphemes** (print symbols or letters) and phonemes.

Normal Language Development

Despite the complexity of language, most children, without any formal instruction, learn to understand language and then to speak during the first few years of life.

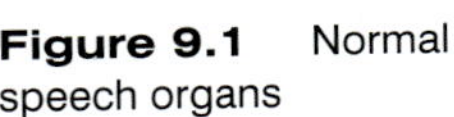
Figure 9.1 Normal speech organs

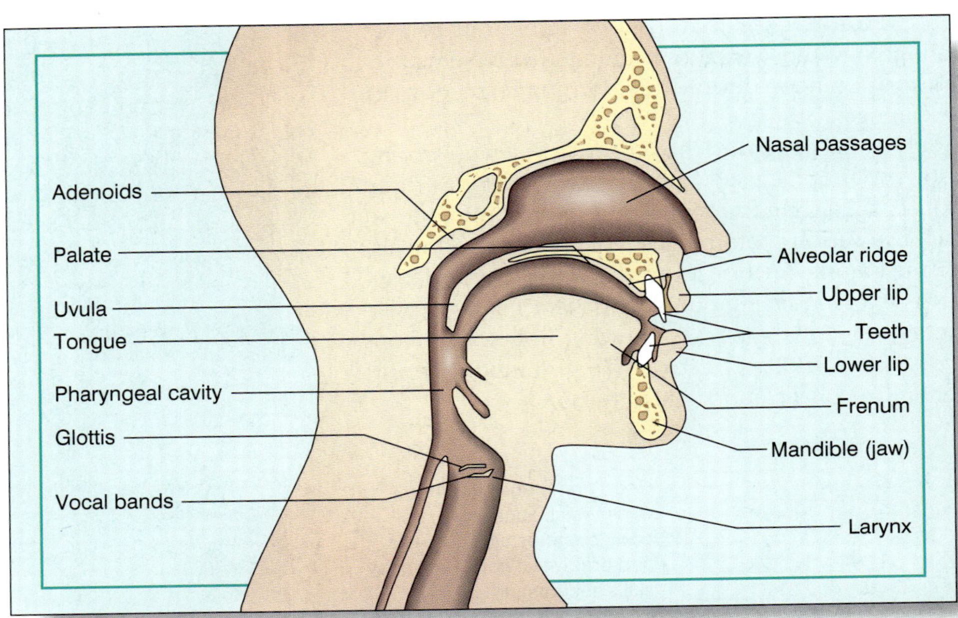

They integrate form, content, and use to communicate. The process of learning language is a remarkable one that is not fully understood. Parents, teachers, and scholars for centuries have been fascinated by the phenomenon of language acquisition in children.

> Whether a child grows up in a "traditional" society or in a "technological" one; whether in a large extended family or in a small nuclear one; whether on a Pacific island, in an urban ghetto, or in a tribal farm compound; whether in a villa, a straw hut, an apartment, or a tent; whether with or without formal schooling; whether in a wet, dry, hot, or cold climate—the child will acquire the language of his community. Humans vary in which languages and dialects they acquire, in how rapidly they acquire them . . . in how talkative they are, in what they use language for, and in how effectively they express themselves in speech and/or writing. But virtually all of them acquire at least one linguistic system for relating meanings. . . . Further, there is striking similarity in how all children learn their language. (Lindfors, 1987, p. 91)

Children with hearing impairments have a special set of problems in learning language. See Chapter 10.

Understanding how young, normally developing children acquire language is helpful to the teacher or specialist working with children who have delayed or disordered communication. Knowledge of normal language development can help the specialist determine whether a particular child is simply developing language at a slower-than-normal rate or whether the child shows an abnormal pattern of language development. Figure 9.2 identifies some of the key features of speech and language development of a typically developing child. As we consider normal language development, remember that the ages at which a normal child acquires certain speech and language skills are not rigid and inflexible. Children's abilities and early environments vary widely, and all of these factors affect language development. Nevertheless, most children follow a relatively predictable sequence in development of speech and language.

Children whose expressive vocabularies consist of fewer than 50 words and/or produce limited word combinations at 24 months of age are considered late talkers. Kelly (1998) reviews the "late talker" literature and makes recommendations for serving this population of children.

As the descriptions in Figure 9.2 indicate, children's words and sentences often differ from adult forms while the children are learning language. Lindfors (1987) points out that children who use structures such as "All gone sticky" and "Where he is going?"; pronunciations such as "cwackers" and "twuck"; or word forms such as "comed," "goed," or "sheeps" gradually learn to replace them with acceptable adult forms. The early developmental forms drop out as the child matures, usually without any special drilling or direct instruction.

It is also worth noting that children often produce speech sounds inconsistently. The clarity of a sound may vary according to factors such as where the sound occurs in a word and how familiar the word is to the child. Although speech sounds generally become clearer as the child grows older, there are exceptions to this rule of gradual progress. Kenney and Prather (1986), for example, found that 3½-year-old children made fewer errors on the /s/ sound than did children ages 4 to 5½. The reasons for these reversals in accuracy are not clear.

Defining Communication Disorders

As we have already noted, the development of speech and language is a highly individual process. No child conforms exactly to precise developmental norms; some are advanced, some are delayed, and some acquire language in an unusual sequence. Unfortunately, some children deviate from the normal to such an extent that they have serious difficulties in learning and interpersonal relations. Children who are not able to make themselves understood or who cannot comprehend ideas that are spoken to them by others are likely to be greatly handicapped in virtually all aspects of education and personal adjustment.

Check your ongoing understanding of Chapter 9 concepts by using the Guided Review Module at http://www.prenhall.com/heward.

Birth to 6 months

- Infant first communicates by crying, which produces a reliable consequence in the form of parental attention.
- Different types of crying develop — a parent can often tell from the baby's cry whether she is wet, tired, or hungry.
- Comfort sounds—coos, gurgles, and sighs—contain some vowels and consonants.
- Comfort sounds develop into babbling, sounds that in the beginning are apparently made for the enjoyment of feeling and hearing them.
- Vowel sounds, such as /i/ (pronounced "ee") and /e/ (pronounced "uh"), are produced earlier than consonants, such as /m/, /b/, and /f/.
- Infant does not attach meaning to words she hears from others but may react differently to loud and soft voices.
- Infant turns eyes and head in the direction of a sound.

6 to 12 months

- Babbling becomes differentiated before the end of the first year and contains some of the same phonetic elements as the meaningful speech of 2-year-olds.
- Baby develops **inflection**—her voice rises and falls.
- She may respond appropriately to "no," "bye-bye," or her own name and may perform an action, such as clapping her hands, when told to.
- She will repeat simple sounds and words, such as "mama."

12 to 18 months

- By 18 months, most children have learned to say several words with appropriate meaning.
- Pronunciation is far from perfect; baby may say "tup" when you point to a cup or "goggie" when she sees a dog.
- She communicates by pointing and perhaps saying a word or two.
- She responds to simple commands such as "Give me the cup" and "Open your mouth."

18 to 24 months

- Most children go through a stage of **echolalia**, in which they repeat, or echo, the speech they hear. Echolalia is a normal phase of language development, and most children outgrow it by about the age of 2½.
- There is a great spurt in acquisition and use of speech; baby begins to combine words into short sentences, such as "Daddy bye-bye" and "Want cookie."
- Receptive vocabulary grows even more rapidly; at 2 years of age she may understand more than 1,000 words.
- Understands such concepts as "soon" and "later" and makes more subtle distinctions between objects such as cats and dogs, and knives, forks, and spoons.

Figure 9.2 Overview of normal language development

2 to 3 years

- The 2-year-old child talks, saying sentences like "I won't tell you" and asking questions like "Where my daddy go?"
- She may have an expressive vocabulary of up to 900 different words, averaging three to four words per sentence.
- She participates in conversations.
- She identifies colors, uses plurals, and tells simple stories about her experiences.
- She can follow compound commands such as "Pick up the doll and bring it to me."
- She uses most vowel sounds and some consonant sounds correctly.

3 to 4 years

- The normal 3-year-old has lots to say, speaks rapidly, and asks many questions.
- Sentences are longer and more varied: "Cindy's playing in water"; "Mommy went to work"; "The cat is hungry."
- She uses speech to request, protest, agree, and make jokes.
- She understands children's stories; grasps such concepts as funny, bigger, and secret; and can complete simple analogies such as "In the daytime it is light; at night it is. . . . "
- She substitutes certain sounds, perhaps saying "baf" for "bath" or "yike" for "like."
- Many 3-year-olds repeat sounds or words ("b-b-ball," "l-l-little"). These repetitions and hesitations are normal and do not indicate that the child will develop a habit of stuttering.

4 to 5 years

- The child has a vocabulary of more than 1,500 words and uses sentences averaging five words in length.
- She begins to modify her speech for the listener; for example, she uses longer and more complex sentences when talking to her mother than when addressing a baby or a doll.
- She can define words like "hat," "stove," and "policeman" and can ask questions like "How did you do that?" or "Who made this?"
- She uses conjunctions such as "if," "when," and "because."
- She recites poems and sings songs from memory.
- She may still have difficulty with such consonant sounds as /r/, /s/, and /z/ or with blends like "tr," "gl," "sk," and "str."

After 5 years

- Language continues to develop steadily, though less dramatically, after age 5.
- A typical 6-year-old uses most of the complex forms of adult English.
- Some consonant sounds and blends are not mastered until age 7 or 8.
- Grammar and speech patterns of child in first grade usually match those of her family, neighborhood, and region.

Figure 9.2 *continued*

When does a communication difference become a communication disorder? In making such judgments, Emerick and Haynes (1986) emphasize the impact that a communication pattern has on one's life. A communication difference would be considered a disability, they note, when any one of these criteria is met:

- The transmission and/or perception of messages is faulty
- The person is placed at an economic disadvantage
- The person is placed at a learning disadvantage
- The person is placed at a social disadvantage
- There is a negative impact on the person's emotional growth
- The problem causes physical damage or endangers the health of the person (pp. 6–7)

The American Speech-Language-Hearing Association (ASHA, 1993) defines a communication disorder as "an impairment in the ability to receive, send, process, and comprehend concepts or verbal, nonverbal and graphic symbols systems. A communication disorder may be evident in the processes of hearing, language, and/or speech" (p. 40).

To be eligible for special education services, a child's communication disorders must have an adverse effect on learning. The definition of speech or language impairments in IDEA reads: "a communication disorder, such as stuttering, impaired articulation, a language impairment, or voice impairment which adversely affects . . . educational performance."

Most specialists in the field of communication disorders make a distinction between speech disorders and language disorders. Children with *impaired speech* have difficulty producing sounds properly, maintaining an appropriate flow or rhythm in speech, or using the voice effectively. Children with *impaired language* have problems understanding or using the symbols and rules people use to communicate with each other. Speech and language are obviously closely related to each other. Some people find it helpful to view speech as the means by which language is most often conveyed. A child may have a speech impairment, a language disorder, or both.

What Are Speech Disorders?

A child's speech is considered impaired when it deviates so far from the speech of other people that it calls attention to itself, interferes with communication, or causes the speaker or his listeners to be uncomfortable (Van Riper & Erickson, 1996). A general goal of specialists in communication disorders is to help the child speak as clearly and pleasantly as possible so that a listener's attention will focus on what the child says rather than how he says it.

The three basic types of speech disorders are articulation, voice, and fluency. Each type is discussed later in the chapter.

It is always important to keep the speaker's age, education, and cultural background in mind when determining whether speech is impaired. A 4-year-old girl who says, "Pwease weave the woom" would not be considered to have a speech impairment, but a 40-year-old woman would surely draw attention to herself with that pronunciation because it differs markedly from the speech of most adults. A traveler unable to articulate the /l/ sound would not be clearly understood in trying to buy a bus ticket to Lake Charles, Louisiana. A male high school student with an extremely high-pitched voice might be reluctant to speak in class for fear of being mimicked and ridiculed by his classmates.

What Are Language Disorders?

Some children have serious difficulties in understanding language or in expressing themselves through language. A child with a *receptive language disorder* may be unable to learn the days of the week in proper order or may find it impossible to follow a sequence of commands, such as "Pick up the paint brushes, wash them in the sink, and then put them on a paper towel to dry." A child with an *expressive lan-*

Leadership Roles Encourage Language in the Classroom

Young children with impaired speech or language are often frustrated by the difficulty they experience in asking questions, expressing their needs, or conveying their wishes to other people. When unable to make themselves understood, some children may resort to physical communication (e.g., pulling, pushing, or hitting classmates), whereas others become so frustrated that they stop trying to communicate.

Judith Hurvitz, Sarah Pickert, and Donna Rilla believe that teachers can help children develop language skills by encouraging them to assume leadership roles in the classroom. Activities that carry responsibility, power, and prestige, they maintain, are useful in promoting language and social interaction. Here are some suggestions developed for Karen, a hypothetical 5-year-old with a communication disorder:

- Ask Karen to sit on a chair while the rest of the children are seated on the floor.
- Allow Karen to wear a special hat or badge.
- Give Karen the authority to distribute rewards, such as stars or tokens, to other children.
- Let Karen lead circle-time activities by taking attendance, directing group songs, and greeting others ("Hi, Judy").
- Allow Karen to assign daily classroom jobs to other children ("Barry, mats." "Ron, get snack.").
- Have Karen act as class messenger, especially when the recipient of the message is familiar with the meaning to be conveyed. (She might say to the librarian, "Need book.")
- Permit Karen to choose how class members will participate in a particular activity—for example, designating whether boys or girls will go first in line ("Boys first.").
- Give Karen a picture to hold up and ask her to call on a child to describe the picture ("Donna, what this?").
- Let Karen lead the group in a movement activity by calling out actions ("March!" "Walk!" "Sit!").
- Suggest words that Karen can use to solve a problem herself when she asks for teacher intervention. Say, "Go to Anthony and tell him, 'I want my block'" or "Take your puzzle to Glen and say, 'Help me.'"
- Encourage Karen to work with another child in tasks such as cleaning up after snack time or moving a bulky table.
- Invite Karen to talk with a classmate by using a pair of toy telephones (this often generates enthusiasm).

Activities such as these can help children use language more effectively and with greater variety. They also enable children to experience the pleasure and power of using language to control their environments.

Source: From Hurvitz, J. A., Pickert, S. M., & Rilla, D. C. (1987). Promoting children's language interaction. *Teaching Exceptional Children, 19*(3), 12-15. Published by the Council for Exceptional Children, Reston, VA. Adapted by permission.

guage disorder may have a limited vocabulary for her age, be confused about the order of sounds or words (e.g., "hostipal," "aminal," "wipe shield winders"), and use tenses and plurals incorrectly (e.g., "Them throwed a balls"). Children with difficulty in expressive language may or may not also have difficulty in receptive language. For instance, a child may be able to count out six pennies when asked and shown the symbol *6,* but she may not be able to say the word "six" when shown the symbol. In that case, the child has an expressive difficulty, but her receptive language is adequate. She may or may not have other disorders of speech or hearing.

ASHA (1993) defines a language disorder as "impaired comprehension and/or use of spoken, written, and/or other symbol systems. The disorder may involve (1) the form of language (phonology, morphology, and syntax), (2) the content of language (semantics), and/or (3) the function of language in communication (pragmatics) in any combination" (p. 40).

Leonard (1986) has noted that children with impaired language frequently play a passive role in communication. They may show little tendency to initiate conversations. When language-disordered children are asked questions, "their replies rarely provide new information related to the topic" (p. 114).

Language is so important to academic performance that it can be impossible to differentiate a learning disability from a language disorder (Wallach & Butler, 1994). Again, the emphasis should be on remediating a child's skill deficits rather than on labeling them.

Children with serious language disorders are almost certain to have problems in school and social development. It is often difficult to detect children with language disorders; their performance may lead people to mistakenly classify them with disability labels such as mental retardation, hearing impairment, or emotional disturbance, when in fact these descriptions are neither accurate nor appropriate. For example, an 11-year-old girl with a neurological impairment that affected her speech and language production was perceived by her fifth- and sixth-grade peers as "frightened, nervous, tense, and unlovable." These perceptions "obviously could have a negative impact on her self-concept" (Gies-Zaborowski & Silverman, 1986, p. 143).

A child may also be markedly delayed in language development. Even though a relatively wide range of language patterns and age milestones is considered normal, some children do not acquire the ability to express and to understand language until much later than normally expected. We would regard a 6-year-old child who cannot use such pronouns as "I," "you," and "me" as having a serious delay in language development. In rare cases, children who have no other impairment may even fail to speak at all.

Dialects and Differences

Taylor and Payne (1994) consider the following myths about dialect and regional language use:

> *Myth:* A speech-language pathologist accepts a position in a Head-start facility on a Native American reservation. On his first day, he notices that all of the children appear to be uncommunicative. They do not initiate conversation, and they do not respond to direct questions such as "What is your name?" He reports to the director that the children are severely language delayed.
>
> *Reality:* The speech-language pathologist is unaware of many of the cultural rules of communication for the community. The children's behavior is normal for communication with a stranger or outsider. In addition, cultural rules dictate that members do not speak their own names.
>
> *Myth:* A 15-year-old black female from suburban Cleveland omits some final consonants and reduces final consonant clusters. She should not be considered for therapy since these are features of Black English Vernacular.
>
> *Reality:* After consideration of the child's speech community, it is not likely that Black English Vernacular features are a part of her middle income, highly educated environment. A possible articulation disorder or hearing loss should be considered. (p. 137)

Kambi, Pollock, and Harris (1996) address issues specific to African American English and to communication disorders in African American children.

The way children speak reflects their culture. Before entering school, most children have learned patterns of speech and language appropriate to their families and neighborhoods. Every language contains a variety of forms, called **dialects,** that result from historic, geographical, and social factors. The English language, for example, includes such variations as Standard American English (as used by most teachers, employers, and public speakers), African American English, Appalachian English, Southern English, a New York dialect, and Spanish-influenced English. A child who uses these variations should not be treated as having a communication disorder (Battle, 1998; Seymour, Bland-Stewart, & Green, 1998).

Most children learn patterns of speech and language appropriate to their families and neighborhoods before they enter school.

It is certainly possible, however, for a child to have a communication disorder within his dialect. ASHA (1983) considers it essential for a specialist to be able to "distinguish between dialectal differences and communicative disorders" and to "treat only those features or characteristics that are true errors and not attributable to the dialect" (p. 24). A speech or language difference from the majority of children, then, is not necessarily a communication disorder in need of treatment. Some major factors in creating speech and language differences are race and ethnicity, social class, education, occupation, geographical region, and peer group identification (Taylor & Payne, 1998). Problems may arise in the classroom and in parent-teacher communication if the teacher does not accept natural communication differences among children and mistakenly assumes that a speech or language impairment is present (Battle, 1998; Reed, 1998).

For children whose native language is not English, the distinction between a language difference and a communication disorder is critical (Roseberry-McKibbin, 1995). Chapter 3 offers guidelines for assessing learners from culturally and linguistically diverse backgrounds.

Prevalence

Estimates of the prevalence of communication disorders in children vary widely. Reliable figures are hard to come by because investigators often employ different definitions of speech and language disorders and sample different populations. One review of various prevalence studies of school-age populations concluded that speech impairments serious enough to warrant special attention are present in approximately 4% of children (Fein, 1983). A 4% prevalence rate would mean that between 2 and 3 million school-age children in the United States have communication disorders. In the 1996–1997 school year, 1,050,975 children ages 6 to 21 received special education services under the IDEA category of "speech or language impairments" (U.S. Department of Education, 1998). This number represents about 2.3% of the resident population and 21.6% of all students receiving special education services, which makes speech or language impairments the second largest category after learning disabilities.

ASHA estimates that speech, language, and related disorders affect 14 million Americans.

A recent study designed to estimate the prevalence of language impairment in kindergarten children reported that 26.2% of the 7,218 children failed an initial screening test and were administered a diagnostic battery that identified 7.4% of the children as having a specific language impairment (Tomblin et al., 1997). This figure contrasts with the estimate that about 1% of school-age children are considered to have language disorders (Matthews & Frattali, 1998). Two factors likely explain most of the difference. First, some children who exhibit language delays at a young age are late bloomers and catch up to their peers (Roberts, Rescorla, Giroux, & Stevens, 1998). Second, a sizable percentage of children who are served in special education programs for students with learning disabilities can also be regarded as having language disorders (Wallach & Butler, 1994).

Speech and language impairments tend to be more prevalent among males than females and are about the same in each of the major geographical regions of the United States. ASHA (1998) states that approximately two-thirds of schoolchildren who have problems understanding language are boys. The prevalence of communication disorders does not remain the same throughout the life span. The percentage of children with speech and language disorders, though rather high, decreases significantly from the earlier to the later school grades. For example, Hull, Mielke, Willeford, and Timmons (1976) found that about 7% of all first-grade boys were reported as having extreme articulation deviations, but only 1% of 3rd-grade boys and 0.5% of 12th-grade boys fell into that category.

Types and Causes of Communication Disorders

Many types of communication disorders and numerous possible causes are recognized. A speech impairment may be *organic*—that is, attributable to a specific physical cause. Examples of physical factors that frequently result in communication disorders are cleft palate, paralysis of the speech muscles, absence of teeth, craniofacial abnormalities, enlarged adenoids, and neurological impairments. Organic speech impairments may be a child's primary disability or may be secondary to other disabilities, such as delayed intellectual development, impaired hearing, and cerebral palsy.

Most communication disorders are not considered organic but are classified as functional. A *functional* communication disorder cannot be ascribed to a specific physical condition, and its origin is not clearly known. McReynolds (1990) points out that decades of research on the causes of many speech and language impairments have produced few answers. A child's surroundings provide many opportunities to learn appropriate and inappropriate communication skills; some specialists believe that functional communication disorders derive mainly from environmental influences. It is also possible that some speech impairments are caused by disturbances in the motor control system and are not fully understood.

Regardless of whether a communication disorder is considered organic or functional, a child with speech or language substantially different from that of others in the same age and cultural group requires systematic intervention to correct or improve the impairment.

Articulation Disorders

Articulation disorders—atypical production of speech sounds—are the most prevalent type of speech impairment among school-age children. The correct articulation, or utterance, of speech sounds requires us to activate a complicated system of muscles, nerves, and organs. Haycock (1933), who compiled a classic manual on teaching speech, describes how the speech organs are manipulated into a variety of shapes and patterns, how the breath and voice must be "molded to form words." Here is Haycock's description of how the /v/ sound is correctly produced: "The lower lip must be drawn upwards and slightly inwards, so that the upper front teeth rest lightly on the lip. Breath must be freely emitted between the teeth and over the lower lip, and voice must be added to the breath" (n.p.). If any part of this process functions imperfectly, a child will have difficulty articulating the /v/. Clearly, in such a complicated process, many types of errors are possible.

There are of four basic kinds of articulation errors:

- Children may *substitute* one sound for another, as in saying "train" for "crane" or "doze" for "those." Children with this problem are often certain they have said the correct word and may resist correction. Substitution of sounds can cause considerable confusion for the listener.

- Children may *distort* certain speech sounds while attempting to produce them accurately. The /s/ sound, for example, is relatively difficult to produce; children may produce the word "sleep" as "schleep," "zleep," or "thleep." Some speakers have a lisp; others a whistling /s/. Distortions can cause misunderstanding, though parents and teachers often become accustomed to them.
- Children may *omit* certain sounds, as in saying "cool" for "school." They may drop consonants from the ends of words, as in "pos" for "post." Most of us leave out sounds at times, but an extensive omission problem can make speech impossible to understand.
- Children may also *add* extra sounds, making comprehension difficult. They may say "buhrown" for "brown" or "hamber" for "hammer."

Dysarthria *and* apraxia *refer to two groups of articulation disorders caused by neuromuscular impairments. Lack of precise motor control needed to produce and sequence sounds causes distorted and repeated sounds.*

Degree of Severity Like all communication disorders, articulation problems vary widely in degree of severity. Many children have mild or moderate articulation disorders. Usually their speech can be understood, but they may mispronounce certain sounds or use immature speech, like that of younger children. These problems often disappear as a child matures. If a mild or moderate articulation problem does not seem to be improving over an extended period or if it appears to have an adverse

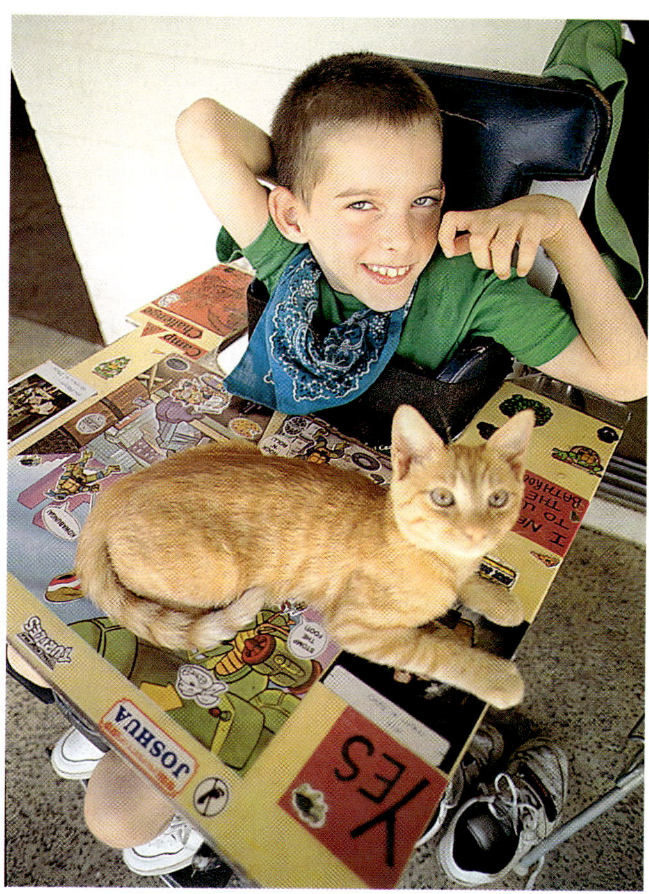

Although Joshua's physical disabilities make it difficult for him to articulate speech sounds well enough to be understood, his communication board has opened up social interaction for him.

effect on the child's interaction with others, referral to a speech-language pathologist is indicated.

A severe articulation disorder is present when a child pronounces many sounds so poorly that her speech is unintelligible most of the time; even the child's parents, teachers, and peers cannot easily understand him. The child with a severe articulation disorder may say, "Yeh me yuh a wido," instead of "Let me look out the window," or perhaps, "Do foop is dood" for "That soup is good." The fact that articulation disorders are prevalent does not mean that teachers, parents, and specialists should regard them as simple or unimportant. On the contrary, as Emerick and Haynes (1986) observe, "an articulation disorder severe enough to interfere significantly with intelligibility is . . . as debilitating a communication problem as many other disorders. . . . articulation disorders are not simple at all, and they are not necessarily easy to diagnose effectively" (p. 153).

Fluency Disorders

Normal speech makes use of rhythm and timing. Words and phrases flow easily, with certain variations in speed, stress, and appropriate pauses. ASHA (1993) defines a *fluency disorder* as an "interrupt in the flow of speaking characterized by atypical rate, rhythm, and repetitions in sounds, syllables, words, and phrases. This may be accompanied by excessive tension, struggle behavior, and secondary mannerisms" (p. 40).

One type of fluency disorder is known as *cluttering,* a condition in which speech is very rapid, with extra sounds or mispronounced sounds. The clutterer's speech is garbled to the point of unintelligibility.

The best-known (and probably least understood) fluency disorder, however, is **stuttering.** This condition is marked by "rapid-fire repetitions of consonant or vowel sounds, especially at the beginning of words; and complete verbal blocks" (Jonas, 1976, p. 7). The cause of stuttering remains unknown, although the condition has been studied extensively with some interesting results (Bloodstein, 1995). Stuttering is far more common among males than females, and it occurs more frequently among twins. The prevalence of stuttering is about the same in all Western countries: regardless of what language is spoken, about 1% of the general population has a stuttering problem. Stuttering is much more commonly reported among children than adults; prevalence estimates in school-age populations are around 5% (Ham, 1986; Martin & Lindamood, 1986). Stuttering is considered a disorder of childhood. Although found on all age levels beginning with the onset of speech, the older the child, the less likely the development of stuttering (Bloodstein, 1995).

Stuttering is situational; that is, it appears to be related to the setting or circumstances of speech. A child may be likely to stutter when talking with the people whose opinions matter most to him, such as parents and teachers, and in situations like being called on to speak in front of the class. Most people who stutter are fluent about 95% of the time; a child with a fluency disorder may not stutter at all when singing, talking to a pet dog, or reciting a poem in unison with others. Reactions and expectations of parents, teachers, and peers clearly have an important effect on any child's personal and communicative development.

Culture-based considerations for the treatment of African American children who stutter are offered by Robinson and Crowe (1998).

All children experience some dysfluencies—repetitions and interruptions—in the course of developing normal speech patterns. It is important not to overreact to dysfluencies and to insist on perfect speech; some specialists believe that stuttering can be caused by pressures placed on a child when parents and teachers react to normal hesitations and repetitions by labeling the child a stutterer. Several researchers and clinicians have explored the effects of social pressures on stuttering by examining its incidence in cultures other than our own. Gerald Jonas, who himself was affected by stuttering, derives insights from a comparison of American Indian tribes. He observes that certain tribes, such as the Utes and the Bannocks of the Rocky Mountain region, have an unusually permissive attitude toward children's speech and have virtually no stuttering problems. Other tribes, such as the Cowichans of the Pacific Northwest, are highly competitive, expecting children to take part in complicated rituals at a young age, and have a high incidence of stuttering. Jonas (1976) suggests that the reason the Ute and Bannock children do not stutter may be that no one ever tries to make them speak correctly. But he acknowledges that this theory fails to explain "why in so many other cultures some children of nagging parents turn into stutterers while others do not" (p. 14).

Voice Disorders

A *voice disorder* is characterized by "the abnormal production and/or absences of vocal quality, pitch, loudness, resonance, and/or duration, which is inappropriate for an individual's age and/or sex" (ASHA, 1993, p. 40).

Voice disorders are more common in adults than in children. Considering how often some children shout and yell without any apparent harm to their voices, it is evident that the vocal cords can withstand heavy use. In some cases, however, a child's voice may be difficult to understand or may be considered unpleasant. Moore and Hicks (1998) use the term *dysphonia* to describe any condition of poor or unpleasant voice quality and note that a voice—whether good, poor, or in between—is closely identified with the person who uses it.

The two basic types of voice disorders involve phonation and resonance. A *phonation disorder* causes the voice to sound breathy, hoarse, husky, or strained most of the time. In severe cases, there is no voice at all. Phonation disorders can have organic causes, such as growths or irritations on the vocal cords, but hoarseness most frequently comes from chronic vocal abuse, such as yelling, imitating noises, or habitually talking while under tension. A breathy voice is unpleasant because it is low in volume and fails to make adequate use of the vocal cords.

A voice with a *resonance disorder* suffers from either too many sounds coming out through the air passages of the nose (*hypernasality*) or, conversely, not enough resonance of the nasal passages (*hyponasality*). The hypernasal speaker may be perceived as talking through her nose or having an unpleasant twang. A child with hypernasality has speech that is excessively nasal, neutral, or central-sounding rather than oral, clear, and forward-sounding (Cole & Paterson, 1986). A child with hyponasality (sometimes called *denasality*) may sound as though he constantly has a cold or a stuffed nose, even when he does not. As with other voice disorders, the causes of nasality may be either organic (e.g., cleft palate, swollen nasal tissues, hearing impairment) or functional (perhaps resulting from learned speech patterns or behavior problems).

Language Disorders

Some professionals view learning disabilities (see Chapter 7) and autism (see Chapter 13) primarily as language disorders.

Language disorders are usually classified as either receptive or expressive. As described earlier, a receptive language disorder interferes with the understanding of language. A child may, for example, be unable to comprehend spoken sentences or to follow a sequence of directions. An expressive language disorder interferes with production of language. The child may have a very limited vocabulary, may use incorrect words and phrases, or may not even speak at all, communicating only through gestures. A child may have good receptive language when an expressive disorder is present or may have both expressive and receptive disorders in combination.

To say that a child has a language delay does not necessarily mean that the child has a language disorder. As Reed (1998) explains, a language delay implies that a child is slow to develop linguistic skills but acquires them in the same sequence as normal children. Generally, all features of language are delayed at about the same rate. A language disorder, however, suggests a disruption in the usual rate and sequence of specific emerging language skills. A child who consistently has difficulty in responding to who, what, and where questions but who otherwise displays language skills appropriate for her age would likely be considered to have a language disorder.

Factors that can contribute to spoken language disorders in children include cognitive limitations or mental retardation, hearing impairments, behavioral disorders, structural abnormalities of the speech mechanism, and environmental deprivation (Chaney & Frodyma, 1982). Environmental influences play an important part in delayed, disordered, or absent language. The communication efforts of some children are reinforced; other children, unfortunately, are punished for talking, gesturing, or otherwise attempting to communicate. A child who has little stimulation at home and few chances to speak, listen, explore, and interact with others will probably have little motivation for communication and may well experience delays in language development. Children who have had little exposure to words and experiences may need the teacher's help in encouraging communication. Active participation in experiences gives children the opportunity to learn and use appropriate vocabulary.

Aphasia Some severe disorders in expressive and receptive language result from impairments of the brain. **Aphasia** describes a "breakdown in the ability to formulate, or to retrieve, and to decode the arbitrary symbols of language" (Holland & Reinmuth, 1982, p. 428). Aphasia is one of the most prevalent causes of language disorders in adults, most often occurring suddenly, following a cardiovascular event (stroke). Aphasia can also occur in children, however, as either a congenital or an acquired condition. Head injury is considered a significant cause of aphasia in children. Aphasia may be either expressive or, less commonly, receptive. Children with mild aphasia have language patterns that are close to normal but may have difficulty retrieving certain words and tend to need more time than usual to communicate (Linebaugh, 1986). Children with severe aphasia, however, are likely to have a markedly reduced storehouse of words and language forms. They may not be able to "use language for successful communicative interchange" (Horner, 1986, p. 892).

Identification and Assessment

Consider the following remarks:

"Don't worry, she'll grow out of it."
"Speech therapists can't help a child who doesn't talk."
"He'll be all right once he starts school."

These are common examples of misguided, inaccurate, and widely held attitudes toward communication disorders. Thompson (1984) contends that such attitudes are "at best worrying and annoying, at worst positively destructive to the child's social, emotional, and intellectual development" (p. 86).

To avoid the consequences of unrecognized or untreated speech and language impairments, it is especially important for children to receive professional assessment and evaluation services.

Case History and Physical Examination

Most professional speech and language assessments begin with the creation of a case history about the child. This typically involves completing a biographical form that includes diverse information such as the child's birth and developmental history, illness, medications taken, scores on achievement and intelligence tests, and adjustment to school. The parents may be asked when the child first crawled, walked, and uttered words. Social skills, such as playing readily with other children, may also be considered.

The specialist carefully examines the child's mouth, noting any irregularities in the tongue, lips, teeth, palate, or other structures that may affect speech production. If the child has an organic speech problem, the child is referred for possible medical intervention.

Evaluation Components

Testing procedures vary according to the suspected type of disorder. Often the specialist conducts broad screenings to detect areas of concern and then moves to more detailed testing in those areas. A comprehensive evaluation to detect the presence of a communication disorder would likely include the following components:

- *Articulation test.* Speech errors by the child are assessed. A record is kept of the sounds that are defective, how they are being mispronounced, and the number of errors. Examples of articulation tests include the Photo Articulation Test (Pendergast, Dickey, Selmar, & Soder, 1984), the Test of Minimal Articulation Competence (Secord, 1981), and the Goldman-Fristoe Test of Articulation (Goldman & Fristoe, 1986).
- *Hearing test.* Hearing is usually tested to determine whether a hearing problem is causing the speech disorder.
- *Auditory discrimination test.* This test is given to determine whether the child is hearing sounds correctly. If unable to recognize the specific characteristics of a given sound, the child will not have a good model to imitate. The Auditory Discrimination Test (Wepman, 1973) and the Test of Auditory Discrimination (Goldman, Fristoe, & Woodcock, 1990) are two examples.

Audiometry, *a formal procedure for testing hearing, is discussed in Chapter 10.*

- *Vocabulary and language development test.* This test is administered to help determine the amount of vocabulary the child has acquired because vocabulary is generally a good indicator of intelligence. Frequently used tests of language development include the Peabody Picture Vocabulary Test and the Tests of Language Development (Newcomber & Hammill, 1988). An overall language test, such as the Clinical Evaluation of Language Functions (Semel & Wiig, 1980), assesses the child's understanding and production of language structures (e.g., important syntactical elements like conjunctions showing causal relationships).
- *Language samples.* An important part of any evaluation procedure is obtaining an accurate example of the child's expressive speech and language. The examiner considers factors such as intelligibility and fluency of speech, voice quality, and use of vocabulary and grammar. Some speech-language pathologists use structured tasks to evoke language samples. They may, for example, ask a child to describe a picture, tell a story, or answer a list of questions. Most specialists, however, use informal conversation as their preferred procedure to obtain language samples (Atkins & Cartwright, 1982). They believe that the child's language sample will be more representative if the examiner uses natural conversation rather than highly structured tasks. Emerick and Haynes (1986) advise examiners to tape-record language samples instead of taking notes, which can be distracting to the child. Open-ended questions, such as "Tell me about your family," are suggested rather than yes-no questions or questions that can be answered with one word, such as "What color is your car?"

Hadley (1998) describes two procedures for obtaining language samples of young children: a conversational interview and a story retelling/generating procedure.

- *Observation in natural settings.* Behavioral observation is becoming increasingly important in assessing communication disorders. Objective recording of

McCormick and Schiefelbusch (1990) note the importance of gathering data on both the child's and the adult's behavior in the language interaction. The extent to which the child learns and uses language effectively in the classroom depends to a large extent on the teacher's language behavior.

children's language competence in social contexts has added much to our knowledge of language acquisition. It is imperative that the observer have experience in reliably recording speech and language and sample the child's communication behavior across various settings rather than limit it to a clinic or examining room. A parent-child observation is frequently arranged for young children. The specialist provides appropriate toys and activities and requests the parent to interact normally with the child.

Arena Assessment

When multiple members of a transdisciplinary team are involved in planning and carrying out an intervention for a child with a communication disorder, a strategy known as **arena assessment** may prove beneficial. Arena assessment is a group assessment procedure in which parents, teachers, speech-language pathologists, and other involved participants seat themselves in a circle or semicircle around the child. Wolery and Dyk (1984) suggest five advantages for the arena assessment approach. First, because many similar or even identical test items appear on the tests given by different specialists, redundancy is eliminated, and both the child and parents are spared responding repeatedly to the same item. Second, unnecessary handling of the child by various professionals is reduced. Third, team members observe the child perform across a wider range of performance domains and end up with a more holistic view of the child. Fourth, team members have an opportunity to observe and learn from one another. Finally, consensus regarding the child's status and intervention needs is more likely because each team member observes the same set of child behaviors.

For a description of a parent involvement program developed by speech-language pathologists to promote academic achievement by focusing on communication skills, see Farber and Goldstein (1998).

After the assessment procedures have been completed, the speech-language pathologist reviews the results of the case history, formal and informal tests, language samples, behavioral observations, medical records, and other available data. A treatment plan is then developed in cooperation with the child's parents and teachers to set up realistic communication objectives and to determine the methods that will be used. Kelly and Rice (1986) suggest giving parents an opportunity to question and react to the recommendations and to discuss their willingness to follow through with the treatment plans. It is also appropriate, they note, to inform parents of the frequency of therapy, the costs involved, and the availability of resources in the community.

A comprehensive assessment of communication disorders includes articulation, auditory discrimination, vocabulary tests, and a language sample.

Educational Approaches

Various approaches are employed in the treatment of speech and language impairments. The profession of speech-language pathology addresses both organic and functional causes and encompasses practitioners with numerous points of view and a wide range of accepted intervention techniques. Medical, dental, and surgical procedures can help many children whose speech problems result from organic causes. Some specialists employ structured exercises and drills to correct speech sounds; others emphasize speech production in natural language contexts. Some prefer to work with children in individual therapy sessions; others believe that group sessions are advantageous for language modeling and peer support. Some encourage children to imitate the therapist's speech; others prefer to have the child listen to tapes of his own speech. Some specialists follow a structured, teacher-directed approach in which targeted speech and language behaviors are precisely prompted, recorded, and reinforced; others favor less structured methods. Some speech-language therapists focus on a child's expressive and receptive communication; others devote attention to other aspects of the child's behavior and environment, such as self-confidence and interactions with parents and classmates. Clearly, many possible options may be explored in devising an appropriate treatment plan.

Treating Articulation Disorders

Some speech-language pathologists, according to Bernthal and Bankson (1986), feel more comfortable and competent when dealing with articulation disorders than with other types of speech and language impairments. This response is probably attributable, they note, to the fact that articulation disorders can be broken down into identifiable segments more readily than can disorders of voice, fluency, or language. Also, a child can logically progress from articulating simple sounds in isolation to syllables, words, phrases, sentences, and sustained conversation. A large percentage of functional articulation disorders either are treated successfully or simply fade away as the child matures.

Four models of treatment are widely used for articulation disorders (Bernthal & Bankson, 1986; Creaghead, Newman, & Secord, 1989):

- The *discrimination model* emphasizes developing the child's ability to listen carefully and detect the differences between similar sounds (e.g., the /t/ in "take," the /c/ in "cake"). The child learns to match his speech to that of a standard model by using auditory, visual, and tactual feedback.
- The *phonologic model* seeks to identify the pattern of sound production and to teach the child to produce gradually more acceptable sounds. A child who tends to omit final consonants, for example, might be taught to recognize the difference between word pairs—for example, "two" and "tooth"—and then to produce them more accurately.
- The *sensorimotor model* emphasizes the repetitive production of sounds in various contexts, with special attention to the motor skills involved in articulation; frequent exercises are employed to produce sounds with differing stress patterns.
- The *operant conditioning model* seeks to define antecedent events, present specific stimuli, and shape articulatory responses by providing reinforcing consequences.

These four models to the remediation of articulation disorders are not mutually exclusive. The interventions planned by many speech-language pathologists involve a combination of the four approaches.

A generally consistent relationship exists between children's ability to recognize sounds and their ability to articulate them correctly (Creaghead et al., 1989). Whatever treatment models are used, the specialist may have the child carefully watch how sounds are produced and then use a mirror to monitor his own speech production. Children are expected to accurately produce problematic sounds in syllables, words, sentences, and stories. They may tape-record their own speech and listen carefully for errors. It is sometimes helpful for children to learn to recognize the difference between the way they produce a sound and the way other people produce it. As in all communication training, it is important for the teacher, parent, or specialist to provide a good language model, to reinforce the child's improving performance, and to encourage the child to talk.

Treating Fluency Disorders

The treatment of stuttering and other fluency disorders varies widely according to the orientation of the client and the therapist. Throughout history, people who stutter have been subjected to countless treatments—some of them unusual, to say the least. Past treatments included holding pebbles in the mouth, sticking fingers into a light socket, talking out of one side of the mouth, eating raw oysters, speaking with the teeth clenched, taking alternating hot and cold baths, and speaking on inhaled rather than exhaled air (Ham, 1986). For many years, it was widely thought that stuttering was caused by a tongue that was unable to function properly in the mouth. It was common for early physicians to prescribe ointments to blister or numb the tongue or even to remove portions of the tongue through surgery!

Application of behavioral principles has strongly influenced recent practices in the treatment of fluency disorders. A therapist using this methodology regards stuttering as a learned response and seeks to eliminate it by establishing and encouraging fluent speech. For example, one stuttering treatment program, called the Lidcombe Program, trains parents to positively reinforce their child's fluent utterances in the home. Packman and Onslow (1998) cite six different studies in which the effectiveness of the Lidcombe Program has been demonstrated.

Children may learn to manage their stuttering by deliberately prolonging certain sounds or by speaking slowly to get through a "block." They may increase their confidence and fluency by speaking in groups, where pressure is minimized and successful speech is positively reinforced. They may learn to monitor their own speech and to reward themselves for periods of fluency. They may learn to speak to a rhythmic beat or with the aid of devices that mask or delay their ability to hear their own speech. Tape recorders are often used for drills, simulating conversations, and documenting progress.

When interacting with a child who stutters, a teacher should pay primary attention to what the child is saying rather than to his difficulties in saying it. This focus helps the child develop a more positive attitude toward himself and communication with others. When the child experiences a verbal block, the teacher should be patient and calm, say nothing, and maintain eye contact with the child until he finishes speaking.

For specific suggestions for how classroom teachers can help children with speech dysfluencies, see "Helping the Child Who Stutters in the Classroom" on the next page.

Children often learn to control their stuttering and produce increasingly fluent speech as they mature. No single method of treatment has been recognized as most effective. Stuttering frequently decreases when children enter adolescence, regardless of which treatment method was used. Often, the problem disappears with no treatment at all. Results from studies of the phenomenon of spontaneous recovery from stuttering have reported that 65% to 80% of children diagnosed as stutterers

Helping the Child Who Stutters in the Classroom

There is no single treatment for stuttering because the causation, type, and severity of nonfluencies vary from child to child. Despite this variability, teachers can significantly help a child who stutters by providing a good speech model, improving the child's self-esteem, and creating a good speech environment.

Provide a Good Speech Model

1. *Reduce your rate of speech.* Young children often imitate the speech rate of their parents and other significant adults. This rate may be inappropriately fast for the child's motoric and linguistic competencies. Slower speech provides the child the time needed to organize thoughts, choose vocabulary and grammatical form, and plan the speech act motorically.
2. *Create silences in your interactions.* Pauses placed at appropriate places in conversation help create a relaxed communication environment, slower rate of speech, and a more natural speech cadence. Pause for two to three seconds before responding to a child's questions and statements.
3. *Model simple vocabulary and grammatical forms.* Stuttering is more likely to occur in longer words, words that are used less frequently, and more grammatically complex sentences.
4. *Model normal nonfluencies.* You may need to make a conscious effort to use normal nonfluencies, such as interjections ("um" or "ah") or an occasional whole-word repetition, phrase repetition, or pause. Knowing that even fluent speech contains nonfluencies will help children accept nonfluencies and reduce the fear of speaking.

Improve the Child's Self-Esteem

1. *Disregard moments of nonfluency.* Reinforce occurrences of fluency and ignore nonfluencies. Do not give instructions such as "Slow down," "Take a deep breath," or "Stop and start over," which imply that the child is not doing enough. This might increase guilt and diminish self-confidence.
2. *Show acceptance of what the child expresses rather than how it is said.* Ask the child to repeat only the parts of the utterance that were not understood rather than those that were nonfluent. This request indicates that you did listen and that the message is important.
3. *Treat the child who stutters like any other child in the class.* Do not reduce your expectations because of the nonfluencies.
4. *Acknowledge nonfluencies without labeling them.* Do not refer to the problem of stuttering. Instead, use words that the child uses to describe her speech, such as "bumpy" or "hard." Assure the child that it is okay to have dysfluencies; everyone does.
5. *Help the child feel in control of speech.* Follow the child's lead in conversation. Speech will more likely be fluent if the child can talk about areas of interest.
6. *Accept nonfluencies.* Try not to be overly concerned about normal nonfluencies because you see the child as a stutterer. Maintain eye contact and remain patient.

Create a Good Speech Environment

1. *Establish good conversational rules.* Interruptions may distract the child and increase nonfluencies. Ensure that no one interrupts and that everyone gets a chance to talk.
2. *Listen attentively.* Active listening lets the child know that content is important. Use naturalistic comments (e.g., "Yes, Johnny, that is a large blue truck.") in place of absentminded "uh-huhs" and generic statements (e.g., "Good talking!").
3. *Suggest that the child cease other activities while speaking.* It is sometimes difficult to perform two different motoric acts, such as coloring and talking, simultaneously. Asking the child to stop other activities while speaking may improve fluency.
4. *Prepare the child for upcoming events.* The emotionality of birthdays, holidays, field trips, and changes in the daily schedule may cause apprehension and increase stuttering. Discussing upcoming events can reduce fear associated with the unknown and should enhance the child's fluency.

Source: From LaBlance, G. R., Steckol, K. F., & Smith, V. L. (1994). Stuttering: The role of the classroom teacher. *Teaching Exceptional Children, 26*(2), 10–12. Adapted by permission.

apparently outgrow or get over their dysfluencies without formal intervention (Curlee & Yairi, 1998). Nevertheless, a speech-language pathologist should be contacted when a child exhibits signs of stuttering or when the parents are concerned about speech fluency. Although some children who stutter get better without help, many do not. Early intervention may prevent the child from developing a severe stutter. In its initial stages, stuttering can almost always be treated successfully by teachers, parents, and a speech-language pathologist working together.

For a review of research on the effectiveness of treatments for voice disorders, see Pannbacker (1998).

Treating Voice Disorders

A thorough medical examination should always be sought for a child with a voice disorder. Organic causes can often be treated by surgery or other medical interventions. In addition, speech-language pathologists sometimes recommend environmental modifications; a person who is consistently required to speak in a noisy setting, for example, may benefit from the use of a small microphone to reduce vocal straining and shouting (Moore & Hicks, 1994). Most remedial techniques, however, offer direct vocal rehabilitation, which helps the child with a voice disorder gradually learn to produce more acceptable and efficient speech. Depending on the type of voice disorder and the child's overall circumstances, vocal rehabilitation may include activities such as exercises to increase breathing capacity, relaxation techniques to reduce tension, or procedures to increase or decrease the loudness of speech.

Visi-pitch is an example of a visual speech display. It can be used with Apple and IBM-compatible computers.

Applied behavior analysis has contributed to the treatment of voice disorders in recent years (Johnson, 1986). Because many voice problems are directly attributable to vocal abuse, behavioral principles can be used to help children and adults break habitual patterns of vocal misuse. Computer technology has also been successfully applied in the treatment of voice disorders. Some instruments enable speakers to see visual representations of their voice patterns on a screen or printout; speakers are thus able to monitor their own vocalizations visually as well as auditorily and to develop new patterns of using their voices more naturally and efficiently (Bull & Rushakoff, 1987).

Treating Language Disorders

Treatments for language disorders are also extremely varied. Some programs focus on precommunication activities that encourage the child to explore and that make the environment conducive to the development of receptive and expressive language. Clearly, children must have something they want to communicate. And because children learn through imitation, it is important for the teacher or specialist to talk clearly, use correct inflections, and provide a rich variety of words and sentences.

Go to the Resources Module for Chapter 9 at http://www.prenhall.com/heward. Click on Special Ed Resource Page and link to "teacher resources." Find and adapt a lesson plan where you could employ naturalistic interventions.

Speech-language pathologists are increasingly employing naturalistic interventions to help children develop and use language skills. *Naturalistic interventions* occur in real or simulated activities that naturally occur in the home, school, or community environments in which a child normally functions. Goldstein, Kaczmarek, and Hepting (1994) offer this definition of and rationale for the development and use of naturalistic interventions:

> Naturalistic interventions vary in the extent to which they depart from the didactic teaching strategies historically implemented in "pull-out" models of treatment for communications disorders. Typically, naturalistic interventions are characterized by their use of dispersed learning trials, attempts to base teaching on the child's attentional lead within the context of normal conversational interchanges, and orientation toward teaching the form and content of language in the context of normal use. Didactic intervention approaches, on the other hand, have been conducted using substitute stimuli (e.g., pictures, puppets) or simulation settings that are amenable to teaching specific skills using mass trials. Naturalistic approaches were developed as an alternative to didactic language intervention,

because children often experienced difficulties in generalizing new skills to everyday contexts where they were needed. (p. 102)

Kaiser (in press) makes the following recommendations about naturalistic interventions, which are also known as **milieu teaching strategies:**

- They should be brief and positive.
- They should be carried out in the natural environment as opportunities for teaching functional communication occur.
- They should be occasioned by student interest in the topic.

Naturalistic interventions involve structuring the environment to create numerous opportunities for desired child responses (e.g., holding up a toy and asking, "What do you want?") and structuring adult responses to a child's communication (e.g., the child points outside and says, "Go wifth me," and the teacher says, "Okay, I'll go with you."). Good milieu teaching should "more closely resemble a conversation than a rote instructional episode" (Kaiser, in press). However, good naturalistic teaching does not mean the teacher should wait patiently to see whether and when opportunities for meaningful and interesting language use by children occur. Environments in which language teaching takes place should be designed to catch students' interest and increase the likelihood of communicative interactions that can be used for teaching purposes. Six strategies for arranging environments that create naturally occurring language teaching opportunities are described in Figure 9.3.

No matter what the approach to treatment, clearly children with language disorders need to be around children and adults with something interesting to talk about. As Reed (1998) points out, it was assumed for many years that a one-to-one setting was the most effective format for language intervention. Emphasis was on eliminating distracting stimuli and focusing a child's attention on the desired communication task. Today, however, it is generally recognized that language is an interactive, interpersonal process and that naturally occurring intervention formats should be used to expose children with language disorders to a wide range of stimuli, experiences, contexts, and people that can not be replicated in one-to-one therapy.

Whatever intervention methods they use, effective speech-language pathologists establish specific goals and objectives, keep precise records of their students' behaviors, and arrange the learning environment so that each child's efforts at communication will be rewarded and enjoyable.

To join in the discussion, "Why are naturalistic interventions more likely to result in maintenance and generalizations of a child's new speech and language skills?" go to the Message Board Module at http://www.prenhall.com/heward.

See "Active Learning Dialogues for Students with Language Learning Disabilities" on the next page.

Augmentative and Alternative Communication

Augmentative and alternative communication (AAC) refers to a diverse set of strategies and methods to assist individuals who are unable to meet their communication needs through speech or writing. AAC has three components (Lloyd, Quist, & Windsor, 1990):

1. A representational symbol set or vocabulary
2. A means for selecting the symbols
3. A means for transmitting the symbols

Each of the three components of AAC may be unaided or aided. *Unaided techniques* do not require a physical aid or device (Lloyd & Kangas, 1994). They include oral speech, gestures, facial expressions, general body posture, and manual signs. Of course, individuals without disabilities use a wide range of unaided augmentative communication techniques. *Aided techniques* of communication involve an external device or piece of equipment.

The Crestwood Company publishes a catalog of AAC devices for children and adults. See "For More Information" at the end of this chapter. Parette and Angelo (1996) suggest 20 questions that should be asked to assess the impact of ACC on the family.

Active Learning Dialogues for Students with Language Learning Disabilities

by Elaine R. Silliman and Jill L. Beasman, University of South Florida

Dramatic changes have occurred in how speech-language pathologists (SLPs) work in schools. Traditionally, the SLP was seen as an outside expert who intervened with children having language and communication disabilities. Children's needs were typically addressed by pulling them out of the classroom; they were brought to the services. But studies show that pullout services are not an effective or efficient way to facilitate real language learning in relation to the curriculum (ASHA, 1996). For example, separating speech and language goals from how communication is used every day in the classroom results in poor transfer of learning. Thus, more SLPs are working as educational partners in the classroom, mediating between students' communication needs and the communication demands of the curriculum (Duchan, 1997). Language and speech goals can be integrated into daily curriculum activities when SLPs become classroom collaborators. The advantage is that services are brought to the child and teacher and communication connections with the curriculum are made more directly.

The major purpose of verbal communication is to create understanding between people. This understanding is made possible through dialogue, the exchange of messages between speakers and listeners or writers and readers. All classroom teaching and learning consists of dialogue between teachers (or SLPs) and students. But not all dialogue is good teaching and learning.

SLP:	Boys and girls, remember this morning when we went to go visit this worker? (Points to picture on board of cafeteria worker.)
Lily:	The chef.
SLP:	The chef—the chef, and who can tell me what the chef's job is to do?
Group:	To cook food.
SLP:	To make food. What else? Remember when we went to the cafeteria and we saw the chefs in our cafeteria? They did a couple of jobs.
Mary:	Made food.
SLP:	They made food, and after they've made the food and you eat your food and you put your trays up, what else do they do?

Figure A Sample of instructional dialogue from "The Chef Lesson"

Passive Learning Dialogues The dialogue in Figure A is an excerpt from a lesson on community workers taught by an SLP. The SLP was the classroom teacher for this kindergarten-grade 1 special education group of eight children with a language learning disability (LLD). This lesson characterizes traditional language learning activities: the dialogue creates the illusion that real learning is taking place (Silliman & Wilkinson, 1991, 1994; Sturm & Nelson, 1997).

Learning through language is presented in fragmented, discrete skills. Students are involved in "language experience time," which treats language and communication as a subject area rather than a learning tool that can be applied across the curriculum.

Learning is a one-way activity in which the SLP is a knowledge transmitter. Students are expected to pay attention and respond to the adult's frame of reference. The purpose of adult communication is to assess continually what students know by asking known-answer questions such as, "Who can tell me what the chef's job is to do?" and "What else does a chef do?" Students' contributions are limited to short responses, such as "To cook food" and "Make food."

The SLP assumes a power role. The SLP controls who can talk, when talking can take place, and what will be talked about. Language learning tends to be reduced to students recalling what they know apart from any real communication purposes.

Passive learning dialogues teach students that learning means giving the right answer, creating the illusion that meaningful learning occurs. For example, the major reason for students to participate in the dialogue is to provide accurate answers to the knowledge testing questions. In contrast, active learning dialogues teach students that learning through language and communication is a process of discovering possible answers to questions.

Active Learning Dialogues Active learning dialogues are guided by theme-based learning in which the communication goals for a student with an LLD are integrated across the curriculum and into all classroom activities. Active learning dialogues are linked to students' real-world experience through problem solving. Outcomes are functional. Children learn that listening, speaking, reading, and writing always have real purposes, such as understanding what others have to say and communicating to others what they want to say. "Lesson talk should sound like conversation, . . . not recitation" (Englert, Tarrant, Mariage, & Oxer, 1994, p. 167).

In the active learning dialogue in Figure B, students have just read a science book on spiders. They are developing a semantic web to organize their reading comprehension. Tom, who has a severe LLD, is attempting to write about what he has learned and becomes orally engaged in persuading Jerry, another student with an LLD, about the importance of having specific knowledge about spiders. The SLP facilitates. This dialogue demonstrates some of the shared interactional features that build active learning contexts (Brookes & Brookes, 1993; Silliman, Mills, & Murphy, 1997):

Integrating primary sources of information and good literature into curriculum/intervention activities. Students draw on a variety of information sources, from the Internet to scientific literature.

Viewing students as critical thinkers. The SLP mediates the many ways that students can think, analyze, and communicate about what they are learning (e.g., through discussion, cooperative writing, drawing). Responsibility for learning is shared between the SLP and the students. This division of power communicates to students that, first, they must take responsibility for what is learned and how, and, second, they are viewed as competent to do so.

Using dialogue that promotes instructional conversations. Students' reasons for decisions are sought, relative to their individual comprehension levels, to advance cognitive, linguistic, and communicative abilities. Jimmy challenges Tom to explain how spiders can "live in dinky little tubes" and "how they [the spiders] can get in there."

Supporting student collaboration. Students often work in cooperative groups to (1) develop ownership of their own learning, (2) explore ideas through talking together, (3) discover similarities that relate concepts, and (4) make new applications (Palincsar, Brown, & Campione, 1993). Tom demonstrates these four outcomes of cooperative learning. He clearly views himself as knowledgeable about the attributes of spiders and their habitats. He attempts to explain his reasoning to Jerry, a process that Amanda and Beatrice reaffirm throughout the interactions with their questions and comments. He draws on real-world knowledge to offer an analogy for Jerry (although the analogy lacks some linguistic clearness—"those play set thingies"). Finally, he can apply what he has learned from reading (and, to a lesser extent, writing) to inform others.

(Participants are the SLP, Tom, age 9 years, 5 months, and Jerry, age 9 years, 6 months, both of whom have an LLD, and Beatrice, age 8 years, 1 month, and Amanda, age 8 years, 3 months, who are typical language learners)

SLP:	Okay, Tom, since Amanda thought of that sentence, do you want to make one of your own?
Tom:	Spiders. Ooooh, you know on swing sets where—where all that stuff is hanging in the little tubes? Inside those. You know what I'm talking about (to SLP).
SLP:	So how are you going to write that, Tom?
Tom:	Spiders live in
Jerry:	in little houses. (overlaps Tom's speaking turn in trying to help him)
Tom:	No, Jerry, no. Spiders live in tubes.
Amanda:	Tubes, huh?
SLP:	What might these tubes be?
Jerry:	How can spiders live in dinky little tubes? They're too large.
Tom:	No, those like play set thingies.
Jerry:	Yeah, but there're too stinky. Dinky.
Tom:	You know on the swing set, the little tunnels. There in the swing set?
Jerry:	How can they get in there? How can they get in there when they're already too high?
Tom:	They climb in them. They have claws.
Jerry:	Then how are they going to get back out?
Amanda:	They don't, Jerry. They live there forever.
Tom:	Jerry, you are the weirdest. Man.
Beatrice:	Forever, forever, and forever.
Tom:	They don't come out. They wait for the food to come in, OK?

Figure B Sample of instructional conversations from "The Spider Dialogue"

1. **Interesting materials.** Students are likely to communicate when things or activities in the environment interest them. *Example:* James lay quietly on the rug, with his head resting on his arms. Ms. Davis sat at one end of the rug and rolled a big yellow ball right past James. James lifted his head and looked around for the ball.
2. **Out of reach.** Students are likely to communicate when they want something that they cannot reach. *Example:* Mr. Norris lifted a drum off the shelf and placed it on the floor between Judy and Annette, who were both in wheelchairs. Mr. Norris hit the drum three times and then waited, looking at his two students. Judy watched and clapped her hands together. Then, she reached for the drum with both arms outstretched.
3. **Inadequate portions.** Students are likely to communicate when they do not have the necessary materials to carry out an instruction. *Example:* Mr. Robinson gave every student except Mary a ticket to get into the auditorium for the high school play. He told his students to give their tickets to the attendant. Mr. Robinson walked beside Mary toward the entrance. When Mary reached the attendant, Mr. Robinson paused and looked at Mary. She pointed to the tickets in his hand and signed "give me." Mr. Robinson gave her a ticket and she handed it to the attendant who said "Thank you. Enjoy the play."
4. **Choice-making.** Students are likely to communicate when they are given a choice. *Example:* Peggy's favorite pastime is listening to tapes on her tape recorder. On Saturday morning, Peggy's father said to her, "We could listen to your tapes" (pointing to the picture of the tape recorder on Peggy's communication board) "or we could go for a ride in the car" (pointing to the picture of the car). "What would you like to do?" Peggy pointed to the picture of the tape recorder. "OK, let's listen to this new tape you like," her father said as he put the tape in and turned on the machine.
5. **Assistance.** Students are likely to communicate when they need assistance in operating or manipulating materials. *Example:* Tammy's mother always places three clear plastic containers with snacks (cookies, crackers, popcorn) on the kitchen table before Tammy returns from school. When Tammy arrives home and is ready for a snack, she goes to the table and chooses what she wants. The containers are hard to open, so Tammy usually brings the container with her chosen snack to her mother. Her mother responds to this nonverbal request by modeling a request form that specifies Tammy's choice (e.g., "Open popcorn.")
6. **Unexpected situations.** Students are likely to communicate when something happens that they do not expect. *Example:* Ms. Esser was helping Kathy put on her socks and shoes after rest time. After assisting with the socks, Ms. Esser put one of the shoes on her own foot. Kathy stared at the shoe for a moment and then looked up at her teacher, who was smiling. "No," laughed Kathy, "my shoe."

Figure 9.3 Six strategies for increasing naturalistic opportunities for language teaching

Source: From Kaiser, A. P. (in press). Teaching functional communication skills. In M. E. Snell & F. Brown (Eds.), *Instruction of students with severe disabilities* (5th ed.). Upper Saddle River, NJ: Merrill/Prentice Hall. Reprinted by permission.

Symbol Sets and Symbol Systems

Individuals who do not speak so that others can understand must have access to vocabulary that matches as nearly as possible the language they would use in various situations if they could speak. Beukelman and Miranda (1998) suggest that decisions about what items to include in a student's augmentative vocabulary should take into account the following:

- Vocabulary that peers in similar situations and settings use
- What communication partners (e.g., teachers, parents) think will be needed
- Vocabulary the student is already using in all modalities
- Contextual demands of specific situations

After selecting the vocabulary for an augmentative communication system, a collection of symbols must be chosen or developed to represent the vocabulary. There are numerous commercially available *symbol sets,* a collection of pictures or drawings in which each symbol has one or more specified meaning, from which a person's AAC vocabulary might be constructed. Symbol sets—such as the Oakland Picture Dictionary (Kirsten, 1981), Picture Communication Symbols (Mayer-Johnson, 1986), and the Pictogram Ideogram Communication symbols (Johnson, 1985)—are graphic, which means that the symbols look like the object or concept they represent as much as possible. Symbol sets may also be homemade, consisting of photos, pictures, and perhaps words and the alphabet.

In contrast to symbol sets, *symbol systems* are structured around an internal set of rules that govern how new symbols are added to the system. One of the best-known symbol systems is Blissymbolics. Bliss symbols were developed in the 1940s by Austrian chemical engineer Charles Bliss as a graphic symbol system for international communication. They were adapted by the Easter Seal Communication Institute in Toronto, Canada, in the early 1970s for use by nonspeaking persons with physical disabilities (McDonald, 1980). Bliss symbols represent concepts through a combination of geometric shapes. The user of Blissymbolics combines multiple symbols to create new meanings (e.g., "school" is communicated by selecting the symbols "house-gives-knowledge"). The system offers a means of greatly expanded communication to the nonspeaking individual who can learn the new language of Blissymbolics. Because many of the Blissymbolics are abstract, however, and do not look like the concept they represent, some individuals have difficulty learning the system. In one study, adolescents with severe physical disabilities quickly learned to use graphic line drawings that directly represented vocabulary objects but developed little functional use of the Bliss symbols (Hurlbut, Iwata, & Green, 1982). Figure 9.4 shows how common concrete and abstract vocabulary can be represented by Bliss symbols and six other symbol sets.

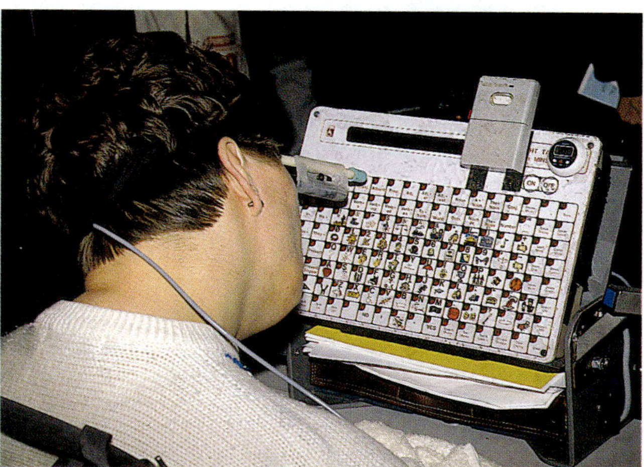

This communication device enables the user to select and transmit synthesized speech via a wand attached to the head.

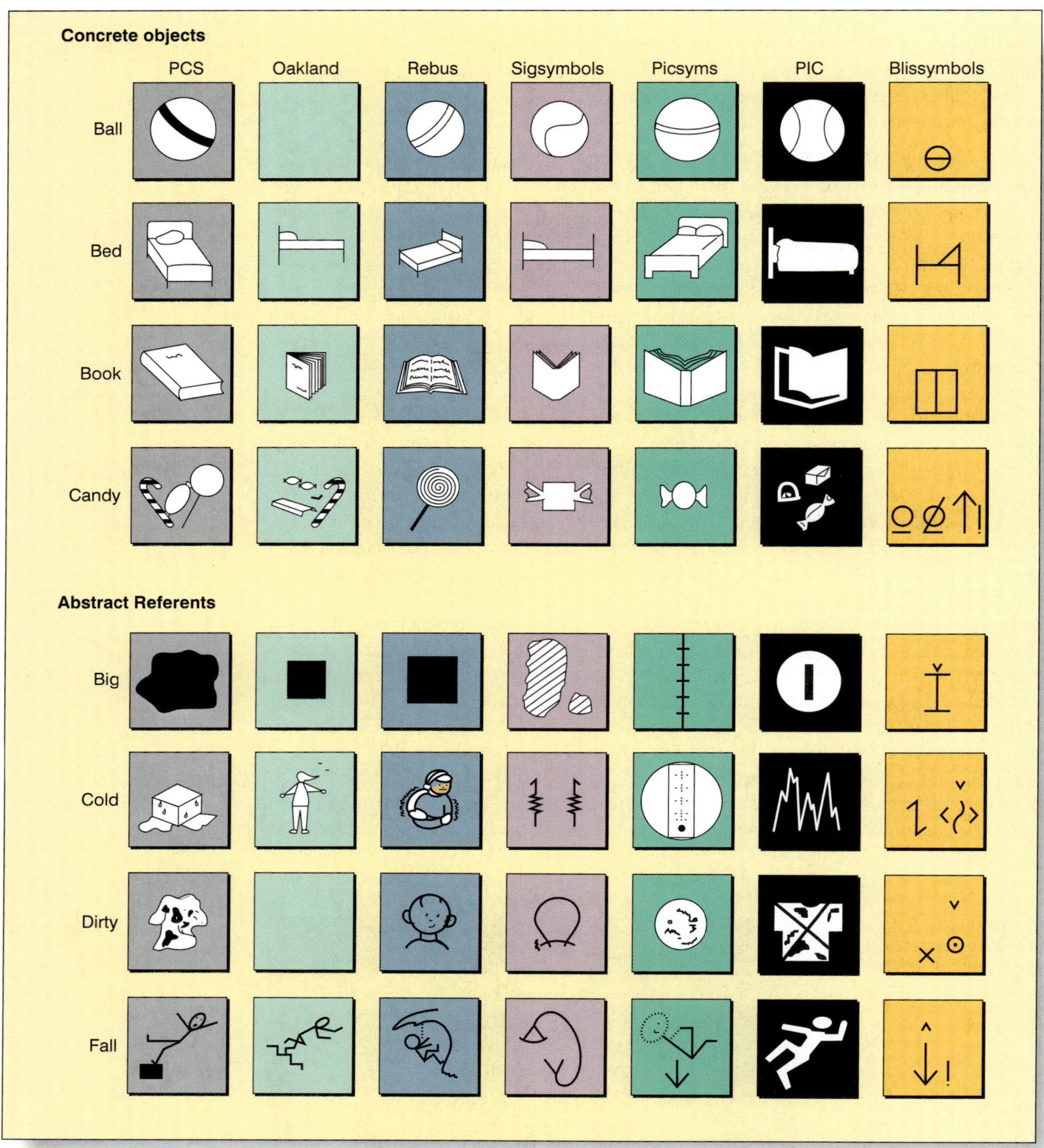

Figure 9.4 Examples from widely used graphic symbol sets (PCS=Picture Communication Symbols; PIC=Pictogram Ideogram Communication)

Source: From Vanderheiden, G. C., & Lloyd, L. L. (1986). Non-speech modes and systems. In S. W. Blackstone (Ed.), *Augmentative communication* (ff. 49–161). Rockville, MD: American Speech-Language-Hearing Association. Reprinted by permission.

Selecting the Symbols

Symbols are selected in augmentative communication by direct selection, scanning, or encoding responses (Lloyd & Kangas, 1994). *Direct selection* involves pointing to the symbol one wishes to express with a finger or fist or sometimes with a wand attached to the head or chin. With a limited number of selections widely spaced from one another, the user can select symbols by "eye pointing." *Scanning* techniques present choices to the user one at a time, and the user makes a response at the proper time to indicate which item or group of selections she wants to communicate. Scanning can be machine- or listener-assisted (e.g., the listener may point to symbols one at a time while watching for the user's eye blink, which signals selection). *Encoding* involves giving multiple signals to indicate the location of the symbol or item to be selected. Usually, the user makes a pair of responses that directs the listener to a specific printed message on a reference list. Encoding can be particularly useful for a student whose severe physical impairments prohibit reliable selection by pointing to an item, unless there are very few symbols and they are widely spaced. In a display in which symbols are organized by color and number, for example, a student can first touch one card (to select the red group of messages) and then make a second pointing response to indicate which number message in the red group is intended.

See Figure 9.5 for suggestions on how to communicate with a person who uses AAC. More ideas for being a good communication partner can be found in the Teaching & Learning box at the end of this chapter.

Transmitting the Symbols

Once vocabulary and a symbol set have been selected, a method of transmitting the symbols must be determined. The most common tool for augmentative communication display and transmission is the *communication board*, a flat area (often a tray

Communicating with someone who does not speak can be a challenging, even unnerving, experience for many natural speakers. Here are 10 suggestions for those who use speech to communicate that will help improve the quality of their conversations with people who use AAC:

- Introduce yourself.
- Ask the person to show you how the communication system works.
- Pause to let the person construct a message. Be patient; it might take a while.
- Relax and give yourself a chance to get used to a slower rhythm of communication. Don't feel like you have to fill all the silent spaces by talking all the time.
- Be sure to give your new friend a chance to ask you questions or to make comments.
- Even though you might guess what's coming next from context, don't finish the person's sentences unless given permission or prompted to do so.
- Interact at eye-to-eye level if you can. If the person's in a wheelchair, you might grab a chair and sit across from her.
- Pay attention to facial expressions and gestures, just as you would with someone who communicates by speech.
- Don't be afraid to say you don't understand something and to ask to have it repeated.
- Talk directly to the person; don't communicate with her through someone else.

Figure 9.5 How to talk with a person who uses AAC
Source: Adapted from Blackstone, S. W. (1991). Beyond public awareness: The road to involvement! *Augmentative Communication News, 4*(2), 6. Used by permission of Augmentative Communication, Inc., Monterey, CA.

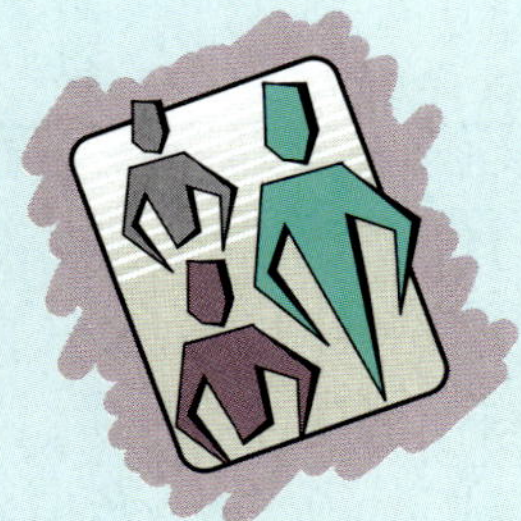

PROFILES AND PERSPECTIVES

My Communication System

by Stephen W. Hawking

Stephen W. Hawking is Lucasian Professor of Mathematics and Theoretical Physics at the University of Cambridge. He has amyotrophic lateral sclerosis (ALS). Sometimes called Lou Gehrig's disease, after one of its most famous victims, ALS is a motor neuron disease of middle or late life that involves progressive degeneration of nerve cells that control voluntary motor functions. Initial symptoms usually entail difficulty in walking, clumsiness of the hands, slurred speech, and an inability to swallow normally. The muscles of the arms and legs waste away; eventually, walking is impossible and control of the hands is lost, although sensation remains normal. There is no known cause or cure for ALS. Professor Hawking responded to our request to describe the augmentative communication system he uses by writing the following story.

In my third year at Oxford, I noticed that I seemed to be getting clumsier, and I fell over once or twice for no apparent reason. Shortly after my 21st birthday, I went into the hospital for tests. I was in for two weeks, during which I had a wide variety of tests. After all that, they didn't tell me what I had, except that it was not multiple sclerosis and that I was an atypical case. I didn't feel like asking for more details because they were obviously bad.

The realization that I had an incurable disease that was likely to kill me in a few years was a bit of a shock. But I didn't die. In fact, although there was a cloud hanging over my future, I found, to my surprise, that I was enjoying life in the present more than before. I began to make progress with my research.

Up to 1974, I was able to feed myself and get in and out of bed. However, things were getting more difficult, so in 1980 we changed to a system of community and private nurses, who came in for an hour or two in the morning and evening. This lasted until I caught pneumonia in 1985 and had to have a tracheotomy operation. After this, I had to have 24-hour nursing care.

Before the operation, my speech had been getting more slurred, so only a few people who knew me well could understand me. But at least I could communicate. I wrote scientific papers by dictating to a secretary, and I gave seminars through an interpreter, who repeated my words more clearly. However, the tracheotomy removed my ability to speak altogether. For a time, the only way I could communicate was to spell out words letter by letter, by raising my eyebrows when someone pointed to the right letter on a spelling card. It is pretty difficult to carry on a conversation like that, let alone write a scientific paper.

Today, I communicate with a computer system. A computer expert in California, Walter Woltosz, sent me a program he had written called Equalizer. This program allowed me to select words from a series of menus on the screen by pressing a switch in my hand. The program could also be controlled by a switch operated by head or eye movement. When I have built up what I want to say, I can send it to a

To learn how the Dynavok and other assistive technology was used to help an 11-year-old boy who was unable to speak participate in the regular classroom, see Erickson and Koppenhaver (1998).

or table attached to a wheelchair) on which the symbols are arranged for the user to select. A student may have a basic communication board of common words, phrases, numbers, and so forth for use across many situations. He may also have various situational boards, or miniboards, with specific vocabulary for certain situations (e.g., at a restaurant, in science class). Symbols can also be transported and displayed in a wallet or photo album.

Recent technological advances have resulted in several electronic devices that offer a wide range of alternatives for transmitting communication symbols. Dedicated communication aids—such as the Prentke Romich Intro Talker, the Prentke Romich Liberator, DECtalk by Digital Equipment Company, and Sentinent System's Dynavok—offer computerized speech selection and transmission.

speech synthesizer. At first, I just ran the Equalizer program through a desktop computer. However, David Mason, of Cambridge Adaptive Communications, who is also the husband of one of my nurses, put together the system I now use. I have a Datavue 25 computer mounted to the back of my wheelchair that runs from a battery under the chair's seat. The screen is mounted where I can see it, though you have to view it from the right angle. I run a program called Living Center, written by a company called Words Plus of Sunnyvale, California. A cursor moves across the upper part of the screen. I can stop it by pressing a switch in my hand. In this way, I can select words that are printed on the lower part of the screen. This system allows me to communicate much better than I could before; I can manage up to 15 words a minute. I can either speak what I have written or save it on a disk. I can then print it out or call it back and speak it sentence by sentence, like I'm doing now. Using this system, I have written a book and a dozen scientific papers. I have also given a number of scientific and popular talks. They have been well received. I think that is in large part due to the quality of my speech synthesizer, made by Speech Plus, also of Sunnyvale, California.

Physicist Stephen W. Hawking

One's voice is very important. If you have a slurred voice, people are likely to treat you as mentally deficient: "Does he take sugar?" This synthesizer is by far the best I have heard because it varies the intonation and doesn't speak like a Dalek. The only trouble is that it gives me an American accent; however, the company is working on a British version.

I have had motor neuron disease for practically all my adult life, and I am often asked, "How do you feel about having ALS?" The answer is, "Not a lot." I try to lead as normal a life as possible and not think about my condition or regret the things it prevents me from doing, which are not that many. It has not prevented me from having a very attractive family and being successful in my work. This is thanks to the help I have received from my wife, my children, and a large number of other people and organizations. I have been lucky, in that my condition has progressed more slowly than is often the case. But it shows that one need not lose hope.

Educational Placement Alternatives

Most speech-language professionals believe it is impossible to adequately serve the child with a speech or language impairment with an isolated, pullout approach (two or three 30-minute sessions each week with a specialist). In fact, this approach has been described as a futile attempt to "sweep back a river with a broom" (Hatten & Hatten, 1975). Because communication is seen as occurring most appropriately in the natural environment, remedial procedures are increasingly carried out in the regular classroom during ongoing routines rather than in a special speech room. Speech-language pathologists who work in school settings more often function as team members concerned with children's overall education and development. The speech-language pathologist often provides training and consultation for the regular classroom teacher, who may do much of the direct work with a child with communication disorders.

Although some self-contained special classes are specifically designed for children with speech or language impairments, the regular classroom is by far the most prevalent setting for school-age children with communication disorders. During the 1995–1996 school year, approximately 89% of children with speech or language impairments were served in the regular classroom—6.5% in resource rooms, 4.5% in separate classes (U.S. Department of Education, 1998). There is an increasing tendency for communication disorders specialists to serve as consultants for regular and special education teachers (and parents) rather than spend most of their time providing direct services to individual children. The specialist concentrates on assessing communication disorders, evaluating progress, and providing materials and techniques. Teachers and parents are encouraged to follow the specialist's guidelines.

ASHA can provide further information about the training, qualifications, and responsibilities of speech-language pathologists. The address of ASHA appears in "For More Information" at the end of this chapter.

Surveys of members of the American Speech-Language-Hearing Association (Mansour, 1985; Shewan, 1986) have found that speech-language pathologists are employed in a wide variety of settings, with the largest single group (about 37%) working in schools. Other settings include hospitals, speech and hearing clinics, nursing homes, physicians' offices, and private practices. The caseloads of these professionals vary widely according to the setting and the types and severity of communication disorders among their clients. The most prevalent pattern of service delivery in schools is a specialist who works with a child for two sessions each week. The most prevalent communication disorders among children served by school speech-language pathologists are, in order of frequency, language disorders (52.2% of a typical caseload), articulation disorders (34.8%), hearing impairments (4.5%), fluency disorders (4.1%), and voice disorders (2.4%) (Shewan, 1986).

Sometimes the specialist visits schools according to a regular schedule and gives individual or group therapy to the children, but this approach is becoming somewhat less common.

Links to more information about communication disorders can be found by accessing the Resources Module for Chapter 9 at http://www.prenhall.com/heward and linking to "general and disability info" on the Special Ed Resource Page.

Current Issues and Future Trends

In the future, specialists in communication disorders will probably function even more indirectly than they do today. They will continue to work as professional team members, assisting teachers, parents, physicians, and other specialists in recognizing potential communication disorders and in facilitating communication skills. Inservice training will become an ever more important aspect of the specialist's responsibilities.

Changing Populations

Speech-language pathologists who work in schools are likely to find themselves working with an increasing percentage of children with severe and multiple disabilities who previously did not receive specialized services from speech-language pathologists. Caseloads have grown in many school districts, and financial restrictions make it virtually impossible for all students with speech or language impairments to receive adequate services from the relatively few specialists who are employed. Even though all students with disabilities are entitled to receive all of the special education and related services they need, the schools' limited resources necessitate difficult decisions at the local level. Some programs may choose to provide special services only to those students with the most severe speech and language impairments. Others may concentrate their professional resources on higher-functioning students who are considered

Teaching & Learning Video Connections

LOOK

SMALL DIFFERENCES

LOOKing at *Small Differences*

"I like him a lot, but he does have a disability."

If you heard someone make this statement, what thoughts and images would go through your mind? Would you see that person's physical disability, or sensory impairment, or learning difficulty, and assume it to be a predominant feature that overshadows that person's life? Would you consider that person as happy or sad? Would you see him dependent on others or self-directed and self-sufficient? Would you picture a classmate, friend, or co-worker? Would you think of a faceless stranger or someone you admire?

In the video *Small Differences*, a group of kids with disabilities share what they hope you see when you see them—kids. Kids, enjoying each other's company and acting quite typically. Kids with interests and hobbies, talents and abilities, strengths and weaknesses. Yes, the children in *Small Differences* have disabilities, but the physical, sensory, and/or learning problems they face do not define who are they are. In *Small Differences*, we see children who want us to understand that people reach their goals and make their own choices regardless of their disability. We see Chaz and his friends who want the same opportunities as everyone else for learning, socializing, and dreaming for the future.

As you watch this video, think about Chaz, Kelly, Amber, and Dante, who put this video together to show you that their disabilities make a small difference in the goals they have for their own futures. Chaz, Kelly, Amber, and Dante want their disabilities to make no more than a small difference to you—in how you perceive their abilities and how you perceive the abilities of others. How does this message match your own expectations of relatives, classmates, friends, or acquaintances with disabilities? Do you see yourself as someone without prejudices or preconceived perceptions of individuals with disabilities?

LEARNing about Your Own Perceptions of People with Disabilities

Think about the perceptions and expectations you have of Richie as you read the following two descriptions.

Richie #1. Richie Hughes is a charming, handsome seventeen-year-old who attends a large suburban high school in central Ohio. He is a sports fanatic and attends all of his school's football and basketball games. One of the stars on the football team is Richie's best friend. Richie also likes to hang out at the movies, talk on the phone, and listen to his favorite heavy metal bands. He doesn't like to do the "club thing," so participating in organized groups at school does not appeal to him. During the summer, Richie works as an usher at a local outdoor concert theater where last year he got to hear his favorite group, Metallica. When asked if he liked his job, Richie replied, "Well, you have to have a real high tolerance for some kinds of people."

Richie #2. Because he was born with a spinal injury and cerebral palsy, Richie Hughes uses a wheelchair to get around. He attends a large suburban high school but is included in all regular education classes. As other seventeen-year-olds, Richie likes going to movies, talking to friends on the telephone, and listening to his favorite rock groups. He is a big sports fan and likes going to high school football and basketball games. At lunch, Richie usually sits with his friend, Brandon, a rising star on the football team. During the summer, Richie works at an outdoor concert theater where he is ever reminded that the "customer is always right."

Anthony Magnacca/Merrill

Richie Hughes

Self-Assessment

Take a moment and examine the picture you had when you read about Richie #1. Did you see someone not unlike yourself at seventeen, someone you might have hung out with and considered a friend? Now think about your response to Richie #2. You no doubt realized that you were reading about the same young man, but do you think you would have related to him in the same way if the first description immediately identified Richie as someone with a disability? When you read about Richie #2, what thoughts crossed your mind? What key words or phrases described your perceptions and expectations of him? In either case, what images did you have of the interactions the two Richies might have had with people at the outdoor concerts?

Advice from Richie Hughes

A personable young man, Richie Hughes has something to share with all of us. His way of accepting others and developing relationships is worth telling.

Perhaps Richie's positive attitude is a product of numerous opportunities from an early age to interact with his peers in an inclusive school environment. Or, perhaps his family's expectations and confidence in him instilled his positive perceptions. Whatever the reason, Richie tells us why he thinks some students, with or without disabilities, sometimes struggle with making friends.

Richie's direct and positive approach to connecting with people has made a difference in overcoming the challenges which his physical disabilities might present. And his advice is well taken. **How do you measure up to Richie's advice? Do you look to yourself first when you find yourself struggling with forming a relationship? Or, do you always blame others for their failure to understand or compromise?**

"I make friends easily. I have never met anyone I didn't like. Well, hardly ever. (He smiles.) When I go up to someone new or introduce myself, I might have to say, 'This is it. This is what I've got to work with; let's see what we can do.' "

"I think it is your own attitude that makes a difference. If you think 'nobody's gonna like me,' then nobody's gonna like you. Nine times out of ten, people will react to you negatively if that's what you expect of them. The bottom line is you're going to have to do it yourself."

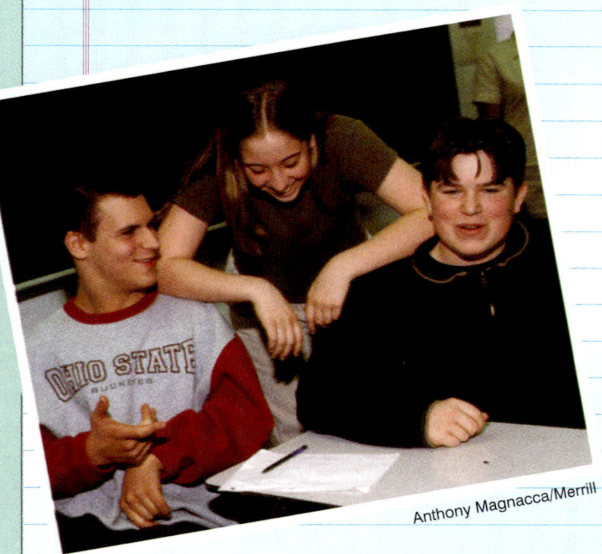

Anthony Magnacca/Merrill

Richie, clowning around with classmates.

TEACH

TEACHing Positive Images and Attitudes

Not only do we need to examine our own preconceptions of others, but we need to take time to help children with disabilities connect with others. What are some ways that persons without disabilities can help one another develop positive attitudes about people with disabilities? I think that Richie and Chaz and his friends would approve of these three follow-up activities. Choose one to try out now. Then, see if you can think of other ideas and pass them on to a peer for review.

* ***Introduce a friend.*** Have you ever had to describe one friend to another who doesn't know the first friend? Let's try it. Write one or two paragraphs describing a good friend of yours. Be realistic and write it just as you would share it with another friend. Then write one or two paragraphs describing a child or adult with disabilities whom you know. Read your two descriptions to another friend and ask for his or her impressions of the two people you described.

* ***About me.*** Help a child or adult with disabilities develop a script for (1) introducing himself to another person, (2) asking questions about the other person, (3) describing and answering questions about his disability, (4) asking for help if and when needed, and (5) letting someone know he appreciates their offer of assistance but wishes to do it himself. Practice role playing the script and encourage the person to try it. Discuss the results and what the two of you learned about making relationships.

* ***Creating positive expectations.*** Find a children's book featuring a person or persons with disabilities. Write a lesson plan with follow-up activities detailing how the book could be used in an elementary general education classroom to help children without disabilities better understand and develop positive expectations about their peers with disabilities.

Anthony Magnacca/Merrill

to have the best potential for developing communication skills. Parents, advocates, and professional organizations will play an instrumental role in determining which children will receive specialized speech and language services.

Paraprofessional personnel may, in the future, be more widely trained to work directly with children who have speech and language disorders, while professionals concentrate on diagnosis, prescriptive programming, evaluation, and the use of technology. Peer tutoring or therapy approaches using students without disabilities as language models are likely to become more prevalent. These approaches may allow more students to receive specialized help.

Currently, speech and language intervention programs are heavily oriented toward the preschool and school-age population. Although early detection and intervention will clearly remain a high priority among communication disorders specialists, there is a need for long-term studies to document the effectiveness of early intervention on later speech and language development. Professionals are also becoming increasingly aware of the special speech and language needs of adolescents and adults, many of whom have untreated communication problems. The future will likely see greater attention to the assessment and treatment of speech and language disorders caused by the aging process.

Across-the-Day Interventions

The traditional role of the speech-language pathologist will probably continue to change, from that of offering direct therapy to students to "facilitating the implementation of communication interventions in the classroom environment" (Goldstein et al., 1994, p. 106). As we have discussed, naturalistic interventions that take place in the actual environments in which children use language are gradually becoming the norm.

But naturalness is no guarantee of effectiveness. As Goldstein et al. (1994) point out, the real challenge lies in designing and implementing across-the-day interventions that can be used effectively by teachers and other significant persons in the child's life. The most effective communication disorders specialist of the future will be expert not only in designing interventions that can be implemented in the classroom and home but also in training and supporting teachers and parents in carrying out those interventions.

Use the self-tests at http://www.prenhall.com/heward to assess your knowledge of the content of Chapter 9.

Communication Partners: Strategies for Opening Doors to Communication

Effective communication requires two people who work as partners. When one of the partners has little or no understandable speech, communication is often limited and frustrating for both. But if the two work together and the normally speaking person learns to employ several strategies for systematic communication, significant information can be exchanged. June Bigge (1991) describes nine strategies that will open doors to help individuals with severe speech impairments enjoy increased communication effectiveness.

Establish and use "yes," "no," and other fundamental signals. A primary goal is to have the student use, or at least approximate, the spoken words or traditional head signals for "yes" and "no." If necessary, signals may be given by using the head in a nontraditional way. An upward glance can mean "yes," a glance to the side "no," a drop of the head or a shrug "I don't know." If a student's technique is not obvious, ask for a demonstration: "Please show me how you say 'yes.'" This unaided communication system can go anywhere with the student. Aided signals may consist of a smiling face or the word "yes" printed on one wheelchair arm, a frowning face or the word "no" on the opposite arm. Or the teacher may write "yes" on one end of the chalkboard, "no" on the other. To respond, the student looks at one end of the board. When reliable signals for indicating messages have been established, post them and tell others.

Use of these responses should accompany other components of a student's communication system; they should not be the only components. Each student must have access to communication components that also allow access to the language she would use if she were able. Otherwise, students will not be able to generate their own language and must always remain somewhat dependent and passive.

Provide opportunities for initiation. When attempting to interact with individuals with physical and speech differences, people tend to lead the interaction. They fail to wait long enough for the person to initiate requests and other communications. This leads to learned helplessness or passivity. Instead of anticipating students' needs and providing fillers for silence in communicative interactions, set up potential communicative opportunities and *wait* for the student to initiate.

Present a range of choices and repeat them one at a time. To avoid ambiguity in asking questions, present a range of choices: "Do you want a drink of water or milk?" Then repeat each question separately: "Water?" "Milk?" Adding the option "neither of these" to any list of choices is a more advanced strategy and is very helpful to the nonspeaking person.

Wait for the expression and expansion of ideas. Allow students with physical and speech disabilities time to think about what they want to convey, to make the necessary motor movements to relay their message, and to add more information. The motor response itself may be very slow for some children. They may need time to think of ways to change the direction of the conversation to reflect their original intent or to add information.

Narrow the options to find the category about which the person has something to say. Sometimes it is not clear what an individual is trying to tell or ask. First, narrow the options by finding a category. Ask, "Are you thinking of telling something? Or asking something?" "Telling?" "Asking?" Once that is decided, ask, "Do you want to talk about somebody, someplace, some things, or some feelings, or none of these?" If the answer is a place, for example, narrow the options by asking, "Is it about home, or school, or someplace else?" Then repeat each category one at a time to allow the individual to indicate a choice.

Clarify and verify to assure that messages are received correctly. It is tempting to ask an individual only dead-end and fact-level yes-and-no questions when he does not speak intelligibly. But speakers with unclear speech have ideas, feelings, and reactions to share with those who will listen. These kinds of exchanges depend on clarification strategies of communication partners. To clarify and verify, communication partners repeat the perceived messages in their entirety or by segments to see whether the message was received correctly. The strategy involves stating first what they think has been communicated so far. If the message was received correctly and verified by a positive answer to the question "Is this exactly right?" then the conversation may move on. If the message is not verified as correct, then more clarification is necessary. The strategy now involves repeating the message in segments and asking questions after each segment: "Am I close?" "Is there more to it than that?" "Do you want to change part of what I said?" "Is this too specific or too general?"

Talk up to, not down to, the person. It is tempting to talk down to a person with a disability. Be aware of your own behavior in this respect. Attempt to stimulate the student's intellect and not bore her or fill in communication silences with just anything. Finding out about a student's needs, feelings, interests, and problems is an important skill. Too often, individuals who do not speak so that others can understand repeatedly answer questions about the same topics: age, family, school, pets. How dull and frustrating to be denied the opportunity for variety and depth in conversations! Regardless of age, do the student a favor and allow her to try to experience higher levels of understanding and a greater variety of messages and information in the conversation.

Recognize deadlocks. In communication breakdowns, partners can use conversational repair strategies (Blackstone, Cassatt-James, & Bruskin, 1988). For example, the student may wish to say something, but a partner does not reflect the correct message. Sometimes the student may realize that a block has been reached over an unimportant topic and would rather drop the subject than waste time pursuing it. The opposite may also be true; the message may be very important. The partner can help by saying, "I'm really stuck. Do you want to go on trying?" Be certain the student does not feel pressured into changing topics. Partners should persist if the student indicates it is important to do so. If the conversation must be terminated before both partners are satisfied, they can keep the communication open by saying, "I have to leave, but I'll think about it. You think too, and maybe you'll find another way of telling me."

Teach these strategies to other communication partners. Teachers and communication specialists should provide opportunities for persons to expand their conversational interactions to include new people inside and outside school. Signs and signals must be taught to others so that consistent procedures are used. It is advisable for parents to teach baby-sitters, family friends, relatives, and neighborhood children. Teachers must teach schoolmates, classroom aides, and other teachers.

Responsibility for opening doors to communication does not lie only with communication partners. Individuals with communication disorders must learn to cue prospective communication partners, including those in the community at large. Nonspeaking students can direct communication partners to the location of brief and easily accessible written cues for effecting satisfying communications for both parties.

Source: From Bigge, J. (1991). *Teaching students with physical disabilities* (3rd ed., pp. 231–244). Upper Saddle River, NJ: Merrill/Prentice Hall. Adapted by permission.

Summary

Communication, Language, and Speech

- Communication is any interaction that transmits information. Narrating, explaining, informing, and expressing are major communicative functions.
- A language is an arbitrary symbol system that enables a group of people to communicate. Each language has rules of phonology, morphology, syntax, semantics, and pragmatics that describe how users put sounds together to convey meaning.
- Speech is the vocal response mode of language and the basis on which language develops.
- Normal language development follows a relatively predictable sequence. Most children learn to use language without instruction; by the time they enter first grade, their grammar and speech patterns match those of the adults around them.

Defining Communication Disorders

- A child has a speech disorder if his speech draws unfavorable attention to itself, interferes with the ability to communicate, or causes social or interpersonal problems.
- Some children have trouble understanding language (receptive language disorders); others have trouble using language to communicate (expressive language disorders); still others have language delays.
- Speech or language differences based on cultural dialects are not communication disorders. However, children with dialects may also have speech or language disorders.

Prevalence

- As many as 5% of school-age children may have speech impairments serious enough to warrant attention.

- Nearly twice as many boys as girls have speech impairments.
- Children with articulation problems represent the largest category of speech-language impairments.

Types and Causes of Communication Disorders

- Although some speech disorders have physical (organic) causes, most are functional disorders that cannot be directly attributed to physical conditions.
- Types of communication disorders include articulation, voice, fluency, and language disorders.
- Stuttering is the most common fluency disorder.

Identification and Assessment

- Assessment of a suspected communication disorder may include some or all of the following components:
  - Case history
  - Physical examination
  - Articulation test
  - Hearing test
  - Auditory discrimination test
  - Language development test
  - Overall language test
  - Conversation with the child or language sample
  - Behavioral observations of child's language competence in social contexts

Educational Approaches

- Different types of communication disorders call for different approaches to remediation; behavioral approaches are frequently used.
- Articulation disorders may be treated by one of four common models: the discrimination model, the phonological model, the sensorimotor model, or the operant conditioning model.
- Voice disorders can sometimes be treated medically or surgically if there is an organic cause, but the most common remediation is direct vocal rehabilitation.
- Treatment of fluency disorders emphasizes either symptom modification or fluency reinforcement.
- Language disorders are treated by either individual or group approaches.

Augmentative and Alternative Communication

- Augmentative and alternative communication (AAC) may be unaided or aided and consists of three components:
  - A representational symbol set, or vocabulary
  - A means for selecting the symbols
  - A means for transmitting the symbols

Educational Placement Alternatives

- Most children with speech and language problems attend regular classes.

Current Issues and Future Trends

- In the future, communication disorders specialists will probably provide largely consultative services and in-service training rather than direct one-to-one therapy. They will help train parents, teachers, and paraprofessionals to work with most children, while they concentrate on diagnosis, programming, and direct intensive services to a few children with special needs.
- Further service needs to be directed toward older youths and adults with untreated speech and language problems.
- Use of special devices to help individuals with communication disorders will expand. Electronic devices are now widely used to analyze children's speech and language and to provide instruction.
- Efforts to develop and implement across-the-day interventions programs for children with communication disorders will increase.

For More Information

Journals

- *Augmentative and Alternative Communication.* Published by the International Society for Augmentative and Alternative Communication, P.O. Box 1762, Station R, Toronto, Ontario M4G 4A3, Canada.
- *Communication Outlook.* Published quarterly by Artificial Language Laboratory, Computer Science Department, Michigan State University, East Lansing, MI 48824. Emphasizes the use of augmentative communication techniques and technology.
- *Journal of Childhood Communication Disorders.* Published twice yearly by CEC's Division for Children with Communication Disorders (DCCD). (See "Organizations.")
- *Journal of Speech and Hearing Disorders.* Published quarterly by the American Speech-Language-Hearing Association (ASHA). Includes articles dealing with the nature, assessment, and treatment of communication disorders. (See "Organizations.")
- *Language, Speech, and Hearing Services in the Schools.* Published quarterly by ASHA. Focuses on practical applications of speech and language training and provides activities for teachers and specialists consistent with current research and theory. (See "Organizations.")

Books

- Adler, S., & King, D. A. (Eds.). (1994). *Oral communication problems in children and adolescents*. Boston: Allyn & Bacon.
- Battle, D. E. (Ed.). (1998). *Communication disorders in multicultural populations* (2nd ed.). Boston: Butterworth-Heinemann.
- Bernstein, D. K., & Tiegerman, E. (1993). *Language and communication disorders in children* (3rd ed.). New York: Macmillan.
- Beukelman, D. R., & Miranda, P. (1998) *Augmentative and alternative communication: Management of severe communication disorder in children and adults* (2nd ed.). Baltimore: Brookes.
- Blackstone, S. W. (Ed.). (1989). *Augmentative communication: Implementation strategies.* Rockville, MD: American Speech-Language-Hearing Association.
- Hegde, M. N. (1993). *Treatment procedures in communicative disorders.* Austin, TX: PRO-ED.
- Johnson, J., Baumgart, D., Helmstetter, E., & Curry, C. A. (1996). *Augmenting basic communication in natural contexts*. Baltimore: Brookes.
- Kent, R. D. (1994). *Reference manual for communicative sciences and disorders.* Austin, TX: PRO-ED.
- Owens, R. E. (1996). *Language development: An introduction* (4th ed.). Boston: Allyn & Bacon.
- Reed, V. A. (1998). *An introduction to children with language disorders* (3rd ed.). Boston: Allyn & Bacon.
- Shames, G. H., Wiig, E. H., & Secord, W. A. (1998). *Human communication disorders* (5th ed.). Boston: Allyn & Bacon.
- Wallach, G. P., & Butler, K. G. (1994). *Language learning disabilities in school-age children and adolescents.* Boston: Allyn & Bacon.

Organizations

- *American Speech-Language-Hearing Association,* 10801 Rockville Pike, Rockville, MD 20852; website: http//:www.asha.org/. The major professional organization concerned with speech and language. Serves as a certifying agency for professionals who provide speech, language, and hearing services. Publishes several journals, sponsors research in communication disorders, and provides a comprehensive *Guide to Professional Services,* which also includes information on accredited training programs. Also sponsors the National Student Speech-Language-Hearing Association, which has chapters on many college and university campuses.
- *Crestwood Company,* 6625 North Sidney Place, Milwaukee, WI 53209-3259; (414) 352-5678. Publishes a catalog featuring a wide range of augmentative and alternative communication devices for children and adults.
- *Division for Children with Communication Disorders* (DCCD), Council for Exceptional Children, 1920 Association Drive, Reston, VA 22091. Includes teachers and communication disorders specialists who work with exceptional children. Sponsors sessions at state, provincial, and national conferences.

Chapter 10

Hearing Loss

Focus Questions

- In what important ways do the child who is deaf and the child who is hard of hearing differ?
- Why can reading not simply replace hearing speech as a means of learning and understanding language?
- How do members of the Deaf culture view hearing loss?
- How do advocates of oral/aural, total communication, and bilingual-bicultural approaches to educating students who are deaf differ in philosophies and teaching methods?
- Why do you think American Sign Language (ASL) has not been fully accepted as the language of instruction in school programs for deaf children?

As Lou Ann Walker, the child of deaf parents, observes in her autobiography, people who have normal hearing usually find it difficult to fully appreciate the enormous importance of the auditory sense in human development and learning: "Nature attaches an overwhelming importance to hearing. As unborns we hear before we can see. Even in deep comas, people often hear what is going on around them. For most of us, when we die, the sense of hearing is the last to leave the body" (Walker, 1986, p. 165).

Many of us have simulated blindness by closing our eyes or donning a blindfold, but it is virtually impossible to switch off our hearing. From the moment of birth, babies respond to sound by startling and blinking. Throughout life, hearing persons obtain information about the world around them, from all directions, 24 hours a day.

The typical hearing child enters school with a vocabulary of more than 5,000 words, the product of perhaps 100 million meaningful contacts with language (Napierkowski, 1981).

Hans Furth (1973), a psychologist who devoted much of his career to studying the language development of people with hearing loss, suggests that a good way to approximate the experience of a child who is deaf from birth or early childhood is to watch a television program in which a foreign language is being spoken—with the sound on the TV set turned off. You would face the double problem of being unable to read lips and understand an unfamiliar language.

Hearing plays the lead role in the natural, almost effortless manner by which most children acquire speech and language. Newborns respond to sounds by startling or blinking. At a few weeks of age, infants with normal hearing can listen to quiet sounds, recognize their parents' voices, and pay attention to their own gurgling and cooing sounds. At 1 month, hearing infants prefer natural speech sounds over nonlanguage sounds (Mehler et al., 1988). By 6 months, hearing infants can discriminate the speech sounds of the language to which they have been exposed from the sounds of other languages (Werker & Lalonde, 1988). By the time they are 1 year old, hearing children have a well-developed ability to discriminate between the phonological sounds of the language used around them (Jusczyk, Friederici, Wessels, Svenkerud, & Jusczyk, 1993).

By the end of their first year, hearing children can produce many of the sounds of their language and are beginning to speak their first words (Ingram, 1989). Children develop language by constantly hearing people talk and by associating these sounds with innumerable activities and events. They attach meaning to sound and quickly learn that people convey information and exchange their thoughts and feelings by speaking and hearing.

For children who cannot hear speech sounds, however, learning a spoken language is anything but natural or effortless. Children who are deaf simply do not have access to an auditorally based language. As we will see, however, when children who are deaf are exposed to a visual, sign-based language as their first language, they acquire language and communication skills in a manner quite similar to the acquisition of speech by hearing children. Some children with hearing loss can hear speech with hearing aids or other technologies, and techniques such as speech training and speechreading enable many children with hearing loss to communicate effectively. Whether a child's hearing loss is mild or profound, early identification and assessment are key to providing needed special education services.

Defining Hearing Loss

When we speak of a person with normal hearing, we generally mean that he has enough hearing to understand speech. Assuming that listening conditions are adequate, a person with normal hearing can interpret speech in everyday situations without using any special device or technique. *Hearing impairment* is the disability category label used in IDEA indicating a hearing loss for which special education and related services are needed. Hearing loss exists on a continuum from mild to profound, and most special educators distinguish between children who are deaf and those who are hard of hearing.

A child who is **deaf** is not able to use hearing to understand speech. Even with a hearing aid, the hearing loss is too great to allow a deaf child to

It may be impossible for a person with normal hearing to fully comprehend the immense difficulties a prelingually deaf child faces trying to learn language.

understand speech through the ears alone. Although a deaf person may perceive some sounds through **residual hearing**, she uses vision as the primary modality for learning and communication.

A child who is **hard of hearing** has a significant hearing loss that makes some special adaptations necessary. The child who is hard of hearing responds to speech and other auditory stimuli. In other words, the child's speech and language skills, though they may be delayed or deficient, are developed mainly through the auditory channel. Children who are hard of hearing are able to use their hearing to understand speech, generally with the help of a hearing aid. "Communicatively, the hard of hearing child is more like the normal hearing child than like the deaf child, because both use audition rather than vision as the primary mode for speech and language development" (Berg, 1986, p. 3).

Go to the companion website at http://www.prenhall.com/heward and select Chapter 10 to review the chapter objectives.

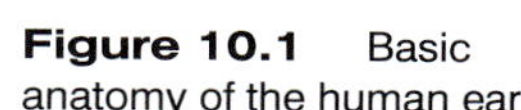

Many deaf persons do not view their hearing loss as a disability and consider terms such as hearing impairment *inappropriate because they suggest a deficiency or pathology. They prefer disability-first terms, such as* teacher of the deaf, school for the deaf, *and* Deaf person. *Like other cultural groups, these members of the Deaf community (who themselves spell* Deaf *with a capital* D) *share a common language and social practices.*

How We Hear

For most people, hearing is automatic. But **audition,** the act or sense of hearing, is a complex and not completely understood process. The function of the ear is to gather sounds (acoustical energy) from the environment and to transform that energy into a form (neural energy) that can be interpreted by the brain (Zemlin, 1995). Figure 10.1 shows the major parts of the human ear. The *outer ear* consists of the external ear and the auditory canal. The part of the ear we see, the **auricle,** functions to collect sound waves into the **auditory canal (external acoustic meatus).**

When sound waves enter the external ear, they are slightly amplified as they move toward the **tympanic membrane** (eardrum). Variations in sound pressure cause the eardrum to move in and out. These movements of the eardrum change the acoustical energy into mechanical energy, which is transferred to the three tiny bones of the *middle ear* (the *hammer, anvil,* and *stirrup*). The base (called the *footplate*) of the third bone in the sequence, the stirrup, rests in an opening called the *oval window,* the path through which sound energy enters the inner ear. The vibra-

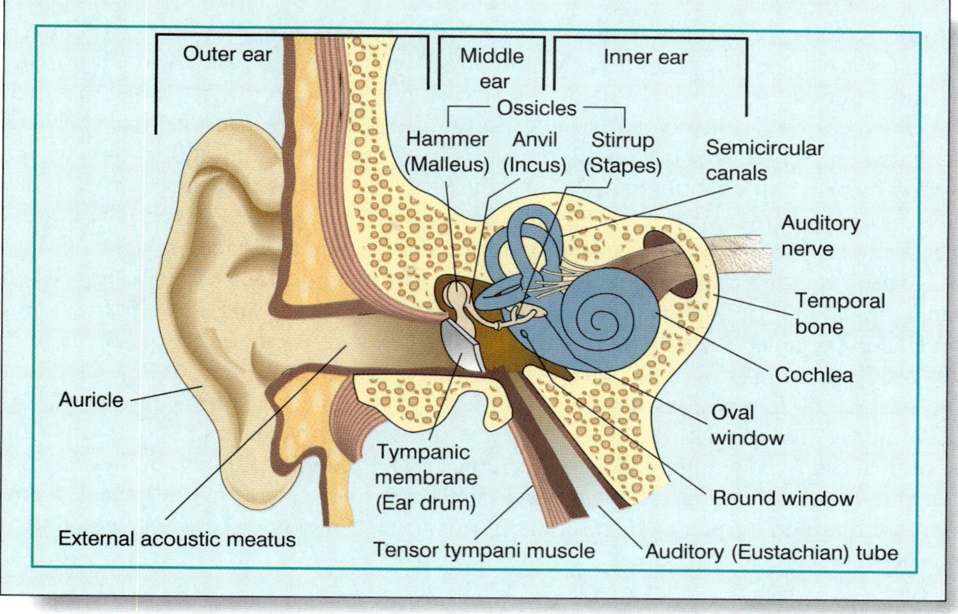

Figure 10.1 Basic anatomy of the human ear

A person without external ears could still hear quite well, losing perhaps only 5 to 7 decibels in sound volume. The intensity or loudness of sound is measured in ***decibels (dB)***.

tions of the three bones (together called the **ossicles**) transmit energy from the middle ear to the inner ear with little loss. The most critical and complex part of the entire hearing apparatus is the *inner ear,* which is covered by the temporal bone, the hardest bone in the entire body. The inner ear contains the **cochlea,** the main receptor organ for hearing, and the *semicircular canals,* which control the sense of balance. The cochlea, which resembles the coiled shell of a snail, consists of two fluid-filled cavities. When energy is transmitted by the ossicles, the fluid in the cochlea moves. Tiny hairs within the cochlea change the motion of the fluid into neural impulses that are transmitted along the auditory nerve to the brain.

The Nature of Sound

Sound is measured in units that describe its intensity and frequency. Both dimensions of sound are important in considering the needs of a child with a hearing loss. Zero dB represents the smallest sound a person with normal hearing can perceive, which is called the *zero hearing-threshold level* (HTL), or **audiometric zero.**

Also within the inner ear is the vestibular mechanism, *which controls the sense of balance by movement-sensitive fluid in the semicircular canals.*

Larger dB numbers represent increasingly louder sounds. A low whisper 5 feet away registers about 10 dB, a running automobile about 65 dB, and Niagara Falls about 90 dB. Conversational speech 10 to 20 feet away registers 30 to 65 dB. A sound of about 125 dB or louder will cause pain to the average person. A person may have a loss of up to 25 dB (not be able to hear any sound of less than 25 dB) and still be considered to have hearing within the normal range. The 25 dB level is often used in screening school children for hearing loss, although, as Berg (1986) warns, such one-shot tests may fail to identify a sizable percentage of hard of hearing children.

Decibel, *the unit of measure for the intensity of sound, is named for Alexander Graham Bell.*

In addition to dB loss, it is important to consider the listening environment. Northern and Lemme (1982) observe that speech needs to be only 10 to 15 dB louder than background noise for normally hearing adults to listen and understand comfortably. For children who are hard of hearing, speech may need to be significantly louder than background noise for them to be able to understand the message being transmitted.

The frequency, or pitch, of sound is measured in cycles per second, or **hertz (Hz);** 1 hertz equals 1 cycle per second. The lowest note on a piano has a frequency of about 30 Hz, middle C about 250 Hz, and the highest note about 4,000 Hz. Humans are able to hear frequencies ranging from about 20 to 20,000 Hz, but many of these audible sounds are outside the speech range, the frequency range in which ordinary conversation takes place. Although a person who cannot hear very low sounds (e.g., a foghorn) or very high sounds (e.g., a piccolo) may suffer some inconvenience, she will encounter no significant problems in the classroom or everyday life. A person with a severe hearing loss in the speech range, however, is at a great disadvantage in acquiring and communicating in a spoken language.

A hearing loss of only 15 dB may negatively affect a child's learning to read because some speech sounds are missed (Schirmer, 1998).

The frequency range generally considered most important for hearing spoken language is 500 to 2,000 Hz. The sounds of English speech vary in their frequency level. For example, the /s/ phoneme (as in the word "sat") is a high-frequency sound, typically occurring between 4,000 and 8,000 Hz (Northern & Lemme, 1982). A student whose hearing loss is more severe at the higher frequencies will thus have particular difficulty in discriminating the /s/ sound. Conversely, phonemes such as /dj/ (the sound of the "j" in "jump") and /m/ occur at low frequencies and will be more problematic for a student with a low-frequency hearing loss. As you might expect, a student with a high-frequency hearing loss tends to hear men's voices more easily than women's voices.

Check your ongoing understanding of Chapter 10 concepts by using the Guided Review Module at http://www.prenhall.com/heward.

Prevalence

According to ASHA (1999), 95 of every 1,000 people have a chronic hearing loss, and about 28 million Americans experience some difficulty in receiving and processing aural communication. The large majority of persons with hearing loss are adults; Stein (1988) estimates that almost 40% of persons over age 75 experience some limitations in hearing.

During the 1996–1997 school year, 68,766 students ages 6 to 21 received special education services under the disability category of hearing impairments (U.S. Department of Education, 1998). This represents 1.3% of all school-age students who received special education services and about 0.14% of the resident student population. The actual number of school-age children with hearing loss in special education programs is somewhat higher because some children with hearing impairments are counted under another primary disability category (e.g., mental retardation, cerebral palsy, and deaf-blind). It is not known precisely the percentage of these students who are deaf or hard of hearing. A national survey of early intervention programs serving children with hearing loss reported that 46% of the children were deaf and 54% hard of hearing (Meadow-Orlans, Mertens, Sass-Lehrer, & Scott-Olson, 1997).

More information about ASHA can be found by accessing the Resources Module for Chapter 10 at http://www.prenhall.com/heward and linking to the Special Ed Resource Page and "associations."

Table 10.1 highlights some key historical events and implications for the education of students with hearing loss.

Types and Causes of Hearing Loss

Types and Age of Onset

The two main types of hearing loss are conductive and sensorineural. **Conductive hearing loss** results from abnormalities or complications of the outer or middle ear. A buildup of excessive wax in the auditory canal can cause a conductive hearing loss, as can a disease that leaves fluid or debris. Some children are born with incomplete or malformed auditory canals. A hearing loss can also be caused if the eardrum or ossicles do not move properly. As its name implies, a conductive hearing loss involves a problem with conducting, or transmitting, sound vibrations to the inner ear. Because the rest of the auditory system is generally intact, conductive hearing losses can often be corrected through surgical or medical treatment. Hearing aids are usually beneficial to persons with conductive impairments.

Sensorineural hearing loss refers to damage to the auditory nerve fibers or other sensitive mechanisms in the inner ear. The cochlea converts the physical characteristics of sound into corresponding neural information that the brain can process and interpret (Berg, 1986); impairment of the cochlea may mean that sound is delivered to the brain in a distorted fashion or not delivered at all. Amplification (making the source of sound louder) may or may not help the person with a sensorineural hearing loss. Most sensorineural hearing loss cannot be corrected by surgery or medication. The combination of both conductive and sensorineural impairments is called a *mixed hearing loss.*

Hearing loss is also described in terms of being *unilateral* (present in one ear only) or *bilateral* (present in both ears). Most students who receive special education for hearing loss have bilateral losses, although the degree of impairment may not be the same in both ears. Children with unilateral hearing loss generally learn speech and language without major difficulties, although they tend to have problems localizing sounds and listening in noisy or distracting settings.

It is important to consider the *age of onset*—whether a hearing loss is **congenital** (present at birth) or **adventitious** (acquired later in life). The terms *prelingual hearing loss* and *postlingual hearing loss* refer to whether a hearing loss is sustained

Table 10.1 A history of the education of children who are deaf or hard of hearing: Key events and implications

Date	Historical Event	Educational Implications
Late 16th century	Pedro Ponce de Leon (1520–1584), an Augustinian monk and scholar, established in Spain a school for the deaf children of noble families.	This was the first educational program for exceptional children of any kind.
18th century	Schools for children who were deaf were set up in England, France, Germany, Holland, and Scotland.	Both oral and manual methods of instruction were used.
1817	The American Asylum for the Education of the Deaf and Dumb (renamed the American School for the Deaf) opened in Hartford, CT, under the leadership of Thomas Gallaudet and Laurent Clerc, a deaf French educator.	Children with hearing loss were among the first in the United States to receive special education. Gallaudet and Clerc used sign language as their method of instruction at the school. Some consider Clerc to be the father of deaf education in the United States.
Early 19th century	Students who were deaf were considered to be most appropriately served in asylums or special sanctuaries and removed from normal society.	The prevailing philosophy of the early 19th century was that persons who were deaf were incapable of benefiting from oral instruction.
Mid- to late 19th century	Instruction in speech and speech reading became widely available to students who were deaf throughout the United States. Several day schools were established for deaf children. Alexander Graham Bell criticized residential schools and the use of sign language, which he believed contributed to the segregation of deaf people.	Oral approaches dominated to such a great degree that the use of sign language in schools was officially prohibited at an international conference in 1880. It was not until many years later that schools relaxed their restrictions against the use of sign language. This era marked the beginning of what some have called "the Hundred Years War" over what methods of communication are best for deaf children.
Mid- to late 20th century	The majority of students whose deafness was caused by the rubella epidemics of the mid-1960s departed from the school-age population.	Enrollments in public residential schools for children with hearing impairments in the United States declined sharply as public school programs became more widely available.
1968	Congress funded the National Technical Institute for the Deaf (NTID) at the Rochester Institute for Technology.	NTID offers technical and vocational degree programs for deaf students.
1970s	Total communication (TC) was adopted as the method of communication and instruction by the majority of deaf education programs.	TC attempts to present instructional content via simultaneous use of speech and sign language. While TC is still used frequently today, it has not raised the academic achievement of deaf students.
1986	In response to concerns about the academic and employment outcomes of deaf students, Congress established the Commission on Education of the Deaf (CED) with the Education of the Deaf Act of 1986.	CED began its 1988 report to Congress: "The present state of education for persons who are deaf in the United States is unsatisfactory. Unacceptably so" (p. viii). The report included 52 recommendations for improving the education of students with hearing loss.
1988	Students at Gallaudet University protested the hiring of a hearing president at their college in the Deaf President Now movement.	The movement led to the hiring of I. King Jordan as the first deaf president of Gallaudet, galvanized the deaf community, and increased the awareness of many in hearing society of the concerns and issues facing the deaf culture.

before or after the development of spoken language. A child who, from birth or soon after, is unable to hear the speech of other people will not learn speech and language spontaneously, as do children with normal hearing. A child who acquires a hearing loss after speech and language are well established, usually after age 2, has educational needs very different from the prelingually deaf child. The educational program for a child who is prelingually deaf usually focuses on acquisition of language and communication, whereas the program for a child who is postlingually deaf usually emphasizes the maintenance of intelligible speech and appropriate language patterns.

Although several hundred causes of hearing loss have been identified, the exact cause is listed as "unknown" for up to 50% of children with hearing loss in some studies (Gallaudet University, 1998; Moores, 1996).

Of the deaf and hard of hearing children served in special education programs, 95% have a prelingual hearing loss (Commission on Education of the Deaf, 1988).

Prelingual Causes

Maternal Rubella Although rubella (also known as German measles) has relatively mild symptoms, it has been shown to cause deafness, visual impairment, heart disorders, and a variety of other serious disabilities in the developing child when it affects a pregnant woman, particularly during the first trimester. A major epidemic of rubella in the United States and Canada between 1963 and 1965 accounted for more than 50% of the students with hearing loss in special education programs in the 1970s and 1980s. Since an effective vaccine was introduced in 1969, the incidence of hearing loss caused by rubella has decreased significantly.

Each year, new cases of hearing loss caused by rubella are recorded. All women of child bearing age should receive the vaccine.

Heredity With the exception of periods of rubella epidemics, the leading cause of deafness is genetic factors (Schildroth, Ralings, & Allen, 1989). Between 150 and 175 types of hereditary or genetic deafness have been identified. There is strong evidence that congenital hearing loss runs in some families. Even though 90% of children who are deaf are born to hearing parents, about 30% of the school-age population of students who are deaf have relatives with hearing loss (Moores, 1996). Most hereditary deafness, however, is the result of recessive genetic traits, and the marriage of two deaf persons results in only a "slightly increased risk of deafness in their children because there is a small chance that both parents would be affected by the same exact genetic deafness" (Northern & Downs, 1991, p. 90).

Hearing loss occurs at a higher-than-usual incidence rate among certain groups of individuals with other disabilities. Down syndrome often involves irregularities in the auditory canal and a tendency for fluid to accumulate in the middle ear; as many as 75% of children with Down syndrome may also have significant hearing loss (Northern & Lemme, 1982). There is also a substantially higher-than-normal incidence of hearing loss among children with cerebral palsy. A hearing test should be part of the assessment of any child who is referred for special education services.

Prematurity and Complications of Pregnancy It is difficult to precisely evaluate the effects of prematurity on hearing loss, but early delivery and low birth weight are more common among children who are deaf than among the general population. Complications of pregnancy arise from a variety of causes.

Congenital Cytomegalovirus (CMV) Cytomegalovirus (CMV), a viral infection affecting 1% to 2% of all newborns, can result in several conditions, including mental retardation, visual impairment, and, most often, hearing impairment. One study estimated that CMV is the causal factor for as many as 50% of children who are deaf or hard of hearing (Schildroth et al., 1989). At present, there is no known prevention or treatment for CMV, although it may be detected by amniocentesis (Moaven, Gilbert, Cunningham, & Rawlinson, 1995).

Postlingual Causes

Meningitis The leading cause of postlingual hearing loss is meningitis, a bacterial or viral infection of the central nervous system that can, among its other effects, destroy the sensitive acoustic apparatus of the inner ear. Children whose deafness is caused by meningitis generally have profound hearing losses. Difficulties in balance and other disabilities may also be present.

Otitis Media An infection or inflammation of the middle ear, **otitis media** is the most common reason for a visit to the doctor for children under the age of 6 (Bess & Humes, 1995). Nearly 90% of all children will experience otitis media at least once, and about one-third of children have three episodes (Roberts, Wallace, & Henderson, 1997). Antibiotics usually are an effective treatment, but if untreated, otitis media can result in a buildup of fluid and a ruptured eardrum, which causes permanent conductive hearing loss.

Noise Noise pollution—repeated exposure to loud sounds, such as industrial noise, jet aircraft, guns, and amplified music—is increasingly recognized as a cause of hearing loss. Exposure to excessive noise is likely the cause of a significant portion of the 28 million Americans with permanent hearing loss (ASHA, 1999).

Identification and Assessment

The earlier a hearing loss is identified, the better a child's chances are for receiving early intervention and treatment and developing good language and communication skills. Unfortunately, hearing loss goes undetected in many children. A national survey of parents of preschool children with hearing loss found that parents suspected their baby had a hearing loss at an average age of 17 months and had the diagnosis confirmed at a mean age of 22 months (Meadow-Orlans et al., 1997). Half of the hard of hearing children in this study did not have their hearing loss diagnosed until they were 2.5 years old. More discouraging are the data on the lag time between diagnosis and intervention: children waited an average of 8 months for a hearing aid, 10 months for speech and auditory services, and 11 months to begin sign language.

All infants, hearing and deaf alike, babble, coo, and smile. Later on, children who are deaf tend to stop babbling and vocalizing because they cannot hear themselves or their parents, but the baby's increasing silence may go unnoticed for a while and then be mistakenly attributed to other causes. Figure 10.2 lists some common auditory behaviors emitted by infants with normal hearing. Failure to demonstrate these responses may mean that an infant has a hearing loss, and an audiological exam is recommended.

Pure-Tone Audiometry

Hearing is formally assessed by a testing procedure called *pure-tone audiometry*. The examiner uses an **audiometer,** an electronic device that generates sounds at different levels of intensity and frequency. The child, who receives the sound either through earphones (air conduction) or through a bone vibrator (bone conduction), is instructed to hold up a finger when he hears a sound and to lower it when he hears no sound. The test seeks to determine how loud sounds at various frequencies must be before the child is able to hear them. Most audiometers deliver tones in 5 dB increments from 0 to 120 dB, with each dB level presented in various frequencies, usually starting at 125 Hz and increasing in octave intervals (doubling in frequency) to 8,000 Hz. The results of the test are plotted on a chart called an **audiogram** (see Figure 10.3 later in this chapter.)

To obtain a hearing level on an audiogram, the child must be able to detect a sound at that level at least 50% of the time. For example, a child who has a 60 dB hearing loss cannot detect a sound until it is at least 60 dB loud, in contrast to a child with normal hearing, who would detect that same sound at a level between 0 and 10 dB.

In determining whether an infant has a hearing loss, it is helpful for parents and teachers to know the normal sequence of auditory development. Audiologist Linda Cleeland has provided the following guide to behaviors that may be expected at certain ages. If a young child is not displaying these behaviors, it is advisable to have the child's hearing professionally tested.

1 Month

- Jumps or startles in response to loud noises
- Begins making gurgling sounds

3 Months

- Makes babbling sounds
- Is aware of voices
- May quiet down to familiar voices close to ear
- Stirs or awakens from sleep when there is a loud sound relatively close

6 Months

- Makes vocal sounds when alone
- Turns head toward sounds or when name is called and speaker is not visible
- Vocalizes when spoken to directly

9 Months

- Responds differently to a cheerful versus angry voice
- Tries to copy the speech sounds of others

12 Months

- Locates a sound source by turning head (whether the sound is at the side, above, or below level)
- Ceases activity when parent's voice is heard
- Recognizes own name
- Uses single words correctly
- Vocalizes emotions
- Laughs spontaneously
- Disturbed by nearby noise when sleeping
- Attempts imitation of sounds and words
- Understands some familiar phrases or words
- Responds to music or singing
- Increases babbling in type and amount

24 Months

- Has more than 50 words in vocabulary
- Uses two words together
- Responds to rhythm of music
- Uses voice for a specific purpose
- Shows understanding of many phrases used daily in life
- Plays with sound-making object
- Uses well-inflected vocalization
- Refers to himself/herself by name

Figure 10.2 Expected auditory behaviors

Source: From Cleeland, L. K. (1984). The function of the auditory system in speech and language development. In R. K. Hull & K. I. Dilka (Eds.), *The hearing-impaired child in school* (pp. 15–16). Orlando, FL: Grune & Stratton. Reprinted by permission.

Deaf President Now!

Gallaudet University in Washington, DC, is the world's only university dedicated exclusively to the education of deaf students. (Students with normal hearing are admitted into some of its programs.) A federally funded institution chartered by Congress in 1864, Gallaudet had never had a deaf president. When a presidential vacancy occurred in 1988, many Gallaudet students, faculty, and alumni expected that a deaf person would be appointed; however, an educator with normal hearing, who was unable to use sign language, was initially selected for the position. A week of turbulent protests and demonstrations ensued, with calls for a "Deaf President Now," focusing national and international attention on Gallaudet. We asked Bridgetta Bourne and Jerry Covell, two of the protest's four primary student leaders, to tell us the dramatic story.

Bridgetta Bourne When I identify myself as a deaf person, it's much like a black person identifying herself as black. All members of minority groups face certain challenges, and for the deaf the challenge is communication. As a deaf person, I feel disabled, even among groups including people with other disabilities. I still can't communicate with them without an interpreter.

There was recently a march from the White House to the Capitol in support of the Americans with Disabilities Act. There were many people with disabilities, but I didn't really feel like part of that community. Without an interpreter, I was basically lost. So the concept of oppression is one in which people in power are making decisions for me—about my life, about what I should do. Oppressed people have no voice.

Oppression is dangerous and pervasive. We even had it at Gallaudet, our own institution. Obviously, we should have a hand in running our own school, and that's why the Deaf President Now protest happened and was so successful. There had been so many years of struggle, so many years of deaf people being told they could not make decisions for themselves. You either have to release your anger at this oppression or just hold it in, as so many deaf people did in the past.

Jerry Covell Before the Deaf President Now movement, Gallaudet went through six presidents, all of them hearing men. These presidents served useful purposes, such as founding the college, expanding programs and services, creating new educational fields, and changing Gallaudet from college to university status. When the sixth president resigned and the board of trustees began a search for a new one, we all felt that the time was right for a deaf president.

Gallaudet is universally recognized and respected for its leadership in educating the deaf. Now we needed a deaf person to truly represent Gallaudet and the Deaf community. We needed a deaf person who could prove to hearing people that he or she was capable of carrying out the duties of a university president, thus opening the door to further opportunities for deaf people. There were qualified deaf people out there, with good backgrounds of education and experience. All but 4 of the 21 members of the board of trustees were hearing people. Many had good backgrounds in business, fund-raising, and public relations, and they contributed to Gallaudet in that way, but they had little or no understanding of deafness and Deaf culture. They needed to be convinced! So we held rallies. We got letters of support from many well-known people, including U.S. presidential candidates and senators. Public awareness grew. We felt confident, especially after the three finalists in the presidential search were announced: two deaf men and a hearing woman. Then the final selection was announced in a press release: "Gallaudet University Appoints First Woman President." We couldn't believe our eyes! We were shocked and upset. Please keep in mind, we didn't see this as a gender issue at all. It was strictly a hearing-deaf issue; a deaf woman president would have been great.

Bridgetta We marched downtown to the hotel where the chairman of the board of trustees was staying. We wanted a personal explanation of why they'd selected a hearing person over a deaf person. There was a reception going on at the hotel to introduce the new president. We hadn't planned a demonstration or a sit-in, but people were so angry! Sitting in the street was spontaneous. We didn't have a permit or anything; we just marched. The police came out with cars, barriers, and bullhorns to try to stop us. Signs and banners appeared. I remember a deaf couple who had a dog wearing a sign: "I understand sign language better than the new president of Gallaudet."

Jerry It was late by the time we got to the hotel, chanting and cheering. I remember seeing lights being turned on all over the hotel and people looking out the windows, wondering what was going on. Finally, the chairman came out. She couldn't understand sign language either. She said, "We felt this was the best decision for Gallaudet." We went round and round asking questions. We asked, "When will a deaf person get the chance to be president of Gallaudet?" "When will you allow this?" Eventually the chairman said, "Deaf people are not ready to function in a hearing world." Ooooh, that hurt! Everyone was stunned—even the interpreter. We were ready for real action after that. The infamous quote really pulled us together; it lit a flame under us. So in a way, we should thank the chairman.

We set out to shut Gallaudet down. On Monday morning, we put bike locks on the campus gates and parked cars in front of them. Students told everyone—administrators, faculty, staff, even board of trustees members—"Don't come in today. Go home. The campus is closed." When we took control of the campus, it showed how serious we were about the board's selection and the chairman's statement. The news media came in, and of course we took advantage of that.

Bridgetta As Jerry says, the protest brought people together. Before the protest, Gallaudet consisted of many different groups of deaf people. We came from various backgrounds. Some were interested in academics, others in sports, politics, or whatever. Some had gone to mainstream schools, others to deaf schools. Some were oral; others signed. But all rallied around the Deaf President Now movement, and our efforts were truly coordinated.

Bridgetta Bourne

Jerry Our chants, in sign and speech, were important to the Deaf President Now movement. One of our chants was "Four! Four! Four!" We had four demands before we would release the university back. First, the hearing president had to be replaced by a deaf person. Second, the chairman of the board had to resign because of her statement. Third, a majority of the board had to consist of deaf people. Fourth, there must be no reprisals against faculty, staff, or students involved in the protest.

Toward the end of the week, the new president resigned or "stepped aside," as she put it. But she hadn't been replaced. So we changed our chant to "Three and a half! Three and a half!" That kept the motivation alive. We also chanted "Deaf and Proud!" and "Deaf Power!" We adapted that last one from the Black Power movement. We made the chant by putting one hand over an ear and raising the fist high in the air.

The media began to call us "the deaf civil rights movement." Deaf people came in from all over the country. There was a large crowd, perhaps as many as 7,000. We marched toward the Capitol to try to have Congress recognize our movement. As we marched, we chanted: "We are—standing tall! United, strong, and walking proud to be deaf! Shouting to the world—time is now!"

The rest is history. Dr. I. King Jordan, a deaf man, was appointed president of Gallaudet. The chairman of the board was replaced by a deaf person. We accepted a verbal agreement that the board of trustees would have a deaf majority within five years and that there would be no reprisals. So we released the university. We changed our chant from "Deaf President Now" to "Deaf President Forever!" And when Dr. Jordan first appeared before a huge crowd, we chanted, "King! King! King!" It was the most inspirational and the best thing that ever happened to us when King Jordan said, "Deaf people can do anything—except hear."

Bridgetta What happened at Gallaudet has had an international impact. And with your help, things are going to continue to get better and better for deaf people.

Jerry Covell

Speech Audiometry

Speech audiometry tests a person's detection and understanding of speech. A list of one- and two-syllable words is presented at different dB levels. The **speech reception threshold (SRT),** the dB level at which the individual can understand half of the words, is measured and recorded for each ear. It is important to recognize that while a child might identify single words 50% of the time when spoken at a given volume and frequency, that does not always translate into ability to follow conversational speech (Woolsey, 1999).

Alternative Audiometric Techniques

Alternative techniques have been developed for testing the hearing of very young children and individuals with severe disabilities who are not able to understand and follow conventional audiometry procedures (Roeser & Yellin, 1987). In **play audiometry,** the child is taught to perform simple but distinct activities, such as picking up a toy or putting a ball into a cup, whenever she hears the signal, either pure tones or speech. A similar procedure is **operant conditioning audiometry,** in which the child is reinforced with a token or small candy when he pushes a lever in the presence of a light paired with a sound. No reinforcer is given for pushing the lever when the light and sound are off. Next, the sound is presented without the light. If the child pushes the lever in response to the sound alone, the examiner knows the child can hear that

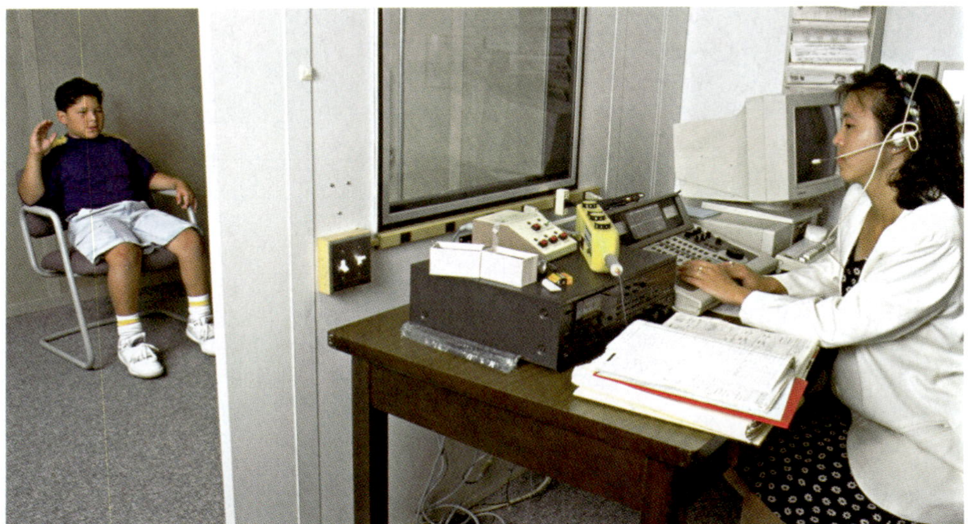

An audiometer generates tones of precise intensity and frequency.

sound. The intensity and frequency of the sound are then varied to determine which levels of sound the child can hear (Lloyd, Spradlin, & Reid, 1968). **Behavior observation audiometry** is a passive assessment procedure in which the child's reactions to sounds are observed. A sound is presented at an increasing level of intensity until a response, such as head turning, eye blinking, or cessation of play, is reliably observed.

Two other techniques rely on physiological reactions to assess hearing. **Evoked-response audiometry** uses electrodes to sense slight electric signals that the auditory nerve generates in response to sound stimulation. Thus, the audiologist can detect hearing loss in infants or others who may not respond to conventional testing because a voluntary response is not required. **Impedance audiometry** tests a child's middle ear function by inserting a small probe and pump to detect sound reflected by the eardrum. It is especially useful in detecting middle ear problems that can result in temporary or permanent conductive hearing loss (MacCarthy & Connell, 1984).

Degrees of Hearing Loss

Hearing loss is usually described by the terms *slight, mild, moderate, severe,* and *profound,* depending on the average hearing level, in decibels, throughout the frequencies most important for understanding speech (500 to 2,000 Hz). It is important to recognize, however, that no two children have exactly the same pattern of hearing, even if their responses on a hearing test are similar. Just as a single intelligence test cannot provide sufficient information to plan a child's educational program, the special education needs of a child with hearing loss cannot be determined from an audiometric test alone. Success in communication and school achievement cannot be predicted simply by looking at an audiogram. Children hear sounds with differing degrees of clarity, and the same child's hearing ability may vary from day to day. Some children with very low levels of measurable hearing are able to benefit from hearing aids and can learn to speak. On the other hand, some children with less apparent hearing loss are less able to function well through the auditory channel and must rely on vision as their primary means of communication. Figure 10.3 shows the audiograms of four children with mild, moderate, severe, and profound hearing loss and describes some of the effects.

To join in the discussion "How do members of the Deaf culture view hearing loss?" go to the Message Board Module at http://www.prenhall.com/heward.

Mild Loss (41 to 55 dB)

Vicki:

- Is able to understand face-to-face conversation with little difficulty
- Misses much of the discussion that goes on in her classroom–particularly if several children are speaking at once or if she cannot see the speaker clearly
- Has some classmates who are unaware she has a hearing loss
- Benefits from wearing a hearing aid
- Receives occasional speech and language assistance from a speech-language pathologist

Audiogram for Vicki, who has a mild hearing loss

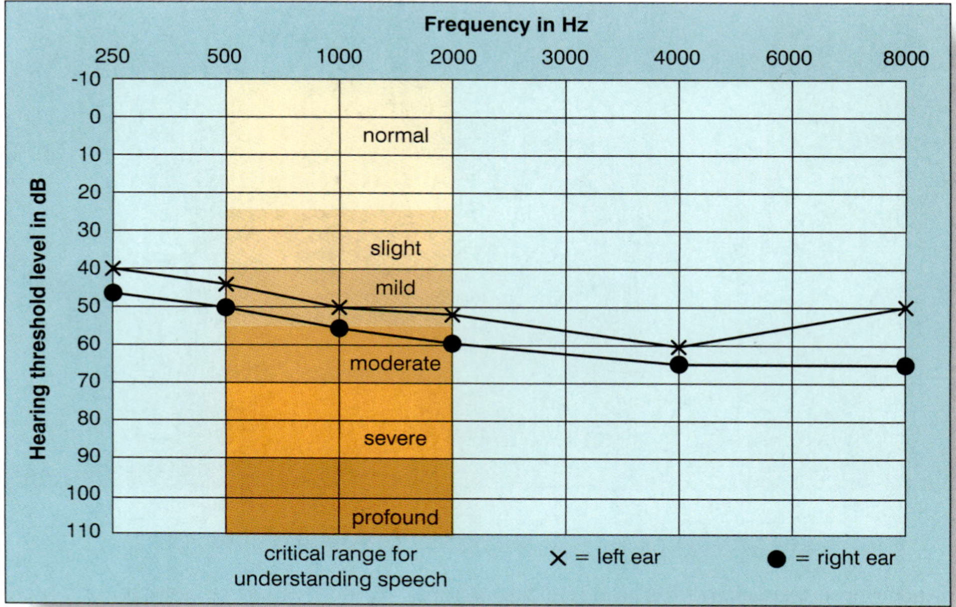

Moderate Loss (56 to 70 dB)

Ahmed:

- Without a hearing aid can only hear conversation if it is loud and clear
- Can hear male voices more easily than female voices (loss is less pronounced in the lower frequencies)
- Finds it impossible to follow most class discussions, even though his teacher arranges favorable seating for him
- Has impaired but intelligible speech
- Attends a part-time special class for children with hearing loss and is in a regular classroom for part of the day

Audiogram for Ahmed, who has a moderate hearing loss

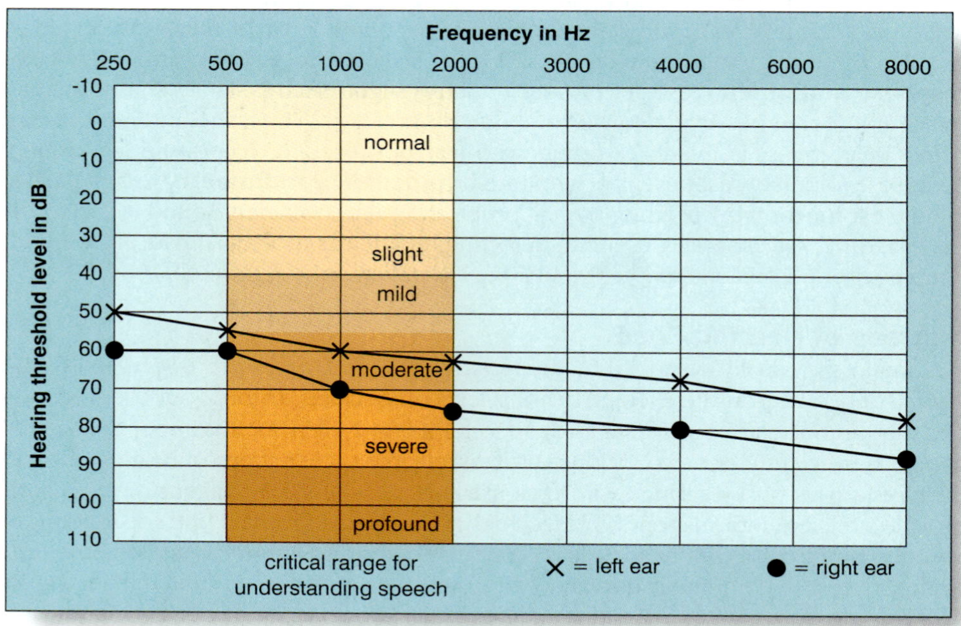

Figure 10.3 Effects of different degrees of hearing loss on speech and language and probable educational needs

Severe Loss (71 to 90 dB)

Chan:

- Can hear voices only if they are very loud and 1 foot or less from his ear
- Wears a hearing aid, but it is unclear how much he gains from it
- Can distinguish most vowel sounds but hears only a few consonants
- Can hear a door slamming, a vacuum cleaner, and an airplane flying overhead
- Communicates by speech and signs
- Must always pay close visual attention to a person speaking with him
- Splits his school day between a special class and a regular classroom with an educational interpreter

Audiogram for Chan, who has a severe hearing loss

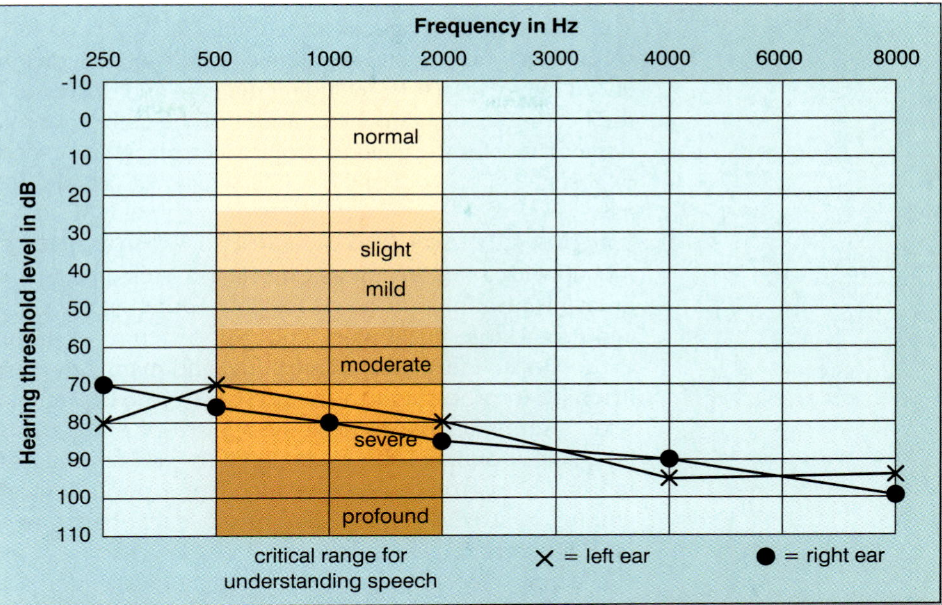

Profound Loss (91 dB or more)

Steve:

- Cannot hear conversational speech at all
- Has a hearing aid that helps him be aware of certain loud sounds, such as a fire alarm or a bass drum
- Uses vision as his primary modality for learning
- Uses American Sign Language as his first language and principal means of communication
- Has not developed intelligible speech
- Attends a residential school for the deaf

Audiogram for Steve, who has a profound hearing loss

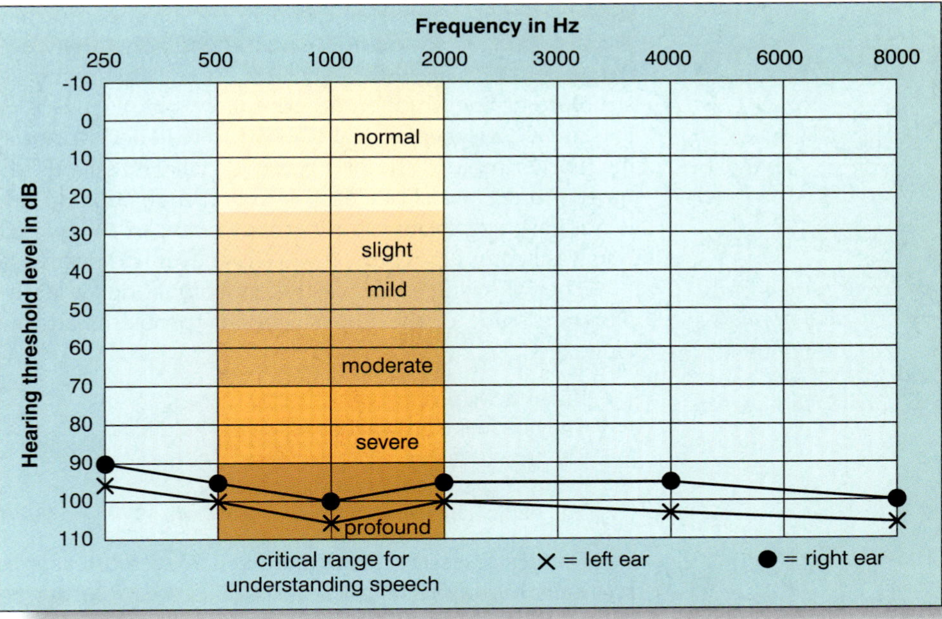

Figure 10.3 *continued*

Effects of Hearing Loss

The effects of hearing loss are complex and pervasive. The educational achievement, social development, and vocational success of an individual with a hearing loss is influenced by many factors, including the type and degree of hearing loss, the age at which the hearing loss began, the attitudes of the child's parents and siblings, the opportunities available for the child to acquire a first language (speech or sign), and the presence or absence of other disabilities (Marschark & Clark, 1998; Paul & Quigley, 1990, 1994).

English Literacy and Academic Achievement

A child with a hearing loss—especially a prelinguistic loss of 90 dB or greater—is at a great disadvantage in acquiring English language skills. Hearing children typically acquire a large vocabulary and a knowledge of grammar, word order, idiomatic expressions, fine shades of meaning, and many other aspects of verbal expression by listening to others and to themselves from early infancy. A child who, from birth or soon after, is unable to hear the speech of other people will not learn speech and language spontaneously, as do children with normal hearing. Since reading and writing involve graphic representations of a phonologically based language, the deaf child must strive to decode and produce text based on a language for which she may have little or no understanding.

When standard measures of reading and writing achievement are used with students who are deaf, examiners typically find that the students' vocabularies are smaller and their sentence structures simpler and more rigid than those of hearing children of the same age or grade level (Meadow, 1980). Many students who are deaf tend to write sentences that are short, incomplete, or improperly arranged. They may have difficulty differentiating questions from statements. They may omit endings of words, such as the plural "-s," "-ed," or "-ing." As Norris (1975) points out, because the grammar and structure of English often do not follow logical rules, a person with prelingual hearing loss must exert a great deal of effort to read and write with acceptable form and meaning. For example, if the past tense of "talk" is "talked," then why doesn't "go" become "goed"? If the plural of "man" is "men," then shouldn't the plural of "pan" be "pen"? It is not easy to explain the difference between the expressions "He's beat" (tired) and "He was beaten" to a person who has never had normal hearing.

Suggestions for teaching writing to deaf students can be found in Kluwin (1996) and "Writer's Workshop" later in this chapter.

The following sentences taken from stories written by elementary deaf students illustrate some of the English literacy problems attributable to not hearing spoken language:

Bobby is walked.
The boy sees a brown football on the hold hand.
The trees is falling a leaves.
Sandy is give Cat in the bootpack.
The happy children is friending. (Heward, 1974, pp. 136–137, 151–153)

Studies assessing the academic achievement of students with hearing loss have routinely found them to lag far behind their hearing peers. Several national surveys of the academic achievement of students with hearing loss have been carried out and reported by the Center for Assessment and Demographic Studies (CADS) at Gallaudet University (DiFrancesca, 1972; Gentile & DiFrancesca, 1969; Trybus & Karchmer, 1977). The results were essentially the same: students with severe and profound hearing loss (students who were deaf) were reading at about a fourth-grade level or lower, and their mathematics performance was around the fifth-grade level. Growth in reading achievement was between 0.2 and 0.3 grade levels per year of schooling. The most recent CADS survey repeated the findings of the earlier studies:

for the oldest group of students (16 to 18 years), the median grade level for reading comprehension ranged from 2.9 to 3.2; for arithmetic computation, it ranged from 7.0 to 7.5 (Allen, 1986). Holt (1993) reported that the average reading level of 18-year-old deaf or hard of hearing students was between the third and fourth grade.

Paul and Quigley (1990) summarize the dismal state of affairs:

> No general improvement in achievement in most students who are severely to profoundly hearing-impaired has been observed since the . . . early years of the 20th century. The average student completing a secondary education program is still reading and writing at a level commensurate with the average 9- to 10-year-old hearing student. Achievement in mathematics is about one or two grades higher. Since the beginning of formal achievement testing, two enduring patterns have been reported: *low levels* and *small gains* in achievement despite 12 to 13 years of education. (p. 227)

We must not, however, equate academic performance with intelligence. Most children who are deaf have normal intellectual capacity, and it has been repeatedly demonstrated that their scores on nonverbal intelligence tests are approximately the same as those of the general population. Deafness imposes no limitations on the cognitive capabilities of individuals (Moores, 1996). The problems that students who are deaf often experience in education and adjustment are largely attributable to a bad fit between their perceptual abilities and the demands of spoken and written English (Hoemann & Briga, 1981). Command of English—particularly when it is a person's second language—is only one indicator of a person's intelligence and ability.

Sign language is the first language for many persons who are deaf. It is a visual-spatial language. Attempting to assess the intelligence of a deaf individual by his understanding and use of English—a phonologically based second language to which this person has had limited access because of its phonological base—is just as inappropriate as using an English language assessment battery to test a child whose first language is Spanish.

Social and Psychological Factors

Impaired hearing can influence a child's behavior and socioemotional development. Research has not provided clear insights into the effects of hearing loss on behavior; however, it appears that the extent to which a child with hearing loss successfully interacts with family members, friends, and people in the community depends largely on others' attitudes and the child's ability to communicate in some mutually acceptable way (Marschark & Clark, 1998). Children who are deaf with deaf parents are thought to have higher levels of social maturity, adjustment to deafness, and behavioral self-control than do children who are deaf with hearing parents, largely because of the early use of manual communication between parent and child that is typical in homes with deaf parents.

Deaf of Deaf *is the term used in the Deaf community to refer to children who are deaf with deaf parents.*

Persons with hearing loss frequently express feelings of depression, withdrawal, and isolation, particularly those who experience adventitious loss of hearing (Meadow-Orlans, 1985). A study of more than 1,000 deaf adolescents who were considered disruptive in the classroom (Kluwin, 1985) found that the most frequently related factor was reading ability; that is, students who were poorer readers were more likely to exhibit problem behaviors in school.

The correlation between poor reading skills and classroom behavior problems is not limited to students with hearing loss.

Many individuals who are deaf choose to associate primarily with other deaf people; this may be mistakenly viewed as clannishness by members of hearing society. Certainly, communication plays a major role in anyone's adjustment. Most individuals with hearing loss are fully capable of developing positive relationships with their hearing peers when a satisfactory method of communication can be used. Generalizations about how people who are deaf are supposed to act and feel should be viewed with

Writer's Workshop: Teaching Process Writing to Students Who Are Deaf

by Barbara R. Schirmer

Reading and writing are so integral to educational success, social interaction, and economic opportunities that it is hard to imagine what it would be like to struggle with written language. For students who are deaf, reading and writing present tremendous challenges. Regardless of how effectively the deaf child can communicate about complex issues person to person, reading and writing about these issues require that the child be able to manipulate the surface structure of English. This is a daunting task for children who are not fluent in oral English.

Traditional approaches for teaching writing emphasize student learning of writing skills and rules, frequent practice in mastering techniques, and evaluation methods that promote error-free compositions as the goal of writing instruction (McAnally, Rose, & Quigley, 1998). These approaches have been widely viewed as unsuccessful in helping students who are deaf become motivated writers who can effectively use writing to interact with others, communicate feelings, explore ideas, give and ask for help, direct the behavior of others, provide information, and create imaginative worlds (Schirmer, 2000).

Current approaches to teaching writing are called *process writing* because they emphasize what individuals think about and do from inception of idea to finished product. Many teachers believe that stressing process over product allows children to develop as writers in much the same way as they develop as speakers and signers.

Writer's Workshop is a teaching model based on the principles of teaching the writing process. The model can be implemented effectively in small self-contained classrooms with a relatively homogeneous group of students who are deaf or in large heterogeneous general education classrooms with one or a few students who are deaf. It has worked successfully with students who are deaf in kindergarten through high school (Andrews & Gonzalez, 1992; Haydon, Mann, & Fugate, 1995; Johnson, 1992; Kluwin & Kelly, 1992; Sturdivant, 1992).

The following qualities characterize the learning environment of Writer's Workshop:

- *Choice*. Students have complete freedom to make decisions about their compositions—from topic to genre, vocabulary to sentence structure, voice to organization, even whether to complete or not complete any given piece of writing.
- *Audience*. Students know that their writing will reach individuals who are genuinely interested in reading and responding to their in-progress and completed pieces.
- *Time*. Periods are substantial enough for students to engage in sustained effort without interruptions and are important enough to be regularly scheduled within each school week.
- *Stages in the writing process*. Students are taught and encouraged to apply the stages in the writing process that researchers had observed in skilled writers: planning, writing, and revising (see Figure A).

Guidelines for Implementation

- Set aside 30 to 45 minutes for each Writer's Workshop period and don't allow interruptions. It is better to have three 35-minute periods each week than five 20-minute periods.

Figure A Illustration drawn by a high school student in response to the assignment "Illustrate the steps you go through when you write"

- Use 5- to 10-minute mini-lessons at the opening of each period to provide direct instruction in a skill or concept with which the children have been grappling in their writing. Mini-lessons can cover the stages of the writing process, how to choose a topic, questions to ask and the kinds of comments that are helpful during peer or teacher conferences, techniques for planning, strategies for revising, how to edit, qualities of good writing, and how to decide which pieces to publish. For children who are deaf in general education classrooms, the educational interpreter or classroom teacher of children who are deaf can interpret the presentation.
- Teach the children how to use conferences for helping them make decisions about their writing. Conferences should be directed by the children and should support them in figuring out what to write about, what they already know about the topic and need to find out, what they should change, what the reader might be thinking and wondering, and how to make the idea clearer. In classrooms with hearing children, conferences with children who are deaf who communicate through sign can be facilitated with the assistance of a sign language interpreter or teacher of deaf children who circulates around the class.
- Provide an author's folder for each child to keep as a portfolio. The folder should contain a list of topic ideas that the child has generated, drafts of writing-in-progress, list of revision suggestions, editing checklist, names and dates of completed pieces, and rules of the Writer's Workshop class period.
- Keep revision of ideas separate from revision of English sentence structures and mechanics. Because of the difficulty that children who are deaf have with English syntax, their written language is often nongrammatical. The writing of children who are deaf whose native language is ASL often follows the word order of ASL (which is significantly different from English), and English morphemes are either left out or used inappropriately. If the teacher focuses all of the deaf child's attention on syntax, the child will see writing as a negative and even hopeless activity. But if syntax is placed in the context of editing, the final step of revision, the child can be guided to use English syntax as a model for written language.

Barbara R. Schirmer is Professor of Special Education at Kent State University. She is the author of *Language and Literacy Development in Children Who Are Deaf* (Allyn & Bacon, 2000).

extreme caution. Lane (1988), for example, makes a strong case against the existence of the so-called psychology of the deaf. He shows the similarity of the traits attributed to deaf people in the professional literature to traits attributed to African people in the literature of colonialism and suggests that those traits do not "reflect the characteristics of deaf people but the paternalistic posture of the hearing experts making these attributions" (p. 8). In addition, he argues that the scientific literature on the psychology of the deaf is flawed in terms of test administration, test language, test scoring, test content and norms, and its description of subject populations, arguments that have been noted by other researchers as well (Moores, 1996; Paul & Quigley, 1990).

To read more from and about Deaf culture, see the Profiles & Perspectives features later in this chapter.

Educational Approaches

Over the years, many special methods and materials have been developed for and used with deaf and hard of hearing children. Techniques, theories, and controversies have proliferated, often with passionate proponents. Regardless of instructional approach or method, the primary objective and focus of teachers of children with hearing loss is helping children develop and use language and communication skills.

> For the teacher of deaf and hard-of-hearing students, language is the curricular foundation on which the school day is built. The child's acquisition of language in face-to-face communication, reading, and writing is the focal point of instruction. The opportunity that content

Numerous resources and ideas for designing and implementing effective instruction for students who are deaf or hard of hearing can be obtained via the Internet at the Deaf Education website. See "For More Information" at the end of this chapter.

area instruction provides deaf and hard of hearing students to use language expressively and receptively is at least as important, and often considerably more important, than the specific concepts taught within individual subject areas. (Schirmer, 1997, p. 53)

Three classroom communication methods used with deaf and hard of hearing students are oral/aural approach, total communication, and bilingual-bicultural education.

Oral/Aural Approaches

Educational programs with an oral/aural emphasis view speech as essential if students who are deaf are to function in the hearing world. Training in producing and understanding speech and language is incorporated into virtually all aspects of the child's education. Used widely in the United States before the 1970s, a purely oral approach without any manual communication is now used by only about one-fourth of educational programs for students with hearing loss (Meadow-Orlans et al., 1997).

A child who attends a program with an oral emphasis typically uses several means to develop residual hearing and the ability to speak as intelligibly as possible. Auditory, visual, and tactile methods of input are frequently used. Much attention is given to amplification, auditory training, speechreading, the use of technological aids, and, above all, talking. Oral education tends to emphasize parent and family involvement. A few schools and classes maintain a purely oral environment and may even prohibit children from pointing, using gestures, or spelling out words to communicate. Children in these programs must express themselves and learn to understand others through speech alone. Other programs also emphasize speech but are more flexible. They may use a variety of approaches to help students produce and understand spoken language.

Educators who use an oral approach acknowledge that teaching speech to children who are deaf is difficult, demanding, and time-consuming for the teacher, the parents, and—most of all—the student. Speech comes hard to the deaf child, and no recent development has made the task any easier: "There has been neither a clear record of steady improvement in teaching methods nor significant breakthroughs that have either markedly reduced the level of effort or significantly increased the quality of the result for 400 years" (Calvert, 1986, p. 167).

The rewards of successful oral communication, however, are thought to be worth the effort. And indeed, most students with hearing losses no worse than severe can learn speech well enough to communicate effectively with hearing people. Paul and Quigley (1990) point out that the best results are obtained with students with hearing loss who are enrolled in indisputably comprehensive oral programs or who are integrated most of the school day into regular education programs.

Cued Speech **Cued speech** is a method of supplementing oral communication. It seeks to supply a visual representation of spoken language by adding cues, in the form of hand signals near the chin, to assist the deaf person in identifying sounds that cannot be distinguished through speechreading. The hand signals must be used in conjunction with speech; they are neither signs nor manual alphabet letters and cannot be read alone. Eight hand shapes are used to identify consonant sounds, and four locations identify vowel sounds. A hand shape coupled with a location gives a visual indication of a syllable.

According to Cornett (1974), who developed the system, cued speech can give intensive language input to young children because it clarifies the patterns of spoken English and does not disrupt the natural rhythm of speech. Although cued speech is advocated by a number of active parent groups and is widely used in educational programs for children with hearing loss in Australia, it has not become popular in the United States (Calvert, 1986).

Total Communication

Educational programs with an emphasis on **total communication** (also called *simultaneous communication*) advocate the use of a variety of forms of communication to teach language to students with hearing loss. Practitioners of total communication maintain that simultaneous presentation of manual communication (by signs and fingerspelling) and speech (through speechreading and residual hearing) makes it possible for children to use either one or both types of communication (Ling, 1984). Since its introduction as a teaching philosophy in the 1960s, total communication has become "the predominant method of instruction in schools for the deaf" (Luterman, 1986, p. 263). A recent survey of 137 early intervention programs for deaf and hard of hearing students in 39 states found that 66% of the programs used total communication (Meadow-Orlans et al., 1997).

Roy Holcomb, a deaf graduate of the Texas School for the Deaf and Gallaudet University, coined the term and is credited as the father of total communication (Gannon, 1981).

Sign Language Sign language uses gestures to represent words, ideas, and concepts. Some signs are *iconic;* that is, they convey meaning through hand shapes or motions that look like or appear to imitate or act out their message. In making the "cat" sign, for example, the signer seems to be stroking feline whiskers on her face; in the sign for "eat," the hand moves back and forth into an open mouth. Most signs, however, have little or no iconicity; they do not resemble the objects or actions they represent. If sign language were simply a form of pantomime, then most nonsigners would be able to understand it with relatively little effort. But several studies have shown that the majority of signs cannot be guessed by people who are unfamiliar with that particular sign language (Klima & Bellugi, 1979).

Teachers who practice total communication generally speak as they sign and make a special effort to follow the form and structure of spoken English as closely as possible. Several sign language systems have been designed primarily for educational purposes, with the intention of facilitating the development of reading, writing, and other language skills in students with hearing loss. *Manually Coded English* is the term applied to several educationally oriented sign systems, such as Seeing Essential

Some signs, such as "cat" (left) and "eat" (right) are iconic; they look like the objects or actions they represent.

English (Anthony, 1971), Signing Exact English (Gustason, Pfetzing, & Zawolkow, 1980), and Signed English (Bornstein, 1974). These sign systems incorporate many features of American Sign Language and also seek to follow correct English usage and word order. Unfortunately, deaf students must often learn and use two or more sign language systems, depending on the person with whom they are communicating.

Fingerspelling is also used by many people who are both deaf and visually impaired. The manual alphabet can be used at close distances or felt with the hand if a person is totally blind.

Fingerspelling *Fingerspelling,* or the manual alphabet, is often used in conjunction with other methods of communication. It consists of 26 distinct hand positions, one for each English letter. A one-hand manual alphabet is used in the United States and Canada (see Figure 10.4). Some manual letters—such as "C," "L," and "W"—resemble the shape of printed English letters, whereas others—such as "A," "E," and "S"—have no apparent similarity. As in typewriting, each word is spelled out letter by letter. A user of sign language relies on fingerspelling to spell out proper names for which no signs exist and to clarify meanings.

Some educators have expressed concern over the consistency and quality of signing that occurs in many total communication classrooms:

> Having ridden a wave of popularity to become the most prominent communication approach in the field, total communication appears to be advancing to its own judgment day. Programs that advocate the use of signs have been characterized by linguistic incon-

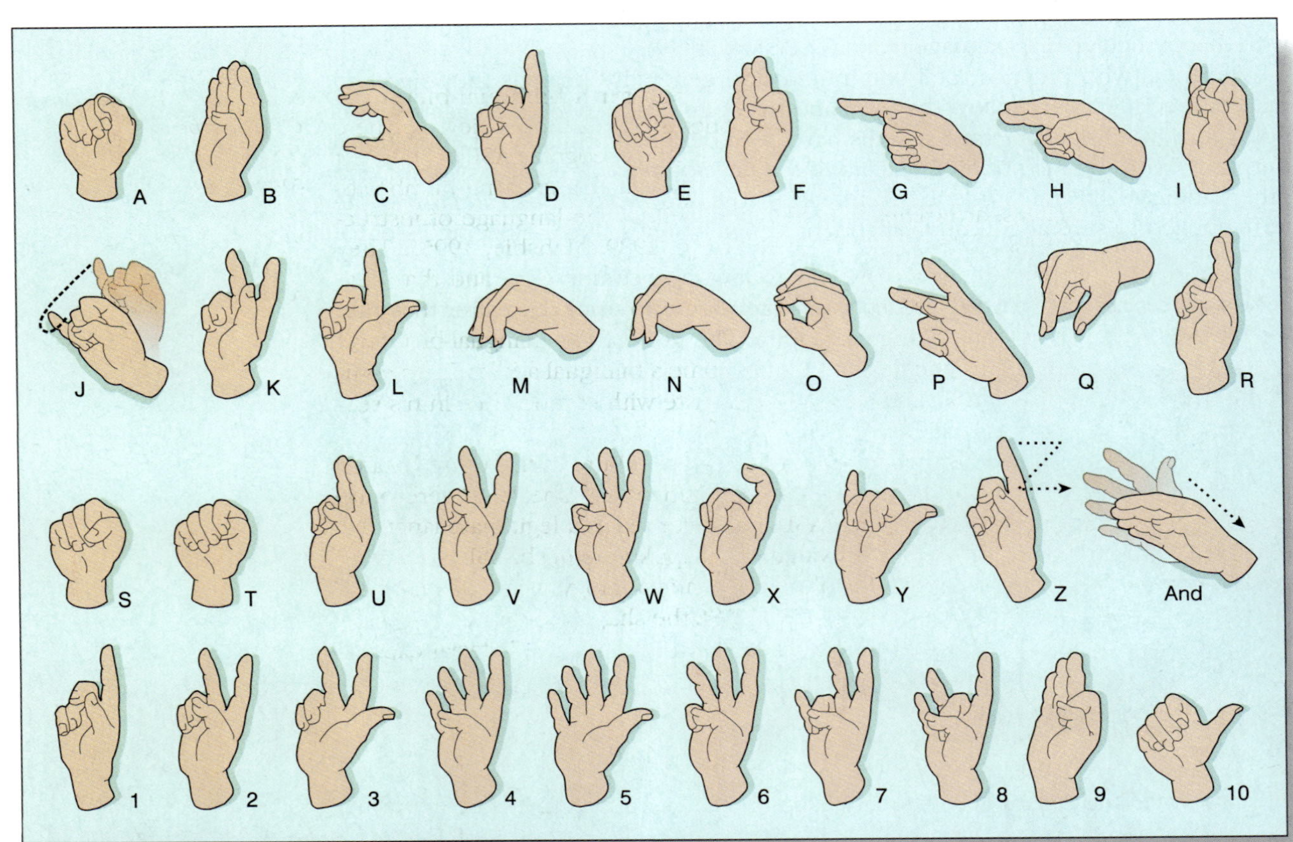

Figure 10.4 The manual alphabet used to fingerspell English in North America

> sistency in the signing behavior of teachers. . . . whereas English, and to a lesser extent American Sign Language (ASL), might be promoted as the primary language base in total communication programs, Pidgin English (PSE) best describes the way most teachers tend to sign. . . . Most teachers of the deaf have spent the first 20 years of their lives using only speech and English skills as their primary means of communication. Then after a couple of sign courses, several field experiences, and limited background information on the pedagogical implications of signing, these teachers are given classrooms and expected to become effective as instructors in what is essentially a foreign medium of communication. (Stewart, 1992, pp. 69, 82)

Many educators believe that total communication facilitates parent-child and teacher-child communication and enhances children's self-esteem, but these supposed gains cannot be easily documented. Luterman (1986) regards the effects of the movement toward total communication as unproven and observes that "total communication has not made any substantial changes in the depressingly low academic achievement of children who are deaf" (p. 263). Schirmer (1998) believes that total communication is an approach that is going out of favor:

> One reason is that the idea of using every communication technique and mode available seems unrealistic. Teaching typically emphasizes speech and audition at the expense of sign language, or vice versa. And students attend more to one mode than the other. A second reason total communication as a method has become controversial is because it was predicated on having the teacher use speech and sign language simultaneously, and . . . it is not possible to speak and use ASL at the same time. (p. 641)

Bilingual-Bicultural Approach

For an excellent discussion of ASL as the deaf child's first language, as well as some recommendations for implementing bilingual-bicultural education programs for deaf children, see Drasgow (1998).

Currently, there is growing interest in and advocacy for a bilingual-bicultural approach to the education of deaf children. Proponents of this model view deafness as a cultural and linguistic difference, not a disability, and recognize ASL as the deaf child's natural language. Both the Deaf community, as well as a growing number of hearing special educators, are calling for the use of ASL as the language of instruction (e.g., Drasgow, 1998; Johnson, Liddell, & Erting, 1989; Mahshie, 1995). They believe that ASL provides a natural pathway to linguistic competence and that English is better learned in the context of a bilingual-bicultural education after the child has mastered his native or first language (ASL). The goal of the bilingual-bicultural education approach is to help the deaf student become a bilingual adult who is competent in his first language, ASL, and can read and write with competence in his second language, English.

American Sign Language is the language of the Deaf culture in the United States and Canada. Although the sign languages used by native deaf speakers were once thought to be nonlanguages (alinguistic), ASL is now viewed as a legitimate language in its own right rather than an imperfect variation of spoken English. ASL is a visual-gestural language with its own rules of phonology, morphology, syntax, semantics, and pragmatics (Drasgow, 1998; Wilbur, 1987). In ASL the shape, location, and movement pattern of the hands; the intensity of motions; and the signer's facial expressions all communicate meaning and content.

Several researchers have found that children as young as 5 months of age are able to produce and understand signs effectively (e.g., Maestas y Moores & Moores, 1980; Orlansky & Bonvillian, 1985; Prinz & Prinz, 1979). "When deaf children have full visual access to a natural signed language, they acquire it in the same effortless manner as hearing children acquire a spoken language" (Drasgow, 1998, p. 334). Empirical support for the bilingual-bicultural approach comes from some recent research finding that early exposure to and development of fluency in ASL are associ-

American Sign Language (ASL) is a legitimate language with its own vocabulary, syntax, and grammatical rules. It does not correspond to spoken or written English.

ated with increased competence and English literacy (reading and writing) (Prinz, Strong, Kuntze, Vincent, Friedman, Moyers, & Helman, 1996; Strong & Prinz, 1997).

Because ASL has its own vocabulary, syntax, and grammatical rules, it does not correspond to spoken or written English. Articles, prepositions, tenses, plurals, and word order are expressed differently from standard English. It is difficult to make precise word-for-word translations between ASL and English, just as it is difficult to translate many foreign languages into English word for word.

Lane (1988) views hearing educators' insistence on imposing a manual form of English on students who are deaf as another sign of the ethnocentrism and paternalism often displayed by the hearing establishment toward students who are deaf.

> This ethnocentric misunderstanding about the nature and status of sign language leads teachers to "fix up" the children's "arbitrary gestures" to make them more like English. New signs are invented by hearing people for English function words and suffixes that have no place, of course, in American Sign Language, and the grammatical order of the signs is scrambled in an attempt to duplicate English word order. No deaf child has ever learned such a system as a native language and indeed could not, for it violates the principles of the manual-visual channel of communication. No deaf adult uses such ways of communicating. But the system is widely used in classrooms with the claim that it assists the deaf child in learning English. (p. 10)

Controversy and Choices

Educators, scientists, philosophers, and parents—both hearing and deaf—have for many years debated the most appropriate instructional methods for children who are deaf. The controversy continues today. In the past, however, fundamental disagreement focused on the extent to which deaf children should express language through speech and perceive the communication of others through speechreading and residual hearing. Today, the focal point has switched to which language modality—auditory or visual—best suits a child's acquisition of an initial language. Research has yet to provide (and perhaps never will provide) a definitive answer to the question of which communication method is best. There is general agreement, however, that educational programs for students who are deaf leave much room for improvement.

Different children communicate in different ways. Some children with hearing loss, unfortunately, have experienced deep frustration and failure because of rigid adherence to an oral-only program. They have left oral programs without having developed a usable avenue of communication. Equally unfortunate is the fact that other children with hearing loss have not been given an adequate opportunity to develop their auditory and oral skills because they were placed in educational programs that did not provide good oral instruction. In both cases, children have been unfairly penalized. Every child who is deaf should have access to an educational program that uses a communication method best suited to her unique abilities and needs. Mahshie (1995) recommends letting the child chose her first language:

> In environments where the Deaf child encounters both spoken and signed language separately—as whole languages—during the course of natural interactions, it has become apparent to both parents and professionals that the child will be the guide regarding his or her predisposition toward a more oral or more visual language. In this win-win situation, the choice of a first language is clearly the child's. (p. 73)

Assistive Listening Devices and Other Support Technologies

In years past, it was assumed that individuals who were deaf simply did not hear at all. But hearing loss occurs in many degrees and patterns, and nearly all children who are deaf have some amount of residual hearing. Modern methods of testing hearing and improved electronic technology for the amplification of sound enable many children with hearing loss to use their residual hearing productively. Even children with severe and profound hearing loss can benefit from hearing aids in the classroom, home, and community, regardless of whether they communicate primarily in an oral or manual mode. Ross (1986) considers residual hearing to be the "biologic birthright" of every hearing-impaired child, one that "should be used and depended on to whatever extent possible" (p. 51).

Amplification Instruments

A hearing aid is an amplification instrument; that is, it functions to make sounds louder. Levitt (1985) describes the hearing aid as "the most widely used technological aid of all. . . . a low cost, acoustic amplification system that can be programmed to best match the needs of each user" (pp. 120–121). There are dozens of kinds of hearing aids; they can be worn behind the ear, in the ear, on the body, or incorporated into eyeglass frames. Children can wear hearing aids in one or both ears (monaural or binaural aids). Whatever its shape, power, or size, a hearing aid picks up sound, magnifies its energy, and delivers this louder sound to the user's ear and brain. In many ways, the hearing aid is like a miniature public address system, with a microphone, an amplifier, and controls to adjust volume and tone (Clarke & Leslie, 1980).

Although hearing aids help many children increase their awareness of sound, it is important to understand that aids make sounds louder but not necessarily clearer. Thus, children who hear sounds with distortion will still experience distortion with hearing aids. The effect is similar to turning up the volume on an old transistor radio: you can make the music louder, but you cannot make the words clearer. Even the most powerful hearing aids generally cannot enable children with severe and profound hearing losses to hear speech sounds beyond a distance of a few feet. No hearing aid can cure a hearing loss or by itself enable a child who is deaf to function

Teachers should check daily to see that a child's hearing aid is functioning properly. The Ling Five Sound Test is a quick and easy way to determine whether a child can detect the basic speech sounds (Ling, 1976). With the child's back to the teacher (to ensure that visual clues do not confound the results), the child repeats each of five sounds spoken by the teacher: /a/, /oo/, /e/, /sh/, and /s/. Ling states that these five sounds are representative of the speech energy in every English phoneme and that a child who can detect these five sounds should be able to detect every English speech sound.

Ho (1991) describes the Easy Listener Freefield Sound System, which functions as a specialized portable PA system to increase auditory attention for all students, and the Easy Listener Personal FM System, in which students with mild hearing loss wear a receiver and headphones.

Teachers should help parents recognize and take advantage of the many opportunities for auditory training and learning around the house.

normally in a regular classroom. In all cases, it is the wearer of the hearing aid, not the aid itself, who does most of the work in interpreting conversation.

The earlier in life a child can be fitted with an appropriate hearing aid, the more effectively he will learn to use hearing for communication and awareness. Today, it is not at all unusual to see infants and preschool children wearing hearing aids; the improved listening conditions become an important part of the young child's speech and language development. To derive the maximum benefit from a hearing aid, a child should wear it throughout the day. Residual hearing cannot be effectively developed if the aid is removed or turned off outside the classroom. It is important for the child to hear sounds while eating breakfast, shopping in the supermarket, and riding the school bus. One study found that the academic performance of students with hearing loss was positively correlated with the length of time they had worn their hearing aids (Blair, Peterson, & Viehweg, 1985).

Group assistive listening devices can solve the problems caused by distance, noise, and reverberation in the classroom, which often interfere with a student's ability to discriminate the desired auditory signal with a personal hearing aid. In most systems, a radio link is established between the teacher and the children with hearing loss, with the teacher wearing a small microphone transmitter (often on the lapel, near the lips) and each child wearing a receiver that doubles as a personal hearing aid (Ross, 1986). An FM radio frequency is usually employed, and wires are not required, so teacher and students can move freely around the classroom area. The FM device creates a listening situation comparable to the teacher's "being only 6 inches away from the child's ear at all times" (Ireland, Wray, & Flexer, 1988, p. 17). Classroom amplification systems are used in both special classes and regular classroom settings where students with hearing loss are integrated with hearing students.

Auditory Learning

Auditory training/learning programs help children make better use of residual hearing. All children with hearing loss, regardless of whether their preferred method of communication is oral (speech) or manual (signs), should participate in lessons and activities that help them improve their listening ability. Many children with hearing loss have much more auditory potential than they actually use, and their residual hearing can be most effectively developed in the context of actual communication and daily experiences (Ross, 1981).

A traditional **auditory training** program for young children with hearing loss begins by teaching awareness of sound. Parents might direct their child's attention to sounds such as a doorbell ringing or water running. They might then focus on localization of sound—for example, by hiding a radio somewhere in the room and encouraging the child to look for it. Discrimination of sounds is another important part of auditory training; a child might learn to notice the differences between a man's voice and a woman's voice, between a fast song and a slow song, or between the words "rack" and "rug." Identification of sounds comes when a child is able to recognize a sound, word, or sentence through listening.

The focus today is on *auditory learning*—that is, teaching the child to learn to listen and to learn by listening instead of simply learning to hear (Ling, 1986). Advocates of auditory learning contend that the first three levels of auditory training—detecting, discriminating, and identifying sounds—are important but insufficient for developing the student's residual hearing. Auditory learning emphasizes a fourth and highest level of listening skills—the comprehension of meaningful sounds.

Some teachers find it helpful to conduct formal auditory training/learning sessions in which a child is required to use only hearing: he would have to recognize

To derive maximum benefit from a hearing aid, a child should wear it throughout the day.

sounds and words without looking at the speaker. In actual practice, however, the student gains useful information from vision and the other senses to supplement the information received from hearing. Consequently, all senses should be effectively developed and constantly used.

Speech Reading

Speechreading is the process of understanding a spoken message by observing the speaker's face. Children with hearing loss, whether they have much or little residual hearing and whether they communicate primarily through oral or manual means, use their vision to help them understand speech. Some sounds are readily distinguished by watching the speaker's lips. For example, the word "pail" begins with the lips in a shut position, whereas the lips are somewhat drawn together and puckered at the corners for the word "rail." Paying careful attention to a speaker's lips may help an individual with hearing loss derive important clues—particularly if she is also able to gain some information through residual hearing, signs or gestures, facial expressions, and familiarity with the context or situation.

Speechreading was traditionally called lipreading, *but understanding speech from visual clues involves more than simply looking at the lips.*

Speechreading, however, is extremely difficult and has many limitations. About half of all English words have some other word(s) that appear the same in pronunciation; that is, although they sound quite different, they look alike on the lips. Words

The combination of amplification and auditory training can help a hearing-impaired child make the most of his residual hearing.

such as "bat," "mat," and "pat," for example, look exactly alike and simply cannot be discriminated by watching the speaker's lips. To complicate matters, visual clues may be blocked by a hand or a pencil, chewing gum, or a mustache. Many speakers are virtually unintelligible through speechreading; they may seem not to move their lips at all. In addition, it is extremely tiring to watch lips for a long time, and it may be impossible to do so at a distance, such as during a lecture.

Walker (1986) estimates that even the best speechreaders detect only about 25% of what is said through visual clues alone; "the rest is contextual piecing together of ideas and expected constructions" (p. 19). Shanny Mow (1973), a teacher who is deaf, graphically describes the frustrations of speechreading:

> Like the whorls on his fingertips, each person's lips are different and move in a peculiar way of their own. When young, you build confidence as you guess correctly "ball," "fish," and "shoe" on your teacher's lips. This confidence doesn't last. As soon as you discover there are more than four words in the dictionary, it evaporates. Seventy percent of the words when appearing on the lips are no more than blurs. Lipreading is a precarious and cruel art which rewards a few who have mastered it and tortures the many who have tried and failed. (pp. 21–22)

Speechreading skills of deaf students can be improved by practicing lipreading their own speech and others via computer-assisted video instruction (DeFilippo, Sims, & Gottermeier, 1995; Sims & Gottermeier, 1995).

Despite the problems inherent in speechreading, it can be a valuable adjunct in the communication of a deaf or hard of hearing person. According to Moores (1996), few new techniques have been developed recently, and little research has been done into the most effective ways of teaching speechreading. Although speechreading cannot take the place of hearing, improved methods might well enable many people with hearing loss to make better use of their vision in decoding messages.

Interpreters

Interpreting—signing the speech of a teacher or other speaker for a person who is deaf—began as a profession in 1964 with the establishment of a professional organization called the Registry of Interpreters for the Deaf (RID). Many states have programs for training interpreters, who must meet certain standards of competence to be certified by the RID. The organization was initially comprised primarily of *freelance interpreters,* who interpret primarily for deaf adults in situations such as legal or medical interactions.

The role of the *educational interpreter* (sometimes referred to as an *educational transliterator*) has made it possible for many students with hearing loss to

Tips for Facilitating Communication

Persons with hearing loss are increasingly participating in community life. It is not unusual for a businessperson, bank teller, student, police officer, or anyone else to have the opportunity to communicate with a person who is deaf. Yet many people with normal hearing are unsure of themselves. As a result, they may avoid deaf people altogether or use ineffective and frustrating strategies when they do attempt to communicate.

The following tips for facilitating communication were suggested by the Community Services for the Deaf program in Akron, Ohio. These tips provide basic information about three common ways that deaf persons communicate: through speechreading, with sign language or the assistance of an interpreter, and by written communication. Usually, the person will indicate the approach with which he is most comfortable. If the person relies mainly on *speechreading*, here are things you can do to help.

- Face the person and stand or sit no more than four feet away.
- The room should have adequate illumination, but don't seat yourself in front of a strong or glaring light.
- Try to keep your whole face visible.
- Speak clearly and naturally, and not too fast.
- Don't exaggerate your mouth movements.
- Don't raise the level of your voice.
- Some words are more easily read on the lips than others. If you are having a problem being understood, try substituting different words.
- It may take a while to become used to the deaf person's speech. If at first you can't understand what she is saying, don't give up.
- Don't hesitate to write down any important words that are missed.

If the deaf person communicates best through *sign language* (and you do not), it will probably be necessary to use an interpreter. Here are some considerations to keep in mind:

- The role of the interpreter is to facilitate communication between you and the person who is deaf. The interpreter should not be asked to give opinions, advice, or personal feelings.
- Maintain eye contact with the deaf person and speak directly to him. The deaf person should not be made to take a back seat in the conversation. For example, say, "How are you today?" instead of "Ask him how he is today."
- Remain face-to-face with the deaf person. The best place for the interpreter is behind you and a little your side. Again, avoid strong or glaring light.
- Remember, it is the interpreter's job to communicate everything that you and the deaf person say. Don't say anything that you don't want interpreted.

Written messages can be helpful in exchanging information. Consider the following:

- Avoid the temptation to abbreviate your communication.
- Write in simple, direct language.
- The deaf person's written English may not be grammatically correct, but you will probably be able to understand it. One deaf person, for example, wrote "Pay off yesterday, finish me" to convey the message "I paid that loan off yesterday."
- Use visual aids, such as pictures, diagrams, and business cards.
- Don't be afraid to supplement your written messages with gestures and facial expressions.
- Written communication has limitations, but it is often more effective than no communication at all.

Remember that English is a second language for many deaf people. They are deprived of a great deal of information because they cannot hear. Skills of spoken and written English are not an accurate reflection of a deaf person's intelligence or ability to function independently.

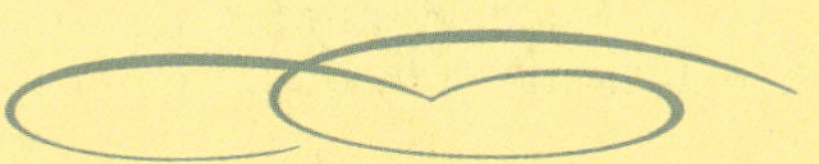

enroll in and successfully complete postsecondary programs. There has also been greater use of educational interpreters in elementary and secondary classrooms (Salend & Longo, 1994). Duties of interpreters vary across schools; they are likely to perform tasks such as tutoring, assisting regular and special education teachers, keeping records, and supervising students with hearing loss (Zawolkow & DeFiore, 1986).

If sign language interpreting sounds interesting, see So You Want to Be an Interpreter *(Humphrey & Alcorn, 1994).*

Text Telephones

The telephone served as a barrier to deaf people in employment and social interaction for many years, but acoustic couplers now make it possible to send immediate messages over conventional telephone lines in typed or digital form. Text telephones (TT) (originally called TTY or TDD systems) enable the user to send a typed message over telephone lines to anyone else who has a TT. As a result of the Americans with Disabilities Act, TTs are now available in most public places such as airports and libraries, and every state has a relay service that enables TT users to communicate with a person on a conventional telephone via an operator who relays the messages. Relay numbers are published in every phone directory.

Another technological development that promises to increase access by deaf persons during live presentations, such as public or classroom lectures, is known as real-time translation. *A trained operator listens to the lecture and types a shorthand code into a laptop computer, and special software produces an instantaneous display of the transcription that can be projected on a screen. After the presentation, the student can obtain a printout of the transcript.*

Television Captioning

Today most regular programming on commercial and public network television, as well as many live newscasts and sporting events, is captioned (printed text appears at the bottom of the screen, similar to watching a film with subtitles), providing access to televised news and entertainment for deaf people. Since 1993, a federal law has required that all new television sets sold in the United States be equipped with an internal device that allows the user to position captions anywhere on the screen. Accessing captions on older television sets requires an external decoder.

Alerting Devices

Some individuals who are deaf or hard of hearing use special devices to alert them to certain sounds or events. For example, to signal the doorbell, a fire alarm, or alarm clock a sound-sensitive switch can be connected to a flashing light or to a vibrator. Hearing ear dogs alert a deaf person to important sounds in the environment.

Educational Placement Alternatives

In most areas of the United States, parents and students now have the option of choosing between local public school programs and residential school placement. Today, approximately 82% of children who are deaf or hard of hearing attend local public schools: 36% receive most of their education in regular classrooms, 19% attend resource rooms for part of the school day, and 27% are served in separate classrooms (U.S. Department of Education, 1998). Most students with hearing loss who are included in regular classrooms are hard of hearing and have hearing losses of less than 90 dB (Karchmer, 1984).

Of the 10% of students with hearing loss who attend residential schools, about one-third live at home with their families and commute to the school (Paul & Quigley, 1990). Over 90% of the students currently enrolled in residential schools have severe and profound prelingual hearing loss. Nearly one-third of the students with hearing loss served in residential schools have additional disabilities.

For a discussion of the challenges facing deaf Hispanic students who are required to be trilingual and tricultural (ASL/English/Spanish) and a proposed model of language instruction and support for such children, see Walker-Vann (1998).

Today, increasing attention is given to the special education needs of students with hearing loss and additional disabilities. Approximately 25% of all students who are deaf or hard of hearing have other disabilities such as mental retardation, learning disabilities, behavioral disorders, visual impairments, and physical disabilities

"Hearing dogs" are trained to alert a deaf person to important sounds in the environment.

(Schildroth & Hotto, 1994). Many programs also seek to meet the needs of the sizable population of children with hearing loss from culturally diverse backgrounds. The challenge of teaching English communication skills to a deaf child when a language other than English is spoken in the home is particularly complex.

Several publications provide helpful guidelines, practical suggestions, and descriptions of programs that have successfully integrated students with hearing loss into regular classrooms (Dale, 1984; Kampfe, 1984; Lynas, 1986; Webster & Ellwood, 1985).

According to Davis (1986), the most important ingredients for the deaf or hard of hearing child's success in the regular classroom are (1) good oral communication skills, (2) strong parental support, (3) average or above-average intelligence, (4) self-confidence and other personal qualities, and (5) adequate support services, such as tutoring, audiological consultation, and speech therapy. As with all learners, we should never overlook the most fundamental factor in determining how successful a student will be in the regular classroom (or any other placement): *quality of instruction.* After studying the math achievement of 215 secondary students with hearing loss who were either in self-contained classrooms or mainstreamed into regular classes with or without an interpreter, Kluwin and Moores (1989) concluded, "Quality of instruction is the prime determinant of achievement, regardless of placement" (p. 327).

There is much debate over where students who are deaf should be educated, with some research evidence—and much strong opinion—to support both residential and inclusive placements. With the increased emphasis on inclusion, some question the effectiveness and appropriateness of residential placements for any student. Research, however, has not found that residential schools for the deaf contribute to academic or social deficits in students. On the contrary, some studies suggest that residential schooling may be the most effective placement for certain students. For example, Braden, Maller, and Paquin (1993) report that the performance IQs of children with hearing loss who were educated in residential schools increased over a three- to four-year period but that the scores of similar students in regular school day programs did not.

PROFILES AND PERSPECTIVES

I Am Not Disabled—I'm Just Deaf

Jesse Thomas was 15 years old when he testified before the National Council on Disabilities. He explained his views on the use of American Sign Language and inclusion. Excerpts from his testimony follow.

I think I have to explain that I am not disabled—I'm just deaf. Deaf persons are a minority group. They use American Sign Language (ASL) and are part of the Deaf Culture. One of the main reasons that mainstreaming is not good is because mainstreaming lacks Deaf Culture and ASL. I can't really explain Deaf Culture. I do know that Deaf Culture makes me proud of who I am—DEAF.

Here are reasons why I think Deaf schools should be favored over the mainstream:

- Learning through an interpreter is very hard. It is pretty tiring for me to keep my eyes on one "place" all day long. After watching an interpreter all morning, I find myself not paying attention in the afternoon.
- It is bad socially in the mainstream situation. I communicate in SIGN, and my peers in my hearing school SPEAK.
- You are ALWAYS outnumbered. There are basically 25 kids in my classes—all hearing but me. That's a ratio of 25:1!
- You don't feel like it's YOUR school; it's like you're along for the ride. I was in one school for sixth grade and got to know some kids, and the junior high was in another town, and I knew nobody there.
- You never know Deaf adults. Once in a while, there is someone who is deaf but thinks hearing, not a Deaf person who is proud to be deaf.
- You don't belong. There are still a lot of people whose faces show sympathy at the word *deaf* and gasp at the thought of a world devoid of hearing. Those people think, "My God, deaf people CAN'T HEAR, there must be something terribly astray with them!"
- You don't feel comfortable as a deaf person. I don't think there should be such a thing as "overcoming deafness." This implies that a person should push being deaf aside and be more hearing. That is absolutely ridiculous. Don't you think that a person should be what he is? I am Deaf; I will succeed as a Deaf person.

I've experienced BOTH kinds of social and educational situations, mainstream and deaf school, and I'll have to say that I favor Deaf schools over mainstreaming. In Deaf schools, the social situation and education is much more normal for Deaf people than in hearing schools.

Source: From Jesse Thomas. (1991). Not disabled—Just deaf. *Let's Talk, 33*(2), p. 30. Published by the American Speech-Language-Hearing Association. Reprinted by permission.

> The results of this study clearly disprove the belief that placement in residential, segregated programs invariably inhibits cognitive abilities. The assumption that children with hearing loss are best served in mainstream settings should be suspended until additional information is available regarding placement effects on such children's cognitive, social and academic development. (p. 432)

In a study of the effects of inclusion on the academic achievement of high school students who are deaf, Kluwin (1993) reported that although those students who were included into regular classrooms for academic content fared better on achievement measures than students who spent all or most of the day in a separate class, the difference may have been the result of curriculum programming and class selection, not the actual placement where instruction took place. In discussing his findings, Kluwin concluded "that for some deaf students, mainstreaming is a good education option; but for others, special classes are more appropriate" (p. 79).

While full inclusion in regular classrooms has benefited some deaf students, all of the professional and parent organizations involved with educating students who are deaf have issued position statements strongly in favor of maintaining a continuum of placement options (e.g., Commission on Education of the Deaf, 1988; Consumer Action Network, 1994). Moores (1993), a respected leader in the field of deaf education, voiced the perspective of many deaf educators and parents when he wrote:

> For many deaf children the concept of total inclusion, as currently promulgated, could in reality be exclusionary in practice. Placing a deaf child in a classroom in physical contiguity to hearing children does not automatically provide equal access to information. In fact, it can be isolating, both academically and socially. (p. 251)

Postsecondary Education

A growing number of educational opportunities are available to students with hearing loss after completion of high school. The oldest and best-known is Gallaudet University in Washington, DC, which offers a wide range of undergraduate and graduate programs in the liberal arts, sciences, education, business, and other fields. The National Technical Institute for the Deaf (NTID), located at the Rochester Institute of Technology, provides wide-ranging programs in technical, vocational, and business-related fields such as computer science, hotel management, photography, and medical technology. Both Gallaudet and NTID are supported by the federal government, and each enrolls approximately 1,500 students who are deaf or hard of hearing.

Gallaudet also has programs to train teachers of deaf children. Both deaf and hearing students are accepted into these programs.

More than 150 other institutions of higher education have developed special programs of supportive services for students with hearing loss. Among these are four regional postsecondary programs that enroll substantial numbers of students with hearing loss: St. Paul (Minnesota) Technical-Vocational Institute, Seattle (Washington) Central Community College, the Postsecondary Education Consortium at the University of Tennessee, and California State University at Northridge.

The percentage of students with hearing loss who attend postsecondary educational programs has risen dramatically in the past 20 years. About 40% of all students with hearing loss go on to receive higher education (Connor, 1986). Enrollment has increased most sharply in areas of study related to business and office careers (Rawlings & King, 1986). It is hoped that the increase in postsecondary programs will expand vocational and professional opportunities for deaf adults.

Current Issues and Future Trends

Given the large percentage of children with hearing loss who are educated in regular classrooms for most of the day, it is likely that oral/aural and total communication methods of instruction will continue to be used (Schildroth & Hotto, 1994). Speech, after all, is the most widely used form of communication among teachers and students in regular classes. At the same time, an increasing percentage of the deaf children served in special schools and self-contained classrooms will be taught with the bilingual-bicultural approach, where ASL is the language of instruction.

Additionally, educators as well as the general public will probably become more aware of ASL and begin to accept its legitimacy as a language separate from English. Training in sign language is already offered to children with normal hearing in some schools, and an increasing number of people who contact the public in the course of their jobs—such as police officers, firefighters, flight attendants, and bank tellers—will learn to communicate manually with individuals who have hearing loss. Television programs, films, concerts, and other media using interpreters or printed captions are becoming more widely available. It is no longer unusual to see a sign language interpreter standing next to a public speaker or performer.

English (1997) has written a book of instructional activities designed to teach self-advocacy skills to students who are deaf or hard of hearing to help them make the transition to adulthood when the safety net of special education disappears.

The Rowley *case is discussed in Chapter 1. It was the first Supreme Court case to be argued by a lawyer who is deaf.*

Many leaders in the deaf community are strong advocates against the development and use of technology designed to "cure" deafness, particularly the use of cochlear implants with deaf children. To learn about their views and a take on society's responsibility to provide services for individuals with disabilities, see "Defiantly Deaf" and "Deafness: The Dilemma," which follow.

The central role that ASL plays in deaf culture, combined with the growing recognition that ASL is the deaf child's first language, will probably heighten the intensity of the longstanding debate over how language should be taught to children with hearing loss. As an illustration of the intensity with which many people who are deaf view this issue, 85 students at the Tennessee School for the Deaf were suspended when they resisted a decree by the school that they sign in English word order instead of being allowed to communicate in ASL (McCracken, 1987).

Despite the recent expansion of postsecondary programs of education and training, many adults with hearing loss still find limited opportunities for appropriate employment and economic advancement. Court decisions regarding the rights of students with hearing loss have had mixed results. In one case (*Barnes v. Converse College,* 1977), a court ordered a private college to provide, at its own expense, an interpreter for a deaf student. In another case (*Southeastern Community College v. Davis,* 1979), the U.S. Supreme Court decided that a college could not be compelled to admit a hearing-impaired student into its nursing program. A widely publicized Supreme Court case (*Board of Education of the Hendrick Hudson Central School District v. Rowley,* 1982) resulted in a local school district's not being required to provide, at its expense, a sign language interpreter for a deaf child who was performing adequately without one in the regular classroom. Similar cases are certain to arise in the future as deaf and hard of hearing people become increasingly aware of their civil rights and seek access to education, employment, and other rights.

Technological advances are already having a significant impact on the lives of many individuals with hearing loss. In addition to the sophisticated techniques that detect hearing losses and make use of even slight amounts of residual hearing, a number of devices known as speech production aids help persons who are deaf monitor and improve their own speech (Calvert, 1986). Cochlear implants have enabled even some persons with profound sensorineural hearing loss to hear speech sounds (Karmody, 1986; Miller & Pfingst, 1984; Yaremko, 1993).

Increasing numbers of deaf children are being taught with bilingual educational approaches in which ASL is the language of instruction.

Defiantly Deaf: Deaf People Live, Proudly, in Another Culture, but Not a Lesser One

by Andrew Soloman

The protest at the Lexington Center, which includes New York's oldest Deaf school, is an important stage in the Deaf struggle for civil rights, and on April 25, the first day of student demonstrations, I ask an African-American from the 11th grade whether she has also demonstrated for race rights. "I'm too busy being Deaf right now," she signs. "My two older brothers aren't Deaf, so they're taking care of being black. Maybe if I have time I'll get to that later."

Another student intercedes. "I am black and Deaf and proud and I don't want to be white or hearing or different in any way from who I am." Her signs are pretty big and clear. The first student repeats the sign "proud"—her thumb, pointing in, rises up her chest—and then suddenly they are overcome with giggles and go back to join the picket line.

This principle is still new to me, but it has been brewing in the Deaf community for some time: while some deaf people feel cut off from the hearing world, or disabled, for others, being Deaf is a culture and a source of pride. ("Deaf" denotes culture, as distinct from "deaf," which is used to describe a pathology.) A steadily increasing number of deaf people have said that they would not choose to be hearing. To them, the word "cure"—indeed the whole notion of deafness as pathology—is anathema.

The Deaf debates are all language debates. "When I communicate in A.S.L., my native language," M. J. Bienvenu, a political activist, said to me, "I am living my culture. I don't define myself in terms of 'not hearing' or of 'not' anything else." A founder of the Bicultural Center (a sort of Deaf think tank), M. J. is gracious, but also famously terrifying: brilliant, striking-looking and self-possessed, with signing so swift, crisp and perfectly controlled that she seems to be rearranging the air in front of her into a more acceptable shape. Deaf of Deaf, with Deaf sisters, she manifests, like many other activists, a pleasure in American Sign Language that only poets feel for English. "When our language was acknowledged," she says, "we gained our freedom." In her hands "freedom"—clenched hands are crossed before the body, then swing apart and face out—is like an explosion.

A "Family" Gathering I attended the National Association of the Deaf convention in Knoxville, Tennessee, with almost 2,000 Deaf participants. At Lexington, I saw Deaf people stand up to the hearing world. I learned how a TTY works, met pet dogs who understood sign, talked about mainstreaming and oralism and the integrity of visual language. I became accustomed to doorbells that flashed lights instead of ringing. But none of this could have prepared me for the immersion that is the NAD convention, where the brightest, most politicized, most committed Deaf gather for political focus and social exchange. There, it is not a question of whether the hearing will accept the existence of Deaf culture, but of whether Deaf culture will accept the hearing.

I arrive the night of the president's reception. There are 1,000 people in the grand ballroom of the Hyatt Regency, the lights turned up because these people are unable to communicate in darkness. The crowd is nearly soundless; you hear the claps that are part of the articulation of A.S.L., the clicks and puffing noises the deaf make when they sign, and occasionally their big uncontrolled laughter. People greet each other as if they have been waiting forever for these encounters—the Deaf community is close, closed and affectionate.

Deaf people touch each other far more than the hearing, and everyone here hugs friends. I, too, find myself hugging people as if I have known them forever. Yet I must be careful of the difference between a friendly and a forward embrace; how you touch communicates a world of meaning in Deaf circles. I must be careful of looking abstractedly at people signing; they will think I am eavesdropping. I do not know any of the etiquette of these new circumstances. "Good luck with the culture shock," more than one person says to me, and I get many helpful hints.

As I look across the room it seems as if some strange human sea is breaking into waves and glinting in the light, as thousands of hands move at stunning speed, describing a spatial grammar with sharply individual voices and accents. The association is host to the Miss Deaf America pageant, and the young beauties, dressed to the nines and sporting their state sashes, are objects of considerable attention. "Look how beautifully she expresses herself," says someone, pointing to one contestant, and then, of another: "Can you believe that blurry Southern signing? I didn't think anyone really signed like that!" (Regional variations of sign can be dangerous: the sign that in New York slang means "cake" in some Southern states means "sanitary napkin.")

The luminaries of the Deaf world—activists, actors, professors—mix comfortably with the beauty queens. I am one of perhaps a dozen hearing people at this party. I have heard Deaf people talk about how their "family" is the Deaf community. Rejected in so many instances by parents with whom they cannot communicate, united by their struggle with a world that is seldom understanding of them, they have formed inviolable bonds of love of a kind that are rare in hearing culture. At the National Association of the Deaf, they are unmistakable. Disconcerting though it may sound, it is impossible, here, not to wish you were Deaf. I had known that Deaf culture existed, but I had not guessed how heady it is.

The Association members are a tiny minority, less than 10 percent of the nation's Deaf; most deaf people are what the Deaf call "grass roots." The week after the convention, the national Deaf bowling championships in Baltimore will attract a much larger crowd, people who go to Deaf clubs, play cards and work in blue-collar jobs. Below them in the Deaf status structure are the peddlers (the Deaf word for the mendicants who "sell" cards with the manual alphabet on subways—the established Deaf community tried as early as the 40's to get them off the streets).

At the V.I.P. party after the radiant Miss Deaf Maryland has won, I am talking to Alec Naiman, a world traveler who was one of the pilots at this year's Deaf fly-in at the Knoxville airport. We are discussing a trip he made to China. "I met some Deaf Chinese people my first day, and went to stay with them. Deaf people never need hotels; you can always stay with other Deaf people. We spoke different signed languages, but we could make ourselves understood. Though we came from different countries, Deaf culture held us together. By the end of the evening we'd talked about Deaf life in China, and about Chinese politics, and we'd understood each other linguistically and culturally. No hearing American could do that in China," he says. "So who's disabled then?"

Making the Irregular Regular How to reconcile this Deaf experience with the rest of the world? Should it be reconciled at all? M. J. Bienvenu has been one of the most vocal and articulate opponents of the language of disability. "I am Deaf," she says to me in Knoxville, drawing out the sign for "Deaf," the index finger moving from chin to ear, as though she is tracing a broad smile. Considerably gentler now than in her extremist heyday in the early 80's, she acknowledges that "for some deaf people, being deaf is a disability. Those who learn forced English while being denied sign emerge semilingual rather than bilingual, and they are disabled people. But for the rest of us, it is no more a disability than being Japanese would be."

I have heard of a couple who opted for an abortion when they heard that their child was hearing, so strong a view did they hold on the superiority of Deaf ways. But I also met many Deaf individuals who objected to the way that the Deaf leadership (focused around the National Association of the Deaf) have presumed to speak for all the deaf people of America. There were plenty who said that being deaf is of course a disability, and that anything you could do about it would be welcome. They were righteously indignant at the thought of a politically correct group suggesting that their problems weren't problems.

It is tempting in the end, to say that there is no such thing as a disability. Equally, one might admit that almost everything is a disability. There are as many arguments for correcting everything as there are for correcting nothing. Perhaps it would be most accurate to say that "disability" and "culture" are really matters of degree. Being Deaf is a disability and a culture in modern America; so is being gay, so is being black; so is being female; so even, increasingly, is being a straight white male. So is being paraplegic, or having Down syndrome. What is at issue is which things are so "cultural" that you wouldn't think of "curing" them, and which things so "disabling" that you must "cure" them—and the reality is that for some people each of these experiences is primarily a disability experience while for others it is primarily a cultural one.

Source: Excerpt from Soloman, A. (1994, August 28). Defiantly deaf. *New York Times.*

Deafness: The Dilemma

by Bonnie Tucker

During the last twenty years, technological advances to assist people with hearing loss surpassed the expectation of many. Hearing aids improved tremendously, both with respect to quality and aesthetics. The newer aids block out background noise and emphasize sound in the speech range, which has enabled some severely hearing-impaired people to benefit from aids for the first time. . . . Cochlear implants have enabled some profoundly deaf people, both children and adults, to understand speech without having to rely on speechreading or interpreters; some cochlear implantees are able to converse on the voice telephone with strangers.

Twenty years ago I, for one, did not foresee these almost Orwellian transformations. Today, however, my vision for the future is unlimited. Given the rapidly advancing state of technology in this area, it is not unrealistic to assume that twenty years hence the technological advances of the past two decades will seem outmoded, even ancient. It is not unrealistic to assume that in twenty years cochlear implants will enable profoundly deaf people to understand speech in most circumstances, including on the telephone. We are not there yet, but we are on our way.

Many members of the Deaf community, including leaders of the National Association of the Deaf (NAD) . . . do not *want* cochlear implants. They do not *want* to hear. They want their children to be Deaf, and to be a part of the Deaf world. "We like being Deaf," they state. "We are proud of our Deafness. . . . " They claim the *right* to their own "ethnicity, with our own language and culture, the same way that Native Americans or Italians bond together"; they claim the right to "personal diversity," which is "something to be cherished rather than fixed and erased. And they *strongly* protest the practice of placing cochlear implants in children. . . . These same individuals, however, are among the strongest advocates for laws and special programs to protect and assist people with hearing loss. They argue fiercely for the need for interpreters, TTYs, telephone relay services, specially funded educational programs, and close-captioning, at no cost to themselves. On the one hand, therefore, they claim that deafness is not a disability, but a state of being, a "right" that should not be altered. On the other hand, they claim that deafness *is* a disability that society should compensate for by providing and paying for services to allow deaf people to function in society. . . .

Do Deaf people have the right to refuse to accept new technology, to refuse to "fix" their Deafness if such repair becomes possible? Yes, absolutely. They *do* have the right, if they wish to exercise that right, to cherish their Deaf culture, their Deaf ethnicity, their "visually oriented" personal diversity. They have *every* right to choose *not* to fix their Deafness. . . . Do Deaf people have the right to demand that society pay for the resulting cost of that choice, however? No, I do not believe they do.

By way of analogy, suppose that blindness and quadriplegia were "curable" due to advanced technology. Blind people could be made to "see" via artificial means such as surgical implantation or three-dimensional eyeglasses; quadriplegic individuals could be made to "walk" and use their arms via artificial means such as surgical nerve implantation or specially built devices. Oh, the blind people might not see as perfectly as sighted people—they might still miss some of the fine print. And the quadriplegic individuals might walk with a limp or move their arms in a jerky fashion. But, for the most part, they would require little special assistance.

Suppose that 10 blind people chose not to make use of available technology for the reason that blindness is not a "disability," not something to be fixed, but that blind people are simply "auditory oriented," and 20 quadriplegic people chose not to make use of available technology for the reason that quadriplegics are simply "out-of-body oriented." How long will society agree to pay for readers, attendants, and other services and devices to assist those blind and quadriplegic individuals who have exercised their right to be diverse? More important, how long *should* society be asked to pay for such services and devices?

When technology advances to the extent that profoundly deaf people could choose to "hear"—which, eventually, it surely will—Deaf people will have to resolve the dilemma, both for reasons of practicality *and* morality. . . . Deaf people will have to decide whether to accept hearing or to remain Deaf. They have every right to choose the latter course. If they do so, however, they must assume responsibility for that choice and bear the resultant cost, rather than thrust that responsibility upon society. . . . As our grandparents used to say, "You can't have your cake and eat it too."

Bonnie Tucker is a professor of law at Arizona State University.

Source: From Tucker, B. (1993). Deafness: 1993–2013—The dilemma. *Volta Review, 95,* 105–108. Reprinted by permission.

Use the self-tests at http://www.prenhall.com/heward to assess your knowledge of the content of Chapter 10.

Among the most intriguing technological concepts is the possibility that an automatic speech recognition system may someday be perfected. Such a system could enable a deaf person to instantly decipher the speech of other people, perhaps through a small portable printout device that would be activated by the speaker's voice. The research required to develop a speech recognition system is highly complex because human speech patterns differ immensely.

Early and continued access to language and communication modality best suited to their individual needs and preferences, effective instruction with meaningful curriculum, and self-advocacy are the keys to increasing the percentage of deaf or hard of hearing people who are able to access and enjoy the full spectrum of educational, social, vocational, and recreational opportunities society has to offer.

Summary

Defining Hearing Loss

- Hearing loss exists on a continuum from mild to profound, and most special educators distinguish between children who are deaf and those who are hard of hearing. A deaf child is not able to understand speech through the ears alone. A hard of hearing child is able to use hearing to understand speech, generally with the help of a hearing aid.
- Sound is measured by its intensity (decibels [dB]) and frequency (Hertz [Hz]); both dimensions are important in considering the special education needs of a child with a hearing loss. The frequencies most important for understanding speech are 500 to 2,000 Hz.

Prevalence

- Students with hearing loss represent about 1.3% of all school-age students receiving special education.

Types and Causes of Hearing Loss

- Hearing loss is described as conductive (outer or middle ear) or sensorineural (inner ear) and unilateral (in one ear) or bilateral (in both ears).
- A prelingual hearing loss occurs before the child has developed speech and language; a postlingual hearing loss occurs after that time.
- Causes of prelingual hearing loss include maternal rubella, heredity, prematurity and complications of pregnancy, and congenital cytomegalovirus (CMV).
- Causes of postlingual hearing loss include meningitis, otitis media, and excessive noise.

Identification and Assessment

- A formal hearing test generates an audiogram, which graphically shows the intensity of the faintest sound an individual can hear 50% of the time at various frequencies.
- Hearing loss is classified as slight, mild, moderate, severe, or profound, depending on the degree of hearing loss.

Effects of Hearing Loss

- Deaf and hard of hearing students leave high school lagging far behind their hearing peers in English literacy and academic achievement.
- Deaf children—especially those with a prelinguistic loss of 90 dB or greater—are at a great disadvantage in acquiring English language skills.
- Many deaf individuals choose membership in the Deaf community and culture.

Educational Approaches

- The oral/aural approach views speech as essential if students are to function in the hearing world; much emphasis is given to amplification, auditory training, speechreading, the use of technological aids, and, above all, talking.
- Total communication uses speech and simultaneous manual communication via signs and fingerspelling in English word order.
- In the bilingual-bicultural approach, deafness is viewed as a cultural and linguistic difference, not a disability, and ASL is used as the language of instruction.

Assistive Listening Devices and Other Support Technologies

- Amplification and auditory training seek to enable students with hearing loss to use their residual hearing more effectively.
- Speechreading can provide useful visual information but has many limitations. Most English sounds cannot be distinguished through vision alone.
- An educational interpreter can help some deaf students participate successfully in the regular classroom.
- Other support technologies used by persons who are deaf or hard of hearing include text telephones, closed television captioning, and a variety of alerting devices.

Educational Placement Alternatives

- Thirty-six percent of children with hearing loss attend regular classrooms, 19% attend resource rooms for part

of the school day, 27% are served in separate classrooms, and 11% go to residential schools.
- All of the professional and parent organizations involved in deaf education have issued position statements strongly in favor of maintaining a continuum of placement options.

Current Issues and Future Trends

- Given the large percentage of children with hearing loss who are educated in regular classrooms for most of the day, it is likely that oral/aural and total communication methods of instruction will continue to be used.
- The bilingual-bicultural approach will probably be used with a growing percentage of the deaf children served in special schools and self-contained classrooms.
- Although technology holds much promise for addressing the communication problems faced by deaf and hard of hearing people, many leaders of the deaf culture do not view deafness as a disability and oppose efforts to "cure" it or make them more like the mainstream hearing culture.
- Access to the language and communication modality best suited to their individual needs and preferences, effective instruction with meaningful curriculum, and self-advocacy are the keys to improving the future for people who are deaf or hard of hearing.

For More Information

Journals

- *American Annals of the Deaf.* Published by the Conference of Educational Administrators Serving the Deaf and the Convention of American Instructors of the Deaf, 814 Thayer Avenue, Silver Spring, MD 20910. Presents articles dealing with education of deaf students and those with hearing loss.
- *Journal of the American Deafness and Rehabilitation Association* (Formerly *Journal of Rehabilitation of the Deaf*), P.O. Box 251554, Little Rock, AR 72225. Focuses on research, innovations, patterns of service, and other topics related to deaf adults.
- *Journal of Deaf Studies and Deaf Education.* Published by Oxford University Press, Great Clarendon Street, Oxford, OX2 6DP, England; website: http://www.oup.co.uk/deafed. Research on cultural, developmental, linguistic, and educational topics related to deaf children and adults.
- *Sign Language Studies.* Published quarterly by Linstok Press, 9306 Mintwood Street, Silver Spring, MD 20901. Contains research and practical articles related to sign language and manual communication.
- *Volta Review.* Published nine times a year by the Alexander Graham Bell Association for the Deaf (see "Organizations"). Encourages teaching of speech, speechreading, and use of residual hearing for deaf persons. Advocates oral approaches.

Books

- Luetke-Stahlman, B., & Luckner, J. (1991). *Effectively educating students with hearing loss.* New York: Longman.
- Mahshie, S. N. (1995). *Educating deaf children bilingually*. Washington, DC: Gallaudet University.
- Marschark, M. (1997). *Raising and educating a deaf child*. New York: Oxford University Press.
- McAnally, P. L., Rose, S., & Quigley, S. P. (1998). *Language learning practices with children who are deaf* (3rd ed.). Austin, TX: PRO-ED.
- Mindel, E. D., & Vernon, M. (1986). *They grow in silence: Understanding deaf children and adults* (2nd ed.). San Diego: College-Hill.
- Moores, D. F. (1996). *Educating the deaf: Psychology, principles, and practices* (4th ed.). Boston: Houghton Mifflin.
- Paul, P. V., & Jackson, D. W. (1993). *Toward a psychology of deafness: Theoretical and empirical perspectives.* Needham Heights, MA: Allyn & Bacon.
- Paul, P. V., & Quigley, S. P. (1990). *Education and deafness.* New York: Longman.
- Paul, P. V., & Quigley, S. P. (1994). *Language and deafness* (2nd ed.). San Diego: College-Hill.
- Ross, M. (Ed.). (1990). *Hearing-impaired children in the mainstream.* Monkton, MD: York.
- Schirmer, B. R. (2000). *Language and literacy development in children who are deaf.* Needham Heights, MA: Allyn & Bacon.
- Van Cleve, J. V. (Ed.). (1986). *Gallaudet encyclopedia of deaf people and deafness.* New York: McGraw-Hill.
- Vernon, M., & Andrews, J. F. (1990). *The psychology of deafness.* New York: Longman.
- Walker, L. A. (1986). *A loss for words: The story of deafness in a family.* New York: Harper & Row.
- Woolsey, M. L. (1998). *Target practice: A teacher's resource for ASL games and activities.* Hillsboro, OR: Butte Publications.

Organizations

- *Alexander Graham Bell Association for the Deaf,* 3417 Volta Place, NW, Washington, DC 20007; phone/TT: (202) 237-5220; website: http://www.agbell.org. Organization for teachers, parents, researchers, and oral deaf adults. Provides brochures, books, software, audiovisual materials, and other information on hearing loss, with an auditory-oral emphasis. Publishes *Volta Review* for professionals, *Our Kids* magazine for parents, and *Newsounds* newsletter.
- *American Society for Deaf Children,* 2848 Arden Way, Suite 210, Sacramento, CA 95825-1373; website: http://www.deafchildren.org. Provides information to families of deaf and hard of hearing children.

- *American Speech-Language-Hearing Association,* 10801 Rockville Pike, Rockville, MD 20852; (800) 638-8255; website: http://www.asha.org/.
- *Gallaudet University,* 800 Florida Avenue, NE, Washington, DC 20002; website: http://www.gallaudet.edu. University's bookstore has one of the most complete collections of professional and popular literature about hearing loss, communication, education, psychology, and related topics. Also has children's sign language books that appeal to many readers. Provides free catalogs of book lists; arranges tours of the Gallaudet campus for visitors.
- *National Association of the Deaf,* 814 Thayer Avenue, Silver Spring, MD 20910; phone/TT: (301) 587-1788; website: http://www.nad.org. A clearinghouse for information about education, employment, legal issues, communication, technological aids, and other topics. Sponsors activities for deaf adults, children, and parents.
- *National Center for Law and the Deaf,* Gallaudet University, 800 Florida Avenue, NE, Washington, DC 20002; phone/TT: (202) 651-5373.
- *National Cued Speech Association,* P.O. Box 31345, Raleigh, NC 27622. Provides information, training, and publications on the cued speech system of identifying sounds and supplementing speechreading skills.
- *National Information Center on Deafness,* Gallaudet University, 800 Florida Avenue, NE, Washington, DC 20002; phone/TT: (800) 672-6720; website: http://www.gallaudet.edu:80/-nicd. Provides information and resource assistance concerning hearing loss.

Websites

- *Deaf Education Website*. Sponsored by the Deaf Education Teacher Preparation Program at Kent State University and the Council on the Education of the Deaf. A central repository of information, resources, and collaborative opportunities focusing on three questions concerning the education of deaf/hard of hearing students: "What should I know?" "What should I teach?" "How should I teach?" www.educ.kent.edu/deafed
- *EDUDEAF Electronic Forum*. To subscribe, send an e-mail message to <listserv@ukcc.uky.edu> with this message: sub EDUDEAF firstname lastname. An internet listserve for discussion of curriculum and instructional issues/strategies that concern teachers of students who are deaf or hard of hearing.
- *Website bibliography*. Simes, K. (1997). World wide web resources for individuals who are deaf or hard of hearing, their families, and the professionals who serve them. *Rural Special Education Quarterly, 16*(2), 44–49. Annotated bibliography of more than 75 websites.

Chapter 11

Blindness and Low Vision

Focus Questions

- In what ways does loss of vision affect learning?
- How does the age at which vision is lost affect the student?
- Normally sighted children enter school with a great deal of knowledge about trees. How can a teacher help the young child who is congenitally blind learn about trees?
- What compensatory skills do students with visual impairment need?
- How do the educational goals and instructional methods for children with low vision differ from those for children who are blind?

Sixteen-year-old Maria is a bright, college-bound student who has been totally blind since birth. She recently took a series of intellectual and psychological tests and performed well, scoring at about her expected age and grade level. Something unusual happened, however, on one of the test items. The examiner handed Maria an unpeeled banana and asked, "What is this?" Maria held the banana and took several guesses but could not answer correctly. The examiner was astonished, as were Maria's teachers and parents. After all, this section of the test was intended for young children. Even though Maria had eaten bananas many times, she had missed out on one important aspect of the banana experience: she had never held and peeled a banana by herself.

This true story (adapted from Swallow, 1978) illustrates the tremendous importance of vision in obtaining information about the world in which we live. Many concepts that children with normal vision seem to acquire almost effortlessly may not be learned at all by children with visual impairments—or may be learned incorrectly—unless someone deliberately teaches them. Teachers who work with children with visual impairments find it necessary to plan and present a great many firsthand experiences, enabling children with visual impairments to learn by doing things for themselves. Good teachers understand, however, that even when a concept is deliberately presented to children with visual impairments, they may not learn it in exactly the same way that children with normal vision would.

This is true because although students with visual impairments may learn to make good use of their other senses (hearing, touch, smell, and taste) as channels for sensory input, they do not totally compensate for loss of vision. Touch and taste cannot tell children much about things that are far away or even just beyond their arms' length. Hearing can tell them a good deal about the near and distant environment, but it seldom provides information that is as complete, continuous, or exact as the information people obtain from seeing their surroundings.

The classroom is one important setting in which vision plays a critical role in learning. For example, in school, normally sighted children are routinely expected to exercise several important visual skills. They must be able to focus on different objects and shift their vision from near to far as needed. They must have good hand-to-eye coordination, maintain visual concentration, discriminate among colors and letters, see and interpret many things simultaneously, and remember what they have seen. Children with visual impairments, however, have deficits in one or more of these abilities. As a result, they need special equipment and/or adaptation in instructional procedures or materials to function effectively in school.

Go to the companion website at http://www.prenhall.com/heward and select Chapter 11 to review the chapter objectives.

Defining Visual Impairment

Unlike other disabilities covered by IDEA, visual impairment has both legal and educational definitions.

Legal Definition of Blindness

The legal definition of blindness is based on visual acuity and field of vision. **Visual acuity**—the ability to clearly distinguish forms or discriminate details at a specified distance—is measured by reading lines of letters, numbers, or other symbols from the Snellen chart. The familiar phrase "20/20 vision" does not, as some people think, mean perfect vision; it simply indicates that at a distance of 20 feet, the eye can see what a normally seeing eye should be able to see at that distance. As the bottom number increases, visual acuity decreases.

Some people, with or without correction, have visual acuity that is better than 20/20. If the vision in one of your eyes is rated as 20/10, for example, you can see from 20 feet what the 20/20 eye must be within 10 feet to see.

A person whose visual acuity is 20/200 or less in the better eye after the best possible correction with glasses or contact lenses is considered **legally blind.** If Jane has 20/200 vision while wearing her glasses, she needs to stand at a distance of 20 feet to see what most people can see from 200 feet away. In other words, Jane must get much closer than normal to see things clearly. Her legal blindness means that she will likely find it difficult to use her vision in many everyday situations. But many children with 20/200, or even 20/400, visual acuity succeed in the regular classroom with special help. Some students' visual acuity is so poor they are unable to perceive fine details at any distance, even while wearing glasses or contact lenses.

A person may also be considered legally blind if his **field of vision** is extremely restricted. When gazing straight ahead, a normal eye is able to see objects within a range of approximately 180 degrees. If David's field of vision is only 10 degrees, he is able to see only a limited area at any one time (even though his visual acuity within that small area may be quite good). Some people with limited fields of vision describe their perceptions as viewing the world through a narrow tube or tunnel; they may have good central vision but poor **peripheral vision** at the outer ranges of the visual field. Conversely, some eye conditions make it impossible for people to see things clearly in the central visual field but allow relatively good peripheral vision.

Whether the visual field impairment is central or peripheral, a person is considered legally blind if she is restricted to an area of 20 degrees or less from the normal 180-degree field. It is common for the visual field to decrease slowly over a period of years and for the decrease to go undetected. A thorough visual examination should always include measurement of the visual field as well as visual acuity.

Children who are legally blind are eligible to receive a wide variety of educational services, materials, and benefits from governmental agencies. They may, for example, obtain Talking Books and playback devices from the Library of Congress. Their schools may be able to buy books and educational materials from the American Printing House for the Blind because the federal quota system allots states and local school districts a certain financial allowance for each legally blind student (Chase, 1986b). A person who is legally blind is also entitled to vocational training, free U.S. mail service, and an additional income tax exemption.

Even though these services and benefits are important to know about, the legal definition of blindness is not especially useful to teachers. Some children who do not meet the criteria for legal blindness have visual impairments severe enough to require special education. Other students, whose visual impairments qualify them as legally blind, have no need for special education services.

Educational Definitions of Visual Impairments

The definition of visual impairments in IDEA is simple and straightforward, emphasizing the relationship between vision and learning: "an impairment in vision that, even with correction, adversely affects a child's educational performance." Students with visual impairments display a wide range of visual abilities—from total blindness to relatively good residual vision. The precise clinical measurements of visual acuity and visual field used to determine legal blindness have limited relevance for educators. Instead, educators classify students with visual impairments based on the extent to which they use vision and/or tactile means for learning (Bishop, 1996; Hazekamp & Huebner, 1989).

- A student who is *totally blind* receives no useful information through the sense of vision and must use tactile and auditory senses for all learning.
- A child who is *functionally blind* has so little vision that she learns primarily through the other senses; however, she may be able to use her limited vision to supplement the information received from auditory and tactile senses and to assist with certain tasks (e.g., moving about the classroom). Most students who are blind use **braille** to read and write. We examine braille later in the chapter.
- A child with **low vision** uses vision as a primary means of learning and generally learns to read print. Students with low vision comprise between 75% and 80% of the school-age visually impaired population (Bryan & Jeffrey, 1982).

To join in the discussion, "In what ways does loss of vision affect learning?" go to the Message Board Module at http://www.prenhall.com/heward.

Age at Onset

Like other disabilities, visual impairment can be congenital (present at birth) or adventitious (acquired). It is useful for a teacher to know the age at which a student acquired a visual impairment. A child who has been blind since birth naturally has quite a different perception of the world than does a child who lost his vision at age 12. The first child has a background of learning through hearing, touch, and the

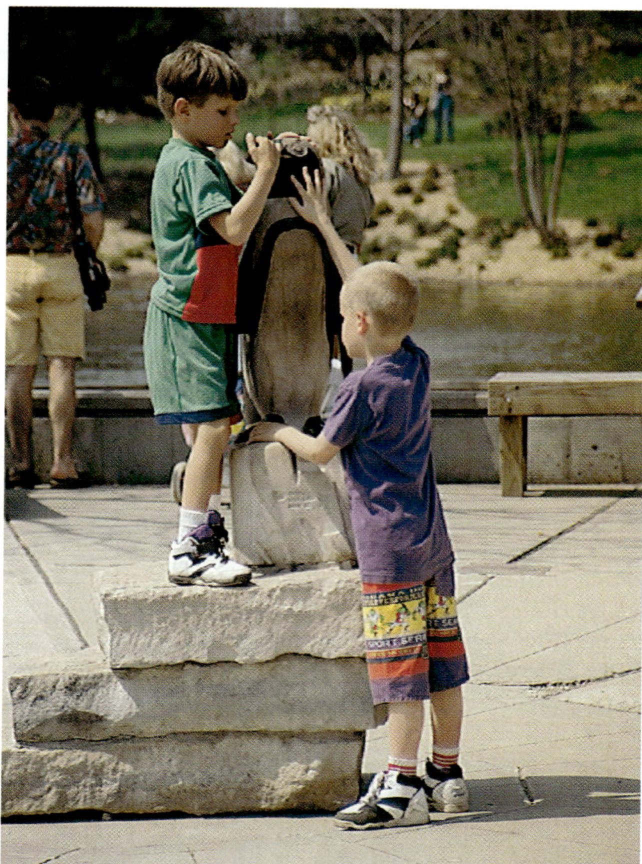

A child who has been blind since birth has a background of learning through hearing, touch, and the other nonvisual senses.

other nonvisual senses, whereas the second child has a large background of visual experiences on which to draw. Most people who are adventitiously blind retain a visual memory of things they formerly saw. This memory can be helpful in a child's education; an adventitiously blind child may, for instance, remember the appearance of colors, maps, and printed letters. At the same time, however, the need for emotional support and acceptance may be greater than that of the congenitally blind child, who does not have to make a sudden adjustment to the loss of vision.

Many persons who have lost their sight report that the biggest difficulty in adapting is dealing with the attitudes and behavior of those around them. Some of those attitudes and behaviors are no doubt influenced by the beliefs, superstitions, and mythology that comprise "the folklore of blindness."

> The influence of the folklore of blindness generally is expressed in attitudes towards (and by) blind people that sound absurd but are genuinely felt. . . . One finds that folk beliefs are divided into two groups. On the negative side of this dichotomy are the beliefs that blind people are either helpless and pathetic or evil and contagious and probably deserve their fate. On the more positive side are the beliefs that blind people have special or even magical abilities, special powers of perception, and deserve special attention. . . . All of us are greatly influenced by what we believe. Irrational beliefs are especially important for a counselor to understand, because they are carried in an idiosyncratic way by each client. An appreciation of superstition and folklore gives the professional a great advantage in understanding the irrational beliefs in both the client and the people he or she must deal with in adapting to the loss of vision. (Wagner-Lampl & Oliver, 1994, pp. 267–268)

Check your ongoing understanding of Chapter 11 concepts by using the Guided Review Module at http://www.prenhall.com/heward.

Prevalence

Children with visual impairments constitute a very small percentage of the school-age population—about 5 children in 10,000. During the 1996–1997 school year, 25,834 children ages 6 to 21 received special education services under IDEA within the category of visual impairments (U.S. Department of Education, 1998). According to Scholl (1986), approximately one-third of the school-age population of students with visual impairments have at least one additional disability. Thus, the total number of students with visual impairments is somewhat higher than the data reported for IDEA because some students with visual impairments are served and counted under other disability categories such as deaf-blindness and multiple disabilities. Still, students with visual impairments make up less than 0.1% of the entire school-age population.

Table 11.1 summarizes key historical events with implications for the education of students with visual impairments.

Even when viewed as a percentage of the population of students who receive special education services, the prevalence of visual impairments is very small: only 0.5% of all school-age children with IEPs are served under the disability category of visual impairments. Educators and parents of children with visual impairments frequently express concern about this low prevalence because they fear that when financial resources are limited, students with visual impairments may not receive adequate services from specially trained teachers. It may be particularly difficult for a local public school to provide comprehensive services for a child with visual impairment who resides in a rural area. Small school districts often cooperate with each other in employing special teachers for students with visual impairments.

Types and Causes of Visual Impairment

The basic function of the eye is to collect visual information from the environment and transmit it to the brain. A simplified diagram of the eye appears in Figure 11.1. The eye is stimulated by light rays reflected from objects in the visual field. In the normal eye, these light rays come to a clear focus on the central part of the **retina.** This multilayered sheet of nerve tissue at the back of the eye has been likened to the film in a camera: for a clear image to be transmitted to the brain, the light rays must come to a precise focus on the retina. The optic nerve is connected to the retina. It conducts visual images to the brain.

In the process of vision, light rays must pass through several structures and substances in the eye itself. Each of these bends the light a little bit to produce the ideal image on the retina. The light first hits the **cornea,** the curved transparent membrane that protects the eye (much as an outer crystal protects a watch face). It then passes through the **aqueous humor,** a watery liquid that fills the front chamber of the eye. Next the light passes through the **pupil,** a circular hole in the center of the colored **iris;** the pupil contracts or expands to regulate the amount of light entering the eye. The light then passes through the **lens,** a transparent, elastic structure suspended by tiny muscles that adjust its thickness so that both the near and far objects can be brought into sharp focus. Finally, the light passes through the **vitreous humor,** a jellylike substance that fills most of the eye's interior. Disturbances of any of these structures can prevent the clear focusing of an image on the retina.

*An **optometrist** specializes in the evaluation and optical correction of refractive errors. An **ophthalmologist** is a physician who specializes in the diagnosis and treatment of eye diseases and conditions.*

Refractive Errors

Refraction is the process of bending light rays when they pass from one transparent structure into another. As just described, the normal eye refracts light rays so that a clear image is perceived on the retina; no special help is needed. However, for many people—perhaps half the general population (Miller, 1979)—the size and shape of the eye prevent refraction from being perfect. That is, the light rays do not focus

Table 11.1 A history of the education of children with visual impairments: Key events and implications

Date	Historical Event	Educational Implications
1784	Shocked at seeing people who were blind performing as jesters or begging on the streets of Paris, Victor Hauy resolved to teach them more dignified ways of earning a living. He started the first school for children who were blind. Hauy's curriculum included reading and writing (using embossed print), music, and vocational skills.	The competence of Hauy's students influenced the establishment of other residential schools in Europe and Russia in the early 19th century.
1821	Samuel Gridley Howe founded the Perkins School for the Blind, the oldest and best-known residential school for students who are blind.	Many methods and materials for teaching students with visual impairments were first developed at Perkins. Anne Sullivan and her famous pupil, Helen Keller, spent several years at Perkins.
Early 1830s	Louis Braille, a young Frenchman who was blind, developed a tactile method of reading using a system of embossed six-dot cells.	Braille's system has proven to be the most efficient method of reading by touch and is still used today.
1862	The Snellen chart was developed by a Dutch ophthalmologist.	The chart provided a fast, standardized test of visual acuity; it is still used today as a visual screening tool for schoolchildren.
1900; 1909⁄1913	The first public school class for children who were blind opened in Chicago; the first classes for children with low vision began in Cleveland and Boston.	Students with visual impairments were educated in public schools; children with low vision were educated in special "sight-saving classes" in which all instruction was conducted orally.
1932	The Library of Congress made Talking Books available to any person who is legally blind.	Availability of recorded books and other print materials enhanced range of curriculum content accessible to students with visual impairments.
1938	The first itinerant teaching program for children with visual impairments attending regular classrooms began in Oakland, California.	This marked the beginning of the long and relatively successful history of including children with visual impairments in regular classrooms.
1940s–1950s	Thousands of children became blind or severely visually impaired by retinopathy of prematurity (ROP) caused by the increased use of oxygen with premature infants.	Residential schools were not able to accommodate the large influx of visually impaired children; thus, special education programs and services for students with visual impairments became much more widely available in the public schools in the 1950s and 60s.
1944	Richard Hoover developed a system for teaching orientation and mobility (O & M) skills to persons with visual impairments. It featured a long white cane.	This system of O&M and the "Hoover cane" become standard parts of the curriculum for students with visual impairments.
1951	The Perkins brailler was invented.	The first fast and easy method for writing braille improved access to and participation in education.
Mid-1960s	Natalie Barraga published research showing that children with low vision do not lose their remaining sight by using it and that visual functioning can be improved by use.	Barraga's (1964, 1970) work was instrumental in ending the sight-saving classes attended by children with low vision for more than 50 years.

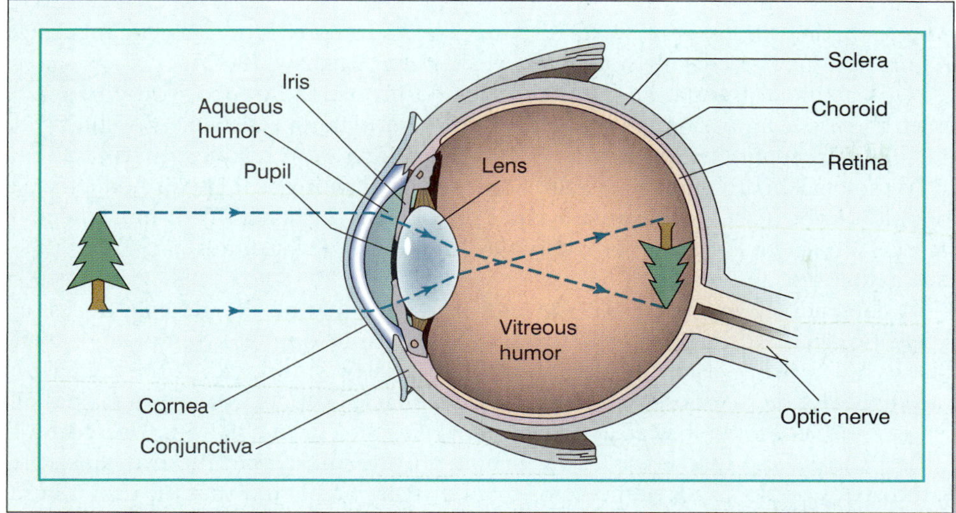

Figure 11.1 Basic parts of the human eye

clearly on the retina. Refractive errors can usually be corrected by glasses or contact lenses, but if severe enough, they can cause permanent visual impairment.

In **myopia,** or nearsightedness, the eye is larger than normal from front to back. The image conducted to the retina is thus somewhat out of focus. A child with myopia can see near objects clearly, but more distant objects, such as a chalkboard or a movie, are blurred or not seen at all. The opposite of myopia is **hyperopia,** commonly called farsightedness. The hyperopic eye is shorter than normal, preventing the light rays from converging on the retina. A child with hyperopia has difficulty seeing near objects clearly but is able to focus well on more distant objects. **Astigmatism** refers to distorted or blurred vision caused by irregularities in the cornea or other surfaces of the eye; both near and distant objects may be out of focus. Glasses or contact lenses can correct many refractive errors by changing the course of light rays to produce as clear a focus as possible.

Other Types of Visual Impairments

Although the most frequently mentioned visual impairments are in visual acuity and field of vision, one's vision may be impaired in several other significant ways. **Ocular motility,** the eye's ability to move, may be hampered. This impairment can cause problems in **binocular vision,** which is the ability of the two eyes to focus on one object and fuse the two images into a single clear image (Ward, 1986). Binocular vision is a complicated process, requiring good vision in each eye, normal eye muscles, and smooth functioning of the coordinating centers of the brain (Miller, 1979).

Several conditions make it difficult or impossible for a child to use the eyes together effectively. **Strabismus** is an inability to focus on the same object with both eyes because of an inward or outward deviation of one or both eyes. If left untreated, strabismus and other disorders of ocular motility can lead to permanent loss of vision. When the two eyes cannot focus simultaneously, the brain avoids a double image by suppressing the visual input from one eye. Thus, the weaker eye (usually the one that turns inward or outward) can actually lose its ability to see. **Amblyopia** refers to this reduction in or loss of vision in the weaker eye from lack of use even though no disease is present. The usual treatment for amblyopia is to place a patch over the stronger eye so that the weaker eye is forced to develop better vision through training and experience. This treatment is most effective if started in early childhood. Eye muscle surgery may also help correct the muscle imbalance and prevent further loss of vision in the weaker eye (Batshaw, 1997).

Other kinds of visual impairments include problems in **accommodation,** in which the eye cannot adjust properly for seeing at different distances. A child with difficulty in accommodation may have trouble shifting from reading a book to looking at the chalkboard and back again. Some children with visual impairments have a condition known as **nystagmus,** a rapid, involuntary back-and-forth movement of the eyes in a lateral, vertical, or rotary direction. Severe nystagmus can cause problems in focusing and reading.

A **cataract** is a cloudiness in the lens of the eye that blocks the light necessary for seeing clearly. Vision may be blurred, distorted, or incomplete. Some people with cataracts liken their vision to looking through a dirty windshield. If the cataract is extremely cloudy or dense, a person may be unable to perceive any details at all. Cataracts are common in older people but may also occur in children. **Glaucoma** is a prevalent disease marked by abnormally high pressure within the eye caused by disturbances or blockages of the fluids that normally circulate within the eye. Central and peripheral vision are impaired or lost entirely when the increased pressure damages the optic nerve. Although glaucoma can be extremely painful in its advanced phase, it frequently goes undetected for long periods, and children may not even be aware of the small, gradual changes in their vision. If detected in its early stages, glaucoma can often be treated successfully with medication or surgery. Figure 11.2 shows how the world might look to someone with cataracts or glaucoma.

Table 11.2 summarizes the most common types and causes of visual impairments. A teacher seldom needs detailed knowledge concerning the etiology of a child's visual impairment, but understanding how a student's particular visual impairment affects classroom performance is important. It is useful to know, for example, that Linda has difficulty reading under strong lights, that Ahmad has only a small amount of central vision in his right eye, or that Yoko sometimes experiences eye pain. Basic knowledge of the conditions described here can help a teacher understand some aspects of a child's learning and behavior and decide when to refer a child for professional vision care.

Figure 11.2 A street scene as it might be viewed by a person with (1) normal vision, (2) cataracts, and (3) advanced glaucoma

Source: From the New York Association for the Blind. *The lighthouse.* New York: Author. Reprinted by permission.

Table 11.2 Types and causes of visual impairments

Condition	Definition/Outcome
Myopia	Nearsightedness; can see near objects clearly, but more distant objects are blurred or not seen at all
Hyperopia	Farsightedness; difficulty seeing near objects clearly but able to focus well on more distant objects
Astigmatism	Distorted or blurred vision caused by irregularities in the cornea or other surfaces of the eye; images on retina not in equal focus
Strabismus	Inability to focus on the same object with both eyes because of an inward or outward deviation of one or both eyes
Amblyopia	Reduction in or loss of vision in the weaker eye from lack of use, even though no disease is present
Nystagmus	Rapid, involuntary back-and-forth movement of the eyes, which makes it difficult to focus on objects
Albinism	Lack of pigmentation in the eyes, skin, and hair; results in moderate to severe visual impairment by reducing visual acuity and causing nystagmus; children with albinism almost always have **photophobia**, a condition in which one's eyes are extremely sensitive to light
Deficient color vision	Difficulty distinguishing certain colors; red-green confusion is most common; usually not an educationally significant visual impairment
Cataract	Cloudiness in the lens of the eye; causes vision to be blurred, distorted, or incomplete; common in older people but may also occur in children
Glaucoma	Abnormally high pressure within the eye due to disturbances or blockages of the fluids that normally circulate within the eye; vision is impaired or lost entirely when the increased pressure damages the retina and optic nerve
Diabetic retinopathy	Individuals with diabetes frequently have impaired vision as a result of hemorrhages and the growth of new blood vessels in the area of the retina; the leading cause of blindness for people ages 20 to 64
Retinitis pigmentosa (RP)	The most common genetic disease of the eye; causes gradual degeneration of the retina; first symptom is usually difficulty seeing at night, followed by loss of peripheral vision
Macular degeneration	Central area of the retina gradually deteriorates, causing loss of clear vision in the center of the visual field and making tasks such as reading and writing difficult; common in older adults but fairly rare in children
Retinopathy of prematurity (ROP)	Caused by administering high levels of oxygen to at-risk infants; when the infants are later removed from the oxygen-rich incubators, the change in oxygen levels can produce an abnormally dense growth of blood vessels and scar tissue in the eyes, leading to visual impairment and often total blindness; formerly called **retrolental fibroplasia**

Go to the Resources Module for Chapter 11 at http://www.prenhall.com/heward. Click on Special Ed Resource Page and link to "multimedia/assistive technology" to review or find additional ideas for technology to assist students with vision impairments.

Bender (1994) describes how individuals who are blind can learn to identify birds in the field by developing their listening skills.

Educational Approaches

Special Adaptations for Students Who Are Blind

Blindness imposes significant obstacles to learning. Because they must frequently teach skills and concepts that most children acquire through vision, teachers of students who are blind must plan and carry out activities that will help their students gain as much information as possible through the nonvisual senses and by participation in active, practical experiences. For example, a blind child may hear a bird singing but get no concrete idea of the bird itself from this sound alone. A teacher interested in teaching such a student about birds might plan a series of activities that have the student touch birds of various species and manipulate related objects such as eggs, nests, and feathers. The student might assume the responsibility for feeding a pet bird at home or in the classroom. Through such experiences, the child with visual impairments can gradually obtain a more thorough and accurate knowledge of birds than she could if her education were limited to reading books about birds, memorizing vocabulary, or feeling plastic models.

Tactile Aids and Manipulatives Manipulatives are generally recognized as effective tools in teaching beginning mathematics skills to elementary students (Parham, 1983). When using most manipulatives, such as Cuisenaire rods, however, sighted students use length and color to distinguish the various numerical values of the rods. Belcastro (1989) has developed a set of rods that enables students who are blind to quickly identify different values by feeling the lengths and tactile markings associated with each number.

Another mathematical aid for students who are blind is the Cranmer abacus. Long used in Japan, the abacus has been adapted to assist students who are blind in learning number concepts and making calculations. Manipulation of the abacus beads is particularly useful in counting, adding, and subtracting.

For more advanced mathematical functions, the student is likely to use the Speech-Plus talking calculator, a small electronic instrument that performs most of the operations of any standard calculator. It "talks" by voicing entries and results aloud and also presents them visually in digital form. This is only one of many instances in which the recent development of synthetic speech technology has helpful implications for people who are blind. Talking clocks and spelling aids are also available.

In the sciences and social studies, several adaptations encourage students who are blind to use their tactile and auditory senses for firsthand manipulation and discovery. Examples are embossed relief maps and diagrams, three-dimensional models, and electronic probes that give an audible signal in response to light. Curriculum

There are virtually no limits to the kinds of activities in which students with visual impairments can participate. This spelunker is totally blind.

modification projects, such as MAVIS (Materials Adaptation for Students with Visual Impairments in the Social Studies) and SAVI (Science Activities for the Visually Impaired), emphasize how students with visual impairments can, with some modifications, participate in learning activities along with normally sighted students.

Technological Aids for Reading Print The Optacon (optical-to-tactile converter) is a small, hand-held electronic device that converts regular print into a readable vibrating form. The Optacon does not convert print into braille but into a configuration of raised pins representing the letter the camera is viewing. When the tiny camera of the Optacon is held over a printed "E," for example, the user feels on the tip of one finger a vertical line and three horizontal lines. Although extensive training and practice are required, many children and adults who are blind are able to read regular print effectively with the aid of the Optacon. The Optacon II enables the user to scan print on computer screens.

The Kurzweil Personal Reader is another technological development with exciting implications for individuals with visual impairments and other disabilities. This sophisticated computer uses an *optical character recognition* (OCR) system that scans and reads printed text with a synthetic voice. The user can regulate the speed (up to 350 words per minute) and tone of the voice and can even have the machine spell out words letter by letter if desired. The "intelligence" of the Kurzweil Personal Reader is constantly being improved, and the machines are currently in use at most residential schools and also in many public school programs, public libraries, rehabilitation centers, and colleges and universities. The first Kurzweil Reading Machine weighed more than 300 pounds and cost $50,000, but the most recent model, Kurzweil Personal Reader/PC, which can be used with a personal computer to convert print to speech, is much smaller and sells for about $4,000.

Although the cost of some assistive technology, such as the Optacon or Kurzweil Personal Reader, is prohibitive for many people, low-interest loans and financial assistance can sometimes be arranged (Uslan, 1992).

Computer Access Assistive technology that provides access to personal computers offers tremendous opportunities for the education, employment, communication, and leisure enjoyment of individuals with visual impairments. These devices fall into two basic categories (Schreier, Leventhal, & Uslan, 1991): (1) devices that magnify screen images through specialized hardware or software and (2) computer screen-access systems that use speech recognition software to enable the user to tell the computer what to do.

Keyboarding is an important means of communication between children who are blind and their sighted classmates and teachers and is also a useful skill for further education and employment. Instruction in keyboarding should begin as early as feasible in the child's school program. Today, handwriting is seldom taught to students who are totally blind, with the noteworthy exception of learning to sign one's name in order to assume responsibilities such as maintaining a bank account, registering to vote, and applying for a job.

The Braille System Braille is the primary means of literacy for people who are blind. Braille is a tactile system of reading and writing in which letters, words, numbers, and other systems are made from arrangements of raised dots (see Figure 11.3). In some ways, braille is like the shorthand that secretaries use. Abbreviations, called *contractions,* help save space and permit faster reading and writing. For example, when the letter "r" stands by itself, it means "rather." The word "myself" in braille is written "myf." Frequently used words, such as "the," "and," "with," and "for," have their own special contractions. For example, the "and" symbol ⠯ appears four times in the following sentence:

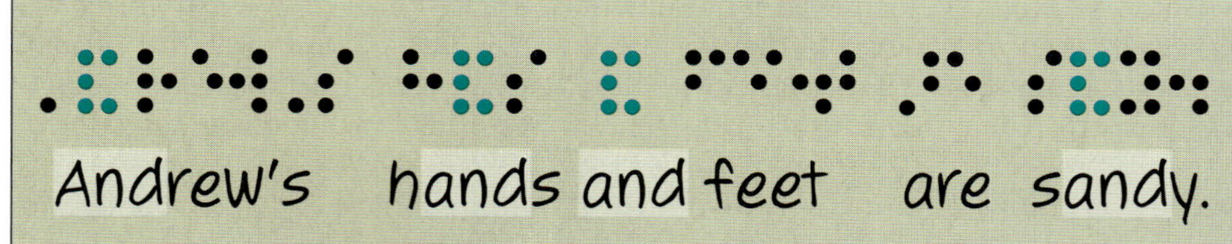

McComiskey (1996) describes a braille readiness grid designed to help early childhood special educators identify skills and activities that will foster enthusiasm for reading and learning braille in preschoolers with visual impairments. Pester (1993) makes recommendations for braille instruction for individuals who are blind adventitiously.

Students who are blind can read braille much more rapidly than they could the raised letters of the standard alphabet. The speed of braille reading varies a great deal from student to student; however, it is almost always much slower (about 100 words per minute for good braille readers) than the speed of print reading. Most children who are blind are introduced to braille at about the first-grade level. The majority of teachers introduce contractions early in the program rather than have the child learn to write out every word, letter by letter, and later unlearn this approach. Of course, it is important for the child who is blind to know the full and correct spelling of words even if every letter does not appear separately in braille. It usually takes several years for children to become thoroughly familiar with the system and its rules.

Young children generally learn to write braille by using a *brailler,* a six-keyed device that somewhat resembles a typewriter. Older students are usually introduced to the slate and stylus, in which the braille dots are punched out one at a time by hand, from right to left. The slate-and-stylus method has certain advantages in note taking; for example, it is much smaller and quieter than the brailler.

Braille Technological Aides Most braille books are large, expensive, and cumbersome. It can be difficult for students to retrieve information quickly when they must tactually review many pages of braille books or notes. Recent technological developments are making braille more efficient, thus enabling many students who are blind to function more independently in regular classrooms, universities, and employment settings. One system, known as VersaBraille II+ (made by Telesensory System, Inc.), is a portable laptop computer on which students can take notes and tests in class and prepare assignments and papers at home. The keyboard has six keys that correspond to the dots in a braille cell, a numeric keypad, and a joystick.

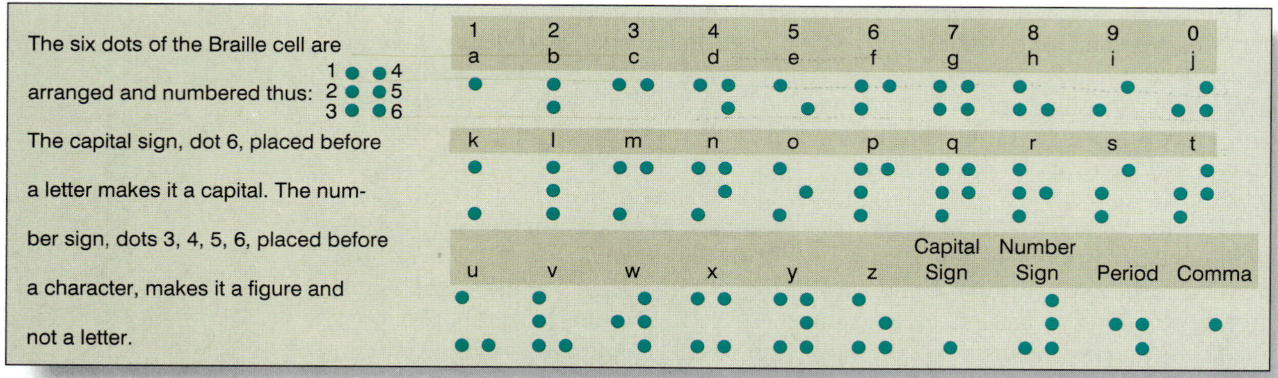

Figure 11.3 The braille system for representing numbers and letters
Source: From the Division for the Blind and Physically Handicapped, Library of Congress, Washington, DC.

Students can check their work by reading a dynamic tactile display on the top of the VersaBraille II+ consisting of 20 braille cells, each made up of small pins that move up and down as the text progresses. Students store their work on a 3.5-inch floppy disk that can be used with a talking word-processing program such as the BRAILLE-EDIT Xpress (BEX) or to produce standard English print copies for teachers to read. A printer by Ohtsuki produces pages with both braille and print formats, enabling both blind and sighted readers to use the same copy.

Declining Braille Literacy The vast majority of employed adults who are blind use braille at work, and research shows that congenitally blind adults who learn to read braille have higher employment rates, educational levels, and income and spend more time reading than those who learn to read print (Ryles, 1996). Nevertheless, there has been a nationwide decline in braille literacy over the years (Wittenstein, 1994). In comparison to the early 1960s, when it was estimated that nearly half of blind students could read and write braille, a national census found that only 10% of legally blind students in grades K through 12 are braille readers (American Printing House for the Blind, 1992). Visual readers, students who primarily use regular or large-print materials, made up the largest group (27%), with 10% being auditory readers, who use recorded or taped materials or are read to aloud. Nonreaders (31%)—students with visual impairments with additional severe disabilities—and prereaders (22%) made up the rest of the student population.

In response to the concern over declining braille literacy, the 1997 amendments to IDEA specified for the first time that IEP teams for students with visual impairments make a determination of the student's preferred reading medium and that instruction in braille must be considered. In addition, at least 27 states have passed legislation, called "braille bills," making braille equipment and instruction available for students if the parents or any other member of the IEP team indicates it is needed and requiring teachers of students with visual impairments to be proficient in braille.

Teachers can determine the most appropriate reading medium for students with visual impairments by conducting the Learning Media Assessment (Koenig & Holbrook, 1993).

Special Adaptations for Students with Low Vision

The great majority of children enrolled in educational programs for visually impaired students have some potentially useful vision. Their learning need not be restricted to touch, hearing, and other nonvisual senses. Corn (1989) believes that curriculum development and instructional planning should be guided by some basic premises about low vision and its effects on a person:

- *Those with congenital low vision view themselves as whole; they do not have remaining or residual vision.* Although it may be proper to speak of residual vision in reference to those who experience adventitious low vision, those with congenital low vision do not have a normal vision reference. They view the world with all of the vision they have ever had.

The brailler is a six-keyed device that punches the raised braille dots in special paper.

- *Those with low vision generally view the environment as stationary and clear.* Although there are exceptions, it is a misconception that people with low vision live in an impressionistic world in which they are continuously wanting to clear the image.
- *Low vision offers a different aesthetic experience.* Low vision may alter an aesthetic experience, but it does not necessarily produce a lesser one.
- *20/20 acuity is not needed for most tasks or for orientation and mobility within most environments.*
- *Clinical measurements do not dictate visual functioning.* Such measurements only provide a ballpark in which to anticipate visual functioning.
- *Those with low vision can enhance visual functioning through the use of optical aids, nonoptical aids, environmental modifications, and/or techniques.*
- *The use of low vision is not in all circumstances the most efficient or preferred method of functioning.* For some individuals or tasks, the use of vision alone or in combination with other senses may reduce one's ability to perform. For example, using vision while pouring salt on food may not be the most efficient method for determining how much salt has been poured.
- *Low vision has unique psychological aspects.* Those with low vision have life experiences not encountered by those without such a condition.
- *Those who have low vision may develop a sense of visual beauty, enjoy their visual abilities, and use vision to learn.*

Visual Functioning **Visual efficiency** and *functional vision* are related terms denoting how well a person uses whatever vision he has. Visual efficiency, as defined by Barraga (1983), includes skills such as controlling eye movements, adapting to the visual environment, paying attention to visual stimuli, and processing visual information rapidly. Corn (1989) defines functional vision as the "visual ability sufficient for utilizing visual information in the planning and execution of a task" (p. 28). Visual efficiency and functional vision cannot be determined by measuring a child's visual acuity or visual field, nor can it be predicted. Some children with severe visual impairments use what vision they have very capably. Other children with relatively minor visual impairments are unable to function as visual learners; they may even behave as though they were blind.

Barraga's Program to Develop Efficiency in Visual Functioning *is available from the American Printing House for the Blind.*

Research has shown that structured programs of visual assessment, training, and evaluation can dramatically improve these abilities and that the earlier in life that such programs begin, the more likely they are to be successful (Corn, 1986; Fellows, Leguire, Rogers, & Bremer, 1986; Ferrell, 1985). The fundamental premise in developing visual efficiency is that children learn to see and must be actively involved in using their own vision. Merely furnishing a classroom with attractive things for children to see is not sufficient. A child with low vision may, without training, be unable to derive much meaningful information through vision. Forms may be perceived as vague masses and shapeless, indistinct blobs. Systematic training in visual recognition and discrimination has helped many children learn to use their visual impressions intelligently and effectively, to make sense out of what they see.

Downing and Bailey (1990) stress the importance of teaching the basic visual skills of attending, localizing, tracking, shifting gaze, scanning, and reaching (moving) toward an object within functional activities for the individual. For example, instead of having the child with low vision practice her visual skills by sorting miscellaneous junk objects, she could use those skills while learning to make a fruit and ice cream drink. Instruction in use of vision skills should not be limited to isolated time periods but incorporated into all parts of the low-vision student's curriculum. For example, a child learning daily living skills might be encouraged to use his vision to identify and reach for his toothbrush.

Corn (1989) suggests that instructional activities in a program for the use of low vision should be based on four goals related to the question "For what purposes do we use vision?"

- *To gain information from directed visual experience.* A 4-year-old child may be asked to count the number of egg yolks in a bowl to see if more are needed to follow a recipe, or a 3-year-old may be asked to repeat a dance step that has been demonstrated.
- *To gain information from incidental visual experiences.* A 12-year-old may notice the symbol of a plumbing company on a truck outside a friend's home and infer that there may be a plumbing problem in the house.
- *To gain an appreciation of visual experiences.* A child may select a video game to play for the enjoyment of watching the target move about the screen.
- *To use vision for the planning or execution of a task.* An adult may observe visually a narrow passage and determine whether it will be necessary to turn her body sideways to go through the opening. Through instruction, she may be able to enhance her ability to use visual observations to plan or execute the task. (adapted from Corn, 1989, pp. 26-38)

Children whose vision is extremely limited are more likely to use monocular (one-eye) than binocular (two-eye) aids, especially for seeing things at a distance. For suggestions to help children become accustomed to their optical aids, see "Helping the Student with Low Vision" later in the chapter.

Optical Devices Today, many ophthalmologists, optometrists, and clinical facilities specialize in the assessment and treatment of low vision. A professional examination can help determine which types of optical aids, if any, can benefit a particular child with low vision. These special devices might include glasses and contact lenses, small hand-held telescopes, and magnifiers placed on top of printed pages. Such aids cannot give normal vision to children with visual impairments but may help them perform better at certain tasks, such as reading small print or seeing distant objects.

Optical aids are usually specialized rather than all-purpose. Juanita might, for example, use her glasses for reading large print, a magnifier stand for reading smaller print, and a monocular (one-eye) telescope for viewing the chalkboard. A usual disadvantage of corrective lenses and magnifiers is that the more powerful they are, the more they tend to distort or restrict the peripheral field of vision. Some field-widening lenses and devices are now available for students with limited visual fields. These

Most optical aids are designed for special purposes. Brock uses his monocular telescope for distance viewing.

include prisms and fish-eye lenses designed to make objects appear smaller so that a greater area can be perceived on the unimpaired portions of a student's visual field. It is usually a good idea to furnish optical aids on a trial or loan basis so that the student can gradually learn to use and evaluate them in natural settings. A follow-up session should then be scheduled.

Closed-circuit television systems are used in some classrooms to enable students with low vision to read regular-sized printed materials. These systems usually include a sliding table on which a book is placed, a television camera with a zoom lens mounted above the book, and a television monitor nearby. The student is able to adjust the size, brightness, and contrast of the material and can select either an ordinary black-on-white image or a negative white-on-black image, which many students prefer. The teacher may also have a television monitor that lets him see the student's work without making repeated trips to the student's desk. A disadvantage of closed-circuit television systems is that they are usually not portable, so the student who uses television as a primary reading medium is largely restricted to the specially equipped classroom or library.

Reading Print Materials Students with low vision use three basic approaches for reading print: (1) *approach magnification* (reducing the distance between the eye and the page of print from 40 cm to 5 cm results in 8x magnification) (Jose, 1983), (2) *lenses* (optical devices), and (3) *large print* (Corn & Ryser, 1989). Large print was first introduced in the Cleveland Public Schools in 1913 in the form of 36-point "clear face" type (Eakin & McFarland, 1960).

Many books and other materials are available in large print for children with low vision. The American Printing House for the Blind produces books in 18-point type. Some states and other organizations produce large-type materials, but the size and style of the print fonts, spacing, paper, and quality of production vary widely. The sentence you are reading now is set in 10-point type. Here are four examples of different large-print type sizes:

This is 14 point type.
This is 18 point type.
This is 20 point type.
This is 24 point type.

Although print size is an important variable, other equally important factors to consider are the quality of the printed material, the contrast between print and page, the spacing between lines, and the illumination of the setting in which the child reads. It is generally agreed that a child with visual impairments should use the smallest print size that she can read comfortably. A child may be able to transfer from large print to smaller print as reading efficiency increases, just as most normally sighted children do.

Table 11.3 compares the advantages and disadvantages of large-print materials and optical devices.

A significant number of children with low vision are able to learn to read using regular-sized print with or without the use of optical aids. This permits a much wider variety of materials and eliminates the added cost of obtaining large-print books or enlarging texts with special duplicating machines. Corn and Ryser (1989) obtained information from the teachers of 399 students with low vision on variables such as reading speed and achievement, fatigue, and access to various materials. They concluded that, in most instances, reading regular print with an optical device is preferable to large-print materials:

Large-Print Materials	Optical Devices
Advantages	**Advantages**
• Little or no instruction is needed to use a large-print book or other materials. • A low vision clinical evaluation is not needed. • Students carry large-print books like other students carry books in their classes. • Funds for large-print books come from school districts that may require parental or other funding for optical devices.	• Users have access to materials of various sizes, such as regular texts, newspapers, menus, and maps. • Optical devices have a lower cost per child than large-print materials do. • Devices are lighter weight and more portable than large-print materials are. • There is no ordering or waiting time for production or availability. • Users have access to distant print and objects, such as chalkboards, signs, and people.
Disadvantages	**Disadvantages**
• Fewer words can be seen at once; large-print materials are more difficult to read smoothly with a natural sweep of eye movements. • Enlarging print by photocopy emphasizes imperfect letters. • Pictures are in black, white, and shades of gray. • Fractions, labels on diagrams, maps, and so forth are enlarged to a print size smaller than 18-point type. • The size and weight of large-print texts make them difficult to handle. • Large-print materials are not readily available after the school years, and students may be nonfunctional readers with regular-size type.	• A low vision clinical evaluation must be obtained for the prescription of optical devices. • Funding for clinical evaluation and optical devices must be obtained. • Instruction in the use of the optical devices is needed • The cosmetics of optical devices may cause self-consciousness. • Optical problems associated with the optics of devices need to be tolerated.

Table 11.3 Large-print materials and optical devices: Advantages and disadvantages

Source: A. Corn & G. Ryser, "Access to Print for Students with Low Vision." *Journal of Visual Impairment & Blindness, 83:* 340–349. Reprinted with permission from American Foundation for the Blind, 15 West 16th St., New York, NY 10011.

> The use of optical devices (for those who can benefit from them) should be viewed as the least restrictive approach to gain access to all regular-print materials for near and distance tasks. The receipt of a prescription for a telescopic device gives the student access to chalkboards, signs, and events in the distance. . . . optical devices are individualized educational tools and are just as important to a child with a low vision as is a brace to a child with a physical handicap or a hearing aid to a hearing-impaired child. (pp. 348–349)

Some students with low vision who read print are also taught to read braille, especially if their visual acuity is expected to decrease because of a degenerative eye condition (Holbrook & Koenig, 1992).

Other Classroom Modifications Other classroom adaptations for students with low vision are often minor but can be very important. Many students benefit from desks with adjustable or tilting tops so that they can read and write at close range without constantly bending over and casting a shadow. Most regular classrooms have adequate lighting, but special lamps may still be helpful for some children. Writing

Helping the Student with Low Vision

What does a child with low vision actually see? It is difficult for us to know. We can obtain some idea of total blindness by wearing a blindfold, but the majority of children with visual impairments are not totally blind. Even when two children share the same cause of visual impairment, it is unlikely that they see things in exactly the same way. And each child may see things differently at different times. We asked a few people with low vision to describe how they see. Here are some excerpts from what they told us.

> Have you ever been out camping in a strange place? When it's dark and you're trying to find your way from the tent to the bathroom, and you can't wear your glasses or contact lenses—that's like the way I see. I'm pretty much nearsighted. I can see a far object, I mean I know the image is there, but I can't distinguish it. I can see a house. It is just a white blob out there. I couldn't tell you what color is the roof trim, or where the windows are.
>
> Put on a pair of sunglasses. Then rub Vaseline all around the central part of each lens. Now try reading a book. Or crossing a street. I never see blackness. . . . If I am looking at a picture, it's not like I see a hole in the middle. I fill something in there, but it wouldn't necessarily be what is really there. That's how I describe it to people—take a newspaper, hold it up, and look straight ahead. Now describe what you see here, off to the side . . . that's what I see all the time. (Orlansky & Heward, 1981, p. 11)

Suggestions for Teachers The following suggestions for teachers of students with low vision are from the Vision Team, a group of specialists in visual impairment who work with regular class teachers in 13 school districts in Hennepin County, Minnesota.

- Using the eyes does not harm them. The more children use their eyes, the greater their efficiency will be.
- Holding printed material close to the eyes may be the child with low vision's way of seeing best. It will not harm the eyes.
- Although eyes cannot be strained from use, a child with low vision's eyes may tire more quickly. A change of focus or activity helps.
- Copying is often a problem for children with low vision. The child may need a shortened assignment or more time to do classwork.
- It is helpful if the teacher verbalizes as much as possible while writing on the chalkboard or using the overhead projector.
- Some children with low vision use large-print books, but many do not. As the child learns to use vision, it becomes more efficient, and the student can generally read smaller print.
- The term *legally blind* does not mean educationally blind. Most children who are legally blind function educationally as sighted children.
- Contrast, print style, and spacing can be more important than the size of the print.
- One of the most important things a child with low vision learns in school is to accept the responsibility of seeking help when necessary rather than waiting for someone to offer help.
- In evaluating quality of work and applying discipline, the teacher best helps the child with low vision by using the same standards that are used with other children.

Using Low-Vision Aids Children who have low-vision aids, such as special eyeglasses, magnifiers, and telescopes, may need instruction and assistance in learning how to use them most effectively. Here are some tips for children to help them become accustomed to low-vision aids:

- *Low-vision aids take time to get used to.* At first, it seems like just a lot more things to take care of and carry around, but each aid you have will help you with a special job of seeing. You will get better with practice. In time, reaching for your telescope to read the chalkboard will seem as natural as picking up a pencil or pen to write. It's all a matter of practice.
- *Lighting is very important.* Always work with the most effective light for you. It makes a big difference in how clear things will look. Some magnifiers come with a built-in light, but most times you will have to use another light. A desk lamp is best. (The overhead light casts a shadow on your book or paper as you get close enough to see it.) Be sure the light is along your side, coming over your shoulder.
- *Be sure to keep your aids clean.* Dust, dirt, and fingerprints are hard to see through. Clean the lenses with a clean, soft cloth (never paper). If you have contact lenses, clean them with a special solution, following

your doctor's instructions carefully. Always be sure your hands are clean to begin with.

- *Keep your aids in their cases when you are not using them.* They will be more protected and always ready for you to take with you wherever you go.
- *Carry your low-vision aids with you.* Most of them are small and lightweight. In that way, you will have them when you need them. If you have aids you use only at school, you may want to ask your teacher to keep them in a safe place for you.
- *Experiment in new situations.* Can you see the menu at McDonald's? Watch the football game? See prices on toys? Find your friend's house number? The more often you use your low-vision aid, the better you will get at using it.
- *Try out different combinations of aids with and without your glasses or contact lenses.* In this way, you will find the combination that works best for you.

Source: Tips for using low-vision aids from Dean, M. *A Closer Look at Low Vision Aids.* Connecticut State Board of Education and Services for the Blind, Division of Children's Services, 170 Ridge Road, Wethersfield, CT 06109. Reprinted by permission.

Low vision aids should be portable and easy to use.

paper should have a dull finish to reduce glare; an off-white color such as buff or ivory is generally better than white. Worksheets photocopied on colored paper can be difficult for students with low vision to use; if needed, an aide or classmate could first go over the worksheet with a dark pen or marker. Some teachers have found it helpful to give students with low vision chairs with wheels so that they can easily move around the chalkboard area or other places in the classroom where instruction is taking place without constantly getting up and down. A teacher can make many other modifications, using common sense and considering the needs of the individual student with low vision.

Gellhaus and Olson (1993) offer numerous suggestions for using color and contrast to improve the educational environment of students with visual impairments with multiple disabilities.

Listening

Children with visual impairments—those who are blind and those with low vision—must obtain an enormous amount of information by listening. They do not automatically develop the ability to listen effectively, nor do they necessarily listen better than their normally sighted peers do. Therefore, systematic development of listening skills is an important component of the educational program of virtually every child with visual impairments.

Listening involves attending to and being aware of sounds, discriminating differences in sounds, and assigning meaning to sound (Heinze, 1986). Good listening skills

These students with visual impairments at a residential school are reading print materials in various large-size type.

Recorded books and magazines and the equipment to use them can be obtained through the Library of Congress, the American Printing House for the Blind, the Canadian National Institute for the Blind, Recordings for the Blind, and various other organizations, usually on a free-loan basis. Each state has a designated library that provides books and materials for blind readers.

broaden a student's vocabulary and support the development of speaking, reading, and writing abilities. Learning-to-listen activities can take an almost unlimited variety of forms. Young children, for example, might learn to discriminate between sounds that are near and far, loud and soft, high-pitched and low-pitched. A teacher might introduce a new word into a sentence and ask the child to identify it. Older students might learn to listen for important details while there are distracting background noises, to differentiate between factual and fictional material, or to respond to verbal analogy questions. Some structured programs for developing listening skills have been developed (Alber, 1974; Stocker, 1973; Swallow & Conner, 1982).

Students with visual impairments make frequent use of recorded materials, particularly in high school. Because many students with visual impairments are able to process auditory information at a faster rate than that of average conversational speech, devices are available to increase the playback rate of tapes without significantly distorting the quality of the speech. The ever-increasing use of synthetic speech equipment means that listening skills will likely become even more important in the future to students with visual impairments. Rhyne (1982) investigated the ability of students who are blind to comprehend synthetic speech; he found that the aural (listening) mode was a generally efficient way to learn and that students' comprehension increased as they gained more experience listening to synthetic speech.

To find out how three secondary students who are blind used tape-recorded prompts to learn to prepare some of their favorite snack foods, see "I Made It Myself, and It's Good!" later in this chapter.

Daily Living and Social Skills

The special education teacher, the regular class teacher, other specialists, the parents, and the student should all participate in planning and providing instruction that will be practical and relevant to the student's current needs and future objectives. Some educators of students with visual impairments are concerned that academic achievement has traditionally been overemphasized at the expense of basic living skills. Specific instruction in skills such as cooking, grooming, shopping, financial management, decision making, recreational activities, personal hygiene, and social behavior will facilitate a student's eventual independence as an adult.

Reviews of the literature on social skills of children with visual impairments indicate that, compared with children with normal sight, they interact less during free time and are often delayed in the development of social skills (Erin, Dignan, & Brown, 1991; Skellenger, Hill, & Hill, 1992). Some young children with sensory impairments experience difficulty in receiving and expressing affection, behaviors that have been shown to facilitate future development in other areas of social competence (Compton & Niemeyer, 1994). Although many adolescents with visual impairments have best friends, many also struggle with social isolation and must work harder than their sighted peers to make and maintain friendships (Rosenblum, 1997; Wolffe & Sacks, 1997).

Don't be afraid to use words such as "look" and "see" when talking with a person who is blind. Individuals with visual impairments use these words too.

One explanation of these differences may be that children with visual impairments are not able to see the social signals given by others and, as a result, are less likely to engage in reciprocal interactions (Rugow, 1984). If necessary, students with visual impairments should also be taught how to deal with strangers, how to interpret and explain their visual impairments to other people, and how to make socially acceptable gestures in conversation. One study of 89 school-age children with visual impairments across 19 states found that only 34% of the children could correctly identify their visual impairment and that only 13% could state which part of their eye was affected (Sacks & Corn, 1996).

Huebner (1986) provides an excellent set of guidelines for teaching social skills. She emphasizes the importance of developing socially acceptable behaviors, which in turn facilitate independence, self-confidence, and acceptance by others in school, community, and employment settings. Even though a child with visual impairment may perform a task safely and independently, he may not do so in a traditional, socially acceptable manner—for example, the child who likes to eat oatmeal by scooping it up to her mouth with her fingers!

Some individuals with visual impairments engage in repetitive body movements or other behaviors, such as body rocking, eye rubbing, hand waving, and head weaving. These behaviors were traditionally referred to in the visual impairment literature as "blindisms" or "blind mannerisms." **Stereotypic behavior (stereotypy)** is a more clearly defined term that subsumes blindisms and mannerisms. It is also a more appropriate term: such behaviors are also exhibited by other children and do not occur among all children who are blind (Gense & Gense, 1994).

Pava (1994) conducted a national survey of 161 women and men with visual impairments to assess their perceived vulnerability to sexual and physical assault. Although women respondents perceived themselves to be at more risk for assault than men, one in three of all respondents reported having been targets of attempted or actual assault at some point in their lives. A curriculum of rape prevention and self-defense training has been developed for women with visual impairments (Pava, Bateman, Appleton, & Glascock, 1991).

Although not necessarily harmful, stereotypic behavior can place a person with visual impairments at a social disadvantage because these actions are conspicuous and may call negative attention to the person. It is not known why many children with visual impairments engage in stereotypic behaviors. However, various behavioral interventions have been used to help individuals with visual impairments reduce stereotypic behaviors such as repetitive body rocking (McAdam, O'Cleirigh, & Cuvo, 1993), head drooping during conversation (Raver, 1984), and off-task behaviors that interfere with learning (Barton & LaGrow, 1985).

Human Sexuality

Sighted children typically learn a great deal about human sexuality through vision. They see people establish social and sexual relationships with each other; they can see their own and others' bodies. Children who are blind, however, may grow up with serious knowledge gaps or misconceptions about sexuality and reproduction, particularly if parents and teachers fail to provide information and explanations. "I know girls have breasts," an adolescent who is blind told his counselor, "but I don't know where they are!" (Elliott, 1979).

In some European countries, live human models are used to familiarize students who are blind with anatomy and sexuality, but this practice has not been widely

I Made It Myself, and It's Good!

For special education to contribute to meaningful lifestyle changes for students, it must help them gain functional skills for postschool environments. Being able to prepare one's own food is a critical skill for independent living. Steve, Lisa, and Carl were 17 to 21 years old and enrolled in a class for students with multiple disabilities at a residential school for the blind. They were living in an on-campus apartment used to teach daily living skills. Several unsuccessful attempts had been made to teach basic cooking skills to the three. None possessed any functional vision or braille skills, and their IQ scores ranged from 64 to 72 on the Perkins Binet Test of Intelligence for the Blind.

To learn new skills, especially those involving long chains of responses such as following the steps of a recipe, students like Steve, Lisa, and Carl require intensive instruction over many trials. Once a skill is learned, its generalization to other settings and situations (e.g., another recipe) and maintenance across time (so that two weeks later the student won't have forgotten) are often lacking. The challenge was to discover a method for teaching cooking skills that would be effective initially but also would enable the students to prepare recipes for which they had not received instruction and that resulted in long-term maintenance of their new skills.

A "Walkman Cookbook" Because Steve, Lisa, and Carl were blind, it was not possible to use picture cookbooks or color-coded recipes, which have been used successfully with learners with mental retardation and other disabilities (Book, Paul, Gwalla-Ogisi, & Test, 1990; Johnson & Cuvo, 1981). Instead, tape-recorded recipes were used. Each student wore a cooking apron on which two pockets had been sewn. One pocket at the waist held a small tape recorder; the second pocket, located at the chest, held a switch that the students pushed to turn the tape player on and off. Each step from the task-analyzed recipes was prerecorded in sequence on a cassette tape. ("Open the bag of cake mix by tearing it at the tab.") A beep signaled the end of each direction.

Performance Measures The number of steps from each recipe that each student independently completed was measured during preinstruction (baseline), instruction, and maintenance phases. To assess generalization, probes were conducted on two classes of recipes on which the students received no training. *Simple generality* recipes could be prepared with the same set of cooking skills learned in a related trained item. *Complex generality* recipes required the use of skills learned in two different trained recipes. The relationship between the trained recipes and the two types of recipes used to assess generality is shown in Figure A. As a measure of social validity, each trial was also scored as to whether the food prepared was edible.

Baseline To objectively assess whether learning has occurred, student performance must be measured before instruction begins. The first baseline trial was conducted without the tape-recorded recipes to determine which food preparation steps, if any, each student could already perform without any assistance or adaptive equipment. It was then necessary to find out whether the students could successfully prepare the food items if they were simply given the tape-

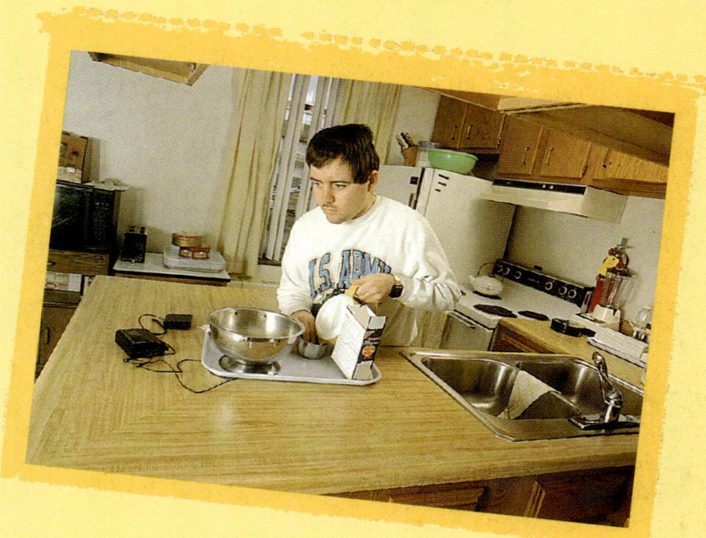

Steve has learned to accurately pour and measure the milk for his cake by placing his fingers in the bowl.

Figure A

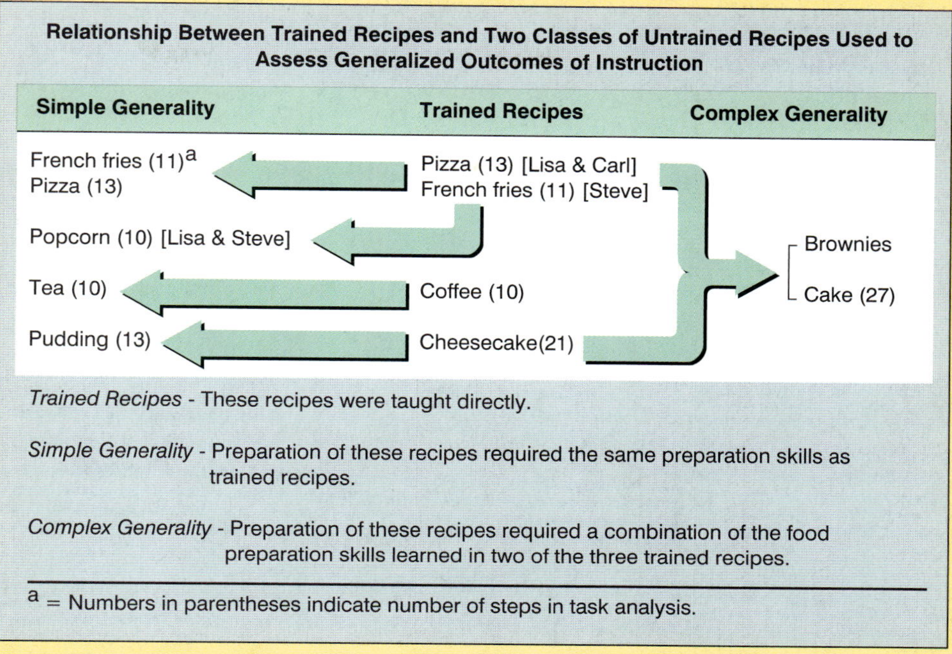

recorded recipes. After being shown how to operate the tape recorder to play back the instructions, each student was asked to prepare each recipe but was given no other prompts, assistance, or feedback.

Relationship Between Trained Recipes and Two Classes of Untrained Recipes Used to Assess Generalized Outcomes of Instruction
Simple Generality
Trained Recipes
Complex Generality
French fries (11)a
Pizza (13)
Pizza (13) [Lisa & Carl]
French fries (11) [Steve]
Popcorn (10) [Lisa & Steve]
Brownies
Tea (10)
Coffee (10)
Cake (27)
Pudding (13)
Cheesecake(21)
Trained Recipes - These recipes were taught directly.
Simple Generality - Preparation of these recipes required the same preparation skills as trained recipes.
Complex Generality - Preparation of these recipes required a combination of the food preparation skills learned in two of the three trained recipes.
a = Numbers in parentheses indicate number of steps in task analysis.

Instruction Students were told that the taped recipes told them exactly what to do and where to find the food items and utensils. They practiced using the remote switch to control the rate of instructions by stopping the tape each time they heard a beep. Training for each step of the task analysis consisted of a three-component least-to-most prompt hierarchy (verbal, physical, and hand-over-hand guidance) following errors and verbal praise for correct responses. Training on a recipe continued until a student correctly performed all steps on two consecutive trials over two sessions.

Results Lisa, Carl, and Steve needed a total of 12, 19, and 35 instructional trials, respectively, to learn the three different recipes. (Steve required a high number of trials to master the coffee and cheesecake recipes due to repeated spills when pouring liquids. This problem was solved by teaching Steve to use his fingers to feel where and how much liquid he was pouring.) Additionally, after they had mastered the trained items, each student was able to prepare both the simple and the complex generality food items with tape-recorded recipes, even though they had not received direct training on those recipes.

The ultimate evaluation measure of cooking skills instruction is whether or not the food prepared can be eaten. A mistake on any one of several crucial steps in the 27-step task analysis for making microwave cake (e.g., not stirring the egg into the batter) would result in a cake no one would want to eat. Before training, none of Steve's 13 attempts to make any of the trained items could be eaten, whereas all 6 of his post-training attempts were edible. Before he learned how to prepare the related items, Steve was unsuccessful in all 20 of his attempts to make the simple generality recipes and on each of 4 attempts to prepare the complex generality recipes. After learning how to make the related items, he was able to follow tape-recorded recipes to successfully prepare the recipes for which he had received no direct training: on 82% of the trials (9 out of 11) with the simple generality recipes and on all 3 trials with the complex generality recipes. In follow-up probes conducted 6 weeks and 4 months after the study ended, Steve was still able to prepare each of the food items successfully. Lisa and Carl showed similar gains in their ability to prepare food for themselves.

Individualized, Normalized, and Self-Determined A self-operated audio prompting system (also see Briggs et al., 1990; Davis, Brady, Williams, & Burta, 1992; Grossi, 1998; Mechling & Gast, 1997; "The Idea Bunny" in Chapter 5) offers several advantages. First, the prerecorded prompts can be individualized for each student—for example:

- Tape-recorded instructions can be as precise or general as necessary, depending on known or probable tasks and environments.
- Vocabulary can be modified, pacing of instructions speeded up or slowed down, and instructions for particularly difficult steps repeated or given in more detail.
- Students might use their own voice to record special prompts or reminders relevant to certain steps of the task (e.g., "Have I checked for spills?").
- Verbal praise and encouragement from teachers, parents, friends, or the student himself could also be included in the instructions.

Second, individuals with disabilities are currently using a variety of assistive devices to increase their independence in domestic, community, and employment settings. Some assistive devices, however, may not be used by the learner in natural settings. A student in a crowded restaurant, for example, may hesitate to remove a laminated ordering card from her pocket or purse because it marks her as different. By contrast, the popularity of Walkman-like personal stereos enables the wearer of audio headphones to listen to a series of self-delivered prompts in a private, unobtrusive, and normalized manner that does not impose on or bother others.

The self-operated feature of the system puts the student in control of the environment, thereby increasing the probability of independent functioning and level of self-determination. As Carl remarked when sharing with his girlfriend the microwave cake he had just made, "I made it myself, and it's good!"

Source: Adapted from Trask-Tyler, S. A., Grossi, T. A., & Heward, W. L. (1994). Teaching young adults with developmental disabilities and visual impairments to use tape-recorded recipes: Acquisition, generalization, and maintenance of cooking skills. *Journal of Behavioral Education, 4,* 283–311. Used by permission.

adopted in North America. In addition to providing accurate biological information, instructional programs should also consider the emotional aspects of sexual experience and possible genetic implications: some kinds of visual impairment can be passed from parents to children.

Issues in Assessment

There is a continuing concern about the use (and possible misuse) of intelligence tests with children with visual impairments. Intelligence tests, standardized on sighted children, are often based largely on visual concepts. They may include questions such as "Why do people have hedges around their homes?" or "What should you do if you see a train approaching a broken track?" The results of these tests may well give an inaccurate picture of the abilities and needs of a child with visual impairments. Regrettably, many children with visual impairments have been placed in inappropriate educational programs because of strict reliance on standardized test performance.

Helpful reviews of assessment procedures and guidelines for appropriate use of tests with children with visual impairments have been provided by Bradley-Johnson and Harris (1990); Chase (1986a, 1986b); and Hall, Scholl, and Swallow (1986). A number of instruments, though not specifically designed for students with visual impairments, may nevertheless be useful in assessing certain aspects of performance. In gathering information that will be helpful in developing educational goals for a child with visual impairment, a variety of formal and informal procedures should be used. The results of any developmental or intelligence test—for all children—should always be supplemented by careful observations of the child's behavior in school and play situations. Teachers and parents are usually in the best position to observe the child's communication, exploration, and social interaction over an extended period. Their contributions should play a major part in planning the educational program of a child with visual impairments.

Orientation and Mobility

Orientation and mobility (O&M) instruction is a well-developed subspecialty in the education and rehabilitation of individuals who are blind and visually impaired. **Orientation** is the ability to establish one's position in relation to the environment through the use of the remaining senses. **Mobility** is the ability to move safely and efficiently from one point to another (Lowenfeld, 1973). Instruction in orientation and mobility is considered a related service by IDEA and is included in the IEP of virtually all children with significant visual impairments.

For most students, more time and effort are spent in orientation training than in learning specific mobility techniques. It is extremely important that, from an early age, children with visual impairments be taught basic concepts that will familiarize them with their own bodies and their surroundings. For example, they must be taught that the place where the leg bends is called a "knee" and that rooms have walls, doors, windows, corners, and ceilings.

In some states, O&M specialists are called peripatologists.

Many specific techniques are involved in teaching students with visual impairments to understand their environment and maneuver through it effectively. Training in such skills should be given by qualified *O&M specialists.* The Association for Education and Rehabilitation of the Blind and Visually Impaired, the professional organization that certifies O&M specialists, also recognizes the important role of O&M assistants (Wiener et al., 1990). The *O&M assistant* is a paid employee who provides selected O&M services under the direction and supervision of a certified O&M specialist.

The long cane is the most widely used device for adults with severe visual impairments who travel independently (Jacobson, 1993). The traveler does not tap the cane but sweeps it lightly in an arc while walking to gain information about the path ahead.

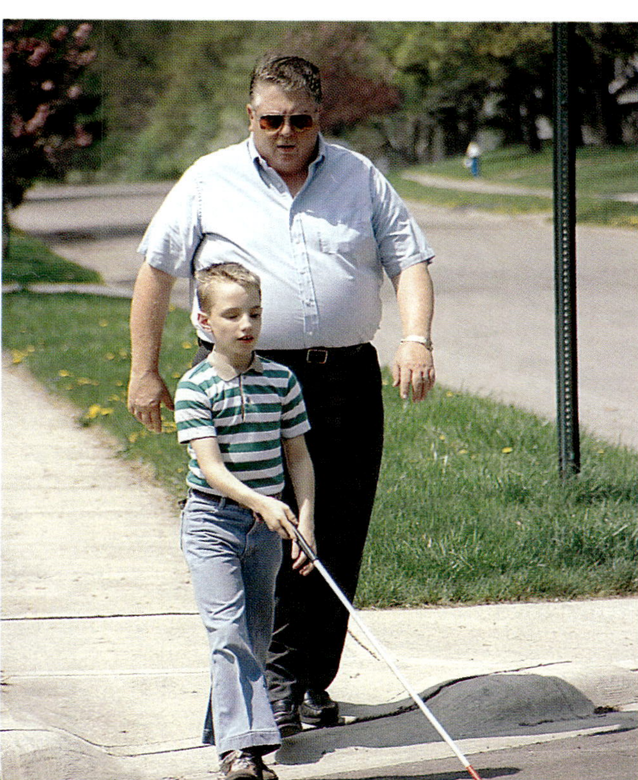

Under the watchful eyes of an orientation and mobility specialist, Matthew is learning how to gain information about the path ahead by sweeping his cane in an arc.

Although the long cane is a relatively simple and sturdy piece of equipment, it takes a beating during training and everyday use. In anticipation of "the inevitable need to repair canes," O&M specialist Tom Langham (1993) always carries a tool kit that includes items such as pliers, hacksaw, pipe cutter, Allen wrenches, red and white reflective tape, wax, and a bent coat hanger.

Clarke (1988) describes a large number of mobility devices for preschoolers with visual impairments and multiple disabilities. She also provides a checklist by which parents, teachers, and O&M specialists can compare and evaluate the relative advantages and disadvantages of the different devices.

Sighted people must realize that guide dogs are not pets but working companions for their owners (Ulrey, 1994). Don't pet a guide dog without first seeking the owner's permission. Don't take hold of the dog's harness as this might confuse the dog and the owner.

Properly used, the cane serves as both a bumper and a probe. It acts as a bumper by protecting the body from obstacles such as parking meters and doors; it is also a probe to detect in advance things such as drop-offs or changes in travel surface (e.g., from grass to concrete or from a rug to a wooden floor).

Even though mastery of cane skills can do much to increase a person's independence and self-esteem, cane use exacts physical effort and poses certain disadvantages (Gitlin, Mount, Lucas, Weirich, & Gramberg, 1997; Tuttle, 1984). The cane cannot detect overhanging obstacles such as tree branches and provides only fragmentary information about the environment, particularly if the person who is blind is in new or unfamiliar surroundings. Unfortunately, many adventitiously blinded persons do not begin learning cane travel skills until one to two years after losing their sight; they mention concern about acceptance by others and the negative stigmas they believe are associated with the cane (Wainapel, 1989).

Until recently, formal O&M instruction, especially for cane use, was seldom given to children younger than about 12 years of age; however, the importance of early development of travel skills and related concepts is now generally recognized (Pogrund & Rosen, 1989). Today, it is not at all unusual for preschool children to benefit from the services of an O&M specialist, but there is disagreement over which, if any, mobility device is most suitable for initial use by very young children (Dykes, 1992). Professionals recognize the long cane's benefits of increased protection and confidence while traveling but question whether preschoolers can handle the motor and conceptual demands of long cane use. These concerns have led to the development of a variety of alternative mobility devices, including modified and smaller canes such as the Connecticut precane (Foy, Von Scheden, & Waiculonis, 1992) and the kiddy cane (Pogrund, Fazzi, & Schreier, 1993).

In an experimental comparison of long cane and precane use by preschoolers, Clarke, Sainato, and Ward (1994) found that the children "were capable of learning to use the long cane . . . for protection with a respectable degree of skill" (p. 29) but that children used the precane device more appropriately overall. This study demonstrates the importance of providing young children with direct, systematic instruction in cane skills. Although the precane has been touted by some as requiring little or no instruction for use (Foy et al., 1992), Clarke et al. (1994) noted the children in their study showed little understanding of the function or use of the device before training: they would drag it behind them, bang it up and down on the floor, or wear it looped around their necks.

A small percentage of people with visual impairments (less than 2%) travel with the aid of guide dogs (Hill, 1986). Like the cane traveler, the guide dog user must have good O&M skills to select a route and to be aware of the environment. The dog wears a special harness and has been trained to follow several basic verbal commands, to provide protection against obstacles, and to ensure the traveler's safety; guide dogs do not take a person where they want to go. Guide dogs are especially helpful when a person must travel over complicated or unpredictable routes, as in large cities. Several weeks of intensive training at special guide dog agencies are required before the person and the dog can work together effectively. They are not usually available to children under 16 years of age or to people with multiple disabilities. Young children, however, should have exposure to and positive experiences with dogs so they are comfortable with them and can make informed choices later about the possibilities of working with a guide dog (Young, 1997).

Most people who are blind find it necessary to rely occasionally on the assistance of others. The *sighted guide technique* is a simple method of helping a person with visual impairments to travel:

- When offering assistance to a person who is blind, speak in a normal tone of voice and ask directly, "May I help you?" This helps the person locate you.
- Do not grab the arm or body of the person who is blind. Permit him to take your arm.
- The person with visual impairment should lightly grasp the sighted person's arm just above the elbow and walk half a step behind in a natural manner.
- The sighted person should walk at a normal pace, describing curbs or other obstacles and hesitating slightly before going up or down. Never pull or push a person who is blind when you are serving as a sighted guide.
- Do not try to push a person who is blind into a chair. Simply place his hand on the back of the chair, and the person will seat himself.

When students with visual impairments attend regular classes, it may be a good idea for one of the students and the O&M specialist to demonstrate the sighted guide technique to classmates. To promote independent travel, however, overreliance on the sighted guide technique should be discouraged once the student has learned to get around the classroom and school.

Several recently developed electronic travel aids may facilitate orientation and independent travel for individuals with visual impairments. These include a laser beam cane, which emits a sound to signal objects in the traveler's path as well as hazards overhead and drop-offs below. Other devices, designed for use in conjunction with a standard cane or guide dog, send out sound waves to bounce off objects and give the trained traveler information about the environment through auditory or tactual channels. Electronic travel aids have even been used with blind infants as young as 6 months in an attempt to enhance their early learning and awareness by enabling them to explore their environment more thoroughly and independently (Ferrell, 1984). Disadvantages of electronic travel aids include high cost, the extensive training required, and possible problems in adverse weather conditions. Hill and Jacobson (1985) note that users of electronic travel aids found them helpful in orienting themselves to new settings but tended to use the aids less after they had become familiar with the environment.

Whatever the preferred method of travel, most students with visual impairments can generally learn to negotiate familiar places, such as school and home, on their own. Many students with visual impairments can benefit from learning to use a systematic method for obtaining travel information and assistance with street crossing (Florence & LaGrow, 1989; LaGrow & Mulder, 1989). Good orientation and mobility skills have many positive effects. A child with visual impairment who can travel independently is likely to develop more physical and social skills and more self-confidence than a child who must continually depend on other people to get around. Good travel skills also expand a student's opportunities for employment and independent living.

Educational Placement Alternatives

There are virtually no limits on the extent to which a child with visual impairments may participate in a full, well-rounded school program. Educators should ensure that a visually impaired student's IEP "includes the full range of instructional areas: those studied with nonhandicapped peers, those that require special instruction, and those outside of the school curriculum that are essential to enable them to compete with their nonhandicapped peers when they move into the adult world" (Scholl, 1987, p. 36).

Go to the Resources Module for Chapter 11 at http://www.prenhall.com/heward. Click on Special Ed Resource Page and link to "teacher resources." Find and adapt a lesson plan for a student with low vision.

Public Schools

In the past, most children with severe visual impairments were educated in residential schools for children. Today, however, two out of three children with visual impairments receive at least some of their education in regular school classrooms: 48% of all school-age students with visual impairments are members of regular classes, and 21% attend resource rooms for part of each day (U.S. Department of Education, 1998). Separate classrooms in public schools serve another 17% of the school-age population of children with visual impairments.

Most students with visual impairments who are included in general education classrooms receive support from *itinerant teacher-consultants,* sometimes called *vision specialists*. These specially trained teachers may be employed by the school district, a nearby residential school, or a regional, state, or provincial education agency. Although their roles and caseloads vary widely from program to program, most itinerant teacher-consultants are expected to assume some or all of the following responsibilities (Flener, 1993; Willoughby & Duffy, 1989):

- Collaboratively develop with the regular classroom teacher curricular and instructional modifications according to the child's individual needs
- Provide direct instruction on compensatory skills to the student with visual impairments (e.g., listening, typing skills)
- Obtain or prepare specialized learning materials
- Adapt reading assignments and other materials into braille, large-print, or tape-recorded form or arrange for readers
- Make referrals for low-vision aids services; train students in the use and care of low-vision aids
- Interpret information about the child's visual impairment and visual functioning to other educators and parents
- Help plan the child's educational goals, initiate and maintain contact with various agencies, and keep records of services provided
- Consult with the child's parents and other teachers

The itinerant teacher-consultant may or may not provide instruction in orientation and mobility. Some schools, particularly in rural areas, employ dually certified teachers who are also O&M specialists. Other schools employ one teacher for educational support and another for O&M training. Students on an itinerant teacher's caseload may range from infants to young adults and may include children who are blind, those with low vision, and students with multiple disabilities.

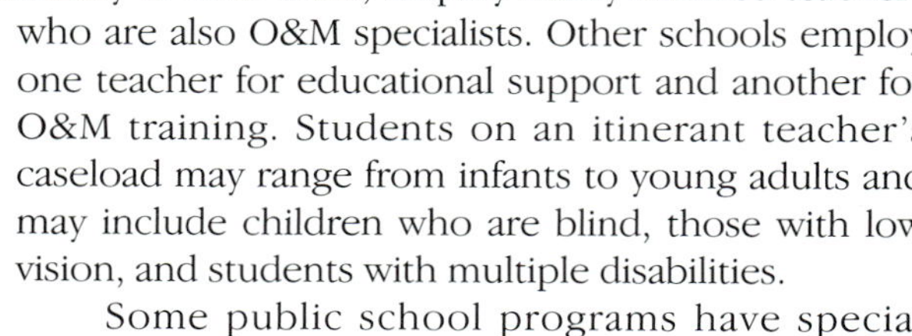

Some public school programs have special resource rooms for students with visual impairments. In contrast with the itinerant teacher-consultant, who travels from school to school, the resource room

Patrick is getting along fine in the regular classroom—thanks to the instructional adaptations jointly planned by his itinerant vision specialist and his classroom teacher.

teacher remains in one specially equipped location and serves students with visual impairments for part of the school day. Usually, only large school districts have resource rooms for students with visual impairments.

The amount of time the itinerant teacher-consultant or resource room teacher spends with a visually impaired student who attends regular classes varies considerably. Some students may be seen every day because they require a great deal of specialized assistance. Others may be seen weekly, monthly, or even less frequently because they are able to function well in the regular class with less support.

To find out how teachers and sighted classmates supported the inclusion of a young child with visual impairment in a community-based preschool, see "Including Ryan."

Inclusive education for students with visual impairments has many advocates. McIntire (1985) writes that "the least restrictive environment for children who are blind is in the local public school regular classroom with nonhandicapped children" (p. 163). Cruickshank (1986) maintains that "the blind child is perhaps the easiest exceptional child to integrate into a regular grade in the public schools" (p. 104). To make inclusion successful, however, a full program of appropriate educational and related services must be provided (Curry & Hatlen, 1988). As Griffing (1986) observes, "no category of handicap requires greater coordination and cooperation among resources than the area of the blind and visually impaired" (p. 5). The key person in the program for a child with visual impairments is the regular classroom teacher. An extensive study of the elements of successful mainstreaming of children with visual impairments in public school classes found that the single most important factor was the regular classroom teacher's flexibility (Bishop, 1986). Other aspects of the school situation found to be highly important were peer acceptance and interaction, availability of support personnel, and adequate access to special supplies and equipment.

Residential Schools

See Chapter 13 for information on children with multiple disabilities, including those who are deaf-blind.

About 9% of school-age children with visual impairments attend residential schools (U.S. Department of Education, 1998). Residential schools continue to meet the needs of a sizable number of children with visual impairments. The current population of residential schools consists largely of children with visual impairments with additional disabilities, such as mental retardation, hearing impairment, behavioral disorders, and cerebral palsy. Some parents are not able to care for their children adequately at home; others prefer the greater concentration of specialized personnel, facilities, and services that the residential school usually offers.

Parents and educators who support residential schools for children with visual impairments frequently point to the leadership that such schools have provided over a long period, with their "wealth and broad range of expertise" (Miller, 1985, p. 160). These supporters argue that a residential school can be the least restrictive environment for some students with visual impairments and multiple disabilities. A follow-up study of students with visual impairments at a state school for the blind found that parents, local education agencies, and the students themselves generally considered the residential school placement to have been appropriate and beneficial (Livingston-White, Utter, & Woodard, 1985). Among the advantages cited were specialized curriculum and equipment, participation in extracurricular activities, individualized instruction, small classes, and improved self-esteem.

The June 1993 issue of the Journal of Visual Impairment and Blindness *is devoted to residential schools.*

Placement in a residential school program need not be regarded as permanent. Many children with visual impairments move from residential schools into public schools (or vice versa) as their needs change. Some students in residential schools attend nearby public schools for part of the school day. Most residential schools encourage parent involvement and have recreational programs that bring students with

Including Ryan: Using Natural Supports to Make Inclusion Natural

Including young children with disabilities in preschool classrooms with their nondisabled peers is widely recognized as a critical component of early childhood special education services. Although efforts have been made to establish more natural preschool settings to accommodate children with disabilities throughout the country, parents of children with visual impairments often have few choices of general early childhood programs that will provide the necessary supports and services for their children. In practice, however, the kinds of inclusive supports of most value are those that are common sense, casual, and unobtrusive. Elizabeth Erwin describes how classroom staff and sighted peers made effective use of natural supports with Ryan, a 3-year-old boy with visual impairments, to facilitate his membership and meaningful participation in a community-based preschool.

The preschool teacher, teacher aides, and Ryan's sighted classmates supported his membership and active participation in the most natural ways possible. We defined *natural supports* as assistance intended to create connections, competence, or teamwork in unobtrusive and individualized ways that lead to the achievement of a task or the provision of important contextual input about the environment. Equally important was acceptance by adults and classmates of the unique adaptive strategies that Ryan used to accomplish tasks and negotiate the classroom environment.

Adult Interventions All three adults in the classroom (the classroom teacher; Kima, the full-time assistant; and Dan, a part-time assistant) provided supports for Ryan in several ways.

Contextual cues. They provided him with frequent and consistent information about the environment and ongoing activities. For example, during snack time, Dan told Ryan, "I put your cup in front of you but not on the place mat. The other kids have it that way, so if the mat moves, the cup won't fall over." When Ryan and four classmates were at the sand table, Kima sat behind Ryan providing verbal information: "You have to put more in your cup; it is still empty." or "Keep your hand inside the table; otherwise, the sand will fall on the floor. Feel the difference?"

Although Kima's responsibilities were to provide assistance to all of the children in the class, she frequently furnished Ryan with information about her physical location. For example, she would alert Ryan that she was returning to or leaving the room or the immediate area and give him contextual information about others in the vicinity (e.g., "Ryan, Sue and Melissa are sitting here.").

Spontaneous events. The staff took advantage of naturally occurring spontaneous events to promote learning and help Ryan make connections between pieces of information that other children acquired visually. For example, during show and tell, Ryan stood in front of the circle with the teacher and answered her questions about the Barney doll he had brought in that day. Toward the end of Ryan's turn, the teacher asked Laurie to come up and stand close to Ryan. She then asked Ryan to look at Laurie's shirt and tell the group what was on it. Ryan bent down and touched Laurie's shirt with his nose because he was so close to her. Then he exclaimed, "It's Barney!" The teacher made a big deal about the fact that the same Barney that Ryan had brought in was also on Laurie's shirt. Ryan and the other children got a big kick out of the coincidence.

Detailed verbal directions and explanations. The adults supported Ryan's independence by providing detailed explanations on how he could accomplish tasks. For example, when Ryan finished painting, the teacher told him, "Walk over to the rug, and when you feel the rug you'll see a bright yellow toy in front of you." Ryan followed the instruction and walked cautiously to the rug. He was a little bent over as if he was looking at the ground for cues. When he found the rug, he sat down to play with the yellow toy.

Simple verbal cues and prompts. Ryan usually needed explicit instructions or a demonstration only when learning a new behavior. After that, the adults used simple verbal cues to help him anticipate what might be happening next. For example, when another song began, Kima provided prompts like "Don't forget: elbows next." or "Now comes the tricky part." Ryan independently carried out the approximate body movements that corresponded to the song.

Physical cues. Physical cues were a natural means to give Ryan specific input about how to carry out a task or activity. He really seemed to like music time. He had a big smile on his face as he moved his body to the music. Kima used physical prompts like positioning his hands straight out in front of him as the song indicated. Once she showed him, he was able to perform the movement correctly and independently the next time the song was played.

Peer Supports Ryan's peers were another viable and natural source of information about and assistance in the environment. At the beginning of the school year, the children did not offer support frequently or spontaneously. Kima said: "At the beginning, they wouldn't come close to Ryan. His movements were a little different at times, and they would just watch him. Eventually, they understood that Ryan was putting his face right into theirs, and I would say this is this person or that person. Now, most of them will say, 'It's me, Ken,' or 'I'm Ronnie.'"

The children did not usually identify themselves to other classmates, but they seemed to recognize that this way of sharing information was useful to Ryan. They also realized that Ryan gained access to certain types of information or needed assistance in ways that might be different from theirs. For example, during show and tell it was Sue's turn to show a toy to the group. She first gave the toy to Ryan. Hillary, who was seated next to Ryan, learned closer to him and guided his hands over the toy, purposely showing him the knobs and buttons.

At other times, the adults orchestrated encounters between Ryan and his classmates to promote positive social and communicative interactions and to reduce the amount of adult intervention. For example, during transitions Kima often enlisted the help of classmates: "I will often say, 'Cathy, can you take Ryan's hand and bring him to the rug?' The children know right away that they need to bring him through a clear path. I have noticed that they don't run him into a chair. They seem to love to do this. He loves it, too. Ryan will take someone's hand and say, 'Well, hi there,' and start a conversation."

Ryan's Adaptive Strategies To compensate for his visual impairment, Ryan used a variety of adaptive strategies that enabled him to move freely within the classroom and gain access to information. His father described one such strategy: "Ryan becomes physically close to people because that is his means of really figuring out what they are doing. He doesn't know how to regard other people's physical space, and he will have to learn that. Right now, he comes very close to other children, and I think that scares them a little bit." Ryan also maintained close physical proximity when he explored objects in his immediate environment. The classroom staff was cognizant of his need to use this distinctive strategy that his sighted peers did not use, and they never discouraged him from bringing objects close to his face or reprimanded him for standing close to others.

The ability to travel independently and make choices were age appropriate and meaningful preschool tasks that Ryan, like his preschool classmates, needed to learn. The difference was in the way the children accomplished those goals. Ryan used familiar landmarks and signals in the classroom to orient himself, which fostered his independent mobility within the environment. Kima said: "He leads himself by touching everything. Lonie [Ryan's vision specialist] told us that he can find the light in the window, so we fostered that right from the beginning. Ryan uses the light from the window to know where the rug is. Also, he can feel the difference when he is on the floor and when he is on the rug. So he can go over and find his toys on the shelf by using the window and rug as guides."

Ryan also used verbal skills to gain information available to his classmates by vision. Kima said: "He will walk over to a group of children, and he always uses his words. If he asks a question, he will not always get an answer. But he will go over and, rather than just join in, say, 'What are you doing?' 'Who are you?' or 'What have you guys got?'"

Source: Adapted from Erwin, E. J. (1996). Meaningful participation in early childhood general education using natural supports. *Journal of Visual Impairment and Blindness, 90,* 400–411. Used by permission.

visual impairments into contact with sighted peers. Independent living skills and vocational training are important parts of the program at virtually all residential schools.

In several states, there is close cooperation between public school and residential school programs that serve children with visual impairments. A residential school for students who are blind has an opportunity to work closely with consumers, parents, professionals, and funding agencies in developing a wide array of community-based services. Cooperative working relationships and creative short- and long-term planning efforts have the potential to generate positive and reality-based services that respond to present-day needs within the context of community integration. Residential schools—primarily because of the expertise of their staff but also because of their location, centralization of resources, and availability of facilities—have the potential to become responsive resource centers on regional and state levels.

Residential schools have long played an important role in training teachers of children with visual impairments on both a preservice and in-service basis. The residential school is usually well equipped to serve as a resource center for instructional materials and as a place where students with visual impairments can receive specialized evaluation services. An increasing number of residential schools now offer short-term training to students with visual impairments who attend regular public schools. One example is a summer workshop emphasizing braille, mobility, and vocational training.

Current Issues and Future Trends

Children with visual impairments constitute a very small portion of the school-age population, but they have many unique needs. Although the current trend toward inclusion of children with visual impairments into regular public school classrooms is generally welcomed, some educators caution against wholesale placement of children with visual impairments in regular schools without adequate support. Many vision professionals tend to resist noncategorical special education programs for students with visual impairments. It is unrealistic, they argue, to expect regular teachers or teachers trained in other areas of special education to be competent in specialized techniques such as braille, orientation and mobility, and visual efficiency.

Specialization of Services

Although financial restrictions may require some public school and residential school programs for children with visual impairments to close down or to consolidate with programs for children with other disabilities, strong support exists for the continuation of highly specialized services. It is likely that both public school and state-run residential programs for children with visual impairments will continue to operate well into the future, occasionally challenging each other for the privilege of serving the relatively small number of available students. The results of this competition may well prove favorable if both types of schools are encouraged to improve the quality of their educational services.

Technology and Research

New technological and biomedical developments will continue to aid students with visual impairments, particularly in the areas of mobility, communication, and use of low vision. In the future, it may even be possible to provide a form of artificial sight to some people who are totally blind by implanting electrodes into the brain and connecting them to a miniature television camera built into an artificial eye. Research in artificial sight is in the early experimental stages but has much promise. Other systems of electronic vision substitution rely on tactile images projected onto an area of the body, such as the back or abdomen, which enable the person who is blind to perceive a visionlike sensation.

Use the self-tests at http://www.prenhall.com/heward to assess your knowledge of the content of Chapter 11.

Fighting against Discrimination and for Self-Determination

Like other groups of individuals with disabilities, people with visual impairments are becoming increasingly aware of their rights as citizens and consumers and are fighting discrimination based on their disabilities. Many people—even some who work with students with visual impairments—tend to underestimate their students' capacities and to deny them a full range of occupational and personal choices. The future will bring a gradual shift away from some of the vocations and settings in which people with visual impairments have traditionally worked (e.g., piano tuning, rehabilitation counseling, sheltered workshops) in favor of a more varied and rewarding range of employment opportunities. These and other trends will be reflected in future special education programs for students with visual impairments.

Summary

Defining Visual Impairment

- Legal blindness is defined as visual acuity of 20/200 or less in the better eye after correction with glasses or contact lenses or a restricted field of vision of 20% or less.
- An educational definition considers the extent to which a visual impairment makes special education materials or methods necessary.
- Children with low vision can learn through the visual channel, and many learn to read print.
- Besides impairments in visual acuity and field of vision, a child may have problems with ocular motility or visual accommodation, photophobia, or defective color vision.
- The age at onset of a visual impairment affects a child's educational and emotional needs.

Prevalence

- Visual impairment is a low-incidence disability affecting approximately 5 of every 10,000 children in the school-age population. About one-third of all students with visual impairments have additional disabilities.

Types and Causes of Visual Impairment

- The eye collects light reflected from objects and focuses the objects' image on the retina. The optic nerve transmits the image to the brain. Difficulty with any part of this process can cause vision problems. Common types of visual impairment include the following:
  - Myopia (nearsightedness)
  - Hyperopia (farsightedness)
  - Astigmatism (blurred vision caused by irregularities in the cornea or other eye surfaces)
  - Cataract (blurred or distorted vision caused by cloudiness in the lens)
  - Glaucoma (loss of vision caused by high pressure within the eye)
  - Diabetic retinopathy, retinitis pigmentosa, macular degeneration, and retinal detachment (all caused by problems with the retina)
  - Retinopathy of prematurity (retrolental fibroplasia) (caused by administration and withdrawal of high doses of oxygen to premature infants in incubators)

Educational Approaches

- Most children who are blind learn to read braille and write with a brailler and a slate and stylus. They may also learn to type and use special equipment for mathematics and social studies as well as listen to or feel regular print.
- Children with low vision should learn to use their residual vision as efficiently as possible. Many use optical aids and large print to read regular type.
- All children with visual impairments need to develop their listening skills.
- Most students with visual impairments also need special instruction in daily living skills, interpersonal skills, and human sexuality.
- Some children with visual impairments need help in reducing or eliminating stereotypic behaviors.
- The teacher should use direct observation and a variety of informal and formal procedures to assess children with visual impairments. Standardized intelligence tests are often inappropriate.
- Orientation and mobility (O&M) instruction is a must for individuals who are blind or have severe visual impairments.

Educational Placement Alternatives

- Most children with visual impairments spend at least part of each school day in regular classes with sighted peers.
- In many districts, a specially trained itinerant vision specialist provides support for students with visual impairments and their regular classroom teachers.
- Some programs also have separate orientation and mobility instructors or separate resource rooms for students with visual impairments.
- About 9% of children with visual impairments, especially those with other disabilities, attend residential schools.
- Most parents can choose between public day and residential schools for their children with visual impairments.

Current Issues and Future Trends

- Children with visual impairments are likely to receive specialized services in the future in both regular and residential schools. Greater emphasis will be placed on intervention with visually impaired infants and young children and on training older students for independence.
- It is hoped that all people with visual impairments will benefit from new technological and biomedical developments. Artificial sight may be possible in the future.
- Career opportunities will likely expand as individuals with visual impairments become more aware of their legal and human rights.

For More Information

Journals

- *Journal of Visual Impairment and Blindness.* Published 10 times per year by the American Foundation for the Blind (see "Organizations"). An interdisciplinary journal for practitioners and researchers concerned with the education and rehabilitation of children or adults who are blind or have visual impairments. Includes regular updates on technological and legislative developments.
- *RE:view* (formerly *Education of the Visually Handicapped*). Published quarterly by the Association for Education and Rehabilitation of the Blind and Visually Impaired (see "Organizations"). Includes practical articles, research studies, interviews, and other features relevant to teachers of students with visual impairments, orientation and mobility specialists, rehabilitation workers, administrators, and parents. Twice a year *RE:view* publishes its *Semi-Annual Listing of Current Literature: Blindness, Visual Impairment, Deaf-Blindness,* an annotated bibliographic listing of articles, books, and other publications designed to "provide a fairly complete and coordinated compilation of professional literature related to serious visual impairment."
- *Sight-Saving Review.* Published quarterly by the National Society to Prevent Blindness, 500 East Remington Road, Schaumburg, IL 60173. Emphasizes new developments in the assessment and treatment of visual impairments, low-vision aids, eye safety, and health education.

Books

- Barraga, N. C., & Erin, J. N. (1992). *Visual handicaps and learning* (3rd ed.). Austin, TX: PRO-ED.
- Best, A. B. (1991). *Teaching children with visual impairments.* Philadelphia: Open University Press.
- Bishop, V. E. (1996). *Teaching visually impaired children* (2nd ed.). Springfield, IL: Thomas.
- Heller, K. W., Alberto, P. A., Forney, P. E., & Schwartzman, M. N. (1996). *Understanding physical, sensory, & health impairments*. Pacific Grove, CA: Brooks/Cole.
- Jose, R. (1983). *Understanding low vision.* New York: American Foundation for the Blind.
- Rugow, S. M. (1988). *Helping the child with visual impairments with developmental problems: Effective practice in home, school, and community.* New York: Teachers College Press.
- Scholl, G. T. (Ed.). (1986). *Foundations of education for blind and visually handicapped children and youth: Theory and practice.* New York: American Foundation for the Blind.
- Torres, I., & Corn, A. L. (1990). *When you have a visually impaired student in your classroom: Suggestions for teachers* (2nd ed.). New York: American Foundation for the Blind.

Organizations

- *American Foundation for the Blind,* 15 West 16th Street, New York, NY 10011; (800) 232-5463; e-mail: afbinfo@afb.org. Provides many publications and films about blindness. Distributes aids and appliances for people with impaired vision. Publishes the *Journal of Visual Impairment and Blindness* and *Directory of Agencies Serving the Visually Handicapped in the United States.*
- *American Printing House for the Blind,* 1839 Frankfort Avenue, Louisville, KY 40206; (800) 223-1839; website: http://www.aph.org. Provides books, magazines, and many other publications in braille, large-print, and recorded form. Distributes educational materials and aids specially designed for the blind and helpful publications for teachers. Attempts to register all U.S. children who are legally blind through state departments of education or residential schools. Also provides recordings and computer materials.
- *Association for Education and Rehabilitation of the Blind and Visually Impaired,* 206 North Washington Street, Alexandria, VA 22314. Emphasizes educational, orientation, mobility, and rehabilitation services. Holds regional and national conferences in the United States and Canada. Publishes *RE:view* and a yearbook compiling recent literature in this field.
- *Canadian National Institute for the Blind,* 1921 Bayview Avenue, Toronto, Ontario M4G 3E8, Canada. The central Canadian agency for information, materials, and supportive services for people with visual impairments. Maintains regional and local offices in all provinces. In its film *Shelley,* effectively depicts the growth and development of a young blind child.
- *Division for the Visually Handicapped (DVH),* Council for Exceptional Children, 1920 Association Drive, Reston, VA 22091; (703) 620-3660. With more than 1,000 members, DVH has promoted appropriate education programs for individuals who have visual disabilities since 1954.
- *National Association for Parents of the Visually Impaired,* 2011 Hardy Circle, Austin, TX 78756. Provides practical information for parents. Sponsors parent groups in several areas. Holds conferences and workshops for parents and teachers.
- *National Federation of the Blind,* 1800 Johnson Street, Baltimore, MD 21230. The largest organization of blind people in the United States, with many state and local chapters. Provides publications and films that emphasize the rights and capabilities of people who are blind. Seeks to involve blind people in education and employment and to avoid discrimination. Also sponsors activities and publications for parents of children who are blind.

Chapter 12

Physical Impairments and Special Health Care Needs

Focus Questions

- In what ways might the visibility of a physical or health impairment affect a child's self-perception, social development, and level of independence across different environments?
- How do the nature and severity of a child's physical disability affect IEP goals and objectives?
- What are some of the problems that members of an interdisciplinary team for a child with severe physical disabilities and multiple health needs must guard against?
- How might an assistive technology device be a hindrance as well as a help?
- Of the many ways in which the classroom environment and instruction can be modified to support the inclusion of students with physical and health impairments, which are most important?

Children with physical impairments and special health care needs are an extremely varied population. Describing them with a single set of characteristics would be impossible, even if we used very general terms. Their physical disabilities may be mild, moderate, or severe. Some children with special health care needs are extremely restricted in their activities and intellectual functioning; others have no major limitations on what they can do and learn. Some appear entirely normal; others have highly visible disabilities. Children may have a single impairment or a combination of disabilities. They may have lived with the physical disability or health impairment since birth or have acquired it recently. Some children must use special assistive devices that call attention to their disability; others display behaviors they cannot control. Some disabilities are always present; others occur only from time to time. Over an extended period, the degree of disability may increase, decrease, or remain about the same.

As you can see, the students whose special education needs we consider in this chapter have a great many individual differences. Linda, for example, has undergone long periods of hospitalization and finds it difficult to keep up with her academic work. Gary takes medication that controls his seizures most of the time, but it also tends to make him drowsy in the classroom. Brian, who uses a wheelchair for mobility, is disappointed that he is unable to compete with his classmates in football, baseball, and track. Yet he participates fully in all other aspects of his high school program with no special modifications other than the addition of a few ramps in the building and a newly accessible washroom. Most of Brian's teachers and friends, in fact, do not think of him as needing special education at all. Janice becomes tired easily and attends school for only three hours per day. Kencel does his schoolwork in a specially designed chair that helps him sit more comfortably in the classroom.

An appropriate education for children with physical and health impairments may require modifications in the classroom environment, use of specialized teaching techniques, assistive devices for communication or mobility, and/or provision of related health services in the classroom. It is important for teachers (and often for other students as well) to understand how a particular condition may affect a child's learning, development, and behavior. Because some physical and health impairments may cause possible complications or emergencies to arise in the classroom, it is equally important for the teacher to know how to manage any situation effectively and when and how to seek help. Although we can make general statements about some physical impairments and health-related conditions, numerous variations occur in the degree and severity of the conditions and how they may affect a child and his educational needs. Thus, general information and suggested guidelines shape our basic approach to the topic of students with physical and health impairments.

Types of Physical Impairments and Special Health Care Needs

WWW

Go to the companion website at http://www.prenhall.com/heward and select Chapter 12 to review the chapter objectives.

This chapter describes some of the physical impairments and special health care needs of children who are eligible for special education in three disability categories included by IDEA: orthopedic impairments, other health impairments, and traumatic brain injury (see Figure 12.1). According to IDEA, a child is entitled to special education services if her educational performance is adversely affected by a physical disability or health condition. Literally hundreds of physical and health impairments can adversely affect children's educational performance. Here we address only those that are encountered most frequently in school-age children. For a more extensive discussion of the many physical impairments and chronic health conditions that may result in special education, see Batshaw (1997) or Hill (1999).

Orthopedic and Neurological Impairments

An orthopedic impairment involves the skeletal system—bones, joints, limbs, and associated muscles. A neurological impairment involves the nervous system, affecting the ability to move, use, feel, or control certain parts of the body. Orthopedic and neurological impairments are two distinct and separate types of disabilities, but they may cause similar limitations in movement. Many of the same educational, therapeutic, and recreational activities are likely to be appropriate for students with orthopedic and neurological impairments (Bigge, 1991; Shivers & Fait, 1985). And there is a close relationship between the two types: for example, a child who is unable to move his legs because of damage to the central nervous system (neurological impairment) may also develop disorders in the bones and muscles of the legs (orthopedic impairment), especially if he does not receive proper therapy and equipment.

Orthopedic impairment—a severe orthopedic impairment that adversely affects a child's educational performance. The term includes impairments caused by congenital anomaly (e.g., clubfoot, absence of some member, etc.), impairments caused by disease (e.g., poliomyelitis, bone tuberculosis, etc.), and impairments from other causes (e.g., cerebral palsy, amputations, and fractures or burns that cause contractures). (C.F.R. Sec. 300.7 [b][7])

Other health impairments—having limited strength, vitality, or alertness due to chronic or acute health problems such as a heart condition, tuberculosis, rheumatic fever, nephritis, asthma, sickle cell anemia, hemophilia, epilepsy, lead poisoning, leukemia, or diabetes that adversely affects a child's educational performance. (20 U.S.C., 1400 et seq.)

Traumatic brain injury—an acquired injury to the brain caused by an external physical force, resulting in total or partial functional disability or psychosocial impairments, or both, that adversely affects a child's educational performance. The term applies to open or closed head injuries resulting in impairments in one or more areas, such as cognition; language; memory; attention; reasoning; abstract thinking; judgment; problem-solving; sensory, perceptual, and motor abilities; psychosocial behavior; physical functions; information processing; and speech. The term does not apply to brain injuries that are congenital or generative, or brain injuries induced by birth trauma. (34 C.F.R. Sec. 300.7 [6][12])

Note the common clause in each definition: *that adversely affects a child's educational performance.* This is the key criterion in determining if a child with a physical disability or illness is eligible for special education.

Figure 12.1 Definitions of children with physical impairments and special health care needs who are eligible for special education services under IDEA

Some children with attention deficit/hyperactivity disorder (ADHD) who meet eligibility requirements for special education are served under the other health impairments category of IDEA; others are served under the specific learning disability or serious emotional disturbance categories. ADHD is discussed in Chapter 7.

Whatever their cause, orthopedic and neurological impairments are frequently described in terms of the affected parts of the body. The term plegia (from the Greek "to strike") is often used in combination with a prefix indicating the location of limb involvement:

- Monoplegia. Only one limb (upper or lower) is affected.
- Hemiplegia. Two limbs on same side of the body are involved.
- Triplegia. Three limbs are affected.
- Quadriplegia. All four limbs (both arms and legs) are involved; movement of the trunk and face may also be impaired.
- Paraplegia. Only legs are impaired.
- Diplegia. Impairment primarily involves the legs, with less severe involvement of the arms.
- Double hemiplegia. Impairment primarily involves the arms, with less severe involvement of the legs.

Maria Serrao, who has paraplegia and has used a wheelchair since age 5, has created a fitness video oriented to people with disabilities (Everyone Can Exercise! by Brentwood Home Video). A photo of Ms. Serrao appears in Chapter 15.

Cerebral Palsy

Cerebral palsy—a disorder of voluntary movement and posture—is the most prevalent physical disability in school-age children. Cerebral palsy is a permanent condition resulting from a lesion to the brain or an abnormality of brain growth. Many diseases can affect the developing brain and lead to cerebral palsy (Batshaw, 1997). Children with cerebral palsy experience disturbances of voluntary motor functions that may include paralysis, extreme weakness, lack of coordination, involuntary convulsions, and other motor disorders. They may have little or no

The children most frequently served in special education programs for orthopedic impairments are those with cerebral palsy. In some programs, half or more of the students considered to have physical or health impairments have cerebral palsy.

control over their arms, legs, or speech, depending on the type and degree of impairment. The more severe forms of cerebral palsy are often diagnosed in the first few months of life. In many other cases, however, cerebral palsy is not detected until the child is 2 to 3 years old when parents notice that their child is having difficulty crawling, balancing, or standing. The motor dysfunction usually does not get progressively worse as a child ages. Cerebral palsy can be treated but not cured; it is not a disease, not fatal, not contagious, and, in the great majority of cases, not inherited.

About one-third of children with cerebral palsy have intelligence within or above the normal range, one-third have mild cognitive impairment, and one-third have moderate to severe mental retardation (e.g., Whaley & Wong, 1995). The probability of mental retardation is greater when a seizure disorder is also present (Smith, 1984).

Seizure disorders are described later in this chapter.

Sensory impairments are also common in children with cerebral palsy; 5% to 15% have hearing loss (Nechring & Steele, 1996), and up to 50% have impaired vision (Dzienkowski, Smith, Dillow, & Yucha, 1996). However, other surveys have estimated that such estimates should be interpreted cautiously. As Levine (1986) points out, students with cerebral palsy often have motor and/or speech impairments that limit the appropriateness of standardized intelligence tests; thus, an IQ score should never serve as the sole descriptor of a child's actual or potential ability. It is also important to bear in mind that no clear relationship exists between the degree of motor impairment and the degree of intellectual impairment (if any) in children with cerebral palsy (or other physical disabilities). A student with only mild motor impairment may experience severe developmental delays, whereas a student with severe motor impairments may be intellectually gifted (Willard-Holt, 1998).

See "I Was Thinking about Black Holes" by theoretical physicist Stephen W. Hawking in Chapter 14.

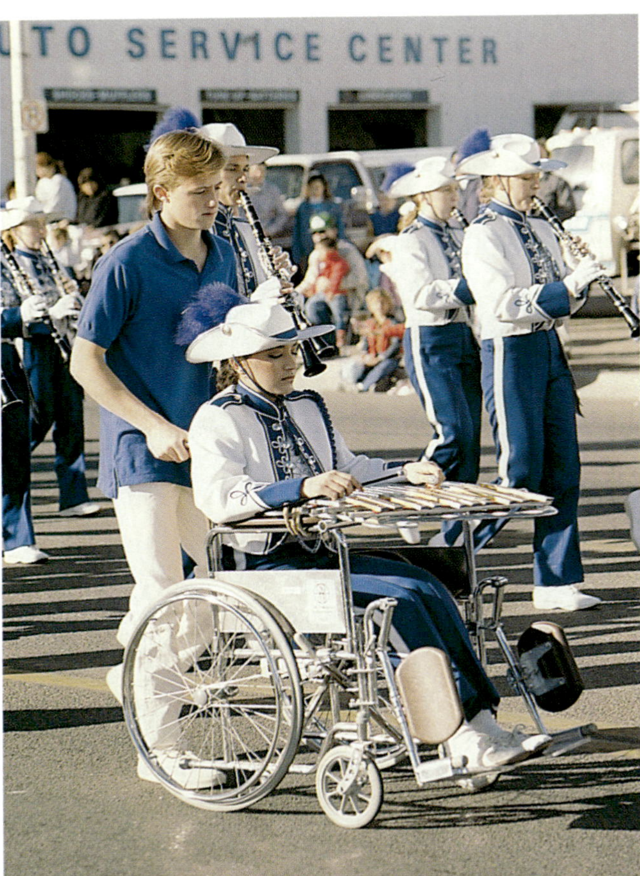

With a little help from a classmate, another musician joins the marching band.

The causes of cerebral palsy are varied and not clearly known (Pellegrino, 1997). It has most often been attributed to the occurrence of injuries, accidents, or illnesses that are *prenatal* (before birth), *perinatal* (at or near the time of birth), or *postnatal* (soon after birth) and that result in decreased oxygen to low birth weight newborns. Recent improvements in obstetrical delivery and neonatal care, however, have not decreased the incidence of cerebral palsy, which has remained steady during the past 20 years or so at about 1.5 in every 1,000 live births (Evans & Smith, 1993). An extensive study of children with cerebral palsy (Nelson & Ellenberg, 1986) found that the factors most likely to be associated with cerebral palsy were mental retardation of the mother, premature birth (gestational age of 32 weeks or less), low birth weight, and a delay of five minutes or more before the baby's first cry. Dzienkowski et al. (1996) reported that 36% of all cases of cerebral palsy occurred in infants weighing less than 2,500 grams at birth.

Types of Cerebral Palsy. Cerebral palsy is divided into several categories according to muscle tone (hypertonia or hypotonia) and quality of motor involvement (athetosis or ataxia) (Pellegrino, 1997). Children may also be described as having mixed cerebral palsy, consisting of more than one of these types, particularly if their impairments are severe.

Because most children with cerebral palsy have diffuse brain damage, "pure" types of cerebral palsy are rare (Jones, 1983).

Approximately 50% to 60% of all individuals with cerebral palsy have **hypertonia** (commonly called *spasticity*), which is characterized by tense, contracted muscles. Their movements may be jerky, exaggerated, and poorly coordinated. They may be unable to grasp objects with their fingers. When they try to control their movements, they may become even more jerky. If they are able to walk, they may use a scissors gait, standing on the toes with knees bent and pointed inward. Deformities of the spine, hip dislocation, and contractures of the hand, elbow, foot, and knee are common.

Most infants born with cerebral palsy have **hypotonia,** or weak, floppy muscles, particularly in the neck and trunk. When hypotonia persists throughout the child's first year without being replaced with spasticity or athetoid involvement, the condition is called *generalized hypotonia.* Hypotonic children typically have low levels of motor activity, are slow to make balancing responses, and may not walk until 30 months of age (Bleck, 1987). Severely hypotonic children must use external support to achieve and maintain an upright position.

The motor impairment of children with cerebral palsy often makes it frustrating, if not impossible, for them to play with toys. See "Adapting Toys for Children with Cerebral Palsy" later in this chapter.

Athetosis occurs in about 20% of all cases of cerebral palsy. Children with athetoid cerebral palsy make large, irregular, twisting movements they cannot control. When they are at rest or asleep, there is little or no abnormal motion. An effort to pick up a pencil, however, may result in wildly waving arms, facial grimaces, and extension of the tongue. These children may not be able to control the muscles of their lips, tongue, and throat and may drool. They may also seem to stumble and lurch awkwardly as they walk. At times their muscles may be tense and rigid; at other times, they may be loose and flaccid. Extreme difficulty in expressive oral language, mobility, and activities of daily living often accompanies this form of cerebral palsy.

Ataxia is noted as the primary type of involvement in only 1% to 10% of cases of cerebral palsy (Hill, 1999). Children with ataxic cerebral palsy have a poor sense of balance and hand use. They may appear to be dizzy while walking and may fall easily if not supported. Their movements tend to be jumpy and unsteady, with exaggerated motion patterns that often overshoot the intended objects. They seem to be constantly attempting to overcome the effect of gravity and stabilize their bodies.

Rigidity and **tremor** are additional but much less common types of cerebral palsy. Children with the rare rigidity type of cerebral palsy display extreme stiffness in the affected limbs; they may be fixed and immobile for long periods. Tremor cerebral palsy, also rare, is marked by rhythmic, uncontrollable movements; the tremors may actually increase when the children attempt to control their actions.

Dormans and Pellegrino (1998) have compiled a detailed handbook to guide the care and education of children with cerebral palsy by interdisciplinary teams.

Treatment of Cerebral Palsy. Gillham (1986) describes cerebral palsy as the result of "not just a brain with a bit missing, but a reorganized brain, working to its own rules" (p. 64). Because cerebral palsy is such a complex condition, it is most effectively managed through the cooperative involvement of physicians, teachers, physical therapists, occupational therapists, communication specialists, counselors, and others who work directly with children and families. Regular exercise and careful positioning in school settings help the child with cerebral palsy move as fully and comfortably as possible and prevent or minimize progressive damage to muscles and limbs. About 80% of children with cerebral palsy are capable of learning to walk although many need to use wheelchairs, braces, and other assistive devices, particularly for moving around outside the home (Bleck, 1979). Orthopedic surgery may increase a child's range of motion or obviate complications such as hip dislocations and permanent muscle contractions.

The term neural tube defect *is sometimes used to describe spina bifida and similar impairments.*

Spina Bifida **Spina bifida** is a general term for a congenital defect in the vertebrae that enclose the spinal cord. As a result, a portion of the spinal cord and the nerves that normally control muscles and feeling in the lower part of the body fail to develop normally. Of the three types of spina bifida, the mildest form is **spina bifida occulta,** in which only a few vertebrae are malformed, usually in the lower spine. The defect is usually not visible externally. It is estimated that up to 10% of the general population may have spina bifida occulta (Liptak, 1997). If the flexible casing (*meninges*) that surrounds the spinal cord bulges through an opening in the infant's back at birth, the condition is called **meningocele.** These two forms do not usually cause any loss of function for the child.

In **myelomeningocele**—the most common and most serious form of spina bifida—the spinal lining, spinal cord, and nerve roots all protrude. The protruding spinal cord and nerves are usually tucked back into the spinal column shortly after birth. This condition carries a high risk of paralysis and infection. In general, the higher the location of the lesion on the spine, the greater the effect on the body and its functioning. About 6 in 10,000 live births in the United States result in myelomeningocele; and it affects girls at a much higher rate than boys (Liptak, 1997).

About 80% to 90% of children born with myelomeningocele develop **hydrocephalus,** the accumulation of cerebrospinal fluid in tissues surrounding the brain (Hill, 1999). Left untreated, this condition can lead to head enlargement and severe brain damage. Hydrocephalus is treated by the surgical insertion of a **shunt,** a one-way valve that diverts the cerebrospinal fluid away from the brain and into the bloodstream. Replacements of the shunt are usually necessary as a child grows older. Teachers who work with children who have shunts should be aware that blockage, disconnection, or infection of the shunt may result in increased intracranial pressure. Warning signs such as drowsiness, vomiting, headache, irritability, and squinting should be heeded because a blocked shunt can be life-threatening (Charney, 1992). Shunts have become safer and more reliable in recent years and can be removed in many school-age children when the production and absorption of cerebrospinal fluid are brought into balance (Gillham, 1986).

Usually children with spina bifida have some degree of paralysis of the lower limbs and lack full control of bladder and bowel functions. In most cases, these children have good use of their arms and upper body (although some children experience fine motor problems). Children with spina bifida usually walk with braces, crutches, or walkers; they may use wheelchairs for longer distances. Some children need special help in dressing and toileting; others are able to manage these tasks on their own.

Because the spinal defect usually occurs above where nerves that control the bladder emerge from the spinal cord, most children with spina bifida have urinary incontinence and need to use a **catheter** (tube) or bag to collect their urine. *Clean intermittent catheterization* (CIC) is taught to children with urinary complications so that they can empty their bladders at convenient times (Liptak, 1997). This technique is effective with both boys and girls, works best if used every three to four hours, and does not require an absolutely sterile environment (Pieper, 1983).

See "Using Dolls to Teach Self-Catheterization Skills to Children with Spina Bifida" later in this chapter. For suggestions on teaching children with spina bifida, see Rowley-Kelly and Teigel (1993).

Muscular Dystrophy **Muscular dystrophy** refers to a group of inherited diseases marked by progressive *atrophy* (wasting away) of the body's muscles. **Duchenne muscular dystrophy (DMD)** is the most common of the 13 types. DMD affects boys (1 in 3,500 male births) much more frequently than girls. The child appears normal at birth, but muscle weakness is usually evident between the ages of 2 and 5, when the child begins to experience difficulty in running or climbing stairs. The child may walk with an unusual gait, showing a protruding stomach and hollow back. The calf muscles of a child with muscular dystrophy may appear unusually large because the degenerated muscle has been replaced by fatty tissue.

Children with muscular dystrophy often have difficulty getting to their feet after lying down or playing on the floor. They may fall easily. By age 10 to 14, the child loses the ability to walk; the small muscles of the hands and fingers are usually the

"Well, I think the best part of the story was when. . . . " Learning self-catheterization has given Kristine more control over her classroom schedule and increased her participation.

last to be affected. Some doctors and therapists recommend the early use of electrically powered wheelchairs; others suggest employing special braces and other devices to prolong walking as long as possible.

Unfortunately, at this time there is no known cure for muscular dystrophy, and in most cases this progressive disease is fatal. Treatment focuses on maintaining function of unaffected muscles for as long as possible, facilitating ambulation, helping the child and family cope with limitations imposed by the disease, and providing emotional support and counseling to the child and family (Hill, 1999). A good deal of independence can be maintained by regular physical therapy, exercise, and the use of appropriate aids and appliances. The child should be encouraged to be as active as possible. However, a teacher should be careful not to lift a child with muscular dystrophy by the arms: even a gentle pull may dislocate the child's limbs.

Most of the approximately 7,000 to 10,000 persons in the United States who are victims of traumatic spinal cord injuries each year are 15 to 25 years old (Laskowski-Jones, 1993).

Spinal Cord Injuries Spinal cord injuries are usually the result of a lesion to the spinal cord caused by a penetrating injury (e.g., gunshot wound), stretching of the vertebral column (e.g., whiplash during an auto accident), fracture of the vertebrae, or compression of the spinal cord (e.g., a diving accident). Vehicular accidents, sports injuries, and violence are the most common causes of spinal cord injuries in school-age children (Apple, Anson, Hunter, & Bell, 1995). Injury to the spinal column is generally described by letters and numbers indicating the site of the damage; for example, a C5-6 injury means the damage has occurred at the level of the fifth and sixth cervical vertebrae, a flexible area of the neck susceptible to injury from whiplash and diving or trampoline accidents. A T12 injury refers to the 12th thoracic (chest) vertebra and an L3 to the 3rd lumbar (lower back) area. In general, paralysis and loss of sensation occur below the level of the injury. The higher the injury on the spine and the more the injury (lesion) cuts through the entire cord, the greater the paralysis (Hill, 1999).

Proper positioning and regular movement are critical for students who use wheelchairs and will be discussed later in this chapter.

Students who have sustained spinal cord injuries usually use wheelchairs for mobility. Motorized wheelchairs, though expensive, are recommended for those with quadriplegia, whereas children with paraplegia can use self-propelled wheelchairs. Children with quadriplegia may have severe breathing problems because the muscles of the chest, which normally govern respiration, are affected. In most cases, children with spinal cord injuries lack bladder and bowel control and need to follow a careful management program to maintain personal hygiene and avoid infection and skin irritation.

Ducharme and Gill (1997) have compiled a question-and-answer format handbook of practical information on sexuality, self-esteem, and many other physical and emotional issues for individuals with spinal cord injury.

Rehabilitation programs for children and adolescents who have sustained spinal cord injuries usually involve physical therapy, the use of adaptive devices for mobility and independent living, and psychological support to help them adjust to a sudden disability. With supportive teachers and peers, students with paralysis can participate fully in school programs. Adolescents and adults are often particularly concerned about sexual function. Even though most spinal cord injuries do affect sexuality, with understanding partners and positive attitudes toward themselves, many people with spinal cord injuries are able to enjoy satisfying sexual relationships.

Limb Deficiency Limb deficiency is the absence or partial loss of an arm or leg. Congenital limb deficiency is rare, occurring in about 1 in every 20,000 births. Acquired limb deficiency (amputations) may be the result of surgery or accident. A **prosthesis** (artificial limb) is often used to facilitate balance, enable the child to participate in a variety of tasks, and create a more normal appearance. Some students or their parents, however, prefer not to use artificial limbs. Most children become quite proficient at using their remaining limbs. Some children who are missing both arms, for example, learn to write, eat, and perform vocational tasks with their feet. They have a much greater feeling of being in contact with objects and people than they would if they used prosthetic limbs. Unless children have other impairments in addition to the absence of limbs, they should be able to function in a regular classroom without major modifications.

Other Health Impairments

Seizure Disorders (Epilepsy) Theoretically, anyone can have a *seizure,* a disturbance of movement, sensation, behavior, and/or consciousness caused by abnormal electrical activity in the brain.

> Regardless of whether an individual is awake or asleep, at a given moment, there is electrical activity occurring in the brain. Some groups of neurons of the brain are actively firing, some are firing but with less vigor, and others are inactive. In some individuals, for a variety of reasons, some known and others unknown, there can be, at certain time, a sudden excessive, disorderly discharge of neuronal excitation in the brain, which may result in an involuntary, transient impairment, of consciousness, sensation, memory, movement, behavior, or autonomic functioning in the human body. Some have likened the event, known as a seizure, to an engine misfiring or to a power surge in a computer. (Hill, 1999, p. 231)

Many unfortunate misconceptions about epilepsy have circulated in the past and are still prevalent even today. Negative public attitudes, in fact, have probably been more harmful to people with epilepsy than has the condition itself.

It is common for a seizure to occur when someone has a high fever, drinks excessive alcohol, or experiences a blow to the head. When seizures occur chronically and repeatedly, however, the condition is known as a *seizure disorder* or, more commonly, **epilepsy.** Epilepsy is not a disease, and it constitutes a disorder only while a seizure is actually in progress. Most students with epilepsy have normal intelligence.

The cause of epilepsy for approximately 30% of cases is identified from among at least 50 different conditions known to result in seizure activity, such as cerebral brain malformations (e.g., cerebral palsy), infections of the brain or central nervous system, metabolic disorders such as hypoglycemia, alcohol or lead poisoning, an underlying lesion caused by scar tissue from a head injury, high fever, or an interruption in blood supply to the brain (Evans & Smith, 1993). In about 70% of cases, the origin of seizure activity cannot be traced to a particular cause or incident (Jones-Saete, 1986). A convulsive disorder can occur at any stage of life but most frequently begins in childhood. A wide variety of psychological, physical, and sensory factors are thought to trigger seizures in susceptible persons—for example, fatigue, excitement, anger, surprise, hyperventilation, hormonal changes (as in menstruation or pregnancy), withdrawal from drugs or alcohol, and exposure to certain patterns of light, sound, or touch.

During a seizure, a dysfunction in the electrochemical activity of the brain causes a person to lose control of the muscles temporarily. Between seizures (that is, most of the time), the brain functions normally. Teachers, school health care personnel, and perhaps classmates need to be aware that a child is affected by a convulsive disorder so that they can be prepared to deal with a seizure if one should occur in school. There are several types of seizures.

The **generalized tonic-clonic seizure** (formerly called *grand mal*) is the most conspicuous and serious type of convulsive seizure. A generalized tonic-clonic seizure can be disturbing and frightening to someone who has never seen one. The affected child has little or no warning that a seizure is about to occur; the muscles become stiff, and the child loses consciousness and falls to the floor. Then the entire body shakes violently as the muscles alternately contract and relax. Saliva may be forced from the mouth, legs and arms may jerk, and the bladder and bowels may be emptied. In most cases, the contractions diminish in two to three minutes, and the child either goes to sleep or regains consciousness in a confused or drowsy state. Generalized tonic-clonic seizures may occur as often as several times a day or as seldom as once a year. They are more likely to occur during the day than at night.

A tonic-clonic seizure, although very frightening to someone who has not witnessed such an episode, is not a medical emergency (Hill, 1999). Figure 12.2 describes procedures for handling seizures in the classroom.

The **absence seizure** (previously called *petit mal*) is far less severe than the generalized tonic-clonic seizure but may occur much more frequently—as often as 100 times per day in some children. Usually there is a brief loss of consciousness, lasting anywhere from a few seconds to half a minute or so. The child may stare blankly, flutter or blink her eyes, grow pale, or drop whatever she is holding. She may be mistakenly viewed as daydreaming or not listening. The child may or may not be aware that she has had a seizure, and no special first aid is necessary. The teacher should keep the child's parents advised of seizure activity and may also find it helpful to explain it to the child's classmates.

A **complex partial seizure** (also called *psychomotor seizure*) may appear as a brief period of inappropriate or purposeless activity. The child may smack her lips, walk around aimlessly, or shout. She may appear to be conscious but is not actually aware of her unusual behavior. Complex partial seizures usually last from two to five minutes, after which the child has amnesia about the entire episode. Some children may respond to spoken directions during a complex partial seizure.

Figure 12.2 Procedures for handling tonic-clonic seizures

Source: Adapted from the Epilepsy Foundation of America. (1987). *Epilepsy school alert.* Washington, DC: Author.

The typical seizure is not a medical emergency, but knowledgeable handling of the situation is important. When a child experiences a generalized tonic-clonic seizure in the classroom, the teacher should follow these procedures:

- Keep calm. Reassure the other students that the child will be fine in a minute.
- Ease the child to the floor and clear the area around him of anything that could hurt him.
- Put something flat and soft (like a folded coat) under his head so it will not bang on the floor as his body jerks.
- You cannot stop the seizure. Let it run its course. Do not try to revive the child and do not interfere with his movements.
- Turn him gently onto his side. This keeps his airway clear and allows saliva to drain away.

  DON'T try to force his mouth open.

  DON'T try to hold on to his tongue.

  DON'T put anything in his mouth.
- When the jerking movements stop, let the child rest until he regains consciousness.
- Breathing may be shallow during the seizure, and may even stop briefly. In the unlikely event that breathing does not begin again, check the child's airway for obstruction and give artificial respiration.

Some students recover quickly after this type of seizure; others need more time. A short period of rest is usually advised. If the student is able to remain in the classroom afterwards, however, he should be encouraged to do so. Staying in the classroom (or returning to it as soon as possible) allows for continued participation in classroom activity and is psychologically less difficult for the student. If a student has frequent seizures, handling them can become routine once teacher and classmates learn what to expect. If a seizure of this type continues for longer than five minutes, call for emergency assistance.

A **simple partial seizure** is characterized by sudden jerking motions with no loss of consciousness. Partial seizures may occur weekly, monthly, or only once or twice a year. The teacher should keep dangerous objects out of the child's way and, except in emergencies, should not try to physically restrain him.

Many children experience a warning sensation, known as an *aura,* a short time before a seizure. The aura takes different forms in different people; distinctive feelings, sights, sounds, tastes, and even smells have been described. The aura can be a useful safety valve enabling the child to leave the class or group before the seizure actually occurs. Some children report that the warning provided by the aura helps them feel more secure and comfortable about themselves.

In some children, absence and partial seizures can go undetected for long periods. An observant teacher can be instrumental in detecting the presence of a seizure disorder and in referring the child for appropriate medical help. The teacher can also assist parents and physicians by noting both the effectiveness and the side effects of any medication the child takes. With proper medical treatment and the support of parents, teachers, and peers, most students with seizure disorders lead full and normal lives. Antiepileptic drugs may largely or wholly control epileptic seizures in 60% to 70% of children (Pedley, Scheuer, & Walczak, 1995). Some children require such heavy doses of medication, however, that their learning and behavior are adversely affected, and some medications have undesirable side effects, such as drowsiness, nausea, weight gain, and thickening of the gums. All children with seizure disorders benefit from a realistic understanding of their condition and accepting attitudes on the part of teachers and classmates. Although the student with seizure disorders may be uncomfortable about letting friends know about the condition, classmates should be aware so that they will know how to, and how not to, respond in the event of a seizure (Hill, 1999).

For more information about record keeping and what to observe before, during, and after a seizure, see Michael (1992).

Diabetes **Juvenile diabetes mellitus**—a chronic disorder of metabolism—is a common childhood disease, affecting about 1 in 600 school-age children, so it is likely that most teachers will encounter students with diabetes at one time or another (Whaley & Wong, 1995). Without proper medical management, the diabetic child's system is not able to obtain and retain adequate energy from food. Not only does the child lack energy, but many important parts of the body—particularly the eyes and the kidneys—can be affected by untreated diabetes. Early symptoms of diabetes include thirst, headaches, weight loss (despite a good appetite), frequent urination, and cuts that are slow to heal.

Diabetic retinopathy *is a leading cause of blindness in adults.*

Children with diabetes have insufficient insulin, a hormone normally produced by the pancreas necessary for proper metabolism and digestion of foods. To regulate the condition, insulin must be injected daily under the skin. Most children with diabetes learn to inject their own insulin—in some cases as frequently as four times per day—and to determine the amount of insulin they need by testing the level of sugar and other substances in their urine. Children with diabetes must follow a specific and regular diet prescribed by a physician or nutrition specialist. A regular exercise program is also usually suggested.

Teachers who have a child with diabetes in their classrooms should learn how to recognize the symptoms of both too little sugar or too much sugar in the child's bloodstream and the kind of treatment indicated by each condition (Yousef, 1995). *Hypoglycemia* (too little sugar), also called *insulin reaction* or *diabetic shock,* can result from taking too much insulin, unusually strenuous exercise, or a missed or delayed meal (the blood sugar level is lowered by insulin and exercise and raised by food). Symptoms of hypoglycemia include faintness, dizziness, blurred vision, drowsiness, and nausea. The child may appear irritable or have a marked personality change. In most cases, giving the child some form of concentrated sugar (e.g., a sugar cube, a glass of fruit juice, a candy bar) ends the insulin reaction within a few minutes. The child's doctor or parents should inform the teacher and school health personnel of the appropriate foods to give in case of insulin reaction.

Hyperglycemia (too much sugar) is more serious; it indicates that too little insulin is present and the diabetes is not under control. Its onset is gradual rather than sudden. The symptoms of hyperglycemia, sometimes called *diabetic coma*, include fatigue; thirst; dry, hot skin; deep, labored breathing; excessive urination; and fruity-smelling breath. A doctor or nurse should be contacted immediately if a child displays such symptoms.

Asthma **Asthma** is a chronic lung disease characterized by episodic bouts of wheezing, coughing, and difficulty breathing. "Asthma is a complex disease in which inflammation of the airways is both the cause and effect of the problem" (Kraemer & Bierman, 1983, p. 160). An asthmatic attack is usually triggered by allergens (e.g., pollen, certain foods, pets), irritants (e.g., cigarette smoke, smog), exercise, or emotional stress, which results in a narrowing of the airways in the lungs. This reaction increases the resistance to the airflow in and out of the lungs, making it harder for the individual to breathe. The severity of asthma varies greatly: the child may experience only a period of mild coughing or extreme difficulty in breathing that requires emergency treatment. Many asthmatic children experience normal lung functioning between episodes.

Asthma is the most common lung disease of children; estimates of its prevalence range from 4% to as high as 11% of school-age children (Hen, 1986; Weitzman, Gortmaker, Sobol, & Perrin, 1992). The causes of asthma are not completely known, though most consider it the result of an interaction of heredity and environment. Symptoms generally begin in early childhood, but sometimes do not develop until late childhood or adolescence. Asthma tends to run in families, which suggests that an allergic intolerance to some stimulus may be inherited. Symptoms of asthma might also first appear following a viral infection of the respiratory system.

Primary treatment for asthma begins with a systematic effort to identify the stimuli and environmental situations that provoke attacks. The number of potential allergens and irritants is virtually limitless, and in some cases it can be extremely difficult to determine the combination of factors that results in an asthmatic episode. Changes in temperature, humidity, and season (attacks are especially common in autumn) are also related to the frequency of asthmatic symptoms. Rigorous physical exercise produces asthmatic episodes in some children. Asthma can be controlled effectively in most children with a

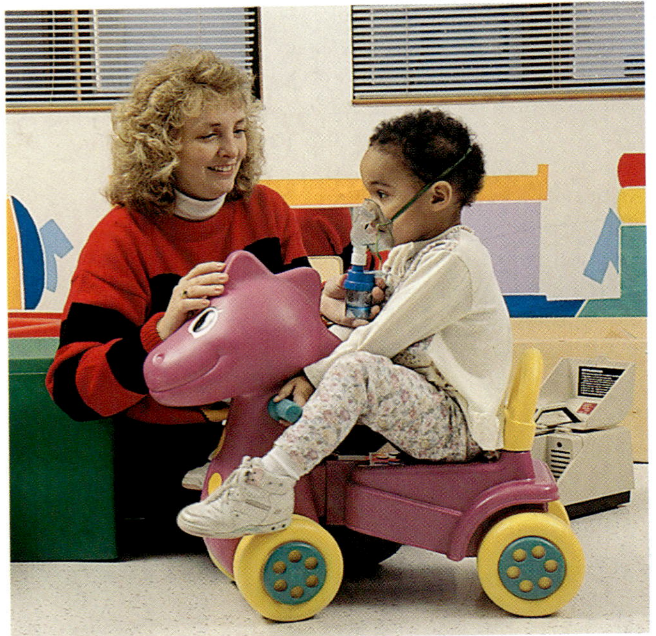

This special educator does not allow Jamika's chronic illness to prevent her from participating in developmentally appropriate play activities.

combination of medications and limiting exposure to known allergens. Most children whose breathing attacks are induced by physical exercise can still enjoy physical exercise and sports through careful selection of activities (e.g., swimming generally provokes less exercise-induced asthma than running) and/or taking certain medications prior to rigorous exercise.

A clear interrelationship also exists between emotional stress and asthma. Periods of psychological stress increase the likelihood of asthmatic attacks, and asthmatic episodes produce more stress. Treatment often involves counseling or an asthma teaching program (Kraemer & Bierman, 1983) in which children and their families are taught ways to reduce and cope with emotional stress.

Asthma is the leading cause of absenteeism in school (Zamula, 1990). Chronic absenteeism makes it difficult for the child with asthma to maintain performance at grade level, and homebound instructional services may be necessary. The majority of children with asthma who receive medical and psychological support, however, successfully complete school and lead normal lives. By working cooperatively with parents and medical personnel to minimize the child's contact with provoking factors and constructing a plan to assist the child during attacks, the classroom teacher can play an important role in reducing the impact of asthma (Getch & Neuharth-Pritchett, 1999).

Estimates of the number of school days lost each year because of asthma range from 10 million (Majer & Joy, 1993) to 130 million if hay fever is included (McLaughlin & Nall, 1994).

Cystic Fibrosis **Cystic fibrosis** is a genetic disorder of children and adolescents in which the body's exocrine glands excrete a thick mucus that can block the lungs and parts of the digestive system. It is a hereditary disease found predominantly in Caucasians—affecting approximately 1 in 3,500 live Caucasian births, 1 in 11,500 Hispanic births, and 1 in 14,500 African American births (FitzSimmons, 1993). Children with cystic fibrosis often have difficulty breathing and are susceptible to pulmonary disease (lung infections). Malnutrition and poor growth are common characteristics of children with cystic fibrosis because of pancreatic insufficiency that causes inadequate digestion and malabsorption of nutrients, especially fats. They often have large and frequent bowel movements because food passes through the system only partially digested. A study found that 40% of children with cystic fibrosis were below the fifth-percentile weight for their age (Cystic Fibrosis Foundation, 1992). The symptoms may result from a missing chemical or substance in the body. Medical research has not determined exactly how cystic fibrosis functions, and no reliable cure has yet been found. Medications prescribed for children with cystic fibrosis include enzymes to facilitate digestion and solutions to thin and loosen the mucus in the lungs.

Many children and young adults with cystic fibrosis are able to lead active lives. During vigorous physical exercises, some children may need help from teachers, aides, or classmates to clear their lungs and air passages. The long-range outlook for children affected by cystic fibrosis is improving, and with current treatment, the average life expectancy of individuals with cystic fibrosis is 29 years (Cystic Fibrosis Foundation, 1992).

Getting children with cystic fibrosis to consume enough calories is critical to their health and development. Stark et al. (1993) used a behaviorally based treatment intervention that included nutrition education, rewards for meeting gradually increasing calorie goals, and relaxation training to successfully increase calorie consumption and growth rates of three children with cystic fibrosis. Increased calorie consumption was maintained at a two-year follow-up.

Hemophilia **Hemophilia** refers to a group of hereditary disorders in which the blood does not coagulate as quickly as it should because one of 13 clotting factors is missing or deficient. Contrary to popular opinion, persons with hemophilia are not in danger of bleeding to death as the result of a minor cut or injury. "Persons with hemophilia do not bleed *faster* but they do bleed *longer* than those with a normal level of clotting factor. Even in the case of a major wound, there is the same amount of time to transport the student to the hospital for treatment as there is for any other student" (Hill, 1999, p. 173).

The most serious consequences are usually internal, rather than external, bleeding. Internal bleeding can cause swelling, pain, and permanent damage to joints, tissues, and internal organs and may necessitate hospitalization for blood transfusions. The primary treatment of hemophilia is *factor replacement therapy*, in which the deficient clotting factor is transfused directly into a vein to stop the bleeding. A student with hemophilia may need to be excused from some physical activities and may use a wheelchair during periods of susceptibility. As with most children who have health-related impairments, however, good physical condition is important for development and well-being, so the restrictions on activities should not be any greater than necessary.

The HIV/AIDS Treatment Information Service provides the most current recommendations concerning the prevention and treatment of HIV/AIDS: (800)448-0440; website: http://www.hivatis.org.

Acquired Immunodeficiency Syndrome (AIDS) Persons with **acquired immunodeficiency syndrome (AIDS)** are not able to resist and fight off infections because of a breakdown in the immune system. In 1983 the virus that causes AIDS was isolated and given the name **human immunodeficiency virus (HIV).** AIDS is contracted when HIV is passed from a carrier (not all persons who have HIV get AIDS) to another person through sexual contact or through the blood (via intravenous drug use with shared needles or transfusions of unscreened contaminated blood). Pregnant women can transmit HIV to their unborn children. At present, there is no known cure or vaccine for the disease, which is fatal. It is estimated that 2 million people in the United States and 20 million people worldwide are infected with HIV (Ungvarski, 1997). The incidence rate for AIDS has increased alarmingly, and projections of the number of people who may contract the disease and die are staggering.

For a discussion of legal issues facing families of children with AIDS, see Gross and Larkin (1996).

Although only a small number of young children diagnosed with AIDS have survived to school age, the continuing development of drug treatments to counter or slow the progression of the disease means it is likely that increasing numbers of children with HIV infection and AIDS will be in the classroom. Children with HIV infection and AIDS are afforded legal protection and the right to a public education under Section 504 of the Rehabilitation Act of 1973, which states that "no otherwise qualified individual with handicaps . . . shall solely by reason of his handicap be excluded from the participation in, be denied the benefits of, or be subjected to discrimination under any program or activity receiving Federal financial assistance." A 1990 memorandum from the Office of Civil Rights clarified that a child with AIDS "generally will be considered 'handicapped' under Section 504 due to the substantial limitation on a major life activity caused by either physical impairment or the reaction of others to the perceived disease."

Significant neurological complications and developmental delays have been noted in children with AIDS (Barnes, 1986; Epstein, Sharer, & Goudsmit, 1988), but we do not yet know what the special education needs of these children might encompass. On the basis of current knowledge about AIDS, however, the following implications and recommendations can be made (Byers, 1989; Hill, 1999):

- Because a minor illness or infection can be life-threatening to a child with AIDS, parents should be informed immediately if their son or daughter has been exposed to a communicable disease at school (e.g., chicken pox, measles, cytomegalovirus, herpes simplex).
- Although children with HIV/AIDS cannot legally be excluded from schools unless they are deemed a direct health risk to other children (e.g., exhibit biting behavior, open sores), it is common for children and their families to face discrimination, prejudice, and isolation. Consequently, teachers and school personnel need to be active in facilitating school/peer acceptance and the social adjustment of a child with AIDS.

- Because no one may know that a particular student has HIV, all school staff must be trained in universal precautions for dealing with blood and bodily fluids from any child (e.g., administering first aid for a cut or tending to a child's nose bleed) (American Academy of Pediatrics, 1991a, 1991b; Porter, Haynie, Bierle, Caldwell, & Palfrey, 1997).
- AIDS prevention must be included in the K–12 curriculum in an effort to prevent the disease from further infiltrating the preadolescent and adolescent populations.

Students receiving special education services may be more prone to contracting HIV because of a lack of knowledge about the disease. For recommendations on developing and implementing an HIV/AIDS prevention and education curriculum for students with disabilities, see Colson and Carlson (1993); Kelker, Hecimovic, & LeRoy (1994); and Lerro (1994).

Traumatic Brain Injury

Injuries to the head are common in children and adolescents. It is estimated that each year 1 in 500 school-age children will be hospitalized with traumatic head injuries, 1 in 30 children will sustain a significant head injury by the age of 15, and 1 in 10,000 children will die as the result of head trauma (Kraus, Fife, & Conroy, 1987; Whaley & Wong, 1995). Traumatic brain injury is the leading cause of death in children, occurring five times more often than leukemia, the second leading cause. Significant causes of head trauma include automobile, motorcycle, and bicycle accidents; falls; assaults; gunshot wounds; and child abuse.

Severe head trauma often results in a *coma,* an abnormal deep stupor from which it may be impossible to arouse the affected individual by external stimuli for an extended period (Michaud & Duhaine, 1992). Temporary or lasting symptoms may include cognitive and language deficits, memory loss, seizures, and perceptual disorders. Victims may display inappropriate or exaggerated behaviors ranging from extreme aggressiveness to apathy. Children may also have difficulty paying attention and retaining new information (see Figure 12.3). The educational and lifelong needs of students with head injuries are likely to require comprehensive programs of academic, psychological, and family support (Savage & Wolcott, 1994). Although few educational programs have been specifically designed for this population, educators have recognized that many of these children need special education services.

When it was originally passed, IDEA did not specifically mention the needs of children who have experienced head trauma and/or coma; however, when the law was amended in 1990 (P.L. 101–476), traumatic brain injury was added as a new disability category under which children could be eligible for special education services.

Students with head injuries reenter school with deficits from their injuries compounded by an extended absence from school. Ylvisaker (1986) recommends that the child with a head injury return to school when she is physically capable, can respond to instructions, and can sustain attention for 10 to 15 minutes. Tyler and Mira (1993) suggest a number of modifications that school programs can make to assist the student with a head injury during the reentry period:

Each year about 65,000 children and adults are treated in hospital emergency rooms for head injuries as a result of bicycle accidents. Most of those injuries would be avoided if riders wore safety helmets (Raskin, 1990).

- A shortened school day, concentrating academic instruction during peak performance periods; frequent breaks; and a reduced class load may be necessitated by the chronic fatigue that some students with head injury experience for a year or more.
- A special resource period at the beginning and end of each school day when a teacher, counselor, or aide helps the student plan or review the day's schedule, keep track of assignments, and monitor progress may be required because of problems with loss of memory and organization.
- Modifications such as an extra set of textbooks at home, a peer to help the student move efficiently from class to class, and early dismissal from class to allow time to get to the next room can help the student who has difficulties with mobility, balance, or coordination. (Adaptive physical education is often indicated.)
- Behavior management and/or counseling interventions may be needed to help with problems such as poor judgment, impulsiveness, overactivity, aggression, destructiveness, and socially uninhibited behavior often experienced by students with head injury.

For more information about students with head injuries and recommendations for successful school reentry, see Bigler (1990), Steensma (1992), and Tucker and Colson (1992).

Physical and sensory changes

- Chronic headaches, dizziness, light-headedness, nausea
- Vision impairments (e.g., double vision, visual field defects, blurring, sensitivity to light)
- Hearing impairment (e.g., increased sensitivity to sound)
- Alterations in sense of taste, touch, and smell
- Sleep problems (e.g., insomnia, day/night confusion)
- Stress-related disorders (e.g., depression)
- Poor body temperature regulation
- Recurrent seizure activity
- Poor coordination and balance
- Reduced speed of motor performance and precision of movement

Cognitive changes and academic problems

- Difficulty keeping up with discussions, instructional presentations, note taking
- Difficulty concentrating or attending to task at hand (e.g., distractible, confused)
- Difficulty making transitions (e.g., home to school, class to class, switching from fractions to decimal problems on same math worksheet)
- Inability to organize work and environment (e.g., difficulty keeping track of books, assignments, lunch box)
- Problems in planning, organizing, pacing tasks and activities
- Extremely sensitive to distraction (e.g., unable to take a test in a room with other students)
- Tendency to perseverate; inflexible in thinking
- Impairments in receptive oral language (e.g., difficulty following directions; misunderstanding what is said by others)
- Inability to perceive voice inflections or nonverbal cues
- Impairments in reading comprehension
- Impairments in expressive oral or written language (e.g., aphasia, difficulty retrieving words, poor articulation, slow speech, difficulty in spelling or punctuation)

Social, emotional, and behavioral problems

- Chronically agitated, irritable, restless, or anxious
- Increased aggressiveness
- Impaired ability to self-manage; lowered impulse control; poor anger control
- Difficulty dealing with change (i.e., rigid); poor coping strategies
- May overestimate own ability (often evidenced as "bragging")
- Decreased insight into self and others; reduced judgment
- Decreased frustration tolerance; frequent temper outbursts and overreactions to events
- May talk compulsively and excessively
- Inability to take cues from the environment (often leading to socially inappropriate behavior)

Figure 12.3 Possible signs and effects of traumatic brain injury

Source: Adapted from Hill, J. L. (1999). *Meeting the needs of children with special physical and health care needs* (pp. 259–260). Upper Saddle River, NJ: Merrill/Prentice Hall. © 1999 by Merrill/Prentice Hall. Used by permission.

- Modifications of instruction and testing procedures such as tape-recording lectures, assigning a note taker, and allowing extra time to take tests may be needed.
- IEP goals and objectives may need to be reviewed and modified as often as every 30 days because of the dramatic changes in behavior and performance by some children during the early stages of recovery.

Prevalence

During the 1996–1997 school year, 66,400 children with orthopedic impairments, 160,824 children with other health impairments, and 10,378 children with traumatic brain injury between the ages of 6 and 21 were served in special education programs (U.S. Department of Education, 1998). Together, these three disability categories represent about 4.6% of all school-age children receiving special education services.

Two factors make the actual number of children with physical impairments and special health needs much higher than the number of children receiving special education services under these three IDEA categories. First, because physical and health impairments often occur in combination with other disabilities, children may be counted under other categories, such as learning disabilities, speech impairment, or mental retardation. For example, for the purpose of special education eligibility, a diagnosis of mental retardation usually takes precedence over a diagnosis of physical impairment. Second, there are numerous children with physical impairments and chronic health conditions that do not adversely affect their educational performance sufficiently to warrant special education (Hill, 1999).

Check your ongoing understanding of Chapter 12 concepts by using the Guided Review Module at http://www.prenhall.com/heward.

Table 12.1 lists some key historical events and their implications for students with physical and health impairments.

Variables Affecting the Impact of Physical Impairments and Chronic Health Conditions

Classifying a child on the basis of the underlying cause of her physical impairment or health condition provides limited guidance in planning needed special education and related services. One student with cerebral palsy may require few special modifications in curriculum, instruction, or environment, while the severe limitations in movement and intellectual functioning experienced by another student with cerebral palsy require a wide array of curricular and instructional modifications, adaptive equipment, and related services. In assessing the effects of a physical impairment or health condition on a child's development and behavior, many factors must be taken into consideration.

A noncategorical system for classifying and understanding children's chronic physical and medical conditions proposed by Perrin et al. (1993) includes 13 dimensions in which the characteristics or effects of the child's condition are judged on a continuum from mild to profound (see Figure 12.4). Three particularly important factors are the age at which the disabling condition was first acquired, the severity with which the condition affects different areas of functioning, and the visibility of the impairment.

Age of Onset

Some conditions are **congenital** (present at birth); other conditions are acquired during the child's development as a result of illness, accident, or unknown cause. As with virtually all disabilities, it is important for the teacher to be aware of the child's age at the time he acquired the physical or health impairment. A child who has not had the use of his legs since birth may have missed out on some important developmental experiences, particularly if early intervention services were not provided. In contrast, a teenager who suddenly loses the use of her legs in an accident has likely had a normal range of experiences throughout childhood but may need considerable support from parents, teachers, specialists, and peers in adapting to life with this newly acquired disability.

Severity

A physical impairment or medical condition can limit a child's ability to engage in age-appropriate activities, mobility, cognitive functioning, social and emotional devel-

Table 12.1 A history of the education of children with physical and health impairments: Key events and implications

Date	Historical Event	Educational Implications
1893	Industrial School for Crippled and Deformed Children was established in Boston.	This was the first special institution for children with physical disabilities in the United States (Eberle, 1922).
Circa 1900	The first special classes for children with physical impairments began in Chicago.	This was the first time children with physical disabilities were educated in public schools (La Vor, 1976).
Early 1900s	There were serious outbreaks of tuberculosis and polio in the United States.	This led to increasing numbers of children with physical impairments being educated by local schools in special classes for the "crippled" or "delicate" (Walker & Jacobs, 1985).
Early 20th century	Winthrop Phelps demonstrated that children could be helped through physical therapy and the effective use of braces. Earl Carlson (who himself had cerebral palsy) was a strong advocate of developing the intellectual potential of children with physical disabilities through appropriate education.	The efforts of these two American physicians contributed to increased understanding and acceptance of children with physical disabilities and to recognition that physical impairment did not preclude potential for educational achievement and self-sufficiency.
Early 20th century to 1970s	Decisions to "ignore, isolate, and institutionalize these children were often based on mental incompetence presumed because of physical disabilities, especially those involving communication and use of upper extremities" (Conner, Scandary, & Tullock, 1988, p. 6).	Increasing numbers of children with mild physical disabilities and health conditions were educated in public schools. Most children with severe physical disabilities were educated in special schools or community agencies (e.g., the United Cerebral Palsy Association).
1975	P.L. 94-142 mandated a free, appropriate public education for all children with disabilities and required schools to provide related services (e.g., transportation services, physical therapy, school health services) necessary for students to be educated in the least restrictive environment.	No longer could a child be denied the right to attend the local public school because there was a flight of stairs at the entrance, bathrooms were not accessible, or school buses were not equipped to transport wheelchairs. The related services provision of IDEA transformed schools from "solely scholastic institutions into therapeutic agencies" (Palfrey, 1995, p. 265).
1984	The Supreme Court ruled in *Independent School District v. Tatro* that schools must provide intermittent catheterization as a supportive or related service if necessary to enable a student with disabilities to receive a public education.	The *Tatro* ruling expanded the range of related services that schools are required to provide and clarified the differences between school health services, which can be performed by a nonphysician, and medical services, which are provided by physicians for diagnostic or eligibility purposes.
1984	The World Institute on Disability was co-founded by Ed Roberts, an inspirational leader for self-advocacy by persons with disabilities.	This was a major milestone in the civil rights and self-advocacy movement by people with disabilities (Stone, 1995).
1990	Americans with Disabilities Act (P.L. 101-336) was passed.	ADA provided civil rights protections to all persons with disabilities in private sector employment and mandated access to all public services, accommodations, transportation, and telecommunications.

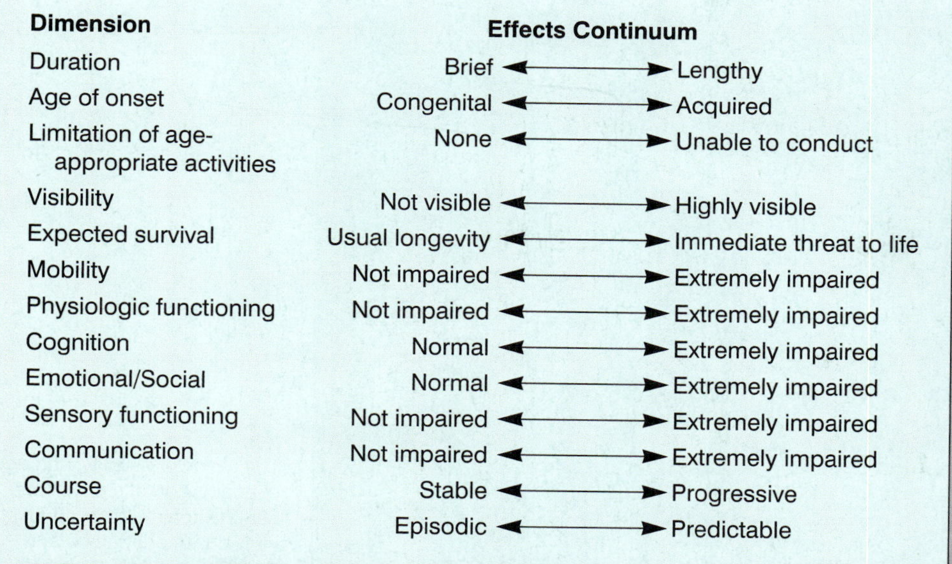

Dimension	Effects Continuum	
Duration	Brief ◄──►	Lengthy
Age of onset	Congenital ◄──►	Acquired
Limitation of age-appropriate activities	None ◄──►	Unable to conduct
Visibility	Not visible ◄──►	Highly visible
Expected survival	Usual longevity ◄──►	Immediate threat to life
Mobility	Not impaired ◄──►	Extremely impaired
Physiologic functioning	Not impaired ◄──►	Extremely impaired
Cognition	Normal ◄──►	Extremely impaired
Emotional/Social	Normal ◄──►	Extremely impaired
Sensory functioning	Not impaired ◄──►	Extremely impaired
Communication	Not impaired ◄──►	Extremely impaired
Course	Stable ◄──►	Progressive
Uncertainty	Episodic ◄──►	Predictable

Figure 12.4 Dimensions of a noncategorical system for classifying and describing the effects of a physical disability or a chronic health condition
Source: Reprinted from Perrin, E. C., Newacheck, P., Pless, B., Drotar, D., Gortmaker, S. L., Leventhal, J., Perrin, J. M., Stein, R. E. K., Walker, D. K., & Weitzman, M. (1993). Issues involved in the definition and classification of chronic health conditions. Reproduced by permission of *Pediatrics,* vol. 91, pp. 787–793. © 1993.

opment, sensory functioning, and communication across a continuum ranging from normal functioning (no impact) to extremely impaired. A minor or transient physical or health impairment, such as those most children experience while growing up, is not likely to have lasting effects; but a severe, chronic impairment can greatly limit a child's range of experiences.

Chronic *conditions are present over long periods and tend not to get better or disappear. An* acute *condition, in contrast, is severe but of limited duration.*

Educators should also be aware of the impact of a child's chronic condition on the family. Some children with chronic health problems need extensive, ongoing assistance that places parents and other family members in the role of caregiver and health services provider. Knoll (1992) gives us a glimpse of the round-the-clock vigilance and stress experienced by the parents of a child with hemophilia.

> There is a monitor when Jacob is in the bathtub to see that he doesn't slip and fall which could start bleeding. Or if he does, so that they will know what to do immediately. Usually pressure and ice are applied. If bleeding continues, an injection of "Factor 8," which controls bleeding, is given. He must be monitored where he plays; e.g., no glass, sharp edges on things, etc. Any kind of cut or fall could affect Jacob's condition. All furniture has been built or rebuilt by the father to have rounded edges. The parents state they didn't take training wheels off Jacob's bicycle for one year after he had the bike for fear he might fall off. The mother states that when he rides it now she watches him. The doctor says the main thing is to protect his head. Any head injury could result in bleeding and you wouldn't always know this. (pp. 31–32)

Many people with disabilities report that their hardware (wheelchairs, artificial limbs, communication devices, and other apparatus) creates a great deal of curiosity and leads to frequent, repetitive questions from strangers. Learning how to explain their physical disabilities or health condition and to respond to questions can be an appropriate component of the educational programs for some children. They may also benefit from discussing concerns such as when to ask for help from others and when to decline offers of assistance.

Visibility Physical impairments and health conditions range from highly visible and conspicuous to not visible. How children think about themselves and the degree to which they are accepted by others often are affected by the visibility of a condition. Some children use a variety of special orthopedic appliances, such as wheelchairs, braces, crutches, and adaptive tables. They may ride to school on a specially equipped bus or van. In school they may need assistance using the toilet or may wear helmets. Although such special devices and adaptations do help children meet important needs, they often have the unfortunate side effect of making the physical impairment more visible, thus making the child look even more different from nondisabled peers.

The severity, visibility, and age of acquisition of a physical or health impairment all affect an individual's adaptation and development.

To join in the discussion "In what ways might the visibility of a physical or health impairment affect a child's self-perception, social development, and level of independence across different environments?" go to the Message Board Module at http://www.prenhall.com/heward.

Educational Approaches

The Interdisciplinary Team

The team approach has special relevance to children with physical impairments and special health needs. No other group of exceptional children comes into contact, both in and out of school, with as many different teachers, physicians, therapists, and other specialists. Because the medical, educational, therapeutic, vocational, and social needs of students with physical and health impairments are often complex and frequently affect each other, it is especially important that educational and health care personnel openly communicate and cooperate with one another. Two particularly important members of the interdisciplinary team for many children with physical and health impairments are the physical therapist and the occupational therapist. Each is a licensed health professional who must complete a specialized training program and meet rigorous standards.

Physical therapists (PTs) are involved in the development and maintenance of motor skills, movement, and posture. They may prescribe specific exercises to help a child increase control of muscles and use specialized equipment, such as braces, effectively. Massage and prescriptive exercises are perhaps the most frequently applied procedures, but physical therapy can also include swimming, heat treatment, special positioning for feeding and toileting, and other techniques. PTs encourage children to be as motorically independent as possible; help develop muscular function; and reduce pain, discomfort, or long-term physical damage. They may also suggest dos and don'ts for sitting positions and activities in the classroom and may devise exercise or play programs that children with and without disabilities can enjoy together.

Occupational therapists (OTs) are concerned with a child's participation in activities, especially those that will be useful in self-help, employment, recreation, communication, and aspects of daily living (e.g., dressing, eating, personal hygiene). They may help a child learn (or relearn) diverse motor behaviors such as drinking from a modified cup, buttoning clothes, tying shoes, pouring liquids, cooking, and typing on a computer keyboard. These activities can enhance a child's physical development, independence, vocational potential, and self-concept. OTs conduct specialized assessments and make recommendations to parents and teachers regarding the effective use of appliances, materials, and activities at home and school. Many OTs also work with vocational rehabilitation specialists in helping students find opportunities for work and independent living after completion of an educational program.

Other specialists who frequently provide related services to children with physical and health impairments include the following:

- *Speech-language pathologists* (SLPs), who provide speech therapy, language interventions, oral motor coordination (e.g., chewing and swallowing), and augmentative and alternative communication (AAC) services
- *Prosthetists,* who make and fit artificial limbs
- *Orthotists,* who design and fit braces and other assistive devices
- *Biomedical engineers,* who develop or adapt technology to meet a student's specialized needs
- *Health aides*, who carry out medical procedures and health care services in the classroom
- *Medical social workers,* who assist students and families in adjusting to disabilities

Environmental Modifications

Environmental modifications are frequently necessary to enable a student with physical and health impairments to participate more fully and independently in school. Environmental modifications include adaptations to provide increased access to a task or activity, modifying the way in which instruction is delivered, and changing the manner in which the task is done (Heller, Dangel, & Sweatman, 1995; Wright & Bigge, 1991). Although barrier-free architecture is the most publicly visible type of environmental modification for making community buildings and services more accessible, some of the most functional adaptations require little or no cost. For example:

- Installing paper cup dispensers near water fountains so they can be used by students in wheelchairs
- Moving a class or an activity to an accessible part of a school building so that a student with a physical impairment can be included
- Providing soft-tip pens that require less pressure for writing
- Providing a head-mounted pointer stick and keyboard guard that enables a student with limited fine motor control to strike one computer key at a time

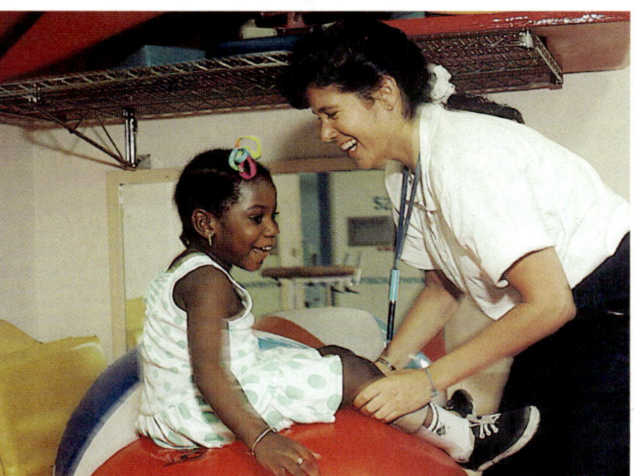

A physical therapist has prescribed specific exercises to increase Tamara's muscular control and range of movement.

Incidentally, a student should not be described as being "confined to a wheelchair." This expression suggests that the person is restrained or even imprisoned. Actually, most students who use wheelchairs leave them from time to time to exercise or to lie down. It is preferable to say that a student "has a wheelchair" or "uses a wheelchair to get around." A working knowledge of techniques associated with wheelchair use can be helpful to a teacher in reducing problems and making classrooms and school buildings accessible (Venn, Morgenstern, & Dykes, 1979).

- Changing desk- and tabletops to appropriate heights for students who are very short or who use wheelchairs
- Providing a wooden pointer to enable a student to reach the upper buttons on an elevator control panel
- Modify the response requirements by allowing written responses instead of spoken responses or vice versa

Special Health Care Needs

Many students with orthopedic and physical disabilities have special health care needs that require specialized procedures such as taking prescribed medication (Harchik, 1994), clean intermittent catheterization (CIC), tracheostomy care, ventilator/respirator care (Lehr & Macurdy, 1994), and managing special nutrition and dietary needs (Harvey Smith, 1994). These special health-related needs are prescribed in an *Individualized Health Care Plan (IHCP),* which is included as part of the student's IEP. According to Poulton (1996), an IHCP is "the written, preplanned and ongoing plan of care for students requiring special health services developed by licensed health personnel and the education team. It includes the nursing process of assessment, nursing diagnosis, planning, intervention, and evaluation. It also includes a plan for emergencies" (p. 1).

Figure 12.5 provides examples of possible IHCP objectives that might be included in a student's IEP. Students who learn to perform all or part of their daily health care needs increase their ability to function independently in normal environments and lessen their dependence on caregivers.

See "Using Dolls to Teach Self-Catheterization Skills to Children with Spina Bifida."

Importance of Positioning, Seating, and Movement Proper positioning, seating, and regular movement are critically important for children with physical disabilities. Proper positioning and movement encourage the development of muscles and bones and help maintain healthy skin (Heller, Alberto, Forney, & Schwartzman, 1996). In addition to the health-related issues, positioning can influence how a child with physical disabilities is perceived and accepted by others. Simple adjustments can contribute to improved appearance and greater comfort and increased health for the child with physical disabilities (Wright & Bigge, 1991):

- Good positioning results in alignment and proximal support of the body.
- Stability positively affects use of the upper body.
- Stability promotes feelings of physical security and safety.
- Good positioning can reduce deformity.
- Positions must be changed frequently.

Students who are able to use their arms should be taught to perform "chair pushups" in which they lift their buttocks off the seat for 5 to 10 seconds. Doing chair pushups every 30 to 60 minutes may prevent pressure sores. Children who cannot perform pushups can shift their weight by bending forward and sideways (Hoeman, 1996).

Proper seating helps combat poor circulation, muscle tightness, and pressure sores, and it contributes to proper digestion, respiration, and physical development. Be attentive to the following (Heller et al., 1996):

- Face should be forward, in midline position.
- Shoulders should be in midline position and not hunched over.
- Trunk should be in midline position; maintain normal curvature of spine.
- Seatbelt, pommel or leg separator, and/or shoulder and chest straps may be necessary for shoulder/upper trunk support and upright positions.
- Pelvic position: hips as far back in the chair as possible and weight distributed evenly on both sides of the buttocks.
- Foot support: both feet level and supported on the floor or wheelchair pedals.

Tube feeding:

- Student will explain (orally, in writing, or through other means) reasons for alternative eating method.
- Student will describe steps necessary in implementing the procedure.
- Student will indicate desire to eat.
- Student will measure feeding liquid to be placed in feeding bag or syringe.
- Student will pour food in feeding bag or syringe.
- Student will direct cleaning of feeding equipment.
- Student will clean equipment.
- Student will feed self.

Tracheostomy suctioning:

- Student will indicate need to be suctioned.
- Student will turn on suction machine.
- Student will hold suction tube while procedure is being implemented.
- Student will describe steps necessary to suction.
- Student will explain to others the indicators of need for suctioning.

Catheterization:

- Student will indicate time to be catheterized.
- Student will self-catheterize.
- Student will describe steps in implementing the process.
- Student will wash materials necessary.
- Student will assemble materials necessary.
- Student will hold catheter steady during procedure.
- Student will describe indicators of problems related to catheterization.

Figure 12.5 Example of IHCP objectives included in an IEP for a student with special health care needs

Source: From Lehr, D. H., & Macurdy, S. (1994). Meeting special health care needs of students. In M. Agran, N. E. Marchand-Martella, & R. C. Martella (Eds.), *Promoting health and safety: Skills for independent living* (p. 82). Pacific Grove, CA: Brooks/Cole. Reprinted by permission.

Lifting and Transferring Students To prevent the development of pressure sores and help students maintain proper seating and positioning, teachers must know how to move and transfer students with physical disabilities. Routines for lifting, transferring, and repositioning children with physical disabilities should be developed for each child and entail standard procedures for (1) making contact with the child, (2) communicating what is going to happen in a manner the child can understand, (3) preparing the child physically for the transfer, and (4) requiring the child to participate in the routine as much as possible (Stremel, Molden, Leister, Matthews, Wilson, Goodall, & Hoston, 1990). Figure 12.6 shows an example of an individualized routine for lifting and carrying a preschool child with physical disabilities and severe auditory impairments. Posting charts and photos of recommended positions for individual students can help remind teachers, paraprofessionals, and

Guidelines for shifting the position of students in their wheelchairs and for moving students to and from a wheelchair to toilets and to the classroom floor are provided by Parette and Hourcade (1986).

Using Dolls to Teach Self-Catheterization Skills to Children with Spina Bifida

Children with physical and health impairments often require regular medical regimens ranging from simple procedures (such as taking prescribed oral medications) to more complex routines (injection of insulin to control diabetes). The ability to self-administer needed medical routines increases the individual's independence to function in normal environments and eliminates reliance on a caretaker. When complex procedures must be performed by children or persons with learning problems, direct systematic instruction is indicated. If the procedures involve invading the body or errors during practice are potentially hazardous, simulation training can be used. This program evaluated the effectiveness of simulation training with a doll.

Children and Setting Cathy and Teresa, ages 4 and 8, two girls with spina bifida whose urinary functions were managed by intermittent catheterization performed by their parents, participated in the training program. Both girls were scheduled to attend regular schools during the fall (preschool and second grade), and their parents had requested they learn self-catheterization to promote independent functioning and adaptation in the classroom.

Task Analysis and Measurement A task analysis of self-catheterization yielded four basic skill components, each with multiple steps: preparation (6 steps); placing and adjusting a compact magnifying mirror (6 steps); catheter insertion and removal (11 steps); and cleanup (9 steps). The children's performance on each step in the task analysis on the doll and then on themselves was observed and recorded during measurement probes before and after training of each of the four skill components. During each doll probe, the child was asked to show how to catheterize the doll; no help or feedback was given. In vivo (self) probes were conducted after each doll probe to determine if training with the doll generalized to self-administration of the procedure. The child was asked to show how to catheterize herself and to do the best she could but to stop whenever she wished.

Simulation Training Each child was taught to perform each step of the procedure on a plastic doll with female genitalia and movable arms and legs. The children were told that they were going to learn to catheterize themselves but that a doll with the same urinary problems needed their help first. The trainer described and modeled on the doll the steps in the skill component under instruction. The child was then asked to demonstrate and verbalize the steps for that component ("Show me how you can help the doll with her catheter, and tell her what you're doing"). To simulate the performance of self-catheterization, the doll was manipulated from a sitting position on the child's lap, facing forward. If the child made an error or performed a step out of sequence, the trainer provided verbal prompts ("Where does that end of the catheter go?"), visual prompts (pointing), and manual guidance as necessary. Correct responses were praised.

Results and Discussion The number of correct responses performed by each child on both doll and self-probes across each skill component is shown in Figure A. During baseline (before training), the children performed few of the steps correctly on either the doll or themselves. After training and practice with the doll, their performance improved both on the doll and on themselves. Cathy required training on herself for several steps of the catheterization insertion and removal component, which she performed correctly on the doll but had trouble with on herself. Follow-up reports from the parents indicated both children were catheterizing themselves independently.

Doll training offers several advantages for teaching children how to self-administer medical procedures. First, because they associate dolls with play activities, children's interest and willingness to participate in training might be increased. Second, children may be reluctant to perform an unfamiliar and intrusive procedure on themselves. Allowing children to achieve mastery on a doll before self-application may desensitize them to the process and decrease the likelihood of making potentially harmful errors while practicing on themselves. Finally, using a doll enables many more opportunities for practice than does the child's normal catheterization schedule. Using dolls also appears to be an efficient means of training. Total training time across a nine-day period was 4 hours and 30 minutes for Cathy and 2 hours and 45 minutes for Teresa.

Source: Adapted from Neef, N. A., Parrish, J. M., Hannigan, K. F., Page, T. J., & Iwata, B. A. (1990, Fall). Teaching self-catheterization skills to children with neurogenic bladder complications. *Journal of Applied Behavior Analysis, 22,* 237–243. Used by permission.

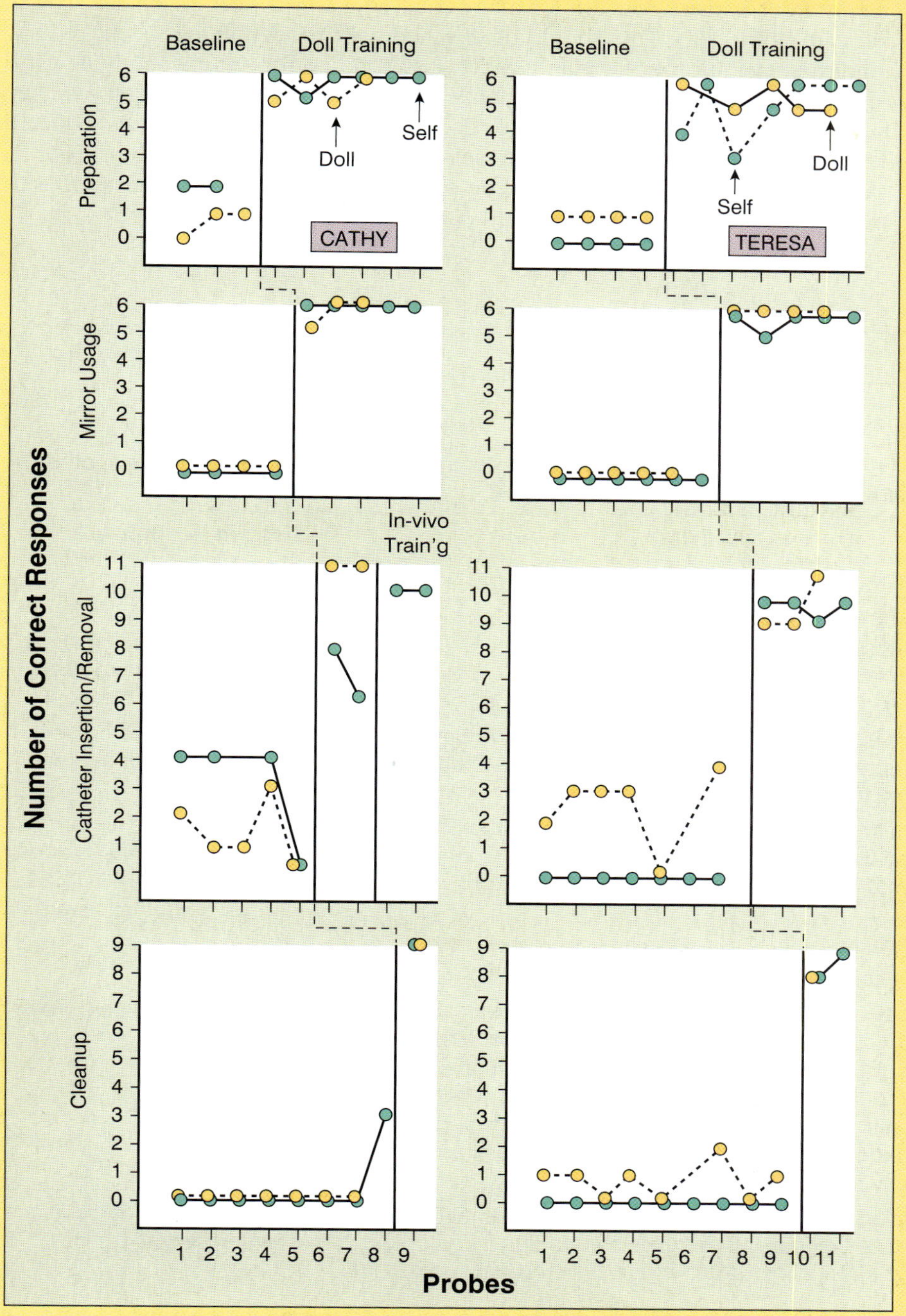

Figure A
Number of correct responses within skill components on simulation (doll) and in vivo (self) probes for each participant

other staff to use proper transferring and positioning techniques (Rikhye, Gothelf, & Appell, 1989).

Skin care is a major concern for many children with physical disabilities. The skin underneath braces or splints should be checked daily to identify persistent red spots that indicate an improper fit. Skin checks should be performed by someone on the student's team at least twice daily. Students who are capable of conducting self-checks of their skin should be taught to do so. Use of a long-handled mirror can reduce the student's dependence on others for this self-care task (Ricci-Balich & Behm, 1996).

A health care professional should be contacted if any spot does not fade within 20 minutes after the pressure is relieved (Campbell, 1993).

Name: Lisa Date: 9/16/00

Lifting and Carrying Routine

Follow these steps each time you pick Lisa up from the floor, move her from one piece of equipment to another, or move her in the classroom from one location or activity to another.

Step	Activity	Desired Response
Contact	Touch Lisa gently. Tell her you are going to move her.	Wait for Lisa to relax.
Communication	Use the appropriate sign to tell Lisa where you are going (i.e., sign toilet for going to the bathroom area).	Wait for Lisa to sign for 3 seconds. If she doesn't make the sign, help her by physically guiding her to make the sign.
Preparation	Make sure Lisa's tone is not stiff before you move her. Use deep pressure and repositioning to attain alignment and reduce tone.	Wait for Lisa's body to come into alignment and for her tone to relax.
Lifting	Place Lisa in a sitting position if she is lying on the floor. She will be lifted from a standing position if in the stander. Tell Lisa that you are going to lift her. Use the sign for lift.	Wait for Lisa to move her arms forward toward you. If she does not reach forward, use facilitation to move her arms forward.
	Place your arms around Lisa's back and under her knees to lift her into your arms.	
Carrying	Turn Lisa away from you so that she is facing away and can see where you are moving. Lean her back against your body to provide support, and hold her with one arm under her pelvis and hips, with her legs in front. If her legs become stiff, use your other arm to hold her legs apart by coming under one leg and between the two legs to hold them gently apart.	Lisa will be able to watch where she is going.
Repositioning	Place Lisa on the floor or in another piece of equipment. Tell her what you are doing by using the correct sign (i.e., sit; stand) and the sign for the activity (i.e., toilet for bathroom).	Lisa will be ready to participate in the next activity.

Figure 12.6 Example of a routine for lifting and carrying a child with physical disabilities

Source: From Ault, M. M., Graff, J. C., & Rues, J. P. (2000). Special health care procedures. In M. E. Snell & F. Brown (Eds.), *Instruction of students with severe disabilities* (5th ed.). Upper Saddle River, NJ: Merrill/Prentice Hall.

Assistive Technology

Although the term *technology* often conjures up images of sophisticated computers and other hardware, technology includes any systematic method for accomplishing a practical task or purpose based on scientific principles. *Assistive technology* is defined in IDEA as "any item, piece of equipment, or product system, whether acquired commercially off the shelf, modified, or customized, that is used to increase, maintain, or improve functional capabilities of individuals with disabilities." Parette (1998) notes that the types of assistive technology used by persons with disabilities are often the same as those used by individuals without disabilities:

> For example, a flexible drinking straw used by persons without disabilities may be viewed as a convenience for drinking purposes. For a student with physical disabilities who cannot grasp and tilt a cup to drink from it, the straw facilitates a functional daily living skill (i.e., drinking from a cup) with little or no assistance from others. A hand-held remote control is viewed by most people as a convenient technology allowing access to a television or VCR from across the room. It is viewed as an alternative to walking to the television set or VCR and making a selection manually. For students with disabilities, a remote control device could be a necessity, that is, the only means of accessing and interacting with modern conveniences. In general then, assistive technology, is a life necessity for many individuals. (Williams, 1991, p. 206)

Individuals with physical disabilities use both low-tech assistive devices (e.g., adapted eating utensils, picture communication books) and high-tech assistive devices (e.g., computerized synthetic speech devices, advanced switches that detect eye movements) for a wide variety of purposes, including mobility, performing daily life skills, improved environmental manipulation and control, better communication, access to computers, recreation and leisure, and enhanced learning (Lewis, 1993; Parette, 1998). Education team members should not view a student's acquisition and use of assistive technology as an educational outcome in itself but as a means of increasing the student's independence and access to various activities and opportunities (Chuch & Glennen, 1992).

Some students are unable to move freely from place to place without the assistance of a mobility device. Advances in wheelchair design have made manual chairs lighter and stronger, powered chairs have been adapted for use in rural areas, and new environmental controls have put the wheelchair user in contact with both immediate and distant parts of their world. Many children as young as 3 to 5 years old can learn to explore their environment with freedom and independence in "energy efficient, creative, wheeled scooter boards and wheeled go-carts that provide mobility without restricting upper or lower extremity functions" (Evans & Smith, 1993, p. 1418). Clarke (1988) describes and compares a variety of mobility devices and suggests that they be selected with the following variables in mind:

- Child's motor capabilities
- Child's physical strength and endurance
- Cost of the device
- Physical layout of the home, school, and community
- Educational and therapy goals

New technological aids for communication are used increasingly by children whose physical impairments prevent them from speaking clearly. For students who are able to speak but have limited motor function, voice input/output products enable them to access computers (Esposito & Campbell, 1987). Such developments allow students with physical impairments to communicate expressively and receptively with others and to take part in a wide range of instructional programs.

Information about multimedia/assistive technology for Chapter 12 can be found by accessing Resources at http://www.prenhall.com/heward and linking to the Special Ed Resource Page.

For a list of websites and other information sources for assistive technology devices, see "For More Information" at the end of this chapter. Several excellent handbooks on designing, selecting, and using assistive technology are also available (e.g., Chuch & Glennen, 1992; Cook & Hussey, 1995; Gray, Quartrano, & Liberman, 1998).

See the section on alternative and augmentative communication in Chapter 9.

Handi-Hams is an international organization of people with and without disabilities who help people with physical disabilities expand their world through amateur radio. To find out about this organization and other sources for adaptive devices and assistive technology, see "For More Information" at the end of this chapter.

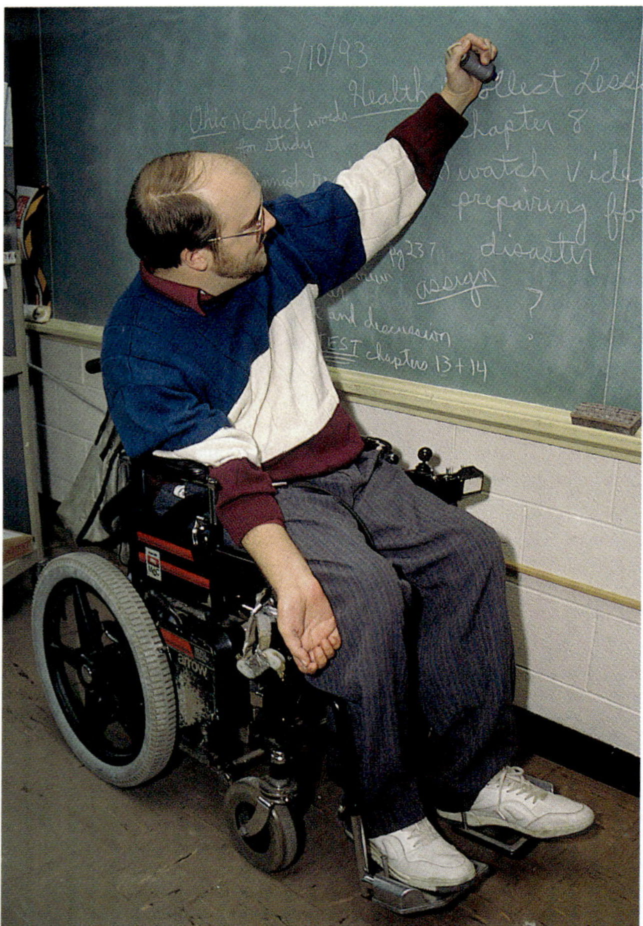

Assistive technology includes low-tech devices such as this simple chalk holder.

Telecommunications technology is used by many individuals with physical disabilities to expand their world, to gain access to information and services, and to meet new people. Electronic mail (e-mail) (Gandell & Laufer, 1993) and amateur (ham) radio are used by many adults with disabilities to communicate with others, to make new friends, and to build and maintain relationships.

Menlove (1996) provides information and suggestions for identifying sources of funding for assistive technology.

Technology can seldom be pulled off the shelf and serve a student with disabilities with maximum effectiveness. Before purchasing and training a child to use any assistive technology device, the education team should carefully consider certain characteristics of the child and of the potential technologies that might be selected as well as the impact of using those technologies on the child's family (Hourcade, Parette, & Huer, 1997; Parette, 1998; Parette, Hourcade, & VanBiervliet, 1993). An assessment of the child's academic skills, social skills, and physical capabilities should help identify the goals and objectives for the technology as well as narrow down the kinds of devices that may be effective. The child's preferences for certain types of technology should also be determined. At that point, the characteristics of potentially appropriate technologies should be considered, including availability, simplicity of operation, initial and ongoing cost, adaptability to meet the changing needs of the child, and the reliability and repair record of the device.

Inclusive Attitudes

After health care objectives are meet, acceptance is the most basic need of children with physical and health impairments. How parents, teachers, classmates, and others react to a child with physical disabilities is at least as important as the disability itself. Many children with physical disabilities suffer from excessive pity, sympathy, and overprotection; others are cruelly rejected, stared at, teased, and excluded from participation in activities with nondisabled children. Turner-Henson, Holaday, Corser, Ogletree, and Swan (1994) conducted interviews with the parents of 365 children with chronic illnesses and reported that one-third (34.5%) of the parents had experienced specific incidences of discrimination concerning their children. Although the study did not focus on the schools, more than half (55%) of the problems cited by the parents occurred at school (e.g., child not allowed to participate in play activities because of a brace or excluded from parties because of food limitations; teacher thinks child is faking low blood sugar). Peers were the second most common source of discrimination (36%).

All children, whether or not they face the challenges presented by a physical disability or chronic health condition, need to develop respect for themselves and to feel that they have a rightful place in their families, schools, and communities. Effective teachers accept and treat children with physical impairments and special health care needs as worthwhile and whole individuals rather than as disability cases. They encourage the children to develop a positive, realistic view of themselves and their physical conditions. They enable the children to experience success, accomplishment, and, at times, failure. They expect the children to meet reasonable standards of performance and behavior. They help the children cope with disabilities wherever possible and realize that, beyond their physical impairments, these children have many qualities that make them unique individuals.

Often, well-meaning teachers, classmates, and parents tend to do too much for a child with a physical or health impairment. It may be difficult, frustrating, and/or time-consuming for the child to learn to care for his own needs, but the confidence and skills gained from independent functioning are well worth the effort in the long run.

Students with physical limitations should be encouraged to develop as much independence as possible. Nevertheless, most persons with physical disabilities find it necessary to rely on others for assistance at certain times, in certain situations. Effective teachers can help students cope with their disabilities, set realistic expectations, and accept help gracefully when it is needed.

Many people without disabilities tend to feel uncomfortable in the presence of a person with a visible disability and react with tension and withdrawal (Allsop, 1980). This response is probably attributable to lack of previous contact with individuals with disabilities: people may fear that they will say or do the wrong thing. A study by Belgrave and Mills (1981) found that when people with physical disabilities specifically mentioned their disabilities in connection with a request for help ("Would you mind sharpening my pencil for me? There are just some things a person can't do from a wheelchair"), they were perceived more favorably than they were when no mention was made of the disability.

Children should be taught to never *equate a person with a disability label, as in "He's a C.P." or "She's an epileptic."*

The classroom can be a useful place to discuss disabilities and to encourage understanding and acceptance of a child with a physical or health impairment. Some teachers find that simulation or role-playing activities are helpful. Classmates might, for example, have the opportunity to use wheelchairs, braces, or crutches to expand their awareness of some barriers a classmate with physical disabilities faces. Pieper (1983) notes that most children with physical and health impairments are "neither saintly creatures nor pitiable objects" (p. 8). She suggests that teachers emphasize cooperation rather than competition by choosing tasks that require students to work together. It is important to give praise when earned but not to make the child with a physical impairment a teacher's pet who will be resented by other students. Factual information can also help build a general understanding of an impairment. Classmates should learn to use accurate terminology and offer the correct kind of assistance when needed.

Adapting Toys for Children with Cerebral Palsy

Spontaneous and independent use of commercially available toys is not possible for many children with cerebral palsy. The toys often require more coordination or strength than these youngsters have. Continuous inability to engage in physical activity and gain mastery over the environment may cause the child to lose motivation and become passive. Because playing is an integral part of intellectual, social, perceptual, and physical development, growth in these areas may be limited when the child cannot actively play.

Fortunately, toys can be adapted to make them more accessible to children with physical disabilities. Six types of modifications are most effective in promoting active, independent use of play materials.

Stabilization Stabilizing a toy enhances its function in two ways. First, it prevents the child's uncontrolled movements and difficulty directing the hand to desired locations from moving objects out of reach or knocking them over. Second, many children with cerebral palsy have difficulty performing tasks that require holding an object with one hand while manipulating it in some way with the other hand. Toys with a base can be clamped to a table. Masking tape is an inexpensive and effective way to secure many toys. Velcro is another. The hook side of Velcro can be placed on the toy, while the loop side is mounted on a clean surface. Suction cups can also stabilize a toy for a short time on a clean, nonwood surface.

Boundaries Restricting the movement of toys such as cars or trains makes it easier for some children to use and retrieve them if pushed out of reach. Boundaries can be created in various ways depending upon how the object is to be moved. For example, push toys can be placed in the top of a cardboard box or on a tray with edges to create a restricted area. Pull toys can be placed on a track, and items that require a banging motion, such as a tambourine, can be held in a wood frame with springs.

Grasping Aids The ability to hold objects independently can be facilitated in a variety of ways. A Velcro strap can be placed around the child's hand, with Velcro also placed on the materials to be held, thus creating a bond between the hand and the object. A universal cuff can be used for holding sticklike objects such as crayons or pointers. Simply enlarging an item by wrapping foam or tape around it may make it easier to hold.

Manipulation Aids Some toys require isolated finger movements, use of a pincer grasp, and controlled movements of the wrist, which are too difficult for a child with physical disabilities. Various adaptations can help compensate for deficits in these movements. Extending and widening pieces of the toy will make swiping and pushing easier. Flat extensions, knobs, or dowels can be used to increase the surface area. A crossbar or dowel, placed appropriately, can compensate for an inability to rotate the wrist.

Switches Some children have such limited hand function that they can only operate toys that are activated by a switch. Commercially available, battery-operated toys can be modified to operate by adapted switches. Teachers can make and adapt their own switches and toys (Burkhardt,

1981; Wright & Momari, 1985) or purchase them from a number of firms that serve persons with disabilities. After determining some physical action (such as moving a knee laterally, lifting a shoulder, or making a sound) that the child can perform consistently and with minimum effort, one selects the type of switch best suited to that movement. The switch is always positioned in the same place, which facilitates automatic switch activation and allows the child to give full attention to the play activity rather than concentrating on using the switch.

An adapted switch makes battery-operated toys accessible and fun for Madelyn.

Positioning An occupational or physical therapist should determine the special positioning needs of each child. Good positioning will maximize freedom of movement, improve the ability to look at a toy, and facilitate controlled, relaxed movement. Placement of the toy is crucial. It should be within easy reach and require a minimum of effort to manipulate. The child should not become easily fatigued or have to struggle. The child must be able to look at the toy while playing.

General Considerations Activities should be interesting and facilitate cognitive growth yet not be beyond the child's conceptual capabilities. Toys should be sturdy and durable. Avoid toys with sharp edges or small pieces that can be swallowed.

These principles for adapting toys can be applied to other devices, such as communication aids, computers, environmental controls, and household items, to make them easier to use. Making an educational environment more accessible gives children with physical disabilities greater control of their surroundings and the opportunity to expand the scope of their learning experiences.

Source: Adapted from Schaeffler, C. (1988, Spring). Making toys accessible for children with cerebral palsy. *Teaching Exceptional Children, 20,* 26–28. Used by permission.

Peckham (1993) provides a lesson plan answering the questions and concerns of classmates of a student with cancer.

For a discussion of ways in which classroom teachers can help themselves, classmates, and parents deal with the death of a student, see Cassini and Rodgers (1989), McHutchion (1991), Peckham (1993), Thornton and Krajewski (1993), and Wrenn (1994).

To find out the percentage of school-age students with orthopedic impairments, other health impairments, and traumatic brain injury served in six different educational environments during the 1995–1996 school year, see Table 1.6 in Chapter 1.

Including Children with Chronic Illness Some students with chronic illnesses are absent from school for extended periods because of flare-ups or scheduled medical treatment. Successful reentry of children who have missed extended periods of school because of illness or the contraction of a disease requires preparation of the child, her parents, classmates, and school personnel (Sexson & Madan-Swain, 1993). A classroom presentation aimed at preparing classmates might be conducted a week or two prior to the child's reentry. Children should be given information and encouraged to ask questions about the child and the disease. Questions that peers often ask about a child with a health problem are listed in Figure 12.7.

There is a need for improved programs of education and counseling for students with terminal illnesses. These programs should give realistic support to the child and family in dealing with death and in making the best possible use of the time available. When a child dies, teachers and classmates may also be seriously affected, and their needs should be considered and talked about.

Educational Placement Alternatives

For no group of exceptional children is the continuum of educational services and placement options more relevant than for students with physical impairments and special health needs. Most children with physical and health impairments today spend at least part of the school day in regular classrooms. During the 1996–1997 school year, about 41% of all school-age students who receive special education services under the disability category orthopedic impairments, 43% of those with other health impairments, and 28% of those with traumatic brain injury were educated in the regular classroom (U.S. Department of Education, 1998). The percentage of students in each disability category served in resource rooms was 21%, 30%, and 25%.

Many children with physical disabilities are also served in special classes in the public schools. During the 1996–1997 school year, about 30% of all school-age students who receive special education services under the disability category orthopedic impairments, 18% of those with other health impairments, and 31% of those with traumatic brain injury were educated in separate classrooms (U.S. Department of Education, 1998). Some districts have entire schools designed or adapted especially for students with physical disabilities, whereas in others special classrooms are housed within regular elementary or secondary school buildings. Special classes usu-

Figure 12.7 Questions that peers often ask about a child's illness or disease

Source: From Sexson, S. B., & Madan-Swain, A. (1993). School reentry for the child with chronic illness. *Journal of Learning Disabilities, 26*(2), 120. © 1993 by PRO-ED, Inc. Reprinted by permission.

- What's wrong with __________?
- Is the disease contagious?
- Will __________ die from it?
- Will he/she lose any more limbs?
- Can __________ still play, visit me at home, drive, date, etc.?
- Should we talk about __________'s illness or should we ignore it?
- What will other kids think if I'm still friends with __________?
- Will __________ be different (look funny, bleed, faint, cough, vomit) when he comes back?

ally provide smaller class size, more adapted equipment, and easier access to the services of professionals such as physicians, physical and occupational therapists, and specialists in communication disorders and therapeutic recreation.

Homebound or hospital education programs are available to children with severe physical and health impairments. If a child's medical condition necessitates hospitalization or treatment at home for a lengthy period (generally 30 days or more), the local school district is obligated to develop an IEP and to provide appropriate educational services to the child through a qualified teacher. Some children need home- or hospital-based instruction because their life-support equipment cannot be made portable. Such *technology-dependent students* are in need of "both a medical device to compensate for the loss of a vital body function and substantial and ongoing nursing care to avoid death or further disability" (Office of Technology Assessment, 1987, p. 3). This is usually regarded as the most restrictive level of special education service because little or no interaction with nondisabled students is possible in a home or hospital setting. Most large hospitals and medical centers employ educational specialists who cooperate with the hospitalized student's home school district in planning and delivering instruction. Homebound children are visited regularly by itinerant teachers or tutors hired by the school district. Some school programs use a closed-circuit TV system to enable children to see, hear, and participate in class discussions and demonstrations from their beds (Kleinberg, 1984).

The term medically fragile *is sometimes used to refer to students who are dependent on life-support medical technology. As Lehr and McDaid (1993) point out, however, many of these children are "incredibly strong—survivors of many adverse conditions, who in fact are not fragile at all, but remarkably strong to be able to rebound from periods of acute illness" (p. 7). They believe the term* medically fragile *frightens school personnel and should not be used.*

One should not assume that a technology-dependent child cannot be educated in the public schools. After examining the experiences of 77 families of children who are ventilator-assisted, the authors of a study on the educational placements of such children concluded that "barriers to the integration of these children into school-based programs are attitudinal more than technological" (Jones, Clatterbuck, Marquis, Turnbull, & Moberly, 1996, p. 47). Wadsworth, Knight, and Balser (1993) propose 15 guidelines for placing a child who is medically fragile into the school environment. Levine (1996) describes a special school program for children who are dependent on ventilators.

Current Issues and Future Trends

Children with physical and health impairments are being included in regular educational programs as much as possible today. No longer do professionals believe that the regular classroom is an inappropriate environment for a child with physical limitations. Although architectural and attitudinal barriers still exist in some areas, integrated public school programs are gradually becoming the norm instead of the exception.

Reviews and discussions of special education law and legal precedents concerning the schools' responsibility for providing assistive technology special health care services can be found in Rapport (1996) and Weiss and Dykes (1995). Reed Martin, an attorney who specializes in special education law, recommends that teachers who perform health care procedures for students have liability insurance (CEC Today, *1998).*

Related Services Support Inclusion

Including students with physical impairments and special health care needs, however, has raised several controversial issues. Many questions center on the extent of responsibility properly assumed by teachers and schools in providing for a child's physical and health needs. In a landmark case (*Irving Independent School District v. Tatro,* 1984), the U.S. Supreme Court decided that a school district was obligated to provide clean intermittent catheterization to a young child with spina bifida. The Court considered catheterization to be a related service, necessary for the child to remain in the least restrictive educational setting and able to be performed by a trained layperson. Some educators and school administrators believe that services such as catheterization are more medical than educational and should not be the school's responsibility. The expense of such services and the availability of insurance pose potential problems for school personnel. Similar questions have been raised with regard to the equipment and special services that children with physical or health impairments may need in regular schools. For example, who should bear the cost of an expensive computerized communication system for a child with cerebral palsy—the parents, the school, both, or some other agency?

We will likely see a continuation of the present trend to serve children with physical and health impairments in regular classrooms as much as possible. Therapists and other support personnel will come into the classroom to assist the teacher, child, and classmates. For example, some school districts in North Carolina employ health aides who carry out medical care plans in the classroom, assist OTs or PTs, help students get lunch trays, or act as teachers' assistants if not needed elsewhere (*CEC Today,* 1998). This appears to be a more effective and economical use of professional time and skill than removing a child with disabilities from the classroom to provide services in an isolated setting. Wherever and by whomever needed health and other related services are carried out, we must heed Orelove and Sobsey's (1991) caution:

> The challenge for the team is to determine how to work with and around the student's medical and physical needs to provide an appropriate education, rather than turning the school day into an extended therapy session. Therapy and specialized health care procedures should facilitate, not replace, instruction. (pp. 3–4)

New and Emerging Technologies for Persons with Severe Physical Disabilities

Over the past several decades, the use of technology to "minimize disadvantages associated with disabilities has blossomed from a promise that benefited a few individuals to a reality that has improved many people's lives" (Sobsey, 1996, p. 207). New and emerging developments in technology and biomedical engineering hold even more exciting implications for many individuals with physical disabilities. People with paralysis resulting from spinal cord injury and other causes are already benefiting from sophisticated microcomputers that can stimulate paralyzed muscles by bypassing damaged nerves. In 1982 Nan Davis became the first human being to walk with permanently paralyzed muscles; she was able to control a computer with her brain and transmit impulses to sensors placed on her paralyzed muscles. Such systems have become more efficient and widespread, helping many people with various kinds of physical impairments. *Myoelectric (bionic) limbs* are battery-powered artificial limbs that pick up electrical signals from the brain and enable the user to perform certain movements and functions. *Robotics* also hold promise for increasing the independent functioning of persons with physical disabilities.

To learn how researchers are developing robots to assist students with physical disabilities in the classroom, see "Grasping the Future with Robotic Aids" later in this chapter.

Animal Assistance

Using animals to assist people with physical disabilities has also generated much recent interest. Animals can help children and adults with physical disabilities in many ways. Nearly everyone is familiar with guide dogs, which can help people who are blind travel independently. Some agencies now train hearing dogs to assist people who are deaf by alerting them to sounds. Another recent and promising approach to the use of animals by people with disabilities is that of a helper or service dog. Depending on a person's needs, dogs can be trained to carry books and other objects (in saddlebags), pick up telephone receivers, turn light switches on or off, and open doors. Dogs can also be used for balance and support—for example, to help a person propel a wheelchair up a steep ramp or to help a person stand up from a seated position. And dogs can be trained to contact family members or neighbors in an emergency.

"Helper" or "service dogs" can be trained to assist with many daily living and work-related tasks.

Monkeys have been trained to perform complex tasks such as preparing food, operating record and tape players, and turning the pages of books (MacFadyen, 1986). Sometimes technological and animal assistance are combined, as when a person uses a laser beam (emitted from a mouth-held device) to show a monkey which light switch to turn on.

In addition to providing practical assistance and enhancing the independence of people with disabilities, animals also appear to have social value as companions. People frequently report that their helper animals serve as ice-breakers in opening up conversations and contacts with nondisabled people in the school and community. In addition, the responsibility of caring for an animal is a worthwhile and rewarding experience for many people, with or without disabilities.

Employment, Life Skills, and Self-Advocacy

A major area of concern is employment, one of the most meaningful aspects of adult life. Many studies show that successful and remunerative work is one of the most important variables in enabling people with disabilities to lead satisfying, productive, and independent lives. Yet negative attitudes persist on the part of many employers. Vocational and professional opportunities must be expanded to include individuals with disabilities more equitably. While children are in school, their education should help them investigate practical avenues of future employment, and there should be ongoing contact between educators and vocational rehabilitation specialists.

The employment and lifestyles of adults with disabilities are examined in detail in Chapter 15.

Self-Advocacy

Traditionally, children and adults with disabilities were viewed as society's responsibility, and it was assumed they should appreciate and be grateful for the services (i.e., charity) bestowed upon them by a benevolent society (Wolfensberger, 1969). Persons with disabilities neither want nor need charity; rather, they need and deserve equal

Grasping the Future with Robotic Aids

by Richard D. Howell

One of the most exciting areas of technological innovation in special education is in the development of new assistive tools for persons with severe physical disabilities. The augmentation or enhancement of human capabilities in communication, mobility, and manipulation is of increasing interest to a new generation of rehabilitation engineers and technologists. An area that has received minimal but growing attention is the use of robots to increase the manipulation potential of persons with severe physical disabilities.

Just What Is a Robot? The word *robot* is derived from a Czech word that means "forced labor," defined in *Webster's New World Dictionary* (1986) as "any mechanical device operated automatically, especially by remote control, to perform in a seemingly human way" (p. 1231). Although most people attribute many more capabilities to robots than they actually possess, they are currently being used in medical surgeries, have come to be associated with state-of-the-art manufacturing processes, and have now entered the area of human services, including rehabilitation and special education.

Robots have great potential as assistive tools for students with disabilities. First, robots can provide opportunities for *independent manipulation* because they are under the exclusive control of the human operator. Second, when properly designed, robots can provide increased *educational access and opportunities* for students with and without disabilities. Given the national trends toward inclusive education, we must design systems that have a broader viability for all students. To be successful, however, every tool must be justified in its use. Personal robotic devices must eventually meet the same demands as other general-purpose tools, including functionality, viability, reliability, and cost-effectiveness.

Robots as New Instructional Tools Once a student has had an educational robotic system properly fitted to her individual capabilities and has received the proper training to establish what the environment is and how it works, she is prepared to address a variety of educational experiences, including physical manipulations of instructional materials. An analysis has revealed that science education provides the content area with the greatest potential for developing a manipulation-rich environment. The key to the increased learning that takes place in an activity-based approach is that students who actively and frequently

Figure A Components of an educational robotic system

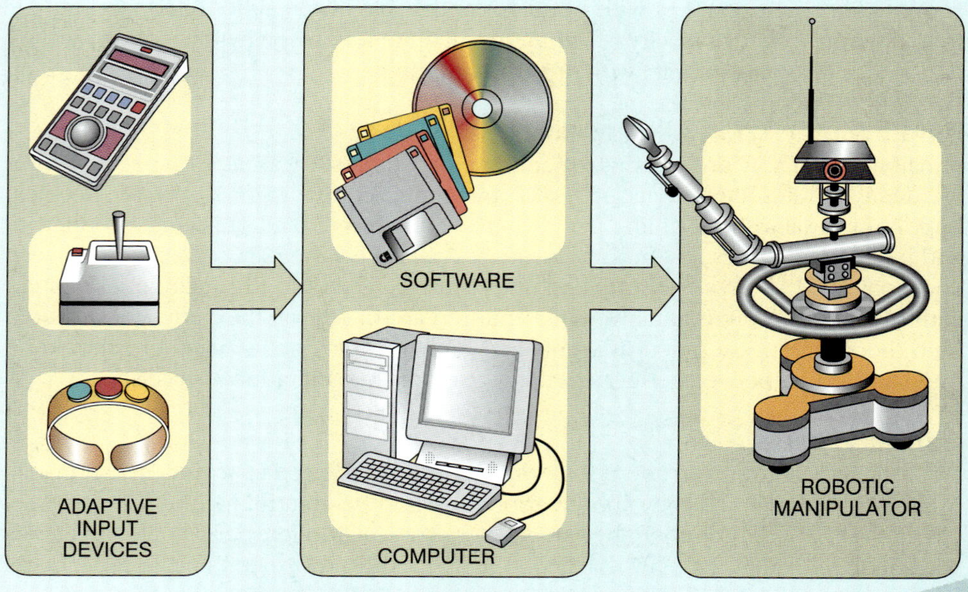

respond to the science materials will be more engaged and motivated than students who must try to imagine what the results of a particular set of experiments might look like and mean.

The story of Troy's use of an educational robot is derived from direct observations during four months in a local public school. As you read, refer to the accompanying diagram to imagine what it is like to use this unique system (see Figure A).

Troy's Story: Grasping His World Some children are so bound up in their own bodies that they cannot direct basic hand movements or communicate their needs. Such a child is Troy, a handsome and willful 10-year-old with severe physical involvement due to cerebral palsy. He is obviously bright and as social as he can be without understandable language. He cannot pick up and hold a block or a ball, and when he does manage to grasp an object, he soon drops it involuntarily or squeezes it tightly in a hand that will not bend or twist at any angle. Without fully functioning hands, his ability to work, learn, play, and take care of himself is so limited that he is almost totally dependent on others.

Which object weighs the most? As his skills at controlling the robot increase, Troy comes into contact with ever more complex and exciting learning experiences.

When Troy heads down the hall at the school to work with the robot, he is expectant and speeds up the motor on his powered wheelchair, forcing us to hustle just to keep up with him. As he moves into place at the table with the robot and science materials, he becomes obviously more powerful. The power is precious because it has been earned. Troy had to work and concentrate hard to learn how to use his new tool effectively, and he knows that new, interesting learning experiences await him.

Troy's robot is actually a light industrial system typically used to test electronic parts and do relatively fine manipulations. It is strong enough to move objects that weigh several pounds and has been adapted for use in many different educational and rehabilitation settings. Currently, only two or three robotic devices have been developed specifically for use by persons with disabilities.

Troy uses a guarded five-switch adaptive input device to control the software that runs the robot. When he was first introduced to the robot, he approached it in a frenzy, pressing switches constantly and randomly. He liked watching the robot move but was unable to understand the linked sequences of actions required to move it purposefully through space, grasp an object, and then present it to Troy for investigation.

The robot moves slowly and deliberately as Troy uses both preprogrammed and directed movements to grasp and move objects through the structured science activities. The computer system is positioned so that Troy can easily see the screen displaying a brightly colored control display. The software gives him discrete control over six joint motors that move the robot in the X, Y, and Z vectors (three-dimensional space), which allows him to move the robot arm to any place within the robot's working space. He also can move the robot to six preprogrammed locations.

Even though the movements are slow and laborious, Troy uses his new tool with growing confidence and independence. He has learned that he can control his environment, albeit more purposefully and slowly than you or I might like—but it is his alone to command.

Robots in Your Future? We are still far from advocating the use of robotic devices as answers to manipulation deficits. Before robots become common in educational and rehabilitation settings, a number of simultaneous developments in both hardware and software must occur: a standard control software that runs the same programs across robot systems, a well-defined set of criteria and procedures for ensuring the user's safety, robots that have been specifically developed for use by humans for personal needs, and a cost-effective system.

Today, researchers and educators are working toward integrating curriculum materials, software tools, and robots into a complete science laboratory environment. This setting will someday enable both students with disabilities and their nondisabled peers to work together within a powerful laboratory-based science setting incorporating the best tools and instructional strategies available.

Source: Richard Howell is a member of the special education faculty and the Biomedical Engineering Center at The Ohio State University. His research focuses on the development of assistive devices and educational robots for persons with severe physical disabilities and sensory impairments. Dr. Howell is also co-author of Chapter 14.

Telethons and other fund-raising activities on behalf of persons with disabilities have become controversial in recent years. Some self-advocacy groups and professionals believe they perpetuate negative stereotypes and portray people with disabilities as objects of pity (see the November 1993 issue of the TASH Newsletter*).*

Use the self-tests at http://www.prenhall.com/heward to assess your knowledge of the content of Chapter 12.

access to the same educational, employment, housing, and recreational opportunities as persons without disabilities (Giangreco, 1996). Legislation and litigation over the past 20 years have mandated equal access and provided funding for improved opportunities, but many of those advancements have been the direct product of self-advocacy.

There are many self-help groups for people with disabilities. These groups can help provide information and support to children affected by similar disabilities. It is usually encouraging for a child and parent to meet and observe capable, independent adults who have disabilities, and worthwhile helping relationships can be established. Teachers can help promote self-knowledge and self-confidence in their students with physical disabilities by introducing them to such adults and groups. Some self-advocacy groups operate centers for independent living, which emphasize adaptive devices, financial benefits, access to jobs, and provision of personal care attendants. Other groups are active as advocates for social change, countering instances in which people with disabilities are excluded from meaningful participation in society.

We all must work to improve the quality of education, increase physical access to public buildings, improve public attitudes, and provide greater support for parents and families. As these needs are met, the opportunity to participate fully in all facets of everyday community life will be open to all people with physical disabilities and health impairments.

Summary

Types of Physical and Health Impairments and Special Health Care Needs

- Children with physical and health impairments are a widely varied population and include those eligible for special education under three disability categories of IDEA: orthopedic impairments, other health impairments, and traumatic brain injury.
- Orthopedic impairments involve the skeletal system; a neurological impairment involves the nervous system. Both are frequently described in terms of the affected parts of the body.
- Cerebral palsy is a long-term condition arising from impairment to the brain and causing disturbances in voluntary motor functions.
- Spina bifida is a congenital condition that may cause loss of sensation and severe muscle weakness in the lower part of the body. Children with spina bifida can usually participate in most classroom activities but need assistance in toileting.
- Muscular dystrophy is a long-term condition; most children gradually lose the ability to walk independently.
- Spinal cord injuries are caused by a penetrating injury, stretching of the vertebral column, fracture of the vertebrae, or compression of the spinal cord and usually

result in some form of paralysis below the site of the injury.

- Other health impairments include the following:
  - Seizure disorders (epilepsy) produce disturbances of movement, sensation, behavior, and/or consciousness.
  - Diabetes is a disorder of metabolism that can often be controlled with injections of insulin.
  - Children with cystic fibrosis, asthma, hemophilia, HIV/AIDS, and other chronic health conditions may require special education and other related services, such as health care services and counseling.
- Traumatic brain injury is a significant cause of neurological impairments and learning problems.

Prevalence

- In 1996–1997, 4.6% of all school-age students who received special education services were reported under the disability categories of orthopedic impairments, other health impairments, and traumatic brain injury. This figure does not include all children with physical or health impairments because some are reported under other disability categories and some do not require special education services.

Variables Affecting the Impact of Physical Impairments and Chronic Health Conditions

- Perrin et al. (1993) have proposed a noncategorical system for classifying and understanding children's chronic physical and medical conditions; it includes 13 dimensions that are judged on a continuum from mild to profound.
- Many factors must be taken into consideration when assessing the effects of a physical impairment or health condition on a child's development and behavior. Three particularly important variables are the age of onset, the severity with which the condition affects different areas of functioning, and the visibility of the impairment.

Educational Approaches

- Children with physical and health impairments typically require services from an interdisciplinary team of professionals.
- Physical therapists (PTs) use specialized knowledge to plan and oversee a child's program in making correct and useful movements. Occupational therapists (OTs) are concerned with a child's participation in activities, especially those that will be useful in self-help, employment, recreation, communication, and other aspects of daily living.
- Students with physical and health impairments can increase their independence by learning to take care of their personal health care routines such as clean intermittent catheterization and self-administration of medication.
- Adaptations to the physical environment and to classroom activities can enable students with physical and health impairments to participate more fully in the school program.
- Proper positioning and seating is important for children with physical disabilities. A standard routine for lifting and moving a child with physical disabilities should be followed by all teachers and other staff.
- Assistive technology is any piece of equipment or device used to increase, maintain, or improve the functional capabilities of individuals with disabilities.
- How parents, teachers, classmates, and others react to a child with physical disabilities is at least as important as the disability itself.
- Successful reentry of children who have missed extended periods of school because of illness or the contraction of a disease requires preparation of the child, his parents, classmates, and school personnel.

Educational Placement Alternatives

- About 40% of students with physical impairments and chronic health conditions are served in regular classrooms.
- The amount of supportive help that may be required to enable a student with physical disabilities to function effectively in a regular class varies greatly according to each child's condition, needs, and level of functioning.
- Special classes usually provide smaller class size, more adapted equipment, and easier access to the services of professionals such as physicians, physical and occupational therapists, and specialists in communication disorders and therapeutic recreation.
- Some technology-dependent children require home- or hospital-based instruction because their life-support equipment cannot be made portable.

Current Issues and Future Trends

- The education of students with physical and health impairments in regular classrooms has raised several controversial issues, especially with regard to the provision of medically related procedures in the classroom.
- New and emerging technologies such as bionic body parts and robot assistants offer exciting possibilities for the future.
- Animals, particularly dogs and monkeys, can assist people with physical disabilities in various ways.
- Children with physical disabilities can gain self-knowledge and self-confidence by meeting capable adults with disabilities and joining self-advocacy groups.

For More Information

Journals

- *ACCENT on Living,* P.O. Box 700, Bloomington, IL 61701. A quarterly journal of practical information, with articles on varied topics, including employment, aids to independent living, architectural barriers, and family concerns. Primarily written by and about people with physical and health impairments. Journal also sponsors an extensive catalog of assistive devices and a computerized information retrieval system.
- *Assistive Technology,* RESNA, 1101 Connecticut Avenue NW, Suite 700, Washington, DC 20036. Information about technology for individuals with disabilities.
- *Disability Rag,* P.O. Box 145, Louisville, KY 40201. Described as "a spicy, irreverent journal." A bimonthly publication tackling controversial issues affecting people with disabilities and serving as a forum for opinion and debate. Features articles on topics such as telethons, legal battles, sexuality, and media portrayals of people with disabilities.
- *Disability Studies Quarterly.* Published by the Department of Sociology, Brandeis University, Waltham, MA 02254. Regularly prints abstracts of current research projects, book reviews, announcements of conferences, resources, and grants. Focuses on social and psychological issues as well as advocacy, economics, and attitudes of and toward persons with physical and other disabilities.
- *Disabled USA.* Published quarterly by the President's Committee on Employment of the Handicapped, 1111 20th Street NW, Suite 600, Washington, DC 20036. Reports on current developments in employment, rehabilitation, and independent living. Seeks to document progress in employment and to encourage new opportunities for workers with disabilities.
- *Physical Disabilities: Education and Related Services* (formerly the *DPH Journal*). Published by the Division for Physical and Health Disabilities, Council for Exceptional Children (see "Organizations").
- *Rehabilitation Literature.* Published monthly by the National Easter Seal Society, 2023 West Ogden Avenue, Chicago, IL 60612. An interdisciplinary publication containing abstracts of current research and practice, with an emphasis on children and adults with orthopedic, neurological, and other physical and health-related impairments. Regularly features reviews of recent books.

Books

- Batshaw, M. L. (Ed.). (1997). *Children with disabilities* (4th ed.). Baltimore: Brookes.
- Bigge, J. L. (1991). *Teaching individuals with physical and multiple disabilities* (3rd ed.). Upper Saddle River, NJ: Merrill/Prentice Hall.
- Bigler, E. D., Clark, E., & Farmer, J. E. (Eds.). (1997). *Childhood traumatic brain injury: Diagnosis, assessment, and intervention*. Austin, TX: PRO-ED.
- Gerring, J. P., & Carney, J. M. (1992). *Head trauma: Strategies for educational reintegration.* San Diego: Singular.
- Goldfarb, L. A., Brotherson, M. J., Summers, J. A., & Turnbull, A. P. (1986). *Meeting the challenge of disability or chronic illness: A family guide.* Baltimore: Brookes.
- Heller, K. W., Alberto, P. A., Forney, P. E., & Schwartzman, M. N. (1996). *Understanding physical, sensory and health impairments*. Pacific Grove, CA: Brooks/Cole.
- Hill, J. L. (1999). *Meeting the needs of students with special physical and health care needs*. Upper Saddle River, NJ: Merrill/Prentice Hall.
- Pieper, E. (1983). *The teacher and the child with spina bifida* (2nd ed.). Rockville, MD: Spina Bifida Association of America.
- Savage, R. C., & Wolcott, G. F. (Eds.). (1994). *Educational dimensions of acquired brain injury.* Austin, TX: PRO-ED.
- Sowers, J., & Powers, L. (1991). *Vocational preparation and employment of students with physical and multiple disabilities.* Baltimore: Brookes.

Organizations

Many national agencies and organizations provide information, educational programs, and community services to children and adults with specific physical and health impairments and to their parents and teachers. Many of these have state and local chapters. Listed here are some of the largest organizations that disseminate publications and encourage research into the causes and treatment of physical and health impairments.

- *American Diabetes Association,* 23 East 26th Street, New York, NY 10010; (800) 232-3472; website: http://www.diabetes.org.
- *Division for Physical and Health Disabilities (DPHD),* Council for Exceptional Children, 1920 Association Drive, Reston, VA 22091-1589.
- *Cystic Fibrosis Foundation,* 6000 Executive Boulevard, Rockville, MD 20852; (800) 378-2233; website: http://www.ceff.ca/~cfwww.
- *Epilepsy Foundation of America,* 4531 Garden City Drive, Landover, MD 20785; (800) 332-1000; website: http://www.efa.org.
- *Muscular Dystrophy Association,* 810 Seventh Avenue, New York, NY 10019; (800) 572-1717; website: http://www.mdausa.org.
- *Spina Bifida Association of America,* 343 South Dearborn Street, Chicago, IL 60604; (800) 621-3141; website: http://www.sbaa.org.
- *United Cerebral Palsy Associations,* 66 East 34th Street, New York, NY 10016; (800) 872-5827; website: http://www.ucpa.org.

Sources for Assistive Technology Devices and Other Information

- *Assistive Technology Sourcebook,* RESNA, 1101 Connecticut Avenue NW, Suite 700, Washington, DC 20036.
- *Handi-Ham System,* Courage HANDI-HAM System (WOZSW), Courage Center, 3915 Golden Valley Road, Golden Valley, MN 55422. An international organization of persons with and without disabilities who help people with disabilities expand their world through amateur radio. The system matches students with one-to-one helpers, provides instruction, and loans radio equipment.
- *Into the Mainstream: A Syllabus for a Barrier-Free Environment,* United States Rehabilitation Services Administration, Superintendent of Documents, Washington, DC 20402.
- *The Disability Bookshop Catalog,* Twin Peaks Press, P.O. Box 129, Vancouver, WA 98666; (800) 637-2256. Information on hundreds of books, tapes, and videos of interest to people with disabilities.
- *The Illustrated Directory of Handicapped Products,* Trio Publications, 3600 West Timber Court, Lawrence, KS 66049. Annually updated descriptions of mobility devices, environmental control devices, adapted sports equipment, clothing, and eating devices.
- *Trace Resource Book,* Trace Research and Development Center, University of Wisconsin, S-151 Waisman Center, 1500 Highland Avenue, Madison, WI 53705. Describes technologies for environmental control and computer access.

Website

- For information on national and state projects related to assistive technology: http://www.ncddr.org/urllist/statetech.html.

Chapter 13

Severe Disabilities

Focus Questions

- Why is a curriculum based on typical developmental stages inappropriate for students with severe disabilities?
- For what reasons is it especially critical to select functional, age-appropriate curriculum objectives for students with severe disabilities?
- How can the principle of partial participation contribute to the quality of life for a student with severe disabilities?
- What are the benefits for students with severe disabilities who are educated in regular, integrated schools? What are potential disadvantages?
- What benefits might students who are not disabled experience from the inclusion of peers with severe disabilities in the regular classroom?

Five-year old Zack is learning to feed himself with a spoon. A teacher shows 13-year-old Toni that it is more appropriate to shake hands than to hug a person when first introduced. Martha, who is 20, is learning to ride a city bus to her afternoon job at the cafeteria, where she clears tables and sorts silverware. Zack, Toni, and Martha have severe disabilities. Except for their general need for ongoing support from others and for instruction in skills that children without disabilities usually acquire at a younger age, these students have little in common with each other.

Students with severe disabilities are a highly diverse population. Each student often has a combination of obvious and not-so-obvious disabilities. Because of differences in their intellectual, physical, and behavioral limitations, each student requires different additions or adaptations in their education. Without direct and systematic instruction, however, many individuals with severe disabilities are not able to perform the most basic, everyday tasks we take for granted, such as eating, toileting, and communicating our needs and feelings to others.

Having a severe disability does not preclude meaningful achievements. Despite the severity and multiplicity of their disabilities, students with severe disabilities can and do learn. And although students with severe disabilities were excluded from education—and from mainstream society—in the past, a philosophy of inclusion now prevails. Laws requiring free, appropriate programs of public education for all students with disabilities; the ever-growing body of evidence demonstrating that individuals with severe disabilities can learn and function effectively in integrated school, work, and community settings; and the belief that inclusion is the right thing to do all support the new philosophy.

Go to the companion website at http://www.prenhall.com/heward and select Chapter 13 to review the chapter objectives.

Defining Severe Disabilities

There is no single, widely accepted definition of severe disabilities. Most definitions are based on tests of intellectual functioning, developmental progress, or the extent of educational need. According to the system of classifying levels of mental retardation previously used by the American Association on Mental Retardation, persons receiving IQ scores of 35 to 40 and below were considered to have severe mental retardation; scores of 20 to 25 and below resulted in a classification of profound mental retardation. In practice, however, the term *severe disabilities* often includes many individuals who score in the moderate level of mental retardation (IQ scores of 40 to 55) (Wolery & Haring, 1994).

See Chapter 6 for discussion of IQ testing and classification of intellectual functioning.

Traditional methods of intelligence testing are virtually useless with children whose disabilities are profound. Imagine the difficulty, as well as the inappropriateness, of giving an IQ test to a student who cannot hold up his head or point, let alone talk. If tested, such students tend to be assigned IQ scores at the extreme lower end of the continuum. Knowing that a particular student has an IQ of 25, however, is of no value in designing an appropriate educational program. Educators of students with severe and profound disabilities tend to focus on the specific skills a child needs to learn rather than on intellectual level.

It was once common to take a developmental approach to the definition of severe disabilities. For example, Justen (1976) proposed that individuals with severe disabilities are "those individuals age 21 and younger who are functioning at a general developmental level of half or less than the level which would be expected on the basis of chronological age" (p. 5). Most educators now maintain that developmental levels have little relevance to this population and instead emphasize that a student with **severe disabilities**—regardless of age—is one who needs instruction in basic skills, such as getting from place to place independently, communicating with others, controlling bowel and bladder functions, and self-feeding. Most children without disabilities are able to acquire these basic skills in the first five years of life, but the student with severe disabilities needs special instruction to do so. The basic-skills definition makes it clear that special education for students with severe disabilities must not focus on traditional academic instruction.

The IDEA regulations governing programs and services for students with severe disabilities refers to the need for "highly specialized" services for students who experience "intense" problems:

> The term "children with severe disabilities" refers to children with disabilities who, because of the intensity of their physical, mental, or emotional problems, need highly specialized education, social, psychological, and medical services in order to maximize their full potential for useful and meaningful participation in society and for self-fulfillment. The term includes those children with disabilities with severe emotional disturbance (including schizophrenia), autism, severe and profound mental retardation, and those who have two or more serious disabilities such as deaf-blindness, mental retarda-

> tion and blindness, and cerebral palsy and deafness. Children with severe disabilities may experience severe speech, language, and/or perceptual-cognitive deprivations, and evidence abnormal behavior such as failure to respond to pronounced social stimuli, self-mutilation, self-stimulation; manifestation of intense and prolonged temper tantrums, and the absence of rudimentary forms of verbal control; and may also have extremely fragile physiological conditions. (Federal Register, 315.4[d])

The inclusion of extremely challenging behavioral problems, such as self-stimulation and self-injurious behavior, in the federal definition is not intended to imply that all children with severe disabilities exhibit such characteristics; most do not. Rather, the inclusion of such examples makes it clear that *all* children are entitled to a free public education in the least restrictive environment no matter how complicated or challenging their learning, behavioral, or medical problems; "even those students who, in the judgment of some people, seem to be 'ineducable'" (Turnbull & Cilley, 1999, p. 9).

The term *severe disabilities* generally encompasses individuals with severe and profound disabilities in intellectual, physical, and social functioning. An increasing number of professionals, however, are making a distinction between individuals with profound disabilities and those with severe disabilities. Sternberg (1994) believes that a distinction between severe and profound disabilities is necessary because the "expectations and implications for each are different. These differences are related not only to one's capability for independent functioning but also to the utility of specific educational or training models and methods" (p. 7). According to Sternberg, an individual with *profound disabilities* is one who

> exhibits profound developmental disabilities in all five of the following behavioral-content areas: cognition, communication, social skills development, motor-mobility, and activities of daily living (self-help skills); and requires a service structure with continuous monitoring and observation. . . . This definition also posits a ceiling of 2 years of age for each area of functioning (6 years of age for those classified as severely disabled). If the individual functions above that level, the individual cannot be classified as profoundly disabled. (p. 6)

Thus, an individual with profound disabilities, according to Sternberg, functions at a level no higher than that of a typically developing 2-year-old in all five areas (whereas the functioning of a student with severe disabilities in one or more of these areas may be less delayed, up to the level of a typical 6-year-old).

The Association for Persons with Severe Handicaps (TASH) defines people with severe disabilities as

> individuals of all ages who require extensive ongoing support in more than one major life activity in order to participate in integrated community settings and to enjoy a quality of life that is available to citizens with fewer or no disabilities. Support may be required for life activities such as mobility, communication, self-care, and learning, as necessary for independent living, employment and self-sufficiency. (Lindley, 1990, p. 1)

The TASH definition not only refers to the level, duration, and focus of support needed by persons with severe disabilities but also specifies the goals and expected outcomes of that support.

Compared with other areas of special education—mental retardation, learning disabilities, and behavioral disorders in particular—there has been less concern and debate over the definition of severe disabilities. This does not indicate that professionals are uninterested in defining the population of students they serve but reflects two inherent features of severe disabilities. First, there is little need for a definition that precisely describes who is and is not to be identified by the term *severe disabilities*. Although the specific criteria a school district uses to define learning disabilities

An extended school year is used to meet the requirements of a free, appropriate public education for some students with severe disabilities. To learn about the legal requirements, judicial rulings, and practical guidelines for educators concerning the extended school year, see Rapport and Thomas (1993).

Some educators question whether children with profound disabilities can benefit from education. See "Are All Children Educable?" later in this chapter. To read more about the educability debate, see Baer (1981b, 1984); Kauffman (1981); Noonan, Brown, Mulligan, and Rettig (1982); Orelove (1984); Tawney (1984); and Ulicny, Thompson, Favell, and Thompson (1985).

Information on TASH can be found in "For More Information" at the end of this chapter. The organization's journal, Journal of the Association for Persons with Severe Handicaps (JASH), *is a primary source for the latest research and conceptual developments in educating learners who are challenged by severe disabilities.*

PROFILES AND PERSPECTIVES

Are All Children Educable?

Some educators, other professionals, and citizens question the wisdom of spending large amounts of money, time, and human resources attempting to train children who have such serious and profound disabilities that they may never be able to function independently. Some would prefer to see resources spent on children with higher apparent potential—especially when economic conditions limit the quality of educational services for all children in the public schools. "Why bother with children who fail to make meaningful progress?" they ask.

> Accelerating a response rate may indeed be a worthy first goal in an educational program if there is reasonable hope of shaping the response into a meaningful skill. Nevertheless, after concerted and appropriate effort by highly trained behavior therapists, for a reasonable period of time, a child's failure to make significant progress toward acquisition of a meaningful skill could reasonably be taken as an indication that the child is ineducable. . . . Granted, all children probably are educable if education is defined as acceleration of any operant response. But such a definition trivializes the meaning of the term education and, even without consideration of benefit, moots the question of educability. Formulating consensual definitions of education, meaningful skill, and significant progress will be difficult, but it is a task we cannot avoid. . . . We suggest that public response to the questions "What is education?" "What skills are meaningful?" "What rate of progress is significant?" and "What cost/benefit ratios are acceptable?" sampled with sufficient care, could be invaluable in deciding who is educable and who is not. (Kauffman & Krouse, 1981, pp. 55–56)

A special educator who is also the parent of a daughter with severe disabilities disagrees:

> If anyone were to be the judge of whether a particular behavior change is "meaningful," it should certainly not be only the general taxpayer, who has no idea how rewarding it is to see your retarded 19-year-old acquire the skill of toilet flushing on command or pointing to food when she wants a second helping. I suspect that the average taxpayer would not consider it "meaningful" to him or her for Karrie to acquire such skills. But in truth, it is "meaningful" to that taxpayer whether he recognizes it or not, in the sense that it is saving him or her the cost of Karrie's being institutionalized, which she certainly would have been by now if she never showed any progress; thus it is functional for the taxpayer even though his or her answer to the question "Is this meaningful?" might well be "No" or "Not enough to pay for."
>
> The complexity, cost, and hopelessness of evaluating fairly the "meaningfulness" of various behavior changes leads me to conclude that no one should be denied an education. . . . I would be very resistant to the idea that we should now, at this infant stage of the science and technology of education for severely retarded students, give up intensive skill training for anyone. (Hawkins, 1984, p. 285)

In many ways, our knowledge of the learning and developmental processes of individuals with severe disabilities is still primitive and incomplete. We do know, however, that children with severe disabilities are capable of benefiting significantly from appropriate and carefully implemented educational programs. Even in cases in which little or no progress has been observed, it would be wrong to conclude that the student is incapable of learning. It may instead be that our teaching methods are imperfect and that the future will bring improved methods and materials to enable that student to learn useful skills (Baer, 1981b). Children, no matter how severe their disabilities, have the right to the best possible public education and training society can offer them.

There are still many unanswered questions in the education of children whose disabilities are complex and pervasive. Even though their opportunities for education and training are expanding rapidly, nobody really knows their true learning potential. What we do know is that students with the most severe disabilities will go no farther than we let them; it is up to us to open doors and to raise our sights, not to create additional barriers.

Don Baer, professor of human development at the University of Kansas and a pioneer in the development of effective teaching methods for persons with severe disabilities, offers this perspective on educability:

> Some of us have ignored both the thesis that all retarded persons are educable and the thesis that some retarded persons are ineducable, and instead have experimented with ways to teach some previously unteachable people. Over a few centuries, those experiments have steadily

reduced the size of the apparently ineducable group relative to the obviously educable group. Clearly, we have not finished that adventure. Why predict its outcome, when we could simply pursue it, and just as well without a prediction? Why not pursue it to see if there comes a day when there is such a small class of apparently ineducable persons left that it consists of one elderly institution resident who is put forward as ineducable. If it comes, that will be a very nice day, and the next day will be even better. (Baer, 1984, p. 299)

have a major impact on who will be eligible for special education services, whether or not special education is needed by any student who might be considered severely disabled is never an issue. Second, because of the tremendous diversity of learning and physical challenges experienced by such students, any single set of descriptors is inadequate. Statements that specify the particular educational goals and support needs of individual students are more meaningful.

Characteristics of Students with Severe Disabilities

Check your ongoing understanding of Chapter 13 concepts by using the Guided Review Module at http://www.prenhall.com/heward.

Throughout this book, we have seen how definitions and lists of characteristics used to describe a disability category have limited meaning at the level of the individual student. And, of course, it is at the level of the individual student where special education takes place, where decisions about what and how to teach should be made. As various physical, behavioral, and learning characteristics associated with severe disabilities are described, keep in mind that students with severe disabilities constitute the most heterogeneous group of all exceptional children. As Guess and Mulligan (1982) point out, the differences among students with severe disabilities are greater than their similarities.

For information on what teachers should know about the special health care needs of students with the most severe and profound disabilities, see Ault, Rues, Graff, and Holvoet (2000).

Most students with severe disabilities exhibit extreme deficits in intellectual functioning. Many need special services and supports because of motor impediments; communication, visual, and auditory impairments; and medical conditions such as seizure disorders. Many have medical and physical problems that require frequent attention. Many students with severe disabilities have more than one disability. Even with the best available methods of diagnosis and assessment, it is often difficult to identify the nature and intensity of a child's multiple disabilities or to determine how combinations of disabilities affect a child's behavior. Some children, for example, do not respond in any observable way to visual stimuli, such as bright lights or moving objects. Is this because the child is blind as a result of eye damage, or is the child unresponsive because of profound mental retardation due to brain damage (Orlansky, 1981)? Such questions arise frequently in planning educational programs for students with severe disabilities.

The one defining characteristic of students with severe disabilities is that they exhibit obvious deficits in multiple life-skill or developmental areas (Sailor & Guess, 1983). No specific set of behaviors is common to all individuals with severe disabilities. Each student presents a unique combination of physical, intellectual, and social characteristics. Educators generally agree, however, that the following behaviors and skill deficits are frequently observed in students with severe disabilities (Brown et al., 1991; Wolery & Haring, 1994):

- *Slow acquisition rates for learning new skills.* Compared to other students with disabilities, students with severe disabilities learn at a slower rate, require more instructional trials to learn a given skill, learn fewer skills in total, and have difficulty learning abstract skills or relationships.
- *Poor generalization and maintenance of newly learned skills.* Generalization refers to the performance of skills under conditions different from those in which they initially were learned. Maintenance refers to the continued use of a new skill after instruction is terminated. For students with severe disabilities, generalization and maintenance seldom occur without instruction that is meticulously planned to facilitate it.
- *Limited communication skills.* Almost all students with severe and multiple disabilities are limited in their abilities to express themselves and to understand others. Some cannot talk or gesture meaningfully and might not respond when communication is attempted; some are not able to follow even the simplest requests.
- *Impaired physical and motor development.* Many children with severe disabilities have limited physical mobility. Many cannot walk; some cannot stand or sit up without support. They are slow to perform such basic tasks as rolling over, grasping objects, and holding up their heads. Physical deformities are common and may worsen without consistent physical therapy.
- *Deficits in self-help skills.* Some children with severe disabilities are unable to independently care for their most basic needs, such as dressing, eating, exercising bowel and bladder control, and maintaining personal hygiene. They usually require special training involving prosthetic devices and/or adapted skill sequences to learn these basic skills.
- *Infrequent constructive behavior and interaction.* Nondisabled children and those whose disabilities are less severe typically play with other children, interact with adults, and seek out information about their surroundings. Some children with severe disabilities do not. They may appear to be completely out of touch with reality and may not show normal human emotions. It may be difficult to capture the attention of or evoke any observable response from a child with profound disabilities.
- *Frequent inappropriate behavior.* Many children with severe disabilities do things that appear to have no constructive purpose. These behaviors may be ritualistic (e.g., rocking back and forth, waving fingers in front of the face, twirling the body), self-stimulatory (e.g., grinding the teeth, patting the body), and/or self-injurious (e.g., head banging, hair pulling, eye poking, hitting or scratching or biting oneself). Although some of these activities may not be considered abnormal in and of themselves, the high frequency with which some children emit these challenging behaviors is a serious concern because they interfere with learning more adaptive behaviors and with acceptance and functioning in integrated settings.

Descriptions of behavioral characteristics, such as those just mentioned, can easily give an overly negative impression. Despite the intense challenges their disabilities impose on them, many students with severe disabilities also exhibit warmth, persistence, determination, a sense of humor, sociability, and various other desirable traits (Forest & Lusthaus, 1990; Stainback & Stainback, 1991). Many teachers find great satisfaction in working with students who have severe disabilities and in observing their progress in school, home, and community settings.

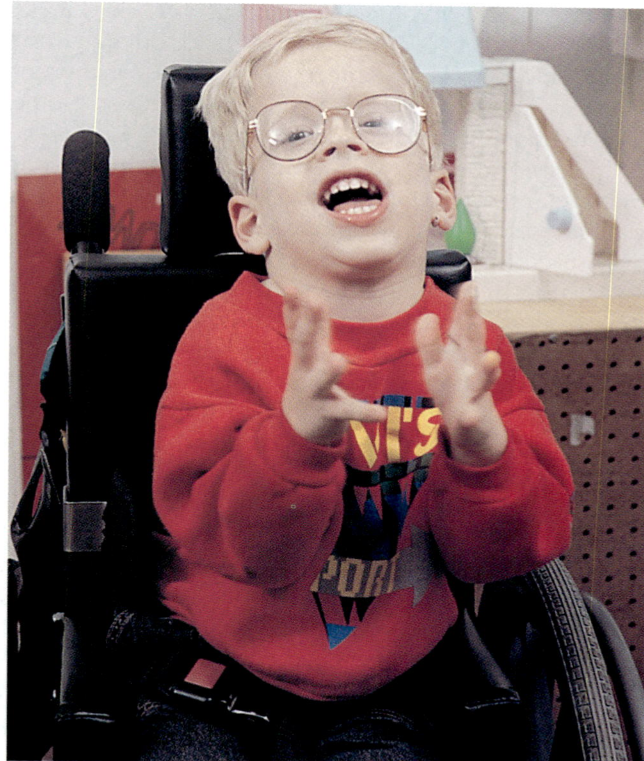

Joey's enthusiasm and determination are evident each time his teacher uses music in a lesson.

Deaf-Blindness

A particularly challenging group of students with severe disabilities includes those with dual sensory impairments. "There is perhaps no condition as disabling as deaf-blindness, the loss of part or all of one's vision and hearing" (Bullis & Otos, 1988, p. 110). IDEA defines **deaf-blindness** as a combination of both auditory and visual disabilities that causes "such severe communication and other developmental and learning needs that the persons cannot be appropriately educated in special education programs solely for children and youth with hearing impairments, visual impairments, or severe disabilities, without supplementary assistance to address their educational needs due to these dual, concurrent disabilities" (IDEA, 1990, sec. 1422).

The intellectual level of students with dual sensory impairments ranges from giftedness (as in the case of Helen Keller) to profound mental retardation.

The majority of children who have both visual and hearing impairments at birth experience major difficulties in acquiring communication and motor skills, mobility, and appropriate social behavior. Helen Keller (1903) once said that blindness separates one from things but that deafness separates one from people.

> Because these individuals do not receive clear and consistent information from either sensory modality, a tendency exists to turn inward to obtain the desired level of stimulation. The individual therefore may appear passive, nonresponsive, and/or noncompliant. Students with dual sensory impairments may not respond to or initiate appropriate interactions with others and often exhibit behavior that is considered socially inappropriate (e.g., hand flapping, finger flicking, head rocking). (Downing & Eichinger, 1990, pp. 98–99)

Although 94% of individuals labeled deaf-blind have some functional hearing and/or vision (Baldwin, 1992), the combined effects of the dual impairments severely impede

It is difficult to assess accurately the degree of sensory impairments in most students with deaf-blindness because additional disabilities or other barriers to communication limit the students' responses to typical testing procedures (Wolf, Delk, & Schein, 1982).

Curricula for assessing and teaching functional communication skills to students who are deaf-blind have been developed by the Perkins School for the Blind (1978) and the Alabama Institute for the Deaf-Blind (1989).

the development of communication and social skills, especially when mental retardation also is involved. An educational program for children who are deaf is often inappropriate for a child who also has limited vision because many methods of instruction and communication rely heavily on the use of sight. On the other hand, programs for visually impaired students usually require good hearing because much instruction is auditory.

Therefore, educational programs for students with dual sensory impairments who require instruction in basic skills are generally similar to those for other students with severe disabilities. Although most students with dual sensory impairments can make use of information presented in visual and auditory modalities, when used in instruction these stimuli must be enhanced and the students' attention directed toward them. Tactile teaching techniques involving the sense of touch are used to supplement the information obtained through visual and auditory modes.

Communication is achieved only with great difficulty by persons who are deaf-blind and requires greater effort on the part of communication partners (Tedder, Warden, & Sikka, 1993). The use of dual communication boards can help students who are deaf-blind discriminate the receptive or expressive functions of responses from a communication partner (Heller, Ware, Allgood, & Castelle, 1994). When a communication partner points to pictures or symbols on her board, a receptive message is provided to the student, requiring a response from the student on his board. The communication partner can point to the student's board and provide imitative prompts or corrective feedback to help the student make expressive messages.

Robert Smithdas (1981), a man who is deaf-blind, vividly describes the importance of supplementing information about the world with other sensory modes:

> The senses of sight and hearing are unquestionably the two primary avenues by which information and knowledge are absorbed by an individual, providing a direct access to the world in which he lives. . . . When these senses are lost or severely limited, the individual is drastically limited to a very small area of concepts, most of which must come to him through his secondary senses or through indirect information supplied by others. The world literally shrinks; it is only as large as he can reach with his fingertips or by using his severely limited sight and hearing, and it is only when he learns to use his remaining secondary senses of touch, taste, smell, and kinesthetic awareness that he can broaden his field of information and gain additional knowledge. (p. 38)

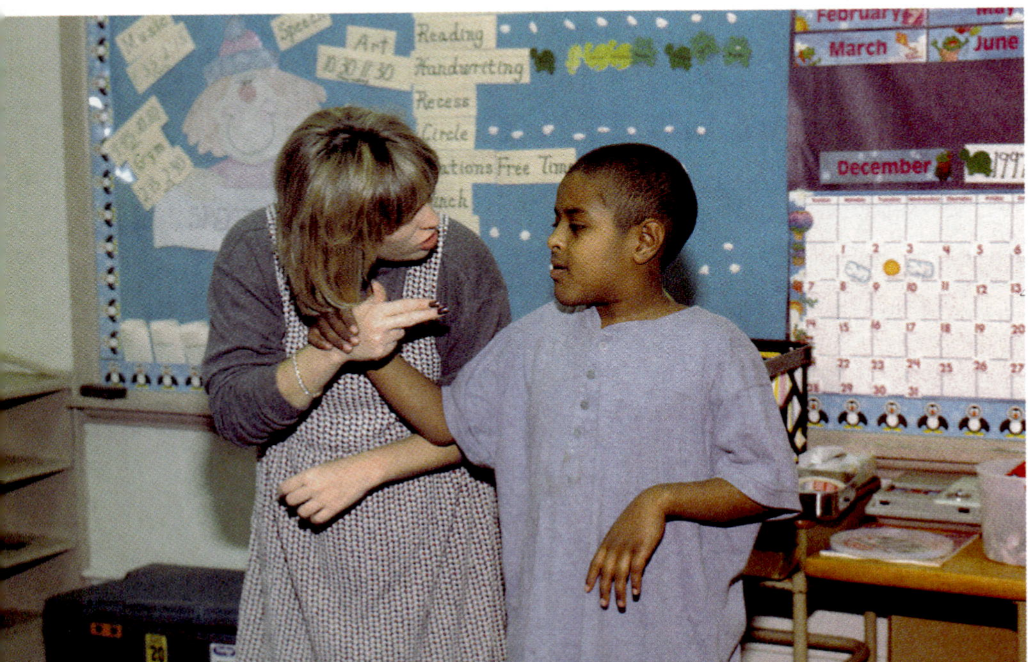

Teaching techniques involving the sense of touch are used to provide and supplement instructional stimuli for students with dual sensory impairments.

Prior to the passage of IDEA in 1975, fewer than 100 children with dual sensory impairments were receiving specialized education services, virtually all of which were located at residential schools for children who are blind. Today, about 6,000 students with dual sensory impairments are being educated in the United States in hundreds of different programs, including those located at schools for children who are deaf, early childhood developmental centers, vocational training centers, and regular public schools (Zambone & Huebner, 1992). Students who are deaf-blind who progress to high school and postsecondary levels usually are integrated into educational programs for students with other disabilities or into programs for nondisabled students, with supportive assistance provided by special teachers, intervenors, interpreters, or tutors. Downing and Eichinger (1990) describe instructional strategies to support the education of students with dual sensory impairments in regular classrooms.

Persons with dual sensory impairments have the potential to achieve success and enjoyment in employment and independent living, but they need systematic instruction to facilitate communication, generalization of skills, and development of appropriate social behaviors (Bullis & Bull, 1986).

Autism

Autism is a disability marked by severe impairment of communication, social, and emotional functioning, usually accompanied by severe intellectual impairment. According to the widely used definition endorsed by the Autism Society of America, the essential features of the condition typically appear prior to 30 months of age and consist of disturbances of (1) developmental rates and/or sequences; (2) responses to sensory stimuli; (3) speech, language, and cognitive capacities; and (4) capacities to relate to people, events, and objects (Sturmey & Sevin, 1994).

Some clinicians use the term pervasive developmental disorder *to describe this set of developmental and behavioral characteristics.*

Autism is defined in IDEA as

> a developmental disability affecting verbal and nonverbal communication and social interaction, generally evident before age 3, that affects a child's performance. Other characteristics often associated with autism are engagement in repetitive activities and stereotyped movements, resistance to environmental change or change in daily routines, and unusual responses to sensory experiences. The term does not apply if a child's educational performance is adversely affected primarily because the child has a serious emotional disturbance. (34 C.F.R., Part 300, 300.7[b][1])

Although autism is quite rare, it is actually more common than blindness in children. It is estimated that autism occurs in approximately 5 to 15 of every 10,000 children (Dawson & Osterling, 1997; Matson, 1994). Boys are affected four to five times more often than girls. In the 1996–1997 school year, 34,101 students ages 6 to 21 received special education services under the IDEA category of autism (U.S. Department of Education, 1998).

Although the precise cause of autism is unknown, recent research suggests a biological or organic origin (Mauk, Reber, & Batshaw, 1997; Rutter & Schopler, 1987).

Parents of children with autism commonly report that their baby developed in typical fashion for the first year or more, acquiring some meaningful communication skills and enjoying cuddling and hugging. But between 12 and 15 months, the child began showing an oversensitivity to certain sounds or touch, no longer seemed to understand even simple words or gestures, and became increasingly withdrawn, aimless, and perseverative (Greenspan, 1992).

Lovaas and Newsom (1976) provide a graphic description of six frequently observed characteristics of children with autism:

- *Apparent sensory deficit.* We may move directly in front of the child, smile, and talk to him, yet he will act as if no one is there. We may not feel that the child is avoiding or ignoring us, but rather that he simply does not seem to see or hear. . . . As we get to

Not all children with autism exhibit each of these characteristics. Many can be "quite loving and caring, thoughtful and creative" (Greenspan & Weider, 1997, p. 88).

Facilitated communication, a controversial method of assisting persons with autism and other nonverbal individuals to communicate, is discussed later in this chapter.

The cognitive ability of about 80% of individuals with autism is similar to that of persons with mental retardation (Ritvo & Freeman, 1978). A very few persons with autism exhibit ***savant syndrome****, an extraordinary ability in an area such as memorization, mathematics, or music while functioning at the mental retardation level in all other areas (Treffert, 1989).*

For a description of this intensive, home-based training program, see Lovaas (1981). Other excellent sources of information on teaching children with autism are Harris and Handleman (1994); Koegel and Koegel (1995); Matson (1994); and Maurice, Green, and Luce (1996).

> know the child better, we become aware of the great variability in this obliviousness to stimulation. For example, although the child may give no visible reaction to a loud noise, such as a clapping of hands directly behind his ears, he may orient to the crinkle of a candy wrapper or respond fearfully to a distant and barely audible siren.
>
> - *Severe affect isolation.* Another characteristic that we frequently notice is that attempts to love and cuddle and show affection to the child encounter a profound lack of interest on the child's part. Again, the parents relate that the child seems not to know or care whether he is alone or in the company of others.
> - *Self-stimulation.* A most striking kind of behavior in these children centers on very repetitive stereotyped acts, such as rocking their bodies when in a sitting position, twirling around, flapping their hands at the wrists, or humming a set of three or four notes over and over again. The parents often report that their child has spent entire days gazing at his cupped hands, staring at lights, spinning objects, etc.
> - *Tantrums and self-mutilatory behavior.* Often the parents report that the child sometimes bites himself so severely that he bleeds, or that he beats his head against walls or sharp pieces of furniture so forcefully that large lumps rise and his skin turns black and blue. He may beat his face with his fists. . . . Sometimes the child's aggression will be directed outward against his parents or teachers in the most primitive form of biting, scratching, and kicking. Some of these children absolutely tyrannize their parents by staying awake and making noises all night, tearing curtains off the window, spilling flour in the kitchen, etc.
> - *Echolalic and psychotic speech.* Most of these children are mute; they do not speak, but they may hum or occasionally utter simple sounds. The speech of those who do talk may be echoes of other people's attempts to talk to them. For example, if we address a child with the question, "What is your name?" the child is likely to answer, "What is your name?" (preserving, perhaps, the exact intonation of the one who spoke to him). At other times the echolalia is not immediate but delayed; the child may repeat statements he has heard that morning or on the preceding day, or he may repeat TV commercials or other such announcements.
> - *Behavior deficiencies.* Although the presence of the behaviors sketched above is rather striking, it is equally striking to take note of many behaviors that the autistic child does not have. At the age of 5 or 10, he may, in many ways, show the behavioral repertoire of a 1-year-old child. He has few if any self-help skills but needs to be fed and dressed by others. (pp. 308–309)

The prognosis for children with autism is generally considered to be extremely poor, with problems persisting into adulthood for more than 90% of cases (Bristol et al., 1996; Matson, 1994). On the brighter side, however, a great deal of exciting and promising research may lead to better futures for children with autism (e.g., Dawson & Osterling, 1997; Green, 1996; Greenspan & Weider, 1997; Panerai, Ferrante, Caputo, & Impellizzeri, 1998). One powerful example of the potential of systematic early intervention on the lives of children with autism is the work of Ivar Lovaas and his colleagues at the University of California at Los Angeles. Lovaas (1987) provided a group of 19 children with autism with an intensive early intervention program of one-to-one behavioral treatment for more than 40 hours per week for two years or more before they reached age 4. Intervention also included parent training and mainstreaming into a regular preschool environment. When compared with a control group of 19 similar children at age 7, children in the early intervention group had gained 20 IQ points and had made major advancements in educational achievement. Nine of the children were able to advance from first to second grade in a regular classroom and were considered by their teachers to be well adjusted.

Follow-up evaluations of the same group of 19 children several years later at the average age of 11.5 years showed that the children had maintained their gains (McEachin, Smith, & Lovaas, 1993). In particular, 8 of the 9 "best outcome" children

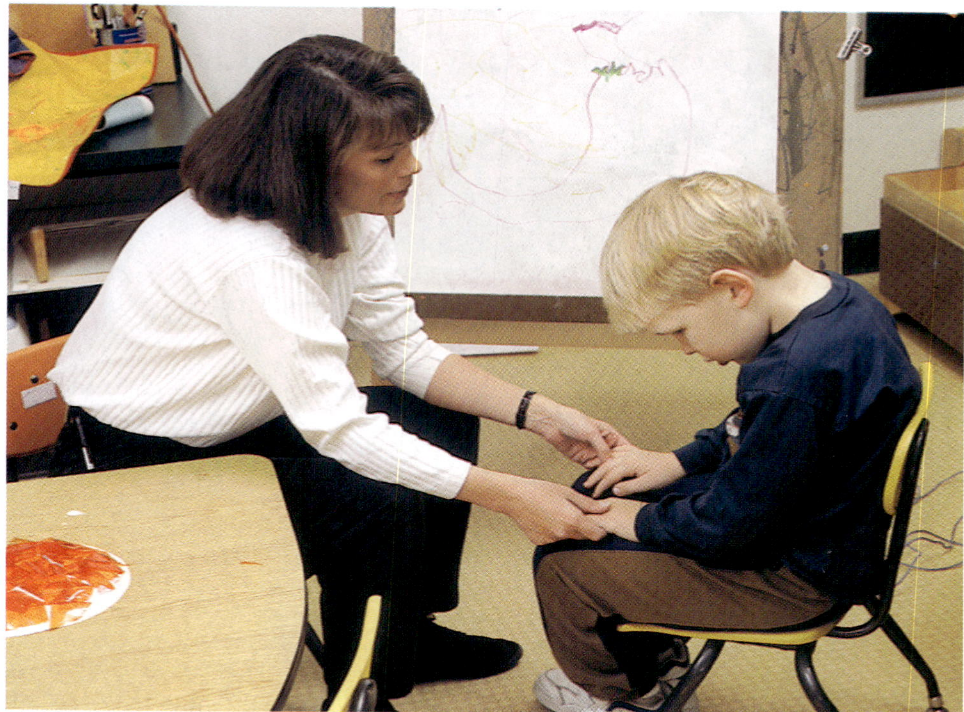

Intensive, behaviorally based early intervention has helped some children with autism learn communication and social skills.

were considered to be "indistinguishable from average children on tests of intelligence and adaptive behavior" (p. 359). In discussing the outcomes of this research, Lovaas (1994) states:

> After 1 year of intensive intervention, fifty percent of the children can be integrated into regular kindergarten classrooms. Then, we have them repeat kindergarten to get a head start on first grade. Successful passing of first grade is the key. Those that pass first grade are likely to obtain normal IQ scores and normal functioning. The children who don't make it into first grade are likely to need intensive supports for their entire life.

Only 12% of school-age children with autism were served in regular classrooms and special schools during the 1995–1996 school year (U.S. Department of Education, 1998).

Although the validity and generality of this research has been questioned by some (e.g., Gresham & MacMillan, 1997), the work of Lovaas and his colleagues represents a landmark accomplishment in the education of children with autism. First, they have discovered and validated at least some of the factors that can be controlled to help children with autism achieve normal functioning in a regular classroom. Second, the successful results offer real hope and encouragement for the many teachers and parents who are desperate to learn how to help children with autism.

For one parent's perspectives on the anguish of trying to separate unsubstantiated claims from scientifically validated treatments for her two children, see "The Autism Wars."

Prevalence

Because there is no universally accepted definition of severe disabilities, there are no accurate and uniform figures on prevalence. Estimates of the prevalence of severe disabilities range from 0.1% to 1% of the population (Ludlow & Sobsey, 1984). Brown (1990) considers students with severe disabilities to be those who function intellectually in the lowest functioning 1% of the school-age population.

Because severe disabilities is not one of the disability categories under which the states make their annual report to the federal government, the number of students with severe disabilities who receive special education services under IDEA cannot be

The Autism Wars

by Catherine Maurice

Many parents I know, as well as many researchers and clinicians, routinely use the phrase "the autism wars." We know what we're talking about, but people unfamiliar with the politics of autism diagnosis and treatment might not. Briefly, "the autism wars" refers to the fierce infighting and conflicting claims of individuals or groups, each of whom claims to know how best to treat children with autism and derides the theories and methods of the other camps. In an environment where funding is scarce, fear and passion run high, and children's futures are at stake, the autism wars can generate much rancor, to say nothing of confusion.

On Monday, for example, a parent may consult one doctor and be told to place her child in a "therapeutic nursery." The doctor will tell the parent to avoid at all costs any program based on behavior analysis because such programs are "manipulative, damaging, and tantamount to dog training." On Tuesday, the parent might be told that therapeutic nurseries have little impact on autistic behaviors and often reinforce such behaviors, in spite of their warm and fuzzy talk about "nurturing the whole child" and "finding the hidden child within the autistic shell." On Wednesday, the parent is informed (say, by another parent writing on the Internet) that massive doses of vitamin B6 can produce meaningful language in the child or that an injection of gamma globulin can repair the child's damaged immune system. In the course of hearing or reading these recommendations, the parent learns that professionals are "not to be trusted" and that parents should always "trust their own instincts" and "follow their hearts" when it comes to selecting autism treatments. On Thursday, the same parent is advised to try "an eclectic approach: a little of this and a little of that." (Soon, because of fear and longing, "a little of this and a little of that" becomes an astonishing array of "treatments" levied onto 3- and 4-year-old children.) Finally, on Friday, the parent is told that there is not a whole lot that anyone can do for autism anyway, so why not come to a weekly support group to discuss "coping" and "feelings" with a "coping facilitator"?

For a parent of a newly diagnosed child or for a young person just starting out in a career in which he wishes to be of service to a child or an adult with autism, the barrage of conflicting messages can produce frustration, fear, and even despair. It is nothing short of outrageous that the organizations and individuals to whom parents and caregivers turn for help have not yet produced a set of clear, strong, discriminatory guidelines based on sound scientific principles as well as humanitarian concerns to lead people through the morass of so-called "options" for autism treatments.

Instead, many experts have tolerated, even encouraged, this frantic, time-consuming, expensive experimentation on our children—perhaps to remain popular with parents, who love anyone who gives them hope. But if my child is diagnosed with cancer, I need hope laced with truth. Otherwise, I will chase every apricot pit and bottle of shark cartilage I can afford as long as there is someone, anyone, who tells me that these things might help. If my child had cancer, I could presumably go to a reputable cancer center and find out which treatments have solid empirical research behind them; which treatments are still experimental; which are "alternative" (an unfortunate euphemism for "no data"); which are known to cause harm. A reputable cancer treatment center, in other words, would give me the objective information I needed to make a truly informed choice for my child's well-being.

But with autism, anything goes. I have had two children diagnosed with autism—meaning that, according to the prevailing opinion, my sweet little girl and my beloved little boy would never hold a meaningful conversation with me; never attend regular schools; never play with other children; never know how to use language to comfort a friend, heal a hurt, or tell a joke. When my daughter received this terrifying diagnosis, many people, both professionals and parents, told me how "expert" they were in autism. I was told about their degrees, their far-flung reputations, and their personal experience. But very few people had ever bothered to read, much less refer me to, published data in reputable, peer-reviewed, science-based journals. All was opinion, all was anecdote, all was theory.

Through the grace of God, I managed to stumble my way through many deviations, mistakes, and wrong turns until I found the program and the people who could truly help my children. Although I was told that applied behavior analysis was cold and harmful, that autism was lifelong, severe, and incurable, I managed somehow to hold onto a little flame of reason in the face of opinion and ideology. The research was there. The data were there. None of the other saviors and experts had anywhere close to the 30-year history of empirical evidence that the field of behavior analysis has accrued. In the end, after trembling through all the tears and the nightmarish uncertainty that other parents have endured, I closed my eyes, said a prayer, and chose to use not only my heart but also that other gift: my head. I chose to believe that sometimes we should follow the gift of reason, the faculty of logic. Men and women in the behavioral sciences have researched for decades how human beings learn, and their exercise of reason and logic have led to monumental strides in understanding how children with autism can learn, sometimes to the point where they can make very significant progress or even recover.

Today, 10 years after they were diagnosed, both my daughter and my son have been reevaluated (by the same people who first diagnosed them) and have been found to have "no significant residua of autism." They attend regular schools where they do not receive any special services. They get good grades, have friends, and have now officially entered the years where they are deeply embarrassed by their mother, especially if I do something mortifying like sing in front of their friends.

No, recovery does not happen to all families who choose intensive behavioral intervention. So far, studies indicate that at best only 30% to 40% of children will reach this level of functioning. However, it does appear that virtually all children can make some appreciable progress if they are treated in a program informed by qualified professionals in the field of applied behavior analysis. Most children will develop some level of meaningful language, even if some behavioral problems remain. Today, I know many families who delight in their children's ever-growing capacity to communicate verbally with them, to learn, and to love. No, their children have not fully recovered, and perhaps they may never do so, but these families have survived the autism wars and have emerged stronger by learning how to sort authority from authoritarianism, fact from opinion.

What do I draw from my own war with autism? Many things, but among them figures the sorrow of a survivor—one who knows that others still endure a dangerous political climate where misinformation and disinformation abound and children do not receive the services they so desperately need. I want other parents to have the same chance that I did: a real chance, with real choices, not bogus "options" that bleed money and time and steal opportunity from their children. There is hope for meaningful improvement in autism, for communication, for true learning—but that hope does not spring from dolphin therapies, facilitated communication, Ouija boards, or pumping our kids full of vitamins or Prozac. That hope springs, at the present time, from the science of applied behavior analysis, and no amount of furious invective about "the training of robots" will succeed for long in blurring the fierce power of that truth.

Do I believe that applied behavior analysis is the only worthwhile treatment for autism? It is not a question of what I or anyone else believes. It is a question of what objective data exist to back up any treatment claim. The education and treatment of children with autism should be based on scientific research, not on belief. Maybe one day science will produce a biomedical intervention that will lead to cure or recovery for most children. I hope so—for the sake of the children I know whose progress under applied behavior analysis is relatively slow, and for the sake of their parents. I hope that careful, responsible research, not media-hyped crazes about substances manufactured from pigs' intestines (cf. the recent "secretin" fad), will one day lead us to that cure. But for today, it is incumbent upon all of us to seek the treatments that can help the children who are alive today. It is incumbent upon us to seek the science—the hard science, not the pseudo-science that abounds in popular books, newsletters, or Internet chat rooms. And for the sake of all our children, we should never just accept at face value what anyone tells us about research. We need to ask for that research, check it out, read it, find out where it was published. Find out the reputation of the journal in which it was published. Find out if there was any peer review of the research. Find out whether or not there were control groups, intake evaluations, outcome data, and independent confirmation of findings.

Reason and tenderness can walk hand in hand. Judgment, intelligence, compassion, and mercy all have their place in autism treatment. We parents love our children. That's a given. We owe it to them to figure out sense from nonsense, hope from hype.

Figuring Out Sense from Nonsense Recommended readings about science, pseudo-science, and discriminatory thinking:

The Demon-Haunted World: Science As a Candle in the Dark by Carl Sagan. Random House: New York, 1995.
Crazy Therapies: What Are They? Do They Work? by Margaret Thaler Singer and Janja Lalich. San Francisco: Jossey-Bass, 1996.
Behavioral Intervention for Young Children with Autism: A Manual for Parents and Professionals edited by C. Maurice, G. Green, and S. C. Luce. Austin, TX: PRO-ED, 1996.

Catherine Maurice, Ph.D., is the author of the best-selling book *Let Me Hear Your Voice: A Family's Triumph over Autism* (Knopf, 1993; Ballantine, 1994). She lectures widely about the importance of bringing more accountability and scientific rigor into the education and treatment of children with autism.

determined from data supplied by the U.S. Department of Education. Students who have severe disabilities are served and reported under other disability categories, including mental retardation, multiple disabilities, other health impairments, autism, and deaf-blindness. The available information, however, shows that this is neither a small nor an isolated population.

Causes of Severe Disabilities

Coulter (1994) states that a brain disorder is "the only condition that will account for the existence of profound disabilities" (p. 41).

Severe intellectual disabilities can be caused by a wide variety of conditions, largely biological, that may occur before (prenatal), during (perinatal), or after birth (postnatal). In almost every case, a brain disorder is involved. Brain disorders are the result of either *brain dysgenesis* (abnormal brain development) or *brain damage* (caused by influences that alter the structure or function of a brain that had been developing normally up to that point). From a review of 10 epidemiological studies (McLaren & Bryson, 1987), Coulter (1994) estimated that prenatal brain dysgenesis accounts for most cases of severe cognitive limitations and that perinatal and postnatal brain damage account for a minority of cases.

A significant percentage of children with severe disabilities are born with chromosomal abnormalities, such as Down syndrome, or with genetic or metabolic disorders that can cause serious problems in physical or intellectual development. Complications of pregnancy—including prematurity, Rh incompatibility, and infectious diseases contracted by the mother—can cause or contribute to severe disabilities. A pregnant woman who uses drugs, drinks alcohol excessively, or is poorly nourished has a greater risk of giving birth to a child with severe disabilities. Because their disabilities tend to be more extreme and more readily observable, children with severe disabilities are more frequently identified at or shortly after birth than are children with mild disabilities.

Severe disabilities can be caused by most of the organic causes of mental retardation (see Chapter 6).

Severe disabilities also may develop later in life from head trauma caused by automobile and bicycle accidents, falls, assaults, or abuse. Malnutrition, neglect, ingestion of poisonous substances, and certain diseases that affect the brain (e.g., meningitis, encephalitis) also can cause severe disabilities. Although hundreds of medically related causes of severe disabilities have been identified, in about one-sixth of all cases, the cause cannot be clearly determined (Coulter, 1994).

Educational Approaches

How does one go about teaching students with severe disabilities? To answer this question, three fundamental and interrelated questions must be considered:

1. What skills should be taught?
2. What methods of instruction should be employed?
3. Where should instruction take place?

Of course, each of these questions must be asked for all students; but when the learner is a student with severe disabilities, the answers take on enormous importance. During the past 25 years, major changes and advancements in the education of students with severe disabilities have led to new responses to the questions of curriculum, teaching methods, and placement.

Curriculum: What Should Be Taught to Students with Severe Disabilities?

Not long ago, a student's so-called "mental age" as determined by norm-referenced tests of development played a significant role in the selection of curriculum content and teaching activities. This practice led to an emphasis on activities thought to be essential prerequisites for higher-level skills because typical children of a given age did such skills. As a result, students with severe disabilities spent many hundreds of hours working on artificially contrived activities that had no immediate value and, because they were not age-appropriate (e.g., teenage students sorting blocks by color or clapping their hands to the rhythm of a song for preschoolers), may have contributed to the perception of students with severe disabilities as eternal children (Bellamy & Wilcox, 1982).

See "My Brother Darryl" later in this chapter.

Today, most educators of individuals with severe disabilities recognize that their students often do not acquire skills in the same way that nondisabled students do and that developmental "ages" should not serve as the basis for determining curriculum activities. For example, a 16-year-old student who is learning to feed and toilet herself should not be taught in the same way or with the same materials as a nondisabled 2-year-old who is learning to feed and toilet herself. Even though both individuals need to learn the same skill, their past experiences, present environments, and future prospects are significantly different and demand different instructional activities and materials. Freagon (1982) offers a thoughtful critique of the developmental sequencing strategy:

> When the developmental curricular strategy is employed, severely handicapped students have considerable impediments to achieving a postschool adult life-style that is similar to those of nonhandicapped persons. In the first place, when instructional activities are based on mental, language and social, and gross and fine motor ages, severely handicapped students rarely, if ever, gain more than 1 or 2 developmental years over the entire course of their educational experience. Therefore, 18-year-old students are relegated to performing infant or preschool or elementary nonhandicapped student activities. They are never seen as ready to engage in 18-year-old activities. In the second place, little, if any, empirical evidence exists to support the notion that severely handicapped students need to learn and grow along the same lines and growth patterns as do nonhandicapped students in order to achieve the same goal of education. (p. 10)

Contemporary curriculum content for students with severe disabilities is characterized by its focus on functional skills that can be used in immediate and future domestic, vocational, community, and recreational/leisure environments. Educational programs are future-oriented in their efforts to teach skills that will enable students with severe disabilities to participate in integrated settings as meaningfully and independently as possible after they leave school.

Functionality Functional skills are immediately useful to a student, frequently required in school and nonschool environments, result in less dependence on others, and allow the student to participate in less restrictive environments (Slaton, Schuster, Collins, & Carnine, 1994). Placing pegs into a pegboard or sorting wooden blocks by color do not

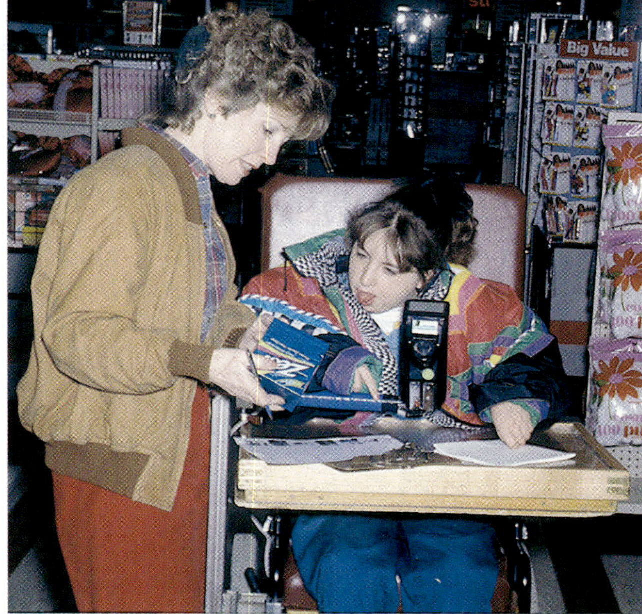

Learning to shop is one of the functional vocational skills identified by Sheila's IEP team.

Several excellent and comprehensive curriculum guides of functional skills and related instructional activities for students with severe disabilities are available (e.g., Falvey, 1989; Ford, Schnorr, Meyer, Davern, Black, & Dempsey, 1989; Fredericks et al., 1980a, 1980b; Giangreco, Cloninger, & Iverson, 1998; Neel & Billingsley, 1989; Wilcox & Bellamy, 1987).

meet any of these criteria. Examples of functional skills for many students with severe disabilities include activities such as learning to dress oneself (McKelvey, Sisson, Van Hasselt, & Hersen, 1992), prepare a snack (Trask-Tyler, Grossi, & Heward, 1994), ride a public bus (Robinson, Griffith, McComish, & Swasbrook, 1984), purchase items from coin-operated vending machines (Sprague & Horner, 1984), and recognize common sight words in community settings (Schloss, Alexander, Hornig, Parker, & Wright, 1995). Whenever possible, functional instructional activities should employ authentic materials (Wolery & Schuster, 1997). For example, students learning to use money to make purchases should practice with real bills and coins instead of simulated money.

Chronological Age-Appropriateness Students with severe disabilities should participate in activities that are appropriate for same-age peers without disabilities. Adolescents with severe disabilities should not use the same materials as young, nondisabled children; in fact, having teenagers sit on the floor and play clap-your-hands games or cutting and pasting cardboard snowmen highlights their differences and discourages integration. It is more appropriate to teach recreational skills, such as bowling and tape recorder operation, or to engage the students in holiday projects, such as printing greeting cards. Teachers of secondary students with severe disabilities should avoid decorating classroom walls with child-oriented characters such as Barney or Mickey Mouse and should not refer to their students as "boys," "girls," or "kids" when "young men," "young women," or "students" are clearly more age-appropriate.

It is critically important to build an IEP for a student with severe disabilities around functional and age-appropriate skills. Because nonschool settings demand such skills and nondisabled peers exhibit them, functional and age-appropriate behaviors are more likely to be reinforced in the natural environment and, as a result, to be maintained in the student's repertoire (Horner, Dunlap, & Koegel, 1988).

Making Choices Imagine going through an entire day without being able to make a choice, any choice at all. Someone else—a teacher, a staff person, a parent—will decide what you will wear, what you will do next, what you will eat for lunch, whom you will sit next to, and so on throughout the day, every day. In the past, students with severe disabilities had few opportunities to express preferences and make choices; the emphasis was on establishing instructional control over students. Traditionally, persons with severe disabilities have simply been cared for and taught to be compliant.

> Some caregivers might feel that to complete tasks for persons with disabilities is easier and faster than allowing them to do it for themselves; while others may have the attitude that the person already has enough problems coping with his or her disability. Regardless of the underlying intention, the result can be to overprotect, to encourage learned helplessness, and to deprive the individual of potentially valuable life experiences. (Guess, Benson, & Siegel-Causey, 1985, p. 83)

Special educators are recognizing the importance of choice making as a way of making activities meaningful and as an indicator of quality of life for students with severe disabilities (Brown & Lehr, 1993; Newton, Horner, & Lund, 1991). Increasing efforts are being made to help students with severe disabilities express their preferences and make decisions about matters that will affect them. For example, Datillo and Mirenda (1987) developed a computerized procedure that enables nonspeaking students with severe disabilities to indicate their preferences and to control access to leisure-time activities (e.g., music, action videos, slides). Other studies have discovered ways to help individuals with severe disabilities express preferences for where

PROFILES AND PERSPECTIVES

My Brother Darryl: A Case for Teaching Functional Skills

by Preston Lewis

Eighteen years old, moderately/severely handicapped. Been in school for 12 years. Never been served in any setting other than an elementary school. He has had a number of years of "individualized instruction." He has learned to do a lot of things! Darryl can now do lots of things he couldn't do before.

He can put 100 pegs in a board in less that 10 minutes while in his seat with 95% accuracy, but he can't put quarters in a vending machine.

Upon command he can "touch" his nose, shoulder, leg, hair, ear. He is still working on wrist, ankle, hips, but he can't blow his nose when needed.

He can do a 12-piece Big Bird puzzle with 100% accuracy and color an Easter bunny and stay in the lines. He prefers music, but has never been taught to use a radio or record player.

He can now fold primary paper in half and even quarters, but he can't sort clothes, white from colors, for washing.

He can roll Play-Doh and make wonderful clay snakes, but he can't roll bread dough and cut out biscuits.

He can string beads in alternating colors and match it to a pattern on a DLM card, but he can't lace his shoes.

He can sing his ABCs and tell me the names of all the letters in the alphabet when presented on a card in upper case with 80% accuracy, but he can't tell Men's room from Ladies' when we go to McDonald's.

He can be told it's cloudy/rainy and take a black felt cloud and put it on the day of the week on an enlarged calendar (with assistance), but he still goes out in the rain without a raincoat or hat.

He can identify with 100% accuracy 100 different Peabody Picture Cards by pointing, but he can't order a hamburger by pointing to a picture or gesturing.

He can walk a balance beam forward, sideways, and backward, but he can't walk up the steps of the bleachers unassisted in the gym or go to basketball games.

He can count to 100 by rote memory, but he doesn't know how many dollars to pay the waitress for a $2.59 McDonald coupon special.

He can put a cube in the box, under the box, beside the box, and behind the box, but he can't find the trash bin in McDonald's and empty his trash into it.

He can sit in a circle with appropriate behavior and sing songs and play Duck Duck Goose, but nobody else in his neighborhood his age seems to want to do that.

I guess he's just not ready yet.

Source: Reprinted from Preston Lewis, Kentucky Department of Education. Used by permission.

they will live (Faw, Davis, & Peck, 1996), what foods they will purchase and eat (Cooper & Browder, 1998; Parsons, McCarn, & Reid, 1993), leisure activities (Browder, Cooper, & Lim, 1998), and whether or not they want to participate in daily routines and activities (Bambara & Ager, 1992; Bannerman, Sheldon, Sherman, & Harchik, 1990).

Gothelf, Crimmins, Mercer, and Finocchiaro (1994) describe a 10-step method for teaching choice making to students who are deaf-blind. For reviews of research on assessing preferences and teaching choice making to persons with severe disabilities, see Hughes, Pitkin, and Lorden (1998) and Lancioni, O'Reilly, and Emerson (1996).

Shevin and Klein (1984) offer several suggestions for incorporating choice-making activities into the classroom programs of students with severe disabilities. For example, a child might be presented with pictures of two activities and asked to point to the one she would rather engage in. Another child might be asked, "Whom would you like for your partner?" Or the teacher might say, "Should we do this again?" Of course, in presenting such choices, the teacher must be prepared to accept whichever alternative the student selects and to follow through accordingly. Bambora and Koger (1996) also describe procedures for providing increased opportunities for choice making throughout the day.

Reichle (1997) describes best practice guidelines for interventions to enhance communication by individuals with severe disabilities.

Rowland and Schweigert (1993) have developed an environmental inventory that enables teachers to analyze specific activities that encourage functional communication. Reichle and Keogh (1986) discuss decision-making rules for selecting the most appropriate methods of communication for students with severe disabilities.

Communication Skills Effective communication is essential to our quality of life, enabling us to express our desires and choices, to obtain and give information, and, most important, to form and maintain relationships with others (Chadsey-Rusch, Drasgow, Reinoehl, Halle, & Collet-Klingenberg, 1993; Ferguson, 1994; Kaiser, 1993). Early research and training in communication for persons with severe disabilities focused on remediation of specific forms of communication, such as the production of speech sounds, words, and descriptive phrases (Kaiser & Goetz, 1993). However, the focus of and methods used to teach communication skills to students with severe disabilities have undergone significant changes during the past 20 years. Two changes in perspective regarding the nature of communication are shaping contemporary research and instructional practices in communication for persons with severe disabilities (Ferguson, 1994; Kaiser & Goetz, 1993):

1. Communication is independent of the specific mode that is used as a channel for communication.
2. Communication occurs when communication partners establish shared meanings.

To be functional, communication must "work"; that is, it must influence the behavior of others to "bring about effects that are appropriate and natural in a given social context" (Calculator & Jorgensen, 1991, p. 204). The responsibility for successful communication rests with both communication partners. However, shared meaning is more likely when the communication partner who is relatively more skilled uses the principles of *responsive interaction,* such as following the lead of the less skilled speaker, balancing turns between conversation partners, and responding with interest and affect (Blackstone, 1981; Fox & Westling, 1991).

Many students with severe disabilities are able to learn to understand and produce spoken language. Speech is always a desirable goal, of course, for those who can attain it. A student who can communicate verbally is likely to have a wider range of educational, employment, residential, and recreational opportunities than a student who is unable to speak.

Ferguson (1994) believes that research and communication training for individuals with severe disabilities eventually will evolve to another level, at which it will be recognized that

> what we really seek is not "socially effective communication repertoires" at all, but membership, specifically participatory, socially valued, image-enhancing membership. The purpose of all of our interventions, programs, indeed, schooling in general, is to enable all students to actively participate in their communities so that others care enough about what happens to them to look for ways to include them as part of that community. (p. 10)

Augmentative and Alternative Communication (AAC) Because of sensory, motor, cognitive, or behavioral limitations, some students with severe disabilities may not learn to speak intelligibly even after

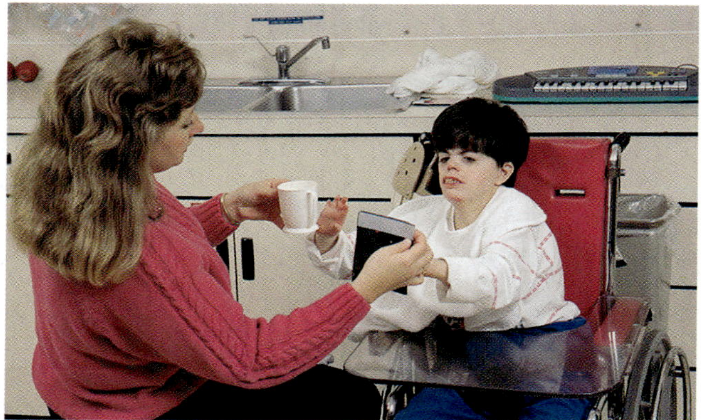

Since she has learned to make choices and express her preferences, Kimberly's quality of life has improved greatly.

extensive instruction. Many systems of augmentative and alternative communication (AAC) have proven useful—including gestures, various sign language systems, pictorial communication boards, symbol systems, and electronic communication aids. Although the specialized forms of communication used by some individuals with severe disabilities limit the number of people with whom they can communicate because the contrived and idiosyncratic nature of their systems requires specialized knowledge by their communication partner (Heller et al., 1994), they do enable many students with severe disabilities to receive and express basic information, feelings, needs, and wants. Sign language and other communication systems also can be learned by a student's teachers, peers, parents, and employers, thus encouraging use outside the classroom. Some students—after learning basic communication skills through sign language, communication boards, or other strategies—later are able to acquire speech skills. Researchers are working to develop partner-friendly forms of communication.

Baumgart, Johnson, and Helmstetter (1990) and Blackstone (1989) describe AAC systems and their use by students with severe disabilities. For more information on AAC and suggestions on how to communicate with a person who uses AAC, see Chapter 9.

Facilitated Communication **Facilitated communication (FC)** is a process by which a communication partner, called a facilitator, provides physical support to assist an individual who cannot speak or whose speech is limited to type on a keyboard or to point at pictures, words, or other symbols on a communication board. Facilitated communication was first developed in Australia for use with persons with cerebral palsy (Crossley, 1988; Crossley & Remington-Guerney, 1992). Biklen brought it to the United States and used it primarily with persons with autism and mental retardation:

> In facilitation a parent, friend, teacher, speech language clinician or other communication partner provides physical and emotional support as the person with a communication disability tries to point in order to communicate. The method can involve pointing at pictures or letters. The physical support may include: assistance in isolating the index finger; stabilizing the arm to overcome tremor; backward resistance on the arm to slow the pace of pointing or to overcome impulsiveness; a touch of the forearm, elbow or shoulder to help the person initiate typing; or pulling back on the arm or wrist to help the person not strike a target repetitively. Emotional support involves providing encouragement but not direction. It is important that the person look at the target. Also, the facilitator must work to avoid influencing the person's selections. . . . Fading physical support causes the typists to pay better attention to looking at the keyboard. (*Syracuse Record,* November 1, 1993, n.p.)

Biklen (1990) has claimed that individuals with autism and other severe disabilities can carry on typed conversations on complex topics such as current events and economics after training with FC. Advocates have reported that FC has produced dramatically more sophisticated language than the user is able to produce by speech, signing, or gestures (Biklen, 1990, 1992; Crossley, 1988), which has led to speculations of an "undisclosed literacy" consistent with "normal intellectual functioning" by individuals previously thought to have severe or profound intellectual disabilities.

FC has produced tremendous interest and controversy, both in the professional literature and in the popular media. Claims of meaningful and extensive communication and vocabulary use by individuals with autism or mental retardation whose use of language had previously been nonexistent or extremely limited generated understandable excitement that a powerful and widely effective new treatment might have been discovered. Even though little or no scientific evidence was available to support these claims, FC was soon being widely implemented in special education and adult human services programs serving individuals with disabilities. State education and mental retardation agencies and school districts hired FC experts and sent their teachers to be trained in the new technique. Many children and adults with disabilities were "facilitated" on a daily basis. All of this was done in the absence of any objective, scientific evaluation of FC.

Although some educators and many parents raised questions from the beginning about the efficacy and appropriateness of FC, asking for some data supporting its use, many more were too excited about the promises of this new wonder therapy to ask too many questions. FC just seemed too good to be true. But as the uniformly negative results of carefully controlled empirical studies on FC have grown (e.g., Oswald, 1994; Simpson & Myles, 1995; Wheeler, Jacobson, Paglieri, & Schwartz, 1993), more people are questioning its use. Research designed to validate FC has repeatedly demonstrated either facilitator influence (correct or meaningful language is produced only when the facilitator "knows" what should be communicated) or no unexpected language competence compared with the participants' measured IQ or a standard language assessment. Green (1992), who reviewed 15 studies in which FC was experimentally evaluated with 138 individuals, concluded that "none of the 138 participants was shown to be the source of the assisted communications. In fact, there is strong evidence in several [studies] that the communications were controlled *entirely* by the assistants" (p. 9).

Advocates of FC contend that objective evaluation of FC is not important because the benefits are potentially large and the procedure carries little risk (e.g., Haskew & Donnellan, 1992). Unfortunately, use of FC has not been without risks; there have been criminal investigations of parents, family members, or other caretakers falsely accused of mistreatment or abuse via FC-produced communications (Johnson, 1994).

After reviewing all 25 scientific evaluations of FC that at the time had been accepted for publication by peer-reviewed professional journals or presented at professional meetings, Shane and Green (1994) concluded that "FC is neither a generally valid nor reliable means for people with disabilities to communicate themselves and that facilitators cannot judge accurately and reliably how much they control FC productions" (p. 157). Proponents, however, claim that conducting objective tests of FC is inherently confrontational and creates an atmosphere of distrust in which the process cannot work (Biklen, 1993; Borthwick, Morton, Crossley, & Biklen, 1992). These same proponents, however, "have been quick to take at face value the few (and questionable) reports of controlled tests that seemed to produce evidence supporting FC's validity" (Green & Shane, 1994, p. 158).

In light of the overwhelming scientific evidence showing that the communication attributed to individuals with severe disabilities during FC was influenced by the facilitator (Rimland, 1993a), several prominent professional organizations have passed resolutions or position statements cautioning that FC is unproven and that no important decisions should be made regarding a student's or client's life that are based on the process unless authorship can be confirmed (e.g., AAMR and the American Psychological Association [APA]) (see Figure 13.1).

Figure 13.1 AAMR policy on facilitated communication

Source: Reprinted from *AAMR News & Notes, 7*(5). (1994, September/October), p. 1. Used by permission of the American Association on Mental Retardation, Washington, DC.

A substantial number of objective clinical evaluation and well-controlled studies indicate that Facilitated Communication, a technique of physically assisting people with autism or mental retardation to communicate through type or communication boards, has not been shown to result in valid messages from the person being facilitated.

Therefore, be it resolved that the Board of Directors of the American Association on Mental Retardation does not support the use of this technique as the basis for making any important decisions relevant to the individual being facilitated without clear, objective evidence as to the authorship of such messages. *Adopted June 1994*

In contrast to AAMR and APA, TASH contends that FC can be an effective means of communication for some individuals with disabilities and believes that limiting its use could violate the individual's right to communicate. According to TASH, FC can be a viable alternative means of expression for some individuals. Therefore, the organization encourages "careful, reflective use" of the technique while recognizing the importance of finding ways to confirm communication competence or authorship (see Figure 13.2).

For extensive discussion and debate by both proponents and critics of FC, see the August 1994 issue of Mental Retardation, *the fall 1994 issue of* JASH, *Donnellan (1996), and Spitz (1996).*

Recreational and Leisure Skills Most children develop the ability to play and later to occupy themselves constructively and pleasurably during their free time. But children with severe disabilities may not learn appropriate and satisfying recreational skills unless they are specifically taught. Teaching appropriate leisure and recreational skills helps individuals with severe disabilities to interact socially, maintain their physical skills, and become more involved in community activities. A survey by Pancsofar and Blackwell (1986) found that many persons with severe disabilities do not use their unstructured time appropriately; rather than participate in enjoyable pursuits, they may spend excessive time sitting, wandering, or looking at television. A variety of programs to teach recreational and leisure skills have recently been developed; this area is now generally acknowledged as an important part of the curriculum for students with severe disabilities.

Horst, Wehman, Hill, and Bailey (1981) describe how several students with severe disabilities, ages 10 to 21, were taught age-appropriate leisure skills. The activities were selected "largely on the basis that many nonhandicapped peers regularly

Therefore Be It Resolved That TASH . . .

- Regards access to alternative means of expression as an individual right.
- Encourages its membership to become informed about the complexities of facilitated communication training and practice and to stay informed of new research and practice throughout the facilitated communication training process.
- Encourages people who decide to become facilitators to seek training in the method.
- Encourages careful, reflective use of facilitated communication.
- Encourages facilitators to work in collaboration with individuals with severe disabilities to find ways of confirming communication competence when using facilitation. To this end, TASH encourages use of multiple strategies, including, for example: controlled designs; portfolio analysis; and transitioning to independent typing.
- Urges that when allegations of abuse or other sensitive communication occur, facilitators and others seek clarification of the communication and work to ensure that users of facilitation are given the same access to legal and other systems that are available to persons without disabilities. It is important not to silence those who could prove their communication competence while using facilitation or any other method of expression.
- Expresses its appreciation to individuals who have disabilities and who have learned to communicate through facilitation and who have been instrumental in discovering ways for themselves and others to demonstrate their communication competence.

Figure 13.2 TASH's resolution on facilitated communication

Source: Reprinted from TASH resolutions. (1994, December; 1995, January). *TASH Newsletter, 20/21,* 7. Used by permission.

engage in these types of activities" (p. 11). Precise teaching procedures were followed in the assessment and teaching of throwing and catching a Frisbee, operating a tape recorder, and playing an electronic bowling game. All students were able to increase their skills in these activities.

Fourteen children ages 6 to 13 with moderate to severe disabilities and 25 fifth- and sixth-grade peers without disabilities enjoyed an integrated aerobic conditioning program (Halle, Gabler-Halle, & Bemben, 1989). Task analysis, picture prompts, and modified game materials were used to help young elementary children with moderate and severe disabilities learn to independently play the board game Candyland (Raschke, Dedrick, Heston, & Farris, 1996).

Modifying the rules by which some team games are played can provide enough supports to enable an individual with severe disabilities to participate (Krebs & Coultier, 1992). For example, Figure 13.3 shows how the rules of a girls' softball league were modified to accommodate the skill limitations of a player with severe disabilities (Bernabe & Block, 1994).

For information and guidelines for selecting and teaching community-based recreational and leisure activities, see Moon (1994); Moon and Bunker (1987); Schlein, Meyer, Heyne, and Brandt (1995); Schlein, Ray, and Green (1997); and Wehman, Renzaglia, and Bates (1985).

Figure 13.3 Modifications that enabled Katie, a player with severe disabilities, to participate in a girls' softball league

Source: Reprinted from Bernabe, E. A., & Block, M. E. (1994). Modifying rules of a regular girls softball league to facilitate the inclusion of a child with severe disabilities. *Journal of the Association for Persons with Severe Handicaps, 19,* 26. Used by permission.

1. Defensively, it was decided to *play Katie in center field.* This was more of a safety decision than a modification because Katie could not field a hit ball. Children at this age have a tendency to make contact with the ball either too early or too late, resulting in more balls being hit toward the left and right fields and fewer to center field. Also, there would be three other outfielders (natural supports) who could back-up and overshadow Katie's position in front, to her left and right (in softball there are four outfield positions: left field, center field, right field, and short center). Thus, the chances of Katie's being hit by the ball would be minimized if she were put into a position where balls are less likely to be hit.
2. Katie is slow and deliberate when she fields the ball, and she rarely stops balls even when they are hit directly to her. Therefore, out of fairness to Katie and her team, *the offense could only advance two bases if the ball were hit directly to her.* It should be noted that this particular modification was suggested by the coaches and approved by 87% of the players without disabilities.
3. Offensively, it was decided to *allow Katie to hit a ball off a tee because she could not hit* a pitched ball. Katie was allowed three attempts to hit the ball from the tee. The possibility, therefore, for a base on balls and being hit by a pitch did not exist for her. If she did not hit the ball in three attempts she was called "out." When Katie hit the ball, she ran unassisted to first base.
4. For baserunning, *the distance to first base was shortened* to account for Katie's running ability. Prior to the beginning of the season, some of Katie's teammates were timed on how fast they could run to first base, and an average time was computed. Using this average time as a standard, Katie was asked to run toward first base. While her teammates could make it all the way to first base in the given time, Katie only made it about halfway. Thus, the distance to first base for Katie was approximately half the distance to regular first base.
5. In consideration of Katie's safety and out of fairness to Katie's hitting and running ability, *the defense had to play at normal depths.* If Katie made contact with the ball and the ball was in fair territory, the fielder had to throw the ball to the first baseman positioned at regulation first base. If the fielder threw the ball to regulation first base before Katie stepped on her modified first base, Katie was called out. Otherwise, she was called "safe." As a result of a safe call, a pinch runner took Katie's place at regulation first base. At this point, Katie was taken back to the dugout.

Prioritizing and Selecting Instructional Targets Teachers must learn good choice-making skills too. Students with severe disabilities present numerous skill deficits often compounded by the presence of challenging behaviors, and each of those could (but not necessarily should) be targeted as an IEP goal or instructional objective. It is seldom, if ever, possible, however, to design and implement a teaching program to deal simultaneously with all of the learning needs and challenging behaviors presented by a student with severe disabilities. (In the rare instance in which the resources to do so might be available, such an all-at-once approach would not be recommended anyway.) One of the greatest responsibilities a special educator undertakes in his role as a member of an IEP team is the selection of instructional objectives.

Judgments about how much a particular skill ultimately will contribute to a student's overall quality of life are difficult to make. In many cases, we simply do not know how useful or functional a behavioral change will prove to be (Baer, 1981b). Whichever skills are chosen for instruction, they ultimately must be meaningful for the learner and her family.

Several methods have been devised to help IEP team members prioritize the relative significance of suggested skills or learning activities (e.g., Cronin & Patton, 1993; Dardig & Heward, 1981; Mount & Zwernick, 1988). For example, Figure 13.4 shows a form on which parents rate and prioritize potential learning outcomes as one step in the IEP planning process developed by Giangreco et al. (1998).

This strategy for involving families in the identification and prioritization of IEP skills and objectives can be used in the development of all IEPs.

Instructional Methods: How Should Students with Severe Disabilities Be Taught?

Care and concern for the well-being of students with severe disabilities and assurance that they have access to educational programs are important. By themselves, however, care and access are not enough. To learn effectively, students with severe disabilities need more than love, care, and a supportive classroom environment. They seldom acquire complex skills through imitation and observation alone; they are not likely to blossom on their own.

The learning and behavioral problems of students with severe disabilities are so extreme and significant that instruction must be carefully planned and executed. Indeed, structure and precision are essential. The teacher must know what skill to teach, why it is important to teach it, how to teach it, and how to recognize that the student has achieved or performed the skill. Careful attention should be given to the following components of an instructional program for a student with severe disabilities:

Several recent texts provide excellent and detailed descriptions of how to plan, conduct, and evaluate instruction for students with severe and profound disabilities (Cipani & Spooner, 1994; Snell & Brown, 2000; Orelove & Sobsey, 1996; Sternberg, 1994; Westling & Fox, 1995).

- *The student's current level of performance must be precisely assessed.* Precise assessment of current performance is necessary to determine which skills to teach and at what level the instruction may start. Is Keeshia able to hold her head up without support? For how many seconds? Under what conditions? In response to what verbal or physical signals? Unlike traditional assessment procedures, which may rely heavily on standardized scores and developmental levels, assessment of students with severe disabilities emphasizes each learner's ability to perform specific, observable behaviors. Assessment should not be a one-shot procedure but should take place at different times, in different settings, and with different persons. The fact that a student with a severe disability does not demonstrate a skill at one particular time or place does not mean that she is incapable of demonstrating that skill.
- *The skill to be taught must be defined clearly.* "Carlos will feed himself" is too broad a goal for many students with severe disabilities. A more appropriate statement might be "When applesauce is applied to Carlos's right index finger, he will

Step 1.2

Mark only one box to indicate if the family wants to discuss this set of learning outcomes in:
Step 1 (Family Interview; priority this year?) ☒; Step 2 (Additional Learning Outcomes) ☐; Skip for Now ☐

Currently, in what ways does the student communicate?

Expressively: *facial expressions, eye movements, vocalizations*

Receptively: *speech*

#	Learning Outcomes	Step 1.3 Circle Score	Step 1.3 Needs Work?	Step 1.4 Rank up to 5 Priorities
1	Expresses Continuation or "More" (e.g., makes sounds or movement when desired interaction stops to indicate he or she would like eating, playing, etc., to continue)	E P (S)	(N) Y	
2	Makes Choices When Given Options	E (P) S	N (Y)	*1*
3	Makes Requests (e.g., for objects, food, interactions, activities, assistance)	(E) P S	N (Y)	*3*
4	Summons Others (e.g., has a way to call others to him or her)	(E) P S	N (Y)	
5	Expresses Rejection/Refusal (e.g., indicates when he or she wants something to stop or does not want something to begin)	E P (S)	(N) Y	
6	Expresses Greetings and Farewells	E (P) S	N (Y)	*4*
7	Follows Instructions (e.g., one step, multistep)	(E) P S	N (Y)	
8	Sustains Communication with Others (e.g., takes turns, attends, stays on topic, perseveres)	E (P) S	N (Y)	*5*
9	Initiates Communication with Others	(E) P S	(N) Y	
10	Responds to Questions (e.g., if asked a question, he or she attempts to answer)	(E) P S	N (Y)	*2*
11	Comments/Describes (e.g., expands vocabulary for events, objects, interactions, feelings)	(E) P S	(N) Y	
12	Asks Questions of Others	(E) P S	(N) Y	
		E P S	N Y	

Comments: *(3) Needs communication system to make requests*
(7) Instructions must be those he can physically do
(8) Yes/no using eye & head movement

Scoring Key (use scores for Step 1.3 alone or in combination):
E = Early/Emerging Skill (1% – 25%) **P** = Partial Skill (25% – 80%) **S** = Skillful (80% – 100%)

Figure 13.4 A method for rating and prioritizing potential learning outcomes in the area of communication skills

Source: Reprinted from Giangreco, M. J., Cloninger, C. J., & Iverson, V. S. (1998). *Choosing outcomes and accommodations for children: A guide to educational planning for students with disabilities* (2nd ed., p. 87). Baltimore: Brookes. Used by permission.

put the finger in his mouth within 5 seconds." A clear statement like this enables the teacher and other observers to determine whether Carlos attains this objective. If, after repeated trials, he has not, a different method of instruction should be tried.

- *The skill may need to be broken down into smaller component steps.* An effective teacher of students with severe disabilities knows how to use task analysis (described in Chapter 6) to break down a skill into a series of specific, observable steps. Assessment of student performance on each step of the task analysis helps the teacher determine where to begin instruction. She can gradually teach each required step until the student can accomplish the entire task independently. Without this sort of structure and precision in teaching, a great deal of time is likely to be wasted.
- *The teacher must provide a clear prompt or cue to the child.* It is important for the child to know what action or response is expected. A cue can be verbal; the teacher might say, "Bev, say apple," to indicate what Bev must do before she will receive an apple. Or a cue can be physical; the teacher might point to a light switch to indicate that Bev should turn on the light. It also may be necessary for the teacher to demonstrate an activity many times and to physically guide the child through some or all of the tasks required in the activity.
- *The student must receive feedback and reinforcement from the teacher.* Students with severe disabilities must receive clear information about their performance; and like all students, they are more likely to repeat an action if it is followed immediately by a reinforcing consequence. Individualized identification of reinforcers is critical for students with severe disabilities (Dyer, 1987). Unfortunately, it is not always easy to determine what items or events a noncommunicative child finds motivating. Many teachers devote extensive efforts to reinforcer sampling; that is, they attempt to find out which items and activities are reinforcing to a particular child, and they keep careful records of what is and is not effective.
- *Strategies that promote generalization and maintenance must be used.* Most students with severe disabilities have difficulty generalizing the skills they learn. As Horner, McDonnell, and Bellamy (1986) note, "education for students with severe disabilities is relevant only to the extent that the knowledge and behaviors that the students acquire become part of their daily routine" (p. 289). Thus, an effective teacher has students perform tasks in different settings and with different instructors, cues, and materials before concluding with confidence that the student has acquired and generalized a skill.
- *The student's performance must be carefully measured and evaluated.* Because students with severe disabilities often make progress in very small steps, it is important to measure performance precisely. Learning is shown most clearly by student performance data collected every day. Some programs keep videotaped records of students' performance on specific tasks. This record can add an important dimension to documenting behavioral changes over extended periods.

For a review of research on methods of delivering and fading instructional prompts to students with severe disabilities, see Doyle, Wolery, Ault, and Gast (1988) and Wolery, Ault, and Doyle (1992).

For a review of methods for assessing stimuli that may serve as reinforcers for individuals with severe disabilities, see Lohrmann-O'Rouke and Browder (1998).

Several strategies for facilitating generalization are discussed in Chapter 6. More detailed information can be found in Baer (1981a); Snell and Brown (2000); Cooper et al. (1987); Haring (1988); Horner et al. (1988); and Stokes and Osnes (1989).

An excellent booklet by Farlow and Snell (1994) shows teachers how to use student performance data to make instruction more effective and efficient.

Partial Participation The principle of **partial participation,** first described by Baumgart et al. (1982), acknowledges that even though some individuals with severe disabilities are not able to independently perform all steps of a given task or activity, they often can be taught to perform selected components or an adapted version of the task. A nonverbal student, for example, may be able to point to pictures of menu items on a laminated card to place an order at a fast-food restaurant. Snell, Lewis,

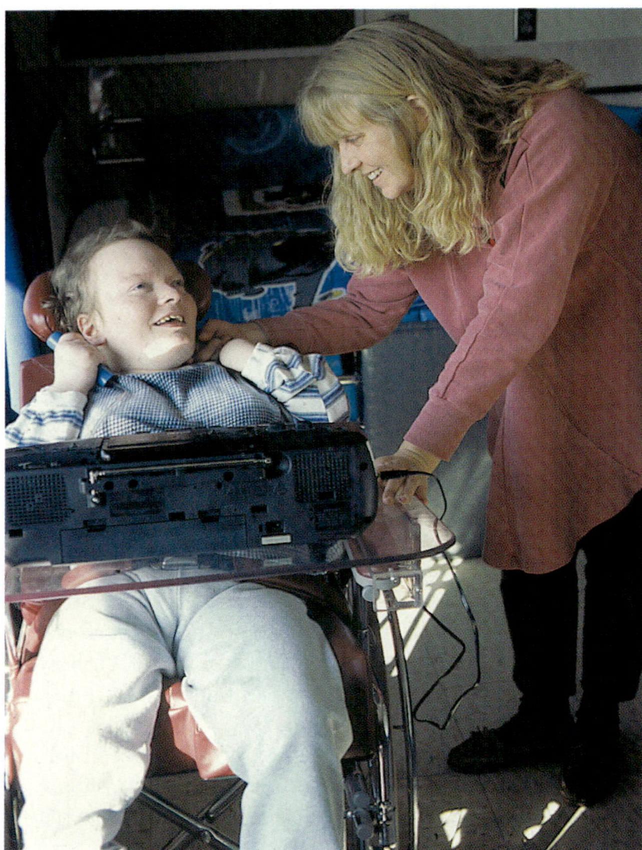

Immediate positive reinforcement is especially critical for students with severe disabilities.

and Houghton (1989) taught three elementary-age students with cerebral palsy and mental retardation to perform selected task analysis components of toothbrushing while the teacher performed the steps the students could not do. Both teachers and parents of two of the three students rated the students' partial participation in the toothbrushing activity as "meaningful" in that they appeared happier and less likely to fuss when they were participating in dental care rather than having their teeth brushed for them. Follow-up data indicated that the toothbrushing skills generalized into the home and were maintained for 19 months following training.

Partial participation can be used to help a learner be more active in a task, make more choices in how the task will be carried out, and provide more control over the activity. Table 13.1 is an example of how partial participation could be used within each step of a task analysis for making a blender drink.

Ferguson and Baumgart (1991) describe and offer suggestions for avoiding four types of errors or common misapplications of partial participation: (1) passive participation—the learner is present but not actively participating; (2) myopic participation—the student's participation is limited to only some parts of the activity that are chosen more for the convenience of others; (3) piecemeal participation—partial participation and the accompanying concepts of functional, activity-based, age-appropriate curriculum activities are only used part of the time; and (4) missed participation—in trying to help students become independent, the point of partial participation is missed altogether.

Positive Behavioral Support Notable changes have occurred in how teachers respond to disruptive, aggressive, or socially unacceptable behaviors by students with severe disabilities. In the not-too-distant past, a student who displayed challenging behaviors, such as stereotypic head weaving, may have been subjected to an unpleasant and undignified procedure, such as having his head restrained or perhaps having a teacher manipulate his head up and down for several minutes (Gast & Wolery, 1987). Some maladaptive behaviors of students with severe disabilities were often "treated" with the application of aversive consequences (e.g., being sprayed with water mist) or with an extended time out from instruction. These were "modes of intervention which most people would reject as absolutely unacceptable if they were used with a person who does not have disabilities" (Center on Human Policy, 1986, p. 4).

Discussion and debate of various viewpoints concerning the use of punishment and aversive consequences with persons with disabilities can be found in Iwata (1988); Mason and Gambrill (1994); Mulick (1990); Repp and Singh (1990); and in the fall 1990 issue of JASH.

With today's emphasis on respect for the individual student and on preparation for independent living, a growing number of special education programs are responding to challenging, excessive, or unacceptable behaviors in more functional and dignified ways by attempting to (1) understand the meaning that a behavior has for a student, (2) offer the student a positive alternative behavior, (3) use nonintrusive intervention techniques, and (4) use strategies that have been validated and are intended for use in integrated community settings (Center on Human Policy, 1986). This nonaversive treatment approach, often called *positive behavioral support*, begins with a functional assessment of the problem behavior.

Several books provide guidelines for developing positive behavioral support plans (e.g., Carr, Levin, McConnachie, Carlson, Kemp, & Smith, 1994; Koegel, Koegel, & Dunlap, 1996; O'Neill et al., 1997).

Although **functional assessment** refers to a variety of behavior assessment methodologies for determining the environmental variables that are setting the occasion for and maintaining challenging behaviors, it usually consists of these three steps (Horner & Carr, 1997):

Table 13.1 Using partial participation within each step of a task analysis for making a blender drink

Task: Making a blender drink | *Learner:* Saundra

Teacher's Assistance	Learner's Participation	Goal
1. Announces activity	Lifts her head to listen	Active
2. Wheels Saundra to the cabinet	—	—
3. Gets out the utensils	Grasps a spoon	Active
4. Wheels Saundra to the table	Releases the spoon on the table	Active
5. Shows fruits	Selects one fruit by grasping it and pushing it to the teacher	Choice
6. Shows beverages	Selects one beverage by grasping it and pushing it to the teacher	Choice
7. Puts the ingredients in the blender	Operates the blender with a switch when the chosen ingredients are in	Control
8. Spoons the blender drink into a glass	Indicates if ready to drink	Control
9. Holds out a straw	Places the straw in the glass and drinks	Active Control

Key: Partial participation may have the goal of encouraging the learner to be more active in the routine (Active), to make more choices (Choice), or to have more control of the routine (Control). These goals are shown for each step of the task analysis.

Source: Reprinted from Browder, D. M., & Snell, M. E. (1993). Daily living and community skills. In M. E. Snell (Ed.), *Instruction for students with severe disabilities* (4th ed.). Upper Saddle River, NJ: Merrill/Prentice Hall. Used by permission.

1. *Structured interviews* are conducted with teachers, family members, and others who know the child well to find out the circumstances that typically surround the occurrence and nonoccurrence of the problem behavior and the reactions the behavior usually evokes from others.
2. *Systematic observations* of the child are conducted to learn (a) the environmental context and events that covary with the problem behavior (e.g., transitions from one classroom or activity to another, task difficulty); (b) the intensity, duration, and form of the problem behavior; and (c) the events that follow the problems behavior and may function to maintain it (e.g., teacher attention, withdrawal of task demands).
3. *Functional analysis* (i.e., experimental manipulation) of the variables identified in steps 1 and 2 is carried out to verify their function in either triggering or maintaining the problem behavior.

See "Positive Behavioral Support in Action" in this chapter and "A Parent-Professional Partnership in Positive Behavioral Support" in Chapter 4. For an extensive collection of research and conceptual papers on functional analysis, see Neef (1994).

Results of functional assessments are used to guide the development of positive behavior support plans. For example, functional assessments conducted by Lalli and colleagues (1993) revealed that the self-injury and aggressive outbursts by three nonvocal students with severe disabilities during instructional activities were maintained by teacher attention (in the form of reprimands) and/or escape (misbehavior often resulted in termination of the academic task). This information led to the design of successful interventions that included frequent positive comments for appropriate behaviors, withholding attention for problem behavior, and teaching the students a socially acceptable behavior for communicating their wishes (e.g., choosing the next activity by pointing to a picture schedule, tapping the teacher on the shoulder).

Functional assessment sometimes suggests how problem behaviors such as noncompliance, aggression, acting out, and self-injury can be reduced through relatively simple modifications of curriculum or the way that learning activities are presented (Ferro, Foster-Johnson, & Dunlap, 1996; Munk & Repp, 1994). For example:

- Providing students with a choice of tasks (Dunlap, Kern-Dunlap, Clark, & Robbins, 1991)
- Interspersing easy or high-probability tasks or requests with more difficult items or low-probability requests (Harchik & Putzier, 1990; Horner, Day, Sprague, O'Brien, & Tuesday-Heathfield, 1991)
- Maintaining a rapid pace of instruction (Dunlap, Dyer, & Koegel, 1983)
- Using a response-prompting procedure that results in fewer errors (Heckaman, Alber, Hooper, & Heward, 1998)
- Reducing task difficulty (Carr & Durand, 1985; Weeks & Gaylord-Ross, 1981)

Positive behavioral support should not be confused with nonintervention interventions, such as "gentle teaching." Gentle teaching is a philosophy and approach for treating problem behaviors by individuals with disabilities that relies on "valuing" the person and "giving warm assistance and protection when necessary" (McGee & Gonzalez, 1990, p. 244). Neither aversive stimulation nor contingent reinforcement is reported to be part of the approach. McGee (1992), the major proponent of gentle teaching, claims, "Behavior problems will evaporate like the morning dew if we express unconditional valuing" (McGee & Menolascino, 1992, p. 109). Although gentle teaching sounds wonderful, examination of the claims made in its behalf yields little scientific evidence of effectiveness (Bailey, 1992; Jones & McCaughey, 1992). Mudford's (1995) review of independent studies of gentle teaching found it unsuccessful with seven of nine individuals, which led him to conclude that gentle teaching "cannot be considered an ethically defensible treatment alternative" (p. 345).

Small-Group Instruction Some educational programs for students with severe disabilities conduct instruction almost entirely on a one-to-one basis; that is, a teacher works with one student at a time. For many years, most professionals believed that one-to-one instruction was the only effective teaching arrangement for students with severe disabilities. When Favell, Favell, and McGimsey (1978) reviewed the literature, they found that about 90% of all articles about teaching or modifying the behavior of students with severe disabilities described a one-to-one approach. The rationale was that one-to-one teaching minimized distractions and increased the likelihood of the student responding only to the teacher.

Although a one-to-one teaching format allows the intensive, systematic instruction known to be effective with students who have severe disabilities, small-group instruction may have several potential advantages over individual instruction (Munk, Laarhoven, Goodman, & Repp, 1998; Snell & Brown, 2000):

For reviews of research on group instruction, see Keel and Gast (1992); Polloway, Cronin, and Patton (1986); Munk et al. (1998); and Reid and Favell (1984).

- Skills learned in small-group instruction may be more likely to generalize to group situations and settings (e.g., Brown, Holvoet, Guess, & Mulligan, 1980).
- Small-group instruction provides opportunities for social interaction and peer reinforcement that are missed when a student is taught alone and isolated from other students (e.g., Alberto, Jobes, Sizemore, & Doran, 1980; Kamps, Dugan, Leonard, & Daoust, 1994).
- Small-group instruction provides no opportunities for incidental or observation learning from other students (e.g., Gast, Wolery, Morris, Doyle, & Meyer, 1990; Orelove, 1982).
- In some instances, small-group instruction may be a more cost-effective use of the teacher's time (e.g., Kamps, Walker, Maher, & Rotholz, 1992; Westling, Ferrell, & Swenson, 1982).

The effectiveness of small-group instruction is enhanced when teachers do the following (Munk et al., 1998; Snell & Brown, 2000):

- Ensure that students possess basic prerequisite skills such as (1) sitting quietly for a period of time, (2) maintaining eye contact, and (3) following simple instructions or imitating simple responses.
- Encourage students to listen and watch other group members and then praise them for doing so.
- Keep instruction interesting by keeping turns short, giving all members turns, giving turns contingent on attending, and using demonstrations and a variety of materials that can be handled. Kamps et al. (1994) and Karsh and Repp (1992) used choral responding so that students could respond concurrently.
- Involve all members by using multilevel instruction individualized to each student's targeted skills and mode of response.
- Use partial participation and material adaptation to enable all students to respond.
- Keep waiting time to a minimum by controlling the group size and limiting the amount of teacher talk and the amount/length of student response in a single turn.
- Promote cooperation among group members.

Choral responding and response cards (see Chapter 8) enable every student in the group to respond to each instructional trial.

Where Should Students with Severe Disabilities Be Taught?

Benefits of the Neighborhood School What is the least restrictive and most appropriate educational setting for a student with severe disabilities? This important question continues to be the subject of much debate and discussion. Some special educators have called for the abolition of all separate placements for students with

Positive Behavioral Support in Action

by John Umbreit

Why would a child suddenly hit another child without being provoked? Or spit at other children? Or bite them? Or scream? Why would a child pick objects off tables and throw them on the floor? Why would he run away sometimes but lay down on the floor and refuse to get up at other times? If this were a typically developing child, we might think he was a brat or a bully, or even disturbed and in need of counseling. But if this were a child with mental retardation or autism, we would be much more likely to think these behaviors were just a part of his disability. After all, a lot of people with developmental disabilities do those kinds of things. At least that is what we thought for many years.

Today, we take a very different approach, one that assumes that challenging behaviors actually are learned behaviors that occur because they produce desirable consequences, such as attention from other people or escape from unpleasant situations. This approach has important implications for treatment. For instance, take the case of the child who hits others to gain attention. With our old way of thinking, we might have "treated" the hitting by ignoring it altogether or by using a negative consequence, such as loss of privileges or time out, that was intended to eliminate the hitting or reduce its frequency. But if we saw that the hitting actually was an effective way for a child with few social skills to gain attention from others, our "treatment" would focus on teaching this child more socially appropriate ways of getting attention.

One of the most interesting children with whom we have used this approach (called functional assessment and positive behavioral support) was Reggie, an 11-year-old boy with moderate to severe retardation, seizures, and behavior disorders. Reggie regularly engaged in a variety of challenging behaviors: he hit, spit, bit, threw objects, screamed, ran away, threw himself on the floor and refused to get up. He did these things frequently throughout the day, including at school, which is where Dr. Kwang-Sun Blair and I worked with him and his teachers.

Reggie began school at age 6 and spent the first three years in a separate class for students with severe emotional disabilities. During that time, he often hit his classmates and teachers. He was then placed in a cross-categorical classroom for a year and then into an inclusion program. In the year before our study began, Reggie's challenging behaviors had escalated so much that school district officials were considering removing him from the program. His teachers had attempted a variety of interventions to reduce these problems, including reinforcing alternative behavior, giving choices, time out, physical restraints, and redirection. None of these procedures had been effective.

We began the process of functional assessment by defining Reggie's challenging behaviors and the appropriate behaviors his teachers wanted him to use instead. Then we conducted structured interviews with 10 people who knew Reggie well (often only two or three people are needed). These people included several of his current and former teachers, the school principal, and both of Reggie's parents. Next, we conducted structured observations to identify the situations in which each challenging behavior occurred and the consequences it produced. These 15-minute observation sessions were conducted in multiple environments: in the classroom, on the playground, in the lunchroom, in the library. The interviews and observations revealed clear and important patterns in Reggie's behavior. Specifically, we learned that Reggie displayed one or more challenging behaviors when an activity was something he didn't like to do, when he was required to engage in an activity (i.e., had no choice in the matter), and when he received little attention from staff. In addition, observational data showed that Reggie's challenging behaviors produced considerably more attention than his appropriate behaviors did.

We hypothesized that Reggie's behavior would improve if he (1) took part in preferred activities, (2) was allowed to choose activities whenever possible, and (3) received frequent social attention from staff for appropriate behavior. Next, we tested each hypothesis within the context of naturally occurring routines and activities at school. To do this, we conducted a series of assessment sessions, ranging from 8 to 15 minutes long. Some were baseline sessions in which the typical conditions that existed before the study were in place. Baseline sessions were alternated with the hypothesis-testing conditions we expected would improve Reggie's behavior. For example, in one session, he might be required to engage in a nonpreferred activity. In the next session, he would be allowed to engage in a preferred activity. Throughout each session, we recorded how often Reggie emitted both challenging and appropriate behaviors. We tested and repeated various combinations of our hypotheses until a clear picture emerged of the situations and consequences that reliably controlled his behavior.

The experimental data supported all three hypotheses: Reggie behaved much better in preferred activities, when he had choices, and when he received frequent attention for appropriate behavior. We used this information to design an intervention package for him consisting of four components. Whenever possible, desired skills were taught through preferred activities that Reggie was allowed to choose, and frequent attention was provided for appropriate behavior. When nonpreferred activities could not be avoided, his teachers tried to give him some choice among these activities and interacted with him frequently when he behaved appropriately.

Instruction in appropriate social and communication skills was included as the fourth component of the intervention because Reggie's teachers and parents told us in the interviews that his limited skills in these areas restricted his ability to interact appropriately with others. This intervention element took two forms. First, the teachers designed a small communication book that included photographs with a written word or phrase related to objects and activities that Reggie encountered during his school day. He carried the book with him wherever he went at school, and his teachers always provided instruction in context (i.e., when the object or activity was encountered naturally). At first, there were only about 10 items in the book, but this number quickly increased to more than 40. Second, the teaching staff was instructed to respond to every occurrence of challenging behavior by immediately teaching Reggie appropriate behavior that he should use instead. For example, he tried to use a computer game in the school's library, but when the game did not boot correctly, he hit the computer screen. Instead of scolding him or using time out, the teacher immediately taught him to ask the school librarian for help, which he got. Thereafter, whenever he needed help, he asked for it independently.

Reggie's communication book helped him interact positively with others

To test the effectiveness of the intervention package, we began with one week of baseline conditions. During the second week, the teachers implemented the intervention only during the afternoon of each day, continuing baseline conditions during the morning. At the end of this week, the afternoon results were very encouraging, so teachers began implementing the intervention throughout the day. They continued to implement the intervention for the remaining five months of the school year.

Figure A on p. 516 shows the power of an intervention that is based on a clear understanding of why a person is engaging in challenging behaviors. Although no formal data have been collected since the study ended, we do know that Reggie's improved behavior continued as he transitioned to middle school and, recently, to high school. During this time, the program we developed has been continued, aided greatly by the school district's willingness to let last year's teachers train Reggie's new teachers at the beginning of each new school year. According to the teachers, the training has focused both on how to work with Reggie and on why it is important to work with him that way.

Now that Reggie is in high school, he spends part of his day at school and part in a community-based program that targets self-sufficiency and the development of work skills. According to his teachers, he would not have been able to participate in the community program if his challenging behaviors had continued.

Data from this study (Umbreit & Blair, 1996) and several others like it are teaching us that challenging behaviors of people with developmental disabilities are functional behaviors that, though inappropriate, give them an effective way to influence their world. Functional assessment and positive behavioral support are two important keys to understanding these behaviors and improving the quality of life for these people and their families, teachers, and friends.

John Umbreit is a professor in the Department of Special Education, Rehabilitation, and School Psychology at the University of Arizona, where he directs the teacher preparation program in severe/multiple disabilities. His research and teaching focus on applied behavior analysis, functional assessment, and positive behavioral support in natural, community-based environments.

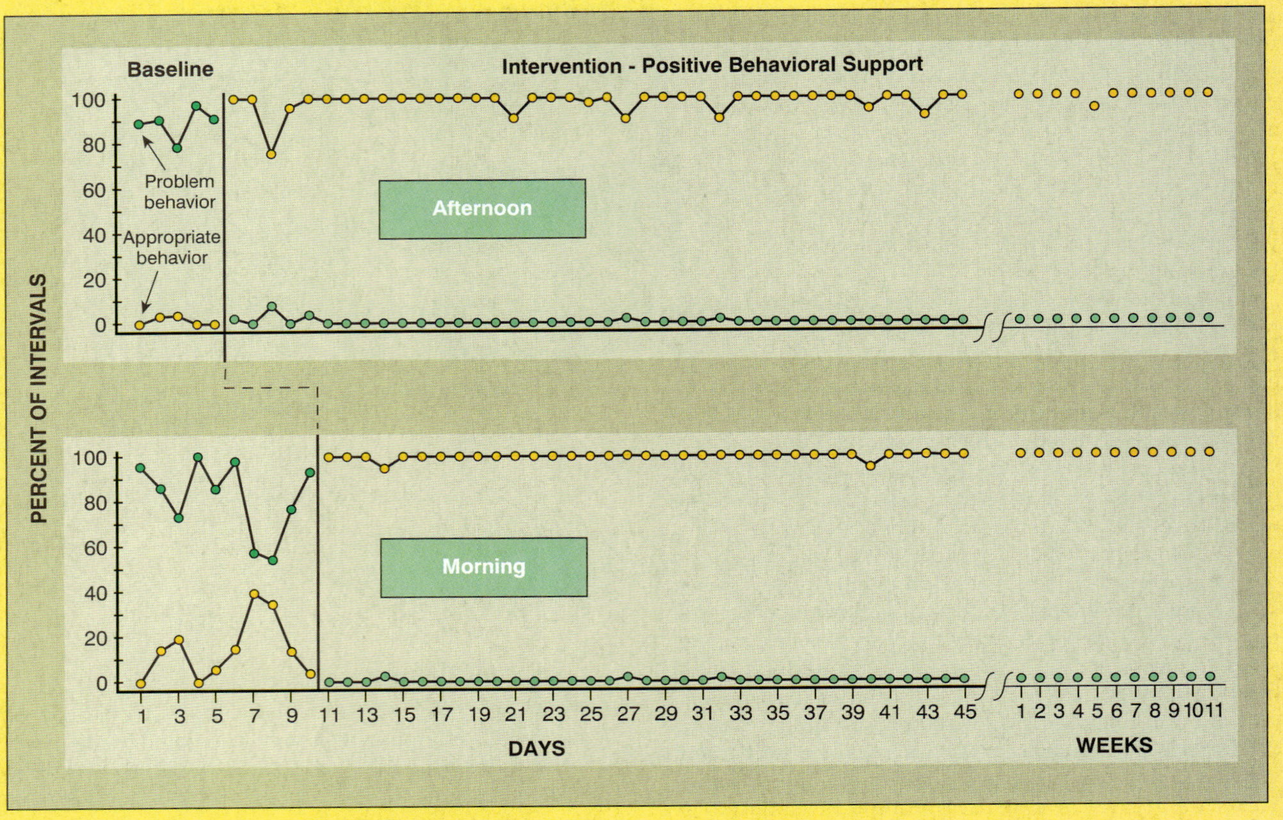

Figure A Percentage of observation intervals in which Reggie exhibited problem and appropriate behaviors in school during baseline and intervention conditions

severe disabilities (e.g., Brown et al., 1989a; Sailor et al., 1989; Stainback & Stainback, 1991). Lou Brown (who has long championed the inclusion of persons with severe disabilities in integrated school, vocational, and community settings) and his colleagues at the University of Wisconsin make a strong case for why students with severe disabilities should attend the same school they would attend if they were not disabled:

> The environments in which students with severe intellectual disabilities receive instructional services have critical effects on where and how they spend their postschool lives. Segregation begets segregation. We believe that when children with intellectual disabilities attend separate schools, they are denied opportunities to demonstrate to the rest of the community that they can function in integrated environments and activities; their nondisabled peers do not know or understand them and too often think negatively of

> them; their parents become afraid to risk allowing them opportunities to learn to function in integrated environments later in life; and taxpayers assume they need to be sequestered in segregated group homes, enclaves, work crews, activity centers, sheltered workshops, institutions, and nursing homes. (Brown et al., 1989a, p. 1)

For a discussion of 10 challenging issues concerning whether students with severe disabilities should be served in regular or separate classrooms in neighborhood schools, see Brown et al. (1989b).

Brown and his colleagues offer four reasons why they believe neighborhood schools should replace segregated and clustered schools. They define a clustered school as "a regular school attended by an unnaturally large proportion of students with intellectual disabilities, but it is not the one any or most would attend if they were not labeled disabled" (1989a, p. 1). First, when students without disabilities go to an integrated school with peers who are disabled, they are more likely to function responsibly as adults in a pluralistic society. Second, various sources of information support integrated schools as more meaningful instructional environments. Hunt, Goetz, and Anderson (1986), for example, compared the IEP objectives for students with severe disabilities who were taught at integrated versus segregated schools. They found the quality of IEP objectives—in terms of age-appropriateness, functionality, and the potential for generalization of what was being taught to other environments—was higher for the students educated in integrated schools. Third, parents and families have greater access to school activities when children are attending their home schools. Further, and perhaps most convincing, is the argument that there are greater opportunities to develop a wide range of social relationships with nondisabled peers when attending one's home school. Table 13.2 presents examples of 11 kinds of social relationships that might develop between students. Table 13.3 presents an assessment of the likelihood that each type of relationship will develop in a home school or in a clustered school.

To join in the discussion "What benefits might students who are not disabled experience from the inclusion of peers with severe disabilities in the regular classrooom?" go to the Message Board module at http://www.prenhall.com/heward.

Social Relationships Establishing and maintaining a network of social relationships is one of the desired outcomes of inclusive educational practices for students with severe disabilities (Billingsley, Gallucci, Peck, Schwartz, & Staub, 1996). Although research has shown that simply placing students with disabilities into regular schools and classrooms does not necessarily lead to increased positive social interactions, regular class participation can provide additional opportunities for positive social contacts and the development of friendships (e.g., Hanline, 1993; Staub, Spaulding, Peck, Gallucci, & Schwartz, 1996).

For example, Kennedy and Itkonen (1994) studied the effects of regular class

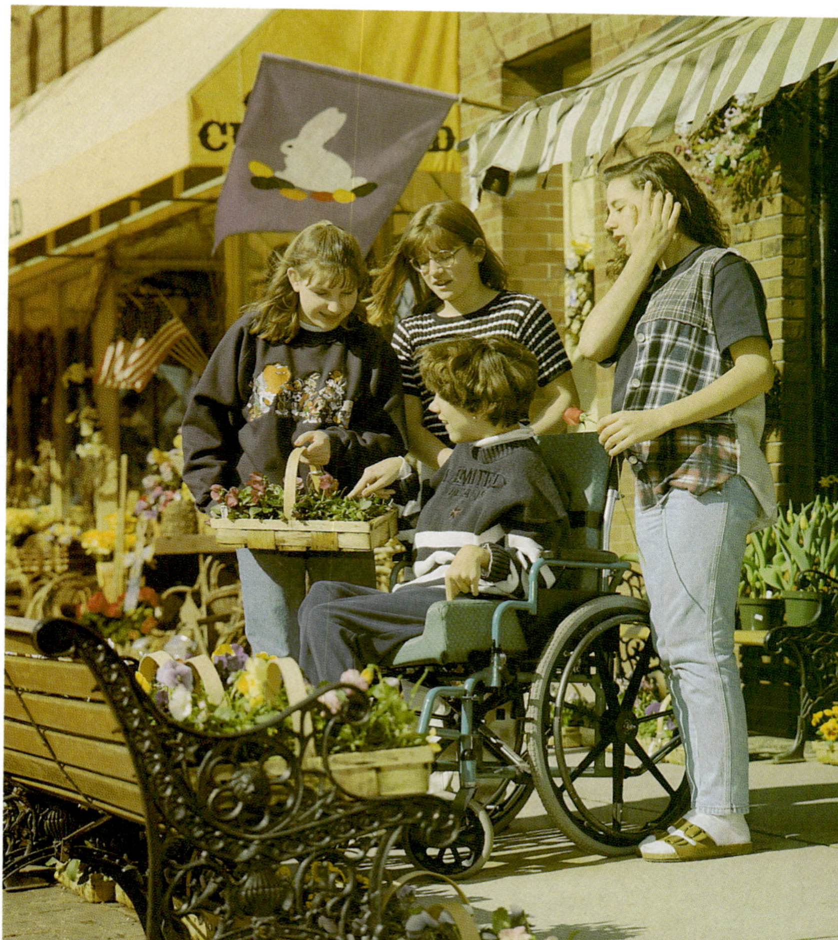

Friendships and after-school relationships between students with disabilities and their nondisabled peers are more likely to develop when all students attend their home school.

Table 13.2 Social relationships that can develop between students with severe disabilities and their nondisabled peers when they attend the same school

Social Relationship	Example
Peer tutor	Leigh role-plays social introductions with Margo, providing feedback and praise for Margo's performance.
Eating companion	Jennifer and Rick eat lunch with Linda in the cafeteria and talk about their favorite music groups.
Art, home economics, industrial arts, music, physical education companion	In art class, students were instructed to paint a sunset. Tom sat next to Dan and offered suggestions and guidance about the best colors to use and how to complete the task.
Regular class companion	A fifth-grade class is doing a "Know Your Town" lesson in social studies. Ben helps Karen plan a trip through their neighborhood.
During-school companion	"Hangs out" and interacts on social level: after lunch and before the bell for class rang, Molly and Phyllis went to the student lounge for a soda.
Friend	David, a member of the varsity basketball team, invites Ralph, a student with severe disabilities, to his house to watch a game on TV.
Extracurricular companion	Sarah and Winona prepare their articles for the school newspaper together and then work on the layout in the journalism lab.
After-school-project companion	The sophomore class decided to build a float for the homecoming parade. Joan worked on it with Maria, a nondisabled companion, after school and on weekends in Joan's garage.
After-school companion	On Saturday afternoon, Mike, who is not disabled, and Bill go to the shopping mall.
Travel companion	David walks with Ralph when he wheels from last-period class to the gym, where Ralph helps the basketball team as a student manager.
Neighbor	Interacts with student in everyday environments and activities. Parents of nondisabled students in the neighborhood regularly exchange greetings with Mary when they are at school, around the neighborhood, at local stores, at the mall, at the grocery.

Source: Adapted from Brown, L., Long, E., Udvari-Solner, A., Davis, L., VanDeventer, P., Ahlgren, C., Johnson, F., Gruenewald, L., & Jorgensen, J. (1989). The home school: Why students with severe disabilities must attend the schools of their brothers, sisters, friends, and neighbors. *Journal of the Association for Persons with Severe Handicaps, 14,* 4. Used by permission.

participation on the social contacts with peers without disabilities for three high school students with severe and multiple disabilities. Don was 18 years old and classified as having severe intellectual retardation, along with paraplegia, cerebral palsy, and visual impairments. He used a wheelchair to move himself for short distances and lived in a 50-person facility for people with multiple disabilities and intensive health care needs. Manny was also 18 years old and classified as having severe retardation. He communicated with two- or three-word sentences and had a 10-year history of hitting and pinching others. Ann was 19 years old with moderate mental retardation. Her communications ranged from a few words to elaborate sentences. She was receiving instruction regarding appropriate topics of conversation and maintaining physical distance when interacting with others. Ann received medication for generalized tonic-clonic seizures and would often yell, run away, and hit others during transitions from one class or activity to another. Contingency contracts were in effect for both Manny and Ann as a preventive behavior management procedure; they could earn privileges for not engaging in problem behaviors.

Table 13.3 Feasibility and likelihood of developing and maintaining 11 kinds of social relationships between students with and without disabilities in home and clustered schools

Social Relationship	Home School				Clustered School			
	Development		Longitudinal		Development		Longitudinal	
	Feasible	Likely	Feasible	Likely	Feasible	Likely	Feasible	Likely
Peer tutor	Yes	Yes	Yes	Yes	Yes	Yes	No	No
Eating companion	Yes	Yes	Yes	Yes	Yes	Yes	No	No
Art, home economics, industrial arts, music, or physical companion	Yes	Yes	Yes	Yes	Yes	Yes	No	No
Regular class companion	Yes	Yes	Yes	Yes	Yes	Yes	No	No
During-school companion	Yes	Yes	Yes	Yes	Yes	Yes	No	No
Friend	Yes	Yes	Yes	Yes	Yes	Yes	No	No
Extracurricular companion	Yes	Yes	Yes	Yes	Yes	No	No	No
After-school-project companion	Yes	Yes	Yes	Yes	Yes	No	No	No
After-school companion	Yes	Yes	Yes	Yes	No	No	No	No
Travel companion	Yes	Yes	Yes	Yes	No	No	No	No
Neighbor	Yes	Yes	Yes	Yes	No	No	No	No

Note: Social relationship refers to a positive personal interaction between a student with severe intellectual disabilities and a peer or other person who is not disabled.

Longitudinal refers to positive personal interactions between a student with severe intellectual disabilities and a peer or others who are not disabled that are developed, maintained, and enhanced across elementary, middle, and high school years.

Home school is the school a student with intellectual disabilities would attend if he were not disabled.

Clustered school is a regular school attended by an unnaturally large proportion of students with intellectual disabilities, but it is not the one any or most would attend if they were not disabled.

Feasible refers to a situation in which all of the structural resources necessary for a particular kind of social relationship to develop are present.

Likely refers to the probability of a particular kind of social relationship occurring, given the reasonable efforts of parents, guardians, professionals, and others.

Companion is a nondisabled person who accompanies, associates with, or assists a student who is severely intellectually disabled.

Source: Adapted from Brown, L., Long, E., Udvari-Solner, A., Davis, L., VanDeventer, P., Ahlgren, C., Johnson, F., Gruenewald, L., & Jorgensen, J. (1989). The home school: Why students with severe disabilities must attend the schools of their brothers, sisters, friends, and neighbors. *Journal of the Association for Persons with Severe Handicaps, 14,* 5. Used by permission.

Increased social contacts and positive social acceptance with peers without disabilities as a result of inclusion have been reported by a number of other researchers as well (e.g., Evans, Salisbury, Palombaro, Berryman, & Hollowood, 1992; Hunt, Farron-Davis, Beckstead, Curtis, & Goetz, 1994; Romer & Haring, 1994). Hunt and Goetz (1997) review 19 studies on the outcomes of inclusion of students with severe disabilities.

To learn about a method for building social supports for students with disabilities in regular classrooms, see "Planning for Inclusion with MAPS" and "The Metropolitan Nashville Peer Buddy Program" later in this chapter.

A social contact was defined as a student with disabilities interacting with a peer(s) within the context of a meaningful activity (e.g., eating lunch, conducting a science project) for a minimum of 15 minutes. Each of the three students participated in a different regular classroom (average size: 25 students) for one period each school day, five days per week. Several aspects of this study deserve special comment. First, regular class participation increased the number of social contacts for each student even though ongoing opportunities to contact nondisabled peers were provided through "friendship" and peer tutoring programs during those weeks when the students were not in the regular classroom. Second, the increases in social contacts were the result of participation for only one class period per day. It might be presumed that additional participation (e.g., two or three periods per day) would result in even more frequent contacts. Third, the increased social contacts were obtained without an elaborate training program or intensive intervention. Each student simply began participating in the regular classroom after a "circle of friends" introduction by the special education teacher to the regular class peers that stressed the similarities among all students, the need for students to support one another, and the importance of social relationships (O'Brien, Forest, Snow, & Hasbury, 1989).

A wide variety of strategies for promoting desired social relationships has been developed. One strategy is to give the student with disabilities a skill for initiating and maintaining interaction. For example, two nonverbal boys with severe and profound mental retardation and multiple physical disabilities learned to initiate play activities with nondisabled peers by showing badges with photographs of activities (Jolly, Test, & Spooner, 1993). Other strategies focus on teaching classmates without disabilities to initiate social contacts during free-time, cooperative learning, or peer tutoring activities (Eichinger, 1990; Hughes, Killian, & Fischer, 1996; Putnam, 1998; Romer, White, & Haring, 1996). Still other approaches involve changes in the roles and responsibilities of instructional faculty, such as teaching teams (Ferguson, Meyer, Jeanchild, Juniper, & Zingo, 1992; Giangreco, 1991; Thousand & Villa, 1990). A large-scale survey of middle and high school students in three states found that most students without disabilities who have experienced inclusive education believed that they should make friends with classmates with severe disabilities and that it is primarily the responsibility of themselves and their teachers to facilitate those friendships (Hendrickson, Shokoohi-Yekta, Hamre-Nietupski, & Gable, 1996). Many of these strategies for facilitating the regular classroom inclusion of students with severe disabilities are compatible with one another, and it is typical for a program to incorporate multiple, concurrent methods for identifying and providing supports for students, their teachers, and their peers.

Experiences and Transformations of General Education Teachers To find out how regular education teachers reacted to having a student with severe disabilities placed in their classrooms, Giangreco, Dennis, Cloninger, Edelman, and Shattman (1993) interviewed 19 K–9 general education teachers. They found that regardless of how the child with severe disabilities was placed in the general education classroom, most teachers initially described the placement in cautious or negative terms (e.g., "reluctant," "nervous," "unqualified," "angry"). Despite their initial negative reactions, 17 of the teachers experienced "increased ownership and involvement" with the child with severe disabilities as the school year progressed. Giangreco et al. refer to this process of changing attitude and perspective as transformation.

> Transformations were gradual and progressive, rather than discrete and abrupt. . . . A number of teachers who had these experiences reportedly came to the realization they could be successful and that including the student was not as difficult as they had origi-

nally imagined. . . . The following quotes typify the comments of teachers who underwent significant transformation.

"I started seeing him as a little boy. I started feeling that he's a person too. He's a student. Why should I not teach him? He's in my class. That's my responsibility. I'm a teacher!"

"I made the full swing of fighting against having Bobbi Sue placed in my room to fighting for her to be in a mainstream classroom working with kids in the way that she had worked with them all year long. I'm a perfect example of how you have to have an open mind."

"I started watching my own regular classroom students. They didn't treat him any differently. They went about their business like everything was normal. So I said, 'If they can do it, I can do it.' He's not getting in their way. They're treating him like everybody else."

"They were always letting me know when I forgot something. 'You didn't remember to include Sarah.' So they were very good at letting me know."

"The kids help you figure it out." (Giangreco et al., 1993, pp. 359–372)

For detailed information about administrative, curricular, and instructional strategies designed to support the education of students with severe disabilities in regular schools, see Downing (1996); Giangreco (1997); Janney and Snell (1998); Sailor et al. (1989); Stainback and Stainback (1996); and Thousand, Villa, and Nevin (1994).

According to Ferguson et al. (1992), the key to successful regular classroom participation for students with severe disabilities is the work of an inclusion facilitator. An effective inclusion facilitator—who is often but not necessarily the special education teacher—plays three roles: (1) a broker, who locates resources and matches them to the student's needs; (2) an adapter, who develops and suggests changes in lesson plans and activities to better accommodate the student with disabilities; and (3) a collaborator, who works effectively with other adults toward shared goals.

Look for information about multimedia assistive technology that can facilitate the inclusion of students with severe disabilities in a regular education classroom by accessing the Resources Module for Chaper 13 at http://www.prenhall.com/heward and linking to the Special Ed Resource page.

How Much Time in the Regular Classroom? Although the social benefits of regular class participation for students with disabilities—as well as for their peers without disabilities—have been clearly shown, the effects of inclusion on the attainment of IEP goals and objectives is not yet known. The functional IEP goals and objectives for students with severe disabilities are seldom reflected in the academic curriculum of the regular classroom (especially at the secondary level). Available instruction time is especially valuable to students who by definition require direct, intensive, and ongoing instruction to acquire basic skills that students without dis-

In the end, the best inclusion facilitators are the students themselves.

Planning for Inclusion with MAPS

by Marsha Forest and Jack Pearpoint

The movement to integrate children with disabilities into ordinary classrooms is founded on a simple yet profound philosophy: everyone belongs. The McGill Action Planning System (MAPS) is a systems approach to problem solving that has helped many schools welcome and support children with disabilities in regular classrooms.

Who Goes to a MAP? Friends! The size of the group that gathers for a MAP session can vary from two to two dozen. The key ingredients for participants are intimate and personal contact with the individual being mapped. A grandmother or neighbor, a friend—all are on equal footing with professionals, who are welcomed and needed, but as individuals, not as therapists. Parents and family members usually have the most to offer. Their perspectives are welcome in a MAP.

Peer participation is critical. Classmates have enormous untapped energy and creative capacity. Their straight talk often offers teachers new ideas. Adults must be careful not to constrain or downgrade the participation of children: they are critical and equal partners in the MAPS process.

Should the individual who is being mapped be present? This is a judgment call; it works both ways. We lean toward full participation. People understand an enormous amount, more than we think. Also, a MAP is a real boost for an individual who previously has been excluded. Full participation also saves time in trying to explain the process later.

What Happens at a MAP? Mapping is a collaborative problem-solving process aided by a facilitator and a recorder. The facilitator, positioned at the open end of a half-circle formed by the participants, presents eight key questions to the group. The facilitator must be skilled in group process and have a problem-solving orientation. Most important, the facilitator must be committed to building an integrated school community. The information and ideas generated during the session are marked by the recorder on a large piece of chart paper. Public charting is vital to the MAPS process: It generates images that help participants visualize the relationships among people and actions, thus promoting the creation of additional problem-solving strategies. It also serves as a permanent record of the plans and commitments made by the group. The recorder need not be an artist, but it is vital that the MAP be printed or written clearly, using the participants' words. The chart should include contributions from everyone in the group.

MAPS planning typically occurs in one or two sessions, and approximately three hours are required to fully address these questions:

1. *What's a MAP?* The facilitator begins the MAPS process by asking participants, "What is a map?" A recent group gave these answers:
   - Something that gives direction
   - A thing that helps you get somewhere
   - Routes to different places
   - A way to find a new way
2. *What is the individual's history?* The participants most intimate with the child being mapped (e.g., parents and family members) are asked to give a 10- to 15-minute history focusing on key milestones and events in the individual's life.
3. *What is your dream for the individual?* This question is intended to get people, especially parents, to imagine their vision for the child's future. Many parents of children with disabilities have lost their ability to dream about what they really want for their child. This question helps the group focus on the direction in which the individual is now heading and encourages concrete action plans for realizing the vision.
4. *What is your nightmare?* This question is the hardest to ask but is very important to get on the table. We must understand the nightmare to prevent it. No parent has ever said, "I'm worried that my child won't attend a university, won't get an *A* on the next test, or won't learn to spell." Instead, the question brings out what is in the heart of virtually every parent of a child with a severe disability: "We're afraid our child will end up in an institution, work in a sheltered workshop, and have no one to care for her when we die."
5. *Who is the individual?* With this question, the MAPS process shifts into a no-holds-barred brainstorming mode. Participants are asked to give words or phrases

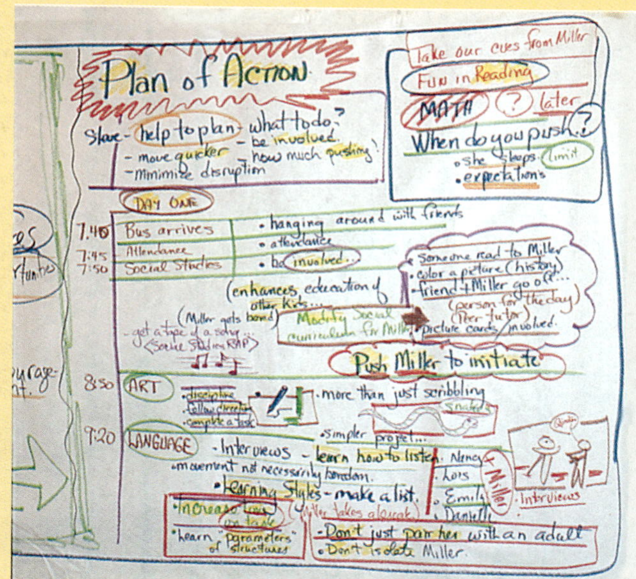

A portion of Miller's MAP.

that describe the person being mapped. The rule is no jargon, no labels; just describe how you see the person. The image of a unique and distinct personality should emerge. Here are examples from a recent MAP for Miller, a 14-year-old who, to some, is "severely handicapped and mentally retarded."

- She has a brother.
- She gets around in a wheelchair.
- She's lots of fun.
- She's active like crazy.
- She's radical/bad (really means good).
- She's temperamental.
- She likes to touch.
- She wants to be involved.
- She looks at you.
- She can talk some.

6. *What are the individual's strengths, abilities, gifts, and talents?* It is vital to build upon strengths and abilities. Yet all too often, we focus on the things a child with a disability cannot do. This can be a difficult question for parents, who have been struggling with negatives for so long. This question also is intended to produce a brainstormed list from the entire group. Here is part of the list generated for Miller:

- She can make us laugh.
- She moves her arms, can throw a ball.
- She likes to listen to music.
- She's persistent, tries real hard.
- She can count and remember numbers.
- She enjoys stories and movies.

7. *What are the individual's needs?* This, too, is a brainstorm. Don't let people stop each other, but don't get bogged down either. Keep it short and record people's words and perceptions. Parents, teachers, and peers often have different perceptions about needs. For Miller, it was decided that what she needed most of all was

- A communication system that lets her express her wants and feelings
- More independence with dressing and other self-care skills
- To be with her own age group
- Places to go and things to do after school
- Teenage clothes

8. *What is the plan of action?* This is the final and most important question of all. The MAPS planning group imagines what the individual's ideal day at school would look like and what must be done to make it a reality. Step by step, the MAPS group goes through an entire day, envisioning the various environments and activities the individual will experience and what kinds of resources, supports, and adaptations can be created to make the day successful. For example, a peer volunteers to meet the taxi that brings Miller to school each morning and to walk with her to the classroom. During language arts period, a classmate will help Miller practice with her communication board. The principle of partial participation will be used on the playground when Miller bats in the softball game and a teammate runs the bases for her.

A MAP Is Not . . .

- A trick, a gimmick, or a quick-fix solution to complex human problems. It is not a one-shot session that blasts a vulnerable person into the everyday life and fabric of school and community. MAPS is a problem-solving process; the plans for action are not set in stone but must be reviewed and changed as often as needed.
- A replacement for an IEP. A MAP session may provide useful information for an IEP, but it is not a substitute for the IEP process and must not be treated as such.

- A tool to make any segregated setting better. MAPS was designed to liberate people from segregated settings; it is for people and organizations who are committed to figuring out together how to get a person fully included in life.
- An academic exercise. It is a genuine, personal approach to problem solving with and on behalf of real individuals who are vulnerable. A MAP produces outcomes that have real implications for how the person will live his life.
- Just talk. MAPS is talk and action. A MAP gives clear directions and action steps for inclusion.

The metaphor for MAPS is a kaleidoscope, a beautiful instrument whose design changes constantly. We see the kaleidoscope as the outcome of each MAP. It is a medley of people working together to make something unique and better happen. It is more than anyone can do alone.

For additional information and training materials on MAPS, write to the Centre for Integrated Education and Community, 24 Thome Crescent, Toronto, Ontario, Canada, M6H 2S5. Forest and Lusthaus (1990) and Vandercook, York, and Forest (1989) also describe the MAPS approach.

Billingsley and Kelley (1994) reported that 39 of 51 instructional methods considered to be best practice for educating students with severe disabilities are considered acceptable and appropriate for use in general education classrooms.

abilities learn without instruction. A major challenge for both special and general educators is to develop models and strategies for including students with severe disabilities in regular classroom activities without sacrificing their opportunities to acquire, practice, and generalize the functional skills they need most.

The question of how much time students with severe disabilities should spend in the regular classroom is an important one. Although a few full inclusion advocates might argue that every student with disabilities should have a full-time regular class placement regardless of the nature of her educational needs, most special educators probably would agree with Brown et al. (1991), whose position is that students with severe intellectual disabilities should be based in the same schools and classrooms they would attend if they were not disabled but that they should also spend some time elsewhere.

> There are substantial differences between being based in and confined to regular education classrooms. "Based in" refers to being a member of a real class, where and with whom you start the school day, you may not spend all your time with your class, but it is still your group and everyone knows it. . . . It is our position that it is unacceptable for students with severe disabilities to spend either 0% or 100% of their time in regular education classrooms. . . . How much time should be spent in regular classes? Enough to ensure that the student is a member, not a visitor. A lot, if the student is engaged in meaningful activities. Quite a bit if she is young, but less as she approaches 21. There is still a lot we do not know. (pp. 40, 46)

The Challenge and Rewards of Teaching Students with Severe Disabilities

Virtually every parent of a child with severe disabilities has heard a host of negative predictions from educators, doctors, and concerned friends and family. Parents often are offered such discouraging forecasts as "Your child will never talk" or "Your child will never be toilet-trained." Yet in many instances those children make gains that far exceed the professionals' original predictions. Despite predictions to the contrary, many children have learned to walk, talk, toilet themselves, and perform other "impossible" tasks.

Teachers—both special and general educators—who are providing instruction to students with severe disabilities can rightfully be called pioneers on an exciting new frontier of education. Professionals who are involved in educating students with severe disabilities "can look back with pride, and even awe, at the advances they have made. In a relatively brief period, educators, psychologists, and other professionals have advocated vigorously for additional legislation and funds, extended the service delivery model into the public schools and community, and developed a training technology" (Orelove, 1984, p. 271).

Future research will increase our understanding of how students with severe disabilities acquire, maintain, and generalize functional skills. Better techniques of measuring and changing behavior are constantly being developed; these are balanced with a growing concern for the personal rights and dignity of individuals with severe disabilities.

Teaching students with severe disabilities is difficult and demanding. The teacher must be well organized, firm, and consistent. He must be able to manage a complex educational operation, which usually involves supervising paraprofessional aides, student teachers, peer tutors, and volunteers. The teacher must be knowledgeable about one-to-one and small-group instruction formats and be able to work cooperatively with other professionals, such as physicians, psychologists, physical therapists, social workers, and language specialists. He must maintain accurate records and be constantly planning for the future needs of the students. Effective communication with parents and families, school administrators, vocational rehabilitation personnel, and community agencies is also vital.

Students with the most severe disabilities sometimes give little or no apparent response, so their teachers must be sensitive to small changes in behavior. The effective teacher is consistent in designing and implementing strategies to improve learning and behavior (even if some of the students' previous teachers were not). The effective teacher should not be too quick to remove difficult tasks or requests that result in noncompliance or misbehavior. It is better to teach students to request assistance (Durand, 1986) and to intersperse tasks that are easy for the student to perform (Munk & Repp, 1994; Sprague & Horner, 1990).

There is a difference between either expecting miracles or being passively patient and simply working each day at the job of designing, implementing, and evaluating systematic instruction and supports. As Lovaas (1981) writes, it can be a mistake to expect a miracle:

> We were expecting a sudden step forward, that possibly somehow we would hit upon some central cognitive, emotional, or social event inside the child's mind that would help him make a sudden and major leap ahead. . . . Such a leap would have been so gratifying, and it would have made our work so much easier. It never happened. Instead, progress followed slow, step-by-step upward progression, with only a few and minor spurts ahead. We learned to settle down for hard work. (p. x)

Use the self-tests at http://www.prenhall.com/heward to assess your knowledge of the content of Chapter 13.

Some might consider it undesirable to work with students with severe disabilities because of their serious and multiple disabilities. Yet working with students who require instruction at its very best can offer many highly rewarding teaching experiences. Much satisfaction can be felt in teaching a child to feed and dress herself independently, helping a student make friends with nondisabled peers, and supporting a young adult's efforts to live, travel, and work as independently as possible in the community. Both the challenge and the potential rewards of teaching students with severe disabilities are great.

The Metropolitan Nashville Peer Buddy Program

by Carolyn Hughes, Carol Guth, Judy Presley, Marilee Dye, and Corie Byers

Most individuals with mental retardation are less socially adept than their peers without disabilities. Consequently, many engage in fewer social interactions (and thus have fewer opportunities to learn and develop social skills), are less accepted by their peers, lack friendships and social relationships, have a limited network of social support at school or work, and experience feelings of loneliness. Fortunately, general education peers can be effective teachers of social skills and have been associated with increased acceptance and participation in everyday life, such as initiating, responding, and attending to conversational interactions (e.g., Hughes, Killian, & Fischer, 1996).

At the secondary level, classroom teachers may find it difficult to get special and general education students together. The typical high school day presents a challenge for extended social interaction between general and special education students. Most high school schedules are broken into 50- to 60-minute class periods—often with no free periods—which makes it difficult to include students with severe disabilities in the mainstream of school life. In addition, many special education students are involved in community-based training, which require longer blocks of time. Scheduling constraints may be one reason why most inclusion projects and research often take place at the preschool and elementary levels.

The Metropolitan Nashville Peer Buddy Program attempts to remove scheduling barriers to inclusion by providing daily class times in which general education and special education students may interact. The program is being implemented in all 11 comprehensive high schools in Nashville, serving 300 students with severe disabilities. An elective, one-credit course allows peer buddies to spend at least one period each day with their special education partners. Peer buddies serve as positive role models for social interaction and provide the support their partners need to be included within general education and vocational classes and the extracurricular activities that make up a typical high school day. Peer buddies report an increase in disability awareness, communication skills, understanding of themselves and others, and appreciation of individual differences. Many of the interactions have developed into friendships with shared experiences in the students' homes and the community.

Seven Steps to Starting a Peer Buddy Program

Step 1: Develop a One-Credit Course

- Incorporate a peer tutoring course into your school's curriculum that allows peer buddies to spend at least one period each day with their special education partners.
- Follow the school district's established procedures when you apply for the new course offering.
- Include the course description in your school's official class schedule.

Step 2: Recruit Peer Buddies

- Present information about the new program at a faculty meeting.
- Actively recruit peer buddies during the first year. After that, peer buddies will recruit for you.
- Include announcements, posters, and articles in the school newspaper and PTO newsletter and videos on the school's closed-circuit television. Have peer buddies speak in school clubs and classes.
- Have guidance counselors refer students who have interest, good attendance, and adequate grades.

Step 3: Screen and Match Students

- Allow students to observe in the special education classroom to learn about the role of a peer buddy and decide if they would be an appropriate match for the class.
- Have students interview with the special education teachers and meet potential partners.
- Have students provide information on past experiences with students with disabilities and clubs or activities they are involved in that their special education partners could join.

Step 4: Teach Instructional Strategies to Peer Buddies

- Conduct a peer buddy orientation that includes people-first language, disability awareness, communication strategies, and suggested activities.
- Communicate teachers' expectations for the peer buddy course, including attendance and grading policies.
- Model prompting and reinforcement techniques.
- Provide suggestions for dealing with inappropriate behavior, setting limits, and modifying general education curricula.

Step 5: Provide Feedback and Evaluate the Program

- Schedule observations and feedback sessions with peer buddies to address their questions or concerns.

- Give peer buddies feedback on their interaction skills, time management, use of positive reinforcement, and activities engaged in with their partners.
- Have peer buddies keep a daily journal of their activities and reflections, which should be reviewed weekly by the classroom teacher.
- Establish a peer buddy club that allows students to share experiences and ideas.

Step 6: Hold a Lunch Bunch

- Invite peer buddies to join special education students in the cafeteria for lunch.
- Encourage buddies to invite their general education friends to join the group, increasing social contacts for special education partners.

Step 7: Establish an Advisory Board

- Develop an advisory board that includes students (buddies and partners), their parents, participating general and special education teachers, administrators, and guidance counselors.
- Include community representatives to expand the peer buddy program to community-based activities, such as work experiences.

A Teacher's Perspective Marilee Dye, special education teacher at McGavock High School:

> My classroom is made up of the entire spectrum of students with severe disabilities: students with multiple disabilities, mental retardation, communication deficits, sensory impairments, and autism. Peer tutors from the peer buddy program have been effective with all of these students. You may wonder exactly what a peer buddy does. In my classroom, they perform a wide variety of activities. But the main thing they do is develop a friendship with the student to whom they are assigned.
>
> Social interaction skills are a deficit for all of my students, and they are the single most difficult set of skills for an adult to teach a teenager. Peer buddies are much more successful at teaching social skills. Often, they are not trying to work on social skills, but through the course of a regular conversation or interaction, it just seems to occur. My first peer buddy, Amy, worked with Melissa on reading skills every day. Also during the school year, personal hygiene issues were often discussed between the two. I had absolutely nothing to do with these conversations. In a period of two months, we were seeing positive changes in Melissa's cleanliness and appearance. I had been working with Melissa for one year on these same issues, as had teachers for the past several years. We had had no impact on her behavior either singly or collectively. It was amazing to me what a peer was able to accomplish in such a short time and with very little effort. By the way, this interaction has had a long-term effect on Melissa. After two years, she is still with us and has maintained the skills she learned from Amy with no prompting, such as keeping her hair washed and combed, brushing her teeth, and wearing clothes that match.
>
> This year I have a student with autism in my class. When Kim first came into my room, she appeared to have no interest in others and only initiated interactions when she wanted to eat or go to the rest room. Then Kim developed a friendship with her peer buddy, Corie. Now she watches the door for Corie everyday. When they are together, Kim makes eye contact with her buddy frequently, laughs often, and even initiates conversations. We never saw her do these behaviors before. Kim also has increased her verbal repertoire from 4 to 11 words. I have been truly amazed at the difference peer buddies have made in the lives of my students.

A Student's Perspective Corie Byers, senior at McGavock High School:

> I heard about the peer buddy program from my guidance counselor and because I really didn't have another class for one of my class periods, I decided to take it. I was kind of interested in it anyway, because I had been a peer tutor in seventh and eighth grade and I wondered how I could get into it again.
>
> I learned a lot about different people and different aspects of handicaps. I really liked just sitting in the classroom and hanging out with everybody. That was my favorite part. My second semester as a peer buddy I spent mostly with Kim in Ms. Dye's room. And that girl—whew! She was a handful. When I first got into the classroom, Kim would just sit there and either sleep all day or cry about something. Or kind of just wander around with her eyes and look and not do anything. After my first semester, I noticed how she wouldn't deal with anybody. She was just always by herself. So I would go over there and tickle her and, all of a sudden, she just livened up! It was like someone had to just talk to her one time and she burst out with life. When I first started talking to her, she really didn't have many words that she could say. Mostly she just said, "Milk," if she wanted milk, or if she had to go to the bathroom, she would tell us. That was about it. Then I got to talking to her, and toward the end of the year, she developed more language and everything.
>
> We played games like hand-slap games and tickled each other. The bean bag chair was the best because she just loved that thing. Kim would just lay on it and wallow all over the floor and just laugh. It was so cool!
>
> Well, that's Kim! She's cool now.

Carolyn Hughes is a faculty member, and Carol Guth and Judy Presley are graduate students, in the Department of Special Education at Peabody College of Vanderbilt University. Marilee Dye is a special education teacher and Corie Byers is a senior at McGavock High School in Nashville.

Summary

Defining Severe Disabilities

- Students with severe disabilities need instruction in many basic skills that most children without disabilities acquire without instruction in the first five years of life.
- Students with profound disabilities have pervasive delays in all domains of functioning at a developmental level no higher than two years.
- TASH defines persons with severe disabilities as "individuals of all ages who require extensive ongoing support in more than one major life activity in order to participate in integrated community settings and to enjoy a quality of life that is available to citizens with fewer or no disabilities."

Characteristics of Students with Severe Disabilities

- Students with severe disabilities frequently have multiple disabilities, including physical problems, and usually look and act markedly different from children without disabilities.
- Children with severe disabilities may show some or all of the following behaviors or skill deficits: slow acquisition rates for learning new skills, difficulty in generalizing and maintaining newly learned skills, severe deficits in communication skills, impaired physical and motor development, deficits in self-help skills, infrequent constructive behavior and interaction, and frequent inappropriate behavior.
- Despite their intense challenges, students with severe disabilities often exhibit many positive characteristics, such as warmth, humor, sociability, and persistence.
- Students with dual sensory impairments cannot be accommodated in special education programs designed solely for students with hearing or visual impairments. Although the vast majority of children labeled deaf-blind have some functional hearing and/or vision, the dual impairments severely impede learning of communication and social skills.
- The essential features of autism typically appear prior to 30 months of age and consist of disturbances of (1) developmental rates and/or sequences; (2) responses to sensory stimuli; (3) speech, language, and cognitive capacities; and (4) capacities to relate to people, events, and objects.
- Although the prognosis for children with autism has traditionally been poor, some children have achieved normal functioning by the primary grades as a result of an intensive, behaviorally oriented program of early intervention and preschool mainstreaming.
- Despite their limitations, children with severe disabilities can and do learn.

Prevalence

- Students with severe and multiple disabilities are served and counted under several disability categories, making prevalence figures hard to determine.
- Estimates of the prevalence of severe disabilities range from 0.1% to 1% of the population.

Causes of Severe Disabilities

- Brain disorders, which are involved in most cases of severe intellectual disabilities, are the result of either brain dysgenesis (abnormal brain development) or brain damage (caused by influences that alter the structure or function of a brain that had been developing normally up to that point).
- Severe and profound disabilities most often have biological causes, including chromosomal abnormalities, genetic and metabolic disorders, complications of pregnancy and prenatal care, birth trauma, and later brain damage.
- In about one-sixth of all cases of severe disabilities, the cause cannot be clearly determined.

Educational Approaches

- A curriculum based on typical developmental milestones is inappropriate for most students with severe disabilities.
- Students with severe disabilities must be taught skills that are functional, age-appropriate, and directed toward the community. Interaction with nondisabled students should occur regularly.
- Students with severe disabilities should be taught choice-making skills.
- The emphasis of research and training in communication for persons with severe disabilities has shifted from the remediation of specific forms of communication to a focus on functional communication in any mode that enables communication partners to establish shared meanings.
- Some students with severe disabilities use augmentative and alternative systems of communication (AAC), such as gestures, various sign language systems, pictorial communication boards, symbol systems, and electronic communication aids.
- Facilitated communication (FC) is a process by which a communication partner, called a facilitator, provides physical support to assist an individual who cannot speak or whose speech is limited to typing on a keyboard or to pointing at pictures, words, or other symbols on a communication board.
- Although proponents claim that FC enables some people with autism and moderate or severe mental retardation to display an "undisclosed literacy" consistent with "normal intellectual functioning," scientific research to date has not confirmed those claims.
- Students with severe disabilities should also be taught age-appropriate recreation and leisure skills.
- Because each student with severe disabilities has many learning needs, teachers must carefully prioritize and

choose IEP objectives and learning activities that will be of most benefit to the student and his family.

- Effective instruction of students with severe disabilities is characterized by these elements:
  - The student's current level of performance is precisely assessed.
  - The skill to be taught is defined clearly.
  - The skills are ordered in an appropriate sequence.
  - The teacher provides clear prompts or cues to the student.
  - The student receives immediate feedback and reinforcement from the teacher.
  - Strategies that promote generalization of learning are used.
  - The student's performance is carefully measured and evaluated.
- Partial participation is both a philosophy for selecting activities and a method for adapting activities and supports to enable students with severe disabilities to actively participate in meaningful tasks they are not able to perform independently.
- The teacher of students with severe disabilities must be skilled in positive, instructionally relevant strategies for assessing and dealing with challenging and problem behaviors.
- Research and practice are providing increasing support for the use of integrated small-group instruction arrangements with students with severe disabilities.
- Students with severe disabilities are more likely to develop and maintain social relationships with students without disabilities if they attend their home school and are included at least part of the time in the regular classroom.
- Although the initial reactions and feelings of many general education teachers who have a student with severe disabilities placed in their classrooms are negative, those apprehensions and concerns often transform into positive experiences as the student becomes a regular member of their classroom.
- Working with students who require instruction at its very best can be highly rewarding to teachers.

For More Information

Journals

- *Focus on Autistic Behavior*. Published bimonthly by PRO-ED, 8700 Shoal Creek Boulevard, Austin, TX 78757. A journal for practitioners who work with individuals with autism and pervasive developmental disabilities. Articles deal with assessment, behavior management, curriculum, instruction, related services, and vocational training.
- *Journal of Autism and Developmental Disorders*. A quarterly journal that publishes multidisciplinary research on all severe psychopathologies in childhood.
- *Journal of the Association for Persons with Severe Disabilities (JASH)*. Published quarterly by the Association for Persons with Severe Disabilities (see "Organizations"). Publishes articles reporting original research, reviews of the literature, and conceptual or position papers that offer new directions for service delivery and program development and effective assessment and intervention methodologies.
- *Journal of Positive Behavior Interventions*. Published by PRO-ED, 8700 Shoal Creek Boulevard, Austin, TX 78757. A new quarterly journal that publishes experimental research, case studies, qualitative research, program descriptions, and literature reviews that contribute to expansion of knowledge and practice of effective behavioral support in school, home, and community.
- *Research in Developmental Disabilities*. Published quarterly by Pergamon Press, Elmsford, NY 10523. Includes articles on theory and behavioral research related to people who suffer from severe and pervasive developmental disabilities.

Books

- Browder, D. M. (1991). *Assessment of individuals with severe disabilities: An applied behavioral approach to life skills assessment* (2nd ed.). Baltimore: Brookes.
- Brown, F., & Lehr, D. H. (1989). *Persons with profound disabilities: Issues and practices*. Baltimore: Brookes.
- Cipani, E. C., & Spooner, F. (Eds.). (1994). *Curricular and instructional approaches for persons with severe disabilities*. Boston: Allyn & Bacon.
- Goetz, L., Guess, D., & Stremel-Campbell, K. (Eds.). (1987). *Innovative program design for individuals with dual sensory impairments.* Baltimore: Brookes.
- Harris, S. L., & Handleman, J. S. (Eds.). (1994). *Preschool programs for children with autism*. Austin, TX: PRO-ED.
- Horner, R. H., Meyer, L. H., & Fredericks, H. D. B. (Eds.). (1986). *Education of learners with severe disabilities: Exemplary service strategies.* Baltimore: Brookes.
- Koegel, R. L., & Koegel, L. (1995). *Teaching children with autism*. Baltimore: Brookes.
- Lovaas, O. I. (1981). *Teaching developmentally disabled children: The ME book*. Austin, TX: PRO-ED.
- Matson, J. L. (Ed.). (1994). *Autism in children and adults: Etiology, assessment, and intervention.* Pacific Grove, CA: Brooks/Cole.
- Maurice, C., Green, G., & Luce, S. G. (Eds.). (1996). *Behavioral intervention for young children with autism: A manual for parents and professionals*. Austin, TX: PRO-ED.

- Meyer, L., Peck, C., & Brown, L. (Eds.). (1990). *Critical issues in the lives of people with severe disabilities*. Baltimore: Brookes.
- Orelove, F. P., & Sobsey, D. (1996). *Educating children with multiple disabilities: A transdisciplinary approach* (3rd ed.). Baltimore: Brookes.
- Rainforth, B., & York-Barr, J. (1997). *Collaborative teams for students with severe disabilities* (2nd ed.). Baltimore: Brookes.
- Snell, M. E., & Brown, F. (Eds.). (2000). *Instruction of students with severe disabilities* (5th ed.). Upper Saddle River, NJ: Merrill/Prentice Hall.
- Sternberg, L. (Ed.). (1994). *Individuals with profound disabilities: Instructional and assistive strategies* (3rd ed.). Austin, TX: PRO-ED.
- Westling, D. L., & Fox, L. (1995). *Teaching persons with severe disabilities*. Upper Saddle River, NJ: Merrill/Prentice Hall.
- Wolery, M., Ault, M. J., & Doyle, P. M. (1992). *Teaching students with moderate to severe disabilities*. New York: Longman.

Organizations

- *ABLENET,* 360 Hoover Street N.E., Minneapolis, MN 55413. Offers information and publications on the use of automated learning devices, microswitches, and other technology with persons who have severe disabilities. Sells a book by Jackie Levin and Lynn Scherfenberg called *Breaking Barriers: How Children and Adults with Severe Disabilities Can Access the World Through Simple Technology*.
- *Autism Society of America*, 8601 Georgia Avenue, Suite 503, Silver Spring, MD 20910. An organization of family members and professionals dedicated to the education and welfare of children and adults with severe disorders of communication and behavior.
- *Department of Specialized Educational Services*, Madison Metropolitan School District, 545 West Dayton Street, Madison, WI 53703. Works in cooperation with the Department of Studies in Behavioral Disabilities at the University of Wisconsin. Especially active in developing programs of instruction for children with severe disabilities and seeking to facilitate integration with nondisabled individuals. Sells a number of curriculum guides and other materials.
- *Helen Keller National Center for Deaf-Blind Youths and Adults*, 111 Middle Neck Road, Sands Point, NY 11050. Offers training programs for persons with impaired vision and hearing and consultation to agencies providing services for this population. Publishes *Directory of Agencies and Organizations Serving Deaf-Blind Individuals,* curriculum manuals, and other informational materials about deaf-blindness.
- *The Association for Persons with Severe Disabilities (TASH),* 29 West Susquehanna Avenue, Suite 210, Baltimore, MD 21204-5201; (410) 828-TASH; TDD: (410) 828-1306; e-mail: info@tash.org; website: www.tash.org. "An organization of professionals in partnership with people with disabilities, their families and others who are dedicated to education, research and advocacy on behalf of individuals of any age who have severe intellectual disabilities and their families, so that these persons may live, learn, work and enjoy life and relationships with dignity, respect and individualized support" (TASH, 1990, p. 1). Through its journal and monthly newsletter, disseminates a wide variety of useful information to teachers, parents, administrators, researchers, and others. Annual convention is a major professional forum for the exchange of new developments relating to the education of persons with severe disabilities. Also sponsors state and local conferences and activities.

Chapter 14

Giftedness and Talent Development

by Richard D. Howell and William L. Heward

Focus Questions

- Why do students who are very bright need special education?
- How has the evolving definition of giftedness changed the ways in which students are identified and served?
- What provisions should be made to accurately identify students with outstanding talents who are from diverse cultural groups or have disabilities?
- How can the regular classroom teacher provide instruction at the pace and depth needed by gifted and talented students while at the same time meeting the needs of other students in the classroom?
- Should gifted students be educated with their same-age peers or with older students who share the same intellectual and academic talents and interests?

Our study of exceptional children thus far has focused on students with intellectual, behavioral, or physical disabilities—children who require specially tailored programs to benefit from education. Gifted and talented students lie on the other end of the continuum of academic, artistic, social, and scientific abilities. Gifted and talented children may also find that a traditional curriculum is inappropriate; it may not provide the advanced and unique challenges they require to learn most effectively. They, too, need special education to reach their potential.

Janie has just completed her report on the solar system and is word-processing it for class tomorrow. She looks out her bedroom window and wonders what might be happening on the countless planets that circle all of those stars. And she thinks about the circumstances that made life possible on the third planet from the star called Sol. What Janie is doing may not seem special; after all, most students type school reports and wonder about extraterrestrial life—until we learn that she is just 6 years old. Janie is functioning years ahead of her peers. She writes in complete sentences, expresses herself exceptionally well, and has a powerful urge to know the answers to many and varied problems.

Toney Jojola saunters down a dusty back road near his home in the Southwest. Toney is excited because today his mentor and great-aunt has promised to teach him the process of applying the rich charcoal slip to the pottery he is making. His people have been making pottery for hundreds of years, but somehow it seems to take on multiple meanings in his hands. He notices and uses small variations in color and texture to embed symbolism into his pieces. Perhaps this one will have the winged serpent that he favors so much, reminding everyone that an immense trade network existed in prehistoric America that reached from present-day Canada to South America. Toney sees much in his pottery, in his ancestors who have inspired him, in the beauty that is the earth made functional, and in a desire for continuity in his life. Toney does not say much in school or express himself very well in writing, but he understands everything that is being said and talked about. He is very patient and seems tentative in his behavior, not wanting to create a disturbance that would draw attention to himself. During class he dreams of the pottery designs he will someday create in the studio that he will inherit from his great-aunt.

Malcolm, a ninth grader, runs from school to the bus stop for the bus that will take him to the local university, where he is taking his second course in creative writing. He is excited about showing his latest short story to the professor. Malcolm's prose brings into focus all of the pain he sees around him, critically analyzing the leadership of his community and nation. He believes he has a message that must be heard; he is powerfully moved to reach out to the disaffected, the disenfranchised, as well as the ambivalent of all races. He has many ideas for changing what he believes is wrong with his government. He believes deeply in his vision and knows he can make a difference once he learns how to communicate his message as effectively as possible. Bursting with energy and desire, Malcolm struggles to sit still while the bus moves him ever closer to his training ground for the future.

Janie, Toney, and Malcolm need special education—in the form of curriculum modifications and specialized instructional activities—to enhance and develop their individual talents. These precocious youngsters, and others like them, will become the outstanding scientists, artists, writers, inventors, and leaders of the future. Understanding and working to develop the talents of these exceptional children is an important undertaking of special educators who work in the area of gifted and talented education.

Go to the companion website at http://www.prenhall.com/heward and select Chapter 14 to review the chapter objectives.

Defining Giftedness and Talent

Intelligence, creativity, and talent have been central to the various definitions of giftedness that have been proposed over the years. Lewis Terman (1925), one of the pioneers of the field, defined the gifted as those who score in the top 2% on standardized tests of intelligence. Guilford (1959) believed creativity was exemplified in the unique solutions and innovations of most gifted scientists and inventors. Witty (1951), recognizing the value of including special skills and talents, described gifted and talented children as those "whose performance is consistently remarkable in any potentially valuable area" (p. 62). These three concepts continue to be reflected in the current and still-evolving definitions of gifted and talented children.

Psychomotor ability—*high performance in gross and fine motor development (e.g., diving, gymnastics)—was included as a sixth area of giftedness in an earlier federal definition (P.L. 91–230). However, Congress believed that schools' existing athletic programs serve such students adequately.*

Federal Definition

According to the Gifted and Talented Children's Act of 1978, gifted and talented children are those

> possessing demonstrated or potential abilities that give evidence of high performance capability in such areas as intellectual, creative, specific academic or leadership ability, or in the performing or visual arts, and who by reason thereof require services or activities not ordinarily provided by the school. (P.L. 95–561, Title IX, Sec. 902)

The areas in which a child can show outstanding performance or unusual potential cover almost the full range of human endeavor. Intellectual ability and specific academic aptitude are only two areas. *General intellectual ability* refers to overall performance on intelligence or achievement tests. Children who meet this criterion usually do or can perform well in most academic areas. Children with *specific academic aptitude* have outstanding ability in one or two areas. For example, Malcolm, who has specific academic aptitude, performs extremely well in English, literature, and history; his work in mathematics and science, however, is no better than that of most of his same-age peers.

The federal definition has fairly widespread acceptance, and most states currently use it as a basis for their efforts to identify and serve gifted and talented students (Passow & Rudnitski, 1994). However, most states limit their definition of giftedness to the three areas of general intellectual ability, creativity, and leadership (Sisk, 1987).

An Emerging Paradigm: From Intelligence to Talent

Feldhusen (1992a) describes an emerging paradigm of giftedness (see Table 14.1), which emphasizes *talent* as the primary defining characteristic of giftedness and focuses on the identification of special talents and aptitudes. This new conception of giftedness represents the growing recognition of the importance of balancing theoretical with practical definitions of giftedness that emphasize situated problem solving (Sternberg, 1988); talents that are context- and domain-related; and the importance of sustained, deliberate practice on the realization of the person's talent (Ericsson & Charness, 1994). The following definitions of gifted and talented students offered by Joseph Renzulli, Jane Piirto, and June Maker are three excellent examples of this contemporary view.

A paradigm *is an overall model or view of a concept or phenomenon.*

Renzulli's Three-Trait Definition

Renzulli's (1978) definition of giftedness is based on an interaction among three basic clusters of human traits: (1) above-average general intellectual abilities, (2) a high level of task commitment, and (3) creativity. Gifted and talented children are those

> possessing or capable of developing this composite set of traits and applying them to any potentially valuable area of human performance. Children who manifest or are capable of developing an interaction among the three clusters require a wide variety of educational

Table 14.1 The emerging paradigm of giftedness

Old	New
Giftedness Is High IQ	Many Types of Giftedness
Trait-Based	Qualities-Based
Subgroup Elitism	Individual Excellence
Innate, "In There"	Based on Context
Test-Driven	Achievement-Driven, "What You Do" Is Gifted
Authoritarian, "You Are or Are Not Gifted"	Collaborative, Determined by Consultation
School-Oriented	Field- and Domain-Oriented
Ethnocentric	Diverse

Source: From Feldman, D. H. (1992). Has there been a paradigm shift in gifted education? In N. Colangelo, S. G. Assouline, & D. L. Ambroson (Eds.), *Talented development: Proceedings from the 1991 Henry and Jocelyn Wallace National Research Symposium on Talent Development* (p. 14). Unionville, NY: Trillium. Reprinted by permission.

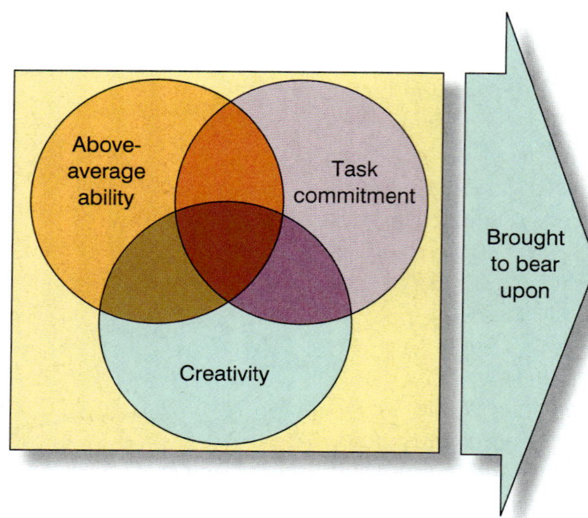

General Performance Areas

Mathematics • Visual Arts • Physical Sciences • Philosophy • Social Sciences • Law • Religion • Language Arts • Music • Life Sciences • Movement Arts

Specific Performance Areas

Cartooning • Astronomy • Public Opinion Polling • Jewelry Design • Map Making • Choreography • Biography • Film Making • Statistics • Local History • Electronics • Musical Composition • Landscape Architecture • Chemistry • Demography • Microphotography • City Planning • Pollution Control • Poetry • Fashion Design • Weaving • Play Writing • Advertising • Costume Design • Meteorology • Puppetry • Marketing • Game Design • Journalism • Electronic Music • Child Care • Consumer Protection • Cooking • Ornithology • Furniture Design • Navigation • Genealogy • Sculpture • Wildlife Management • Set Design • Agricultural Research • Animal Learning • Film Criticism • etc.

Figure 14.1 Renzulli's three-component definition of giftedness
Source: Reprinted from Renzulli, J. S. (1978). What makes giftedness? Reexamining a definition. *Phi Delta Kappan, 60,* 184. Used by permission.

> opportunities and services that are not ordinarily provided through regular instructional programs. (p. 184)

Figure 14.1 illustrates how the three components of ability (actual or potential), task commitment, and creative expression are jointly applied to a valuable area of human endeavor. Like the federal definition, Renzulli's definition provides a great deal of freedom in determining who is considered gifted and talented, depending on the interpretation of "valuable human performance." In a general sense, Renzulli's model merges some acknowledged components of superior performance, including fundamentally high levels of intellectual capability, the ability to innovate and synthesize information, and the motivation necessary to spend a great deal of time working with media and materials.

Piirto's Concept of Talent Development

Piirto (1999) defines the gifted as

> those individuals who, by way of having certain learning characteristics such as superior memory, observational powers, curiosity, creativity, and the ability to learn school-related subject matters rapidly and accurately with a minimum of drill and repetition, have a right to an education that is differentiated according to those characteristics. (p. 28)

Piirto believes such children become apparent early and should be served throughout their educational lives, from preschool through college. While they may or may not become producers of knowledge or makers of novelty, Piirto contends that their education should give them the background to become adults who do produce knowledge or make new artistic and social products.

Maker's Problem-Solving Perspective

Maker's dynamic perspective incorporates the three elements that appear most often within contemporary definitions of the gifted and talented: high intelligence, high creativity, and excellent problem-solving skills. She characterizes a gifted person as

> a problem solver—one who enjoys the challenge of complexity and persists until the problem is solved in a satisfying way. Such an individual is capable of: a) creating a new or more clear definition of an existing problem, b) devising new and more efficient or effective methods, and c) reaching solutions that may be different from the usual, but are recognized as being effective, perhaps more effective, than previous solutions. (Maker, 1993, p. 71)

A New Definition of Outstanding Talent

In *National Excellence: A Case for Developing America's Talent,* the U.S. Department of Education (1993) proposed a new definition of students with exceptional talent, based on new research on cognition and assessment "reflecting today's knowledge and thinking" (p. 3).

> Children and youth with outstanding talent perform or show the potential for performing at remarkably high levels of accomplishment when compared with others of their age, experience, or environment. These children and youth exhibit high performance capability in intellectual, creative, and/or artistic areas, possess an unusual leadership capacity, or excel in specific academic fields. They require services or activities not ordinarily provided by the schools. Outstanding talents are present in children and youth from all cultural groups, across all economic strata, and in all areas of human endeavor.
>
> To put this definition into practice, schools must develop a system to identify gifted and talented students that:

Maker characterizes the gifted person as a creative problem solver who enjoys the challenge of complexity.

1. *Seeks variety*—looks throughout a range of disciplines for students with diverse talents;
2. *Uses many assessment measures*—uses a variety of appraisals so that schools can find students in different talent areas and at different ages;
3. *Is free of bias*—provides students of all backgrounds with equal access to appropriate opportunities;
4. *Is fluid*—uses assessment procedures that can accommodate students who develop at different rates and whose interests may change as they mature;
5. *Identifies potential*—discovers talents that are not readily apparent in students, as well as those that are obvious; and
6. *Assesses motivation*—takes into account the drive and passion that play a key role in accomplishment. (p. 26)

The definition purposely does not use the term *gifted* and implies that environmental factors are at least as critical to the presence of outstanding talent as is genetic predisposition. It asserts that these talents are found across all cultural and socioeconomic groups and other areas of human endeavor. By embracing the terms *outstanding talent* and *exceptional talent,* the framers of this definition avoid the negative commentary and implications of labeling a child as gifted and bring it into line with school programs that are changing their names and focus from the IQ-derived label of "gifted" to talent development (Piirto, personal communication, 1994). This definition presents a new conception of gifted children that radically departs from previous definitions by broadening the understanding of talents, reducing the focus on IQ, and focusing on certain environmental and personality areas as well as on specific talents.

Characteristics of Students Who Are Gifted and Talented

Check your ongoing understanding of Chapter 14 concepts by using the Guided Review Module at http://www.prenhall.com/heward.

The ability to manipulate symbol systems is a key indicator of intellectual giftedness. Although the most common symbol system is language, there are numerous other symbol systems, such as scientific notation, music and dance notation, mathematics, and engineering symbols. These systems can be incorporated into creative endeavors as well as academic and intellectual areas.

Giftedness is a complex human condition covering a wide range of abilities and traits. Some students have special talents, but rarely do these match the stereotypes that many people have of giftedness. These students may not be outstanding in academics, but they may have special abilities in areas such as music, dance, art, or leadership. Gifted and highly talented individuals are found across gender, cultural, linguistic, and even disability groups. Some children may have intellectual abilities found only in 1 child in 1,000 or 1 child in 10,000. Learning and intellectual characteristics in those persons who are considered to be gifted and talented include the following (Clark, 1997; Gallagher & Gallagher, 1994; Maker, 1993; Piirto, 1999):

- The ability to rapidly acquire, retain, and use large amounts of information
- The ability to relate one idea to another
- The ability to make sound judgments
- The ability to perceive the operation of larger systems of knowledge that may not be recognized by the typical person
- The ability to acquire and manipulate abstract symbol systems
- The ability to solve problems by reframing the question and creating novel solutions

Silverman (1995) identifies the following characteristics for the *highly gifted*—children with IQ scores three standard deviations or greater above the mean (IQ > 145):

- Intense intellectual curiosity
- Fascination with words and ideas
- Perfectionism
- Need for precision
- Learning in great intuitive leaps
- Intense need for mental stimulation

- Difficulty conforming to the thinking of others
- Early moral and existential concern
- Tendency toward introversion (pp. 220–221)

We must remember that the characteristics mentioned here are generalizations about the population of gifted and talented students, not the description of any single individual. We may meet a gifted child who does not neatly match these characteristics. It may be the child's giftedness that makes her unique, and the uniqueness may defy any attempt to categorize it into a neat, well-ordered compartment. We must also realize that many lists of gifted characteristics portray gifted children as having only virtues and no flaws. The very attributes by which we identify gifted children, however, can cause problems. High verbal ability, for example, may prompt gifted students to talk themselves out of troublesome situations or allow them to dominate class discussions. High curiosity may give them the appearance of being aggressive or snoopy as they pursue anything that comes to their attention. Table 14.2 identifies both positive and not-so-positive aspects of intellectual giftedness.

See "Making the Earth a Better Place."

For information on the affective dimensions of giftedness, see Swassing (1994).

Table 14.2 Positive characteristics and behaviors of gifted and talented students and possible problems that may arise as a result

Positive Aspects	Not-So-Positive Aspects
1. Expresses ideas and feelings well	1. May be glib, making fluent statements based on little or no knowledge or understanding
2. Develops broad knowledge and an extensive store of vicarious experiences	2. May dominate discussions
3. Wants to learn, explore, and seek more information	3. May be impatient to proceed to next level or task
4. Is sensitive to the feelings and rights of others	4. May be considered nosy
5. Is able to use reading skills to obtain new information	5. May choose reading at the expense of active participation in social, creative, or physical activities
6. Often seeks different, novel ways to accomplish a task	6. May struggle against rules, regulations, and standardized procedures
7. Makes original and stimulating contributions to discussions	7. May lead discussions off the track
8. Sees relationships easily	8. May be frustrated by the apparent absence of logic in activities and daily events
9. Requires little drill for learning	9. May become bored by repetitions
10. Contributes to enjoyment of life for self and others	10. May use humor to manipulate
11. Completes assigned tasks quickly	11. May resist a schedule based on time rather than task
12. Can move at a rapid pace	12. May lose interest quickly

Source: Adapted from a table by R. H. Swassing in Heward, W. L., & Orlansky, D. (1980). *Exceptional children* (p. 310). Upper Saddle River, NJ: Merrill/Prentice Hall.

PROFILES AND PERSPECTIVES

Making the Earth a Better Place

Who Said It? Who do you think made each of these observations? Check your selections with the correct answers at the end.

1. After the strife of war begins the strife of peace.
   a. Napoleon Bonaparte
   b. Carl Sandburg
   c. Dwight Eisenhower
   d. Matthew O'Brien
   e. Abraham Lincoln
2. Global peace is a powerful weapon. If we have it, we can use it to make the earth a better place.
   a. Tom Brokaw
   b. Winston Churchill
   c. Henry David Thoreau
   d. Robert Campbell
   e. Mahatma Gandhi
3. The truth is more important than the facts.
   a. Frank Lloyd Wright
   b. Oscar Wilde
   c. Alyce Jaspers
   d. Albert Einstein
   e. Golda Meir
4. Cooperation is a crucial part of survival. Cooperation is key in human life because humans' needs are so diverse, requiring for their fulfillment more skills, more talents, and more learning than any one individual can possess.
   a. Lester Brown
   b. Buckminster Fuller
   c. Polao Salori
   d. Andrea Goldberg
   e. John Nesbit
5. The only way for earth to even come near perfection is for the people in our society who are in the best position to create a perfect earth to become somewhat competent.
   a. John F. Kennedy
   b. Margaret Mead
   c. John Lennon
   d. Nelson Mandela
   e. Peter Bret Lamphere

Most highly gifted children experience asynchronous development, *in which mental, physical, emotional, and social development occur at dramatically different rates. Their cognitive and intellectual abilities usually outpace their physical development.*

Individual Differences among Gifted and Talented Students

Awareness of individual differences is also important in understanding gifted students. Like other children, gifted children show both inter- and intraindividual differences. For example, if two students are given the same reading achievement test and each obtains a different score, we can speak of interindividual differences in reading achievement. If a student who obtains a high reading achievement score obtains a much lower score on an arithmetic achievement test, we say the student has an intraindividual difference across the two areas of performance. A graph of any student's abilities would reveal some high points and some lower points; scores would not be the same across all dimensions. The gifted student's overall *pattern* of performance, however, may be well above the average for that grade and/or age, as we see in Figure 14.2. Leslie performs higher in vocabulary and social studies than Jackie, however, and Jackie shows higher performance in science and mathematics than Leslie. These are *interindividual* differences. Each student also has *intraindividual* differences in scores. For example, Leslie has the vocabulary of an 11th grader but scores only at a 7th-grade equivalent in mathematics; Jackie earned grade equivalents of 10th grade in science and mathematics and 7th grade in writing.

6. After much deep thinking and evaluation of those thoughts, I have come to the realization that, without a shadow of a doubt, the most crucial global issue today, and for years to come, is arms reduction.
   a. Edward Kennedy
   b. Mikhail Gorbachev
   c. Roy Stoner
   d. Jimmy Carter
   e. George Bush
7. Change lately has given us humans quite a stir. Berlin wall down, democracy up; Noriega down, taxes up. What a fast changing world we live in.
   a. Barbara Walters
   b. Peter Jennings
   c. Walter Cronkite
   d. Connie Chung
   e. Robert Campbell
8. People should feel obligated to leave the world a little better than they found it.
   a. Pippa Bowde
   b. Carl Sagan
   c. Robert Redford
   d. Teddy Roosevelt
   e. Mother Teresa
9. Death in the rain forest used to be a natural part of life. The message was simple: Death was the beginning of a new generation. Now that man has entered the picture, death has come to have a new meaning: An end to birth.
   a. Barry Lopez
   b. Andrea Goldberg
   c. Carl Sagan
   d. Manuel Lujan
   e. Abbie Hoffman
10. If there is no personal concern, nothing happens.
   a. Martin Luther King, Jr.
   b. Carl Rogers
   c. Benjamin Spock
   d. Thomas Jefferson
   e. Danielle Eckert

Answers: (1) Carl Sandburg; (2) Robert Campbell, age 10; (3) Frank Lloyd Wright; (4) Andrea Goldberg, age 9; (5) Peter Bret Lamphere, age 9; (6) Roy Stoner, age 9; (7) Robert Campbell, age 10; (8) Pippa Bowde, age 11; (9) Andrea Goldberg, age 9; (10) Danielle Eckert, age 9. Except for numbers 1 and 3, all the statements were written by gifted students. We are grateful to Sandy Lethem and Dennis Higgins, facilitators for the gifted at the Zuni Elementary Magnet School, Albuquerque, New Mexico, for sharing their students' thoughts on the environment.

Creativity

Many writers and teachers believe that creative ability is central to the definition of giftedness. Clark (1997) calls creativity "the highest form of giftedness" (p. 64), and Sternberg (1988) suggests that "gifted individuals who make the greatest long-range contributions to society are probably those whose gifts involve coping with novelty—specifically, in the area of insight. Creative and insightful individuals make discoveries and devise the inventions that ultimately change society" (p. 74).

Although we all profess to know creativity when we see it, there is no universally accepted definition of creativity. Guilford (1987), who studied the emergence of creativity as one aspect of his overall theorizing concerning human intelligence, describes these dimensions of creative behavior:

- *Fluency.* The creative person is capable of producing many ideas per unit of time.
- *Flexibility.* A wide variety of ideas, unusual ideas, and alternative solutions are offered.
- *Novelty/originality.* Unique, low-probability words and responses are used; the creative person has novel ideas.

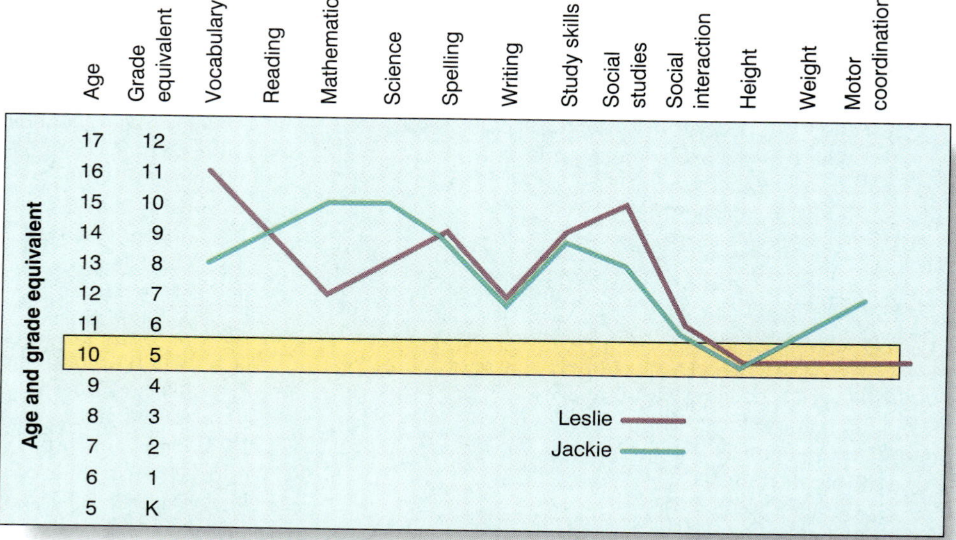

Figure 14.2 Profiles of two gifted and talented students, both age 10 and in fifth grade

- *Elaboration.* The ability to provide details is evidenced.
- *Synthesizing ability.* The person has the ability to put unlikely ideas together.
- *Analyzing ability.* The person has the ability to organize ideas into larger, inclusive patterns. Symbolic structures must often be broken down before they can be reformed into new ones.
- *Ability to reorganize or redefine existing ideas.* The ability to transform an existing object into one of different design, function, or use is evident.
- *Complexity.* The ability to manipulate many interrelated ideas at the same time is shown.

Piirto (1992) studied creative individuals in a variety of areas and summarized the characteristics of highly creative individuals within their fields of creativity, thus linking their high abilities to particular areas of expertise. She reports that (1) each of these fields has specific predictive behaviors in childhood, (2) there is a developmental process in the emergence of talents in various domains, and (3) IQ scores should be minimized in importance and subsumed into a more contextual view of children performing tasks within specific domains.

Torrance (1993) summarized the abilities and achievements of a group of highly creative individuals who were followed for 30 years in a longitudinal study of creativity. He formulated a list of the 10 most common characteristics of high-ability adults who were judged to have achieved far beyond their peers in creative areas. Torrance concluded that the predictive ability of the commonly held measures of creativity is insufficient to predict reliably the emergence of highly creative individuals in later life. His list includes a number of characteristics that do not typically appear in the literature:

1. Delight in deep thinking
2. Tolerance of mistakes
3. Love of one's work
4. Clear purpose
5. Enjoyment in one's work
6. Feeling comfortable as a minority of one

7. Being different
8. Not being well rounded
9. A sense of mission
10. The courage to be creative

Further, Piirto (1999) reminds us that although many gifted and talented students do become scientists, physicians, inventors, and great artists and performers, they have no obligation to do so and that providing them with the differentiated education they need should not be predicated on an expectation that they "owe society."

> These children have no greater obligation than any other children to be future leaders or world-class geniuses. They should just be given a chance to be themselves, children who might like to classify their collection of baseball cards by the middle initial of the players, or who might like to spend endless afternoon hours in dreamy reading of novels, and to have an education that appreciates and serves these behaviors. (pp. 28–29)

Gifted and talented children are most often identified by creativity, talent, and/or extreme intellectual ability that is atypical for their age. See "Precocity As a Hallmark of Giftedness."

It is often difficult to differentiate between the concepts of talent and creativity, perhaps because they may exist on a continuum rather than as separate entities. If we examine the life of a highly talented individual, such as the famous dancer Martha Graham, we can see the relationship between creativity and talent. Her creativity is evident in her pioneering modern dance techniques and her innovative methods of expression in the choreography of the dance. However, her great talent as a dancer, seen in her elegant movements, is equally impressive and serves notice that not only was she a talented dancer but she also created new dances with great meaning and impact on the viewer.

Gifted and talented children can often be identified by their precociousness. Although just 12 years old, Alexandra Nechita is one of the world's most recognized artists. Her unique abstract style was evident at the age of 4.

Precocity As a Hallmark of Giftedness

by Jane Piirto

Four-year-old Maria has been waiting and waiting to go to school. She plays school all the time. She is the teacher, and her dolls are the students. At her day-care center, she is the one who always leads the other kids in games because she is the only one who can read. The other kids look up to her, except when she tries to make them do things they really don't want to do, such as count by twos. The day-care center teacher told Maria's mother that Maria was very bright. When Maria went for her preschool screening, the district recommended that she be tested by the school psychologist. The school psychologist told Maria's mother that Maria had an IQ of 145 on the Stanford-Binet Intelligence Scale, a score that put her in the 99th percentile. This score would qualify her for the district's program for the academically talented, which started at the third grade, although they did have enrichment lessons in first and second grade.

Finally, it is the first day of school; Maria turned 5 in August. She has her new dress and new shoes on. Her mother braids her hair and fastens it with new barrettes. When she gets to school, she is anxious for her mother to leave, yet still she feels shy, with all of these children here. Half of them are crying as their parents leave them. Maria looks around the room and sees a shelf of books. She always reads when she doesn't know what else to do, so she goes over to the shelf and waits for things to calm down. After all of the parents have gone, the teacher tells the children to sit on a line painted on the floor. As the children have come into the room, they have been given large name tags. The teacher sits on a small chair with the children in a semicircle around her and says, "My name is Mrs. Miller, boys and girls. Welcome to kindergarten. In kindergarten, we will learn our letters and our numbers so that we can learn to read in first grade."

"I can read already," Maria says, jumping up.

"That's nice," says Mrs. Miller. "Maria, when we want to talk, first we must stand, and then we must wait until Mrs. Miller calls on us."

"But I can read already!" Maria's voice gets petulant, and tears form in the corners of her eyes.

"Maria, that's nice," said Mrs. Miller. "But in kindergarten, we will learn how to read right. Please sit down now."

Maria is chagrined. Feeling shame and embarrassment, she sits down. She has taken the first step to underachievement.

Underachievement is the prevailing situation in the education of academically talented young children in most schools today. By the time she has been socialized into the kindergarten milieu, Maria will have learned to keep quiet about her abilities and even to suppress that she can read. In first grade, she will comply with the reading tasks in order to fit in. By second grade, even though she will be getting all of her work right, she will have learned that she doesn't have to put forth any effort in school in order to be the best student. By third grade, she will have learned that boredom (as long as she's quietly bored) and waiting (as long as she's not disruptive while she's waiting) are what the school seems to expect of her. By fourth grade, when she gets into a pullout program for academically talented students, she will resent it when the teacher of the academically talented tries to challenge her and, in challenging her, stretches her capabilities. Maria's story, unfortunately, is typical of many young academically talented children who enter the public school system.

This true scenario with Maria indicates the types of *precocious* behavior talented students might display when their abilities are great. Like other young gifted and talented children, Maria can easily do things typically seen only in older children. Even without special testing, their talents can be spotted by teachers who are sensitive to the concept of precocity. In fact, I believe the main way to recognize talented students is by their precocity: achievements resembling those of older children. I call these behaviors *predictive behaviors.* These children are often difficult to locate because they might wish to fit in and not to create disturbances, but their talents can be found by teachers, parents, and educators who look closely.

Jane Piirto is on the education faculty at Ashland University in Ashland, Ohio. She is the author of *Talented Children and Adults* (1999, 2nd ed.), published by Merrill/Prentice Hall.

Prevalence

In 1972, Stanley Marland, the U.S. commissioner of education, reported to Congress on the state of education for gifted students in America's schools. Known as the Marland Report, this study included a minimum estimate of gifted and talented students at 3% to 5% of the total school-age population in the United States at that time. The estimate was derived from the predicted number of individuals with high intellectual ability one would expect to find at the high end of the normal curve, or about two standard deviations above the mean on a standardized intelligence test. Most states that have begun programs for gifted and talented students use the Marland Report's 3% to 5% estimate of the prevalence of giftedness as a guideline for identifying children within their school-age population to serve. If we include those students regarded as highly talented, estimates for the prevalence of giftedness can range as high as 10% to 15% of the total school-age population (Renzulli & Reis, 1997).

There is no "correct" prevalence of gifted and talented children. Because giftedness is a social construct, there are as many gifted and talented students as the definition in use determines.

By 1990, 38 states reported serving more than 2 million students in K–12 gifted programs (U.S. Department of Education, 1993). This number ranks gifted and talented students as the second-largest group of exceptional children receiving special education services. The number and percentage of students identified as gifted and talented vary from state to state; for instance, four states identified more than 10% of the student population as gifted and talented, and 21 states identified less than 5% (U.S. Department of Education, 1993).

The remaining states did not report the numbers of children served. States are not required to provide special services to gifted and talented students or to report the number of children served, although they are required to do so for children with disabilities.

On the basis of an estimate that gifted and talented children comprise 5% of the school-age population, approximately 2.5 million additional gifted and talented children may need special education (Clark, 1997). This discrepancy between need and the level of service may make gifted and talented children the most underserved group of exceptional children.

Identification and Assessment

Richert, Alvino, and McDonnel (1981) contend that the identification of gifted and talented students must take into account six basic principles:

Table 14.3 summarizes some key historical events in the education of gifted students.

1. *Advocacy.* The identification procedures should be for the benefit of all students.
2. *Defensibility.* The best research should be used.
3. *Equity.* The civil rights of all students should be safeguarded, and disadvantaged talented students should be identified.
4. *Pluralism.* A broad definition of talent should be used.
5. *Comprehensiveness.* Various kinds of talented students should be identified and served.
6. *Pragmatism.* The district should be permitted to make local modifications of guidelines and tools.

Feldhusen (1992c) has pressed for the abandonment of attempts to identify gifted students and instead suggests concentrating on (1) searching for talents in all students, (2) searching for those with very high levels of talent or precocity in a worthwhile area of human endeavor, and (3) attempting to use the best instructional methods so that students develop their talent to their highest degrees. Feldhusen and Moon (1995) suggest that all identification efforts should aim to identify talent that represents both precocity and potential: "The student's performance is far ahead of age peers and exhibits potential for continued superior achievements. That momentum is best sustained by continuing opportunities to surge ahead, to develop

"We can find outstanding talent by observing students at work in rich and varied educational settings. Providing opportunities and observing performance give the best information on children's strengths" (U.S. Department of Education, 1993, pp. 25–26).

Table 14.3 A history of the education of gifted and talented students: Key events and implications

Date	Historical Event	Educational Implications
1868	The first special education services for gifted and talented students were offered.	A flexible promotion strategy was applied, followed by acceleration strategies; students were encouraged to complete multiple years of course work in one academic year.
1869	Sir Francis Galton focused on genius.	He was the first to offer a definition of genius that used observable characteristics or outcomes.
1916	The Stanford-Binet Intelligence Scale was published.	Many schools adopted the test as a standard and primary means of identifying gifted students.
1920s	The Progressive Education Movement became important.	Enrichment programs advocated in-depth instruction and ability grouping as appropriate intervention strategies to support giftedness.
1925	Lewis Terman began a longitudinal study tracking 1,500 individuals whose IQ was above 140; he completed the study in 1959 and published *Genetic Studies of Genius.*	The study refuted popular misconceptions of gifted children, including the stereotypical image of gifted children as little adults.
1942	Leta Hollingworth reported the results of 12 case studies of children in the New York City area whose IQs were above 180.	Hollingworth's research revealed that early identification, guidance, personal interest in the children, and differentiated curriculum contributed to adjustment and acceptance of learning as a challenge.
1956	J.P. Guilford analyzed and categorized mental processes.	Guilford challenged the field to look beyond traditional conceptions of intelligence and see IQ score as a small sample of mental abilities.
1957	Russia launched the *Sputnik* satellite, which many in the United States viewed as a risk to national security during the cold war and a challenge to be first in space.	This precipitated concern about the academic and scientific capabilities of Americans and focused attention on the education of the country's academically gifted students.
1958	The National Defense Education Act was passed.	The act was funded to advance students in science, mathematics, and foreign language studies to ensure that American students could compete with the Soviet Union's.
1972	The U.S. commissioner of education submitted a report to Congress titled *Education of the Gifted and Talented* (known as the Marland Report).	The report raised public awareness of the needs of gifted and talented youth in the public schools.
1977	Title IV-C grants were funded.	They provided federal funding for gifted education, which was not included in IDEA (P.L. 94-142).
1983	Howard Gardner published a theory of multiple intelligences.	Some educators use descriptors of Gardner's eight intelligences to account for varying types of giftedness.
1985	Sternberg's triarchic theory identified three kinds of information processing components of intelligence: metacognitive, performance, and knowledge-acquisition.	The theory attempted to balance theoretical with practical definitions of giftedness that emphasize situated problem solving in everyday life.

Date	Historical Event	Educational Implications
1988	The Jacob Javits Gifted and Talented Students Education Act was passed.	The act supported research, teacher preparation, and service delivery concerns.
1993	*National Excellence: A Case for Developing America's Talent* was submitted to Congress.	This report by Secretary of Education Richard Riley warned Americans about "the quiet crisis": neglect of students whose giftedness could otherwise allow Americans to compete in a global economy.

the talents to the highest degree through accelerated and enriched learning experiences that maintain academic challenge and motivation to achieve" (p. 104).

A national survey found that 73% of school districts use IQ and achievement tests as the primary tools for identifying the only category of gifted student that they serve: students with high general intelligence (U.S. Department of Education, 1993). For a comparison of various intelligence tests and suggestions for their use in identifying gifted children, see Bireley (1995) and Silverman (1995).

Within this context, current best practices include intelligence tests as part of the identification process but acknowledge that no single index or procedure can identify all gifted and talented children. A multifactored assessment approach that uses information from a variety of sources is considered to be more accurate and equitable. This approach includes data from a variety of sources, including the following:

- Intelligence tests
- Creativity measures
- Achievement tests
- Portfolios of student work
- Teacher nomination based on reports of student behavior in the classroom
- Parent nomination
- Self-nomination
- Peer nomination

Clark (1997) describes a comprehensive approach for identifying students who require specialized services for their talents. This model employs a progressive filtering process that refines a large pool of potentially gifted students to a smaller, formally identified group (see Figure 14.3). The process is time-consuming and thorough, beginning with the development of a large pool of potentially gifted students in the initial stage (screening); testing, consulting, and analyzing data (development of profile and case study); identification decisions and placement (committee meeting for consideration; placement in gifted program); and finally the development of an appropriate educational program for the child.

We can demonstrate how this process would work with a student thought to have great potential—say, the little girl Janie described at the beginning of this chapter. First, Janie's highly refined intellectual behaviors would have to be noticed by a teacher, parent, her peers, or another person, who would then forward a nomination for additional screening. Figure 14.4 shows questions that Janie's teacher might ask. The teacher's report would contribute to the multidimensional, or multifactored, screening approach that is gaining in popularity among educators of the gifted and talented.

Multidimensional screening also involves a rigorous examination of teacher reports, family history, student inventories, and work samples and perhaps the administration of group achievement or group intelligence tests. The coordinator of gifted services at the school or district level reviews this information and determines

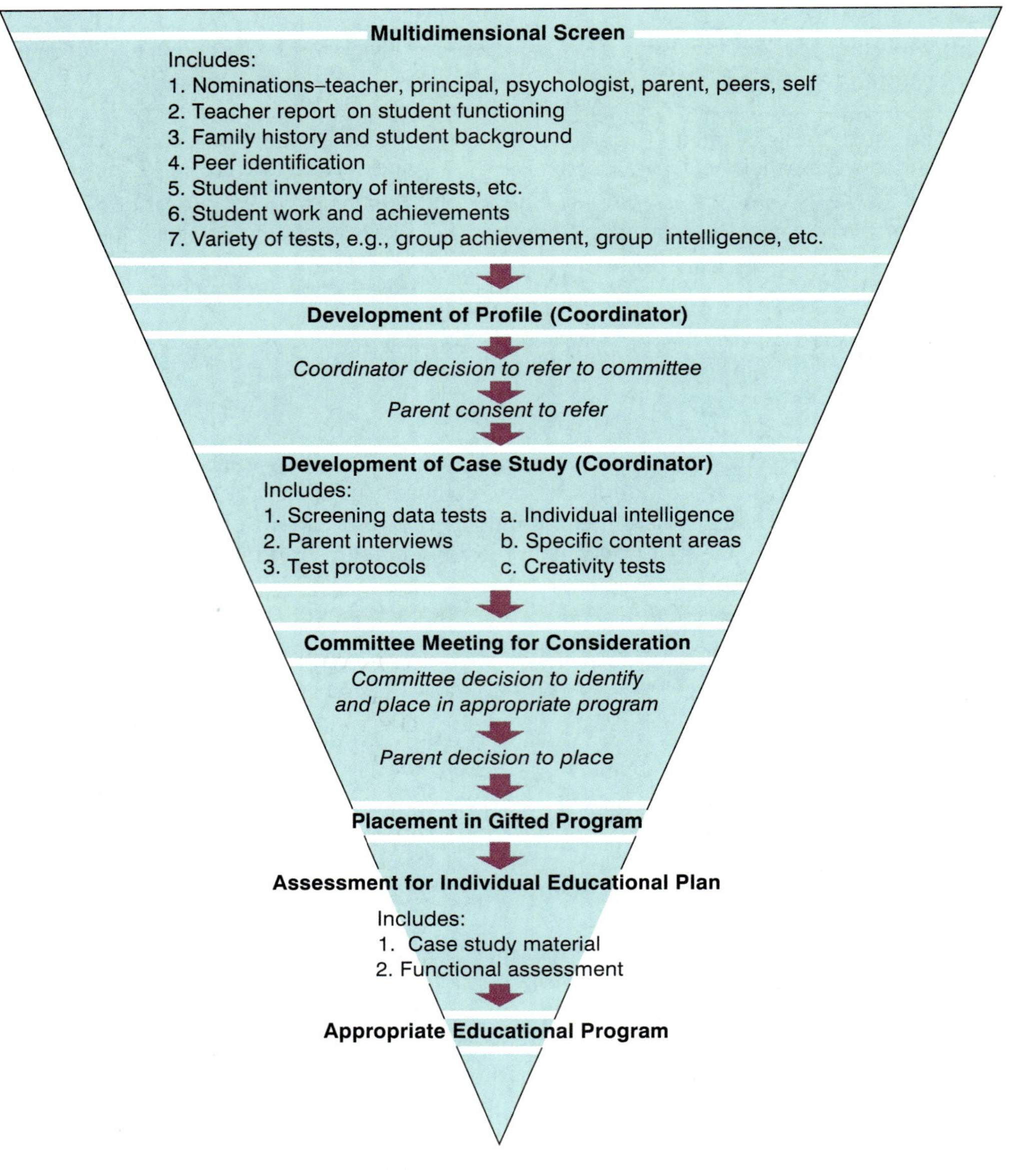

Multidimensional Screen
Includes:
1. Nominations–teacher, principal, psychologist, parent, peers, self
2. Teacher report on student functioning
3. Family history and student background
4. Peer identification
5. Student inventory of interests, etc.
6. Student work and achievements
7. Variety of tests, e.g., group achievement, group intelligence, etc.
Development of Profile (Coordinator)
Coordinator decision to refer to committee
Parent consent to refer
Development of Case Study (Coordinator)
Includes:
1. Screening data tests
2. Parent interviews
3. Test protocols
a. Individual intelligence
b. Specific content areas
c. Creativity tests
Committee Meeting for Consideration
Committee decision to identify and place in appropriate program
Parent decision to place
Placement in Gifted Program
Assessment for Individual Educational Plan
Includes:
1. Case study material
2. Functional assessment
Appropriate Educational Program

Figure 14.3 A model for identifying gifted and talented students
Source: From Clark, B. A. (1997). *Growing up gifted, 5e* (p. 283). Upper Saddle River, NJ: Merrill/Prentice Hall. Reprinted by permission.

whether the results indicate a potential for giftedness and justify the referral of the case to a placement committee. If the coordinator believes there is sufficient evidence to continue, the parents are asked if they would like to refer Janie for more extensive testing to determine whether she qualifies for gifted services. The coordinator then manages the development of a case study that includes screening data, parent interviews, test protocols, an individual intelligence test, tests in specific content areas, and creativity tests. These data are compiled, organized, and presented to the place-

In the classroom does the child

- Ask a lot of questions?
- Show a lot of interest in progress?
- Have lots of information on many things?
- Want to know why or how something is so?
- Become unusually upset at injustices?
- Seem interested and concerned about social or political problems?
- Often have a better reason than you do for not doing what you want done?
- Refuse to drill on spelling, math facts, flash cards, or handwriting?
- Criticize others for dumb ideas?
- Become impatient if work is not "perfect"?
- Seem to be a loner?
- Seem bored and often have nothing to do?
- Complete only part of an assignment or project and then take off in a new direction?
- Stick to a subject long after the class has gone on to other things?
- Seem restless, out of seat often?
- Daydream?
- Seem to understand easily?
- Like solving puzzles and problems?
- Have his or her own idea about how something should be done? And stay with it?
- Talk a lot?
- Love metaphors and abstract ideas?
- Love debating issues?

This child may be showing giftedness cognitively.

Does the child

- Show unusual ability in some area? Maybe reading or math?
- Show fascination with one field of interest? And manage to include this interest in all discussion topics?
- Enjoy meeting or talking with experts in this field?
- Get math answers correct, but find it difficult to tell you how?
- Enjoy graphing everything? Seem obsessed with probabilities?
- Invent new obscure systems and codes?

This child may be showing giftedness academically.

Does the child

- Try to do things in different, unusual, imaginative ways?
- Have a really zany sense of humor?
- Enjoy new routines or spontaneous activities?
- Love variety and novelty?
- Create problems with no apparent solutions? And enjoy asking you to solve them?
- Love controversial and unusual questions?
- Have a vivid imagination?
- Seem never to proceed sequentially?

This child may be showing giftedness creatively.

Does the child

- Organize and lead group activities? Sometimes take over?
- Enjoy taking risks?
- Seem cocky, self-assured?
- Enjoy decision making? Stay with that decision?
- Synthesize ideas and information from a lot of different sources?

This child may be showing giftedness through leadership ability.

Does the child

- Seem to pick up skills in the arts—music, dance, drama, painting, etc.—without instruction?
- Invent new techniques? Experiment?
- See minute detail in products or performances?
- Have high sensory sensitivity?

This child may be showing giftedness through visual or performing arts ability.

Figure 14.4 Questions about classroom behavior that can guide a teacher's efforts to identify students who may be gifted and talented

Source: From Clark, B. A. (1997). *Growing up gifted* (p. 282). Upper Saddle River, NJ: Merrill/Prentice Hall. Reprinted by permission.

ment committee for consideration. The committee determines whether Janie qualifies for services and what type of program would be best suited for her particular pattern of giftedness. The parents are an integral part of this meeting and have to agree with the results and placement decisions that are developed in committee. Janie is then placed in a gifted program, and special services are initiated by the special education teacher or person in charge of the program. This level of assessment is more focused and uses all of the previous case study materials and other assessment data to determine where Janie should start in the program and the overall focus of the special education services she will receive. At this point, Janie begins her new and more appropriate educational program, which provides exciting and innovative experiences designed to increase her intellectual and creative capabilities.

Multicultural Assessment and Identification

Biases inherent in the identification process are primarily to blame for the underrepresentation of students from groups such as African Americans, Latinos, and Native Americans in gifted programs nationally (Ford, 1998; Plummer, 1995; Van Tassel-Baska, Patton, & Prillaman, 1991). In addition, minorities are not entering many important fields requiring mathematics and science skills. For example, although African Americans make up 12% of the population, they earn just 5% of the bachelor's degrees awarded each year in mathematics and science, receive only 1% of the doctoral degrees, and make up just 2% of all employed scientists and engineers in this country. Hispanics comprise 9% of the population but represent just 3% of the bachelor's degrees in science and mathematics, 2% of the doctoral degrees, and 2% of all employed scientists in this country (U. S. Department of Education, 1991).

In response to the prevailing reliance on intelligence testing and the desire to identify underserved and minority students, Feldhusen (1992a) asserts that

> most current identification systems call for multiple measures which are added up to a single composite index of giftedness. Many youth from special populations have not had the extensive opportunities to develop such a broad pattern of giftedness, but they have often developed special talent within a particular domain. The identification process should be designed to find the special talent. Subsequent educational service should focus on facilitating growth in this talent area. (p. 123)

Current best practices for identifying gifted and talented students from diverse cultural groups involve a multifactored, or multidimensional, assessment process that meets these criteria (Clark, 1997; Ford, 1998; Frasier, 1987; Maker, 1994; Ortiz & Gonzales, 1991; Plummer, 1995; Tonemah, 1987; Woliver & Woliver, 1991):

- Identification should have a goal of inclusion rather than exclusion.
- Data should be gathered from multiple sources providing both objective and subjective data (e.g., parent interviews, individual intelligence testing, performance on group problem-solving tasks, motivational and behavioral factors, individual conferences with candidates).
- A combination of formal and informal testing techniques, including teacher referrals, the results of intelligence tests, and individual achievement tests, should be used.
- A generally greater sensitivity to aspects of acculturation and assimilation that allows for multiple perspectives to be identified and honored should be demonstrated.
- Identification procedures should begin as early as possible—before children are exposed to prejudice and stereotyping—and be continuous.

- Unconventional measures involving arts and aesthetic expression such as dance, music, creative writing, and crafts should be used.
- Information gathered during the identification process should be used to help determine the curriculum.

Maker (1997) developed a procedure called DISCOVER, which has been used to assess children from diverse cultural groups and females in an equitable fashion. Based on Gardner's theoretical framework of multiple intelligences, the DISCOVER assessment process involves a series of five progressively more complex problems that provide children with various ways to demonstrate their problem-solving competence by interacting with the content and with one another.

Howard Gardner's theory of multiple intelligences (1983, 1993) proposes an expanded definition of intelligence that entails eight separate domains—linguistic, musical, logical-mathematical, spatial, bodily-kinesthetic, interpersonal, intrapersonal, and naturalist—that operate somewhat independently of one another but that interact at other levels when a person is engaged in active problem solving.

> Problem Types I and II require convergent thinking and are most similar to the types of question found on standardized intelligence and achievement tests. Type I problems are highly structured. The solver knows the solution method and must recall or derive the correct answer and involve convergent thinking. Type II problems also are highly structured, but the solver must decide on the correct method to use. . . . Type III problems are clearly structured, but a range of methods can be used to solve them and they have a range of acceptable answers. Type IV and V problems are more open ended, less structured, and require much more divergent thinking. . . . Type IV problems are commonly found in tests of creativity. Type V problems are extremely ill structured. The solver must explore the possibilities, identify the questions to be answered, and determine the criteria by which an effective solution will be recognized. (Maker, Nielson, & Rogers, 1994, p. 7)

Figure 14.5 shows an example of DISCOVER problem-solving activities for four types of intelligences for children in grades K–2. Children use a Pablo kit, a 21-piece set of tangrams (geometric shapes), to demonstrate their problem-solving abilities with mathematical-spatial problems. Observers record the time used to complete the puzzles, the number of puzzles completed, and particular problem-solving strategies used by the child. A bag of toys provides the materials for assessing the child's linguistic (storytelling) skills.

Assessment of young children's abilities to solve mathematical-spatial problems might include the time used to complete puzzles, the number of puzzles completed, and the particular problem-solving strategies used by the child.

Activities and Intelligences	Problem Type				
	Type I	Type II	Type III	Type IV	Type V
Spatial	Find a piece shaped like a ____. (Teacher shows a shape.)	Find pieces that look like a rainbow. (Observer shows pictures.)	Find pieces and make mountains. (Observer shows pictures.)	Make any animal with as many pieces as you need. Tell about your animal if you want. (Observer provides connectors.)	Make anything you want to make. Tell about it if you wish.
Mathematical-Spatial	Complete simple tangram puzzles with a one-to-one correspondence between the tangram pieces and the puzzles.	Complete simple tangram puzzles with more than one solution that works.	Complete complex tangram puzzles with multiple solutions.	Make a square with as many tangram pieces as you can.	Make a design or a pattern with the pieces.
Mathematical	Complete one- and two-digit addition and subtraction problems.	Complete magic squares using addition and subtraction.	Write correct number sentences using numbers given (in any order).	Write as many correct number problems as you can with an answer of 10.	None
Linguistic	Provide a label for toys given.	Make groups of toys and tell how items in the group are alike. (Some are obvious.)	Make different groups of toys and tell how items in each group are alike. (Encourage going beyond the obvious.)	Tell a story that includes all your toys.	Write a story about a personal experience, something you made up, or anything you wish.

Figure 14.5 Examples of activities for assessing K–2 children's problem-solving competence across four different types of intelligence

Source: From "Giftedness, Diversity, and Problem-Solving" by C. J. Maker, A. B. Nielson, & J. A. Rogers. *Teaching Exceptional Children, 27*(1), 1994, p. 9. © 1994 by the Council for Exceptional Children. Reprinted with permission.

Maker et al. (1994) report positive results from using the DISCOVER model to assess the problem-solving abilities of students from African American, Navajo, Tohono O'Odham, and Mexican American cultural groups: (1) the children identified by the process closely resemble the cultural characteristics of the communities from which they come; (2) equitable percentages of children from various ethnic, cultural, linguistic, and economic groups are identified; (3) the process is equally effective with boys and girls; and (4) students identified through the process make gains equal to or greater than those of students who were identified by traditional standardized tests when placed in special enrichment programs.

Gifted and Talented Girls

Cultural barriers; test and social biases; organizational reward systems; sex-role stereotyping; and conflicts among career, marriage, and family all act as external impediments to the advancement of gifted and talented women (Kerr, 1985). In reviewing the topic of gifted women, Silverman (1986) points out that the history of genius and women's roles has been contradictory (eminent contributions cannot be made from a subservient status) and that identification procedures reflect masculine (product-oriented) versus feminine (development-oriented) concepts of giftedness.

Thus, some of the key issues that appear in the literature concerning the identification and education of females who are gifted and talented involve conflicts concerning role definitions (McCormick & Wolf, 1993), extreme stress related to a lack of self-esteem (Genshaft, Greenbaum, & Borovosky, 1995), poor course selection based on academic choices made in middle school and high school (Clark, 1997), and a lack of parental and general community support for female achievements (Hollinger, 1995).

See the journal Gifted Education International *for a special issue on gifted and talented girls and women (1994, Vol. 9[3]).*

Programs serving gifted and talented females should strive to alter attitudes toward nontraditional career choices, influence the attitudes and behavior of significant others in the girls' environment, change sex-biased instructional practices in the schools, and change the image of math and science to a gender-free domain (Fox, Brody, & Tobin, 1980). Silverman (1986, 1989) makes these recommendations for improving the special education of gifted girls:

- Hold high expectations for girls.
- Believe in their logical and mathematical abilities.
- Expose both boys and girls to female role models.
- Actively recruit girls for advanced placement math and science classes.
- Encourage and deal with girls' multiple interests and talents.
- Use nonsexist texts, language, and communication.
- Form support groups for girls.
- Encourage independence.

Gifted and Talented Students with Disabilities

It may be surprising to learn that the incidence of giftedness and talent among a large proportion of students with disabilities mirrors that of the larger general education population. So we would expect to have almost as many gifted students within the subpopulation of all students with disabilities. However, the combination of a disability and giftedness brings with it an even more complicated set of behaviors and attitudes to challenge educators and parents.

World-famous theoretical physicist Stephen W. Hawking talks about his views of the Big Bang singularity and quantum mechanics in "I Was Thinking about Black Holes" later in this chapter.

Whitmore and Maker (1985) conducted in-depth case studies of the needs and accomplishments of five gifted and talented students with visual, hearing, physical, and learning disabilities. They concluded that teachers and parents can foster the intellectual and talent development of children with disabilities by conveying positive, realistic expectations; encouraging independence; guiding constructive coping strategies; providing daily opportunities to build abilities and enjoy success; and pursuing positive social experiences for the child. Similar implications for practice were drawn by Willard-Holt (1998), who reported case study analyses of the academic and personality characteristics of gifted students with cerebral palsy and no speech.

Reis, Neu, and McGuire (1995) followed twelve young adults with learning disabilities who were successful at the college level. Extensive interviews with these young adults and their parents, as well as a thorough review of available school records, provided a fascinating portrait of the challenges and problems faced by high-ability students with learning disabilities. These researchers offered several specific recommendations for the development of school programs for individuals who were both gifted and learning disabled:

I Was Thinking about Black Holes

by Stephen W. Hawking

Stephen W. Hawking is Lucasian Professor of Mathematics and Theoretical Physics at the University of Cambridge in England. He is considered by many to be the foremost theoretical physicist in the world today. His goal is to develop a grand unifying theory of the entire universe. Such a theory would encompass all known laws of science and describe how the universe began. While a student in college, he was diagnosed with amyotrophic lateral sclerosis (ALS), a degenerative disease of the nervous system sometimes called Lou Gehrig's disease. He uses a wheelchair for mobility and a computer-assisted synthetic speech generator to communicate (see "My Communication System" in Chapter 9).

I was born on January the 8th, 1942, exactly 300 years after the death of Galileo. However, I estimate that about 200,000 other babies were also born that day; I don't know whether any of them were later interested in astronomy.

I was a fairly normal small boy, slow to learn to read, and very interested in how things worked. I was never more than about halfway up the class at school (it was a very bright class). When I was 12, one of my friends bet another friend a bag of sweets that I would never come to anything. I don't know if this bet was ever settled, and, if so, which way it was decided.

My father would have liked me to do medicine. However, I thought that biology was too descriptive and not sufficiently fundamental. Maybe I would have thought differently if I had been aware of molecular biology, but that was not generally known about at the time. Instead, I wanted to do mathematics, more mathematics, and physics. My father thought, however, that there would not be any jobs in mathematics, apart from teaching. He therefore made me do chemistry, physics, and only a small amount of mathematics. Another reason against mathematics was that he wanted me to go to his old College, University College, Oxford, and they did not do mathematics at that time. I duly went to University College in 1959 to do physics, which was the subject that interested me most, because it governs how the universe behaves. To me, mathematics is just a tool with which to do physics.

At that time, the physics course at Oxford was arranged in a way that made it particularly easy to avoid work. I did one exam before I went up and then had 3 years at Oxford, with just the final exam at the end. I once calculated that I did about 1,000 hours of work in the 3 years I was at Oxford, an average of an hour a day. I'm not proud of this lack of work, I'm just describing my attitude of complete boredom and feeling that nothing was worth making an effort for. One result of my illness has been to change all that; when you are faced with the possibility of an early death, it makes one realize that life is worth living and that there are lots of things you want to do.

Because of my lack of work, I had planned to get through the final exam by doing problems in theoretical physics and avoiding any questions that required factual knowledge. However, I didn't sleep the night before the exam because of nervous tension. So I didn't do very well. I was on the borderline between a first- and second-class degree, and I had to be interviewed by the examiners to determine which I should get. In the interview, they asked me about my future plans. I replied I wanted to do research. If they gave me a first, I would go to Cambridge. If I only got a second, I would stay in Oxford. They gave me a first.

I thought there were two possible areas of theoretical physics that were fundamental and in which I might do research. One was cosmology, the study of the very large. The other was elementary particles, the study of the very small. However, I thought that elementary particles were less attractive because, although scientists were finding lots of new particles, there was no proper theory of elementary particles. All they could do was arrange the particles in families, like in botany. In cosmology, on the other hand, there was a well-defined theory, Einstein's General Theory of Relativity.

I had not done much mathematics at school or at Oxford, so I found General Relativity very difficult at first and did not make much progress. Also, during my last year at Oxford, I had noticed that I was getting rather clumsy in my movements. Soon after I went to Cambridge, I was diagnosed as having ALS, amyotrophic lateral sclerosis, or motor neuronic disease, as it is known in England. The doctors could offer no cure or assurance that it would not get worse. The only consolation they could give me was that I was not a typical case.

At first the disease seemed to progress fairly rapidly. There did not seem much point in working at my research because I didn't expect to live long enough to finish my Ph.D. However, as time went by, the disease seemed to slow down. I also began to understand General Relativity and to make progress with my work. However, what really made the difference was that I got engaged to a girl whom I had met about the time I was diagnosed with ALS. This gave me something to live for.

If I were to get married, I had to get a job. And to get a job, I had to finish my Ph.D. I therefore started working hard for the first time in my life. To my surprise, I found I liked it. Maybe it is not really fair to call it work.

My research up to 1970 was in cosmology, the study of the universe on a large scale. My most important work in this period was on singularities. Observations of distant galaxies indicate that they are moving away from us: The universe is expanding. This implies that the galaxies must have been closer together in the past. The question then arises: Was there a time in the past when all of the galaxies were on top of each other and the density of the universe was infinite? Or was there a previous contracting phase, in which the galaxies managed to avoid hitting each other? Maybe they flew past each other and started to move away from each other. To answer this question required new mathematical techniques. These were developed between 1965 and 1970, mainly by Roger Penrose and myself. Penrose was then at Birkbeck College, London. Now he is at Oxford. We used these techniques to show that there must have been a state of infinite density in the past, if the General Theory of Relativity was correct.

This state of infinite density is called the Big Bang singularity. It would be the beginning of the universe. All of the known laws of science would break down at a singularity. This would mean that science would not be able to predict how the universe would begin, if General Relativity is correct. However, my more recent work indicates that it is possible to predict how the universe would begin if one takes into account the theory of quantum mechanics, the theory of the very small.

Stephen W. Hawking

General Relativity also predicts that massive stars will collapse in on themselves when they have exhausted their nuclear fuel. The work that Penrose and I had done showed that they would continue to collapse until they reached a singularity of infinite density. This singularity would be an end of time, at least for the star and anything on it. The gravitational field of the singularity would be so strong that light could not escape from a region around it, but would be dragged back by the gravitational field. The region from which it is not possible to escape is called a black hole, and its boundary is called the event horizon. Anything or anyone who falls into the black hole through the event horizon will come to an end of time at the singularity.

I was thinking about black holes as I got into bed one night in 1970, shortly after the birth of my daughter, Lucy. Suddenly, I realized that many of the techniques that Penrose and I had developed to prove singularities could be applied to black holes. In particular, the area of the event horizon, the boundary of the black hole, could not decrease with time. And when two black holes collided and joined together to form a single hole, the area of the horizon of the final hole would be greater than the sum of the areas of the horizons of the original black holes. This placed an important limit on the amount of energy that could be emitted in the collision. I was so excited that I did not get much sleep that night.

From 1970 to 1974, I worked mainly on black holes. But in 1974, I made perhaps my most surprising discovery: Black holes are not completely black! When one takes the small-scale behavior of matter into account, particles and radiation can leak out of a black hole. The black hole emits radiation as if it were a hot body.

Since 1974, I have been working on combining General Relativity and quantum mechanics into a consistent theory. One result of that has been a proposal I made in 1983 with Jim Hartle, of Santa Barbara: that both space and time are finite in extent but they don't have any boundary or edge. They would be like the surface of the Earth, but with two more dimensions. The Earth's surface is finite in area, but it doesn't have any boundary. In all of my travels, I have not managed to fall off the edge of the world.

If this proposal is correct, there would be no singularities, and the laws of science would hold everywhere, including at the beginning of the universe. The way the universe began would be determined by the laws of science. I would have succeeded in my ambition to discover how the universe began. But I still don't know why it began.

- Many high-ability students who have learning disabilities are not recognized for their gifts and may have negative school experiences.
- Traditional remediation techniques such as special education classification, tutoring, and/or retention offer little challenges to high-ability students with learning disabilities and may perpetuate a cycle of underachievement.
- High-ability students with learning disabilities need support to understand and effectively use their strengths.
- Lack of understanding by school personnel, peers, and self may cause emotional and academic problems for students struggling to cope with learning disabilities and giftedness.
- Parents are often the only ones to offer support to their high-ability children who also have learning disabilities. They can increase their effectiveness by exploring all available options and advocating for their children from an early age.

The intellectual abilities and talents of children with disabilities can be fostered by providing daily opportunities for practicing superior abilities and for enjoying the feelings of success.

Bireley (1995) optimistically predicts, "One of the most positive outcomes of the current movement toward inclusion may be increased appropriate service to such children who need accommodation for their widely disparate abilities" (p. 202). But Clark (1997) reminds educators that students who are gifted with disabilities face daunting odds: "The learning disability will always be there, and the child must learn how to compensate for it. The struggle will always be there; the frustration will always be there" (p. 563).

Educational Approaches

Curricular Goals

The overall goal of educational programs for gifted and talented students should be the fullest possible development of every child's actual and potential abilities. In the broadest terms, the educational goals for these youngsters are no different from those for all children. Feelings of self-worth, self-sufficiency, civic responsibility, and vocational and avocational competence are important for everyone. However, some additional specific educational outcomes are especially desirable for gifted and talented students.

Gallagher (1981) has classified the educational objectives of programs for gifted students into two areas: (1) mastering the knowledge structure of disciplines and (2) heuristic skills. Knowledge structures include both basic principles and systems of knowledge; heuristic skills include problem solving, creativity, and scientific inquiry. In other words, gifted students need both content knowledge and the abilities to develop and use that knowledge effectively.

The finding of one national survey that teachers usually make only minor, if any, changes in curricular content for gifted students is not encouraging in this respect (Archambault, Westberg, Brown, Hallmark, Zhang, & Emmons, 1993). In a related study, the same researchers found that in more than 84% of the instructional activities, gifted and talented children were not provided with any meaningful instructional or curricular differentiation (Westberg, Archambault, Dobyns, & Salvin, 1993).

Most authors and teachers agree that the most important concern in developing appropriate curriculum is to match the students' specific needs with a qualitatively different curricular intervention. According to Kaplan (1988), the differentiated curriculum should do the following:

1. be responsive to the needs of the gifted student as both a member of the gifted population and as a member of the general population.
2. include or subsume aspects of the regular curriculum.
3. provide gifted students with opportunities to exhibit those characteristics that were instrumental in their identification as gifted individuals.
4. not academically or socially isolate these students from their peers.
5. not be used as either a reward or a punishment for gifted students. (p. 170)

Feldhusen and Moon (1995) advocate the development of an individualized growth plan designed to develop a broad program of services for gifted and talented students. The growth plan differs from an IEP along several important dimensions: (1) it is not a requirement for services to be provided; (2) it is more flexible, having no time restrictions, reporting requirements, or physical boundaries; and (3) it is primarily collaboratively planned but essentially student-directed. The growth plan should include assessment information, student-generated goals (in consultation with others), and the recommended activities for accomplishing these goals. A key feature of this approach is that the student is guided toward the establishment of her own goals and is an active participant in all instructional and evaluative activities. This method is consistent with Maker's (1994) contention that "one of the most important goals of these [gifted] programs is to increase the individual learner's control of the learning process and opportunities for decision making in situations involving both learning and other aspects of living" (p. 18).

Piirto (1999) recommends that curriculum and instruction for gifted and talented students should have the following characteristics:

- *Be based on learning characteristics of academically talented students in their area of strength.* These characteristics include "their ability to learn at a faster rate; their ability to think abstractly about content that is challenging; their ability to think productively, critically, creatively, and analytically; and their ability to constantly and rapidly increase their store of knowledge, both knowledge of facts and knowledge of processes and procedures" (p. 365).
- *Possess academic rigor.* The widespread abuse of grading practices, the dumbing down of the curriculum, and the lowered expectations of teachers have all sapped curriculum of its strength and rigor. Research skills, keyboarding and computer use, speed reading, at least one foreign language, and interpersonal and affective development should be systematically taught as part of the curriculum. There is a distinct need to increase the relevance, discipline, and depth of current curriculum, primarily within the regular education setting, where most gifted students are for most of the day.

See "Dumbing Down" later in this chapter.

- *Be thematic and interdisciplinary.* Academically talented students should be exposed to the structures, terminologies, and methodologies of various disciplines. The skills of systematic investigation are fundamental abilities that gifted students use throughout a lifetime of learning. These skills include the use of references, the use of the library, the gathering of information (data), and the reporting of findings in a variety of ways. These skills may ultimately be used in diverse settings, such as law and medical libraries, museums, chemical and electrical laboratories, theatrical archives, and national parks.

Curriculum Organization and Delivery Methods

Gifted and talented students need exposure to a challenging and conceptually rich curriculum. Far too many gifted children are "languishing in the regular classroom, unable to focus their attention on material that was mastered long ago, is unbearably simplistic, and has been reiterated beyond their tolerance level" (Silverman, 1995, p. 220). Because gifted students learn at a faster rate than most students and can absorb and reconfigure more concepts, they benefit from a differentiated curriculum that is modified in both its pace and depth (Piirto, 1999). **Acceleration** is the general term for modifying the pace at which the student moves through the curriculum; **enrichment** means probing or studying a subject at a greater depth than would occur in the regular curriculum.

Technology can be used to provide both acceleration and enrichment opportunities for gifted students. See "New and Emerging Technologies for Gifted and Talented Students" later in this chapter.

Acceleration *Acceleration* means providing a student with opportunities to move through required curriculum at a faster pace. There are many acceleration options, including the following:

- Early admission to school
- Grade skipping/advancement
- Content acceleration in one or two subjects while remaining with age peers
- Testing out of courses
- Curriculum compacting or telescoping
- Concurrent enrollment in both high school and college
- Advanced placement tests
- Early admission to college

Silverman (1995) believes that acceleration is a "necessary response to a highly gifted student's faster pace of learning" (p. 229). Research indicates that when acceleration is practiced wisely, students benefit by having increased interest in school, attaining higher levels of academic achievement, receiving recognition of accomplishment, and completing higher levels of education in less time, which provides increased time for pursuing careers at the end of schooling (Kulick & Kulick, 1984; Robinson & Noble, 1991; Southern & Jones, 1991). Finally, one of the practical benefits of acceleration is that it is both time- and cost-effective for school personnel to implement (Swiatek & Benbow, 1991).

A commonly heard concern is that early admission and grade skipping will lead to social or emotional problems because the child will be in a classroom with older students who are more advanced physically and emotionally. Feldhusen and Moon (1995) state that "ridiculous myths . . . circulate among school personnel" (p. 105) that talented students will suffer from the pressure to achieve at higher levels and will burn out or become social misfits. Although this concern is understandable, research shows that if acceleration is done properly, few, if any, socioemotional problems result (Robinson & Noble, 1991; Southern & Jones, 1991). After reviewing a decade of longitudinal research on the academic acceleration of mathematically precocious youths, Swiatek (1993) found no evidence that acceleration harms willing students either academically or socially/emotionally. Feldhusen (1992b), a strong advocate for acceleration who believes it is "the most powerful educational service we can offer to gifted and talented youth" (n.p.), writes:

To join in the discussion, "Should students who are gifted be educated with their same-age peers or with older students who share the same intellectual and academic talents and interests?" go to the Message Board Module at http://www.prenhall.com/heward.

> A more salient question to ask is what are the risks of *not* advancing the children. The excruciating daily boredom (Feldhusen & Kolloff, 1985), the problems of dealing with peers who are less mature intellectually, and the learning to get by may produce serious emotional problems. For some highly gifted students there can be clear social ostracism because of the child's advanced interests and precocious verbal behaviors. . . . Thus, for a number of reasons the problems of social and/or emotional adjustment for the gifted child may be greater in the age-grade placement than in an advanced grade. (p. 46)

For example, Miranda has been identified and served in gifted classes through elementary school and is a candidate for acceleration in the form of grade skipping to the eighth grade. These are some of the critical questions that her parents and teacher must ask:

- How socially mature is Miranda? Does she prefer to play with children older than herself? What kind of feedback does she generally get from her peers—positive or negative?
- Does the school routinely accelerate advanced students and have a process in place to deal with the transitional needs that Miranda will have? Is there a willingness by the administration and teachers to support Miranda's advanced placement?
- Has the option of accelerating Miranda in only one, or selected, subject areas been considered? Teachers or curriculum specialists can be helpful in determining what aspects of a subject are covered in each grade.

Questions like these must be asked when engaged in the decision-making process involved in accelerating a student. The final decision is best determined by parents, teachers, and student after receiving advice through discussions with the school's coordinator for the gifted and talented, the guidance counselor, and the principal. It helps to have the enthusiastic support and understanding of the teachers who will be working with the accelerated child as well as commitments for continuity and coordination from the school's administration.

For specific guidelines for teachers and parents who are considering early admission or grade advancement, see Feldhusen (1992a) and Feldhusen, Proctor, and Black (1986). The March/April 1992 issue of Gifted Child Today *contains 11 articles on acceleration.*

Curriculum Compacting Many gifted and talented students have already mastered much of the content of the regular curriculum when the school year begins. In fact, one study found that 60% of *all* fourth graders in a certain school district were able to attain a score of 80% correct or higher on a test of mathematics content before they had even opened their books in September (EPIE, 1980). *Curriculum compacting* involves compressing the instructional content and materials so that academically able students have more time to work on more challenging materials. It is a powerful technique for adapting and developing curriculum for talented students in the regular classroom. Curriculum compacting has been shown to be an effective way to not only ensure that gifted and talented students cover the important information and materials within the regular education curriculum but also move beyond it to meet special instructional needs.

Teachers must avoid the temptation and ease of providing gifted students with the MOTS curriculum (More of the Same)—repetitious and unnecessary drill and practice of the same kinds of items or problems the students have already mastered. MOTS activities do not represent differentiated curriculum for gifted and talented students and may be one reason that some students underachieve (Clark, 1997).

Reis, Westberg, Kulikowich, and Purcell (1998) conducted a study that examined the effects of curriculum compacting on the achievement test scores of a national sample of 336 high-ability students from second- through sixth-grade heterogeneous classrooms in rural, suburban, and urban settings. Teachers from treatment and control groups in the study selected one to two students from their classes who demonstrated superior ability and advanced content knowledge prior to instruction. They eliminated 40% to 50% of curriculum content for these students across subject areas. Their results showed that the achievement test scores of students whose curriculum was compacted did not differ significantly from students who did not experience curriculum compacting.

A series of studies on the impact of a progressive staff development program showed some promise in terms of teaching teachers how to adapt their curricula (Reis, 1995). The intervention involved three steps to facilitate curriculum compacting: (1) assess the target content areas, (2) determine the content to be eliminated, and (3) substitute the more appropriate content. Researchers found that the 436 teachers who participated in the study successfully eliminated 40% to 50% of the curricular content without detrimental effects on the academic performance of 783 gifted and talented students. In addition, the gifted and talented students scored significantly higher on tests of mathematics and science concepts after the content was altered.

For curriculum compacting to be effective, teachers must have a substantial understanding of the curricular content and not only condense the material but also modify its presentation, create more meaningful instruction, and evaluate that instruction for individual students. For example, Juan's teacher, Mr. Dominguez, suspects that Juan has already mastered substantial amounts of the mathematics that students are doing in the fourth grade, perhaps by as much as two grade levels. To discover if Juan is a good candidate for curricular compacting, Mr. Dominguez first determines the scope and sequence of the mathematics problems that Juan should be able to do in the fifth and sixth grade. Then he constructs an evaluation process that will accurately determine at what level Juan is able to perform the mathematics problems. If Juan is found to have mastered the content and strategies of the higher-level math, then Mr. Dominguez must design and provide replacement activities that are a more challenging and productive use of Juan's time.

What's more important for gifted and talented students—acceleration or enrichment? "The question of acceleration versus enrichment is irrelevant, because this group of students needs both. They learn at a very accelerated pace, and they need high-level conceptual material outside the regular curriculum" (Silverman, 1995, p. 229).

Enrichment Enriching the content of instruction to include more innovation, novelty, and sophistication is the most common method of differentiating curriculum for academically talented students. The use of new teaching techniques is also advocated, including the use of new technologies for the organization, manipulation, and presentation of student products. Enriching the curriculum generally involves adding new and different information from a variety of disciplines outside the traditional curriculum. This is the strategy of choice by most regular education teachers when attempting to provide additional opportunities for gifted and talented students in their classrooms. It is important to remember that enrichment is meant to be thoughtfully and systematically applied to the educational program of targeted students.

PROFILES AND PERSPECTIVES

Dumbing Down: Pretending That All Students Are Equal Doesn't Make It So

by Robin Marantz Henig

Last summer, I ran into my neighbor when I dropped by the pool for an evening swim. She was sitting in the slanting sunshine, a closed paperback on her lap, and she and the other swim-team mothers waited for practice to end.

I asked how her sons were enjoying the summer and she told me how well they were doing on the team. She even told me their best lap times, in seconds, down to the hundredths. This was not bragging—simply the way things are around here. Yet when she asked about my daughters, I didn't tell her that both had been accepted for the highly selective academic programs in their respective schools. This was also the way things are around here.

My neighbor and I are both products of our national ambivalence about ability: it's O.K. to extol athletic excellence, but there's something elitist, or at least unseemly, about even acknowledging intellectual excellence.

The notion of intellectual accomplishment, as opposed to performance in other spheres, must be uniquely threatening to the American egalitarian spirit. How else to explain the offensive attitude of many public schools—the very places where academic achievement should be cultivated and celebrated—toward our brightest children?

School officials seem to make decisions based on the belief that no child is smarter than any other child. But of course some are smarter, just as some are better athletes or musicians. The school system's lie hurts everyone, but especially the kids with the greatest intellectual promise.

When the boy across the street asked for harder work in sixth-grade math, he was told he couldn't get too far ahead of the rest of the class—it would run counter to the school's group-oriented philosophy. Yet he was capable of working at an eighth-grade level or higher, while some kids in his class were still mastering third-grade skills.

What perverse logic would force him to tread water for an entire year so as not to outdistance the others? If he were a 12-year-old Michael Jordan, would his coach caution him not to make too many baskets so the others would have a chance to score?

Very bright kids are victims of the trend toward "heterogeneous classrooms," which lump together children who perform at, above, and below grade level. And though experts say high achievers are a good influence on slower kids and though teachers may intend to offer "differentiated instruction," in practice this rarely happens. Sometimes simple logistics make it impossible. Sometimes accelerating an individual goes against some inexplicable educational philosophy.

My own daughters, who are now 10 and 14, wasted a lot of time in heterogeneous classrooms while the lesson was repeated again and again until everyone got it.

When my younger one was in third grade, the teacher said she wouldn't call on her when she raised her hand because the teacher knew she knew the answer. So my daughter sat quietly, trying hard to focus on the lesson even though she couldn't participate. Expecting her to blossom intellectually in such a setting is like expecting the young Jordan to get better at basketball just by showing up at a gym.

My older daughter suffered similarly until in fifth grade she moved to a homogeneous class, one of the few our school system still grudgingly offers. Finally, she could learn something each day that she didn't already know. "It's perfect—I love it—everyone's like me," she said after her first day. They weren't, really; they were white and black and Indian and Chinese and Hispanic and Sri Lankan.

By spending all day with intellectual peers, my daughter and her classmates have learned that their brainpower is not only admirable but something to revel in. This is a rare and wonderful lesson in a community that hands out trophies for sports but not for schoolwork. So is the corollary: that intelligence, like the muscles of a powerful swimmer, can be exercised and stretched, so that all kids can achieve their personal best.

Source: Excerpted from Henig, R. M. (1994, October 23). Dumbing down. *New York Times,* pp. 34, 36.

Do gifted and talented students benefit the most by participating in acceleration and enrichment programs with peers who show similar intellectual abilities? See the National Association for Gifted Children's position statement on ability grouping (Figure 14.6).

Contact the site at http://www.asel.udel.edu/sem/programs/telementoring/activities/cyberfair96.

Enrichment experiences let students investigate topics of interest in greater detail than is ordinarily possible with the standard school curriculum. Topics of investigation may be based on the ongoing activities of the classroom but may permit students to go beyond the limits of the day-to-day instructional offerings. However, by allowing the students to help define the area of interest and independently access a variety of information and materials, the teacher can learn to facilitate the development of gifted and talented students' competencies and skills.

An excellent example of an enrichment activity was carried out at the Applied Sciences and Engineering Laboratories of the A. T. duPont Institute (Barner, Howell, & Mahoney, 1996). A special project matched 20 students with disabilities with 20 mentors who all worked together in a virtual project environment aimed at cooperatively creating a website for high school–age students with disabilities. The website was meant to provide college application and funding information for students with disabilities throughout the United States. The website was also envisioned as a means of communicating between and among groups of students with disabilities. The project involved smaller teams of students and mentors working on different components of the page. A great deal of on-line searching, writing, and reporting produced a website that facilitates information exchange among a specific group of students.

Enrichment is not a "do-your-own-thing" approach with no structure or guidance. Children involved in enrichment experiences should not be released to do a random, haphazard project. A basic framework that defines limits and sets outcomes is necessary. Projects should have purpose, direction, and specified outcomes. A teacher should provide guidance where necessary—and to the degree that is necessary—to keep students working efficiently.

Curriculum Differentiation Outside the Classroom For some students with outstanding talents, the things that take place outside the classroom may be more important and rewarding than many of the things that take place within it. The teacher should always attempt to connect with both human and physical resources that are available within the community. Much more flexibility is offered by outside learning environments because of the relaxed scheduling and the lack of physical barriers they offer to students. Options for learning outside the school include the following:

- *Internships and mentor programs.* The value and power of a viable mentor to the realization of talent or creativity have been recognized since the Middle Ages. The importance of mentors cannot be underestimated in certain artistic and scientific fields, where the development of both conceptual and performance skills is critical to success. These opportunities allow students with exceptional talents to be exposed to one of the most powerful and proven educational strate-

A good mentor provides students with exceptional talents opportunities to develop both their conceptual and performance skills in a real-world setting.

NATIONAL ASSOCIATION FOR GIFTED CHILDREN
POSITION PAPER

Ability Grouping

The National Association for Gifted Children (NAGC) periodically issues policy statements that deal with issues, policies, and practices that have an impact on the education of gifted and talented students. Policy statements represent the official convictions of the organization.

All policy statements approved by the NAGC Board of Directors are consistent with the organization's belief that education in a democracy must respect the uniqueness of all individuals, the broad range of cultural diversity present in our society, and the similarities and differences in learning characteristics that can be found within any group of students. NAGC is fully committed to national goals that advocate both excellence and equity for all students, and we believe that the best way to achieve these goals is through *differentiated* educational opportunities, resources, and encouragement for all students.

The practice of grouping, enabling students with advanced abilities and/or performance to be grouped together to receive appropriately challenging instruction, has recently come under attack. NAGC wishes to reaffirm the importance of grouping for instruction of gifted students. Grouping allows for more appropriate, rapid, and advanced instruction, which matches the rapidly developing skills and capabilities of gifted students.

Special attention should be given to the identification of gifted and talented students who may not be identified through traditional assessment methods (including economically disadvantaged individuals, individuals of limited English proficiency, and individuals with handicaps), to help them participate effectively in special grouping programs.

Strong research evidence supports the effectiveness of ability grouping for gifted students in accelerated classes, enrichment programs, advanced placement programs, etc. Ability and performance grouping has been used extensively in programs for musically and artistically gifted students, and for athletically talented students with little argument. Grouping is a necessary component of every graduate and professional preparation program, such as law, medicine, and the sciences. It is an accepted practice that is used extensively in the education programs in almost every country in the western world.

NAGC does not endorse a tracking system that sorts all children into fixed layers in the school system with little attention to particular content, student motivation, past accomplishment, or present potential.

To abandon the proven instructional strategy of grouping students for instruction at a time of educational crisis in the U.S. will further damage our already poor competitive position with the rest of the world, and will renege on our promise to provide an appropriate education for all children.

Figure 14.6 Position statement on ability grouping by the National Association for Gifted Children
Source: National Association for Gifted Children, Washington, DC. Adopted November 1991. Reprinted by permission.

gies—modeling, practice, and direct feedback and reinforcement of important behaviors within a real-world setting.

- *Special courses.* Many specialized courses are offered within most communities, including courses at local colleges and universities, arts and cultural events, museums, and workshops at recreation centers. These courses may or may not have high school or college continuing education credits attached to them. They form a rich variety of additional opportunities for students to encounter mentors, new friends, and expansive concepts that may not be available in the confines of the school curriculum.
- *Odyssey of the Mind.* This is an international program designed to bring together children from every country in a cooperative problem-solving environ-

TEACHING AND LEARNING IN SCHOOL

New and Emerging Technologies for Gifted and Talented Students

Teachers of gifted students must deal with both conceptual and practical issues as they plan for the integration of technology into their classroom instruction. They must first have a clear idea of their own curricular focus and which aspects of technology they wish to use if they are to enhance the student's understanding and use of this information. This is primarily a matching process between the curricular information and the best manner of presenting and manipulating this information by using a technological tool. The results of this process should be (1) a conceptual framework in which instruction will take place and (2) the identification of the technological methods and tools to be used in instructional delivery.

Software Selection and Acquisition The identification of appropriate software for a gifted student depends on the curricular goals for that student. If the curricular demand is to build research and scientific inquiry skills, then the best software might be simulations, data base systems, interactive videodisc programs, and possibly spreadsheets. If the curriculum focuses on expressive writing, then the use of word-processing, desktop publishing, and graphics software are appropriate.

Perry (1989) provides several selection criteria that he believes should be applied when previewing educational software for use in gifted education: (1) the provision for differing levels of ability, (2) branching capabilities, (3) reusability—that is, students can profit from using the software more than one time, (4) an evaluation component, (5) a challenge for students, and (6) accurate and up-to-date content.

Intelligent Computer-Assisted-Instruction (ICAI) ICAI software analyzes and interprets student responses and presents new information to the learner modeled on the student's own cognitive strengths and weaknesses. The critical difference between ICAI and traditional CAI programs is in their ability to collect diagnostic information and act on it; basically, ICAI software "learns" from the user's responses. These programs are able to modify their instructional strategies on the basis of patterns of information they gather from student responses.

An example of an ICAI program is a math tutor that initially presents to a student a group of mathematics problems at a defined difficulty level. After analyzing the student's response patterns to the initial set of problems, the program sets a starting point within a sequenced set of problems for the learner. The student then begins working on this first set, with the ICAI program analyzing the correct solutions and the types and patterns of errors the student makes. The program uses these error patterns to create expert models that will progressively guide the student through problem solution, providing hints and directional cues on student errors. The program thus monitors, evaluates, and constructs problem solutions for each individual student user.

Virtual Reality Three-dimensional simulations provide opportunities for creative development and the exploration of both real and imaginary environments. Virtual reality can concretize formerly highly abstract concepts (Papert, 1980) and thus allow for earlier and more powerful instructional interventions with gifted students. An example of an educational application of virtual reality is a social studies simulation of a medieval village. The student accesses the virtual medieval world through the computer-based simulation and a helmet that transmits the sounds and images to the user. A data glove or joystick allows a limited response capability to manipulate objects in the village/world. For example, the student walks through the streets up to the castle, enters the castle, and takes part in a grand feast in the main hall. The food, entertainment, and interactions can all be modeled in the virtual world to closely approximate those revealed in historic documents and paintings. The student can come to know and experience the reality of medieval life in a manner that is both exciting and educational.

However, there may also be a dark side to virtual reality that has not been fully articulated in the rush to bring this technology into the recreational and entertainment marketplaces. Access to a variety of virtual worlds has the potential to be so engrossing that students may reject other types of learning or play experiences. The potential danger is that children might become isolated within these mental environments that are so easily molded to meet their desires and forsake the somewhat messy real world, where one must work at relationships and life.

Electronic Communities Recent developments in telecommunications allow for greater interactions and sharing among gifted students from across the world. The distant interactions provide new impetus for students to continue their studies and perhaps to reach out and assist in the process of globalizing education for the future. A number of distance learning projects have already been initiated throughout the United States, linking students from across town to across the world with one another. The curricular focus of these projects is as diverse as second language learning and social studies and language arts. Their most important contribution to learning, however, may be in the areas of cultural understanding and interpersonal communications. Students may be able to more fully realize and deal with the realities of a global community through such learning opportunities. The world grows smaller through such contacts, and an understanding of different cultures and peoples will prepare students to deal better with both global competition and cooperation as they mature into adulthood.

Source: Adapted from Howell, R. D. (1994). Technological innovations in the education of gifted and talented students. In J. L. Genshaft, M. Bireley, & C. L. Hollinger (Eds.), *Serving gifted and talented students* (pp. 155–171). Austin, TX: PRO-ED. Used by permission.

ment. Teams are formed in three age divisions: grades K–5, grades 6–8, and grades 9–12. The process begins at the school level and advances through regional, state, national, and finally international levels of competition. Each of the teams is given three types of problems to solve—some that take months to solve, others that require only days, and some that must be solved spontaneously. The problems require a unique blend of creativity, basic knowledge, and cooperative problem solving to distinguish team processes and products from each other.

- *Junior Great Books.* This is a highly structured educational program in which students read selections from a number of areas, including classics, philosophy, fiction, and poetry, and then discuss their meaning with teachers. The teachers must undergo special training and use specific questioning techniques designed to evoke high-quality responses from the students.
- *Summer programs.* Many summer programs are available to gifted and talented students that offer educational experiences as diverse as environmental studies and space and aeronautical studies. A number of new program offerings have been aimed at gifted minority students at the state and local levels. Summer programs are usually relatively brief but intense learning experiences that concentrate on specific areas of intellectual, artistic, or cultural affairs.
- *International curricular experiences.* New Zealanders have a cultural rite of passage they refer to as "the trek," wherein they pack their bags and travel in modest fashion to the far reaches of the planet. It is an eye-opening experience for people from a tiny Pacific island and one that gives them an exceptional opportunity to see and touch the world in an intimate fashion. An international curricular experience can merge this act of exploration with the demands of a structured learning experience such as the International Baccalaureate Program. Numerous international programs offer academic credits for study at participating educational agencies around the world. They are excellent opportunities to develop global interactional skills with academically rigorous studies.

Addresses for Odyssey of the Mind, Junior Great Books, and the Future Problem Solving programs appear in "For More Information" at the end of the chapter.

Go to the Resources Module for Chapter 14 at http://www.prenhall.com/heward and link to the Special Ed Resource Page. Review the general resources sites under "Teacher Resources" for ideas you could use to motivate students who are gifted.

Instructional Models and Methods

Each of the four instructional models described in this section engages students in similar ways, focusing on independent exploration and inquiry, substantial modifications to the individual student's learning environment, and tangible products as an outcome of the learning activities. These models were selected because they offer the best examples of how special education for gifted and talented students can truly be differentiated from the regular curriculum. Although the Schoolwide Enrichment Model (Renzulli & Reis, 1997) is the only model to attempt to provide activities for both typically developing and gifted students, each of the other models includes components that can be modified and applied to a broad range of student abilities and talents within inclusive classrooms.

The Schoolwide Enrichment Model The Schoolwide Enrichment Model (SEM) not only attempts to meet the needs of gifted and talented students within the regular classroom setting but also is meant to be used with the other students in the classroom (Renzulli & Reis, 1986). According to Renzulli (1998):

> The Schoolwide Enrichment Model (SEM) focuses on applying the know-how of gifted education to a systematic plan for total school improvement. This plan is not intended to replace existing services to students who are identified as gifted according to various state or local criteria. Rather, the model should be viewed as an umbrella under which many different types of enrichment and acceleration services are made available to targeted groups of students, as well as all students within a given school or grade level. (p. 1)

The model has undergone several revisions since it was first introduced and now provides new identification procedures, the inclusion of all students in the planned activities, and even more extensive follow-up activities. The process involves first identifying a talent pool of high-ability students (usually about 15% to 20% of the school's enrollment) by using a multifactored assessment approach, including achievement tests, teacher and peer nominations, and creativity assessments. Once the students are identified, they are able to take part in specialized services, many of which are also available and appropriate for other learners in the same classroom. Reis (1995) discusses some of the relevant features of this instructional approach:

- Interest and learning styles assessments are used with talent pool students. Informal and formal methods are used to create and/or identify individual students' interests and to encourage students to further develop and pursue their interests in various ways.
- Curriculum compacting is offered to all eligible students. The regular curriculum of the classroom is modified by eliminating redundant or repetitious information and materials.
- Three types of enrichment activities are offered to students: Type I, general exploratory experiences; Type II, purposefully designed instructional methods and materials; and Type III, advanced-level studies with greater depth and complexity.

Reis and Cellerino (1983) recommend using a "revolving door" identification model (Renzulli, Reis, & Smith, 1981) that allows all children in the talent pool to participate in Type I and Type II enrichment activities. Only students who show serious interest in a specific topic evolve into Type III investigators. Students are never compelled to begin Type III projects; the level remains an open option for them.

When a student indicates a particular area of interest, the teacher must determine whether the interest is serious enough to warrant launching an in-depth investigation or whether it is only a temporary, superficial interest. Reis and Cellerino (1983) interviewed Michael, a second-grade student in their gifted program, who, as a result of Type I and Type II activities, expressed a strong interest in Tchaikovsky. They asked Michael these questions:

1. Michael, will you tell me a little about Tchaikovsky and how you became interested in knowing more about him?
2. Have you read any books about him and his music?
3. How long have you been interested in studying about Tchaikovsky?
4. Do you like looking in different books to find information?
5. Do you have any ideas about what you would like to do with the information you find? (p. 137)

Michael's responses showed his interest in Tchaikovsky to be genuine. After specifying objectives for his research, Michael's teachers helped him set up a management plan for his investigation. Potential sources of information were identified, and a timeline was developed. Then Michael was encouraged to generate a specific idea for a product of his investigation and to consider an audience for his product. Michael's product, a children's book of 30 typed pages and an audiotaped version that plays selections of Tchaikovsky's music, is now part of both his school's and his local public library's collection. On the first page of his book, Michael wrote,

> Some of you may wonder why a second grader would want to write a book about Tchaikovsky. People get interested in different things for different reasons. For example, I got interested in Tchaikovsky because I like his music. I play the piano and have a whole book of his music. At Christmas I saw the ballet of the Nutcracker Suite. His music can be both cheerful and sad at the same time. I wondered how music can be both happy and sad at the same time so I decided to learn about Tchaikovsky's life.
>
> I wondered if when he was sad he wrote sad music, and if when he was happy he wrote happy music. In this book you will get to know a little bit more about Tchaikovsky, how he lived and about the music he wrote. (Reis & Cellerino, 1983, p. 139)

Responsive Learning Environment The Responsive Learning Environment (RLE), developed by Clark (1986), is a flexibly structured learning environment designed to turn the classroom into a laboratory for learning that is closely related to the real world of people and ideas. It is the first, and most important, step in a comprehensive process of instruction that Clark calls the Integrative Educational Model (1997). The RLE has a flexible structure and provides the basis for the highly interactive instruction that gifted and talented students require to achieve. The teacher's role is critical to the establishment of the classroom and community-based experiences. Basically, the teacher assists students in defining their personal and group goals and helps them maintain their motivation for learning. Clark (1997) describes the following as important characteristics of the RLE:

- There is an open, respectful, and cooperative relationship among teachers, students, and parents that includes planning, implementing, and evaluating the learning experience.
- The environment is more like a laboratory or workshop that is rich in materials with simultaneous access to many learning activities. The emphasis is on experimentation and involvement.
- The curriculum is responsive, flexible, and integrative. The needs and interests of the students provide the base from which the curriculum develops.
- There is a minimum of total group lessons. Most instruction is in small groups among individuals.
- The student is an active participant in the learning process. Movement, decision making, self-directed learning, invention, and inquiry are encouraged.

- Assessment, contracting, and evaluation are all used as tools to aid in the growth of the students.
- The physical placement of the furniture, seating of the students, and traffic patterns are planned to support learning.
- There is evidence of student work and input in the physical appearance of the room. (p. 339)

The RLE focuses its attention on the development of a dynamic physical environment both within and without the school walls and a supportive social and emotional environment among peers and students. An example of the RLE in action is the "school within a school" model that allows for small teams of teachers to interact with students in a common undertaking in academic, creative, or artistic areas. Students in this type of program get a rare opportunity to interact with cooperating faculty in a relatively open environment while still within the school walls. Students can attend the regular classroom for the bulk of their day and visit the common areas at different times throughout the day to continue their investigations and relationships with their extended educational family.

Maker's Active Problem Solver Model Maker (1993) builds her curricular interventions around a theoretical conception of the gifted person as "a problem solver—one who enjoys the challenge of complexity and persists until the problem is solved in a satisfying way" (p. 7). The role of the teacher, then, is to facilitate and arrange

Letting students choose the kinds of problems they wish to study and how they will go about their investigations is one method for differentiating curriculum for students with outstanding academic abilities.

the intellectual, emotional, and physical environment to make it possible for high achievement and creativity to take place. Formerly, this differentiation was thought to require a special teacher, a special classroom, and special materials; however, the current realities of fiscal and intellectual retrenchment have modified the demand for such accommodations. The demands of modifying and individualizing curriculum should not be underestimated, given the multitude of other pressing concerns that comprise the day-to-day life in the regular classroom.

Maker (1982) proposes a process by which the key elements of content, process, products, and the environment of a child's learning situation can be modified.

- *Content modifications.* The content of a curriculum is the type of subject matter being taught. In general, the goal is to develop content that is more advanced, complex, innovative, and original than what is usually encountered in the classroom.
- *Process modifications.* The strategies and methods used in delivering the content to learners are key features of instruction. The goal is to provide students with many opportunities to actively respond to the content, including independent research, cooperative learning, peer coaching, simulations, and apprenticeships.
- *Product modifications.* The products of learning are the outcomes associated with instruction. The goal is to encourage a variety of ways that students can present their thoughts, ideas, and results.
- *Environment modifications.* The learning environment is both the physical characteristics of the setting(s) and the ambiance created by the teachers or facilitators. The goal is first to establish a positive working environment and then to rearrange the layout. Such ideas as peer tutoring, learning centers, management sheets, and learning packets can help students take more active control and interest over their learning.

One teacher who uses Maker's model of curriculum design and delivery is Shirly Begay, a high school English teacher at the Rock Point Community School in Rock Point, Arizona. She discusses the way she integrates the various aspects of the curriculum with the underlying theory of multiple intelligences and problem-solving emphasis.

> We follow a problem-solving model. When I presented the first lesson, I wanted the students to become familiar with what I was talking about, so I used illustrations. I said, "You can't be hasty about solving a problem, or you'll be considered a sloppy problem solver. You'll come up with sloppy solutions, sloppy alternatives, and sloppy options." I wanted them to spend plenty of time gathering ideas and thinking about the answers to the questionnaires they sent out.
>
> Most of the time when we introduce problem solving to children, we want them to imagine and make up problems, but this time I wanted them to think of the problems faced by teenagers in this remote area. They brainstormed and then selected problems they didn't want their children to have. We are hoping to remedy some of these problems. I know we can't do away with most of them, but we can lessen the pressure of some, especially if we look at them in different ways. I don't want the students' ideas to stop in the classroom. I want them to write the results for publication in the school's newspaper or to read them to the chapter presidents, chapter officers, or the school board.
>
> For this problem-solving experience, I wanted the students to create a "before" picture and another after they found solutions and remedied the problem. Most Navajo students like to incorporate artwork into whatever they do. I allow them to do artwork and visual/imaginative things with whatever they have read. Most of the students who are gifted hate to write, but a few of them love to write poems and essays, so I encourage them to use both language and visual art. (cited by Maker, Nielson, & Rogers, 1994, p. 16)

Figure 14.7 shows how Krystal, an 8-year-old girl who had been identified by the DISCOVER process, demonstrated her giftedness in logical-mathematical problem solving in response to open-ended math questions. The answers by another 8-year-old girl with the exact same score on a standardized quantitative reasoning test show why Maker and her colleagues considered Krystal gifted in logical-mathematical problem solving. Instead of giving just one answer to question 11 through 14, as the other child did, Krystal provided all possible combinations and showed an early understanding of the reversibility of operations. On the last question, Krystal used a clear logical strategy for generating alternatives (1 + 9, 2 + 8, 3 + 7, etc.), another important aspect of mathematical reasoning. When working with the tangram puzzles, Krystal had taken them apart and solved them without any prompting or clues before anyone else in her group.

The Autonomous Learner Model The Autonomous Learner Model (ALM) was developed by Betts (1985) to meet the cognitive, social, and emotional needs of gifted students. The guiding philosophy of the approach originated in the work of

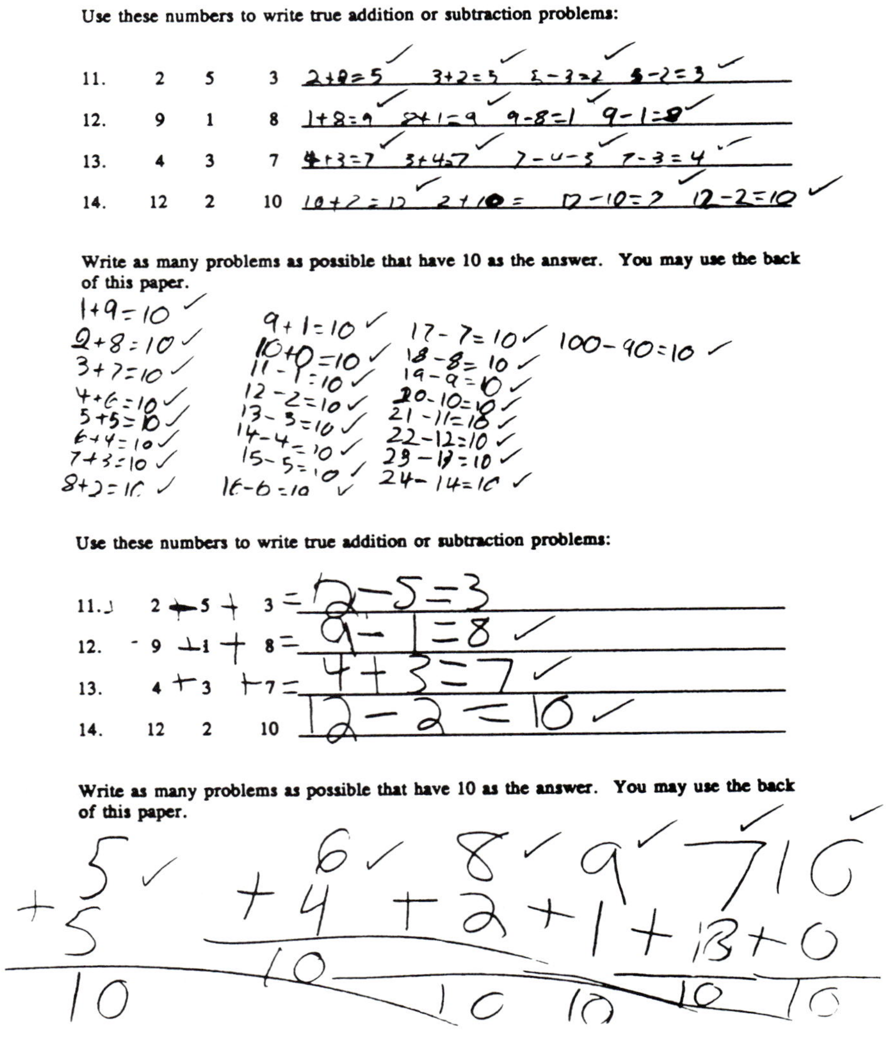

Use these numbers to write true addition or subtraction problems:

11. 2 5 3 — 2+3=5 3+2=5 5−3=2 5−2=3
12. 9 1 8 — 1+8=9 8+1=9 9−8=1 9−1=8
13. 4 3 7 — 4+3=7 3+4=7 7−4=3 7−3=4
14. 12 2 10 — 10+2=12 2+10=12 12−10=2 12−2=10

Write as many problems as possible that have 10 as the answer. You may use the back of this paper.

1+9=10 2+8=10 3+7=10 4+6=10 5+5=10 6+4=10 7+3=10 8+2=10
9+1=10 10+0=10 11−1=10 12−2=10 13−3=10 14−4=10 15−5=10 16−6=10
17−7=10 18−8=10 19−9=10 20−10=10 21−11=10 22−12=10 23−13=10 24−14=10
100−90=10

Use these numbers to write true addition or subtraction problems:

11. 2 5 3 — 2−5=3
12. 9 1 8 — 9−1=8
13. 4 3 7 — 4+3=7
14. 12 2 10 — 12−2=10

Write as many problems as possible that have 10 as the answer. You may use the back of this paper.

5+5=10 6+4=10 8+2=10 9+1=10 7+3=10 10+0=10

Figure 14.7 Logical-mathematical problem solving by an 8-year-old girl identified through the DISCOVER process. Answers by another 8-year-old girl with the same score on a standardized math test are also shown.

Source: From "Giftedness, Diversity, and Problem-Solving" by C. J. Maker, A. B. Nielson, & J. A. Rogers. *Teaching Exceptional Children, 27*(1), 1994, p. 10. © 1994 by the Council for Exceptional Children. Reprinted with permission.

Tannenbaum (1983), who advocated that instruction should go beyond the prescribed role of students as consumers of information to that of producers of knowledge. The ALM was designed to be done in a special class setting by a specially trained teacher, with a great deal of community involvement and support. The program has five sequential steps that move the students from an initial state of awareness to complete (autonomous) control over their learning within a 2½- to 3-year period. These are the five dimensions of the ALM:

- *Orientation* provides a foundation in aspects of the model and expectations for students, educators, parents, and community members.
- *Individual development* gives students the appropriate skills, concepts, and attitudes for lifelong learning as they become autonomous learners.
- *Enrichment activities* develop student-based content as opposed to content prescribed by teachers and other adults. Students explore new content and are given the opportunity to decide what they want to study and how.
- *Seminars* emphasize the production of ideas and topics. Learners work together in small groups and develop a seminar that they use to present their ideas and findings.
- *In-depth study* allows the students long-term opportunities to pursue topics of their choice either alone or in small groups.

The ALM is a combination in- and out-of-school model that attempts to provide a *saturated learning environment* for gifted and talented students. Because the model is designed specifically for gifted and talented students, teachers are able to engage in both highly individualized activities and collaborative group enrichment activities out in the community. A unique feature of this program is the non-negotiable requirement that students engage in service activities in which they must contribute their time and effort for direct involvement with people who need help. This service includes activities such as volunteering at a hospital or clinic for AIDS patients, providing food and other supplies for homeless or disadvantaged families, and tutoring children with learning problems.

Current Issues and Future Trends

The current ethos surrounding the development and provision of special education services to gifted and talented students involves movement on several fronts:

- The conceptual and definitional nature of giftedness is being more intensively questioned.
- There is a possibility that almost all services for gifted and talented students may originate with the regular teacher from within the regular classroom.
- There is increased pressure to identify and serve students from several underserved populations, including different cultural groups, females, students with disabilities, and children from disadvantaged environments.

First, advocates and writers in the field are growing increasingly wary of the term *gifted,* realizing that in some ways it perpetuates the myth that talent is predetermined and not the result of extensive effort on the part of students, teachers, parents, and communities. It simply makes it too easy for society as a whole to ignore these students' needs and to ascribe their growth and development (or lack thereof) to uncontrollable, unseen forces beyond the reach of our instructional interventions. An unintended result is that both individuals and societal institutions can assert that because these students can easily make it on their own, they need no extra help from society. If only the misconception that all of these students make it were true! The available data indicate that large numbers of students who would qualify for gifted and talented services drop out of school and that many more students who are culturally different, disabled, or economically disadvantaged are never even identified. Estimates of this group of underachieving gifted students range from 10% to 20% of all high school dropouts (Davis & Rimm, 1994). An equally disturbing finding is that 40% of the top 5% of the high school graduates do not complete college (DeLeon, 1989).

Second, there is a growing awareness that gifted advocates will need to reconceptualize special services to gifted and talented students in a manner that differs from the traditional model of a gifted teacher in a segregated gifted classroom (Hertzog, 1998). Most of the newer instructional models (e.g., Renzulli's Schoolwide Enrichment Model, Maker's Active Problem Solver Model) occur within the regular classroom and depend heavily on interactions within the community, with few requiring a special teacher or classroom. There are obvious and important impacts on teacher training, classroom management, and curriculum if the regular classroom becomes the dominant educational service setting in U.S. schools. It is likely there will be an increased emphasis on collaboration rather than on independent instruction. This emphasis implies that teachers of the gifted will have to work closely with regular classroom educators to provide services to gifted and talented students. Finally, the increasingly sophisticated use of technological tools and related methods will provide gifted students with greater connectivity and independence in the future. In some cases, this ability to communicate with persons from distant and differing cultures and languages will provide new avenues of expression for gifted and talented students. In addition, the ability to explore topics in greater depth through the use of global data bases and to create interactive presentations about their discoveries will allow gifted and talented students to become more independent and exert greater self-determination over their own learning.

Third, increasing numbers of persons are advocating more accurate and inclusive identification procedures that provide access to special educational services for gifted students who are members of several underserved populations. Persons who have high ability or talent comprise a very different group of exceptional learners, but it is important to remember that all talent, including exceptional talent, can suffer from a lack of quality educational experiences, informative feedback, and emotional support. Students who exhibit high ability and talent are susceptible to the same fears and frustrations that come with a lack of interest or understanding of their needs and abilities regardless of race, gender, socioeconomic status, and disability status.

For information on counseling gifted and talented students, see Delisle (1992); Genshaft, Bireley, and Hollinger (1995); Silverman (1993); and Van Tassel-Baska (1990).

In addition, there is a pressing need to provide counseling services to gifted and talented students. Gallagher (1990) points out that our track record of understanding and then facilitating the emotional growth of gifted and talented students is weak to nonexistent. As with all children and adults, a number of predictable and unpredictable crises will occur throughout their lives. With their heightened sense of social justice and greater awareness of the needs of others, students who are gifted and talented often experience confusion and estrangement with more depth than their peers.

Use the self-tests at http://www.prenhall.com/heward to assess your knowledge of the content of Chapter 14.

Gifted and talented students need special education; they need differentiated curriculum, instructional strategies, materials, and experiences that allow them to realize their potential. As we face increasingly complex problems in the global society of the future, we will need as much help as we can get from our citizenry. There are new approaches and perspectives concerning the manner in which students are identified and services are delivered that reflect insights into the way humans learn and create. These innovations promise to provide students with high ability and talents a brighter learning future that returns benefits to the country and world in which they live.

Summary

Defining Giftedness and Talent

- The federal government defines gifted and talented children as those exhibiting high performance capability in intellectual, creative, and/or artistic areas; possessing an unusual leadership capacity; or excelling in specific academic fields.
- Renzulli's definition of giftedness is based on the traits of above-average general abilities, high level of task commitment, and creativity.
- Feldhusen's definition of giftedness emphasizes talent as the primary defining characteristic.
- Piirto defines the gifted as having superior memory, observational powers, curiosity, creativity, and ability to learn.
- Maker defines the gifted and talented student as a problem solver who is capable of (1) creating a new or clearer definition of an existing problem, (2) devising new and more efficient or effective methods, and (3) reaching solutions that may be different from the usual.

Characteristics of Students Who Are Gifted and Talented

- Learning and intellectual characteristics of gifted and talented students include the ability to do the following:
  - Rapidly acquire, retain, and use large amounts of information
  - Relate one idea to another
  - Make sound judgments
  - Perceive the operation of larger systems of knowledge that may not be recognized by the ordinary citizen
  - Acquire and manipulate abstract symbol systems
  - Solve problems by reframing the question and creating novel solutions
- Gifted children are by no means perfect, and their unusual talents and abilities may make them either withdrawn or difficult to manage in the classroom.
- Gifted students need both basic and advanced content knowledge and the abilities to use and develop that knowledge effectively.
- Many gifted children are creative. Although there is no universally accepted definition of creativity, we know that creative children have knowledge, examine it in a variety of ways, critically analyze the outcomes, and communicate their ideas.
- Guilford includes dimensions of fluency, flexibility, originality, and elaboration in his definition of creativity.

Prevalence

- The most commonly cited prevalence estimate is that gifted students make up 3% to 5% of the school-age population.

Identification and Assessment

- IQ tests are one, but not necessarily the best, means for identifying students with high intellectual ability.
- The usual means of identification include a combination of IQ scores; creativity and achievement measures; teacher, parent, and peer nominations; and self-nomination.
- Maker's DISCOVER procedure can be used to equitably identify gifted and talented females as well as students from diverse cultural groups.
- Teachers and parents can foster the intellectual and talent development of children with disabilities by conveying positive, realistic expectations; encouraging independence; guiding constructive coping strategies; providing daily opportunities to build abilities and enjoy success; and pursuing positive social experiences for the child.

Educational Approaches

- Three approaches to educating gifted and talented students are acceleration, curriculum compacting, and enrichment.
- Four models for teaching gifted students are Renzulli's Schoolwide Enrichment Model, Clark's Responsive Learning Environment, Maker's Active Problem Solver Model, and Betts's Autonomous Learner Model.

Current Issues and Future Trends

- The conceptual and definitional nature of giftedness is being more intensively questioned.
- Most services for gifted and talented students will probably originate from the regular teacher within the regular classroom.
- The importance of identifying gifted and talented students among females, individuals with disabilities, and diverse cultural groups is now recognized. We need better procedures for identifying, assessing, teaching, and encouraging these children.
- As we have seen with other exceptional children, we must improve society's attitudes toward gifted and talented children if we are to improve their futures.

For More Information

Journals

- *Gifted Child Quarterly.* Published four times per year by the National Association for Gifted Children (see "Organizations"). Publishes articles by both parents and teachers of gifted children.
- *Gifted Child Today* (formerly *G/C/T*). Published six times per year by GCT, 350 Weinacker Avenue, Mobile, AL 36604. Publishes articles aimed at parents and teachers of gifted, talented, and creative youngsters.

- *Gifted International.* Published semiannually by the World Council for Gifted and Talented Children, Dr. Dorothy Sisk, Secretariat, Lamar University, College of Education, P.O. Box 10034, Beaumont, TX 77710. Devoted to international communication among educators, researchers, and parents.
- *Journal for the Education of the Gifted.* Published quarterly by the Association for the Gifted (TAG) (see "Organizations"). Presents theoretical, descriptive, and research articles with diverse ideas and points of view on the education of gifted and talented students.
- *Journal of Creative Behavior.* Published by Creative Educational Foundation, State University College, 1300 Elmwood Avenue, Buffalo, NY 14222. Devoted to research reports and program suggestions and designed to understand and enhance creative behavior in children and adults.
- *Roeper Review.* Published quarterly by the Roeper City and Country Schools, 2190 North Woodward, Bloomfield Hills, MI 48013. Publishes articles by teachers, researchers, and students in gifted education.

Books

- Berger, S. L. (1994). *College planning for gifted students* (2nd ed.). Reston, VA: Council for Exceptional Children.
- Clark, B. (1997). *Growing up gifted: Developing the potential of children at home and at school* (5th ed.). Upper Saddle River, NJ: Merrill/Prentice Hall.
- Colangelo, N., & Davis, G. A. (Eds.). (1997). *Handbook of gifted education* (2nd ed.). Needham Heights, MA: Allyn & Bacon.
- Davis, G. A., & Rimm, S. B. (1994). *Education of gifted and talented* (3rd ed.). Boston: Allyn & Bacon.
- Gallagher, J. J., & Gallagher, S. (1994). *Teaching the gifted child* (4th ed.). Needham Heights, MA: Allyn & Bacon.
- Genshaft, J. L., Bireley, M., & Hollinger, C. L. (Eds.). (1995). *Serving gifted and talented students: A resource for school personnel.* Austin, TX: PRO-ED.
- Heller, K. A., Monks, F. J., & Passow, A. H. (Eds.). (1993). *International handbook of research and development of giftedness and talent.* Tarrytown, NY: Pergamon.
- Maker, C. J. (Ed.). (1993). *Critical issues in gifted education: Programs for the gifted in regular classrooms.* Austin, TX: PRO-ED.
- Maker, C. J., & Nielson, A. B. (1995). *Teaching models in education of the gifted* (2nd ed.). Austin, TX: PRO-ED.
- Maker, C. J., & Nielson, A. B. (1996). *Curriculum development and teaching strategies for gifted learners* (2nd ed.). Austin, TX: PRO-ED.
- Piirto, J. (1999). *Talented children and adults: Their development and education* (2nd ed.). Upper Saddle River, NJ: Merrill/Prentice Hall.
- Renzulli, J. S. (1994). *Schools for talent development: A practical plan for total school improvement.* Reston, VA: Council for Exceptional Children.
- Silverman, L. K. (Ed.). (1993). *Counseling the gifted and talented.* Denver: Love.
- Sisk, D. (1987). *Creative teaching of the gifted.* New York: McGraw-Hill.
- Van Tassel-Baska, J. (Ed.). (1990). *A practical guide to counseling the gifted in a school setting* (2nd ed.). Reston, VA: Council for Exceptional Children.
- Van Tassel-Baska, J. (Ed.). (1994). *Comprehensive curriculum for gifted learners* (2nd ed.). Needham Heights, MA: Allyn & Bacon.

Organizations

- *American Creativity Association,* P.O. Box 26068, St. Paul, MN 55126. Promotes creativity in business, education, the arts, sciences, and social and political decision making.
- *Association for the Gifted (TAG),* Council for Exceptional Children, 1920 Association Drive, Reston, VA 22091; (703) 620-3660; website: http://www.cec.sped.org. A growing division of CEC that includes teachers, teacher educators, administrators, and others interested in gifted and talented children.
- *Future Problem Solving International,* 2500 Packard, Suite 110, Ann Arbor, MI 48104-6827; (313) 973-8781 or (800) 256-1499; website: http://www.fpsp.org/toc.htmt. Four-person teams learn and apply a six-step creative thinking process to solve three annually determined problems. Solutions are mailed to trained evaluators, who provide feedback.
- *Gifted Child Society,* Suite 6, 190 Rock Road, Glen Rock, NJ 07452; (210) 444-6530; website: http://www.gifted.org. An organization for parents; also offers information and in-service training for educators.
- *Junior Great Books Foundation,* 40 East Huron, Chicago, IL 60611.
- *Mensa, Gifted Child Program,* 201 Main Street NW; (817) 332-7299; website: http://www.us.mensa.org.
- *National Association for Gifted Children,* 1707 L Street NW, Suite 550, Washington, DC 20036; (202) 785-4268; website: http://www.nagc.org. An organization for parents, professionals, and others interested in gifted and talented children.
- *National Research Center on the Gifted and Talented (NRC/GT),* University of Connecticut, Storrs, CT 06269-2007; (860) 486-4678; website: http://www.ucc.uconn.edu/~wwwgt.
- *Odyssey of the Mind,* OM Association, P.O. Box 547, Glassboro, NJ 08028.
- *World Council for Gifted and Talented Children,* 210 Lindquist Center, University of Iowa, Iowa City, IA 53342; website: http://www.uiowa.edu/-belinctr. Promotes worldwide communication on issues related to the education and development of gifted children.

Chapter 15

Transition to Adulthood

Focus Questions

- How can special education programs for school-age children with disabilities prepare them for successful transition to life as adults?
- What are the most appropriate and effective programs and services for supporting adults with disabilities in their efforts to find and keep meaningful work, to locate a home, or to use community recreation centers?
- How can services such as sheltered employment programs, which are designed and intended to help adults with disabilities, also limit their participation in life activities?
- Does it make sense for society to provide the ongoing supports a person with severe disabilities needs to work and live in the community?
- Why must quality of life be the ultimate outcome measure for special education?

What happens to youth with disabilities when they leave school and enter the adult world? Do graduates of special education programs find work? Where do they live? How do the lives of adults with disabilities compare with the expectations and experiences of most citizens? How do adults with disabilities rate their quality of life: are they happy? How can special education interrelate its goals and services with those of other human service agencies, such as vocational education and rehabilitation, residential services, and community recreation programs to support the successful transition of students with disabilities to the adult world?

Obtaining answers to these questions has become the highest priority for many special educators today. We begin by taking a look at the results of several studies that focus on what is perhaps the most important question of all regarding the ultimate effectiveness of special education: what do students with disabilities do after they leave school?

How Do Former Special Education Students Fare As Adults?

More than 50 studies of graduates and leavers of secondary special education programs provide enlightening information on their experiences as young adults. The research methodology used to determine postschool outcomes for young adults with disabilities consists primarily of *follow-up* and *follow-along* studies that obtain information via interviews, surveys, or direct observation of former students, their parents, and/or employers.

A follow-up study *collects information at a single point in time (e.g., one or two years after a student's graduating class leaves school) and shows a "snapshot" of adult adjustment. A* follow-along study *collects information on postschool outcomes at multiple points in time and enables the assessment of progress over time (Darrow & Clark, 1992).*

Employment Status

Between 50% and 75% of all adults with disabilities are unemployed, "depending on which survey you choose to review" (Wehman, 1992, p. 112). Here are results from some of those studies:

- Data from the National Longitudinal Transition Study (NLTS) show an unemployment rate of 46% for all youth with disabilities who have been out of school for less then two years.
- The unemployment rate for young adults with disabilities drops to 36.5% when they have been out of school for three to five years, but nearly one in five persons (19.6%) states she has given up looking for work (NLTS).
- The employment outcomes outlook is much worse for students with severe and multiple disabilities. According to one study, the unemployment rate for 117 young adults with moderate, severe, or profound mental retardation who had left public school special education programs in Virginia was 78.6% (Wehman, Kregel, & Seyfarth, 1985b). Similarly, NLTS found an employment rate of only 17% for young adults with multiple disabilities three to five years after secondary school.
- Extremely low employment rates three to five years after secondary school have also been reported for young adults with orthopedic impairments (22%) and visual impairments (29%) (NLTS).
- Between one-half and two-thirds of young adults with disabilities who are employed work in part-time jobs (e.g., Scuccimarra & Speece, 1990; Sitlington & Frank, 1990; Sitlington, Frank, & Carson, 1993).

NLTS is an ongoing effort to assess and monitor changes in the adult adjustment of youth with disabilities after they leave secondary special education programs. NLTS has tracked more than 8,000 youths with disabilities who left U.S. secondary special education programs between 1985 and 1987. Several major reports of NLTS findings have been issued (Blackorby & Wagner, 1996; Wagner, 1991; Wagner, D'Amico, Marder, Newman, & Blackorby, 1993).

Go to the companion website at http://www.prenhall.com/heward and select Chapter 15 to review the chapter objectives.

Wages and Benefits

The incomes of many individuals with disabilities hover near the poverty level (Mithaug, Horiuchi, & Fanning, 1985; Scuccimarra & Speece, 1990) and relatively few receive benefits.

- Median hourly wage for all youth with disabilities was $5.72, less than $12,000 per year for full-time, year-round employment (NLTS).
- Of all youth with disabilities who had jobs three to five years after school, only 40% earned more than $6.00 per hour (NLTS).
- Although the employment earnings of high school graduates with learning disabilities is slightly higher than peers without disabilities for the first four years after leaving school (because most of their peers are attending college), by the fifth year the earnings of graduates without disabilities "increasingly outpaced those of their peers with LD" (Goldstein, Murray, & Edgar, 1998, p. 60).
- The average hourly pay for individuals with mental retardation who were working in sheltered workshops three years after graduating from high school was $1.59 (Frank & Sitlington, 1993).
- Less than half of employed youth with mental retardation received health insurance, sick leave, or vacation benefits (Frank & Sitlington, 1993).

Sheltered workshops are discussed later in the chapter.

Postsecondary Education

Attending college and postsecondary vocational programs greatly increases the likelihood of obtaining employment and generally experiencing "success" as an adult. Compared with their peers without disabilities, fewer former special education students pursue postsecondary education.

- Three years after graduation, two out of three young adults with mental retardation who were interviewed by Frank and Sitlington (1993) reported they had participated in no postsecondary training of any kind.
- A follow-up of 1,242 youths with disabilities who had been out of school for one year found that 15% had taken at least one postsecondary course, compared with 56% of youth without disabilities (Fairweather & Shaver, 1991).
- NLTS found that 27% of young adults who had left high school had enrolled in postsecondary education programs within three to five years, compared with 68% of the general same-age population (Blackorby & Wagner, 1996).

The percentage of first-time, full-time freshmen enrolled in college who indicate they have a disability has increased significantly in recent years (Henderson, 1992). The majority are students with learning disabilities. For information on promoting the success of postsecondary education for students with learning disabilities, see Brinckerhoff, Shaw, and McGuire (1993); Garten, Rumrill, and Serebreni (1996); and Skinner (1998).

Dropouts

Students who do not complete high school are likely to face more difficulties in adult adjustment than those who do. Special education students who do not complete school are more likely to have lower levels of employment and wages and higher rates of problems with the criminal justice system than those who finish (Malian & Love, 1998; Wagner, Blackorby, Cameto, & Newman, 1994). A "staggering number" of special education students drop out of school (Patton, Cronin, & Jairrels, 1997, p. 295). Only 58% of the more than 220,000 teenagers and young adults with disabilities who exited from the public schools during the 1991–92 school year graduated with either a diploma or a certificate of completion; 22% of students with disabilities dropped out, and 18% exited for "unknown" reasons before they finished (U.S. Department of Education, 1994). Although many high school dropouts resume their secondary education or obtain a general education development (GED) diploma,

Requirements for graduation and the type of exit document (i.e., standard diploma, modified diploma, or certificate of completion) for students with disabilities vary tremendously from state to state. See Thurlow, Ysseldyke, and Reid (1997) for a review.

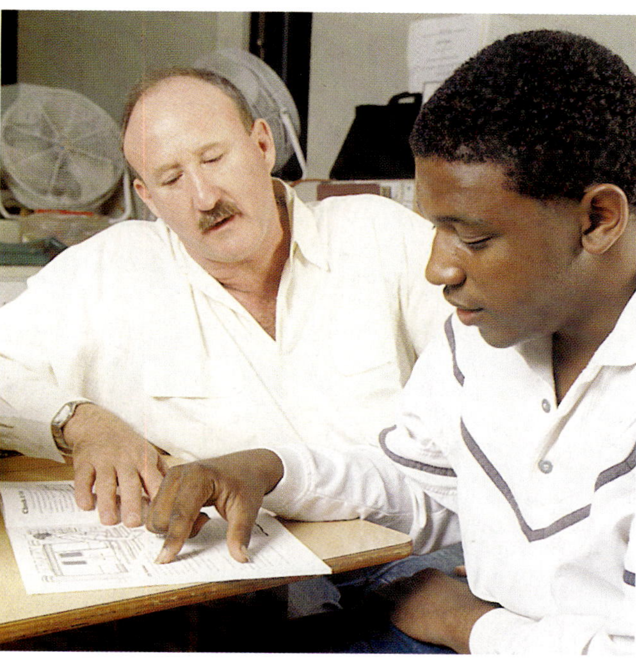

The percentage of students with disabilities attending college and postsecondary education programs has increased significantly in recent years. Most are students with learning disabilities.

TEACHING AND LEARNING IN SCHOOL

A Friendship Program for Future Special Education Teachers

by Jill C. Dardig

Scott and Ted, both big sports fans, attended several local basketball and baseball games together. They cheered for the Pickerington High School Lady Tigers in the state tournament and scarfed frank after frank on Dime-a-Dog Night at a Columbus Clippers game. Kelly and Kami went out to dinner at several of their favorite restaurants. They also spent some quiet nights at home baking brownies, looking at family pictures, and just talking. Paula and Todd attended a concert, went to the mall, and spent an evening with popcorn and a video at Todd's apartment.

Scott, Kelly, and Paula, all college students learning to become special education teachers, were doing their fieldwork for a required course called "Focus on Adults with Disabilities." Each student in this class is paired with an adult with developmental disabilities living in a group home, family home, or supported living apartment in the community. Each student spends time getting to know her new friend on an informal and personal basis and planning some at-home and community-based activities they can enjoy together during the semester. Students function as friends or companions. In this way, they are able to look at their special friends in a different light—not as a school-age child but as a similar-aged peer who is learning to be an independent adult.

After meeting with his friend (and sometimes group home or supported living staff) to determine what the friend might enjoy doing, each college student designs a clear and attractive calendar or schedule of planned activities. The schedule may be written; but if the friend cannot read, the scheduled activities are illustrated by photos, pictures, symbols, or objects (e.g., a menu, a K-Mart ad, a puzzle piece, or a page from *TV Guide*). This schedule allows the friend to anticipate and prepare for each activity and provides cues for friends, family, and caregivers to ask questions and discuss the person's weekly activities.

Date	Time	Icon	Activity
Feb. 19	4:00 - 7:00		Drawing & Painting
Feb. 26	4:00 - 7:00		Winter Hike/Sharon Woods
Mar. 5	4:00 - 7:00		Videos & Popcorn
Mar. 19	4:00 - 7:00	Wal-Mart	Shopping/Dining
Mar. 26	4:00 - 7:00	PUZZLES	Games & Puzzles
Apr. 2	4:00 - 7:00		Movie/Dining
Apr. 9	4:00 - 7:00		Walk in the Park/Dining
Apr. 16	4:00 - 7:00		Popcorn & Video
Apr. 23	4:00 - 7:00		The Mall/Dining
Apr. 30	4:00 - 7:00	Surprise?	?????

Using computer-generated icons, Susan Snyder prepared this schedule of activities for her friend Terry.

We Both Had a Good Time Students also keep a journal. They record and reflect on their activities and pay special attention to identifying which skills their friend is lacking that she could have learned in school to enable the person to become more independent in the home and community settings as an adult. Here are some journal entries from a recent class:

> We visited the Northland Mall, where we wandered in and out of stores. Mary and I tried on a pair of high heels, and we both had a good time laughing as we attempted to walk. (Norma Bernstein)

> Upon returning to his apartment, Ted was very happy, almost ecstatic. He acted out dribbling and shooting a basketball, to let everyone know that he and his "Special Friend" had gone to a game. This made me feel fantastic, and I could sense that we were starting to bond. (Scott Martin)

Scott included Ted in some everyday activities like gassing up and washing his car—both by hand and in an automatic car wash. Ted was thrilled; he had never participated in these activities with a friend before.

I did not know what to expect on my first "date" with Jack. Nothing had been planned, and I expected to stay around the home so that we could get acquainted. Jack must have seen me pull in because he was waiting outside with his hat and jacket on. He wanted to see my truck. I don't just mean looking at my truck, I mean getting in, listening to the radio, and examining everything. It was a good ice-breaker, and we sat outside for some time. (Dean Scheiderer)

After dinner, Kami and I went shopping at the Target department store. Kami picked out a card for her brother's birthday and helped me choose a present for my newborn nephew. After Target, we went to a pet store, since she loves animals. (Kelly Byers)

If Edna Could Redo Her Education Aside from having a good time, students completing this field placement gained many valuable insights. Their most frequent observation and strongest recommendation had to do with many of their friends' lack of social skills. Several students noticed that basic social skills, such as saying "please" when requesting items, greeting the student when she arrived, and shaking hands and saying "thank you" at the end of the evening, were lacking. Students thought that many of these important skills could have been acquired easily and naturally if their friends had experienced early inclusion with their nondisabled peers while participating in informal school and community activities.

Edna and I spent a lot of our time at the City Center Mall—an activity she had expressed an interest in. It turned out to be quite an experience. Edna had a difficult time navigating her way around people; she seemed to just "bulldoze" ahead without going around people or other obstacles. We browsed in many stores and had pizza there too, and Edna had a great time. As soon as we got back to her home, however, she vanished without a word. . . . Later, during a trip to the movies and out to dinner, Edna spoke very loudly and annoyed other customers. Edna can be such a pleasant and nice young woman, but she seems oblivious to others around her. I can't help but think this would not be the case if she had spent some time with her nondisabled peers more while growing up. . . . If Edna could redo her education, I think she would have benefited from spending time, both in and outside school, with her nondisabled peers. (Barbara Miller)

Scott Martin concurred: "Inclusion early on would have been an excellent help with Ted's verbal and social skills."

Another critical skill that many of the friends lacked was the ability to make choices.

Today, Kami and I went to dinner at Pizza Hut. We continued to talk about our families and our work. I noticed Kami waits for me to do everything. Open the door, serve the food, anything that requires a decision. (Kelly Byers)

A really big difference was that [in spending time with Ted] I always took the lead with decision making. I had to be sure to wait and prompt responses from him, or else I would not have known which store he wanted to visit or what flavor of ice cream he preferred. (Scott Martin)

Future teachers can keep this in mind and give students repeated opportunities to choose snacks, books, and leisure-time activities.

Appropriate affect and expression of feelings were other areas in which many adults had some difficulty.

Todd lacks a sense of humor. I usually associate with people who like to have fun and laugh. It was very hard for me to relate to Todd, who hardly ever laughed or seemed to want to have a good time. (Paula Kruer)

Many students observed that their adult friends, even if they were quite verbal, did not have adequate conversation skills. Some adults could answer questions but did not ask questions of the students or initiate conversation.

Edna apparently has little or no concept of friendship. Her life experiences have provided her with the model that adults are "providers." Our conversation was usually one-sided, with me asking her a lot of questions, but rarely was the reverse true. She never asked me when she would see me again. (Barbara Miller)

Money-handling skills were also identified as critically important in making a person more adept in the community, and many of the adults experienced difficulty paying for items independently.

Ben could have been taught basic skills that would have been helpful in integrating him into society. Handling money transactions and telling time could have prevented the need for someone to keep track of Ben's every move in stores and restaurants. (Beth Wahl)

Another area in which some of the adults were weak were self-care skills.

I believe that Mary could have been taught basic hygiene, housekeeping, and social skills during her school years so that she could enjoy more independence and less frustration as she deals with these issues now. (Norma Bernstein)

This placement helped me realize the need for an emphasis in schools to be placed on daily living skills,

skills that students will need when they become adults living in the community. It will be helpful to remember this when I become a teacher. (Beth Wahl)

Thinking Beyond Today's Activities and Experiences Although the students who take this course will be certified to teach K–12 students, spending time with an adult will help them as teachers to become more future-oriented in their instruction—to think beyond the day's activities or the week's goals for a particular child with a disability. This experience will help teachers select and teach functional skills to their school-age students so that eventually they will be as fully integrated into the community as possible.

> This experience will enable me to visualize students as adults and thus to think ahead to behaviors that may or may not be appropriate when my student is 22 years old and beyond. No matter what grade level I teach, I will have a much clearer view of which skills are functional, which are not, and which will allow my students to take full advantage of the world around them. (Janet Fleming)

If your teacher-training program does not offer a course such as this one, you can arrange to get to know a special friend as a volunteer through a local group home or an advocacy agency. Developing a special friendship with an adult with disabilities will help you become a more responsive and effective teacher of children and youth with special needs.

Jill C. Dardig is a professor of education at Ohio Dominican College in Columbus, where she trains special education teachers.

The case studies of four young adults with learning disabilities who had dropped out of high school "cast doubt on the prevailing opinion that school dropouts are 'losers' and 'failures'" (Lichtenstein, 1993, p. 336). Their personal stories reveal both the shortfalls and inadequacies of the secondary special education and transition services they had received and the "considerable resiliency" in the former students' efforts to seek out jobs, develop friendships, gain alternative education credentials, and pursue career ambitions. Case studies describing the transition experiences of four young adults with mental retardation can be found in Lichtenstein and Michaelides (1993).

only 3% of youth with disabilities had completed a program to earn a high school diploma within three to five years after they had dropped out (Wagner et al., 1993).

Factors found to reduce the probability that a student with disabilities will drop out include low absenteeism, job-specific vocational experience, receiving individual attention such as tutoring or counseling, socializing with other students outside school, and joining extracurricular activities (Wagner, 1991). Strategies for combating dropouts among students with disabilities can be found in Cohen and deBettencourt (1991); Diem and Katims (1991); Lovitt (1991); and Thurlow, Christenson, Sinclair, Evelo, & Thornton (1995).

Living Arrangement and Community Participation

Adults with disabilities face numerous obstacles in day-to-day living that affect where and how they live, how well they can use community resources, and their opportunities for social interaction.

- After being out of high school for three to five years, only 37% of youth with disabilities were living independently (alone, with a spouse or roommate, in a college dormitory or military housing, not as a dependent), compared with 60% of the general population (NLTS).
- One of every four young adults with learning disabilities indicated he was "dissatisfied" with his social life two years after leaving high school (Scuccimarra & Speece, 1990).
- After being out of high school for three to five years, 51% of young adults with disabilities were registered to vote, compared with 66% of the general population.
- A survey conducted by Louis Harris and associates and reported to Congress in 1986 found that 56% of adults said their disabilities prevented them from moving about the community, attending cultural or sporting events, and socializing with friends outside their homes.

Overall Adjustment and Success

Although useful, isolated statistics do not provide a complete picture of the overall adjustment to adult life experienced by young people with disabilities. Being a successful adult involves much more than holding a job; it is achieving status as an independent and active member of society. Independence for an adult has been defined as the "ability to participate in society, to work, have a home, raise a family, and share the joys and responsibilities of community life" (Stoddard, 1978, quoted in Fisher, 1989, p. 94).

The ongoing NLTS includes a measure of adult adjustment that assesses independent functioning in three domains: (1) employment (competitively employed in a full-time job or engaged in job training or postsecondary education), (2) residential arrangements (living alone or with a spouse or roommate), and (3) social activities (having friends, belonging to social groups). When assessed at a period less than two years out of school, only 6.4% of all youth with disabilities met these three criteria. When the same measures are assessed after individuals have been out of school for three to five years, 20% were judged to be independent in all three domains (Wagner et al., 1993). Even with this significant improvement after several years, four out of every five former special education students had still not achieved the status of independent adulthood after being out of high school for up to five years.

It is important to note that the very small percentage of young adults who met the criteria for "successful" transition to adult life in this study had graduated *from secondary special education programs. Young adults who leave secondary programs by routes other than graduation do not fare as well as those who do complete school with a diploma or certificate (Blackorby & Wagner, 1996; Malian & Love, 1998).*

A follow-up study of graduates of secondary special education programs in Iowa evaluated whether or not transition to adulthood was "successful" as defined by four criteria: (1) employed (full or part time) in a competitive job, a homemaker, a full-time student, or in a job-training program; (2) buying a home, living independently, or living with a friend or spouse; (3) paying at least a portion of one's living expenses; and (4) being involved in more than three different leisure activities (Sitlington et al., 1993). They found only 5.8% of 737 students with learning disabilities, 5 of 142 students with mental retardation (3.5%), and just 1 of 59 students with behavioral disorders could be judged as having made a "successful adult adjustment" one year after they had completed high school (p. 230).

Check your ongoing understanding of Chapter 15 concepts by using the Guided Review Module at http://www.prenhall.com/heward.

Findings such as these have focused attention on what has become a dominant issue in special education today—the transition from school to adult life in the community. No longer can special educators be satisfied with improved performance by students on classroom-related tasks. We must work equally hard to ensure that the education students receive during their school years plays a direct and positive role in helping them deal successfully with the multifaceted demands of adulthood.

Participating in community recreation and leisure activities with an adult with disabilities is an excellent way to appreciate the importance of a functional curriculum for school-age students. See "A Friendship Program for Future Special Education Teachers" earlier in the chapter.

Transition from School to Adult Life: Models and Services

Will's Bridges Model of School-to-Work Transition

In response to growing concern over the failure of so many young adults with disabilities in the job market and community living, Congress authorized funding for secondary education and transitional services for youth with disabilities (Sec. 626) when it amended IDEA in 1983 (P.L. 98–199). Madeline Will, assistant secretary of the U.S. Department of Education and director of the Office of Special Education and Rehabilitation Services, proposed a model of transition services that encompassed three levels of service, each conceptualized as a bridge between the secondary special education curriculum and adult employment (Will, 1986). Each level differs in terms of the nature and extent of the services an individual with disabilities needs to make a successful transition from school to work. At the first level are students who require no special transition services. On graduation from an appropriate secondary special education curriculum, these young adults, presumably those with mild dis-

To find more information about transitions' needs, go to the Resources Module for Chapter 15 at http://www.prenhall.com/heward and link to "families" on the Special Ed Resource Page.

For a history of the transition movement in special education, see Halpern (1992); Neubert (1997); and Rusch, DeStefano, Chadsey-Rusch, Phelps, and Szymanski (1992).

abilities, would make use of the generic employment services already available to people without disabilities in the community (e.g., job placement agencies). At the second level are persons with disabilities who require the time-limited transitional services offered by vocational rehabilitation or adult service agencies that are specially designed to help individuals with disabilities gain competitive, independent employment. The third level of transitional services consists of ongoing employment services that are necessary to enable persons with severe disabilities to enjoy the benefits of meaningful paid work.

Halpern's Three-Dimensional Model

Because it showed the federal government's recognition of the need to improve the employment outcomes for special education students, Will's bridges model for school-to-work transition was viewed as a move in the right direction. Many special educators, however, thought that it offered a too-limited perspective on transition. Halpern (1985) wrote that it is a mistake to focus on adult employment as the sole purpose and outcome of transition services: "Living successfully in one's community should be the primary target of transitional services" (p. 480). Halpern proposed a transition model that directed Will's generic, time-limited, and ongoing support services toward helping students with disabilities adjust to adult life in the community in three domains: (1) the quality of residential environment, (2) adequacy of social and interpersonal network, and (3) meaningful employment (see Figure 15.1).

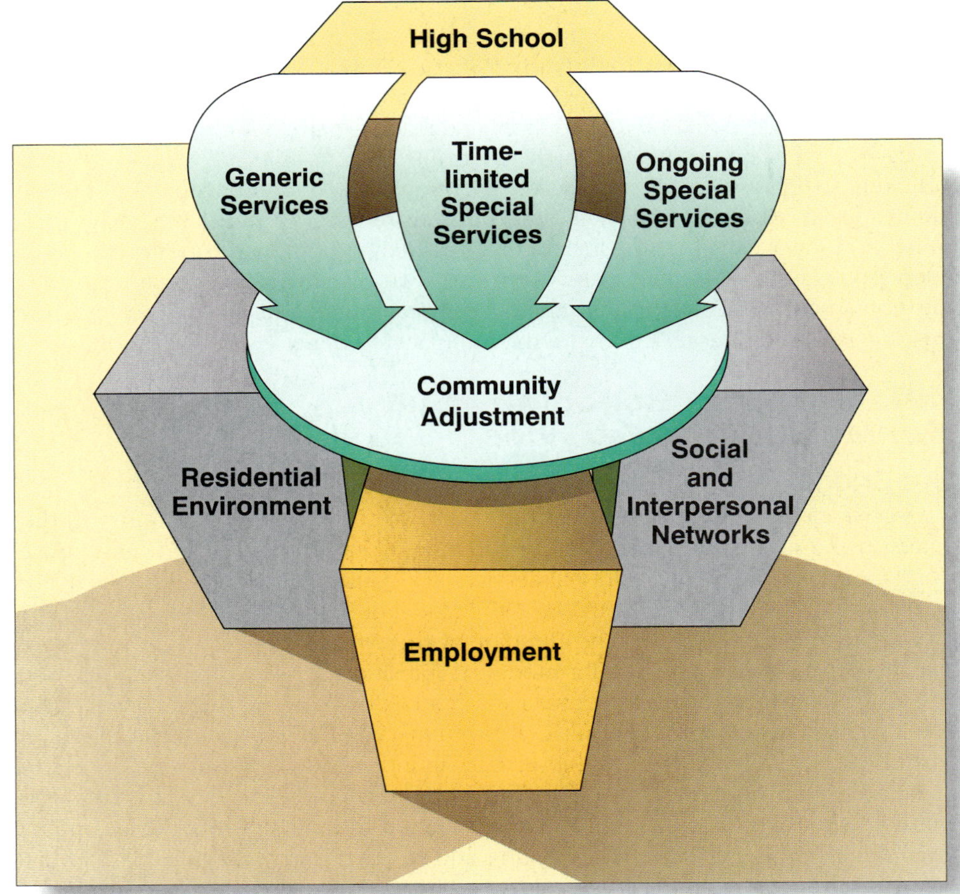

Figure 15.1 Halpern's three-dimensional conceptualization of transition

Source: From "Transition: A Look at the Foundation" by A. S. Halpern. *Exceptional Children, 51,* 1985, p. 481. © 1985 by the Council for Exceptional Children. Reprinted with permission.

The view that transition must focus on all domains of adult functioning characterizes the field today. The 1990 and 1997 amendments to IDEA defined transition services as those aimed at more than employment and mandated that an individualized transition plan would be incorporated into each student's IEP.

Definition of Transition Services

Transition services are defined in IDEA as

> a coordinated set of activities for a student with a disability that:
>
> (a) is designed within an outcome-oriented process, which promotes movement from school to post-school activities, including postsecondary education, vocational training, integrated employment (including supported employment), continuing and adult education, adult services, independent living, or community participation;
> (b) is based upon the individual student's needs, taking into account the student's preferences and interests; and
> (c) includes instruction, related services, community experiences, the development of employment and other post-school adult living objectives, and, when appropriate, acquisition of daily living skills and functional vocational evaluation. (P.L. 105–17, Sec. 602 [30])

Supported employment *is defined and discussed later in the chapter.*

Individualized Transition Plan

To find helpful resources for completing IEPs for planning transitions, go to the Resources Module for Chapter 15 at http://www.prenhall.com/heward and link to "General Disability Info" on the Special Ed Resource Page.

When a student reaches the age of 16, an *individualized transition plan* (ITP) must be developed. The ITP may be written at an earlier age if the IEP team determines it is appropriate for an individual student. Developed and included as part of the IEP process, a student's ITP outlines actions, events, and resources that will affect and support her move from school to adulthood. A well-written ITP details the types of curricular programming and supports that will facilitate a smooth and successful transition to adult life. Here are some key points to remember in developing transition services:

- Postschool outcomes should drive the secondary programming for every student with disabilities over the age of 16.
- Transition plans are designed within an outcome-oriented process based on the student's and family's vision of the future. The student's IEP/ITP team specifies postschool outcomes and goals in four major areas—employment, postsecondary education/training, residential, and recreation/leisure—and then develops an individualized program of instruction and activities designed to reach those outcomes.
- Identify and build the necessary supports and links by developing a transition team consisting of persons who can help in developing or reaching goals, including general education teachers, special education teachers, vocational education teachers, related services personnel, adult agency personnel such as higher education and vocational rehabilitation counselors, and mental retardation/developmental disabilities adult services agencies.
- Transition is a process involving the coordination, delivery, and transfer of services from the secondary school program to receiving agencies (e.g., employers, postsecondary education and vocational training programs, residential service providers; Edgar, 1987). Although work-study and vocational training programs for special education students and vocational rehabilitation services for adults with disabilities have existed in every state for a long time, systematic coordination of and communication between schools and community-based adult services have not typically occurred. Although interagency cooperation is critical to the success of transition, the amendments to IDEA "made it clear that the initial and ultimately most significant transition responsibilities lie with schools" (Moon & Inge, 1993, p. 583).

- After graduation, the ITP can be incorporated into an *individual rehabilitation plan* if the young adult is served by vocational rehabilitation or made part of an *individualized habilitation plan* if the young adult is served by a community adult services agency (e.g., a county program for people with developmental disabilities). A well-written transition plan ensures that parents are aware of available adult services and employment options in the community, improves the chances that adult services will be available with few disruptions to the graduating student, and provides school and adult-service personnel with a set of procedures and timelines to follow.

Examples of ITP formats and transition planning and support activities can be found in Clark and Kolstoe (1995); Gajar, Goodman, and McAfee (1993); Martin and Marshall (1995); Siegel et al. (1993); Szymanski (1994); Udvari-Solner, Jorgenson, and Courchane (1992); Wehman (1998); and West et al. (1992).

Transition plans can take many formats. Figure 15.2 shows the ITP developed for Jeff, an 10th-grader with learning disabilities. Jeff and his parents share a vision for the future in which Jeff has a good job and lives as independently as possible. He is very interested in obtaining his driver's license; and based on some of his community-work experiences, Jeff thinks he might like to work in the heating and air conditioning field. Jeff also sees himself getting married someday, but first he wants to live on his own for a while, probably in an apartment with a roommate or two. He has also expressed the desire to continue his education after high school; therefore, one of the activities on his ITP is to obtain information about community and technical colleges.

The goals and objectives numbers on the ITP refer to the goals and objectives on Jeff's IEP that support the transition plan (IEP objectives follow). Academic goals for Jeff such as reading comprehension use the content area from the transition plan—e.g., heating and air conditioning textbook and the driver's education manual. Jeff frequently relies on adults to assist him in decision making and to request information for days off at work, and he needs to better understand his disability. His self-advocacy goal relates to more self-reliance. Although specific skills will be taught, Jeff will practice his self-advocacy skills at his part-time job.

Jeff's IEP Objectives

1. *Reading comprehension—Goal:* Jeff will increase his reading comprehension skills.
   a. When given a reading passage from the driver's education manual or heating and air conditioning textbook, Jeff will increase his reading comprehension skills by using the SQ3R study skills method.
   b. Given 10 functional vocabulary words from the course text, Jeff will identify and define each word.
   c. Given unfamiliar/unknown words found in the heating and air conditioning text (or other course text), Jeff will decode the word using word attack skills.
2. *Self-advocacy—Goal:* Jeff will increase his self-advocacy skills.
   a. Jeff will increase his understanding of his disability by identifying and stating his strengths and areas of difficulty.
   b. When given various community and work situations, Jeff will identify and demonstrate appropriate decision-making skills.
   c. When given various community and work problem situations, Jeff will identify people who can assist him with difficult or unfamiliar situations.
3. *Money management—Goal:* Jeff will manage his personal finances.
   a. Jeff will construct and use a monthly personal budget for his present income.
   b. Jeff will record personal major income and expenses for three months.

IEP-608b

IEP ADDENDUM:
STATEMENT OF NEEDED TRANSITION SERVICES

Name of Student Jeff Grace **Date** 1-14-99

Person Responsible for Coordinating Transition Services Nancy Long

Title Work Study Coordinator

INSTRUCTION: Goals and objectives for transition should be indicated below in the following areas and be incorporated into the body of the IEP (pages 2 and 3).

See IEP goals and objectives for curriculum modifications and adaptations

EMPLOYMENT & POSTSECONDARY OUTCOME(S): Full-time job in heating/air conditioning

ACTIVITIES AND SERVICES	Goal Number for Transition Goals and Objectives	Responsible Person/Provider	Initiation/Duration
Heating/air cond. voc. class	1.a, 1.b, 1.c	Voc Educ. Teacher	1/99 to 2/00
Explore Technical colleges	NA	Jeff, guidance coun.	1/99 to 6/99
Part-time job	2.a, 2.b, 2.c	Jeff, work study coord.	1/99 to 2/00

POSTSCHOOL/ADULT LIVING OUTCOME(S): Live independently in apartment with roommate

ACTIVITIES AND SERVICES	Goal Number for Transition Goals and Objectives	Responsible Person/Provider	Initiation/Duration
Family Planning Class	1.a, 1.b, 1.c	SPED Teacher/Reg. Teacher	1/99 to 6/99
Money management	3.a 3.b	SPED Teacher	1/99 to 1/00
Self-advocacy skills trn.	2.a, 2.b, 2.c	Jeff, SPED Teacher	1/99 to 2/00

COMMUNITY PARTICIPATION OUTCOME(S): To participate in the community through social relationships and transportation.

ACTIVITIES AND SERVICES	Goal Number for Transition Goals and Objectives	Responsible Person/Provider	Initiation/Duration
Drivers Ed.	1.a 1.b 1.c	Driver Ed Teacher / SPED Teacher	1/99 to 6/00
Register to vote	NA	Jeff and parents	1/99 to 6/00
Interact Club	NA	Jeff	1/99 to 6/00

If appropriate include the following:

Functional Vocational Evaluation YES ☐
(Indicate in Activities/Services in Employment/Postsecondary Outcomes Section)

Daily Living Skills YES ☐
(Indicate in Activities/Services in Postschool/ Adult Living Outcomes Section)

NOTE:

1. If the student does not need instruction, community experiences and the development of employment and other postschool adult living objectives, document the basis upon which this determination was made by the IEP team in the appropriate area above.
2. Activities and services must include community experiences.

A copy of this completed form is part of, and must be attached to, the student's IEP form.

Figure 15.2 Example of an individualized transition plan (ITP)

Source: ITP form from Ohio Department of Education. (1998). *Model policies and procedures for the education of children with disabilities* (p. 608b). Columbus: Author.

The 1997 amendments to IDEA (P.L. 105–17) mandated a new transition-related IEP requirement in addition to the ITP:

> Beginning at age 14, and updated annually, a statement of the transition service needs of the child under the applicable components of the child's IEP that focuses on the child's courses of study (such as participation in advanced-placement courses or a vocational education program). [P.L. 105–17, Sec. 602 [30])

The intent of this provision is to focus attention on curriculum and course planning related to postschool success. It is designed to augment, not replace, the separate transition services requirements under which children beginning no later than age 16 receive transition services.

For recommendations on how transition services can be made more relevant and effective for students and families from culturally diverse backgrounds, see Atkins (1992) and Boone (1992). Cooperation and communication are keys to effective transition planning. See "Removing Transition Hurdles with Effective Communication" later in this chapter.

Beginning Career Development and Transition Activities Early

Numerous models for conceptualizing and guiding the delivery of transition services have been developed. All stress the importance of providing career education at an early age, a functional secondary school curriculum that offers work experience in integrated community job sites, systematic coordination between the school and adult service providers, parental involvement and support, and a written ITP to guide the entire process.

The Council for Exceptional Children's Division on Career Development and Transition (DCDT) believes that career development and transition services should begin in the elementary grades for all children with disabilities. According to DCDT's position statement, three basic principles underlie the provision of career education and transition services:

> 1. *Education for career development and transition is for individuals with disabilities of all ages.* Anyone in our society with a disability that is severe enough to qualify for special education programming or services is much more likely to encounter significant adult adjustment and employment assistance demands after leaving school. The nature of these demands vary, but *every* disability categorical group has problems in employment, independent living, and person-social relationships. . . . The defensibility for earlier intervention in the areas of career development and transition skills is as strong as the longstanding position of special educators for the importance of early educational intervention with children who are at risk or who have identifiable disabilities.
> 2. *Career development is a process begun at birth and continues throughout life.* Career development, from the broad perspective of fostering life-long career competencies in the work world, independent living skills in the community, and personal-social relationships at home and in the community, is actually only different terminology for what some disciplines refer to as normal human growth and development.
> 3. *Early career development is essential for making satisfactory choices later.* A frequent criticism of secondary employment training programs is that there are too few choices and that professionals too often end up making those choices for students. . . . The best way to prepare individuals for self-knowledge (interests, abilities, limiting barriers) and decision-making is to begin the process of self-awareness and choice-making as early as possible. (Clark, Carlson, Fisher, Cook, & D'Alonzo, 1991, pp. 115–116.)

Figure 15.3 shows the career development and transition model developed by Clark and Kolstoe (1995). This model focuses on obtaining work after one leaves school but gives equal importance to competencies that are critical for life as an adult. The four mutually important elements of the model—(1) values, attitudes, and habits; (2) human relationships; (3) occupational information; and (4) acquisition of job and daily living skills—are superimposed over vertical lines that extend upward, undergirding the high school, postsecondary, and adult options for education and training. The relative emphasis of the four elements changes as a student progresses through the elementary and middle school grades and moves into high school and postsecondary education or vocational training opportunities and as individual needs and career goals change.

Developing career awareness and vocational skills during the elementary years does not mean, of course, that 6-year-old children should be placed on job sites for training. Appropriate transition-related objectives should be selected at each age level (Freagon et al., 1986; Wehman, 1983). For example, elementary students might sample different types of jobs through classroom responsibilities such as watering

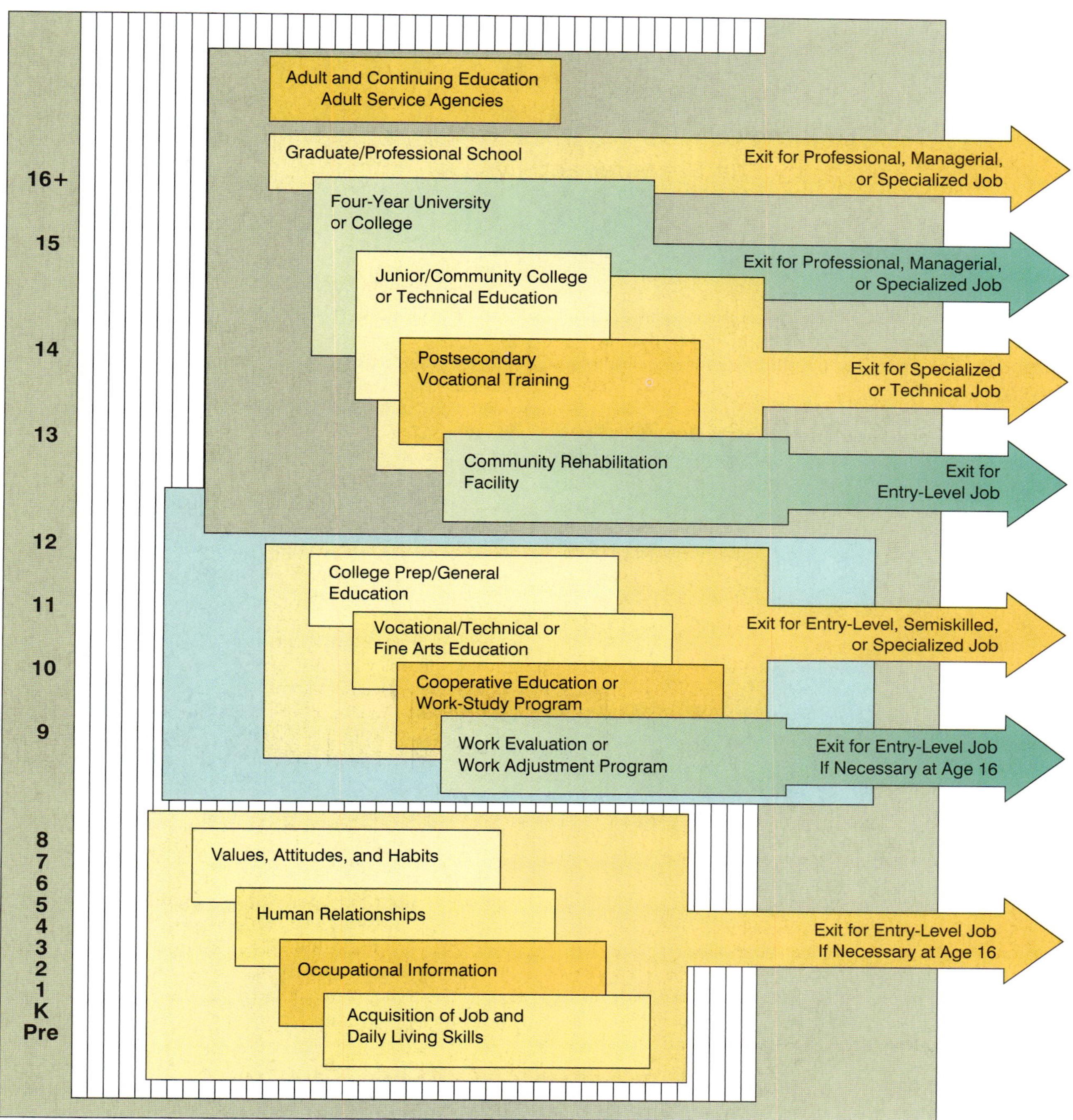

Figure 15.3 A school-based career development and transition education model

Source: Reprinted from Clark, G. M., & Kolstoe, O. P. (1995). *Career development and transition education for adolescents with disabilities* (2nd ed., p. 46). Needham Heights, MA: Allyn & Bacon. Used by permission.

Removing Transition Hurdles with Effective Communication

by Sue Brewster and Lyn Dol

Let us introduce ourselves: Sue is a job-training coordinator and transition specialist for an urban school system; Lyn is the mother of Karen, a young adult with a disability. We would like to share what we learned about helping young adults with disabilities transition from school to adult life from our experience with a transition-planning meeting for Karen.

Karen Karen, challenged by mental retardation, epilepsy, and osteoporosis, which requires her to use a wheelchair, was in her last year of high school. Throughout high school, Karen had participated in a variety of work experiences in the community, such as at a restaurant, a child care facility, two different nursing homes, and a large general department store. Karen's strengths include her desire to work in the community, social skills, and quality of work. Staying on task, poor productivity, and short-term memory were areas of difficulty.

Karen and her family were feeling the many stresses that occur with leaving high school and moving into the adult world. The county board of mental retardation and developmental disabilities (MR/DD), which provides vocational, residential, recreation, and other services to individuals with disabilities, had presented Karen and her family with two options: community-based employment or a sheltered workshop environment. At the time, community-based employment was only an option for persons who could work at least 20 hours per week with minimal support, such as a job coach stopping in every week or so. Individuals whose disabilities prevented them from working the required hours or who needed more support were automatically placed on the waiting list for the sheltered workshop. Karen's seizure disorder and physical disability made it difficult for her to meet the required number of hours for community placement, yet she had frequently expressed her desire to work in the community.

To help prepare Karen for community placement, Sue had found her a nonpaying work experience at a restaurant on a nearby university campus. Karen's duties were to bus tables and clean off trays. Grant funds to increase transition services for youths with disabilities were used to provide transportation to and from the job site and for a maximum of 100 job-coaching hours. Karen and her job coach, Chris, began working at the restaurant for eight hours per week. It was hoped that this nonpaid work experience would lead to paid employment and possibly additional working hours after graduation.

As the 100 hours of grant-funded job coaching neared completion, Chris thought that Karen would continue to need support services on the job. Lyn preferred that Karen work in the community, but she had many questions concerning the feasibility of community work. Sue, who had visited Karen at the job site, thought that things were going pretty well, and the restaurant manager had indicated the possibility of offering Karen competitive employment. Sue was also concerned that the grant funding might be lost for other students if this placement failed. At this point, Sue arranged a transition-planning meeting for all interested parties in an effort to determine what support services Karen would need after graduation and to try to solidify the employment placement.

Karen's Transition Meeting The meeting was held at the restaurant with all interested parties present: Karen; Lyn and Bill, Karen's parents; Mark, Karen's older brother; Sue, the job training coordinator; Chris, the job coach; Jim, the restaurant manager; two people from the county MR/DD program; and a representative from the Bureau of Vocational Rehabilitation (BVR).

After all had introduced themselves, Sue began the meeting by asking Chris, "How is Karen doing since you've been with her for six weeks on the job?" Knowing what the stakes were and who was present around the table (parents and restaurant manager), Chris hesitated and then said something positive while admitting that Karen had some "slow days." When Bill, Karen's father, asked Jim, the restaurant manager, whether he would have to hire somebody else to do the job if Karen didn't get it, he sounded as if he didn't really expect that Karen would ever work in the community.

Throughout the meeting, it seemed that people were saying one thing and meaning another. Everyone seemed to be communicating at cross purposes, to have his own agenda and objective. The meeting ended with everyone feeling very negative, exhausted, and perplexed.

Most important, the meeting ended without a community job for Karen.

Bubble Heads Two months after the meeting, Sue, feeling as though she had failed, met with Lyn to figure out

Figure A Karen's ITP meeting: What people said and what they were really thinking

what went wrong at the meeting. They decided to ask each participant to remember what she was thinking during the meeting and to compare that with the statements they had actually said. After talking with the participants and comparing what was said with what they "were really saying," Sue and Lyn learned some important lessons about effective communication during transition planning. Figure A shows actual statements made by members of the planning team; the bubbles show what each person was really thinking.

Communication Breakdown

- The seating arrangement is important. The meeting had been conducted at a long, narrow table. A round table would have helped ensure that each team member had equal opportunity to talk and be heard by everyone and to see and hear the person speaking.
- Too many people hamper effective communication. Both the family and the employer expressed the feeling of being overwhelmed by the number of people (10) who were present at the meeting.
- Listen to what people are saying they want and need, even if their request differs from what you think should occur. For example, Lyn was saying to Sue that she would like to see Karen working in the community rather than in a sheltered workshop. At the same time, her husband and her son were voicing skepticism and were being "protective" of Karen. Sue did not consider the interactions among the family members and only considered what she thought would be best for Karen. Sue should have met with the family before the transition meeting to help the family sort out and determine what they wanted.
- Because Lyn was surrounded with negative beliefs about Karen's ability to work in the community, she left the meeting thinking that perhaps her husband and son had been right all along. The family gave up hope of community work for Karen. This made it easy for the business to not offer Karen the job.
- Sue may not have been really listening to the family because of her job-placement requirement. She may have been more concerned with meeting her placement quota than with the concerns of the family.
- Not once during the meeting did anyone ask Karen where she wanted to work and what she thought her strengths, weaknesses, and support needs were. Service providers have to step outside their realm and place the individual with a disability in the center of the planning to ensure that her requests and desires are addressed.

Professionals Sometimes Build Their Own Hurdles

- Even though they want to do the right thing, service providers often get trapped by their own rules and regulations and their usual way of doing business. BVR and MR/DD gave up by stating that they could not provide services to Karen if she was not going to get paid at least minimum wage or work at least 20 hours per week.
- Potential employers will avoid getting involved when they deal with too many professionals, bureaucratic tangles, or turf fighting between agencies.

Karen's New Job Everyone except Karen seemed to have given up after that fateful meeting. But Karen persisted in expressing her preference for a job in the community. Sue brought the transition team together again to address the requests and needs of Karen and her family. By being flexible and creative, Sue has worked during the last two years to create jobs for Karen and others with significant challenges. Karen is now doing meaningful work in an integrated job in the community. She is currently working at Anderson's General Store in a group placement (enclave) with three other individuals with significant challenges. Her job entails moving and facing items to the front of the shelves. Karen works three days per week for three hours per day with the support of a job coach. To help alleviate the family's concerns about Karen struggling in the community, Sue arranged for them to observe Karen at work.

Karen's production rate currently keeps her from earning minimum wage, but she has the opportunity to do meaningful work for pay and to interact with nondisabled peers. In the last year, Karen has made another transition. She has moved from her parents' home to a group home with four other adults with disabilities. With her supports and effective communication among service providers and the family, Karen is continuing her transition to independence.

Sue Brewster is a job-training coordinator for the Toledo (Ohio) Public School System. Lyn Dol, a coordinator for the local Interagency Transition Team and a parent mentor for adult issues, ensures that services for individuals with disabilities are family-driven.

plants, cleaning chalkboards, or taking messages to the office. Young children with disabilities might also visit community work sites where adults with disabilities are employed. In addition, assessment and teaching of job performance skills can be accomplished with elementary-age special education students through prevocational work samples, which provide practice on skills (e.g., counting, packaging, following directions) and are related to a variety of potentially available jobs in the community

(Scott, Ebbert, & Price, 1986). Middle school students should begin to spend time at actual community job sites, with an increasing amount of in-school instruction devoted to the development of associated work skills, such as being on time, staying on task, and using interpersonal skills (Beakley & Yoder, 1998; Sulzbacher, Haines, Peterson, & Swatman, 1987).

Developing and operating a school-based business enterprise can help high school students learn functional academic, work, problem-solving, and social skills. For example, Lindstrom, Benz, and Johnson (1997) describe four school-based businesses—an espresso and baked goods bar, a take-out meals operation, a mail-order seed business, and a winter produce garden—that students with disabilities in several high schools in Oregon have helped develop and operate. Secondary students with moderate and severe disabilities should also spend an increasing amount of time receiving instruction at actual community job sites (Goldberger, Kazis, & O'Flanagan, 1994). For example, Test, Grossi, and Keul (1988) describe a procedure for systematically teaching a 19-year-old student with mental retardation janitorial skills in a competitive work setting. The remaining hours of in-school instruction should focus on acquisition of functional skills needed in the adult work, domestic, community, and recreational/leisure environments toward which the student is headed (Benz & Lindstrom, 1997; Patton, Cronin, & Jairrels, 1997). Table 15.1 shows examples of curriculum activities in the domestic, community, leisure, and vocational domains that might be incorporated into a student's IEP.

Brolin's Life-Centered Career Education *(1997) is an excellent career education curriculum. For a description of nine different career education and life skills education models, see Sitlington (1996).*

Project WORK is a field-tested classroom-based employability skills curriculum designed to place students in jobs in six weeks (Patton, de la Graza, & Harmon, 1997).

Employment

Work can be defined as using one's physical and/or mental energies to accomplish something productive. Our society is based on a work ethic; we place a high value on work and on people who contribute. Besides providing economic support, work

Secondary school programs can facilitate the successful transition to the adult world of work by providing functional curricula and real work experiences in integrated community job sites.

Table 15.1 Examples of transition-related curriculum activities in four domains that might be included in a student's IEP

	Domestic	Community	Leisure	Vocational
Elementary	Picking up toys/belongings Washing dishes with family Making bed Dressing Grooming Eating skills Toileting skills Sorting clothing Vacuuming Setting the table at mealtime	Eating meals in a restaurant Using restroom in a local restaurant Putting trash into container Choosing correct change to ride city bus Giving the clerk money to purchase an item Responding appropriately to pedestrian safety signs Going to neighbor's house for lunch	Climbing on monkey bars Playing board games Playing tag with neighbors Scouts Coloring Playing kickball Croquet Riding bicycles Playing with dolls and other age-appropriate toys Community soccer league Nintendo	Returning toys/belongings to appropriate storage space Cleaning the room at the end of the day Working on a task for a designated period (10–15 minutes) Wiping tables after meals Following 2- to 4-step instructions Answering the telephone Emptying trash Taking messages to people
Middle School	Washing clothes Cooking a simple hot meal (soup, salad, and sandwich) Keeping bedroom clean Making snacks Mowing lawn Raking leaves Making a grocery list Purchasing items from a list Vacuuming and dusting Setting an alarm clock at night and turning it off when waking Using deodorant	Crossing streets safely Purchasing an item from a department store Purchasing a meal at a restaurant Using local transportation system to get to and from recreational facilities Participating in local scout troop Going to a neighbor's house for lunch on Saturday Riding the city bus with family or school friends	Playing volleyball Taking aerobics classes Playing checkers with a friend Playing miniature golf Cycling Attending high school or local college basketball games Hanging out at local mall Swimming Attending crafts class at city recreation center	Mopping/waxing floors Cleaning windows Hanging and bagging clothes Busing tables Working for 1–2 hours with family on weekends Cleaning sinks, bathtubs, and fixtures Operating machinery (such as dishwasher, buffer) Internship with school janitor Internship with school office staff Following a daily schedule
High School	Cleaning all rooms in place of residence Developing a weekly budget Cooking meals Operating thermostat to regulate heat or air Doing yard maintenance Maintaining personal needs Caring for and maintaining clothing Taking care of menstrual needs	Utilizing bus system to move about the community Depositing checks into bank account Using community department stores Using community grocery stores Using community health facilities (physician, pharmacist)	Jogging Boating Watching college basketball Video games Card games YMCA swim class Gardening Going on a vacation Collecting tapes or CDs Reading magazines or comics Hanging out/sleeping over with friends	Janitorial duties (at J. C. Penney) Housekeeping duties (at Days Inn) Grounds keeping duties at local college campus Food service at mall cafeteria Laundry duties at local laundromat Photography at local bank Food-stocking duties at large grocery store Messenger/reception duties at local business

Source: Adapted from Wehman, P., Moon, M. S., Wood, J. M., & Barcus, J. M. (1988). *Transition from school to work: New challenges for youth with severe disabilities* (pp. 140–142). Baltimore: Brookes. Used by permission.

offers opportunities for social interaction and a chance to use and enhance skills in a chosen area. Work generates the respect of others and provides a sense of pride and self-satisfaction (Terkel, 1974).

All young adults face important questions about what to do with their lives—whether to attend college or technical school, whether to work as a bricklayer or an accountant—but for the person without disabilities, answering those questions involves choosing from a number of options. By contrast, the young adult with disabilities often has few, if any, options from which to choose. Occupational choices decrease if the person with disabilities has limited skills; they may decrease even more due to the nature of the disability and still further because of employers' (needless) prejudices and misconceptions about people with disabilities. For most adults with disabilities, obtaining and holding a job is a major life challenge and goal.

Competitive Employment

A person who is competitively employed performs work valued by an employer, functions in an integrated setting with nondisabled co-workers, and earns at or above the federal minimum wage (Rusch, Chadsey-Rusch, & Lagomarcino, 1987). Wehman and Hill (1985) further specify that a person who is truly competitively employed receives no subsidized wages of any kind. Virtually all special educators who have studied the transition of students with disabilities from school to adult life believe that only through significant revision of the public school curriculum and improved coordination of school and adult vocational habilitation services can the prospect of competitive employment be enhanced for young adults with disabilities (e.g., Bellamy & Horner, 1987; Clark & Kolstoe, 1995; Patton, Cronin, & Jairrels, 1997).

Wehman, Kregel, and Barcus (1985) consider three characteristics critical to good secondary school programs. First, the curriculum must stress functional skills; that is, students must learn vocational skills that they will actually need and use in local employment situations. Second, school-based instruction must be carried out in integrated settings as much as possible. Students with disabilities must be given ample opportunities to learn the interpersonal skills necessary to work effectively with co-workers in integrated work sites. Third, community-based instruction should begin as early as about age 12 for students with severe disabilities and must be used for progressively extended periods as students near graduation. While on work sites in the community, students should receive direct instruction in areas such as specific job skills, ways to increase production rates, and transportation to and from employment sites. "Students should train and work in the community whenever possible. This is not only to expose them to the community and work expectations, but to expose future employers and co-workers to their potential as reliable employees" (Wehman, Kregel, & Barcus, 1985, p. 29).

Several follow-up studies have found a positive correlation between paid work experiences during high school and postschool employment (e.g., Benz, Yovanoff, & Doren, 1997; D'Amico, 1991; Hasazi, Gordon, & Roe, 1985; Hasazi, Johnson, Hasazi, Gordon, & Hull, 1989; Kohler, 1994; Scuccimarra & Speece, 1990). The NLTS, however, found that only 39% of young adults with disabilities had been enrolled in work experience programs during high school.

Supported Employment

For adults with disabilities, especially those with severe intellectual and/or physical disabilities, the opportunity to earn real wages for real work has been almost nonexistent in this country. A new type of vocational opportunity has emerged that is aimed at helping individuals with severe disabilities who have historically been unemployed or restricted to sheltered settings. Supported employment enables persons with severe disabilities to participate successfully in integrated work environments.

The supported employment movement recognizes that many adults with severe disabilities require ongoing, often intensive support to obtain, learn, and hold a job. The incorporation of supported employment into the Rehabilitation Act Amendments of 1986 (P.L. 99–506) has led to a proliferation of federally assisted supported employment programs throughout the country.

Supported employment is

- competitive work in integrated work settings;
- for persons with the most severe disabilities;
- for whom competitive employment has not traditionally occurred;
- or for whom competitive employment has been interrupted or intermittent as a result of a severe disability; and
- who, because of the severity of their disability, need intensive support services; or
- extended services in order to perform such work. (P.L. 102–569, Sec. 635[b][6][c][iii])

An integrated work setting requires regular contact with nondisabled co-workers.

Supported employment has grown rapidly since its inception. In 1986, fewer than 10,000 individuals were working in federally assisted supported employment demonstration projects in 20 states. Just two years later, the supported employment movement had grown to a total of 32,342 participants nationally, and the cumulative wages these workers earned grew from $1.4 million to $12.4 million in the 15 states that reported earnings data (Wehman, Kregel, Shafer, & West, 1989). By 1995, it was estimated that more than 140,000 persons with disabilities were working through supported employment with an average hourly wage of $4.53 and monthly earnings of $464.10 (Wehman, Revell, & Kregel, 1996).

The individual placement (job coach) model is the most widely used supported employment approach (79.7%), followed by work enclaves (14.5%), mobile work crews (5.3%), and small business enterprises (0.1%) (Revell et al., 1994).

Types of Supported Employment Four distinct placement models have been developed and widely reported in the supported employment literature. Although other models have been used and proposed, a national survey of supported employment programs found that more than 99% of individuals are served by one of these four models (Revell, Wehman, Kregel, West, & Rayfield, 1994).

- Individual placement model
- Work enclave (or workstation) model
- Mobile work crew model
- Small business enterprise model

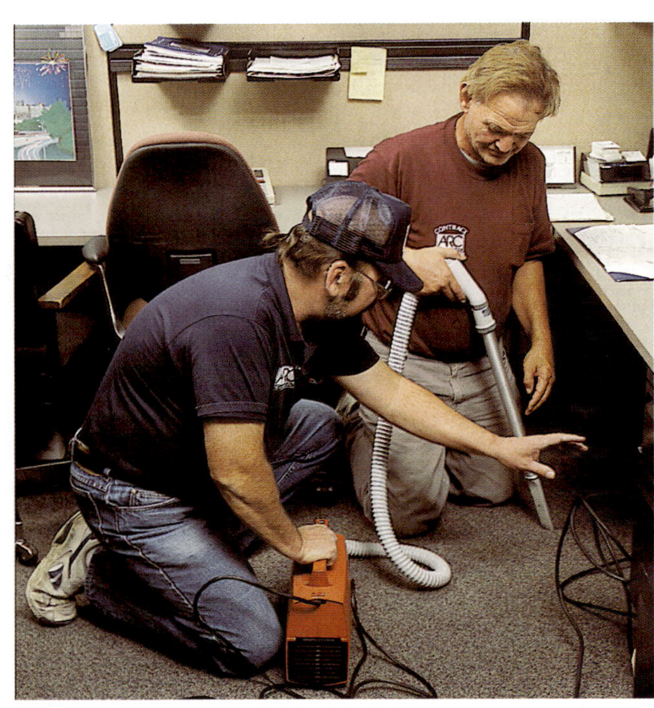

The supported employment movement is enabling tens of thousands of individuals like Barry to experience, for the first time in their lives, the benefits of real work for real wages.

Individual Placement Model. Wehman and Kregel (1985) describe an individual placement model for supported employment that consists of four components:

1. A comprehensive approach to job placement
2. Intensive job-site training and advocacy
3. Ongoing monitoring of client performance
4. A systematic approach to long-term job retention and follow-up

The supported employment specialist is the key to making a supported work program effective. The supported employment specialist, sometimes called a *job coach,* is a community-based professional who works in a nonprofit job placement program, a public vocational or adult services program, or a secondary special education program. The job coach is "the most integral aspect in making supported employment work" (Wehman & Revell, 1997, p. 630). Figure 15.4 identifies the major activities and responsibilities of a supported employment specialist in each component of the supported work model. Although all participants in supported employment continue to receive support and services as needed, the amount of direct on-the-job assistance from the supported employment specialist is gradually reduced as the new employee acquires greater competence in completing the job requirements independently (Kregel, Hill, & Banks, 1988).

For details on developing supported employment programs, see Bellamy, Rhodes, Mank, and Albin (1988) and Rusch (1990). The winter 1989 issue of the Journal of Applied Behavior Analysis *is devoted to research on supported employment.*

Wehman, Hill, Hill, Brooke, Pendleton, and Britt (1985) report the employment status of 167 adults who were placed in part- and full-time paid jobs with the individual placement model. The employees ranged in age from 18 to 66 years old and had a median IQ score of 49.

> The great majority (86%) were receiving regular financial aid from the government at the time of placement. In fact, 81% earned under $200 as an annual salary the year prior to placement, which indicates the level of economic independence exhibited by these individuals prior to intervention. A total of 71% lived with their parents or family and 90% lacked skills to use public transportation at the time of their initial placement. (p. 275)

A total of 252 job placements, most in entry-level minimum-wage positions, were made with more than 100 employers, representing primarily service occupations, such as cleaning and custodial work in hotels, restaurants, and hospitals. The average length of employment for all 167 of the persons in the study was 19 months. At the time of the report, 72 clients were still employed. The authors note that the 8.1 months of employment during their clients' first year on the job compares favorably with the results of a study by the National Hotel and Restaurant Association (1983) that found more than 2,300 individuals without disabilities had retained their comparable entry-level positions for an average of only five months. They also point out that the average total cost of $5,255 per client for the supported work program, which resulted in an average of 19 months of paid employment per client, compares favorably with the average annual cost of $4,000 per year for adult day programs (sheltered workshops and work activity centers). This comparison is especially favorable when one takes into account the total client wages earned and income taxes contributed.

For a thought-provoking examination and debate of the issues concerning whether adults with severe disabilities should be permitted to perform meaningful work without pay in community-based integrated work sites while undergoing extended training, see Bellamy et al. (1984) and Brown et al. (1984).

Enclave (or Workstation) Model. In this model of supported employment, a small group of no more than eight persons with disabilities performs work with special training or job supports within a normal business or industry. The work enclave provides a useful alternative to traditional segregated sheltered employment, offering many of the benefits of community-based integrated employment as well as the ongoing support necessary for long-term job success.

The success of supported employment depends in large part on job development, *the identification and creation of community-based employment opportunities for individuals with disabilities. For suggestions on how job developers can improve their "sales pitch" to the business community, see Fabian, Luecking, and Tilson (1994); Hagner and Daning (1993); and Nietupski, Verstegen, and Hamre-Nietupski (1992).*

Rhodes and Valenta (1985) report the preliminary results of a work enclave that resulted in the employment of six persons with severe disabilities. They established a working agreement with Physio Control Corporation of Redmond, Washington, to create a separate production line within the company to employ persons with severe disabilities. Physio Control employs 900 people in its Redmond facility, where it manufactures biomedical equipment, primarily heart defibrillators. A nonprofit organization called Trillium Employment Services was created to provide the employment training and ongoing support the workers with severe disabilities needed. The work enclave employees have become part of a production line that does subassemblies

Job Description: Employment Specialist

General Description

The employment specialist is involved in all aspects of community-based vocational training, placement, and follow-along for persons with an array of severe disabilities as part of the Excel Rehabilitation Program. The successful candidate will meet the employers to secure placements, provide one-on-one training for job and other related skills, and maintain systematic and regular contact with employers after job training has been completed. The employment specialist will work as part of a team and will interact frequently with other professionals related to specific cases.

Specific Duties/Responsibilities

1. Job Development. The employment specialist will complete job market screening activities and regularly present the employment program to prospective employers until adequate numbers of appropriate open positions have been identified. The specialist will analyze job duties and requirements of potential jobs.
2. Consumer Assessment. The employment specialist will complete and/or secure assessment and evaluation information as necessary to assist the consumer with informed decision making. This may include referral to other professionals/agencies and subsequent interpretation of reports, observations, and interviewing persons knowledgeable about the consumer.
3. Job Placement. The employment specialist will complete activities to secure placement of individuals with disabilities that include vocational guidance, assistance with application procedures, support during interview processes, advice regarding job offers and negotiation, and initial planning for work.
4. Job Site Training. The employment specialist will work with the consumer on and off the job site until the consumer can maintain employment without regular or frequent assistance from the specialist. These duties may include development and implementation of instructional and/or behavioral programming strategies, conferences with the employer, co-workers, and/or consumer, and collection of performance information such as measures of quality and rate of work.
5. Follow-Along. The employment specialist will establish and maintain periodic contact with consumers, employers, and others as necessary to facilitate continued successful placement of the employee with disabilities. The employment specialist will be on call to assist in the resolution of obstacles to continued employment.
6. Other. The employment specialist will perform other related duties including but not limited to participating in agency meetings, attending training and professional development meetings, developing materials, coordinating consumer services as necessary for continued placement, and maintaining accurate consumer case files.

Figure 15.4 Sample description of a job coach's responsibilities

Source: Reprinted from Wehman, P., & Revell, W. G., Jr. (1997). Transition from school to adulthood: Looking ahead. In P. Wehman (Ed.), *Exceptional individuals in school, community, and work* (p. 631). Austin, TX: PRO-ED. Used by permission.

of defibrillator components, such as chest paddles and wire harnesses. As much as possible, tasks are selected that are of the same type performed by other employees of the company. The work enclave employees are supervised by Physio Control, although legal employment responsibility rests with the support organization (Trillium) until an individual's three-month productivity averages 65% of the productivity of other Physio Control employees. At that time, the individual is hired as a Physio

Control employee. Work enclave employees receive wages commensurate with their productivity rates. Training and supervision procedures use a behavioral model, incorporating task analysis and direct instruction of specific job skills as well as arrangement of the physical and social aspects of the work environment to encourage improved work rates (Bellamy et al., 1979).

At the end of one year, all of the enclave employees were producing at or above 50% of the productivity standard of other Physio Control employees. Total wages earned by all program employees for the first year were $20,207, including $2,425 paid by the employees in federal income tax. Total public costs for the program were $15,945 for the first year, with the majority of those costs incurred during the first five months of the program. With respect to interaction with nondisabled co-workers, Rhodes and Valenta (1985) warn that program developers and industrial managers contemplating this model must ensure that

> employees not become segregated from the rest of the working community (much like the "handicapped wing" of a public school). A balance must be attained in providing the structure to support training interventions, to address low productivity, and insure adaptability to changing work demands, without sacrificing the advantages of a normal industrial environment. (p. 18)

Although measures such as the number of persons placed, hours worked, wages earned, and taxes paid are important outcomes in evaluating supported employment programs, so, too, is job satisfaction. When 34 supported employees were interviewed (22 who were in individual placements and 12 in the workstation model), the majority said they (1) liked their jobs, (2) were satisfied with the supports they received from their job coach, (3) had had input into selecting their jobs, (4) would rather work in the community than in a sheltered workshop, and (5) had friends at work (Test, Hinson, Solow, & Keul, 1993).

Mobile Work Crew Model. A mobile work crew involves a small group of supported employees organized around a small single-purpose business, such as building or grounds maintenance, working in an integrated community employment setting. A general manager may be responsible for finding and coordinating the work of several small crews of three to eight individuals, with each crew supervised by a supported employment specialist. Mobile work crews are organized as not-for-profit corporations; the extra costs the organizations incur because their employees do not work at full productivity levels are covered by public funds. Such costs are usually less than would be needed to support the work crew employees in activity centers, which provide little or no real work or reimbursement.

Small Business Enterprise Model. This model provides supported employment for persons with disabilities by establishing a business that takes advantage of existing commercial opportunities within a community. The business hires a small number of individuals with disabilities as well as several employees without disabilities. One example of this model is the Port Townsend Baking Company, a commercial bakery in Port Townsend, Washington.

Learning Independence and Adaptability on the Job

The complexity of competitive and supported work environments requires employees to use a wide range of vocational and social skills. Consider the following list of work performance expectations that can be used to evaluate the performance of employees with disabilities.

Performance Measures

1. Works independently
2. Completes all assigned tasks
3. Attends to job tasks consistently
4. Meets company standards for quality of work
5. Meets company standards for rate of work performance
6. Follows company procedures
7. Maintains good attendance and punctuality

8. Takes care of equipment and materials
9. Maintains acceptable appearance

Adaptability Measures

1. Obtains/returns materials for tasks
2. Adjusts rate of performance according to job demands
3. Works safely
4. Follows a schedule
5. Manages time properly
6. Is able to adjust to changes in routine
7. Solves work-related problems independently

Social Skills Measures

1. Follows directions
2. Accepts criticism
3. Asks for assistance when necessary
4. Gets along with fellow workers
5. Interacts appropriately with customers (Lagomarcino, Hughes, & Rusch, 1989, p. 143)

To earn high marks in most of these areas, an employee must display some degree of independence and adaptability in the workplace. Successful employees independently solve minor problems (e.g., clear off an obstructed work area before beginning) instead of calling their supervisor. Successful employees are sensitive to cues in the work setting that signal changing demands, and they adjust their performance accordingly (e.g., a dishwasher increases his rate of pot scrubbing during the busy lunch hour).

In a typical supported employment program, the employment specialist provides direct, on-site job training to the employee with disabilities and serves as the primary source of support and assistance to the supported employee. Although the job coach gradually reduces the time spent in direct, on-site training and support, this model of outside assistance has several inherent drawbacks (Curl, 1990; Hughes, Rusch, & Curl, 1990; Mithaug, Martin, Agran, & Rusch, 1988):

- The arrival and presence of the job coach can be disruptive to the natural work setting.
- The supported employee may perform differently in the presence of her job coach.
- It is difficult for the employment specialist to be sensitive to the changing demands of the job over time and to provide continued support and training consistent with those changes.
- The cost of providing training and support by an employment specialist who must travel to the job site is higher and the efficiency of the approach is lower than one that takes advantage of the natural interactions of co-workers.
- The always-on-call job coach may also prevent the employer and co-workers from figuring out and implementing natural solutions to problems.
- This approach fosters too much dependence on the job coach, working against the supported employee's learning how to solve problems on the job and assuming responsibility for her own management.

For a critical review of the literature on natural supports in supported employment, see Test and Wood (1996).

Natural Supports The role of the employment specialist/job coach is evolving from one of primary supporter for the employee with disabilities to one who works with the employer and co-workers to help identify, develop, and facilitate the typical or indigenous supports of the workplace (Rogan, Hagner, & Murphy, 1993). Rogan et al. define *natural support* as "any assistance, relationships or interactions that allow a person to secure or maintain a community job . . . in a way that corresponds to the typical work routines and social interactions of other employees" (p. 275).

The Importance of Co-Workers Social interaction is a natural feature of a typical workplace. Social interaction provides an important source of support for any employee, with or without disabilities, and it is associated with job performance and job satisfaction (Nisbet & Hagner, 1988). Because of their consistent presence in the work environment, co-workers can be a potentially powerful source of natural support for workers with disabilities (Rusch & Minch, 1988). Rusch, Hughes, McNair, and Wilson (1990) define a co-worker as an employee who works in the proximity of the supported employee, performs the same or similar duties, and/or takes breaks or eats meals in the same area as the supported employee. Six types of co-worker involvement beneficial to supported employees are described in Figure 15.5. McNair and Rusch (1992) have developed and field-tested the Co-worker Involvement Instrument, a 10-item assessment device for measuring co-worker involvement with supported employees.

Rusch, Johnson, and Hughes (1990) found fairly extensive involvement with nondisabled co-workers by supported employees working in individual or work-station placements regardless of the supported employees' level of disability. Supported employees working in mobile work crews, however, experienced far less co-worker involvement.

A skilled and friendly co-worker can provide information, answer questions, demonstrate job tasks, provide assistance and repeat instructions as needed, give social praise and feedback for performance, and serve as an important contact point for the supported employee's entry into the social fabric of the workplace (Baumgart & Askvig, 1992). Although some co-workers provide support naturally, observations in the workplace indicate that some formal training is usually necessary to make co-workers' "help" effective in maintaining successful employment. For example, Curl, Lignugaris/Kraft, Pawley, and Salzberg (1988) found that co-workers typically presented more than 100 instructions in the first two hours of employment training—a frequency likely to overwhelm a newly hired employee with disabilities. Several approaches for co-worker training have been developed recently. Co-workers can be taught how to provide support during brief, 15- to 20-minute sessions during breaks or before or after work. Curl (1990) has developed a program in which co-workers learn to use a simple four-step procedure in which they (1) provide instructions, (2) demonstrate the job task, (3) observe the supported employee performing the same task, and (4) deliver praise and evaluative feedback on the trainee's performance.

1. **Advocating.** A co-worker advocates for a supported employee by optimizing, backing, and supporting a supported employee's employment status. *Optimizing* refers to encouraging a supervisor to assign high-status and relevant tasks to a supported employee; *backing* refers to supporting a supported employee's rights, for example, by attempting to prevent practical jokes aimed at her. It also includes speaking up for a supported employee or offering explanations during differences of opinion. *Supporting* relates to providing emotional support to a supported employee in the form of friendship, association, etc.
2. **Associating.** A co-worker interacts socially with a supported employee at the workplace.
3. **Befriending.** A co-worker interacts socially with a supported employee outside the workplace.
4. **Collecting data.** A co-worker collects data by observing and recording social and/or work performance.
5. **Evaluating.** A co-worker appraises a supported employee's work performance and provides (written/oral) feedback to him.
6. **Training.** A co-worker supports a supported employee by providing on-the-job skill training.

Figure 15.5 Six types of co-worker involvement
Source: Adapted from Rusch, F. R., Hughes, C., McNair, J., & Wilson, P. G. (1990). *Co-worker involvement scoring manual and index.* Champaign: University of Illinois Press. Used by permission.

A paid co-worker was used to support the employment of two individuals with severe and multiple disabilities as hotel laundry attendants (Hood, Test, Spooner, & Steele, 1996).

Mithaug, Martin, and Agran (1987) describe an approach they call the adaptability model *designed to help students learn independence in the workplace. Instructional activities are designed to foster four kinds of skills inherent in self-determination: decision making, independent performance, self-evaluation, and making adjustments the next time they perform the task.*

Agran and Moore (1994) provide training scripts and monitoring forms for teaching self-instruction of job skills to students with mental retardation. Additional information on how to increase the independence and problem-solving skills of secondary students with disabilities can be found in Agran (1997) and Wehmeyer, Agran, and Hughes (1998).

A study by Likins, Salzberg, Stowitschek, Lignugaris/Kraft, and Curl (1989) demonstrates the potential of co-workers as job trainers for supported employees. Three women with mental retardation who were employed in the food preparation area of a self-service cafeteria were taught a 19-step sequence by co-workers for preparing a chef salad and how to conduct quality-control checks of their salads.

Self-Management The belief that employees with disabilities should be taught independence in the workplace has gained widespread acceptance among supported employment professionals and has spawned an exciting and promising area of research. Hughes et al. (1990) suggest identifying natural cues in the work environment that can be used to promote independent performance. For example, clocks or whistles may signal going to a job station; co-workers stopping work and leaving the job station might be the prompt for break time; and a growing pile of dirty dishes should be the cue to increase the rate of dish washing. The job specialist's role expands from training the employee how to perform various vocational and social skills to teaching the supported employee how to respond independently to the cues that occur naturally in the workplace. When naturally occurring cues are insufficient to prompt the desired behavior, the supported employee can be taught to respond to contrived cues, such as picture prompts depicting individual steps in a multiple-step task (Wilson, Schepis, & Mason-Main, 1987) or prerecorded verbal prompts interspersed within favorite music that the employee listens to on a Walkman-type cassette player (Barfels, Al-Attrash, & Heward, 1999; Grossi, 1998; West, Rayfield, Clements, Unger, & Thornton, 1994).

Self-monitoring, which has proven so successful in the classroom, can also be effectively used in employment training. Research has shown that employees with disabilities can use self-monitoring (observing and recording one's performance) and self-evaluation (comparing self-monitored performance with a goal or production criterion) to increase their job productivity and independence (Grossi & Heward, 1998; Sowers, Verdi, Bourbeau, & Sheehan, 1985; Wheeler, Bates, Marshall, & Miller, 1988). For example, Allen, White, and Test (1992) developed a picture/symbol form that employees with disabilities can use to self-monitor their performance on the job (see Figure 15.6).

Employees with disabilities can also learn to self-manage their work performance by providing their own verbal prompts and self-instructions (Hughes, 1997). For example, Salend, Ellis, and Reynolds (1989) used a self-instructional strategy to teach four adults with severe mental retardation to "talk while you work." Productivity increased dramatically and error rates decreased when the women verbalized to themselves, "Comb up, comb down, comb in bag, bag in box" while packaging combs in plastic bags. Hughes and Rusch (1989) taught two supported employees working at a janitorial supply company how to solve problems by using a self-instructional procedure consisting of four statements:

1. Statement of the problem (e.g., "Tape empty")
2. Statement of the response needed to solve the problem (e.g., "Need more tape")
3. Self-report (e.g., "Fixed it")
4. Self-reinforcement (e.g., "Good")

Sheltered Employment

A **sheltered workshop** is the most common type of vocational setting for adults with disabilities. Sheltered workshops serve individuals with a wide variety of disabilities, although about half are persons with mental retardation. Sheltered workshops

Task Sheet

Student: ______________ Week of: __________ Observer: ____________________

	M	*T*	*W*	*Th*	*Comments*
1. Job needs (e.g., name tag, lunch).					
2. Get work assignment.					
3. Get cart.					
4. Find and enter room.					
5. Check drapes.					
6. Check TV.					
7. Make bed.					
8. Dust.					
9. Stock amenities.					
10. Empty wastebaskets.					
11. Clean bathroom.					
12. Vacuum.					
13. Fill out hotel checklist					

Figure 15.6 A picture/symbol form that a student or employee with disabilities could use to self-monitor job performance

Source: From "Using a Picture/Symbol Form for Self-Monitoring within a Community-Based Training Program" by C. P. Allen, J. White, J., & D. W. Test. *Teaching Exceptional Children, 24*(2), 1992, p. 55. © 1992 by the Council for Exceptional Children. Reprinted with permission.

provide one or more of three types of programs: (1) evaluation and training for community-based employment (commonly referred to as transitional workshops), (2) extended or long-term employment, and (3) work activities.

A **work activity center** offers programs of activities for individuals whose disabilities are viewed by local decision makers as too severe for productive work. Rehabilitation and training revolve around concentration and persistence at a task. Intervals of work may be short, perhaps only an hour long, interspersed with other activities—such as training in social skills, self-help skills, household skills, community skills, and recreation. It is estimated that approximately 100,000 adults with disabilities attend work activity centers, with about 40,000 being excluded from an opportunity to earn wages (Will, 1986). The remaining 60,000 earn an average of $1.00 per day, or $288 per year.

Many sheltered work programs offer both transitional and extended employment within the same building. Transitional workshops continually try to place their employees in community-based jobs. Extended employment workshops are operated to provide whatever training and support services are necessary to enable individuals with severe disabilities to work productively within the sheltered environment. The Wage and Hour Division of the U.S. Department of Labor requires that persons working in an extended sheltered workshop receive at least 50% of the minimum wage; they may be paid an hourly wage or a piecework rate.

All sheltered workshops have at least two elements in common. First, they offer rehabilitation, training, and—in some instances—full employment. Second, to provide meaningful work for clients, a sheltered workshop must operate as a business. Sheltered workshops generally engage in one of three types of business ventures: contracting, prime manufacturing, or reclamation.

Contracting is the major source of work in most workshops. A contract is an agreement that a sheltered workshop will complete a specified job (e.g., assembling and packaging a company's product) within a specified time for a given price. Most sheltered workshops have one or more professional staff members, called contractors or contract procurement persons, whose sole job is to obtain and negotiate contracts with businesses and industries in the community.

Prime manufacturing involves the designing, producing, marketing, and shipping of a complete product. The advantage of prime manufacturing over contracting, assuming a successful product is being manufactured, is that the workshops do not have problems with downtime when they are between contracts. They can plan their training and labor requirements more directly. Most sheltered workshops, however, are neither staffed nor equipped to handle the more sophisticated business venture of prime manufacturing.

In a *reclamation,* or salvage, operation, a workshop purchases or collects salvageable material, performs the salvage or reclamation operation, and then sells the reclaimed product. Salvage and reclamation operations have proven successful for many sheltered workshops because they require a lot of labor, are low in overhead, and can usually continue indefinitely.

The average wage of all persons with mental retardation who worked in sheltered employment settings in 1987 was $1.02 per hour (Lakin, Hill, Chen, & Stephens, 1989).

Problems with Sheltered Workshops Sheltered workshops and work activity centers have come under intense criticism. The theoretical purpose of sheltered workshops is to train individuals in specific job-related skills that will enable them to obtain competitive employment; however, few employees of sheltered workshops are ever placed in jobs in the community. Only about 10% of sheltered workshop employees were placed in community jobs from 1977 to 1987 (U.S. Congress, 1987; U.S. Department of Labor, 1979), and many who are placed do not keep their jobs for long (Brickey, Campbell, & Browning, 1985). By contrast, approximately 50% of all supported employees are still earning wages and paying taxes one year after placement alongside nondisabled co-workers (Rusch, 1990).

Some professionals believe that the poor competitive employment record of sheltered workshop graduates may be more indicative of limitations inherent in sheltered workshops than of the employment potential of persons with disabilities

(Mank, Cioffi, & Yovanoff, 1998; McLoughlin, Garner, & Callahan, 1987). Rusch and Schutz (1981) concluded that "training" in sheltered workshops often consists of no more than "supervision with vague instructions and occasional prompts to stay on task" (p. 287). After conducting 9,000 hours of observation in a workshop for adults with mental retardation, Turner (1983) found that "the average individual in workshop society spends less than 50% of his or her time on the lines actually working" (p. 153). Turner found that on-task behavior varied tremendously as a function of the availability of subcontracts and that workers decreased their productivity rates to accommodate times when little subcontracted work was available.

Nisbet and Vincent (1986) compared the behavior of employees with moderate and severe mental retardation in sheltered and community work environments. They found that inappropriate behavior (e.g., hostility, aggression, inactivity, self-stimulation) was exhibited 8.8 times more frequently in sheltered environments than in the community work environments.

For a discussion of the challenges faced by agencies that operate sheltered work programs in converting their programs to supported employment, see West, Revell, and Wehman (1998).

> In sheltered environments, inactivity accounted for 61% of the inappropriate behavior and in nonsheltered environments, it accounted for 3%. The lack of meaningful work or absence of work altogether due to contract procurement difficulties may, in part, account for the inactivity rather than the inability of the worker with a disability to perform at an acceptable rate over a measurable duration of time. (Nisbet & Vincent, 1986, p. 26)

Because sheltered workshop employment is conducted in segregated settings, affords limited opportunities for job placement in the community, and provides extremely low pay, it has been called a "dead-end street" for individuals with mental retardation (Frank & Sitlington, 1993; Frank et al., 1992). Brown et al. (1984) are particularly critical of the lack of real work in sheltered workshops and work activity centers:

> Thousands of workers . . . are confined to activity centers and sheltered workshops where they are required to perform "simulated work," "prework," "could be work some day," and "looks like work" year after year. In the process, they are systematically and categorically denied access to the real world of work. (p. 266)

Residential Alternatives

Where one lives determines a great deal about how one lives. Where a person lives influences where she can work, what community services and resources will be available, who her friends will be, what the opportunities for recreation and leisure will be, and, to a great extent, what feelings of self and place in the community will develop. Not long ago, the only place someone with severe disabilities could live, if she did not live with family, was a large state-operated institution. Although she had done no wrong to society, an institution was considered the best place for the person. There were no other options—no such thing as residential alternatives.

Today, most communities provide a variety of residential options for adults with disabilities. Increased community-based residential services have meant a greater opportunity for adults with severe disabilities to live in a more normalized setting. Three residential alternatives for adults with mental retardation and related developmental disabilities—group homes, foster homes, and apartment living—help complete a continuum of possible living arrangements between the highly structured and typically segregated public institution and fully independent living. First, however, we consider the number of persons with mental retardation in large public institutions.

Institutions

Most of our nation's public institutions were founded in the 19th or early 20th century, when it was generally believed that people with mental retardation could not be educated or trained. Large custodial institutions (many institutions once housed hundreds or even a thousand or more people with mental retardation and other disabilities) kept people with disabilities segregated from the rest of society; the institutions were never designed to help people learn to live in the community. In the 1960s and 1970s, these institutions came under intense criticism for their inability to provide individualized residential services in a comfortable, humane, and normalized environment (Blatt, 1976; Blatt & Kaplan, 1966; Kugel & Wolfensberger, 1969; Wolfensberger, 1969). The complaints were not leveled against the concept of residential programs; there will probably always be persons whose disabilities are so severe that they require the kind of 24-hour support that residential facilities can offer. The problem lies with the inherent inability of an institutional environment to allow a person to experience a normal lifestyle.

During the past 35 years, tremendous improvements have been made in the abysmal living conditions in institutions that Blatt and Kaplan exposed in their book *Christmas in Purgatory* (1966). During the 1970s, the U.S. Department of Health, Education, and Welfare and the Joint Commission on the Accreditation of Hospitals developed extensive standards for residential facilities for individuals with mental retardation. A residential facility must meet these standards—which cover topics as diverse as building construction, staffing, and habilitative and educational programming—to qualify for federal and state Medicaid funding. Residential units that meet the standards are referred to as ICF-MR Medicaid facilities. Although the ICF-MR Medicaid system of rules and regulations has eliminated the inhumane and filthy conditions and the overcrowding that had been defining features of institutional life, the system has become the target of increasing criticism in terms of residents' quality of life and the high cost (e.g., Stancliffe & Hayden, 1998; Stancliffe & Lakin, 1998). Holburn's (1990) assessment is indicative of the sentiments of many:

Today, an ICF-MR facility serving 16 or more residents is considered an institution.

> If Burton Blatt could spend a day in an ICF-MR today, he would likely see a smaller, more livable residence. It would be clean, well-appointed, even homelike. The people who live there would be appropriately dressed, and a few might be interacting with direct-care staff members. Professional staff members would probably be found absorbed in paperwork or in a meeting. Voluminous records would detail individualized programmatic goals and procedures, but there would be questions as to which programs are actually being implemented and working. Further observation might reveal that the staff, as a whole, is not as organized or adept in teaching as the paperwork and expertise might suggest. However, the staff members might be quite sensitive and oriented to their own ICF-MR accountability requirements, giving the impression that regulation compliance is the predominant focus . . . , whereas habilitation and enhancing the quality of life are secondary. (p. 65)

Deinstitutionalization—the movement of people with mental retardation out of large institutions and into smaller community-based living environments, such as group homes or apartments—furthers the degree of normalization of persons who have previously resided in institutions. Deinstitutionalization is more than a philosophy or goal of concerned individuals; it has been an active reality during the past 30 years. The number of persons with mental retardation living in state institutions has decreased steadily from a high of 194,650 in 1967 to 58,320 persons in 1996 (Lakin, Prouty, Braddock, & Anderson, 1997; Lakin, Prouty, Smith, & Braddock, 1996). Evidence of this is the dramatic decline in the percentage of persons with mental retardation living in large public institutions. Whereas 85% of all people with mental retardation in the residential services system lived in large state-run institutions in 1967, only 32% were still in institutions by 1995 (Lakin, Braddock, & Smith, 1996).

But what about the experiences of those who transfer from institutions to smaller community residences? Does the quality of their lives improve? Given the complexity and variety of community residential programs and the many variables that play a part in determining quality of life and developmental progress, answering these important questions in a definitive, scientific manner is nearly impossible. Several studies, however, indicate generally positive outcomes for residents transferred from institutions to group homes to smaller community-based living arrangements (Larson & Lakin, 1989). One of the most comprehensive and widely cited studies was reported by Conroy and Bradley (1985), who monitored over a five-year period the adjustment of 176 persons with mental retardation who were deinstitutionalized from the Pennhurst State School and Hospital in Pennsylvania and placed in community residences. Measures of the adaptive behavior growth of the individuals placed in the community showed gains 10 times greater than those of a matched comparison group remaining in the institution.

A person who has just left an institution needs support in the community. Some former residents of state institutions experience "relocation syndrome" (Cochran, Sran, & Varano, 1977) or "transition shock" (Coffman & Harris, 1980) as a result of being dumped into the community without the necessary skills to cope successfully in their new environment and without easy access to support and follow-up services to see that the transition was successful.

In another study, Conroy (1996) compared 35 quality-of-life measures over a five-year period for individuals living in "small institutions" serving an average of eight people with outcomes for persons living in community-based living apartments or group homes of three people. Higher quality was found in the community living arrangements on 10 of the indicators (e.g., choice making, normalization, individualized treatment, family satisfaction). Higher quality was not found in the ICF-MR facilities on any of the indicators Conroy concluded:

> It was remarkable that the ICFs/MR did not provide more programming time than did community living arrangements in view of the ICF/MR standards' insistence on constant, aggressive, "active" treatment. Correspondingly, the difference in adaptive behavior developing over a 5-year period was unexpected, with the average ICF/MR resident losing in the performance of independent behaviors and the average community living arrangement resident *gaining*. (p. 24).

Group Homes

Group homes provide family-style living for a small group of individuals, usually three to six persons. Most group homes serve adults with mental retardation, although some have residents with other disabilities. Some group homes are principally residential and represent a permanent home for their residents. Staff persons in this type of home help the people who live there develop self-care and daily living skills, form interpersonal relationships, and participate in recreation and leisure skills. During the day, most residents work in the community or in a sheltered workshop.

More than half of all adults with mental retardation who receive residential services live in community group homes of fewer than six residents (Lakin, Braddock, & Smith, 1996), and the number is growing each year as closure of institutions continues.

Other group homes operate more as halfway houses. Their primary function is to prepare individuals with disabilities for a more independent living situation, such as a supervised apartment. These transitional group homes typically serve residents who have recently left institutions, bridging the gap between institutional and community living.

Two key aspects of group homes make them a much more normalized place to live than an institution: their size and their location. Most people grow up in a typical family-sized group, where there is opportunity for personal attention, care, and privacy. The congregate-living arrangement of an institution cannot offer a typical, normalized lifestyle, no matter how much effort a hardworking, caring staff makes. By keeping the number of people in a group home small, there is a greater chance for a family-like atmosphere (Bronston, 1980). Size is also directly related to the neighborhood's ability to assimilate the members of the group home into typical activities within the community (Cooke, 1981). Large groups tend to become self-sufficient, orienting inward and thereby resisting movement outward into the community; and in groups larger than six or eight, care providers can no longer relate properly to individuals. Indeed, some evidence suggests that quality of life is better for persons residing in smaller rather than larger group homes (Rotegard, Hill, & Bruininks, 1983).

The location and physical characteristics of the group home itself are also vital determinants of its ability to provide a normalized lifestyle. A group home must be located within the community, in a residential area, not in a commercially zoned district. It must be in an area where the people who live there can conveniently access shopping, schools, churches, public transportation, and recreational facilities. In other words, a group home must be located in a normal residential area where any one of us might live. And it must look like a home, not conspicuously different from the other family dwellings on the same street.

The Home Observation for Measurement of the Environment (HOME) is a 100-item scale that measures various aspects of a home environment and daily care practices of care providers (Bradley & Caldwell, 1979). The Home Quality Rating Scale (HQRS) is an attempt to measure the sense of love and attachment shown by care providers to the person with disabilities in a foster care setting and family participation in providing care (Meyers, Mink, & Nihira, 1981).

Recent research has shown that the architectural features of the home not only influence the degree to which residents and others give it a high rating of "homelikeness" but that some interior design features of a home correlate with the frequency of some adaptive and maladaptive behaviors by residents (Thompson, Robinson, Dietrich, Farris, & Sinclair, 1996a, 1996b). For example, a laundry room located in the basement may present challenges for residents that create behavioral problems, and a cafeteria-style dining room table is not conducive to conversations during meals. The most well known and widely used method for evaluating the degree to which service programs such as community residential programs meet various criteria of normalization is the Program Analysis of Service Systems (PASS) (Wolfensberger & Thomas, 1983). Pieper and Cappuccilli (1980) suggest a set of 15 questions, based on PASS, as a means of determining how appropriate a given residential setting may be.

New group homes are opening almost every day all across the country; however, they continue to encounter obstacles. Many communities have been slow to accept group homes into their neighborhoods. Most agencies, service groups, and individuals who have started (or attempted to start) group homes for persons with disabilities have encountered harsh resistance (Gelman, Epp, Downing, Twark, & Eyerly, 1989). Convinced that people with disabilities are dangerous or crazy, that they will have a bad influence on neighborhood children, or that property values will go down if a group home comes into the area, neighborhood associations have too often been effective in keeping group homes from starting.

Two studies analyzing real estate transaction data have found that neighborhood property values were not adversely affected by group homes. One study examined the sale prices of 525 homes sold around 13 group homes in and around Omaha, Nebraska (Ryan & Coyne, 1985); a second study analyzed the sale of 388 properties near 19 group homes in the Pittsburgh, Pennsylvania, area (Gelman et al., 1989).

In 1985, the U.S. Supreme Court unanimously ruled that communities cannot use a discriminatory zoning ordinance to prevent the establishment of group homes for persons with mental retardation in an area already zoned for apartment and other congregate living facilities (*City of Cleburne v. Cleburne Living Center,* 1985). Lawyers for the city of Cleburne, Texas, argued that the nearby presence of a junior high school and the fact that the group home site was located on a 500-year flood plain permitted the city to exclude the group home from that site. City administrators also claimed concerns about the legal responsibility for actions that "the mentally retarded might take," fire safety, congestion, and the serenity of the neighborhood. In their analysis of the Cleburne decision, the attorneys who prepared a brief on behalf of the group home for the AAMD, CEC, TASH, and four other national disability groups said:

> In each instance, the Supreme Court concluded that the city's purported concerns were a smokescreen for prejudice and unconstitutional discrimination. . . . [This case] is a useful precedent for arguments that zoning laws cannot be used as a device to discriminate against the housing needs of people who are mentally retarded, and in particular that the fears and irrational prejudices of neighbors who may be opposed to such a group home will not justify its exclusion from the community. (Ellis & Luckasson, 1985, p. 250)

Foster Homes

When a family opens its home to an unrelated person for an extended period, the term *foster home* applies. Although foster homes have provided temporary residential services and family care for children (usually wards of the court) for many years, more and more families have begun to share their homes with adults with disabilities. In return for providing room and board for their new family member, foster families receive a modest financial reimbursement.

To learn more about foster family care for persons with mental retardation, see Borthwick-Duffy, Widaman, Little, and Eyman (1992).

Life in a foster family home can have numerous advantages for an adult with disabilities. Instead of interacting with paid group home staff, who may or may not actually live at the same address, the person with disabilities lives in a residence that is owned or rented by individuals or families as their primary domicile. The person can participate and share in day-to-day family activities, receive individual attention from people vitally interested in his continued growth and development, and develop close interpersonal relationships. As part of a family unit, the adult with disabilities also has more opportunities to interact with and be accepted by the community at large. In their survey of small group homes and foster homes, Hill et al. (1989) found that 80% of foster home caregivers perceived residents with disabilities primarily as family members. In contrast, group home staff were more likely to view persons with disabilities as trainees or friends.

"What's for dinner?" Judy and Kathy, who spent most of their lives in a state institution for people with mental retardation, have shared an apartment for the past eight years.

Apartments and small group homes are the fastest-growing living arrangement for adults with disabilities. One-third of individuals with mental retardation who receive residential support services now live in community residences with one to three persons (Anderson, Lakin, Polioster, & Prouty, 1998).

It is estimated that 85% of persons with mental retardation or developmental delays live with their families or on their own without support from the public residential care system (Amado, Lakin, & Menke, 1990). The cost to society to support families in caring for their adult offspring with disabilities is small compared with the cost of providing public out-of-home residential services (Fujiura, Roccoforst, & Braddock, 1994). These individuals, however, do not experience the same level of independence and self-determination that characterize typical adulthood.

For information on how to help individuals with disabilities learn domestic and daily living skills, see Browder and Snell (in press) and Spooner and Test (1994).

Apartment Living

A rented apartment is one of the most common living arrangement for people without disabilities in our society. Today, an increasing number of adults with disabilities are enjoying the freedom and independence that apartment living offers. Apartment living offers individuals with disabilities an even greater opportunity for integration into the community than do group homes. Whereas the resident of a group home interacts primarily with other persons with disabilities, in an apartment-living arrangement (assuming the apartment is in a regular apartment complex), the likelihood of interacting with persons without disabilities is greater. Burchard, Hasazi, Gordon, and Yoe (1991) found that people who lived in supervised apartments had about twice as many social and leisure activities in the community than did individuals who lived in small group homes or with their natural parents. They also found that persons living in supervised apartments were more likely to be accompanied in the community by peers who are not disabled than those living in group homes. Another study followed up on seven young adults with mental retardation who had moved from a campus-type residential setting to community-based apartments (Rose, White, Conroy, & Smith, 1993). Assessments of the young adults' social/communication skills, community-living skills, and general independence conducted at 6 and 12 months after the move found significant and continued gains over pre-move measures.

Three types of apartment living for adults with disabilities are most common: the apartment cluster, the co-residence apartment, and the maximum-independence apartment. An *apartment cluster* consists of a small number of apartments housing persons with disabilities and another nearby apartment for a support person or staff member. An apartment cluster allows for a great deal of flexibility in the amount and degree of support needed by residents in the various apartments. Whereas some people might require direct help with such things as shopping, cooking, or even getting dressed, others need only limited assistance or suggestions and prompts. To facilitate social integration, some apartments in an apartment cluster may also be occupied by persons without disabilities.

A *co-residence apartment* is shared by an individual with disabilities and a roommate without disabilities. Although this arrangement is sometimes permanent, most co-residence apartments are used as a step toward independent living. The live-in roommates are often unpaid volunteers.

Two to four adults with disabilities usually cohabit *maximum-independence apartments.* These adults have all of the self-care and daily living skills required to take care of themselves and their apartment on a day-to-day basis. A supervisory visit is made once or twice a week to help them deal with any special problems they may be having.

Supported Living

Most professionals agree that no one type of residential setting is best for all adults with disabilities; just like the least restrictive environment in schools, a continuum of residential options is needed. But the continuum-of-services approach, with residential options ranging from most restrictive (ICF-MR) to least restrictive (independent living), is not without its problems and critics. The typical continuum of residential options does not guarantee there will be no gaps between one option and the next, nor does it recognize the possibility that other, perhaps more innovative, alternatives are appropriate for some individuals (Cooke, 1981). Also, continuum-of-service models usually assume that someone moves into the residential service system at the more restrictive end and must "earn the right to live in an integrated setting" (Hitzing, 1980, p. 84).

Several innovative models for residential services for adults with disabilities—based on the belief that residential placements must be adapted to the needs of the person with disabilities, not vice versa—have been developed (Apolloni & Cooke, 1981; Klein, 1994; Provencal, 1980). **Supported living** is the term used to describe a growing movement of helping people with disabilities live in the community as independently and normally as they possibly can. Similar to the way that supported employment provides ongoing, individualized supports to help a person with disabilities perform meaningful work in real community-based employment setting, supported living involves a personalized network of various kinds and levels of natural supports. Supported living is neither a place nor a single set of procedures to be provided for a person with disabilities.

To join in the discussion, "Does it make sense for society to provide the ongoing supports a person with severe disabilities needs in order to work and live in the community?" go to the Message Board Module at http://www.prenhall.com/heward.

Klein (1994) explains what supported living is by describing what it is not. Supported living does not revolve around a professional program. People should not live in a place referred to by an agency name or provider name (e.g., UCP Group Home, New Life Center). There are no criteria for participation (e.g., persons in this program must be able to cook for themselves, have a physical disability, need more or less than three hours per day of attendant care, have visual impairments). Supported living is not based on readiness and movement through a continuum. Participation in traditional residential services is based on a professional's assessment of the person's readiness or ability to live in a particular program, and a person must perform well (learn new skills on her individual habilitation plan) in order to move ("earn" the right) to the next, less restrictive rung on the continuum.

Supported living, according to Klein (1994), is guided by these nine principles:

1. *Individualization.* Supported living must be something that is for one person without exception. This does not mean that everyone has to live alone. It does mean that if people want to live with someone else, they choose with whom they live. The magic number becomes one.
2. *Everybody is ready.* There are no criteria to receive support because what occurs is individually designed. We must give up trying to make people ready by simulating how it is to live in a home and begin supporting people to have that home.
3. *Future planning.* People who are assisting others must get to know the individuals they are supporting. What are their desires and preferences? What would an ideal living situation look like for each person? After answers to these questions are determined, the people who care about the person get together regularly to develop a plan for getting as close as possible to that ideal living situation.
4. *Use of connections.* Traditional residential services rely on system solutions to problems, referring to the procedures and policy manual to find out what rules and regulations suggest. Supported living relies on the assistance of all who want to and can help. This means that professional care providers and staff are replaced by friends, family members, and neighbors whenever possible. "Who do we know who can help?" becomes a key question for planning and arranging needed supports.
5. *Flexible supports.* Supports are based and provided on the individual's schedule and needs, not on a program's schedule. Persons receive support where, when, how, and with whom it is needed. Supports must be flexible enough to be adjusted on the basis of the individual's changing needs, preferences, and desires.
6. *Combining natural supports, learning, and technology.* As much as possible, supports used are natural to the time, place, and person. Individuals are given opportunities to learn to provide their own support and to use technology to gain control over their environment as much as possible.
7. *Focusing on what people can do.* Traditional residential programs often focus on what people cannot do and design treatment programs to try to remediate those skill deficiencies. Supportive living focuses on what people can do, provides support

The supports needed by a person with severe disabilities to make an important difference in the quality of her social life at home may be as simple as help with a personal schedule, introductions, and a photo activity file with which to indicate preferences (Werner, Horner, & Newton, 1997).

for things they cannot do, and provides opportunities for them to learn how to do the things they want to do.

8. *Using language that is natural to the setting.* The language of supported living is natural and promotes inclusion in the community. The places where people live are described as Joe's home or Mary's home. People clean their homes and do their laundry rather than learn programs; people live with roommates, not with staff or care providers; friends, not volunteers, come over to visit; and people with disabilities are referred to as neighbors, friends, and citizens rather than as clients, consumers, and residents.
9. *Ownership and control.* Last and most important, the home is the person's, and that person controls the support that is received. Home ownership does not mean that most individuals with disabilities who do not have many financial resources will hold the mortgage to a home. It does mean, however, that they sign the lease, that things in the home belong to them, and that the place is their home. Roommates sublet from the person, support people are hired by the person, and support people respond to the need for assistance when, where, and how it is needed as determined by the person. (adapted from Klein, 1994, pp. 17–18)

Rather than a single approach or model, supported living is a philosophy about the kind of living experiences appropriate for citizens with disabilities and about commitment to figuring out how to best approximate the ideal for each individual. Supported living, supported employment, and inclusion of school-age students in regular classrooms share four fundamental philosophical positions and procedural features:

1. Individuals with disabilities have the right to live, work, and learn in the same settings as everyone else.
2. When meaningful inclusion occurs, benefits accrue to individuals with disabilities, to persons without disabilities, and to society at large.
3. Individuals with disabilities must be given opportunities to choose and self-determine the kinds of settings in which they wish to live, work, and learn and the kinds of lifestyle, job, and learning activities they wish to pursue.

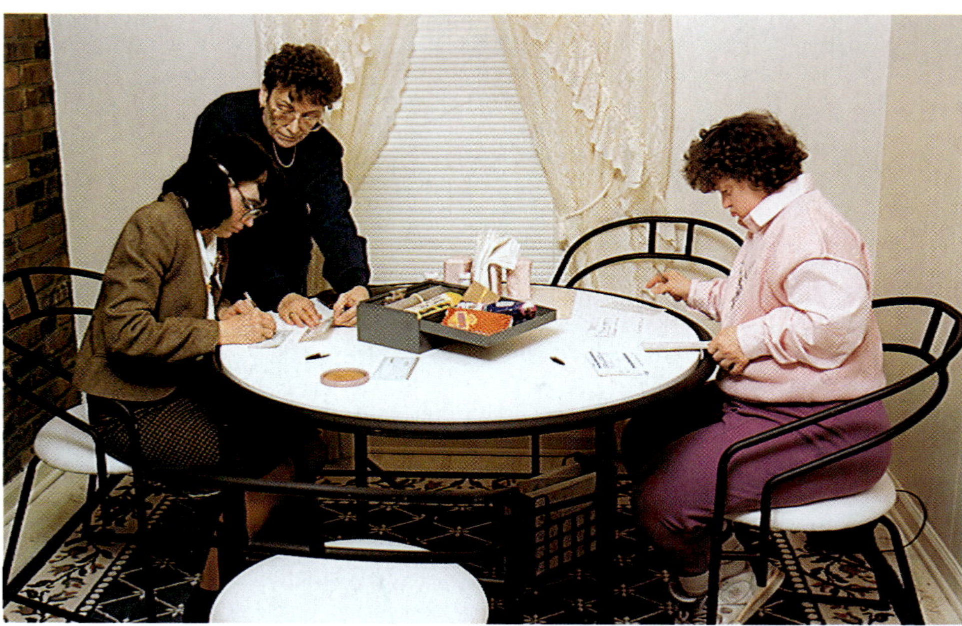

Supported living provides flexible supports when and as they are needed. Twice per month, Judy and Kathy pay their bills and review their budget with the help of a support person.

4. The kinds and levels of supports necessary to accomplish fully integrated and meaningful living, working, and learning must be determined and provided on an individual basis.

Recreation and Leisure

Recreation and the enjoyable use of leisure time are important components of a self-satisfying lifestyle. Most of us take for granted our ability to pursue leisure and recreational activities. We benefit from a lifetime of learning how to play and how to enjoy personal hobbies or crafts.

But appropriate recreation and leisure activities do not come easily for many adults with disabilities. To use community recreational resources, one must have transportation, the physical ability or skills to play the game, and, usually, other willing and able friends to play with. These three variables, alone or in combination, often work to limit the recreation and leisure activities available to the adult with disabilities. Transportation is not available; the person's disability does not allow him to swim, bowl, or play tennis; and he has no friends with similar skills and interests. Because of these problems, the majority of recreation and leisure experiences for many adults with disabilities have consisted of segregated, "disabled only" outings.

For examples of teaching secondary students and adults with mild to severe mental retardation to make choices and decisions during leisure, see Browder, Cooper, and Lim (1998) and Mahon and Bullock (1992).

Professionals must also realize the importance that leisure activities hold for adults with disabilities, especially those who are unemployed (Fain, 1986). Too often, their so-called leisure activities consist of watching great amounts of television, listening to music in the solitude of their rooms, and spending discretionary time socially isolated (Shannon, 1985). As Bigge (1991) says,

> Choice is the most crucial element. Without choice, activities become simply tasks rather than providing elements of control that lead to leisure satisfaction. If television is the only choice, choice is neglected. Thus, awareness of options through leisure education must precede development of specific recreation-related skills. (p. 429)

Tom loves to fish. Choice is crucial to the enjoyment of leisure activities.

Special educators must realize the importance of including training for recreation and leisure in curricula for school-age children with disabilities (Bigge, 1991; Peterson & Gunn, 1984). Bigge describes how numerous games, hobbies, crafts, and projects can be adapted to become enjoyable, worthwhile leisure-time pursuits for persons with disabilities. Areas she suggests include raising guinea pigs, music appreciation and study, photography, card games, and nature study. Suggestions are also available for adapting leisure activities for young adults who are deaf-blind, such as using permanent tactile prompts (e.g., attaching fabric to the flipper buttons of a pinball machine), adequately stabilizing materials, enhancing the visual or auditory input provided by the materials (e.g., using large-print, low-vision playing cards), and simplifying the requirements of the task (e.g., raising the front legs on a pinball machine, thereby reducing the speed with which the ball approaches the flippers) (Hamre-Nietupski, Nietupski, Sandvig, Sandvig, & Ayres, 1984).

Figure 15.7 discusses criticism leveled against the Special Olympics and some of the integrated sports activities that program has begun in recent years.

Learning appropriate leisure skills is particularly important for adults with severe disabilities. Most persons with severe disabilities have ample free time but do not use it constructively, often engaging in inappropriate behaviors such as body rocking, hand flapping, or bizarre vocalizations (Wehman & Schleien, 1981). A number of promising studies have been reported in which age-appropriate leisure skills have been taught to secondary students and adults with moderate and severe mental retardation (Collins, Hall, & Branson, 1997; Johnson & Bailey, 1977; Nietupski & Svoboda, 1982; Schleien, Kiernan, & Wehman, 1981). Schleien, Wehman, and Kiernan

Figure 15.7 Special Olympics: Opportunities for sports and physical development or segregated program?

Founded in 1968, Special Olympics is the largest sports and physical development program for individuals with mental retardation in the world, with more than 1 million athletes participating (Special Olympics, 1991). Some special educators have criticized Special Olympics for offering a segregated program only for athletes with mental retardation, which invites sympathy and limits opportunities for interaction with nondisabled peers, and for holding competitive events that are nonfunctional (Orelove, Wehman, & Wood, 1982; Polloway & Smith, 1978). These early criticisms were mostly on target because the Special Olympics program of the 1960s and 1970s was out of step with the changing philosophies in special education of integration and functional curriculum.

In recent years, however, Special Olympics has developed several innovative approaches toward promoting the inclusion of persons with disabilities in mainstream community recreation and sports activities. Two examples are the Unified Sports Program, in which teams made up of athletes with mental retardation and nondisabled teammates of similar age and skill levels compete in the local community, and Sports Partnerships, in which athletes with mental retardation become members of their local high school or club team and practice and receive training alongside nondisabled teammates. Block and Moon (1992) recommend that present-day critics of the Special Olympics "quit talking about what 'they' should do and start doing it themselves. . . . at this point in time, the organization so many of us have criticized may be doing as much as any of us to provide integrated recreation options" (p. 385). A national survey of agencies that provide services to individuals with disabilities found that while Special Olympics continues to be a leader in the area of sports for people with disabilities, respondents recommended that Special Olympics increase its emphasis on inclusion activities and provide opportunities to participate to individuals with a wider variety of disabilities (Porretta, Gillespie, & Jansma, 1996).

Teaching & Learning Video Connections

LOOK

LEARNING TO LIVE ON MY OWN

LOOKing at *LifeLink*: A Transition Lab

There is perhaps no greater transition in life than leaving high school and living at home to entering the world of work and independent living. The video *LifeLink* shows one school district's efforts to help students make this transition to adulthood a smooth one. In this project, educators in State College, Pennsylvania, allow students with disabilities to experience apartment living while they are still in high school so they can practice the skills and responsibilities that independent living requires.

Special educators have often used classroom simulations to teach daily living skills, sometimes with great success (e.g., van den Pol, Iwata, Ivancic, Page, Neef, & Whitley, 1981). But by conducting training in an actual apartment setting in the community, the *LifeLink* program provides learning opportunities that simply cannot be duplicated in the classroom. Students participate in such real-life activities as making beds, doing laundry, cleaning bathrooms, getting along with roommates, planning leisure time activities, shopping for groceries, and handling money—skills that will enable them to live as independently as possible in the community when the time comes. In addition, the *LifeLink* program gives parents (who otherwise might do most tasks for their children or expect to have to do them for the rest of their children's lives) a glimpse of how happy and successful their children can be on their own or in a supported living situation.

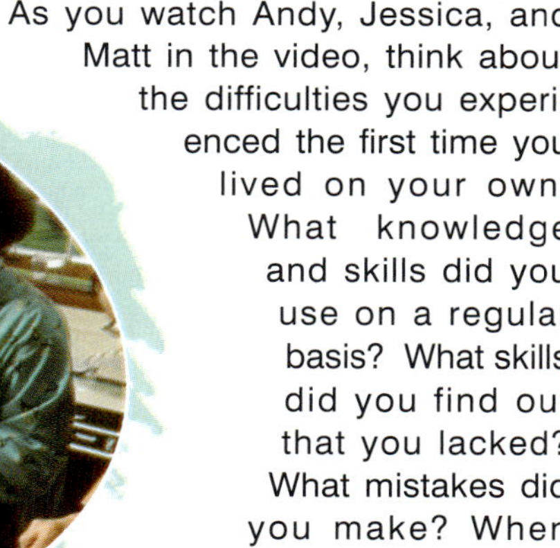

Greenlar/The Image Works

As you watch Andy, Jessica, and Matt in the video, think about the difficulties you experienced the first time you lived on your own. What knowledge and skills did you use on a regular basis? What skills did you find out that you lacked? What mistakes did you make? When and how did you have to problem solve?

LEARN

LEARNing about Effective Transition Programming

How do we ensure that students with disabilities leave high school with the ability to function in the adult world as employees, as homeowners or apartment dwellers, and as friends, neighbors, and citizens in their community? The young people who participated in the *LifeLink* program are confident of their new abilities and are excited about the prospects of living on their own. Andy now sorts whites and darks before doing his laundry, Jessica is more sociable with her peers, and Matt has learned to pay his utility bills on time. And at least some of their parents' anxiety about their future has been replaced by a newfound pride in their children's accomplishments and growing independence. Three components of the *LifeLink* program that contribute to these positive outcomes are self-determination, interactive teaming, and naturalistic teaching.

* ***Self-determination.*** The importance of self-determination has been stressed throughout this text. When provided with the training and support to help direct their own programs, students with disabilities often show increased motivation and dedication to learning. As a result, they attain levels of competence and independence previously considered beyond their capabilities. *LifeLink* students picked the apartment in which they would live, created advertisements for program staff, interviewed applicants, and helped decide who would be hired. Later, they checked out the amenities offered by a new apartment complex under construction and decided to move. A critical element of transition programming is the students' right and responsibility to make important decisions about their education—including the freedom to fail, to get knocked down and get back up again.

* ***Interactive Teaming.*** *LifeLink* students benefit greatly from the collaboration among classroom teachers, apartment support staff, community agencies, and their parents. The program is an excellent example of the kind of interactive teaming described in the Teaching & Learning box on pages 55–56 in Chapter 2.

* ***Naturalistic Teaching and Learning.*** Real-life tasks of day-to-day living define the *LifeLink* curriculum. The staff teaches critical skills as problems are encountered (e.g., what to do if you don't have enough money to pay for the groceries), and students are allowed to experience the natural consequences of their behavior (e.g., if the bill isn't paid on time, the phone will be disconnected). Knowledge and skills learned through such naturalistic instruction have a high probability of maintenance and generalization.

As part of naturalistic teaching, you may want to teach students how to locate useful information on the Internet, such as this site (http://www.ilusa.com/news.html) from Independent Living USA. Through the Internet, students can be alerted to legislation and forums that address disability issues.

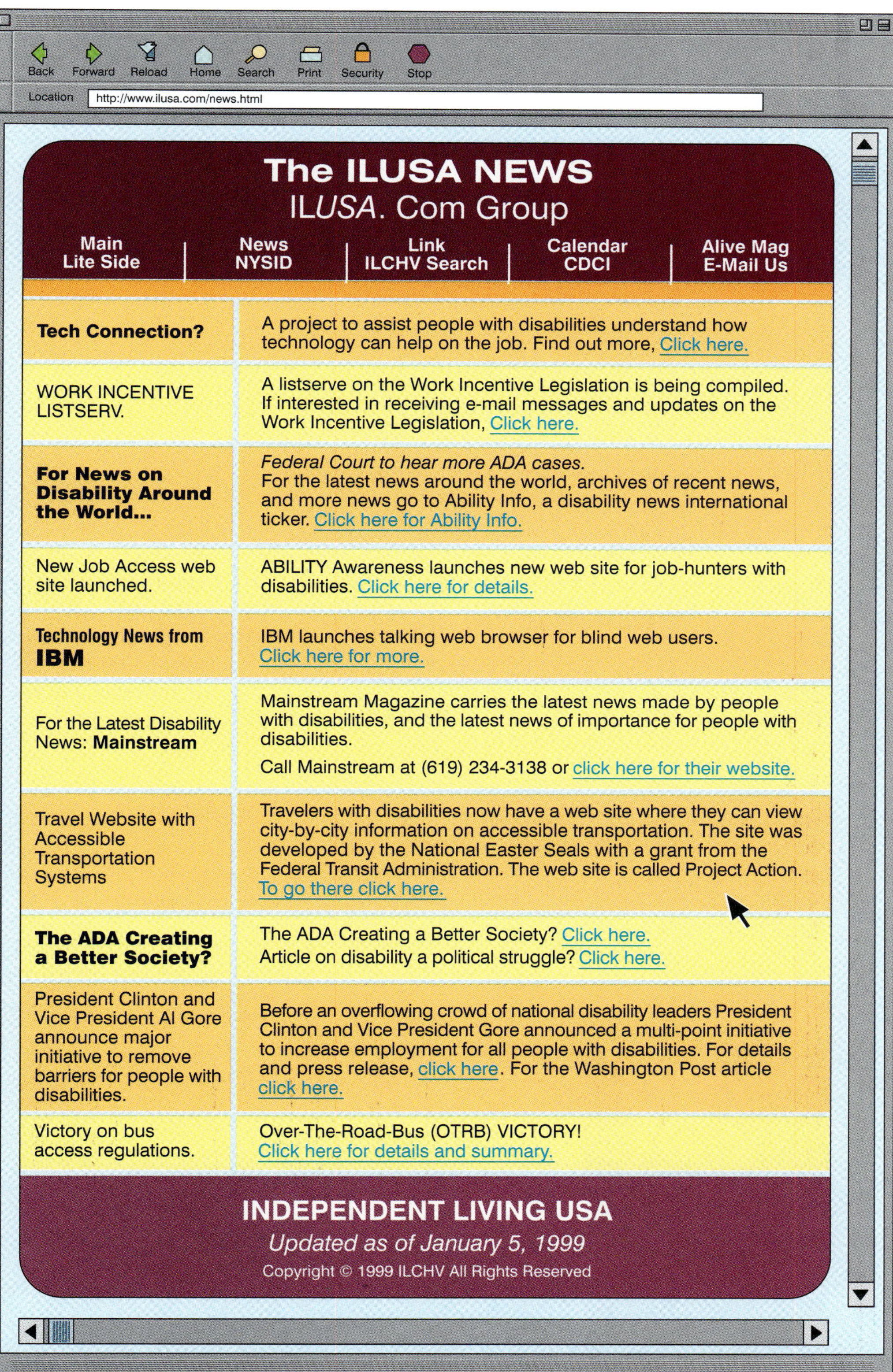

Back Forward Reload Home Search Print Security Stop

Location http://www.ilusa.com/news.html

The ILUSA NEWS

ILUSA. Com Group

Main | News | Link | Calendar | Alive Mag
Lite Side | NYSID | ILCHV Search | CDCI | E-Mail Us

Tech Connection?	A project to assist people with disabilities understand how technology can help on the job. Find out more, Click here.
WORK INCENTIVE LISTSERV.	A listserve on the Work Incentive Legislation is being compiled. If interested in receiving e-mail messages and updates on the Work Incentive Legislation, Click here.
For News on Disability Around the World...	*Federal Court to hear more ADA cases.* For the latest news around the world, archives of recent news, and more news go to Ability Info, a disability news international ticker. Click here for Ability Info.
New Job Access web site launched.	ABILITY Awareness launches new web site for job-hunters with disabilities. Click here for details.
Technology News from IBM	IBM launches talking web browser for blind web users. Click here for more.
For the Latest Disability News: **Mainstream**	Mainstream Magazine carries the latest news made by people with disabilities, and the latest news of importance for people with disabilities. Call Mainstream at (619) 234-3138 or click here for their website.
Travel Website with Accessible Transportation Systems	Travelers with disabilities now have a web site where they can view city-by-city information on accessible transportation. The site was developed by the National Easter Seals with a grant from the Federal Transit Administration. The web site is called Project Action. To go there click here.
The ADA Creating a Better Society?	The ADA Creating a Better Society? Click here. Article on disability a political struggle? Click here.
President Clinton and Vice President Al Gore announce major initiative to remove barriers for people with disabilities.	Before an overflowing crowd of national disability leaders President Clinton and Vice President Gore announced a multi-point initiative to increase employment for all people with disabilities. For details and press release, click here. For the Washington Post article click here.
Victory on bus access regulations.	Over-The-Road-Bus (OTRB) VICTORY! Click here for details and summary.

INDEPENDENT LIVING USA

Updated as of January 5, 1999

TEACH

TEACHing for Transition to a Place of Your Own

Transition planning begins with thinking and talking and dreaming about the future. What are the student's strengths and abilities that will contribute to that future? What new knowledge and skills must be acquired to make that future a reality? Here are three follow-up activities that will provide some insight and practice in transition planning and programming in the area of independent living.

Futures Planning. Transition planning is all about the future. Talk with a high school student with disabilities to find out her hopes or plans for living arrangements after leaving school. Make up your own set of interview questions, but include the following:

- Where do you want to live when you finish high school?
- Do you think you can live on your own? Why or why not?
- What will be the best thing about living on your own?
- What do think will be the most difficult or scariest thing about living on your own?
- Do you want a roommate? Why or why not?

How do the student's answers compare with how you might have responded as a high school student? If you now live away from your parents in an apartment or dorm, think about how prepared (or unprepared) you were for living on your own. Ask the same questions of the student's parents. Find out what experiences or opportunities their child has had that might prepare her to live on her own. Ask about their hopes and concerns, and if it will be hard for them to "let go."

Transition Teaming. With a group of your peers, create a mock transition team for the student and family who shared with you their dreams and expectations for the future. Assign roles for one another: the student, parents and family members, special and general education teachers, related service providers, community agency personnel, and school district administrator. Hold a team meeting and write a transition plan to help the student and family reach their goals in the area of independent living.

Teaching for Transition Success. Develop a lesson plan for teaching a high school student the following skills:

Teaching basic life skills does not need to wait until students are in high school. Students who are younger benefit from learning practical skills earlier and can transition to more challenging skills when they are older.

Todd Yarrington/Merrill

- prepare a box of macaroni and cheese
- sort, wash, dry, fold, and put away a load of laundry
- respond to telephone solicitations to purchase various items or services
- clean a bathroom
- invite and host one or more friends for an evening of watching videos

Evaluate your plan in terms of the naturalistic qualities described above. If the student who needs and wants to learn these skills does not participate in a community-based program like *LifeLink*, how might you design instruction to promote generalization and maintenance?

(1981) successfully taught three adults with severe and multiple disabilities to throw darts; Hill, Wehman, and Horst (1982) taught a group of young adults with severe disabilities to play pinball machines. Vandercook (1991) taught five high school students with severe mental retardation and physical disabilities to play pinball and bowl with nondisabled peer partners. In another study, four teenagers and young adults with severe and profound mental retardation learned to perform a basic dance step (Lagomarcino, Reid, Ivancic, & Faw, 1984).

The Ultimate Goal: A Better Life

Quality of Life

Without question, significant strides have been made in the lives of many people with disabilities. Tens of thousands of people who previously were relegated to life in an institution now live in real homes in regular neighborhoods. Many thousands who never had an opportunity to learn meaningful job skills go to work each day and bring home a paycheck each week. But living in a community-based residence and having a job in an integrated setting do not translate automatically into a better life (Landesman, 1986).

Most advocates and professionals now realize that the physical presence of individuals with disabilities in integrated residential, work, and community settings is an important first step but that the only truly meaningful outcome of human service programs must be an improved quality of life. How highly would we rate the quality of life for a woman who always sits alone during lunch and breaks at work because she has not developed a social relationship with her co-workers? Recent research on social interaction patterns in integrated work settings suggests that this is an all-too-common scenario. Several studies have found that the majority of contact between employees with disabilities and their nondisabled co-workers involves task performance; disabled workers are less involved in good-natured teasing and joking; and few workers with disabilities are befriended by their co-workers (e.g., Lignugaris/Kraft, Rule, Salzberg, & Stowitscheck, 1988; Rusch, Johnson, & Hughes, 1990; Shafer, Rice, Metzler, & Haring, 1989).

Belfiore and Toro-Zambrana (1994) offer step-by-step instructions to help care providers recognize and provide choice-making opportunities for persons with disabilities in community settings. For research and recommendations on the supports needed to improve the quality of life of older citizens with disabilities, see Seltzer, Krauss, and Janicki (1994) and Sutton, Factor, Hawkins, Heller, and Seltzer (1993).

And what is the quality of life for a young man who lives in a small group home in a residential neighborhood but who seldom or never gets to choose what will be served for dinner or when he will go to bed and whose only "friends" are the paid staff responsible for supervising him on his weekly trip to the shopping mall? One measure of the quality of a person's life is the extent to which he can make choices (Meyer, 1986). The choices we make play a significant role in defining our individual identities—from everyday matters, such as what to eat or wear, to the choices we make on larger matters, such as where to live or what kind of work to do (O'Brien, 1987). Opportunities to make choices for persons living in residential programs, however, "are generally absent from the daily routines" (Bercovici, 1983, p. 42). One study comparing the everyday choices and choice-making opportunities of 24 adults with mental retardation living in group homes with 42 adults without disabilities found the group home residents had significantly fewer choices about fundamental matters of daily living (e.g., what television show to watch, whether to make a phone call) (Kishi, Teelucksingh, Zollers, Park-Lee, & Meyer, 1988).

Schalock, Keith, Hoffman, and Karan (1989) have proposed an objective measure of quality of life. Figure 15.8 shows the 28 criterion-referenced questions that comprise the Quality of Life Index. The questions are organized under three aspects: control of one's environment, involvement in the community, and social relationships. This approach to assessing the quality of life differs from facility, or program-level, evaluations such as the Program Analysis of Service Systems (PASS) (Wolfens-

Maria Serrao won't let paraplegia get in the way of her quality of life. In her video "Everyone Can Exercise!" Maria shows individuals with disabilities how to achieve fitness and enjoy a more active lifestyle.

There are numerous conceptions and definitions of quality of life, debates over how or whether it can be measured, and recommendations of what should or must be done to improve it (e.g., Dennis, Williams, Giangreco, & Cloninger, 1993; Halpern, 1993; Hatton, 1998; Sands & Kozleski, 1994; Schalock & Bogale, 1990; Wehmeyer, 1994).

berger & Thomas, 1983). The authors' goal is to "develop an instrument that can be used easily by (re)habilitation personnel to assess, monitor, and improve a person's quality of life" (p. 27). They note the Quality of Life Index is more appropriate for living rather than work environments and that generalizations across all types of living environments are not possible.

Handicapism

A continuing problem for many adults with disabilities is lack of acceptance as full members of our society, with all the rights, privileges, and services granted to any citizen. Progress has been made in this regard (witness the litigation and legislation on behalf of persons with disabilities that have been discussed throughout this book), but we still have a long way to go. Courts can decree and laws can require, but neither can alter the way individuals treat people with disabilities. People with disabilities often "seem to be in the community but not of it" (Birenbaum, 1986, p. 145).

To read about the personal experiences of living and working in the community as described by people with disabilities, see Taylor, Bogdan, and Lutfiyya (1995).

Most adults with disabilities believe the biggest barriers to full integration into society are not inaccessible buildings or the actual restrictions imposed by their disabilities but the differential treatment afforded them by nondisabled people. Just as the terms *racism* and *sexism* indicate prejudiced, discriminatory treatment of racial groups and women, the term **handicapism** has been coined to describe biased reactions toward a person with a disability. Those reactions are not based on an individual's qualities or performance but on a presumption of what the disabled person must feel or must be like because of the disability.

Factor 1: Environmental Control	Factor 2: Community Involvement	Factor 3: Social Relations
1. How many people sleep in your bedroom?	14. Does your job make you feel good?	3. How about your neighbors? How do they treat you?
2. How much control do you have when you go to bed and when you get up?	15. Do you think that your work is important to your employer?	4. How do you like this town?
7. Who plans your meals?	17. How often do you use public transportation? (handibus, taxi, city bus, etc.)	5. How often do you talk with the neighbors, either in the yard or in their home?
8. Who shops for groceries?	18. Do you earn enough money to pay for all the things you need?	6. If there are staff or family where you live, or if you live with another client or spouse, do they eat meals with you?
9. Who chose the decorations in your bedroom?	19. Do you have friends over to visit your home?	10. Do you have any pets?
11. If you have a regular doctor, who chose your doctor?	27. How frequently do you spend time in recreational activities in town?	21. Are there people living with you who have dangerous or annoying behavior problems?
12. If you take medicines, who gives you the medicine?		25. What type of educational program are you involved in at the present time?
13. Who makes your doctor and dentist appointments?		
16. How do you usually get to work?		
20. Do you have a guardian or conservator?		
22. Do you have a key to your house?		
23. How many rooms or areas in your house are locked so that you cannot get in them?		
24. Can you do what you want to do?		
26. Who decides how you spend your money?		
28. When can friends visit your home?		

Note: Each of the 28 questions is anwered or scored on a 1- to 3-point scale. A person's Quality of Life Index can range from 28 (low) to 84 (high).

Note: Numbering reflects sequence of items on questionnaire.

Figure 15.8 The Quality of Life Index

Source: Reprinted from Schalock, R. L., Keith, K. D., Hoffman, K., & Karan, O. C. (1989). Quality of life: Its measurement and use. *Mental Retardation, 27,* 27. Used by permission.

Handicapism occurs on personal, professional, and societal levels. Biklen and Bogdan (1976) describe seven forms of handicapism in personal relations:

> First, there is a tendency to presume sadness on the part of the person with a disability. For example, one woman who has a physical disability, and who, incidentally, smiles a lot, told us of an encounter with a man who said, "It's so good that you can still smile. Lord knows, you don't have much to be happy for."
>
> Second, there is the penchant to pity. You might have heard, "It is a tragedy that it had to happen to her; she had so much going for her." Or people sometimes tell us, "It is so good of you to give up your lives to help the poor souls." Or "My, you must be so patient to work with them. I could never do it."
>
> Third, people without disabilities sometimes focus so intensely on the disability as to make it impossible to recognize that the person with the disability is also simply another person with many of the same emotions, needs, and interests as other people. This attitude is reflected in the perennial questions, "What is it like to be deaf?" "It must be hard to get around in a wheelchair," and "You must really wish you could see sometimes."
>
> Fourth, people with disabilities are often treated as children. Notice, for example, that feature films about people with mental retardation and physical handicaps are so frequently titled with first names: "Joey," "Charley," "Larry," and "Walter." We communicate this same message by calling disabled adults by first names when full names and titles would be more appropriate and by talking in a tone reserved for children.
>
> Fifth is avoidance. Having a disability often means being avoided, given the cold shoulder, and stared at from a distance. The phrases "Sorry, I have to go now," "Let's get together sometime [but not now and not any specific time]," and, "I'd like to talk but I have to run" are repeated too consistently for mere coincidence.
>
> Sixth, we all grow up amidst a rampage of handicapist humor. It must take a psychological toll. "Did you hear the one about the moron who threw the clock out the window?" "There was a dwarf with a sawed-off cane. . . . " "Two deaf brothers went into business with each other . . . and a blind man entered the store."
>
> Seventh, people with disabilities frequently find themselves spoken for, as if they were not present or were unable to speak for themselves. In a similar vein, people without disabilities sometimes speak about people with disabilities in front of them, again as if they were objects and not people.
>
> In terms of personal relations, then, if you are labeled "handicapped," handicapism is your biggest burden. It is a no-win situation. You are not simply an ordinary person.

Only when a man or woman with a disability is allowed to be simply an ordinary person—given the opportunity to strive and perhaps succeed but also allowed the freedom and dignity to strive and sometimes fail—can normalization become a reality. Only then can people with disabilities enjoy a quality of life that citizens without disabilities take for granted.

Self-Advocacy

Advocacy on behalf of children and adults with disabilities has had tremendous impact, especially during the past 30 years. Indeed, most of the pervasive changes in education, employment opportunities, and residential services have occurred because of the efforts of advocates. Advocacy for persons with disabilities has traditionally been undertaken by family members, friends, professionals, and attorneys. Bigge (1991), however, is among a growing number of professionals and individuals with disabilities who believe that

> the age of "doing for" a person with a disability is rapidly diminishing. Increasingly, our society is viewing individuals with disabilities as integral and contributing members of the community in which they are a part. Federal and state legislation have provided and supported equal access of individuals with disabilities into all walks of life. . . . Along with the

acquisition of these equal rights has come the responsibility for the utilization and protection of these rights. It is now necessary for those with disabilities, as individuals and as groups, to assert themselves as self-advocates. (p. 493)

Internet addresses for several disability rights and self-advocacy organizations are provided in "For More Information" at the end of the chapter.

Persons with disabilities have begun to assert their legal rights, challenging the view that persons with disabilities are incapable of speaking for themselves. Perhaps most conspicuous has been the self-advocacy of individuals with physical disabilities, who have been highly effective in their lobbying as part of the independent living movement. Individuals with sensory impairments have also engaged in self-advocacy. A striking and successful example is the refusal by students at Gallaudet University to accept the appointment of a hearing president who did not know American Sign Language. Persons with mental retardation, however, have engaged in little self-advocacy, perhaps because many have not learned to recognize when their rights are being violated and because they lack the verbal skills to advocate on their behalf.

Despite the importance of self-advocacy and the efforts of persons with disabilities to assert their rights, little research has been conducted on how to teach self-advocacy skills. A study by Sievert, Cuvo, and Davis (1988) is a notable exception. They taught eight adults with a variety of mild disabilities (mental retardation, learning disability, cerebral palsy, speech impairment) to discriminate whether or not possible violations of legal rights occurred in up to 200 hypothetical scenarios involving 30 specific rights (e.g., right to help when voting) across four general areas: personal, community, human services, and consumer. Through role playing, the participants learned a three-step procedure for redressing a violation that involved (1) asserting their rights directly to the person who violated them, (2) if this person did not resolve the problem, complaining to that person's supervisor, and (3) if the problem remained unsolved, seeking the assistance of a community advocacy agency. Participants were given a handbook describing each of the legal rights and the procedure for redressing violations. With one exception, the participants demonstrated generalization and maintenance of their newly learned self-advocacy skills by responding accurately to simulations and depictions of legal rights violations in natural settings.

Self-advocacy: responsibility for the utilization and protection of one's rights.

Giving students the responsibility of directing and managing their own IEP is an excellent way to help them learn self-determination and independence (Martin & Marshall, 1995).

Self-advocacy requires self-determination:

> Self-determined people know how to choose. They know what they want and use their self-advocacy skills to get it. From an awareness of personal needs, self-determined individuals choose goals and doggedly pursue those goals. This involves asserting their presence, making their needs known, evaluating progress toward meeting their goals, adjusting their performance, and creating unique approaches to solve problems. (Martin, Marshall, & Maxson, 1993, p. 55)

This is a tall order for anyone, with or without disabilities. But along with these skills comes freedom.

> Freedom to choose, what kind of job to have, where to live, to have relationships, to make all of the everyday decisions (big and small), and the freedom to make mistakes. Dignity of failure.
>
> Tony Coehlo, Chairperson of the President's Committee on Employment of People with Disabilities, opened the 1994 National Self-Advocacy Conference: Voices for Choices with these remarks:
>
> We want everything we are entitled to as citizens, nothing more, but nothing less. We want the privileges of full citizenship, but we also welcome its responsibilities. We want the respect we deserve, and we demand the rights we have been denied. We now recognize that empowerment is not a gift to be given, but a right to be demanded. (in Cone, 1994, p. 445)

Still a Long Way to Go

In general, the quality of life for most adults with disabilities today is better than it has ever been. Not only do more adults with disabilities live, work, and play in community-based, integrated environments, but more adults with disabilities have acquired or are acquiring the personal, social, work, and leisure skills that enable them to enjoy the benefits of those settings. But more persons with disabilities does not mean *all* persons with disabilities. And individuals don't live life "in general"; they experience specific instances of joy and sadness, success and failure. There is still a long way to go.

WWW

Use the self-tests at http://www.prenhall.com/heward to assess your knowledge of the content of Chapter 15.

True, the quality of life for someone who now has his own bedroom in a group home and works for wages in a sheltered workshop may be appreciably better than it was before he left the institution where he ate and slept communally and his "work" consisted of an endless series of arts-and-crafts projects. But do the unacceptable standards of the past mean that a relatively better quality of life today is therefore good? Would it be good enough for you?

PROFILES AND PERSPECTIVES

Sebine: Twelve Years Later— "I Need a Vacation"

When we took her picture for the cover of the second edition of this textbook, Sebine Johnson was 10 years old and in the third grade. Now, she's 22 years old and experiencing the joys and responsibilities and facing the changes that lie ahead for any young adult. She works two jobs, juggles her checkbook, takes dance lessons, and hangs out with friends. Sebine is still living with her parents but will soon be moving into her own home as part of a supported living program. Before reading what Sebine has to say about her busy life, here's a brief biography of her educational experiences that helped prepare her for where she is today.

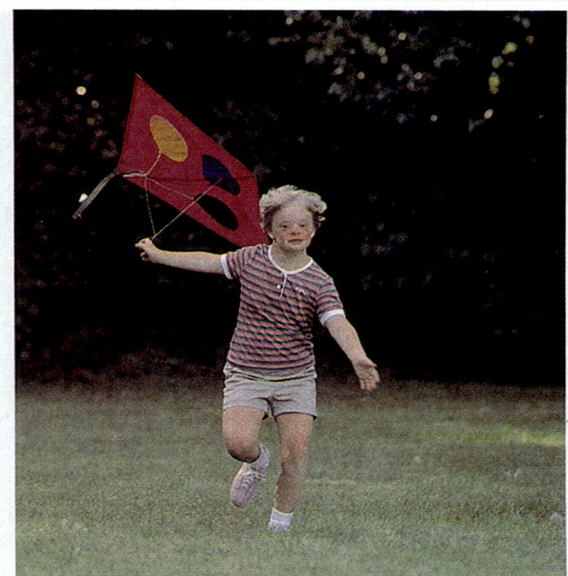

Sebine on the cover of the second edition.

Early Childhood Sebine was born in Minneapolis and diagnosed with Down syndrome. The doctor strongly encouraged her parents to place her in an institution. When she was 1½ months old, her parents began taking her once a week to an infant stimulation program, where they also received training on how to work with Sebine at home. At about 18 months of age, Sebine began attending a full-time (five hours per day, five days per week), center-based, early intervention program. Even though this was before P.L. 94–142, the center had IEPs for every child and offered multidisciplinary, family-oriented services, including a speech therapist and a social worker.

When Sebine was 5 years old, her family moved to Columbus, Ohio, and she was enrolled in a half-day integrated preschool. When she was 6, her parents met with the principal, school psychologist, and teaching staff of her neighborhood school to write her first IEP. There was some initial reluctance to having Sebine in the school because the school had never before had a child with Down syndrome and a county program operated separate schools for children with such disabilities. Nevertheless, school personnel agreed to create a full-day kindergarten program for Sebine. She spent mornings in the regular kindergarten classroom and afternoons going back and forth between the regular class, a resource room, music, art, the library, and gym. Sebine "sold herself" with her outgoing personality and was soon a regular part of the school. During that kindergarten year, the resource room teacher taught Sebine how to read with a phonics-based approach.

Elementary School During her elementary years, Sebine spent about half of each school day with her regular classroom peers, being mainstreamed for music and art and some academic activities. In first grade, Sebine and her classmates participated in a research study evaluating a classwide peer tutoring system. Sebine did so well that she was featured in a journal article describing how peer tutoring could be used as a means to include children with disabilities in both the academic and social life of a regular classroom (Cooke, Heron, Heward, & Test, 1982). Several of her elementary teachers took the initiative to plan and adapt academic activities to include Sebine, particularly in social studies, creative writing, plays, and community activities. In fifth grade, Sebine started playing drums in the school band.

Sebine's elementary school had only one resource room, and it served children in grades 1 to 6. Because of the large differences in the students' ages, skills, and special education needs, it was difficult to keep track of all of their schedules. The resource room teacher developed laminated, color-coded cards. Sebine learned to follow her own schedule, independently getting herself from the resource room, to the regular classroom, to the gym, to the music room, back to the resource room, and so on. Her parents believe this opportunity to be independent laid the foundation for the high level of self-determination and responsibility that Sebine displays as a young adult.

With two jobs and a busy social life, Sebine is on the go.

Junior High To facilitate the transition to junior high school, Sebine's mother and her elementary special education teacher met with each of the teachers and staff members that Sebine would come into contact with: the gym teacher, art teacher, librarian, cooks, school secretary, custodian, and so on. They told of Sebine's experiences and success in elementary school, answered questions about her strengths and weaknesses, and suggested ways that people might support her inclusion in the school.

Sebine spent between one-third and one-half of her time in regular classes, went to school dances and sports events, and was generally a part of the school. She was treated well by her peers. Teachers reported that if a new student laughed or stared at Sebine, he would be "talked to" and corrected by those who knew Sebine.

Sebine began attending her IEP meetings during junior high. The meetings were sometimes difficult for her—as they would be for anyone who is listening to a group of people who are important in your life talk about you and rehash every flaw and thing you cannot do as well as some that you can.

High School In high school, Sebine attended regular classes for health, art, music, gym, and home economics. Her extracurricular activities included taking part in several clubs, participating on the gymnastics team, and participating in the band for two years. She attended football and basketball games and went to the prom.

In her sophomore and junior years, Sebine's IEP included community-based job experiences; and she spent half of each school day working at different jobs—dishwasher, laundry, supply room, etc.—at a local hospital. Sebine's transition program during her senior year included training at a Bob Evans Restaurant, which eventually led to competitive employment.

Here are some of the things Sebine has to say about her life today.

Work

> Before I left school, I had an interview down at the Bob Evans on Olentangy River Road. They hired me for busing tables. I have worked there for over three years. Dave, the manager, has also trained me how to do tank [dish washing].
>
> A cab takes me to work. I tell the driver my schedule. Sometimes they are late or forget to come, so I call the dispatcher. When I finish work, they give me a ride home.

When Sebine first started at the restaurant, she only worked during the afternoon, when it wasn't very busy. Her supervisor was concerned that she might not be able to keep up the pace required for the busy lunch or dinner hours. A job coach was brought in to help increase her productivity. But after two years, Sebine was only working 19 hours per week, so she decided to get a second job. Her parents helped her prepare a résumé.

I wrote the address on the envelope and mailed it to other restaurants. The owner called me, and I had an interview.

The second job was at Nickleby's Bookstore & Cafe, where Sebine worked as a "tanker." For several months, Sebine worked seven days per week: Monday through Friday afternoons at Bob Evans and Saturday and Sunday afternoons at Nickleby's. Then trouble happened at Nickleby's. The concern was about Sebine's work rate and that she wasn't following her supervisor's directions to put dishes and other items in the right places.

I got fired. I was arguing. I put things not in the right place. I just put it where I felt like.

A week later, Sebine went back to apologize, on her own volition and by herself, even though she had already found another job.

I rode my bike to the Spaghetti Shop. It was a store where I mailed my résumé before. The manager still had my résumé. He just gave me an application form and I signed it. Then he asked me what's my schedule at Bob's. I started there a couple months ago. First they had me bus, but I'm really good at it, and so now they send me in the back to help wash dishes too. Now, Mondays and Tuesdays I work from 11–2, no, no, Mondays and Tuesday I work from 11 to 1, and Wednesday, Thursday and Friday I work 11 to 2.

In the meantime, Sebine's supervisor at Bob Evans gave her the additional hours she'd been asking for, increasing her work week there to 32 hours.

And I work late at Bob's now. Friday they have me work 5 to 9, Saturday 2 to 9, Sunday 2 to 9, Monday 2 to 9, Tuesday 2 to 9. Sometimes they change my schedule, have me come in on Wednesdays or holidays or to make up for someone who's missing.

Friends Sebine's entire family, including her grandparents, recently had dinner at Bob Evans when she was on duty. Sebine proudly introduced them to all of her co-workers.

Yeah, I got friends there. I've got lots of friends from work, from church and dance too. We usually go out to eat, see a movie. If it's someone's birthday, I usually take them out. Sometimes we have a party.

Some of Sebine's friends have disabilities, and some do not.

I got lots of friends now. Well, I have some with handicaps, but some are not. I got some friends who are in college, Jenny at Wittenberg. We mostly have dinner or a movie, or whatever. Susan lives in Cincinnati, and Kristin is in South America. I talk to her mom on the phone. Sometimes I write letters to my friends. My friend Barb is going to have her first baby. I talked to her last night. She said she's going to the hospital because her baby's coming soon.

Sebine chooses to participate in some of the recreation and leisure activities and outings offered by the community parks and recreation program.

Mostly I hang out with a few people who have handicaps. The adult group does activities. This fall we went to an Amish farm. We go to movies, have parties and dinners, baseball games. After they give me a flier, I usually look at them and pick the ones I want to go, and then take off from work. On the 12th, I have to find someone to work for me. We have a new guy at work, his name is Francis, and he's going to work for me on Monday and I can work for him on Tuesday.

I like to dance. Now this year I take only ballet, jazz, and tap. So I'm just taking three this year instead of four. Ballet is only two people, but jazz is lots of people. Mostly I dance ballet and jazz with kids, but mostly I am taking tap with adults.

A Busy Life Sebine goes to the grocery store, deposits her own paychecks at the bank, visits the hair salon, checks books out of the library, goes to the dance studio, and eats at fast-food restaurants by herself or with friends. All in all, she's a very busy young lady. She even spent three years working as a volunteer at a local nursing home, which recently recognized her for accumulating more than 500 service hours.

I'm a volunteer there. I go there early in the morning, and I stay there until 11:00. I got friends over there. Mostly the residents and mostly people who work there. I don't know exactly how many. Mostly old people, but not that old I don't think. I come in the mornings and there are activities going on, like music. I push the wheelchairs and take my friends to their activities. Yeah. I did go there, but since I got my job at the Spaghetti Shop, there's no time anymore.

Saving for the Future

Well, Spaghetti Shop don't pay me that much because I get short hours there, but I get more at Bob's. I put most of it in the bank. I pay Irene for my dance lessons.

I go shopping. I save for a baby gift. I save for a flight ticket to Minnesota to see my relatives and to go to Disney World. One time my checkbook got messed up and I got in big trouble with my mom. I'm paying for my rent when I move. I'll be moving into my own house pretty soon. Not too far away. It's kind of like crummy right now. They didn't fix it up yet. I'll have two roommates, Cristal and Lisa.

There's two things I'm wondering about now. One big and other one just little. The big one is I will miss my mom, mostly. The little one is, I met this kid, this boy, he's from Worthington. I haven't seen him that much, but I'm thinking about him.

I need a vacation.

"I like to dance."

Agreed. Sebine's busy life is pretty normal for these days: a hectic schedule, bills to pay, things to do, people to see, plans to make, and things to worry and wonder about. Sebine's full life represents the ultimate outcome for special education. She has learned the necessary skills, is sufficiently self-determined, and has access to the natural supports needed. Sebine has achieved significant autonomy, is an active and valued member of her community, and can prepare for and cope with the changes she will experience as an adult. Sebine was fortunate to have parents who spent time with her, were interested and actively involved with her schooling, and who encouraged her from an early age to be as independent as she could be. But Sebine's success as a young adult is also due, at least in part, to a special education that included

- Intensive early intervention that began when she was an infant, that included integrated preschool classes, and continued until she entered school
- Regular home-school communication and cooperation between teachers and parents
- Being a regular member of inclusive academic and social activities of her home school throughout her elementary, junior high, and high school years
- Systematic, direct instruction in functional academic and daily living skills throughout her school years
- Early and frequent opportunities to make choices and to participate in the decision making that would affect her life
- Early career education and a systematic plan for the transition from school to adult life that included experience and training in real community-based jobs while she was still in school

An earlier edition of this textbook began with a picture of 10-year-old Sebine on the cover. During the years since, both Sebine and special education have come a long way. Sebine is one of special education's success stories, but her story is not unique; there are many success stories like hers. But Sebine's story is as good a story as any with which to end this book.

Summary

How Do Former Special Education Students Fare As Adults?

- Data from the National Longitudinal Transition Study (NLTS) show an unemployment rate of 46% for all youth with disabilities who have been out of school for less then two years; most of the young adults who had found competitive employment were working in part-time, low-paying jobs.
- The unemployment rate for young adults with disabilities drops to 36.5% when they have been out of school for three to five years, but nearly one in five (19.6%) states she has given up looking for work (NLTS).
- Only 58% of teenagers and young adults with disabilities who exited from the public schools during the 1991–92 school year graduated with a diploma or received a certificate of completion, and it is estimated that 30% of students with disabilities who enroll in high school drop out before they finish.
- Although the percentage of college students who indicate they have a disability has increased in recent years, compared to their peers without disabilities, fewer former special education students pursue postsecondary education.
- NLTS reported that four out of every five former special education students had still not achieved the status of independent adulthood after being out of high school for up to five years.

Transition from School to Adult Life: Models and Services

- Transition from school to life in the community has become perhaps the most challenging issue in special education today. Models for school- to adult-life transition stress the importance of a functional secondary school curriculum that provides work experience in integrated community job sites, systematic coordination between the school and adult service agencies, parental involvement and support, and a written individualized transition plan (ITP) to guide the entire process.
- Development of career awareness and vocational skills should begin in the elementary grades for children with severe disabilities.
- Middle school students should begin to spend time on actual community job sites.
- Secondary students should spend more time on actual community job sites, with in-school instruction focusing on the functional skills needed in the adult work, domestic, community, and recreational/leisure environments.

Employment

- Secondary school programs can enhance the competitive employment prospects for young adults with disabilities by (1) stressing functional, vocational skills; (2) conducting school-based instruction in integrated settings as much as possible; and (3) beginning community-based instruction as early as about age 12 for students with severe disabilities and for progressively extended periods as the student nears graduation.
- Supported employment is a relatively new concept that recognizes that many adults with severe disabilities require ongoing support to obtain and hold a job. Supported employment is characterized by performance of real paid work in regular, integrated work sites; it requires ongoing support from a supported work specialist.
- The role of the employment specialist/job coach is evolving from one of primary supporter for the employee with disabilities to one who works with the employer and co-workers to create innovative and natural support networks.
- Self-monitoring, self-evaluation, learning how to respond independently to naturally occurring cues in the workplace, and self-instructions are four ways that employees with disabilities can increase their independence and job productivity in the workplace.
- Many adults with severe disabilities work in sheltered workshops that provide one or a combination of three kinds of programs: training for competitive employment in the community, extended or long-term employment, and work activities.

Residential Alternatives

- More community-based residential services mean greater opportunities for adults with severe disabilities to live in more normalized settings.
- Despite deinstitutionalization—movement of persons with mental retardation out of large public institutions and into smaller community-based residences such as group homes—approximately 60,000 persons, mostly adults with severe or profound mental retardation, still live in large institutions.
- Foster home placement allows the adult with disabilities to participate in day-to-day activities of family life, to receive attention from people interested in his development, and to experience close personal relationships.
- Apartment living offers the greatest opportunities for integration into the community and interaction with people without disabilities. Three common forms of apartment living for adults with disabilities are the apartment cluster, the co-residence apartment, and the maximum-independence apartment.
- Supported living is an approach toward helping people with disabilities live in the community as independently and normally as they can by providing a network of various kinds and levels of natural supports.

Recreation and Leisure

- Learning to participate in age-appropriate recreation and leisure activities is necessary for a self-satisfying lifestyle.

The Ultimate Goal: A Better Quality of Life

- Adults with disabilities continue to face lack of acceptance as full members of society.
- Handicapism—discriminatory treatment and biased reactions toward someone with a disability—occurs on personal, professional, and societal levels. It must be eliminated before normalization can become a reality for every man and woman with a disability.
- Persons with disabilities have begun to assert their legal rights, challenging the view that persons with disabilities are incapable of speaking for themselves.

For More Information

Journals

- *Career Development for Exceptional Individuals.* Published two times per year by the Division on Career Development and Transition (DCDT) of the Council for Exceptional Children (see "Organizations"). Focuses on education and other programs for complete life experiences—including vocational, residential, and leisure activities—for children and adults with disabilities.
- *Journal of Vocational Rehabilitation.* Quarterly journal of research and ideas for practitioners published by Andover Medical Publishers, 80 Montvale Avenue, Stoneham, MA 02180.
- *Mainstream: Magazine of the Able-Disabled.* Published by Exploding Myths, P.O. Box 370598, San Diego, CA 92137-0598. A monthly magazine with articles and advertising directed toward persons with disabilities.
- *Mouth: The Voice of Disability Rights,* 61 Brighton Street, Rochester, NY 14607. A satirical and hard-hitting newsletter published by disability rights activists and aimed at human services professionals and the rehabilitation industry. Six issues per year.

Books

- Bellamy, G. T., Rhodes, L. E., Mank, D. M., & Albin, J. M. (1988). *Supported employment: A community implementation guide.* Baltimore: Brookes.
- Benz, M. R., & Lindstrom, L. E. (1997). *Building school-to-work programs: Strategies for youth with special needs*. Austin, TX: PRO-ED.
- Brinkerhoff, L. C., Shaw, S. F., & McGuire, J. M. (1993). *Promoting postsecondary education for students with learning disabilities.* Austin, TX: PRO-ED.
- Brolin, D. E. (1995). *Career education: A functional life skills approach* (3rd ed.). Upper Saddle River, NJ: Merrill/Prentice Hall.
- Clark, G. M., & Kolstoe, O. P. (1995). *Career development and transition education for adolescents with disabilities* (2nd ed.). Needham Heights, MA: Allyn & Bacon.
- Edgerton, R. B., & Gaston, M. A. (1990). *"I've seen it all!" Lives of older persons with mental retardation in the community.* Baltimore: Brookes.
- Halpern, A. S., Close, D. W., & Nelson, D. J. (1986). *On my own: The impact of semi-independent living programs for adults with mental retardation.* Baltimore: Brookes.
- Ludlow, B. L., Turnbull, A. P., & Luckasson, R. (Eds.). (1988). *Transitions to adult life for people with mental retardation: Principles and practices.* Baltimore: Brookes.
- Moon, M. S., Inge, K. J., Wehman, P., Brooke, V., & Barcus, M. (1990). *Helping persons with severe mental retardation get and keep employment.* Baltimore: Brookes.
- Rusch, F. R. (1990). *Supported employment: Models, methods, and issues.* Pacific Grove, CA: Brooks/Cole.
- Rusch, F. R., DeStefano, L., Chadsey-Rusch, J., Phelps, A., & Szymanski, E. (1992). *Transition from school to adult life: Models, linkages, and policy.* Pacific Grove, CA: Brooks/Cole.
- Siegel, S., Robert, M., Greener, K., Meyer, G., Halloran, W., & Gaylord-Ross, R. (1993). *Career ladders for challenged youths in transition from school to adult life.* Austin, TX: PRO-ED.
- Smith, J. D. (1995). *Pieces of purgatory: Mental retardation in and out of institutions.* Pacific Grove, CA: Brooks/Cole.
- Smith, M. D., Belcher, R. G., & Juhrs, P. D. (1995). *A guide to successful employment for individuals with autism.* Baltimore: Brookes.
- Wehman, P. (Ed.). (1996). *Life beyond the classroom: Transition for youth with disabilities* (2nd ed.). Baltimore: Brookes.
- Wehman, P. (Ed.). (1998). *Developing transition plans*. Austin, TX: PRO-ED.
- Wehman, P., & Kregel, J. (Eds.). (1998). *More than a job: Securing satisfying careers for people with disabilities.* Baltimore: Brookes.
- Wehman, P., Moon, M. S., Everson, J. M., Wood, W., & Barcus, J. M. (Eds.). (1988). *Transition from school to work: New challenges for youth with severe disabilities.* Baltimore: Brookes.
- West, L. L., Corbey, S., Boyer-Stephens, A., Jones, B., Miller, R. J., & Sarkees-Wircenski, M. (1992). *Integrating transition planning into the IEP process.* Reston, VA: Council for Exceptional Children.

Organizations

- *American Coalition of Citizens with Disabilities* (ACCD), 346 Connecticut Avenue NW, Washington, DC 20201.
- *Association on Handicapped Student Service Programs in Post-Secondary Education,* P.O. Box 21192, Columbus, OH 43221. An association devoted to providing accessibility and equal opportunities for college and university students with disabilities. Includes special interest groups on deafness, learning disabilities, community colleges, and rural institutions.
- *Clearinghouse on Disability Information,* Office of Special Education and Rehabilitation Services, U.S. Department of Education, Room 3132, Switzer Building, Washington, DC 20202-1904.
- *Disability Rights Education and Defense Funds,* 2212 Sixth Street, Berkeley, CA 94710.
- *Division on Career Development and Transition* (DCDT), Council for Exceptional Children, 1920 Association Drive, Reston, VA 22091. A relatively new division of CEC that focuses on career and lifestyle education for persons with disabilities.

Websites

- *Ability Network Magazine,* http://www.ability.ns.ca/anet.html. An on-line magazine of articles written primarily by people with disabilities.
- *Association of Disability Advocates,* http://www.icanect.net/fpa/. Provides information and assistance to individuals with disabilities regarding the exercise of their civil rights as provided by the Americans with Disabilities Act.
- *Electric Edge,* http://www.ragged-edge-mag.com/. On-line edition of *Ragged Edge Magazine*. Cutting-edge articles about the disability experience and what "it means to be a crip at the turn of the millennium."
- *The Disability Rights Activist,* http://www.disrights.org. Information from various sources to enable anyone to advocate for the rights of people with disabilities. Includes tools for activists, announcements and action alerts, and links to several disabilities rights organizations and publications.
- *International Leadership Forum for Women with Disabilities,* http://www.prodworks.com/ilf/. Provides a support network with an emphasis on technical assistance for women with disabilities.
- *The National Home of Your Own Alliance,* http://www.alliance.unh.edu. A partnership between the federal government and disability advocacy groups whose goal is to create housing and support networks so that people with disabilities can have choice and control over where and how they live.
- *World Institute on Disability,* http://www.igc.apc.org/wid/. International public policy center dedicated to carrying out research on disability issues and overcoming barriers to independent living.

Postscript: Developing Your Own Personal View of Special Education

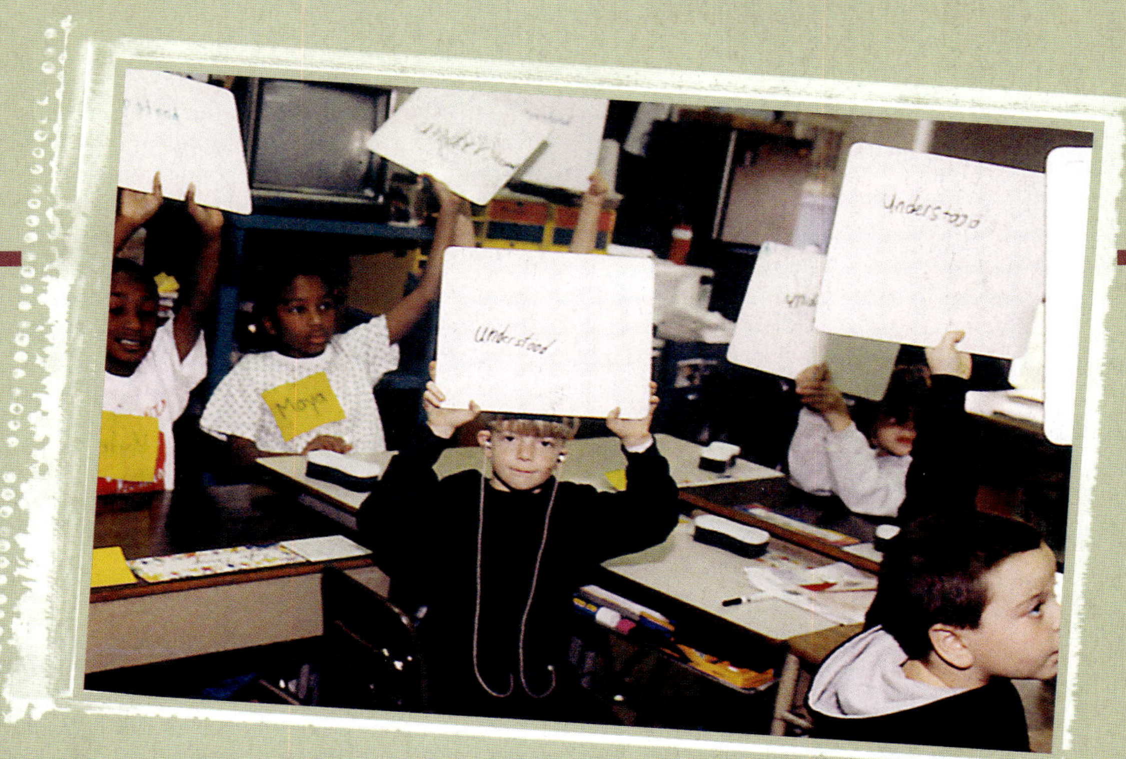

All introductory textbooks contain a great deal of information. In that respect, this book is no different from others. I hope, however, that you have gained more than just some basic facts and information about learners with exceptional educational needs and special education, the discipline dedicated to meeting those needs. I hope you have examined your own attitudes toward and relationships with children and adults with disabilities. At the beginning of the book, I shared eight fundamental beliefs that underlie my personal, but by no means unique, view of special education. I would like to repeat those beliefs.

- People with disabilities have a fundamental right to live and participate in the same settings and programs—in school, at home, in the workplace, and in the community—as do people without disabilities. People with and without disabilities have a great deal to contribute to and learn from one another. We cannot do that in the absence of regular, meaningful interaction.
- Individuals with disabilities have the right to as much independence as we can help them achieve. Special educators have no more important teaching task than helping children and adults with disabilities learn how to increase the level of decision making and control over their own lives.
- Special education must continue to expand its efforts to recognize and respond appropriately to all learners with exceptional educational needs. These include the gifted and talented child, the preschooler with a disability; the infant or toddler who is at risk for a future learning problem; the exceptional child from a different cultural, ethnic, or linguistic background; and the adult with disabilities.
- Special education is enhanced by a working partnership between schools and families.
- Special educators' efforts are most effective when they incorporate the input and services of all of the disciplines in the helping professions.
- All students have the right to an effective education. As educators, our primary responsibility is to design and implement effective instruction for personal, social, vocational, and academic skills. Instruction is ultimately effective when it helps the individuals we serve acquire and maintain positive lifestyle changes. Or to put it another way, the proof of the process is in the product. Therefore . . .
- Teachers must demand effectiveness from their instructional approaches. The belief that special educators require unending patience is a disservice to students with special needs and to the educators—both special and general education teachers—whose job it is to teach them. Teachers should not wait patiently for exceptional children to learn but should modify the instructional program to improve its effectiveness.
- Finally, the future for individuals with disabilities holds great promise. We have only begun to discover the ways to improve teaching, to increase learning, to prevent some of the conditions that lead to disabilities, to encourage acceptance, and to use technology to compensate for disabilities. We have not come as far as we can in learning how to help exceptional individuals build and enjoy fuller, more independent lives in the school, community, and workplace.

As a Member of the Profession

If you consider yourself a prospective special educator, view special education as a profession and yourself as a professional. View yourself as someone with special skills and knowledge; you are different from people without your special training. This has nothing to do with arrogance, but everything to do with the recognition that each of us must develop and responsibly use as much professional competence as we can muster.

Professional competence begins with an objective sense of the job to be done. Be wary of the conception of disabilities as merely socially constructed phenomena: that all children who are identified as disabled would achieve success and behave well if others simply viewed them more positively. This romantic ideology is seldom, if ever, promoted by individuals with disabilities themselves or by their parents and families. Children with disabilities have skill deficits and difficulties in acquiring and generalizing new knowledge and skills—real disabilities that won't be "deconstructed" away. Don't let the needs of exceptional children and their families get lost in such postmodern ideologies. They need and deserve systematic, effective special education.

It is commendable that you have a commitment and a desire to help children with exceptional educational needs. You will probably hear often that you are "wonderful" or "patient" because of this. Good intentions are fine, but desire and commitment are only a beginning. What learners with disabilities need more than anything are teachers who are *impatient*—impatient with lack of progress; impatient with methods, materials, and policies that do not help their students acquire and subsequently use the knowledge and skills required for successful functioning in the home, school, workplace, and community. So don't be patient; be effective.

You will increase your effectiveness as a teacher by using only instructional materials and methods backed by sound, empirical research evidence. Teaching not only *can* but *must* be informed by science if students with disabilities are to learn as much as they can. When considering a new curriculum, program, or instructional method, teachers should ask questions such as the following:

"Has this program been tested in the classroom?"
"What is the evidence showing this program works?"
"What measures of student performance were used to evaluate this program?"
"Has any research on this program been published in peer-reviewed journals?"
"Is there any evidence to suggest the program will be successful if modified to meet the skill levels and ages of my students?"

Teaching students with disabilities requires systematic instruction. It is demanding work. Prepare yourself for that work the best way you can. Demand relevant, up-to-date information and hands-on practical experiences from your teacher-education program. Continue your education and training throughout your career. Stay on top of the continual developments in special education by reading professional journals, participating in in-service training opportunities, and attending conferences. Even better, experiment with instructional methods and share the results of your research with colleagues through presentations and publications.

Special education is not a grim, thankless business. Quite the opposite: special education is an exciting, dynamic field that offers personal satisfaction and feelings of accomplishment unequaled in most areas of endeavor. Welcome aboard!

As a Member of the Community

The degree of success and happiness that a person with disabilities enjoys in the normal routines of everyday life does not depend solely on his skills and abilities. In large measure, the integration of people with disabilities into contemporary society depends on the attitudes and actions of citizens with little knowledge of or experience with exceptional learners. How can people come to accept and support a group they do not know?

Society controls who enters and who is kept out, much as a gatekeeper lets some visitors pass but refuses others. For a particular individual, society's gatekeeper may have been a doctor who urged parents to institutionalize their child or a teacher who resisted having any difficult-to-teach kids in class. It may have been a school psychologist who imposed a label of "trainable mentally retarded" or an employer who refused to hire workers with disabilities. It may have been a social worker, a school board member, a voter. Saddest of all, it may have been a parent whose low expectations kept the gate closed.

How society views people with disabilities influences how individual members of the community respond. Society's views are changing gradually for the better—they are being changed by people who believe that our past practices of exclusion and denial of opportunities were primitive and unfair. But to have maximum impact, the movement toward integration and opportunities described in this book must ultimately translate into personal terms for those of you who will not choose careers in special education. People with disabilities and people without disabilities do experience certain aspects of life differently, but they are more like one another than they are different. And the conclusion I hope you have reached is this: every child and adult with disabilities must be treated as an individual, not as a member of a category or a labeled group.

In Sum

Viewing every individual with disabilities first as a person and second as a person with disabilities may be the most important step in integrating the individual into the mainstream of school and community life. But a change in attitude will not diminish the disability. What it will do is give us a new outlook—more objective and more positive—and allow us to see a disability as a set of special needs. Viewing exceptional people as individuals with special needs tells us much about how to respond to them—and how we respond is the essence of special education.

Glossary

Absence seizure A type of epileptic seizure in which the individual loses consciousness, usually for less than half a minute; can occur very frequently in some children.

Acceleration An educational approach that provides a child with learning experiences usually given to older children; most often used with gifted and talented children.

Accommodation The adjustment of the eye for seeing at different distances; accomplished by muscles that change the shape of the lens to bring an image into clear focus on the retina.

Acquired immune deficiency syndrome (AIDS) A fatal illness in which the body's immune system breaks down. At present there is no known cure for AIDS or a vaccine for the virus that causes it (see *human immunodeficiency virus*).

Acquisition stage of learning The initial phase of learning when the student is learning how to perform a new skill or use new knowledge; feedback should focus on accuracy and topography of the student's response.

Active student response (ASR) A frequency-based measure of a student's active participation during instruction; measured by counting the number of observable responses made to an ongoing lesson or to curriculum materials.

Adaptive device Any piece of equipment designed to improve the function of a body part. Examples include standing tables and special spoons that can be used by people with weak hands or poor muscle control.

Adventitious A disability that develops at any time after birth, from disease, trauma, or any other cause; most frequently used with sensory or physical impairments (contrasts with *congenital*).

Advocate Someone who pleads the cause of a person with disabilities or group of people with disabilities, especially in legal or administrative proceedings or public forums.

Albinism A congenital condition marked by deficiency in, or total lack of, pigmentation. People with albinism have pale skin; white hair, eyebrows, and eyelashes; and eyes with pink or pale blue irises.

Amblyopia Dimness of sight without apparent change in the eye's structures; can lead to blindness in the affected eye if not corrected.

American Sign Language (ASL) A visual-gestural language with its own rules of syntax, semantics, and pragmatics; does not correspond to written or spoken English. ASL is the language of the Deaf culture in the United States and Canada.

Amniocentesis The insertion of a hollow needle through the abdomen into the uterus of a pregnant woman. Used to obtain amniotic fluid in order to determine the presence of genetic and chromosomal abnormalities. The sex of the fetus can also be determined.

Anencephaly Congenital malformation of the skull with absence of all or part of the brain.

Anoxia A lack of oxygen severe enough to cause tissue damage; can cause permanent brain damage and mental retardation.

Aphasia Loss of speech functions; often, but not always, refers to inability to speak because of brain lesions.

Applied behavior analysis "The science in which procedures derived from the principles of behavior are systematically applied to improve socially significant behavior to a meaningful degree and to demonstrate experimentally that the procedures employed were responsible for the improvement in behavior" (Cooper, Heron, & Heward, 1987, p. 14).

Aqueous humor Fluid that occupies the space between the lens and the cornea of the eye.

Arena assessment A group assessment procedure sometimes used with infants and preschoolers; professionals from different disciplines (e.g., early childhood specialist, speech-language pathologist, psychologist, physical therapist) seat themselves in a circle around the child and conduct simultaneous evaluations while the child interacts with parent or play materials.

Articulation The production of distinct language sounds by the vocal organs.

Assistive technology Any item, piece of equipment, or product system, whether acquired commercially off the shelf, modified, or customized, that is used to increase, maintain, or improve the functional capabilities of children with disabilities. (IDEA regulations, 34 C.F.R. § 300.5)

Asthma A chronic respiratory condition characterized by repeated episodes of wheezing, coughing, and difficulty breathing.

Astigmatism A defect of vision usually caused by irregularities in the cornea; results in blurred vision and difficulties in focusing. Can usually be corrected by lenses.

At risk A term used to refer to children who are not currently identified as handicapped or disabled but are considered to have a greater-than-usual chance of developing a disability. Physicians use the terms *at risk* or *high risk* to refer to pregnancies with a greater-than-normal probability of producing a baby with disabilities.

Ataxia Poor sense of balance and body position and lack of coordination of the voluntary muscles; characteristic of one type of cerebral palsy.

Athetosis A type of cerebral palsy characterized by large, irregular, uncontrollable twisting motions. The muscles may be tense and rigid or loose and flaccid. Often accompanied by difficulty with oral language.

Attention deficit disorder (ADD) See *attention deficit/hyperactivity disorder (ADHD).*

Attention deficit/hyperactivity disorder (ADHD) Diagnostic category of the American Psychiatric Association for a condition in which a child exhibits developmentally inappropriate inattention, impulsivity, and hyperactivity.

Audiogram A graph of the faintest level of sound a person can hear in each ear at least 50% of the time at each of several frequencies, including the entire frequency range of normal speech.

Audiologist A professional who specializes in the evaluation of hearing ability and the treatment of impaired hearing.

Audiology The science of hearing.

Audiometer A device that generates sounds at specific frequencies and intensities; used to examine hearing.

Audiometric zero The smallest sound a person with normal hearing can perceive; also called the zero hearing-threshold level (HTL).

Audition The act or sense of hearing.

Auditory canal (external acoustic meatus) Slightly amplifies and transports sound waves from the external ear to the middle ear.

Auditory training A program that works on listening skills by teaching individuals with hearing impairments to make as much use as possible of their residual hearing.

Augmentative and alternative communication (AAC) A diverse set of nonspeech communication strategies and methods to assist individuals who are unable to meet their communication needs through speech; includes sign language, symbol systems, communication boards, and synthetic speech devices.

Auricle External part of the ear; collects sound waves into the auditory canal.

Autism A pervasive developmental disorder marked by severe impairment of intellectual, social, and emotional functioning. The essential features of the condition typically appear prior to 30 months of age and consist of disturbances of (1) developmental rates and/or sequences; (2) responses to sensory stimuli; (3) speech, language, and cognitive capacities; and (4) capacities to relate to people, events, and objects (Autism Society of America; Ritvo & Freeman, 1978).

Baseline A measure of the level or amount of a specific target behavior prior to implementation of an intervention designed to change the behavior. Baseline data are used as an objective measure against which to compare and evaluate the results obtained during intervention.

Behavior observation audiometry A method of hearing assessment in which an infant's reactions to sounds are observed; a sound is presented at an increasing level of intensity until a response, such as head turning, eye blinking, or cessation of play, is reliably observed.

Behavioral contract A written agreement between two parties in which one agrees to complete a specified task (e.g., a child agrees to complete a homework assignment by the next morning) and in return the other party agrees to provide a specific reward (e.g., the teacher allows the child to have 10 minutes of free time) upon completion of the task.

Behavioral disorder A disability characterized by behavior that differs markedly and chronically from current social or cultural norms and adversely affects educational performance.

Bilingual special education Using the child's home language and home culture along with English in an individually designed program of special education.

Binocular vision Vision using both eyes working together to perceive a single image.

Blind Having either no vision or only light perception; learning occurs through other senses.

Blindness, legal See *legally blind*.

Braille A system of writing letters, numbers, and other language symbols with a combination of six raised dots. A person who is blind reads the dots with his fingertips.

Cataract A reduction or loss of vision that occurs when the crystalline lens of the eye becomes cloudy or opaque.

Catheter A tube inserted into the body to permit injections or withdrawal of fluids or to keep a passageway open; often refers to a tube inserted into the bladder to remove urine from a person who does not have effective bladder control.

Cerebral palsy Motor impairment caused by brain damage, which is usually acquired during the prenatal period or during the birth process. Can involve a wide variety of symptoms (see *ataxia, athetosis, rigidity, spasticity,* and *tremor*) and range from mild to severe. Neither curable nor progressive.

Choral responding Each student in the class or group responding orally in unison to a question, problem, or item presented by the teacher.

Chorion villus sampling (CVS) A procedure for prenatal diagnosis of chromosomal abnormalities that can be conducted during the first 8 to 10 weeks of pregnancy; fetal cells are removed from the chorionic tissue, which surrounds the fetus, and directly analyzed.

Cleft palate A congenital split in the palate that results in an excessive nasal quality of the voice. Can often be repaired by surgery or a dental appliance.

Cochlea Main receptor organ for hearing located in the inner ear; tiny hairs within the cochlea transform mechanical energy into neural impulses that then travel through the auditory nerve to the brain.

Communication An interactive process requiring at least two parties in which messages are encoded, transmitted, and decoded by any means, including sounds, symbols, and gestures.

Complex partial seizure A type of seizure in which an individual goes through a brief period of inappropriate or purposeless activity (also called psychomotor seizure). Usually lasts from two to five minutes, after which the person has amnesia about the entire episode.

Conduct disorder A group of behavior disorders including disobedience, disruptiveness, fighting, and tantrums, as identified by Quay (1975).

Conductive hearing loss Hearing loss caused by obstructions in the outer or middle ear or malformations that interfere with the conduction of sound waves to the inner ear. Can often be corrected surgically or medically.

Congenital Any condition that is present at birth (contrasts with *adventitious*).

Constant time delay A procedure for transferring stimulus control from teacher-provided response prompts to the instructional item itself. The teacher begins by simultaneously presenting the stimulus being taught and a controlling response prompt (e.g., as the teacher holds up a flashcard with the word "ball" printed on it, she says, "Ball"). After a number of zero-second-delay trials the teacher waits for a fixed amount of time (e.g., four seconds) between presentation of the instructional stimulus and the response prompt. Practice trials are repeated with the constant delay until the student begins to respond correctly prior to the teacher's prompt.

Contingency contract A document that specifies an if-then relationship between performance of a specified behavior(s) and access to or delivery of a specified reward.

Continuum of services The range of different placement and instructional options that a school district can use to serve children with disabilities. Typically depicted as a pyramid, ranging from the least restrictive placement (regular classroom) at the bottom to the most restrictive placement (residential school or hospital) at the top.

Convulsive disorder See *epilepsy*.

Cornea The transparent part of the eyeball that admits light to the interior.

Cri-du-chat syndrome A chromosomal abnormality resulting from deletion of material from the fifth pair of chromosomes. It usually results in severe retardation. Its name is French for "cat cry," named for the high-pitched crying of the child due to a related larynx dysfunction.

Cued speech A method of supplementing oral communication by adding cues in the form of eight different hand signals in four different locations near the chin.

Cultural pluralism The value and practice of respecting, fostering, and encouraging the cultural and ethnic differences that make up society.

Cultural-familial mental retardation See *psychosocial disadvantage*.

Culture The established knowledge, ideas, values, and skills shared by a society; its program of survival and adaptation to its environment.

Curriculum-based assessment Evaluation of a student's progress in terms of her performance on the skills that comprise the curriculum of the local school.

Cystic fibrosis An inherited disorder that causes a dysfunction of the pancreas, mucus, salivary, and sweat glands. Cystic fibrosis causes severe, long-term respiratory difficulties. No cure is currently available.

Deaf The result of a hearing loss severe enough so that speech cannot be understood through the ears alone, even with a hearing aid; some sounds may still be perceived.

Decibel (dB) The unit of measure for the relative intensity of sound on a scale beginning at zero. Zero dB refers to the faintest sound a person with normal hearing can detect.

Deinstitutionalization The social movement to transfer individuals with disabilities, especially persons with mental retardation, from large institutions to smaller, community-based residences and work settings.

Diabetes See *juvenile diabetes mellitus*.

Diabetic retinopathy Visual impairment caused by hemorrhages on the retina and other disorders of blood circulation in people with diabetes.

Dialect A variety within a specific language; can involve variation in pronunciation, word choice, word order, and inflected forms.

Differential reinforcement of other behavior (DRO) A procedure in which any behavior except the targeted inappropriate response is reinforced; results in a reduction of the inappropriate behavior.

Diplegia Paralysis that affects the legs more often than the arms.

Disability Condition characterized by functional limitations that impede typical development as the result of a physical or sensory impairment or difficulty in learning or social adjustment.

Double hemiplegia Paralysis of the arms, with less severe involvement of the legs.

Down syndrome A chromosomal anomaly that often causes moderate to severe mental retardation, along with certain physical characteristics such as a large tongue, heart problems, poor muscle tone, and a broad, flat bridge of the nose.

Duchenne muscular dystrophy The most common form of muscular dystrophy, a group of long-term diseases that progressively weaken and waste away the body's muscles.

Due process Set of legal steps and proceedings carried out according to established rules and principles; designed to protect an individual's constitutional and legal rights.

Duration (of behavior) Measure of how long a person engages in a given activity.

Dyslexia A specific language-based disorder of constitutional origin characterized by difficulties in single word decoding, usually reflecting insufficient phonological processing. These difficulties, which are not the result of generalized developmental disability or sensory impairment, are often unexpected in relation to age and other cognitive and academic abilities and severely impair the individual's ability to read (Orton Dyslexia Society Research Committee, 1994).

Echolalia The repetition of what other people say as if echoing them; characteristic of some children with delayed development, autism, and communication disorders.

Electroencephalograph (EEG) Device that detects and records brain wave patterns.

Encephalitis Inflammation of the brain; can cause permanent damage to the central nervous system and mental retardation.

Endogenous Refers to an inherited cause of a disability or impairment.

Enrichment Educational approach that provides a child with extra learning experiences that the standard curriculum would not normally include. Most often used with gifted and talented children.

Epilepsy A condition marked by chronic and repeated seizures, disturbances of movement, sensation, behavior, and/or consciousness caused by abnormal electrical activity in the brain (see *generalized tonic-clonic seizure, complex partial seizure, simple complex seizure,* and *absence seizure*). Can usually be controlled with medication, although the drugs may have undesirable side effects. May be temporary or lifelong.

Equal protection Legal concept included in the 14th Amendment to the Constitution of the United States, stipulating that no state may deny any person equality or liberty because of that person's classification according to race, nationality, or religion. Several major court cases leading to the passage of P.L. 94-142 (IDEA) found that children with disabilities were not provided with equal protection if they were denied access to an appropriate education solely because of their disabilities.

Ethnocentrism The view that the practices of one's own culture are natural and correct, while perceiving the practices of other cultures as odd, amusing, inferior, and/or immoral.

Etiology The cause(s) of a disability, impairment, or disease. Includes genetic, physiological, and environmental or psychological factors.

Evoked-response audiometry A method of testing hearing by measuring the electrical activity generated by the auditory nerve in response to auditory stimulation. Often used to measure the hearing of infants and children considered difficult to test.

Exceptional children Children whose performance deviates from the norm, either below or above, to the extent that special educational programming is needed.

Exogenous Refers to a cause of a disability or impairment that stems from factors outside the body such as disease, toxicity, or injury.

Extinction A procedure in which reinforcement for a previously reinforced behavior is withheld. If the actual reinforcers that are maintaining the behavior are identified and withheld, the behavior will gradually decrease in frequency until it no longer, or seldom, occurs.

Facilitated communication (FC) A type of augmentative communication in which a "facilitator" provides assistance to someone in typing or pointing to vocabulary symbols; typically involves an alphanumeric keyboard on which the user types out his message one letter at a time. To date, research designed to validate FC has repeatedly demonstrated either facilitator influence (correct or meaningful language is produced only when the facilitator "knows" what should be communicated) or no unexpected language competence compared to the participants' measured IQ or a standard language assessment.

Fetal alcohol effects (FAE) Term used to identify the suspected etiology of developmental problems experienced by infants and toddlers who have some but not all of the diagnostic criteria for fetal alcohol syndrome (FAS) and have a history of prenatal alcohol exposure.

Fetal alcohol syndrome (FAS) A condition sometimes found in the infants of alcoholic mothers; can involve low birth weight, developmental delay, and cardiac, limb, and other physical defects. Caused by excessive alcohol use during pregnancy; often produces serious physical defects and developmental delays; diagnosed when the child has two or more craniofacial malformations and growth is below the 10th percentile for height and weight. FAS is one of the leading known causes of mental retardation. In addition to physical problems, many children with FAS have neurological damage that contributes to cognitive and language delays.

Field of vision The expanse of space visible with both eyes looking straight ahead, measured in degrees; 180 degrees is considered normal.

Fluency A performance measure that includes both the accuracy and the rate with which a skill is performed; a fluent performer is both accurate and fast. In communication, the term refers to the rate and smoothness of speech; stuttering is the most common fluency disorder in speech.

Foster home A living arrangement in which a family shares its home with a person who is not a relative. Long used with children who for some reason cannot live with their parents temporarily, foster homes are now being used with adults with disabilities as well.

Fragile-X syndrome A chromosomal abnormality associated with mild to severe mental retardation. Thought to be the most common known cause of inherited mental retardation. Affects males more often and more severely than females; behavioral characteristics are sometimes similar to individuals with autism. Diagnosis can be confirmed by studies of the X chromosome.

Functional analysis Refers to a variety of behavior assessment methodologies for determining the environmental variables that are setting the occasion for and maintaining challenging behaviors such as self-injury (see Iwata et al., 1994).

Generalization Using previously learned knowledge or skill under conditions other than those under which it was originally learned. Stimulus generality occurs when a student performs a behavior in the presence of relevant stimuli (people, settings, instructional materials) other than those that were present originally. For instance, stimulus generality occurs when a child who has learned to label baseballs and beach balls as "ball" identifies a basketball as "ball." Response generality occurs when a person performs relevant behaviors that were never directly trained but are similar to the original trained behavior. For example, a child may be taught to say, "Hello, how are you?" and "Hi, nice to see you," as greetings. If the child combines the two to say, "Hi, how are you?" response generality has taken place.

Generalized tonic-clonic seizure The most severe type of seizure, in which the individual has violent convulsions, loses consciousness, and becomes rigid. Formerly called grand mal seizure.

Genetic counseling A discussion between a specially trained medical counselor and persons who are considering having a baby about the chances of having a baby with a disability, based on the prospective parents' genetic backgrounds.

Glaucoma An eye disease characterized by abnormally high pressure inside the eyeball. If left untreated, it can cause total blindness, but if detected early most cases can be arrested.

Grand mal seizure See *generalized tonic-clonic seizure*.

Group home A community-based residential alternative for adults with disabilities, most often persons with mental retardation, in which a small group of people live together in a house with one or more support staff.

Group-oriented contingency A type of behavior management and motivation procedure in which consequences (rewards and/or penalties) are applied to the entire group or class of students and are contingent upon the behavior of selected students or the entire group.

Guided notes A handout that guides students through a lecture, presentation, or demonstration by providing a format that includes basic information and cues students to note key points.

Handicap Refers to the problems a person with a disability or impairment encounters in interacting with the environment. A disability may pose a handicap in one environment but not in another.

Handicapism Prejudice or discrimination based solely on a person's disability, without regard for individual characteristics.

Hard of hearing Level of hearing loss that makes it difficult, although not impossible, to comprehend speech through the sense of hearing alone.

Hearing impaired Describes anyone who has a hearing loss significant enough to require special education, training, and/or adaptations; includes both deaf and hard-of-hearing conditions.

Hemiplegia Paralysis of both the arm and the leg on the same side of the body.

Hemophilia An inherited deficiency in blood-clotting ability, which can cause serious internal bleeding.

Hertz (Hz) A unit of sound frequency equal to one cycle per second; used to measure pitch.

Human immunodeficiency virus (HIV) The virus that causes acquired immune deficiency syndrome (AIDS).

Hydrocephalus An enlarged head caused by cerebral spinal fluid accumulating in the cranial cavity; often causes brain damage and severe retardation. A condition present at birth or developing soon afterward. Can sometimes be treated successfully with a shunt.

Hyperactive Excessive motor activity or restlessness.

Hyperopia Farsightedness; condition in which the image comes to a focus behind the retina instead of on it, causing difficulty in seeing near objects.

Hypertonia Muscle tone that is too high; tense, contracted muscles.

Hypotonia Muscle tone that is too low; weak, floppy muscles.

Immaturity Group of behavior disorders, including short attention span, extreme passivity, daydreaming, preference for younger playmates, and clumsiness, as identified by Quay (1975).

Impedance audiometry Procedure for testing middle ear function by inserting a small probe and pump to detect sound reflected by the eardrum.

Incidence The percentage of people who, at some time in their lives, will be identified as having a specific condition. Often reported as the number of cases of a given condition per 1,000 people.

Individualized education program (IEP) Written document required by the Individuals with Disabilities Education Act (P.L. 94-142) for every child with a disability; includes statements of present performance, annual goals, short-term instructional objectives, specific educational services needed, relevant dates, regular education program participation, and evaluation procedures; must be signed by parents as well as educational personnel.

Individualized family services plan (IFSP) A requirement of P.L. 99-457, Education of the Handicapped Act Amendments of 1986, for the coordination of early intervention services for infants and toddlers with disabilities from birth to age 3. Similar to the IEP, which is required for all school-age children with disabilities.

Inflection Change in pitch or loudness of the voice to indicate mood or emphasis.

In-service training Any educational program designed to provide practicing professionals (e.g., teachers, administrators, physical therapists) with additional knowledge and skills.

Inter-observer agreement The degree to which two or more independent observers record the same results when observing and measuring the same target behavior(s); typically reported as a percentage of agreement.

Inter-rater agreement See *inter-observer agreement.*

Interdisciplinary team Group of professionals from different disciplines (e.g., education, psychology, speech and language, medicine) who work together to plan and implement an individualized education program (IEP) for a child with disabilities.

Interindividual differences Differences between two or more people in one skill or set of skills.

Intervention Any effort made on behalf of children and adults with disabilities; may be preventive (keeping possible problems from becoming a serious disability), remedial (overcoming disability through training or education), or compensatory (giving the individual new ways to deal with the disability).

Intraindividual differences Differences within one individual on two or more measures of performance.

Iris The opaque, colored portion of the eye that contracts and expands to change the size of the pupil.

Juvenile diabetes mellitus A children's disease characterized by inadequate secretion or use of insulin and the resulting excessive sugar in the blood and urine. Managed with diet and/or medication but can be difficult to control. Can cause coma and, eventually, death if left untreated or treated improperly. Can also lead to visual impairments and limb amputation. Not curable at the present time.

Kinesics The study of bodily movement, particularly as it relates to and affects communication.

Klinefelter syndrome A chromosomal anomaly in which males receive an extra X chromosome; associated with frequent social retardation, sterility, underdevelopment of male sex organs, development of secondary female sex characteristics, and borderline or mild levels of mental retardation.

Language A system used by a group of people for giving meaning to sounds, words, gestures, and other symbols to enable communication with one another. Languages can use vocal (speech sounds) or nonvocal symbols, such as American Sign Language, or use movements and physical symbols instead of sounds.

Learning channel A description of the modes with which a learner receives and sends information in performing a given learning task. Orally reading sight words, for example, uses the "see/say" learning channel; the "hear/write" learning channel is involved in taking a spelling test.

Learning trial Consists of three major elements: (1) antecedent (i.e., curricular) stimuli, (2) the student's response to those stimuli, and (3) consequent stimuli (i.e., instructional feedback) following the response; serves as a basic unit of analysis for examining teaching and learning from both the teacher's perspective, as an opportunity to teach, and the student's perspective, as an opportunity to learn (Heward, 1994). Sometimes called a *practice trial* or *learn unit.*

Least restrictive environment (LRE) The educational setting that most closely resembles a regular school program and also meets the child's special educational needs. For many students with disabilities, the regular classroom is the LRE; however, the LRE is a relative concept and must be determined for each individual student with disabilities.

Legally blind Visual acuity of 20/200 or less in the better eye after the best possible correction with glasses or contact lenses, or vision restricted to a field of 20 degrees or less. Acuity of 20/200 means the eye can see clearly at 20 feet what the normal eye can see at 200 feet.

Lens The clear part of the eye that focuses rays of light on the retina.

Longitudinal study A research study that follows one subject or group of subjects over an extended period of time, usually several years.

Low vision Visual impairment severe enough so that special educational services are required. A child with low vision is able to learn through the visual channel and generally learns to read print.

Low-incidence disability A disability that occurs relatively infrequently in the general population; often used in reference to sensory impairments, severe and profound mental retardation, autism, and multiple disabilities.

Macular degeneration A deterioration of the central part of the retina, which causes difficulty in seeing details clearly.

Magnitude (of behavior) The force with which a response is emitted.

Mainstreaming The process of integrating children with disabilities into regular schools and classes.

Manifestation determination A review of the relationship between a student's misconduct and her disability conducted by the IEP team and other qualified personnel. Required by the IDEA amendments of 1997 when school officials seek to discipline a student with disabilities in a manner that would result in a change of placement, suspension, or expulsion in excess of 10 days.

Meningitis An inflammation of the membranes covering the brain and spinal cord; can cause problems with sight and hearing and/or mental retardation.

Meningocele Type of spina bifida in which the covering of the spinal cord protrudes through an opening in the vertebrae but the cord itself and the nerve roots are enclosed.

Mental retardation Substantial limitations in present functioning; characterized by significantly subaverage intellectual functioning, existing concurrently with related limitations in two or more of the following applicable adaptive skill areas: communication, self-care, home living, social skills, community use, self-direction, health and safety, functional academics, leisure, and work. Mental retardation manifests before age 18 (AAMR, 1992).

Microcephalus A condition characterized by an abnormally small skull with resulting brain damage and mental retardation.

Milieu teaching strategies A variety of strategies used to teach speech and language that naturally occur during real or simulated activities in the home, school, or community environments in which a child normally functions; characterized by dispersed learning trials, following the child's attentional lead within the context of normal conversational interchanges, and teaching the form and content of language in the context of normal use.

Minimal brain dysfunction A once-popular term used to describe the learning disabilities of children with no clinical (organic) evidence of brain damage.

Mobility The ability to move safely and efficiently from one point to another.

Model program A program that implements and evaluates new procedures or techniques in order to serve as a basis for development of other similar programs.

Monoplegia Paralysis affecting one limb.

Morpheme The smallest element of a language that carries meaning.

Multicultural education An educational approach in which a school's curriculum and instructional methods are designed and implemented so that all children acquire an awareness, acceptance, and appreciation of cultural diversity and recognize the contributions of many cultures.

Multifactored assessment Assessment and evaluation of a child with a variety of test instruments and observation procedures. Required by IDEA when assessment is for educational placement of a child who is to receive special education services. Prevents the misdiagnosis and misplacement of a student as the result of considering only one test score.

Multiple-gating screening A multistep process for screening children who may have disabilities. The initial step casts the broadest net (e.g., a multiple-gated screening for children who may have emotional and behavior problems might begin with teacher nominations); children identified in the first step are assessed more closely in a second step (e.g., a behavior checklist); children who have passed through the first two "gates" are screened further (e.g., direct observations in the classroom).

Muscular dystrophy A group of diseases that gradually weakens muscle tissue; usually becomes evident by the age of 4 or 5.

Myelomeningocele A protrusion on the back of a child with spina bifida, consisting of a sac of nerve tissue bulging through a cleft in the spine.

Myopia Nearsightedness; results when light is focused on a point in front of the retina, resulting in a blurred image for distant objects.

Neurologic impairment Any physical disability caused by damage to the central nervous system (brain, spinal cord, ganglia, and nerves).

Normal curve A mathematically derived curve depicting the theoretical probability or distribution of a given variable (such as a physical trait or test score) in the general population. Indicates that approximately 68.26% of the population will fall within one standard deviation above and below the mean; approximately 27.18% will fall between one and two standard deviations either above or below the mean; and less than 3% will achieve more extreme scores of more than two standard deviations in either direction.

Normalization As a philosophy and principle, the belief that individuals with disabilities should, to the maximum extent possible, be physically and socially integrated into the mainstream of society regardless of the degree or type of disability. As an approach to intervention, the use of progressively more normal settings and procedures "to establish and/or maintain personal behaviors which are as culturally normal as possible" (Wolfensberger, 1972, p. 28).

Nystagmus A rapid, involuntary, rhythmic movement of the eyes that may cause difficulty in reading or fixating on an object.

Occupational therapist A professional who programs and/or delivers instructional activities and materials to help children and adults with disabilities learn to participate in useful activities.

Ocular motility The eye's ability to move.

Operant conditioning audiometry Method of measuring hearing by teaching the individual to make an observable response to sound. For example, a child may be taught to drop a block into a box each time a light and a loud tone are presented. Once this response is learned, the light is no longer presented and the volume and pitch of the tone are gradually decreased. When the child no longer drops the block into the box, the audiologist knows the child cannot hear the tone. Sometimes used to test the hearing of nonverbal children and adults.

Ophthalmologist A physician who specializes in the diagnosis and treatment of diseases of the eye.

Optic nerve The nerve that carries impulses from the eye to the brain.

Optometrist A vision professional who specializes in the evaluation and optical correction of refractive errors.

Oral approach A philosophy and approach to educating deaf children that stresses learning to speak as the essential element for integration into the hearing world.

Orientation The ability to establish one's position in relation to the environment.

Orthopedic impairment Any disability caused by disorders to the musculoskeletal system.

Ossicles Three small bones (hammer, anvil, and stirrup) that transmit sound energy from the middle ear to the inner ear.

Osteogenesis imperfecta A hereditary condition in which the bones do not grow normally and break easily; sometimes called brittle bones.

Otitis media An infection or inflammation of the middle ear that can cause a conductive hearing loss.

Otologist A physician who specializes in the diagnosis and treatment of diseases of the ear.

Overcorrection A procedure in which the learner must make restitution for, or repair, the effects of his undesirable behavior and then put the environment in even better shape than it was prior to the misbehavior. Used to decrease the rate of undesirable behaviors.

Paraplegia Paralysis of the lower part of the body, including both legs; usually results from injury to or disease of the spinal cord.

Paraprofessionals (in education) Trained classroom aides who assist teachers; may include parents.

Partial participation Teaching approach that acknowledges that even though an individual with severe disabilities may not be able to independently perform all the steps of a given task or activity, she can often be taught to do selected components or an adapted version of the task.

Perceptual handicap A term formerly used to describe some conditions now included under the term *learning disabilities;* usually referred to problems with no known physical cause.

Perinatal Occurring at or immediately after birth.

Peripheral vision Vision at the outer limits of the field of vision.

Personality disorder A group of behavior disorders, including social withdrawal, anxiety, depression, feelings of inferiority, guilt, shyness, and unhappiness, as identified by Quay (1975).

Petit mal seizure See *absence seizure*.

Phenylketonuria (PKU) An inherited metabolic disease that can cause severe retardation; can now be detected at birth and the detrimental effects prevented with a special diet.

Phoneme The smallest unit of sound that can be identified in a spoken language. There are 45 phonemes, or sound families, in the English language.

Photophobia Extreme sensitivity of the eyes to light; occurs most notably in albino children.

Physical therapist (PT) A professional trained to help people with disabilities develop and maintain muscular and orthopedic capability and make correct and useful movement.

Play audiometry A method for assessing a child's hearing ability by teaching the child to perform simple but distinct activities, such as picking up a toy or putting a ball into a cup whenever he hears the signal, either pure tones or speech.

Positive reinforcement Presentation of a stimulus or event immediately after a behavior has been emitted, which has the effect of increasing the occurrence of that behavior in the future.

Postlingual Occurring after the development of language; usually used to classify hearing losses that begin after a person has learned to speak.

Postnatal Occurring after birth.

Practice stage of learning After the student has learned how to perform a new skill, she should work to develop fluency with the target skill. Feedback during the practice stage of learning should emphasize the rate or speed with which the student correctly performs the skill.

Prader-Willi syndrome A condition linked to chromosomal abnormality that is characterized by delays in motor development, mild to moderate mental retardation, hypogenital development, an insatiable appetite that often results in obesity, and small features and stature.

Pragmatics Study of the rules that govern how language is used in a communication context.

Precision teaching An instructional approach that involves (1) pinpointing the skills to be learned; (2) measuring the initial fluency with which the student can perform those behaviors; (3) setting an aim, or goal, for the child's improvement; (4) using direct, daily measurement to monitor progress made under an instructional program; (5) charting the results of those measurements; and (6) changing the program if progress is not adequate.

Prelingual Describes a hearing impairment acquired before the development of speech and language.

Prenatal Occurring before birth.

Prenatal asphyxia A lack of oxygen during the birth process usually caused by interruption of respiration; can cause unconsciousness and/or brain damage.

Prevalence The number of people who have a certain condition at any given time.

Projective tests Psychological tests that require a person to respond to a standardized task or set of stimuli (e.g., draw a picture or interpret an ink blot). Responses are thought to be a projection of the test taker's personality and are scored according to the given test's scoring manual to produce a personality profile.

Prosthesis Any device used to replace a missing or impaired body part.

Psychomotor seizure See *complex partial seizure*.

Psychosocial disadvantage Category of causation for mental retardation that requires evidence of subaverage intellectual functioning in at least one parent and one or more siblings (when there are siblings). Typically associated with impoverished environments involving poor housing, inadequate diets, and inadequate medical care. Often used synonymously with cultural-familial retardation; suggests that mental retardation can be caused by a poor social and cultural environment.

Pupil The circular hole in the center of the iris of the eye, which contracts and expands to let light pass through.

Quadriplegia Paralysis of all four limbs.

Rate (or *frequency of behavior*) A measure of how often a particular action is performed; usually reported as the number of responses per minute.

Refraction The bending or deflection of light rays from a straight path as they pass from one medium (e.g., air) into another (e.g., the eye). Used by eye specialists in assessing and correcting vision.

Regular education initiative (REI) A position advocated by some special educators that students with disabilities can and should be educated in regular classrooms under the primary responsibility of the general education program.

Rehabilitation A social service program designed to teach a newly disabled person basic skills needed for independence.

Reinforcement See *positive reinforcement*.

Related services Developmental, corrective, and other supportive services required for a child with disabilities to benefit from special education. Includes special transportation services, speech and language pathology, audiology, psychological services, physical and occupational therapy, school health services, counseling and medical services for diagnostic and evaluation purposes, rehabilitation counseling, social work services, and parent counseling and training.

Remediation An educational program designed to teach a person to overcome a disability through training and education.

Residual hearing The remaining hearing, however slight, of a person who is deaf.

Resource room Classroom in which special education students spend part of the school day and receive individualized special education services.

Response cards Cards, signs, or items that are simultaneously held up by all students to display their response to a question or problem presented by the teacher; response cards enable every student in the class to respond to each question or item.

Response cost A procedure for reducing the frequency of inappropriate behavior by withdrawing a specific amount of reinforcement contingent upon occurrence of the behavior.

Retina A sheet of nerve tissue at the back of the eye on which an image is focused.

Retinitis pigmentosa (RP) An eye disease in which the retina gradually degenerates and atrophies, causing the field of vision to become progressively more narrow.

Retinopathy of prematurity (ROP) A condition characterized by an abnormally dense growth of blood vessels and scar tissue in the eye, often causing visual field loss and retinal detachment. Usually caused by high levels of oxygen administered to premature infants in incubators. Also called retrolental fibroplasia (RLF).

Retrolental fibroplasia (RLF) See *retinopathy of prematurity*.

Reye's syndrome A relatively rare disease that appears to be related to a variety of viral infections; most common in children over the age of 6. About 30% of children who contract it die; survivors sometimes show signs of neurological damage and mental retardation. The cause is unknown, although some studies have found an increased risk after the use of aspirin during a viral illness.

Rigidity A type of cerebral palsy characterized by increased muscle tone, minimal muscle elasticity, and little or no stretch reflex.

Rubella German measles; when contracted by a woman during the first trimester of pregnancy, may cause visual impairments, hearing impairments, mental retardation, and/or other congenital impairments in the child.

Schizophrenic Describes a severe behavior disorder characterized by loss of contact with one's surroundings and inappropriate affect and actions.

Screening A procedure in which groups of children are examined and/or tested in an effort to identify children who are most likely to have a disability; identified children are then referred for more intensive examination and assessment.

Selective mutism Speaking normally in some settings or situations and not speaking in others.

Self-contained class A special classroom, usually located within a regular public school building, that includes only exceptional children.

Self-monitoring A behavior change procedure in which an individual observes and records the frequency and/or quality of his own behavior.

Semantics The study of meaning in language.

Sensorineural hearing loss A hearing loss caused by damage to the auditory nerve or the inner ear.

Severe disabilities Term used to refer to challenges faced by individuals with severe and profound mental retardation, autism, and/or physical/sensory impairments combined with marked developmental delay. Persons with severe disabilities exhibit extreme deficits in intellectual functioning and need systematic instruction for basic skills such as self-care and communicating with others.

Shaping A process for teaching new behavior through reinforcement of successive approximations of targeted performance.

Sheltered workshop A structured work environment where persons with disabilities receive employment training and perform work for pay. May provide transitional services for some individuals (e.g., short-term training for competitive employment in the community) and permanent work settings for others.

Shunt Tube that diverts fluid from one part of the body to another; often implanted in people with hydrocephalus to remove extra cerebrospinal fluid from the head and send it directly into the heart or intestines.

Simple partial seizure A type of seizure characterized by sudden jerking motions with no loss of consciousness. Partial seizures may occur weekly, monthly, or only once or twice a year.

Snellen chart A chart used to test visual acuity; developed by a Dutch ophthalmologist in 1862 and still used today. Consists of rows of letters, or Es facing up, down, left, or right; each row corresponds to the distance that a normally sighted person can discriminate the letters.

Social validity A desirable characteristic of the objectives, procedures, and results of intervention, indicating their appropriateness for the learner. For example, the goal of riding a bus independently would have social validity for students residing in most cities but not for those in small towns or rural areas.

Socialized aggression A group of behavior disorders, including truancy, gang membership, theft, and delinquency, as identified by Quay (1975).

Spasticity A type of cerebral palsy characterized by tense, contracted muscles.

Special education Individually planned, specialized, intensive, outcome-directed instruction. When practiced most effectively and ethically, special education is also characterized by the systematic use of research-based instructional methods, the application of which is guided by frequent measures of student performance.

Speech A system of using breath and muscles to create specific sounds for communicating.

Speech audiometry Tests a person's detection and understanding of speech by presenting a list of two-syllable words at different decibel (sound volume) levels.

Speech reception threshold (SRT) The decibel (sound volume) level at which an individual can understand half of the words during a speech audiometry test; the SRT is measured and recorded for each ear.

Speechreading Process of understanding a spoken message by observing the speaker's lips in combination with information gained from facial expressions, gestures, and the context or situation.

Spina bifida A congenital malformation of the spine in which the vertebrae that normally protect the spine do not develop fully; may involve loss of sensation and severe muscle weakness in the lower part of the body.

Spina bifida occulta A type of spina bifida that usually does not cause serious disability. Although the vertebrae do not close, there is no protrusion of the spinal cord and membranes.

Standard celeration chart Chart for graphically displaying a student's learning progress from day to day in terms of changes in the frequency of correct and incorrect responses per minute.

Standard deviation A descriptive statistic that shows the average amount of variability among a set of scores. A small standard deviation indicates that the scores in the sample are distributed close to the mean; a larger standard deviation indicates that more scores in the sample fall farther from the mean.

Stereotype An overgeneralized or inaccurate attitude held toward all members of a particular group, on the basis of a common characteristic such as age, sex, race, or disability.

Stereotypic behavior (stereotypy) Repetitive, nonfunctional movements (e.g., hand flapping, rocking).

Stimulus control Occurs when a behavior is emitted more often in the presence of a particular stimulus than it is in the absence of that stimulus.

Strabismus A condition in which one eye cannot attain binocular vision with the other eye because of imbalanced muscles.

Stuttering A complex fluency disorder of speech, affecting the smooth flow of words; may involve repetition of sounds or words, prolonged sounds, facial grimaces, muscle tension, and other physical behaviors.

Supported employment Providing ongoing, individualized supports to persons with disabilities to help them find, learn, and maintain paid employment at regular work sites in the community.

Syntax The system of rules governing the meaningful arrangement of words in a language.

Systematic replication A strategy for extending and determining the generality of research findings by changing one or more variables from a previous study to see if similar results can be obtained. For example, testing a particular instructional method with elementary students that a previous study found effective with secondary students.

Task analysis Breaking a complex skill or chain of behaviors into smaller, teachable units.

Tay-Sachs disease A progressive nervous system disorder causing profound mental retardation, deafness, blindness, paralysis, and seizures. Usually fatal by age 5. Caused by a recessive gene; blood test can identify carrier; analysis of enzymes in fetal cells provides prenatal diagnosis.

Time out A behavior management technique that involves removing the opportunity for reinforcement for a specific period of time following an inappropriate behavior; results in a reduction of the inappropriate behavior.

Time trials A fluency-building procedure in which a student performs a new skill as many times as she can during a short period of time; one-minute time trials are effective for most academic skills.

Token economy (token reinforcement system) An instructional and behavior management system in which students earn tokens (e.g., stars, points, poker chips) for performing specified behaviors. Students accumulate their tokens and turn them at prearranged times for their choice of activities or items from a menu of backup rewards (e.g., stickers, hall monitor for a day).

Topography (of behavior) The physical shape or form of a response.

Total communication An approach to educating deaf students that combines oral speech, sign language, and fingerspelling.

Tremor A type of cerebral palsy characterized by regular, strong, uncontrolled movements. May cause less overall difficulty in movement than other types of cerebral palsy.

Triplegia Paralysis of any three limbs; relatively rare.

Turner's syndrome A sex chromosomal disorder in females, resulting from an absence of one of the X chromosomes; lack of secondary sex characteristics, sterility, and short stature are common. Although not usually a cause of mental retardation, it is often associated with learning problems.

Tymphonic membrane (eardrum) Located in the middle ear, the eardrum moves in and out to variations in sound pressure, changing acoustical energy to sound energy.

Usher's syndrome An inherited combination of visual and hearing impairments. Usually, the person is born with a profound hearing loss and loses vision gradually in adulthood because of retinitis pigmentosa, which affects the visual field.

Visual acuity The ability to clearly distinguish forms or discriminate details at a specified distance.

Visual efficiency A term used to describe how effectively a person uses his vision. Includes such factors as control of eye movements, near and distant visual acuity, and speed and quality of visual processing.

Vitreous humor The jellylike fluid that fills most of the interior of the eyeball.

Vocational rehabilitation A program designed to help adults with disabilities obtain and hold employment.

Work activity center A sheltered work and activity program for adults with severe disabilities; teaches concentration and persistence, along with basic life skills, for little or no pay.

References

Abbot, D. A., & Meredith, W. H. (1986). Strengths of parents with retarded children. *Family Relations, 35,* 371–375.

Achenbach, T. M., & Edelbrock, C. S. (1991). *Manual for the child behavior checklist*. Burlington: University of Vermont, Department of Psychiatry.

Adams, G., & Engelmann, S. (1996). *Research on Direct Instruction: 25 years beyond Distar*. Seattle: Educational Achievement Systems.

Adelman, H. S. (1994). Intervening to enhance home involvement in schooling. *Intervention in School and Clinic, 29*(5), 276–284.

Adelman, H. S. (1996). Appreciating the classification dilemma. In W. Stainback & S. Stainback (Eds.), *Controversial issues confronting special education: Divergent perspectives* (2nd ed.) (pp. 96–111). Boston: Allyn & Bacon.

Affleck, J. Q., Madge, S., Adams, A., & Lowenbraun, S. (1988). Integrated classroom vs. resource model: Academic viability and effectiveness. *Exceptional Children, 54,* 339–348.

Afzali-Nomani, E. (1991). Education conditions related to successful full inclusion programs involving deaf/hard of hearing children. *American Annals of the Deaf, 140,* 396–401.

Agran, M. (1997). *Student directed learning: Teaching self-determination skills*. Pacific Grove, CA: Brooks/Cole.

Agran, M., & Moore, S. C. (1994). *How to teach self-instruction of job skills*. Washington, DC: American Association on Mental Retardation.

Aiello, B. (1976, April 25). Up from the basement: A teacher's story. *New York Times,* p. 14.

Alabama Institute for the Deaf and Blind. (1989). *Helping kids soar*. Talladega: Author.

Alber, M. B. (1974). *Listening: A curriculum guide for teachers of visually impaired students.* Springfield: Illinois Office of Education.

Alber, S. R., & Heward, W. L. (1997). Recruit it or lose it! Training students to recruit contingent teacher attention. *Intervention in School and Clinic, 5,* 275–282.

Alber, S. R., & Heward, W. L. (in press). Teaching students to recruit positive attention: A literature review with recommendations for practice and future research. *Journal of Behavioral Education*.

Alber, S. R., Heward, W. L., & Hippler, B. J. (1999). Training middle school students with learning disabilities to recruit positive teacher attention. *Exceptional Children, 65,* 253–270.

Alberg, J., Petry, C., & Eller, S. (1994). *A social skills planning guide*. Longmont, CO: Sopris West.

Alberto, P. A., & Troutman, A. C. (1995). *Applied behavior analysis for teachers* (4th ed.). Upper Saddle River, NJ: Merrill/Prentice Hall.

Alberto, P. A., & Troutman, A. C. (1999). *Applied behavior analysis for teachers* (5th ed.). Upper Saddle River, NJ: Merrill/Prentice Hall.

Alberto, P., Jobes, N., Sizemore, A., & Doran, D. (1980). A comparison of individual and group instruction across response tasks. *Journal of The Association for Persons with Severe Handicaps, 5,* 285–293.

Alberto, P., Sharpton, W., Briggs, A., & Stright, M. (1986). Facilitating task acquisition through the use of a self-operated auditory prompting system. *Journal of The Association for Persons with Severe Handicaps, 11,* 85–91.

Algozzine, B., & Korinek, L. (1985). Where is special education for students with high prevalence handicaps going? *Exceptional Children, 51,* 388–394.

Algozzine, B., Christenson, S., & Ysseldyke, J. E. (1982). Probabilities associated with the referral to placement process. *Teacher Education and Special Education, 5,* 19–23.

Algozzine, B., Ysseldyke, J. E., & Christenson, S. (1983). An analysis of the incidence of special class placement: The masses are burgeoning. *Journal of Special Education, 17,* 141–147.

Allen, C. P., White, J., & Test, D. W. (1992). Using a picture/symbol form for self-monitoring within a community-based training program. *Teaching Exceptional Children, 24*(2), 54–56.

Allen, D. A., & Affleck, G. (1985). Are we stereotyping parents? A postscript to Blacher. *Mental Retardation, 23,* 200–202.

Allen, K. E. (1980a). The language impaired child in the preschool: The role of the teacher. *Directive Teacher, 2*(3), 6–10.

Allen, K. E. (1980b). *Mainstreaming in early childhood education.* Albany, NY: Delmar.

Allen, K. E., & Schwartz, I. S. (1996). *The exceptional child: Inclusion in early childhood education*. Albany, NY: Delmar.

Allen, T. (1986). Patterns of academic achievement among hearing impaired students: 1974 and 1983. In A. Schildroth & M. Karchmer (Eds.), *Deaf children in America* (pp. 161–206). San Diego: Little, Brown.

Allsop, J. (1980). Mainstreaming physically handicapped students. *Journal of Research and Development in Education*, *13*(4), 37–44.

Alzate, G. (1978). Analysis of testing problems in Spanish-speaking children. In A. H. Fink (Ed.), *International perspectives on future special education* (pp. 77–79). Reston, VA: Council for Exceptional Children.

Amado, A. N., Lakin, K. C., & Menke, J. M. (1990). *1990 chartbook of services for people with developmental disabilities.* Minneapolis: University of Minnesota, Center for Residential and Community Services.

American Academy of Pediatrics. (1991a). Human immunodeficiency virus [acquired immunodeficiency syndrome (AIDS) virus] in the athletic setting. *Pediatrics, 88,* 640–641.

American Academy of Pediatrics. (1991b). Task force on pediatric AIDS. *Pediatrics, 88,* 645–648.

American Council on Science and Health. (1979, May). *Diet and hyperactivity: Is there a relationship?* New York: Author.

American Printing House for the Blind. (1992). *Annual report*. Louisville, KY: Author.

American Psychiatric Association. (1994). *Diagnostic and statistical manual of mental disorders* (4th ed.). Washington, DC: Author.

American Speech-Language-Hearing Association (1996, Spring). Inclusive practices for children and youths with communication disorders: Position statement and technical report. *ASHA, 38* (Suppl. 16), 33–44.

American Speech-Language-Hearing Association. (1983). Position paper on social dialects. *ASHA*, *25*(9), 23–27.

American Speech-Language-Hearing Association. (1993). Definitions of communication disorders and variations. *ASHA, 35* (Suppl. 10), 40–41.

American Speech-Language-Hearing Association. (1999). [http://www.asha.org/]

Ammer, J. J., & Littleton, B. R. (1983, April). Parent advocacy: Now more than ever, active involvement in education decisions. Paper presented at the 61st annual international convention of the Council for Exceptional Children, Detroit.

Anderegg, M. L., Vergason, G. A., & Smith, M. C. (1992). A visual representation of the grief cycle for use by teachers with families of children with disabilities. *Remedial and Special Education*, *13*(2), 17–23.

Anderson, C., & Katsiyannis, A. (1997). By what token economy: A classroom learning tool for inclusive settings. *Teaching Exceptional Children, 29*(4), 65–67.

Anderson, K. M., & Anderson, C. L. (1997). Helpful web sites for parents of children with disabilities. *Intervention in School and Clinic, 33*(1), 40–42.

Anderson, L., Lakin, K. C., Polioster, B., & Prouty, R. (1998). One third of residential service recipients live in homes with three or fewer residents. *Mental Retardation, 36,* 249.

Anderson, W., Chitwood, S., & Hayden, D. (1997). *Negotiating the special education maze: A guide for parents and teachers*. Reston, VA: Council for Exceptional Children.

Anderson-Inman, L., Walker, H. M., & Purcell, J. (1984). Promoting the transfer of skills across settings: Transenvironmental programming for handicapped students in the mainstream. In W. L. Heward, T. E. Heron, D. S. Hill, & J. Trap-Porter (Eds.), *Focus on behavior analysis in education* (pp. 17–37). Upper Saddle River, NJ: Merrill/Prentice Hall.

Andrews, J. F., & Gonzalez, K. (1992). Free writing of deaf children in kindergarten. *Sign Language Studies, 74,* 63–78.

Anthony, D. (1971). *Seeing essential English.* Anaheim, CA: Anaheim School District.

Antonak, R. F., Fiedler, C. R., & Mulick, J. A. (1989). Misconceptions relating to mental retardation. *Mental Retardation*, *27*, 91–97.

Apolloni, T., & Cooke, T. P. (Eds.). (1981). California housing resources for persons with special developmental needs. Unpublished manuscript, California Institute on Human Services at Sonoma State University.

Apple, D. F., Anson, C. A., Hunter, J. D., & Bell, R. B. (1995). Spinal cord injury in youth. *Clinical Pediatrics, 34,* 90–95.

Archambault, F. X., Jr., Westberg, K. L., Brown, S. W., Hallmark, B. W., Zhang, W., & Emmons, C. L. (1993). Classroom practices used with gifted third and fourth grade students. *Journal for the Education of the Gifted*, *16*, 103–119.

Armstrong v. Kline, 476 F. Supplement 583 (E.D. PA 1979).

Arnold, K. M., & Hornett, D. (1990). Teaching idioms to children who are deaf. *Teaching Exceptional Children*, *22*(4), 14–17.

Arnold, L. E., Christopher, J., Huestis, R. D., & Smeltzer, D. J. (1978). Megavitamins for minimal brain dysfunction: A placebo controlled study. *Journal of the American Medical Association*, *240*, 2642–2643.

Artiles, A. J., & Trent, S. C. (1994). Overrepresentation of minority students in special education: A continuing debate. *Journal of Special Education*, *27*, 410–437.

Artiles, A., & Zamora-Durán, G. (1997). *Reducing disproportionate representation of culturally diverse students in special and gifted education*. Reston, VA: Council for Exceptional Children.

Atkins, B. J. (1992). Transition for individuals who are culturally diverse. In F. R. Rusch, L. DeStefano, J. Chadsey-Rusch, L. Allen Phelps, & E. Szymanski (Eds.), *Transition from school to adult life* (pp. 443–457). Pacific Grove, CA: Brooks/Cole.

Atkins, C. P., & Cartwright, L. R. (1982). National survey: Preferred language elicitation procedures used in five age categories. *Journal of the American Speech and Hearing Association, 24,* 321–323.

Ault, M. J., Gast, D. L., Wolery, M., & Doyle, P. M. (1992). Data collection and graphing method. *Teaching Exceptional Children, 24*(2), 28–33.

Ault, M. M., Graff, J. C., & Rues, J. P. (in press). Physical management and handling procedures. In M. E. Snell & F. Brown (Eds.), *Instruction of students with severe disabilities* (5th ed.). Upper Saddle River, NJ: Merrill/Prentice Hall.

Ault, M. M., Rues, J. P., Graff, J. C., & Holvoet, J. F. (in press). Special health care procedures. In M. E. Snell & F. Brown (Eds.), *Instruction of students with severe disabilities* (5th ed.). Upper Saddle River, NJ: Merrill/Prentice Hall.

Baca, L. M., & Cervantes, H. T. (1998). *The bilingual special education interface* (3rd ed.). Upper Saddle River, NJ: Merrill/Prentice Hall.

Baer, D. M. (1981a). *How to plan for generalization.* Lawrence, KS: H & H Enterprises.

Baer, D. M. (1981b). A hung jury and a Scottish verdict: "Not proven." *Analysis and Intervention in Developmental Disabilities, 1,* 91–97.

Baer, D. M. (1984). We already have multiple jeopardy; why try for unending jeopardy? In W. L. Heward, T. E. Heron, D. S. Hill, & J. Trap-Porter (Eds.). *Focus on behavior analysis in education* (pp. 296–299). Upper Saddle River, NJ: Merrill/Prentice Hall.

Baer, D. M., & Fowler, S. A. (1984). How should we measure the potential of self-control procedures for generalized educational outcomes? In W. L. Heward, T. E. Heron, D. S. Hill, & J. Trap-Porter (Eds.), *Focus on behavior analysis in education* (pp. 145–161). Upper Saddle River, NJ: Merrill/Prentice Hall.

Bagnato, S. J., Neisworth, J. T., & Capone, A. (1986). Curriculum-based assessment of the young exceptional child: Rationale and review. *Topics in Early Childhood Special Education, 6,* 97–110.

Bagnato, S. J., Neisworth, J. T., & Munson, S. M. (1997). *LINKing assessment and early intervention: An authentic curriculum-based approach.* Baltimore: Brookes.

Bailey, D. B., & Simeonsson, R. J. (1988a). *Family assessment in early intervention.* Upper Saddle River, NJ: Merrill/Prentice Hall.

Bailey, D. B., & Simeonsson, R. J. (1988b). Home-based early intervention. In S. L. Odom & M. B. Karnes (Eds.), *Early intervention for infants & children with handicaps* (pp. 199–215). Baltimore: Brookes.

Bailey, D. B., & Wolery, M. (1984). *Teaching infants and preschoolers with handicaps.* Upper Saddle River, NJ: Merrill/Prentice Hall.

Bailey, D. B., & Wolery, M. (1992). *Teaching infants and preschoolers with disabilities* (2nd ed.). Upper Saddle River, NJ: Merrill/Prentice Hall.

Bailey, D., Skinner, D., Rodriguez, P., & Correa, V. I. (in press). Awareness, use, satisfaction with services for Latino parents of young children with disabilities. *Exceptional Children.*

Bailey, J. S. (1992). Gentle teaching: Trying to win friends and influence people with euphemism, metaphor, smoke, and mirrors. *Journal of Applied Behavior Analysis, 25,* 879–883.

Baker, B. L, & Brightman, A. J. (1997). *Steps to independence: Teaching everyday skills to children with special needs* (3rd ed.). Baltimore: Brookes.

Baker, B. L. (1989). *Parent training and developmental disabilities.* Washington, DC: American Association on Mental Retardation.

Baker, J., & Zigmond, N. (1990). Are regular education classes equipped to accommodate students with learning disabilities? *Exceptional Children, 56,* 515–526.

Baker, J. M., & Zigmond, N. (1995). The meaning and practice of inclusions for students with learning disabilities: Themes and implications for the five cases. *Journal of Special Education, 29,* 163–180.

Baker, L., & Lombardi, B. R. (1985). Students' lecture notes and their relation to test performance. *Teaching of Psychology, 12,* 28–32.

Baldwin, V. (1995). *Annual deaf-blind census.* Monmouth: Western Oregon State College, Teacher Research.

Bambara, L. M., & Ager, C. (1992). Using self-scheduling to promote self-directed leisure activity in home and community settings. *Journal of The Association for Persons with Severe Handicaps, 17,* 67–76.

Bambora, L., & Koger, F. (1996). *Innovations: Providing opportunities for choice throughout the day.* Washington, DC: American Association on Mental Retardation.

Banbury, M. M., & Hebert, C. R. (1992). Do you see what I mean? *Teaching Exceptional Children, 24*(2), 34–38.

Banks, J. A., & Banks, C. A. M. (Eds.). (1997). *Multicultural education: Issues and perspectives* (3rd ed.). Boston: Allyn & Bacon.

Banks, J.A. (1994a). *An introduction to multicultural education.* Boston: Allyn & Bacon.

Banks, J.A. (1994b). *Multiethnic education: Theory and practice* (3rd ed.). Boston: Allyn & Bacon.

Bannerman, D. J., Sheldon, J. B., Sherman, J. A., & Harchik, A. E. (1990). Balancing the right to habilitation with the right to personal liberties: The rights of people with developmental disabilities to eat too many doughnuts and take a nap. *Journal of Applied Behavior Analysis, 23,* 79–89.

Barbetta, P. M. (1990a). GOALS: A group-oriented adapted levels system for children with behavior disorders. *Academic Therapy, 25,* 645–656.

Barbetta, P. M. (1990b). Red light—green light: A classwide management system for students with behavior disorders in the primary grades. *Preventing School Failure, 34*(4), 14–19.

Barbetta, P. M. (1991, February). Personal communication.

Barbetta, P. M., & Heron, T. E. (1991). Project SHINE: Summer home instruction and evaluation. *Intervention in School and Clinic, 26,* 276–281.

Barbetta, P. M., & Heward, W. L. (1993). Effects of active student response during error correction on the acquisition and maintenance of geography facts by elementary students with learning disabilities. *Journal of Behavioral Education, 3,* 217–233.

Barbetta, P. M., Heron, T. E., & Heward, W. L. (1993). Effects of active student response during error correction on the acquisition, maintenance, and generalization of sight words by students with developmental disabilities. *Journal of Applied Behavior Analysis, 26,* 111–119.

Barbetta, P. M., Heward, W. L., & Bradley, D. M. C. (1993). Relative effects of whole-word and phonetic error correction on the acquisition and maintenance of sight words by students with developmental disabilities. *Journal of Applied Behavior Analysis, 26,* 99–110.

Barbetta, P. M., Heward, W. L., Bradley, D. M. C., & Miller, A. D. (1994). Effects of immediate and delayed error correction on the acquisition and maintenance of sight words by students with developmental disabilities. *Journal of Applied Behavior Analysis, 27,* 177–178.

Barfels, M., Heward, W. L., & Al-Attrash, M. (1999). Using audio prompts to improve work performance by adults with developmental disabilities in an enclave supported employment setting. Manuscript submitted for publication.

Barner, K., Howell, R. D., & Mahoney, R. (1996). Telementoring and collaborative learning for students with disabilities. *Proceedings of the 20th Annual Meeting of the Society for Advancement of Rehabilitation Technologies* (pp. 176–179). Salt Lake City, UT.

Barnes, D. M. (1986). Brain function decline in children with AIDS. *Science, 232,* 1196.

Barnett, W. S. (1986). Definition and classification of mental retardation: A reply to Zigler, Balla, and Hodapp. *American Journal of Mental Deficiency, 91,* 111–116.

Barraga, N. C. (1983). *Visual handicaps and learning* (rev. ed.). Austin, TX: Exceptional Resources.

Barton, L. E., & LaGrow, S. J. (1985). Reduction of stereotypic responding in three visually impaired children. *Education of the Visually Handicapped, 6,* 145–181.

Bateman, B. D., & Linden, M. L. (1998). *Better IEPs: How to develop legally correct and educationally useful programs* (3rd ed.). Longmont, CO: Sopris West.

Batshaw, M. L. (Ed.). (1997). *Children with disabilities* (4th ed.). Baltimore: Brookes.

Batshaw, M. L., & Perret, Y. M. (1992). *Children with disabilities: A medical primer* (3rd ed.). Baltimore: Brookes.

Battle, D. E. (Ed.). (1998). *Communication disorders in multicultural populations* (2nd ed.). Boston: Butterworth-Heinemann.

Bauer, M. S., & Balius, F. A., Jr. (1995). Storytelling. *Teaching Exceptional Children, 27*(2), 24–28.

Baumgart, D., & Askvig, B. (1992). Job-related social skills interventions: Suggestions from managers and employees. *Education and Training in Mental Retardation, 27,* 345–353.

Baumgart, D., & Giangreco, M. F. (1996). Key lessons learned about inclusion. In D. H. Lehr & F. Brown (Eds.), *People with disabilities who challenge the system* (pp. 79–97). Baltimore: Brookes.

Baumgart, D., Johnson, J., & Helmstetter, E. (1990). *Augmentative and alternative communication systems for persons with moderate and severe disabilities.* Baltimore: Brookes.

Bayley, N. (1993). *Bayley Scales of Infant Development manual—Second edition manual.* San Antonio, TX: Psychological Corporation.

Beach Center on Families and Disability. (1996). *Parent handbook for individualized education programs* (Product No. 71). Lawrence, KS: Author.

Beakley, B. A., & Yoder, S. L. (1998). Middle schoolers learn community skills. *Teaching Exceptional Children, 30*(3), 16–21.

Beare, P. L. (1991). Philosophy, instructional methodology, training, and goals of teachers of teachers of the behaviorally disordered. *Behavioral Disorders, 16,* 211–218.

Beatty, L. S., Madden, R., Gardner, E. F., Karlsen, B. (1995). *Stanford Diagnostic Mathematics Test—Fourth Edition.* San Antonio, TX: Harcourt Brace Educational Measurement.

Beck, J., Broers, J., Hogue, E., Shipstead, J., & Knowlton, E. (1994). Strategies for functional community-based instruction and inclusion for children with mental retardation. *Teaching Exceptional Children, 26*(2), 44–48.

Beck, R., Conrad, D., & Anderson, P. (1995). *Skill builders handbook.* Longmont, CO: Sopris West.

Becker, W. C. (1971/1998). *Parents are teachers.* Champaign, IL: Research Press.

Becker, W. C. (1992). Direct Instruction: A 20-year review. In R. P. West & L. A. Hamerlunck (Eds.), *Designs for excellence in education* (pp. 71–112). Longmont, CA: Sopris West.

Becker, W. C., Engelmann, S., & Thomas, D. R. (1971). *Teaching: A course in applied psychology.* Chicago: Science Research Associates.

Beckley, C. G., Al-Attrash, M., Heward, W. L., & Morrison, H. (1999). Using guided notes in an eighth-grade social studies class: Effects on next-day quiz scores and notetaking accuracy. Manuscript submitted for publication.

Behr, S. K., Murphy, D. L., & Summers, J. A. (1992). *User's manual: Kansas Inventory of Parental Perceptions (KIPP)*. Lawrence: University of Kansas, Beach Center on Families and Disability.

Beirne-Smith, M., Ittenbach, R., & Patton, J. R. (1998). *Mental retardation* (5th ed.). Upper Saddle River, NJ: Merrill/ Prentice Hall.

Belcastro, F. P. (1989). Use of Belcastro Rods to teach mathematical concepts to blind students. *RE:view, 21*, 71–79.

Belfiore, P. J., & Toro-Zambrana, W. (1994). *Recognizing significant choices in community settings by people with significant disabilities*. Washington, DC: American Association on Mental Retardation.

Belgrave, F. Z., & Mills, J. (1981). Effect upon desire for social interaction with a physically disabled person of mentioning the disability in different contexts. *Journal of Applied Social Psychology, 11,* 44–57.

Bellamy, G. T., & Horner, R. H. (1987). Beyond high school: Residential and employment options after graduation. In M. Snell (Ed.), *Systematic instruction of persons with severe handicaps* (3rd ed.) (pp. 491–510). Upper Saddle River, NJ: Merrill/Prentice Hall.

Bellamy, G. T., & Wilcox, B. (1982). Secondary education for severely handicapped students: Guidelines for quality services. In K. P. Lynch, W. E. Kiernan, & J. A. Stark (Eds.), *Prevocational and vocational education for special needs youth: A blueprint for the 1980s.* Baltimore: Brookes.

Bellamy, G. T., Horner, R. H., & Inman, D. (1979). *Vocational training of severely retarded adults.* Baltimore: Brookes.

Bellamy, G. T., Rhodes, L. E., Mank, D. M., & Albin, J. M. (1988). *Supported employment: A community implementation guide*. Baltimore: Brookes.

Bender, E. K. (1994). A birding program for the blind. *RE:view, 26,* 92–96.

Bender, W. N. (1997). *Understanding ADHD: A practical guide for teachers and parents*. Upper Saddle River, NJ: Merrill/Prentice Hall.

Beninghof, A. M. (1998). *Ideas for inclusion: The classroom teacher's guide to integrating students with severe disabilities*. Longmont, CO: Sopris West.

Benjamin, S. (1989). An ideascape for education: What futurists recommend. *Educational Leadership, 47*, 8–14.

Bennett, C. I., (1990). *Comprehensive multicultural education; Theory and practice*. Needham Heights, MA: Allyn & Bacon.

Bennett, L. M., & Hensen, F. O. (1977). *Keeping in touch with parents: The teacher's best friend.* Hingham, MA: Teaching Resources.

Bennett, W. J. (1986). *First lessons: A report on elementary education in America.* Washington, DC: U.S. Department of Education.

Benz, M. R., & Lindstrom, L. E. (1997). *Building school-to-work programs: Strategies for youth with special needs*. Austin, TX: PRO-ED.

Benz, M. R., Yovanoff, P., & Doren, B. (1997). School-to-work components that predict postschool success for students with and without disabilities. *Exceptional Children, 63,* 151–165.

Bercovici, S. M. (1983). *Barriers to normalization: The restrictive management of retarded persons.* Austin, TX: PRO-ED.

Berg, F. S. (1986). Characteristics of the target population. In F. S. Berg, J. C. Blair, S. H. Viehweg, & A. Wilson-Vlotman (Eds.), *Educational audiology for the hard of hearing child* (pp. 1–24). Orlando, FL: Grune & Stratton.

Berman, J. L., & Ford, R. (1970). Intelligence quotients and intelligence loss in patients with phenylketonuria and some variant states. *Journal of Pediatrics, 77*, 764–770.

Bernabe, E. A., & Block, M. E. (1994). Modifying rules of a regular girls softball league to facilitate the inclusion of a child with severe disabilities. *Journal of The Association for Persons with Severe Handicaps, 19*, 24–31.

Bernthal, J. E., & Bankson, N. W. (1986). Phonologic disorders: An overview. In J. M. Costello & A. L. Holland (Eds.), *Handbook of speech and language disorders* (pp. 3–24). San Diego: College-Hill.

Bess, F. H., & Humes, L. E., (1995). *Audiology: The fundamentals* (2nd ed.). Baltimore: Williams & Wilkins.

Betts, G. (1985). *The autonomous learner model*. Greeley, CO: Autonomous Learning Publications Specialists.

Beukelman, D. R., & Miranda, P. (1998) *Augmentative and alternative communication: Management of severe communication disorder in children and adults* (2nd ed.). Baltimore: Brookes.

Bigge, J. L. (1991). *Teaching individuals with physical and multiple disabilities* (3rd ed.). Upper Saddle River, NJ: Merrill/Prentice Hall.

Bigge, J. L., Stump, C. S., Spagna, M. E., & Silberman, R. K. (1999). *Curriculum, assessment, and instruction for students with disabilities*. Belmont, CA: Wadsworth.

Biglan, A. (1995). Translating what we know about the context of antisocial behavior into a lower prevalence of such behavior. *Journal of Applied Behavior Analysis, 28,* 479–492.

Bigler, E. D. (Ed.). (1990). *Traumatic brain injury: Mechanisms of damage, assessment, intervention and outcome*. Austin, TX: PRO-ED.

Bijou, S. W. (1966). A functional analysis of retarded development. In N. R. Ellis (Ed.), *International review of research in mental retardation* (vol. 1). New York: Academic Press.

Biklen, D. (1988). The myth of clinical judgment. *Journal of Social Issues, 44*, 127–140.

Biklen, D. (1990). Communication unbound: Autism and praxis. *Harvard Educational Review*, *60*, 291–314.

Biklen, D. (1992). Typing to talk: Facilitated communication. *American Journal of Speech-Language Pathology*, *1*(2), 15–17.

Biklen, D. (1993). *Communication unbound: How facilitated communication is challenging traditional views of autism and ability-disability.* New York: Teachers College Press.

Biklen, D., & Bogdan, R. (1976). *Handicapism in America.* Syracuse, NY: WIN.

Biklen, D., & Zollers, N. (1986). The focus of advocacy in the LD field. *Journal of Learning Disabilities*, *19*, 579–586.

Billingsley, F. F., & Kelley, B. (1994). An examination of the acceptability of instructional practices for students with severe disabilities in general education settings. *Journal of The Association for Persons with Severe Handicaps*, *19*, 75–83.

Billingsley, F. F., Gallucci, C., Peck, C. A., Schwartz, I. S., & Staub, D. (1996). "But those kids can't even *do* math": An alternative conceptualization of outcomes for inclusive education. *Special Education Leadership Review, 3*(1), 43–55.

Billingsley, F. F., Liberty, K. A., & White, O. R. (1994). The technology of instruction. In E. C. Cipani & F. Spooner (Eds.), *Curricular and instructional approaches for persons with severe disabilities* (pp. 81–116). Boston: Allyn & Bacon.

Binder, C. (1996). Behavioral fluency: Evolution of a new paradigm. *Behavior Analyst, 19,* 163–197.

Binder, C., Haughton, E., & Van Eyk, D. (1990). Increasing endurance by building fluency: Precision teaching attention span. *Teaching Exceptional Children, 22*, 24–27.

Bireley, M. (1995). The special characteristics and needs of gifted students with disabilities. In J. L. Genshaft, M. Bireley, & C. L. Hollinger (Eds.), *Serving gifted and talented students: A resource for school personnel* (pp. 201–215). Austin, TX: PRO-ED.

Birenbaum, A. (1986). Symposium overview: Community programs for people with mental retardation. *Mental Retardation*, *24*, 145–146.

Bishop, V. E. (1986). Identifying the components of successful mainstreaming. *Journal of Visual Impairment and Blindness*, *80*, 939–946.

Bishop, V. E. (1996). *Teaching visually impaired children* (2nd ed.). Springfield, IL: Thomas.

Blacher, J. (1984). A dynamic perspective on the impact of a severely handicapped child on the family. In J. Blacher (Ed.), *Severely handicapped children and their families* (pp. 3–50). Orlando, FL: Academic Press.

Blackorby, J., & Wagner, M. (1996). Longitudinal postschool outcomes of youth with disabilities: Findings from the National Longitudinal Transition Study. *Exceptional Children, 62,* 399–413.

Blackstone, M. (1981). How parents can affect communitization, or, what do you mean I'm a troublemaker? In C. H. Hansen (Ed.), *Severely handicapped persons in the community* (pp. 29–52). Seattle: University of Washington, PDAS.

Blackstone, S. W., Cassatt-James, E. L., & Bruskin, D. M. (1988). *Augmentative communication implementation strategies.* Rockville, MD: American Speech-Language-Hearing Association.

Blair, J., Peterson, M., & Viehweg, S. (1985). The effects of mild hearing loss on academic performance of young school-age children. *Volta Review*, *87*, 87–93.

Blalock, G. (1991). Paraprofessionals: Critical team members in our special education programs. *Intervention in School and Clinic*, *26*(4), 200–214.

Blatt, B. (1976). *Revolt of the idiots: A story.* Glen Ridge, NJ: Exceptional Press.

Blatt, B. (1987). *The conquest of mental retardation.* Austin, TX: PRO-ED.

Blatt, B., & Kaplan, F. (1966). *Christmas in purgatory: A photographic essay on mental retardation.* Boston: Allyn & Bacon.

Bleck, E. E. (1979). Integrating the physically handicapped child. *Journal of School Health*, *49*, 141–146.

Bleck, E. E. (1987). *Orthopedic management of cerebral palsy—Clinics in developmental medicine No. 99/100.* Philadelphia: Lippincott.

Bloodstein, O. (1995). *A handbook on stuttering* (5th ed.). San Diego: Singular.

Bloom, B. S. (1980). The new direction in educational research: Alterable variables. *Phi Delta Kappan*, *61*, 382–385.

Bloom, L., & Lahey, M. (1978). *Language development and language disorders.* New York: Wiley.

Board of Education of the Hendrick Hudson Central School District v. Rowley, 102 S. Ct. 3034 (1982).

Bock, G., Stebbins, L., & Proper, E. C. (1996). Excerpts from the Abt reports: Descriptions of the models and the results. *Effective School Practices, 15*(1), 10–16.

Boe, E. E., Cook, L. H., Bobbitt, S. A., & Terhanian, G. (1998). The shortage of fully certified teachers in special and general education. *Teacher Education and Special Education, 21,* 1–21.

Bogdan, R., & Talylor, S. J. (1994). *The social meaning of mental retardation*. New York: Teachers College Press.

Bondy, A., & Frost, L. (1994). PECS: The picture exchange communication system. *Focus on Autistic Behavior, 9,* 1–9.

Book, D., Paul, T. L., Gwalla-Ogisi, N., & Test, D. W. (1990). No more bologna sandwiches. *Teaching Exceptional Children*, *22*(2), 62–64.

Boone, R. S. (1992). Involving culturally diverse parents in transition planning. *Career Development for Exceptional Individuals*, *15*, 205–221.

Bornstein, H. (1974). Signed English: A manual approach to English language development. *Journal of Speech and Hearing Disorders, 3,* 330–343.

Borthwick, C., Morton, M., Crossley, R., & Biklen, D. (1992). Facilitated communication and disclosures of abuse. *Facilitated Communication Digest*, *1*(1), 5–6.

Borthwick-Duffy, S. (1994). Review of mental retardation: Definition, causes, and systems of supports. *American Journal on Mental Retardation*, *98*, 541–544.

Borthwick-Duffy, S. A., Widaman, K. F., Little, T. D., & Eyman, R. K. (1992). *Foster family care for persons with mental retardation*. Washington, DC: American Association on Mental Retardation.

Boudah, D. J., Schumaker, J. B., & Deshler, D. D. (1997). Collaborative instruction: Is it an effective option for inclusion in secondary classrooms? *Learning Disability Quarterly, 4,* 293–316.

Bowen, J., Olympia, D., & Jensen, W. (1996). *Study buddies: Parent tutoring tactics*. Longmont, CO: Sopris West.

Bower, E. M. (1960). *Early identification of emotionally handicapped children in the schools.* Springfield, IL: Thomas.

Bower, E. M. (1981). *Early identification of emotionally handicapped children in school* (3rd ed.). Springfield, IL: Thomas.

Bower, E. M. (1982). Defining emotional disturbance: Public policy and research. *Psychology in the Schools*, *19*, 55–60.

Braaten, S., Kauffman, J. M., Braaten, B., Polsgrove, L., & Nelson, C. M. (1988). The Regular Education Initiative (REI): Patent medicine for behavioral disorders. *Exceptional Children*, *55*, 21–27.

Braden, J. P., Maller, S. J., & Paquin, M. M. (1993). The effects of residential versus day placement on the performance IQs of children with hearing impairment. *Journal of Special Education*, *26*, 423–433.

Bradley, D. F., & Calvin, M. B. (1998). Grading modified assignments: Equity or compromise? *Teaching Exceptional Children, 31*(2), 24–29.

Bradley, R. H., & Caldwell, B. M. (1979). Home observation for measurement of the environment: A revision of the preschool scale. *American Journal of Mental Deficiency, 84*, 235–244.

Bradley, V. J., Knoll, J., & Agosta, J. M. (Eds.). (1992). *Emerging issues in family support*. Washington, DC: American Association on Mental Retardation.

Bradley-Johnson, S., & Harris, S. (1990). Best practices in working with students with a visual loss. In A. Thomas & J. Grimes (Eds.), *Best practices in school psychology—II* (pp. 871–885). Washington, DC: National Association of School Psychologists.

Brandt, J. (1992). Idea Bunny: Teaching special needs preschool children independent work skills with an audio prompt recording device. Unpublished master's thesis, The Ohio State University, Columbus.

Bredekamp, S. (1987). *Developmentally appropriate practice in early childhood programs serving children from birth through age 8.* Washington, DC: National Association for the Education of Young Children.

Bredekamp, S. (1993). The relationship between early childhood education and early childhood special education: Healthy marriage or family feud? *Topics in Early Childhood Special Education*, *13*, 258–273.

Bredekamp, S., & Copple, C. (Eds.). (1997). *Developmentally appropriate practice in early childhood programs*. Washington, DC: National Association for the Education of Young Children.

Brewer, J., & Kieff, J. (1996). Fostering mutual respect for play at home and school. *Childhood Education, 7,* 92–96.

Bricker, D. (1993). *AEPS measurement for birth to three years*. Baltimore: Brookes.

Bricker, D., & Pretti-Frontczak, K. (1996). *AEPS measurement for three to six years*. Baltimore: Brookes.

Bricker, D., & Squires, J. (1999). *Ages & stages questionnaires: A parent-completed, child-monitoring system* (2nd ed.). Baltimore: Brookes.

Bricker, D., & Waddell, M. (1996). *AEPS curriculum for three to six years*. Baltimore: Brookes.

Bricker, D., Pretti-Frontczak, K., & McComas, N. (1998). *An activity-based approach to early intervention* (2nd ed.). Baltimore: Brookes.

Bricker, D. D. (1986). An analysis of early intervention programs: Attendant issues and future directions. In R. J. Morris & B. Blatt (Eds.), *Special education: Research and trends* (pp. 28–65). New York: Pergamon.

Brickey, M. P., Campbell, K. M., & Browning, L. J. (1985). A five-year follow-up of sheltered workshop employees placed in competitive jobs. *Mental Retardation*, *23*, 67–73.

Brigance, A. (1983). *Brigance Diagnostic Inventory of Basic Skills.* N. Billerica, MA: Curriculum Associates.

Briggs, A., Alberto, P., Sharpton, W., Berlin, K., McKinley, C., & Ritts, C. (1990). Generalized use of a self-operated audio prompt system. *Education and Training in Mental Retardation*, *25*, 381–389.

Briggs, S. J. (1991). The multilingual/multicultural classroom. *Kappa Delta Pi Record*, *28*, 11–14.

Brigham, F. J., & Kauffman, J. M. (1998). Creating supportive environments for students with emotional or behavioral disorders. *Effective School Practices, 17*(2), 25–35.

Brinker, R. P. (1985). Interactions between severely mentally retarded students and other students in integrated and segregated public school settings. *American Journal of Mental Deficiency*, *89*, 587–594.

Brinker, R. P. (1992). Family involvement in early intervention: Accepting the unchangeable, changing the changeable, and knowing the difference. *Topics in Early Childhood Special Education, 12*(3), 307–332

Brinkerhoff, L. C., Shaw, S. F., & McGuire, J. M. (1993). *Promoting postsecondary education for students with learning disabilities*. Austin, TX: PRO-ED.

Bristol, M., Cohen, D., Costello, J., Denckla, M., Eckberg, T., Kallen, R., Kraemer, H., Lord, C. Maurer, R., McIlvane, W., Minshew, N. Sigman, M., & Spence, M. (1996). State of the science in autism: Report to the National Institute of Health. *Journal of Autism and Developmental Disorders, 26,* 121–154.

Brolin, D. E. (1995). *Career education: A functional life skills approach* (3rd ed.). Upper Saddle River, NJ: Merrill/Prentice Hall.

Brolin, D. E. (1997). *Life-centered career education: A competency based approach* (5th ed.). Reston, VA: Council for Exceptional Children.

Bronicki, G. J., & Turnbull, A. P. (1987). Family-professional interactions. In M. E. Snell (Ed.), *Systematic instruction of persons with severe handicaps* (3rd ed.) (pp. 9–35). Upper Saddle River, NJ: Merrill/Prentice Hall.

Bronston, W. (1980). Matters of design. In T. Apolloni, J. Cappuccilli, & T. P. Cooke (Eds.), *Achievements in residential services for persons with disabilities: Toward excellence.* Baltimore: University Park Press.

Brookes, J., & Brookes, M. (1993). In search of understanding: The case for constructivist classrooms. Alexander, VA: Association for Supervision and Curriculum Development.

Brophy, J. (1986). Teacher influences on student achievement. *American Psychologist*, *41*, 1069–1077.

Brophy, J., & Good, T. (1986). Teacher behavior and student achievement. In M. C. Wittrock (Ed.), *Handbook on research on teaching* (3rd ed.) (pp. 328-375). Upper Saddle River, NJ: Merrill/Prentice Hall.

Browder, D. M., & Snell, M. E. (in press). Daily living and community skills. In M. E. Snell & F. Brown (Eds.), *Instruction of students with severe disabilities* (5th ed.). Upper Saddle River, NJ: Merrill/Prentice Hall.

Browder, D. M., Cooper, K. J., & Lim, L. (1998). Teaching adults with severe disabilities to express their choice of settings for leisure activities. *Education and Training in Mental Retardation and Developmental Disabilities, 33,* 228–238.

Browder, D. M., Lim, L., Lin, C. H., & Belfiore, P. J. (1993). Applying therbligs to task analytic instruction: A technology to pursue? *Education and Training in Mental Retardation*, *28*, 242–251.

Browder, D., Lentz, F. E., Knoster, T., & Wilansky, C. (1988). Determining extended school year eligibility: From esoteric to explicit criteria. *Journal of The Association for Persons with Severe Handicaps*, *13*, 235–243.

Brower, I. C. (1983). Counseling Vietnamese. In D. R. Atkinson, G. Morten, & D. W. Sue (Eds.), *Counseling American minorities* (2nd ed.) (pp. 107–121). Dubuque, IA: Brown.

Brown v. Board of Education of Topeka, 347 U.S. 483 (1954).

Brown, F., & Lehr, D. H. (1993). Making activities meaningful for students with severe multiple disabilities. *Teaching Exceptional Children*, *25*(4), 12–16.

Brown, F., Holvoet, J., Guess, G., & Milligan, M. (1980). The individualized curriculum sequencing model (III): Small group instruction. *Journal of The Association for Persons with Severe Handicaps*, *5*, 352-367.

Brown, J. R. (1982). Assessment of the culturally different and disadvantaged child. In G. Ulrey & S. J. Rogers (Eds.), *Psychological assessment of handicapped infants and young children* (pp. 163–171). New York: Thieme-Stratton.

Brown, L. (1990). Who are they and what do they want? An essay on TASH. *TASH Newsletter*, *16*(9), 1.

Brown, L. L., & Hammill, D. D. (1990). *Behavior rating profile: An ecological approach to behavioral assessment* (2nd ed.). Austin, TX: PRO-ED.

Brown, L., Long, E., Udvari-Solner, A., Davis, L., VanDeventer, P., Ahlgren, C., Johnson, F., Gruenewald, L., & Jorgensen, J. (1989a). The home school: Why students with severe disabilities must attend the schools of their brothers, sisters, friends, and neighbors. *Journal of The Association for Persons with Severe Handicaps*, *14*, 1–7.

Brown, L., Long, E., Udvari-Solner, A., Davis, L., VanDeventer, P., Ahlgren, C., Johnson, F., Gruenewald, L., & Jorgensen, J. (1989b). Should students with severe intellectual disabilities be based in regular or in special education classrooms in home schools? *Journal of The Association for Persons with Severe Handicaps*, *14*, 8–12.

Brown, L., Schwartz, P., Udvari-Solner, A., Kampschroer, E. F., Johnson, F., Jorgensen, J., & Gruenewald, L. (1991). How much time should students with severe intellectual disabilities spend in regular education classrooms and elsewhere? *Journal of The Association for Persons with Severe Handicaps*, *16*, 39–47.

Brown, L., Shiraga, B., York, J., Kessler, K., Strohm, B., Rogan, P., Sweet, M., Zanella, K., VanDeventer, P., & Loomis, R. (1984). Integrated work opportunities for adults with severe handicaps: The extended training option. *Journal of The Association for Persons with Severe Handicaps*, *9*, 262–269.

Brown, V. L., Cronin, M. E., & McEntire, E. (1994). *Test of Mathematical Abilities—2*. Austin, TX: PRO-ED.

Brown, W., Thurman, S. K., & Pearl, L. W. (1993). *Family-centered intervention with infants and toddlers:*

Innovative cross-disciplinary approaches. Baltimore: Brookes.

Bryan, T. (1997). Assessing the personal and social status of students with learning disabilities. *Learning Disabilities Research and Practice, 12,* 63–76.

Bryan, W. H., & Jeffrey, D. L. (1982). Education of visually handicapped students in the regular classroom. *Texas Tech Journal of Education*, *9*, 125–131.

Buchanan, L., & Kochar, C. (1989). *The right to a free & appropriate public education (for some?): The case of Timothy vs. Rochester School District* (Policy Briefs in Special Education, Paper No. 1). Washington, DC: George Washington University, School of Education and Human Development.

Bull, G. L., & Rushakoff, G. E. (1987). Computers and speech and language disordered individuals. In J. D. Lindsey (Ed.), *Computers and exceptional individuals* (pp. 83–104). Upper Saddle River, NJ: Merrill/Prentice Hall.

Bullis, M., & Bull, B. (1986). *Review of research on adolescents and adults with deaf-blindness.* Washington, DC: Catholic University of America, DATA Institute.

Bullis, M., & Otos, M. (1988). Characteristics of programs for children with deaf-blindness: Results of a national survey. *Journal of The Association for Persons with Severe Handicaps*, *13*, 110–115.

Bullivant, B. M. (1993). Culture: Its nature and meaning for educators. In J. A. Banks & C. A. M. Banks (Eds.), *Multicultural education: Issues and perspectives* (2nd ed.) (pp. 29–47). Boston: Allyn & Bacon.

Burchard, S. N., Hasazi, J. S., Gordon, L. R., & Yoe, J. (1991). An examination of lifestyle and adjustment in three community residential alternatives. *Research in Developmental Disabilities*, *12*, 127–142.

Burd, L., & Martsolf, J. T. (1989). Fetal alcohol syndrome: Diagnosis and syndrome variability. *Physiology and Behavior*, *46*, 39–43.

Burgess, D. M., & Steissguth, A. P. (1992). Fetal alcohol syndrome and fetal alcohol effects: Principles for educators. *Phi Delta Kappan*, *74*, 24–29.

Burkhardt, L. J. (1981). *Homemade battery powered toys and educational devices for severely disabled children.* Millville, PA: Burkhardt.

Bursuck, W., Polloway, E. A., Plante, L., Epstein, D. H., Jayanthi, M., & McConeghy, J. I. (1996). Report card grading and adaptations: A national survey of classroom practices. *Exceptional Children, 62,* 301–318.

Bushell, D., Jr., & Baer, D. M. (1994). Measurably superior instruction means close, continual contact with the relevant outcome data. Revolutionary! In R. Gardner III, D. M. Sainato, J. O. Cooper, T. E. Heron, W. L. Heward, J. Eshleman, & T. A. Grossi (Eds.), *Behavior analysis in education: Focus on measurably superior instruction* (pp. 3–10). Pacific Grove, CA: Brooks/Cole.

Butterfield, N., Arthur, M., & Sigafoos, J. (1995). *Partners in everyday communicative exchanges: A guide for promoting interaction involving people with severe intellectual disability.* Baltimore: Brookes.

Byers, J. (1989). AIDS in children: Effects on neurological development and implications for the future. *Journal of Special Education*, *23*, 5–16.

Calculator, S. N., & Jorgensen, C. M. (1991). Integrating augmentative and alternative communication instruction into regular education settings: Expounding on best practices. *Augmentative and Alternative Communication*, *7*, 204–214.

Calhoun, M. L., & Kuczera, M. (1996). Increasing social smiles of young children with disabilities. *Perceptual and Motor Skills, 82,* 1265–1266.

Calhoun, M. L., Rose, T. L., & Prendergast, D. E. (1991). *The Charlotte Circle intervention guide for parent-child interactions*. Tucson, AZ: Communication Skill Builders.

Calhoun, M. L., Rose, T. L., Hanft, B. & Sturkey, C. (1991). Social reciprocity interventions: Implications for developmental therapists. *Physical and Occupational Therapy in Pediatrics, 11,* 45–46.

Callahan, K., Rademacher, J. A., & Hildreth, B. L. (1998). The effect of parent participation in strategies to improve the homework performance of students who are at risk. *Remedial and Special Education, 19*(3), 131–141.

Callister, J. P., Mitchell, L., & Talley, G. (1986). Profiling family preservation efforts in Utah. *Children Today*, *15*, 23–25, 36–37.

Calvert, D. R. (1986). Speech in perspective. In D. M. Luterman (Ed.), *Deafness in perspective* (pp. 167–191). San Diego: College-Hill.

Campbell, P. H. (1993). Physical management and handling procedures. In M. E. Snell, *Instruction of students with severe disabilities* (4th ed.) (pp. 248–263). Upper Saddle River, NJ: Merrill/Prentice Hall.

Campbell, V., Smith, R., & Wool, R. (1982). Adaptive Behavior Scale differences in scores of mentally retarded individuals referred for institutionalization and those never referred. *American Journal of Mental Deficiency*, *86*, 425–428.

Caputo, R. A. (1993). Using puppets with students with emotional and behavioral disorders. *Intervention in School and Clinic*, *29*, 26–30.

Cardon, L. R., Smith, S. D., Fulker, D. W., Kimberling, B. F., Pennignton, B. F., & DeFries, J. C. (1994) Quantitative trait locus for reading disability on chromosome 6. *Science, 226,* 276–279.

Carmichael Olson, H. (1994). The effects of prenatal alcohol exposure on child development. *Infants and Young Children*, *6*(3), 10–25.

Carnine, D. (1976). Effects of two teacher presentation rates on off-task behavior, answering correctly, and participation. *Journal of Applied Behavior Analysis, 9,* 199–206.

Carnine, D. (1997). Bridging the research to practice gap. *Exceptional Children, 63,* 513–521.

Carnine, D. W., Dixon, R. C., & Silbert, J. (1998). Effective strategies for teaching mathematics. In D. W. Carnine & E. J. Kameenui (Eds.). *Effective teaching strategies that accommodate diverse learners* (pp. 93–112). Upper Saddle River, NJ: Merrill/Prentice Hall.

Carnine, D. W., Grossen, B., & Silbert, J. (1995). Direct instruction to accelerate cognitive growth. In J. Block, S. Everson, & T. Guskey (Eds.), *School improvement programs: A handbook for educational leaders* (pp. 129–152). New York: Scholastic.

Carnine, D. W., Silbert, J., & Kameenui, E. J. (1998). *Direct instruction reading* (3rd ed). Upper Saddle River, NJ: Merrill/Prentice Hall.

Carnine, D., Jones, E., & Dixon, R. (1994). Mathematics: Educational tools for diverse learners. *School Psychology Review, 23,* 406–427.

Caro, P., & Derevensky, J. L. (1997). An exploratory study using the sibling interaction scale: Observing interactions between siblings with and without disabilities. *Education and Treatment of Children, 20*(4), 383–403.

Carr, E. G., & Durand, V. M. (1985). Reducing behavior problems through functional communication training. *Journal of Applied Behavior Analysis, 18,* 111–126.

Carr, E. G., Levin, L., McConnachie, G., Carlson, J. I., Kemp, D. C., & Smith, C. E. (1994). *Communication-based intervention for problem behavior: A user's guide for producing positive change*. Baltimore: Brookes.

Carr, S. C., & Punzo, R. P. (1993). The effects of self-monitoring of academic accuracy and productivity on the performance of students with behavioral disorders. *Behavioral Disorders, 18,* 241–250.

Carroll, M. E., Burnworth, C., Chambers, J., Cousino, D., Mahaney, P., & Trent, D. (1991). Classroom companies: The buck starts here. *Intervention in School and Clinic, 27(*2), 97–100.

Carta, J. J., Atwater, J. B., Schwartz, I. S., & McConnell, S. R. (1993). Developmentally appropriate practices and early childhood special education: A reaction to Johnson and McChesney Johnson. *Topics in Early Childhood Special Education, 13,* 243–254.

Carta, J. J., Atwater, J. B., Schwartz, I. S., & Miller, P. A. (1990). Applications of ecobehavioral analysis to the study of transitions across early education settings. *Education and Treatment of Children, 13,* 298–315.

Carter, J., & Sugai, G. (1989). Survey on prereferral practices: Responses from state departments of education. *Exceptional Children, 55,* 298–302.

Cartledge, G., & Cochran, L. L. (1993). Developing cooperative learning behavior in students with behavior disorders. *Preventing School Failure, 37,* 5–10.

Cartledge, G., & Milburn, J. F. (1995). *Teaching social skills to children and youth: Innovative approaches* (3rd ed.). Boston: Allyn & Bacon.

Case, L. P., Harris, K. R., & Graham, S. (1992). Improving the mathematical problem-solving skills of students with learning disabilities: Self-regulated strategy development. *Journal of Special Education, 26,* 1–19.

Cassini, K. K., & Rodgers, J. L. (1989). *Death in the classroom: A teacher's guide to assist grieving students*. Cincinnati, OH: Griefwork of Cincinnati.

Cavalier, A. R., & Brown, C. C. (1998). From passivity to participation: The transformational possibilities of speech-recognition technology. *Teaching Exceptional Children, 30*(6), 60–65.

Cavanaugh, R. A. (1990). "I don't have any homework, and even if I did I don't remember what it was." *American Secondary Education, 19*(1), 2–8.

Cavanaugh, R. A., Heward, W. L., & Donelson, F. (1996). Effects of response cards during lesson closure on the academic performance of secondary students in an earth science course. *Journal of Applied Behavior Analysis, 29,* 403–406.

Cazden, C. B. (1992). *Whole language plus: Essays on literacy in the United States and New Zealand.* New York: Teachers College Press.

CEC Today. (1998). Growing challenge for teachers—Providing medical procedures for students. *5*(3), 1, 5, 15.

Center, D. B. (1990). Social maladjustment: An interpretation. *Behavioral Disorders, 15,* 141–148.

Center on Human Policy. (1986, December). Positive interventions for challenging behavior. *The Association for Persons with Severe Handicaps Newsletter, 12*(12), 4.

Chadsey-Rusch, J., Drasgow, E., Reinoehl, B., Halle, J., & Collet-Klingenberg, L. (1993). Using general-case instruction to teach spontaneous and generalized requests for assistance to learners with severe disabilities. *Journal of The Association for Persons with Severe Handicaps, 18,* 177–187.

Chaikind, S., Danielson, L. C., & Brauen, M. L. (1993). What do we know about the costs of special education? A selected review. *Journal of Special Education, 26,* 344–370.

Champagne, J. F. (1993). Decisions in sequence: How to make placements in the least restrictive environment. *EdLaw Briefing Paper, 9 & 10,* 1–16.

Chandler, L. K. (1993). Steps in preparing for transition: Preschool to kindergarten. *Teaching Exceptional Children, 25*(4), 52–55.

Chaney, C., & Frodyma, D. A. (1982). A noncategorical program for preschool language development.

Teaching Exceptional Children, *14*, 152–155.

Charney, E. B. (1992). Neural tube defects: Spina bifida and myelomeningocele. In M. L. Batshaw & Y. M. Perret, *Children with disabilities: A medical primer* (3rd ed.) (pp. 471–488). Baltimore: Brookes.

Chase, J. B. (1986a). Application of assessment techniques to the totally blind. In P. J. Lazarus & S. S. Strichart (Eds.), *Psychoeducational evaluation of children and adolescents with low-incidence handicaps* (pp. 75–102). Orlando, FL: Grune & Stratton.

Chase, J. B. (1986b). Psychoeducational assessment of visually-impaired learners. In P. J. Lazarus & S. S. Strichart (Eds.), *Psychoeducational evaluation of children and adolescents with low-incidence handicaps* (pp. 41–74). Orlando, FL: Grune & Stratton.

Chesapeake Institute. (1994, September). *National agenda for achieving better results for children and youth with serious emotional disturbance*. Washington, DC: U.S. Department of Education.

Chesley, G. M., & Calaluce, P. D. (1997). The deception of inclusion. *Mental Retardation, 35,* 488–490.

Chinn, P. C., & Hughes, S. (1987). Representation of minority students in special education classes. *Remedial and Special Education, 8*, 41–46.

Chinn, P. C., & Kamp, S. H. (1982). Cultural diversity and exceptionality. In N. G. Haring (Ed.), *Exceptional children and youth* (3rd ed.) (pp. 371–390). Upper Saddle River, NJ: Merrill/Prentice Hall.

Christensen, C. M. (1992). Multicultural competencies in early intervention: Training professionals for a pluralistic society. *Infants and Young Children*, *4*, 49–83.

Christensen, J., & Vogel, J. R. (1998). A decision model for grading students with disabilities. *Teaching Exceptional Children, 31*(2), 30–35.

Christenson, S. L., Ysseldyke, J. E., & Thurlow, M. L. (1989). Critical instructional factors for students with mild handicaps: An integrative interview. *Remedial and Special Education*, *10*, (5), 21–23.

Chuch, G., & Glennen, S. (1992). *The handbook of assistive technology*. San Diego: Singular.

Cipani, E. (1998). *Classroom management for all teachers: 11 effective plans*. Upper Saddle River, NJ: Merrill/ Prentice Hall.

Cipani, E. C., & Spooner, F. (Eds.). (1994). *Curricular and instructional approaches for persons with severe disabilities*. Boston: Allyn & Bacon.

Clark, B. (1986). The integrative education model. In J. S. Renzulli (Ed.), *Systems and models for developing programs for the gifted and talented* (pp. 57–91). Mansfield Center, CT: Creative Learning Press.

Clark, B. (1997). *Growing up gifted: Developing the potential of children at home and at school* (5th ed.). Upper Saddle River, NJ: Merrill/Prentice Hall.

Clark, G. M. (1994). Is a functional curriculum approach compatible with an inclusive education model? *Teaching Exceptional Children*, *26*(2), 36–39.

Clark, G. M., & Kolstoe, O. P. (1995). *Career development and transition education for adolescents with disabilities* (2nd ed.). Needham Heights, MA: Allyn & Bacon.

Clark, G. M., & Patton, J. R. (1997). *Transition planing inventory*. Austin, TX: PRO-ED.

Clark, G. M., Carlson, B. C., Fisher, S., Cook, I. D., & D'Alonzo, B. J. (1991). Career development for students with disabilities in elementary schools: A position statement of the division on career development. *Career Development for Exceptional Individuals*, *14*, 109–120.

Clarke, B., & Leslie, P. (1980). Environmental alternatives for the hearing handicapped. In J. W. Schifani, R. M. Anderson, & S. J. Odle (Eds.), *Implementing learning in the least restrictive environment: Handicapped children in the mainstream* (pp. 199–240). Baltimore: University Park Press.

Clarke, K. L. (1988). Barriers or enablers? Mobility devices for visually impaired and multihandicapped infants and preschoolers. *Education of the Visually Handicapped*, *20*, 115–132.

Clarke, K. L., Sainato, D. M., & Ward, M. E. (1994). Travel performance of preschoolers: The effects of mobility training with a long cane versus a precane. *Journal of Visual Impairment and Blindness*, *88*, 19–30.

Cleburne Living Center, Inc., v. City of Cleburne, Texas, 735 F. 2d 832 (5th Cir. 1984).

Clements, S. D. (1966). *Minimal brain dysfunction in children* (NINDS Monograph No. 3, Public Health Service Bulletin No. 1415). Washington, DC: U.S. Department of Health, Education, and Welfare.

Cline, D. H. (1990). Interpretations of emotional disturbance and social maladjustment as policy problems: A legal analysis of initiatives to exclude handicapped/disruptive students from special education. *Behavioral Disorders*, *15*, 159–173.

Cochran, L., Feng, H., Cartledge, G., & Hamilton, S. (1993). The effects of cross-age tutoring on the academic achievement, social behaviors, and self-perceptions of low-achieving African-American males with behavioral disorders. *Behavioral Disorders*, *18*, 292–302.

Cochran, W. E., Sran, P. K., & Varano, G. A. (1977). The relocation syndrome in mentally retarded individuals. *Mental Retardation*, *15*, 10–12.

Coffman, T. L., & Harris, M. C. (1980). Transition shock and adjustments of mentally retarded persons. *Mental Retardation*, *18*, 28–32.

Cohen, S. B., & deBettencourt, L. V. (1991). Dropout: Intervening with the reluctant learner. *Intervention in School and Clinic*, *26*(5), 263–271.

Cohen, S., Agosta, J., Cohen, J., & Warren, R. (1989). Supporting families of children with severe disabilities.

Journal of The Association for Persons with Severe Handicaps, *14*, 155–162.

Cole, E. B., & Paterson, M. M. (1986). Assessment and treatment of phonologic disorders. In J. M. Costello & A. L. Holland (Eds.), *Handbook of speech and language disorders* (pp. 93–127). San Diego: College-Hill.

Coleman, J. M., & Minnett, A. M. (1992). Learning disabilities and social competence: A social ecological perspective. *Exceptional Children, 59,* 234–246.

Coleman, M., & Webber, J. (1988). Behavior problems? Try groups! *Academic Therapy*, *23*, 265–274.

Collins, B. C., Hall, M., & Branson, T. A. (1997). Teaching leisure skills to adolescents with moderate disabilities. *Exceptional Children, 63,* 499–512.

Colson, S. E., & Carlson, J. K. (1993). HIV/AIDS education for students with special needs. *Intervention in School and Clinic*, *28*, 262–274.

Colvin, G., Kameenui, E., & Sugai, G. (1993). Reconceptualizing behavior management and school-wide discipline in general education. *Education and Treatment of Children, 16,* 361–381.

Commission on Education of the Deaf. (1988). *Toward equality: Education of the deaf*. Washington, DC: U.S. Government Printing Office.

Compton, M. V., & Niemeyer, J. A. (1994). Expressions of affection in young children with sensory impairments: A research agenda. *Education and Treatment of Children*, *17*, 68–85.

Condon, M. E., York, R., Heal, L. W., & Fortschneider, J. (1986). Acceptance of severely handicapped students by nonhandicapped peers. *Journal of The Association for Persons with Severe Handicaps*, *11*, 216–219.

Cone, A. A. (1994). Reflections on "Self-advocacy: Voices for choices." *Mental Retardation*, *32*, 444–445.

Cone, J. D., Delawyer, D. D., & Wolfe, V. V. (1985). Assessing parent participation: The Parent/Family Involvement Index. *Exceptional Children*, *51*, 417–424.

Cone, T. E., Wilson, L. R., Bradley, C. M., & Reese, J. H. (1985). Characteristics of LD students in Iowa: An empirical investigation. *Learning Disability Quarterly*, *8*, 211–220.

Connell, M. C., Carta, J. J., & Baer, D. M. (1993). Programming generalization of in-class transition skills: Teaching preschoolers with developmental delays to self-assess and recruit contingent teacher praise. *Journal of Applied Behavior Analysis, 26,* 345–352.

Conner, E. P., Scandary, J., & Tullock, D. (1988). Education of physically handicapped and health impaired individuals: A commitment to the future. *DPH Journal, 10*(1), 5–24.

Conners, F. A. (1992). Reading instruction for students with moderate mental retardation: Review and analysis of research. *American Journal on Mental Retardation*, *96*, 577–597.

Connolly, A. J. (1988). *KeyMath—Revised: A Diagnostic Inventory of Essential Skills*. Circle Pines, MN: American Guidance Service.

Connor, L. E. (1986). Oralism in perspective. In D. M. Luterman (Ed.), *Deafness in perspective* (pp. 116–129). San Diego: College-Hill.

Connors, C. K., Goyette, C., Southwick, D., Lees, J., & Andrulonis, P. (1976). Food additives and hyperkinesis: A controlled double blind study. *Pediatrics*, *58*, 154–166.

Conroy (1996). The small ICF/MR program: Dimensions of quality and cost. *Mental Retardation, 34,* 13–26.

Conroy, J. W., & Bradley, V. J. (1985). *The Pennhurst longitudinal study: A report on five years of research and analysis.* Philadelphia: Temple University Developmental Disabilities Center.

Conte, R., & Andrews, J. (1993). Social skills in the context of learning disability definitions: A reply to Gresham and Elliott and directions for the future. *Journal of Learning Disabilities*, *26*, 146–153.

Cook, A. M., & Hussey, S. M. (1995). *Assistive technologies: Principles and practice*. St. Louis: Mosby.

Cook, P. S., & Woodhill, J. M. (1976). The Feingold dietary treatment of the hyperkinetic syndrome. *Medical Journal of Australia*, *2*, 85–90.

Cooke, N. L., Heron, T. E., Heward, W. L., & Test, D. W. (1982). Integrating a Down syndrome student into a classwide peer tutoring system. *Mental Retardation*, *20*, 22–25.

Cooke, N. L., Heward, W. L., Test, D. W., Spooner, F., & Courson, F. H. (1991). Student performance data in the special education classroom: Measurement and evaluation of student progress. *Teacher Education and Special Education*, *13*, 155–161.

Cooke, N. L., Test, D. W., Heward, W. L., Spooner, F., & Courson, F. H. (1993). Teachers' opinions of research and instructional analysis in the classroom. *Teacher Education and Special Education, 16,* 319–329.

Cooke, T. P. (1981). Your place or mine? Residential options for people with developmental disabilities. In C. L. Hansen (Ed.), *Severely handicapped persons in the community* (pp. 103–145). Seattle: University of Washington, PDAS.

Cooper, C. S., & McEvoy, M. A. (1996) Group friendship activities. *Teaching Exceptional Children, 28*(3), 67–69.

Cooper, J. O., Heron, T. E., & Heward, W. L. (1987). *Applied behavior analysis.* Upper Saddle River, NJ: Merrill/Prentice Hall.

Cooper, K. J., & Browder, D. M. (1998). Enhancing choice and participation for adults with severe disabilities in community-based instruction. *Journal of The Association for Persons with Severe Handicaps, 23,* 252–260.

Corn, A. L. (1986). Low vision and visual efficiency. In G. T. Scholl (Ed.), *Foundations of education for blind and visually handicapped children and youth: Theory and practice* (pp. 99–117).

New York: American Foundation for the Blind.

Corn, A. L. (1989). Instruction in the use of vision for children and adults with low vision: A proposed program model. *RE:view, 21*, 26–38.

Corn, A., & Ryser, G. (1989). Access to print for students with low vision. *Journal of Visual Impairment and Blindness, 83*, 340–349.

Cornett, R. O. (1974). What is cued speech? *Gallaudet Today, 5*(2), 3–5.

Correa, V. I. (1992). Cultural accessibility of services for culturally diverse clients with disabilities and their families. *Rural Special Education Quarterly, 7*, 6–12.

Correa, V. I., Blanes-Reyes, M., & Rapport, M. J. (1995). Minority issues. In H. R. Turnbull & A. P. Turnbull (Eds.), *A compendium report to Congress*. Lawrence, KS: Beach Center.

Correa, V. I., Gollery, T., & Fradd, S.. (1988). The handicapped undocumented alien student dilemma: Do we advocate or abdicate? *Journal of Educational Issues of Language Minority Students, 3*, 41–47.

Cott, A. (1972). Megavitamins: The orthomolecular approach to behavioral disorders and learning disabilities. *Academic Therapy, 7*, 245–258.

Coulter, D. L. (1994). Biomedical conditions: Types, causes, and results. In L. Sternberg (Ed.), *Individuals with profound disabilities: Instructional and assistive strategies* (3rd ed.) (pp. 41–58). Austin, TX: PRO-ED.

Coulter, D. L. (1996). Prevention as a form of support: Implications for the new definition. *Mental Retardation, 34,* 108–116.

Council for Children with Behavioral Disorders. (1989). Best assessment practices for students with behavioral disorders: Accommodation to cultural diversity and individual differences. *Behavioral Disorders, 14*, 263–278.

Council for Learning Disabilities (1993). Concerns about the full inclusion of students with learning disabilities in regular education classrooms. *Journal of Learning Disabilities, 26*, 595.

Council for Learning Disabilities. (1986). Use of discrepancy formulas in the identification of learning disabled individuals. *Learning Disabilities Quarterly, 9*, 245.

Courson, F. H. (1989). Comparative effects of short- and long-form guided notes on social studies performance by seventh grade learning disabled and at-risk students. Unpublished doctoral dissertation, The Ohio State University, Columbus.

Courson, F. H., & Hay, G. H. (1996). Parents as partners. *Beyond Behavior, 7*(3), 19–23.

Courson, F. H., & Heward, W. L. (1988). Increasing active student response through the effective use of paraprofessionals. *Pointer, 33*(1), 27–31.

Craft, M. A., Alber, S. R., & Heward, W. L. (1998). Teaching elementary students with developmental disabilities to recruit teacher attention in a general education classroom: Effects on teacher praise and academic productivity. *Journal of Applied Behavior Analysis, 31,* 399–415.

Cramer, S., Erzkus, A., Mayweather, K., Pope, K., Roeder, J., & Tone, T. (1997). Connecting with siblings. *Teaching Exceptional Children, 30*(1), 46–51.

Crank, J. N., & Bulgren, J. A. (1993). Visual depictions as information organizers for enhancing achievement of students with learning disabilities. *Learning Disabilities Research and Practice, 8*, 140–147.

Creaghead, N. A., Newman, P. W., & Secord, W. (1989). *Assessment and remediation of articulatory and phonological disorders* (2nd ed.). Upper Saddle River, NJ: Merrill/Prentice Hall.

Cremins, J. J. (1983). *Legal and political issues in special education.* Springfield, IL: Thomas.

Cripe, J., Slentz, K., & Bricker, D. (1993). *AEPS curriculum for birth to three years*. Baltimore: Brookes.

Cronin, M. E., Slade, D. L., Bechtel, C., & Anderson, P. (1992). Home-school partnerships: A cooperative approach to intervention. *Intervention in School and Clinic, 27*, 286–292.

Cronin, M. S., & Patton, J. R. (1993). *Life skills instruction for all students with special needs: A practical guide for integrating real-life content into the curriculum.* Austin, TX: Pro-Ed.

Cronin, M., Slade, D. L., Bechtel, C., & Anderson, P. (1992). Home-school partnerships: A cooperative approach to intervention. *Intervention in School and Clinic, 27,* 286–292.

Crosse, S. B., Kaye, E., & Ratnofsky, A. C. (1993). *A report on the maltreatment of children with disabilities.* Washington, DC: Westat, National Center on Child Abuse and Neglect.

Crossley, R. (1988). *Unexpected communication attainments by persons diagnosed as autistic and intellectually impaired.* Caulfield, Victoria: Deal Communication Centre.

Crossley, R., & Remington-Guerney, J. (1992). Getting the words out: Facilitated communication training. *Topics in Language Disorders, 12*(4), 29–45.

Cruickshank, W. M. (1986). *Disputable decisions in special education.* Ann Arbor: University of Michigan Press.

Cullinan, D., Epstein, M. H., & Kauffman, J. M. (1984). Teachers' ratings of students behaviors: What constitutes behavior disorders in schools? *Behavioral Disorders, 10*, 9–19.

Cullinan, D., Epstein, M. H., & Lloyd, J. W. (1991). Evaluation of conceptual models of behavior disorders. *Behavioral Disorders, 16*, 148–157.

Cullinan, D., Epstein, M. H., & Sabornie, E. J. (1992). Selected characteristics of a national sample of seriously emotionally disturbed adolescents. *Behavioral Disorders, 17*, 273–280.

Cummins, J. (1989). A theoretical framework for bilingual special education. *Exceptional Children, 56,* 111–119.

Curl, R. M. (1990). A demonstration project for teaching entry-level job skills: The Co-Worker Transition Model for Youths with Disabilities. *Exceptional News, 13*(3), 3–7.

Curl, R. M., Lignugaris/Kraft, B., Pawley, J. M., & Salzberg, C. L. (1988). "What's next?" A quantitative and qualitative analysis of the transition for trainee to valued worker. Unpublished manuscript.

Curlee, R., & Yairi, E. (1998). Treatment of early childhood stuttering: Advances and research needs. *American Journal of Speech-Language Pathology, 7,* 20–26.

Curry, S., & Hatlen, P. (1988). Meeting the unique educational needs of visually impaired pupils through appropriate placement. *Journal of Visual Impairment and Blindness, 82,* 417–424.

Cusher, K., McClelland, A., & Safford, P. (1992). *Human diversity in education*. New York: McGraw-Hill.

Cutler, B. C. (1993). *You, your child, and "special" education: A guide to making the system work*. Baltimore: Brookes.

D'Amico, R. (1991). The working world awaits. In M. Wagner, L. Newman, R. D'Amico, E. D. Jay, P. Butler-Nalin, C. Marder, & R. Cox (Eds.), *Youth with disabilities: How are they doing? A comprehensive report from Wave 1 of the National Longitudinal Transition Study of special education students*. Menlo Park, CA: SRI International.

Dale, D. M. C. (1984). *Individualized integration: Studies of deaf and partially-hearing children and students in ordinary schools and colleges.* London: Hodder & Stoughton.

Dalrymple, A. J., & Feldman, M. A. (1992). Effects of reinforced directed rehearsal on expressive sign language learning by persons with mental retardation. *Journal of Behavioral Education*, 2, 1–16.

Danforth, S., & Navarro, V. (1998). Speech acts: Sampling the social construction of mental retardation in everyday life. *Mental Retardation, 36,* 31–43.

Dangle, R. F., & Polster, R. A. (Eds.). (1984). *Parent training: Foundations of research and practice.* New York: Guilford.

Darch, C., Gersten, R., & Taylor, R. (1987). Evaluation of Williamsburg County Direct Instruction program: Factors leading to success in rural elementary programs. *Research in Rural Education, 4,* 111–118.

Dardig, J. C., & Heward, W. L. (1981). A systematic procedure for prioritizing IEP goals. *Directive Teacher, 3,* 6–8.

Darrow, M. A., & Clark, G. M. (1992). Cross-state comparisons of former special education students: Evaluation of a follow-along model. *Career Development for Exceptional Individuals, 15,* 83–99.

Datillo, J., & Mirenda, P. (1987). An application of a leisure preference assessment protocol for persons with severe handicaps. *Journal of The Association for Persons with Severe Handicaps, 12,* 306–311.

Davis, C. A., Brady, M. P., Williams, R. E., & Burta, M. (1992). The effects of self-operated auditory prompting tapes on the performance fluency of persons with severe mental retardation. *Education and Training in Mental Retardation, 27,* 39–50.

Davis, G. A., & Rimm, S. B. (1994). *Education of gifted and talented* (3rd ed.). Boston: Allyn & Bacon.

Davis, J. M. (1986). Academic placement in perspective. In D. M. Luterman (Ed.), *Deafness in perspective* (pp. 205–224). San Diego: College-Hill.

Dawson, G., & Osterling, J. (1997). Early intervention in autism. In M. J. Guralnick (Ed.), *The effectiveness of early intervention* (pp. 307–326). Baltimore: Brookes.

De La Paz, S. (1997). Strategy instruction in planning: Teaching students with learning and writing disabilities to compose persuasive and expository essays. *Learning Disability Quarterly, 20*(3), 227–248.

De La Paz, S., & Graham, S. (1997). Strategy instruction in planning: Effects on the writing performance and behavior of students with learning difficulties. *Exceptional Children, 63,* 167–181.

DeAvila, E. (1976). Mainstreaming ethnically and linguistically different children: An exercise in paradox or a new approach? In R. I. Jones (Ed.), *Mainstreaming and the minority child* (pp. 93–108). Reston, VA: Council for Exceptional Children.

DeFilippo, C. L., Sims, D. G., & Gottermeier, L. (1995). Linking visual and kinesthetic imagery in lipreading instruction. *Journal of Speech and Hearing Research, 38,* 244–256.

DeLeon, J. (1989). Cognitive style differences and the underrepresentation of Mexican-Americans in programs for the gifted. *Journal for the Education of the Gifted, 19*(3), 52–53.

Delisle, J. (1992). *Social and emotional needs of the gifted*. Boston: Longman.

Delpit, L. (1995). *Other people's children: Cultural conflict in the classroom*. New York: New Press.

Delquadri, J., Greenwood, C. R., Whorton, D., Carta, J. J., & Hall, R. V. (1986). Classwide peer tutoring. *Exceptional Children, 52,* 535–542.

Dennis, R. E., & Giangreco, M. F. (1996). Creating conversation: Reflections on cultural sensitivity in family interviewing. *Exceptional Children, 53,* 103–116.

Dennis, R. E., Williams, W., Giangreco, M. F., & Cloninger, C. J. (1993). Quality of life as context for planning and evaluation of services for people with disabilities. *Exceptional Children, 53,* 499–512.

Deno, S. L. (1985). Curriculum-based measurement: The emerging alternative. *Exceptional Children, 52,* 219–232.

Deno, S. L. (1997). Whether thou goest . . . perspectives on progress monitoring. In J. W. Lloyd, E. J. Kameenui, & D. Chard (Eds.), *Issues in educating students with disabilities* (pp. 77–99). Mahwah, NJ: Erlbaum.

Derby, L. M., Wacker, D. P., Berg, W., DeRaad, A., Ulrich, S., Asmus, J., Harding, J., Prouty, A., Laffey, P., & Stoner, E. A. (1997). The long-term effects of functional communication training in home settings. *Journal of Applied Behavior Analysis, 30*(3), 507–531.

Deshler, D. D. (1998, October 1). *Comments during teleconference seminar: Contemporary issues in special education*. Columbus: The Ohio State University.

Deshler, D. D., & Lenz, B. K. (1989). The strategies instructional approach. *International Journal of Disability, Development, and Education, 6*(3), 203–244.

Deshler, D. D., & Schumaker, J. B. (1993). Strategy mastery by at-risk students: Not a simple matter. *Elementary School Journal, 94,* 153–157.

Dever, R. B. (1988). *Community living skills: A taxonomy*. Washington, DC: American Association on Mental Retardation.

Dever, R. B. (1989). A taxonomy of community living skills. *Exceptional Children, 55*, 395–404.

Dever, R. B. (1990). Defining mental retardation from an instructional perspective. *Mental Retardation, 28*, 147–153.

Diamond, K. E., & Squires, J. (1993). The role of parental report in the screening and assessment of young children. *Journal of Early Intervention, 17*, 107–115.

Diem, R., & Katims, D. S. (1991). Handicaps and at risk: Preparing teachers for a growing populace. *Intervention in School and Clinic, 26*(5), 272–275.

DiFrancesca, S. (1972). *Academic achievement test results of a national testing program for hearing-impaired students* (Series D, No. 9). Washington, DC: Gallaudet University, Center for Assessment and Demographic Studies.

DiGangi, S. A., & Maag, J. W. (1992). A component of self-management training with behaviorally disordered youth. *Behavioral Disorders, 17,* 281–290.

Division for Early Childhood. (1993). *DEC Recommended Practices*. Reston, VA: Council for Exceptional Children, Division for Early Childhood.

Division for Learning Disabilities of the Council for Exceptional Children. (1993). *Inclusion: What does it mean for students with learning disabilities*? Reston, VA: Author.

Dodd, A. W. (1996). Involving parents, avoiding gridlock. *Educational Leadership, 53*(7), 50–54.

Dodge, K. (1993). The future of research on conduct disorder. *Development and Psychopathology, 5*(1/2), 311–320.

Doll, E. A. (1965). *Vineland Social Maturity Scale.* Circle Pines, MN: American Guidance Service.

Donley, C. R., & Williams, G. (1997). Parents exhibit children's progress at a poster session. *Teaching Exceptional Children, 29*(4), 46–51.

Donnellan, A. M. (1996). A comment on Spitz's comment. *American Journal on Mental Retardation, 101,* 100–103.

Doren, B., Bullis, M., & Benz, M. R. (1996a). Predicting the arrest status of adolescents with disabilities in transition. *Journal of Special Education, 29,* 363–380

Doren, B., Bullis, M., & Benz, M. R. (1996b). Predictors of victimization experiences of adolescents with disabilities in transition. *Exceptional Children, 63,* 7–18.

Dormans, J. P., & Pellegrino, L. (Ed.) (1998). *Caring for children with cerebral palsy: A team approach*. Baltimore: Brookes.

Downing, J. E. (1996). *Including students with severe and multiple disabilities in typical classrooms*. Baltimore: Brookes

Downing, J., & Bailey, B. (1990). Developing vision use within functional daily activities for students with visual and multiple disabilities. *RE:view, 21*, 209–221.

Downing, J., & Eichinger, J. (1990). Instructional strategies for learners with dual sensory impairments in integrated settings. *Journal of The Association for Persons with Severe Handicaps, 15*, 98–105.

Downs, J., & Morin, S. (1990). Improving reading fluency with precision teaching. *Teaching Exceptional Children, 22,* 38–40.

Doyle, P. M., Wolery, M., Ault, M. J., & Gast, D. L. (1988). System of least prompts: A literature review of procedural parameters. *Journal of The Association for Persons with Severe Handicaps, 13*, 28–40.

Drasgow, E. (1998). American Sign Language as a pathway to linguistic competence. *Exceptional Children, 64,* 329–342.

Drevno, G. E., Kimball, J. W., Possi, M. K., Heward, W. L., Gardner, R., III, & Barbetta, P. M. (1994). Effects of active student response during error correction on the acquisition, maintenance, and generalization of science vocabulary by elementary students: A systematic replication. *Journal of Applied Behavior Analysis, 27*, 179–180.

Duchan, J. F. (1997). A situated pragmatics approach for supporting children with severe communication disorders. *Topics in Language Disorders, 17 (2),* 1–18.

Ducharme, S. H., & Gill, K. M. (1997). *Sexuality after spinal cord injury: Answers to your questions*. Baltimore: Brookes.

Dudley-Marling, C. C., & Edmiaston, R. (1985). Social status of learning disabled children and adolescents: A review. *Learning Disability Quarterly, 8*, 189–204.

Dumas, J. E. (1989). Treating antisocial behavior in children: Child and family approaches. *Clinical Psychology Review, 9,* 197–222.

Dunlap, G., & Fox, L. (1996). Early intervention and serious problem behavior: A comprehensive approach. In L. K. Koegel, R. L. Koegel, & G. Dunlap (Eds.), *Positive behavioral support: Including people with difficult behavior in the community* (pp. 31–50). Baltimore: Brookes.

Dunlap, G., Clarke, S., Jackson, M., Wright, S., Ramos, E., & Brinson, S. (1995). Self-monitoring of classroom behaviors with students exhibiting emotional and behavioral challenges. *School Psychology Quarterly, 10,* 165–177.

Dunlap, G., Dyer, K., & Koegel, R. L. (1983). Autistic self-stimulation and intertrial interval duration. *American Journal of Mental Deficiency, 88,* 194–204.

Dunlap, G., Kern-Dunlap, L., Clarke, S., & Robbins, F. K. (1991). Functional assessment, curricular revision, and severe behavior problems. *Journal of Applied Behavior Analysis*, *24*, 387–397.

Dunlap, G., Robbins, F. R., & Darrow, M. A. (1994). Parents' reports of their children's challenging behaviors: Results of a statewide survey. *Mental Retardation, 32,* 206–212.

Dunst, C. J., Trivette, C. M., & Deal, A. G. (1988). *Enabling and empowering families: Principles and guidelines for practice*. Cambridge, MA: Brookline Books.

DuPaul, G. J., Stoner, G., Tilly, W. D., & Putnam, D. (1991). Interventions for attention problems. In G. Stoner, M. Shinn, & H. M. Walker (Eds.), *Interventions for achievement and behavior problems* (pp. 685–713). Silver Spring, MD: National Association for School Psychologists.

Durand, V. M. (1986). Review of strategies for educating students with severe handicaps. *Journal of The Association for Persons with Severe Handicaps*, *11*, 140–142.

Durrell, D. D., & Catterson, J. H. (1980). *Durrell Analysis of Reading Difficulty* (3rd ed.). San Antonio, TX: Harcourt Brace Educational Measurement.

Dyer, K. (1987). The competition of autistic stereotyped behavior with usual and special assessed reinforcers. *Research in Developmental Disabilities, 8,* 607–626.

Dykes, J. (1992). Opinions of orientation and mobility instructors about using the long cane with preschool-age children. *RE:view*, *24*, 85–92.

Dyson, L. L. (1996). The experiences of families of children with learning disabilities: parental stress, family functioning, and sibling self-concept. *Journal of Learning Disabilities, 29*(3), 280–286.

Dyson, L., Edgar, E., & Crnic, K. (1989). Psychological predictors of adjustment by siblings of developmentally disabled children. *American Journal of Mental Retardation*, *94*, 292–302.

Dzienkowski, R. C., Smith, K. K., Dillow, K. A., & Yucha, C. B. (1996). Cerebral palsy: A comprehensive review. *Nurse Practitioner, 21*(2), 45–59.

Eakin, W. M., & McFarland, T. L. (1960). *Type, printing, and the partially seeing child.* Pittsburgh: Stanwix.

Eastman, M. (1978). The Eden express doesn't stop here anymore. *American Pharmacy*, *40*, 12–17.

Eberle, L. (1922). The maimed, the halt and the race. Reprinted in R. H. Bremner (Ed.), *Children and youth in America: A documentary history. Vol. 2: 1866–1832* (pp. 1026–1028). Cambridge: Harvard University Press.

Eden-Piercy, G. V. S., Blacher, J. B., & Eyman, R. K. (1986). Exploring parents' reactions to their young child with severe handicaps. *Mental Retardation*, *24*, 285–291.

Edens, J. F. (1997). Home visitation programs with ethnic minority families: Cultural issues in parent consultation. *Journal of Educational and Psychological Consultation, 8*(4), 373–383.

Edgar, E. (1987). Secondary programs in special education: Are many of them justifiable? *Exceptional Children*, *53*, 555–561.

Education Trust. (1996). *Education watch: The 1996 Education Trust state and national data book.* Washington, DC: Author.

Eichinger, J. (1990). Effects of goal structure on social interaction between elementary level nondisabled students and students with severe disabilities. *Exceptional Children*, *56*, 408–417.

Eikeseth, S., & Lovaas, O. I. (1992). The autistic label and its potentially detrimental effect on the child's treatment. *Journal of Behavioral Therapy and Experimental Psychiatry*, *23*(3), 151–157.

Eklind, D. (1998). Behavioral disorders: A postmodern perspective. *Behavioral Disorders, 23,* 153–159.

Ellett, L. (1993). Instructional practices in mainstreamed secondary classrooms. *Journal of Learning Disabilities*, *26*, 57–64.

Elliott, B. (1979). Look but don't touch: The problems blind children have learning about sexuality. *Disabled USA*, *3*(2), 14–17.

Ellis, E. S., Deshler, D. D., Lenz, B. K., Schumaker, J. B. & Clark, F. L. (1991). An instructional model for teaching learning strategies. *Focus on Exceptional Children, 24*(1), 1–14.

Ellis, J. W., & Luckasson, R. A. (1985). Discrimination against people with mental retardation: A comment on the Cleburne decision. *Mental Retardation*, *23*, 249–252.

Emerick, L. L., & Haynes, W. O. (1986). *Diagnosis and evaluation in speech pathology* (3rd ed.). Upper Saddle River, NJ: Merrill/Prentice Hall.

Engelmann, S. (1977). Sequencing cognitive and academic tasks. In R. D. Kneedler & S. G. Tarver (Eds.), *Changing perspectives in special education* (pp. 46–61). Upper Saddle River, NJ: Merrill/Prentice Hall.

Engelmann, S. (1997). Theory of mastery and acceleration. In J. W. Lloyd, E. J. Kameenui, & D. Chard (Eds.), *Issues in educating students with disabilities* (pp. 177–195). Mahwah, NJ: Erlbaum.

Engelmann, S., & Bruner, E. C. (1988). *Reading mastery: Fast cycle (DISTAR)*. Chicago: Science Research Associates.

Engelmann, S., & Carnine, D. (1992). *Connecting math concepts*. Chicago: Science Research Associates.

Engelmann, S., & Carnine, D. W. (1982). *Theory of instruction:*

Principles and applications. New York: Irvington.

Engelmann, S., & Silbert, J. (1993). *Reasoning and writing D*. Chicago: Science Research Associates.

Engelmann, S., Haddox, P., & Bruner, E. (1983). *Teach your child to read in 100 easy lessons*. New York: Simon & Schuster.

Englert, C. S., Mariage, T. V., Garmon, M. A., & Tarrant, K. L. (1998). Accelerating reading progress in early literacy project classrooms. *Remedial and Special Education, 19,* 142–159, 180.

Englert, C. S., Tarrant, K. L., Mariage, T. V., & Oxer, T. (1994). Lesson talk as the work of reading groups: The effectiveness of two interventions. *Journal of Learning Disabilities, 27*, 165–186.

Englert, C., Raphael, T., Anderson, L., Anthony, H., Stevens, D., & Fear. (1991). Making writing strategies and self-talk visible: Cognitive strategy instruction in writing in regular and special educaiton classrooms. *American Educational Research Journal, 28,* 337–373.

English, K. M. (1997). *Self-advocacy for students who are deaf or hard of hearing*. Austin, TX: PRO-ED.

English, K., Goldsten, H., Kaczmarek, L., & Shafer, K. (1996). "Buddy skills" for preschoolers. *Teaching Exceptional Children, 28*(3), 62–66.

Epstein, L. G., Sharer, L. R., & Goudsmit, J. (1988). Neurological and neuropathological features of human immunodeficiency virus infection in children. *Annals of Neurology*, *23*, 19–23.

Epstein, M. H., Bursuck, W., & Cullinan, D. (1985). Patterns of behavior problems among the learning disabled. II: Boys aged 12–18, girls aged 6–11. *Learning Disability Quarterly*, *8*, 123–131.

Epstein, M. H., Cullinan, D., & Lloyd, J. W. (1986). Behavior-problem patterns among the learning disabled. III: Replication across age and sex. *Learning Disability Quarterly*, *9*, 43–54.

Epstein, M. H., Cullinan, D., & Rosemier, R. (1983). Patterns of behavior problems among the learning disabled: Boys aged 6–11. *Learning Disability Quarterly*, *6*, 305–312.

Epstein, M. H., Foley, R. M., & Cullinan, D. (1992). National survey of educational programs for adolescents with serious emotional disturbance. *Behavioral Disorders*, *17*, 202–210.

Erickson, K. A., & Koppenhaver, D. A. (1998). Using the "write talk-nology" with Patrick. *Teaching Exceptional Children, 31*(1), 58–64.

Ericsson, K. A., & Charness, N. (1994). Expert performance. Its structure and acquisition. *American Psychologist*, 49(8), 725–747.

Erin, J. (1996). Children with multiple and visual disabilities. In *Children with visual impairments: A parents' guide* (pp. 287–316). Bethesda, MD: Woodbine House.

Erin, J. N., Dignan, K., & Brown, P. A. (1991). Are social skills teachable? A review of the literature. *Journal of Visual Impairment and Blindness*, *85*, 58–61.

Erwin, E. J. (1993). Social participation of young children with visual impairments in specialized and integrated environments. *Journal of Visual Impairment and Blindness, 87,* 138–142.

Erwin, E. J. (1996). Meaningful participation in early childhood general education using natural supports. *Journal of Visual Impairment and Blindness, 90,* 400–411.

Espe-Sherwindt, M., & Crable, S. (1993). Parents with mental retardation: Moving beyond the myths. *Topics in Early Childhood Special Education*, *13*, 154–174.

Espin, C. A., & Deno, S. L. (1989). The effects of modeling and prompting feedback strategies on sight word reading of students labeled learning disabled. *Education and Treatment of Children, 12*, 219–231.

Esposito, B. G., & Reed, T. M. (1986). The effects of contact with handicapped persons on young children's attitudes. *Exceptional Children, 54*, 224–229.

Esposito, L., & Campbell, P. H. (1987). Computers and severely and physically handicapped individuals. In J. D. Lindsey (Ed.), *Computers and exceptional individuals* (pp. 105–124). Upper Saddle River, NJ: Merrill/Prentice Hall.

Evans, I. M., Salisbury, C. L., Palombaro, M. M., Berryman, J., & Hollowood, T. M. (1992). Peer interactions and social acceptance of elementary-age children with severe disabilities in an inclusive school. *Journal of The Association for Persons with Severe Handicaps*, *17*, 205–212.

Evans, J. C., & Smith, J. (1993). Nursing planning, intervention, and evaluation for altered neurologic function. In D. B. Jackson & R. B. Saunders (Eds.), *Child health nursing: A comprehensive approach to the care of children and their health* (pp. 1353–1430). Philadelphia: Lippincott.

Fabian, E. S., Luecking, R. G., & Tilson, G. P., Jr. (1994). *A working relationship: The job development specialist's guide to successful partnerships with business*. Baltimore: Brookes.

Fain, G. S. (1986). Leisure: A moral imperative. *Mental Retardation*, *24*, 261–263.

Fairweather, J. S., & Shaver, D. M. (1991). Making the transition to postsecondary education and training. *Exceptional Children*, *57*, 264–270.

Falvey, M. A. (1989). *Community-based curriculum: Instructional strategies for students with severe handicaps*. Baltimore: Brookes.

Farber, J. G., & Goldstein, M. K. (1998). Parents working with speech-language pathologists to foster partnerships in education. *Language, Speech and Hearing Services in the School, 29,* 24–34.

Farlow, L. J., & Snell, M. E. (1994). *Making the most of student performance data*. Washington, DC: American Association on Mental Retardation.

Farrington, D. P. (1995). The development of offending and antisocial behavior from childhood: Key findings from the Cambridge Study in Delinquent Development. *Journal of Child Psychology and Psychiatry, 36,* 929–964.

Favell, J. E., Favell, J. E., & McGimsey, J. F. (1978). Relative effectiveness and efficiency of group vs. individual training of severely retarded persons. *American Journal of Mental Deficiency, 83,* 104–109.

Faw, G. D., Davis, P. K., & Peck, C. (1996). Increasing self-determination: Teaching people with mental retardation to evaluate residential options. *Journal of Applied Behavior Analysis, 29,* 173–188.

Fein, D. J. (1983). The prevalence of speech and language impairments. *ASHA, 25,* 37.

Feingold, B. F. (1975a). Hyperkinesis and learning disabilities linked to artificial food flavors and colors. *American Journal of Nursing, 75,* 797–803.

Feingold, B. F. (1975b). *Why your child is hyperactive.* New York: Random House.

Feingold, B. F. (1976). Hyperkinesis and learning disabilities linked to ingestion of artificial food colors and flavorings. *Journal of Learning Disabilities, 9,* 551–559.

Feldhusen, J. F. (1992a). Early admission and grade advancement. *Gifted Child Today, 15,* 45–49.

Feldhusen, J. F. (1992b). On acceleration. *Gifted Child Today, 15*(2), 1–3.

Feldhusen, J. F. (1992c). *Talent identification and development in education (TIDE).* Sarasota, FL: Center for Creative Learning.

Feldhusen, J. F., & Moon, S. (1995). The educational continuum and delivery of services. In J. L. Genshaft, M. Bireley, & C. L. Hollinger (Eds.), *Serving gifted and talented students: A resource for school personnel* (pp. 103–121). Austin, TX: PRO-ED.

Feldhusen, J., & Kolloff, P. (1985). The Purdue three-stage enrichment model for gifted education at the elementary level. In J. Renzulli (Ed.), *Systems and models for developing programs for the gifted and talented.* Mansfield Center, CT: Creative Learning Press.

Feldhusen, J., Proctor, T. B., & Black, K. N. (1986). Guidelines for grade advancement of precocious children. *Roeper Review, 9,* 25–27.

Fellows, R. R., Leguire, L. E., Rogers, G. L., & Bremer, D. L. (1986). A theoretical approach to vision stimulation. *Journal of Visual Impairment and Blindness, 80,* 907–909.

Ferguson, D. L. (1994). Is communication really the point? Some thoughts on interventions and membership. *Mental Retardation, 1,* 7–18.

Ferguson, D. L., & Baumgart, D. (1991). Partial participation revisited. *Journal of The Association for Persons with Severe Handicaps, 16,* 218–227.

Ferguson, D. L., Meyer, G., Jeanchild, L., Juniper, L., & Zingo, J. (1992). Figuring out what to do with the grownups: How teachers make inclusion "work" for students with disabilities. *Journal of The Association for Persons with Severe Handicaps, 17,* 218–226.

Ferrell, K. A. (1984). A second look at sensory aids in early childhood. *Education of the Visually Handicapped, 16,* 83–101.

Ferrell, K. A. (1985). *Reach out and teach.* New York: American Foundation for the Blind.

Ferro, J., Foster-Johnson, L., & Dunlap, G. (1996). Relations between curricular activities and problem behaviors of students with mental retardation. *American Journal on Mental Retardation, 101,* 184–194.

Fewell, R. R. (1986). Supports from religious organization and personal beliefs. In R. R. Fewell & P. F. Vadasy (Eds.), *Families of handicapped children: Needs and supports across the life span* (pp. 297–316). Austin, TX: PRO-ED.

Fiedler, J. F., & Knight, R. R. (1986). Congruence between assessed needs and IEP goals of identified behaviorally disabled students. *Behavioral Disorders, 12,* 22–27.

Field, S., Hoffman, A., & Spezia, S. (1998). *Self-determination strategies for adolescents in transition.* Austin, TX: PRO-ED.

Field, S., Martin, J., Miller, R., Ward, M., & Wehmeyer, M. L. (1998). *A practical guide for teaching self-determination.* Reston, VA: Council for Exceptional Children.

Figueroa, R. A. (1989). Psychological testing of linguistic-minority students: Knowledge gaps and regulations. *Exceptional Children, 56,* 145–152.

Figueroa, R. A., Fradd, S. H., & Correa, V. I. (1989). Bilingual special education and this special issue. *Exceptional Children, 56,* 174–178.

Finlan, T. G. (1992). Do state methods of quantifying a severe discrepancy result in fewer students with learning disabilities? *Learning Disability Quarterly, 15,* 129–134.

Finn, J. D., & Achilles, C. M. (1990). Answers and questions about class size: A statewide experiment. *American Educational Research Association, 27,* 557–577.

Fish, M. C. (1990). Family-school conflict: Implications for the family. *Journal of Reading, Writing, and Learning Disabilities International, 6,* 71–97.

Fisher, A. T. (1989). Independent living. In D. L. Harnish & A. T. Fisher (Eds.), *Transition literature review: Educational, employment, and independent living outcomes.* Champaign: University of Illinois.

Fisher, C. W., & Berliner, D. C. (Eds.). (1985). *Perspectives on instructional time.* New York: Longman.

Fitzgerald, E. (1929). *Straight language for the deaf.* Washington, DC: Alexander Graham Bell Association for the Deaf.

FitzSimmons, S. C. (1993). The changing epidemiology of cystic fibrosis. *Journal of Pediatrics, 122,* 1–9.

Flener, B. S. (1993). The consultative-collaborative teacher for students with visual handicaps. *RE:view, 25,* 173–182.

Fletcher, J. M., Francis, D. J., Shaywitz, S. E., Lyon, G. R., Foorman, B. R., Stuebing, K. K., & Shaywitz, B. A. (1998). Intelligent testing and the discrepancy model for children with learning disabilities. *Learning Disabilities Research and Practice, 13,* 186–203.

Fletcher, J. M., Shaywitz, S. E., Shankweiler, D. P., Katz, L., Liberman, I. Y., Fowler, A., Francis, D. J., Stuebing, K. K., & Shaywitz, B. A. (1994). Cognitive profiles of reading disability: Comparisons of discrepancy and low achievement definitions. *Journal of Educational Psychology, 86,* 1–18.

Florence, I. J., & LaGrow, S. J. (1989). The use of a recorded message for gaining assistance with street crossings for deaf-blind travelers. *Journal of Visual Impairment and Blindness*, *83*, 471–472.

Florian, V. (1987). Cultural and ethnic aspects of family support services for parents of a child with a disability. In D. K. Libsky (Ed.), *Family supports for families with a disabled member* (pp. 37–52). New York: World Rehabilitation Fund.

Flynn, L. L., & McCollum, J. (1989). Support systems: Strategies and implications for hospitalized newborns and families. *Journal of Early Intervention*, *13*, 173–182.

Foorman, B., Francis, D., Fletcher, J., Schatschneider, C., & Mehta, P. (1998). Early interventions for children with reading problems: Study designs and preliminary findings. *Journal of Educational Psychology, 90*(1), 1–12.

Ford, A., Schnorr, R., Meyer, L., Davern, L., Black, J., & Dempsey, P. (Eds.). (1989). *The Syracuse community-referenced curriculum guide for students with moderate and severe disabilities*. Baltimore: Brookes.

Ford, C. S., Silliman, E. R., Beasman, J., & Evans, D. (in press). An inclusion model for children with language learning disabilities: Building classroom partnerships. *Topics in Language Disorders, 19*(3).

Ford, D. Y. (1998). The underrepresentation of minority students in gifted education. *Journal of Special Education, 32*(1), 4–14.

Forest, M., & Lusthaus, E. (1990). Everyone belongs with the MAPS Action Planning System. *Teaching Exceptional Children*, *22*(2), 32–35.

Forness, S. R., & Kavale, K. A. (1997). Defining emotional or behavioral disorders in school and related services. In J. W. Lloyd, E. J. Kameenui, & D. Chard (Eds.), *Issues in educating students with disabilities* (pp. 45–61). Mahwah, NJ: Erlbaum.

Forness, S., & Knitzer, J. (1992). A new proposed definition and terminology to replace "serious emotional disturbance" in the Individuals with Disabilities Education Act. *School Psychology Review*, *21*, 12–20.

Fowler, S. A., Dougherty, S. B., Kirby, K. C., & Kohler, F. W. (1986). Role reversals: An analysis of therapeutic effects achieved with disruptive boys during their appointments as peer monitors. *Journal of Applied Behavior Analysis*, *19*, 437–444.

Fowler, S. A., Schwartz, I., & Atwater, J. (1991). Perspectives on the transition from preschool to kindergarten for children with disabilities and their families. *Exceptional Children*, *58*, 136–145.

Fox, L., & Westling, D. (1991). A preliminary evaluation of training parents to use facilitated strategies with their children with profound disabilities. *Journal of The Association for Persons with Severe Handicaps*, *16*, 168–176.

Fox, L., Brody, L., & Tobin, D. (Eds.). (1980). *Women and the mathematical mystique*. Baltimore: Johns Hopkins University Press.

Fox, L., Dunlap, G., & Philbrick, L. A. (1997). Providing individual supports to young children with autism and their families. *Journal of Early Intervention, 21,* 1–14.

Foy, C. J., Von Scheden, M., & Waiculonis, J. (1992). The Connecticut precane: Case study and curriculum. *Journal of Visual Impairment and Blindness*, *86*, 178–181.

Fradd, S. H., & McGee, P. L. (1994). *Instructional assessment: An integrative approach to evaluating student performance*. Reading, MA: Addison-Wesley.

Frank, A. R., & Sitlington, P. L. (1993). Graduates with mental disabilities: The story three years later. *Education and Training in Mental Retardation*, *28*, 30–37.

Frank, D. A., Zuckerman, B. S., Amaro, H., Aboagye, K., Baucher, H., Cabral, H., Fried, L., Hingson, R., Kayne, H., Levenson, S. M., Parker, S., Reece, H., & Vinvi, R. (1988). Cocaine use during pregnancy: Prevalence and correlates. *Pediatrics*, *82*, 888–895.

Frankenberger, W., & Fronzaglio, K. (1991). States' definitions and procedures for identifying children with mental retardation: Comparison over nine years. *Mental Retardation*, *29*, 315–321.

Frankenburg, W. K., & Dodds, J. B. (1990). *The Denver II training manual*. Denver: Denver Developmental Materials.

Frankenburg, W. K., Dodds, J., & Fandal, A. (1975). *Denver Developmental Screening Test.* Denver: LADOCA Project and Publishing Foundation.

Frasier, M. (1987). The identification of gifted black students: Developing new perspectives. *Journal for the Education of the Gifted*, *10*(3), 155–180.

Freagon, S. (1982). Present and projected services to meet the needs of severely handicapped children [Keynote address]. In *Proceedings of the National Parent Conference on Children Requiring Extensive Special Education Programming.* Washington, DC: U.S. Department of Education, Special Education Programs.

Freagon, S., Smith, B., Costello, C., Bay, J., Ahlgren, C., & Costello, D. (1986). *Procedures and strategies for program development leading to employment of students with moderate and severe handicaps.* DeKalb: Northern Illinois University Press.

Fredericks, H. D., Hanks, S., Makohon, L., Fruin, C., Moore, W., Piazza-Templeman, T., Blair, L., Dalke, B., Hawkins, P., Coen, M., Renfroe-Burton, S., Bunse, C., Farnes, T., Moses, C., Toews, J., McGuckin, A. M., Moore, B., Riggs, C., Baldwin, V., Anderson, V., Ashbacher, V., Carter, V., Gage, M. A., Rogers, G., & Samples, B. (1980a). *The teaching research curriculum for moderately and severely handicapped: Gross and fine motor*. Springfield, IL: Thomas.

Freeman, D. E., & Freeman, Y. S. (1993). Strategies for promoting the primary language of all students. *Reading Teacher, 46,* 552–558.

Freeman, G., & Haughton, E. (1996). *Learning success: Segmentation and blending of syllables and words.* Napa, CA: Haughton Learning Center.

French, N. K. (in press). Working together: Resource teachers and paraeducators. *Remedial and Special Education*.

French, N. K., & Pickett, A. L. (1997). Paraprofessionals in special education: Issues for teacher educators. *Teacher Education and Special Education, 20,* 61–73.

Frey, K. S., Fewell, R. R. & Vadasy, P. F. (1989). Parental adjustment and changes in child outcomes among families of young handicapped children. *Topics in Early Childhood Special Education, 8*(4), 38–57.

Frey, K. S., Greenberg, M. T., & Fewell, R. R. (1989). Stress and coping among parents of handicapped children: A multidimensional approach. *American Journal on Mental Retardation*, *94*, 240–249.

Friend, M., & Bursuck, W. D. (1999). *Including students with special needs: A practical guide for classroom teachers* (2nd ed.). Needham Heights, MA: Allyn & Bacon.

Fuchs, D., & Fuchs, L. S. (1994). Inclusive schools movement and the radicalization of special education reform. *Exceptional Children*, *60*, 294–309.

Fuchs, D., Fuchs, L. S., & Bahr, M. W. (1990). Mainstream assistance teams: A scientific basis for the art of consultation. *Exceptional Children*, *57*, 128–139.

Fuchs, D., Fuchs, L. S., Bahr, M. W., Fernstrom, P., & Stecker, P. (1990). Prereferral intervention: A prescriptive approach. *Exceptional Children*, *56*, 493–513.

Fuchs, L. S., & Fuchs, D. (1986). Effects of systematic formative evaluation: A meta-analysis. *Exceptional Children*, *53*, 199–209.

Fuchs, L. S., & Fuchs, D. (1996). Combining performance assessment and curriculum-based measurement to strengthen instructional planning. *Learning Disabilities Research and Practice, 11*(3), 183–192.

Fuchs, L. S., & Fuchs, D. (1998). Treatment validity: A unifying concept for reconceptualizing the identification of learning disabilities. *Learning Disabilities Research and Practice, 13,* 204–219.

Fuchs, L. S., Fuchs, D., & Bishop, N. (1992). Teacher planning for students with learning disabilities: Differences between general and special education. *Learning Disabilities Research and Practice*, *7*, 120–128.

Fujiura, J. E., & Yamaki, K. (1997). Analysis of ethnic variations in developmental disability prevalence and household economic status. *Mental Retardation, 35,* 286–294.

Furth, H. G. (1973). *Deafness and learning: A psychosocial approach.* Belmont, CA: Wadsworth.

Gadow, K. D. (1986). *Children on medication.* Vol. 1: *Hyperactivity, learning disabilities, and mental retardation.* San Diego: College-Hill.

Gajar, A., Goodman, L., & McAfee, J. (1993). *Secondary schools and beyond: Transition of individuals with mild disabilities*. Upper Saddle River, NJ: Merrill/Prentice Hall.

Galagan, J. E. (1985). Psychoeducational testing: Turn out the lights, the party's over. *Exceptional Children, 53,* 288–299.

Gallagher, J. J. (1981). Differential curriculum for the gifted. In A. H. Kramer, D. Bitan, N. Butler-Por, A. Eryatar, & E. Landau (Eds.), *Gifted children: Challenging their potential* (pp. 136–154). New York: World Council for Gifted and Talented Children.

Gallagher, J. J. (1984). The evolution of special education concepts. In B. Blatt & R. J. Morris (Eds.), *Perspectives in special education: Personal orientations* (pp. 210–232). Glenview, IL: Scott, Foresman.

Gallagher, J. J. (1990). Editorial: The public and professional perception of the emotional status of gifted children. *Journal for the Education of the Gifted*, *13*, 202–211. [Special issue]

Gallagher, J. J. (1994). The pull of societal forces on special education. *Journal of Special Education*, *27*, 521–530.

Gallagher, J. J. (1997). We do make a difference: No Nobel prizes though. *Journal of Early Intervention, 21,* 88–91.

Gallagher, J. J., & Gallagher, S. (1994). *Teaching the gifted child* (4th ed.). Boston: Allyn & Bacon.

Gallaudet University. (1998). *1996–1997 annual survey of deaf and hard-of-hearing children and youth.* Washington, DC: Gallaudet University, Center for Assessment and Demographic Studies.

Gallimore, R., Boggs, J., & Jordan, C. (1974). *Culture, behavior, and education.* Beverly Hills, CA: Sage.

Gallimore, R., Weisner, T. S., Bernheimer, L. P., Guthrie, D., & Nihira, K. (1993). Family responses to young children with developmental delays: Accommodation activity in ecological and cultural context. *American Journal on Mental Retardation*, *98*, 185–206.

Gallivan-Fenlon, A. (1994). Integrated transdisciplinary teams. *Teaching Exceptional Children*, *26*(3), 16–20.

Gandell, T. S., & Laufer, D. (1993). Developing a telecommunications curriculum for students with physical disabilities. *Teaching Exceptional Children*, *25*(2), 26–28.

Gannon, J. (1981). *Deaf heritage: A narrative history of deaf America.* Silver Spring, MD: National Association of the Deaf.

Garber, H. L. (1988). *The Milwaukee Project: Preventing mental retardation in children at risk.* Washington, DC: American Association on Mental Retardation.

Garber, H., & Heber, R. (1973). *The Milwaukee Project: Early intervention as a technique to prevent mental retardation* [Technical paper]. Storrs: University of Connecticut.

Gardner, H. (1983). *Frames of mind*. New York: Basic Books.

Gardner, H. (1993). *Multiple intelligences: The theory in practice*. New York: Basic Books.

Gardner, R., III, Heward, W. L., & Grossi, T. A. (1994). Effects of response cards on student participation and academic achievement: A systematic replication with inner-city students during whole-class science instruction. *Journal of Applied Behavior Analysis*, *27*, 63–71.

Garten, B. C., Rumrill, P., & Serebreni, R. (1996). The higher education transition model: Guidelines for facilitating college transition among college-bound students with disabilities. *Teaching Exceptional Children, 29*(3), 30–33.

Gartland, D. (1993). Elementary teacher-parent partnerships: Effective communication strategies. *LD Forum, 18*(3), 40–42.

Gast, D. L., & Wolery, M. (1987). Severe maladaptive behaviors. In M. E. Snell (Ed.), *Systematic instruction of persons with severe handicaps* (3rd ed.) (pp. 300–332). Upper Saddle River, NJ: Merrill/Prentice Hall.

Gast, D. L., Wolery, M., Morris, L. L., Doyle, P. M., & Meyer, L. L. (1990). Teaching sight word reading in a group instructional arrangement using constant time delay. *Exceptionality, 1,* 81–96.

Gates, A. I., McKillop, A. S., & Horowitz, R. (1981). *Gates-McKillop-Horowitz Reading Diagnostic Tests*. New York: Teachers College Press.

Gelb, S. A. (1997). The problem of typological thinking in mental retardation. *Mental Retardation, 35,* 448–457.

Gellhaus, M. M., & Olson, M. R. (1993). Using color and contrast to improve the education environment of students with visual impairments with multiple disabilities. *Journal of Visual Impairment and Blindness*, *87*, 19–20.

Gelman, S. R., Epp, D. J., Downing, R. H., Twark, R. D., & Eyerly, R. W. (1989). Impact of group homes on the values of adjacent residential properties. *Mental Retardation*, *27*, 127–134.

Gense, M. H., & Gense, D. J. (1994). Identifying autism in children with blindness and visual impairments. *RE:view*, *26*, 55–62.

Genshaft, J. L., Bireley, M., & Hollinger, C. L. (Eds.). (1995). *Serving gifted and talented students: A resource for school personnel*. Austin, TX: PRO-ED.

Genshaft, J. L., Greenbaum, S., & Borovosky, S. (1995). Stress and the gifted. In J. L. Genshaft, M. Bireley, & C. L. Hollinger (Eds.), *Serving gifted and talented students: A resource for school personnel* (pp. 257–268). Austin, TX: PRO-ED.

Gentile, A., & DiFrancesca, S. (1969). *Academic achievement test performance of hearing-impaired students: United States, Spring, 1969.* (Series D, No. 1). Washington, DC: Gallaudet University, Center for Assessment and Demographic Studies.

George, J. D. (1988). Therapeutic intervention for grandparents and extended family of children with developmental delays. *Mental Retardation*, *26*, 369–375.

Gersten, R. (1998). Recent advances in instructional research for students with learning disabilities: An overview. *Learning Disabilities Research and Practice, 13,* 162–170.

Gersten, R., Carnine, D., & White, W. A. T. (1984). The pursuit of clarity: Direct instruction and applied behavior analysis. In W. L. Heward, T. E. Heron, D. S. Hill, & J. Trap-Porter (Eds.), *Focus on behavior analysis in education* (pp. 38–57). Upper Saddle River, NJ: Merrill/Prentice Hall.

Getch, Y. Q., & Heuharth-Pritchett, S. (1999). Children with asthma: Strategies for educators. *Teaching Exceptional Children, 31*(3), 30–36.

Giangreco, M. F. (1991). Curriculum in inclusion-oriented schools: Trends, issues, challenges, and potential solutions. In S. Stainback & W. Stainback (Eds.). *Teaching in the inclusive classroom: Curriculum design, adaptation and delivery.* Baltimore: Brookes.

Giangreco, M. F. (1996). "The stairs don't go anywhere!" A self-advocate's reflections on specialized services and their impact on people with disabilities [An invited interview]. *Physical Disabilities and Related Services, 14*(2), 1–12.

Giangreco, M. F. (1997). *Quick-guides to inclusion: Ideas for educating students with disabilities*. Baltimore, MD: Brookes

Giangreco, M. F. (1998). *Ants in his pants: Absurdities and realities of special education*. Minnetonka, MN: Peytral.

Giangreco, M. F., Cloninger, C. J., & Iverson, V. S. (1998). *Choosing options and accommodations for children: A guide to educational planning for students with disabilities* (2nd ed.). Baltimore: Brookes.

Giangreco, M. F., Cloninger, C. J., Dennis, R. E., & Edelman, S. W. (1994). Problem-solving methods to facilitate inclusive education. In J. S. Thousand, R. A. Villa, & A. I. Nevin (Eds.), *Creativity and collaborative learning* (pp. 321–346). Baltimore: Brookes.

Giangreco, M. F., Dennis, R., Cloninger, C., Edelman, S., & Schattman, R. (1993). "I've counted Jon": Transformational experiences of teachers educating students with disabilities. *Exceptional Children, 59*, 359–372.

Giangreco, M. F., Edelman, S., & Dennis, R. (1991). Common professional practices that interfere with the integrated delivery of related services. *Remedial and Special Education, 12*(2), 16–24.

Giangreco, M. F., York, J., & Rainforth, B. (1989). Providing related services to learners with severe handicaps in educational settings: Pursuing the least restrictive option. *Pediatric Physical Therapy, 1*(2), 55–63.

Gibbs, J. (1994). *Tribes: A new way of learning together*. Santa Rosa, CA: Center Source.

Giek, K. A. (1992). Monitoring student progress through efficient record keeping. *Teaching Exceptional Children, 24*(3), 22–26.

Gies-Zaborowski, J., & Silverman, F. H. (1986). Documenting the impact of a mild dysarthria on peer perception. *Language, Speech, and Hearing Services in the Schools, 17*, 143.

Gillham, B. (Ed.). (1986). *Handicapping conditions in children.* London: Croom Helm.

Gitlin, L. N., Mount, J., Lucas, W., Weirich, L. C., & Gramberg, L. (1997). The physical costs and psychosocial benefits of travel aids for persons who are visually impaired or blind. *Journal of Visual Impairment and Blindness, 91,* 347–359.

Glover, N. M., & Glover, S. J. (1996). Ethical and legal issues regarding selective abortion of fetuses with Down syndrome. *Mental Retardation, 34,* 207–214.

Goddard, Y. I., & Heron, T. E. (1998). Please teacher: Help me learn to spell better, teach me self-correction. *Teaching Exceptional Children, 30*(6), 38–43.

Gold, M. W. (1980). An alternative definition of mental retardation. In M. W. Gold (Ed.), *"Did I say that?" Articles and commentary on the Try Another Way System.* Champaign, IL: Research Press.

Goldberger, S., Kazis, R., & O'Flanagan, M. (1994). *Learning through work: Designing and implementing worksite learning for high school students*. New York: Manpower Demonstration Research Corporation. [ERIC Document Reproduction Service No. ED 369 940]

Golden, G. (1980). Nonstandard therapies in developmental disabilities. *American Journal of Diseases of Children, 134*, 487–491.

Goldman, R., & Fristoe, M. (1986). *Goldman-Fristoe Test of Articulation*. Austin, TX: PRO-ED.

Goldman, R., Fristoe, M., & Woodcock, R. W. (1990). *Goldman-Fristoe-Woodcock Test of Auditory Discrimination*. Austin, TX: PRO-ED.

Goldstein, D. E., Murray, C., & Edgar, E. (1998). Employment earnings and hours of high school graduates with learning disabilities through the first decade after graduation. *Learning Disabilities Research and Practice, 13,* 53–64.

Goldstein, H. (1993). Use of peers as communication intervention agents. *Teaching Exceptional Children, 25*(2), 37–40.

Goldstein, H., Kaczmarek, L., & Hepting, N. (1994). Communication interventions: The challenges of across-the-day implementation. In R. Gardner III, D. M. Sainato, J. O. Cooper, T. E. Heron, W. L. Heward, J. Eshleman, & T. A. Grossi (Eds.), *Behavior analysis in education: Focus on measurably superior instruction* (pp. 101–113). Pacific Grove, CA: Brooks/Cole.

Gollnick, D. M., & Chinn, P. C. (1994). *Multicultural education in a pluralistic society* (4th ed.). Upper Saddle River, NJ: Merrill/Prentice Hall.

Gollnick, D. M., & Chinn, P. C. (1998). *Multicultural education in a pluralistic society* (5th ed.). Upper Saddle River, NJ: Merrill/Prentice Hall.

Gonder, S. (1997).What are special education teachers made of? *Teaching Exceptional Children, 29*(5), 19–26.

Gonzalez, V., Brusca-Vega, R., & Yawkey, T. (1997). *Assessment and instruction of culturally and linguistically diverse students with or at-risk of learning problems: From research to practice*. Boston: Allyn & Bacon.

Goodman, G., & Poillion, M. J. (1992). ADD: Acronym for any dysfunction or difficulty. *Journal of Special Education, 26*, 37–56.

Goodman, L. V. (1976). A bill of rights for the handicapped. *American Education, 12*(6), 6–8.

Gothelf, C. R., Crimmins, D. B., Mercer, C. A., & Finocchiaro, P. A. (1994). Teaching choice-making skills to students who are deaf-blind. *Teaching Exceptional Children, 26*(4), 13–15.

Gradel, K., Thompson, M. S., & Sheehan, R. (1981). Parental and professional agreement in early childhood assessment. *Topics in Early Childhood Special Education, 1*, 31–39.

Graden, J. L. (1989). Redefining "prereferral" intervention as intervention assistance: Collaboration between general and special education. *Exceptional Children, 56*, 227–231.

Graham, S., & Harris, K. R. (1988). Instructional recommendations for teaching writing to exceptional students. *Exceptional Children, 54,* 506–512.

Graham, S., & Harris, K. R. (1993). Self-regulated strategy development: Helping students with learning problems develop as writers. *Elementary School Journal, 94,* 169–181.

Grant, C. A., & Sleeter, C. E. (1989). Race, class, gender, exceptionality, and educational reform. In J. A. Banks & C. A. M. Banks (Eds.), *Multicultural education: Issues and perspectives* (pp. 46–65). Boston: Allyn & Bacon.

Grant, G., & McGrath, M. (1990). Need for respite-care services for caregivers of persons with mental retardation. *American Journal on Mental Retardation, 94*, 638–648.

Gray, D. B., Quartrano, L. A., & Liberman, M. L. (1998). *Designing and using assistive technology*. Baltimore: Brookes.

Green, G. (1992, October). Facilitated communication: Scientific and ethical issues. Research symposium for the E. K. Shriver Center University Affiliated Program, Waltham, WA.

Green, G. (1996). Early behavioral intervention for autism: What does research tell us? In C. Maurice (Ed.), *Behavioral intervention for young children with autism: A manual for parents and professionals* (pp. 29–44). Austin, TX: PRO-ED.

Green, G., & Shane, H. C. (1994). Science, reason, and facilitated communication. *Journal of The Association for Persons with Severe Handicaps, 19*, 151–172.

Green, S. K., & Shinn, M. R. (1995). Parent attitudes about special education and reintegration: What is the role of student outcomes? *Exceptional Children, 61*, 269–281.

Greenspan, S. (1994). Review of mental retardation: Definition, classification, and systems of supports. *American Journal on Mental Retardation, 98*, 544–549.

Greenspan, S. I. (1992). Reconsidering the diagnosis and treatment of very young children with autistic spectrum or pervasive developmental disorder. *Zero to Three, 13*(2), 1–9.

Greenspan, S. I., & Weider, S. W. (1997). Developmental patterns and outcomes in infants and children with disorders in relating and communicating: A chart review of 200 cases of children with autistic spectrum diagnoses. *Journal of Developmental and Learning Disorders, 1,* 87–141.

Greenwood, C. R., & Maheady, L. (1997). Measurable change in student performance: Forgotten standard in teacher preparation? *Teacher Education and Special Education, 20,* 265–275.

Greenwood, C. R., Carta, J. J., Hart, B., Kamps, D., Terry, D., Delquadri, J. C., Walker, D., & Risley, T. (1992). Out of the laboratory and into the community: Twenty-six years of applied behavior analysis at the Juniper Gardens Children's Center. *American Psychologist, 47*, 1464–1474

Greenwood, C. R., Carta, J. J., Hart, B., Thurston, L. P., & Hall, R. V. (1989). A behavioral approach to research on psychosocial retardation. *Education and Treatment of Children, 12*, 330–346.

Greenwood, C. R., Delquadri, J., & Carta, J. J. (1997). *Together we can: Classwide peer tutoring to improve basic academic skills*. Longmont, CO: Sopris West.

Greenwood, C. R., Delquadri, J., & Hall, R. V. (1984). Opportunity to respond and student academic achievement. In W. L. Heward, T. E. Heron, D. S. Hill, & J. Trap-Porter (Eds.), *Focus on behavior analysis in education* (pp. 58–88). Upper Saddle River, NJ: Merrill/Prentice Hall.

Greenwood, C. R., Hart, B., Walker, D., & Risley, T. (1994). The opportunity to respond and academic performance revisited: A behavioral theory of developmental retardation and its prevention. In R. Gardner III, D. M. Sainato, J. O. Cooper, T. E. Heron, W. L. Heward, J. Eshleman, & T. A. Grossi (Eds.), *Behavior analysis in education: Focus on measurably superior instruction* (pp. 213–223). Pacific Grove, CA: Brooks/Cole.

Greer, R. D. (1994). The measure of a teacher. In R. Gardner III, D. M. Sainato, J. O. Cooper, T. E. Heron, W. L. Heward, J. W. Eshleman, & T. A. Grossi (Eds.), *Behavior analysis in education: Focus on measurably superior instruction* (pp. 161–171). Belmont, CA: Wadsworth.

Gresham, F. M. (1982). Misguided mainstreaming: The case for social skills training with handicapped children. *Exceptional Children, 48*, 422–433.

Gresham, F. M., & MacMillan, D. L. (1997). Autistic recovery? An analysis and critique of the empirical evidence on the Early Intervention Project. *Behavioral Disorders, 22,* 185–201.

Gresham, F. M., & Reschly, D. J. (1986). Social skill deficits and low peer acceptance of mainstreamed learning disabled children. *Learning Disability Quarterly, 9*, 23–32.

Griffing, B. L. (1986). Planning for the future: Programs and services for the blind and visually impaired children. In *Yearbook of the Association for Education and Rehabilitation of the Blind and Visually Impaired* (vol. 3) (pp. 2–11). Alexandria, VA: Association for Education and Rehabilitation of the Blind and Visually Impaired.

Griffith, D. R. (1992). Prenatal exposure to cocaine and other drugs: Developmental and educational prognoses. *Phi Delta Kappan, 74*(1), 30–34.

Gross, E. J., & Larkin, M. H. (1996). The child with HIV in day care and school. *Nursing Clinics of North America, 31,* 231–241.

Grossen, B. (1997). *30 years of NICHD research: What we now know about how children learn to read*. Santa Cruz: Center for the Future of Teaching and Learning. [http://www.cftl.org/]

Grossen, B. (1998). *Child-directed teaching methods: A discriminatory practice of western education*. [http://darkwing.uoregon.edu/~bgrossen/cdp.htm]

Grossi, T. A. (1998). Using a self-operated auditory prompting system to improve the work performance of two employees with severe disabilities. *Journal of The Association for Persons with Severe Handicaps, 23,* 149–154.

Grossi, T. A., & Heward, W. L. (1998). Using self-evaluation to improve the work productivity of trainees in a community-based restaurant training program. *Education and Training in Mental Retardation and Developmental Disabilities, 33,* 248–263.

Grossman, H. (1995). *Teaching in a diverse society*. Boston: Allyn & Bacon.

Grossman, H. J. (Ed). (1983). *Classification in mental retardation*. Washington, DC: American Association on Mental Deficiency.

Groves, B. M. (1997). Growing up in a violent world: The impact of family and community violence on young children and their families. *Topics in Early Childhood Special Education, 17*(1), 74–102.

Guess, D., & Mulligan, M. (1982). The severely and profoundly handicapped. In E. L. Meyen (Ed.), *Exceptional children and youth: An introduction* (2nd ed.). Denver: Love.

Guess, D., Benson, H. A., & Siegel-Causey, E. (1985). Concepts and issues related to choice-making and autonomy among persons with severe disabilities. *Journal of The Association for Persons with Severe Handicaps*, *10*, 79–86.

Guilford, J. P. (1959). Traits of creativity. In H. H. Anderson (Ed.), *Creativity and its cultivation* (pp. 142–161). New York: Harper.

Guilford, J. P. (1987). Creativity research: Past, present and future. In S. Isaksen (Ed.), *Frontiers of creativity research* (pp. 33–66). Buffalo, NY: Bearly.

Gunter, P. L., Denny, R. K., Jack, S. L., Shores, R. E., & Nelson, C. M. (1993). Aversive stimuli in academic interactions between students with serious emotional disturbance and their teachers. *Behavioral Disorders*, *18*, 265–274.

Gunter, P. L., Hummel, J. H., & Conroy, M. A. (1998). Increasing correct academic responding: An effective intervention strategy to decrease behavior problems. *Effective School Practices, 17*(2), 55–62.

Guralnick, M. J. (1990). Social competence and early intervention. *Journal of Early Intervention*, *14*, 3–14.

Guralnick, M. J. (1997). *The effectiveness of early intervention*. Baltimore: Brookes.

Guralnick, M. J. (1998). Effectiveness of early intervention for vulnerable children: A developmental perspective. *American Journal of Mental Retardation, 102*(4), 319–345.

Guskey, T. R., Passaro, P. D., & Wheeler, W. (1995). Mastery learning. *Teaching Exceptional Children*, *27*(2), 15–18.

Gustason, G. (1985). Interpreters entering public school employment. *American Annals of the Deaf, 130*, 265–266.

Gustason, G., Pfetzing, D., & Zawolkow, E. (1980). *Signing exact English*. Los Alamitos, CA: Modern Signs.

Haager, D., & Vaughn, S. (1995). Parent, teacher, peer, and self-reports of the social competence of students with learning disabilities. *Journal of Learning Disabilities, 28*, 205–231.

Hadden, S., & Fowler, S. A. (1997). Preschool: A new beginning for children and parents. *Teaching Exceptional Children, 30*(1), 36–39.

Hadley, P. A. (1998). Language sampling protocols for eliciting text-level discourse. *Language, Speech, and Hearing Services in the Schools, 29*, 132–147.

Hagner, D., & Daning, R. (1993). Opening lines: How job developers talk to employers. *Career Development for Exceptional Individuals, 16*, 123–134.

Halgren, D. W., & Clarizio, H. F. (1993). Categorical and programming changes in special education services. *Exceptional Children*, *59*, 547–555.

Hall, A., Scholl, G. T., & Swallow, R. M. (1986). Psychoeducational assessment. In G. T. Scholl (Ed.), *Foundations of education for blind and visually handicapped children and youth: Theory and practice* (pp. 187–214). New York: American Foundation for the Blind.

Hallahan, D. P. (1992). Some thoughts on why the prevalence of learning disabilities has increased. *Journal of Learning Disabilities*, *25*, 523–528.

Hallahan, D. P. (1998). Teach. Don't flinch. *DLD Times, 16*(1), 1, 4.

Hallahan, D. P. (1998, September). *Comments on LD-Online's "Ask the expert."* [http://www.ldonline.org/bulletin_boards/main_inclusion_sept98.html]

Hallahan, D. P., & Kauffman, J. M. (1994). Toward a culture of disability in the aftermath of Deno and Dunn. *Journal of Special Education, 27*, 496–508.

Halle, J. W., Gabler-Halle, D., & Bemben, D. A. (1989). Effects of a peer-mediated aerobic conditioning program on fitness measures with children who have moderate and severe disabilities. *Journal of The Association for Persons with Severe Handicaps*, *14*, 33–47.

Hallenbeck, B. A., & Kauffman, J. M. (1995). How does observational learning affect the behavior of students with emotional or behavioral disorders? A review of research. *Journal of Special Education, 29*, 43–71.

Halpern, A. S. (1985). Transition: A look at the foundations. *Exceptional Children*, *51*, 479–486.

Halpern, A. S. (1992). Transition: Old wine in new bottles. *Exceptional Children*, *58*, 202–211.

Halpern, A. S. (1993). Quality of life as a conceptual framework for evaluating transition outcomes. *Exceptional Children*, *59*, 486–498.

Halpern, A. S., Herr, C. M., Wolf, N. K., Doren, B., Johnson, M. D., & Lawson, J. D. (1997). *Next S.T.E.P.: Student transition and educational planning*. Austin, TX: PRO-ED.

Ham, R. (1986). *Techniques of stuttering therapy.* Upper Saddle River, NJ: Prentice Hall.

Hamayan, E. V., & Damico, J. S. (1991). *Limiting bias in the assessment of bilingual students.* Austin, TX: PRO-ED.

Hammill, D. D. (1990). On defining learning disabilities: An emerging consensus. *Journal of Learning Disabilities*, *23*, 74–84.

Hammill, D. D., & Larsen, S. (1978). The effectiveness of psycholinguistic training: A reaffirmation of position. *Exceptional Children*, *44*, 402–417.

Hammill, D. D., & Larsen, S. (1988). *Test of Written Language—2*. Austin, TX: PRO-ED.

Hamre-Nietupski, S., Nietupski, J., Sandvig, R., Sandvig, M. B., & Ayres, B. (1984). Leisure skills instruction in a community residential setting with young adults who are deaf/ blind severely handicapped. *Journal of The Association for Persons with Severe Handicaps*, *9*, 49–54.

Hancock, L. (1996, March 18). Mother's little helper. *Newsweek*, *137*(12), 50–56.

Hanline, M. F. (1993). Inclusion of preschoolers with profound disabilities: An analysis of children's interactions. *Journal of The Association for Persons with Severe Handicaps*, *18*, 28–35.

Harchik, A. E. (1994). Self-medication skills. In M. Agran, N. E. Marchand-Martella, & R. C. Martella (Eds.), *Promoting health and safety: Skills for independent living* (pp. 55–69). Pacific Grove, CA: Brooks/Cole.

Harchik, A. E., & Putzier, V. S. (1990). The use of high-probability requests to increase compliance with instructions to take medication. *Journal of The Association for Persons with Severe Handicaps*, *15*, 40–43.

Harchik, A. E., Harchik, A. J., Luce, S. C., & Sherman, J. A. (1990). Teaching autistic and severely handicapped children to recruit praise: Acquisition and generalization. *Research in Developmental Disabilities*, *11*, 77–95.

Hardin, D. M., & Littlejohn, W. (1995). Family-school collaboration: Elements of effectiveness and program models. *Preventing School Failure*, *39*(1), 4–8.

Hardman, M. L., McDonnell, J., & Welch, M. (1997). Perspectives on the future of IDEA. *Journal of The Association for Persons with Severe Handicaps*, *22*, 61–77.

Haring, N. G. (Ed.). (1988). *Generalization for students with severe handicaps: Strategies and solutions*. Seattle: University of Washington Press.

Haring, N. G., & Romer, L. T. (Eds.). (1995). *Welcoming students who are deaf-blind into typical classrooms: Facilitating school participation, learning, and friendships*. Baltimore: Brookes.

Harris, S. L., & Handleman, J. S. (Eds.). (1994). *Preschool programs for children with autism*. Austin, TX: PRO-ED.

Harry, B. (1992a). *Cultural diversity, families, and the special education system: Communication and empowerment*. New York: Teachers College Press.

Harry, B. (1992b). Making sense of disability: Low-income, Puerto Rican parents' theories of the problem. *Exceptional Children*, *59*, 27–40.

Harry, B. (1992c). Restructuring the participation of African-American parents in special education. *Exceptional Children*, *59*, 123–131.

Harry, B. (1994). *The disproportionate representation of minority students in special education: Theories and recommendations*. Alexandria, VA: National Association of State Directors of Special Education.

Hart, B. M. (1985). Naturalistic language training strategies. In S. F. Warren & A. Rogers-Warren (Eds)., *Teaching functional language* (pp. 63–88). Baltimore: University Park Press.

Hart, B. M., & Risley, T. R. (1980). In vivo language intervention: Unanticipated general effects. *Journal of Applied Behavior Analysis*, *12*, 407–432.

Hart, B., & Risley, T. R. (1995). *Meaningful differences in the everyday experience of young American children*. Baltimore: Brookes.

Harvey Smith, M. A. (1994). Nutrition and diet. In M. Agran, N. E. Marchand-Martella, & R. C. Martella (Eds.), *Promoting health and safety: Skills for independent living* (pp. 33–53). Pacific Grove, CA: Brooks/Cole.

Hasazi, S. B., Gordon, L. R., & Roe, C. A. (1985). Factors associated with the employment status of handicapped youth exiting high school from 1979 to 1983. *Exceptional Children*, *51*, 455–469.

Hasazi, S. B., Johnson, R. E., Hasazi, J. E., Gordon, L. R., & Hull, M. (1989). Employment of youth with and without handicaps following high school: Outcomes and correlates. *Journal of Special Education*, *23*, 243–255.

Haskew, P., & Donnellan, A. M. (1992). *Emotional maturity and well-being: Psychological lessons of facilitated communication*. Danbury, CT: DRI.

Hassett, M. E., Engler, C., Cooke, N. L., Test, D. W., Weiss, A. B., Heward, W. L., & Heron, T. E. (1984). A telephone-managed, home-based summer writing program for LD adolescents. In W. L. Heward, T. E. Heron, D. S. Hill, & J. Trap-Porter (Eds.), *Focus on behavior analysis in education* (pp. 89–103). Upper Saddle River, NJ: Merrill/Prentice Hall.

Hatten, J. T., & Hatten, P. W. (1975). *Natural language*. Tucson, AZ: Communication Skill Builders.

Hatton, C. (1998). What is quality of life anyway? Some problems with the emerging quality of life consensus. *Mental Retardation*, *36*, 104–115.

Hawkins, R. P. (1984). What is "meaningful" behavior change in a severely/ profoundly retarded learner? The view of a behavior analytic parent. In W. L. Heward, T. E. Heron, D. S. Hill, & J. Trap-Porter (Eds.), *Focus on behavior analysis in education* (pp. 282–286). Upper Saddle River, NJ: Merrill/Prentice Hall.

Hawkins, R. P., & Hawkins, K. K. (1981). Parental observations on the education of severely retarded children: Can it be done in the classroom? *Analysis and Intervention in Development Disabilities*, *1*, 13–22.

Haworth, A. M., Hill, A. E., & Glidden, L. M. (1996). Measuring religiousness in parents of children with developmental disabilities. *Mental Retardation*, *34*, 271–279.

Haycock, G. S. (1933). *The teaching of speech*. Stoke-on-Trent, England: Hill & Ainsworth.

Haydon, D. M., Mann, N., & Fugate, G. (1995). Using conversation to enhance learning. *Volta Review, 97,* 129–138.

Hazekamp, J., & Huebner, K. M. (1989). *Program planning and evaluation for blind and visually impaired students: National guidelines for excellence*. New York: American Foundation for the Blind.

Hebbeler, K. M., Smith, B. J., & Black, T. L. (1991). Federal early childhood special education policy: A model for the improvement of services for children with disabilities. *Exceptional Children, 58,* 104–112.

Heber, R. F. (1961). A manual on terminology and classification in mental retardation (rev. ed.). Monograph Supplement, *American Journal of Mental Deficiency*, p. 64.

Heber, R. F., & Garber, H. (1971). An experiment in prevention of cultural-familial mental retardation. In D. A. Primrose (Ed.), *Proceedings of the Second Congress of the International Association for the Scientific Study of Mental Deficiency.* Warsaw: Polish Medical Publishers.

Heckaman, K. A., Alber, S. R., Hooper, S., & Heward, W. L. (1998). A comparison of least-to-most prompts and progressive time delay on the disruptive behavior of students with autism. *Journal of Behavior Education, 8,* 171–201.

Heinze, T. (1986). Communication skills. In G. T. Scholl (Ed.), *Foundations of education for blind and visually handicapped children and youth: Theory and practice* (pp. 301–314). New York: American Foundation for the Blind.

Heller, I., Manning, D., Pavur, D., & Wagner, K. (1998). Enhancing language development in an inclusive preschool. *Teaching Exceptional Children, 30*(3), 50–53.

Heller, K. W., Alberto, P. A., Forney, P. E., & Schwartzman, M. N. (1996). *Understanding physical, sensory and health impairments*. Pacific Grove, CA: Brooks/Cole.

Heller, K. W., Dangel, H., & Sweatman, L. (1995). Systematic selection of adaptations for students with muscular dystrophy. *Journal of Developmental and Physical Disabilities, 7,* 253–265.

Heller, K. W., Ware, S., Allgood, M. H., & Castelle, M. (1994, July/August). Use of dual communication boards with students who are deaf-blind. *Journal of Visual Impairment and Blindness*, pp. 368–376.

Heller, T., Markwardt, R., Rowitz, L., & Farber, B. (1994). Adaptation of Hispanic families to a member with mental retardation. *American Journal of Mental Retardation, 99,* 289–300.

Hen, J. (1986). Office evaluation and management of pediatric asthma. *Pediatric Annals, 15,* 111–123.

Henderson, A. T., Marburger, C. L., & Odoms, T. (1986). *Beyond the bake sale: An educator's guide to working with parents*. Columbia, MD: National Committee for Citizens in Education.

Henderson, C. (1992). *College freshmen with disabilities: A statistical profile*. Washington, DC: American Council on Education, HEATH Resource Center. (ERIC No. ED354792).

Henderson, L. W., & Meisels, S. J. (1994). Parental involvement in the developmental screening of their young children: A multiple-source perspective. *Journal of Early Intervention, 18,* 141–154.

Hendrickson, J. M., Shokoohi-Yekta, M., Hamre-Nietupski, S., & Gable, R. A. (1996). Middle and high school students' perceptions on being friends with peers with severe disabilities. *Exceptional Children, 63,* 19–28.

Henggler, S. (1989). *Delinquency in adolescence*. Beverly Hills, CA: Sage.

Heron, T. E., & Harris, K. C. (in press). *The educational consultant: Helping professionals, parents, and mainstreamed students* (4th ed.). Austin, TX: PRO-ED.

Heron, T. E., Heward, W. L., Cooke, N. L., & Hill, D. S. (1983). Evaluation of a classwide peer tutoring system: First graders teach each other sight words. *Education and Treatment of Children, 6,* 137–152.

Hertzog, N. B. (1998). The changing role of the gifted education specialist. *Teaching Exceptional Children, 30*(3), 39–43.

Heward, W. L. (1974). The acquisition of prenominal adjectives and adverbs to sentences written by deaf-aphasic children. Unpublished doctoral dissertation, University of Massachusetts, Amherst.

Heward, W. L. (1987). Self-management. In J. O. Cooper, T. E. Heron, & W. L. Heward, *Applied behavior analysis* (pp. 515–549). Upper Saddle River, NJ: Merrill/Prentice Hall.

Heward, W. L. (1994). Three "low-tech" strategies for increasing the frequency of active student response during group instruction. In R. Gardner III, D. M. Sainato, J. O. Cooper, T. E. Heron, W. L. Heward, J. Eshleman, & T. A. Grossi (Eds.), *Behavior analysis in education: Focus on measurably superior instruction* (pp. 283–320). Pacific Grove, CA: Brooks/Cole.

Heward, W. L., & Cavanaugh, R. A. (1997). Educational equality for students with disabilities. In J. A. Banks & C. A. M. Banks (Eds.), *Multicultural education: Issues and perspectives* (3rd ed.) (pp. 301–333). Needham Heights, MA: Allyn & Bacon.

Heward, W. L., & Chapman, J. E. (1981). Improving parent-teacher communication through recorded telephone messages: Systematic replication in a special education classroom. *Journal of Special Education Technology, 4,* 11–19.

Heward, W. L., Courson, F. H., & Narayan, J. S. (1989). Using choral responding to increase active student response during group instruction. *Teaching Exceptional Children, 21*(3), 72–75.

Heward, W. L., Gardner, R., III, Cavanaugh, R. A., Courson, F. H., Grossi, T. A., & Barbetta, P. M. (1996). Everyone participates in this class: Using response cards to increase active student response. *Teaching Exceptional Children, 28*(2), 4–10.

Heward, W. L., Heron, T. E., & Cooke, N. L. (1982). Tutor huddle: Key element in a classwide peer tutoring system. *Elementary School Journal, 83*, 115–123.

Heward, W. L., Heron, T. E., Gardner, R., III, & Prayzer, R. (1991). Two strategies for improving students' writing skills. In G. Stoner, M. R. Shinn, & H. M. Walker (Eds.), *A school psychologist's interventions for regular education* (pp. 379–398). Washington, DC: National Association of School Psychologists.

Hewett, F. M., & Taylor, F. D. (1980). *The emotionally disturbed child in the classroom: The orchestration of success* (2nd ed.). Boston: Allyn & Bacon.

Hidalgo, N. M., Siu, S. F., Bright, J. A., Swap, S. M., & Epstein, J. L. (1995). Research on families, schools, and communities: A multicultural perspective. In J. A. Banks & C. A. M. Banks (Eds.), *Handbook of research on multicultural education* (pp. 498–524). New York: Simon & Schuster Macmillan.

Higbee Mandlebaum, L. (1992). Frequently recommended books for students in preschool through high school. *Intervention in School and Clinic, 27*, 170–184.

Hill, B. K., Lakin, K. C., Bruininks, R. H., Amado, A. N., Anderson, D. J., & Copher, J. I. (1989). *Living in the community: A comparative study of foster homes and small group homes for people with mental retardation* (Report No. 28). Minneapolis: University of Minnesota, Center for Residential and Community Services.

Hill, E. W. (1986). Orientation and mobility. In G. R. Scholl (Ed.), *Foundations of education for blind and visually handicapped children and youth: Theory and practice* (pp. 315–340). New York: American Federation for the Blind.

Hill, E. W., & Jacobson, W. H. (1985). Controversial issues in orientation and mobility: Then and now. *Education of the Visually Handicapped, 17*, 59–70.

Hill, J. L. (1999). *Meeting the needs of students with special physical and health care needs*. Upper Saddle River, NJ: Merrill/Prentice Hall.

Hill, J. W., Wehman, P., & Horst, G. (1982). Toward generalization of appropriate leisure and social behavior in severely handicapped youth: Pinball machine use. *Journal of The Association for the Severely Handicapped, 6*(4), 38–44.

Hilliard, A. G. (1975). The strengths and weaknesses of cognitive tests for young children. In J. D. Andrews (Ed.), *One child indivisible* (pp. 17–33). Washington, DC: National Association for the Education of Young Children.

Hilliard, A. G. (1980). Cultural diversity and special education. *Exceptional Children, 46*, 584–588.

Hilton, A., & Ringlaben, R. (1998). *Best and promising practices in developmental disabilities*. Austin, TX: PRO-ED.

Hitzing, W. (1980). ENCOR and beyond. In T. Apolloni, J. Cappuccilli, & T. P. Cooke (Eds.), *Achievements in residential services for persons with disabilities: Total excellence.* Baltimore: University Park Press.

Ho, Y. (1991). The easy listener FM system: A new strategy for students with LD. *Intervention in School and Clinic, 27*(1), 56–59.

Hobbs, N. (1966). Helping the disturbed child: Psychological and ecological strategies. *American Psychologist, 21*, 1105–1115.

Hock, M. F., Schumaker, J. B., & Deshler, D. D. (in press). Closing the gap to success in secondary schools: A model for cognitive apprenticeship. In D. D. Deshler & J. B. Schumaker (Eds.), *Teaching every adolescent every day: Learning in diverse schools and classrooms*. Cambridge, MA: Brookline.

Hoemann, H. W., & Briga, J. I. (1981). Hearing impairments. In J. M. Kauffman & D. P. Hallahan (Eds.), *Handbook of special education.* Upper Saddle River, NJ: Prentice Hall.

Holbrook, M. C., & Koenig, A. J. (1992). Teaching braille reading to students with low vision. *Journal of Visual Impairment and Blindness, 86*, 44–48.

Holburn, C. S. (1990). Symposium overview: Our residential rules—have we gone too far? *Mental Retardation, 28*, 65–66.

Holland, A. L., & Reinmuth, O. M. (1982). Aphasia in adults. In G. H. Shames & E. H. Wiig (Eds.), *Human communication disorders: An introduction* (pp. 561–593). Upper Saddle River, NJ: Merrill/Prentice Hall.

Hollinger, C. L. (1995). Counseling gifted young women about educational and career choices. In J. L. Genshaft, M. Bireley, & C. L. Hollinger (Eds.), *Serving gifted and talented students: A resource for school personnel* (pp. 269–283). Austin, TX: PRO-ED.

Holt, J. (1993). Stanford Achievement Test—8th edition: Reading comprehension subgroup results. *American Annals of the Deaf, 138*, 172–175.

Hood, E. J., Test, D. W., Spooner, F., & Steele, R. (1996). Paid co-worker support for individuals with severe and multiple disabilities. *Education and Training in Mental Retardation and Developmental Disabilities, 31*, 251–265.

Hoover, H. D., Hieronymus, A. N., Frisbie, D. A., & Dunbar, S. B. (1993). *Iowa Tests of Basic Skills*. Chicago: Riverside.

Hoover, J. J. (1989). Study skills and the education of students with learning disabilities. *Journal of Learning Disabilities, 22,* 452–455.

Horner, R. H., & Carr, E. G. (1997). Behavioral support for students with severe disabilities: Functional assessment and comprehensive intervention. *Journal of Special Education, 31,* 84–104.

Horner, R. H., Day, H. M., Sprague, J. R., O'Brien, M., & Tuesday-Heathfield, L. (1991). Interspersed requests: A non-aversive procedure for reducing aggression and self-injury during instruction. *Journal of Applied Behavior Analysis, 24,* 265–278.

Horner, R. H., Dunlap, G., & Koegel, R. L. (1988). *Generalization and maintenance: Life-style changes in applied settings.* Baltimore: Brookes.

Horner, R. H., Eberhard, J. M., & Sheehan, M. R. (1986). Teaching generalized table bussing. *Behavior Modification, 10*(4), 457–471.

Horner, R. H., McDonnell, J. J., & Bellamy, G. T. (1986). Teaching generalized skills: General case instruction in simulation and community settings. In R. H. Horner, L. H. Meyer, & H. D. B. Fredericks (Eds.), *Education of learners with severe handicaps: Exemplary service strategies* (pp. 289–314). Baltimore: Brookes.

Horner, R. H., Williams, J. A., & Steveley, J. D. (1987). Acquisition of generalized telephone use by students with moderate and severe mental retardation. *Research in Developmental Disabilities, 8,* 229–247.

Horst, G., Wehman, P., Hill, J. W., & Bailey, C. (1981). Developing age-appropriate leisure skills in severely handicapped adolescents. *Teaching Exceptional Children, 14,* 11–16.

Horton, S. V., Lovitt, T. C., & Bergerud, D. (1990). The effectiveness of graphic organizers for three classifications of secondary students in content area classes. *Journal of Learning Disabilities, 23,* 12–22.

Hourcade, J. J., Parette, H. P., & Huer, M. B. (1997). Family and cultural alert! Considerations in assistive technology assessment. *Teaching Exceptional Children, 30*(1), 40–44.

Howard, V. F., Williams, B. F., & McLaughlin, T. F. (1994). Children prenatally exposed to alcohol and cocaine: Behavioral solutions. In R. Gardner III, D. M. Sainato, J. O. Cooper, T. E. Heron, W. L. Heward, J. Eshleman, & T. A. Grossi (Eds.), *Behavior analysis in education: Focus on measurably superior instruction* (pp. 131–146). Pacific Grove, CA: Brooks/Cole.

Howell, K. W. (1998). *Curriculum-based evaluation: Teaching and decision making* (3rd ed.). Monterey, CA: Brooks/Cole.

Howell, K. W., & Lorson-Howell, K. A. (1990). What's the hurry? Fluency in the classroom. *Teaching Exceptional Children, 22*(3), 20–23.

Howell, K. W., Evans, D., & Gardiner, J. (1997). Medications in the classroom: A hard pill to swallow. *Teaching Exceptional Children, 29*(6), 58–61.

Howell, K. W., Fox, S. L., & Morehead, M. K. (1993). *Curriculum-based evaluation: Teaching and decision making* (2nd ed.). Pacific Grove, CA: Brooks/Cole.

Hrydowy, E. R., Stokes, T. F., & Martin, G. L. (1984). Training elementary students to prompt teacher praise. *Education and Treatment of Children, 7,* 99–108.

Hudson, P., Lignugaris/Kraft, B., & Miller, T. (1993). Using content enhancements to improve the performance of adolescents with learning disabilities in content classes. *Learning Disabilities Research and Practice, 8,* 106–126.

Huebner, K. M. (1986). Social skills. In G. T. Scholl (Ed.), *Foundations for education for blind and visually handicapped children and youth: Theory and practice* (pp. 341–362). New York: American Foundation for the Blind.

Hughes, C. (1994). Teaching generalized skills to persons with disabilities. In R. Gardner III, D. M. Sainato, J. O. Cooper, T. E. Heron, W. L. Heward, J. Eshleman, & T. A. Grossi (Eds.), *Behavior analysis in education: Focus on measurably superior instruction* (pp. 335–348). Pacific Grove, CA: Brooks/Cole.

Hughes, C. (1997). Self-instruction. In M. Agran (Ed.), *Student directed learning: Teaching self-determination skills* (pp. 144–170). Pacific Grove, CA: Brooks/Cole.

Hughes, C., & Rusch, F. R. (1989). Teaching supported employees with severe mental retardation to solve problems. *Journal of Applied Behavior Analysis, 22,* 365–372.

Hughes, C., Killian, D. J., & Fischer, G. M. (1996). Validation and assessment of a conversational interaction intervention. *American Journal on Mental Retardation, 100,* 493–509.

Hughes, C., Pitkin, S. E., & Lorden, S. W. (1998). Assessing preferences and choices of persons with severe and profound mental retardation. *Education and Training in Mental Retardation and Developmental Disabilities, 33,* 299–316.

Hughes, C., Rusch, F. R., & Curl, R. M. (1990). Extending individual competence, developing natural support, and promoting social acceptance. In F. Rusch (Ed.), *Supported employment: Models, methods, and issues* (pp. 181–197). Sycamore, IL: Sycamore.

Hughes, F., Elicker, J., & Veen, L. (1995, January). A program of play for infants and their caregivers. *Young Children,* 52–58.

Hulit, L. M., & Howard, M. R. (1993). *Born to talk: An introduction to speech and language development.* Upper Saddle River, NJ: Merrill/Prentice Hall.

Hull, F. M., Mielke, P. W., Willeford, J. A., & Timmons, R. J. (1976). *National speech and hearing survey* (Final report; Project No. 50978; Grant No. OE-32-15-0050-5010 [607]). Washington, DC: U.S. Department of Health, Education, and Welfare.

Humphrey, J. H., & Alcorn, B. J. (1994). *So you want to be an interpreter: An introduction to sign language interpreting*. Amarillo, TX: H & H.

Hunsucker, P. F., Nelson, R. O., & Clark, R. P. (1986). Standardization and evaluation of the Classroom Adaptive Behavior Checklist for school use. *Exceptional Children*, *53*, 69–71.

Hunt, P., & Goetz, L. (1997). Research on inclusive educational programs, practices, and outcomes for students with severe disabilities. *Journal of Special Education, 31,* 3–29.

Hunt, P., Farron-Davis, F., Beckstead, S., Curtis, D., & Goetz, L. (1994). Evaluating the effects of placement of students with severe disabilities in general education versus special education classes. *Journal of The Association for Persons with Severe Handicaps*, *19*, 200–214.

Hunt, P., Goetz, L., & Anderson, J. (1986). The quality of IEP objectives associated with placement on integrated versus segregated school sites. *Journal of The Association for Persons with Severe Handicaps*, *11*, 125–130.

Hurlbut, B. I., Iwata, B. A., & Green, J. D. (1982). Nonvocal language acquisition in adolescents with severe physical disabilities: Blissymbol versus iconic stimulus formats. *Journal of Applied Behavior Analysis*, *15*, 241–258.

Hutinger, P. L., Marshall, S., & McCarten, K. (1983). *Core curriculum: Macomb 0–3 regional project* (3rd ed.). Macomb: Western Illinois University.

Hynd, G. W., Marshall, R., & Gonzalez, J. (1991). Learning disabilities and presumed central nervous system dysfunction. *Learning Disabilities Quarterly, 14,* 283–296.

Ingram, D. (1989). *First language acquisition: Method, description, and explanation*. New York: Cambridge University Press.

Ireland, J. C., Wray, D., & Flexer, C. (1988). Hearing for success in the classroom. *Teaching Exceptional Children*, *20*(2), 15–17.

Irving Independent School District v. Tatro, 104 S. Ct. 3371, 82 L.Ed. 2d 664 (1984).

Iscoe, I., & Payne, S. (1972). Development of a revised scale for the functional classification of exceptional children. In E. P. Trapp & P. Himelstein (Eds.), *Readings on the exceptional child* (pp. 7–29). New York: Appleton-Century-Crofts.

Ishil-Jordan, S. (1997). When behavior differences are not disorders. In A. Artiles & G. Zamora-Durán (Eds.), *Reducing disproportionate representation of culturally diverse students in special and gifted education* (pp. 27–46). Reston, VA: Council for Exceptional Children.

Iwata, B. A. (1988). The development and adoption of controversial default technologies. *Behavior Analyst*, *11*, 149–157.

Jacobsen, J. J., & Mulick, J. (in press). *APA manual on mental retardation*. Washington, DC: American Psychological Association.

Jacobsen, J. W., & Mulick, J. A. (1992). A new definition of mentally retarded or a new definition of practice. *Psychology in Mental Retardation and Developmental Disabilities*, *18*(2), 9–14.

Jacobson, W. H. (1993). *The art and science of teaching orientation and mobility to persons with visual impairments*. New York: American Federation for the Blind.

Janney, R. E., & Snell, M. E. (1996). Using peer interactions to include students with extensive disabilities in elementary general education classes. *Journal of The Association for Persons with Severe Handicaps, 21*, 72–80.

Janney, R. E., & Snell, M. E. (1997). How teachers include students with moderate and severe disabilities in elementary classes: The means and meaning of inclusion. *Journal of The Association for Persons with Severe Handicaps, 42*(3), 159–169.

Janney, R. E., & Snell, M. E. (1998). *Teacher's guides to inclusive practices: Instructional modifications*. Baltimore: Brookes

Jayanthi, M., Bursuck, W., Epstein, M. H., & Polloway, E. A. (1997). Strategies for successful homework. *Teaching Exceptional Children, 30*(1), 4–7.

Jenkins, J. R., Speltz, M. L., & Odom, S. L. (1985). Integrating normal and handicapped preschoolers: Effects on child development and social interaction. *Exceptional Children*, *52*, 7–17.

Jensen, W. R., Sheridan, S. M., Olympia, D., & Andrews, D. (1994). Homework and students with learning disabilities and behavior disorders: A practical, parent-based approach. *Journal of Learning Disabilities, 27*(9), 538–548.

Jitendra, A. K., & Kameenui, E. J. (1993). Dynamic assessment as a compensatory assessment approach: A description and analysis. *Remedial and Special Education*, *14*(5), 6–18.

Johnson, B., & Cuvo, A. (1981). Teaching mentally retarded adults to cook. *Behavior Modification*, *12*, 69–73.

Johnson, C. (1994, September). The nightmare of facilitated communication: A survivor fights back. Paper presented at the annual meeting of the Florida Association for Behavior Analysis, Orlando.

Johnson, H. L. (1993). Stressful family experiences and young children: How the classroom teacher can help. *Intervention in School and Clinic, 28*(3), 165–171.

Johnson, J., Baumgart, D., Helmstetter, E., & Curry, C. A. (1996). *Augmenting basic communication in natural contexts*. Baltimore: Brookes.

Johnson, K. M., & Johnson, J. E. (1993). Rejoinder to Carta, Atwater, Schwartz, and McConnell. *Topics in Early Childhood Special Education*, *13*, 255–257.

Johnson, L. J., LaMontagne, M. J., Elgas, P. M., & Bauer, A. M. (1998). *Early childhood education: Blending theory, blending practice*. Baltimore: Brookes.

Johnson, M. J. (1992). What's basic in a student-centered reading, writing, and thinking approach: One teacher's perspective. *Volta Review*, *94*, 389–394.

Johnson, M., & Bailey, J. (1977). The modification of leisure behavior in a halfway house for retarded women. *Journal of Applied Behavior Analysis*, *10*, 273–282.

Johnson, R. (1985). *The picture communication symbols—Book II.* Solana Beach, CA: Mayer-Johnson.

Johnson, R. E., Liddell, S. K., & Erting, C. J. (1989). Unlocking the curriculum: Principles for achieving access in deaf education. *Gallaudet Research Institute Working Paper 89-3.* Washington, DC: Gallaudet University.

Johnson, T. P. (1986). *The principal's guide to the educational rights of handicapped students.* Reston, VA: National Association of Secondary School Principals.

Johnson-Martin, N. M., Attermeier, S. M., & Hacker, B. (1990). *The Carolina Curriculum for preschoolers with special needs*. Baltimore: Brookes.

Johnston, K. R., & Layng, T. V. J. (1994). The Morningside model of generative instruction. In R. Gardner III, D. M. Sainato, J. O. Cooper, T. E. Heron, W. L. Heward, J. Eshleman, & T. A. Grossi (Eds.), *Behavior analysis in education: Focus on measurably superior instruction* (pp. 173–197). Pacific Grove, CA: Brooks/Cole.

Jolly, A. C., Test, D. W., & Spooner, F. (1993). Using badges to increase initiations of children with severe disabilities in a play setting. *Journal of The Association for Persons with Severe Handicaps*, *18*, 46–51.

Jonas, G. (1976). *Stuttering: The disorder of many theories.* New York: Farrar, Straus, & Giroux.

Jones, B. E., Clark, G. M., & Soltz, D. F. (1997). Characteristics and practices of sign language interpreters in inclusive education programs. *Exceptional Children, 63,* 257–268.

Jones, D. E., Clatterbuck, C. C., Marquis, J., Turnbull, H. R., & Moberly, R. L. (1996). Educational placements for children who are ventilator assisted. *Exceptional Children, 63,* 47–57.

Jones, K. H., & Bender, W. N. (1993). Utilization of paraprofessionals in special education: A review of the literature. *Remedial and Special Education*, *14*(1), 7–14.

Jones, M. H. (1983). Cerebral palsy. In J. Umbreit (Ed.), *Physical disabilities and health impairments: An introduction* (pp. 41–58). Upper Saddle River, NJ: Merrill/Prentice Hall.

Jones, R. S. P., & McCaughey, R. E. (1992). Gentle teaching and applied behavior analysis: A critical review. *Journal of Applied Behavior Analysis*, *25*, 853–867.

Jones, T. M., Garlow, J. A., Turnbull, H. R., & Barber, P. A. (1996). Family empowerment in a family support program. In G. H. S. Singer, L. E. Powers, & A. L. Olson (Eds.), *Redefining family support: Innovations in public-private partnerships* (p. 91). Baltimore: Brookes.

Jones-Saete, C. (1986). The student with epilepsy. In G. Larson (Ed.), *Managing the school age children with a chronic health condition* (pp. 113–122). Wayzata, MN: DCI.

Jose, R. (1983). *Understanding low vision*. New York: American Foundation for the Blind.

Jusczyk, P. W., Friederici, A. D., Wessels, J., Svenkerud, V. Y., & Jusczyk, A. M. (1993). Infants' sensitivity to sequential and prosodic characteristics in their native language. *Journal of Memory and Language, 32,* 402–420.

Justen, J. E. (1976). Who are the severely handicapped? A problem in definition. *AAESPH Review*, *1*(2), 1–12.

Kairys, S. (1996). Family support in cases of child abuse and neglect. In G. H. S. Singer, L. E. Powers, & A. L. Olson (Eds.), *Redefining family support: Innovations in public-private partnerships* (pp. 171–188). Baltimore: Brookes.

Kaiser, A. P. (1993). Functional language. In M. E. Snell (Ed.), *Instruction of students with severe disabilities* (4th ed.) (pp. 347–379). Upper Saddle River, NJ: Merrill/Prentice Hall.

Kaiser, A. P. (2000). Teaching functional communication skills. In M. E. Snell & F. Brown (Eds.), *Instruction of students with severe disabilities* (5th ed.). Upper Saddle River, NJ: Merrill/Prentice Hall.

Kaiser, A. P., & Goetz, L. (1993). Enhancing communication with persons labeled severely disabled. *Journal of The Association for Persons with Severe Handicaps*, *18*, 137–142.

Kameenui, E. J., & Carnine, D. W. (1998). *Effective teaching strategies that accommodate diverse learners*. Upper Saddle River, NJ: Merrill/Prentice Hall.

Kameenui, E. J., & Darch, C. B. (1995). *Instructional classroom management: A proactive approach to behavior management*. White Plains, NY: Longman.

Kameenui, E. J., & Simmons, D. C. (1990). *Designing instructional strategies: The prevention of academic learning problems.* Upper Saddle River, NJ: Merrill/Prentice Hall.

Kamhi, A. G., Pollock, K. E., & Harris, J. L. (1996). *Communication development and disorders in African American children*. Baltimore: Brookes.

Kampfe, C. M. (1984). Mainstreaming: Some practical suggestions for teachers and administrators. In R. H. Hill & K. I. Dilka (Eds.), *The hearing-impaired child in school* (pp. 99–112). Orlando, FL: Grune & Stratton.

Kamps, D. M., Dugan, E. P., Leonard, B. R., & Daoust, P. M. (1994). Enhanced small group instruction using choral responding and student interactions for children with autism and developmental disabilities. *American Journal on Mental Retardation, 99,* 60–73.

Kamps, D. M., Walker, D., Maher, J., & Rotholz, D. (1992). Academic and environmental effects of small group instruction arrangements in classrooms for students with autism and developmental disabilities. *Journal of Autism and Developmental Disorder, 22,* 277–293.

Kaplan, S. (1988). Maintaining a gifted program. *Roeper Review, 11*(1), 35–37.

Karagiannis, A., Stainback, W., & Stainback, S. (1996). Rationale for inclusive schooling. In S. Stainback & W. Stainback (Eds.), *Inclusion: A guide for educators* (pp. 3–16). Baltimore: Brookes.

Karchmer, M. (1984). Hearing impaired students and their education: Population perspectives. In W. Northcott (Ed.), *Introduction to oral interpreting: Principles and practices* (pp. 41–59). Baltimore: University Park Press.

Karmody, C. S. (1986). Otology in perspective. In D. M. Luterman (Ed.), *Deafness in perspective* (pp. 1–13). San Diego: College-Hill.

Karnes, K. B., Beauchamp, K. D. F., & Pfaus, D. B. (1993). PEECH: A nationally validated early childhood special education model. *Topics in Early Childhood Special Education, 13,* 120–135.

Karsh, K. G., & Repp A. C. (1992). The Task Demonstration Model: A concurrent model for teaching groups of students with severe disabilities. *Exceptional Children, 59,* 54–67.

Katsiyannis, A., & Maag, J. W. (1998). Disciplining students with disabilities: Issues and considerations for implementing IDEA '97. *Behavioral Disorders, 23,* 276–289.

Kauffman, J. M. (1982). Social policy issues in special education and related services for emotionally disturbed children and youth. In M. M. Noel & N. G. Haring (Eds.), *Progress of change: Issues in educating the emotionally disturbed.* Vol. 1: *Identification and program planning* (pp. 1–10). Seattle: University of Washington Press.

Kauffman, J. M. (1985). An interview with James M. Kauffman. *Directive Teacher, 7*(1), 12–14.

Kauffman, J. M. (1996). The challenge of nihilism. *Behavioral Disorders, 19,* 205–206.

Kauffman, J. M. (1998a). How we prevent prevention of emotional and behavioral disorders. Manuscript submitted for publication.

Kauffman, J. M. (1998b). Commentary: Today's special education and its messages for tomorrow. *Journal of Special Education, 32*(3), 127–137.

Kauffman, J. M. (Ed.). (1981). Special issue: Are all children educable? *Analysis and Intervention in Developmental Disabilities, 1*(1).

Kauffman, J. M., & Hallahan, D. K. (1994). *The illusion of full inclusion: A comprehensive critique of a current special education bandwagon.* Austin, TX: PRO-ED.

Kauffman, J. M., & Krouse, J. (1981). The cult of educability: Searching for the substance of things hoped for; the evidence of things not seen. *Analysis and Intervention in Developmental Disabilities, 1*(1), 53–61.

Kauffman, J. M., Cullinan, D., & Epstein, M. H. (1987). Characteristics of students placed in special programs for the seriously emotionally disturbed. *Journal of Special Education, 13,* 283–295.

Kauffman, J. M., Hallahan, D. P., & Ford, D. Y. (Guest Eds.). (1998). Special section: Disproportionate representation of minority students in special education. *Journal of Special Education, 32,* 3–54.

Kavale, K. A., & Forness, S. R. (1996). Social skills deficits and learning disabilities: A meta-analysis. *Journal of Learning Disabilities, 29,* 226–237.

Kavale, K. A., & Forness, S. R. (1997). Defining learning disabilities: Consonance and dissonance. In J. W. Lloyd, E. J. Kameenui, & D. Chard (Eds.), *Issues in educating students with disabilities* (pp. 3–25). Mahwah, NJ: Erlbaum.

Kavale, K. A., & Reese, J. H. (1992). The character of learning disabilities: An Iowa profile. *Learning Disability Quarterly, 15,* 74–94.

Kavale, K., & Mattson, P. D. (1983). One jumped off the balance beam: Meta-analysis of perceptual-motor training. *Journal of Learning Disabilities, 16,* 165–173.

Kay, P. J., & Fitzgerald, M. (1997). Parents + teachers + action research = Real parent involvement. *Teaching Exceptional Children, 30*(1), 8–11

Kazak, A. E., & Marvin, R. S. (1984). Differences, difficulties and adaptation: Stress and social networks in families with a handicapped child. *Family Relations, 33,* 67–77.

Keel, M. C., & Gast, D. L. (1992). Small-group instruction for students with learning disabilities: Observational and incidental learning. *Exceptional Children, 58,* 357–368.

Kelker, K., Hecimovic, A., & LeRoy, C. H. (1994). Designing a classroom and school environment for students with AIDS: A checklist for teachers. *Teaching Exceptional Children, 26*(4), 52–55.

Keller, H. (1903). *The story of my life.* New York: Dell.

Kelly, D. J. (1998). A clinical synthesis of the "late talker" literature: Implications for service delivery. *Language, Speech and Hearing Services in the School, 29,* 76–84

Kelly, D. J., & Rice, M. L. (1986). A strategy for language assessment of young children: A combination of two approaches. *Language, Speech, and Hearing Services in the Schools, 17,* 83–94.

Kelly, M. L. (1990). *School-home notes.* New York: Guilford.

Kennedy, C. H., & Itkonen, T. (1994). Some effects of regular class participation on the social contacts and social network of high school students with disabilities. *Journal of*

The Association for Persons with Severe Handicaps, *19*, 1–10.

Kenney, K. W., & Prather, E. M. (1986). Articulation development in preschool children: Consistency of productions. *Journal of Speech and Hearing Research*, *29*, 29–36.

Keogh, B. K. (1990). Narrowing the gap between policy and practice. *Exceptional Children*, *57*, 186–190.

Kerr, B. (1985). Smart girls, gifted women: Special guidance concerns. *Roeper Review*, *8*(1), 30–33.

Kerr, M. M., & Nelson, C. M. (1998). *Strategies for managing behavior problems in the classroom* (3rd ed.). Upper Saddle River, NJ: Merrill/Prentice Hall.

Kershner, J., Hawks, W., & Grekin, R. (1977). Megavitamins and learning disorders: A controlled double-blind experiment. Unpublished manuscript, Ontario Institute for Studies in Education.

Kirsten, I. (1981). *The Oakland picture dictionary.* Wauconda, IL: Johnston.

Kishi, G., Teelucksingh, B., Zollers, N., Park-Lee, S., & Meyer, L. (1988). Daily decision-making in community residences: A social comparison of adults with and without mental retardation. *American Journal on Mental Retardation*, *92*, 430–435.

Klein, J. (1994). Supported living: Not just another "rung" on the continuum. *TASH Newsletter*, *20*(7), 16–18.

Kleinberg, S. (1984). Facilitating the child's entry to school and coordinating school activities during hospitalization. In *Home care for children with serious handicapping conditions* (pp. 67–77). Washington, DC: Association for the Care of Children's Health.

Kleinman, D., Heckaman, K. A., Kimball, J. W., Possi, M. K., Grossi, T. A., & Heward, W. L. (1994, May). A comparative analysis of two forms of delayed feedback on the acquisition, generalization, and maintenance of science vocabulary by elementary students with learning disabilities. Poster presented at the 20th annual convention of the Association for Behavior Analysis, Atlanta.

Klima, E., & Bellugi, U. (1979). *The signs of language.* Cambridge: Harvard University Press.

Klingner, J. K., Vaughn, S., Hughes, M. T., Schumm, J. S., & Elbaum, B. (1998). Outcomes for students with and without learning disabilities in inclusive classrooms. *Learning Disabilities Research and Practice, 13,* 153–161

Kluwin, T. N. (1985). Profiling the deaf student who is a problem in the classroom. *Adolescence*, *20*, 863–875.

Kluwin, T. N. (1993). Cumulative effects of mainstreaming on the achievement of deaf adolescents. *Exceptional Children*, *60*, 73–81.

Kluwin, T. N. (1996). Getting hearing and deaf students to write to each other through dialogue journals. *Teaching Exceptional Children, 28*(2), 50–53.

Kluwin, T. N., & Kelly, A. B. (1992). Implementing a successful writing program in the public schools for students who are deaf. *Exceptional Children, 59,* 41–53.

Kluwin, T. N., & Moores, D. F. (1989). Mathematics achievement of hearing impaired adolescents in different placements. *Exceptional Children*, *55*, 327–335.

Knapczyk, D. R. (1992). Effects of developing alternative responses on the aggressive behavior of adolescents. *Behavioral Disorders*, *17*, 247–263.

Knitzer, J., Sternberg, Z., & Fleisch, B. (1990). *At the school house door: An examination of programs and policies for children with behavioral and emotional problems.* New York: Bank Street College of Education Press.

Knoll, J. (1992). Being a family: The experience of raising a child with a disability or chronic illness. In V. J. Bradley, J. Knoll, & J. M Agosta (Eds.), *Emerging issues in family support* (pp. 9–56). Washington, DC: American Association on Mental Retardation.

Knowlton, E. (1998). Considerations in the design of personalized curricula supports for students with developmental disabilities. *Education and Training in Mental Retardation and Developmental Disabilities, 33,* 95–107.

Koegel, L. K., Koegel, R. L., & Dunlap, G. (1996). *Positive behavioral support: Including people with difficult behavior in the community*. Baltimore: Brookes.

Koegel, L. K., Stiebel, D., & Koegel, R. L. (1998). Reducing aggression in children with autism toward infant or toddler siblings. *Journal of The Association for Persons with Severe Handicaps, 23,* 111–118.

Koegel, R. L., & Koegel, L. (1995). *Teaching children with autism*. Baltimore: Brookes.

Koenig, A. J., & Holbrook, M. C. (1993). *Learning media assessment of students with visual impairments: A resource guide for teachers*. Austin: Texas School for the Blind.

Kohler, F. W., & Greenwood, C. R. (1986). Toward a technology of generalization: The identification of natural contingencies of reinforcement. *Behavior Analyst*, *9*, 19–26.

Kohler, F. W., & Strain, P. S. (1993). The early childhood social skills program. *Teaching Exceptional Children*, *25*(2), 41–42.

Kohler, P. D. (1994). On-the-job training: A curricular approach to employment. *Career Development for Exceptional Individuals*, *17*, 29–40.

Koyanagi, C., & Gaines, S. (1993). *All systems failure: An examination of the results of neglecting the needs of children with serious emotional disturbance*. Alexandria, VA: National Mental Health Association.

Kraemer, M. J., & Bierman, C. W. (1983). Asthma. In J. Umbreit (Ed.), *Physical disabilities and health impairments* (pp. 159–166). Upper Saddle River, NJ: Merrill/Prentice Hall.

Kratzer, D. A., Spooner, F., Test, D. W., & Koorland, M. A. (1993). Extending the application of constant time delay: Teaching a requesting skill to students with severe multiple disabilities. *Education and Treatment of Children*, *16*, 235–253.

Kraus, J. E., Fife, D., & Conroy, D. (1987). Pediatric brain injuries: The nature, clinical course, and early outcomes in a defined United States population. *Pediatrics*, *79*, 501–507.

Krauss, M. W., Seltzer, M. M., Gordon, R., & Fiedman, D. H. (1996). Binding ties: The roles of adult siblings of persons with mental retardation. *Mental Retardation, 34,* 83–93.

Krebs, P., & Coultier, G. (1992). Unified sports: I've seen the light. *Palaestra*, *8*(2), 42–45.

Kregel, J., Hill, M., & Banks, P. D. (1988). Analysis of employment specialist intervention time in supported competitive employment. *American Journal on Mental Retardation*, *93*, 200–208.

Krim, M. (1969). Scientific research and mental retardation. In *President's Committee on Mental Retardation message* (No. 16). Washington, DC: U.S. Government Printing Office.

Kroth, R. L., & Edge, D. (1997). *Strategies for communicating with parents of exceptional children* (3rd ed.). Denver: Love.

Krug, D. A., Arick, J., & Almond, P. (1980). Behavior checklist for identifying severely handicapped individuals with high levels of autistic behavior. *Journal of Child Psychology and Psychiatry, 21,* 221–229.

Kubina, R. M., & Cooper, J. O. (in press). Changing learning channels: An efficient strategy to facilitate instruction and learning. *Intervention in School and Clinic*.

Kugel, R. B., & Wolfensberger, W. (Eds.). (1969). *Changing patterns in residential services for the mentally retarded.* Washington, DC: Superintendent of Documents.

Kuhlman, F. (1924). Mental deficiency, feeble-mindedness, and defective delinquency. *American Association for the Study of the Feeble-Minded*, *29*, 58–70.

Kuhn, T. S. (1970). *The structure of scientific revolutions* (2nd ed.). Chicago: University of Chicago Press.

Kulick, J. A., & Kulick, C. L. (1984). Effects of accelerated instruction on students. *Review of Educational Research*, *54*(3), 409–425.

Kusserow, R. P. (1990, February). *Crack babies: A report of the Office of Inspector General, Department of Health and Human Services.* Washington, DC.

La Vor, M. L. (1976). Federal legislation for exceptional persons: A history. In F. J. Weintraub, A. Abeson, J. Ballard, & M. L. La Vor (Eds.), *Public policy and the education of exceptional children* (pp. 96–111). Reston, VA: Council for Exceptional Children.

Labov, W. (1975). The logic of nonstandard English. In P. Stoller (Ed.), *Black American English: Its background and its usage in the schools and in literature.* New York: Dell.

Lagomarcino, A., Reid, D. H., Ivancic, M. T., & Faw, G. D. (1984). Leisure-dance instruction for severely and profoundly retarded persons: Teaching an intermediate community-living skill. *Journal of Applied Behavior Analysis*, *17*, 71–84.

Lagomarcino, T. R., Hughes, C., & Rusch, F. R. (1989). Utilizing self-management to teach independence on the job. *Education and Training of the Mentally Retarded*, *24*, 139–148.

LaGrow, S. J., & Mulder, L. (1989). Structured solicitation: A standardized method for gaining travel information. *Journal of Visual Impairment and Blindness*, *83*, 469–471.

Lahey, M. (1988). *Language disorders and language development.* Upper Saddle River, NJ: Merrill/Prentice Hall.

Lakin, K. C., Braddock, D., & Smith, G. (1996). Majority of MR/DD residential service recipients now in homes of 6 or fewer residents. *Mental Retardation, 34,* 198.

Lakin, K. C., Hill, B. K., Chen, T., & Stephens, S. A. (1989). *Persons with mental retardation and related conditions in mental retardation facilities: Selected findings for the 1987 National Medical Expenditure Survey.* Minneapolis: University of Minnesota, Center for Residential and Community Services.

Lakin, K. C., Prouty, B., & Braddock, D. & Anderson, L. (1997). State institution populations smaller, older, more impaired. *Mental Retardation, 35,* 231–232.

Lakin, K. C., Prouty, B., Smith, G., & Braddock, D. (1996). Nixon goal surpassed—twofold. *Mental Retardation, 34,* 67.

Lalli, J. S., Browder, D. M., Mace, F. C., & Brown, D. K. (1993). Teacher use of descriptive analysis data to implement interventions to decrease students' problem behaviors. *Journal of Applied Behavior Analysis, 26,* 227–238.

Lambert, N., Nihira, K., & Leland, H. (1993). *Adaptive Behavior Scale—School* (2nd ed.). Austin, TX: PRO-ED.

Lancioni, G. E., O'Reilly, M. F., & Emerson, E. (1996). A review of choice research with people with severe and profound developmental disabilities. *Research in Developmental Disabilities, 17,* 391–411.

Landesman, S. (1986). Quality of life and personal life satisfaction: Definition and measurement issues. *Mental Retardation*, *24*, 141–143.

Landesman, S., & Ramey, C. T. (1989). Developmental psychology and mental retardation: Integrating scientific principles with treatment practices. *American Psychologist*, *44*, 409–415.

Lane, H. L. (1988). Is there a "psychology of the deaf"? *Exceptional Children*, *55*, 7–19.

Langham, T. (1993). Tools of the trade. *RE:view*, *25*, 137–141.

Larson, S. A., & Lakin, K. C. (1989). Deinstitutionalization of persons with mental retardation. *Journal of The Association for Persons with Severe Handicaps, 14*, 324–332.

LaSasso, C. J., & Mobley, R. T. (1997). National survey of reading instruction for deaf or hard-of-hearing students in the U.S. *Volta Review, 99*(1), 31–58.

Laskowski-Jones, L. (1993). Acute SCI: How to minimize the damage. *American Journal of Nursing, 93*(12), 23–31.

Lazarus, B. D. (1996). Flexible skeletons: Guided notes for adolescents with mild disabilities. *Teaching Exceptional Children, 28*(3), 37–40.

Leach, D. J., & Siddall, S. W. (1992). Parental involvement in the teaching of reading: A comparison of Hearing Reading, Paired Reading, Pause, Prompt, Praise and Direct Instruction methods. *ADI News, 11*(2), 14–19.

Lehr, D. H., & Macurdy, S. (1994). Meeting special health care needs of students. In M. Agran, N. E. Marchand-Martella, & R. C. Martella (Eds.), *Promoting health and safety: Skills for independent living* (pp. 71–84). Pacific Grove, CA: Brooks/Cole.

Lehr, D. H., & McDaid, P. (1993). Opening the door further: Integrating students with complex health needs. *Focus on Exceptional Children, 25*(6), 1–7.

Lenz, B. K., & Bulgren, J. A. (1995). Promoting learning in content classes. In P. A. Cegelka & W. H. Berdine (Eds.), *Effective instruction for students with learning problems* (pp. 385–417). Needham Heights, MA: Allyn & Bacon.

Leonard, L. B. (1986). Conversational replies of children with specific language impairments. *Journal of Speech and Hearing Research, 29*, 114–119.

Leone, P. E. (1994). Education services for youth with disabilities in a state-operated juvenile correctional system: Case study and analysis. *Journal of Special Education, 28*, 43–58.

Leone, P. E., Rutherford, R. B., & Nelson, C. M. (1991). *Special education and juvenile corrections*. Reston, VA: Council for Exceptional Children.

Leone, P., Lovitt, T. C., & Hansen, C. (1981). A descriptive follow-up study of learning disabled boys. *Learning Disability Quarterly, 4*, 152–162.

Lerner, J. W. (1993). *Learning disabilities: Theories, diagnosis, and teaching strategies* (6th ed.). Boston: Houghton Mifflin.

Lerro, M. (1994). Teaching adolescents about AIDS. *Teaching Exceptional Children, 26*(4), 49–51.

Leung, E. K. (1988). Cultural and acultural commonalities and diversities among Asian Americans: Identification and programming considerations. In A. A. Ortiz & B. A. Ramirez (Eds.), *Schools and the culturally diverse exceptional student: Promising practices and future directions* (pp. 86–95). Reston, VA: Council for Exceptional Children.

Levine, J. M. (1996). Including children dependent on ventilators in school. *Teaching Exceptional Children, 28*(3), 25–29.

Levine, M. N. (1986). Psychoeducational evaluation of children and adolescents with cerebral palsy. In P. J. Lazarus & S. S. Stirchart (Eds.), *Psychoeducational evaluation of children and adolescents with low incidence handicaps* (pp. 267–284). Orlando, FL: Grune & Stratton.

Levitt, H. (1985). Technology and the education of the hearing impaired. In F. Powell, T. Finitzo-Hieber, S. Friel-Patti, & D. Henderson (Eds.), *Education of the hearing impaired child* (pp. 119–129). San Diego: College-Hill.

Lewis, R. B. (1993). *Special education technology: Classroom applications*. Pacific Grove, CA: Brooks/Cole.

Lewis, R. B., & Doorlag, D. H. (1991). *Teaching special students in the mainstream* (3rd ed.). Upper Saddle River, NJ: Merrill/Prentice Hall.

Lewis, R. B., & Doorlag, D. H. (1995). *Teaching special students in the mainstream* (4th ed.). Upper Saddle River, NJ: Merrill/Prentice Hall.

Lichtenstein, S. (1993). Transition from school to adulthood: Case studies of adults with learning disabilities who dropped out of school. *Exceptional Children, 59*, 336–347.

Lichtenstein, S., & Michaelides, N. (1993). Transition from school to young adulthood: Four case studies of young adults labeled mentally retarded. *Career Development for Exceptional Individuals, 16*, 183–195.

Lieberman, L. M. (1982). The nightmare of scheduling. *Journal of Learning Disabilities, 15*, 57–58.

Lignugaris/Kraft, B., Rule, S., Salzberg, C. L., & Stowitschek, J. J. (1988). Social-vocational skills of handicapped and nonhandicapped adults at work. *Journal of Employment Counseling, 23*, 20–31.

Likins, M., Salzberg, C. L., Stowitschek, J. J., Lignugaris/Kraft, R., & Curl, R. (1989). Co-worker implemented job training: The use of coincidental training and quality-control checking on the food preparation skills of trainees with mental retardation. *Journal of Applied Behavior Analysis, 22*, 381–393.

Lindfors, J. W. (1987). *Children's language and learning* (2nd ed.). Upper Saddle River, NJ: Prentice Hall.

Lindley, L. (1990, August). Defining TASH: A mission statement. *TASH Newsletter, 16*(8), 1.

Lindsley, O. R. (1971). From Skinner to precision teaching: The child knows best. In J. B. Jordan & L. S. Robbins (Eds.), *Let's try doing something else kind of thing* (pp. 1–11). Arlington, VA: Council for Exceptional Children.

Lindsley, O. R. (1996). The four free-operant freedoms. *Behavior Analyst, 19*, 199–210.

Lindstrom, L. E., Benz, M. R., & Johnson, M. D. (1997). From school grounds to coffee grounds: An introduction to school-based enterprises. *Teaching Exceptional Children, 29*(4), 20–24.

Linebaugh, C. W. (1986). Mild aphasia. In J. M. Costello & A. L. Holland (Eds.), *Handbook of speech and language disorders* (pp. 871–889). San Diego: College-Hill.

Ling, D. (1976). *Speech and the hearing-impaired child: Theory and practice.* Washington, DC: Alexander Graham Bell Association for the Deaf.

Ling, D. (1986). Devices and procedures for auditory learning. *Volta Review, 88*(5), 19–28.

Ling, D. (Ed.). (1984). *Early intervention for hearing-impaired children: Total communication options.* San Diego: College-Hill.

Lipsky, D. K., & Garter, A. (1991). Restructuring for quality. In J. W. Lloyd, A. C. Repp, & N. N. Singh (Eds.), *The regular education initiative: Alternative perspectives on concepts, issues, and models* (pp. 43–56), Sycamore, IL: Sycamore.

Liptak, G. S. (1997). Neural tube defects. In M. L. Batshaw (Ed.), *Children with disabilities* (4th ed.) (pp. 529–552). Baltimore: Brookes.

Little Soldier, L. (1990). The education of Native American students: Where makes a difference. *Equity and Excellence, 24*(4), 66–69.

Livingston-White, D., Utter, C., & Woodard, Q. E. (1985). Follow-up study of visually impaired students of the Michigan School for the Blind. *Journal of Visual Impairment and Blindness, 79*, 150–153.

Lloyd, J. W., Weintraub, F. J., & Safer, N. D. (1997). A bridge between research and practice: Building consensus. *Exceptional Children, 63,* 535–538.

Lloyd, L. L., & Kangas, K. A. (1994). Augmentative and alternative communication. In G. H. Shames & E. H. Wiig (Eds.), *Human communication disorders* (4th ed.) (pp. 606–657). Upper Saddle River, NJ: Merrill/Prentice Hall.

Lloyd, L. L., Quist, R. W., & Windsor, J. (1990). A proposed augmentative and alternative communication model. *Augmentative and Alternative Communication, 6*, 172–183.

Lloyd, L., Spradlin, J., & Reid, M. (1968). An operant audiometric procedure for difficult-to-test patients. *Journal of Speech and Hearing Disorders, 33*, 236–245.

Lohrmann-O'Rouke, S., & Browder, D. M. (1998). Empirically based methods to assess the preferences of individuals with severe disabilities. *American Journal on Mental Retardation, 103,* 146–161.

Lou, M. W. (1988). The history of language use in the education of the deaf in the United States. In M. Strong (Ed.), *Language learning and deafness* (pp. 75–98). New York: Cambridge University Press.

Lovaas, O. I. (1981). *Teaching developmentally disabled children: The ME book*. Austin, TX: PRO-ED.

Lovaas, O. I. (1987). Behavioral treatment and normal educational and intellectual functioning in young autistic children. *Journal of Consulting and Clinical Psychology, 55*, 3–9.

Lovaas, O. I. (1994, October). Comments made during Ohio State University teleconference on applied behavior analysis, The Ohio State University, Columbus.

Lovaas, O. I., & Newsom, C. D. (1976). Behavior modification with psychotic children. In H. Leitenberg (Ed.), *Handbook of behavior modification and behavior therapy* (pp. 303–360). Upper Saddle River, NJ: Prentice Hall.

Lovitt, T. C. (1977). *In spite of my resistance . . . I've learned from children.* Upper Saddle River, NJ: Merrill/Prentice Hall.

Lovitt, T. C. (1979). What should we call them? *Exceptional Teacher, 1*(1), 5–7.

Lovitt, T. C. (1982). *Because of my persistence . . . I've learned from children.* Upper Saddle River, NJ: Merrill/Prentice Hall.

Lovitt, T. C. (1989). *Introduction to learning disabilities*. Boston: Allyn & Bacon.

Lovitt, T. C. (1991). *Preventing school dropouts*. Austin, TX: PRO-ED.

Lovitt, T. C. (1995). *Tactics for teaching* (2nd ed.). Upper Saddle River, NJ: Prentice Hall.

Lowenfeld, B. (Ed.). (1973). *The visually handicapped child in school.* New York: Day.

Luckasson, R., Coulter, D. L., Polloway, E. A., Reiss, S., Schalock, R. L., Snell, M. E., Spitalnik, D. M., & Stark, J. A. (1992). *Mental retardation: Definition, classification, and systems of supports* (9th ed.). Washington, DC: American Association on Mental Retardation.

Luckner, J. (1994). Developing independent and responsible behaviors in students who are deaf or hard of hearing. *Teaching Exceptional Children, 26*(2), 13–17.

Ludlow, B. L., & Sobsey, R. (1984). *The school's role in educating severely handicapped students.* Bloomington, IN: Phi Delta Kappa Educational Foundation.

Lund, K. A., & Bos, C. S. (1981). Orchestrating the preschool classroom: The daily schedule. *Teaching Exceptional Children, 14*, 120–125.

Luterman, D. M. (Ed.). (1986). *Deafness in perspective.* San Diego: College-Hill.

Lutzker, J. R., & Campbell, R. (1994). *Ecobehavioral family interventions in developmental disabilities*. Pacific Grove, CA: Brooks/Cole.

Lutzker, J. R., & Newman, M. R. (1986). Child abuse and neglect: Community problem, community solutions. *Education and Treatment of Children, 9,* 344–354.

Lynas, W. (1986). *Integrating the handicapped into ordinary schools: A study of hearing-impaired pupils.* London: Croom Helm.

Lynch, E., & Hanson, M. (1998). *Developing cross-cultural competence* (2nd ed.). Baltimore: Brookes

Lyon, G. R. (1995). Toward a definition of dyslexia. *Annals of Dyslexia, 45,* 3–27

Lyon, G. R., & Chhabra, V. (1996). The current state of the science and the future of specific reading disability. *Mental Retardation and Developmental Disabilities, 2,* 2–9.

MacCarthy, A., & Connell, J. (1984). Audiological screening and assessment. In G. Lindsay (Ed.), *Screening for children with special needs* (pp. 63–85). London: Croom Helm.

MacFadyen, J. T. (1986). Educated monkeys help the disabled to help themselves. *Smithsonian, 17*(7), 125–133.

Macht, J. (1998). *Special education's failed system: A question of eligibility*. Westport, CT: Bergin & Garvey.

Macmann, G. M., & Barnett, D. W. (1992). Redefining the WISC-R: Implications for professional practice and public policy. *Journal of Special Education, 26,* 139–161.

MacMillan, D. L. (1982). *Mental retardation in school and society* (2nd ed.). Boston: Little, Brown.

MacMillan, D. L. (1989). Mild mental retardation: Emerging issues. In G. A. Robinson, J. R. Patton, E. A. Polloway, & L. R. Sargent (Eds.), *Best practices in mild mental disabilities* (pp. 3–20). Reston, VA: Council for Exceptional Children.

MacMillan, D. L., & Reschly, D. J. (1998). Overrepresentation of minority students: The case for greater specificity or reconsideration of the variables examined. *Journal of Special Education, 32,* 15–24.

MacMillan, D. L., Gresham, F. M., & Siperstein, G. N. (1993). Conceptual and psychometric concerns about the 1992 AAMR definition of mental retardation. *American Journal on Mental Retardation, 98,* 325–335.

MacMillan, D. L., Gresham, F. M., Bocian, K. M., & Lambros, K. M. (1998). Current plight of borderline students: Where do they belong? *Education and Training in Mental Retardation and Developmental Disabilities, 33,* 83–94.

MacMillan, D. L., Gresham, F. M., Siperstein, G. N., & Bocian, K. M. (1996). The labyrinth of IDEA: School decisions on referred students with subaverage general intelligence. *American Journal on Mental Retardation, 101,* 161–174.

MacMillan, D. L., Jones, R., & Aloia, G. (1974). The mentally retarded label: A theoretical analysis and review of the literature. *American Journal on Mental Retardation, 79,* 241–261.

MacMillan, D. L., Siperstein, G. N., & Gresham, F. M. (1996). Mild mental retardation: A challenge to its viability as a diagnostic category. *Exceptional Children, 62,* 356–371.

Maestas y Moores, J., & Moores, D. F. (1980). Language training with the young deaf child. In D. Bricker (Ed.), *Early language intervention with handicapped children.* San Francisco: Jossey-Bass.

Maheady, L., Mallete, B., Harper, G. F., & Saca, K. (1991). Heads together: A peer-mediated option for improving the academic achievement of heterogeneous learning groups. *Remedial and Special Education, 12*(2), 25–33.

Mahon, M. J., & Bullock, C. C. (1992). Teaching adolescents with mild mental retardation to make decisions in leisure through the use of self-control techniques. *Therapeutic Recreation Journal, 26,* 9–26.

Mahshie, S. N. (1995). *Educating deaf children bilingually*. Washington, DC: Gallaudet University Press.

Majer, L. H., & Joy, J. H. (1993). A principal's guide to asthma. *Principal, 73*(2), 42–44.

Maker, C. J. (1982). Teaching models in education of the gifted. Rockville, MD: Aspen.

Maker, C. J. (1993). Creativity, intelligence, and problem solving: A definition and design for cross-cultural research and measurement related to giftedness. *Gifted Education International, 9*(2), 68–77.

Maker, C. J. (1997). DISCOVER problem solving assessment. *Quest, 8*(1), 3, 4, 7.

Maker, C. J., Nielson, A. B., & Rogers, J. A. (1994). Giftedness, diversity, and problem-solving. *Teaching Exceptional Children, 27*(1), 4–19.

Malian, I. M., & Love, L. L. (1998). Leaving high school: An ongoing transition study. *Teaching Exceptional Children, 30*(3), 4–10.

Mank, D. M., & Horner, R. H. (1987). Self-recruited feedback: A cost-effective procedure for maintaining behavior. *Research in Developmental Disabilities, 8,* 91–112.

Mank, D., Cioffi, A., & Yovanoff, P. (1998). Employment outcomes for people with severe disabilities: Opportunities for improvement. *Mental Retardation, 36,* 205–216.

Mann, D. (1996). Serious play. *Teachers College Record, 97*(3), 447–469.

Mannix, D. (1992). *Life skills activities for special children*. West Nyack, NY: Center for Applied Research in Education.

Mansour, S. L. (1985). 1985 ASHA demographic update. *ASHA, 27*(7), 55.

Margolis, H., & Brannigan, G. (1990). Calming the storm. *Learning, 18,* 40–42.

Markwardt, F. C. (1989). *Peabody Individual Achievement Test*. Circle Pines, MN: American Guidance Service.

Marschark, M., & Clark, M. D. (Eds.) (1998). *Psychological perspectives on deafness* (Vol. 2). Mahwah, NJ: Erlbaum.

Marsh, L. G., & Cooke, N. L. (1996). The effects of using manipulatives in teaching math problem solving to students with learning disabilities. *Learning Disabilities Research and Practice, 11*(1), 58–65.

Martin, E. W. (1993). Learning disabilities and public policies: Myths and outcomes. In G. R. Lyon, D. B. Gray, J. F. Kavanaugh, & N. A. Krasnegor (Eds.), *Better understanding learning disabilities: New views from research and their implications for education and public policies* (pp. 325–342). Baltimore: Brookes.

Martin, J. E., & Marshall, L. H. (1995). ChoiceMaker: A comprehensive self-determined transition program. *Intervention in School and Clinic, 30,* 147–156.

Martin, J. E., Marshall, L. H., & Maxson, L. L. (1993). Transition policy: Infusing self-determination and self-advocacy into transition programs. *Career Development for Exceptional Individuals, 16,* 53–61.

Martin, J. E., Marshall, L. H., Maxson, L., & Jerman, P. (1993). *Self-directed IEP*. Colorado Springs: University of Colorado Press.

Martin, J. R. (1985). *Reclaiming a conversation: The ideal of the educated woman*. New Haven: Yale University Press.

Martin, R. R., & Lindamood, L. P. (1986). Stuttering and spontaneous recovery: Implications for the speech-language pathologist. *Language, Speech, and Hearing Services in the Schools, 17*, 207–218.

Martin, S. L., Ramey, C. T., & Ramey, S. L. (1990). The prevention of intellectual impairment in children of impoverished families: Findings of a randomized trial of educational daycare. *American Journal of Public Health, 80*, 844–847.

Mason, M. A., & Gambrill, E. (1994). *Debating children's lives*. Hollywood, CA: Sage.

Mastropieri, M. A., & Scruggs, T. E. (1998). Constructing more meaningful relationships in the classroom: Mnemonic research into practice. *Learning Disabilities Research and Practice, 13*(3), 138–145.

Mastropieri, M. A., Scruggs, T. E., & Whedon, C. (1997). Using mnemonic strategies to teach information about U.S. presidents: A classroom-based investigation. *Learning Disabilities Quarterly, 20*, 13–21.

Matson, J. L. (Ed.). (1994). *Autism in children and adults: Etiology, assessment, and intervention*. Pacific Grove, CA: Brooks/Cole.

Mattes, L. J., & Omark, D. R. (1984). *Speech and language assessment for the bilingual handicapped.* San Diego: College-Hill.

Mauk, J. E., Reber, M., & Batshaw, M. L. (1997). Autism. In M. L. Batshaw (Ed.), *Children with disabilities* (pp. 425–448). Baltimore: Brookes.

Maurice, C., Green, G., & Luce, S. G. (Eds.). (1996). *Behavioral intervention for young children with autism: A manual for parents and professionals*. Austin, TX: PRO-ED.

Mayer, G. R. (1995). Preventing antisocial behavior in schools. *Journal of Applied Behavior Analysis, 28,* 467–478.

Mayer-Johnson, R. (1986). *The Picture Communications Symbols* (Book 1). Solana Beach, CA: Mayer-Johnson.

McAdam, D. B., O'Cleirigh, C. M., & Cuvo, A. J. (1993). Self-monitoring and verbal feedback to reduce stereotypic body rocking in a congenitally blind adult. *RE:view, 24*, 163–172.

McAnally, P. L., Rose, S., & Quigley, S. P. (1998). *Language learning practices with children who are deaf* (3rd ed.). Austin, TX: PRO-ED.

McComiskey, A. V. (1996). The Braille Readiness Grid: A guide to building a foundation for literacy. *Journal of Visual Impairment and Blindness, 90,* 190–193.

McConnell, S. R. (1994). Social context, social validity, and program outcome in early intervention. In R. Gardner III, D. M. Sainato, J. O. Cooper, T. E. Heron, W. L. Heward, J. Eshleman, & T. A. Grossi (Eds.), *Behavior analysis in education: Focus on measurably superior instruction* (pp. 75–85). Pacific Grove, CA: Brooks/Cole.

McConnell, S. R., McEvoy, M. A., & Odom, S. L. (1992). Implementation of social competence interventions in early childhood special education classes. In S. L. Odom, S. R. McConnell, & M. A. McEvoy (Eds.), *Social competence of young children with disabilities: Nature, development and intervention* (pp. 277–306). Baltimore: Brookes.

McCormick, L., & Schiefelbusch, R. L. (1990). *Early language intervention: An introduction* (2nd ed.). New York: Merrill/Prentice Hall.

McCormick, L., & Schiefelbusch, R. L. (1990). *Early language intervention: An introduction* (2nd ed.). Upper Saddle River, NJ: Merrill/Prentice Hall.

McCormick, M. E., & Wolf, J. S. (1993). Intervention programs for gifted girls. *Roeper Review, 16*, 85–88.

McCracken, K. (1987, October 5). 85 at TSD suspended in sign language dispute. *Knoxville Journal,* pp. 1, 10.

McCuin, D., & Cooper, J. O. (1994). Teaching keyboarding and computer skills to persons with developmental disabilities. *Behaviorology, 2*(1), 63–78.

McDermott, S. (1994). Explanatory model to describe school district prevalence rates for mental retardation and learning disabilities. *American Journal on Mental Retardation, 99*, 175–185.

McDonald, E. T. (1980). *Using and teaching Blissymbolics.* Toronto: Blissymbolics Communication Institute.

McEachin, J. J., Smith, T., & Lovaas, I. O. (1993). Long-term outcome for children with autism who received early intensive behavioral treatment. *American Journal on Mental Retardation, 97*, 359–372.

McEvoy, M. A., & Yoder, P. (1993). Interventions to promote social skills and emotional development. In *DEC Recommended Practices* (pp. 77–81). Reston, VA: Council for Exceptional Children, Division for Early Childhood.

McGee, J. J. (1992). Gentle teaching's assumptions and paradigm. *Journal of Applied Behavior Analysis, 25*, 869–872.

McGee, J. J., & Gonzalez, L. (1990). Gentle teaching and the practice of human interdependence: A preliminary group study of 15 persons with severe behavioral disorders and their caregivers. In A. C. Repp & N. N. Singh (Eds.), *Current perspectives on the use of nonaversive and aversive interventions for persons with developmental disabilities* (pp. 237–254). Sycamore, IL: Sycamore.

McGee, J. J., & Menolascino, F. J. (1991). *Beyond gentle teaching: A nonaversive approach to helping those in need*. New York: Plenum.

McGregor, G., & Vogelsberg, R. T.(1998). *Inclusive schooling practices: Pedagogical and research foundations.* Philadelphia:

Allegheny University of the Health Sciences.

McHutchion, M. E. (1991). Student bereavement: A guide for school personnel. *Journal of School Health, 61,* 363–366.

McIntire, J. C. (1985). The future role of residential schools for visually impaired students. *Journal of Visual Impairment and Blindness*, *79*, 161–164.

McIntosh, R., Vaughn, S., Schumm, J. S., Haager, D., & Lee, O. (1993). Observations of students with learning disabilities in general education classrooms. *Exceptional Children, 60*, 249–261.

McIntyre, T. (1992). The culturally sensitive disciplinarian. In R. B. Rutherford, Jr., & S. R. Mathur (Eds.), *Severe behavior disorders of children and youth* (vol. 15, pp. 112–120). Reston, VA: Council for Children with Behavior Disorders.

McIntyre, T. (1993a).Behaviorally disordered youth in correctional settings: Prevalence, programming, and teacher training. *Behavioral Disorders*, *18*, 167–176.

McIntyre, T. (1993b). Reflections on the new definition for emotional or behavioral disorders: Who still falls through the cracks and why. *Behavioral Disorders*, *18*, 148–160.

McIntyre, T. (1995). Culturally sensitive and appropriate assessment for EBD. *CCBD Newsletter*. Reston, VA: Council for Children with Behavioral Disorders.

McIntyre, T., & Forness, S. R. (1996). Is there a new definition yet or are kids still seriously emotionally disturbed? *Beyond Behavior, 7*(3), 4–9.

McKelvey, J. L., Sisson, L. A., Van Hasselt, V. B., & Herson, M. (1992). An approach to teaching self-dressing to a child with dual-sensory impairment. *Teaching Exceptional Children*, *25*(1), 12–15.

McLaren, J., & Bryson, S. E. (1987). Review of recent epidemiological studies of mental retardation: Prevalence, related disorders and etiology. *American Journal on Mental Retardation*, *92*, 243–254.

McLaughlin, J. A., & Nall, M. (1994). Allergies and learning/behavioral disorders. *Intervention in School and Clinic, 20,* 198–207.

McLean, M., Bailey, D. B., & Wolery, M. (1996). *Assessing infants and preschoolers with special needs* (2nd ed.) Upper Saddle River, NJ: Merrill/Prentice Hall.

McLeskey, J. (1992). Students with learning disabilities at primary, intermediate, and secondary grade levels: Identification and characteristics. *Learning Disability Quarterly*, *15*, 13–19.

McLoughlin, C. S., Garner, J. B., & Callahan, M. (1987). *Getting employed, staying employed: Job development and training for persons with severe handicaps*. Baltimore: Brookes.

McLoughlin, J. A., & Lewis, R. B. (1994). *Assessing special students* (4th ed.). Upper Saddle River, NJ: Merrill/Prentice Hall.

McNair, J., & Rusch, F. R. (1992). The co-worker involvement instrument: A measure of indigenous workplace support. *Career Development for Exceptional Individuals*, *15*, 23–36.

McNeish, T. J., & Naglieri, J. A. (1993). Identification of individuals with serious emotional disturbance using the Draw a Person: Screening procedure for emotional disturbance. *Journal of Special Education*, *27*, 115–121.

McReynolds, L. V. (1990). Articulation and phonological disorders. In G. H. Shames & E. H. Wiig (Eds.), *Human communication disorders* (3rd ed.) (pp. 30–73). Upper Saddle River, NJ: Merrill/Prentice Hall.

Meadow, K. P. (1980). *Deafness and child development.* Berkeley: University of California Press.

Meadow-Orlans, K. P. (1985). Social and psychological effects of hearing loss in adulthood: A literature review. In H. Orlans (Ed.), *Adjustment to adult hearing loss* (pp. 35–57). San Diego: College-Hill.

Meadow-Orlans, K. P., Mertens, D. M., Sass-Lehrer, M. A., & Scott-Olson, K. (1997). Support services for parents and their children who are deaf or hard of hearing. *American Annals of the Deaf, 142,* 278–288.

Meadows, N. B., Neel, R. S., Scott, C. M., & Parker, G. (1994). Academic performance, social competence, and mainstream accommodations: A look at mainstreamed and nonmainstreamed students with serious behavioral disorders. *Behavioral Disorders*, *19*, 170–180.

Mechling, L. C., & Gast, D. L. (1997). Combination audio/visual self-prompting system for teaching chained tasks to students with intellectual disabilities. *Education and Training in Mental Retardation and Developmental Disabilities, 32,* 138–153.

Meddin, B. M., & Rosen, A. L. (1987). Child abuse and neglect: Prevention and reporting. *Education Digest, 52,* 52–55.

Mehler, J., Jusczyk, P. W., Lambertz, G., Halsted, N., Bettoncini, J. & Ameil-Tison, C. (1988). A precursor of language acquisition in young infants. *Cognition, 29,* 143–178.

Meichenbaum, D., & Goodman, J. (1971). Training impulsive children to talk to themselves: A means of developing self-control. *Journal of Abnormal Psychology, 77,* 116–126.

Menlove, M. (1996). A checklist for identifying funding sources for assistive technology. *Teaching Exceptional Children, 28*(3), 20–24.

Mercer, C. D. (1997). *Students with learning disabilities* (5th ed.). Upper Saddle River, NJ: Merrill/Prentice Hall.

Mercer, C. D., Jordan, L., Allsopp, D. H., & Mercer, A. R. (1995). Learning disabilities definitions and criteria used by state education departments. Unpublished manuscript.

Mercer, J. R. (1973a). *Labelling the mentally retarded.* Berkeley: University of California Press.

Mercer, J. R. (1973b). The myth of 3% prevalence. In R. K. Eymon, C. E. Meyers, & G. Tarjon (Eds.), *Sociobehavioral studies in mental retardation* (No. 1, pp. 1–18). American Association on Mental Deficiency.

Meyer, D. J., Vadasy, P. F., & Fewell, R. R. (1994). *Sibshops: Workshops for siblings of children with special needs*. Baltimore: Brookes.

Meyer, L. H. (1986, June). Creating options and making choices. *TASH Newsletter*, p. 1.

Meyer, L. H., Cole, D. A., McQuarter, R., & Reichle, J. (1990). Validation of the Assessment of Social Competence (ASC) for children and young adults with developmental disabilities. *Journal of The Association for Persons with Severe Handicaps*, *15*, 57–68.

Meyer, L., Gersten, R., & Gutkin, J. (1983). Direct Instruction: A project follow through success story in an inner-city school. *Elementary School Journal, 84,* 241–252.

Meyers, C. E., Mink, I. T., & Nihira, K. (1981). *Home Quality Rating Scale: User's manual*. Los Angeles: University of California, Neuropsychiatric Institute.

Michael, R. J. (1992). Seizures: Teachers' observations and record keeping. *Intervention in School and Clinic*, *27*, 211–214.

Michaud, L. J., & Duhaime, A. (1992). Traumatic brain injury. In M. L. Batshaw & Y. M. Perret (Eds.), *Children with disabilities: A medical primer* (3rd ed.) (pp. 525–546). Baltimore: Brookes.

Miller, A. D., Barbetta, P. M., & Heron, T. E. (1994). START tutoring: Designing, training, implementing, adapting, and evaluating tutoring programs for school and home settings. In R. Gardner III, D. M. Sainato, J. O. Cooper, T. E. Heron, W. L. Heward, J. Eshleman, & T. A. Grossi (Eds.), *Behavior analysis in education: Focus on measurably superior instruction* (pp. 75–85). Pacific Grove, CA: Brooks/Cole.

Miller, A. D., Hall, S. W., & Heward, W. L. (1995). Effects of sequential 1-minute time trials with and without intertrial feedback and self-correction on general and special education students' fluency with math facts. *Journal of Behavioral Education*, *5*, 319–345.

Miller, D. (1979). *Ophthalmology: The essentials.* Boston: Houghton Mifflin.

Miller, J., & Pfingst, B. (1984). Cochlear implants. In C. Berlin (Ed.), *Hearing science* (pp. 309–339). San Diego: College-Hill.

Miller, L. J., Strain, P. S., Boyd, K., McKinley, J., Hunsicker, S., & Wu, A. (1992). *Preschool mainstreaming: Outcomes for children with disabilities and typical children*. Pittsburgh: Allegheny-Singer Research Institute.

Miller, S. P., & Hudson, P. (1994). Using structured parent groups to provide parental support. *Intervention in School and Clinic*, *29*, 151–155.

Miller, W. (1989, July). Obstetrical issues. Paper presented at the Conference on Drugs, Alcohol, Pregnancy and Parenting: An Intervention Model, Spokane, WA.

Miller, W. H. (1985). The role of residential schools for the blind in educating visually impaired students. *Journal of Visual Impairment and Blindness*, *79*, 160.

Minner, S., Beane, A., & Prater, J. (1986). Try telephone answering machines. *Teaching Exceptional Children, 19*(1), 62–63.

Mithaug, D. E., Horiuchi, C. N., & Fanning, P. N. (1985). A report on the Colorado statewide follow-up survey of special education students. *Exceptional Children*, *51*, 397–404.

Mithaug, D. W., Martin, J. E., & Agran, M. (1987). Adaptability instruction: The goal of transitional programming. *Exceptional Children*, *53*, 500–505.

Mithaug, D. W., Martin, J. E., Agran, M., & Rusch, F. R. (1988). *Why special education graduates fail: How to teach them to succeed.* Colorado Springs: Ascent.

Moaven, L. D., Gilbert, G. L., Cunningham, A. L., & Rawlinson, W. D. (1995). Amniocentesis to diagnose congenital cytomegalovirus infection. *Medical Journal of Australia, 162,* 334–335.

Moll, L. C. (1992). Bilingual classroom studies and community analysis: Some recent trends. *Educational Researcher, 21*(2), 20–24.

Monda-Amaya, L. E., Dieker, L., & Reed, F. (1998). Preparing students with learning disabilities to participate in inclusive classrooms. *Learning Disabilities Research and Practice, 13*(3), 171–182.

Moon, M. S. (1994). *Making school and community recreation fun for everyone: Places and ways to integrate*. Baltimore: Brookes.

Moon, M. S., & Bunker, L. (1987). Recreation and motor skills programming. In M. E. Snell (Ed.), *Systematic instruction of persons with severe handicaps* (3rd ed.) (pp. 214–244). Upper Saddle River, NJ: Merrill/Prentice Hall.

Moon, M. S., & Inge, K. (1993). Vocational preparation and transition. In M. E. Snell (Ed.), *Instruction of students with severe disabilities* (4th ed.) (pp. 556–587). Upper Saddle River, NJ: Merrill/Prentice Hall.

Moore, P., & Hicks, D. M. (1994). Voice disorders. In G. H. Shames & E. H. Wiig (Eds.), *Human communication disorders* (4th ed.) (pp. 292–335). Upper Saddle River, NJ: Merrill/Prentice Hall.

Moore, P., & Hicks, D. M. (1998). Voice disorders. In G. H. Shames & E. H. Wiig (Eds.), *Language disorders: A functional approach to assessment and intervention* (2nd ed., pp. 292–335). Needham Heights, MA: Allyn & Bacon.

Moores, D. F. (1991). The great debate: Where, how, and what to teach deaf children. *American Annals of the Deaf, 136,* 35–37.

Moores, D. F. (1993). Total inclusion/zero rejection models in general education: Implication for deaf children. *American Annals of the Deaf, 138,* 251.

Moores, D. F. (1996). *Educating the deaf: Psychology, principles, and practices* (4th ed.). Boston: Houghton Mifflin.

Morgan, C. D., & Murray, H. A. (1935). A method for investigating fantasies: The Thematic Apperception Test. *Archives of Neurology and Psychiatry, 34*, 289–306.

Morgan, D. P., & Jensen, W. R. (1988). *Teaching behaviorally disordered students*. Upper Saddle River, NJ: Merrill/Prentice Hall.

Morgan, D., Young, K. R., Goldstein, S. (1983). Teaching behaviorally disordered students to increase teacher attention and praise in mainstreamed classrooms. *Behavioral Disorders, 8*, 265–273.

Morgan, S. R. (1987). *Abuse and neglect of handicapped children*. San Diego: College-Hill.

Morrison, G. S. (1998). *Early childhood education today* (7th ed.). Upper Saddle River, NJ: Merrill/Prentice Hall.

Morrison, R. S. (1999). Effects of correspondence training with photographic activity schedules on toy play by young children with pervasive developmental disorders. Unpublished doctoral dissertation, The Ohio State University, Columbus.

Morse, W. C. (1976). Worksheet on lifespace interviewing for teachers. In N. Long, W. Morse, & R. Newman (Eds.), *Conflict in the classroom* (pp. 337–341). Belmont, CA: Wadsworth.

Morse, W. C. (1985). *The education and treatment of socioemotionally impaired children and youth*. Syracuse, NY: Syracuse University Press.

Morten, W. L., Heward, W. L., & Alber, S. R. (1998). When to self-correct?: A comparison of two procedures on spelling performance. *Journal of Behavioral Education, 8*, 321–335.

Mount, B., & Zwernick, K. (1988). *It's never too early, it's never too late: A booklet about personal futures planning*. St. Paul, MN: St. Paul Metropolitan Council.

Mow, S. (1973). How do you dance without music? In D. Watson (Ed.), *Readings on deafness* (pp. 20–30). New York: New York University School of Education, Deafness Research and Training Center.

Moyer, J. R., & Dardig, J. C. (1978). Practical task analysis for special educators. *Teaching Exceptional Children, 11*(1), 1–16.

Mudford, O. C. (1995). Review of the gentle teaching data. *American Journal on Mental Retardation, 99*, 345–355.

Mulick, J. A. (1990). The ideology and science of punishment in mental retardation. *American Journal on Mental Retardation, 95*, 142–156.

Mulick, J. A., & Antonak, R. (Eds.). (1994). *Life styles: Transitions in mental retardation* (vol. 5). Norwood, NJ: Ablex.

Munk, D. D., & Repp, A. C. (1994). The relationship between instructional variables and problem behavior: A review. *Exceptional Children, 60*, 390–401.

Munk, D. D., Van Laarhoven, T., Goodman, S., & Repp, A. C. (1998). Small-group Direct Instruction for students with moderate to severe disabilities. In A. Hilton & R. Ringlaben (Eds.), *Best and promising practices in developmental disabilities* (pp. 127–138). Austin, TX: PRO-ED.

Myers, P. I., & Hammill, D. D. (1990). *Learning disabilities: Basic concepts, assessment practices, and instructional strategies* (3rd ed.). Austin, TX: PRO-ED.

Nagel, D., Schumaker, J. B., & Deshler, D. D. (1986). *The learning strategies curriculum: The FIRST-letter mnemonic strategy*. Lawrence, KS: Excel Enterprises.

Naglieri, J. A., & Pfeiffer, S. I. (1992). Performance of disruptive behavior by behavior disordered and normal samples on the Draw a Person: Screening Procedure for Emotional Disturbance. *JCCP: Psychological Assessment, 4*, 156–159.

Naglieri, J. A., McNeish, T. J., & Bardos, A. N. (1991). *Draw a Person: Screening Procedure for Emotional Disturbance*. Austin, TX: PRO-ED.

Napierkowski, H. (1981). The role of language in the intellectual development of the deaf child. *Teaching Exceptional Children, 14*, 106–109.

Narayan, J. S., Heward, W. L., Gardner, R., III, Courson, F. H., & Omness, C. (1990). Using response cards to increase student participation in an elementary classroom. *Journal of Applied Behavior Analysis, 23*, 483–490.

National Center for Education Statistics. (1997, December 17). Dropout rates remain stable over last decade. [http://nces.ed.go/pressrelease/dropout.html]

National Center for Juvenile Justice. (1998). Crime statistics. [http//:www.ncjj.org/]

National Hotel and Restaurant Association. (1983). Personal communication with Dr. Philip Nelen, Washington, DC.

National Joint Committee on Learning Disabilities (1989, September 18). Letter from NJCLD to member organizations. Topic: Modifications to the NJCLD definition of learning disabilities.

National Joint Committee on Learning Disabilities. (1994). *Collective perspectives on issues affecting learning disabilities: Position papers and statements*. Austin, TX: PRO-ED.

National Joint Committee on Learning Disabilities. (1998). Operationalizing the NJCLD definition of learning disabilities for ongoing assessment in schools. *Learning Disabilities Quarterly, 21*, 186–193.

Nechring, W. M., & Steele, S. (1996). Cerebral palsy. In P. L. Jackson & J. A. Vessey (Eds.), *Primary care of the child with a chronic condition* (2nd ed.) (pp. 232–254). St. Louis: Mosby.

Neef, N. A. (Guest Ed.). (1994). *Journal of Applied Behavior Analysis, 27*(2) [Special issue], 196–418.

Neef, N. A., et al. (1998). *Caring for persons with developmental disabilities: A training program for respite care providers*. Champaign, IL: Research Press.

Neef, N. A., Parrish, J. M. Egel, A. L., & Sloan, M. E. (1986). Training respite care providers for families with handicapped children: Experimental analysis and validation of an instructional package. *Journal of Applied Behavior Analysis, 19,* 105–124.

Neel, R. S., & Billingsley, F. F. (1989). *IMPACT: A functional curriculum for students with moderate to severe disabilities*. Baltimore: Brookes.

Neisworth, J. T., & Smith, R. M. (Eds.). (1978). *Retardation: Issues, assessment, and intervention.* New York: McGraw-Hill.

Nelson, C. M., Rutherford, R. B., Jr., & Wolford, B. I. (1987). *Special education in the criminal justice system.* Upper Saddle River, NJ: Merrill/Prentice Hall.

Nelson, J. R., Smith, D. J., Young, R. K., & Dodd, J. M. (1991). A review of self-management outcome research conducted with students who exhibit behavioral disorders. *Behavioral Disorders*, *16*, 169–179.

Nelson, K. B., & Ellenberg, J. H. (1986). Antecedents of cerebral palsy: Multivariate analysis of risk. *New England Journal of Medicine*, *315*, 81–86.

Neubert, D. A. (1997). The history—and future—of preparing youth for adult roles in society. *Teaching Exceptional Children, 29*(5), 5–17.

Nevin, A., McCann, S., & Semmel, M. I. (1983). An empirical analysis of the regular classroom teacher's role in implementing IEPs. *Teacher Education and Special Education*, *6*, 235–246.

Newborg, J., Stock, J., Wnek, J., Guidubaldi, & Suinicki, J. (1988). *Battelle Developmental Inventory*. Chicago: Riverside.

Newcomber, P. L., & Hammill, D. D. (1988). *Tests of language development* (2nd ed.). Austin, TX: PRO-ED.

Newcomer, P. L., & Barenbaum, E. M. (1991). The written composing ability of children with learning disabilities: A review of the literature from 1980 to 1990. *Journal of Learning Disabilities, 24,* 578–593.

Newman, R. S., & Golding, L. (1990). Children's reluctance to seek help with school work. *Journal of Educational Psychology, 82,* 92–100.

Newton, J. S., Horner, R. H., & Lund, L. (1991). Honoring activity preferences in individualized plan development. *Journal of The Association for Persons with Severe Handicaps*, *16*, 207–212.

Nietupski, J., & Svoboda, R. (1982). Teaching a cooperative leisure skill to severely handicapped adults. *Education and Training of the Mentally Retarded*, *17*, 38–43.

Nietupski, J., Verstegen, D., & Hamre-Nietupski, S. (1992). Incorporating sales and business practices into job development in supported employment. *Education and Training in Mental Retardation*, *27*, 207–218.

Nihira, K., Leland, H. & Lambert, N., K. (1993). *Adaptive Behavior Scale—Residential and Community* (2nd ed.). Austin, TX: PRO-ED.

Nisbet, J., & Hagner, D. (1988). Natural supports in the workplace: A reexamination of supported employment. *Journal of The Association for Persons with Severe Handicaps*, *13*, 260–267.

Nisbet, J., & Vincent, L. (1986). The differences in inappropriate behavior and instructional interactions in sheltered and nonsheltered work environments. *Journal of The Association for Persons with Severe Handicaps*, *11*, 19–27.

Noonan, M. J., & McCormick, L. (1993). *Early intervention in natural environments.* Pacific Grove, CA: Brooks/Cole.

Noonan, M. J., Brown, F., Mulligan, M., & Rettig, M. A. (1982). Educability of severely handicapped persons: Both sides of the issue. *Journal of The Association for the Severely Handicapped*, *7*(1), 3–12.

Norris, C. (Ed.). (1975). *Letters from deaf students.* Eureka, CA: Alinda.

Northern, J. L., & Downs, M. P. (1991). *Hearing in children* (4th ed.). Baltimore: Williams & Wilkins.

Northern, J. L., & Lemme, M. (1982). Hearing and auditory disorders. In G. H. Shames & E. H. Wiig (Eds.), *Human communication disorders: An introduction.* Upper Saddle River, NJ: Merrill/Prentice Hall.

Northup, J., Fusilier, I., Swanson, V., Roane, H., & Borrero, J. (1997). An evaluation of methylphenidate as a potential establishing operation for some common classroom reinforcers. *Journal of Applied Behavior Analysis, 30,* 615–625.

Norton, L. S., & Hartley, J. (1986). What factors contribute to good examination marks? The role of notetaking in subsequent examination performance. *Higher Education*, *15*, 355-371.

Notari-Syverson, A. R., & Shuster, S. L. (1995). Putting real-life skills into IEP/IFSPs for infants and young children. *Teaching Exceptional Children*, *27*(2), 29–32.

O'Brien, J. (1971). How we detect mental retardation before birth. *Medical Times*, *99*, 103.

O'Brien, J. (1987). A guide to life-style planning: Using the activity catalog to integrate services and natural life support systems. In B. Wilcox & G. T. Bellamy (Eds.), *A comprehensive guide to the activities catalog: An alternative curriculum for youth and adults with severe disabilities* (pp. 175–189). Baltimore: Brookes.

O'Brien, J., Forest, M., Snow, J., & Hasbury, D. (1989). *Action for inclusion*. Toronto: Frontier College Press.

O'Connell, J. C. (1986). Managing small group instruction in an integrated preschool setting. *Teaching Exceptional Children*, *18*, 166–171.

O'Neill, R. E., Horner, R. H., Albin, R. W., Sprague, J. R., Storey, K., & Newton, J. S. (1997). *Functional assessment and program development for problem behavior: A practical handbook*. Pacific Grove, CA: Brooks/Cole.

O'Shea, L. J., Sindelar, P. T., & O'Shea, D. J. (1985). The effects of repeated readings and attentional cues on reading fluency and comprehension. *Journal of Reading Behavior, 17*, 129–142.

Obiakor, F. E., Algozzine, B., & Ford, B. A. (1993). Urban education, the General Education Initiative, and service delivery to African-American students. *Urban Education, 28*, 313–327.

Ochoa, S. H., & Palmer, D. J. (1995). A meta-analysis of peer rating sociometric studies with learning disabled pupils. *Journal of Special Education, 29*, 1–9.

Odom, S. L. & McClean, M. E. (Eds.). (1996). *Early intervention/early childhood special education: Recommended practices*. Austin, TX: PRO-ED.

Odom, S. L., McConnell, S. R. & McEvoy, M. M. (1992). *Social competence of young children with disabilities: Nature, development, and intervention*. Baltimore: Brookes.

Office of Technology Assessment. (1987). *Technology-dependent children: Hospital v. home care—A technical memorandum.* OTA-TM-H-38. Washington, DC: Author.

Olympia, D., Andrews, D., Valum, L., & Jensen, W. (1993). *Homework teams: Homework management strategies for the classroom*. Longmont, CO: Sopris West.

Orelove, F. P. (1982). Acquisition of incidental learning in moderately and severely handicapped adults. *Education and Training of the Mentally Retarded, 17*, 131–136.

Orelove, F. P. (1984). The educability debate: A review and a look ahead. In W. L. Heward, T. E. Heron, D. S. Hill, & J. Trap-Porter (Eds.), *Focus on behavior analysis in education* (pp. 271–281). Upper Saddle River, NJ: Merrill/Prentice Hall.

Orelove, F. P., & Sobsey, D. (1996). *Educating children with multiple disabilities: A transdisciplinary approach* (3rd ed.). Baltimore: Brookes.

Orlansky, M. D. (1981). The deaf/blind and the severely/profoundly handicapped: An emerging relationship. In S. R. Walsh & R. Holzberg (Eds.), *Understanding and educating the deaf-blind/severely profoundly handicapped* (pp. 5–24). Springfield, IL: Thomas.

Orlansky, M. D., & Bonvillian, J. D. (1985). Sign language acquisition: Language development in children of deaf parents and implications for other populations. *Merrill-Palmer Quarterly, 31*, 127–143.

Orlansky, M. D., & Heward, W. L. (1981). *Voices: Interviews with handicapped people.* Upper Saddle River, NJ: Merrill/Prentice Hall.

Orr, L. E., Craig, G. P., Best, J., Borland, A., Holland, D., Knodel, H., Lehman, A., Mathewson, C., Miller, M., & Pequignot, M. (1997). Exploring developmental disabilities through literature: An annotated bibliography. *Teaching Exceptional Children, 29*(6), 14–15.

Ortiz, A. A. (1991a). *AIM for the BESt: Assessment and intervention model for the bilingual exceptional student. A technical report for the Innovative Approaches Research Project*. Austin: University of Texas (ERIC Document No. 341 194).

Ortiz, A. A. (1991b). *AIM for the BESt: Assessment and intervention model for the bilingual exceptional student. A handbook for teachers and planners from the Innovative Approaches Research Project*. Austin: University of Texas (ERIC Document No. 341 195).

Ortiz, A. A., & Garcia, S. (1988). A prereferral process for preventing inappropriate referrals of Hispanic students to special education. In A. Ortiz & B. A. Ramirez (Eds.), *Schools and the culturally diverse exceptional student: Promising practices and future directions* (pp. 6–18). Reston, VA: Council for Exceptional Children.

Ortiz, V., & Gonzales, A. (1991). Gifted Hispanic adolescents. In M. Bireley & J. Genshaft (Eds.), *Understanding the gifted adolescent* (pp. 240–247). New York: Teachers College Press.

Oswald, D. P. (1994). Facilitator influence in facilitated communication. *Journal of Behavioral Education, 4*, 191–200.

Owens, R. E. (1995). Development of communication, language, and speech. In G. H. Shames & E. H. Wiig (Eds.), *Language disorders: A functional approach to assessment and intervention* (2nd ed., pp. 36–81). Needham Heights, MA: Allyn & Bacon.

Owens, R. E. (1996). *Language development: An introduction* (4th ed.). Boston: Allyn & Bacon.

Packman, A., & Onslow, M. (1998). What is the take-home message from Curlee and Yairi? *American Journal of Speech-Language Pathology, 7*, 5–9.

Pados, G. (1989). A comparison of the effects of students' own notes and guided notes on the daily quiz performance of fifth-grade students. Unpublished master's thesis, The Ohio State University, Columbus.

Page, E. B. (1972). Miracle in Milwaukee: Raising the IQ. *Educational Researcher, 15*, 8–16.

Palincsar, A. L. (1998). Keeping the metaphor of scaffolding fresh. *Journal of Learning Disabilities, 31*, 370–373.

Palincsar, A. S., Brown, A. L., & Campione, J. C. (1993). First grade dialogues for knowledge acquisition and use. In E. A. Forman, N. Minick, & C. A. Stone (Eds.), *Contexts for learning: Sociocultural dynamics in children's development* (pp. 43–57). New York: Oxford University Press.

Pancsofar, E., & Blackwell, R. (1986). *A user's guide to community entry for the severely handicapped.* Albany: State University of New York Press.

Panerai, S., Ferrante, L., Caputo, V., & Impellizzeri, C. (1998). Use of structured teaching for the treatment of children with autism and severe and profound mental retardation. *Education and Training in Mental Retardation and Developmental Disabilities, 33,* 367–374.

Parette, H. P. (1998). Assistive technology effective practices for students with mental retardation and developmental disabilities. In A. Hilton and R. Ringlaben (Eds.), *Best and promising practices in developmental disabilities* (pp. 205–224). Austin, TX: PRO-ED.

Parette, H. P., & Angelo, D. H. (1996). Augmentative and alternative communication impact on families: Trends and future directions. *Journal of Special Education, 30,* 77–98.

Parette, H. P., & Brotherson, M. J. (1996). Family participation in assistive technology assessment for young children with mental retardation and developmental disabilities. *Education and Training in Mental Retardation and Developmental Disabilities, 31,* 29–43.

Parette, H. P., Jr., & Hourcade, J. J. (1986). Management strategies for orthopedically handicapped students. *Teaching Exceptional Children, 18*(4), 282–286.

Parette, H. P., Jr., Hourcade, J. J., & VanBiervliet, A. (1993). Selection of appropriate technology for children with disabilities. *Teaching Exceptional Children, 25*(3), 18–22.

Parette, H. R., & Bartlett, C. S. (1996). Collaboration and ecological assessment: Bridging the gap between medical and educational environments for students who are medically fragile. *Physical Disabilities: Education and Related Services, 15*(1), 33–47.

Parham, J. L. (1983). A meta-analysis of the use of manipulative materials and student achievement in elementary school mathematics. Doctoral dissertation, Auburn University, Auburn, AL. (*Dissertation Abstracts International,* 96, 44A)

Parsons, M. B., McCarn, J. E., & Reid, D. H. (1993). Evaluating and increasing meal-related choices throughout a service setting for people with severe disabilities. *Journal of The Association for Persons with Severe Handicaps, 18,* 253–260.

Passow, A. H., & Rudnitski, R. A. (1994). Transforming policy to enhance educational services for the gifted. *Roeper Review, 16*(4), 271–275.

Patterson, G. R. (1979/1998). *Living with children: New methods for parents and teachers*. Champaign, IL: Research Press.

Patterson, G. R. (1980). Mothers: The unacknowledged victims. *Monographs of the Society for Research in Child Development, 45*(5). (Serial No. 186)

Patterson, G. R. (1982). *Coercive family process*. Eugene, OR: Castilia.

Patterson, G. R., Cipaldi, D., & Bank, L. (1991). An early starter model for predicting delinquency. In D. J. Pepler & K. H. Rubin (Eds.), *The development and treatment of childhood aggression* (pp. 139–168). Hillsdale, NJ: Erlbaum.

Patterson, G. R., Reid, J. B., & Dishion, T. J. (1992). *Antisocial boys.* Vol. 4: *A social interactional approach*. Eugene, OR: Castalia.

Patterson, J. M., & Leonard, B. J. (1994). Caregiving and children. In E. Kahan, D. Biegel, & M. Wykle (Eds.), *Family caregiving across the lifespan* (pp. 133–158). Beverly Hills, CA: Sage.

Patton, J. M. (1992). Assessment and identification of African-American learners with gifts and talents. *Exceptional Children, 59,* 150–159.

Patton, J. R., Cronin, M. E., & Jairrels, V. (1997). Curricular implications of transition: Life-skills instruction as an integral part of transition education. *Remedial and Special Education, 18,* 294–306.

Patton, J. R., Polloway, E. A., Smith, T. E. C., Edgar, E., Clark, G. M., & Lee, S. (1996). Individuals with mild mental retardation: Postsecondary outcomes and implications for educational policy. *Education and Training in Mental Retardation and Developmental Disabilities, 31,* 75–85

Patton, P. L., de la Graza, B., & Harmon, C. (1997). Successful employment. *Teaching Exceptional Children, 29*(3), 4–10.

Paul, P. V., & Quigley, S. P. (1990). *Education and deafness.* New York: Longman.

Paul, P. V., & Quigley, S. P. (1994). *Language and deafness* (2nd ed.). San Diego: Singular.

Pava, W. S. (1994). Visually impaired persons' vulnerability to sexual and physical assault. *Journal of Visual Impairment and Blindness, 88,* 103–112.

Pava, W. S., Bateman, P., Appleton, M. K., & Glascock, J. (1991). Self-defense training for visually impaired women. *Journal of Visual Impairment and Blindness, 85,* 397–401.

Peacock Hill Working Group. (1991). Problems and promises in special education and related services for children and youth with emotional or behavioral disorders. *Behavioral Disorders, 16,* 299–313.

Pearson, S. (1996). Child abuse among children with disabilities. *Teaching Exceptional Children, 29*(1), 34–37.

Peck, C. A., Odom, S. L., & Bricker, D. D. (1993). *Integrating young children with disabilities into community programs*. Baltimore: Brookes.

Peckham, V. C. (1993). Children with cancer in the classroom. *Teaching Exceptional Children, 26*(1), 27–32.

Pedley, T. A., Scheuer, M. L., & Walczak, T. S. (1995). Epilepsy. In L. P. Rowland (Ed.), *Merritt's textbook of neurology* (9th ed.) (pp. 845–868). Baltimore: Williams & Wilkins.

Pellegrino, L. (1997). Cerebral palsy. In M. L. Batshaw (Ed.), *Children with disabilities* (4th ed.) (pp. 499–528). Baltimore: Brookes.

Pendergast, K., Dickey, S., Selmar, J., & Soder, A. (1984). *Photo Articulation Test*. Austin, TX: PRO-ED.

Pennhurst State School and Hospital v. Halderman, 446 F. Supp. 1295 (E. D. Pa. 1981).

Pennington, B. F. (1995). Genetics of learning disabilities. *Journal of Child Neurology, 10,* 69–77.

Pennsylvania Association for Retarded Children v. Commonwealth of Pennsylvania, 343 F. Supp. 279 (1972).

Pennypacker, H. S., Koenig, C., & Lindsley, O. (1972). *Handbook of the standard behavior chart*. Kansas City, MO: Precision Media.

Perkins School for the Blind. (1978). *Sign language curricula*. Watertown, MA: Author.

Perlmutter, J., & Burrell, L. (1995, January). Learning through play as well as work. *Young Children,* pp. 14–21.

Perrin, E. C., Newacheck, P., Pless, B., Drotar, D., Gortmaker, S. L., Leventhal, J., Perrin, J. M., Stein, R. E. K., Walker, D. K., & Weitzman, M. (1993). Issues involved in the definition and classification of chronic health conditions. *Pediatrics, 91,* 787–793,

Pester, E. (1993). Braille instruction for individuals who are blind adventitiously: Scheduling, expectation, and reading interests. *RE:view*, *25*, 83–87.

Peterson, C. A., & Gunn, S. L. (1984). *Therapeutic recreation* (2nd ed.). Upper Saddle River, NJ: Prentice Hall.

Peterson, R., Benson, D., Edwards, L., Rosell, J., & White, M. (1986). Inclusion of socially maladjusted children and youth in the legal definition of the behaviorally disordered population: A debate. *Behavioral Disorders*, *11*, 213–222.

Pieper, B., & Cappuccilli, J. (1980). Beyond the family and the institution: The sanctity of liberty. In T. Apolloni, J. Cappuccilli, & T. P. Cooke (Eds.), *Achievements in residential services for persons with disabilities: Toward excellence.* Baltimore: University Park Press.

Pieper, E. (1983). *The teacher and the child with spina bifida* (2nd ed.). Rockville, MD: Spina Bifida Association of America.

Piirto, J. (1992). *Understanding those who create*. Dayton: Ohio Psychology Press.

Piirto, J. (1999). *Talented children and adults* (2nd ed.). Upper Saddle River, NJ: Merrill/Prentice Hall.

Plummer, D. (1995). Serving the needs of gifted children from a multicultural perspective. In J. L. Genshaft, M. Bireley, & C. L. Hollinger (Eds.), *Serving gifted and talented students: A resource for school personnel* (pp. 285–300). Austin, TX: PRO-ED.

Pogrund, R. L., & Rosen, S. J. (1989). The preschool child can be a cane user. *Journal of Visual Impairment and Blindness*, *83*, 431–439.

Pogrund, R. L., Fazzi, D. L., & Schreier, E. M. (1993). Development of a preschool "kiddy cane." *Journal of Visual Impairment and Blindness*, *87*, 52–54.

Polloway, E. A. (1984). The integration of mildly retarded students in the schools: A historical review. *Remedial and Special Education*, *5*(4), 18–28.

Polloway, E. A., Cronin, M. E., & Patton, J. R. (1986). The efficacy of group versus one-to-one instruction: A review. *Remedial and Special Education*, *7*(1), 22–30.

Polloway, E. A., Patton, J. R., Smith, T. E. C., & Buck, G. H. (1997). Mental retardation and learning disabilities: Conceptual and applied issues. *Journal of Learning Disabilities, 30,* 297–308.

Polloway, E. A., Smith, J. D., Patton, J. R., & Smith, T. E. C. (1996). Historic changes in mental retardation and developmental disabilities. *Education and Training in Mental Retardation and Developmental Disabilities, 31,* 3–12.

Porretta, D. L., Gillespie, M., & Jansma, P. (1996). Perceptions about Special Olympics from service delivery groups in the United States: A preliminary investigation. *Education and Training in Mental Retardation and Developmental Disabilities, 31,* 44–54.

Porter, S., Haynie, M., Bierle, T., Caldwell, T. H., & Palfrey, J. S. (1997). *Children and youth: Assisted by medical technology in educational settings: Guidelines for care* (2nd ed.). Baltimore: Brookes.

Potts, L., Eshleman, J. W., & Cooper, J. O. (1993). Ogden R. Lindsley and the historical development of precision teaching. *Behavior Analyst*, *16*, 177–189.

Poulton, S. (1996). Guidelines to writing individualized healthcare plans. [http://www.nursing.uiowa.edu/www/nursing/courses/96-22/students/sp1996/96-222WEguideline/htm]

Powell, D. S., Batsche, C. J., Ferro, J., Fox, L., & Dunlap, G. (1997). A strength-based approach in support of multi-risk families: Principles and issues. *Topics in Early Childhood Special Education, 17*(1), 1–26.

Poyadue, F. S. (1993). Cognitive coping at Parents Helping Parents. In A. P. Turnbull, J. M. Paterson, S. K. Behr, D. L. Murphy, J. G. Marquis, & M. J. Blue-Banning (Eds.), *Cognitive coping, families, and disability* (pp. 95–110). Baltimore: Brookes.

Prendergast, D. E. (1995). Preparing for children who are medically fragile in educational programs. *Teaching Exceptional Children*, *27*(2), 37–41.

Prinz, P. M., & Prinz, E. A. (1979). Simultaneous acquisition of ASL and spoken English in a hearing child of a deaf mother and hearing father. *Sign Language Studies*, *25*, 283–296.

Prinz, P. M., Strong, M., Kuntze, M., Vincent, J., Friedman, J., Moyers, P. P., & Helman, E. (1996). A path to literacy through ASL and English for deaf children. In C. E. Johnson & J. H. V. Gilbert (Eds.), *Children's language* (Vol. 9) (pp. 235–251). Mahwah, NJ: Erlbaum.

Provencal, G. (1980). The Macomb-Oakland regional center. In T. Apolloni, J. Cappucilli, & T. P. Cooke (Eds.), *Achievements in residential services for persons with disabilities: Toward excellence* (pp. 19–43). Baltimore: University Park Press.

Public Law 95-561. Gifted and Talented Children's Education Act. *Congressional Record* (1978, October 10). H-12179.

Pueschel, S. M. (1991). Ethical considerations relating to prenatal diagnosis of fetuses with Down syndrome. *Mental Retardation, 29*, 185–190.

Pugach, M. C., & Johnson, L. J. (1989). Prereferral interventions: Progress, problems, and challenges. *Exceptional Children, 56*, 217–226.

Pugach, M. C., & Warger, C. L. (1993). Curriculum considerations. In J. I. Goodlad & T. C. Lovitt (Eds.), *Integrating general and special education* (pp. 125–148). Upper Saddle River, NJ: Merrill/Prentice Hall.

Putnam, J. W. (1998). *Cooperative learning and strategies for inclusion: Celebrating diversity in the classroom* (2nd ed.). Baltimore: Brookes.

Ramey, C. T., & Ramey, S. L. (1992). Effective early intervention *Mental Retardation, 30*, 337–345.

Ramey, C. T., Bryant, D. M., Wasik, B. H., Sparling, J. J., Fendt, K. H., & LaVange, L. M. (1992). The Infant Health and Development Program for low birthweight, premature infants: Program elements, family participation, and child intelligence. *Pediatrics, 89*, 454–465.

Ramirez, M., & Casteñeda, A. (1974). *Cultural democracy, bicognitive development, and education*. New York: Academic Press.

Rand, M. (1994). Using thematic instruction to organize an integrated language arts curriculum. In L. M. Morrow, J. Smith, & L. C. Wilkinson (Eds.), *The integrated language arts: Controversy to consensus* (pp. 177–192). Needham Heights, MA: Allyn & Bacon.

Rapport, M. J. K., & Thomas, S. B. (1993). Extended school year: Legal issues and implications. *Journal of The Association for Persons with Severe Handicaps, 18*, 16–27.

Rapport, M. J., K. (1996). Legal guidelines for the delivery of health care services in schools. *Exceptional Children, 62,* 537–549.

Raschke, D. B., Dedrick, C. V. L., Heston, M. L., & Farris, M. (1996). Everyone can play! Adapting the Candy Land board game. *Teaching Exceptional Children, 28*(4), 28–33.

Raskin, D. (1990). Fast brakes. *American Health, 9*(6), 24.

Raver, S. (1984). Modification of head droop during conversation in a 3-year-old visually impaired child: A case study. *Journal of Visual Impairment and Blindness, 78,* 307–310.

Raver, S. A. (1999). *Intervention strategies for infants and toddlers with special needs: A team approach* (2nd ed). Upper Saddle River, NJ: Merrill/Prentice Hall.

Rawlings, B. W., & King, S. J. (1986). Postsecondary educational opportunities for deaf students. In A. N. Schildroth & M. A. Karchmer (Eds.), *Deaf children in America* (pp. 231–257). San Diego: College-Hill.

Reed, V. A. (1998). *An introduction to children with language disorders* (3rd ed.). Needham Heights, MA: Allyn & Bacon.

Reichle, J. (1997). Communication intervention with persons who have severe disabilities. *Journal of Special Education, 31,* 110–134.

Reichle, J., & Keogh, W. J. (1986). Communication instruction for learners with severe handicaps: Some unresolved issues. In R. H. Horner, L. H. Meyer, & H. D. B. Fredericks (Eds.), *Education of learners with severe handicaps: Exemplary service strategies* (pp. 189–219). Baltimore: Brookes.

Reid, D. H., & Favell, J. (1984). Group instruction with persons who have severe disabilities: A critical review. *The Journal of The Association for Persons with Severe Handicaps, 9*, 167–177.

Reid, R., Maag, J. W., & Vasa, S. F. (1994). Attention deficit hyperactivity disorder as a disability category: A critique. *Exceptional Children, 60*, 198–214.

Reiff, H. B., Gerber, P. J, & Ginsberg, R. (1993). Definitions of learning disabilities from adults with learning disabilities: The insiders' perspectives. *Learning Disability Quarterly, 16*, 114–125.

Reis, S. (1995). What gifted education can offer the reform movement: Talent development. In J. L. Genshaft, M. Bireley, & C. L. Hollinger (Eds.), *Serving gifted and talented students: A resource for school personnel* (pp. 371–387). Austin, TX: PRO-ED.

Reis, S. M., & Cellerino, M. (1983). Guiding gifted students through independent study. *Teaching Exceptional Children, 15*, 136–139.

Reis, S. M., Neu, T. W., & McGuire, J. M. (1995). *Talents in two places: Case studies of high ability students with learning disabilities who have achieved* (Research Monograph 95114). Storrs: University of Conneticut, National Research Center on the Gifted and Talented.

Reis, S. M., Westberg, K. L., Kulikowich, J. M., & Purcell, J. H. (1998). Curriculum compacting and achievement: What does the research say? *Gifted Child Quarterly, 42*(2), 41–45.

Reiss, S. (1994). Issues in defining mental retardation. *American Journal on Mental Retardation, 99*, 1–7.

Renzulli, J. (1998). *Relationship between gifted programs and total school improvement using the schoolwide enrichment model*. Storrs: University of Connecticut, National Resource Center on the Gifted and Talented.

Renzulli, J. S. (1978). What makes giftedness?: Reexamining a definition. *Phi Delta Kappan, 61*, 180–184.

Renzulli, J. S., & Reis, S. M. (1997). The schoolwide enrichment model: New directions for developing high-end learning. In N. Colangelo & G. A. Davis (Eds.), *Handbook of gifted education* (2nd ed.) (pp. 136–154) Needham Heights, MA: Allyn & Bacon.

Renzulli, J., & Reis, S. (1986). The enrichment triad/revolving door model: A schoolwide plan for the development of creative productivity. In J. Renzulli (Ed.), *Systems and models for developing programs for the gifted and talented*. Mansfield Center, CT: Creative Learning Press.

Renzulli, J., Reis, S., & Smith, L. (1981). *The revolving door identification model.* Mansfield Center, CT: Creative Learning Press.

Repp, A. C., & Singh, N. N. (Eds.). (1990). *Perspectives on the use of nonaversive and aversive interventions for persons with developmental disabilities.* Sycamore, IL: Sycamore.

Repucci, N. D., Britner, P. A., & Wollard, J. L. (1997). *Preventing children abuse and neglect through parent education*. Baltimore: Brookes.

Reschly, D. J. (1996). Identification and assessment of students with disabilities. *Future of Children, 6*(1), 40–53.

Revell, W. G., Wehman, P., Kregel, J., West, M., & Rayfield, R. (1994). Supported employment for persons with severe disabilities: Positive trends in wages, models, and funding. *Education and Training in Mental Retardation*, *29*, 256–264.

Reynolds, C. R. (1992). Two key concepts in the diagnosis of learning disabilities and the habilitation of learning. *Learning Disability Quarterly*, *15*, 2–12.

Reynolds, M. C. (1989). An historical perspective: The delivery of special education to mildly disabled and at-risk students. *Remedial and Special Education*, *10*(6), 7–11.

Reynolds, M. C., & Heistad, D. (1991). Classification and labeling. In J. W. Lloyd, N. N. Singh, & A. C. Repp (Eds.), *The regular education initiative: Alternative perspectives on concepts, issues, and models* (pp. 29–42). Sycamore, IL: Sycamore.

Reynolds, M. C., & Heistad, D. (1997). 20/20 analysis: Estimating school effectiveness in serving students at the margins. *Exceptional Children, 63,* 439–449.

Reynolds, M. C., Wang, M. C., & Walberg, H. J. (1987). The necessary restructuring of special and regular education. *Exceptional Children*, *53*, 391–398.

Reynolds, M. C., Zetlin, A. G., & Heistad, D. (1996). *A manual for 20/20 analysis*. Philadelphia: Temple University, Center for Research in Human Development and Education. [ERIC Document Reproduction Service No. ED 358 183]

Reynolds, M. C., Zetlin, A. G., & Wang, M. C. (1993). 20/20 analysis: Taking a close look at the margins. *Exceptional Children*, *59*, 294–300.

Rhoads, G. G., Jackson, L. G., Schlesselman, S. E., de la Cruz, F. F., Desnick, R. J., Golbus, M. S., Ledbetter, D. H., Lubs, H. A., Mahoney, M. J., Pergament, E., Simpson, J. L., Carpenter, R. J., Elias, S., Ginsberg, N. A., Goldberg, J. D., Hobbins, J. C., Lynch, L., Shiono, P. H. K., Wapner, R. J., & Zachary, J. M. (1989). The safety and efficacy of chorionic villus sampling for early prenatal diagnosis of cytogenetic abnormalities. *New England Journal of Medicine*, *320*, 609–617.

Rhode, G., Jensen, W. R., & Reavis, H. K. (1998). *The tough kid book: Practical classroom management strategies.* Longmont, CO: Sopris West.

Rhode, G., Morgan, D. P., & Young, K. R. (1983). Generalization and maintenance of treatment gains of behaviorally handicapped students from resource rooms to regular classrooms using self-evaluation procedures. *Journal of Applied Behavior Analysis*, *16*, 171–188.

Rhodes, L. E., & Valenta, L. (1985). Industry-based supported employment: An enclave approach. *Journal of The Association for Persons with Severe Handicaps*, *10*, 12–20.

Rhodes, W. C., & Head, S. (Eds.). (1974). *A study of child variance.* Vol. 3: *Service delivery systems.* Ann Arbor: University of Michigan Press.

Rhodes, W. C., & Tracy, M. L. (Eds.). (1972a). *A study of child variance.* Vol. 1: *Theories.* Ann Arbor: University of Michigan Press.

Rhodes, W. C., & Tracy, M. L. (Eds.). (1972b). *A study of child variance.* Vol. 2: *Interventions.* Ann Arbor: University of Michigan Press.

Rhyne, J. M. (1982). Comprehension of synthetic speech by blind children. *Journal of Visual Impairment and Blindness*, *76*, 313–316.

Ricci-Balich, J., & Behm, J. A. (1996). Pediatric rehabilitation nursing. In S. P. Hoeman (Ed.), *Rehabilitation nursing: Process and application* (pp. 660–682). St. Louis: Mosby.

Richardson, P., & Schwartz, I. S. (1998). Making friends in preschool: Friendship patterns of young children with disabilities. In L. Meyer, H. Park, M. Grenot-Scheyer, I. Schwartz, & B. Harry (Eds.), *Making friends: The influences of culture and development* (pp. 65–80). Baltimore: Brookes.

Richert, E. S., Alvino, J., & McDonnel, R. (1981). *The national report on identification: Assessment and recommendations for comprehensive identification of gifted and talented youth*. Sewell, NJ: U.S. Department of Education, Educational Information and Resource Center.

Richman, G. S., Harrison, K. A., & Summers, J. A. (1995). Assessing and modifying parent responses to their children's noncompliance. *Education and Treatment of Children, 18*(2), 105–116.

Rikhye, C. H., Gothelf, C. R., & Appell, M. W. (1989). A classroom environment checklist for students with dual sensory impairments. *Teaching Exceptional Children*, *22*(1), 44–46.

Rimland, B. (1993a). Beware the advozealots: Mindless good intentions injure the handicapped. *Autism Research Review International*, *7*(4), 1.

Rimland, B. (1993b). Inclusive education: Right for some. *Autism Research Review International*, *7*(1), 3.

Rindfuss, J. B., Al-Attrash, M., Morrison, H., & Heward, W. L. (1998,

May). Using guided notes and response cards to improve quiz and exam scores in an eighth grade American history class. Paper presented at the 24th annual convention of the Association for Behavior Analysis, Orlando, FL.

Ritvo, E. R., & Freeman, B. J. (1978). National Society of Autistic Children definition of the syndrome of autism. *Journal of Autism and Developmental Disorders, 8,* 162–170.

Roberts, J. E., Wallace, I. F., & Henderson, F. W. (1997). *Otitis media in young children: Medical, developmental, and education considerations.* Baltimore: Brookes.

Roberts, J., Rescorla, L., Giroux, J., & Stevens, L. (1998). Phonological skills of children with specific expressive language impairment (SLI-E). *Journal of Speech, Language, and Hearing Research, 41,* 374–384.

Robins, L. (1966). *Deviant children grown up.* Baltimore: Williams & Wilkins.

Robins, L. N. (1979). Follow-up studies. In H. C. Quay & J. S. Werry (Eds.), *Psychopathological disorders of childhood* (2nd ed., pp. 483–513). New York: Wiley.

Robinson, N. M., & Noble, K. D. (1991). Social-emotional development and adjustment of gifted children. In M. C. Wang, M. C. Reynolds, & H. J. Walberg (Eds.), *Handbook of special education: Research and practice.* Vol. 4: *Emerging programs* (pp. 57–76). New York: Pergamon.

Robinson, T. L., Jr., & Crowe, T. A. (1998). Culture-based considerations in programming for stuttering intervention with African American clients and their families. *Language, Speech, and Hearing Services in the Schools, 29,* 172–179.

Rockwell, S., & Guetzloe, E. (1996). Group development for students with emotional/behavioral disorders. *Teaching Exceptional Children, 29*(1), 38–43.

Rodden-Nord, K., & Shinn, M. R. (1991). The range of reading skills within and across general education classrooms: Contributions to understanding special education for students with mild handicaps. *Journal of Special Education, 24,* 441–453.

Roeser, R., & Yellin, W. (1987). Pure-tone tests with preschool children. In F. Martin (Ed.), *Hearing disorders in children: Pediatric audiology* (pp. 217–264). Austin, TX: PRO-ED.

Rogan, P., Hagner, D., & Murphy, S. (1993). Natural supports: Reconceptualizing job coach roles. *Journal of The Association for Persons with Severe Handicaps, 18,* 275–281.

Rogers, C. (1983). *Freedom to learn for the 80's.* Upper Saddle River, NJ: Merrill/Prentice Hall.

Rogers-Dulan, J. (1998). Religious connectedness among urban African-American families who have a child with disabilities. *Mental Retardation, 36,* 91–103.

Rogers-Warren, A., & Warren, S. (1980). Mands for verbalization: Facilitating the generalization of newly trained language in children. *Behavior Modification, 4,* 320–345.

Romer, L. T., & Haring, N. G. (1994). The social participation patterns of students with deaf-blindness in educational settings. *Education and Training in Mental Retardation and Developmental Disabilities, 29,* 134–144.

Romer, L. T., White, J., & Haring, N. G. (1996). The effect of peer mediated social competency training on the type and frequency of social contacts with students with deaf-blindness. *Education and Training in Mental Retardation and Developmental Disabilities, 31,* 324–338.

Rooney, K. J. (1991). Controversial therapies: A review and critique. *Intervention in School and Clinic, 26,* 134–142.

Roos, P. (1985). Parents of mentally retarded children—misunderstood and mistreated. In A. P. Turnbull & H. R. Turnbull (Eds.), *Parents speak out: Views from the other side of the two-way mirror* (2nd ed.) (pp. 245–257). Upper Saddle River, NJ: Merrill/Prentice Hall.

Rorschach, H. (1942). *Rorschach psychodiagnostic plates.* New York: Psychological Corporation.

Rosales, J., & Baer, D. M. (1998). *How to plan for generalization* (2nd ed.). Austin, TX: PRO-ED.

Rose, K. C., White, J. A., Conroy, J., & Smith, D. M. (1993). Following the course of change: A study of adaptive and maladaptive behaviors in young adults living in the community. *Education and Training in Mental Retardation, 28,* 149–154.

Rose, T. L., & Calhoun, M. L. (1990). The Charlotte Circle Project: A program for infants and toddlers with severe/profound disabilities. *Journal of Early Intervention, 14,* 175–185.

Roseberry-McKibbin, C. (1995, Summer). Distinguishing language differences from language disorders. *Multicultural Education,* pp. 12–15.

Rosenblum, L. P. (1997). Adolescents with visual impairments who have best friends: A pilot study. *Journal of Visual Impairment and Blindness, 91,* 225–235.

Rosenshine, B., & Stevens, R. (1986). Teaching functions. In M. C. Wittrock (Ed.), *Handbook on research in teaching* (3rd ed.) (pp. 376–391). New York: Macmillan

Ross, M. (1981). Review, overview, and other educational considerations. In M. Ross & L. W. Nober (Eds.), *Educating hard of hearing children* (pp. 102–116). Reston, VA: Council for Exceptional Children.

Ross, M. (1986). A perspective on amplification: Then and now. In D. M. Luterman (Ed.), *Deafness in perspective* (pp. 35–53). San Diego: College-Hill.

Rotegard, L. L., Hill, B. K., & Bruininks, R. H. (1983). Environmental characteristics of residential facilities for mentally retarded persons in the

United States. *American Journal of Mental Deficiency*, *88*, 49–56.

Rowitz, L. (1981). A sociological perspective on labeling and mental retardation. *Mental Retardation*, *19*, 47–51.

Rowland, C., & Schweigert, P. (1993). Analyzing the communication environment to increase functional communication. *Journal of The Association for Persons with Severe Handicaps*, *18*, 161–176.

Rowley-Kelly, F. L., & Teigel, D. H. (1993). *Teaching the student with spina bifida*. Baltimore: Brookes.

Rubin, R. A., & Balow, B. (1978). Prevalence of teacher identified behavior problems: A longitudinal study. *Exceptional Children*, *45*, 102–111.

Rueda, R. (1997). Changing the context of assessment: The move to portfolios and authentic assessment. In A. Artiles & G. Zamora-Durán (Eds.), *Reducing disproportionate representation of culturally diverse students in special and gifted education* (pp. 7–26). Reston, VA: Council for Exceptional Children.

Rugow, S. (1984). The uses of social routines to facilitate communication in visually impaired and multihandicapped children. *Topics in Early Childhood Special Education*, *3*(4), 67–70.

Rumberger, R. W., Ghatak, R., Polous, G., Ritter, P. L., & Dornbush, S. M. (1990). Family influences on dropout behavior in one California high school. *Sociology of Education, 63*, 283–299.

Rusch, F. (1990). *Supported employment: Models, methods, and issues.* Sycamore, IL: Sycamore.

Rusch, F. R., & Minch, K. E. (1988). Identification of co-worker involvement in supported employment: A review and analysis. *Research in Developmental Disabilities*, *9*, 247–254.

Rusch, F. R., & Schutz, R. P. (1981). Vocational and social work behavior: An evaluative review. In J. L. Matson & J. R. McCartney (Eds.), *Handbook of behavior modification with the mentally retarded* (pp. 247–280). New York: Plenum.

Rusch, F. R., Chadsey-Rusch, J., & Lagomarcino, T. (1987). Preparing students for employment. In M. E. Snell (Ed.), *Systematic instruction of persons with severe handicaps* (3rd ed.) (pp. 471–490). Upper Saddle River, NJ: Merrill/Prentice Hall.

Rusch, F. R., DeStefano, L., Chadsey-Rusch, J., Phelps, A., & Szymanski, E. (1992). *Transition from school to adult life: Models, linkages, and policy*. Pacific Grove, CA: Brooks/Cole.

Rusch, F. R., Hughes, C., McNair, J., & Wilson, P. G. (1990). *Co-worker involvement scoring manual and instrument.* Champaign: University of Illinois, Board of Trustees.

Rusch, F. R., Johnson, J. R., & Hughes, C. (1990). Analysis of co-worker involvement in relations to level of disability versus placement approach among supported employees. *Journal of The Association for Persons with Severe Handicaps*, *15*, 32–39.

Rutherford, R., Chipman, J., DiGangi, S., & Anderson, K. (1992). *Teaching social skills: A practical instructional approach*. Reston, VA: Council for Exceptional Children.

Rutter, M. (1976). *Helping troubled children.* New York: Plenum.

Rutter, M., & Schopler, E. (1987). Autism and pervasive developmental disorders: Concepts and diagnostic issues. *Journal of Autism and Developmental Disorders*, *17*, 159–186.

Ryan, C. S., & Coyne, A. (1985). Effects of group homes on neighborhood property values. *Mental Retardation*, *23*, 241–245.

Ryles, R. (1996). The impact of braille reading skills on employment, income, education, and reading habits. *Journal of Visual Impairment and Blindness, 90,* 219–226.

Sabornie, E. J., & Kauffman, J. M. (1986). Social acceptance of learning disabled adolescents. *Learning Disability Quarterly*, *9*, 55–60.

Sack, J. (1997, April 16). Disruptive special education students get own school. *Education Week on the Web*, 1–7.

Sacks, S. Z., & Corn, A. L. (1996). Students with visual impairments: Do they understand their disability? *Journal of Visual Impairment and Blindness, 90,* 412–422.

Safer, D. J., & Krager, J. M. (1988). A survey of medication treatment for hyperactive/inattentive students. *Journal of the American Medical Association*, *260*, 2256–2258.

Safford, P. L., & Safford, E. J. (1996). *A history of childhood disability*. New York: Teachers College Press.

Sailor, W., & Guess, D. (1983). *Severely handicapped students: An instructional design*. Boston: Houghton Mifflin.

Sailor, W., Anderson, J. L., Halvorsen, A. T., Doering, K., Filler, J., & Goetz, L. (1989). *The comprehensive local school: Regular education for all students with disabilities.* Baltimore: Brookes.

Sainato, D. M., & Lyon, S L. (1989). Promoting successful mainstreaming transitions for handicapped preschool children. *Journal of Early Intervention, 13*(4), 305–314.

Sainato, D. M., & Strain, P. S. (1993). Increasing integration success for preschoolers with disabilities. *Teaching Exceptional Children*, *25*(2), 36.

Sainato, D. M., Goldstein, H., & Strain, P. S. (1992). Effects of self-evaluation on preschool children's use of social interaction strategies with their autistic peers. *Journal of Applied Behavior Analysis*, *25*, 127–141.

Sainato, D. M., Strain, P. S., & Lyon, S. L. (1987). Increasing academic responding of handicapped preschool children during group instruction. *Journal of the Division of Early Childhood Special Education*, *12*, 23–30.

Salend, S. (1998). *Effective mainstreaming: Creating inclusive classrooms* (3rd ed.). Upper Saddle River, NJ: Merrill/Prentice Hall.

Salend, S. J. (1998). Using portfolios to assess student performance. *Teaching Exceptional Children, 31*(2), 36–43.

Salend, S. J., & Longo, M. (1994). The roles of the education interpreter in mainstreaming. *Teaching Exceptional Children, 26*(4), 22–28.

Salend, S. J., Ellis, L. L., & Reynolds, C. J. (1989). Using self-instruction to teach vocational skills to individuals who are severely retarded. *Education and Training of the Mentally Retarded, 24*, 248–254.

Salend, S. J., Jantzen, N. R., & Giek, K. (1992). Using a peer confrontation system in a group setting. *Behavioral Disorders, 17*, 211–218.

Salvia, J., & Hughes, C. (1990). *Curriculum-based assessment: Testing what is taught.* Upper Saddle River, NJ: Merrill/Prentice Hall.

Salvia, J., & Ysseldyke, J. E. (1995). *Assessment in special and remedial education* (6th ed.). Boston: Houghton Mifflin.

Sameroff, A. J., & Chandler, M. J. (1975). Reproductive risk and the continuum of caretaking casualty. In F. D. Horowitz (Ed.), *Review of child development research* (vol. 4) (pp. 187–244). Chicago: University of Chicago Press.

Sandler, A. G., & Mistretta, L. A. (1998). Positive adaptation in parents of adults with disabilities. *Education and Training in Mental Retardation and Developmental Disabilities, 33,* 123–130.

Sandler, A. G., Arnold, L. B., Gable, R. A., & Strain, P. S. (1987). Effects of peer pressure on disruptive behavior of behaviorally disordered students. *Behavioral Disorders, 16*, 9–22.

Sands, D. J., & Kozleski, E. B. (1994). Quality of life differences between adults with and without disabilities. *Education and Training in Mental Retardation, 29*, 90–101.

Sansone, J., & Zigmond, N. (1986). Evaluating mainstreaming through an analysis of students' schedules. *Exceptional Children, 52*, 452–458.

Santelli, B., Turnbull, A., Marquis, J., & Lerner, E. (1997). Parent-to-parent programs: A resource for parents and professionals. *Journal of Early Intervention, 21,* 73–83.

Santos, K. E. (1992). Fragile X syndrome: An educator's role in identification, prevention, and intervention. *Remedial and Special Education, 13*, 32–39.

Saski, J., Swicegood, P., & Carter, J. (1983). Notetaking formats for learning disabled adolescents. *Learning Disability Quarterly, 6*, 265–270.

Savage, R. C., & Wolcott, G. F. (Eds.). (1994). *Educational dimensions of acquired brain injury*. Austin, TX: PRO-ED.

Scarcella, R. (1990). *Teaching language minority students in the multicultural classroom.* Upper Saddle River, NJ: Merrill/Prentice Hall.

Schalock, R. L. (1996). *Quality of life: Application to persons with disabilities*. Washington, DC: American Association on Mental Retardation.

Schalock, R. L., Harper, R. S., & Carver, G. (1981). Independent living placement: Five years later. *American Journal of Mental Deficiency, 86*, 170–177.

Schalock, R. L., Keith, K. D., Hoffman, K., & Karan, O. C. (1989). Quality of life: Its measurement and use. *Mental Retardation, 27*, 25–31.

Schalock, R. L., Stark, J. A., Snell, M. E., Coulter, D. L., Polloway, E. A., Luckasson, R., Reiss, S., & Spitalnik, D. M. (1994). The changing conception of mental retardation: Implications for the field. *Mental Retardation, 32,* 181–193.

Schalock, R., & Bogale, M. J. (Eds.) (1990). *Quality of life: Perspectives and issues*. Washington, DC: American Association on Mental Retardation.

Schenck, S. (1980). The diagnostic/instructional links in individualized education programs. *Journal of Special Education, 14*, 337–345.

Schildroth, A. N., Rawlings, B. W., & Allen, R. E. (1989). Hearing-impaired children under age 6: A demographic analysis. *American Annals of the Deaf, 134,* 63–69.

Schirmer, B. R. (1997). Boosting reading success: Language, literacy, and content area instruction for deaf and hard-of-hearing students. *Teaching Exceptional Children, 30*(1), 52–55.

Schirmer, B. R. (1998). Hearing loss. In A. Turnbull, R. Turnbull, M. Shank, & D. Leal (Eds.), *Exceptional lives: Special education in today's schools* (pp. 620–660). Upper Saddle River, NJ: Merrill/Prentice Hall.

Schirmer, B. R. (2000). *Language and literacy development in children who are deaf* (2nd ed.). Needham Heights, MA: Allyn & Bacon.

Schirmer, B. R., & Woolsey, M. L. (1997). Effect of teacher questions on the reading comprehension of deaf children. *Journal of Deaf Studies and Deaf Education, 2,* 47–56.

Schleien, S. J., Kiernan, J., & Wehman, P. (1981). Evaluation of an age-appropriate leisure skills program for moderately retarded adults. *Education and Training of the Mentally Retarded, 16*, 13–19.

Schleien, S. J., Meyer, L. H., Heyne, L. A., & Brandt, B. B. (1995). *Lifelong leisure skills and lifestyles for persons with developmental disabilities*. Baltimore: Brookes.

Schleien, S. J., Wehman, P., & Kiernan, J. (1981). Teaching leisure skills to severely handicapped adults: An age-appropriate darts game. *Journal of Applied Behavior Analysis, 14*, 513–519.

Schleien, S., Ray, M., & Green, F. (1997). *Community recreation and persons with disabilities: Strategies for inclusion* (2nd ed.). Baltimore: Brookes.

Schloss, P. J., Alexander, N., Hornig, E., Parker, K., & Wright, B. (1993). Teaching meal preparation vocabulary and procedures to individuals with mental retardation. *Teaching Exceptional Children, 25*(3), 7–12.

Schloss, P. J., Alper, S., Young, H., Arnold-Reid, G., Aylward, M., &

Dudenhoeffer, S. (1995). Acquisition of functional sight words in community-based recreation settings. *Journal of Special Education, 29,* 84–96.

Schneider, B. H., & Leroux, J. (1994). Educational environments for the pupil with behavioral disorders: A "best evidence" synthesis. *Behavioral Disorders, 19,* 192–204.

Scholl, G. T. (1986). Multicultural considerations. In G. T. Scholl (Ed.), *Foundations of education for blind and visually handicapped children and youth* (pp. 165–182). New York: American Foundation for the Blind.

Scholl, G. T. (1987). Appropriate education for visually impaired students. *Teaching Exceptional Children, 19*(2), 33–36.

Scholl, G. T. (Ed.). (1986). *Foundations of education for blind and visually handicapped children and youth: Theory and practice.* New York: American Foundation for the Blind.

Schonert-Reichl, K. A. (1993). Empathy and social relationships in adolescents with behavioral disorders. *Behavioral Disorders, 18,* 189–204.

Schopler, E., Reichler, R. J., & Renner, B. R. (1988). *The Childhood Autism Rating Scale.* Los Angeles: Western Psychological Services.

Schreier, E. M., Leventhal, J. D., & Uslan, M. M. (1991). Access technology for blind and visually impaired persons. *Technology and Disability, 1*(1), 19–23.

Schroeder, S. (Ed.). (1987). *Toxic substances and mental retardation: Neurobiological toxicology and teratology.* Washington, DC: American Association on Mental Retardation.

Schulz, J. B. (1985). The parent-professional conflict. In H. R. Turnbull & A. P. Turnbull (Eds.), *Parents speak out: Then and now* (pp. 3–11). Upper Saddle River, NJ: Merrill/Prentice Hall.

Schumaker, J. B., & Deshler, D. D. (1992). Validation of learning strategy interventions for students with learning disabilities: Results of a programmatic research effort. In B. Y. L. Wong (Ed.), *Contemporary intervention research in learning disabilities* (pp. 22–46). New York: Springer-Verlag.

Schumaker, J. B., & Sheldon, J. (1985). *The sentence writing strategy.* Lawrence: University of Kansas Press.

Schumm, J. S., Vaughn, D., Haager, D., McDowell, J., Rothlein, L., & Saumell, L. (1995). General education teacher planning: What can students with learning disabilities expect? *Exceptional Children, 61,* 335–352.

Schwartz, I. S., & Baer, D. M. (1991). Social validity assessments: Is current practice state of the art? *Journal of Applied Behavior Analysis, 24,* 189–204.

Schwartz, I. S., Billingsley, F. F., & McBride, B. M. (1998). Including children with autism in inclusive preschools: Strategies that work. *Young Exceptional Children, 1*(2), 19–26.

Schwartz, I. S., Garfinkle, A. N., & Bauer, J. (1998). The picture exchange communication system: Communication outcomes for young children with disabilities. Manuscript submitted for publication.

Scott, M. L., Ebbert, A., & Price, D. (1986). Assessing and teaching employability skills with prevocational work samples. *Directive Teacher, 8*(1), 3–5.

Scruggs, T. E., & Mastropieri, M. A. (1992). Classroom applications of mnemonic instruction: Acquisition, maintenance, and generalization. *Exceptional Children, 58,* 219–229.

Scruggs, T. F., & Mastropieri, M. A. (1995). What makes special education special? Evaluating inclusion programs with the PASS variables. *Journal of Special Education, 29,* 224–233.

Scuccimarra, D. J., & Speece, D. L. (1990). Employment outcomes and social integration of students with mild handicaps: The quality of life two years after high school. *Journal of Learning Disabilities, 23,* 213–219.

Secord, W. (1981). *Test of Minimal Articulation Competence.* Upper Saddle River, NJ: Merrill/Prentice Hall.

Seltzer, M. M., Krauss, M. W., & Janicki, M. P. (1994). *Life course perspectives on adulthood and old age.* Washington, DC: American Association on Mental Retardation.

Semel, E. M., & Wiig, E. H. (1980). *Clinical evaluation of language functions.* Upper Saddle River, NJ: Merrill/Prentice Hall.

Serna, L. (1993). Social skills instruction. In E. A. Polloway & J. R. Patton, *Strategies for teaching learners with special needs* (5th ed.) (pp. 437–458). Upper Saddle River, NJ: Merrill/Prentice Hall.

Sexson, S. B., & Madan-Swain, A. (1993). School reentry for the child with chronic illness. *Journal of Learning Disabilities, 26,* 115–125.

Sexton, M., Harris, K. R., & Graham, S. (1998). Self-regulated strategy development and the writing process: Effects on essay writing and attributions. *Exceptional Children, 64,* 295–311.

Seymour, F. W., & Stokes, T. F. (1976). Self-recording in training girls to increase work and evoke staff praise in an institution for offenders. *Journal of Applied Behavior Analysis, 9,* 41–54.

Seymour, H. N., Bland-Stewart, L., & Green, L. J. (1998). Difference versus deficit in child African American English. *Language, Speech, and Hearing Services in the Schools, 29,* 96–108.

Shade, B. J., & New, C. A. (1993). Cultural influences on learning: Teaching implications. In J. A. Banks & C. A. M. Banks (Eds.), *Multicultural education: Issues and perspectives* (2nd ed.) (pp. 317–331). Needham Heights, MA: Allyn & Bacon.

Shafer, M. S., Rice, M. L., Metzler, H. M. D., & Haring, M. (1989). A survey of nondisabled employees' attitudes toward supported employees with mental retardation. *Journal of The Association for Persons with Severe Handicaps*, *14*, 137–146.

Shames, G. H., Wiig, E. H., & Secord, W. A. (1998). *Human communication disorders* (5th ed.). Boston: Allyn & Bacon.

Shannon, G. (1985). Characteristics influencing current recreational patterns of persons with mental retardation. Unpublished doctoral dissertation, Brandeis University, Waltham, MA.

Shapiro, J. P., Loeb, P., & Bowermaster, D., & Toch, T. (1993, December 13). Separate and unequal: How special education programs are cheating our children and costing taxpayers billions of dollars. *U.S. News and World Report*, *115*(23), 46–60.

Shaywitz, S. E., Shaywitz, B. A., Pugh, K. R., Skudlarski, P., Fulbright, R. K., Constable, T., Bronen, R. A., Fletcher, J. M., Liberman, A. M., Shankweiler, D. P., Katz, L., Lacadi, C., & Gore, J. C. (in press). The neurobiology of developmental reading disorders as viewed through the lens of neuroimaging technology. In G. R. Lyon & J. Ramsey (Eds.), *Neuroimaging: A window to the neurological foundations of learning and behavior*. Baltimore: Brookes.

Shearer, M. S., & Shearer, D. E. (1972). The Portage Project: A model for early childhood education. *Exceptional Children*, *39*, 210–217.

Shelton, T. L., & Barkely, R. A. (1994). Critical issues in the assessment of attention deficit disorders in children. *Journal of Learning Disabilities, 14,* 26–41.

Shevin, M., & Klein, N. K. (1984). The importance of choice-making skills for students with severe disabilities. *Journal of The Association for Persons with Severe Handicaps, 9,* 159–166.

Shewan, C. M. (1986). Characteristics of clinical services provided by ASHA members. *ASHA*, *28*(1), 29.

Shields, J., & Heron, T. E. (1989). Teaching organizational skills to students with learning disabilities. *Teaching Exceptional Children*, *21*(2), 8–13.

Shildroth, A. N., & Hotto, S. A. (1994). Inclusion or exclusion? Deaf students and the inclusion movement. *American Annals of the Deaf, 139,* 239–242.

Shildroth, A. N., Rawlings, B. W., & Allen, T. E. (1989). Hearing impaired children under age 6: A demographic analysis. *American Annals of the Deaf, 134,* 63–69.

Shivers, J. S., & Fait, H. F. (1985). *Special recreational services: Therapeutic and adapted.* Philadelphia: Lea & Febiger.

Shonkoff, J. P., & Meisels, S. J. (1990). Early childhood intervention: The evaluation of a concept. In S. J. Meisels & J. P. Shonkoff (Eds.), *Handbook of early childhood intervention* (pp. 3–32). New York: Cambridge University Press.

Shonkoff, J. P., & Meisels, S. J. (1991). Defining eligibility for services under PL 99-457. *Journal of Early Intervention*, *15*, 21–25.

Shores, R. E., Gunter, P. L., & Jack, S. L. (1993). Classroom management strategies: Are they setting events for coercion? *Behavioral Disorders*, *18*, 92–102.

Siccone, F. (1995). *Celebrating diversity: Building self-esteem in today's multicultural classrooms*. Boston: Allyn & Bacon.

Sicley, D. (1993). Effective methods of communication: Practical interventions for classroom teachers. *Intervention in School and Clinic*, *29*, 105–108.

Sidman, M. (1989). *Coercion and its fallout*. Boston: Authors Group.

Siegel, B. (1996). *The world of the autistic child*. New York: Oxford University Press.

Siegel, L. J., & Senna, J. J. (1991). *Juvenile delinquency: Theory, practice, and law* (5th ed.). St. Paul, MN: West.

Siegel, S., Robert, M., Greener, K., Meyer, G., Halloran, W., & Gaylord-Ross, R. (1993). *Career ladders for challenged youths in transition from school to adult life*. Austin, TX: PRO-ED.

Sievert, A. L., Cuvo, A. J., & Davis, P. K. (1988). Training self-advocacy skills to adults with mild handicaps. *Journal of Applied Behavior Analysis*, *21*, 299–309.

Silliman , E. R., & Wilkinson, L. C. (1991). *Communicating for learning: Classroom observation and collaboration*. Gaithersburg, MD: Aspen.

Silliman, E. R. & Wilkinson, L. C. (1994). Discourse scaffolds for classroom intervention. In G. P. Wallach & K. G. Butler (Eds.), *Language learning disabilities in school-age children and adolescents: Some principles and applications* (pp. 27–52). Needham Heights, MA: Allyn & Bacon.

Silliman, E. R., Mills, L. R., & Murphy, M. M. (1997). How to start? One story of change in a middle school. In N. W. Nelson & B. Hoskins (Eds.), *Strategies for supporting classroom success* (pp. 1–22). San Diego: Singular.

Silver, L. B. (1990) Attention-deficit-hyperactivity disorder: Is it a learning disability or a related disorder? *Journal of Learning Disabilities, 23,* 394–397.

Silver, L. B. (1993). On the occasion of the 30th anniversary of LDA: Learn from the past, look to the future. *LDA Newsbrief*, *28*(2), 12–13.

Silverman, L. K. (1986). Parenting young gifted children. *Journal of Children in Contemporary Society*, *18*, 73–87.

Silverman, L. K. (1989). The highly gifted. In J. F. Feldhusen, J. VanTassel-Baska, & K. Seeley (Eds.), *Excellence in educating the gifted* (pp. 71–83). Denver: Love.

Silverman, L. K. (1993). *Counseling the gifted and talented*. Denver: Love.

Silverman, L. K. (1995). Highly gifted children. In J. L. Genshaft, M. Bireley, & C. L. Hollinger (Eds.), *Serving gifted and talented students: A resource for school personnel* (pp. 124–160). Austin, TX: PRO-ED.

Simes, K. J. (1997) World wide web resources for individuals who are deaf or hard of hearing, their families, and the professionals who serve them. *Rural Special Education Quarterly, 16*(2), 44–49.

Simmons, D. C., Fuchs, D., & Fuchs, L. S., Hodge, J. P., & Mathes, P. G. (1994). Inclusive schools movement and the radicalization of special education reform. *Learning Disabilities: Research and Practice*, *9*, 203–212

Simmons, D. C., Kameenui, E. J., & Chard, D. J. (1998). General education teachers' assumptions about learning and students with learning disabilities: Design-of-instruction analysis. *Learning Disability Quarterly, 21,* 6–21.

Simon, R. (1987). *After the tears: Parents talk about raising a child with a disability.* San Diego: Harcourt Brace Jovanovich.

Simons, J. A. (1998). Response to Chesley and Calaluce on inclusion. *Mental Retardation, 35,* 322–324.

Simpson, R. L. (1996). *Working with families and parents of exceptional children and youth: Techniques for successful conferencing and collaboration* (3rd ed.). Austin, TX: PRO-ED.

Simpson, R. L., & Myles, B. S. (1995). Effectiveness of facilitated communication with children and youth with autism. *Journal of Special Education, 28,* 424–439.

Sims, D. G., & Gottermeier, L. (1995). Computer-assisted, interactive video methods for speechreading instruction: A review. In K. Erik-Spens & G. Plant (Eds.), *Speech, communication and profound deafness* (pp. 220–241). London: Whurr.

Sinclair, E., Del'Homme, M., & Gonzalez, M. (1993). Systematic screening for preschool behavioral disorders. *Behavioral Disorders*, *18*, 177–188.

Singer, G. H. S., & Powers, L. E. (1993). *Families, disability, and empowerment: Active coping skills and strategies for family interventions*. Baltimore: Brookes.

Singh, N. N., & Ellis, C. R. (1993). *Effects of school, child and family variables on drug responsiveness of children with ADHD* (Proposal funded by the Office of Special Education and Rehabilitative Services: CFDA No. 84.023C). Washington, DC.

Sisk, D. (1987). *Creative teaching of the gifted*. New York: McGraw-Hill.

Sitlington, P., & Frank, A. (1990). Are adolescents with learning disabilities successfully crossing the bridge into adult life? *Learning Disability Quarterly*, *13*, 97–111.

Sitlington, P. L. (1996). Transition to living: The neglected component of transition programming for individuals with learning disabilities. *Journal of Learning Disabilities, 29,* 31–39, 52.

Sitlington, P. L., Frank, A. R., & Carson, R. (1993). Adult adjustment among high school graduates with mild disabilities. *Exceptional Children*, *59*, 221–233.

Skeels, H. M. (1966). Adult status of children with contrasting early life experiences. *Monographs of the Society for Research in Child Development*, *31* (No. 3).

Skeels, H. M., & Dye, H. B. (1939). A study of the effects of differential stimulation on mentally retarded children. *Convention Proceedings, American Association on Mental Deficiency*, *44*, 114–136.

Skellenger, A., Hill, E., & Hill, M. (1992). The social functioning of children with visual impairments. In S. L. Odom, S. R. McConnell, & M. A. McEvoy (Eds.), *Social competence of young children with disabilities: Issues and strategies for intervention* (pp. 165–188). Baltimore: Brookes.

Skinner, B. F. (1974). *About behaviorism*. New York: Knopf.

Skinner, M. (1998). Promoting self-advocacy among college students with learning disabilities. *Intervention in School and Clinic, 33*(5), 278–283.

Skinner, M. E., & Schenck, S. J. (1992). Counseling the college-bound student with a learning disability. *School Counselor, 39*(5), 369–376.

Slade, J. C., & Conoley, C. W. (1989). Multicultural experiences for special educators. *Teaching Exceptional Children*, *22*(1), 60–64.

Slaton, D. E., Schuster, J., Collins, B., & Carnine, D. (1994). A functional approach to academic instruction. In E. Cipani & F. Spooner (Eds.), *Curricular and instructional approaches for persons with severe disabilities* (pp. 149–183). Boston: Allyn & Bacon.

Smith, D. D., & Luckasson, R. (1995). *Introduction to special education: Teaching in an age of challenge* (2nd ed.). Boston: Allyn & Bacon.

Smith, J. D. (1994). The revised AAMR definition of mental retardation: The MRDD position. *Education and Training in Mental Retardation*, *29*, 179–183.

Smith, J. D., & Hilton, A. (1997). The preparation and training of the educational community for the inclusion of students with developmental disabilities: The MRDD position. *Education and Training of Mental Retardation and Developmental Disabilities, 32,* 3–10.

Smith, L., & Fowler, S. A. (1984). Positive peer pressure: The effects of peer monitoring on children's disruptive behavior. *Journal of Applied Behavior Analysis*, *17*, 213–227.

Smith, O. S. (1984). Severely and profoundly physically handicapped students. In P. J. Valletutti & B. M. Sims-Tucker (Eds.), *Severely and profoundly handicapped students: Their nature and needs* (pp. 85–152). Baltimore: Brookes.

Smith, S. W. (1990a). Comparison of Individualized Education Programs (IEPs) of students with behavioral disorders and learning disabilities. *Journal of Special Education*, *24*(1), 85–100.

Smith, S. W. (1990b). Individualized Education Programs (IEPs) in special education—From intent to acquiescence. *Exceptional Children, 57*, 6–14.

Smith, S. W., & Farrell, D. T. (1993). Level system use in special education: Classroom intervention with prima facie appeal. *Behavioral Disorders, 18*, 251–264.

Smith, S. W., & Simpson, R. L. (1989). An analysis of individualized education programs (IEPs) for students with behavioral disorders. *Behavioral Disorders, 14*, 107–116.

Smith, S., Bone, R., & Higgins, K. (1998). Expanding the writing process to the web. *Teaching Exceptional Children, 30*(5), 22–26.

Smith, T. E. C., & Hilton, A. (1994). Program design for students with mental retardation. *Education and Training in Mental Retardation, 29*, 3–8.

Smithdas, R. (1981). Psychological aspects of deaf-blindness. In S. R. Walsh & R. Holzberg (Eds.), *Understanding and educating the deaf-blind/severely and profoundly handicapped: An international perspective.* Springfield, IL: Thomas.

Snarr, R. W., & Wolford, B. I. (1985). *Introduction to corrections.* Dubuque, IA: Brown.

Snell, M. E. (1991). Schools are for all kids: The importance of integration for students with severe disabilities and their peers. In J. W. Lloyd, A. C. Repp, & N. N. Singh (Eds.), *The regular education initiative: Alternative perspectives on concepts, issues, and models* (pp. 133–148). Sycamore, IL: Sycamore.

Snell, M. E. (in press). Characteristics of elementary school classrooms where children with moderate and severe disabilities are included: A compilation of findings. In D. Mithaug & S. J. Vitello (Eds.), *Inclusive schooling: National and international perspectives*. New York: Erlbaum.

Snell, M. E., & Beckman-Brindley, S. (1984). Family involvement in intervention with children having severe handicaps. *Journal of The Association for Persons with Severe Handicaps, 9*, 213–230.

Snell, M. E., & Brown, F. (Eds.). (2000). *Instruction of students with severe disabilities* (5th ed.). Upper Saddle River, NJ: Merrill/Prentice Hall.

Snell, M. E., Lewis, A. P., & Houghton, A. (1989). Acquisition and maintenance of toothbrushing skills by students with cerebral palsy and mental retardation. *Journal of The Association for Persons with Severe Handicaps, 14*, 216–226.

Sobsey, D. (1994). *Violence and abuse in the lives of people with disabilities: The end of silent acceptance?* Baltimore: Brookes.

Sobsey, D. (1996). Review of assistive technologies: Principles and practice by A. M. Cook & S. M. Hussey. *Journal of The Association for Persons with Severe Handicaps, 21,* 207–209.

Sontag, E., & Haring, N. G. (1996). The professionalization of teaching and learning for children with severe disabilities: The creation of TASH. *Journal of The Association for Persons with Severe Handicaps, 21,* 39–45.

Sontag, E., Sailor, W., & Smith, J. (1977). The severely/profoundly handicapped: Who are they? Where are we? *Journal of Special Education, 11*(1), 5–11.

Sontag, J. C., & Schacht, R. (1994). An ethnic comparison of parent participation and information needs in early intervention. *Exceptional Children, 60*, 422–433.

Soodak, L. C., & Podell, D. M. (1994). A response to Reynolds, Zetlin, and Wang's "20/20 analysis: Taking a closer look at the margins." *Exceptional Children, 60*, 276–277.

Southeastern Community College v. Davis, 442 U.S. 397 (1979).

Southern, W. T., & Jones, E. (1991). *The academic acceleration of gifted children.* New York: Teachers College Press.

Sowers, J., Verdi, M., Bourbeau, P., & Sheehan, M. (1985). Teaching job independence to mentally retarded students through the use of a self-control package. *Journal of Applied Behavior Analysis, 18,* 81–85.

Spache, G. D. (1963). *Diagnostic Reading Scales.* Monterey, CA: California Test Bureau.

Spache, G. D. (1981). *Diagnostic Reading Scales*. Monterey, CA: CTB McGraw-Hill.

Sparrow, S. S., Balla, D. A., & Cicchetti, D. V. (1984). *Vineland Adaptive Behavior Scales.* Circle Pines, MN: American Guidance Service.

Special Olympics. (1991). *Special Olympics International official media guide*. Washington, DC: Author.

Speece, D. L., & Harry, B. (1997). Classification for children. In J. W. Lloyd, E. J. Kameenui, & D. Chard (Eds.), *Issues in educating students with disabilities* (pp. 63–73). Mahwah, NJ: Erlbaum.

Spenciner, L. J. (1972). Differences between blind and partially sighted children in rejection by sighted peers in integrated classrooms, grades 2–8. In B. W. Tuckman (Ed.), *Conducting educational research.* New York: Harcourt Brace Jovanovich.

Spitz, H. H. (1996). Comment on Donnellan's review of Shane's (1994) "Facilitated Communication: The clinical and social phenomenon." *American Journal on Mental Retardation, 101,* 96–100.

Spivak, M. P. (1986). Advocacy and legislative action for head-injured children and their families. *Journal of Head Trauma Rehabilitation, 1*, 41–47.

Spooner, F. H., & Test, D. W. (1994). Domestic and community living skills. In E. Cipani & F. H. Spooner (Eds.), *Curricular and instructional approaches for persons with severe disabilities* (pp. 149–183). Boston: Allyn & Bacon.

Sprague, J. R., & Horner, R. H. (1984). The effects of single instance, multiple instance, and general case training on generalized vending machine used by moderately and severely handicapped students. *Journal of Applied Behavior Analysis*, *17*, 273–278.

Spratt, R. H. (1999, January). Personal communication.

Sprick, R. S., & Howard, L. M. (1997). *The teacher's encyclopedia of behavior management: 100 problems/500 plans*. Longmont, CO: Sopris West.

Spring, C., & Sandoval, J. (1976). Food additives and hyperkinesis: A critical evaluation of the evidence. *Journal of Learning Disabilities*, *9*, 560–569.

Stainback, S., & Stainback, W. (1992). *Curriculum considerations in inclusive classrooms: Facilitating learning for all students*. Baltimore: Brookes.

Stainback, S., & Stainback, W. (Eds.). (1991). *Teaching in the inclusive classroom: Curriculum design, adaptation and delivery.* Baltimore: Brookes.

Stainback, S., & Stainback, W. (Eds.). (1992). *Inclusion: A guide for educators*. Baltimore: Brookes.

Stainback, S., & Stainback, W. (Eds.) (1996). *Inclusion: A guide for educators* (2nd ed.). Baltimore: Brookes.

Stancliffe, R. J., & Hayden, C. (1998). Longitudinal study of institutional downsizing: Effects on individuals who remain in the institution. *American Journal on Mental Retardation, 102,* 500–510.

Stancliffe, R. J., & Lakin, K. C. (1998). Analysis of expenditures and outcomes of residential alternatives for persons with developmental disabilities. *American Journal on Mental Retardation, 102,* 552–568.

Stanovich, K. E. (1991). Conceptual and empirical problems with discrepancy definitions of reading disability. *Learning Disability Quarterly*, *14*, 269–280.

Stanovich, K. E. (1993). The construct validity of discrepancy definitions of reading disability. In G. R. Lyon, D. Gray, J. Kavanagh, & N. Krasnegor (Eds.), *Better understanding of learning disabilities: New views on research findings and their implications for public policies*. Baltimore: Brookes.

Stanovich, K. E., & Siegel, L. S. (1994). The phenotypic performance profile of reading-disabled children: A regression-based test of the phonological-core variable-difference model. *Journal of Educational Psychology, 86,* 24–53.

Stanovich, K., & Stanovich, P. (1995). How research might inform the debate about early reading acquisition. *Journal of Reading Research, 18*(2), 87–105.

Stark, L. J., Knapp, L. G., Bowen, A. M., Powers, S. W., Jelalian, E., Evans, S., Passero, M. A., Mulvihill, M. M., & Hovell, M. (1993). Increasing calorie consumption in children with cystic fibrosis: Replication with 2-year follow-up. *Journal of Applied Behavior Analysis*, *26*, 435–450.

Starr, J. (1989). The great textbook war. In H. Holtz, I. Marcus, J. Dougherty, J. Michaels, & R. Peduzzi (Eds.), *Education and the American dream: Conservatives, liberals, and radicals debate the future of education* (pp. 96–109). Granby, MA: Bergin & Garvey.

Staub, D., & Peck, C. A. (1995). What are the outcomes for nondisabled students? *Educational Leadership, 52*(4), 36–40.

Staub, D., Schwartz, I. S., Gallucci, C., & Peck, C.A. (1994). Four portraits of friendship at an inclusive school. *Journal of The Association for Persons with Severe Handicaps, 19,* 314–325.

Staub, D., Spaulding, M., Peck, C. A., Gallucci, C., & Schwartz, I. S. (1996). Using nondisabled peers to support the inclusion of students with disabilities at the junior high school level. *Journal of The Association for Persons with Severe Handicaps, 21,* 194–205.

Steensma, M. (1992). Getting the student with head injuries back in school: Strategies for the classroom. *Intervention in School and Clinic*, *27*, 207–210.

Stein, L. (1988). Hearing impairment. In V. B. Van Hasselt, P. S. Strain, & M. Hersen (Eds.), *Handbook of developmental and physical disabilities* (pp. 271–294). New York: Pergamon.

Stein, M., Silbert, J., & Carnine, D. W. (1997). *Designing effective mathematics instruction: A Direct Instruction approach* (3rd ed.). Upper Saddle River, NJ: Merrill/Prentice Hall.

Stemley, J. (1993). Idea Puppy: Teaching preschool age children with disabilities to build independent work skills with the use of a self-operated audio prompt recording device. Unpublished master's thesis, The Ohio State University, Columbus.

Stephens, T. M., & Wolf, J. S. (1989). *Effective skills in parent/teacher conferencing* (2nd ed.). Columbus: The Ohio State University, College of Education, School Study Council of Ohio.

Sternberg, L. (Ed.). (1994). *Individuals with profound disabilities: Instructional and assistive strategies*. Austin, TX: PRO-ED.

Sternberg, R. (1988). *The triarchic mind: A new theory of human intelligence*. New York: Viking.

Stevenson, R. E., Massey, P. S., Schroer, R. J., McDermott, S., & Richter, B. (1996). Preventable fraction of mental retardation: Analysis based on individuals with severe mental retardation. *Mental Retardation, 34,* 182–188.

Stewart, D. A. (1992). Initiating reform in total communication programs. *Journal of Special Education*, *26*, 68–84.

Stewart, J. L. (1977). Unique problems of handicapped Native Americans. In *The White House Conference on Handicapped Individuals* (vol. 1) (pp. 438–444). Washington, DC: U.S. Government Printing Office.

Stocker, C. S. (1973). *Listening for the visually impaired: A teaching manual.* Springfield, IL: Thomas.

Stokes, T. F., Fowler , S. A., & Baer, D. M. (1978). Training preschool children to recruit natural communities of reinforcement. *Journal of Applied Behavior Analysis, 11,* 285–303.

Stokes, T. F., & Baer, D. M. (1977). An implicit technology of generalization. *Journal of Applied Behavior Analysis, 10*, 349–367.

Stokes, T. F., & Osnes, P. G. (1989). An operant pursuit of generalization. *Behavior Therapy*, *20*, 337–355.

Stone, C. A. (1998). The metaphor of scaffolding: Its utility for the field of learning disabilities. *Journal of Learning Disabilities, 31*, 344–364.

Stoner, G., Carey, S. P., Ikeda, M. J., & Shinn, M. R. (1994). The utility of curriculum-based measurement for evaluating the effects of methylphenidate on academic performance. *Journal of Applied Behavior Analysis*, *27,* 101–113.

Stowell, L. J., & Terry, C. (1977). Mainstreaming: Present shock. *Illinois Libraries, 59,* 475–477.

Strain, P. S., & Odom, S. L. (1986). Peer social initiations: Effective intervention for social skills development of exceptional children. *Exceptional Children*, *52*, 543–551.

Strain, P. S., & Smith, B. J. (1986). A counter-interpretation of early intervention effects: A response to Casto and Mastropieri. *Exceptional Children*, *53*, 260–265.

Straus, M. A., Gelles, R. J., & Steinmetz, S. K. (1980). *Behind closed doors: Violence in the American family.* New York: Anchor.

Strauss, A. A., & Lehtinen, L. E. (1947). *Psychopathology and education of the brain-injured child*. New York: Grune & Stratton.

Streissguth, A. P., Aase, J. M., Clarren, S. K., Randels, S. P., La Due, R. A., & Smith, D. F. (1991). Fetal alcohol syndrome in adolescents and young adults. *Journal of the American Medical Association*, *265*, 1961–1967.

Stremel, K., Molden, V., Leister, C., Matthews, J., Wilson, R., Goodall, D. V., & Hoston, J. (1990). *Communication systems and routines: A decision making process*. Washington, DC: U.S. Office of Special Education.

Strickland, B. B., & Turnbull, A. P. (1993). *Developing and implementing Individualized Education Programs* (3rd ed.). Upper Saddle River, NJ: Merrill/Prentice Hall.

Strickland, S. P. (1971). Can slum children learn? *American Education*, *7*(6), 3–7.

Strong, M., & Prinz, P. M. (1997). A study of the relationship between American Sign Language and English literacy. *Journal of Deaf Studies and Deaf Education, 2,* 36–46.

Stuart v. Nappi, 443 F. Supp. 1235 (D. Conn. 1978).

Stump, C. S., Lovitt, T. C., Fister, S., Kemp, K., Moore, R., & Schroeder, B. (1992). Vocabulary intervention for secondary-level youth. *Learning Disability Quarterly*, *15*, 207–222.

Sturdivant, C. (1992). Ownership, risk-taking, and collaboration in an elementary language arts classroom. *Volta Review, 94,* 371–375.

Sturm, J., & Nelson, N. W. (1997). Formal classroom lessons: New perspectives on a familiar discourse event. *Language, Speech, and Hearing Services in Schools, 28,* 255–273.

Sturmey, P., & Sevin, J. A. (1994). Defining and assessing autism. In J. L. Matson (Ed.), *Autism in children and adults: Etiology, assessment, and intervention* (pp. 13–36). Pacific Grove, CA: Brooks/Cole.

Sugai, G., & Horner, R. H. (in press). Discipline and behavioral support: Preferred processes and practices. *Effective School Practices*.

Sugai, G., Horner, R. H., & Sprague, J. R. (in press). Functional assessment-based behavior support planning: Research-to-practice-to-research. *Education and Treatment of Children*.

Sullivan, P. M., & Knutson, J. F. (1994). *The relationship between child abuse and neglect and disabilities: Implications for research and practice*. Omaha, NE: Boys Town National Research Hospital.

Sulzbacher, S., Haines, R., Peterson, S. L., & Swatman, F. M. (1987). Encourage appropriate coffee break behavior. *Teaching Exceptional Children*, *19*(2), 8–12.

Sulzer-Azaroff, B., & Mayer, G. R. (1991). *Behavior analysis for Lasting change*. New York: Holt, Rinehart, & Winston.

Summers, M., Bridge, J., & Summers, C. R. (1991). Sibling support groups. *Teaching Exceptional Children*, *23*(4), 20–25.

Suritsky, S. K., & Hughes, C. A. (1991). Benefits of notetaking: Implications for secondary and postsecondary students with learning disabilities. *Learning Disability Quarterly*, *14*, 7–18.

Sutton, E., Factor, A. R., Hawkins, B. A., Heller, T. & Seltzer, G. B. (1993) *Older adults with developmental disabilities: Optimizing choice and change*. Baltimore: Brookes.

Swallow, R. M. (1978, May). Cognitive development. Paper presented at the North American Conference on Visually Handicapped Infants and Preschool Children, Minneapolis.

Swallow, R. M., & Conner, A. (1982). Aural reading. In S. S. Mangold (Ed.), *A teacher's guide to the special educational needs of blind and visually handicapped children* (pp. 119–135). New York: American Foundation for the Blind.

Swanson, J. M., McBurnett, K., Wigal, T., Pfiffner, L. J., Lerner, M. A., Williams, L., Christian, D. L., Tamm, L., Willcutt, E., Crowley, K., Clevenger, W., Khouzam, N., Woo, C., Crinella, F. M., & Fisher, T. D. (1993). Effect of stimulant medication on children with attention deficit disorder: A "review of reviews." *Exceptional Children*, *60*, 154–161.

Swassing, R. (1994). (Guest Ed.). Affective dimensions of being gifted. *Roeper Review, 17*(2).

Swiatek, M. A. (1993). A decade of longitudinal research on academic acceleration through the study of mathematically precocious youth. *Roeper Review*, *15*(3), 120–123.

Swiatek, M. A., & Benbow, C. P. (1991, November). Acceleration: Does it cause academic or psychological harm? Paper presented at the meeting of the National Association for Gifted Children, Little Rock, AR.

Syracuse University Center on Human Policy. (1987). *A statement on support of families and their children*. Syracuse, NY: Author.

Szymanski, E. M. (1994). Transition: Life-span and life-space considerations for empowerment. *Exceptional Children*, *60*, 402–410.

Tam, B. K. Y., & Heward, W. L. (1999). Effects of vocabulary instruction, error correction, and fluency-building on oral reading rate and reading comprehension by students with limited English proficiency. Manuscript submitted for publication.

Tannenbaum, A. (1983). *Gifted children: Psychological and educational perspectives*. Upper Saddle River, NJ: Merrill/Prentice Hall.

Tarver, S. G. (1998). Myths and truths about Direct Instruction. *Effective School Practices, 17*(1), 18–22.

Tawney, J. W. (1984). The pragmatics of the educability issue: Some questions which logically precede the assumption of ineducability. In W. L. Heward, T. E. Heron, D. S. Hill, & J. Trap-Porter (Eds.), *Focus on behavior analysis in education* (pp. 287–295). Upper Saddle River, NJ: Merrill/Prentice Hall.

Taylor, O. L., & Payne, K. T. (1994). Language and communication differences. In G. H. Shames & E. H. Wiig (Eds.), *Human communication disorders* (4th ed.) (pp. 136–173). Upper Saddle River, NJ: Merrill/Prentice Hall.

Taylor, S. J. (1988). Caught in the continuum: A critical analysis of the principle of the least restrictive environment. *Journal of The Association for Persons with Severe Handicaps*, *13*, 41–53.

Taylor, S. J., Bogdan, R., & Lutfiyya, Z. M. (1995). *The variety of community experience: Qualitative studies of family and community life*. Baltimore: Brookes.

Teacher Education Division. (1986). *The national inquiry into the future of education for students with special needs.* Reston, VA: Council for Exceptional Children.

Tedder, N. E., Warden, K., & Sikka, A. (1993). Prelanguage communication of students who are deaf-blind and have other severe impairments. *Journal of Visual Impairment and Blindness*, *87*, 302–307.

Terkel, S. (1974). *Working: People talk about what they do all day and how they feel about what they do.* New York: Pantheon.

Terman, L. (Ed.). (1925). *Genetic studies of genius* (vol. 1). Stanford, CA: Stanford University Press.

Terrell, S. L, & Terrell, F. (1993). African-American cultures. In D. E. Battle (Ed.), *Communications disorders in multicultural populations* (pp. 3–37). Boston: Andover Medical Publishers.

Test, D. W., & Spooner, F. (1996). *Community-based instructional support*. Washington, DC: American Association on Mental Retardation.

Test, D. W., & Spooner, F. (1996). *Task analysis*. Washington, DC: American Association on Mental Retardation.

Test, D. W., & Wood, W. M. (1996). Natural supports in the workplace: The jury is still out. *Journal of The Association for Persons with Severe Handicaps, 21,* 155–173.

Test, D. W., Cooke, N. L., Weiss, A. B., Heward, W. L., & Heron, T. E. (1986). A home-school communication system for special education. *Pointer*, *30*, 4–7.

Test, D. W., Grossi, T., & Keul, P. (1988). A functional analysis of the acquisition and maintenance of janitorial skills in a competitive work setting. *Journal of The Association for Persons with Severe Handicaps*, *13*, 1–7.

Test, D. W., Hinson, K. B., Solow, J., & Keul, P. (1993). Job satisfaction of persons in supported employment. *Education and Training in Mental Retardation*, *28*, 38–46.

Test, D. W., Spooner, F. H., Keul, P. K., & Grossi, T. A. (1990). Teaching adolescents with severe disabilities to use the public telephone. *Behavior Modification*, *14*, 157–171.

Tharp, R. G. (1994). Research knowledge and policy issues in cultural diversity and education. In B. McLeod (Ed.), *Language and learning: Educating linguistically diverse students* (pp. 129–167). Albany: State University of New York Press.

Thomas, C. C., Correa, V. I., & Morsink, C. V. (1995). *Interactive teaming: Consultation and collaboration in special programs* (2nd ed.). Upper Saddle River, NJ: Merrill/Prentice Hall.

Thomas, G., & Jackson, G. (1986). The whole-school approach to integration. *British Journal of Special Education*, *13*(1), 27–29.

Thompson, K. (1984). The speech therapist and language disorders. In G. Lindsay (Ed.), *Screening for children with special needs: Multidisciplinary approaches* (pp. 86–97). London: Croom Helm.

Thompson, T., Robinson, J., Dietrich, M., Farris, M., & Sinclair, V. (1996a). Architectural features and perceptions of community residences for people with mental retardation. *American Journal on Mental Retardation, 101,* 292–314.

Thompson, T., Robinson, J., Dietrich, M., Farris, M., & Sinclair, V. (1996b). Interdependence of architectural features and program variables in community residences for people with mental retardation. *American Journal on Mental Retardation, 101,* 315–327.

Thorndike, R. L., Hagen, E. P., & Sattler, J. M. (1986). *Technical man-*

ual, the Stanford-Binet Intelligence Scale: Fourth edition. Chicago: Riverside.

Thornton, C., & Krajewski, J. (1993). Death education for teachers: A refocused concern relative to medically fragile children. *Intervention in School and Clinic, 29*, 31–35.

Thousand, J. S., & Villa, R. A. (1990). Sharing expertise and responsibilities through teaching teams. In S. Stainback & W. Stainback (Eds.), *Support networks for inclusive schooling: Interdependent integrated education* (pp. 151–166). Baltimore: Brookes.

Thousand, J. S., Villa, R. A., & Nevin, A. I. (1994). *Creativity and collaborative learning: A practical guide to empowering students and teachers*. Baltimore: Brookes.

Thurlow, M. L., Christenson, S., Sinclair, M., Evelo, D., & Thornton, H. (1995). *Staying in school: Strategies for middle school students with learning and emotional disabilities*. Minneapolis: Institute of Community Integration.

Thurlow, M. L., Ysseldyke, J. E., & Reid, C. L. (1997). High school graduation requirements for students with disabilities. *Journal of Learning Disabilities, 30,* 608–616.

Thurston, L. P., & Dasta, K. (1990). An analysis of in-home parent tutoring in children's academic behavior at home and in school and on parents' tutoring behaviors. *Remedial and Special Education, 11*(4), 41–52.

Todd, A. W., Horner, R. H., & Sugai, G. (in press). Effects of self-monitoring and self-recruited praise on problem behavior, academic engagement and work completion in a typical classroom. *Journal of Positive Behavior Interventions*.

Todis, B., Severson, H. H., & Walker, H. M. (1990). The critical events scale: Behavioral profiles of students with externalizing and internalizing behavior disorders. *Behavioral Disorders, 15*, 75–86.

Tolan, P. H., & Thomas, P. (1995). The implications of age of onset for delinquency risk II: Longitudinal data. *Journal of Abnormal Child Psychology, 23,* 157–181.

Tomblin, J. B., Records, N. L., & Zhang, X. (1996). A system for the diagnosis of specific language impairment in kindergarten children. *Journal of Speech and Hearing Research, 39,* 1284–1294.

Tomblin, J. B., Records, N. L., Buckwalter, P., Zhang, X., Smith, E., & O'Brien, M. (1997). Prevalence of specific language impairment in kindergarten children. *Journal of Speech, Language, and Hearing Research, 40,* 1245–1260

Tonemah, S. A. (1987). Assessing American Indian gifted and talented student's abilities. *Journal for the Education of the Gifted, 10*, 181–194.

Torgesen, J. K. (in press). Phonologically based reading disabilities: Toward a coherent theory of one kind of learning disabilities. In R. J. Sternberg & L. Spear-Swerling (Eds.), *Perspectives on learning disabilities*. Mahwah, NJ: Erlbaum.

Torgesen, J. K., & Wagner, R. K. (1998). Alternative diagnostic approaches for specific developmental reading disabilities. *Learning Disabilities Research and Practice, 13,* 220–232.

Torgeson, J. K., Wagner, R. K., & Rashotte, C. A. (1997). Prevention and remediation of severe reading disabilities: Keeping the end in mind. *Scientific Studies of Reading, 1,* 217–234.

Torrance, E. P. (1993). The beyonders in a 30 year longitudinal study of creative achievement. *Roeper Review, 15*(3), 131–135.

Trammel, D. L., Schloss, P. J., & Alper, S. (1994). Using self-recording, evaluation, and graphing to increase completion of homework assignments. *Journal of Learning Disabilities, 27*, 75–81.

Trask-Tyler, S. A., Grossi, T. A., & Heward, W. L. (1994). Teaching young adults with developmental disabilities and visual impairments to use tape-recorded recipes: Acquisition, generalization, and maintenance of cooking skills. *Journal of Behavioral Education, 4*, 283–311.

Treffert, D. A. (1989). *Extraordinary people: Understanding "idiots savants."* New York: Harper & Row.

Trent, J. (1995). *Inventing the feeble mind: A history of mental retardation in the United States*. Berkeley: University of California Press.

Trybus, R., & Karchmer, M. (1977). School achievement scores of hearing impaired children: National data on achievement status and growth patterns. *American Annals of the Deaf, 122*, 62–69.

Tucker, B. F., & Colson, S. E. (1992). Traumatic brain injury: An overview of school re-entry. *Intervention in School and Clinic, 27*, 198–206.

Tucker, J. A. (1985). Curriculum-based assessment: An introduction. *Exceptional Children, 52,* 199–204.

Turnbull, A. P. (1983). Parent-professional interactions. In M. E. Snell (Ed.), *Systematic instruction of the moderately and severely handicapped* (2nd ed.) (pp. 18–43). Upper Saddle River, NJ: Merrill/Prentice Hall.

Turnbull, A. P., & Bronicki, G. J. (1986). Changing second graders' attitudes toward people with mental retardation: Using kid power. *Mental Retardation, 24*, 44–45.

Turnbull, A. P., & Ruef, M. (1996). Family perspectives on problem behavior. *Mental Retardation, 34,* 280–293.

Turnbull, A. P., & Turnbull, H. R. (1982). Parent involvement in the education of handicapped children: A critique. *Mental Retardation, 20*, 115–122.

Turnbull, A. P., & Turnbull, H. R. (1997). *Families, professionals, and exceptionality: A special partnership* (3rd ed.). Upper Saddle River, NJ: Merrill/Prentice Hall.

Turnbull, A. P., Turnbull, H. R., Shank, M., & Leal, D. (1995). *Exceptional lives: Special education in today's schools*. Upper Saddle River, NJ: Merrill/Prentice Hall.

Turnbull, H. R. (1986). Appropriate education and Rowley. *Exceptional Children, 52,* 347–352.

Turnbull, H. R., & Turnbull, A. P. (1985). *Parents speak out: Then and now* (2nd ed.). Upper Saddle River, NJ: Merrill/Prentice Hall.

Turnbull, H. R., & Turnbull, A. P. (1998). *Free appropriate public education: The law and children with disabilities* (5th ed.). Denver: Love.

Turnbull, K., & Bronicki, G. J. (1989). Children can teach other children. *Teaching Exceptional Children, 21*(3), 64–65.

Turnbull, R., & Cilley, M. (1999). *Explanations and implications of the 1997 amendments to IDEA.* Upper Saddle River, NJ: Merrill/Prentice Hall.

Turner, J. (1983). Workshop society: Ethnographic observations in a work setting for retarded adults. In K. Kernan, M. Begab, & R. Edgerton (Eds.), *Environments and behavior: The adaptation of mentally retarded persons* (pp. 147–171). Austin, TX: PRO-ED.

Turner-Henson, A., Holaday, B., Corser, N., Ogletree, G., & Swan, J. H. (1994). The experiences of discrimination: Challenges for chronically ill children. *Pediatric Nursing, 20,* 571–577.

Tuttle, D. W. (1984). *Self-esteem and adjusting with blindness: The process of responding to life's demands.* Springfield, IL: Thomas.

Tyler, J. S., & Mira, M. P. (1993). Educational modifications for students with head injuries. *Teaching Exceptional Children, 25*(3), 24–27.

U.S. Congress. (1987). *Promotion opportunities for blind and handicapped workers in sheltered workshops under the Javitz-Wagner-O'Day act.* Washington, DC: U.S. Government Printing Office.

U.S. Department of Commerce. (1990a). Persons arrested by crime, sex, and age: 1988. In *Statistical abstracts of the U.S.* (110th ed.) (p. 177). Washington, DC: Author.

U.S. Department of Commerce. (1990b). *Statistical abstracts of the United States* (110th ed.). Washington, DC: Author.

U.S. Department of Education. (1986). *Eighth annual report to Congress on the implementation of the Education of the Handicapped Act.* Washington, DC: Author.

U.S. Department of Education. (1989). *Eleventh annual report to Congress on the implementation of the Education of the Handicapped Act.* Washington, DC: Author.

U.S. Department of Education. (1990). *Twelfth annual report to Congress on the implementation of the Education of the Handicapped Act.* Washington, DC: Author.

U.S. Department of Education. (1991). *America 2000, an Education strategy sourcebook.* Washington, DC: Author.

U.S. Department of Education. (1992). *To assure the free appropriate public education of all children with disabilities: Fourteenth annual report to Congress on the implementation of the Individuals with Disabilities Education Act.* Washington, DC: U.S. Government Printing Office.

U.S. Department of Education. (1993). *To assure the free appropriate public education of all children with disabilities: Fifteenth annual report to Congress on the implementation of the Individuals with Disabilities Education Act.* Washington, DC: Government Document Service.

U.S. Department of Education. (1994). *Sixteenth annual report to Congress on the implementation of the Individuals with Disabilities Education Act.* Washington, DC: Author.

U.S. Department of Education. (1996). *Eighteenth annual report to Congress on the implementation of the Individuals with Disabilities Education Act.* Washington, DC: Author.

U.S. Department of Education. (1997). *Nineteenth annual report to Congress on the implementation of the Education of the Handicapped Act.* Washington, DC: Author.

U.S. Department of Education, Office of Civil Rights. (1994). *Annual report to Congress.* Washington, DC: Author.

U.S. Department of Health and Human Services. (1998). *Child maltreatment 1996: Reports from the states to the National Child Abuse and Neglect Data System.* Washington, DC: U.S. Government Printing Office.

U.S. Department of Labor. (1979). *Study of handicapped clients in sheltered workshops* (vol. 2). Washington, DC: Author.

U.S. Office of Education. (1977a). Implementation of Part B of the Education of the Handicapped Act. *Federal Register, 42,* 42474–42518.

U.S. Office of Education. (1977b). Procedures for evaluating specific learning disabilities. *Federal Register, 42,* 65082–65085.

Udvari-Solner, A., Jorgenson, J., & Courchane G. (1992). Longitudinal vocational curriculum: The foundations for effective transition. In F. R. Rusch, L. DeStefano, J. Chadsey-Rusch, L. Allen Phelps, & E. Szymanski (Eds.), *Transition from school to adult life* (pp. 285–320). Pacific Grove, CA: Brooks/Cole.

Ulicny, G. R., Thompson, S. K., Favell, J. E., & Thompson, M. S. (1985). The active assessment of educability: A case study. *Journal of The Association for Persons with Severe Handicaps, 10,* 111–114.

Ulrey, P. (1994). When you meet a guide dog. *RE:view, 26,* 143–144.

Umbreit, J. (1995). Functional assessment and intervention in a regular classroom setting for the disruptive behavior of a student with attention deficit hyperactivity disorder. *Behavioral Disorders, 20,* 267–278.

Umbreit, J., & Blair, K. C. (1996). The effects of preference, choice, and attention on problem behavior at school. *Education and Training in Mental Retardation and Developmental Disabilities, 31,* 151–161.

Ungvarski, P. J. (1997). Update on HIV infection. *American Journal of Nursing, 97,* 44–51.

Upshar, C. (1982). Respite care for mentally retarded and other disabled populations: Program models and family needs. *Mental Retardation, 20,* 2–6.

Uslan, M. M. (1992). Barriers to acquiring assistive technology: Cost and lack of information. *Journal of Visual Impairment and Blindness*, *86*, 402–407.

Utley, C. (1995). Culturally and linguistically diverse students with mild disabilities. In C. A. Grant (Ed.), *Educating for diversity: An anthology of multicultural voices* (pp. 301–324). Boston: Allyn & Bacon.

Utley, C. A., Lowitzer, A. C., & Baumeister, A. A. (1987). A comparison of the AAMD's definition, eligibility criteria, and classification schemes with state department of education guidelines. *Education and Training in Mental Retardation*, *22*, 35–43.

Valdes, K. A., Williamson, C. L., & Wagner, M. (1990). *The national longitudinal transition study of special education students.* Vol. 3: *Youth categorized as emotionally disturbed*. Palo Alto, CA: SRI International.

van den Pol, R. A., Iwata, B. A., Ivancic, M. T., Page, T. J., Neef, N. A., & Whitley, F. P. (1981). Teaching the handicapped to eat in public places: Acquisition, generalization and maintenance of restaurant skills. *Journal of Applied Behavior Analysis*, *14*, 61–69.

Van Houten, R. (1980). *Learning through feedback: A systematic approach for improving academic performance.* New York: Human Sciences Press.

Van Houten, R. (1984). Setting up performance feedback systems in the classroom. In W. L. Heward, T. E. Heron, D. S. Hill, & J. Trap-Porter (Eds.), *Focus on behavior analysis in education* (pp. 114–125). Upper Saddle River, NJ: Merrill/Prentice Hall.

Van Reusen, A. K., & Bos, C. (1994). Facilitating student participation in individualized education programs through motivation strategy instruction. *Exceptional Children*, *60*, 466–475.

Van Reusen, A. K., & Bos, C. S. (1990). IPLAN: Helping students communicate in planning conferences. *Teaching Exceptional Children*, *22*(4), 30–32.

Van Riper, C., & Erickson, R. L. (1996). *Speech correction: An introduction to speech pathology and audiology* (9th ed.). Boston: Allyn & Bacon.

Van Tassel-Baska, J. (Ed.). (1990). *A practical guide to counseling the gifted in a school setting* (2nd ed.). Reston, VA: Council for Exceptional Children.

Van Tassel-Baska, J., Patton, J. M., & Prillaman, D. (1991). *Gifted youth at risk: A report of a national study*. Reston, VA: Council for Exceptional Children.

Vandercook, T. (1991). Leisure instruction outcomes: Criterion performance, positive interactions, and acceptance by typical high school peers. *Journal of Special Education*, *25*, 320–339.

Vandercook, T., York, J., & Forest, M. (1989). The McGill Action Planning System (MAPS): A strategy for building the vision. *Journal of The Association for Persons with Severe Handicaps*, *14*, 205–215.

Vaughn, B. J., Clarke, S., & Dunlap, G. (1997). Assessment-based intervention for severe behavior problems in a natural family context. *Journal of Applied Behavior Analysis, 30,* 713–716.

Vaughn, B. J., Fox, L., Dunlap, G., Fox, L., Clarke, S., & Bucy, M. (1997). Parent-professional partnership in behavioral support: A case study in community-based intervention. *Journal of The Association for Persons with Severe Handicaps, 22,* 186–197.

Vaughn, S., Elbaum, B. E., & Schumm, J. S. (1996). The effects of inclusion on the social functioning of students with learning disabilities. *Journal of Learning Disabilities, 29,* 598–608.

Vaughn, S., McIntosh, R., Schumm, J. S., Haager, D., & Callwood, D. (1993). Social status, peer acceptance, and reciprocal friendships revisited. *Learning Disabilities Research and Practice*, *8*, 82–88.

Vaughn, S., Schumm, J. S., & Brick, J. B. (1998). Using a rating scale to design and evaluate inclusion programs. *Teaching Exceptional Children, 30*(4), 41–45.

Venn, J. (1994). *Assessment of students with special needs*. Upper Saddle River, NJ: Merrill/Prentice Hall.

Venn, J., Morgenstern, L., & Dykes, M. K. (1979). Checklists for evaluating the fit and function of orthoses, prostheses, and wheelchairs in the classroom. *Teaching Exceptional Children*, *11*, 51–56.

Vergason, G. A., & Anderegg, M. L. (1997). The ins and outs of special education terminology. *Teaching Exceptional Children, 29*(5), 35–39.

Vig, S., & Jedrysek, E. (1996). Application of the 1992 AAMR definition: Issues for preschool children. *Mental Retardation, 34,* 244–246.

Villaronga, P. (1995). The so called. In C. A. Grant (Ed.), *Educating for diversity: An anthology of multicultural voices* (pp. 255–260). Boston: Allyn & Bacon.

Villegas, A. M. (1988). School failure and cultural mismatch: Another view. *Urban Review, 20*(4), 253–265.

Voltz, D. L. (1994). Developing collaborative parent-teacher relationships with culturally diverse parents. *Intervention in School and Clinic, 29*(5), 288–291.

Voltz, D. L., & Damiano-Lantz, M. (1993). Developing ownership in learning. *Teaching Exceptional Children, 25,* 18–28.

Wadsworth, D. E., Knight, D., & Balser, V. (1993). Children who are medically fragile or technology dependent: Guidelines. *Intervention in School and Clinic*, *29*, 102–104.

Wagner, M. (1991). *Dropouts: What do we know? What can we do*? Menlo Park, CA: SRI International.

Wagner, M., Blackorby, J., Cameto, R., & Newman, L. (1994). *What makes a difference? Influences on postschool outcomes of youth with disabilities*. Menlo Park, CA: SRI International.

Wagner, M., D'Amico, R., Marder, C., Newman, L., & Blackorby, J. (1993). *What happens next? Trends in postschool outcomes of youth with disabilities: The second comprehensive report from the national longitudinal transition study of special education students*. Menlo Park, CA: SRI International.

Wagner-Lampl, A., & Oliver, G. W. (1994). Folklore of blindness. *Journal of Visual Impairment and Blindness*, *88*, 267–276.

Wahler, R. G., & Dumas, J. E. (1986). "A chip off the old block": Some interpersonal characteristics of coercive children across generations. In P. S. Strain, M. J. Guralnick, & H. M. Walker (Eds.), *Children's social behavior: Development, assessment, and modification* (pp. 49–91). Orlando, FL: Academic Press.

Wainapel, S. F. (1989). Attitudes of visually impaired persons toward cane use. *Journal of Visual Impairment and Blindness*, *83*, 446–448.

Walker, D. K., & Jacobs, F. H. (1985). Where there is a way, there is not always a will: Technology, public policy, and the school integration of children who are technology-assisted. *Children's Health Care, 20,* 68–74.

Walker, H. M. (1997). *The acting out child: Coping with classroom disruption* (2nd ed.). Longmont, CO: Sopris West.

Walker, H. M., & Fabre, T. R. (1987). Assessment of behavior disorders in the school setting: Issues, problems and strategies revisited. In N. G. Haring (Ed.), *Assessing and managing behavioral disabilities* (pp. 198–243). Seattle: University of Washington Press.

Walker, H. M., & Rankin, R. (1983). Assessing the behavioral expectations and demands of less restrictive settings. *School Psychology Review*, *12*(3), 274–284.

Walker, H. M., & Severson, H. H. 1990. Systematic Screening for Behavior Disorders. Longmont, CO: Sopris West.

Walker, H. M., & Sylvester, R. (1998). Reducing student refusal and resistance. *Teaching Exceptional Children, 30*(6), 52–57.

Walker, H. M., Colvin, G., & Ramsey, E. (1995). *Antisocial behavior in schools: Strategies and best practices*. Pacific Grove, CA: Brooks/Cole.

Walker, H. M., Severson, H. H., & Feil, E. G. (1994). *The Early Screening Project: A proven child-find process*. Longmont, CO: Sopris West.

Walker, H. M., Stieber, S., Ramsey, E., & O'Neill, R. E. (1991). Longitudinal prediction of the school achievement, adjustment, and delinquency of antisocial versus at-risk boys. *Remedial and Special Education*, *12*(4), 41–51.

Walker, L. A. (1986). *A loss for words: The story of deafness in a family.* New York: Harper & Row.

Walker-Vann, C. (1998). Profiling Hispanic deaf students. *American Annals of the Deaf, 143,* 46–54.

Wallach, G. P., & Butler, K. G. (1994). *Language learning disabilities in school-age children and adolescents.* Needham Heights, MA: Allyn & Bacon.

Ward, M. C. (1994). Effects of a self-operated auditory prompt system on the acquisition, maintenance and generalization of independent work skills of preschoolers with developmental disabilities. Unpublished doctoral dissertation, The Ohio State University, Columbus.

Ward, M. E. (1986). The visual system. In G. T. Scholl (Ed.), *Foundations of education for blind and visually handicapped children and youth: Theory and practice* (pp. 35–64). New York: American Foundation for the Blind.

Warger, C. L., Aldinger, L. E., & Okun, K. A. (1983). *Mainstreaming in the secondary school: The role of the regular teacher.* Bloomington, IN: Phi Delta Kappa Educational Foundation.

Warren, S. F., & Gazdag, G. (1990). Facilitating early language development with milieu intervention procedures. *Journal of Early Intervention, 14*, 62–86.

Warren, S. F., McQuarter, R. J., & Rogers-Warren, A. K. (1984). The effects of teacher mands on the speech of unresponsive language-delayed children. *Journal of Speech and Hearing Research*, *49*, 43–52.

Wasik, B. H., Ramey, C. T., Bryant, D. M., & Sparling, J. J. (1990). A longitudinal study of two early intervention strategies: Project CARE. *Child Development*, *61*, 1682–1692.

Watkins, C. L. (1996). Follow through: Why didn't we? *Effective School Practices, 15*(1), 57–66.

Wayman, K., Lynch, E., & Hanson, M. (1990). Home based early childhood services: Cultural sensitivity in a family systems approach. *Topics in Early Childhood Special Education*, *10*, 56–75.

Webber, J., Scheuermann, B., McCall, C., & Coleman, M. (1993). Research on self-monitoring as a behavior management technique in special education classrooms: A descriptive review. *Remedial and Special Education*, *14*(2), 38–56.

Weber, C., Behl, D., & Summers, M. (1994). Watch them play—watch them learn. *Teaching Exceptional Children, 27*(1), 30–35

Webster, A., & Ellwood, J. (1985). *The hearing-impaired child in the ordinary school.* London: Croom Helm.

Webster's New World Dictionary of the American Language (2nd ed.). (1986). New York: Simon & Schuster.

Wechsler, D. (1974). *Manual for the Wechsler Intelligence Scale for Children—Revised.* New York: Psychological Corporation.

Wedel, J. W., & Fowler, S. A. (1984). "Read me a story, Mom": A home-tutoring program to teach prereading skills to language-delayed children. *Behavior Modification*, *8*, 245–266.

Weeks, M., & Gaylord-Ross, R. (1981). Task difficulty and aberrant behavior in severely handicapped students. *Journal of Applied Behavior Analysis*, *14*, 449–463.

Wehby, J. H., Dodge, K. A., & Valente, E. (1993). School behavior of first grade children identified as at-risk for development of conduct problems. *Behavioral Disorders, 19,* 67–78.

Wehman, P. (1983). Toward the employability of severely handicapped children and youth. *Teaching Exceptional Children*, *15*, 220–225.

Wehman, P. (1992). Transition for young people with disabilities: Challenges for the 1990's. *Education and Training in Mental Retardation*, *27*, 112–118.

Wehman, P. (Ed.). (1998). *Developing transition plans*. Austin, TX: PRO-ED.

Wehman, P., & Hill, J. W. (Eds.). (1985). *Competitive employment for persons with mental retardation.* Richmond: Virginia Commonwealth University, Rehabilitation Research and Training Center.

Wehman, P., & Kregel, J. (1985). A supported work approach to competitive employment of individuals with moderate and severe handicaps. *Journal of The Association for Persons with Severe Handicaps*, *10*, 3–11.

Wehman, P., & Kregel, J. (1997). *Functional curriculum for elementary, middle, and secondary age students with special needs*. Austin, TX: PRO-ED.

Wehman, P., & Revell, G. (1997). Transition from school to adulthood: Looking ahead. In P. Wehman (Ed.), *Exceptional individuals in school, community, and work* (pp. 597–648). Austin, TX: PRO-ED,

Wehman, P., & Schleien, S. J. (1981). *Leisure programs for handicapped persons: Adaptations, techniques, and curriculum.* Baltimore: University Park Press.

Wehman, P., Hill, M., Hill, J. W., Brooke, V., Pendleton, P., & Britt, C. (1985). Competitive employment for persons with mental retardation: A follow-up six years later. *Mental Retardation*, *23*, 274–281.

Wehman, P., Kregel, J., & Seyfarth, J. (1985a). Employment outlook for young adults with mental retardation. *Rehabilitation Counseling Bulletin*, *5*, 343–354.

Wehman, P., Kregel, J., & Seyfarth, J. (1985b). Transition from school to work for individuals with severe handicaps: A follow-up study. *Journal of The Association for Persons with Severe Handicaps*, *10*, 132–136.

Wehman, P., Kregel, J., Shafer, M., & West, M. (1989). *Emerging trends in supported employment: A preliminary analysis of 27 states.* Richmond: Virginia Commonwealth University, Rehabilitation Research and Training Center.

Wehman, P., Renzaglia, A. M., & Bates, P. (1985). *Functional living skills for moderately and severely handicapped individuals.* Austin, TX: PRO-ED.

Wehman, P., Revell, G., & Kregel, J. (1996). Supported employment for 1986–1993: A national program that works. Manuscript submitted for publication.

Wehmeyer, M. L. (1994). Perceptions of self-determination and psychological empowerment of adolescents with mental retardation. *Education and Training in Mental Retardation*, *29*, 9–21.

Wehmeyer, M. L., & Kelchner, K. (1998). *The Arc's self-determination scale*. Arlington, TX: The Arc National Headquarters.

Wehmeyer, M. L., Agran, M., & Hughes, C. (1998). *Teaching self-determination to students with disabilities*. Baltimore: Brookes.

Wehmeyer, M. L., Kelchner, K., & Richards, S. (1996). Essential characteristics of self-determined behavior of individuals with mental retardation. *American Journal on Mental Retardation, 100,* 632–642.

Weinstein, G., & Cooke, N. L. (1992). The effects of two repeated reading interventions on generalization of fluency. *Learning Disability Quarterly*, *15*, 21–28.

Weintraub, F. J., & Abeson, A. (1974). New education policies for the handicapped: The quiet revolution. *Phi Delta Kappan*, *55*, 526–529, 569.

Weisberg, P. (1994). Helping preschoolers from low-income backgrounds make substantial progress in reading through Direct Instruction. In R. Gardner III, D. M. Sainato, J. O. Cooper, T. E. Heron, W. L. Heward, J. Eshleman, & T. A. Grossi (Eds.), *Behavior analysis in education: Focus on measurably superior instruction* (pp. 115–129). Pacific Grove, CA: Brooks/Cole.

Weisman, M. L. (1994). When parents are not in the interest of the child. *Atlantic Monthly, 274* (1), 43–44, 46–47, 50–54, 56–60, 62–63.

Weisner, T. S., Beizer, L., & Stolze, L. (1991). Religion and families of children with developmental delays. *American Journal of Mental Retardation, 95*, 647–662.

Weiss, K. W., & Dykes, M. K. (1995). Legal issues in special education: Assistive technology and supportive services. *Physical Disabilities: Education and Related Services, 14*(1), 29–36.

Weisz, J. R. (1981). Effects of the "mentally retarded" label on adult judgments about child failure. *Journal of Abnormal Psychology*, *4*, 371–374.

Weisz, J. R., Bromfield, R., Vines, D. L., & Weiss, B. (1985). Cognitive development, helpless behavior, and labeling effects in the lives of the mentally retarded. *Applied Developmental Psychology*, *2*, 129–167.

Weitzman, M., Gortmaker, S. L., Sobol, A. M., & Perrin, J. M. (1992). Recent trends in the prevalence and severity of childhood asthma. *Journal of the American Medical Association, 268,* 2673–2677.

Wepman, J. M. (1973). *Auditory discrimination test*. Chicago: Language Research Associates.

Werker, J. E., & Lalonde, C. E. (1988). Cross language speech perception: Initial capabilities and developmental change. *Developmental Psychology, 24,* 672–683.

Werle, M. A., Murphy, T. B., & Budd, K. S. (1993). Treating chronic food refusal in young children: Home-based parent training. *Journal of Applied Behavior Analysis, 26,* 421–433.

Werner, K., Horner, R. H., & Newton, J. S. (1997). Reducing structural barriers to improve the social life of three adults with severe disabilities. *Journal of The Association for Persons with Severe Handicaps, 22,* 138–150.

Werts, M. G., Wolery, M., Venn, M. L., Demblowski, D., & Doren, H. (1996). Effects of transition-based teaching with instructive feedback on skill acquisition by children with and without disabilities. *Journal of Behavioral Research, 90,* 75–86.

Werts, M., Wolery, M., Gast, D. L., & Holcombe, A. (1996). Sneak in some extra learning by using instructive feedback. *Teaching Exceptional Children, 28*(3), 70–71.

Wesson, C. L., & King, R. P. (1996). Portfolio assessment and special education students. *Teaching Exceptional Children, 28*(2), 44–48.

Wesson, C. L., King, R. P., & Deno, S. L. (1984). Direct and frequent measurement of student performance: If it's good for us, why don't we do it? *Learning Disability Quarterly*, 7, 45–48.

Wesson, C., Wilson, R., & Higbee Mandlebaum, L. (1988). Learning games for active student responding. *Teaching Exceptional Children, 20*(2), 12–14.

West, J. F., & Idol, L. (1990). Collaborative consultation in the education of mildly handicapped and at-risk students. *Remedial and Special Education*, *11*(1), 22–31.

West, L. L., Corbey, S., Boyer-Stephens, A., Jones, B., Miller, R. J., & Sarkees-Wircenski, M. (1992). *Integrating transition planning into the IEP process*. Reston, VA: Council for Exceptional Children.

West, M. D., Rayfield, R. G., Clements, C., Unger, D., & Thornton, T. (1994). An illustration of positive behavioral support in the workplace for individuals with severe mental retardation. *Journal of Vocational Rehabilitation*, *4*(4), 265–271.

West, M., Revell, G., & Wehman, P. (1998). Conversion from segregated services to supported employment: A continuing challenge to the VR service system. *Education and Training in Mental Retardation and Developmental Disabilities, 33,* 239–247.

West, R. P., Young, K. R., & Spooner, F. (1990). Precision teaching: An introduction. *Teaching Exceptional Children, 22,* 4–9.

Westberg, K. L., Archambault, F. X., Jr., Dobyns, S. M., & Salvin, T. J. (1993). The classroom practices observation study. *Journal for the Education of the Gifted*, *16,* 120–146.

Westling, D. L. (1996). What do parents of children with moderate and severe mental disabilities want? *Education and Training in Mental Retardation and Developmental Disabilities, 31,* 86–104.

Westling, D. L., & Fox, L. (1995). *Teaching persons with severe disabilities*. Upper Saddle River, NJ: Merrill/Prentice Hall.

Westling, D. L., Ferrell, K., & Swenson, K. (1982). Intraclassroom comparison of two arrangements for teaching profoundly mentally retarded children. *American Journal of Mental Deficiency*, *86*, 601–608.

Weyhing, M. C. (1983). Parental reactions to handicapped children and familial adjustments to routines of care. In J. A. Mulick & S. M. Pueschell (Eds.), *Parent-professional partnerships in developmental disabilities* (pp. 125–138). Cambridge, MA: Ware.

Whaley, L. F., & Wong, D. L. (1995). *Nursing care of infants and children* (5th ed.). St. Louis: Mosby.

Wheeler, D. L., Jacobson, J. W., Paglieri, R. A., & Schwartz, A. A. (1993). An experimental assessment of facilitated communication. *Mental Retardation*, *31*, 49–60

Wheeler, J. J., Bates, P., Marshall, K. J., & Miller, S. R. (1988). Teaching appropriate social behaviors to a young man with moderate mental retardation in a supported competitive employment setting. *Education and Training in Mental Retardation*, *23*, 105–116.

White, B. L. (1975). *The first three years of life*. Upper Saddle River, NJ: Prentice Hall.

White, K. R., Bush, D., & Casto, G. (1986). Let the past be prologue: Learning from previous reviews of early intervention efficacy research. *Journal of Special Education*, *19*(4), 417–428.

White, R. B., & Koorland, M. A. (1996). What can we do about cursing? *Teaching Exceptional Children, 28*(4), 48–52.

Whitmore, J. R., & Maker, C. J. (1985). *Intellectual giftedness in disabled persons.* Rockville, MD: Aspen.

Widerstrom, A. H., Mowder, B. A., & Willis, W. G. (1989). The school psychologist's role in the early childhood special education program. *Journal of Early Intervention*, *13*, 239–248.

Wiederholt, J. L., & Bryant, B. R. (1992) *Gray Oral Reading Tests—3rd edition*. Austin, TX: PRO-ED.

Wiederholt, J. L., & Chamberlain, S. P. (1989). A critical analysis of resource programs. *Remedial and Special Education*, *10*(6), 15–37.

Wiederholt, J. L., Hammill, D. D., & Brown, V. (1983). *The resource teacher: A guide to effective practice* (2nd ed.). Boston: Allyn & Bacon.

Wiener, W. R., Deaver, K., DiCorpo, D., Hayes, J., Hill, E., Manzer, D., Newcomver, J., Pogrund, R., Rosen, S., & Uslan, M. (1990). The orientation and mobility assistant. *RE:view*, *22*, 69–77.

Wikler, L. D. (1986). Periodic stresses of families of older mentally retarded children: An exploratory study. *American Journal of Mental Deficiency*, *90*, 703–706.

Wilbur, R. (1987). *American Sign Language: Linguistic and applied dimensions* (2nd ed.). Boston: Little, Brown.

Wilcox, B., & Bellamy, G. T. (1987). *A comprehensive guide to "The Activities Catalog": An alternative curriculum for youth and adults with severe disabilities*. Baltimore: Brookes.

Wilkinson, G. S. (1989). *Wide Range Achievement Test—3*. Wilmington, DE: Jastak.

Will, M. C. (1986). Educating children with learning problems: A shared responsibility. *Exceptional Children*, *52*, 411–415.

Willard-Holt, C. (1998). Academic and personality characteristics of gifted students with cerebral palsy: A multiple case study. *Exceptional Children, 65,* 37–50.

Williams, B. F., & Howard, V. F. (1993). Children exposed to cocaine: Characteristics and implications for research and intervention. *Journal of Early Intervention*, *17*, 61–72.

Williams, J. (1977). The impact and implication of litigation. In G. Markel (Ed.), *Proceedings of the University of Michigan Institute on the Impact and Implications of State and Federal Legislation Affecting Handicapped Individuals.* Ann Arbor: University of Michigan, School of Education.

Williams, R. R. (1991). Assistive technology and people with disabilities: Separating fact from fiction. *A. T. Quarterly, 2*(3), 6–7.

Williams, V. L., & Cartledge, G. (1997). Passing notes to parents. *Teaching Exceptional Children, 30*(1), 30–34.

Williamson, G. G. (1978). The individualized education program: An interdisciplinary endeavor. In B. Sirvis, J. W. Baken, & G. G. Williamson (Eds.), *Unique aspects of the IEP for the physically handicapped, homebound, and hospitalized.* Reston, VA: Council for Exceptional Children.

Willoughby, D. M., & Duffy, S. (1989). *Handbook for itinerant and resource teachers of blind and visually impaired students.* Baltimore: National Federation of the Blind.

Wilson, C. L. (1995). Parents and teachers: "Can we talk?" *LD Forum, 20*(2), 31–33.

Wilson, C. L., & Hughes, M. (1994). Involving linguistically diverse parents. *LD Forum, 19*(3), 25–27.

Wilson, J., Blacher, J., & Baker, B. L. (1989). Siblings of children with severe handicaps. *Mental Retardation*, *27*, 167–173.

Wilson, P. G., Schepis, M. M., & Mason-Main, M. (1987). In vivo use of picture prompt training to increase independent work at a restaurant. *Journal of The Association for Persons with Severe Handicaps*, *12*, 145–150.

Winton, P. J., & Turnbull, A. P. (1981). Parent involvement as viewed by parents of preschool handicapped children. *Topics in Early Childhood Special Education*, *1*, 11–19.

Winzer, M. A., & Mazurek, K. (1998). *Special education in multicultural contexts*. Upper Saddle River, NJ: Merrill/Prentice Hall.

Wittenstein, S. H. (1994). Braille literacy: Preservice training and teachers' attitudes. *Journal of Visual Impairment and Blindness, 88,* 516–524.

Witty, P. A. (Ed.). (1951). *The gifted child*. Boston: Heath.

Wolery, M., & Dyk, L. (1984). Arena assessment: Description and preliminary social validity data. *Journal of The Association for Persons with Severe Handicaps*, *9*, 231–235.

Wolery, M., & Haring, T. G. (1994). Moderate, severe, and profound disabilities. In N. G. Haring, L. McCormick, & T. G. Haring (Eds.), *Exceptional children and youth* (6th ed.) (pp. 258–299). Upper Saddle River, NJ: Merrill/Prentice Hall.

Wolery, M., & Sainato, D. M. (1993). General curriculum and intervention strategies. In *DEC Recommended Practices* (pp. 50–57). Reston, VA: Council for Exceptional Children, Division for Early Childhood.

Wolery, M., & Sainato, D. M. (1996). General curriculum and intervention strategies. In S. L. Odom & M. McClean (Eds.), *Recommended practices in early intervention* (pp. 125–158). Austin, TX: PRO-ED.

Wolery, M., & Schuster, J. W. (1997). Instructional methods with students who have significant disabilities. *Journal of Special Education, 31,* 61–79.

Wolery, M., & Wilbers, J. S. (1994). *Including young children with special needs in early childhood programs*. Washington, DC: National Association for the Education of Young Children.

Wolery, M., Anthony, L., & Heckathorn, J. (1998). Transition-based teaching: Effects on transitions, teachers' behavior, and children's learning. *Journal of Early Intervention, 21,* 117–131.

Wolery, M., Ault, M. J., & Doyle, P. M. (1992). *Teaching students with moderate to severe disabilities*. New York: Longman.

Wolery, M., Werts, M. G., Snyder, E. D., & Caldwell, N. K. (1994). Efficacy of constant time delay implemented by peer tutors in general education classrooms. *Journal of Behavioral Education, 4,* 415–436.

Wolf, E. G., Delk, M. T., & Schein, J. D. (1982). *Needs assessment of services to deaf-blind individuals* (Contract No. 300-81-0426). Silver Spring, MD: REDEX.

Wolf, M. M. (1978). Social validity: The case for subjective measurement, or how behavior analysis is finding its heart. *Journal of Applied Behavior Analysis, 11*, 203–214.

Wolfensberger, W. (1969). The origin and nature of our institutional models. In R. B. Kugel & W. Wolfensberger (Eds.), *Changing patterns in residential services for the mentally retarded* (pp. 59–71). Washington, DC: President's Committee on Mental Retardation.

Wolfensberger, W. (1972). *Normalization: The principle of normalization in human services.* Toronto: National Institute on Mental Retardation.

Wolfensberger, W. (1983). Social role valorization: A proposed new term for the principle of normalization. *Mental Retardation*, *21*, 234–239.

Wolfensberger, W., & Thomas, S. (1983). *Program analysis of service systems implementation of normalization goals: Normalization criteria and ratings manual* (vol. 2). Toronto: National Institute on Mental Retardation.

Wolffe, K., & Sacks, S. Z. (1997). The lifestyles of blind, low vision, and sighted youths: A quantitative comparison. *Journal of Visual Impairment and Blindness, 91,* 245–257.

Woliver, R., & Woliver, G. M. (1991). Gifted adolescents in the emerging minorities: Asians and Pacific Islanders. In M. Bireley & J. Genshaft (Eds.), *Understanding the gifted adolescent* (pp. 248–258). New York: Teachers College Press.

Wolman, C., Thurlow, M. L., & Bruininks, R. H. (1989). Stability of categorical designation for special education students: A longitudinal study. *Journal of Special Education*, *23*, 213–222.

Wolraich, M. L., Lindgren, S., Stromquist, A., Milich, R., Davis, C., & Watson, D. (1990). Stimulant medications use by primary care physicians in the treatment of attention deficit hyperactivity disorder. *Pediatrics*, *86*, 95–101.

Wood, B. A., Frank, A. R., & Hamre-Nietupski, S. M. (1996). How do you work this lock? Adaptations for teaching combination lock use. *Teaching Exceptional Children, 28*(2), 35–39.

Wood, D. A., Rosenberg, M. S., & Carran, D. T. (1993). The effects of tape-recorded self-instruction cues on the mathematics performance of students with learning disabilities. *Journal of Learning Disabilities*, *26*, 250–258.

Wood, J. W. (1998). *Adapting instruction for mainstreamed students and at-risk students* (3rd ed.). Upper Saddle River, NJ: Merrill/Prentice Hall.

Wood, S. J., Murdock, J. Y., Cronin, M. E., Dawson, N. M., & Kirby, P. C. (1998). Effects of self-monitoring on on-task behaviors of at-risk middle school students. *Journal of Behavioral Education, 8,* 263–279.

Woodcock, R. W. (1987).*Woodcock Reading Mastery Tests*. Circle Pines, MN: American Guidance Service.

Woodcock, R. W., & Johnson, M. B. (1989). *Woodcock-Johnson Psycho-Educational Battery—Revised*. Chicago: Riverside.

Woodruff, G., & McGonigel, M. J. (1988). Early intervention team approaches: The transdisciplinary model. In J. B. Jordon, J. J. Gallagher, P. L. Hutinger, & M. B. Karnes (Eds.), *Early childhood special education: Birth to three* (pp. 163–181). Reston, VA: Council for Exceptional Children.

Woolsey, M. L. (1999, January). Personal communication.

Wrenn, R. L. (1994). A death at school: Issues and interventions. *Counseling and Human Development, 26*(7), 1–7.

Wright, C., & Bigge, J. L. (1991). Avenues to physical participation. In J. L. Bigge (Ed.), *Teaching individuals with multiple and physical disabilities* (3rd ed.) (pp. 132–174). Upper Saddle River, NJ: Merrill/Prentice Hall.

Wright, C., & Momari, M. (1985). *From toys to computers: Access for the physically disabled child.* San Jose, CA: Wright.

Yaremko, R. L. (1993). Cochlear implants and children under the age of three. *Volta Review*, *95*, 51–61.

Yell, M. L. (1995). Least restrictive environment, inclusion, and students with disabilities: A legal analysis. *Journal of Special Education*, *28*, 389–404.

Yell, M. L. (1998). *The law and special education*. Upper Saddle River, NJ: Merrill/Prentice Hall.

Ylvisaker, M. (1986). Language and communication disorders following pediatric head injury. *Journal of Head Trauma Rehabilitation*, *1*, 48–56.

Young, J. L. (1997). Positive experiences with dogs: An important addition to the curriculum for blind and visually impaired children. *RE:view, 29*(2), 55–61.

Young, K. R., West, R. P., Smith, D. J. & Morgan, D. P. (1997). *Teaching self-management strategies to adolescents.* Longmont, CO: Sopris West.

Yousef, J. M. S. (1995). Insulin-dependent diabetes mellitus: Education implications. *Physical Disabilities: Education and Related Services, 13*(2), 43–53.

Zambone, A. M., & Huebner, K. M. (1992). Service for children and youths who are deaf-blind: An overview. *Journal of Visual Impairment and Blindness*, *86*, 287–290.

Zamora-Durán, G., & Reyes, E. (1997). From tests to talking in the classroom: Assessing communicative competence. In A. Artiles & G. Zamora-Durán (Eds.), *Reducing disproportionate representation of culturally diverse students in special and gifted education* (pp. 45–58). Reston, VA: Council for Exceptional Children.

Zamula, E. (1990). Childhood asthma: More than snuffles. *FDA Consumer, 24*(6), 10–13.

Zaragoza, N., Vaughn, S., & McIntosh, R. (1991). Social skills intervention and children with behavior problems: A review. *Behavioral Disorders*, *16*, 260–275.

Zawaiza, T. W. (1995). Stand and deliver: Multiculturalism and special education report in the early 21st century. In S. Walker, K. A. Turner, M. Haile-Michael, A. Vincent, & M. D. Miles (Eds.), *Disability and diversity: New leadership for a new era*. Washington, DC: President's Committee on Employment of People with Disabilities.

Zawolkow, E., & DeFiore, S. (1986). Educational interpreting for elementary- and secondary-level hearing-impaired students. *American Annals of the Deaf, 131,* 26–28.

Zeece, P. D., & Wolda, M. K. (1995). Let me see what you say; let me see what you feel! *Teaching Exceptional Children, 27*(2), 4–9.

Zemlin, W. B. (1998). *Speech and hearing science: Anatomy and physiology* (4th ed). Needham Heights, MA: Allyn & Bacon.

Zetlin, A., & Murtaugh, M. (1990). What ever happened to those with borderline IQs? *American Journal on Mental Retardation, 94,* 463–469.

Zigler, E., Balla, D., & Hodapp, R. (1984). On the definition and classification of mental retardation. *American Journal of Mental Deficiency, 89,* 215–230.

Zigmond, N. (1997). Educating students with disabilities: The future of special education. In J. W. Lloyd, E. J. Kameenui, & D. Chard (Eds.), *Issues in educating students with disabilities* (pp. 377–390). Mahwah, NJ: Erlbaum.

Zigmond, N., & Baker, J. M. (1995). Concluding comments: Current and future practices in inclusive schooling. *Journal of Special Education, 29,* 245–250.

Zirpoli, T. J. (1987). Child abuse and children with handicaps. *Remedial and Special Education, 7*(2), 39–48.

Zirpoli, T. J. (1990). Physical abuse: Are children with disabilities at greater risk? *Intervention in School and Clinic, 26*(1), 6–11.

Zirpoli, T. J., & Melloy, K. J. (1997). *Behavior management: Applications for teachers and parents* (2nd ed.). Upper Saddle River, NJ: Merrill/Prentice Hall.

Name Index

Subject Index

Photo Credits

Kevin Fitzsimons/Merrill: ii; Jill Dardig: vi; Larry Hamill/Merrill: xxiii, 36, 255, 313, 321, 429; Sylvia Plachy: 1; Elizabeth Crews: 3, 253, 327; Laura Dwight: 7, 58, 71, 78, 161, 449, 463; Paul Conklin/Photo Edit: 13, 33, 65, 237; Scott Cunningham/Merrill: 17, 19, 51, 73, 85, 93, 108, 118, 123, 134, 157, 179, 185, 196, 201, 203, 210, 222, 227, 234, 245, 248, 267, 280, 297, 329, 337, 344, 365, 366, 391, 392, 407, 410, 419, 421, 425, 431, 454, 473, 479, 491, 497, 502, 510, 517, 521, 551, 555, 609, 612, 613, 621, 623; Stacy Pick/Stock Boston: 31; Dennis MacDonald/Photo Edit: 39; Richard Hutchings/Photo Edit: 47, 153, 289; Mary Kate Denny/Photo Edit: 83, 302, 315; Paul A. Souders: 90; Gale Zucker: 100; Bob Daemmrich/The Image Works: 110, 436; Frank Siteman/Omn-Photo Communications: 117; Michael Newman/Photo Edit: 130, 372, 485, 579; Anthony Magnacca/Merrill: 141, 251, 492, 515, 629; Kay Shaw: 145; Courtesy of National Lekotek Center: 155; Gail Meese/Meese Photo Research: 162, 175, 353, 443, 470, 477; Jacques Chenet/Woodfin Camp & Assoc.: 170; Terry Wild Studios: 191; Paul Conklin/Monkmeyer Press: 213; Mug Shots/The Stock Market: 314; Bill Bachman: 339; Manni Mason's Pictures: 357, 556; Bill Heward: 375, 376, 385; Sullivan/TexasStock: 388; San Francisco SPCA Hearing Dog Program: 394; Bill Aron/Photo Edit: 401; Courtesy The Lighthouse, Inc.: 414; Boroff/TexasStock: 416; Janis Miglaus/Image Source: 426; Tony Freeman/Photo Edit: 446; M. Richards/Photo Edit: 462, 620; James Shaffer: 499; Jim Cronk: 533; David Young-Wolff/Photo Edit: 537; International Art Publishers: 544; Susan Burger: 562; Lawrence Migdale/Photo Researchers, Inc.: 568; John MacPherson/Monkmeyer: 577; Todd Yarrington/Merrill: 596; Blair Seitz: 616; John Kringas/Chicago Tribune: 619.